Winner's Electoral College Vote %	Winner's Popular Vote %	Congress	House		Senate	
			Majority Party	Minority Party	Majority Party	Minority Party
**	No popular vote	1st	38 Admin †	26 Opp	17 Admin	Opp
		2nd	37 Fed ††	33 Dem-R	16 Fed	13 Dem-R
**	No popular vote	3rd	57 Dem-R	48 Fed	17 Fed	13 Dem-R
		4th	54 Fed	52 Dem-R	19 Fed	13 Dem-R
**	No popular vote	5th	58 Fed	48 Dem-R	20 Fed	12 Dem-R
		6th	64 Fed	42 Dem-R	19 Fed	13 Dem-R
HR**	No popular vote	7th	69 Dem-R	36 Fed	18 Dem-R	13 Fed
		8th	102 Dem-R	39 Fed	25 Dem-R	9 Fed
92.0	No popular vote	9th	116 Dem-R	25 Fed	27 Dem-R	7 Fed
		10th	118 Dem-R	24 Fed	28 Dem-R	6 Fed
69.7	No popular vote	11th	94 Dem-R	48 Fed	28 Dem-R	6 Fed
		12th	108 Dem-R	36 Fed	30 Dem-R	6 Fed
59.0	No popular vote	13th	112 Dem-R	68 Fed	27 Dem-R	9 Fed
		14th	117 Dem-R	65 Fed	25 Dem-R	11 Fed
84.3	No popular vote	15th	141 Dem-R	42 Fed	34 Dem-R	10 Fed
		16th	156 Dem-R	27 Fed	35 Dem-R	7 Fed
99.5	No popular vote	17th	158 Dem-R	25 Fed	44 Dem-R	4 Fed
		18th	187 Dem-R	26 Fed	44 Dem-R	4 Fed
HR	39.1 †††	19th	105 Admin	97 Dem-J	26 Admin	20 Dem-J
		20th	119 Dem-J	94 Admin	28 Dem-J	20 Admin
68.2	56.0	21st	139 Dem	74 Nat R	26 Dem	22 Nat R
		22nd	141 Dem	58 Nat R	25 Dem	21 Nat R
76.6	54.5	23rd	147 Dem	53 AntiMas	20 Dem	20 Nat R
		24th	145 Dem	98 Whig	27 Dem	25 Whig
57.8	50.9	25th	108 Dem	107 Whig	30 Dem	18 Whig
		26th	124 Dem	118 Whig	28 Dem	22 Whig
79.6	52.9					
–	52.9	27th	133 Whig	102 Dem	28 Whig	22 Dem
		28th	142 Dem	79 Whig	28 Whig	25 Dem
61.8	49.6	29th	143 Dem	77 Whig	31 Dem	25 Whig
		30th	115 Whig	108 Dem	36 Dem	21 Whig
56.2	47.3	31st	112 Dem	109 Whig	35 Dem	25 Whig
–	–	32nd	140 Dem	88 Whig	35 Dem	24 Whig
85.8	50.9	33rd	159 Dem	71 Whig	38 Dem	22 Whig
		34th	108 Rep	83 Dem	40 Dem	15 Rep
58.8	45.6	35th	118 Dem	92 Rep	36 Dem	20 Rep
		36th	114 Rep	92 Dem	36 Dem	26 Rep
59.4	39.8	37th	105 Rep	43 Dem	31 Rep	10 Dem
		38th	102 Rep	75 Dem	36 Rep	9 Dem
91.0	55.2					
–	–	39th	149 Union	42 Dem	42 Union	10 Dem
		40th	143 Rep	49 Dem	42 Rep	11 Dem
72.8	52.7	41st	149 Rep	63 Dem	56 Rep	11 Dem
		42nd	134 Rep	104 Dem	52 Rep	17 Dem
81.9	55.6	43rd	194 Rep	92 Dem	49 Rep	19 Dem
		44th	169 Rep	109 Dem	45 Rep	29 Dem
50.1	47.9 †††	45th	153 Dem	140 Rep	39 Rep	36 Dem
		46th	149 Dem	130 Rep	42 Dem	33 Rep
58.0	48.3	47th	147 Rep	135 Dem	37 Rep	37 Dem
–	–	48th	197 Dem	118 Rep	38 Rep	36 Dem
54.6	48.5	49th	183 Dem	140 Rep	43 Rep	34 Dem
		50th	169 Dem	152 Rep	39 Rep	37 Dem

Source for election data: Svend Peterson, *A Statistical History of American Presidential Elections.* New York: Frederick Ungar Publishing, 1963. Updates: Richard Scammon, *America Votes* 19. Washington D.C.: Congressional Quarterly, 1991; *Congressional Quarterly Weekly Report*, Nov. 7, 1992, p. 3552.

Abbreviations:

Admin = Administration supporters
AntiMas = Anti-Masonic
Dem = Democratic
Dem-R = Democratic-Republican
Fed = Federalist

Dem-J = Jacksonian Democrats
Nat R = National Republican
Opp = Opponents of administration
Rep = Republican
Union = Unionist

EIGHTH EDITION

American Government

SUSAN WELCH
The Pennsylvania State University

JOHN GRUHL
University of Nebraska—Lincoln

JOHN COMER
University of Nebraska—Lincoln

SUSAN M. RIGDON
University of Illinois at Urbana-Champaign

WADSWORTH ™

THOMSON LEARNING

Australia • Canada • Mexico • Singapore • Spain • United Kingdom • United States

WADSWORTH
THOMSON LEARNING

Political Science Publisher: Clark Baxter

Senior Development Editor: Sharon Adams Poore

Assistant Editor: Jennifer Ellis

Executive Marketing Manager: Diane McOscar

Print Buyer: Barbara Britton

Permissions Editor: Joohee Lee

Production Service: Penmarin Books

Text Designer: Carolyn Deacy

Art Editor: Hal Lockwood

Photo Researcher: Connie Hathaway

Copy Editor: Laura Larson

Cover Designer: Randall Goodall/Seventeenth Street Studios

Cover Image: © 2001 David J. Sams/Stone

Cover Printer: Phoenix Color

Compositor: Carlisle Communications

Printer: R.R. Donnelley and Sons Company, Willard

For permission to use material from this text, contact us by
Web: http://www.thomsonrights.com
Fax: 1-800-730-2215
Phone: 1-800-730-2214

ISBN: 0-534-57105-0

Wadsworth/Thomson Learning
10 Davis Drive
Belmont, CA 94002-3098
USA
For more information about our products, contact us:
Thomson Learning Academic Resource Center
1-800-423-0563
http://www.wadsworth.com

International Headquarters
Thomson Learning
International Division
290 Harbor Drive, 2nd Floor
Stamford, CT 06902-7477
USA

UK/Europe/Middle East/South Africa
Thomson Learning
Berkshire House
168-173 High Holborn
London WC1V 7AA
United Kingdom

Asia
Thomson Learning
60 Albert Street, #15-01
Albert Complex
Singapore 189969

Canada
Nelson Thomson Learning
1120 Birchmount Road
Toronto, Ontario M1K 5G4
Canada

Brief Contents

Contents

PART TWO

Links between People and Government

Institutions

Preface

Popular esteem for American political institutions continues to decline. The public alternates between curiosity about, and revulsion toward, politics and politicians. Yet beneath the scandals, and the attempts of elected officials to gain political advantage or minimize political disadvantage from these scandals, the role of government in our lives remains crucial. The eighth edition of our text, *American Government,* tries, as did the previous editions, to demonstrate to students why government is important, and to interest students in learning about the exciting, important, and controversial issues in American public life. We believe an introductory course succeeds if most students develop an understanding of major ideas, an interest in learning more about American government, and an ability to begin to understand and evaluate the news they hear about American political issues. Although a firm grounding in the essential "nuts and bolts" of American government is crucial, other approaches are helpful in motivating students' interest in government.

We offer the essential "nuts and bolts" of American government, but we also want the student to understand why (and sometimes how) these important features have evolved, their impact on government and individuals, and why they are controversial (if they are) and worth learning. For example, we prefer students to leave the course remembering why campaign finance laws were created and why they are generally ineffective than to memorize specific dollar limitations on giving for different types of candidates from different types of organizations. The latter will change or will soon be forgotten, but understanding the "whys" will help the student understand the campaign finance issue long after the course is over.

We have also tried to interest students by describing and discussing the impact of various features of govern-

ment. For example, students who do not understand why learning about voter registration laws is important may "see the light" when they understand the link between such laws and low voter turnout. Therefore, a particular emphasis throughout the book is on the *impact* of government: how individual features of government affect its responsiveness to different groups (in Lasswell's terms, "Who gets what and why?"). We realize that nothing in American politics is simple; rarely does one feature of government produce, by itself, a clear outcome. Nevertheless, we think that students will be more willing to learn about government if they see some relationships between how government operates and the impact it has on them as American citizens.

Changes in the Eighth Edition

This edition is again substantially revised. We cover the 2000 national elections, although our publication deadlines gave little time for postelection reflection.

We have added a new feature in each chapter: a timeline of important events. This timeline, found near the end of each chapter, is designed to help students remember key events and developments in the topic addressed in the chapter and to get a better sense of chronology of these events. Given national studies that show that a majority of college graduates are woefully ignorant about the chronology of even important events such as major wars and pathbreaking presidential administrations, we thought that students needed assistance in visualizing key points in the development of the American polity.

We have retained the feature box added in the seventh edition labelled *What Government Does Right.* In an era when it is fashionable to run against government when running for public office, and at a time when

Instructor's Manual

Features an extensive resource guide section correlating each chapter's content to other components of the ancillary package (for example: *InfoTrac College Edition* articles, transparencies, PowerPoint® slides, CNN video clips, the *America at Odds* CD-ROM, and others). Corresponding to each text chapter, every chapter in the manual also contains a chapter outline, lecture ideas and suggested activities, and recommended Web sites.

Test Bank

A large selection of test items, including multiple-choice, fill-in-the-blank, short-answer, and essay questions.

ExamView® Computerized Testing for Windows and Macintosh

Create, deliver, and customize tests and study guides (both print and online) in minutes with this easy-to-use assessment and tutorial system. Test appears on screen just as it will in print. You can easily edit and import your own questions and graphics, change test layout, and move questions. Also offers flexible delivery and the ability to test and grade online.

Wadsworth Political Science Video Library

So many exciting, new videos . . . so many great ways to enrich your lectures and spark discussion of the material in this text! Your Wadsworth/Thomson representative will be happy to provide details on our video policy by adoption size.

American Government Transparency Acetate Package, 2001 Edition

Includes more than seventy full-color acetates (tables, charts, and figures from the text and additional sources).

For instructors and students . . .

Book-Specific Web Site

Easily accessible from the Wadsworth Political Science Resource Center at http://politicalscience.wadsworth.com, this site is the ultimate in interactive learning. Linking online material to the text at every opportunity, it includes:

- Interactive quizzes for each chapter where students can self-assess and review their knowledge
- Hypercontents for each chapter—an extensive hypertext list of sites that provide reviews of related

material, supplemental media, and chapter-related news and research

- Online instructor resources—password protected, of course!

PLUS: quick access to The Wadsworth Political Science Resource Center and "Election Central"—featuring the latest election updates, information, and links to election Web sites. The Political Science Resource Center also includes *InfoTrac College Edition* activities, links to general political Web sites, a career center, online news, a discussion forum, and much more.

InfoTrac® College Edition . . .

FREE access to an extensive online library of current articles! Available exclusively from Wadsworth/Thomson Learning, four months of access to the *InfoTrac College Edition* library is included *FREE* to adopters and their students. Featuring thousands of full-length articles (not abstracts) from such publications as *National Review, Washington Monthly,* and many others, this online resource opens new worlds of information for your students. At the end of chapters students will find lists of suggested topic-related articles that they can access in *InfoTrac College Edition*'s extensive library of important political science and other popular sources.

Thomson Learning WebTutor™ 2.0 . . .

takes your course beyond classroom boundaries! Rich with content for your American government course, this Web-based teaching and learning tool includes course management, study/mastery, and communication tools. Use *WebTutor* to provide virtual office hours, post your syllabi, and track student progress with *WebTutor's* quizzing material.

For students, *WebTutor* offers real-time access to interactive online tutorials and simulations, practice quizzes, and Web links—all correlated to *American Government* and *Understanding American Government*. Available on WebCT and Blackboard.

Student Resources

New!

American Government: An Introduction Using MicroCase ExplorIt, Sixth Edition

Includes CD-ROM and Workbook. Students make their own decisions about the issues as they analyze and interpret current NES and GSS data.

America at Odds CD-ROM

Your students actually participate in American politics with the twenty interactive modules in this CD-ROM as they research the issues, discuss ideas, formulate opinions, and interpret data! Features a rich mix of media, including digital video and audio, photos, graphics, and Internet technology.

New!
American Government: Readings and Responses

By Monica Bauer. A wonderful collection of readings from prominent writers, plus "Chat Room" conversations with students who debate the topics in the readings.

Study Guide

Features (in each chapter) a chapter summary; key terms, and fill-in-the blank, true/false, multiple-choice, and short essay questions.

Readings in American Government, Third Edition

Spark lively debate in your classroom with this on-target reader, updated with the latest issues in American government. More than sixty readings. Edited by Steffen W. Schmidt and Mack C. Shelley.

Thinking Globally, Acting Locally

By John Soares. A concise book offering specific guidance for getting involved as an active citizen.

American Government Internet Activities, Third Edition

Contains activities for all major topics in the text. Students are asked to surf the Web to obtain answers to thought-provoking questions.

The Handbook of Selected Court Cases

Includes more than thirty Supreme Court cases.

The Handbook of Selected Legislation and Other Documents

Features excerpts from twelve laws passed by the U.S. Congress that have had a significant impact on American politics.

An Introduction to Critical Thinking and Writing in American Politics

Introduces a number of critical thinking and writing techniques, helping students make better use of the information they receive in class and in the text.

Acknowledgments

We would like to thank the many people who have aided and sustained us during the lengthy course of this project. We first acknowledge the work of Margery Ambrosius, the coauthor of Chapters 12 and 17, for her intellectual contribution to this book. Our current and former University of Nebraska and Penn State colleagues have been most tolerant and helpful. We thank them all. In particular, we appreciate the assistance of John Hibbing, Philip Dyer, Robert Miewald, Beth Theiss-Morse, Louis Picard, John Peters, David Rapkin, Peter Maslowski, David Forsythe, W. Randy Newell, and Steven Daniels, who provided us with data, bibliographic information, and other insights that we have used here. We are especially grateful to Philip Dyer, Alan Booth, Louis Picard, Robert Miewald, and John Hibbing, who read one or more chapters and saved us from a variety of errors.

We are also grateful to the many other readers of our draft manuscript, as listed below. Without their assistance the book would have been less accurate, less complete, and less lively.

We are also grateful to those instructors who have used the book and relayed their comments and suggestions to us. Our students at the University of Nebraska have also provided invaluable reactions to the previous editions.

Others too have been of great assistance to us. Jeff Walz, Staci Beavers, and Michael Moore provided essential service and help in producing the ancillary materials for the book.

Several people at Wadsworth Publishing also deserve our thanks. Clark Baxter has been a continual source of encouragement and optimism from the beginning of the first edition through the last decision on the eighth. We are greatly in debt to Carolyn Deacy, who designed this edition of the book, and to Hal Humphrey and Hal Lockwood, who produced it.

Reviewers

REVIEWERS OF THE NEW EDITION

Alan D. Buckley,
Santa Monica College
Kay Hofer
Southwest Texas State University
Joseph F. Jozwiak, Jr.
Texas A & M University—Kingsville

Kenneth M. Mash
  East Stroudsburg University
Michael K. Moore
  University of Texas at Arlington

REVIEWERS OF PREVIOUS EDITIONS

Alan Abramowitz
  State University of New York at Stony Brook
Larry Adams
  Baruch College—City University of New York
Danny M. Adkison
  Oklahoma State University
James Alt
  Harvard University
Margery Marzahn Ambrosius
  Kansas State University
Kevin Bailey
  North Harris Community College
Kennette M. Benedict
  Northwestern University
Timothy Bledsoe
  Wayne State University
Jon Bond
  Texas A&M University
Paul R. Brace
  New York University
Joseph V. Brogan
  La Salle University
James R. Brown, Jr.
  Central Washington University
Chalmers Brumbaugh
  Elon College
Richard G. Buckner, Jr.
  Santa Fe Community College
Ronald Busch
  Cleveland State University
Carl D. Cavalli
  Memphis State University
Richard A. Champagne
  University of Wisconsin, Madison
Michael Connelly
  Southwestern Oklahoma State University
Gary Copeland
  University of Oklahoma
George H. Cox, Jr.
  Georgia Southern College
Paige Cubbison
  Miami-Dade University
Landon Curry
  Southwest Texas State University

Jack DeSario
  Case Western Reserve University
Robert E. DiClerico
  West Virginia University
Ernest A. Dover, Jr.
  Midwestern State University
Georgia Duerst-Lahti
  Beloit College
Ann H. Elder
  Illinois State University
Ghassan E. El-Eid
  Butler University
C. Lawrence Evans
  College of William and Mary
Murray Fischel
  Kent State University
Bobbe Fitzhugh
  Eastern Wyoming College
Marianne Fraser
  University of Utah
Jarvis Gamble
  Owens Community College
David Garrison
  Collin County Community College
Phillip L. Gianos
  California State University—Fullerton
Doris A. Graber
  University of Illinois—Chicago
Ruth M. Grubel
  University of Wisconsin—Whitewater
Stefan D. Haag
  Austin Community College
Larry M. Hall
  Belmont University
Edward Harpham
  University of Texas—Dallas
Peter O. Haslund
  Santa Barbara City College
Richard P. Heil
  Fort Hays State University
Peggy Heilig
  University of Illinois at Urbana
Craig Hendricks
  Long Beach City College
Marjorie Hershey
  Indiana University
Samuel B. Hoff
  Delaware State College
Robert D. Holsworth
  Virginia Commonwealth University

Jesse C. Horton
San Antonio College

Gerald Houseman
Indiana University

Peter G. Howse
American River College

David W. Hunt
Triton College

Pamela Imperato
University of North Dakota

Jerald Johnson
University of Vermont

Loch Johnson
University of Georgia

Evan M. Jones
St. Cloud State University

Henry C. Kenski
University of Arizona

Matt Kerbel
Villanova University

Marshall R. King
Maryville College

Orma Lindford
Kansas State University

Peter J. Longo
University of Nebraska—Kearney

Roger C. Lowery
University of North Carolina—Wilmington

H. R. Mahood
Memphis State University

Jarol B. Manheim
The George Washington University

A. Nick Minton
University of Massachusetts—Lowell

Matthew Moen
University of Maine

Michael Nelson
Vanderbilt University

Bruce Nesmith
Coe College

Walter Noelke
Angelo State University

Thomas Payette
Henry Ford Community College

Theodore B. Pedeliski
University of North Dakota

Jerry Perkins
Texas Tech University

Toni Phillips
University of Arkansas

C. Herman Pritchett
University of California—Santa Barbara

Charles Prysby
University of North Carolina—Greensboro

Sandra L. Quinn-Musgrove
Our Lady of the Lake University

Donald R. Ranish
Antelope Valley Community College

Linda Richter
Kansas State University

Jerry Sandvick
North Hennepin Community College

James Richard Sauder
University of New Mexico

Eleanor A. Schwab
South Dakota State University

Earl Sheridan
University of North Carolina—Wilmington

Edward Sidlow
Northwestern University

Cynthia Slaughter
Angelo State University

John Squibb
Lincolnland Community College

M. H. Tajalli-Tehrani
Southwest Texas State University

Kristine A. Thompson
Moorehead State University

R. Mark Tiller
Austin Community College

Gordon J. Tolle
South Dakota State University

Susan Tolleson-Rinehart
Texas Tech University

Bernadyne Weatherford
Rowan College of New Jersey

Richard Unruh
Fresno Pacific College

Jay Van Bruggen
Clarion University of Pennsylvania

Kenny Whitby
University of South Carolina

Donald C. Williams
Western New England College

Clifford J. Wirth
University of New Hampshire

Ann Wynia
North Hennepin Community College

Mary D. Young
Southwestern Michigan College

About the Authors

SUSAN WELCH received her A.B. and Ph.D. degrees from the University of Illinois at Urbana-Champaign. She is currently Dean of the College of the Liberal Arts and Professor of Political Science at The Pennsylvania State University. Her teaching and research areas include legislatures, state and urban politics, and women and minorities in politics. She has edited the *American Politics Quarterly.*

JOHN GRUHL, a Professor of Political Science, received his A.B. from DePaul University in Greencastle, Indiana, and his Ph.D. from the University of California at Santa Barbara. Since joining the University of Nebraska faculty in 1976, he has taught and done research in the areas of judicial process, criminal justice, and civil rights and liberties. He won University of Nebraska campus-wide distinguished teaching awards in 1979 and 1986 for excellence in undergraduate teaching, and became a charter member of the University's Academy of Distinguished Teachers in 1995.

JOHN COMER is a Professor of Political Science at the University of Nebraska. He received his A.B. in political science from Miami University of Ohio in 1965 and his Ph.D. from the Ohio State University in 1971. His teaching and research focus on interest groups, public opinion, voting behavior, and political parties.

SUSAN RIGDON received A.B. and Ph.D. degrees in political science from the University of Illinois in 1966 and 1971. She has taught American Government at several institutions in the U.S. and China, and has other teaching and research interests in foreign policy, comparative government, and political development. She is a Research Associate in Anthropology at the University of Illinois at Urbana-Champaign.

American Government

American Democracy

YOU ARE THERE

Is Politics Futile?

In this section of following chapters, you will be asked to step into the shoes of decision makers and analyze how and why they made certain key decisions. But here you are asked to be, well—*you.*

You are sitting there reading your American government text but wondering how much you are really interested in government or politics. You know that every two years there is a national election, every four years one to elect a president, and that, on or between these dates, there are a host of state and local elections for governors, mayors, city councils, and school, library, and county board members. Perhaps in the next election you will be a first-time voter, or maybe you already have several campaigns under your belt. Yet each time an election approaches, you ask yourself whether it is worth the effort. Maybe you are one of those people who shares Groucho Marx's observation that "politics is the art of finding trouble everywhere, diagnosing it incorrectly, and applying the wrong remedy."

If you are going to vote, you will have to make decisions on dozens of candidates. Do you have the time to get to know something about each of them and

to read up on the issues? Maybe you should vote only for those candidates whose positions you know and only in those elections you think will have a significant impact on your life. And what about the campaigns leading up to election day? Should you become active in a political party, write letters in support of an issue, make campaign contributions, attend rallies, or campaign for candidates? And what about all the other efforts to influence policy outcomes that do not involve electoral politics? Should you join one or more of the many interest groups that lobby unelected officials such as bureaucrats, political appointees, and federal judges?

You are a busy person, so why bother to get involved in politics? Surely, if you vote, you will have done your civic duty. You look at the news and see dog-eat-dog, negative campaigning, character attacks, investigations into the most intimate aspects of the lives of public figures, gridlock caused by party conflict in Congress and state legislatures, and huge campaign donations buying access to candidates or officials. You know that interest groups and legislators spend years debating issues, such as government's role in health care, yet all they appear to

| | Middle Eastern | Italian | African | Vietnamese | Anglo-Saxon | Chinese | Hispanic |

America is more a melting pot than ever, with increasing population diversity and increasing rates of intermar-riage among different racial and ethnic groups. This computer-generated matrix from Time magazine reflects the changing face of America. Move across from the left and down from the top to see resulting progeny.

Photographs: Ted Thai/*Time* magazine, computer morphing: Kin Wah Lam, design: Walter Bernard and Milton Glaser.

achieve is a standoff. Who needs it? After all, government works: your mail comes, your grandparents' Social Security checks arrive on time, your state issued you a driver's license, the roads are paved, the bridges and dams hold up, the schools are open, and we have a large military establishment, local law enforcement, a great-looking capital city, and a massive infrastructure. America has social stability and a well-functioning economy. Government is doing the basics. Why should you get involved in politics?

One obvious argument that you are well aware of is that if you do not, others will, and they may not agree with your idea of what government should be doing to solve the country's problems and prepare for the future. This is a huge country—it is economically, ethnically, and religiously diverse and becoming more so every year. There will always be divergent views and therefore competing interests trying to shape government policy. If you opt out, and candidates are elected and policies made that you disagree with, quite frankly, you will not have much basis for complaint. Furthermore, you know that participation is integral to the concept on which our form of government is founded. Americans have fought for generations to expand rights to the point where virtually every citizen eighteen or older who is not a convicted felon has full rights of participation. Why did they make the effort?

What will you do? Are you going to vote in some, all, or none of the upcoming local, state, and federal elections? Do you believe the major parties and candidates differ sufficiently on the issues or philosophically to make your vote worth casting? If your candidates are elected, do you think they will be able to move government in the direction you want it to go? Do you care enough about some issues that you might be willing to invest time and effort, beyond voting, to influence policy? Do you think that if you do get involved, you as an ordinary citizen will have any chance of reaching policymakers with your views? What would it take to get you involved in government and the political process?

There may be conflict in our political life, but Americans are members of one community. We are parties to a single legal contract, the Constitution, and are all equally subject to the protections and obligations of a common set of laws. We also share an economic system, and although the Constitution has little to say about its nature, our government is deeply implicated in its successes and failures. In fact, government's role in managing the economy is sufficient to link the level of confidence we have in government to how well the economy is doing, or at minimum to how well we are doing. Our economic well-being also affects how much we participate and how much access we have to policymakers.

If government is the instrument for forging one interest out of many in order to legislate and to speak for the country as a whole in matters of national interest, then **politics** is a means through which individual and group interests compete to shape government's impact on society's problems and goals. Interests compete through political parties and many other extragovernmental organizations. The institutions of government were also created to represent competing interests as well as to mediate among them. So politics is also the art of governing.

Inconsistencies dominate American political life. Americans cherish the symbols of democracy but deplore its realities.[1] We visit Washington to marvel at the Washington Monument, the Jefferson and Lincoln Memorials, the Capitol, and the White House. We show these symbols of our democracy to our children, hoping they will revere them. We cherish the Declaration of Independence and the Constitution.

But at the same time that we prize these symbols of democracy, we condemn the reality of democracy. We refer to debates over issues as quarrels or "bickering"; we call compromises "selling out"; we label conflict as mere self-interest; we tag interest groups and political parties as "special interests." We have little tolerance for the slow pace at which government deals with the nation's problems. In other words, we love the concept of democracy but hate the rough and tumble, the give and take, and the conflict of democracy in action.[2]

How do people, politics, government, and the economy come together to form the "American system"? How might these relationships change as we move through the twenty-first century? This chapter provides short answers to these questions by profiling the American people, identifying the political values we share, and describing how they are expressed in our form of government. It also briefly describes how democracy, when practiced by people who are ethnically, economically, and religiously diverse and scattered across a vast and varied landscape, is destined to be characterized as much by competition and conflict as by cooperation and community. All of these topics will be developed in greater detail in later chapters.

The American People

When the poet Walt Whitman wrote, "Here is not merely a nation but a teeming Nation of nations," he said a lot about our country and its politics.[3] It is a cliché, yet true, that the United States is a land of immigrants, peopled by individuals from all over the world. Americans are a conglomeration of religions, races, ethnicities, cultural traditions, and socioeconomic groups, or what one historian calls "a collision of histories."[4]

Cultural Diversity

From its beginnings the American population has been characterized by diversity. Anthropologists are still debating the timing and points of origin of North America's first settlers, but many probably arrived after crossing a land bridge from Asia thousands of years ago. Although sometimes characterized by a single term such as Indians or Native Americans, they went on to found many different civilizations, both agricultural and hunting/gathering. Their nations were competitive and at times at war, and their differences substantial enough to doom eighteenth-century efforts to form pan-Indian alliances against European colonization.[5] Today the Census Bureau recognizes 554 different tribes, many fewer than two hundred years ago, but still suggestive of the wide array of cultures that predated European settlement.

The umbrella term *European* is itself somewhat deceptive in that European settlers emigrated from countries that not only differed linguistically, religiously, and politically but also had often been at war with one

Immigrants crowd a New York City neighborhood in 1900.
UPI/Corbis-Bettmann

another. Migrants carried some of these conflicts with them to America. Because the colonies were ruled from England and its language and culture were dominant, we tend to think of early Americans as Anglos and Protestants. But the earliest European settlers of the southeastern and southwestern territories were more likely to be Roman Catholics from France and Spain than Anglo-Protestants. And over time, Germany, a distinctly non-Anglo country and one evenly split between Catholics and Protestants, provided more immigrants to America than England. By preference, or to avoid discrimination by earlier-arriving or more dominant settlers, immigrants often self-segregated into territories (Quakers to Pennsylvania, Catholics to Maryland), which later became states. At the time the Constitution was adopted, six of the thirteen original states had established religions.[6] These different beliefs and traditions contributed to the rise of distinctive local cultures and to the varying character of state governments and politics.

Like European settlers, Africans, too, came from a huge continent that encompassed many languages and cultures. Even though the European slave trade was con-

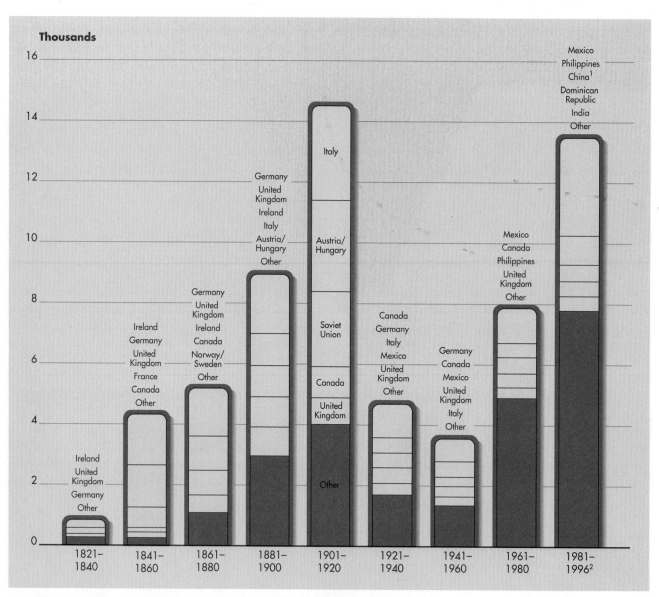

FIGURE 1 ■ *Immigrants Admitted to the United States from the Top Five Countries of Last Residence: 1821 to 1996*

1. Includes People's Republic of China and Taiwan.
2. Sixteen-year period.
SOURCE: 1996 *Statistical Yearbook of the Immigration and Naturalization Service,* p. 14.

centrated in coastal areas of Africa, the men and women forcibly removed to the Americas did not share a common tradition. Their experience in the American colonies, however, united most of them in a common condition as noncitizens lacking all political and economic rights.

The ethnic, racial, and religious composition of the American population broadened further in the mid to late nineteenth century as new waves of settlers came from southern and eastern Europe, China, and Japan, as well as Ireland and Germany (Figure 1). They included large numbers of Roman Catholics, Eastern and Russian Orthodox, Jews, and some Buddhists. Immigration continued at high levels into the twentieth century before peaking in the decade 1905–1914, when more than ten million immigrants entered the country.

Not all immigrants who came, stayed. In addition to deportations, almost 30 percent of arrivals in the early 1900s returned voluntarily to their home countries each year (compared to about 20 percent of today's arrivals). For a few years during the Great Depression of the 1930s, more people left the United States than entered.[7] Then, following the peak years of the second decade until the end of World War II, a deliberate effort was made to slow the rate of new arrivals. It was not until the decade 1987–1996 that immigration reached its peak level to date (1991).

By 1998, 10 percent of all residents of the United States were foreign-born, less than the 15 percent in the peak year 1910 but of greater political and economic impact than the numbers suggest. Five of eight immigrants settle in only five states (California, New York, Florida, Texas, and New Jersey) with California alone accepting one-quarter of all new arrivals. One of every three immigrants heads for New York City, Los Angeles, Miami, Chicago, or Washington, D.C.[8] Still, the 14 percent of Chicago's population that was foreign born in 1996 compares to about half in 1910; the 20 percent of foreign born among New York City's residents compares to 40 percent in 1910, when another 40 percent had foreign-born parents.[9]

Of the more than ten million who arrived between 1987 and 1996, the majority came from Asia, Latin America, and eastern Europe. Of those entering in 1997, more were born in Mexico than any other country (18 percent), while 33 percent were from Asia.[10] This shift in national origin of immigrants was due in part to significant changes in immigration law in the 1960s (see the box "Immigration: The Law, the Ideal"). The Census Bureau predicts that, if current trends continue, the 72 percent population share held by white non-Hispanics in 1999 will fall to 53 percent by the middle of the next century. This prediction is increasingly challenged for its failure to take into account the rising rate of intermarriage: one of every twenty-five marriages for the country as a whole and one in ten in California, in 1997. Should this pattern continue, the only majority in the United States by 2050 would be white/mixed race.[11]

Americans' religious profile is also changing. Although a large majority still identify themselves as Christians (87 percent), Americans now claim affiliation with 1,600 different religions and denominations, including 5.5 million Jews, 750,000–1,000,000 Buddhists and about the same number of Hindus, and as many Muslims as Presbyterians (3.5 million).[12] To some these figures may represent the potential for social fragmentation, but by Voltaire's standards, a proliferation in religious affiliation is an indicator of increased liberty. A nation with one church, Voltaire wrote, will have oppression; with two, civil war; with a hundred, freedom.[13]

Immigration and Political Cleavage

Much is made of racial and ethnic conflict in American history. But some of the most intense political cleavages have arisen between older and new immigrants. There have always been some native-born Americans who fear economic competition from newcomers or perceive non-English-speaking people or anyone with different traditions and religious practices as a cultural threat. So throughout our history there has been antiforeign, or nativist, sentiment, even by first-generation immigrants, but the political impact of antiforeign sentiment is typically greatest when immigration levels are high. Hence, strong nativist sentiments influenced the politics of the mid-1800s, the 1920s, and the 1990s.

The "Know-Nothings" won popularity in the 1840s by spreading fear of a Catholic takeover. Patriotic fervor during World War I produced hostility toward Americans of German birth or descent. In 1918, Iowa's governor required all groups of two or more people to speak only English, even when using the telephone.[14] From 1924 to 1965, federal law limited immigration from most areas outside western Europe.

In 1991, Republican presidential candidate Patrick Buchanan complained that immigration is about to "submerge" our "predominantly Caucasian Western society" and warned about a "dilution" of our European heritage.[15] A newspaper criticized immigrants who "bring with them their non-Christian Third World cultures, poverty-mindedness and a tendency toward crime."[16]

"Give me your tired, your poor, your huddled masses yearning to breathe free. . . ." These words from Emma Lazarus's poem—engraved on the Statue of Liberty—capture the ideal of the United States as a refuge for the world's outcasts: political and religious dissidents and the economically downtrodden. Despite the high-flown rhetoric, U.S. law has not always reflected the ideals in Lazarus's poem. Not all newcomers have been made welcome on arrival, and some were not even invited to apply. Yet the ideal remains that America's doors are open to those fleeing persecution and to industrious people looking for new opportunities. But since these categories potentially encompass hundreds of millions of people, only a small fraction of refugees and opportunity seekers can settle in the United States. Thus, rules must be established to determine who qualifies for an immigration visa, who is entitled to refugee status, and how many people will be allowed to take up residency in the United States each year.

Few people would argue with the proposition that every country has the right to control its borders, but many disagree over the standards used to regulate immigration. For most of its history, the United States has used immigration law to populate the country, stimulate the economy, give refuge to political and religious dissidents, and, until fairly recently, regulate the ethnic and racial composition of the population. It has not always been able to pursue these goals simultaneously.

Regulation of immigration began in 1798 when Congress gave the president power to deport people he deemed "dangerous to the peace and safety" of the country. An 1807 law, implementing a provision in the new constitution, prohibited the migration or "importation" of people for purposes of slavery. Then, for almost seventy years, there was no new federal regulation, but some state governments, especially those in the underpopulated interior, did pass laws encouraging immigration. During this period tens of thousands of laborers were brought into the country to build railroads, canals, and other large infrastructure projects; settle the West; and work in the new factories.

State laws became invalid in 1876 when the Supreme Court ruled that regulating immigration was the provenance of Congress. About this time Congress began passing laws restricting immigration by category of person, putting criminals and prostitutes first on the list. In 1882, the prohibition was extended to the mentally ill and incompetent and all who were unable to support themselves. Laws passed up through the end of World War II added new categories of people prohibited entry: anarchists and revolutionaries, members of communist parties or affiliated groups, polygamists, alcoholics, vagrants, stowaways, and those with contagious diseases or convicted of "moral depravity."

As immigration law evolved during these decades, it also had the clear purpose of maintaining the ethnic balance of the country: immigration was largely restricted to the countries already represented in the American population. For example, in the Exclusion Act of 1882, Congress suspended immigration of Chinese laborers, many of whom had come in the mid–nineteenth century to mine gold and to help build the railroads. It barred reentry to those who had gone back to China to visit their families and citizenship to those who were here. (It was not until 1943 that Congress allotted entry quotas to Chinese, who at the time were our World War II allies.) Restrictive policies never worked exactly as intended, however, because too few people in the preferred countries of western Europe had motive to emigrate. This led to periods of labor shortfalls and an influx of eastern and southern Europeans, as well as large numbers of nonEuropeans, such as Japanese (many of whom entered indirectly through Hawaii, then a U.S. territory) and Mexican agricultural laborers.

Ethnic and racial restrictions were not eliminated until the Immigration and Naturalization Act of 1965 replaced them with a preference system that targets family reunification and specific job skills. During the past thirty years, this system has undergone considerable tinkering, including an amnesty that gave permanent residency to 2.6 million illegal residents between 1989 and 1992, but the priority system remains in place. A 1990 law set a flexible cap of 675,000 on annual admissions. Almost 500,000 of these slots are reserved each year for family-sponsored immigrants (close relatives who are *not* members of the immediate family), and 140,000 are reserved for those with in-demand job skills.

To ensure that people from all parts of the world have a chance to apply, the Immigration and Naturalization Service (INS) divides the world into regions and assigns quotas to countries within each region, which it adjusts annually. There is also a "diversity" quota, which sets aside fifty-five thousand slots per year for people in countries where a low number of visa requests had been granted in the previous five years.

Despite the ceiling placed on annual admissions, the actual number of legal entries fluctuates substantially because, even after the numerical cap is reached, an unlimited number of additional persons can qualify for residency if they fall into one of the off-quota categories: asylees and refugees, for example, and immediate family members of U.S. citizens. Thus, the actual number of legal immigrants who entered in 1996 was 915,900. During much of the Cold War, anyone fleeing a communist country was pretty much guaranteed refugee or asylee status. In this way several million Cubans, Russians, eastern Europeans, Vietnamese, Cambodians, and Laotians emigrated, and thousands of Chinese were granted permanent residency under an amnesty following the 1989 Tiananmen Square massacre.

When these permanent residents become citizens, all immediate members of their families living outside the United States automatically qualify for residency visas. The percentage of new residents who are family sponsored has been increasing and in 1998 accounted for about two-thirds of all legal immigrants admitted.[1]

In the mid-1990s, immigration policy took a turn toward tighter control. Overall admissions fell, the family preference quota was lowered, and the rules under which asylum can be granted were overhauled. Some of the changes came in reaction to the high levels of new arrivals in the preceding decade. But increasing fear of terrorism, especially af-

ter the bombing of the World Trade Center in New York City and a wave of bad publicity about abuses of the lax admission policies for asylees, was also a contributing factor. In 1996, Congress passed laws that make much easier the detention and deportation of illegal entrants without judicial review, and the federal court later ruled the INS can, on its own authority, revoke the citizenship of any naturalized American who lied about a criminal record on an immigration application.[2] In 1997 and 1998, the INS set new records for deportations, while also turning back roughly 1.5 million people apprehended at U.S. borders each year.[3] The Coast Guard even began picking up Cubans in international waters and returning them to the island.

The number of legal immigrants also began falling in the late nineties. In 1998, INS granted permanent residency to 660,477 foreigners (well over half of whom were already living here), a 17 percent decrease from 1997 and a 28 percent drop from 1996. The decline is attributed to the agency's inability to keep up with the backlog of cases and the lowering of some of the family preference allotments.[4]

Another sign of changing immigration policy is the increasing use of temporary admissions to satisfy domestic business demands. Even though the job preference quota for permanent residency has not been filled in the past few years, both the White House and Congress have favored issuing six-year work visas for college graduates (up to 195,000 a year) to fill slots in high-tech industries. Critics of this policy claim it is a way of making use of highly trained foreigners while offering them little or

no hope of citizenship. The majority of the visas will be awarded to Chinese and Indians whose chances of converting them to permanent residency are small. No country is allotted more than 7 percent of the job preference admissions in any given year, so most temporary workers would have to leave the country before qualifying for permanent residency.

Overall, immigration law is an example of how laws passed by Congress reflect principle, as well as competition and compromise. To the extent that the post-1965 laws eliminated racial and ethnic barriers to immigration, they allow for a fuller realization of the sentiments in Lazarus's poem. But the emphasis on family reunification, priority job skills, and diversity also reflects a realignment in the political process, illustrating how Congress responds to the demands of business, new voters, and the growing power of race- and ethnic-based interest groups.

1. "Legal Immigration, Fiscal Year 1997," Immigration and Naturalization Service, Office of Policy and Planning, Annual Report, no. 1, January 1999, p. 4.
2. The 1995 changes in asylum law can be found at www.ins.usdoj.gov/graphics/aboutins/history/jan95.html.
3. In 1998, the INS deported 171,154 illegal residents, one-third of whom had criminal records. This was a 50 percent increase over the 1997 record of 114,383. Mexican nationals accounted for 81 percent of all removals. "Illegal Aliens Deported in Record Numbers in 1998," *Champaign-Urbana News-Gazette*, January 9, 1999, p. A-5.
4. "Legal Immigration, Fiscal Year, 1997." OTHER SOURCES: *1997 Statistical Yearbook of the Immigration and Naturalization Service*; Immigration and Nationality Act, Title II (available at the INS Web site: http://www.ins.usdoj.gov/); Dick Kirschten, "American Dreamers," *National Journal*, July 5, 1997, pp. 1364–1369.

Every ten years the U.S. government takes a census of the American population. This should be a fairly straightforward statistical procedure, but it has often been a contentious political issue. This is largely because the census does much more than establish the size and geographic distribution of the population; its findings have important political and economic consequences. Of special significance are the figures that establish the racial and ethnic breakdown of the population. These data have become essential for implementation of the Voting Rights Act and court rulings stemming from the modern civil rights movement, as well as for "a smorgasbord of set-asides and entitlements and affirmative-action programs."[1]

Unlike in the past, today the collection of information on the racial heritage of Americans has greater significance for inclusion than for exclusion. Racial categories have been used since the first census was taken in 1790, when Americans were identified as white males, white females, other (free blacks, and Indians living off reservations, for example), and slaves (obviously not a racial category, but since only people of African descent were enslaved, *slave* became synonymous with *black*). Some states classified as "black" people

with as little as 1/32 African ancestry, consigning them to political and economic exclusion. Chinese and American Indian became census categories in 1860; Japanese was added in 1870, and other Asian "races" in 1910. For one census taking only (1930), "Mexican" was defined as a race, before quickly being reabsorbed into the whites category.

From this it should be apparent that over time little has been fixed about how race and color classifications have been used. They reflect "common or social usage" rather than scientifically determined biological differences. Through the 1950 census, race was established solely by the census taker's observation, which usually resulted in people of mixed white and other heritage being counted as "other." It was not until the 1980 census that an individual's ethnicity and race were established entirely by self-classification.[2]

While Canada has long since stopped categorizing citizens by race in its census, the United States has switched to broader categories. Each person counted in the 1990 census was asked to self-identify with one of four racial groups: black; white; American Indian or Native Alaskan; Asian or Pacific Islander; and, where applicable, also to claim a Hispanic/Latino ethnic heritage. (A large

percentage of Hispanic Americans are of mixed-race ancestry: European, Native American, African, or Asian.) Complaints about this classificatory scheme have intensified as immigration and interracial marriage have steadily increased the number of multiracial Americans, many of whom object to characterizing their heritage in a single census category. The archetypal representative of this dilemma is golf pro Tiger Woods, who describes himself as a "Cablinasian," a person of white, African, American Indian, and Asian ancestry. Why, Woods asks, should he be asked to identify himself with only one part of his ancestry, and how would he decide which one to choose?[3]

In response to these considerations, the census for the year 2000 offered five racial categories (Native Hawaiians and Pacific Islanders were split off from Asians), while retaining the Hispanic ethnic designation. A "multiracial" category was rejected in favor of letting each person check more than one box—even if, as in the case of Tiger Woods, that turns out to be four boxes. The new method permits up to sixty-three variations in reporting race and ethnicity. This approach may allow more Americans to identify their ancestry accurately, but it could create a host of problems for census analysts. In

white by survey researchers. A study of infant deaths showed that many infants were classified by a different race at death than on their birth certificates. A quarter of those who identified themselves as American Indian on the census did not claim American Indian ancestry.

Interracial marriages and interracial children are becoming increasingly common. In the 1990 census, nearly a third of all native-born Hispanic women and men reported having non-Hispanic spouses; 45 percent of native-born Asian women and 36 percent of native-born Asian men had white spouses. Blacks and whites are also intermarrying with greater frequency. By 1999, there were more than 1.46 million intermarriages in the United States.[19]

All of these examples indicate that once seemingly clear notions of "race" as either black or white are becoming confused as we become an increasingly multiracial society. One survey showed that one-third of African Americans believe that blacks are not a single race, and almost half of both black and white respondents believed

"We've thought and thought, but we're at a loss about what to call ourselves. Any ideas?"

determining what percentage of Americans belongs to each category, will a data analyzer count Tiger Woods and others who check multiple boxes more than once, divide them into fractions, or just assign them to a single category? This may seem ridiculous, but it is a very real problem to the Census Bureau. Laws guaranteeing equal access and representation have meant, in practice, that the racial or ethnic composition of the population affects who is admitted to universities, how the boundaries of legislative districts are drawn, whether school districts need to submit desegregation plans, and whether minorities are adequately represented among workers hired on federally funded projects and among business owners receiving federal contracts.

The new categories are therefore of great concern to interest groups representing American minorities. The National Association for the Advancement of Colored People (NAACP), for example, does not want the political clout and greater opportunities it has worked decades to win diminished just because people who were classified as black for purposes of exclusion under the old "one-drop-of-blood" standard now are counted as white or Asian because they self-identify as multiracial. One NAACP official said, "Let those mixed race people check all the boxes they want—but *count* them as black."[4] One Hispanic American organization has asked that "Hispanic" be categorized as a race rather than an ethnicity, and the Arab American Institute wants a special protected category to be created for people of Middle Eastern ancestry. An official of an Asian American interest group said she opposed the multiple-choice approach because racial and ethnic data are collected for a reason, and "If you can't tabulate it, you've undermined the ability of the federal government to provide information that will help set policy and help ensure that the civil rights laws are effectively enforced. That is the bottom line."[5] Or, as it was more bluntly put by a member of the House committee that oversees the Census Bureau, "The numbers drive the dollars."[6]

1. Lawrence Wright, "One Drop of Blood," *New Yorker,* July 25, 1994, p. 47.
2. Campbell J. Gibson and Emily Lennon, "Historical Census Statistics on the Foreign-born Population of the United States: 1850–1990," Census Bureau, Population Division Working Paper, no. 29 (February 1999), p. 9. This report can be found at www.census.gov/population/www/documentation/twps0029/twps0029.html.
3. Rochelle L. Stanfield, "Multiple Choice," *National Journal,* November 22, 1997, pp. 2352–2355.
4. Stanfield, p. 2355.
5. Ibid.
6. Representative Thomas C. Sawyer (D.-Ohio) quoted in Wright, p. 47.
OTHER SOURCES: Jack E. White, "I'm Just Who I Am," *Time,* May 5, 1997, pp. 30–36.

that government should not collect information on race at all (see the box "Census and Sensibility").[20]

Political Culture

In recent years diversity has become a political catchword and has been raised to the level of a civic virtue. Yet our motto is "E Pluribus Unum"—"One Out of Many"—referring to the union of many states and the molding of one people from many traditions. There is a popular saying that Americans are people of many cultures united by a single idea. But what is that single idea, and is it, however fundamental, sufficient to form a political culture? A **political culture** is a shared body of values and beliefs that shapes perception and attitudes toward politics and government and, in turn, influences political behavior.

Governments rely for their stability and vitality on the positive affect of citizens: their identity with the country and its method of governing, and their adoption

Illegal immigrants wait to cross the border to California.
© Don Barletti, *Los Angeles Times*

of political values and behavior necessary to sustain the system. The only alternatives are for government to be ineffective or to gain compliance through force or other punitive measures. So it is essential for Americans to share a basic belief in the founding principles and institutions of government, including the individual's relationship to government and role in the political process.

In a democracy, sharing a political culture does not mean that citizens must agree on specific issues or even generally on what government's role should be in dealing with the country's problems. Democracy embraces conflict and competition just as it requires cooperation and a sense of community. A basic function of government is to establish the rules under which interests can compete. So the essence of political culture is not agreement on issues but the common perception of the rights and obligations of citizenship and of the rules for participating in the political process. These shared values reduce the strains produced by our differences and allow us to compete intensely on some issues while cooperating on others.

The significance of political culture—even its definition—has long been a topic of debate. Some argue that every country in the world, regardless of its level of de-

velopment, is composed of "competing political cultures, not a single political culture."[21] While American society has often been characterized as a melting pot, it has been a slow melt. It is easy to forget that not long ago people's identity as Virginians or Pennsylvanians was much more important to them than being an American. And it was not until the Civil War, under the influence of Lincoln's powerful reference at Gettysburg to the "unfinished work" of preserving the Union, that Americans began referring to the United States with the singular "is" rather than the plural "are."[22] Our "nation of nations" is crosscut with cultural, political, and economic cleavages, but despite our sometimes overwhelming diversity, most Americans do share some basic goals and values.

American Democracy: The Core Values

The words Americans use to characterize their form of government are less likely to come from the Constitution than from the second paragraph of the Declaration

Kentucky Fried Chicken follows a Korean American parade in Los Angeles.
Alon Reininger/Contact Press Images

of Independence: "We hold these Truths to be self-evident, that all Men are created equal, that they are endowed by the Creator with certain unalienable Rights, that among these are Life, Liberty, and the Pursuit of Happiness."

These words suggest the basic assumptions, or core beliefs, on which the American system was founded: universal truths that can be known and acted upon, equality before the law, belief in a higher power that transcends human law, and rights that are entitlements at birth and therefore can be neither granted nor taken away by government. The fundamental concept is liberty, especially the freedom to pursue one's livelihood and other personal goals that lead to a "happy" life.

The Declaration was primarily a political argument for separation from Great Britain and, as such, was concerned with the basic principles and philosophy of government.[23] Guaranteeing the rights of individuals, the Declaration postulated, was the primary reason for government to exist. The Constitution reinforced the Declaration's emphasis on equality, while specifying other core principles of American democracy: majority rule exercised through elected representatives, and minority rights (a reference to political or religious minorities, not to racial or ethnic minorities). But unlike the Declaration, the Constitution had to deal with the practical problems of governing and of creating institutions that would protect the rights and pursuits of the individual while balancing them against the public interest. Thus,

while the Declaration is all principle, the Constitution, of necessity, is founded on political compromise.

In this section we look briefly at each of the core principles of American democracy. A more detailed description of their legal expression in the Constitution is provided in Chapter 2.

Individual Liberty

Our belief in individual liberty has roots in the Judeo-Christian belief that every individual is equal and has worth before God. It has also been shaped by the works of the English philosophers Thomas Hobbes and John Locke. Briefly, they wrote that individuals give some of their rights to government so it can protect them from each other. Individuals then use their remaining liberties to pursue their individually defined visions of the good life. These ideas are part of social contract theory, which we discuss in Chapter 2.

Influenced by these ideas, early Americans emphasized individual liberty over other goals of government. James Madison, for example, justified the Constitution by writing that government's job is to protect the "diversity" of interests and abilities that exists among individuals. Liberty is also reflected in our long tradition of rights, deriving from Great Britain's. Usually, these rights are framed as powers *denied* to government—for example, government shall not deny freedom of assembly nor engage in unreasonable searches and seizures. Essentially, this means the overall right to be left alone by the government. Such individualistic values have molded popular expectations. Immigrants often came and still come to America to be their own bosses. The other side of this coin is that we are also at liberty to fail and accept the consequences. Although the opportunities for many individuals to get ahead in America are limited by prejudice and poverty, living in a society with an explicit commitment to individual liberty can be exciting and liberating.

Political Equality

The Judeo-Christian belief that all people are equal in the eyes of God reflects one type of equality, but it led logically to other types, such as political equality. The ancient Greek emphasis on the opportunity and responsibility of all citizens to participate in ruling their city-states also contributed to our notion of political equality. Thus, the Declaration of Independence proclaimed that "all Men are created equal." This did not mean that all people are born with equal talents or abilities. It meant that all citizens are born with equal standing before government and are entitled to equal rights.

In the early years of our country, however, as in the ancient Greek city-states, full rights of citizenship were conferred only on those thought to have the intellectual and moral judgment to act in the public interest. This wisdom could be acquired from experience in the public arena, such as through one's work, not just by formal education. In both Greece and the United States, such thinking denied political rights to slaves, who were believed incapable of independent judgment, and women, whose knowledge was seen as limited to the private or domestic sphere. This left a deep tension between the value of the individual conferred by religious belief and the secular concept of political rights rooted in circumstances of birth or acquired experience. Over time, this conflict was resolved in favor of the inherent worth of every individual and hence the political equality of all.

Americans have long considered themselves relatively equal politically and socially if not economically. Or, at minimum, they believe they are inherently equal, even when that condition cannot be realized in the political arena. Alexis de Tocqueville, a perceptive Frenchman who traveled through the United States in the 1830s, observed that Americans felt more equal than Europeans did. He attributed this feeling to the absence of a hereditary monarchy and aristocracy in this country. There was no tradition in America of looking up to kings and queens and aristocrats as one's "betters."

A belief in political equality leads to **popular sovereignty,** or rule by the people. Abraham Lincoln expressed this concept when he spoke of "government of the people, by the people and for the people." If individuals are equal, no one person or small group has the right to rule others. Instead, the people collectively rule themselves. And so we arrive at our form of government, a **democracy.** The word *democracy,* derived from the Greek, means "authority of the people." If all political authority resides in the people, then the people have the right to govern themselves.

"We can't come to an agreement about how to fix your car, Mr. Simons. Sometimes that's the way things happen in a democracy."

Majority Rule

If political authority rests in the people collectively, and if all people are equal, then the majority should rule. That is, when there are disagreements over policies, majorities rather than minorities should decide. If individuals are equal, then policies should be determined according to the desires of the greater number. Otherwise, some individuals would be bestowed with more authority than others.

Majority rule helps provide the support necessary to control the governed. Those in the minority go along because they accept this principle and expect to be in the majority on other issues. At a minimum, the minority expects those in the majority to respect their basic rights. If these expectations are not fulfilled, the minority is less likely to accept majority rule and tolerate majority decisions. Thus, majority rule necessarily entails minority rights.

Minority Rights

While majority rule is important, it sometimes conflicts with minority rights. Majorities make decisions *for* "the people" but in doing so do not *become* "the people." "The people" includes members of the majority *and* members of the minority. As a result, majorities that harm minority rights diminish everyone's rights. Sadly, as James Madison and other writers of the Constitution feared, majorities in the United States have sometimes forgotten this principle, the most egregious example being the enslavement of African Americans. At various times in our history, ethnic, political, and religious minorities have been denied basic rights. The idea that everyone loses when minority rights are trampled is a lesson that does not stay learned.

Thus, democratic principles sometimes contradict each other. These principles are goals more than reality. Americans have struggled for two centuries to reconcile practice with democratic aims and to perfect a system of government that was revolutionary for its time.

Economic Rights

The centrality of private property rights in the Founders' thinking about government is a subject we leave to Chapter 2. Here we call attention to the relationship between the political principles briefly described above and economic rights. Everyone is familiar with the idea that the American Revolution was triggered by what the colonists saw as unfair taxation and other economic burdens placed on them by the British Parliament. To a certain extent, Americans fought the Revolution to be left alone to pursue their livelihoods and to ensure that they would not have to give up any part of their wealth without their consent.

Economic freedom, specifically the right to own property, is an adjunct to our concepts of individual liberty and the "pursuit of happiness." But just as tension exists between majority and minority rights and between individual liberty and the good of all, so also there is potential conflict between the political equality the Declaration avows and the property rights it protects. Inevitably, some people, through inheritance, luck, or initiative, amass more wealth and power than others and come to exercise more influence over government. The ancient Greeks feared that democracy could not tolerate extremes of wealth and poverty. They thought a wealthy minority, out of smugness, and an impoverished minority, out of desperation, would try to act independently of the rest of the people and consequently would disregard the public interest. Early Americans worried less about this. They thought they could create a government that would protect individual diversity, including economic disparity, and still survive. But the pursuit of the goal of political equality in a real world of great economic inequities has led government to a much greater role in regulating economic activity than the Founders anticipated.

American Democracy in Practice

Democratic principles come alive only when people participate in government. But the principle of rule by the people can be implemented in various forms. In a large and complex society, as ours already was in 1789, direct democracy is not practical.

A **direct democracy** permits citizens to vote on most issues. The best example of a direct democracy is the town meeting, which has been the form of governance of many New England towns for over 350 years. Although town meetings today are often attended by relatively small numbers of citizens, they still offer one of the few opportunities people have to govern themselves directly. Citizens attending town meetings make their own decisions (for example, whether to put parking meters on the main street) and elect officers to enforce them (such as the police chief and city clerk).

Our national government is an **indirect democracy,** or a **republic.** Citizens have an indirect impact on government because they select policymakers to make decisions for them. Members of Congress, not rank-and-file citizens, vote bills into law. But these officials are not rulers; they are the representatives of the people and draw their authority from law sanctioned by the people.

Classical Democracy

The Greek philosopher Aristotle's definition of democracy emphasized the importance of citizen participation in government through debating, voting, and holding office. We call this vision **classical democracy.** In a classical democracy, citizens are committed to learning about and participating in government. They are well informed, discuss public affairs regularly, tell public officials what they think, and they vote. Some political theorists think that, compared to individuals who do not take their roles as democratic citizens seriously, those who do are more likely to see the complexities in issues and, while disagreeing with each other, still share common goals and work together to accomplish them.[24]

Political scientists initially accepted the classical democratic view as a fairly accurate picture of the American political process. By the 1940s, however, as they used information from surveys and voter turnout records, they discovered that far fewer citizens take advantage of their democratic rights than classical democratic theory predicts. For example, voting is a routine political activity. It is the easiest way to participate in politics and the least costly in terms of time and energy. Yet only one-half of Americans vote in presidential elections, and only one-third have voted in recent congressional elections. Even fewer vote in local elections. Instead of being motivated to participate in politics as in a classical democracy, most citizens are little involved. In fact, one-fifth of the electorate does nothing at all political; they do not even discuss politics.[25]

Only about one-tenth of the population takes full advantage of opportunities to participate. These activists give money to candidates, make phone calls, distribute leaflets, write letters to legislators, attend meetings, or join neighbors to work for a common end (such as improving local schools).

Why does the reality of political participation fall short of classical democratic expectations? One recent analysis argues that many Americans do not participate because they are turned off by, among other things, long political campaigns in which sound bites and negative campaigning replace meaningful dialogue about issues.[26] Another and more enduring explanation is that political participation is class based: people who partici-

pate tend to have more money and education. The working class and America's poorest, unlike their counterparts in many European countries, lack strong trade unions and political parties to represent them. American trade unions represent only about 14 percent of civilian employees and involve mostly middle-class and better-off workers. American political parties appeal more to middle-class than working-class interests, too.

The poor tend to belong to fewer organizations of any kind (civic groups, labor unions, or issue-oriented groups) than do the middle or upper classes. Political participation requires both time and money. Many poor adults are single heads of families with little spare time for political activity or resources for transportation and baby-sitters. As a result, they have fewer opportunities to be drawn into political action through such associations and in turn have no strong organizations to promote their political participation.

Race and ethnicity explain political participation, too, but not as well. Overall, blacks and Hispanics participate less than others, but this is due primarily to their average lower education and income levels. At each education and income level, blacks and Hispanics participate at about the same rates as whites.

Age also explains participation in politics. Young people participate much less than their elders. The middle-aged, who have the highest participation rate, are more apt to be established in a career and family life and have more time and money to devote to political activities. They are also less apt to be infirm than older people.

Thus, American government is not a classical democracy. Only a small minority of citizens fully participate in politics. Majorities cannot rule when most people do not take advantage of their rights by voting or trying to influence government or each other.[27] Furthermore, those who do participate are not representative of the whole population in class and other social characteristics. This can have an important impact on the kind of public policy we have. Elected officials chosen by people with more money and education are unlikely to have the same perspectives as those chosen by people with less money and education.

Pluralism

In the 1950s, many political scientists sought to reconcile democratic principles with the evidence that most people do not participate actively in politics. They thought they had an alternate explanation of how American democracy operated. In a theory called **pluralism,** they argued that enough people belong to interest groups to ensure that government ultimately hears everyone.[28] Individuals join others with like beliefs, and their group leaders and paid staff represent rank-and-file members to decision makers. According to pluralist theory, this process produces a kind of balance in which no group loses so often that it stops competing. As a result, no group or small number of groups can dominate government. This encourages people to continue to "play the game" by finding ways to compromise with each other. It also leads government to avoid major policy changes to maintain the balance and the popular support that comes with it.

Pluralist theory is attractive because it says democracy can work without everyone participating in politics. There is some validity to this theory. Thousands of interest groups in Washington employ experts to represent them in congressional corridors, bureaucratic agencies, and courtrooms.

As Chapter 6 shows, however, many people and issues fall through the cracks of interest group representation. The poor are especially unlikely to be organized or to have sufficient resources to fight political battles.

Groups may not always even represent the interests of their members. In 1915, Robert Michels formulated the "iron law of oligarchy."[29] This "law" says that effective power in a group, no matter what its size, usually goes to a few, an oligarchy or an elite. In fact, groups do create elites by electing officers and hiring staffs. As they spend more time on group affairs and develop ties to public officials, group leaders may come to see group interests differently than do many members. In addition, there is no guarantee that every issue can be resolved through competition. Intense competition between well-organized groups on some issues—such as abortion and gun control—sometimes makes compromise difficult.

Pluralism Reconsidered

The failure of pluralist theory to acknowledge the limited power of citizens with average or below-average incomes has led some political scientists to argue that American democracy is much less democratic than pluralists believed. Some theorists maintain that the holders of a few top jobs in key parts of the society dominate governmental decision making. These leaders include the chief officials of major corporations, universities, foundations, and media outlets, as well as the heads of important agencies of government, such as the Defense Department.

One political scientist identified 7,314 key jobs in major organizations such as these.[30] Some especially important jobs led to memberships on the boards of directors of other organizations. In addition, he found that about 4,300 elite business leaders controlled well over 50 percent of America's corporate wealth and that almost 40 percent of them had once held a government post. If this is right, relatively few people share the most powerful jobs and make some of the most important decisions in America.

There is another very different interpretation of elitism. In contrast to the conception of a malignant power elite who conspire against reform and in support of policies keeping economic and political power in their hands, others argue that throughout the twentieth century groups of elites acted primarily to promote the general welfare. This view holds that without the academics and intellectuals from the Ivy League, think tanks, and foundations like the Brookings Institution and Ford Foundation, we would not have had the sweeping social welfare and redistributive policies of Franklin Roosevelt's New Deal or the War on Poverty legislation of the Kennedy and Johnson administrations. Elites are often best situated to win these battles, the argument maintains, because they occupy "A position of independence, between the wealthy and the people . . . prepared to curb the excesses of either."[31]

But the argument that government is run by the few rather than the many continues to find credibility with the public. Fifty-four percent of respondents to a 1999 poll said government of, by, and for the people no longer applies.[32]

It is often hard to know what is *really* going on in Washington and easy to be frustrated when the process yields outcomes we do not like. It is misleading, however, to think that a few powerful people determine everything. America's diversity produces too many different interests and opinions to permit this. And political power is dispersed among local, state, and federal decision makers as well as across the private sector in corporate boardrooms and the leadership councils of interest groups and trade unions. There is abundant evidence that these decision makers are often in conflict or competition with one another. Nevertheless, theories of power elites are useful because they remind us that tremendous inequalities of resources exist, enabling some parts of society to influence government more than others.

Gradually, most political scientists have come to agree that interest groups do not represent everyone, especially the poor, the working class, and the apathetic. Yet a handful of people in powerful positions do not decide everything either. Policy often reflects a compromise of competing interests.

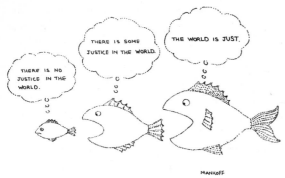

Current perspectives on how government works stress the "veto" many interest groups can exercise on issues affecting them. Some political scientists have labeled this **hyperpluralism,** suggesting a pluralist system run wild. With so many interests, it is difficult to find common ground to work out solutions to problems. The close ties of many interests to congressional committees and subcommittees considering legislation allow them to stop policy ideas they dislike. And modern technology heightens their impact. A witness to congressional hearings on tax reform reported that lobbyists used cellular phones to produce floods of protest by phone or fax the instant anyone "even *thought*" about something they opposed.[33] So many powerful groups with clout exist that attempts to alter the status quo or change national priorities are extremely difficult. Presidents Carter, Reagan, and Clinton found this out when they tried to make major changes in energy, budget, and health care policy, respectively. The Clinton White House tried to work with over 1,100 interest groups on health care reform, to no avail.[34] Efforts to bring about major changes in national domestic priorities are extremely difficult. It is telling that one of the most sweeping changes in entrenched policy was the overhaul of the welfare system, a reform whose impact will be felt primarily by the poorest and least politically active Americans.

The difficulties created by interest group vetoes often contribute to gridlock and what one observer calls the "blame game."[35] Gridlock occurs when policies are not enacted or administered effectively because the president and Congress cannot agree on what to do. Politicians representing different interests often blame each other for this inaction, or play the "blame game," when they see that gridlock is likely to keep them from getting what they want. The blame game encourages elected officials to distrust each other and furthers public cynicism about government's responsiveness and effectiveness.

Given the presence of many strong groups and their veto opportunities, passing a law means fashioning compromises out of competing group views.[36] In addition to being slow, the process often leads to vaguely worded laws giving actual policymaking authority to bureaucrats who work less visibly with interest group help. In effect, agencies and interest groups, not Congress, often legislate. Thus, chemical industry lobbyists help write regulations on hazardous waste, and military contractors help the Pentagon write weapons contracts.

The growth of bureaucratic policymaking makes our democracy more indirect than the writers of the Constitution intended. Most citizens cannot monitor and influence the actions of the president and 535 members of Congress organized into over three hundred committees, subcommittees, *and* bureaucratic agencies. The leaders of major interest groups can, and this gives them considerable power. The possibility that these leaders may be relatively independent of their rank-and-file memberships makes them even more important.

These views challenge the pluralist explanation by concluding that government responds to many but not all groups. This suggests a hybrid explanation of American government stressing the clout of more powerful groups, whose leaders may belong to a larger, more diversified elite.

Conclusion: Is Government Responsive?

America has a split political personality. Most people have a low opinion of Congress, yet we reelect most of its members. We love the idea that the average person has a say in government, yet half of us do not vote, even in presidential elections. We criticize big government while complaining that it does not do very much. As one newspaper columnist put it, "All the evidence suggests that when Americans look at Washington they see a conniving bunch of hustlers playing an insider's game at the expense of the nation."[37] Most people feel that government is out of their control and unrepresentative of their interests.

Why do we act as if we dislike democracy in action? Has government failed? Are the laws it enacts not what the people want? Is it the fault of the media, emphasizing mostly the negative side of government? Are average citizens actually shut out of the process? Or is the problem really the fault of citizens, and not government at all?

For all their anger with government over the years, many Americans are not well informed about it. That many are not helps explain the public's attraction to quick fixes and seemingly easy solutions. Thus, many Americans continue to demand tax cuts but oppose spending cuts that affect them (half of all households receive some sort of federal financial payment).[38] They want democracy but no arguments or compromises.

Quick fixes look good to those who are poorly informed about government and who resent the debating, compromises, and slowness of democracy. But a quick fix and a free lunch are a lot alike: there are no such things.

American government is characterized by conflict and compromise because Americans do not agree on either the nature of the problems that confront us or their solutions. If we all agreed, there would be no need for debate, bargaining, compromise, or delays.

Although we are not equally well situated to influence policymakers, more avenues for political participation are available now than ever before.

In contemporary America, the number of organized interests and their effectiveness in making their views known have multiplied so dramatically that government officials are besieged by a cacophony of views. And this development has occurred in an era when the workings of government are increasingly in public view.

"Remember when people had only themselves to blame?"

We have argued that much of this is a necessary component of a democratic system in a large and diverse nation. Nonetheless, to say we must live with debate, compromise, and slowness in our system does not mean we cannot improve and speed the workings of government. In coming chapters, we will carefully examine the major institutions and processes of our democracy to see whether we can shed light on how they contribute to public dissatisfaction and how they might be improved.

EPILOGUE

What Will You Do?

This is the only epilogue where the authors cannot provide the outcome of the decision-making process. But we can speculate. Based on present evidence, there is only one chance in two that you cast your vote in the presidential election in 2000—that chance is much less if you are under twenty-five years of age. The chance that you will vote in any local elections is from 10 percent to 20 percent, and that you will become politically active beyond voting, only 20 percent. Where do you fit into this pattern?

Collectively, Americans have been accused of practicing "couch potato politics," refusing to accept the responsibilities of national citizenship.[39] Most of us, even those highly dissatisfied with the way government works, do not want a king, a dictator, or an emperor to make decisions for us. Indeed, democracy assumes that majorities control government and indirect democracy assumes that citizens control their representatives. This means that people need to get up off their couches and participate. It does not appear to be happening. In 1999, nearly half of all eighteen- to twenty-four-year-olds said they felt disconnected from government.[40] Yet the razor-thin 2000 election margin illustrated that the participation and votes of every citizen can be crucial.

About their unwillingness to get involved in issue debates or the electoral process, Americans often say, "It's all politics." Of course! Issue debates and elections are political because the competition to determine what policy will be is essential to government. Politics is inescapable because divergence of interests is unavoidable.

More than two thousand years ago, Aristotle wrote that politics is the most noble endeavor in which people can engage, partly because it helps them know themselves and partly because it forces them to relate to others. Through political participation individuals pursue their own needs and interests, but not without consideration for the needs of other citizens. In other words, it is through politics that we learn to balance our own needs and interests against the good of the political community as a whole.

Today Americans are less inclined to share Aristotle's conception of politics than the cynical view of novelist Gore Vidal that "who collects what money from whom in order to spend on what is all there is to politics."[41]

In a 1999 poll asking "What's wrong with government?," 38 percent of respondents named special interests, 29 percent said the media, while elected officials and political parties were each tabbed by 24 percent.[42] No one blamed the voters. The same poll had eight out of ten respondents saying they believed government will be as or more important in improving people's lives in the next century as it has been in the past. If this is what we believe, then dropping out of the political process because we think it is futile or controlled by special interests is like cutting off our noses to spite our faces.

Politics is necessary to govern a democratic society. Ignoring politics and the institutions we have to represent ourselves, such as political parties and interest groups, will not eliminate politics. Rather, it would eliminate the most effective ways yet developed for the public to influence government's decisions.

Key Terms

politics
indifference
identity politics
political culture
popular sovereignty
democracy

direct democracy
indirect democracy
republic
classical democracy
pluralism
hyperpluralism

Further Reading

Joyce Appleby, *Inheriting the Revolution* (Cambridge, Mass.: Harvard University Press, 2000). A historian looks at what the first generation of Americans made of their new government and how they invented a new culture and identity. Special emphasis is given to the rise of a community of free Black Americans.

John E. Chubb and Paul E. Peterson, *Can the Government Govern?* (Washington, D.C.: Brookings Institution, 1989). A collection of case studies showing how the public interest often suffers when elected officials and bureaucrats avoid hard policy choices by playing the blame game with each other and "special interests."

Edward Countryman, *Americans: A Collision of Histories* (New York: Hill & Wang, 1996). A historian traces the history of the dominant ethnic groups in America from 1600 to 1900. He argues that the very different experiences of Native, African, and European Americans mean that there is no unified American history and no one "type" who can be identified as American.

William Greider, *Who Will Tell the People: The Betrayal of American Democracy* (New York: Simon & Schuster, 1992). A populist perspective that views Washington politics as a "grand bazaar" where wealthy interest groups exchange favors with public officials who want to maintain their power.

John B. Judis, *The Paradox of American Democracy: Elites, Special Interests and the Betrayal of Public Trust* (New York: Pantheon, 1999). A counterargument to the malignant interpretation of elitism, this book attributes the twentieth century's great waves of reform and social welfare legislation to small groups of Ivy League and think tank elites.

Harold Lasswell, *Politics: Who Gets What, When, How* (New York: New World, 1958). A classic treatment of some very practical political problems.

Pauline Maier, *American Scripture: The Making of the Declaration of Independence* (New York: Knopf, 1997). A historian offers a revisionist view of the importance of the Declaration by arguing that its language was not original but rather was almost identical in content to that of ninety other declarations written in the colonies at the same time. Given the widespread agreement on language and principles in all these documents, she judges the Declaration "an expression of the American mind."

Michael J. Sandel, *Democracy's Discontent: America in Search of a Public Philosophy* (Cambridge, Mass.: Harvard University Press, Belknap, 1996). A political theorist argues that American politics is "ill-equipped to allay discontent" over the unraveling moral fabric of the country and suggests that one reason is the supremacy of individual rights over community interests.

Hedrick Smith, *The Power Game: How Washington Works* (New York: Random House, 1988). A Pulitzer Prize–winning journalist's account of the colorful personalities and complex alliances that shape national policymaking. Loaded with good anecdotes.

Electronic Resources

In each chapter we will provide a few addresses to the Internet for particularly useful or interesting sites relevant to the chapter. Today, you can access information, including statistics and information about public officials, that was formerly accessible only in libraries. Unlike library call numbers, however, Internet addresses sometimes change.

www.census.gov/
The primary source for results of the 2000 census.

www.fedstats.gov/index20.html
This site of the Immigration and Naturalization Service leads you to official statistics on immigration flows to the United States. http://www.fedstats.gov is a central link to all federal statistics.

www.firstgov.gov/
This is a central federal government site providing links to 27 million government Web pages, including all branches of government, federal agencies and commissions, and important policy areas.

lcweb.loc.gov/exhibits/religion
A rich source on the role of religion in the founding of the American republic and on the relationship between organized religion and the state governments. Contains many original documents on the relationship between church and state.

InfoTrac College Edition

"We Can Play a Big Part"
"Imminent Immigration"
"What Voters Want"
"Situating Social Attitudes Toward Cultural Pluralism"

Notes

1. See John Hibbing and Beth Theiss-Morse, *Congress as Public Enemy: Public Attitudes toward American Political Institutions* (Cambridge: Cambridge University Press, 1995); Hibbing and Theiss-Morse, "Civics Is Not Enough; Teaching Barbarics in K-12," forthcoming in *PS;* Gabriel A. Almond and Sidney Verba, *The Civic Culture* (Boston: Little, Brown, 1965), p. 64.

2. Hibbing and Theiss-Morse, *Congress.*

3. Walt Whitman, *Leaves of Grass and Selected Prose,* ed. Lawrence Buell (New York: Random House, 1981), p. 449.

4. Edward Countryman, *Americans: A Collision of Histories* (New York: Hill & Wang, 1996), pp. 3–22.

5. John Sugden, *Tecumseh: A Life* (New York: Holt, 1998).

6. Michael J. Sandel, *Democracy's Discontent: America in Search of a Public Philosophy* (Cambridge, Mass.: Harvard University Press, Belknap, 1997). Sandel points out that the Constitution prohibited only the federal government, not the states, from establishing an official religion.

7. Dick Kirschten, "American Dreamer," *National Journal,* July 5, 1997, p. 1364; Susan Welch and Timothy Bledsoe, *Urban Reform and Its Consequences* (Chicago: University of Chicago Press, 1988), p. 2.

8. "Legal Immigration, Fiscal Year 1997," Immigration and Naturalization Service, Office of Policy and Planning, Annual Report, no. 1, January 1999, pp. 4–5 and Table 3, p. 10.

9. *1996 Statistical Abstract of the Immigration and Naturalization Service,* p. 11.

10. "Legal Immigration, Fiscal Year 1997," p. 5.

11. Michael Lind, "The Beige and the Black," *New York Times Magazine,* August 16, 1998, p. 38.

12. "Belief by the Numbers," *New York Times Magazine,* December 7, 1997, pp. 60–61; Gustav Niebur, "Makeup of American Religion Is Looking More like Mosaic, Data Say," *New York Times,* April 12, 1998, p. 12.

13. Quoted by James Q. Wilson in "The History and Future of Democracy," lecture delivered at the Reagan presidential library November 15, 1999 (reprinted by School of Public Policy, Pepperdine University), p. 3.

14. Robert Reinhold, "Resentment against New Immigrants," *New York Times,* October 26, 1986, p. 6E.

15. George F. Will, "Buchanan Takes Aim," *Washington Post National Weekly Edition,* December 16–22, 1991, p. 28.

16. The *Christian American,* quoted in Dick Kirschten, "Building Blocs," *National Journal,* September 26, 1993, p. 2173.

17. Walter Benn Michaels, *Our America: Nativism, Modernism, and Pluralism* (Durham, N.C.: Duke University Press, 1997).

18. Bureau of the Census, *General Social and Economy Characteristics: U.S. Summary* (Washington, D.C.: U.S. Government Printing Office, 1990), Part 1, Table 12.

19. Steven A. Holmes, "The Politics of Race and the Census," *New York Times,* March 19, 2000, section 4, p. 4.

20. Reported in Tom Morganthau, "What Color Is Black?" *Newsweek,* February 13, 1995, p. 64. Data on black-white intermarriage are found in Susan Kalish "Interracial Baby Boomlet in Progress?" *Population Today* 20 (December 1992), pp. 1–2.

21. Michael Thompson, Richard Ellis, and Aaron Wildavsky, *Cultural Theory* (Boulder, Colo.: Westview, 1990), p. 216.

22. Garry Wills, *Lincoln at Gettysburg: The Words That Remade America* (New York: Simon & Schuster, 1992), p. 145.

23. For a discussion of the Declaration of Independence's origins in pragmatism versus the political philosophy of the Founders, see Pauline Maier, *American Scripture: Making the Declaration of Independence* (New York: Knopf, 1997).

24. For a discussion of this see Mark Warren, "Democratic Theory and Self-Transformation," *American Political Science Review* 86 (March 1992), pp. 8–23.

25. This discussion draws on Sidney Verba and Norman Nie, *Participation in America* (New York: Harper & Row, 1972), and Stephen Earl Bennett and Linda L. M. Bennett, "Political Participation," in *Annual Review of Political Science,* ed. Samuel Long, (Norwood, N.J.: Ablex, 1986).

26. E. J. Dionne Jr., *Why Americans Hate Politics* (New York: Simon & Schuster, 1991).

27. Robert A. Dahl, *A Preface to Democratic Theory* (Chicago: University of Chicago Press, 1956), p. 142.

28. See Arthur F. Bentley, *The Process of Government* (Chicago: University of Chicago Press, 1908), and David Truman, *The Governmental Process* (New York: Knopf, 1951).

29. Robert Michels, *Political Parties* (New York: Collier, 1915).

30. Thomas R. Dye, *Who's Running America? The Bush Era* (Englewood Cliffs, NJ: Prentice Hall, 1990), p. 12.

31. John B. Judis, *The Paradox of American Democracy: Elites, Special Interests and the Betrayal of Public Trust* (New York: Pantheon, 1999). Judis is senior editor of *The New Republic.*

32. David S. Broder, "Where Did Our Government Go?" *Washington Post National Weekly Edition,* July 19–26, 1999, p. 37.

33. Reported in Robert Wright, "Hyper Democracy," *Time,* January 23, 1995, p. 18.

34. David S. Broder, "Can We Govern?" *Washington Post National Weekly Edition,* January 31–February 6, 1994, p. 23.

35. Hedrick Smith, *The Power Game: How Washington Works* (New York: Random House, 1988), chapter 17.

36. For example, see Theodore J. Lowi, *The End of Liberalism,* 2d ed. (New York: Norton, 1979).

37. *New York Times* columnist Russell Baker, reprinted in the *Champaign-Urbana News-Gazette,* August 29, 1997, p. A4.

38. Michael Wines, "Taxpayers Are Angry. They're Expensive, Too," *New York Times,* November 20, 1994, p. E5.

39. This was the headline on an op-ed piece by the sociologist Alan Wolfe in the *New York Times,* March 15, 1998, section 4, p. 17. He was summarizing the results of a survey of middle-class opinion he published in *One Nation, After All* (New York: Viking, 1997).

40. Broder, "Where Did Our Government Go?"

41. Gore Vidal, "Coached by Camelot," *New Yorker,* December 1, 1997, p. 88.

42. E. J. Dionne Jr., "Preferring Policies over Politics," *Washington Post National Weekly Edition,* February 7, 2000, p. 22.

The Constitution

YOU ARE THERE

The Case of the Confidential Tapes

In June 1972, a security guard for the Watergate building in Washington, D.C., noticed that tape had been placed across the latch of a door to keep it from locking. The guard peeled off the tape. When he made his rounds later, he noticed that more tape had been placed across the latch. He called the police.

The police encountered five burglars in the headquarters of the Democratic National Committee. Wearing surgical gloves and carrying tear gas guns, photographic equipment, and electronic gear, they had been installing wiretaps on the Democratic Party's phones.

No one expected this break-in to lead to the White House. The *Washington Post* assigned two young reporters who usually covered local matters to the story. But the unlikely pair of Bob Woodward, a Yale graduate, and Carl Bernstein, a college dropout, were ambitious, and they uncovered a series of bizarre connections. The burglars had links to President Richard Nixon's Committee to Reelect the President (CREEP).

The administration dismissed the break-in as the work of overzealous underlings. Even the press called it a "caper." Indeed, it was hard to imagine that high officials in the administration

could be responsible. In public opinion polls, Nixon enjoyed an enormous lead, almost 20 percent, over the various Democrats vying for their party's nomination to challenge him in the fall election. Risky tactics seemed unnecessary.

But Woodward and Bernstein discovered that White House staff members had engaged in other criminal and unethical actions to sabotage the Democrats' campaign. They had forged letters accusing some of the Democrats' candidates of homosexual acts. Later they had obtained and publicized psychiatric records, causing the Democrats' vice presidential nominee to resign.

Nixon won reelection handily, but the revelations forced his two top aides to resign and prompted the Senate to establish a special committee to investigate what was being called the **Watergate scandal.** When investigators happened to ask a lower-level aide to the president whether there was a taping device in the Oval Office, he said, "I was hoping you fellows wouldn't ask me about that." Then he revealed what only a handful of aides had known—that Nixon had secretly tape-recorded conversations in nine locations in the White House, the Executive Office Building across the street, and Camp David

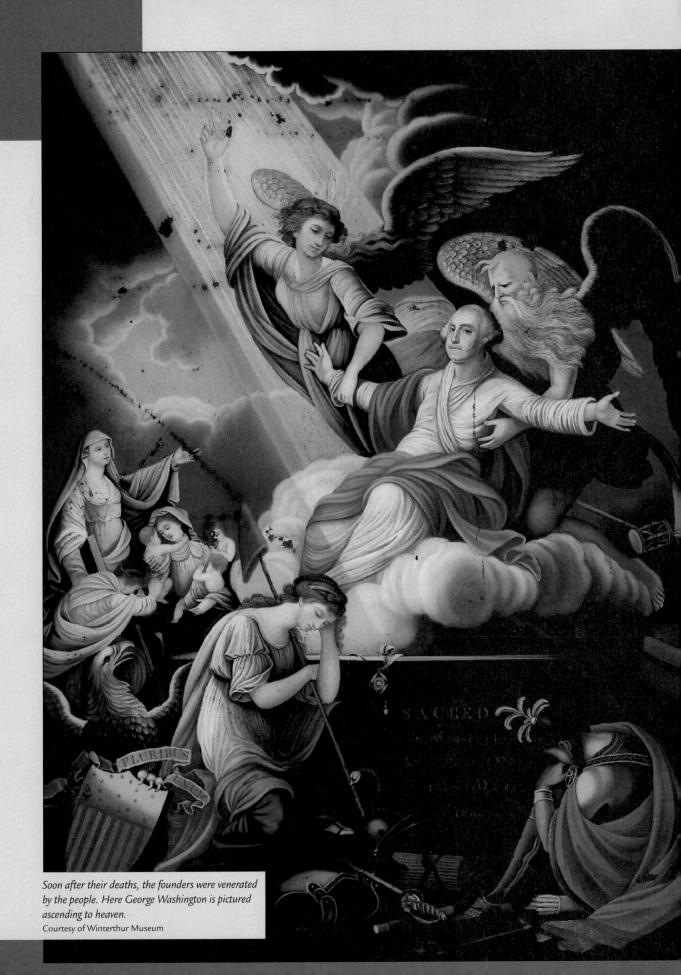

Soon after their deaths, the founders were venerated by the people. Here George Washington is pictured ascending to heaven.
Courtesy of Winterthur Museum

Washington Post *reporters Carl Bernstein (left) and Bob Woodward uncovered the Watergate scandal.*

Dennis Brack Ltd./Black Star

in Maryland. Nixon had intended to create a comprehensive record of his presidency to demonstrate his greatness.[1]

The tapes could confirm or refute charges of White House complicity in the break-in and cover-up, but Nixon refused to release them. Special Prosecutor Archibald Cox filed suit to force Nixon to do so, and federal trial court Judge John Sirica ordered him to do so. After the federal appeals court affirmed the trial court's decision, Nixon demanded that his attorney general fire Cox. The attorney general and deputy attorney general both refused and resigned in protest. Then the third-ranking official in the Justice Department, Robert Bork, fired the special prosecutor. (Bork later would be nominated to the Supreme Court by President Reagan.)

The public furor over this "Saturday Night Massacre" was so intense that Nixon finally did release some tapes. But one crucial tape contained a mysterious eighteen-minute gap that a presidential aide speculated was caused by "some sinister force."

To mollify critics, Nixon appointed a new special prosecutor, Leon Jaworski. After his investigation, Jaworski presented evidence to a grand jury that indicted seven of the president's aides for the cover-up, specifically for obstruction of justice, and even named the president as an "unindicted coconspirator."

The House Judiciary Committee considered impeaching the president, and Jaworski subpoenaed more tapes. Nixon issued edited transcripts of the conversations but not the tapes themselves. As a compromise he proposed that one person listen to the tapes—a senator who was seventy-two years old and hard of hearing. Frustrated, Jaworski went to court, where Judge Sirica ordered Nixon to release the tapes. When Nixon refused, Jaworski appealed directly to the Supreme Court.

You are Chief Justice Warren Burger, appointed to the Court by President Nixon in 1969 partly because of your calls for more law and order. Three of your brethren also were appointed by Nixon. In the case of *United States v. Nixon,* you are

faced with a question that could lead to a grave constitutional showdown with the president. Special Prosecutor Jaworski claims he needs the tapes because they contain evidence pertaining to the upcoming trial of the president's aides indicted for the cover-up. Without all relevant evidence, which possibly could vindicate the aides, the trial court might not convict them.

President Nixon claims he has **executive privilege**—authority to withhold information from the courts and Congress. Although the Constitution does not mention such a privilege, Nixon claims the privilege is inherent in the powers of the presidency. Without it presidents could not guarantee confidentiality in conversations with other officials or even foreign leaders. This could make it difficult for them to govern.

You have few precedents to guide you. Many past presidents exercised executive privilege when pressed for information by Congress. In these instances, Congress ordinarily acquiesced rather than sued for the information, so the courts did not rule on the existence of the privilege. Once, in 1953, the Eisenhower administration invoked the privilege, and the Supreme Court upheld the claim. However, that case involved national security.[2]

In addition to considering the merits of the opposing sides, you also need to consider the extent of the Court's power. The Court lacks strong means to enforce its rulings. It has to rely on its authority as the highest interpreter of the law in the country. Therefore, if the Court orders Nixon to relinquish the tapes and Nixon refuses, there would be little the Court could do. The refusal would show future officials they could disregard your orders with impunity.

In this high-stakes contest, do you and your brethren on the Court order Nixon to turn over the tapes, or do you accept his claim of executive privilege?

Early settlers came to America for many reasons. Some came to escape religious persecution, others to establish their own religious orthodoxy. Some came to get rich, others to avoid debtors' prison. Some came to enrich their families or companies in the Old World, others to flee the closed society of that world. Some came as free persons, others as indentured servants or slaves. Few came to practice self-government. Yet the desire for self-government was evident from the beginning.[3] The settlers who arrived in Jamestown in 1607 established the first representative assembly in America. The pilgrims who reached Plymouth in 1620 drew up the Mayflower Compact in which they vowed to "solemnly & mutually in the presence of God, and one of another, covenant and combine our selves together into a civill body politick." They pledged to establish laws for "the generall good of the colonie" and in return promised "all due submission and obedience."[4]

During the next century and a half, the colonies adopted constitutions and elected representative assemblies. Of course, the colonies lived under British rule; they had to accept the appointment of royal governors and the presence of British troops. But a vast ocean separated the two continents. At such a distance, Britain could not wield the control it might at closer reach. Consequently, it granted the colonies a measure of autonomy, with which they practiced a degree of self-government.

These early efforts toward self-government led to conflict with the mother government. In 1774, the colonies established the Continental Congress to coordinate their actions. Within months the conflict reached flashpoint, and the Congress urged the colonies to form their own governments. In 1776, the Congress adopted the Declaration of Independence.

After six years of war, the Americans accepted the British surrender. At the time it seemed they had met their biggest test. Yet they would find fomenting a revolution easier than fashioning a government and drafting a declaration of independence easier than crafting a constitution.

The Articles of Confederation

Even before the war ended, the Continental Congress passed a constitution, and in 1781 the states ratified it. This first constitution, the **Articles of Confederation,** formed a "league of friendship" among the states. As a

confederation, it allowed each state to retain its "sovereignty" and "independence." That is, it made the states supreme over the national government.

Under the Articles, however, Americans would face problems with both their national and state governments.

National Government Problems

The Articles established a Congress, with one house in which each state had one vote. But they strictly limited the powers that Congress could exercise, and they provided no executive or judicial branch.

The Articles reflected the colonial experience under the British government. The leaders feared a powerful central government with a powerful executive like a king. They thought such a government would be too strong and too distant to guarantee individual liberty. Additionally, the Articles reflected a lack of national identity among the people. Most did not view themselves as Americans yet. As Edmund Randolph remarked, "I am not really an American, I am a Virginian."[5] Consequently, the leaders established a very decentralized government that left most authority to the states.

The Articles satisfied many people. Most people were small farmers, and although many of them sank into debt during the depression that followed the war, they felt they could influence the state governments to help them. They realized they could not influence a distant central government as readily.

But the Articles frustrated bankers, merchants, manufacturers, and others in the upper classes. They envisioned a great commercial empire replacing the agricultural society that existed in the late eighteenth century. More than local trade, they wanted national and even international trade. For this they needed uniform laws, stable money, sound credit, and enforceable debt collection. They needed a strong central government that could protect them against debtors and against state governments sympathetic to debtors. The Articles provided neither the foreign security nor the domestic climate necessary to nourish these requisites of a commercial empire.

After the war the army disbanded, leaving the country vulnerable to hostile forces surrounding it. Britain maintained outposts with troops in the Northwest Territory (now the Midwest), in violation of the peace treaty, and an army in Canada. Spain, which had occupied Florida and California for a long time and had claimed the Mississippi River valley as a result of a treaty before the war, posed a threat. Barbary pirates from North Africa seized American ships and sailors.

Although the Articles gave the federal government authority to print money, the states circulated their own currencies as well.
Corbis-Bettmann

Congress could not raise an army, because it could not draft individuals directly, or finance an army, because it could not tax individuals directly. Instead, it had to ask the states for soldiers and money. The states, however, were not always sympathetic to the problems of the distant government. And although Congress could make treaties with foreign countries, the states made, or broke, treaties independently of Congress. Without the ability to establish a credible army or negotiate a binding treaty, the government could not get the British troops out of the country. Neither could it get the British government to ease restrictions on shipping or the Spanish government to permit navigation on the Mississippi River.

In addition to an inability to confront foreign threats, the Articles demonstrated an inability to cope with domestic crises. The country bore a heavy war debt that brought the government close to bankruptcy. Since Congress could not tax individuals directly, it could not shore up the shaky government.

The states competed with each other for commercial advantage. As independent governments, they imposed tariffs on goods from other states. The tariffs slowed the growth of businesses.

In short, the government under the Articles seemed too decentralized to ensure either peace or prosperity. The Articles, one leader concluded, gave Congress the privilege of asking for everything, while reserving to each state the prerogative of granting nothing.[6] A similar situation exists today in the United Nations, which must rely on member countries to furnish troops for its peacekeeping forces and dues for its operating expenses.

The government under the Articles, however, could boast of one major accomplishment. The Northwest Ordinance, adopted in 1787, provided for the government and future statehood of the land west of Pennsylvania (land that would become most of the Great Lakes states). The law also banned slavery in this territory.

State Government Problems

Other conflicts arose closer to home. State constitutions adopted during the Revolution made the state legislatures more representative than the colonial legislatures had been. Most state legislatures also began to hold elections every year. The result was heightened interest among candidates and turnover among legislators. In the eyes of national leaders, there was much pandering to voters and horsetrading by politicians as various factions vied for control. The process seemed up for grabs. According to the Vermont Council of Censors, laws were "altered—realtered—made better—made worse; and kept in such a fluctuating position that persons in civil commission scarce know what is law."[7] In short, state governments were experiencing more democracy than any other governments in the world at the time. National leaders, stunned by the changes in the few years since the Revolution, considered this development an "excess of democracy."

Moreover, state constitutions made the legislative branch the most powerful. Some state legislatures began to dominate the other branches, and national leaders called them "tyrannical."

The national leaders, most of whom were wealthy and many of whom were creditors, pointed to the laws passed in some states that relieved debtors of some of their obligations. The farmers who were in debt pressed the legislatures for relief that would slow or shrink the payments owed to their creditors. Some legislatures granted such relief.

While these laws worried the leaders, **Shays's Rebellion** in western Massachusetts in 1786 and 1787 scared them. Boston merchants who had loaned Massachusetts money during the war insisted on being repaid in full so they could trade with foreign merchants. The state levied steep taxes that many farmers could not pay during the hard times. The law authorized foreclosure—sale of the farmers' property for the taxes—and jail for the debtors. The law essentially transferred wealth from the farmers to the merchants. The farmers protested the legislature's refusal to grant any relief from the law. Bands of farmers blocked entrances to courthouses where judges were scheduled to hear cases calling for foreclosure and jail. Led by Daniel Shays, some marched to the Springfield arsenal to seize weapons. Although they were defeated by the militia, their sympathizers were victorious in the next election, and the legislature did provide some relief from the law.

Both the revolt and the legislature's change in policy frightened the wealthy. To them it raised the specter of "mob rule." Nathaniel Gorham, the president of the Continental Congress and a prominent merchant, wrote Prince Henry of Prussia, announcing "the failure of our free institutions" and asking whether the prince would agree to become king of America (the prince declined).[8] Just months after the uprising, Congress approved a convention for "the sole and express purpose of revising the Articles of Confederation."

To a significant extent, then, the debate at the time reflected a conflict between two competing visions of the future American political economy—agricultural or commercial.[9] Most leaders espoused the latter, and the combination of national problems and state problems prompted them to push for a new government.

The Constitution

The Constitutional Convention

The Setting

The **Constitutional Convention** convened in Philadelphia, then the country's largest city, in 1787. That year the Industrial Revolution was continuing to sweep Europe and beginning to reach this continent. The first American cotton mill opened in Massachusetts, and the first American steamboat plied the Delaware River.[10]

State legislatures chose seventy-four delegates to the convention; fifty-five attended. They met at the Pennsylvania State House—now Independence Hall—in the same room where some of them had signed the Declaration of Independence eleven years before. (See also the box "Founding Mothers.")

Delegates came from every state except Rhode Island. That state was controlled by farmers and debtors who feared that the convention would weaken states' powers to relieve debtors of their debts.

The delegates were distinguished by their education, experience, and enlightenment. Benjamin Franklin, of Pennsylvania, was the best-known American in the world. He had been a printer, scientist, and diplomat. At 81 he was the oldest delegate. George Washington, of Virginia, was the most respected American in the country. As the commander of the revolutionary army, he was a national hero. He was chosen to preside over the convention. The presence of men like Franklin and Washington gave the convention legitimacy.

The delegates quickly determined that the Articles were hopeless. Rather than revise them, as instructed by Congress, the delegates decided to start over and draft a new constitution.[11] But what would they substitute for the Articles?

The Predicament

The delegates came to the convention because they complained about a government that was too weak. Yet previously Americans had fought a revolution because they chafed under a government that was too strong. "The nation lived in a nearly constant alternation of fears that it would cease being a nation altogether or become too much of one."[12] People feared both anarchy and tyranny.

This predicament was made clear by the diversity of opinions among the leaders. At one extreme was Patrick Henry, of Virginia, who had been a firebrand of the Revolution. He felt the government would become too strong, perhaps even become a monarchy, in reaction to the current problems with the Articles. He said he "smelt a rat" and did not attend the convention. At the other extreme was Alexander Hamilton, of New York, who had been an aide to General Washington during the war and had seen the government's inability to supply and pay its own troops. Since then he had called for a stronger national government. He wanted one that could veto the laws of the state governments. He also wanted one person to serve as chief executive for life and others to serve as senators for life. He did attend the convention but, finding little agreement with his proposals, participated infrequently.

Charles Francis Adams, a grandson of President John Adams and Abigail Adams, declared in 1840, "The heroism of the females of the Revolution has gone from memory with the generation that witnessed it, and nothing, absolutely nothing remains upon the ear of the young of the present day."[1] That statement is still true today; in the volumes written about the revolutionary and Constitution-making eras, much is said of the "Founding Fathers" and very little about the "Founding Mothers." Although no women were at the Constitutional Convention, in many other ways women contributed significantly to the political ferment of the time. The political role of women during the Constitution-making era was probably greater than it would be again for a century.

Before the Revolutionary War, women were active in encouraging opposition to the British. Groups of women, some called the "daughters of liberty," led boycotts of British goods as part of the protest campaign against taxation without representation. A few women were political pamphleteers, helping increase public sentiment for independence. One of those pamphlet writers, Mercy Otis Warren, of Massachusetts, was thought to be the first person to urge the Massachusetts delegates to the Continental Congress to vote for separation from Britain.[2] Throughout the period before and after the Revolution, Warren shared her political ideas in personal correspondence with leading statesmen of the time, such as John Adams and Thomas Jefferson. Later she wrote a three-volume history of the American Revolution.

Many women were part of the American army during the battles for independence. Most filled traditional women's roles as cooks, seamstresses, and nurses, but some disguised themselves as men (this was before a military bureaucracy mandated preenlistment physical exams)

and fought in battle. One such woman, wounded in action in 1776, is the only Revolutionary War veteran buried at West Point. Still other women fought to defend their homes using hatchets, farm implements, and pots of boiling lye in addition to muskets.

Following independence, some women continued an active political role. Mercy Warren, for example, campaigned against the proposed Constitution because she felt it was not democratic enough.

Independence did not bring any improvement in the political rights of women. In fact, after the Constitution was adopted, some rights that women had held before were gradually lost, such as the right of some women to vote. It was to be another century before the rights of women became a full-fledged part of our national political agenda.

1. Quoted in Linda Grant DePauw and Conover Hunt, *Remember the Ladies* (New York: Viking, 1976), p. 9.
2. Alice Felt Tyler, *Freedom's Ferment* (New York: Harper & Row, 1962).

A SOCIETY of PATRIOTIC LADIES, AT EDENTON in NORTH CAROLINA.

This English political cartoon satirizes a gathering of leading women in North Carolina who drew up a resolution to boycott taxed English goods and tea.
The Metropolitan Museum of Art, Bequest of Charles Allen Munn, 1924 (24-90-35)

In between were those like James Madison, of Virginia. Small and frail, timid and self-conscious as a speaker, he was nonetheless intelligent and savvy as a politician. He had operated behind the scenes to convene the convention and to secure Washington's attendance. (He publicized that Washington would attend without asking Washington first. Washington, who was in retirement, did not plan to attend and only reluctantly agreed to do so because of the expectation that he would.[13]) Madison had secretly drafted a plan for a new government, one that was a total departure from the government under the Articles and set the agenda for the convention. During the convention and the ratification process, Madison was "up to his ears in politics, advising, persuading, softening the harsh word, playing down this difficulty and exaggerating that, engaging in debate, harsh controversy, polemics, and sly maneuver."[14] In the end, his views more than anyone else's would prevail, and he would be called the Father of the Constitution.

Consensus

Despite disagreements, the delegates did see eye to eye on the most fundamental issues. They agreed that the government should be a republic—an indirect democracy—in which people could vote for at least some of the officials who would represent them. This was the only form of government they seriously considered. They also agreed that the national government should be stronger than before. At the same time, they thought the government should be limited, with checks to prevent it from exercising too much power.

They agreed that the national government should have three separate branches—legislative, executive, and judicial—to exercise separate powers. They thought both the legislative and executive branches should be strong.

Conflict

Although there was considerable agreement over the fundamental principles and elemental structure of the new government, the delegates quarreled about the specific provisions concerning representation, slavery, and trade.

Representation Sharp conflict was expressed between delegates from large states and those from small states over representation. Large states sought a strong central government that they could control; small states feared a government that would control them.

When the convention began, Edmund Randolph introduced the Virginia Plan drafted by Madison. According to this plan, the central government would be strong. The legislature would have more power than under the Articles, and a national executive and national judiciary also would have considerable power. The legislature would be divided into two houses, with representation based on population in each.

But delegates from the small states calculated that the three largest states—Pennsylvania, Virginia, and Massachusetts—would have a majority of the representatives and could control the legislature. These delegates countered with the New Jersey Plan, introduced by William Paterson. According to this plan, the central government would be relatively strong, although not as strong as under the Virginia Plan. But the primary difference was that the legislature would be one house, with representation by states, which would have one vote each. This was exactly the same as the structure of Congress under the Articles, also designed to prevent the large states from controlling the legislature.

To complicate matters, some states claimed vast territory to their west, while other states feared such expansion that would make frontier states even larger.

The convention deadlocked. George Washington wrote that he almost despaired of reaching agreement. To ease tensions, Benjamin Franklin suggested that the delegates begin each day with a prayer, but they could not agree on this either; Alexander Hamilton insisted they did not need "foreign aid."

Faced with the possibility that the convention would disband without a constitution, the delegates compromised. Delegates from Connecticut and other states proposed a plan in which the legislature would have two houses. In one, representation would be based on population, and members would be elected by voters. In the other, representation would be by states, and members would be selected by state legislatures. Presumably, the large states would dominate the former, the small states the latter. The delegates narrowly approved this **Great Compromise,** or Connecticut Compromise. Delegates from the large states still objected, but those from the small states made it clear that such a compromise was necessary for their agreement and, in turn, their states' ratification. The large states, though, did extract a concession that all taxing and spending bills must originate in the house in which representation was based on population. This provision would allow the large states to take the initiative on these important measures. The compromise was "great" in that it not only resolved this critical issue but paved the way for resolution of other issues.

This plan of a slave ship shows the overcrowding that led to inhumane conditions, rampant disease, and high mortality.
Historical Society of Pennsylvania

This decision began a pattern that continues to this day. When officials face implacable differences, they try to compromise, but the process is not easy, and a resolution is not inevitable. It is an apt choice of words to say that officials "hammer out" a compromise; it is not a coincidence that we use *hammer* rather than a softer metaphor.

Slavery In addition to conflict between large states and small states over representation, conflict emerged between northern states and southern states over slavery, trade, and taxation.

With representation in one house based on population, the delegates had to decide how to apportion the seats. They agreed that Indians would not count as part of the population but differed about slaves. Delegates from the South, where slaves were one-third of the population, wanted slaves to count fully in order to boost the number of their representatives. They argued that their use of slaves produced wealth that benefited the entire nation. Delegates from the North, where most states had outlawed slavery or at least the slave trade after the Revolution, did not want slaves to count at all. Gouverneur Morris, of Pennsylvania, said the southerners' position

> comes to this: that the inhabitant of Georgia and South Carolina who goes to the coast of Africa, and in defiance of the most sacred laws of humanity tears away his fellow creatures from their dearest connections and damns them to the most cruel bondages, shall have more votes in a government instituted for the protection of the rights of mankind

> than the citizen of Pennsylvania or New Jersey who views with a laudable horror so nefarious a practice.[15]

Others pointed out that slaves were not considered persons when it came to rights such as voting. Nevertheless, southerners asserted that they would not support a constitution if slaves were not counted at least partially. In the **Three-fifths Compromise,** the delegates agreed that three-fifths of the slaves would be counted in apportioning the seats.

As a result, the votes of southern whites would be worth more than those of northerners in electing members to the House of Representatives and presidents (because the Electoral College would be based on membership in Congress). Between 1788 and 1860, nine of the fifteen presidents, including all five who served two terms, were slaveowners.[16]

Although northerners had to accept this compromise to win southerners' support for the Constitution, northerners apparently did not contest two other provisions addressing slavery. Southerners pushed through one provision forbidding Congress to ban the importation of slaves before 1808 and another requiring free states to return any escaped slaves to their owners in slave states. In these provisions southerners won most of what they wanted; even the provision permitting Congress to ban the slave trade in 1808 was hardly a limitation because by then planters would have enough slaves to fulfill their needs by natural population increases rather than importation. In return, northerners, representing most shippers, got authority for Congress to regulate commerce by a simple majority rather than a two-thirds majority. Thus, northerners conceded two provisions reinforcing slavery in order to benefit shippers.[17]

Yet the framers were embarrassed by the hypocrisy of claiming to have been enslaved by the British while allowing enslavement of blacks. The framers' embarrassment is reflected in their language. The three provisions reinforcing slavery never mention "slavery" or "slaves"; one gingerly refers to "free persons" and "other persons."

The unwillingness to tackle the slavery issue more directly has been called the "Greatest Compromise" by one political scientist.[18] But an attempt to abolish slavery would have caused the five southern states to refuse to ratify the Constitution.

Trade and Taxation Slavery also underlay a compromise on trade and taxation. With a manufacturing economy, northerners sought protection for their businesses. In particular, they wanted a tax on manufactured goods imported from Britain. Without a tax, these goods would be cheaper than northern goods; but with a tax, northern goods would be more competitive—and prices for southern consumers more expensive. With an agricultural economy, southerners sought free trade for their plantations. They wanted a guarantee that no tax would be levied on agricultural products exported to Britain. Such a tax would make their products less competitive abroad and, they worried, amount to an indirect tax on slavery—the labor responsible for the products. The delegates compromised by allowing Congress to tax imported goods but not exported ones. Tariffs on imported goods would become a point of controversy between the North and South in the years leading up to the Civil War.

After seventeen weeks of debate, the Constitution was ready. On September 17, 1787, thirty-nine of the original fifty-five delegates signed it. Some delegates had left when they saw the direction the convention was taking, and three others refused to sign, feeling that the Constitution gave too much authority to the national government. Most of the rest were not entirely happy with the result (even Madison, who was most responsible for the content of the document, was despondent that his plan for a national legislature was compromised by having one house with representation by states), but they thought it was the best they could do. Benjamin Franklin had some qualms, but he was more optimistic. Referring to the sun painted on the back of George Washington's chair, he remarked that throughout the proceedings he had wondered whether it was a rising or a setting sun. "But now . . . I have the happiness to know that it is a rising and not a setting sun."

Features of the Constitution

William Gladstone, a British prime minister in the nineteenth century, said the American Constitution was "the most wonderful work ever struck off at a given time by the brain and purpose of man."[19] To see why it was unique, it is necessary to examine its major features.

A Written Constitution

The Founders established the idea of a written constitution, first in the Articles of Confederation and then more prominently in the Constitution itself. Other Western countries had constitutions that served as their supreme law, but these constitutions were not written or, if written, not as a single document. For example, the British constitution, which consisted of various customs, declarations, acts of Parliament, and precedents of courts, was partly unwritten and partly written. To Americans this was no constitution at all. They felt that a constitution should be a fundamental law above all other laws—not a mixture of customs and laws.

This belief is reflected in Americans' use of social contract theory. A **social contract,** not a literal contract like a business contract, is an implied agreement between the people and their government. The people give up part of their liberty to the government, which in exchange protects the remainder of their liberty. The Mayflower Compact was a very general form of social contract, whereas the written Constitution, stipulating the powers and limits of government, was a more specific form of social contract.

A Republic

The Founders distinguished between a democracy and a republic. For them a "democracy" meant a **direct democracy,** which permits citizens to vote on most issues, and a "republic" meant an **indirect democracy,** which allows citizens to vote for their representatives who make governmental policies.

The Founders opposed a direct democracy for the whole country. Many individual towns in New England had a direct democracy (and some still do), but these communities were small and manageable. Some city-states of ancient Greece and medieval Europe had a direct democracy, but they could not sustain it. The Founders thought a large country would have even less ability to do so because people could not be brought together in one place in order to act. The Founders also believed human nature was such that people could not withstand the passions of the moment and would

Democracy is "the worst of all political evils."

—Elbridge Gerry

"[T]he people have ever been and ever will be unfit to retain the exercise of power in their own hands."

—William Livingston

"[T]he people [should] have as little to do as may be about the government."

—Roger Sherman

"Notwithstanding the oppression and injustice experienced among us from democracy, the genius of the people is in favor of it, and the genius of the people must be consulted."

—George Mason

"It seems indispensable that the mass of citizens should not be without a voice in making the laws which they are to obey, in choosing the magistrates who are to administer them."

—James Madison

In part, these statements reflect the Founders' support for republicanism and opposition to democracy, as they defined the terms. But in a more general sense, these statements reflect the Founders' ambivalence about "the people." Rationally, they believed in popular sovereignty, but emotionally they feared it. Perhaps no statement illustrates this ambivalence more than the one by New England clergyman Jeremy Belknap: "Let it stand as a principle that government originates from the people; but let the people be taught . . . that they are not able to govern themselves."

© 1986 by Sidney Harris

SOURCE: Richard Hofstadter, *The American Political Tradition and the Men Who Made It* (New York: Vintage, 1948), pp. 3–17.

---

be swayed by a demagogue to take unwise action. Eventually, democracy would collapse into tyranny. "Remember," John Adams wrote, "democracy never lasts long. It soon wastes, exhausts, and murders itself. There never was a democracy yet that did not commit suicide."[20]

The Founders favored an indirect democracy—a republic—because they firmly believed the people should have some voice in government for it to be based on the consent of the governed. So the Founders provided that the people could elect representatives to the House and that the state legislators, themselves elected by the people, could select senators and members of the Electoral College, who would choose the president. In this way the people would have a voice but one filtered through their presumably wiser representatives. (See the box "The Founders and the People.")

The Founders considered a democracy radical and a republic only slightly less radical. Because they believed the country could not maintain a democracy, they worried that it might not be able to maintain a republic either. When the Constitutional Convention closed, Benjamin Franklin was approached by a woman who asked, "Well, Doctor, what have we got, a republic or a monarchy?" Franklin responded, "A republic, madam, if you can keep it."

Fragmentation of Power

Other countries assumed that government must have a concentration of power to be strong enough to govern. However, when the Founders made our national government more powerful than it had been under the Articles, they feared they also had made it more capable of oppression, and therefore they fragmented its power.

The Founders believed people were selfish, coveting more and more property, and that leaders lusted after more and more power. They assumed such human nature was unchangeable. Madison speculated, "If men were angels, no government would be necessary." But, alas, Madison said, men are not angels. Therefore, "In framing a government which is to be administered by men over men, the great difficulty lies in this: you must first enable the government to control the governed; and in the next place oblige it to control itself."[21] (Madison's views are reflected in two of the Federalist Papers included in the appendix). The Founders decided the way to oblige government to control itself was to structure it to prevent any one leader, group of leaders, or factions of people from exercising power over more than a small part of it. Thus, the Founders fragmented government's power. This is reflected in three concepts they built into the structure of government: federalism, separation of powers, and checks and balances.

Federalism The first division of power was between the national government and the state governments. This division of power is called **federalism.** Foreign governments had been "unitary"; that is, the central government wielded all authority. At the other extreme, the U.S. government under the Articles had been "confederal," which meant that although there was some division of power, the state governments wielded almost all authority. The Founders wanted a strong national government, but they also wanted, or at least realized they would have to accept, reasonably strong state governments as well. They invented a federal system as a compromise between the unitary and confederal systems. (Chapter 3 explains these types of government further.)

Separation of Powers The second division of power was within the national government. The power to make, administer, and judge the laws was split into three branches—legislative, executive, and judicial (see Figure 1). In the legislative branch, the power was split further into two houses. This **separation of powers** contrasts with the British parliamentary system in which the legislature, Parliament, is supreme. Both executive and judicial officials are drawn from it and responsible to it. Madison expressed the American view of such an arrangement when he said that "the accumulation of all powers, legislative, executive, and judiciary, in the same hands . . . may justly be pronounced the very definition of tyranny."[22]

To reinforce the separation of powers, officials of the three branches were chosen by different means. Representatives were elected by the people (at that time mostly white men who owned property), senators were selected by the state legislatures, and the president was selected by the Electoral College, whose members were selected by the states. Only federal judges were chosen by officials in the other branches. They were nominated by the president and confirmed by the Senate. Once appointed, however, they were allowed to serve for "good behavior"—essentially life—so they had much independence. (Since the Constitution was written, the Seventeenth Amendment has provided for election of senators by the people, and the state legislatures have provided for election of members of the Electoral College by the people.)

Officials of the branches were also chosen at different times. Representatives were given a two-year term,

Branch:	Legislative Congress		Executive Presidency	Judicial Federal Courts
	House	Senate	President	Judges
Officials chosen by:	People	People, (originally, state legislatures)	Electoral College, whose members are chosen by the people (originally, by state legislatures)	President, with advice and consent of Senate
For term of:	2 years	6 years	4 years	Life
To represent primarily:	Common people	Wealthy people	All people	Constitution
	Large states	Small states		

FIGURE 1 ■ *Separation of Powers* *Separation of powers, as envisioned by the Founders, means not only that government functions are to be performed by different branches but also that officials of these branches are to be chosen by different people, for different terms, and to represent different constituencies.*

senators a six-year term (with one-third of them up for reelection every two years), and the president a four-year term. These staggered terms would make it less likely that temporary passions in society would bring about a massive switch of officials or policies.

The Senate was designed to act as a conservative brake on the House, due to senators' selection by state legislatures and their longer terms. After returning from France, Thomas Jefferson met with George Washington over breakfast. Jefferson protested the establishment of a legislature with two houses. Washington supposedly asked, "Why did you pour that coffee into your saucer?" "To cool it," Jefferson replied. Similarly, Washington explained, "We pour legislation into the senatorial saucer to cool it."[23]

Checks and Balances To guarantee separation of powers, the Founders built in overlapping powers called **checks and balances** (see Figure 2). Madison suggested that "the great security against a gradual concentration of the several powers in the same department consists in giving those who administer each department the necessary constitutional means and personal motives to resist encroachments by the others. . . . *Ambition must be made to counteract ambition.*"[24] To that end, each branch was given some authority over the others. If one branch abused its power, the others could use their checks to thwart it.

Thus, rather than a simple system of separation of powers, ours is a complex, even contradictory, system of both separation of powers and checks and balances. The principle of separation of powers gives each branch its own sphere of authority, but the system of checks and balances allows each branch to intrude into the other branches' spheres. For example, because of separation of powers, Congress makes the laws, but due to checks and balances, the president can veto them and the courts can rule them unconstitutional. In these ways all three branches are involved in legislating. One political scientist calls ours "a government of separated institutions sharing powers."[25]

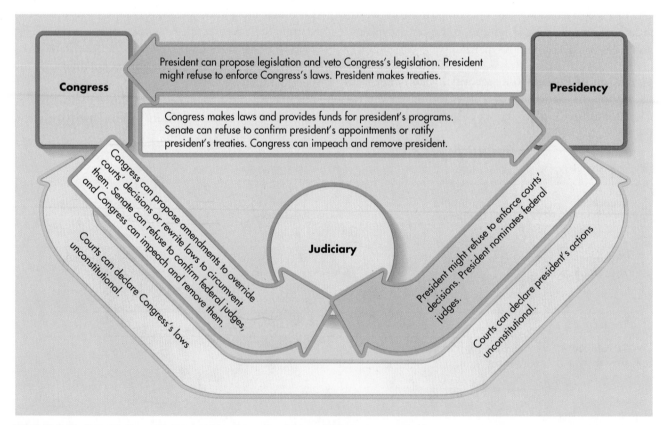

FIGURE 2 ■ *Checks and Balances* Most of the major checks and balances between the three branches are explicit in the Constitution, though some are not. For example, the courts' power to declare congressional laws or presidential actions unconstitutional—their power of "judicial review"—is not mentioned. The president's power to refuse to enforce congressional laws or judicial decisions is also not mentioned or even implied. In fact, it contradicts the Constitution, but sometimes it is assertd by the president nonetheless.

With federalism, separation of powers, and checks and balances, the Founders expected conflict. They invited the parts of government to struggle against each other to limit each other's ability to dominate all. At the same time, the Founders hoped for "balanced government." The national and state governments would represent different interests, and the branches within the national government would represent different interests. The House would represent the "common" people and the large states; the Senate, the wealthy people and the small states; the president, all the people; and the Supreme Court, the Constitution. The parts of government would have to compromise to get anything accomplished. Although each part would struggle for more power, it could not accumulate enough to dominate the others. Eventually, its leaders would have to compromise and adopt policies in the interest of all of the parts and their constituencies. Paradoxically, then, the Founders expected narrow conflict to produce broader harmony.

Motives of the Founders

To understand the Constitution better, it is useful to consider the motives of the Founders. Were they selfless patriots, sharing their wisdom and experience? Or were they selfish property owners, protecting their interests? To answer these questions it is necessary to look at the philosophical ideas, political experience, and economic interests that influenced these men.

Philosophical Ideas

The Founders were exceptionally well-educated intellectuals who incorporated philosophical ideas into the Constitution. At a time when the average person did not dream of going to college, a majority of the Founders graduated from college. As learned men, they shared a common library of writers and philosophers.

The framers of the Constitution reflected the ideals of the Enlightenment, a pattern of thought emphasizing the use of reason, rather than tradition or religion, to solve problems; they studied past governments to determine why they had failed in the hope they could apply these lessons to the present.

From all accounts the framers engaged in a level of debate at the convention that was rare in politics, citing philosophers ranging from the ancient Greeks to the modern British and French. Even when they did not mention them explicitly, their comments seemed to reflect the writings of particular philosophers.

The views of John Locke, a seventeenth-century English philosopher, underlay many of the ideas of the Founders. In fact, his views permeate the Declaration of Independence and Constitution more than those of any other single person.

Locke, like some previous philosophers, believed people had **natural rights.** These rights were inherent; they existed from the moment people were born. They were inalienable; they were given by God so they could not be taken away. One of the most important was the right to property. When people worked the land, clearing it and planting it, they mixed their labor with it. This act, according to Locke, made the land their property. Some people, due to more work or better luck, would accumulate more property than others. Thus, the right to property would result in inequality of wealth. Yet he thought it would lead to greater productivity for society. This view of property appealed to Americans who saw an abundance of land in the new country.

"Religious freedom is my immediate goal, but my long range plan is to go into real estate."

Did the Iroquois Influence the Founders?

For many years, popular writers portrayed Native Americans as simple savages. To some they were "bloodthirsty savages." To others they were "noble savages." But to almost all writers, Indians were so preoccupied by surviving that they had little time for anything but hunting and fighting. Yet these Native Americans had far more sophisticated societies than most writers, until recently, gave them credit for.

Although most Americans are aware that the colonists adopted the tactics of Indian warfare—the forerunner of modern guerrilla warfare—to defeat the British in the Revolutionary War, few Americans realize that the colonists mirrored several other Indian practices in founding the country. In fact, the colonists used some concepts similar to those of the Iroquois in the Declaration of Independence, Articles of Confederation, and Constitution.

The Iroquois, who inhabited what is now New York State, included the Cayugas, Mohawks, Oneidas, Onondagas, and Senecas. (After the early 1700s, they also included the Tuscaroras, who migrated from the Carolinas.) After generations of bloody warfare, the "Five Nations" formed the **Iroquois Confederacy** sometime between 1000 and 1450, according to various estimates.[1]

Iroquois Government

The Confederacy adopted a constitution called the "Great Law of Peace." Although some provisions were not written, others were recorded on "wampum belts," constructed of shells sewn in intricate patterns on hides. Few white Americans realized that the Iroquois constitution was partly written until it was transcribed into English in the late nineteenth century.

The Great Law provided for a union with federalism, checks and balances, restrictions on the power of the leaders, opportunities for participation by the people, and some natural rights and equality for the people.

Federalism was most apparent. Each of the Five Nations was essentially a state within a state. Each was allowed to govern its internal affairs. (Even non-Iroquois nations conquered by the Iroquois were allowed to keep their form of government as long as they did not make war on other nations.)

Checks and balances were incorporated in several ways. The Confederacy established a system of clans that overlapped the boundaries of the nations. Members of clans were considered relatives despite living in different nations. Thus, the system of clans was designed to operate like the system of checks and balances in the U.S. Constitution: Where checks and balances were intended to prevent the dominance of one branch of government or one faction that got control of a branch of government, clans were intended to prevent the dominance of one nation in the Confederacy.

The Confederacy used governing procedures that also entailed checks and balances. The "older brothers"—Mohawks and Senecas—were on "one side of the house." The "younger brothers"—Cayugas and Oneidas—were on the "opposite side of the house." The "firekeepers"— Onondagas—would break the tie if the two sides disagreed. If the two sides agreed, the firekeepers could veto the measure, but then the two sides could override the veto. Thus, the governing council was analogous to a two-house legislature and an executive with a limited veto.

The Great Law had elaborate provisions for the selection and obligations of the chiefs who sat on the governing council. Most chiefs were selected by women from extended families that had hereditary power. Thus, these women were permitted to participate in making these important political decisions, although they themselves were not permitted to serve on the council.

The chiefs were obligated to communicate with the people—send messages to them and consider requests from them. The chiefs were expected to tolerate anger and criticism by the people and to reflect "endless patience" and "calm deliberation." The chiefs were to be the people's servants rather than their masters. As such, they were not supposed to accumulate more wealth than the people. (In fact, there was some pressure to give away their material possessions, so they would be poorer than the people.) If the chiefs failed to follow these rules, they could be recalled or impeached.

The Great Law also provided for

Locke wrote that people came together to form government through a social contract that established a **limited government,** strong enough to protect their rights but not too strong to threaten these rights. This government should not act without the consent of the governed. To make its decisions, this government should follow majority rule. (Locke never resolved the conflict between majority rule and natural rights—that is, between majority rule and minority rights for those who disagree with the majority.)

The views of Charles de Montesquieu, an eighteenth-century French philosopher, also influenced the debate at

some natural rights and equality. There was significant separation of church and state. There was no state religion, and the duties of the civil chiefs were distinct from those of the religious leaders. The Great Law upheld freedom of expression in religious and political matters, and it reflected tolerance of different races and national origins. For example, its adoption rules included no restrictions on the basis of race or national origin. Even some Anglo-Americans received full citizenship in the Confederacy.

Thus, in various ways the Iroquois government, unlike the Indian civilizations in Central and South America, reflected characteristics we consider democratic.[2] As one historian concludes, "all these things were part of the American way of life before Columbus landed."[3]

Iroquois Influence on American Government?

In colonial times, the Iroquois occupied land between the English on the Atlantic coast and the French in what is now southern Canada. The Iroquois controlled the only level mountain pass and the best communication and trade route between the English and the French. The Iroquois were the balance of power between these settlers, whose nations were at war with each other.

Britain tried to forge an alliance with the Iroquois. Colonial envoys and Indian chiefs held treaty councils to establish the alliance. As early as 1744 one chief,

Canassatego, advised the colonies to unite, as the Iroquois had, for the colonists' protection (and for the Indians' convenience—to reduce the confusion of dealing with separate colonies). Benjamin Franklin, who served as an envoy and as the printer of the proceedings of the councils, was fascinated by the Iroquois and seemed influenced by Canassatego's advice. He, too, urged the colonies to unite, and he proposed a plan very similar to the Iroquois Confederacy. But the plan was not adopted by the colonies, which fretted that it would deny their individual independence. It was not accepted by the Crown either, which feared that it would establish the colonies' joint independence from the mother country. The colonies would not unite until the Crown imposed the Stamp Act and other measures two decades later.

Many colonists were intrigued by Iroquois ways. Franklin found a market eager for his accounts of the treaty councils. He printed accounts of thirteen councils in twenty-six years. An official in New York's colonial government published a systematic description of Iroquois government in 1727 and expanded it in 1747. Other officials asked the Iroquois for information about their confederacy's structure.

Over the years there was much intermingling between European and Native American cultures. (At least one colonial official was adopted by the Mohawks, and another was allowed to serve on their councils and even lead their war parties at

times.) Some Founders admired certain Indian practices and ideas. Besides Franklin, Thomas Jefferson and Thomas Paine, for example, were attracted to the Iroquois' emphasis on natural rights and their restrictions on their leaders' power and wealth. Thus, "the American frontier became a laboratory for democracy precisely at a time when colonial leaders were searching for alternatives to what they regarded as European tyranny and class stratification."[4]

Historians debate whether the Iroquois actually influenced the Founders. The parallels between the Iroquois government and our Declaration of Independence, Articles of Confederation, and Constitution could be coincidental. Political ideas can take root in more than one society simultaneously. But the parallels are striking, and the possibilities are intriguing. The roots of our political ideas might be more numerous and complex than we have assumed.[5]

SOURCE: Bruce E. Johansen, *Forgotten Founders* (Ipswich, MA: Gambit, 1982). Additional sources are cited, especially in Chapter 1.
1. Johansen, p. 22.
2. Johansen, pp. 17–18.
3. Felix Cohen, quoted in Johansen, p. 13.
4. Johansen, p. xv.
5. At least fragments of evidence suggest that Native Americans influenced European philosophers, such as Locke, Montesquieu, and Rousseau, who in turn influenced the colonists. Some Iroquois chiefs had been to Europe, and the Europeans were as intrigued by their ways as the colonists were. Johansen, pp. 14, 52.

the convention and the provisions of the Constitution itself. Others had suggested separation of powers before, but Montesquieu refined the concept and added that of checks and balances. Referring to him as "the celebrated Montesquieu," the Founders cited him more than any other thinker.[26] (Presumably, they cited him more than

Locke because by this time Locke's views had so permeated American society that the Founders considered them just "common sense."[27])

The principles of the system of mechanics formulated by Isaac Newton, a British mathematician of the late seventeenth and early eighteenth centuries, also

Constitutional Provisions Protecting Property

Numerous constitutional provisions, some obvious and others not, were designed to protect property:

"The Times, Places and Manner of holding Elections for Senators and Representatives, shall be prescribed in each State by the Legislature thereof."

Allows state to set property qualifications to vote.

"The Congress shall have Power . . . To coin Money."

Centralizes currency.

"No State shall . . . emit bills of credit."

Prevents states from printing paper money.

"Congress shall have Power . . . To establish uniform Laws on the subject of Bankruptcies."

Allows Congress to prevent states from relieving debtors of obligation to pay.

"No State shall . . . pass any . . . Law impairing the Obligation of Contracts."

Prevents states from relieving debtors of obligation to pay.

"The United States shall guarantee to every State [protection] against domestic Violence."

Protects states from debtor uprisings.

"Congress shall have Power . . . To provide for calling forth the Militia to execute the Laws of the Union, suppress insurrections."

Protects creditors from debtor uprisings.

---

pervaded the provisions of the Constitution. As Newton viewed nature as a machine, so the Founders saw the constitutional structure as a machine, with different parts having different functions and balancing each other. Newton's principle of action and reaction is manifested in the Founders' system of checks and balances. Both the natural environment and the constitutional structure were viewed as self-regulating systems.[28]

Political Experience

Although the Founders were intellectuals, they were also practical politicians. According to one interpretation, they were "first and foremost superb democratic politicians" and the convention was "a nationalist reform caucus which had to operate with great delicacy and skill in a political cosmos full of enemies."[29]

The Founders brought extensive political experience to the convention: eight had signed the Declaration of Independence; thirty-nine had served in Congress; seven had been governors; many had held other state offices; some had helped write their state constitutions. The framers drew upon this experience. For example, while they cited Montesquieu in discussing separation

of powers, they also referred to the experience of colonial and state governments that already had some separation of powers. (See also the box "Did the Iroquois Influence the Founders?")

As practical politicians, "no matter what their private dreams might be, they had to take home an acceptable package and defend it—and their own political futures—against predictable attack."[30] So they compromised the difficult issues and ducked the stickiest ones. Ultimately, they pieced together a Constitution that allowed each delegate to go home and announce that his state had won something.

Economic Interests

Historian Charles Beard sparked a lively debate when he published *An Economic Interpretation of the Constitution* in 1913.[31] Beard argued that those with money and investments in manufacturing and shipping dominated the Constitutional Convention and state ratification conventions and that they produced a document that would increase their wealth. (After Beard published his conclusions, an Ohio newspaper proclaimed, "Scavengers, hyena-like, desecrate the graves of the dead patriots we revere."[32]) Later scholars questioned Beard's facts and interpretations, pointing out that support for the Constitution was not based strictly on wealth.[33]

Although some of Beard's specific points do not hold up, his underlying position that the Founders represented an elite that sought to protect its property from the masses seems more valid. The delegates to the Constitutional Convention were an elite. They included prosperous planters, manufacturers, shippers, and lawyers. About one-third were slaveowners. Most came from families of prominence and married into other families of prominence. Not all were wealthy, but most were at least well-to-do. Only one, a delegate from Georgia, was a yeoman farmer like most men in the country. In short, "this was a convention of the well-bred, the well-fed, the well-read, and the well-wed."[34]

The Founders supported the right to property. The promise of land and perhaps riches enticed most immigrants to come to America.[35] A desire for freedom from arbitrary taxes and trade restrictions spurred some colonists to fight in the Revolution.[36] And the inability of the government under the Articles to provide a healthy economy prompted the Founders to convene the Constitutional Convention. They probably agreed with Madison that "the first object of government" is to protect property.[37]

The Founders' emphasis on property was not as elitist as it might seem, however. Land was plentiful, and, with westward expansion, even more would be available. Already most men were middle-class farmers who owned some property. Many who owned no property could foresee the day when they would, so most Americans wanted to protect property.

The Founders diverged from the framers in their desire to protect other property in addition to land, such as wealth and credit. Of the fifty-five delegates, forty were owners of government bonds that had depreciated under the Articles, and twenty-four were moneylenders.[38] So the delegates included provisions to protect commerce, including imports and exports, contracts, and debts, and provisions to regulate currency, bankruptcy, and taxes. (See the box, "Constitutional Provisions Protecting Property.")

Political scientists and historians disagree about which of these three influences on the Founders—philosophical, political, or economic—was most important. Actually, the influences are difficult to separate because they reinforce each other; the framers' ideas point to the same sort of constitution that their political experience and economic interests do.[39]

The Federalist Papers

Out of the great debate over ratification came a series of essays considered the premier example of American political philosophy. Titled the *Federalist Papers,* these essays were written by Alexander Hamilton, James Madison, and John Jay. At the urging of Hamilton,[1] the authors wrote eighty-five essays that appeared in New York newspapers during the ratification debates there. The authors tried to convince delegates to the convention to vote for ratification.

In the fashion of the time, the papers were published anonymously—by "Publius" (Latin for "Public Man"). They were so unified in approach that few of the authors' contemporaries could

discern their pens at work. Given the arguments and compromises at the Constitutional Convention, one political scientist speculated that the framers who read the essays "must have discovered with some surprise what a coherent and well-thought-out document they had prepared."[2]

Despite the unity of the papers, political scientists have identified the authors of individual ones. Hamilton wrote most of those describing the defects of the Articles, Madison most of those explaining the structure of the new government, including the famous #10 and #51 (reprinted in the appendix). Before he became sick, Jay, who was

secretary of foreign affairs, wrote a few concerning foreign policy.

Actually, there is little evidence that the essays swayed any of the delegates. Yet they have endured because readers see them as an original source of political thinking and as a useful guide to the intentions of the framers, and because judges consult them when they interpret various provisions of the Constitution.

1. Although Hamilton worried that the Constitution would not establish a strong enough government, he thought it was preferable to the Articles, which he despised.
2. John P. Roche, ed., *Origins of American Political Thought* (New York: Harper & Row, 1967), p. 163.

Ratification of the Constitution

The Constitution specified that ratification would occur through conventions in the states and that the document would take effect with approval of conventions in nine of the thirteen states. The framers purposely did not provide for approval by the state legislatures because they feared that some legislatures would reject the Constitution because it reduced their power. In addition, the framers wanted the broader base of support for the new government that ratification conventions would provide.

Technically, the procedures for ratification were illegal. According to the Articles of Confederation, which were still in effect, any changes had to be approved by all thirteen states. However, the framers suspected that they would not find support in all states.

Indeed, ratification was uncertain. Many people opposed the Constitution, and a lively campaign against it appeared in newspapers, pamphlets, and mass meetings. Although the procedures required ratification by only nine states, the framers realized they needed support from all of the largest states and much of the public to lend legitimacy to the new government.

Knowing opponents would charge them with setting up a national government to dominate the state governments, those who supported the Constitution ingeniously adopted the name **Federalists** to emphasize a real division of power between the national and state governments. They dubbed their opponents **Antifederalists** to imply that they did not want a division of power between the governments. (See the box "The Federalist Papers.")

The Antifederalists faulted the Constitution for lacking a bill of rights. The Constitution did contain some protection for individual rights, such as the provision that the writ of habeas corpus, which protects against arbitrary arrest and detention, cannot be suspended except during rebellion or invasion, and the provision that a criminal defendant has a right to a jury trial. But the framers made no effort to include most of the rights people believed they had, because most states already had a bill of rights in their own constitutions. The framers also thought that by fragmenting power no branch could become strong enough to deny individual rights. Yet critics demanded provisions protecting various rights of criminal defendants and freedom of the press. In response, the Federalists promised to propose amendments guaranteeing these rights as soon as the government began.

The Antifederalists also criticized the Constitution for other reasons. Localists at heart, they were wary of entrusting power to officials far away; they correctly claimed that republics historically worked only in small geographic areas where the population was more homogeneous and the officials were closer to the people. They worried that the central government, to function effectively, would accumulate too much power and the presidency would become a monarchy or Congress an aristocracy. One delegate to the Massachusetts convention blasted the Federalists:

> These lawyers, and men of learning and moneyed men, that talk so finely, and gloss over matters so smoothly, to make us poor illiterate people swallow down the pill, expect to get into Congress themselves; they expect to . . . get all the power and all the money into their own hands, and then they will swallow up all us little folks . . . just as the whale swallowed up Jonah![40]

But the Antifederalists had no alternative plan. They were divided; some wanted to amend the Articles, while others wanted to reject both the Articles and the Constitution in favor of some yet undetermined form of government. Their lack of unity on an alternative was instrumental in their inability to win support.[41]

Ratification was quick in some states, a bitter struggle in others. Within three months after the Constitutional Convention, Delaware became the first state to ratify, and six months later New Hampshire became the necessary ninth. The Constitution took effect, and the new government began in 1788, with George Washington becoming president. Within one year, North Carolina and Rhode Island, both of which initially rejected the Constitution, became the last states to approve it.

Changing the Constitution

The framers expected their document to last; Madison wrote, "We have framed a constitution that will probably be still around when there are 196 million people."[42] Yet because the framers realized it would need some changes, they drafted a Constitution that can be changed either formally by constitutional amendment or informally by judicial interpretation or political practice. In doing so, they left a legacy for later governments. "The example of changing a Constitution, by assembling the wise men of the state, instead of assembling armies," Jefferson noted, "will be worth as much to the world as the former examples we had given them."[43]

By Constitutional Amendment

That the Articles of Confederation could be amended only by a unanimous vote of the states posed an almost

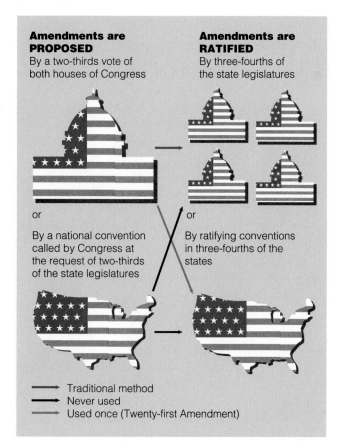

Amendments are PROPOSED
By a two-thirds vote of both houses of Congress

or

By a national convention called by Congress at the request of two-thirds of the state legislatures

Amendments are RATIFIED
By three-fourths of the state legislatures

or

By ratifying conventions in three-fourths of the states

— Traditional method
— Never used
— Used once (Twenty-first Amendment)

FIGURE 3 ■ *Avenues for Constitutional Amendment*

insurmountable barrier to any amendment at all. The framers of the Constitution made sure this experience would not repeat itself. Yet they did not make amendment easy; the procedures do not require unanimity, but they do require widespread agreement.

Procedures The procedures for amendment entail action by both the national government and the state governments. Amendments can be proposed in either of two ways: by a two-thirds vote of both houses of Congress or by a national convention called by Congress at the request of two-thirds of the state legislatures. Congress then specifies which way amendments must be ratified—either by three-fourths of the state legislatures or by ratifying conventions in three-fourths of the states.[44] Among these avenues, the usual route has been proposal by Congress and ratification by state legislatures (see Figure 3).

Amendments In the first Congress under the Constitution, the Federalists fulfilled their promise to support a bill of rights. Madison drafted the amendments, Congress proposed them, and the states ratified ten of them in 1791. This **Bill of Rights** includes freedom of expression—speech, press, assembly, and religion (First Amendment). It also includes numerous rights for those accused of crimes—protection against unreasonable searches and seizures (Fourth), protection against compulsory self-incrimination (Fifth), guarantee of due process of law (Fifth), the right to counsel and a jury trial in criminal cases (Sixth), and protection against excessive bail and fines, and cruel and unusual punishment (Eighth). It also includes a jury trial in civil cases (Seventh).

In addition to these major rights, the Bill of Rights includes two amendments that grew out of the colonial experience with Great Britain—the right to bear arms for a militia (Second) and the right not to have soldiers quartered in homes during peacetime (Third). The Bill of Rights also includes two general amendments—a statement that the listing of these rights does not mean these are the only ones people have (Ninth) and a statement that the powers not given to the national government are reserved to the states (Tenth).

Among the other seventeen amendments to the Constitution, the strongest theme is the expansion of citizenship rights:[45]

- Abolition of slavery (Thirteenth, 1865)
- Equal protection, due process of law (Fourteenth, 1868)
- Right to vote for black men (Fifteenth, 1870)
- Direct election of senators (Seventeenth, 1913)
- Right to vote for women (Nineteenth, 1920)
- Right to vote in presidental elections for District of Columbia residents (Twenty-third, 1960)
- Abolition of poll tax in federal elections (Twenty-fourth, 1964)
- Right to vote for persons eighteen and older (Twenty-sixth, 1971)

Another theme is the increase of federal power. Many amendments, notably those regarding voting, take authority away from the states and authorize Congress to enforce these rights by "appropriate legislation."

Most amendments proposed by Congress were ratified by the states, although some were not. Recently, two proposed amendments were not ratified. One would have provided equal rights for women (this amendment will be discussed in Chapter 15), and the other would have given congressional representation to the District of Columbia, as though it were a state.

Did Lincoln Amend the Constitution at Gettysburg?

After the battle at Gettysburg, Pennsylvania, in 1863, President Abraham Lincoln was invited to deliver "a few appropriate remarks" during the dedication of the battlefield and burial ground. Although the battle was inconclusive, it was considered a Union victory and the turning point in the Civil War. Similarly, Lincoln's remarks may be considered the turning point in public thinking about the importance of equality.[1]

Lincoln was not the main speaker, and his speech was not long. While the main speaker took two hours, Lincoln took three minutes—less time than a minister spent for a prayer. While the main speaker explained the battle and cited the names of the leaders and even some of their soldiers, Lincoln mentioned no specifics about the battle, the war, or the Union. Instead, he used the occasion to advance his ideal of equality. He began: "Four score and seven years ago our fathers brought forth on this continent, a new nation, conceived in liberty and dedicated to the proposition that all men are created equal."

Lincoln, of course, borrowed this phrase from the Declaration of Independence, which he admired as a permanent ideal. He considered the

Constitution an early effort to implement the goals of the Declaration. He thought the Constitution was unfinished because it tolerated slavery.

In this speech, however, Lincoln did not mention slavery or the Emancipation Proclamation; these were divisive. A shrewd politician, he wanted people to focus on the Declaration, which was revered.

Like most Americans at the time, Lincoln did not believe in genuine equality for blacks. In the years leading up to the war, he had made ambiguous, even contradictory, statements about slavery and racial equality.[2] But even then he had invoked the Declaration to undermine slavery. He had drawn parallels between a king's control over servants and a master's control over slaves to point out the inconsistency between supporting the Declaration and at the same time accepting slavery.

Thus, in his speech at Gettysburg, the president essentially added the Declaration's promise of equality to the Constitution. According to historian Garry Wills, "he performed one of the most daring acts of open-air sleight-of-hand ever witnessed by the unsuspecting. . . . The crowd departed with a

new thing in its ideological luggage, that new constitution Lincoln had substituted for the one they brought with them."[3]

The **Gettysburg Address**, as it came to be called, was heard by an audience of perhaps fifteen thousand, but its language was spread to countless others through word of mouth and newspapers, and eventually by politicians and teachers. Although some critics perceived what Lincoln was attempting—the *Chicago Times* quoted the Constitution to the president and charged him with betraying the document he swore to uphold—most citizens came to accept Lincoln's addition. Their acceptance ultimately led to more explicit guarantees of equality in the Constitution, through amendments and changes in interpretations and practices.

SOURCE: Garry Wills, *Lincoln at Gettysburg* (New York: Simon & Schuster, 1992).
1. Much more so than the Emancipation Proclamation. Wills, pp. 135–145.
2. For a critical perspective of Lincoln's racial views, see Lerone Bennett, Jr., *Forced into Glory: Abraham Lincoln's White Dream* (Chicago: Johnson, 2000).
3. Wills, p. 38. Wills insists this was not a coincidence and debunks the notion that Lincoln hastily dashed off his remarks while on his way to the town or to the speech itself (pp. 27–31).

These and other recent amendments have had time limits for ratification—usually seven years—set by Congress. But an amendment preventing members of Congress from giving themselves a midterm pay raise, written by Madison and passed by Congress in 1789, had no time limit. Once Michigan ratified it in 1992, it reached the three-fourths mark and became the Twenty-seventh Amendment.

Although the Constitution expressly provides for change by amendment, its ambiguity about some sub-

jects and silence about others virtually guarantee change by interpretation and practice as well.

By Judicial Interpretation

If there is disagreement about what the Constitution means, who is to interpret it? Although the Constitution does not say, the judicial branch has taken on this role. To decide disputes before them, the courts must determine what the relevant provisions of the Constitution mean. By saying the provisions mean one thing rather than another, the courts can, in effect, change the Constitution. Woodrow Wilson called the Supreme Court "a constitutional convention in continuous session." The Court has interpreted the Constitution in ways that bring about the same results as new amendments. (Chapters 13, 14, and 15 provide many examples.)

By Political Practice

Political practice has accounted for some very important changes. These include the rise of political parties and the demise of the Electoral College as an independent body. They also include the development of the cabinet to advise the president and the development of the committee system to operate the two houses of Congress. (Chapters 7, 8, and 10 explain these changes.)

The Founders would be surprised to learn that only seventeen amendments, aside from the Bill of Rights, have been adopted in over two hundred years. In part this is due to their wisdom, but in part it is due to changes in judicial interpretation and political practice, which have combined to create a "living Constitution."

It is common to think of the Founders as geniuses and succeeding generations as simply imitators and followers. Yet succeeding generations have altered the Constitution a lot more than the small number of amendments suggests. During the Civil War, new attitudes about an equality among people and a union of states led to the Thirteenth, Fourteenth, and Fifteenth Amendments, which not only protected the rights of newly freed slaves but also fundamentally altered the relationship between the nation and the states. From this point on, we would emphasize equality more, and we would emphasize the national government more than we had before. (See the box "Did Lincoln Amend the Constitution at Gettysburg?") During the Great Depression, new attitudes about the relationship between employers and employees and the regulation of businesses led to new laws and new interpretations of constitutional provisions. Both sets of changes—from the Civil War and the Great Depression—can be considered constitutional "revolutions."[46] At other times evolving attitudes prompted less noticed constitutional changes. We will see these changes as we proceed through the book. So, succeeding generations of American people should be given credit as well as the Founders.

Late in life, Jefferson observed:

Some men look at constitutions with sanctimonious reverence, and deem them like the ark of the covenant, too sacred to be
touched. They ascribe to the men of the preceding age a wisdom more than human, and suppose what they did to be beyond amendment. I knew that age well; I belonged to it, and labored with it. It deserved well of its country. It was very like the present, but without the experience of the present; and 40 years of experience in government is worth a century of book-reading; and this they would say themselves, were they to rise from the dead.[47]

The Constitution in Time

1776	Continental Congress adopts Declaration of Independence.
1781	Continental Congress adopts Articles of Confederation, the first U.S. constitution.
1783	Revolutionary War ends, as British surrender.
1786–87	Shays's Rebellion of farmers and debtors scares merchants and wealthy.
1787	Congress approves convention to revise the Articles. Constitutional Convention convenes.
1787	Constitutional Convention creates and adopts new constitution.
1788	New government begins, as the ninth state ratifies the Constitution.
1791	Bill of Rights—the first ten amendments to the Constitution—is adopted.
1863	Lincoln's Gettysburg Address begins to incorporate the idea of equality into the Constitution.
1865	Civil War ends, and alters relationship between nation and state.
1865–70	Post–Civil War amendments—Thirteenth, Fourteenth, and Fifteenth—are adopted. These further alter the relationship between nation and state and the relationship between blacks and whites.
1930s	Depression leads to changes in constitutional interpretations and alters the relationship between government and business and the relationship between employees and employers.
1972	Watergate scandal reveals crimes by officials in the Nixon administration that challenge the electoral process and the Constitution.
1974	*U.S. v. Nixon.* Supreme Court rejects President Nixon's claim of executive privilege to withhold the Watergate tapes from the courts.
1974	President Nixon resigns to avoid impeachment, seventeen days after the Supreme Court's ruling.

Conclusion: Does the Constitution Allow Government to Be Responsive?

Soon after ratification, the Constitution became accepted by the people. It took on the aura of a secular Bible. People embraced it, consulted it for guidance, cited it for support, and debated the meaning of its provisions.

The Constitution has proved so popular that many countries have copied parts of it. Almost all of the nations in the world today have a constitution written as a single document. Many have provisions similar to those in our Constitution. The Kenyan constitution speaks of "freedom of expression," the Costa Rican gives the "right to petition," and the German says that "all persons shall be equal before the law." Officials and groups in eastern European countries, emerging from communist governments, and South Africa, transforming its apartheid regime, considered provisions in our Constitution as they changed theirs.[48]

But the brevity of our Constitution remains unique; with just eighty-nine sentences, it is far shorter than those of other nations. Because it is short, it is necessarily general; because it is general, it is necessarily ambiguous; because it is ambiguous, it is necessarily open to interpretation. This provides succeeding generations the opportunity to adapt the Constitution to changing times. The longer, more detailed, and less flexible constitutions of other nations become outdated and periodically need complete revision.

In 1987, our Constitution celebrated its bicentennial as the oldest written constitution in the world. During the same two hundred years, France, for example, had ten distinct constitutional orders, including five republics, two empires, one monarchy, one plebiscitary dictatorship, and one puppet dictatorship during World War II. Since 1932, Thailand has had seventeen constitutions.[49]

Although our Constitution and the institutions it established have been responsive enough to survive, are they responsive enough to allow us to solve our problems? Can a constitution written by a small circle of men whose fastest mode of travel was horseback continue to serve masses of diverse people, some of whom have traveled by spaceship?

Intended to construct a government responsive to the masses of people to a limited extent, the Constitution set up a republic, which allowed the people to elect some representatives who would make their laws. This gave the people more say in government than people in other countries enjoyed at the time.

But the Constitution was intended to construct a government unresponsive to the masses of people to a large extent. It was expected to filter the public's passions and purify their selfish desires. Consequently, the Founders limited participation in government, allowing people to vote only for members of the House of Representatives—not for members of the Senate or the president.

Moreover, the Founders fragmented the power of government. Federalism, separation of powers, and checks and balances combine to make it difficult for any one group to capture all of government. Instead, one faction might control one branch, another faction another branch, and so on, with the result a standoff. Then the factions must compromise to accomplish anything.

Since the time of the founding, changes in the Constitution, whether by amendment, interpretation, or practice, have expanded opportunities for participation in government. But the changes have done little to modify the fragmentation of power, which remains the primary legacy of the Founders.

This structure has prevented many abuses of power, though it has not always worked. During the Vietnam War, for example, one branch—the presidency—exercised vast power while the others acquiesced. This structure also has provided the opportunity for one branch to pick up the slack when the others became sluggish. The overlapping of powers ensured by checks and balances allows every branch to act on virtually every issue it chooses to. In the 1950s, President Eisenhower and Congress were reluctant to push for civil rights for blacks, but the Supreme Court did so by declaring segregation unconstitutional in a series of cases.

But the system's very advantage has become its primary disadvantage. In their efforts to fragment power so that no branch could accumulate too much, the Founders divided power to the point where the branches sometimes cannot wield enough. In their efforts to build a government that requires a national majority to act, they built one that allows a small minority to block action. This problem has become increasingly acute as society has become increasingly complex. Like a mechanical device that operates only when all of its parts function in harmony, the system moves only when there is consensus or compromise. Consensus is rare in a large heterogeneous society; compromise is common, but it requires a long time as well as the realization by competing interests that they cannot achieve much of what they want without compromise. Even then, compromise often results in only a partial solution.

At best the system moves inefficiently and incrementally. At worst it moves hardly at all; the Constitution has established a government that is slow to respond to change. One political scientist characterizes it as a "negative, do-nothing system."[50] Although other political scientists consider this characterization an exaggeration, virtually all agree that the system is structured to preserve the status quo and to respond to the groups that want to maintain it.

Yet some political scientists believe the American people actually prefer this arrangement. Because the people are suspicious of government, they may be reluctant to let one party dominate it and use it to advance that party's policies. In surveys many people—a quarter to a third of those polled—say they think it is good for one party to control the presidency and the other to control Congress.[51] In presidential and congressional elections, more than a quarter of the voters split their ticket between the two major parties.[52] As a result, between 1968 and 2000 opposing parties controlled the executive and legislative branches for all but six years.

Another disadvantage of the fragmentation of power is that it makes it difficult, if not impossible, for citizens to pin responsibility on particular officials and parties for the decisions and policies of government. "If no individual or institution possesses the authority to act without the consent of everybody else in the room, then nobody is ever at fault if anything goes wrong. Congress can blame the President, the President can blame the Congress or the Supreme Court, the Supreme Court can blame the Mexicans or the weather in Ohio."[53] If citizens cannot determine who is responsible for what, they cannot hold them accountable and make them responsive. In this way, the fragmentation of power reduces the responsiveness of government.

EPILOGUE

The President Complies

Chief Justice Warren Burger announced the unanimous decision in the case of *United States v. Nixon:* The president must turn over the tapes.[54] The Court acknowledged the existence of executive privilege in general but rejected it in this situation because another court needed the information for an upcoming trial and because the information did not relate to national security.

The Court emphasized that courts would determine the legitimacy of claims of executive privilege, not presidents, as Nixon wanted. Because of separation of powers, Nixon argued, neither the judicial nor legislative branch should involve itself in this executive decision. However, this president, who as a high school student in Whittier, California, had won a prize from the Kiwanis Club

for the best oration on the Constitution, ignored the system of checks and balances, which limits separation of powers. In this case, checks and balances authorized the courts to conduct criminal trials of the president's aides and Congress to conduct impeachment proceedings against the president. To do so, the courts and Congress needed the information on the tapes.

Within days of the Court's decision, the House Judiciary Committee passed three articles of impeachment. These charged Nixon with obstruction of justice, by covering up a crime; defiance of the committee's subpoenas for the tapes; and abuse of power. Nevertheless, some Republicans maintained there was no "smoking gun"—that is, no clear evidence of crimes. They said the impeachment effort was strictly political.

Regardless, Nixon's support in Congress dwindled, and he found himself caught between a rock and a hard place: releasing the tapes would furnish more evidence for impeachment, but not releasing them would spur impeachment. He reportedly considered disregarding the decision but, after twelve days of weighing his options, complied with the order.

Releasing the tapes did reveal a smoking gun. Although the tapes did not show that Nixon participated in planning the break-in, they did show that he participated in covering it up. When the burglars blackmailed the administration, Nixon approved paying them hush money. He ordered the head of his reelection committee to "stonewall it" and "cover up." He and an aide formulated a plan to have the

CIA thwart the FBI in its investigation of the scandal. When his top aides were subpoenaed to appear before the grand jury, he encouraged them to lie.

In addition to this evidence of crimes, the tapes revealed profanity, vulgarity, and derogatory remarks about women, Catholics, Jews, blacks, Hispanics, and various ethnic groups. ("The Italians . . . they're not like us . . . they smell different, they look different, act different. . . . Of course, the trouble is . . . you can't find one that is honest."[55]) Such language repelled the public and undercut the image Nixon had tried to project.

As his presidency came collapsing all around him, White House insiders began telling people privately that Nixon was dazed, like a "wind-up doll" or a "madman." They said that he was drinking heavily, "going bananas," talking to portraits of past presidents, and showing other signs of cracking under the strain. Some worried that he was considering suicide. One day he said to his chief of staff, General Alexander Haig, "You fellows, in your business [the army], you have a way of handling problems like this. Somebody leaves a pistol in the drawer." He paused, then added sadly, "I don't have a pistol." Afterward, Haig notified Nixon's doctors and had Nixon's sleeping pills and tranquilizers taken away.[56]

When it became clear that public opinion would force the House to impeach him and the Senate to remove him, Nixon decided to resign. On August 9, 1974—just seventeen days after the Supreme Court's ruling—he became the first American president to do so. Vice President Gerald Ford became the new president.

Although the smoking gun had been found, some people thought Nixon should not have been driven from office. But Watergate was not just a break-in. It was a series of acts, more than can be de-

tailed here, to subvert the Constitution and democratic elections. As the magnitude of these acts came to light, Nixon lost some support. Then, as the cover-up of these acts came to light, he lost even more support. He had campaigned for president on a platform calling for "law and order" and had sworn an oath promising to "take care that the laws be faithfully executed." When Watergate revelations appeared in the media, he had proclaimed his innocence. Ultimately, the hypocrisy and the lying became too much for the public to stomach. Nixon no longer could lead the public he had misled for so long.

President Nixon at a press conference.
©1971, *The Washington Post*. Reprinted with permission.

Despite depression and cynicism about the scandal, many people saw that the system had worked as it was supposed to. The Founders had divided power to make it difficult for any one branch to amass too much power. In the face of the president's efforts to exercise vast power, the courts, with their orders to turn over the tapes, and Congress, with its Senate Watergate Committee hearings and House Judiciary Committee impeachment proceedings, checked the president's abuse of power. In addition, the media, with its extensive publicity, first prompted and then reinforced the actions of the courts and Congress.

However, although the system worked, it worked slowly. More than two years elapsed between the break-in and the resignation. For more than half the length of a presidential term, the president and many of his aides were so preoccupied with Watergate they could not devote sufficient attention to other problems facing the country.

When the affair was over, twenty-one of the president's men were con-

victed and sentenced to prison for their Watergate crimes. Except for one, a burglar who was most uncooperative and who served fifty-two months (G. Gordon Liddy, who now hosts a radio talk show), the men served from four to twelve months. Nixon, who could have and probably would have been prosecuted after leaving office, received a pardon from President Ford before any prosecution could begin.

Nine years after the resignation, the security guard who discovered the break-in was convicted for shoplifting in Augusta, Georgia. Unemployed, he had stolen a pair of shoes for his son. Unlike the president's men, he received the maximum sentence—twelve months for the $12 shoes.

Congress passed a law mandating that other, unreleased tapes and documents be turned over to the National Archives, which was to make public any that related to Watergate or had "general historic significance." The Archives has slowly released these materials. On one tape, Nixon is heard remarking to his chief of staff, "I always wondered about that taping equipment, but I'm damn glad we have it, aren't you?"[57]

Not only does Nixon's voice remain, but the effects of Watergate linger. The public has become less trustful of government officials, and the media have become more suspicious of them. The parties have become more aware of the benefits of a scandal involving their opponents. In the wake of Watergate, the Democrats captured the White House and gained many seats in Congress. These results have prompted both parties to point accusing fingers and to launch congressional investigations—though only against members of the other party— even when the alleged transgressions have been far less serious than those in Watergate. Thus, Watergate contributed to the culture of scandal that afflicts American politics today.

Key Terms

Watergate scandal
executive privilege
Articles of Confederation
Shays's Rebellion
Constitutional Convention
Great Compromise
Three-fifths Compromise
social contract
direct democracy
indirect democracy
federalism

separation of powers
checks and balances
natural rights
limited government
Iroquois Confederacy
Federalists
Antifederalists
Federalist Papers
Gettysburg Address
Bill of Rights

Further Reading

Leonard W. Levy, ed., *Essays on the Making of the Constitution* (New York: Oxford University Press, 1969). These essays address the question, Was the Constitution an undemocratic document framed and ratified by an undemocratic minority for an undemocratic society?

Clinton Rossiter, *1787: The Grand Convention* (New York: Macmillan, 1966). A lively account of the Constitutional Convention and the ratification campaign.

Theodore H. White, *Breach of Faith* (New York: Atheneum, 1975). A chronicle of the Watergate scandal as a Greek tragedy in which actors on both sides behaved in such ways as to fulfill their destinies.

Bob Woodward and Carl Bernstein, *All the President's Men* (New York: Simon & Schuster, 1974). A riveting account of journalistic sleuthing by the two reporters who broke the Watergate story.

Electronic Resources

lcweb.loc.gov/exhibits/declara/declaral.html
At this site, you can learn more about how the Declaration of Independence was written and see a special Library of Congress exhibit on the Declaration.

etext.virginia.edu/jefferson/quotations/jeffsite.html
This home page, sponsored by the University of Virginia, links to a variety of sites where you can access Jefferson's writings, autobiography, and other related Jeffersonia.

www.yahoo.com/Arts/Humanities/History/ U_S_History/20th_Century/1970s/Watergate/ Watergate_25th_Anniversary/
Links to documents concerning the Watergate affair, compiled twenty-five years later.

www.nwbuildnet.com/nwbn/usconstitutionsearch. html
Even the Constitution has a home page. Here it is, with links to other historical documents and to PBS Project Democracy. Another Constitution page with interesting links is www.usconstitution.net/, a site originally set up by a political science student as a class project.

InfoTrac College Edition

"The Legacy of Slavery Lingers"
"Keep Your Amendments Off My Constitution"

Notes

1. Nixon thought he might be considered an American Disraeli. (Benjamin Disraeli, a British prime minister in the nineteenth century, was a Tory who had progressive ideas.) Nixon praised Robert Blake's biography of Disraeli, and one cabinet secretary remarked in 1971, "The similarities are great, Mr. President, but what a pity that Blake could not quote Disraeli's conversations." Nixon did not destroy the tapes, even after they became a liability, apparently for this reason. Sidney Blumenthal, "The Longest Campaign," *New Yorker,* August 8, 1994, p. 37.

2. *United States v. Reynolds,* 345 U.S. 1 (1953).

3. The Indians, of course, had their own governments, and the Spanish may have established St. Augustine, Florida, or Santa Fe, New Mexico, before the English established Jamestown. These Spanish settlements were extensions of Spanish colonization of Mexico and were governed by Spanish officials in Mexico City.

4. This is not to suggest that the Pilgrims believed in democracy. Apparently, they were motivated to draft the compact by threats from some on the *Mayflower* that when the ship landed they would "use their owne libertie; for none had power to command them." Thus, the compact was designed to bind them to the laws of the colony. Richard Shenkman, *"I Love Paul Revere, Whether He Rode or Not"* (New York: HarperCollins, 1991), pp. 141–142.

5. David Hawke, *A Transaction of Free Men* (New York: Scribner's, 1964), p. 209.

6. Louis Fisher, *President and Congress* (New York: Free Press, 1972), p. 14.

7. Gordon S. Wood, "The Origins of the Constitution," *This Constitution: A Bicentennial Chronicle* (Summer 1987), pp. 10–11.

8. Eric Black, *Our Constitution* (Boulder, Colo.: Westview, 1988), p. 6. Shays, eventually pardoned by Massachusetts, settled in New York and became a staunch Federalist (Black, p. 8).

9. For development of this idea, see Kenneth M. Dolbeare and Linda J. Medcalf, "The Political Economy of the Constitution," *This Constitution: A Bicentennial Chronicle* (Spring 1987), pp. 4–10.

10. Black, *Our Constitution,* p. 59.

11. The Constitution, however, would reflect numerous aspects of the Articles. See Donald S. Lutz, "The Articles of Confederation as the Background to the Federal Republic," *Publius* 20 (Winter 1990), pp. 55–70.

12. Robert McCloskey, *The American Supreme Court* (Chicago: University of Chicago Press, 1960), p. 29.

13. Fred Barbash, "James Madison: A Man for the '80s," *Washington Post National Weekly Edition,* March 30, 1987, p. 23.

14. Robert A. Dahl, *A Preface to Democratic Theory* (Chicago: University of Chicago Press, 1956), p. 5. Yet, according to a poll in 1987, the bicentennial of the Constitution, only 1 percent of the public identified Madison as the one who played the biggest role in creating the Constitution. Most—31 percent—said Thomas Jefferson, who was a diplomat in France during the convention. Black, *Our Constitution,* p. 15.

15. Paul Finkelman, "Slavery at the Philadelphia Convention," *This Constitution: A Bicentennial Chronicle* (1987), pp. 25–30.

16. Finkelman, "Slavery at the Philadelphia Convention," p. 29.

17. Finkelman, "Slavery at the Philadelphia Convention."

18. Theodore J. Lowi, *American Government* (Hinsdale, Ill.: Dryden, 1976), p. 97.

19. C. Herman Pritchett, *Constitutional Law of the Federal System* (Englewood Cliffs, N.J.: Prentice Hall, 1984), p. xi.

20. Richard Hofstadter, *The American Political Tradition and the Men Who Made It* (New York: Random House, 1948), p. 13.

21. *Federalist Paper* #51.

22. *Federalist Paper* #47.

23. Max Farrand, *The Framing of the Constitution of the United States* (New Haven, Conn.: Yale University Press, 1913).

24. *Federalist Paper* #51.

25. Richard E. Neustadt, *Presidential Power and the Modern Presidents* (New York: Macmillan, 1990), p. 29.

26. Donald S. Lutz, "The Relative Influence of European Writers on Later Eighteenth-Century American Political Thought," *American Political Science Review* 78 (March 1984), pp. 139–197.

27. Alpheus T. Mason and Richard H. Leach, *In Quest of Freedom: American Political Thought and Practice,* 2d ed. (Englewood Cliffs, N.J.: Prentice Hall, 1973), p. 51.

28. For development of this idea, see Martin Landau, "A Self-Correcting System: The Constitution of the United States," *This Constitution: A Bicentennial Chronicle* (Summer 1986), pp. 4–10.

29. John P. Roche, "The Founding Fathers: A Reform Caucus in Action," *American Political Science Review* 56 (March 1962), pp. 799–816.

30. Ibid.

31. Charles Beard, *An Economic Interpretation of the Constitution* (New York: Macmillan, 1913).

32. Ellen Nore, "Charles A. Beard's Economic Interpretation of the Origins of the Constitution," *This Constitution* (Winter 1987), p. 39.

33. R. E. Brown, *Charles Beard and the Constitution* (Princeton, N.J.: Princeton University Press, 1956); Forrest MacDonald, *We the People* (Chicago: University of Chicago Press, 1976).

34. James MacGregor Burns, *The Vineyard of Liberty* (New York: Knopf, 1982), p. 33.

35. Bernard Bailyn, *Voyagers to the West* (New York: Knopf, 1986), p. 20.

36. The Boston Tea Party, contrary to myth, was not prompted by higher taxes on British tea. Parliament lowered the taxes to give the British East India Company, facing bankruptcy, an advantage in the colonial market. This threatened American shippers who smuggled tea from Holland and controlled about three-fourths of the market. The shippers resented Parliament's attempt to manipulate the economy from thousands of miles away. Shenkman, *"I Love Paul Revere, Whether He Rode or Not,"* p. 155.

37. *Federalist Paper* #10.

38. Black, *Our Constitution,* p. 21.

39. Calvin C. Jillson and Cecil L. Eubanks, "The Political Structure of Constitution Making," *American Journal of Political Science* 29 (August 1984), pp. 435–458.

40. Jonathan Elliot, *The Debates in the Several State Conventions on the Adoption of the Federal Constitution as Recommended by the General Convention at Philadelphia, in 1787,* 2d ed., 5 vols. (Philadelphia, 1896), vol. 2, p. 102; as quoted in Cecilia M. Kenyon, "Men of Little Faith," in *Origins of American Political Thought,* ed. John P. Roche (New York: Harper & Row, 1967), pp. 197–198.

41. For Antifederalist thinking, see W. B. Allen and Gordon Lloyd, eds., *The Essential Antifederalist* (Lanham, Md.: University Press of America, 1985); John F. Manley and Kenneth M. Dolbeare, *The Case against the Constitution* (Armonk, N.Y.: Sharpe, 1987).

42. "A Fundamental Contentment," *This Constitution: A Bicentennial Chronicle* (Fall 1984), p. 44.

43. Charles Warren, *The Making of the Constitution* (Boston: Little, Brown, 1928), p. xiv. Jefferson made this observation from afar, as he was ambassador to France during the Constitutional Convention.

44. These procedures posed problems for adoption of the Fourteenth Amendment after the Civil War. The amendment, which included the due process and equal protection clauses, was designed to protect the rights of the newly freed slaves. But the defeated Confederate states would not have ratified it, so the Radical Republican sponsors made their readmission to the Union contingent upon their approval of the amendment. This process may well have been a violation of the Constitution, as the process of adopting the Constitution itself had been a violation of the Articles of Confederation. Yet the people accepted the change. Bruce Ackerman, *We the People: Transformations* (Cambridge, Mass.: Harvard University Press, 1998).

45. Alan P. Grimes, *Democracy and the Amendments to the Constitution* (Lexington, Mass.: 1978). Grimes also shows how the adoption of new amendments reflects the rise of new power blocs in society.

46. Ackerman, *We the People,* discusses these "revolutions" at length. See also Theodore J. Lowi, *The End of Liberalism,* 2d ed. (New York: Norton, 1979), and *The Personal President* (Ithaca, N.Y.: Cornell, 1985).

47. William O. Douglas, *The Record of the Association of the Bar of the City of New York,* vol. 4 (1949), p. 152.

48. "South Africa Looks at U.S. Constitution," *Lincoln Sunday Journal-Star (New York Times),* October 7, 1990; David Remnick, "'We, the People,' from the Russian," *Washington Post National Weekly Edition,* September 10–16, 1990, p. 11.

49. Since Thailand became a constitutional monarchy in 1932. Anthony DePalma, "Constitutions Are the New Writers' Market," *New York Times,* November 30, 1997, Week in Review, p. 3.

50. Harold J. Spaeth, *Supreme Court Policy Making* (San Francisco: Freeman, 1979), p. 13.

51. Richard Morin, "Happy Days Are Here Again," *Washington Post National Weekly Edition,* August 25, 1997, p. 35.

52. About 25 percent split their ticket between candidates for president and representative. In addition, others split their vote between candidates for president and senator or between candidates for representative and senator. For an examination of the research about divided government, see Morris Fiorina, *Divided Government,* 2d ed. (Boston: Allyn & Bacon, 1996), p. 153.

53. Lewis Lapham, "Get Me Rewrite!" *New York Times Book Review* (February 4, 1996), p. 11.

54. 418 U.S. 683 (1974).

55. Tip O'Neill with William Novak, *Man of the House* (New York: Random House, 1987). The tapes did contain some useful advice for future presidents. Unfortunately, this advice, on tapes not released until 1999, came too late for President Clinton: "Frankly, we shouldn't have had those interns. They're a pain in the ass." "Verbatim," *Time* (October 18, 1999), p. 35.

56. Bob Woodward and Carl Bernstein, *The Final Days* (New York: Simon & Schuster, 1976), pp. 343, 403–404, 423.

57. "Tapes Confirm Nixon Approved Hush Money," *Lincoln Journal* (AP), June 5, 1991. For a survey of presidents' efforts to record their conversations, see William Doyle, *Inside the Oval Office: White House Tapes from FDR to Clinton* (New York: Kodansha, 1999).

CHAPTER 3

Federalism and the Growth of Government

YOU ARE THERE

Should the President Expand Federal Lands?

You are Bill Clinton, the lame duck president of the United States. It is 2000, and in this your last year in office you are facing a legacy problem. You will leave behind eight years of prosperity, balanced budgets, and the reform of welfare and entitlement programs. But the economy runs in cycles, prosperity is not forever, and the outcome of your welfare reform is still unknown. You want to leave something permanent for the American people as part of your legacy. Having served during one of the most partisan eras of the twentieth century, you have found it impossible to get most of your legislative program through Congress. So you have to look elsewhere, to areas where you can act on executive authority.

In your first term you discovered, as did many presidents before you, how to use the 1906 Antiquities Act to further your environmental goals without congressional approval.[1] The act allows presidents to safeguard objects or lands of historic, scientific, or archaeological significance by declaring them national monuments. Conferring this status on land or natural wonders limits access to them and prohibits their sale or develop-ment. Only three presidents since Teddy Roosevelt—Nixon, Reagan, and Bush—have chosen not to use the act to set aside some spectacular piece of publicly held land for posterity. Carter, another president famously frustrated by Congress, used the act to conserve fifty-four million acres of wilderness in Alaska, making him the all-time champion of land set-asides.

You have used the act four times since 1996: to create the Grand Staircase Escalante National Monument in Utah, the Grand Canyon Parashant and Agua Fria national monuments in Arizona, and the California Coastal National Monument, thousands of offshore rocks and tiny islands that run the length of the California coast. All of these are in western states where the federal government already owns and manages huge tracts of land, to the consternation of governors, legislators, and local business interests.

Now your agriculture secretary is recommending that you use your executive powers to confer national monument status on 355,000 acres of the Sequoia National Forest in California that contain seventy-five groves of giant sequoias. You do not have to consult state or local

After efforts of residents of Quincy, Missouri, failed to prevent a flood, the federal government worked with state and local governments to provide disaster relief.
Ron Haviv/SABA

officials. All you have to do is issue an executive order. There are good reasons to do it. Giant sequoias, the world's largest trees, used to grow as far east as Colorado but now are found only on the west slope of the Sierra Nevadas. About half are already protected because they are inside national parkland, but the trees in national forests are subject to fewer restrictions. And these trees are in an area with a history of fires.

Politically, making this declaration would improve your image with environmentalists. Although your environmental record has not been bad, you can point to few specific actions that would endear you to ecology-minded citizens. On the other hand, many residents of the communities surrounding the sequoia groves will resent your action. Declaring the area a national monument would put an end to further development and limit recreational use. More important, many will see your action as another example of the federal government using its power to impose its will on the states. The federal government already owns almost 45 percent of California land. Indeed, in other western states (Idaho, Oregon, Utah), the federal government owns over 50 percent of the land. In Nevada, it owns 80 percent.[2]

State and local governments have little control over how federal land is used. Through the Bureau of Land Management and the Forest Service, the federal government limits the number of cattle that can graze the land, the amount of timber that can be cut from forested lands, and, in some areas, the kind of vehicles that can drive on the land. Although the bureau tries to balance the interests of farmers, ranchers, loggers, and miners with environmental concerns, any regulation arouses angry protests. As one irate state legislator noted, "The federal government has a stranglehold on the rural West."[3]

The antagonism of many westerners to federal regulation is growing. At least thirty-five counties in the West have said that federally owned lands in their counties fall under their jurisdiction.[4] Such disputes strike at the heart of federal authority and our federalist structure.

You also worry that you will be accused of political opportunism. Even if there are good reasons for declaring the area a national monument, opponents are likely to criticize your motives. If people believe that you acted only to beef up your legacy, you will have saved the trees but undermined your political goal. But this may be a time when political motives coincide with genuine policy concerns. You know that kind of convergence of motives occurs much more frequently than cynics would admit.

On the other hand, you recall that when you were governor of Arkansas, you would have deeply resented a president shutting you out of a decision so important to your state. A middle ground might be to ask Congress to preserve the sequoias. Although this would still be a federal action, at least California's representatives and senators could help make the decision. If you make the declaration alone, the state and the affected communities will be kept out of the decision-making process.

Your time in office is running out. What do you do? Do you declare the giant sequoias a national monument, or do you pass up this opportunity to make a gift to the American people and avoid antagonizing local interests?

M ost Americans claim to believe that state governments are more responsive to them than the federal government (Table 1), but over the past sixty years they have asked the federal government to get involved in almost every policy issue imaginable. Many Americans decry the growth of big government, and yet few realize that over the past twenty-five years, the size of state governments has doubled while the number of federal employees has fallen. Most Americans want small government, but they also want a government powerful enough to keep the peace abroad and responsive to their needs at home.

These issues of the size and scope of the federal government relative to the states are not new. They are the same issues that the Founders debated at the Constitutional Convention in 1787. Conflict over whether the states or the national government have the final say in domestic policy sparked the Civil War (1861–1865). The victory of the Union over secessionist states determined that the national government, not the states, was supreme.

Table 1	The Public Trusts the States More		
		State	Federal
Which government do you trust to:			
do a better job running things?		70%	27%
establish rules about who can receive welfare?		70	25
set rules for workplace safety?		55	42
set Medicare and Medicaid regulations?		52	43
set environmental rules for clean air?			
and clean water?		51	47
protect civil rights?		35	61

SOURCE: Washington Post-ABC Poll, reported in Richard Morin, "Power to the States," *Washington Post National Weekly Edition*, March 27–April 2, 1995, p. 37.

Because of this outcome, because of our expectations of government and the sheer size of the country and its role in world affairs, we live in a nation with a strong central government. Yet we vigorously disagree about just how strong that government should be. Critics accuse the national government and its programs of being too large, too expensive, and too intrusive on the rights of the states and the people. Yet when members of Congress suggest cutting programs severely or transferring responsibilities back to the states, the public outcry is vociferous. And even though our system of powers at both the national and state levels contributes to the messiness of democracy that the public dislikes, there is little support for streamlining or centralizing powers at the national level.

These contradictions are perhaps endemic to a federal system. In this chapter we will examine the nature of American federalism and how it has changed as government has grown.

Federal and Other Systems

Federal Systems

The term **federalism** describes a system in which power is constitutionally divided between a central government and subnational or local governments (in the United States the subnational governments are the states). Both

Federalism is the only domestic issue in the United States over which several million Americans fought. Between 1861 and 1865, half a million combatants died. This photograph shows the remains of Richmond, Virginia, after a Civil War battle.
Corbis-Bettmann

levels of government receive their grants of power from a higher authority—the will of the people as expressed in a constitution. Power granted to each level is not necessarily exclusive. In the United States, each level has the power to tax, regulate, and provide benefits.

While the national government is not the creation of the states (as it was under the Articles of Confederation), neither can the national government abolish a state or alter its boundaries without its consent. That power is an essential element in federalism.

Nations that have federal systems—Germany, Canada, India, and Brazil, for example—vary greatly in their basic economic and political characteristics. They are similar only in that each has a written constitution allocating some powers to the national and some to the subnational governments.

Unitary Systems

In contrast to the federal system, in a **unitary system** the national government creates subnational governments and gives them what power it wishes. Thus, the national government is supreme. In Britain, for example, the national government can give or take away any power of the subnational governments or can even abolish them, as it did with some city governments in the 1980s. And, in unitary Sweden, the national parliament abolished 90 percent of its local governments from 1952 to 1975. Nearly 90 percent of all nations have unitary systems.

In the United States, the fifty states are each unitary with respect to their local governments; cities, counties, and school districts can be altered or even eliminated by state governments.

The distinction between unitary and federal is not at all related to the distinction between democracy and authoritarianism. Some unitary systems are among the most democratic in the world (Britain and Sweden); others are authoritarian (Egypt and China). Nor are only federal systems decentralized. All modern governments have to decentralize power because a central government, even in a unitary system, cannot run every local service or deal with every local problem.

Confederal Systems

The third arrangement between central and subnational governments is confederal. In a **confederal system,** the central government has only those powers given to it by the subnational governments; it cannot act directly on citizens. Two examples of confederal systems are the United States under the Articles of Confederation and

the United Nations. The lack of central authority in such systems makes them basically unworkable in modern nations.

The Political Bases of Federalism

Why do some nations choose a federal form of government while others do not? The Founders of the United States chose federalism as one means of limiting governmental power. Federalism also allowed the Founders to incorporate the states into the new government; no one thought seriously about abolishing the states. Another reason for choosing federalism was that it could help deal with national diversity. Federal systems are often, though not always, ethnically, linguistically, religiously, or racially diverse. We in the United States are not as diverse as the peoples of India, for example, but we are a nation of many ethnic groups, races, religions, and political traditions.

Our nation remains diverse, and our states reflect that diversity. Despite our national media networks, franchises and chains bringing the same products to all parts of the country, and transportation systems that carry us across the nation in only a few hours, there are still significant differences among us, and not just whether we prefer Texas chili or New England clam chowder. Different states and regions have developed somewhat different political styles and attitudes. Candidates for state office would not run the same campaign in Pennsylvania, for example, as they would in Idaho. Ways of looking at politics, partisan preferences, ideology, political style, and what appeals to voters vary across our nation.

In Chapter 1, we defined *political culture* as a shared body of values and beliefs that shapes perceptions and attitudes toward politics and government and, in turn, influences behavior. For much of the twentieth century, the United States was said to have three geographically based political subcultures or distinctive ways of looking at and participating in politics.[5] The *moralistic* political culture characterized the New England and the Upper Midwest view of politics as a way of improving life and the strong believe they should participate. In the *individualistic* political culture, said to be typical of the industrial Midwest and the East, the ultimate objective of politics was not to create a better life for all but to get benefits for oneself and one's group. In the *traditionalistic* political culture, associated with the states of the Deep South, politics was seen not as a way to further the public good but as a way to maintain the status quo, and little value was placed on participation.

Today the industrial Midwest is all but gone; only 2 percent of the population live on farms, and the Deep South, having been the site of intense grassroots political mobilization during the modern civil rights movement, today continues as a center of grassroots activity, especially among the religious right. The economic transformation of the United States from an industry- and agriculture-based economy to a high-tech and service economy has had an inevitable impact on political culture. Mass communication, especially television and the spread of Internet access, has radically altered political style. Also, the mobility of the American population means that fewer people are likely to have a political orientation rooted in a state or regional identity.

It is not that the three archetypal political subcultures have been homogenized but rather that the content of subcultures inevitably evolves in response to socioeconomic change. The country has no less diversity of interests; indeed, it is ethnically and racially more diverse. The fact that immigrants tend to settle in clusters in a handful of states and big cities concentrates regional differences, as does the contemporary emphasis on identity politics.

In addition states *want* to be different from one another. Each has its own constitution, flag, motto, symbols of state, not to mention its very own official state bird and flower. Each state is basically a political actor competing for a share of the nation's resources. Just as individuals organize around identity issues, so states compete with one another on the basis of their distinctive profiles. Geography, natural resources, political history, and demographic factors all shape a state's politics.

In New Mexico, for instance, 40 percent of the population is of Hispanic origin, while in Maine non-Hispanic whites make up over 98 percent of the population, and in Mississippi African Americans make up over 35 percent. In Florida, almost as many people are over age sixty-five (18 percent of the population) as are under seventeen (22 percent), but in Utah, young people outnumber senior citizens by more than four to one.[6] And in New Jersey, the median family income is almost 80 percent higher than in Arkansas ($48,021 versus $26,162).[7]

These disparities make for different politics in the states. The priorities of older people (health care, for instance) are different than those of younger people (education, for example). In states with larger numbers of Latinos and black Americans, civil rights issues are more salient than in states with predominantly white popula-

tions. And states whose citizens are poorer face greater demands for services and have correspondingly fewer resources to provide them.

States also vary in how liberal their policies are. One way to measure this is to determine how much the states spend on various activities such as education and health care and how restrictive or lenient their policies are toward gambling and crime.[8] The map in Figure 1 illustrates the results of one such analysis. The differences among the states can be explained by how "liberal" (see Chapter 4) each state's citizens are and by the kind of political culture the state has. State policies reflect the different views and social and economic circumstances of their citizens.

Thus, state boundaries mean something beyond identifying the government to which state taxes are paid. In policy areas as diverse as economic development, welfare, and regulation of personal morality (such as gambling and prostitution), states vary widely. Federalism, even with a strong national government, provides sufficient autonomy for states to adopt and maintain policies consistent with their own political cultures.

The Constitutional Bases of Federalism

Major Features of the System

As we saw in Chapter 2, the Founders were unsure how to solve the problem of national versus state powers. All wanted limited government. Although they saw federalism as one way to limit government power by dividing it, there was little debate over the concept of federalism, and the main outlines emerged only as the Founders dealt with other issues. The major features of nation-state relationships outlined by the Constitution include a strong national government, prohibition of certain powers to the states, and some limitations on national powers.

Strong National Government

Although the Founders did not all agree on how strong the national government should be, all did agree that they wanted a national government stronger than that of the Articles of Confederation. They wanted a national government able to tax without the permission of the states and one able to carry out foreign and domestic policies without the states' consent. Thus, the Constitution grants many specific powers to Congress, including taxation

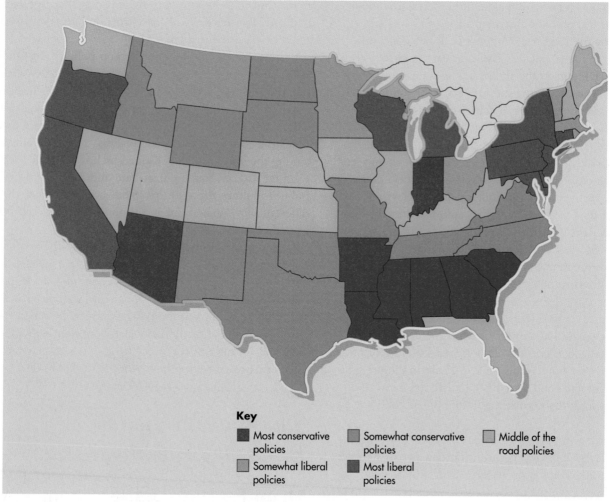

Key

- ■ Most conservative policies
- ■ Somewhat conservative policies
- □ Middle of the road policies
- ■ Somewhat liberal policies
- ■ Most liberal policies

FIGURE 1 ■ *States Vary in How Liberal or Conservative Their Policies Are*

SOURCE: Robert S. Erikson, Gerald C. Wright, and John P. McIver, *Statehouse Democracy: Public Opinion and Policy in the American States* (New York: Cambridge University Press, 1993), Table 4.2, p. 77.

and regulation of interstate commerce, which gives tremendous power to the national government and allows it to be independent of the will of the state governments. The clause granting Congress the power to make all laws **"necessary and proper"** for carrying out its specific powers—sometimes called the **implied powers clause**—also strengthened the national government. This grant of power soon was interpreted to mean that Congress could legislate in almost any area it wished.

In addition, the decision to make the president independent of Congress and the state legislatures also strengthened the federal government by giving the occupant a base from which to exercise independent national leadership. The president's role as commander in chief and principal executor of the laws of the United States further enlarged national powers. Finally, the **supremacy clause** established the predominance of the national government over the states. It says that treaties, the Constitution, and "laws made in pursuance thereof" are to be the supreme law of the land whenever they come into conflict with state laws or state actions.

Restrictions of States' Powers

The Constitution forbids states to undertake actions that might conflict with the power of the national government; they cannot enter into treaties, keep standing armies or navies, make war, print or coin money, or levy import or export taxes on goods. These prohibitions reaffirmed that the national government was to be supreme in making foreign policy and regulating interstate commerce. Under the Articles, the national government was limited in both these areas. The new Constitution also forbade states to infringe on certain rights of individuals. For example, a state cannot pass a law making an action a crime and then punish citizens who committed the "crime" before it was made illegal (an *ex post facto* or after-the-fact law).

Limitations on National Powers

The Constitution prohibits the creation of new states within existing states, the combination of two states, or the change of existing state boundaries without the approval of the legislatures of the affected states.

The Tenth Amendment granted to the states and to the people those powers not granted by the Constitution to the national government. At the time, this was considered a significant limit on national powers. But the broad construction of Congress's "necessary and proper" powers established by many federal court rulings over the decades weakened the Tenth Amendment. Yet the wording remains open to more restrictive interpretations, and in the 1990s there were attempts to breathe life into this amendment, with some success.[9]

These three features—a strong national government, prohibition of certain powers to the states, and some limitations on national powers—ensured a strong national government as well as a significant role for the states. The Founders believed that this arrangement would limit the ability of any one government to tyrannize its citizens and that the diversity of interests in the system would prevent the formation of a national majority that could trample minority rights. Similarly, a central government would ensure that states could protect the rights of their citizens against arbitrary local majorities. Many believed that the primary virtue of a federal system was that the authority of government was limited because it was divided between two levels.

Interpretations of Federalism

The Founders left the exact details of the nation-state relationship vague because they could not agree on specifics. It is not surprising that different views of federalism emerged.[10] (See also the box "Federalism and the 'Mischiefs of Faction.'")

Nation-Centered Federalism

In the *Federalist Papers,* Alexander Hamilton clearly articulated the view that national power was to be supreme. This nation-centered view of federalism rests on the assumption that the Constitution is a document ratified by the people. The states have many powers, but

---

Federalism and the "Mischiefs of Faction"

One of the most influential works of American political theory is James Madison's *Federalist Paper* 10 (reprinted in the appendix to this book). This essay helps explain the attraction of a federal system for Madison and many of the other Founders.

In *Federalist* 10, Madison asserted that it is inevitable that factions—groups of citizens seeking some goal contrary to the rights of other citizens or to the well-being of the whole country—will threaten the stability of nations. To cure the **"mischiefs of faction"** Madison said government has either to remove the causes of factionalism or to control its effects. The first, Madison believed, was unrealistic because it would require the impossible changing of selfish human nature. It also would require taking away freedom by outlawing opinions and strictly regulating behavior. People inevitably have different ideas and beliefs, and government, he thought, should not try to prevent this.

Because the causes of faction could not be removed without placing too many restrictions on freedom, its effects had to be controlled by a properly constructed government. If a faction were less than a majority, Madison believed it could be controlled through majority rule, the majority defeating the minority faction. If the faction were a majority, however, a greater problem arose, but one for which Madison had an answer.

To control a majority faction, one had only to limit the ability of a majority to carry out its wishes. Madison believed this was impossible in a small democracy, where there is little to check a majority determined to do something. But in a large federalist system, there are many checks on a majority faction—more interests competing with each other and large distances to separate those who might scheme to deprive others of liberty. As Madison noted, "The influence of factious leaders may kindle a flame within their particular States, but will be unable to spread a general conflagration through the other States." Having many states and having them spread over a large territory were, in Madison's view, major checks against majority tyranny.

---

the national government has the ultimate responsibility for preserving the nation and the viability of the states as well. Nation-centered federalism was the view used by northerners to justify a war to prevent the southern states from seceding in 1861.

State-Centered Federalism

An alternative view, used by southerners to justify their defiance of the central government before the Civil War, held that the Constitution is a product of state action. In this view, the states created the union. State-centered federalists argue that the grant of powers to Congress is limited to those items specifically mentioned in Article I. Madison said, "The powers delegated . . . to the federal government are few and defined. Those which are to remain in the state governments are numerous and indefinite."[11] In this view, any attempt by Congress to go beyond these explicitly listed powers violates state authority.

Dual Federalism

Yet a third interpretation of the division of powers rests on the argument that the Constitution created a system in which the national government and the states each have separate grants of power, with each supreme in its own sphere. In this view, called **dual federalism,** the two levels of government are essentially equal. Their differences derive from their separate jurisdictions, not from inequality of power.

Federalism and the Growth of Government

In just over two hundred years, our national government has grown from a few hundred people with relatively limited impact on the residents of thirteen small states to a government employing several millions, affecting the daily lives of most of the population of more than 270 million people in fifty states. This transformation to a large complex nation has changed the way in which our federal system functions.

Over the years, the dominant interpretations of power sharing in our form of federalism have shifted among the nation-centered, state-centered, and dual views. Interpretations reflect changing court composition, economic conditions, the philosophies of those in the executive and legislative branches, and changing public demands. There has been a general trend away from state-centered and toward nation-centered federalism, but significant shorter-term shifts have occurred back toward the states.

Early Nationalist Period

Very soon after the Constitution was ratified, the federal courts became the arbiters of the Constitution. (Note that we are using *federal* to mean "national," a confusing but common usage. "Federal government" is used interchangeably with "national government.") John Marshall, chief justice of the United States from 1801 to 1835, was a firm believer in the need for a strong national government and the decisions of his Court supported this view. The Marshall-led Supreme Court not only held that decisions of the state courts could be overturned by the federal courts, it also, in the case of *McCulloch v. Maryland,* gave approval to the broad interpretation of Congress's implied powers in the Constitution.

McCulloch v. Maryland

The broad interpretation of the clause giving Congress the right to make all laws "necessary and proper" to carry out the powers that the Constitution gives it, grew out of a case involving the establishment of a national bank. Because the Constitution does not explicitly grant Congress the authority to charter banks, many people thought Congress may have been infringing on rights the Constitution left to the states. Ironically, it was John Calhoun, later to become the leading states' rights advocate, who introduced a bill to charter a Bank of the United States.

Once established, the bank was immediately unpopular because it competed with smaller banks operating under state laws and because some of its branches engaged in reckless and even fraudulent practices. When the government of Maryland levied a tax on the notes—what we would now call currency—issued by the Baltimore branch of the bank, the constitutionality of the bank was called into question and a case was brought to the Supreme Court.

In 1819 in **McCulloch v. Maryland,** John Marshall wrote one of his most influential decisions.[12] Pronouncing the tax unconstitutional, Marshall wrote that "the power to tax involves the power to destroy." The states should not have the power to destroy the bank, he stated, because the bank was "necessary and proper" to carry out Congress's powers to collect taxes, borrow money, regulate commerce, and raise an army. Marshall argued that if the goal of the legislation is legitimate and constitutional, "all means which are appropriate, which are plainly adapted to that end, which are not prohibited, but consistent with the letter and spirit of the Constitution, are constitutional."

Thus, Marshall interpreted "necessary" quite loosely. The bank was probably not necessary, but it was "use-

In a spirit of optimism amid the turmoil of the Civil War, Congress in 1862 established federal support for the land grant colleges, a striking example of intergovernmental cooperation in the nineteenth century. Today many of these institutions are among our finest universities. Here, students plow on the campus of the Pennsylvania State University, one of the first land grant colleges.
U.S. Department of Agriculture

ful." This interpretation of the implied powers clause allowed Congress, and thus the national government, to wield much more authority than the Constitution gave it explicitly.

Although there was some negative reaction—"a deadly blow has been struck at the sovereignty of the states," cried one Baltimore newspaper—the Court maintained its strong nation-centered position as long as Marshall was chief justice.

Early Growth of Government

At the same time the courts were interpreting national powers broadly, the national government was exercising its powers on a rather small scale. The federal government had only one thousand employees in the administration of George Washington, and this number had increased only to thirty-three thousand by the presidency of James Buchanan seventy years later. The national government also raised relatively little revenue. But state

governments were also small and had limited functions. There were only a few federal-state cooperative activities. For example, the federal government gave land to the states to support education and participated in joint federal-state-private ventures, such as canal-building projects initiated by the states.

Thus, the early nationalist period was characterized by the growth of nation-centered federalism in legal doctrine, by small-scale state and national government, and by a few intergovernmental cooperative activities responding to the needs of an expanding nation.

Pre–Civil War Period

In 1836, the Court began to interpret the Tenth Amendment as a strict limitation on federal powers, holding that powers to provide for public health, safety, and order were *exclusively* powers of the state governments, not of the national government. This dual federalism interpretation eroded some of the nation-centered federal interpretations of the Marshall Court while continuing to uphold the rights of the federal courts to interpret the Constitution.

At the same time, champions of the state-centered view of federalism were gaining ascendance in the South. Southern leaders feared that the federal government, dominated by the increasingly populous North, would regulate or even abolish slavery. John Calhoun, one of the leading proponents for the state-centered view, even went so far as to say that a state could nullify laws of Congress (the doctrine of nullification). According to Calhoun, a state could withdraw from the Union if it wished. When the South did secede from the Union in 1861, it called itself the Confederate States of America, emphasizing the supremacy of the states embedded in a confederal system. After the Civil War, the vision of state-centered federalism largely lost its credibility.

The Civil War to the New Deal

After the Civil War, vast urbanization and industrialization took place throughout the United States. Living and working conditions for many city dwellers were appalling. Adults as well as children who moved into the cities often took jobs in sweatshops—factories where they worked long hours in unsafe conditions for low pay.

Spurred by revelations of these unsafe and degrading conditions, states and sometimes Congress tried to regulate working conditions, working hours, and pay through such means as child labor and industrial safety laws. Beginning in the 1880s, a conservative Supreme Court used the dual federalism doctrine to rule unconstitutional many federal attempts to regulate. But it often ruled that the states had overstepped their powers as well, displaying more of an antigovernment, pro-business stance than a commitment to dual federalism. From 1874 to 1937, the Supreme Court found fifty federal and four hundred state laws unconstitutional.[13] Before the Civil War, in contrast, the Court overturned only two congressional and sixty state laws.

At the same time that the Court was limiting both state and national action in regulating business and industry, both levels of government were slowly expanding. The revenues of both grew—the United States through an income tax finally ratified in 1913, the states and localities through gasoline and cigarette taxes, higher property taxes, and some state income taxes. Federal support for state programs also grew through land and case grants given by the federal government to the states.[14] By the late 1920s, however, most governmental functions still rested primarily in state and local hands.

The states were clearly the dominant partner in providing most services, from health and sanitation to police and fire protection. The federal government provided few direct services to individuals, nor did it regulate their behavior. The Great Depression signaled a dramatic shift in this arrangement.

The New Deal

To grasp the scope of the changes that have taken place in our federal structure between 1930 and today, consider the report of a sociologist who studied community life in Muncie, Indiana.[15] In 1924 the federal govern-

President Roosevelt's confidence, along with the hopes people had in his New Deal programs, led to public support for the expansion of the role of the federal government.
AP/Wide World Photos

ment in Muncie was symbolized by little more than the post office and the American flag. Today, two-thirds of the households in Muncie depend in part on federal funds—federal employment, Social Security and other income support, veterans benefits, student scholarships and loans, Medicare and Medicaid, and many other smaller programs.

In large part, the Great Depression brought about these changes. During the stock market crash of 1929, wealthy people became poor overnight. In the depths of the Depression one-fourth of the workforce was unemployed, and banks failed daily.

Unlike today, there was no systematic national program of relief for the unemployed then—no unemployment compensation, no food stamps, no welfare, nothing to help put food on the table and pay the rent. Millions were hungry, homeless, and hopeless. States and localities, which had the responsibility for providing relief to the poor, were overwhelmed; they did not have the funds or organizational resources to cope with the millions needing help. And private charities did not have enough resources to assume the burden.

The magnitude of the economic crisis led to the election of Franklin Delano Roosevelt in 1932. He formulated, and Congress passed, a program called the **New Deal** (see the box on "New Deal Legislation"). Its purpose was to stimulate economic recovery and aid those who were unemployed, hungry, and in ill health. New Deal legislation regulated many activities of business and labor, set up a welfare system for the first time, and began large-scale federal-state cooperation in funding and administering programs through federal grants-in-aid. Grants-in-aid provided federal money to states (and occasionally to local governments) to set up programs to help people—for example, the aged poor or the unemployed.

These measures had strong popular support, although they were opposed by many business and conservative groups and initially by the Supreme Court. But after the reelection of Roosevelt in 1936, the Court became more favorable toward New Deal legislation, and later resignations of two conservative judges ensured that the Court would be sympathetic to the New Deal (see Chapter 13 for more on the Court and the New Deal.)

The Court decisions approving New Deal legislation were, in a sense, a return to the nation-centered federalism of John Marshall's day. But although the Supreme Court ratified much of the New Deal, it also approved more sweeping *state* regulations of business and labor than had the more conservative pre–New

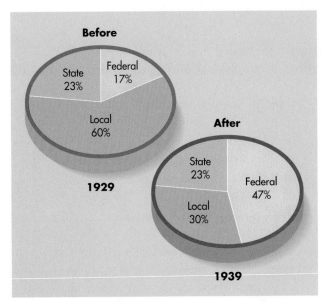

FIGURE 2 ■ *The New Deal Increased Federal and State Spending* Share of nonmilitary spending by each level of government, before and after New Deal legislation.

SOURCE: "Significant Features of Fiscal Federalism," *Advisory Commission on Intergovernmental Relations* (Washington, D.C.: U.S. Government Printing Office, 1979), 7.

Deal Court. Thus, the change in Court philosophy did not enlarge the federal role at the expense of the powers of the states. *It enlarged the powers of both state and federal government.* In doing so, the Court responded to preferences on the part of taxpayers for a more active government to cope with the tragedy of the Great Depression. The limited government desired by the Founders became less limited as both state and national government grew.

Changes in patterns of taxing and spending soon reflected the green light given to federal involvement with the states and localities. As Figure 2 indicates, the federal share of spending for domestic needs (exclusive of military spending) nearly tripled, from 17 percent in 1929, before the New Deal, to 47 percent in 1939, a decade later. The state share stayed constant while the local share dropped dramatically. The federal government raised more revenue and in turn gave much of it to the states and localities in the form of grants-in-aid to carry out programs such as unemployment compensation, free school lunches, emergency welfare relief, farm surpluses to the needy, and other programs.

The New Deal brought a dramatic change in the relationship of the national government to its citizens. Before this, when the national government directly touched the lives of citizens, it usually was to give or sell them something, such as land for settlers or subsidies for

March 9, 1933	Emergency Banking Act				
March 31, 1933	Civilian Conservation Corps created				
May 12, 1933	Agricultural Adjustment Act				
May 12, 1933	Federal Emergency Relief Act				
May 18, 1933	Tennessee Valley Authority created				
June 5, 1933	Nation taken off gold standard				
June 13, 1933	Home Owners Loan Corporation created				
June 16, 1933	Federal Deposit Insurance Corporation created				
June 16, 1933	Farm Credit Administration created				
June 16, 1933	National Industrial Recovery Act				
January 30, 1934	Dollar devalued				
June 6, 1934	Securities and Exchange Commission authorized				
June 12, 1934	Reciprocal Tariff Act				
June 19, 1934	Federal Communications Commission created	April 8, 1935	Works Progress Administration created	August 30, 1935	National Bituminous Coal Conservation Act
June 27, 1934	Railroad Retirement Act	July 5, 1935	National Labor Relations Act	February 19, 1936	Soil Conservation and Domestic Allotment Act
June 28, 1934	Federal Housing Administration authorized	August 14, 1935	Social Security Act		
		August 26, 1935	Federal Power Commission created		

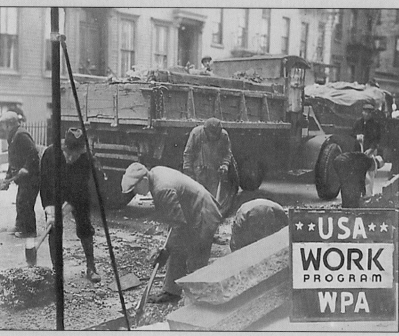

Franklin Roosevelt took office on March 4, 1933. He immediately sent to Congress a group of legislative proposals, many of which Congress passed within one hundred days. Roosevelt's program, known as the New Deal, enlarged the role of the federal government. Shown in the photo are civilians employed in the Works Progress Administration (WPA), a New Deal agency that built schools, roads, airports, and post offices in many towns in the late 1930s. Though the term boondoggle *was coined in reference to some WPA projects, the agency was successful in putting millions to work and improving the nation's public buildings, roads, and bridges.*
National Archives

SOURCE: List compiled by Lee Epstein and Thomas Walker, *Constitutional Law for a Changing America: Institutional Powers and Constraints* (Washington, D.C.: CQ Press, 1992), 283.

businesses helping develop the frontier.[16] With New Deal programs the federal government directly affected the lives of its citizens through its regulations (of banks and working conditions, for example) and its redistributive policies designed to protect the poor (such as Social Security and Aid to Dependent Children).

From the New Deal to the Great Society

During the years that followed the initiation of the New Deal, federal aid to states increased steadily but not dramatically. But federal support to the states carried conditions. For example, local administrators of Aid to Dependent Children programs had to be hired through a merit system, not because of political or personal connections. Construction funds for highways could be spent only on highways whose designs met professional standards. Thus, federal "strings" accompanied federal money.

By the 1950s, some public officials became uneasy about the growing size of the federal government and its involvement in so many state and local programs. Yet under President Dwight D. Eisenhower, a Republican concerned about the growth of federal involvement, many new federal grants-in-aid to the states were added, ranging from the massively expensive interstate highway program to collegiate programs in science, engineering, and languages. Federal grants-in-aid spending nearly tripled during his administration (1952–1960).

The 1960s witnessed an explosion in federal programs. Most were initiated by President Lyndon Johnson's massive social welfare program called the Great Society. Federal support was extended to many areas that were formerly state and local preserves such as law enforcement, urban mass transit, public education, and fire protection.

Johnson's concept of federalism was born in the New Deal era; his was a centralizing approach in which program areas were identified by, funded from, and monitored at the national level yet allowed for local input on which projects got funded. A new feature of the Great Society era was the increasing number of grants that went directly to localities, bypassing states. Urban and other local officials, believing the state legislatures were unresponsive to their interests, now demanded, and got, direct federal support.

From 1960 to 1968, as the number of federal programs grew from 132 to 379 and federal aid more than tripled, state and local governments became increasingly dependent on federal funding.[17] The vast increase in programs and the multiplying requirements and conditions of the grants made federal aid ever more complex. State and local officials soon felt hamstrung by the increasingly burdensome regulations.

New Federalism

When Richard Nixon (1969–1974) came into office he wanted to make government "more effective as well as more efficient." Nixon took a managerial rather than ideological approach to streamlining the cumbersome structure created by the profusion of Great Society programs. He saw a messy bureaucratic problem and an overconcentration of decision making at the federal level, and he tried to find a solution through more efficient management.[18]

Nixon's plan had two primary elements. One was to consolidate the several hundred grant programs into six major functional areas. Instead of trying to micromanage hundreds of types of grants from the federal level, Washington would make block grants to the states and localities and leave it to them to determine how to fund programs in these functional areas. This greater leeway in how to spend grant money gave local officials more opportunity to target projects to local needs. It also meant administrative streamlining at the federal level.

The second major aspect of Nixon's **new federalism** was general revenue sharing. Under this program tax money paid into the federal government was returned to the states to fund local projects and services. It was a way of encouraging state activism in the hope that it would decrease the need for federal programs. The main restriction on use was that the way money was spent had to be consistent with federal civil rights and equal opportunity laws.

In contrast to Nixon's managerial approach, Ronald Reagan's (1981–1988) new federalism had a more ideological purpose, as he made clear when he declared in his first inaugural address: "Government is not the solution to our problems. Government is the problem." Reagan said he was seeking a "quiet revolution" to bring people closer to government. Thus, his new federalism was aimed at reducing the power and influence of government rather than at improving intergovernmental management and effectiveness. Instead of seeing block grants as a way to encourage states to provide services the federal government would fund, Reagan saw them as a step toward ending all federal involvement in these program areas. He opposed general revenue sharing and ended the program.

Reagan's critics have a more pragmatic explanation for his new federalism; they said it was driven as much or more by fiscal as ideological considerations. They say he chose to cut federal funding for state and local programs to reduce the size of the budget deficits created by his increased military spending. While this may well have been a factor, it is hard to deny that Reagan's federalism was much more ideologically driven than Nixon's managerial approach to reform. It is also true that Reagan's new federalism was rooted not so much in state-centered or dual federalism as it was in his opposition to government. Reagan's ultimate goal was to

Problems get all the publicity, or so it seems. When federal officials accept favors from industries they are supposed to regulate or when the government buys hammers at outrageous prices, we hear about it. There are a lot of these stories out there, and the media have little trouble bringing them to us. We don't hear nearly as many stories about government doing its job well.

Nevertheless, our government does work. And it does some things exceedingly well. Tom Hanks's HBO miniseries, "From the Earth to the Moon," dramatized a spectacularly successful 1960s project—putting a man on the moon. Less spectacularly, government every day performs thousands of tasks and performs them responsibly and effectively. Despite the popular saying "Close enough for government work," government's standards are as high, if not higher, than those in the private sector. In this and succeeding chapters, we will highlight some examples where government indeed works well.

Disaster Relief and Federalism

One of the roles of the national government is to undertake tasks that the states cannot handle themselves. Providing "for the common defence," in the words of the Preamble to the Constitution, is the classic example. Only the national government can effectively protect the nation from foreign enemies.

Assisting states in times of natural disaster is another example. The destruction caused by a hurricane, flood, tornado, or earthquake may be so severe and widespread that the resources of the affected states and localities are over-

whelmed. And if the damage is not quickly repaired, the local economy slows, people lose jobs, and recovery is difficult. Paradoxically, when the need for state and local government action is the greatest, local resources are stretched to the breaking point. Just when they need to spend money to rebuild roads, bridges, buildings, and houses, their tax revenues dip significantly. Just when people can't work, no income taxes are withheld; when people can't shop, because stores are destroyed, sales taxes are not collected. When a state decides it cannot deal with a natural disaster on its own it can ask the president to declare it a federal disaster area.

The national government helps out in these situations through the Federal Emergency Management Agency (FEMA). Originally set up in 1979 to cope with the effects of a nuclear attack,[1] the agency has in recent years been called to assist in areas struck by natural disasters by providing financial help, temporary shelters, and a host of other aid.

Created for one purpose and diverted to another, the agency got off to a rough start. It was especially criticized for an inadequate response to Hurricane Andrew in south Florida in 1992. It took three days for the agency to begin distributing emergency food and water, and medical help was delayed, too. Senator Ernest Hollings (D-S.C.) once described FEMA as "the sorriest bunch of bureaucratic jackasses I've ever known."[2] The agency's response to Hurricane Andrew reinforced that image.

The widespread criticism FEMA received from both Republicans and Democrats led to some major changes.

The agency got new appointees with significant disaster relief experience. And FEMA changed its approach, from reactive ("Let's see if they ask for help") to proactive ("Let's see what we can do right now"). Red tape was cut, and agency response time was drastically reduced. For instance, a FEMA advance team arrived in Oklahoma City about five hours after the bombing of the Alfred P. Murrah Federal Office Building in 1995, and a search and rescue team was on the scene by 2:30 A.M. the following morning.[3]

The agency responded with similar success to the devastating floods in the Midwest in 1993. When the Des Moines (Iowa) Water Works was on the verge of collapse, FEMA set up water distribution centers and water purification systems within a day. FEMA provided clean water to Des Moines residents for over two weeks.

The rejuvenated Federal Emergency Management Agency stands as a clear example of federalism in action. No matter how much independent autonomy we want states to have, states cannot always respond adequately to disasters of catastrophic proportions. But the national government can help alleviate local distress without undermining the independence of the states. When the national government rolls up its sleeves to help out, it underlines that we are all part of the same nation, sharing its benefits and helping to carry one another's burdens no matter which state we live in.

1. Ted Gup, "How FEMA Learned to Stop Worrying about Civilians and Love the Bomb," *Mother Jones* (January/February 1994): 28.
2. Quoted in Daniel Franklin, "The FEMA Phoenix," *Washington Monthly* (July/August 1995): 38.
3. Ibid., 32.

reduce the role of government at all levels (except for national defense) and increase "society's reliance on private markets" and private institutions.[19] This approach—cutting federal spending on local and state programs to downsize government at all levels—has been called *instrumental federalism* in contrast with Nixon's "rationalizing" approach, in which making government more efficient and effective was an end in itself.

While Reagan had an ideological commitment to smaller government, he had no significant programmatic approach to achieve it, and he was often more preoccupied with the Cold War than with his domestic program. In fact, the size and expenditures of the federal government grew during his administration, and states gained few new powers. Reagan took a more indirect approach in rolling back government power by slowing enforcement or blocking implementation of rules he thought were an abuse of federal power.

The New New Federalism

Like Reagan, Bill Clinton came to office with a wary view of Washington and a commitment to working in partnership with governors. Clinton was a multiterm governor from a southern state where the states' rights tradition held sway; reforming state-federal relations had been a special interest when he chaired the national organization of governors and a reform group within the Democratic Party. Except in the area of civil rights policy, Clinton claimed to be a supporter of state activism. On this issue there was partial convergence of interest with the Contract with America Republicans who gained control of Congress midway through Clinton's first term. Their goal, Speaker Newt Gingrich said, was "to rethink the entire structure of American society, and the entire structure of American government. . . . This is a real revolution."[20]

Unlike the Gingrich Republicans, Clinton was not an advocate of state-centered federalism or smaller government for its own sake. But he was committed to the idea of the states as laboratories (earlier articulated by Justice Louis Brandeis)—that is, as places for policy experimentation. He used the phrase frequently, wrote it into executive orders, and eventually based his welfare, health care, and education policies around it.[21] During the period from 1994 through the end of his administration, Clinton and congressional Republicans supported policies that delegated more powers to the states than either Nixon's or Reagan's new federalism had. Overall, Clinton's federalism policies were much closer to Nixon's than to Reagan's in that both Clinton and

Nixon were primarily interested in "rationalizing intergovernmental relations" and making government more efficient.

The Gingrich Republicans, on the other hand, shared Reagan's view of government and put forward a legislative program for downsizing the federal government. The return of, or delegation of powers to, subunits or lower levels of government from a higher level is called **devolution.** Here we use it to refer to the delegation, by the national to state and local governments, of the authority to make and implement policy in specific areas. In contrast to Nixon's new federalism, which was a piecemeal attempt to give states sharply restricted areas of decision-making authority, devolution meant the return of functional areas of policymaking to subnational units of government. What happened during the Clinton years was by no means a wholesale surrender of policymaking authority because the federal government was still telling the states that there were specific areas, such as welfare, in which they had to provide services. Another aspect of the devolutionary trend has been a more deferential stance toward the states in implementation of federal rules and regulations, especially regulation of business and the environment. (See the discussion on unfunded mandates in the later "Conflict" section.)

Despite the new emphasis on devolution, Congress appears to have few advocates of pure state-centered federalism. While delegating some authority, Congress continues to supersede the states in rule making whenever it thinks necessary. In recent years, bills have been introduced to supplant state laws on drunk driving with a national standard, allow property owners to bypass state courts and go directly to federal courts to protest local zoning laws, and override state laws on late-term abortions and assisted suicides.[22] In 1998 Congress even restricted state taxation powers by passing a three-year moratorium on taxing e-commerce and other Internet activity, an act states claim will cost them $20 billion in lost revenue.[23] One congressman said of his colleagues that they "don't really believe in states' rights; they believe in deciding the issue at whatever level of government they think will do it their way. They want to be Thomas Jefferson on Monday, Wednesday and Friday and Alexander Hamilton on Tuesday and Thursday and Saturday."[24]

A more consistent trend toward empowering the states at the expense of the national government can be found in the last decade of rulings by the Supreme Court. Between 1992 and 1999, it handed down five key decisions that restrict Congress's ability to impose rules

Table 2 — Number of Government Units in the United States

Part of the reason that intergovernmental relations in the United States are so complex is that there are so many units of government. Though the number of school districts has decreased dramatically in the last 40 years, and the number of townships has declined slowly, the number of "special districts"—created for a single purpose, such as parks, airports, or flood control management—continues to grow.

	States	Counties	Municipalities	Townships and Towns	School Districts	Special Districts
1942	48	3,050	16,220	18,919	108,579	8,299
1997	50	3,043	19,372	16,629	13,726	34,683

SOURCE: *Statistical Abstract of the United States, 1999* (Washington, D.C.: U.S. Government Printing Office, 1999), Table 500.

and regulations on state governments and prevent litigants from bypassing state courts to seek remedies in federal courts. In a 1995 decision the Court ruled for the first time since the New Deal that Congress had exceeded its authority to regulate interstate commerce. While the rulings do not try to reinterpret or limit the areas in which Congress can legislate, the Court has overturned a number of obligations Congress had placed on the states to implement federal laws. The current Court's interpretation of federal relations has been summarized as "Rights without Remedies," or one that permits Congress to confer rights on citizens but not to tell the states how to enforce them.[25] Now that the direction of the thinking of the Court's majority is known, dozens of other federalism suits are being filed.

To a great extent, the increased activism of states since the 1980s has come about *because* of the growth of government. The fiscal restraints imposed by decades of spiraling federal budget deficits made it difficult for Congress or the president to propose new initiatives or to fund existing programs. At the same time, the Vietnam War and the Watergate, Iran-Contra, and Clinton scandals all contributed to increased partisanship and gridlock at the federal level and to declining trust among the public. State governments now look less often to Washington and instead launch their own policy initiatives. In the 1990s the states experimented with charter schools, vouchers for private schools, rolling back affirmative action and bilingual programs, new ways of teaching religion in schools, and a variety of crime laws such as mandatory sentencing, three-strikes laws, and victims' compensation. A few states adopted term limits and tax caps and passed their own campaign financing laws. Some have placed restrictions on gay rights, while a few have passed laws strengthening them, supporting health benefits for gay partners. Since the states have gained control over welfare, they have tried many different job training and work programs.[26] The states have

also become more bold in challenging or refusing to enforce federal regulations affecting business and the environment and have in one case refused to implement federal gun laws.

A telling measure of the general turning away from Washington is the increasing use of the ballot initiative. Interest groups now try to bypass not only Congress but state legislatures as well by getting policy questions placed on state ballots and having them decided directly by voters. In 1998, of sixty-six statewide initiatives that made it onto ballots, thirty-nine became law; overall, about 40 percent of all initiatives become law, while only a tiny percentage of bills submitted to legislatures get passed into law.[27] Doing an end run around their elected representatives, voters have approved initiatives that kill state laws on affirmative action, sanction medical use of marijuana, impose limits on campaign spending and contributions, expanding casino gambling, and give adopted children the right to know the names of their biological parents.

It is important to remember that through all these policy changes, nothing has changed in the constitutional relationship between the national and state governments. Authority delegated can be taken back by the center. This is where the divergence of views occurs among contemporary supporters of devolution. Advocates of state-centered and dual federalism believe Washington has only surrendered powers that by right belong to the states, whereas the more pragmatic supporters of devolution see it as a practical measure to bring more efficiency to policymaking and implementation. Welfare policy, for example, was long thought of by many Americans as a bungled federal program. But welfare was always jointly funded and implemented by Washington and the states and localities. In fact, much of the old program was administered at the county level. In Clinton's approach to federal-state relations, it was both a rationalization of the process and smart politics to put accountability at the level where the decisions are made.

The Practice of Federalism

Today's federalism is a mixture of cooperation and conflict. One expert calls it "competitive federalism," because states and the federal government are competing for leadership of the nation's domestic policy.[28] In this section, we review some of the mechanics of today's federalism that make it possible for more than eighty-seven thousand units to coordinate the day-to-day work of government.

Federal-State Relations

Cooperative Federalism

Much federal-state activity is cooperative. Given the large number of governments in the United States (Table 2), cooperation is essential. States and the federal government work together in a myriad of activities in almost every area of policy. (See also the boxes "Are States Really Closer to the People?" and "Who, Me?")

The term *cooperative federalism* describes the day-to-day joint activities and continuing cooperation among federal, state, and local officials in carrying out the business of government. The term encompasses the relationship of federal and state officials when distributing payments to farmers, providing welfare services, planning highways, organizing centers for the elderly, and carrying out all the functions that the national and state governments jointly fund and organize. It also refers to informal cooperation in locating criminals, tracking down mysterious diseases, and many other activities.

One example of informal but intensive cooperation is the Centers for Disease Control in Atlanta, which helps state and local governments meet health emergencies and prevent the spread of contagious diseases. National and state police and other crime-fighting agencies share data on crimes and criminals. The federal government and the states also jointly regulate in several areas, including occupational safety and the environment.

Another important area of federal-state cooperation is federal grants to states (Figure 3). The federal government returns tax revenues to states to help pay for essential services provided by state and local governments. Mass transit, community development and unemployment compensation are good examples. Grants to help states collect child support money from nonpaying divorced or unmarried fathers is another. Despite some inefficiency, federal funding has succeeded in helping state

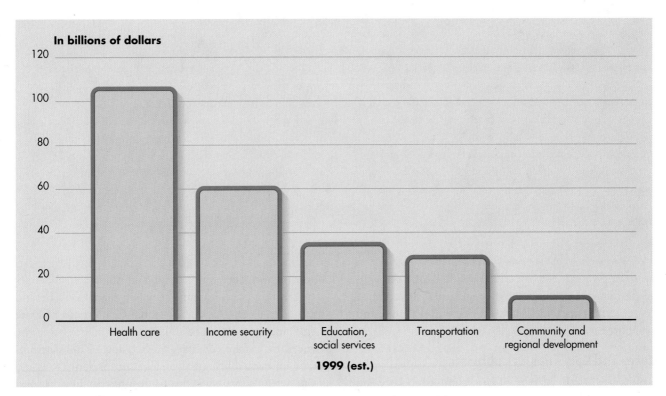

FIGURE 3 ■ *What Does the Federal Government Give the States Money to Do?* *Most of the $245 billion the federal government gave to the states went for programs in these areas.*

SOURCE: *Statistical Abstract of the United States, 1999,* Washington, D.C.: U.S. Government Printing Office, 1999, Table 508.

Are States Really Closer to the People?

In an address to the American people in 1995, Newt Gingrich sounded an old and familiar theme in American politics: "This country is too big and too diverse for Washington to have the knowledge to make the right decisions on local matters; we've got to return the power back to you—to your families, your neighborhoods, your local and state governments."[1] It is an oft-made claim that many federal government programs, such as health care, welfare, education, and environmental protection, could be more effectively run at the state level because the states are closer to the people.

This claim rests on several assumptions. Because state governments are smaller than the national government, it should be easier both for citizens to influence policy and for policymakers to have a sense of the public mood. This is important because economic conditions and political culture vary from state to state, resulting in different policy preferences. Moreover, local officials may have a better grasp of local conditions and are better situated to shape policy to fit these preferences. Advocates of returning power to the states also argue that smaller is in itself better because it increases the possibility for efficiency in management and implementation of

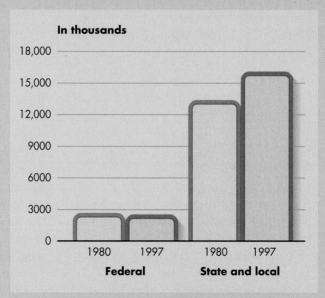

In thousands

Number of Full- and Part-Time Civilian Employees in the Federal and State Governments, 1980–1997

SOURCE: *Statistical Abstract of the United States, 1999*, Tables 534 and 535.

policy. It also makes government and its decision makers more accessible to the voters and more vulnerable to their specific preferences.

Is there evidence for any of these assumptions? Of course state governments *are* smaller than the national government. While the United States has more than 270 million residents, thirty-two states have populations under five million. But the average person is not necessarily better informed about state

officials; most local candidates get far less media exposure than national candidates, partly because there are so many of them. Of 87,504 government units in the United States, all but fifty-one exist below the level of state government. Small may be beautiful, but it can also be very confusing. In 1990, California's citizens had to wade through a 222-page pamphlet outlining their ballot choices. Two years earlier in San Francisco, facing a ballot containing more than one hun-

and local governments meet real needs. Along the way, the performance standards and regulations attached to the grants have increased the professionalism of state and local bureaucrats.

States and Localities as Lobbyists

Lobbying is a crucial part of the relationship between the states and the federal government. The importance of federal money to states and localities and the need for

coordination between federal and state bureaucracies have stimulated the organization of groups of state and local officials, such as the National Conference of State Legislatures, the National League of Cities, and the American Public Welfare Association. These groups lobby for favorable legislation for states and localities and work with federal agencies to ensure that new regulations are implemented in a way acceptable to the states. Most of these organizations have multimillion-dollar

dred items, voters passed one proposition for public financing of campaigns while simultaneously passing another measure outlawing it.[2]

The increasing use of ballot initiatives is in itself a sign, according to one study, that many citizens do not feel all that close to their state governments.[3] Moreover, states are no less vulnerable than the national government to special interests. Huge sums of money are flowing into states from outside organizations to support or defeat initiatives. When an initiative to undo a gay rights law was put on the ballot in Maine, for example, money from national antigay rights groups poured in to defeat it.

Turning programs over to the states will not necessarily make them more efficient, inexpensive, or responsive to local needs either. In Wisconsin, after the turnback of welfare to the states, the cost of the programs actually rose because of that state's intensive approach to reintegrating the unemployed in the job market.[4] So many new programs were created they were described as a mini-New Deal.[5] Since welfare reform was enacted, many qualified children and poor families have gone without health insurance or food stamps because their state governments did not spend money allocated by the federal government, or they diverted it to other programs favored by the middle class.[6]

States are not bureaucracy-free. Collectively state and local governments account for almost 85 percent of all civilian governmental employees, 33 percent of all governmental spending, and more than 13 percent of the gross domestic product.[7] By one calculation, "if every last thing the federal government does, aside from defense and foreign affairs and writing checks for entitlements and state and local grants, were transferred to the states (such as national parks, museums, air-traffic control, the FBI and Border Patrol, the National Weather Service, student loans), and the states could do it all a full 10% more efficiently, the cost of government would fall by less than half of one percent."[8]

Finally, there is no evidence that state governments are less corrupt than the federal government.[9] A nationwide survey showed that between 18 and 25 percent of all state legislators do not abide by conflict-of-interest laws. They regulate businesses in which they have an interest, and they have financial ties to lobbyists. Indeed, federal pressure has been a major influence in the professionalization of state bureaucracies.

These problems with state governments do not mean that turning some federal programs back to the states is a bad idea. But it does mean that devolving decision making on the states is no guarantee of greater efficiency, honesty, or responsiveness or that the public will be better informed on the issues or trust more in their government.

1. Quoted in Timothy Conlan, *From Federalism to Devolution: Twenty-five Years of Intergovernmental Reform* (Washington, D.C.: Brookings Institution, 1998), 11.
2. Garry Wills, "The War between the States . . . and Washington," *New York Times Magazine,* July 5, 1998, p. 27.
3. David Broder, "Take Back the Initiative," *Washington Post National Weekly Edition,* April 10, 2000, p. 6.
4. Wills, "The War between the States," p. 27.
5. "States Sitting on Unspent Welfare Funds, Group Says," *Champaign-Urbana News Gazette,* February 24, 2000, p. A-4; "Audit: States Denying Medicaid," *Champaign-Urbana News Gazette,* December 15, 1999; Robert Pear, "Cash to Ensure Health Coverage for the Poor Goes Unused," *New York Times,* May 21, 2000, pp. 18, A6.
6. Raymond Hernandez, "Federal Welfare Windfall Frees New York Money for Other Uses," *New York Times,* April 23, 2000, p. 1; "7 Million Eligible Kids Uninsured," *Champaign-Urbana News-Gazette,* August 9, 2000, p. A-3.
7. *Statistical Abstract of the United States, 1999,* Table 500.
8. John D. Donahue, "The Disunited States," *Atlantic Monthly* (May 1997): 20.
9. See for recent discussions, Richard Cohen, "States Aren't Saints Either," *Washington Post National Weekly Edition,* April 3–9, 1995, p. 28; R. W. Apple, "You Say You Want a Devolution," *New York Times,* January 29, 1995, Section 4, p. 1; "Study: Legislators Mix Personal, State Affairs," *Champaign-Urbana News-Gazette,* p. A-9.

budgets and employ sizable staffs of lobbyists and researchers. Many individual states and cities have their own Washington lobbyists, and these lobbyists appear to have some positive effect on increasing federal aid.[29]

But why should states lobby when they are all represented in the House and Senate? For one thing, lobbying organizations can help coordinate legislators' efforts by contacting large numbers of members at the same time. Moreover, the members of Congress may not always agree with the state leaders, or they may belong to different parties. Or a state may have an urban majority while the members of Congress disproportionately represent rural and suburban areas.

Conflict

Current federal-state relations are also characterized by conflict. One of the sharpest clashes concerns so-called **unfunded mandates.** When Congress passes laws requiring states to do something, usually to regulate, it often transfers money to the states to cover part of the cost of the activity, but not always. A law or regulation imposed on the states unaccompanied by sufficient funding to implement it is an unfunded mandate. For example, the federal government requires the states to deduct child support from the wages of parents who fall behind on payments. The state is also to deduct payments automatically from paychecks of fathers of children whose mothers are on welfare.[30] States that fail to carry out these mandates risk losing federal contributions to their welfare funds.

Environmental regulations are, overall, the most expensive federal mandates costing billions annually. Other costly mandates order states and localities to educate the children of illegal immigrants and to make public buildings, sidewalks, and transportation accessible to people with disabilities.

The fiscal burden of these and other mandates led to state and local officials joining together in 1993 to mount a national campaign to restrict the use of mandates. In 1995 Congress passed a bill reforming procedures under which unfunded or underfunded mandates, especially regulatory mandates, are sent to the states, but it stopped short of prohibiting them. The law does require the federal government to provide information on the adminis-trative and other costs of implementing laws and regulatory statutes before Congress or an executive branch agency, such as the EPA, can adopt them. Federal agencies are required to consult with the states and localities before imposing mandates and to adopt regulations that impose the smallest burden for implementation.[31]

Interstate Relations

Constitutional Requirements

The Constitution established rules governing states' relationships with each other. One important provision is the **full faith and credit clause,** which requires states to recognize contracts. No matter in which state you contract your marriage, every state must recognize it. The Constitution also provides that if a fugitive from justice flees from one state to another, he or she is supposed to be extradited—that is, sent back to the state with jurisdiction.

Normally, meeting full faith and credit requirements is rather routine. However, now that Vermont has become the only state to register unions between gays, we can expect controversy when out-of-state couples who have their relationship registered in Vermont test the validity of that status in their home state on such issues as partner benefits and estate planning.

Voluntary Cooperation

Most state-to-state interaction is informal and voluntary, with state officials consulting with officials in other states about common problems and states borrowing ideas from one another. Sometimes states enter into formal agreements, called interstate compacts, to deal with a common problem—operating a port or allocating water from a river basin, for example.

Interstate Competition

Changing economic patterns and an overall loss of economic competitiveness by the United States in the world market have stimulated vigorous competition among the states to attract new businesses and jobs. They advertise the advantages of their states to prospective new businesses: low taxes, good climate, a skilled workforce, low wages, and little government regulation.

Federalism in Time

1787	Constitutional Convention meets in Philadelphia and dissolves the confederal system created by the Articles of Confederation in favor of a federal system that would strengthen the national government.
1791	Ratification of the Bill of Rights, including the Tenth Amendment, which reserves for individuals and the states all powers not explicitly granted to the national government by the Constitution.
1801	John Marshall becomes chief justice of the Supreme Court and for the next thirty-seven years plays major role in writing decisions that expand power of federal government.
1819	*McColloch v. Maryland* decision handed down by Supreme Court; interprets the "necessary and proper" clause of Article 1 in Constitution to give Congress broad legislative powers.
1835	End of Marshall era on Supreme Court; composition shifts to a panel more favorable to states' rights.
1861	Southern states secede from Union and establish an independent confederal system, setting off the Civil War. Union victory four years later establishes supremacy of national over state governments.
1876	Lack of electoral majority in presidential election leads to House compromise to give election to the northerner Rutherford B. Hayes in return for easing Reconstruction policies in the former states of the confederacy. Sets stage for adoption of Jim Crow laws and states' rights era in the Deep South.
1901	Teddy Roosevelt enters presidency and uses it as bully pulpit "for the people" by advocating strong federal role in conservation, child welfare, and regulation of business.
1913	Sixteenth Amendment enhances power of federal government by giving Congress the power to levy a national income tax.
1913	Seventeenth Amendment removes power of state legislatures to elect U.S. senators by providing for direct election.
1933	Franklin Delano Roosevelt assumes presidency and initiates a massive legislative agenda to deal with

	Great Depression, including grants-in-aid to state governments. Begins shift of primary responsibility for general welfare programs from state and local to the federal government.
1941	United States enters World War II and leaves four years later as world leader, further expanding power and size of national government.
1955	Onset of modern civil rights movement that targets federal courts to spearhead reform. Establishes federal government as primary guarantor of civil rights and the federal courts as major players in political change.
1963	Lyndon Johnson succeeds John Kennedy and launches massive social welfare legislative agenda called the Great Society. Federal activism reaches new high.
1964	Passage of voting rights act and adoption of Twenty-fourth Amendment to the Constitution outlawing poll tax. Together they put final nails in coffin of Jim Crow laws and power of southern states to limit civil rights of minorities.
1969	Richard Nixon enters office with New Federalism policy to rationalize federal-state relations; restructures grants-in-aids into block grants and initiates general-revenue sharing with the states.
1981	Ronald Reagan takes office with more ideological version of New Federalism that cuts funding for block grants, ends revenue sharing, and tries to decrease power of government at all levels in favor of private sector institutions.
1994	Republicans gain control of Congress offering a "Contract with America" to downsize federal government and return power to states.
1995	For first time since the New Deal, Supreme Court rules a congressional law has exceeded the boundaries of its authority to legislate under interstate commerce clause.
1998	Initiatives make it onto in twenty state ballots, and many municipalities and citizens make policy by direct vote, bypassing state legislatures.

A little-known example of federal-state-local cooperation is firefighting in wilderness areas. In the dry summer of 2000, firefighters battled blazes across the West. Here, Sioux Indian firefighters head toward a forest fire in Montana.

AP/Wide World Photos

This growing competition prompts states to give tax advantages and other financial incentives to businesses willing to relocate there.

Critics believe that these offers serve mostly to erode a state's tax base and have little impact on most business relocation decisions. Evidence indicates that low taxes are not the primary reason for business relocation.[32] Nevertheless, without offering some special break, states now feel at a competitive disadvantage in recruiting new businesses.

State-Local Relations

Another important feature of contemporary federalism is the relationship of states to their localities—counties, cities, and special districts. These relationships are defined by state constitutions; they are not dealt with in the federal constitution. States differ in the autonomy they grant to their localities. In some states, **home rule** charters give local governments considerable autonomy in such matters as setting tax rates, regulating land use, and choosing their form of local government. In many states, cities of different sizes have different degrees of autonomy. Although localities are creatures of their states, whereas states exist independently of the national government, some of the same problems that affect national-state relations also affect state-local relations. City and county officials often wish for more authority and fewer mandates from the state.

Conclusion: Is Federalism Responsive?

Across the United States, our beliefs in democracy, freedom, and equality bind us together. In many ways we are becoming more alike, as rapid transportation, television and other forms of instant communication, fast-food franchises, hotel chains, and other nationwide businesses bring about increasing similarity. But to say that Alabama is more like New York than it used to be is certainly not to say they are alike. Our federal system helps us accommodate this diversity by allowing both state and federal governments a role in policymaking.

Our Founders probably did not foresee a national government that would surpass the states in power and scope of action in domestic policy. Yet one of the paradoxes of our system is that as the national government has gained extraordinary power, so have the states and localities. All levels of government are stronger than in the eighteenth century. Federal power *and* state power have grown hand in hand.

It is probably foolish to pretend to know how the Founders might deal with our complex federal system. However, many of them were astute politicians who would undoubtedly recognize that our system had to evolve along with population and territorial growth and social and economic change. Yet we continue to believe in local control and grassroots government. This is a paradox built into our form of government, one that Thomas Jefferson discovered very early. He called his election a revolution, abolished all internal taxes, and set about making government as small, simple, and informal as possible. He tried to keep the United States out of war in Europe and closed down ports and foreign trade but soon found he needed federal policing to enforce his policy.[33] He also had a vision for the country, and with or without formal authority, purchased the Louisiana Territory, instantly setting the country down the road from a small coastal agrarian republic to a vast continental empire where his idea of small government would no longer be possible.

Is such a complex system responsive? It is very responsive in that groups and individuals whose demands are rejected at one level of government can go to another level. The federal system creates multiple points of access, each with power to satisfy political demands by making policy rejected at another level. Or, as one cynic put it a little less idealistically, for those times when "we have wrecked one level of government, the Founding Fathers had the foresight to provide a spare."[34]

Yet many Americans still believe government cannot be trusted and is not sufficiently responsive. Part of what is happening is that during the post–Cold War, prosperous 1990s, people turned away from government at all levels because they did not have a sense of pressing problems they wanted government to solve. But declining trust is also a factor. In late 1997 only 39 percent of Americans polled said they trusted the federal government, and 74 percent said the federal government should be running only those things that cannot be run at the local level.[35] Yet Americans are not that enamored of state governments, either, as indicated by the increasing use of ballot initiatives to bypass both national and local legislators.

A contemporary observer reading Madison's caveat about "the propensity of mankind to fall into mutual animosities" sees a potential danger in too much devolution during this time in American politics "when passions run high and interests are in sharp competition." She sees today's politics as an example of the divisiveness of factions that can plague a country made up of contentious states that Madison warned about in *Federalist Paper* 10.[36] Others clearly see the move toward greater state autonomy and more direct democracy as taking us nearer to the Founders' ideal of a government close to the people. The increasing use of grassroots initiatives, however, is not necessarily a move toward the kind of government the Founders envisioned. The Founders feared policymaking getting too close to the people and government being too responsive to popular demands. They saw the potential for overheating the political process through too much direct democracy, which is why they chose an indirect or republican form of democracy. The issue is how to keep a balance in this division of power to prevent a tyranny of factions while maintaining a sense of national unity and purpose.

EPILOGUE

Clinton Creates a New National Monument

In April 2000, ninety-two years to the day after Teddy Roosevelt designated the Grand Canyon a national monument, Bill Clinton used his authority under the Antiquities Act to protect virtually all remaining sequoia groves not already lying within national parkland. By changing their designation from national forest to national monument, Clinton has protected the giant sequoias "for eternity." The Agriculture Secretary recommended creation of a science advisory panel to draw up guidelines for management of the area. Existing logging agreements and property owners' water and grazing rights will be honored, but hunting is banned, recreational access restricted, and further development prohibited.

Three members of California's congressional delegation introduced a bill to block the action, but Clinton acted before it came to a vote. One of the bill's sponsors accused Clinton of "declaring war" on the communities surrounding the forest. Local officials said the new designation would cost their communities millions of dollars in lost logging jobs. In addition, they argued, the protection was not needed. Thinning the areas around the groves through logging had helped protect the sequoias from fires and pest infection.

With nine months still remaining in his term, Clinton had committed 3.1 million acres to his "land legacy," the most land set aside in the lower forty-eight states by any president since Teddy Roosevelt. The Antiquities Act gained sufficient celebrity to serve as a plot line in the popular *West Wing* television series. But Clinton was not finished: he ordered a study of fifty million additional acres in thirty-eight states for possible designation as wilderness areas. A reporter said Clintons' resolve to use the act was "like a golfer who has just discovered the power of a titanium driver."[37]

There is no way for us to know exactly Clinton's reasons for his decision. The political costs to him were probably small since he will not stand again for election to national office and opposition to land

President Clinton looks over seeds from sequoia trees while touring Sequoia National Park.
AP/Wide World Photos

set-asides is greatest in the affected areas. States will never be equally affected by the creation of federal parks because wilderness areas and spectacular land formations are not evenly distributed across the country.

Yet Clinton's actions illustrate well the political dynamics of our federal system. The national government can override the wishes of a state when there is a national majority supporting its actions. Willing to face opposition from western governors, ranchers, and others, the president was responding to a broader national constituency of those who love their national parks and believe more should be done to conserve wilderness areas and natural landmarks. No one but the president, or the president and Congress acting together, could have saved the giant sequoias for all the people for eternity.

Key Terms

federalism
unitary system
confederal system
"necessary and proper"
implied powers clause
supremacy clause
"mischiefs of faction"
dual federalism

McCulloch v. Maryland
New Deal
new federalism
devolution
cooperative federalism
unfunded mandates
full faith and credit clause
home rule

Further Reading

David S. Broder, *Democracy Derailed: Initiative Campaigns and the Power of Money* (New York: Harcourt Brace, 2000). A senior Washington correspondent and nationally syndicated columnist takes a look at the rise in use of the ballot initiative to legislate and explains why he believes it is a threat to our republican form of government.

Daniel Elazar, *American Federalism: A View from the States,* 3d ed. (New York: Harper & Row, 1984). Explores the development of intergovernmental relations and examines American political cultures.

John Ferejohn and Barry R. Weingast, eds., *The New Federalism: Can the States Be Trusted?* (Stanford, Calif.: Hoover Institution Press, 1997). Seven scholars of federalism look at interstate competition to attract new business and how the states are handling welfare reform and environmental regulation.

Jeffrey Pressman and Aaron Wildavsky, *Implementation* (Berkeley: University of California Press, 1973). A classic look at the difficulties of translating federal laws into working programs when dealing with a multiplicity of state and local governments.

Alice Rivlin, *Reviving the American Dream: The Economy, the States, and the Federal Government* (Washington, D.C.: Brookings Institute, 1992). An analysis of the fiscal relations between the federal government and the states by Clinton's budget director.

John Steinbeck, *The Grapes of Wrath* (New York: Viking, 1939). A novel portraying the conditions facing the country that set the stage for the New Deal.

David Walker, *The Rebirth of Federalism* (Chatham, N.J.: Chatham House, 1995). A look at contemporary trends in federal-state relations.

Electronic Resources

www.ncsl.org/public/guide.htm
The home page of the National Council of State Legislatures. The council promotes reform and increased efficiency in state legislatures, helps facilitate interstate cooperation, and lobbies for state issues. Its home page also provides information about current issues of relevance to states.

InfoTrac College Edition

"Sequoia National Forest"
"Government Slowly Getting Bigger Because"
"Process Direct Democracy"
"Undermining Quality Care"

Notes

1. This segment is based in part on Timothy Egan, "Putting Some Space between His Presidency and History," *New York Times,* January 16, 2000, section 4, p. 3; "President Expands Protection of Sequoias," *New York Times,* April 16, 2000, p. 25; Michael Janofsky, "U.S. Readies a Major Land Protection Initiative," *New York Times,* November 21, 1999, p. 17; Barbara Whitaker, "A Plan to Preserve Giant Sequoias, World's Biggest Trees," *New York Times,* April 9, 2000, p. 18; "President Gives Land in Four Areas New Status," *Champaign-Urbana News-Gazette,* January 12, 2000, p. A3.

2. *Statistical Abstract of the United States, 1999* (Washington, D.C.: U.S. Government Printing Office, 1999), Table 394.

3. Christopher John Farley, "The West Is Wild Again," *Time,* March 20, 1995, p. 46.

4. Erik Larson, "Unrest in the West," *Time,* October 23, 1995, p. 54.

5. Daniel Elazar, *American Federalism: A View from the States,* 3d ed. (New York: Harper & Row, 1984).

6. George E. Hall and Deirdre A. Gagnin, eds., *1997 County and City Extra: Annual Metro, City, and County Data Book* (Lanham, Md.: Bernan, 1997).

7. *Statistical Abstract of the United States, 1999,* Table 748.

8. Robert S. Erikson, Gerald C. Wright, and John P. McIver, *Statehouse Democracy: Public Opinion and Policy in the American States* (New York: Cambridge University Press, 1993).

9. A 1976 Supreme Court decision used the Tenth Amendment as a reason to forbid the federal government to extend minimum wage and hour laws to state and local government employees. See *National League of Cities v. Usery,* 426 U.S. 833 (1976). This decision was partially overruled in 1985. See *Garcia v. San Antonio Metropolitan Transit Authority,* 469 U.S. 528 (1985).

10. The following discussion is drawn from Richard Leach, *American Federalism* (New York: Norton, 1970), chap. 1. See also Christopher Hamilton and Donald Wells, *Federalism, Power and Political Economy: A New Theory of Federalism's Impact on American Life* (Englewood Cliffs, N.J.: Prentice Hall, 1990).

11. *Federalist Paper* 45.

12. *McCulloch v. Maryland,* 4 Wheat. 316 (1819).

13. Alfred Kelly and Winfred Harbeson, *The American Constitution: Its Origins and Development* (New York: Norton, 1976).

14. Daniel Elazar, *The American Partnership* (Chicago: University of Chicago Press, 1962).

15. Perhaps because he is a sociologist (!), Theodore Caplan did not fully appreciate the extent of federal involvement in Muncie, even in 1924—the support of veterans, schools, roads, and hospitals by federal land grants. Nevertheless, his major point is valid: The federal presence there was nothing compared to now. Caplan is quoted in Daniel Walker, *Toward a Functioning Federalism* (Cambridge, Mass.: Winthrop, 1981), 3–4.

16. Theodore Lowi, *The Personal President* (Ithaca, N.Y.: Cornell University Press, 1985).

17. Timothy Conlan, *From Federalism to Devolution: Twenty-five Years of Intergovernmental Reform* (Washington, D.C.: Brookings Institution, 1998), 6.

18. On Nixon's managerial approach to federalism, see Lawrence D. Brown, *New Policies, New Politics: Government's Response to Government's Growth* (Washington, D.C.: Brookings Institution, 1983). The comparative discussion of Lyndon Johnson's, Richard Nixon's, and Ronald Reagan's federalism policies draws on Conlon, *From New Federalism to Devolution,* chaps. 1, 6, and 13.

19. Conlon, *From New Federalism to Devolution,* 109.

20. Quoted in ibid., 1.

21. See, for example, William J. Clinton, "Federalism," Executive Order 13132, *Federal Register* 54, no. 163 (August 10, 1999), pp. 43255–43259. Clinton discussed his views on state activism and federalism in general with the historian Gary Wills in "The War between the States . . . and Washington," *New York Times Magazine,* July 5, 1998, pp. 26–29.

22. David Broder, "Take Back the Initiative," *Washington Post National Weekly Edition,* April 10, 2000, p. 6.

23. James W. Brosnan, "Not Taxing Internet Sales Hurts," *Champaign-Urbana News-Gazette,* February 21, 2000, p. A6.

24. Barney Frank (D-Mass.) quoted in Michael Grunwald, "Everybody Talks about State's Rights . . . ," *Washington Post National Weekly Edition,* November 1, 1999, p. 29. Frank was referring to Republicans only, but the quote fits Democrats as well.

25. Dan Carney, "Latest Supreme Court Rulings Reinforce the Federalist Trend," *Congressional Quarterly,* June 26, 1999, p. 1528; Linda Greenhouse, "High Court Faces Moment of Truth in Federalism Cases," *New York Times,* March 28, 1999, p. 20.

26. Wills, "The War between the States . . . and Washington," p. 26.

27. Broder, "Take Back the Initiative," p. 6; John Maggs, "Ballot Boxing," *National Journal,* July 1, 2000, p. 2147.

28. Alice Rivlin, *Reviving the American Dream: The Economy, the States and the Federal Government* (Washington, D.C.: Brookings Institute, 1992).

29. Neil Berch, "Why Do Some States Play the Federal Aid Game Better than Others?" *American Politics Quarterly* 20 (July, 1992): 366–377.

30. See Mary Ann Glendon, *Abortion and Divorce in Western Law* (Cambridge, Mass.: Harvard University Press, 1987), 87–88; see also Susan Welch, Sue Thomas, and Margery Ambrosius, "Family Policy," in *State Politics and Policy,* 5th ed., Virginia Gray and Herbert Jacob (Boston: Little, Brown, 1995).

31. For a review of the politics surrounding the law, its provisions, and limitations see Conlon, *From New Federalism to Devolution,* chap. 13, pp. 257–292.

32. Enid F. Beaumont and Harold Hovey, "State, Local and Federal Development Policies: New Federalism Patterns, Chaos, or What?" *Public Administration Review* 45 (March/April 1985): 327–332; Barry Rubin and C. Kurt Zorn, "Sensible State and Local Development," *Public Administration Review* 45 (March/April 1985): 333–339.

33. Richard Neustadt, *American Presidency* series, episode 5 (PBS broadcast, April 2000).

34. John D. Donahue, "The Disunited States," *Atlantic Monthly* (May 1997): 20.

35. Eliza Newlin Carney, "Power Grab," *National Journal,* April 11, 1998, pp. 798–800.

36. Katherine Sullivan, "In Defense of Federal Power," *New York Times Magazine,* August 18, 1996, p. 36.

37. Egan, "Putting Some Space between His Presidency and History," p. 3.

Public Opinion

YOU ARE THERE

Should a Pollster Make Public Details of His Polls?

It is 1996 and you are Frank Luntz, leading pollster, consultant, and strategist for the Republican Party.[1] After receiving your doctorate in political science at Oxford University, you started Luntz Research Companies in Arlington, Virginia. In the short time you have been in the business, you have become something of a personality, appearing regularly on a number of television shows such as *Nightline, Crossfire, The NewsHour, Good Morning America,* and others. *Time* magazine recently named you one of America's most promising leaders under forty. *USA Today* describes you as one of the most influential minds in the Republican Party. You won the *Washington Post* "Crystal Ball" award for being the most accurate pundit. You were the first pollster to predict Republican success in winning control of Congress in 1994.

Your research was the basis for the Republican Contract with America, ten proposals that the party promised to consider if it won control of Congress in 1994. Your polls showed that each element of the Contract was supported by 60 percent or more of the American people. Majority support for proposals such as a balanced budget, welfare reform, and a middle-class tax cut were important in getting Republican candidates for the House to sign the Contract and agree to bring the proposals up for consideration should the party win a majority.

The Contract became the centerpiece of the 1994 campaign. You and others pushed it on the talk show circuit and evening news. You also discussed the poll results that suggested the Contract was a sure winner. When the election results were finally in, you looked like a political genius. For the first time since 1954, the Republicans won control of both the Senate and the House.

Your rising star quality was only partially diminished by a complaint registered with the Committee on Standards of the American Association for Public Opinion Research (AAPOR) concerning the polls you did on the Contract. The AAPOR, an organization of research professionals in government, universities, and commercial polling firms, monitors polls to ensure that pollsters follow accepted procedures in conducting and reporting polls. Although the organization has no legal authority, it can censure or publicly reprimand pollsters who

Robb Kendrik Photography

violate professional standards. The organization cannot stop anyone from polling, but censure can hurt a pollster's professional reputation.

In response to the complaint, the AAPOR asked you to report the questions and other details of your Contract polls. Most pollsters comply with AAPOR standards and provide information on how their polls are conducted. It is a way for other pollsters, the press, government officials, and the public to evaluate the reliability of a poll. To report a poll publicly but withhold information on how the poll was conducted, in the words of the AAPOR, "undermines the credibility of all polls." It also undermines the public agenda because poll results influence which issues get attention. The public can be misled into thinking that some issues are seen as more important than they really are.

How do you respond to the AAPOR? Do you satisfy the organization and others in the polling community by releasing the information? Doing so is likely to maintain your professional standing by demonstrating that you abide by the professional and ethical standards of the profession. Although the Republican Party technically owns the poll, the Contract received a great deal of attention in the campaign. You and others have been discussing the poll results for more than two years. Other than the information requested by the AAPOR, little regarding the polls is still private. Moreover, if the items in the Contract are as popular as you say, the information may spur added interest in the Contract and help influence Congress to pass it.

Or do you withhold the information? You are not a member of the AAPOR. Censure is unlikely to damage your reputation a great deal. In time, everyone may simply forget the whole thing. Moreover, you know that, in fact, your questions were loaded to get the results you wanted, exactly the kind of polling methods the AAPOR finds unprofessional. For example, to show that the majority of Americans favored legal reform, you reported responses to the statement "We should stop excessive legal claims, frivolous lawsuits, and overzealous lawyers." It would be hard for anyone to disagree with this statement. Revealing these sorts of questions would be embarrassing even though the polls have served the purposes you wanted. What do you do and why?

Feelings about public opinion are contradictory. In a democracy we want leaders to be responsive to public opinion. Yet often we complain that elected officials do not lead but simply follow the latest trends in public opinion polls. The polls are contradictory, too. Many Americans are angry with government. They do not trust it; they think it is too big and spends too much money. At the same time, they like the services government provides them, and very few Americans are willing to cut spending so drastically as to eliminate their favorite service or program.

In this chapter we will explore public opinion to better understand these contradictions. We will describe how public opinion is formed and measured, discuss the pattern of public opinion on some important issues, and assess the extent to which government is responsive to public opinion. Because political science is primarily interested in opinions that affect government, the focus of this chapter is public opinion about political issues, personalities, institutions, and events.

Nature of Public Opinion

We can define **public opinion** as the collection of individual opinions toward issues or objects of general interest—that is, those that concern a significant number of people. Public opinion can be described in terms of direction, intensity, and stability. Direction refers to whether public opinion is positive or negative. Generally, it is mixed: Some individuals have positive opinions, others negative. Intensity refers to the strength of opinion. Intense opinions often give rise to behavior. Pro-life and pro-choice advocates, for example, are likely to act on their opinions and vote against members of Congress opposed to their positions.

Most public issues are not of interest to most people. Individuals may feel intensely about one or two issues that directly affect them, but not everyone, or even a majority, is intense about the same issues. The relative absence of severe economic and social divisions in the United States explains the lack of intense opinions. With the possible exception of the racial and states' rights issues that almost destroyed the nation in the 1860s, there has been nothing like the long-standing, divisive class and religious conflicts of many European nations.

Opinions also differ in stability. An opinion is more likely to change when an individual lacks intensity or information about an issue. For example, the opinions of citizens toward abortion are more stable than their opinions toward candidates running for president, especially at the beginning of the campaign. Opinion polls following the party nominating conventions in 1992 showed Bill Clinton's margins over George Bush seesawing back and forth from day to day (Figure 1). At this stage of the campaign, many voters were undecided. Some opposed

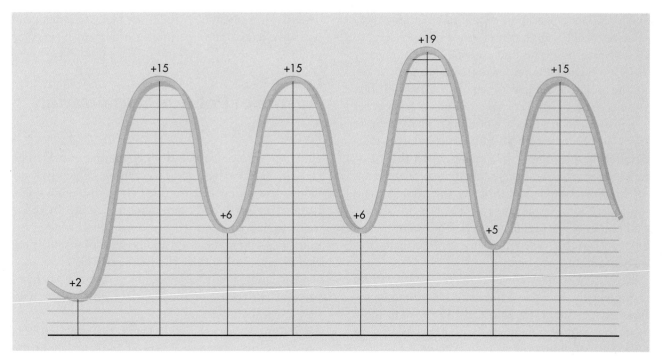

FIGURE 1 ■ *The Presidential "Poller Coaster"* *Clinton's margins over Bush rose and fell dramatically early in the 1992 campaign.*

SOURCE: *USA Today,* October 3, 1992. Polls taken August 20 to September 2, 1992. The term *poller coaster* was coined by Richard Morin, "The Ups and Downs of Political Poll-Taking." *Washington Post National Weekly Edition,* October 5, 1992, p. 37.

Bush but did not know enough about Clinton to support him firmly. They would see something on television or read something in the press favorable to Clinton and report a preference for him, and then see something unfavorable and shift to Bush.[2] In 2000, voters knew more about Al Gore and George W. Bush than Clinton in 1992, and their opinions were less likely to be moved by new information.[3]

Formation of Public Opinion

People have opinions about issues and objects because they learn them in a process called **political socialization.**

As with other types of learning, individuals learn about politics by being exposed to new information from parents, peers, schools, the media, political leaders, and the community. These sources are referred to as **agents of political socialization.** Individuals also can learn about politics through direct personal experience.

Political learning begins at an early age and continues through life. Reasoning capacity as well as the demands placed on an individual influences what is learned.[4] Very young children are unable to distinguish the political from the nonpolitical world. If fact, young children have difficulty separating political figures from cartoon characters. Some confuse the political with the religious. Twenty-five percent of a sample of five- and six-year-olds reported that the president takes his orders directly from God.[5] By first grade, however, children begin to see government as distinct and unique.[6]

The inability to understand abstract concepts or complex institutions means the child's conception of government is limited. Most identify government with the president.[7] Children can recognize the president—they see him on television—and understand that he is a leader of the nation much as the parent is a leader of the family. In general, experiences with parents and other adult figures provide children with a basis for understanding remote authority figures such as the president.[8] Positive feelings toward parents are also responsible for positive feelings toward the president. Children describe the president as good and helpful[9] and view him as more powerful than he really is.[10]

With age, children are introduced to political ideas and institutions by parents, teachers, peers, and the media. Their conception of government broadens to include Congress and such things as voting, freedom, and democracy. The idealization of the president gives way to a more complex and realistic image. The process can be accelerated by events and parental and community reaction to them. Children were much less positive toward the president and government in the 1970s than in the 1960s. The 1970s were a period when support for government among adults was declining. The Watergate scandal in 1973 lowered both adults' and children's evaluations of the president.[11] We might expect that Clinton's sexual scandals and the impeachment proceedings of 1998 also lowered evaluations of the president and government. This was not the case, however. In fact, approval ratings of the president reached record levels and confidence in the executive branch remained unchanged from the year before.[12]

Even when scandals lower children's evaluations of government, the effect does not last. Although those socialized in the late 1960s and early 1970s were more cynical toward government, as they aged, they became less cynical and more positive.[13]

In adolescence, political understanding expands still further. Children discuss politics with family and friends. Political activity, however limited, begins. By their middle teens, individuals begin to develop positions on issues.[14] Some fifteen- and sixteen-year-olds have political opinions similar to many adults'. They begin to recognize faults in the system but still believe the United States is better than other countries. They rate the country low in limiting violence and fostering political morality, but they rate it high in providing educational opportunities, a good standard of living, and science and technology.[15] For most, the positive feelings toward American government learned earlier are reinforced.

In adulthood, opinions toward specific policies and personalities develop, and political activity becomes more serious. Most Americans do not develop a critical perspective toward government, and few are asked or pushed to criticism, other than in superficial ways, by the schools, press, or political leaders.[16] Though many are disillusioned, their negative feelings are passive and directed toward leaders rather than institutions or toward symbolic issues, which make Americans angry but rarely lead to major institutional changes. One study in the 1990s showed that Americans have developed surprisingly ambivalent attitudes toward major national institutions. In general, the public seems to distrust most those aspects of our institutions that involve the overt workings of democracy. They dislike conflict, bargaining, and lobbying. Still, in the absence of a major upheaval, depression, or war, for most, the positive feelings developed toward government early in life are likely to remain and perhaps even cushion the impact of such events if they occur.[17]

Agents of Political Socialization

Family

Children are not born little Republicans and Democrats. Most learn these allegiances from the family. Individuals are influenced by the family throughout life. Families are particularly important in shaping the opinions of children, however, because of the strong emotional ties among members and because of parents' near exclusive control of their children's early lives.

The family influences opinions in several ways. First, parents share their opinions directly with children, who may adopt them.

Second, parents say or do things that children imitate. They may overhear parents' comments about the Republican or Democratic Party, for example, and repeat what they hear. Many initially learn a party identification in this way.

Third, children may transfer or generalize opinions from parents to other objects. When children are less positive toward parents, they are also less positive toward the president and other authority figures.[18]

Fourth, the family shapes the personality of the child, which may affect the child's political opinions. For example, the family contributes to self-esteem, and self-esteem is related to having political opinions and a willingness to express them.

Fifth, the family places children in a network of social and economic relationships that influences how they view the world and how the world views them. Children who live in middle-class suburbs view themselves and the world around them differently than children who live in poor inner-city areas:

The influence of the family is strongest when children clearly perceive what the parents' opinion is and that the matter is important to the parents. In the case of party identification, cues are frequent and unambiguous. In one study, 72 percent of a sample of high school seniors could identify their parents' party identification, whereas no more than 36 percent could identify their parents' opinion on any other issue.[19]

Parental influence is not immutable, however. As young adults leave their parents' circle, correspondence between their opinions, including party identification, and those of their parents declines. New people, institutions, and experiences come into play in shaping opin-

This boy, at a white supremacist rally, likely was socialized in these views by his parents.
Black Star

ions.[20] Even among younger children, parental influence may decline over time. Parents no longer have exclusive control during a child's preschool years, and the number of households with both parents working or with a single parent who works means that children have fewer daily contact hours with parents. Consequently, other agents of socialization are becoming more influential. For example, we turn more often to the schools to deal with problems the family dealt with in the past.

School

A child of our acquaintance who came to the United States at the age of five could not speak English and did not know the name of his new country. After a few months of kindergarten, he knew that George Washington and Abraham Lincoln were good presidents, he was able to recount stories of the Pilgrims, he could draw the flag, and he felt strongly that the United States was the best country in the world. This child illustrates the importance of the school in political socialization and how values and symbols of government are explicitly taught in American schools, as they are in schools in all nations.[21]

Schools promote patriotic rituals, such as beginning each day with the Pledge of Allegiance, and include pa-

triotic songs and programs in many activities. In the lower grades, children celebrate national holidays such as Presidents' Day and Thanksgiving and learn the history and symbols associated with them. Such exercises foster awe and respect for government.

In the upper grades, mock conventions, elections, Girls' and Boys' State, and student government introduce students to the operation of government. School clubs often operate with democratic procedures and reinforce the concepts of voting and majority rule. The state of Illinois even let the state's elementary school children vote to select the official state animal, fish, and tree, conveying the message that voting is the way things are decided.

Textbooks often foster commitment to government and the status quo. Those used in elementary grades emphasize compliance with authority and the need to be a "good" citizen. Even textbooks in advanced grades present idealized versions of the way government works and exaggerate the role of citizens in holding public officials accountable and in shaping public policy. They are less likely, however, to emphasize the need for citizens to participate in politics and uphold democratic values. Nor do they help students understand that conflicts and differences of opinion are inevitable in a large and diverse society.

Civic courses and teachers do not make much difference in fostering participation or support for democratic values, either.[22] Only a minority of a sample of seventeen-year-olds could list four or more ways to influence politics. Sixty percent of a sample of high school seniors favored allowing the police and other groups to censor books and movies.[23]

The failure of the schools to foster political participation and commitment to democratic values is attributed by some to the "hidden curriculum."[24] They point out that schools are not democratic institutions in which students are encouraged to participate in a meaningful way. In such an environment, the values of participation and democracy are unlikely to develop.

Education—the skills that it provides and experiences it represents—does make a difference, however. People who have more years of formal education are generally more interested in and knowledgeable about politics.[25] They are also more likely to participate in politics and to be politically tolerant. But educated Americans are no more likely than others to appreciate that democratic politics and government involves disagreements, arguments, bargaining, and compromise—in other words, to understand the reality of politics in a democratic society.

The major impact of schooling (kindergarten through high school) is that it helps create "good" citizens. Citizens are taught to accept political authority and the institutions of government and to channel political activity in legitimate and supportive ways. Thus, the schools provide a valuable service to the government, its leaders, and institutions.

Studies show that a college education alters one's outlook and opinions. Many go to college to get a job that pays a high salary. Some attend to expand their knowledge and understanding of the world. Others enroll because their parents want them to or simply because everyone else does. No one goes to develop more liberal opinions, but this is often the result.[26] (Liberal attitudes are discussed in more detail later in the chapter.)

College students are more liberal than the population as a whole, and the longer they are in college, the more liberal they become. Seniors are more liberal than freshmen, and graduate students are more liberal than undergraduates.

Some argue that college professors indoctrinate students. A Carnegie Commission survey showed that 64 percent of the social science faculty in the nation's colleges identified themselves as liberal, and only 20 percent regarded themselves as conservative. Faculty in other disciplines are much less likely to be liberal, however. For example, 30 percent of the business faculty identified themselves as liberal. Although the potential for influence exists, faculty impact is probably not great.

For example, during the height of the Vietnam War (1968–1971), students were more likely to identify themselves as liberal in outlook than students before and after the war. During the same period, college faculty changed very little. Thus, students are not simply a reflection of their college classroom teachers. At large universities, where the largest percentage of students attend college, the environment is sufficiently diverse to reinforce many points of view. Indeed, it is college that provides students with the self-confidence and independence that enable them to resist indoctrination.

It is possible that college students are liberal in outlook because college attracts those who are more liberal in the first place. Although this may have been true in the early 1970s when 38 percent of college freshmen identified themselves as liberal compared to 26 percent for the nation as a whole, today 24 percent of college freshmen identify themselves as liberal compared to 25 percent of the nation.[27] At the same time, there has been only a slight increase in the percentage of conservatives among freshmen. The biggest shift has been from liberal to middle of the road. Whereas 45 percent of college

freshmen in 1970 were moderate, this figure increased to 60 percent in the 1980s, before falling to 56 percent in 1999.[28]

On issues, college freshmen look much like the population as a whole, liberal on some issues but conservative on others. They are liberal in wanting the government to do more to control pollution and the sale of handguns and provide national health care to cover everyone's medical costs. They are conservative in wishing to retain the death penalty, believing that the courts show too much concern for the rights of criminals, and asserting that racial discrimination is no longer a problem. They are divided on abortion and affirmative action in college admissions (Table 1).

The most distinctive characteristic of college freshmen in recent years has been their lack of interest in politics. Only 12 percent said that they had discussed politics in the past year, and only 21 percent voted in a school election. Only 27 percent of college freshmen in 1997 considered it very important to keep up with politics. These figures, which have been declining since the 1960s, represent an all-time low.[29] In many respects, the political apathy that has gripped adults is also reflected in college freshmen. On the other hand, 47 percent participated in an organized demonstration, and 79 percent performed volunteer work. College freshmen are involved in their local communities, but this involvement does not extend to politics. College freshmen are likely to become more politically active as they age, but not to achieve high levels of activism.

Table 1	Opinions of College Freshmen
	Percentage Who Agree
Federal government is not doing enough to control pollution (1997).	81
Federal government needs to do more to control sale of handguns.	82
National health care is needed to cover everyone's medical costs (1997).	72
Affirmative action in college admissions should be abolished.	48
Abortion should be abolished.	53
Courts show too much concern for rights of criminals.	72
The death penalty should be abolished.	25
Racial discrimination is no longer a problem.	23

SOURCE: Linda Sax, Alexander Astin, William Korn, and Kathryn Mahoney, *The American Freshman: National Norms for Fall 1999* (Los Angeles: Higher Education Research Institute, Graduate School of Education and Information Studies, 1999).

Issues that involve moral questions have the greatest potential to be divisive. Slavery was a moral issue that almost destroyed the nation. In the first decades of this century, prohibition—banning the sale of alcoholic beverages—was a divisive moral issue. In the 1990s and early 2000s, the rights of gays and lesbians has become a moral issue.

Abortion emerged as a moral issue in the 1970s. There are two dimensions to

public opinion on this issue. One involves the health and safety of the mother or child. The vast majority of Americans endorse legal abortion when the mother's health may be endangered, the child is likely to have a serious defect, or the pregnancy is the result of rape or incest. This pattern of opinion has been reasonably stable over the past decade.

The other dimension relates to the personal preferences of the mother.

Americans are divided on whether a legal abortion is acceptable when the family has a low income and does not want any more children or when the mother is unmarried and does not want to marry the father.

Although the accompanying graphs do not reveal intensity, the patterns in boxes a, b, and c show agreement, or consensus, whereas boxes d, e, and f reveal disagreement, or conflict.

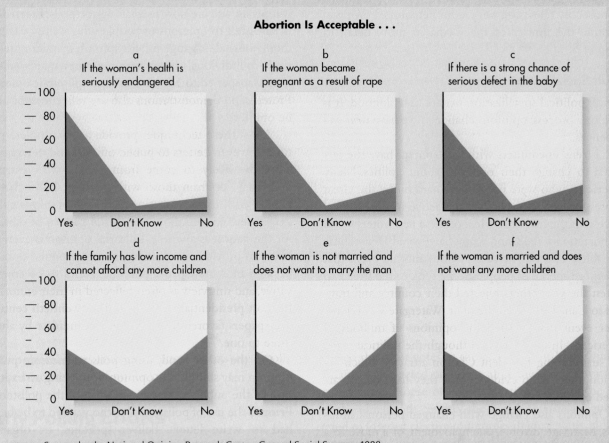

Abortion Is Acceptable . . .

a
If the woman's health is seriously endangered

b
If the woman became pregnant as a result of rape

c
If there is a strong chance of serious defect in the baby

d
If the family has low income and cannot afford any more children

e
If the woman is not married and does not want to marry the man

f
If the woman is married and does not want any more children

SOURCE: Surveys by the National Opinion Research Center, General Social Surveys, 1998.

Peers

In many instances, peers simply reinforce the opinions of the family or school. When there is a conflict between peer and parental socialization, peers sometimes win but

only on issues of special relevance to youth. For example, peer influence is more important than family influence on the issue of whether eighteen-year-olds should be allowed to vote, but parental influence appears to be

telephone numbers for listeners to call—one for yes, one for no. The votes are then electronically recorded.

The major problem with straw polls is that there is no way to ensure that the sample of individuals giving opinions is representative of the larger population. Generally speaking, they are not.

The famed *Literary Digest* poll is a good example. This magazine conducted polls of presidential preferences between 1916 and 1936. As many as eighteen million ballots were mailed out to persons drawn from telephone directories and automobile registration lists. Although the purpose was less to measure public opinion than to boost subscriptions, the *Digest* did have a pretty good record. It predicted the winners in 1924, 1928, and 1932. In 1936, however, the magazine predicted Alfred Landon would win, but Franklin Delano Roosevelt won by a landslide. The erroneous prediction ended the magazine's polling, and in 1938 the *Digest* went out of business.

A bias in the *Digest*'s polling procedure that the editors failed to consider led to an erroneous prediction. At the time, owners of telephones and automobiles were disproportionately middle- and high-income individuals who could afford a telephone or car in the depths of the Great Depression; these people were much more likely to vote for Landon (a Republican) than were lower-income people.[39] Since the survey was drawn from telephone directories and auto registrations, lower-income people were disproportionately excluded from the poll.

Emergence of Scientific Polling

Scientific polling began after World War I, inspired by the new field of business known as *marketing research*. After the war, demand for consumer goods rose, and American business, no longer engaged in the production of war materials, turned to satisfying consumer demand. Businesses used marketing research to identify what consumers wanted and, perhaps more important, how products should be packaged so consumers would buy them. For example, the American Tobacco Company changed from a green to a white package during World War II because it found that a white package was more attractive to women smokers.[40]

The application of mathematical principles of probability was also important to the development of scientific polling. To check the rates of defects in manufactured products, random or spot inspections of a few items, called a *sample,* were made. From these, projections of defects among the entire group of items could be made. From this use of sampling, it was a small step to conclude that sampling a small number of individuals could provide information about a larger population.

In the early 1930s, George Gallup and several others, using probability-based sampling techniques, began polling opinions on a wide scale. In 1936, Gallup predicted that the *Literary Digest* would be wrong and that Roosevelt would be reelected with 55.7 percent of the vote. Though Gallup underestimated Roosevelt's actual vote (he won 62.5 percent), his correct prediction of a landslide lent credibility to probability-based polls.

Increasingly, government used polls. In 1940, Roosevelt became the first president to use polls on a regular basis, employing a social scientist to measure trends in public opinion about the war in Europe. Most major American universities have a unit that does survey research, and there are hundreds of commercial marketing research firms, private pollsters, and newspaper polls.

Polls and Politics

For politicians, polls have become what the oracle of Delphi was to the ancient Greeks and Merlin was to King Arthur: a divine source of wisdom. During the

Doonesbury © G. B. Trudeau. Reprinted with permission of Universal Press Syndicate. All rights reserved.

budget debate between President Clinton and congressional Republicans, Republicans used polls that told them that promising to "put the government on a diet" would be popular in the upcoming 1996 election. Polls directed Clinton to counter by accusing the Republicans of trying to cut Medicare. When the media wanted to make sense out of the debate, they conducted still more polls.[41]

John Kennedy commissioned sixteen polls during his three years as president. Richard Nixon conducted 233 over six years in the White House. Bill Clinton spent $4.5 million on polls in his first two and a half years in office, enough to buy 150 polls.[42] Clinton was even advised on his vacation plans based on a poll. Rather than vacation on Martha's Vineyard and play golf, Clinton was advised by pollster and consultant Dick Morris that golf was a Republican sport and the voters he needed to win over where those who went camping. Morris sent Clinton off hiking in the Rockies. In addition, members of Congress, state officeholders, political parties, political candidates, and media poll.

Pollsters can conduct a poll at a moment's notice and have the results within a few hours. But can polls be taken at face value?

On clearly defined issues that the public has thought about carefully and on which they hold strong views, such as how they will vote in tomorrow's election, a well-designed poll can accurately reflect the winner. For example, all eight of the election eve polls in the 1996 presidential election predicted the winner. One got it exactly right, finding Clinton with a 9 percent advantage over Dole. The president's actual margin of victory was 8.4 percent. The average error of these presidential election polls in 1996 was a remarkably low 1.7 percent.[43]

On issues that the public has not thought much about and where choices are less clearly defined, polls rarely provide a meaningful guide to what the public thinks. For example, poll results reflecting support for candidates seeking office for the first time often jump up and down simply because voters do not know much about the candidates.

Even when issues are well defined and opinions are fairly stable, it is increasingly difficult to obtain a sample that provides a representative picture of public opinion. Many respondents refuse to be interviewed,[44] some because they do not want to be bothered, others because they fear they will be asked to buy something or contribute money. Nonrespondents, those who refuse or cannot be reached, number from one-half to 80 percent of those called, and these people are more likely to be better educated, more affluent, and live in suburbs rather than cities and rural areas.[45] Many of these nonrespondents are more likely to vote Republican.

Another problem for pollsters is the tendency of some respondents to express an opinion when they do not have one. No one wants to appear ignorant. Some respondents volunteer an answer even though they know little or nothing about a subject. The problem is getting worse as pollsters increasingly probe topics on which the public has no opinion and on which there is little reason to believe it should. For example, pollsters have asked whether the public thought President Reagan's colon cancer was serious and whether the bloody glove originally fit O. J. Simpson.[46]

Although polls can be biased because of these problems, some pollsters and politicians consciously distort poll results. Today, many pollsters come from political consulting backgrounds and poll exclusively for members of one political party. Rather than provide accurate information about public opinion, their goal is to present their client in the most favorable light.[47]

An example of misuse is the "push poll." A pollster asks whether the person called is for John Jones, Mary Smith, or undecided in the upcoming congressional election. If the answer is Smith or undecided, the person is asked, "If you were told that Smith's hobby is driving a high-powered sports car at dangerous speeds through residential neighborhoods to see how many children and pets she can run over, would that make a difference in your vote?" You are asked your preference again. The idea is to see if certain "information" can "push" voters away from a candidate or a neutral opinion toward the candidate favored by those doing the poll.[48] Learning the weaknesses of the opposition has always been a part of politics, but push polls seek to manipulate opinion, rarely focus on a candidate's issue positions, and often distort a candidate's record and the facts.

An even more vicious tactic is to pump thousands of calls into a district or state under the guise of conducting a poll but with the intent of spreading false information about a candidate. John McCain accused the Bush campaign of spreading false information in the guise of a poll in the South Carolina primary when both were seeking the Republican presidential nomination in 2000. Similarly, Bush chided McCain for using a push poll in the Michigan presidential primary. Both the push poll and the phony poll are corruptions of the political process as well as violations of polling ethics. (See also the box "SLOP Surveys Are Sloppy Surveys.")

In spite of problems and abuses, polls still provide a valuable service to the nation. If direct democracy like the New England town meeting is the ideal, the use of public opinion polls is about as close as the modern state is likely to get to it. Polls help interpret the meaning of elec-

SLOP Surveys Are Sloppy Surveys

SLOP is an acronym for self-selected listener opinion polls. SLOP surveys are telephone call-in polls, which are being used increasingly by radio and television stations and even by newspapers. Why attach such a negative label to call-in polls? The answer is simple: the results are meaningless because those who call in do not reflect the views of the general public.

An example was CBS's survey to gauge public reaction to President Bush's 1992 State of the Union address. The program allowed viewers to dial and then respond to a series of recorded questions by pushing buttons on their telephone. CBS recorded the views of more than three hundred thousand respondents. In an effort to measure representativeness, at the same time, CBS also conducted a survey of 1,241 adults. A comparison of the two polls revealed that the results differed by 10 percent or more on seven of the nine questions. One question asked whether respondents were better off or worse off than four years ago. In the call-in poll, 54 percent said they were worse off, compared to 32 percent in the scientific survey. Viewers who felt they were worse off called in greater proportions than viewers who felt they were better off. In other words, viewers who are angrier or more concerned may be more likely to use their telephones to express their opinions.

Another problem with call-in polls is that people can call in more than once. *Parade* magazine conducted a call-in poll on abortion and received more than three hundred thousand responses. It later acknowledged that 21 percent of the callers may have voiced their opinion more than once. Obviously, if the views of some people are counted two or more times, the results will not be representative of the general public.

Despite these problems, SLOP surveys are likely to continue. As one pollster put it, "it's a good show. And who's going to give up a good show just for the truth?"

SOURCES: Richard Morin, "Another Contribution to SLOPpy Journalism," *Washington Post National Weekly Edition*, February 10, 1992, p. 38; Richard Morin, "Numbers from Nowhere: The Hoax of the Call-in 'Polls,'" *Washington Post*, February 9, 1992, p. B3.

Harry Truman exults in incorrect headlines, based on poll results and early returns, the morning after the 1948 election.

From the collection of the St. Louis Mercantile Library

tions. When voters cast their ballots for one candidate over another, all anyone knows for sure is that a majority preferred one candidate. Polls can help reveal what elections mean in terms of policy preferences and thus help make the government more responsive to voters. For example, the Republicans claimed their victory in the 1994 congressional elections was an indication that voters supported the party's Contract with America. However, polls showed that most Americans had never heard of it.

Polls, however, have a down side. Poor standing in the polls may discourage otherwise viable candidates from entering a race, leaving the field to others who have less chance of winning or who lack the skills necessary to govern effectively. George Bush's standing in the polls in January 1991, at the start of the Gulf War, made him appear a sure winner in the 1992 presidential election. In 2000, several potential Republican candidates passed up the presidential race when early polls suggested that George W. Bush was the odds-on favorite to win the Republican nomination. However, John McCain was able to effectively challenge him in the early primaries, and had he or someone else entered the race earlier, Bush may not have won the nomination.

Polls also have a negative effect on political campaigns. Prior to polling, the purpose of campaigns was to reveal the candidates' views on the issues and their solutions to the pressing problems of the day. Instead, polls focus attention on the electorate and what they think. Polls find out what the voters want, and the candidates develop images to suit the market.

The ease of polling also means that judgment and leadership often give way to the sentiments expressed in public opinion polls. Politicians rarely make a decision without one. Rather than educate the public regarding the merits of particular policies, many politicians seem to follow the polls blindly.

For example, when Rodney King, a black man who was stopped for speeding, was beaten by four white police officers in Los Angeles in 1992, the incident created a furor, and when the officers' first trial resulted in a verdict of not guilty, it led to a riot. President Bush was in a quandary about what to do. His aides were divided. Some said he should give speeches emphasizing the need for racial harmony, and some said he should propose programs providing urban renewal for big cities. But others said he should do neither. So he tried to follow the polls. At first, he defended the police and called their chief "an American hero." After the first trial he declared, "The system has worked." But in a couple of days, he said he was "stunned" and felt "a deep sense of personal frustration and anguish" about the verdict. As the public changed their responses in the polls, he changed his messages to the public. Ultimately, analysis of the polls showed no clear mandate, so Bush did not do anything except approve some emergency aid to cope with the destruction from the riots.[50]

Former senator Daniel Patrick Moynihan (D-N.Y.) decried politicians' addiction to poll results, suggesting that it had caused Congress to adopt popular causes, such as the line item veto, that were later found by the Supreme Court to be unconstitutional. "We've lost our sense of ideas that we stand by, principles that are important to us."[51]

As the number of polls, both good and bad, increases, their importance for the public and perhaps politicians may decline. The sheer number of polls may lead everyone to take them less seriously. Moreover, if politicians allow themselves to be driven by poll results, no one will gain an advantage from the information the polls provide.[52] Still, it is unlikely that ambitious politicians bent on winning at all costs will abandon something that may help them win.

How Informed Is Public Opinion?

Many Americans are uninformed or misinformed concerning government and politics. Only one-fourth can name their two senators,[53] and only one-third can name their U.S. representative.[54] More than one-third do not know the party of their representative,[55] and 40 percent do not know which party controls Congress.[56]

Many Americans are unable to identify prominent political personalities (see Table 2). Six years after he was elected vice president, 24 percent could not identify George Bush. More people can identify the judge on the television show *The People's Court* than can identify the chief justice of the United States.[57] In spite of increases in education, levels of knowledge regarding politics have not changed much since the 1940s.[58]

Although Americans revere the Constitution and see it as a blueprint for democracy, many do not know what is in it. One-third think it established English as the country's official language, and one in six thinks it established America as a Christian nation. One-fourth cannot name a single First Amendment right, and only 6 percent can name all four.[59]

Only a small percentage of Americans can identify a single piece of legislation passed by Congress.[60] Nearly 60 percent were ignorant of a plan passed by the House of Representatives in 1995 to balance the federal budget.[61]

Misperception regarding government policies is widespread. While polls show Americans in favor of reducing the size of the federal government, more than 70 percent are unaware that the number of federal employees has decreased in recent years.[62] Seven out of ten feel that the country spends too much on foreign aid, and two out of three say the country should cut spending on foreign aid. However, one-half estimate foreign aid to be about fifteen times greater than it is. Asked what an appropriate spending level would be, the average answer is eight times more than the country actually spends. Thus, 70 percent think the country spends too much on foreign aid but many would support an amount substantially higher.[63]

Another example of Americans not knowing what they think they know is that 24 percent agreed and 19 percent disagreed that the Public Affairs Act of 1975 should be repealed. The problem is that they offered an opinion on something that does not exist.[64] The *Washington Post* included the exact same question in a 1995 survey and found the same thing. The question was a ploy to see how many would volunteer an answer when they have no opinion.

Most Americans do not think much about politics. Their major concerns are family and work. Lack of concern for government means that politicians can sometimes ignore what the public wants and what it needs. That is, politicians can be less responsive to the public.

Although the public may not pay much attention to politics and is uninformed on many things, some political scientists argue that average citizens know what they need to know to make sound political judgments.[65] Most do take an active interest in politics when their personal stake is affected. Eighty percent know that Congress passed a law requiring employers to provide family leave following the birth of a child or a family emergency. Family leave touches people directly.

Although many can no doubt make sound political judgments, others are unable to do so. Polls show that those who are less politically knowledgeable find it difficult to sort through the claims and counterclaims of politicians. Some support candidates and policies that work against their self-interest.[66]

Adding to the problem are public officials who fail to educate the public on issues. Politicians often do not like to discuss issues, especially controversial ones. When they do, public awareness increases. After President Reagan made an issue of American support for the Nicaraguan Contras, for example, awareness of the issue and the side the United States was supporting jumped from 25 percent to 59 percent.[67]

Public Opinion

Public opinion polls cover virtually every aspect of American life. Polls have reported the number of California drivers with paraphernalia hanging from their rearview mirrors and Iowans with ornaments on their

Table 2	Political Ignorance of the Public
	Percentage Unable to Identify
Who is in Washington:	
Vice president	40
Speaker of the House	46
Their Senate representatives	54
Majority leader in Senate	66
Their House representative	67
What goes on in Washington:	
That the number of federal employees decreased in past three years	72
That the government spends more on Medicare than on foreign aid	73
That the House passed a plan to balance the budget	75
That the Senate passed a plan to balance the budget	78

SOURCE: Richard Morin, "Tuned Out, Turned Off," *Washington Post National Weekly Edition*, February 5–11, 1996, pp. 6–8.

Focus Groups: Measuring or Manipulating Public Opinion?

Ever wonder where the ideas for political ads come from? Many come from people like you, meeting in focus groups. A *focus group* is a dozen or so ordinary people who are brought together to share their opinions on everything from grocery products to television sitcoms. They are also used by political candidates to examine voters' attitudes. Focus group leaders ask questions such as, "If Bill Clinton came to your house for dinner, what would you talk about?" or "If the candidate were a color, what would he be?" Sessions are taped, and consultants spend hours poring over every word and gesture in an effort to find out what is on voters' minds.

Unlike in public opinion polls, the samples are not drawn scientifically, nor is a great deal of time spent ensuring that questions used to measure opinions are fair and unbiased. The only requirement is that participants feel comfortable enough with each other to share their thoughts. It is considered risky to mix people of different social characteristics—for example, blue- with white-collar workers, blacks with whites, even men with women.

The objective in using focus groups is to identify feelings that lurk below the surface, rarely being voiced publicly but nevertheless affecting votes. Yes-no-I don't know answers in public opinion polls reveal the substance but not the texture of public opinion. Feelings censored from public comments often rise to the surface in focus groups. These feelings are likely to come into play when people vote.

The 1992 presidential campaigns illustrate the growing reliance on focus groups. Every ad was tested with a focus group. The Clinton campaign began holding focus groups in New Hampshire even before the candidate announced. Personal responsibility and welfare reform, centrist themes from Clinton's earlier days, bombed when tested in focus groups. With high unemployment and depressed real estate values, New Hampshire residents did not want to hear about personal responsibility. And instead of viewing welfare recipients as freeloaders, they recognized them as people who had lost their jobs to the recession and could no longer make it—people very much like themselves. In response to this information, Clinton abandoned his message and developed a new one, tailored to New Hampshire.

Between New Hampshire and the convention, the Clinton campaign convened focus groups at every major crisis. And focus groups were behind the idea to profile Clinton's humble beginnings at the Democratic National Convention. His Georgetown, Yale, and Oxford education had given many voters the impression that he was a Bush-style blue blood.

Focus groups continued to be a staple of Clinton's strategy following his election. Findings from focus groups assisted him in dealing with his personal scandals and the impeachment process.

The Republican revolution in 1994 that led to their capturing control of Congress was crafted in focus groups. Rather than "restructure" and "modernize" Medicare, which focus groups suggested was too "techie," or "reform," which was too frightening, focus groups led Newt Gingrich and the House Republicans to "preserve, protect, and strengthen" Medicare.

Focus group participants invariably come away with a sense of empowerment, a feeling that someone is genuinely interested in their opinions. Most forget what they suspected at the beginning, that they are being used for the $50 fee. To be sure, politicians are interested in their opinions, but not to make the system more responsive to them. Rather, politicians use their opinions to produce a potent message that will influence their vote. As a former Perot pollster put it, "They're the guinea pigs allowing us to exploit the electorate."

SOURCE: Elizabeth Kolbert, "Test-Marketing a President," *New York Times Magazine*, August 30, 1992, p. 18.

---

lawns. Political polls examine opinions about political issues and political candidates, whether the American people are liberal or conservative, and whether this influences their positions on issues and preferences for political candidates. (See also the box on focus groups.) Although it is important to know how Americans stand on current issues and how they feel about political candidates, it is also important to know what they think about government: its founding principles, political institutions, and political leaders. This is especially true when large numbers of Americans see government and politics as unimportant or even feel hostile toward them.

We begin by discussing ideology—what it is, what the labels liberal and conservative mean, and whether Americans identify themselves as liberal or conservative. We then look at how ideology relates to opinions on specific issues such as social welfare, social issues, and race. We also explore how ideology is related to political tolerance, whether Americans are willing to extend rights and liberties to individuals who do not share their opinions. Finally, we look at trust in government: Do Americans trust their government to do the right thing, and are liberals more trusting than conservatives?

Ideology

The term **ideology** refers to a highly organized and coherent set of opinions. In the extreme, one who is ideological takes a position on all issues consistent with his or her ideology. *Liberalism* and *conservatism* are terms used to describe the current major ideologies in American politics. Liberals are sometimes identified by the label "left" or "left wing" and conservatives by the label "right" or "right wing." These terms date from the French National Assembly of the early nineteenth century in which conservatives occupied the right side of the chamber and liberals occupied the left side.

Liberalism, as a set of ideas, endorses the notion that government has an obligation to help individuals, groups, and communities that are economically disadvantaged by providing them with such things as health care, education, and income. In the New Deal era, liberal ideas were the justification for using government to expand opportunities and improve the quality of life for all. With this as their platform, the Democrats came to power in the 1930s and dominated American politics through the 1960s. During the 1960s, liberalism came to be identified with the civil rights policies of the Democrats. These policies threatened the white-dominated social order in the South and white ethnic communities in the North. Blacks increased their support for the Democratic Party, and many whites, especially in the South, increased their support for the Republican Party. Liberalism was also linked to anti–Vietnam War protests and to Supreme Court decisions that expanded the rights of persons accused of crimes, legalized abortion, and barred mandatory prayer in schools. These less popular policies led to conservative attacks on liberalism and government activism.

Today, liberalism has lost some of the stigma associated with the unpopular policies of the 1960s and 1970s, but it still faces major opposition from conservatives who, having lost their voice from the 1930s through 1970s, gained renewed energy in the 1980s and 1990s. Liberalism is still identified with government assistance for the poor and, in different forms, working- and middle-class Americans. It is also associated with support for Social Security, universal health care, a progressive income tax, abortion rights, affirmative action, and gun control. Liberals generally oppose the death penalty and oppose expansion of military spending.

Conservatism, on the other hand, identifies a set of ideas emphasizing that individuals are responsible for their own well-being and that the government has little or no obligation to help or improve individuals or communities. Whereas liberalism seeks answers to social and economic problems in government solutions, conservatism relies on the "invisible hand" of the economic marketplace. Conservatism would, for example, scale back or eliminate welfare payments to the poor and create incentives for the private sector to employ them. However, since the 1960s, conservatism has also come to embrace a moralistic component, which, in contrast to the hands-off approach with regard to income redistribution, endorses government-imposed solutions in the realm of social behavior.

Contemporary conservatism would outlaw abortion and require prayer in school. It would place restrictions on labor's right to organize and bargain collectively. It would opt for a flat income tax and look to the market to deal with issues of health care, public education, and Social Security.

Do the labels liberal and conservative describe Americans' opinions? One way to find out is to ask. Slightly more Americans identify themselves as conservative than liberal, and this pattern has changed very little in the past fifteen years. However, most Americans identify themselves as moderate or centrist. Moderates can be those who fall in the middle on most issues—that is, those who are neither liberal nor conservative or those who are liberal on some issues and conservative on others.

Self-identifications are helpful, but one cannot be sure that individuals actually know what the label means or that they support the positions identified with the label. Although liberals and conservatives do take different positions on a number of issues, on most issues a majority of liberals and conservatives take the same position. On social welfare issues, for example, most liberals and conservatives endorse increased spending for health care, education, and the environment and to combat drugs. Majorities of liberals and conservatives have similar feelings on issues of race and are supportive of civil liberties for all Americans whatever their views. Both tend to agree on the failings of the government. All of this means that most Americans are not very ideological. While many call themselves liberals and conservatives, these groups do not represent cohesive blocs of citizens with opposing issue positions seeking to control the government to enact their position into law.

Why aren't Americans more ideological? First, we are not very interested in politics. Much of what we find important in life falls outside politics. We are concerned about our families and jobs, which for the most part are not directly and immediately affected by government.

Lack of interest leads to lack of intensity. Even where majorities of liberals and conservatives disagree—as, for example, on abortion and prayer in school—the feelings of most are not very intense, perhaps because most are not touched by these issues.

Second, political candidates and parties do not usually mobilize their followings with ideological or issue appeals. Both candidates and parties try to be all things to all people, for reasons we will discuss more fully in Chapter 7, and often blunt the ideological or issue content of their message to attract support from both the right and the left. Evidence also indicates that candidates, at least those running for president, are more successful the closer they are to the middle compared to their opponent. President Clinton received his highest approval ratings following movement to the center when he supported welfare reform, free trade, and a balanced budget. His ratings declined when he advocated removing restrictions on gays in the military and health care reform.[68]

Nonetheless, political leaders of both parties are more ideological than the rank and file. Obviously, political leaders are more interested in politics, which contributes to the intensity of their feelings. And whereas a few years ago scholars talked of "the end of ideology," today they remark on its increase in American political debates.

Social Welfare and the Proper Role of Government

Government programs to help individuals deal with economic hardship started during the Great Depression in the 1930s. These included programs to provide aid for the elderly (Social Security), unemployed, and poor (Aid to Families with Dependent Children). Most Americans supported government assistance of this kind in the 1930s and support it today (see Figure 2).

Still, Americans have mixed feelings about social welfare spending. Support is high for Social Security and for helping the poor. About 60 percent feel that the nation is spending too little to assist the poor and poor children, and nearly the same number feel we spend too little on Social Security.[69] Nearly 85 percent favored provisions of the Clinton health care plan that would have subsidized medical costs for low-income families and the unemployed.

On the other hand, support for "welfare," especially Aid to Families with Dependent Children, is much lower. Polls show most (60 to 80 percent) supported the reforms that require persons on welfare to work and get off welfare after two years. Over 50 percent feel, however, that it is unfair for the government to cut off payments after two years if there is no other source of income. Most Americans (75 percent) believe the answer to welfare is job training and are willing to pay more in the short term to provide it. Americans appear to favor helping the poor, but they do not like "welfare," which for decades has been the target of both government officials and the media. They believe that requiring work and training for jobs are the keys to welfare reform.

Americans approve increased spending for education, health care, the environment, drug rehabilitation, and crime and law enforcement. For example, two-thirds favor increased spending for improving and protecting the nation's health. Nearly 40 percent favor increases in spending for the nation's highways and bridges, mass transportation, and parks; less than 10 percent oppose additional funding in these areas.

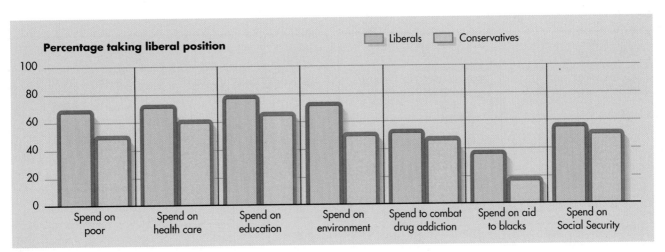

FIGURE 2 ■ *Self-Identified Liberals and Conservatives Differ Modestly on Spending for Social Services*

SOURCE: 1998 General Social Survey.

In spite of these sentiments, two-thirds report that their federal income taxes are too high, and 84 percent indicate that taxes are very important when deciding among candidates for Congress. However, only a third would use the budget surplus to cut taxes rather than fund increases in education, defense, Medicare, and other programs.[70] Other things equal, Americans want lower taxes and smaller government, but they are also concerned about the well-being of people in the country and about caring for the disadvantaged.

Consistent with Republican goals to devolve functions of government from the national to state levels, 75 percent want the states to take over many of the responsibilities performed by the national government.[71] Only 12 percent say that the national government does the best job of spending tax dollars in an efficient and constructive manner. Thirty-two percent say that state governments do the best job.

The preference for state over national government is linked to greater confidence in state government. Complaints include that the government wastes money, spends too much on the wrong things, takes too long to solve problems, and offers ineffective solutions to problems. It is possible (indeed likely) that the greater visibility of the national government compared to state governments in turn leads to this relative lack of confidence. If our state legislatures were covered by television to the extent that Congress is, the evaluations by the public would probably be quite different.

Americans have not, however, given up on the national government. They want it managed better and want to see better performance from government employees. Few want to see the government made smaller by cutting spending and programs.

Social Issues

Beginning in the 1960s, so-called social issues, those relating to morality, became topics of political debate. Examples include abortion, prayer in schools, restrictions on pornography, tolerance of homosexuals, capital punishment, and the role of women in society. Not all surfaced at the same time, but by the 1990s all were included in what some described as the family values agenda.

Social issues represent a clash of values between those seeking to impose traditional moral standards on society and those who are less willing to do so. Many of these cleavages stem from the 1960s and 1970s, a period of rapid social change. Conventional ways of doing things were challenged by a number of social movements, including civil rights, women's, and environmental movements. Many people believed that government decisions, particularly court decisions, favored the agenda of these groups. The Supreme Court approved abortion, outlawed mandated prayer in school, extended rights to persons accused of crimes, and raised questions about capital punishment. Women moved into the workforce in large numbers, aided by affirmative action policies. Homosexuals became more visible as a group and more outspoken regarding their civil rights. Some people, particularly Christian conservatives, believed these developments were evidence of a decline in moral standards.

The division over values, fueled in part by religious conservatives, continued until the end of the century. This division was reflected in opinions of Americans toward the impeachment of President Clinton. Some religious conservatives accused Clinton of subverting honesty and decency to such a degree that he should not be

Doonesbury © G. B. Trudeau. Reprinted with permission of Universal Press Syndicate. All rights reserved.

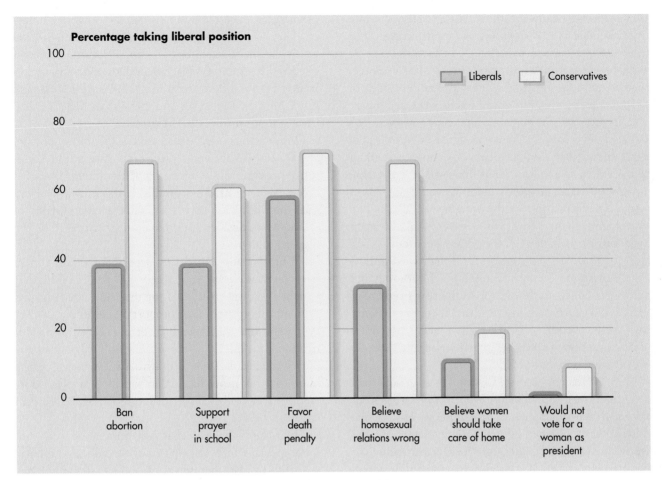

Percentage taking liberal position

Legend: Liberals / Conservatives

FIGURE 3 ■ *Self-Identified Liberals and Conservatives Differ on Many Social Issues*

SOURCE: 1998 General Social Survey.

allowed to continue in office; on the other side, others accused the president's opponents of practicing "sexual McCarthyism" (see Chapter 14), trampling civil liberties and invading people's privacy.[72] While most found the president's actions lacking in morality and ethics, nearly one-half felt it was unimportant as long as he was doing a good job running the country.

The position of liberals and conservatives on social issues is opposite of what it is on social welfare. On social welfare issues, liberals are likely to support government action, but on social issues, they reject government involvement. Liberals generally prefer to leave questions of religious belief and sexual morality to individuals to decide for themselves, while conservatives are more willing to call on government to enforce particular standards of behavior.

Conservatives, for example, are more likely to favor a ban on abortion and to require prayer in public schools (see Figure 3). They are more willing to support capital punishment and traditional roles for women. For example, conservatives are slightly more likely to feel that

women should take care of the home and leave running the country to men. The vast majority of both liberals and conservatives, however, are open to men and women running the country and would support a woman for president.

Conservatives are considerably more likely than liberals to respond that homosexual relations are always wrong. A significant generational divide suggests that society will become more tolerant in the future. Seven out of ten of those over sixty-five say homosexual behavior is wrong, but only five in ten of those eighteen to twenty-nine have this view.[73] Eight out of ten Americans, including both liberals and conservatives, think homosexuals should have equal rights in job opportunities and housing.

Race

Public opinion has influenced as well as responded to the progress of the black struggle for equality. Although the historical record extends to colonial times, the polling record begins in the 1940s. It shows white America increasingly opposed to discrimination and segregation, at least in principle.[74] In fact, the change might be characterized as revolutionary. For example, whereas only one-third of whites accepted the idea of black and white children going to the same schools in 1942, in the 1980s more than 90 percent approved. Today nearly everyone (98 percent) agrees. Over 80 percent respond that they have no objection to sending their children to schools where more than half of the students are black. Nearly two-thirds would not object to schools where most of the students are black. The percentage believing that whites have a right to keep blacks out of their neighborhood has been cut in half since 1963, and a 1996 survey found that two-thirds of white Americans live in integrated neighborhoods and that 70 percent claim they have a fairly close friend who is black (83 percent of blacks claim they have a fairly close white friend).[75] Thirty-eight percent of whites were against laws forbidding intermarriage in 1963; 85 percent were opposed in 1998.[76]

Only 37 percent expressed a willingness to vote for a black candidate for president in 1958; in 1996, 92 percent expressed such willingness. These findings suggest that white America is becoming much more tolerant of racial diversity (see Figure 4). Although the North continues to be more supportive of black rights than the South, whites in both regions show increased acceptance of blacks.

Public opinion can change because individuals change or because older individuals with one set of opinions are replaced by a new generation with a different set. Changes in whites' racial opinions through 1960 occurred for both reasons. In the 1970s, most changes occurred because of replacement. Differences in socialization between those born in the 1920s and 1930s and those born in the 1950s and 1960s have led to much greater support for racial integration.

More change can be expected in the future as white and black teens age and replace older Americans. A majority of white adults agree that the failure of blacks to take advantage of opportunities is more of a problem than discrimination by whites, while a large plurality of white teens consider discrimination by whites to be the bigger problem.[77]

While white Americans accept integration, they have been much slower to accept government initiatives to achieve it. In some issues, the direction of change has shifted from greater to less support. For example, 38 percent approved the federal government's ensuring fair treatment for blacks in jobs in 1964; only 28 percent endorsed the idea in 1996. Busing to achieve racial balance in schools has never had much appeal to whites. Thirteen percent endorsed the idea in 1972, and 33 percent did so in 1996.

Two-thirds believe that government should not make special efforts to help minorities and that minorities need to help themselves. In some cases, unwillingness on the part of whites to endorse government initiatives to end segregation reflects racist sentiments.[78] Although only 10 percent of white Americans respond

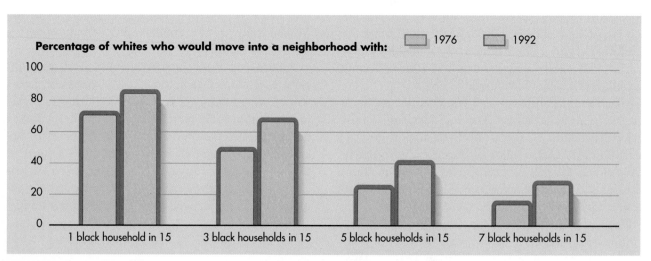

FIGURE 4 ■ *Whites Have Grown More Accepting of Neighborhood Integration* *Residential segregation is the linchpin of racial separation in America. Such segregation influences the quality and nature of schools, employment opportunities, and the amenities of daily life. In the past twenty years, American cities have become somewhat less segregated, stimulated in part by whites' changing attitudes about residential segregation.*

SOURCE: Douglas Massey and Nancy Denton, *American Apartheid* (Cambridge, Mass.: Harvard University Press, 1993).

that differences in jobs, housing, and income between whites and blacks are the result of biological differences,[79] 43 percent cling to the racist belief that it is lack of motivation and will power on the part of blacks.[80] Thus, anywhere from 10 to 40 percent of white Americans harbor racist beliefs in spite of their willingness to accept blacks, live in integrated neighborhoods, and have their children attend integrated schools.

However, some whites oppose government help for blacks on principle. They object to being told what to do by government or feel government assistance for blacks is discrimination against whites. For some, government help violates their sense that individuals have a responsibility to provide for themselves.

Another reason that some white Americans are reluctant to accept government intervention is that some do not believe that racial prejudice exists. Most whites (64 percent) reject the idea that differences in jobs, housing, and income between whites and blacks are the result of discrimination. Even among those who are aware of discrimination, most reject racial preferences to redress discrimination. Three out of four Americans reject affirmative action programs that give preferences to blacks.[81] A majority of whites believe affirmative action hurts white men. It is not only Republicans and conservatives who oppose racial preferences, but Democrats and liberals as well.[82] (We will explore affirmative action in more detail in Chapter 15.)

Blacks see things quite differently. About a third believe that there is discrimination in education, about half believe discrimination exists in housing and getting an unskilled job, and about two-thirds see discrimination in getting a skilled job or managerial position.[83] Forty-four percent indicate that they have been denied a job or promotion because of race, more than three times the percentage of whites.[84]

What do blacks believe should be done about race discrimination? Although the polling record for blacks does not extend as far back as it does for whites, blacks have overwhelmingly endorsed integration. Nearly all blacks have responded consistently that blacks and whites should go to the same schools and that blacks have a right to live anywhere they want to. Intermarriage is approved by three out of four blacks.

Like whites, blacks have become somewhat less supportive of government initiatives. In 1964, 92 percent thought the national government should ensure blacks fair treatment in jobs; by 1996, only 64 percent did. Support for government assistance in school integration has also declined, from 82 percent in 1964 to 57 percent in 1994. Some blacks fear that government initiatives will only antagonize whites. Others believe government aid hurts blacks by making them too dependent. Still others believe government is ineffective in bringing about an end to discrimination.

Self-identified liberals and conservatives also differ on race issues. Liberals are somewhat more likely to oppose laws that ban racial intermarriage, to disagree that whites have a right to keep blacks out of their neighborhood, and to be willing to send their children to a school where most are a different race. However, differences are fairly small (5 to 9 percentage points), and majorities of both liberals and conservatives take the pro-equality position on each issue. Nevertheless, because there are gaps between abstractions about equality and concrete issues such as affirmative action and between survey questions and real-life dilemmas, issues of race remain the most vexing in our society.

Political Tolerance

Political tolerance is the willingness of individuals to extend procedural rights and liberties to people with whom they disagree. Tolerance is important because it embodies many elements essential to democratic government, such as freedom of speech and assembly.

J. William Fulbright, the former senator from Arkansas, once said, "Americans believe in the right to free speech until someone tries to exercise it." In other words, people are tolerant in the abstract but not when called upon to support speakers they disagree with. More than 85 percent of Americans claim to believe in free speech for all,[85] yet a 1954 nationwide survey found that only 37 percent of the respondents would allow a person opposed to churches and religion to speak in their communities.[86] Even fewer would permit an admitted communist to speak. More highly educated people were more tolerant than those with less education, and political elites were more tolerant than the general public.

The finding that elites were more tolerant than the general public was reassuring. After all, many elites are in a position to deprive people of rights, and elites help shape public opinion. Later studies have revealed, however, that elites are more tolerant than the general public largely because they are better educated.[87] Elites, however, do influence the opinions of the general public on civil liberties. When elites agree among themselves, the general public is more likely to reflect this consensus.[88]

More recent studies suggest that Americans have become substantially more tolerant of communists, socialists, and atheists.[89] However, overall levels of tolerance may not have increased that much.

In the 1950s, people perceived communists and socialists as a major threat. As the perception of the threat diminished, so did people's fears. Research on tolerance, therefore, has first asked people which groups they dislike and then assessed their tolerance toward those groups.[90] Two-thirds or more thought that members of their least-liked group should be banned from being president and from teaching in the public schools. Many responded that the group should be outlawed, indicating a high degree of intolerance. On the other hand, in the 1970s, the public was more willing to allow their least-liked group to speak and teach than they were to allow communists to do so in 1954.[91] This suggests that tolerance may have increased. Thus, although intolerance remains, it seems that the public has grown more tolerant since the 1950s.

While increased levels of political tolerance since the 1950s are a reason to be positive, economic insecurity in the 1980s and early 1990s helped promote negative feelings toward minorities and immigrants and others outside the mainstream. A majority of whites, for example, agree that equal rights for racial minorities have gone too far. Eighty-two percent agree that people coming to live in the United States should be restricted and controlled more than they are now.[92] Such sentiments are not likely to lead to a loss of civil liberties unless political elites direct citizens' fears in an attempt to gain political advantage.

In general, liberals tend to be more tolerant than conservatives, at least toward communists, atheists, racists, and those who would support a military government. For example, in 1996, 74 percent of those who identified themselves as liberals in a national survey indicated a willingness to allow a communist to speak in their community; 64 percent of the conservatives took this position.[93] The difference, however, may reflect that conservatives view communists as a bigger threat than liberals do. Liberals may be equally intolerant toward groups they perceive as threatening. In general, intolerance is not caused by ideology, but by personality, the tendency to see the world as a dangerous place, specific beliefs about individuals and groups, and lack of support for the principles of democracy.[94]

Trust in Government

An important dimension of public opinion is the trust or support citizens have for their government, its institutions and officials, and their fellow citizens. With high levels of trust, citizens might do everything government

demands. They would pay their taxes and, if called upon to do so, defend the government. They might also gullibly accept anything officials tell them. At low levels of trust, citizens would be more skeptical; they might even disobey the law. At the lowest levels, they might try to overthrow the government or commit violent acts against it, as with the Oklahoma City bombing. Thus, democratic government "depends on a fine balance between trust and distrust."[95]

Public trust of government has declined significantly in the last forty years. In the early 1960s, Americans were supportive of the government. A comparison of five nations—the United States, Britain, West Germany, Italy, and Mexico—found Americans to be the most positive about the responsiveness and performance of government; 95 percent of the Americans sampled pointed to the government when asked what aspects of the nation they were proud of.[96] The picture that emerged was one of trust and confidence.

The pattern, however, changed sometime in the mid-1960s. Trust in government declined after 1964 and continued to decline through 1980 (see Figure 5). The pattern was characteristic not only of opinions toward government but of opinions toward all major institutions in society, including the medical profession, business, and the press. Government responsiveness also was rated less positively during the 1960s and 1970s.

Why did levels of trust and confidence in government decline? One answer is the performance of government itself. In the mid to late 1960s, the nation was divided over a number of issues, including what to do about the war in Vietnam and the civil rights demands of blacks. Many people wanted the government to do everything possible to win the war in Vietnam, whereas others wanted an immediate withdrawal of U.S. forces;

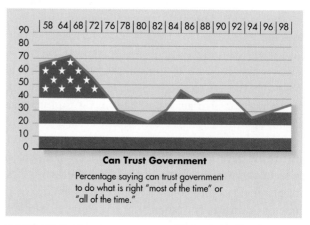

Can Trust Government

Percentage saying can trust government to do what is right "most of the time" or "all of the time."

FIGURE 5 ■ *Trust in Government Declined During the 1960s and 1970s*

SOURCE: National Election Studies, the Center for Political Studies.

the Johnson and Nixon policies of limited and prolonged war were unresponsive to both sides.

The civil rights struggle also divided the nation. Some wanted government to do more to speed the progress of blacks and other minorities, whereas others thought government was moving too fast. Once more, government chose a middle course fully responsive to neither side.[97]

Following on the heels of these seemingly intractable problems, the early 1970s brought news of Watergate and corruption in government, and after 1973 the nation experienced economic problems, inflation, high interest rates, and unemployment. The government was little more successful in dealing with these than it was with the problems of the 1960s. Levels of trust again declined.

Between 1980 and 1984, levels of trust and confidence in government increased modestly. People seemed to respond to what appeared to be an improved economy and a few foreign policy successes. President Reagan's personal popularity seemed to inspire confidence on the part of the American people.

Reagan's involvement in the Iran-Contra scandal, a sense that his administration lacked compassion, and popular dissatisfaction with domestic and foreign policy diminished his appeal, however, and no doubt contributed to a decline in trust between 1984 and 1986.[98] In the 1990s, trust has remained low.[99] Following the 1994 election, President Clinton and the Republican majority deadlocked over health care reform, welfare, and the budget deficit. Resolution of the welfare debate and a balanced budget agreement raised public assessments of both the president and Congress prior to the 1998 election, but trust remained low compared to the 1960s. Negative reaction to the Lewinsky scandal and impeachment process in Congress did not affect trust in government. In fact, the level just prior to the election in 1998 jumped. Although it is possible that the scandals will have a longer-term consequence, so far there is no evidence of it.[100]

As we have suggested, one explanation for declining trust is policy failure. Citizens have become increasingly oriented to government in terms of the services (jobs and high standard of living) they expect government to provide. When performance falls short of expectations, trust in government falls.[101] One study documents the link between confidence in government and the state of the economy. Between 1966 and 1980, every percentage increase in unemployment lowered confidence in government by almost 3 percent.[102]

Expressions of trust in government may involve more than evaluations of government performance, however. Societal problems may also cause declining

trust. Recent studies have found that trust in government is tied to public concern about declining morality and values, something over which government has limited control.[103] Declining levels of trust may have less to do with failed government performance than with the public's sense that the nation is doing badly on a number of fronts. If this is so, an improving economy is unlikely to make a big difference in levels of trust.

Another theory for declining trust focuses on process.[104] Declining trust is highly correlated with the increasing visibility of government. As Americans see more of their federal government on a day-to-day basis, through C-Span and newscasts, they like and trust it less. Talk radio and television interpret what are normal parts of the democratic process—lobbying, bargaining, negotiating, and compromise—as cynical acts done only for the self-interest of an individual, interest group, or political party. Of course, there is plenty of self-interest in politics, as in any other form of human endeavor, but compromise and negotiation are a necessary part of a democratic process. Since most Americans seem neither to understand nor to like that part of the process, the more exposure the process gets, the less the public likes it.

Both policy and process have contributed to declining trust in government. Moreover, the two reinforce each other. Policy deadlock contributes to negative reactions to process, but even when the process yields significant policies, the public visibility of the mechanics of the policy process, with its negotiations and deals, still contributes to cynicism and mistrust.

What would it take to restore public trust? This is a very difficult question. Most of the public think the country would be better off if the nation's leaders followed public opinion more closely. When asked whether the decisions of five hundred Americans selected to represent the nation would be better than the decisions of Congress, two-thirds said yes. Only 18 percent of Americans believe Congress would make the same decision they personally would most of the time. Two out of three would like public officials to consult the polls to find out what Americans think.[105] However, following the polls, which often reveal a divided public, will not provide policymakers with clear direction. Nor is it likely to produce high levels of trust.

Levels of trust among liberals and conservatives are frequently influenced by the party that occupies the White House. During Republican administrations, liberals tend to be less trusting; when Democrats hold office, liberals are more trusting.[106]

Negative feelings toward government and society in general are not unique to the United States.[107] Seventy

1824 The *Harrisburg Pennsylvanian* dispatches reporters to conduct a straw poll assessing candidate preferences of voters among the field of presidential contenders.

1916 The magazine *Literary Digest* begins polling, selecting respondents from telephone directories and automobile registration lists. It begins a run of successfully predicting the winner of the presidential election.

1935 An early poll shows that 89 percent of Americans favor old-age pensions for needy persons.

1936 The *Literary Digest* poll wrongly predicts that Landon will defeat Roosevelt. George Gallup, using probability sampling techniques, correctly predicts that the *Digest* will be wrong and that Roosevelt will win.

1939 Sixty-three percent of the public disapproves of a third term for President Roosevelt, but he easily wins reelection.

1948 Virtually every major pollster predicts that Dewey, the Republican candidate, will defeat Truman in the presidential election. Truman surprises them all by winning.

1955 While the overwhelming majority of Americans outside the South endorse the Supreme Court's edict to integrate the nation's public schools with "all deliberate speed," only 20 percent of southerners do.

1960 Thirty-nine percent of the public express no interest in watching John Kennedy and Richard Nixon engage in the first televised presidential debate.

1965 Twenty-five percent believe sending troops to Vietnam is a mistake.

1971 Sixty-one percent believe sending troops to Vietnam is a mistake.

1974 Fifty-seven percent of the public believe that President Nixon should resign the presidency because of his involvement in the Watergate scandal. Nixon subsequently resigns.

1984 The Democrats nominate Geraldine Ferraro for vice president. Seventy-eight percent of Americans indicate they would vote for a qualified woman for president, up from 66 percent in 1971 and 31 percent in 1937.

1991 Following U.S. success in the Gulf War, President Bush's approval rating hits 89 percent, the highest ever for a president. It sinks to 50 percent by December and bottoms out at 29 percent by the end of his term in 1992.

1998 A week after President Clinton is accused of having a sexual affair with a White House intern, 67 percent of the public approve of the way he is doing his job, the highest rating of his presidency.

1998 Thirty-six percent favor impeaching Clinton on the eve of an impeachment vote in the House.

percent of Canadians responded in a survey that their country was moving in the wrong direction. Forty-four percent in Japan responded the same way, and given that country's recent economic woes, this number is probably higher today.

Companies can move operations and individuals can transfer capital across national boundaries at will. While this creates economic opportunity, it also creates anxiety. Individuals are unclear what they need or should do to protect themselves and their families.

In the United States, a prosperous economy and expanded job opportunities in recent years have increased citizen confidence. Nevertheless, competition and technological change continue, and an economic downturn is likely to undermine the recent rise in public confidence.

At the same time, however, Americans as well as citizens in other industrialized countries report that they are content with the lives they lead. Citizens' lack of trust and concern for the future may result from what they read and see in the news and the feeling that government is being run in the interests of other people and groups with more resources.[108] Thus, citizens' nega-

tivism may be due to the expanding scope of the media in developed countries.

Conclusion: Is Government Responsive to Public Opinion?

Our interest in public opinion stems in part from the belief that in a democracy government should be responsive to the wishes of the people. But is it? Political scientists have had only limited success answering this question because of the difficulty in measuring influence.

The most direct way to assess whether public policy is responsive to public opinion is to compare changes in policy with changes in opinion. The largest study of this type examined several hundred public opinion surveys done between 1935 and 1979. From these surveys, the researchers culled hundreds of questions, each of which dealt with a particular policy and had been asked more than one time. On more than three hundred of these questions, public opinion had changed. The authors of the study compared changes in these three hundred opinions with changes, if any, in public policy. They found congruence between opinion changes and policy changes in more than two-thirds of the opinions. Congruence was most likely when the opinion change was large and stable and when the opinion moved in a liberal direction.

The authors acknowledged that in about one-half of the cases, the policy change may have caused the opinion change, but in the other half the opinion change probably caused the policy change or they both affected each other. Although in many instances policy was not congruent with public opinion, on important issues, when changes in public opinion were clear-cut, policy usually became consistent with opinion.[109]

Although policy usually changes with changes in opinions, sometimes it does not. One reason is that re-election does not rest with the entire public but with the voting public, and those who vote often differ in their policy preferences from those who do not.[110] To the extent that elected public officials are responsive to voters, and voters differ from nonvoters, public policy will not reflect public opinion.

Then, too, elected public officials must pay attention not only to the direction of public opinion but also to its intensity. It may be advantageous for an elected official to vote in support of a minority opinion that is intensely held. A minority with intense feelings is more likely to vote against a candidate who does not support its position than is a group with weak preferences. When elected officials are confronted with an intense minority, public policy may not reflect public opinion.

Moreover, public opinion is not the only influence on public policy, nor is it necessarily the most important. Interest groups, political parties, other institutions of government, and public officials' own preferences also influence policy, and they may or may not agree with public opinion. Where the preferences of the various influences do not agree, policy generally will reflect a compromise among them.

Finally, there is nothing sacred about public opinion. Even when a majority of the public favors a course of action, one should not assume that this is the most desirable course; the public can be wrong. This possibility led the Founders to establish a government that was partially insulated from the influence of public opinion. In other words, we do not have complete and immediate correspondence between opinion and policy because the Founders did not want instant government responsiveness. They built a federal system with separation of powers and many checks and balances to ensure that the majority could not steamroll the minority. Thus, one should not expect public policy to reflect public opinion perfectly. The fact that policy usually comes to reflect large and stable majorities does indicate, however, that government is eventually responsive on important issues. Indeed, some observers think politicians pay too much attention to public opinion, to the point that leaders are fearful of leading or of offending the competing groups pulling in opposite directions. The result is gridlock.

By Heller for the *Green Bay Press Gazette*, WI

Luntz Eventually Reveals Loaded Questions

Initially, Luntz ignored the AAPOR's request. After a year, he provided some information, including sample sizes, interviewing dates, and how respondents were selected, but would not provide question wording or results of questions he said measured popular support for the Contract. He argued that such information was the property of the Republican Party and implied that while he would like to supply the information, he would not betray a client's trust. Although the AAPOR rarely issues a public reprimand against nonmembers, because of Luntz's continued refusal to provide information and because his polls had received so much publicity, the AAPOR voted to censure him.

Luntz later admitted that his polls were flawed. The results were based on loaded questions, designed by him to ensure support for the Contract. Luntz's polling was designed to manipulate the public rather than to find out what the public thought.

Luntz remains a highly sought-after consultant and strategist. In spite of his playing fast and loose with his Contract polls, he continues to advise Republicans on how to win elections.

Key Terms

public opinion

political socialization

agents of political socialization

straw polls

ideology

liberalism

conservatism

political tolerance

Further Reading

Herbert Asher, *Polling and the Public: What Every Citizen Should Know* (Washington, D.C.: CQ Press, 1998). An introduction to polling methodology and the influence of polls on American politics as well as advice to citizens on how to evaluate polls.

Paul Brace and Barbara Hinckley, *Follow the Leader: Opinion Polls and the Modern President* (New York: Basic Books, 1992). A survey of how recent presidents have allowed the results of public opinion polls to influence their position on issues.

Susan Herbst, *Numbered Voices: How Opinion Polling Has Shaped American Politics* (Chicago: University of Chicago Press, 1993). A historical review of the way public opinion has been measured and the way the evolution of measurement techniques has affected the definition of public opinion.

Celinda Lake, *Public Opinion Polling: A Handbook for Public Interest and Citizen Advocacy Groups* (Washington, D.C.: Island, 1987). A step-by-step treatment for lay audiences on how to conduct a public opinion poll.

Thomas E. Mann and Gary R. Orren, eds., *Media Polls and American Politics* (Washington, D.C.: Brookings, 1992). Several essays focusing on the influence of media-conducted polls on American political institutions and elections.

Benjamin I. Page and Robert Y. Shapiro, *The Rational Public: Fifty Years of Trends in American's Policy Preferences* (Chicago: University of Chicago Press, 1992). An examination of the influence of public opinion on public policy using public opinion polling information generated over the past fifty years.

Electronic Resources

Many polling firms have homepages. Here is a sampling of some of the more reputable ones.

www.ropercenter.uconn.edu
The Roper Center Web site contains information on the current and past presidents' job performance and a listing of current Roper surveys.

www.irss.unc.edu/data_archive/pollsearch.html
The Louis Harris Center archive Web site links to current and past Harris surveys. Frequencies are available for all questions, and information can be downloaded and analyzed.

www.icpsr.umich.edu.gss/home.htm
The General Social Survey provides data on a variety of political and social issues gathered in surveys from 1972 to 1996. Data from one or more years can be analyzed on-line.

www.gallup.com
The Gallup Center does weekly national surveys on political and social issues. The Web site links to past Gallup newsletters, special reports, and trends in public opinion including the public support for the president and Congress and the public mood.

www.umich.edu/~nes/
The National Election Studies of the University of Michigan Web site provides access to the most recent national election study. This information can be analyzed on-line.

www.usatoday.com/elect/eg/equidex.htm
The Web site links to surveys carried in USA Today.

www.people-press.org./
The Pew Center Web site provides recent polling information.

InfoTrac College Edition

"Old, New Make Up Today's Surveys"
"Boutique Liberalism"
"Does School Integration Work?"
"Psychological Underpinnings of Democracy"

Notes

1. Richard Morin, "A Pollster's Peers Cry Foul," *Washington Post National Weekly Edition,* April 28, 1997, p. 13; American Association for Public Opinion Research, "Major Opinion Research Association Finds Pollster Frank Luntz Violated Ethics Code," news release, April 23, 1997; Ceci Connolly, "For the Republicans, a Campaign Primer," *Washington Post National Weekly Edition,* September 15, 1997, p. 13.

2. Richard Morin, "The Ups and Downs of Political Poll-Taking," *Washington Post National Weekly Edition,* October 5, 1992, p. 37.

3. Gallup Poll, "Bush Continues to Enjoy Single-Digit Lead over Gore in Presidential Race," May 3, 2000.

4. T. E. Cook, "The Bear Market in Political Socialization and the Costs of Misunderstood Psychological Theories," *American Political Science Review* 79 (December 1985): 1079–1093.

5. S. W. Moore et al., "The Civic Awareness of Five- and Six-Year-Olds," *Western Political Quarterly* 29 (August 1976): 418.

6. R. W. Connell, *The Child's Construction of Politics* (Carlton, Victoria: Melbourne University Press, 1971).

7. F. I. Greenstein, *Children and Politics* (New Haven, Conn.: Yale University Press, 1965), 122; see also F. I. Greenstein, "The Benevolent Leader Revisited: Children's Images of Political Leaders in Three Democracies," *American Political Science Review* 69 (December 1975): 1317–1398; R. D. Hess and J. V. Torney, *The Development of Attitudes in Children* (Chicago: Aldine, 1967).

8. Hess and Torney, *Development of Attitudes in Children;* Connell, *Child's Construction of Politics.*

9. Greenstein, *Children and Politics;* Greenstein, "The Benevolent Leader"; and Hess and Torney, *Development of Attitudes in Children.*

10. Connell, *Child's Construction of Politics.*

11. F. C. Arterton, "The Impact of Watergate on Children's Attitudes toward the President," *Political Science Quarterly* 89 (June 1974): 269–288; also F. Haratwig and C. Tidmarch, "Children and Political Reality: Changing Images of the President," paper presented at the 1974 Annual Meeting of the Southern Political Science Association; J. Dennis and C. Webster, "Children's Images of the President and Government in 1962 and 1974," *American Politics Quarterly* 4 (October 1975): 386–405; R. P. Hawkins, S. Pingree, and D. Roberts, "Watergate and Political Socialization," *American Politics Quarterly* 4 (October 1975): 406–436.

12. Gallup Poll, "Public Trust in Federal Government Remains High," January 8, 1999.

13. M. A. Delli Carpini, *Stability and Change in American Politics: The Coming of Age of the Generation of the 1960s* (New York: New York University Press, 1986), 86–89.

14. R. Merelman, *Political Socialization and Educational Climates* (New York: Holt, Rinehart & Winston, 1971), 54.

15. R. Sigel and M. Hoskin, *The Political Involvement of Adolescents* (New Brunswick, N.J.: Rutgers University Press, 1981).

16. J. Citrin, "Comment: The Political Relevance of Trust in Government," *American Political Science Review* 68 (September 1974): 973–1001; J. Citrin and D. P. Green, "Presidential Leadership and the Resurgence of Trust in Government," *British Journal of Political Science* 16 (1986): 431–453.

17. John Hibbing and Elizabeth Theiss-Morse, *Congress as Public Enemy: Public Attitudes toward American Political Institutions* (Cambridge: Cambridge University Press, 1995). It is plausible to assume that the content of early political socialization influences what is learned later, but the assumption has not been adequately tested. Thus, we might expect the positive opinions toward government and politics developed early in childhood to condition the impact of traumatic events later in life. D. Easton and J. Dennis, *Children and the Political System: Origins of Regime Legitimacy* (New York: McGraw-Hill, 1969); R. Weissberg, *Political Learning, Political Choice and Democratic Citizenship* (Englewood Cliffs, N.J.: Prentice Hall, 1974). See also D. D. Searing, J. J. Schwartz, and A. E. Line, "The Structuring Principle: Political Socialization and Belief System," *American Political Science Review* 67 (June 1973): 414–432.

18. D. Jaros, H. Hirsch, and F. Fleron, Jr., "The Malevolent Leader: Political Socialization in an American Subculture," *American Political Science Review* 62 (June 1968): 564–575.

19. K. Tedin, "The Influence of Parents on the Political Attitudes of Adolescents," *American Political Science Review* 68 (December 1974): 1579–1592.

20. M. Kent Jennings, *Generations and Politics* (Princeton, N.J.: Princeton University Press, 1981).

21. On the impact of the public schools and teachers on political socialization, particularly in the area of loyalty and patriotism, see Hess and Torney, *Development of Attitudes in Children.*

22. K. Langton and M. K. Jennings, "Political Socialization and the High School Civics Curriculum," *American Political Science Review* 62 (September 1968): 852–877; D. Goldenson, "An Alternative View about the Role of the Secondary School in Political Socialization: A Field Experimental Study of the Development of Civil Liberties Attitudes," *Theory and Research in Social Education* 6 (March 1978): 44–72.

23. The study of seventeen-year-olds is reported by E. Shantz, "Sideline Citizens," in *Political Youth, Traditional Schools,* ed. Byron Massiales (Englewood Cliffs, N.J.: Prentice-Hall, 1972), 69–70; the study of high school seniors is reported by H. H. Remmers and R. D. Franklin, "Sweet Land of Liberty," in *Anti-Democratic Attitudes in American Schools,* ed. H. H. Remmers (Evanston, Ill.: Northwestern University Press, 1963), 62.

24. R. Merelman, "Democratic Politics and the Culture of American Education," *American Political Science Review* 74 (June 1980): 319–332.

25. G. Almond and S. Verba, *Civic Culture* (Boston: Little, Brown, 1965); John R. Hibbing and Elizabeth Theiss-Morse, "Civics Is Not Enough: Teaching Barbarics in K–12," *P.S* (March 1992): 12.

26. Material for this section is drawn from E. C. Ladd and S. M. Lipset, *The Divided Academy* (New York: McGraw-Hill, 1975); C. Kesler, "The Movement of Student Opinion," *The National Review,* November 23, 1979, p. 29; E. L. Boyer, *College: The Undergraduate Experience in America* (New York: Harper & Row, 1986); "Fact File: Attitudes and Characteristics of This Year's Freshman," *Chronicle of Higher Education,* January 11, 1989, pp. A33–A34; General Social Survey, National Opinion Research Center, 1984, p. 87.

27. Alexander W. Astin, W. S. Korn, and Linda Sax, *The American Freshman: Thirty Year Trends* (Los Angeles: Higher Education Research Institute, Graduate School of Education and Information Studies, 1997).

28. Linda Sax, Alexander W. Astin, and W. S. Korn, *The American Freshman: National Norms for Fall 1998* (Los Angeles: Higher Education Research Institute, Graduate School of Education and Information Studies, 1998).

29. Ibid.

30. M. K. Jennings and R. G. Niemi, *The Political Character of Adolescence* (Princeton, N.J.: Princeton University Press, 1974), p. 243.

31. M. McCombs and D. Shaw, "The Agenda Setting Function of the Media," *Public Opinion Quarterly* 36 (Summer 1972): 176–187.

32. B. I. Page, R. Shapiro, and G. R. Dempsey, "What Moves Public Opinion?" *American Political Science Review* 81 (March 1987): 23–44.

33. H. Weissberg, "Marital Differences in Voting," *Public Opinion Quarterly* 51 (1987): 335–343.

34. P. R. Abramson, *Political Attitudes in America* (San Francisco: Freeman, 1983), 150, 213; see also Paul R. Abramson, *The Political Socialization of Black Americans* (New York: Free Press, 1977).

35. P. E. Converse, A. R. Clausen, and W. Miller, "Electoral Myth and Reality," *American Political Science Review* 59 (1965): 321–326.

36. J. P. Robinson, "The Press as Kingmaker: What Surveys Show from the Last Five Campaigns," *Journalism Quarterly* 49 (Summer 1974): 592.

37. Susan Herbst, *Numbered Voices: How Opinion Polling Has Shaped American Politics* (Chicago: University of Chicago Press, 1993); Benjamin Ginsberg, "How Polling Changes Public Opinion" in *Manipulating Public Opinion,* ed. Michael Margolis and Gary Mauser (Pacific Grove, Calif.: Brooks/Cole, 1989).

38. For a review of the history of polling, see Bernard Hennessy, *Public Opinion,* 4th ed. (Monterey, Calif.: Brooks/Cole, 1983), 42–44, 46–50. See also C. Roll and A. Cantril, *Polls: Their Use and Misuse in Politics* (New York: Basic Books, 1972), 3–16.

39. P. Squire, "The 1936 Literary Digest Poll, " *Public Opinion Quarterly* 52 (1988): 125–133; see also Don Cahalan, "The Digest Poll Rides Again," *Public Opinion Quarterly* 53 (1989): 107–113.

40. Hennessy, *Public Opinion,* 46.

41. "Consulting the Oracle," *U.S. News and World Report,* December 4, 1995, pp. 52–55.

42. Ibid.

43. Claudia Deane, "And Why Haven't You Been Polled," *Washington Post National Weekly Edition,* January 18, 1999, p. 34; Richard Morin, "The Election Post-Mortem," *Washington Post National Weekly Edition,* January 13, 1997, p. 34; Richard Morin, "Standing on the Record," *Washington Post National Weekly Edition,* September 30, 1996, p. 37.

44. "All Things Considered," National Public Radio, October 30, 1992.

45. "Consulting the Oracle," p. 53.

46. Ibid.

47. R. Morin, "Surveying the Surveyors," *Washington Post National Weekly Edition,* March 2, 1992, p. 37.

48. David Broder, "Push Polls Plunge Politics to a New Low," *Lincoln Star,* October 9, 1994, p. 5E.

49. Ibid.

50. Ann Devroy, "George Bush's Identity Crisis," *Washington Post National Weekly Edition,* August 24–30, 1992, pp. 6–7.

51. *New Yorker Magazine,* March 20, 1999, p. 18.

52. Richard Morin, "When the Method Becomes the Message," *Washington Post National Weekly Edition,* December 19–25, 1994, p. 33.

53. Richard Morin, "Tuned Out, Turned Off," *Washington Post National Weekly Edition,* February 5–11, 1996, pp. 6–8.

54. Ibid.

55. Ibid.

56. Richard Morin, "They Know Only What They Don't Like," *Washington Post National Weekly Edition,* October 3–9, 1994, p. 37.

57. 1986 National Election Study, Center for Political Studies, University of Michigan; "Wapner Top Judge in Recognition Poll," *Lincoln Star,* June 23, 1989, p. 1 (*Washington Post* syndication).

58. Michael X. Delli Carpini and Scott Keeter, "U.S. Public Knowledge of Politics," *Public Opinion Quarterly* (Winter 1991): 583–612.

59. Richard Morin, "We Love It—What We Know of It," *Washington Post National Weekly Edition,* September 22, 1997, p. 35.

60. Morin, "They Know Only What They Don't Like."

61. Morin, "Tuned Out, Turned Off."

62. Ibid.

63. Richard Morin, "Foreign Aid: Mired in Misunderstanding," *Washington Post National Weekly Edition,* March 20–26, 1995, p. 37.

64. Richard Morin, "What Informed Public Opinion?" *Washington Post National Weekly Edition,* April 10–16, 1995, p. 36.

65. V. O. Key, *The Responsible Electorate* (Cambridge, Mass.: Harvard University Press, 1966); N. Nie, S. Verba, and J. R. Petrocik, *The Changing American Voter* (Cambridge, Mass.: Harvard University Press, 1976), chapter 18.

66. Morin, "Tuned Out, Turned Off."

67. B. Sussman, "When Politicians Talk about Issues People Listen," *Washington Post National Weekly Edition,* August 18, 1986, p. 37.

68. John Zaller, "Monica Lewinsky's Contribution to Political Science," *PS: Political Science and Politics* (June 1998): 182–189.

69. Data in this section are summarized in *The Public Perspective* 6, no. 2 (February/March 1995): 39–46.

70. Gallup Poll, January 13–16, 2000.

71. Data here are from Peter Hart Research Associates Survey for the Council for Excellence in Government, March 16–18, 1995.

72. David Broder and Richard Morin, "A Question of Values," *Washington Post National Weekly Edition,* January 11, 1999, pp. 6–7.

73. Richard L. Berke, "Chasing the Polls on Gay Rights," *New York Times,* August 2, 1998, p. 3.

74. This section draws heavily on H. Schuman, C. Steeh, and L. Bobo, *Racial Attitudes in America* (Cambridge, Mass.: Harvard University Press, 1985); data summaries are drawn from the General Social Surveys of the National Opinion Research Center, University of Chicago, and National Elections Studies of CPS, University of Michigan; see also L. Sigelman and S. Welch, *Black Americans' Views of Racial Inequality* (Cambridge, Mass.: Cambridge University Press, 1991).

75. General Social Survey, 1996; *Washington Post National Weekly Edition,* October 30, 1989, p. 37.

76. General Social Surveys, 1996; "Whites Retain Negative Views of Minorities, a Survey Finds," *New York Times,* January 10, 1991, p. C19; M. Jackman, "General and Applied Tolerance: Does Education Increase Commitment to Racial Inequality?" *American Journal of Political Science* 22 (1978): 302–324; M. Jackman, "Education and Policy Commitment to Racial Equality," *American Journal of Political Science* 25 (1981): 256–269; D. Kinder and D. Sears, "Prejudice and Politics," *Journal of Personality and Social Psychology* 40 (1981): 414–431.

77. Richard Morin, "We've Moved Forward, but We Haven't," *Washington Post National Weekly Edition,* October 5, 1998, p. 34.

78. "Whites Retain Negative Views."

79. General Social Survey, 1998; see also Donald Kinder and Lynn Saunders, *Divided by Color: Racial Politics and Democratic Ideals* (Chicago: University of Chicago Press, 1996); H. Schuman and L. Bobo, "Survey-Based Experiments on White Attitudes toward Residential Integration," *American Journal of Sociology* 94 (1988): 272–294; W. R. Merriman and E. Carmines, "The Limits of Liberal Tolerance: The Case of Racial Politics," *Polity* 20 (1988): 519–526; see also Schuman, Steeh, and Bobo, *Racial Attitudes.*

80. General Social Survey, 1998.

81. Richard Morin, "No Place for Calm and Quiet Opinions," *Washington Post National Weekly Edition,* April 24–30, 1994, p. 34.

82. Martin Gilens and Paul Sniderman, "Affirmative Action and the Politics of Realignment." Paper presented at the Midwest Political Science Association Meeting, Chicago, 1995; Paul Sniderman

and Thomas Piazza, *The Scar of Race* (Cambridge, Mass: Harvard University Press, 1993).

83. ABC/*Washington Post* Poll, 1981 and 1986.

84. General Social Survey, 1998.

85. J. Sullivan, G. Marcus, S. Feldman, and J. Pierson, "Sources of Political Tolerance: A Multivariate Analysis," *American Political Science Review* 75 (March 1981): 92–106.

86. S. Stouffer, *Communism, Conformity, and Civil Liberties* (New York: Wiley, 1954).

87. R. W. Jackman, "Political Elites, Mass Publics, and Support for Democratic Principles," *Journal of Politics* 34 (August 1972): 753.

88. H. McClosky and J. Zaller, *The American Ethos: Public Attitudes toward Capitalism and Democracy* (Cambridge, Mass.: Harvard University Press, 1986).

89. C. Z. Nunn, H. H. Crockett, Jr., and J. A. Williams, *Tolerance for Nonconformity* (San Francisco: Jossey-Bass, 1976).

90. J. Sullivan, J. Pierson, and G. Marcus, "An Alternative Conceptualization of Tolerance: Illusory Increases 1950s–1970s," *American Political Science Review* 73 (September 1979): 781–794. For a critique of this study, see P. M. Sniderman, P. E. Tetlock, J. M. Glaser, D. P. Gress, and M. Hout, "Principled Tolerance and the American Mass Public," *British Journal of Political Science* 19 (January 1989): 25–46.

91. P. Abramson, "Comments on Sullivan, Pierson, and Marcus," *American Political Science Review* 74 (June 1980): 780–781.

92. "Polls Find Americans Angry, Anxious, Less Altruistic," *Lincoln Journal* (September 21, 1994): 9.

93. General Social Survey, 1996.

94. George E. Marcus (ed.), John L. Sullivan, and Elisabeth Theiss-Morse, *With Malice toward Some: How People Make Civil Liberties Judgments* (Cambridge: Cambridge University Press, 1995).

95. Judith Shklar, quoted in Paul Taylor, "In Watergate's Wake: The Good, the Bad, and the Ugly," *Washington Post National Weekly Edition,* June 22, 1992, p. 25.

96. Almond and Verba, *Civic Culture,* 64–68.

97. A. Miller, "Political Issues and Trust in Government, 1964–1970," *American Political Science Review* 68 (September 1974): 951–972.

98. A. Miller and S. Borrelli, "Confidence in Government during the 1980s," *American Politics Quarterly* 19 (April 1991): 147–173.

99. "Clinton's High Victory Rate Conceals Disappointments," *Congressional Quarterly Weekly Reports* (December 31, 1994), pp. 3619–3623.

100. David Broder and Dan Balz, "Who Wins?" *Washington Post National Weekly Edition,* February 15, 1999, pp. 6–7.

101. T. J. Lowi, *The Personal President* (Ithaca, N.Y.: Cornell University Press, 1995).

102. S. M. Lipset and W. Schneider, *The Confidence Gap* (New York: Free Press, 1983).

103. Richard Morin, "Less Than Meets the Eye," *Washington Post National Weekly Edition,* March 16, 1998, p. 35.

104. Hibbing and Theiss-Morse, *Congress as Public Enemy.*

105. Richard Morin, "Is Anyone Listening?," *Washington Post National Weekly Edition,* February 15, 1999, p. 34.

106. General Social Survey, 1990.

107. Richard Morin, "I'm OK; My Government's Not," *Washington Post National Weekly Edition,* July 26–August 1, 1993, p. 37.

108. Ibid.

109. Benjamin Page and Robert Shapiro, "Effects of Public Opinion on Policy," *American Political Science Review* 77 (March 1983): 175–190.

110. Sidney Verba and Norman H. Nie, *Participation in America: Political Democracy and Social Equality* (New York: Harper & Row, 1972), chap. 15.

News Media

YOU ARE THERE

Should You Torpedo the Admiral?

You are Evan Thomas, the Washington bureau chief of *Newsweek* magazine, and it is 1996. One of your contributors is proposing an exposé about an admiral who has worn medals he is not authorized to wear. The story could make a big splash in military, political, and publishing circles. You have to decide whether to pursue it.[1]

Admiral Mike Boorda is chief of naval operations (CNO)—the highest-ranking admiral in the United States Navy. The son of Ukrainian immigrants, he enlisted as a seventeen-year-old in 1956, and almost four decades later he reached the top. His appointment by President Clinton broke precedents. Boorda became the first CNO who had been an enlisted man, the first who had not graduated from the Naval Academy, and the first who was Jewish.

Boorda is devoted to his sailors. Every time he visits a ship or base, he holds a session to respond to the sailors' questions and complaints. He tries to show the sailors that he understands their jobs. He learned how to handle the ships, from small boats to battleships, even in choppy waters, and he learned how to fly helicopters and fighter planes.

Boorda also knows how to navigate the treacherous waters of politics. He has forged ties with members of Congress and has developed skills in negotiating. Before becoming CNO, he demonstrated his talent for diplomacy by persuading UN, NATO, and U.S. commands to work together in Bosnia. (In Sarajevo he once slipped away from UN officials and showed up in the trenches and buildings of the Serb and Muslim fighters. To their surprise, he explained, "It's the American way. We talk to each other.")

But the admiral has come under attack from traditionalists in the navy. In the aftermath of the Tailhook convention in 1991, when several dozen women were assaulted by drunken aviators, he was expected to improve the climate for women. But when he implemented new policies developed by civilians in Washington, such as allowing women to serve on combat ships and fly combat planes and encouraging toleration of homosexuals (under the "don't ask, don't tell" policy, which will be explained in Chapter 14), he was criticized for trying to make the policies work rather than trying to resist them.

He has been criticized by retired

Photographers crush Monica Lewinsky, her father, and her stepmother.
Mylan Ryba/Globe Photos 1998

Admiral Mike Boorda.
Steve Barrett/Contact Press Images

admirals, who wield clout like an interest group, and by current officers for helping enlisted sailors with their problems. They say he is usurping the authority of ship and base commanders. And he has even been criticized for driving his own car, rather than using a chauffeur as other admirals do. They say he is eroding the prestige of the admirals.

A former secretary of the navy in the Reagan administration who opposed women attending the Naval Academy and serving in combat units gave a fiery speech at the academy accusing Boorda of sacrificing navy traditions for political correctness. Excerpts were printed in the *Washington Times,* a conservative newspaper, and the *San Diego Union-Tribune,* a prominent newspaper covering navy issues. Then a former captain of a ship who was shifted to a desk job after an investigative report accused him of physically and verbally abusing his crew wrote a letter ridiculing Boorda and demanding he resign. The letter was published, anonymously, in the *Navy Times,* a newspaper circulating throughout the navy.

After two years as CNO, Boorda has been under so much pressure that he recently told his family he will not finish the two years remaining in his term.

Amid this controversy, a Washington correspondent for the National Security News Service, which, like similar organizations with a political agenda and foundation funding, locates specialized information that it passes on to bigger media, received a tip that Boorda had worn medals he might not have been authorized to wear. The correspondent contacted a friend, David Hackworth, a retired army officer who was highly decorated and who has sharply criticized the military's medal inflation (as some college professors have complained about grade inflation). After Hackworth had written a popular autobiography, he had been appointed a contributing editor of *Newsweek.* In competition with *Time* for readers, *Newsweek* had sought prominent people, like Hackworth, who would contribute occasional articles.

Hackworth examined photos of Boorda in his uniform and concluded that the admiral should not have worn a small *V* on two ribbons from the Vietnam War. Although he was entitled to wear the ribbons, he might not have been entitled to wear the *V,* which stands for valor and is reserved for troops who face fire in combat. Yet later photos of Boorda show that he stopped wearing the *V.* Still, Hackworth, who is motivated by a desire to expose wrongdoing by generals and admirals, thinks he has a story. Researching regulations at the Pentagon, he confided to some officers that he is working on a story that will bring down an admiral.

Hackworth contacted the editor of *Newsweek,* informing him of the story and telling him that it could be "a real career ender" for the admiral. The editor referred the story to you, as Washington bureau chief of the magazine, and reserved a page in the next issue if you decide to run it. You met with the correspondent for the National Security News Service, who showed the photos

and explained the navy's regulations to you.

You are uneasy, wary of both the correspondent for the National Security News Service and Hackworth. Neither is a regular reporter in your bureau. Neither, in fact, is an experienced reporter. You told a fellow editor, "There's something about this story that is too good to be true. Stories are never this neat." You consulted with a senior correspondent who specializes in national defense for the magazine. He noted that the navy's regulations concerning the *V* had changed during the war, perhaps reflecting the navy's confusion over its regulations, so perhaps Boorda had not worn the *V* improperly or had not done so intentionally.

Do you run Hackworth's article exposing Boorda?

Or do you seek clarification from the navy to determine whether the *V* was actually improper? Or do you question Boorda to determine whether he was honestly mistaken? If so, do you still run the article?

If you run the article, do you balance your findings of wrongdoing with information about Boorda's contributions to the navy in his forty years of service?

Or do you just forget the article, because Boorda no longer wears the *V?*

You are mindful of the competition with *Time* and realize that this story would be a real scoop and could make a big splash for *Newsweek.* You also realize that the editor has reserved a page for this story, yet you do have discretion.

A "medium" transmits something. The mass media—which include newspapers, magazines, books, radio, television, movies, and records—transmit communications to masses of people.

Although the media do not constitute a branch of government or even an organization established to influence government, such as a political party or interest group, they have an impact on government. In addition to providing entertainment, the media provide information about government and politics. This chapter focuses on the news media—the part of the media that delivers the news about government and politics.

The Media State

The media have developed and flourished to an extent the Founders could not have envisioned. As one political scientist noted, the media have become "pervasive ... and atmospheric, an element of the air we breathe."[2] Without exaggeration, another observer concluded, "Ancient Sparta was a military state. John Calvin's Geneva was a religious state. Mid–nineteenth century England was Europe's first industrial state, and the contemporary United States is the world's first media state."[3]

Americans spend more time being exposed to the media than doing anything else. In a year, according to one calculation, the average full-time worker puts in 1,824 hours on the job, 2,737 hours in bed, and 3,256 hours exposed to the media (almost 9 hours a day).[4] Seventy-seven percent of adults read newspapers; the average person does so for three and a half hours a week. The average person also reads two magazines for one and a half hours a week.[5] Ninety-eight percent of American homes have a radio, and the same percentage have a television. More homes have a television than have a toilet.[6] The average adult or child watches television three hours a day.[7] By the time the average child graduates from high school, he or she has spent more time in front of the tube than in class.[8] By the time the average American dies, he or she has spent one and a half years just watching television commercials.[9]

The rest of this section will examine three continuing trends in journalism: the shifting roles of the media, the increasing concentration of the media, and the increasing atomization of the media.

Roles of the Media

American newspapers originated in colonial times, and political magazines appeared in the 1800s, but there were no "mass media" until the advent of the broadcast media. Radio, which became popular in the 1920s, and television, which became popular in the 1950s, reached people who could not or would not read. Television would become so central and influential in American life that one scholar has speculated that the second half of the twentieth century will go down in history as "the age of television."[10]

Although people bought television sets to watch entertainment programs, they also began to watch newscasts. At first the newscasts, lasting only fifteen minutes and consisting solely of an anchor and a few correspondents reading news in front of a camera, were not compelling. In 1963 the networks expanded the time to thirty minutes and altered the format to emphasize visual interest. That year, for the first time, people said they got more political information from television than from any other source.

As television grew in popularity, newspapers waned. People did not need to read their headlines anymore, and some people did not care to read their more indepth coverage. Newspapers have struggled for readers and advertisers, and some have folded. Since 1970 the number of adults and the number of households have increased significantly, but the circulation of daily newspapers has remained stagnant.[11] The percentage of regular readers has declined (from 78 percent of adults in 1970 to 59 percent in 1997).[12] The percentage of young adults who are regular readers has declined the most. (In 1966 58 percent of first-year college students said "keeping up-to-date with political affairs" was an "essential" or "very important" goal. In 1998 only 26 percent held this view.[13])

Consequently, television has become the most important of the media for politics. According to surveys, people pay more attention to it and put more faith in it than in other media. This makes positive coverage on television essential for politicians.

While television offers more immediate and dramatic coverage, newspapers provide more thorough and thoughtful coverage. Because newspapers require more effort and provide more depth, they leave a longer-lasting impression. People remember the news they read in newspapers better than the news they watch on television.[14]

Moreover, national newspapers such as the *New York Times* and *Washington Post,* which blanket the country with in-depth international and national news, influence opinion leaders who, in turn, influence other persons.

Now the Internet is challenging the established media. It allows people to get the news when they want it around the clock, rather than at a specified schedule, and

Table 1	Where Do You Get Most of Your News?
Source	**Percentage**
Television	50
Newspaper	25
Radio	11
News magazine	5
Internet	5
Other	4

SOURCE: Responses from a survey of randomly selected American adults, published in Frank Luntz, "Public to Press: Cool It," *Brill's Content* (March 2000): 76.

to get more news if they want it, rather than the brief newscasts of radio and television. Although the Internet is still in its infancy, already a significant number of adults, mostly young and well educated, get most of their news from this source (see Tables 1 and 2).

These trends will likely continue: newspapers and radio will lose more readers and listeners, while television will lose its dominance, and the Internet will gain new users.[15]

Concentration of the Media

Journalism is a big business. The media industry is the nation's ninth largest, above the electronics industry and just below the aerospace industry.[16]

Although journalism has been a business since the nineteenth century, with media organizations seeking a profit, it became a bigger business in the second half of the twentieth century. First, small media organizations owned by local families or local companies were taken over by chains (owning multiple newspapers, radio stations, or television stations) or conglomerates (owning multiple newspapers, radio stations, and television sta-

Table 2	Number of Years after Introduction to Attract 50 Million Users
Medium	**Years**
Radio	38
Television	13
Internet	4

SOURCE: "Ticker," *Brill's Content* (March 1999): 128.

tions). Then, large media organizations were taken over by chains or conglomerates. Finally, chains and conglomerates were bought out by larger chains and conglomerates. (See the box "The Deals of the Decade.")

The largest merger of media in history occurred when America Online (AOL) bought Time Warner in 2000. AOL was the dominant Internet corporation, with half the market for the services that link computer users to the Internet, and Time Warner was the largest media conglomerate. The new company has over eighty thousand employees and $30 billion in annual revenues. It boasts 50 percent of the on-line business, 20 percent of the cable television business, 18 percent of the movie business, and 16 percent of the record business in the country. It also boasts thirty-three magazines, five publishing houses, and "Looney Tunes" cartoons.[17] The chairman of the new company (formerly the head of AOL), who had no journalistic experience except on his high school newspaper, is now a media mogul.[18] The deal stunned many people in the business. A Silicon Valley venture capitalist called it "the single most transformational event I've seen in my career."[19]

In addition, other large corporations—telecommunications companies, such as AT&T, and computer software companies, such as Microsoft—established alliances with the media conglomerates. Microsoft formed an alliance with General Electric, which owns NBC, to launch a twenty-four-hour cable news channel (MSNBC) and an interactive on-line news service. The latter, which is in development, will allow people with computers to retrieve more information, data, and pictures about events covered on the news channel. It will also enable Microsoft, which has already conquered the software industry, to extend its reach into the news business.

While an immediate goal of the mergers was to expand the companies' markets, the long-range goal of both the mergers and the alliances is to control the information and entertainment markets of the future. Analysts expect the media conglomerates that survive will be those that offer all types of media—newspapers, magazines, radio stations, television stations, books, movies, records, and computer services—in various formats, including through such devices as Palm Pilots, at all times of the day. Then they will use each type of media to promote other types they own. For example, they will use their newspapers, magazines, radio stations, and television stations to promote their movies and then use their movies to spin off new television programs, records, books, and merchandise.

This trend toward concentration of the media is certain to continue. It will provide much more conve-

The Deals of the Decade

Media mergers of the past decade show the trend toward media concentration.

1990 Warner Communications and Time complete $14.1 billion merger, creating the world's biggest media conglomerate.

1993 *New York Times* buys the parent company of the *Boston Globe* for $1.1 billion.

1995 Westinghouse Electric buys CBS for $5.4 billion.

1996 Walt Disney buys Capital Cities/ABC for $19 billion.
Time Warner and Turner Broadcasting System complete $7.6 billion merger.

1999 Viacom announces deal to buy CBS for $34.5 billion.

2000 America Online announces deal to buy Time Warner in $183 billion merger, history's biggest media deal.
Tribune Company announces deal to buy Times Mirror Company for $8 billion.

SOURCE: "Media Mergers," *Washington Post National Weekly Edition*, March 20, 2000, p. 19.

nience, allowing much easier access, at somewhat more cost for consumers, but it will pose problems for a democracy that relies on the media to inform its citizens. Already this trend toward concentration makes these problems apparent.

The news comes from fewer sources than it used to. Although there are many media in the United States—approximately 1,500 daily newspapers, 10,800 radio stations, and 1,600 television stations[20]—these numbers are misleading. Chains and conglomerates own the newspapers and magazines with most of the readers, the radio stations with most of the listeners, and the television stations with most of the viewers.[21] In fact, eight or nine massive corporations plus twelve to fifteen large corporations dominate the media industry now. According to one media analyst, "These two dozen profit-driven companies, owned and managed by billionaires operating in barely competitive markets, account for nearly the entirety of the U.S. media culture."[22] Yet numerous media observers predict a shakeout that will further reduce this small number.

Moreover, just one wire service—AP—supplies the international and national news for most of the newspapers. Only four radio networks—ABC, CBS, NBC, and Mutual—furnish the news for most of the radio stations, and only four television networks—ABC, CBS, NBC, and CNN—furnish the news for most of the television stations.

With fewer sources of news, there is less of a range of views—less of a marketplace of ideas—than is healthy for a democracy. A small number of powerful people provide information—essentially, define reality—for all the rest of the people.

Another problem resulting from concentration of the media is corporate pressure to avoid some topics if the coverage would affect corporate interests. Will NBC launch an investigation of its partner Microsoft? Will ABC air negative reports of its owner Disney? Indeed, in 1998 ABC's president killed a story that Disney's practices allowed the employment of convicted pedophiles at its parks. Apparently ABC, a comparatively small division of the huge Disney company, got mouseke*fear*.[23]

Although other media might pick up a story killed by one organization, what if some story would affect the interests of multiple corporations? In 1996 Congress passed the Telecommunications Act, which set aside a portion of the nation's airwaves for new digital television broadcasts. Although the frequencies were valued at $70 billion, the act handed them to broadcasters for free. When the bill was proposed, Senator John McCain (R-Ariz.) predicted, "You will not see this story on any television or hear it on any radio broadcast because it directly affects them."[24] Indeed, during the nine months in which the bill was pending, there was little coverage of the bill or the lobbying by the broadcasters. ABC, CBS, and NBC television news shows devoted an average of just six and a half minutes to the bill and virtually none to this provision.[25] If citizens had been more aware of this legislation, they might have demanded that Congress, rather than giving the broadcasters a windfall, charge the market value for the frequencies and use the $70 billion to bolster popular governmental programs.

Another problem resulting from concentration of the media is financial pressure to reduce the quality of

Steven Benson. Reprinted by permission of United Features Syndicate, Inc.

news coverage. Media organizations are under pressure to show sizable profits each year; some are under pressure to show expanding profits each year. Media organizations are expected to match other divisions in their corporations. Corporate officers feel pressure from Wall Street analysts and major stockholders, such as managers of mutual funds, retirement funds, and insurance companies, who are more concerned with the value of the stock than the quality of the journalism. As a result, costs are cut and profits are not reinvested in more staff training or investigative reports. A reporter for a midsize newspaper in Illinois learned, "If a story needs a real investment of time and money, we don't do it anymore." He lamented, "Who the hell cares about corruption in city government, anyway . . . ?"[26]

The trend toward concentration of the media is potentially harmful for everyone but stockholders. Some observers foresee "the free-enterprise equivalent of a Ministry of Culture"[27]—the government office that regulates the media in small countries that lack a free press. In fact, the financial value of some American conglomerates is greater than the entire economy of some foreign countries whose monopolistic policies we condemn as hostile to a democratic society.

Atomization of the Media

Despite the growing concentration of the media during the twentieth century, a contrary trend—an atomization of the media—has also developed in recent years. Whereas concentration has led to a national media, atomization has fragmented the influence of this national media. The major newspapers and broadcast networks have lost their dominance, while other media, some not even considered news organizations, have started to play a significant role in politics.

This trend is partly the result of technological changes. First the national networks lost viewers to the local stations, as the local stations linked with other local stations, via satellite, to share coverage of national and international events. Then the traditional stations lost viewers to cable television. With its multiplicity of channels, cable can offer competing newscasts and more specialized programs. Although much of cable's menu duplicates the networks' (and reflects Bruce Springsteen's complaint, "57 Channels, and Nothin' On"), its offerings are becoming more focused—"narrowcasting" to appeal to small segments of the audience in contrast to the networks' broadcasting to appeal to the overall audience. For example, C-SPAN covers Congress on three channels and, unlike the networks, lingers on members' speeches and committees' hearings. Even MTV covers presidential campaigns in formats that attract young viewers.

Other national cable networks cater to blacks and Hispanics. A cable system in Los Angeles and New York caters to Jews. A cable channel in California broadcasts in Chinese, one in Hawaii broadcasts in Japanese, and one in Connecticut and Massachusetts broadcasts in Portuguese. Stations in New York also provide programs in Greek, Hindi, Korean, and Russian.

Cable has led to twenty-four-hour news. CNN, created as a twenty-four-hour news network, has a large audience. Now it is being challenged by Fox and MSNBC.

The Internet has led to additional news sites. Major newspapers post their articles on Web sites before the papers themselves are delivered. On-line "magazines" also address politics. During the congressional impeachment of President Clinton, one on-line magazine—Salon—revealed that the Republican representative spearheading the effort (Henry Hyde of Illinois) had had an adulterous relationship. Self-styled "journalists" even post their "news" as well. Matt Drudge offers political gossip on his own Web site, the Drudge Report, from his one-bedroom apartment in Hollywood.[28]

With such proliferation of newscasts, the audience for the traditional nightly news has sunk to its lowest level since 1961[29]—two years before the networks attracted a mass audience by expanding the newscast and emphasizing visual interest (see Figure 1).

The trend toward atomization of the media is also partly the result of the populist backlash against government officials and established journalists, perceived as "Washington insiders," that characterized American politics in the 1980s and 1990s. This is reflected in the popularity of radio and television talk shows. Many radio stations have some talk shows, and about 10 percent of the stations have an all-talk format.[30] According to

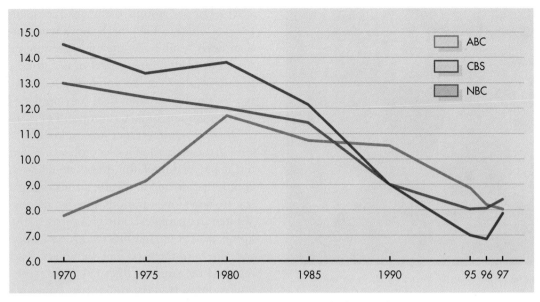

FIGURE 1 ■ *The Decline of Network Newscast Ratings* *Ratings for the networks' evening newscasts show a decline in viewers since the 1970s.*

SOURCE: Nielsen Media, published in Michael J. Wolf and Geoffrey Sands, "Fearless Predictions," *Brill's Content* (July/August 1999): 110.

one survey, 17 percent of the public say they listen to these shows regularly; 25 percent more say they listen sometimes. (Eleven percent have tried to call in; 6 percent have gotten on the air.)[31] With millions of people listening, talk radio is a force in politics. It attracts a middle-class audience that serves as a national jury on governmental controversies.

The populist backlash is also reflected in the increasing attention paid to fringe media by the public. In the 1992 presidential campaign, *The Star,* a supermarket tabloid, published allegations by Gennifer Flowers, a former nightclub singer, that she had a twelve-year affair with Bill Clinton while he was governor of Arkansas. The major media hesitated to repeat the *Star's* story—they had nothing but scorn for the tabloids, which, they insisted, did not practice true journalism—but within days most gave in, under the pretense of debating the propriety of reporting personal matters. The Clintons appeared on "60 Minutes" to refute the allegations (while sidestepping the question whether he had committed adultery). Flowers then appeared on "A Current Affair," a syndicated television show, rated Clinton as a lover on a scale from 1 to 10, and sang "Stand by Your Man." Thus, Flowers did not need to take her story to the major media; she got the tabloid media to tell it and pay her for it ($150,000 from the *Star* and $25,000 from "A Current Affair").[32]

During the impeachment of President Clinton, Larry Flynt, the publisher of *Hustler* magazine, was of-

fended by the hypocrisy of some of the president's adversaries. Seeking information about affairs they had, he ran an ad in the *Washington Post* offering to pay for such information. He published an article about an affair involving the Speaker of the House–designate, Robert Livingston (R-La.). Although the article appeared in a raunchy magazine read by relatively few men, Flynt was called a "pornalist," and his techniques were considered sleazy by professional journalists, the revelation received publicity in other media and caused Livingston to resign. (The major media, while attacking Flynt, did not criticize the *Post* for taking his money—an estimated $85,000—and running the ad.)[33]

Because the public pays attention to the fringe media more, politicians have begun to use these media more than they used to. Instead of announcing their candidacy at a press conference, as they traditionally have done, in the 1990s some politicians announced their candidacy on a television talk show. During the campaign, they appeared on other television shows. Clinton fielded questions on the "Phil Donahue Show" and MTV and played the saxophone on the "Arsenio Hall Show." Candidates swapped jokes with Jay Leno and David Letterman, hoping they would not be made to look silly.

Candidates use these shows to reach people who do not follow the major media and to communicate their messages without having them "filtered"—that is, condensed, simplified, distorted, or challenged—by

Bill Clinton plays his saxophone on the "Arsenio Hall Show" during the 1992 election campaign.
AP/Wide World Photos

professional reporters. Candidates also buy television time for "electronic town meetings," shows in which they take questions from voters in several cities without any journalists present.

All this blurs the line between politics and entertainment. When Senator Bill Bradley (D-N.J.) appeared at a Houston radio station, ranked number one among men in the area, he expected to discuss his new book. Instead, the disc jockeys had two women disrobe from the waist up to report his reaction.[34]

Because of the expanding role of fringe media, mainstream journalists envision a shrinking role for themselves. They no longer monopolize the market of political information; they no longer control the gates through which such information must pass.

In fact, according to one journalism professor, many citizens see no purpose in having journalists intervene in politics. "Max in Seattle feels as well represented by Julie's question from Houston as he would be by Sam Donaldson's inquiry from New York." (Actually, Max might prefer Julie's to Sam Donaldson's. Many citizens are annoyed by the "cult of toughness" among journalists that leads them to challenge public figures with "a level of shamelessness and aggression that ordinary people cannot manage."[35])

This trend toward atomization of the media has significant implications beyond its impact on the established media and their professional journalists. Although this trend makes the news more accessible to more people, it makes the news less factual and less analytical.

The mainstream media have allowed their standards of reporting to slip. With proliferation of news outlets and newscasts around the clock, competition among them is intense. They have more space or time to fill than news to fill it. So they feel pressure to locate new stories or identify new angles of old stories. In the rush to publish, they put less emphasis on assessing the accuracy of this information than they used to. The result is a "commingling of fact, rumor, and opinion."[36]

Interest groups eager to exploit the competition among the media add to the problem. When Vince Foster, deputy counsel for President Clinton, apparently committed suicide in a park, a right-wing group sent a fax to news organizations linking the suicide to the Whitewater land deal. The group passed the rumor that Foster died at an administration "safe house" and later was moved to the park. Talk show host Rush Limbaugh reported the rumor. Other talk show hosts repeated it, while some added the rumor that Foster was murdered. A few financial speculators spread the rumors as a way to manipulate the stock market, and the next day newspaper business sections repeated the rumors in articles about their effect on the stock market. Thus, through announcement and repetition by the media, the rumors came to seem true to many people—yet they remained just rumors[37] (and false ones, according to two independent counsels).

A similar pattern occurred when a conservative magazine, *Insight,* charged that the Clinton administration was "selling" burial plots in Arlington National Cemetery to "dozens of big-time political donors or friends of the Clintons." Because the cemetery is reserved for military veterans, anonymous officials were quoted as saying this was "corruption of the worst kind." The charge was repeated on talk radio, then aired in Congress when some members demanded an investigation. Within forty-eight hours it was reported by the mainstream media. Yet there was no truth to it.[38]

The mainstream media have been uncertain how to act in such situations. They are reluctant to report rumors they are unable to verify. But they fear they will lose their audience if they fail to report stories other media report. Usually, they decide to report the stories but in a different context—under the guise of addressing the political ramifications of the accusation or the journalistic ethics of publicizing it. Nevertheless, the effect is nearly the same—the accusation winds up in the mainstream media, and the public believes it. As a result, unscrupulous groups realize they can use the fringe media to manipulate the mainstream media into publicizing bogus charges. Thus, they can drag the mainstream media down to their level. President Clinton's lawyer said it reminds him of when he lived with a bunch of guys in college: four were neat and one was a slob; by the end of the year, they were all slobs.[39]

The fringe media aggravate the problem. Their goal is entertainment and their audience is politically unsophisticated, so the fringe media are less careful about the accuracy of the information they disseminate. Some pay for stories, possibly encouraging people to lie for the money; many sensationalize stories, possibly distorting the truth. Of course, the mainstream media also are commercial enterprises subject to the pressures of the marketplace (as will be addressed later in the chapter). Yet these established media are subject to the pressures of tradition. Reporters at major newspapers and broadcast networks often speak of their responsibility to follow certain journalistic norms, while members of the fringe media sometimes reflect the views of radio talk show host Don Imus, who asserts, "The news isn't sacred to me. It's entertainment . . . designed to revel in the agony of others."[40]

The Internet aggravates the problem even more. With no editors, any person with a computer and a phone line can deliver any "fact," however erroneous, to the whole world. In 1997 Pierre Salinger, the respected press secretary to President Kennedy and then correspondent for ABC, announced in a speech to an airline association that the TWA flight that crashed off the coast of Long Island had been accidentally shot down by a navy missile and that this fact was being covered up by the U.S. government. The cause of the crash had been listed as "unknown," so Salinger's speech was reported prominently worldwide. When doubters asked how he learned this, Salinger replied that he received the information from a top intelligence agent in France. Salinger was hoodwinked. The information originated in the fertile imagination of a retired pilot in Florida who hypothesized this scenario and posted it on the Internet, where it eventually reached the intelligence agent in France.[41]

Meanwhile, the public is lost in this factual free-for-all. Most citizens are not well versed in the issues or very knowledgeable about the politicians. Without the help of professional journalists, many are not able to separate the blarney from the gospel truth when candidates and officials speak.

In sum, two opposite trends—concentration of the media and atomization of the media—are occurring. It is not clear how they are going to interact. Now they are developing side by side. But strong financial pressures persist, and very powerful corporations are working to dominate the media business. In the future, the huge conglomerates might dominate more than they do now, particularly on issues that do not have a human interest angle. Occasional independent voices from the Internet may from time to time break through to have an impact. It seems unlikely that this will happen on most issues that affect the economic well-being of the public (such as the telecommunication legislation mentioned earlier) in which there are few human interest angles to break through the conglomerates' dominance.

Relationship between the Media and Politicians

"Politicians live—and sometimes die—by the press. The press lives by politicians," according to a former presidential aide. "This relationship is at the center of our national life."[42]

Politicians and journalists need each other. Politicians need journalists to reach the public and to receive feedback from the public. They scan the major newspapers in the morning and the network newscasts in the evening. President Lyndon Johnson watched three network newscasts on three televisions simultaneously. Journalists need politicians to cover government. They seek a steady stream of fresh information to fill their news columns and newscasts. Just two days after the election of Bill Clinton, a chorus of reporters complained of a "news blackout" by the incoming administration.[43] A week later the chorus forced the president-elect to call a press conference to pacify the press corps, though he had no news yet and hardly any voice after the long campaign.[44]

The close relationship between the media and politicians is both a **symbiotic relationship,** meaning they use each other for their mutual advantage, and an **adversarial relationship,** meaning they fight each other.

Symbiotic Relationship

President Lyndon Johnson told individual reporters, "You help me and I'll help make you a big man in your profession." He gave exclusive interviews, told outrageous tales, and invited reporters to bunk overnight at his Texas ranch.[45] In return he expected favorable coverage.

Reporters get information from politicians in various ways. Some reporters are assigned to monitor beats. Washington beats include the White House, Congress, Supreme Court, State Department, Defense Department, and some other departments and agencies. Other reporters are assigned to cover specialized subjects, such as economics, en-

the president rehearses appropriate answers. (Former press secretaries admit that they predicted at least 90 percent of the questions asked and often the exact reporters who asked them.[61]) Aides prepare a seating chart, and during the conference the president calls on the reporters he wants. Although he cannot ignore those from the major media, he can call disproportionately on those he knows will lob soft questions. Consequently, the conference usually helps the president.

Beaming the conference to the nation results in less news than having a casual exchange around the president's desk, which used to reveal his thinking on programs and decisions. Appearing in millions of homes, the president cannot be as open and cannot allow himself to make a gaffe in front of the huge audience.

Televising the conference does not even provide much accountability, because one is scheduled when the administration wants and nearly every aspect is scripted or predicted in advance. Televising the conference only offers an illusion of accountability.

The transformation of the conference frustrates reporters and prompts them to act as prosecutors. As one press secretary observed, they play a game of "I gotcha."[62] After Clinton's first conference, one reporter criticized him because "he didn't say a single thing he didn't mean to."[63] The reporter considered the conference a game in which the press tries to beat the presi-

dent, and this time the press had lost because it could not trick him into saying something imprudent.

Still, reporters value the conference. Editors consider the president's remarks news, so the conference helps reporters do their job. It also gives them a chance to bask in the limelight. According to a former press secretary, it gives them "fame, power in the eyes of their peers, recognition by their families, ego gratification, and lecture fees from the Storm Door and Sash Associations of the world."[64] (Business and professional associations pay well-known journalists handsome fees to speak at their annual meetings.)

Media events also show the symbiotic nature of the media-politician relationship. Staged for television, these events usually pair a photo opportunity and a speech to convey a particular impression of a politician's position on an issue.

The "photo op" frames the politician against a backdrop of things that symbolize clear values—for example, children or flags. Photo ops for economic issues often use factories, whether bustling to represent a success or abandoned to represent a failure. The backdrop is designed to be visually interesting to attract the cameras. The strategy is the same as that for advertisements of merchandise: Combine the product (the politician) with the symbols in the hope that the potential buyers (voters) will link the two.[65] In the 1992 campaign, President Bush peered into the Grand Canyon to demonstrate his

Independent Counsel Kenneth Starr saw a photo opportunity when it was time to deliver his report on the Clinton investigation to Congress. Although the report was just 445 pages long, Starr staged a caravan of vehicles with an escort of police to make a show for the photographers.
Photo by Ray Lustig © 1998 The *Washington Post*. Reprinted with permission.

credentials as an environmentalist, despite his limited record; Governor Clinton appeared at a bowling alley to demonstrate his credentials as an average "Joe," despite his Yale and Oxford education.

The speech at a media event is not a classical oration or even a cogent address with a beginning, middle, and end. It is an informal talk that emphasizes a few key words or phrases or sentences—almost slogans, because television editors allot time only for a short **sound bite.** And the amount of time is less and less. In 1968 the average sound bite of a presidential contender on the evening news was 42.3 seconds, but in 1988 it was just 9.8 seconds and in 1992 only 7.3 seconds.[66]

Speech writers plan accordingly. "A lot of writers figure out how they are going to get the part they want onto television," a former presidential aide explained. "They think of a news lead and write around it. And if the television lights don't go on as the speaker is approaching that news lead, he skips a few paragraphs and waits until they are lit to read the key part."[67] This approach does not produce coherent speeches, but the people watching on television will not know, and the few watching in person do not matter because they are just props. But such writing does not provide either group of people with an adequate explanation.

Perhaps more than any other source of news, media events illustrate the reliance of politicians on television, and of television on politicians. The head of CBS News said, "I'd like just once to have the courage to go on the air and say that such and such a candidate went to six cities today to stage six media events, none of which had anything to do with governing America."[68] Yet television fosters these events, and despite occasional swipes by correspondents, networks continue to show them.

Adversarial Relationship

Although the relationship between the media and politicians is symbiotic in some ways, it is adversarial in others. Since George Washington's administration, when conflicts developed between Federalists and Jeffersonians, the media have attacked politicians and politicians have attacked the media. In John Adams's administration, Federalists passed the Sedition Act of 1798, which prohibited much criticism of the government. Federalists used the act to imprison Jeffersonian editors. Not long after, President Andrew Jackson proposed a law to allow the government to shut down "incendiary" newspapers. Even now, a former press secretary commented, "There are very few politicians who do not cherish privately the notion that there should be some regulation of the news."[69]

The conflict stems from a fundamental difference in perspectives. Politicians want the media to help them accomplish their goals, so they hope the media will pass along their messages to the public exactly as they deliver them. But journalists see themselves as servants not of the government but of the public. They question officials until the public knows enough about a matter to hold the officials accountable. According to correspondent Sam Donaldson, "My job is not to say here's the church social with the apple pie, isn't it beautiful?"[70] But some go beyond skepticism to cynicism. In the eyes of a Clinton aide, they walk in the door "assuming that something is wrong and asking, 'What are you hiding?' "[71]

In contemporary society, information is power. The media and the government, especially the president, with the huge bureaucracy at his disposal, are the two primary sources of information. To the extent that the administration controls the flow of information, it can achieve its policy goals. To the extent that the media disseminate contradictory information, they can ensure that the administration's policy goals will be subject to public debate.

Inevitably, politicians fall short of their goals, and many blame the media for their failures. They confuse the message and the messenger, like Czar Peter the Great, who, when notified that the Russian army had lost a battle in 1700, promptly ordered the messenger strangled.

When President Kennedy became upset by the *New York Times* coverage of Vietnam, he asked the paper to transfer the correspondent out of Vietnam. (The paper refused.) When President Nixon became angry with major newspapers and networks, he had Vice President Agnew lash out at them. He also ordered the Department of Justice to investigate some for possible antitrust violations and the Internal Revenue Service to audit some for possible income tax violations.

However, it would be incorrect to think that the relationship between the media and politicians is usually adversarial. Normally, it is symbiotic. Although journalists like to think of themselves and try to portray themselves as adversaries who stand up to politicians, most rely upon politicians most of the time.[72]

Yet the relationship has become more adversarial since the Vietnam War and the Watergate scandal fueled cynicism about government's performance and officials' honesty. After Watergate, Congress became more willing to launch investigations of administration officials, and reporters became more aggressive in reporting possible scandals.[73] Many reporters, according to the editor of the

Doonesbury © G. B. Trudeau. Reprinted with permission of Universal Press Syndicate. All rights reserved.

Des Moines Register, "began to feel that no journalism is worth doing unless it unseats the mighty."[74] New reporters especially began to feel this way. Senator Alan Simpson (R-Wy.) asked the daughter of old friends what she planned to do after graduating from journalism school. "I'm going to be one of the hunters," she replied. When he asked, "What are you going to hunt?" she answered, "People like you!"[75] With this attitude, "young reporters, without a sense of history, context, or proportion, saw scandal where none existed or at least treated any mistake, no matter how minor, as worthy of being called a 'gate.'"[76] During the Clinton years alone, reporters talked about "Travelgate," "Filegate," "Koreagate," "Paulagate," and "Monicagate," as well as "Whitewatergate." Yet none of these rivaled Watergate (or the Iran-Contra affair) in scope or significance.

In response, politicians have restricted access for reporters, out of fear that they will say something that will be used against them. Then reporters have complained that politicians are not accessible and that they cannot get the information to do their job.

At the same time, politicians have become more sophisticated in their efforts to "spin" the media—to portray themselves and their programs in the most favorable light, regardless of the facts, and to shade the truth where necessary. Then reporters have become more cynical. "They don't explicitly argue or analyze what they dislike in a political program but instead sound sneering and supercilious about the whole idea of politics."[77]

This prompts politicians to increase their efforts to spin the media, which, in turn, prompts reporters to escalate their comments that politicians are insincere or dishonest. And so the cycle continues.

After Vice President Al Gore announced his candidacy for president from his family's farm in Carthage, Tennessee, ABC correspondent Diane Sawyer, while smiling and oozing charm, conducted an interview replete with disrespect. She began, "Are you really a country boy?" He replied, "I grew up in two places. I grew up in Washington, D.C. [as the son of a senator from Tennessee], and I grew up here. My summers were here. Christmas was here." Sawyer taunted Gore, "You mucked pigpens?" Gore answered, "I cleaned out the pigpens . . . and raised cattle and planted and plowed and harvested and took in hay." Sawyer, not satisfied, challenged Gore in an attempt to show that he was a hypocrite: "I have a test for you. Ready for a pop quiz? . . . How many plants of tobacco can you have per acre? . . . What is brucellosis? . . . What are cattle prices roughly now? . . . When a fence separates two farms, how can you tell which farm owns the fence?" By announcing from his family's farm, Gore was trying to convey his rural roots; by interviewing him in this manner, Sawyer was trying to question his sincerity.[78]

In this poisoned relationship, "the most embarrassing, humiliating thing" for a journalist, according to one, is not to have accused someone falsely but to have been perceived by one's peers as getting taken.[79] During the

1992 presidential campaign, Bush aides complimented a *New York Times* reporter for a fair article. "He looked at us like we had the plague. . . . The next thing we heard, a bunch of other reporters were grousing about [him] and accusing him of being a shill for Bush, of being 'in the tank.' By paying him a compliment we had compromised him."[80]

The increasing adversariness is also due to other factors mentioned earlier. There are so many media, with so much space to fill, that they have a voracious appetite for news and a strong incentive to compete against each other for something "new." As a result, they often magnify trivial things. And because the fringe media play a more prominent role, and because their stories eventually appear in the mainstream media, the media pay more attention to politicians' personal shortcomings with sex, drugs, and alcohol and raise more questions about politicians' "character" than they ever used to.[81] In 1977 one of every two hundred stories on network newscasts was about a purported scandal; in 1997 (*before* the Monica Lewinsky affair was revealed), one of every seven stories was![82]

Yet the apparent toughness usually is "a toughness of demeanor," rather than a toughness of substantive journalism.[83] Reporters exhibit tough attitudes rather than conduct thorough investigations and careful analyses. In fact, few engage in investigative journalism. An examination of 224 incidents of criminal or unethical behavior by Reagan administration appointees found that only 13 percent were uncovered by reporters. Most were discovered through investigations by executive agencies or congressional committees, which then released the information to the press. Only incidents reflecting personal peccadillos of government officials, such as sexual offenses, were exposed first by reporters.[84]

Few reporters engaged in investigative journalism of the Clinton administration, either. For the Whitewater scandal, reporters got most of their tips from a Republican Party operation run by officials from Republican presidential campaigns.[85] For the sexual matters, reporters got most of their tips from prosecutors for the independent counsel, lawyers for Paula Jones, or a book agent for Linda Tripp. "The big difference between this and Watergate," Bob Woodward said, "is that in Watergate Carl [Bernstein] and I went out and talked to people whom the prosecutors were ignoring or didn't know about. . . . And we were able to look these people in the eye and decide if they were credible and get the nuances of what they were saying. . . . Here, the reporting is all about lawyers telling reporters what to believe and write."[86]

Relationship between the Media and Recent Administrations

Franklin Roosevelt created the model that most contemporary presidents follow when interacting with the media. Newspaper publishers had no use for Roosevelt and his policies. In fact, a former correspondent recalls, "The publishers didn't just disagree with the New Deal. They hated it. The reporters, who liked it, had to write as though they hated it, too."[87] Roosevelt saw he was not going to get favorable coverage, but he still wanted to reach the public. He used press conferences to provide a steady stream of news. This tactic enabled him to sidestep the publishers but gain access to their readers. He also used radio, giving a series of **fireside chats,** to advocate his policies and reassure his listeners in the throes of the Great Depression. He had a fine voice and a superb ability to speak informally—he commented about his family, even his dog, in a way to appeal to average people. (He drew so many listeners that he was granted as much airtime as he wanted, but he was shrewd enough to realize that too much would result in overexposure.) This tactic enabled him to avoid the filters of reporters and editors and take his case directly to the people.

Reagan Administration

As a young man, Reagan idolized FDR and developed an imitation of him that included an appropriate accent and even a cigarette holder.[88] As president, Reagan duplicated Roosevelt's success in using the media, which dubbed him the "Great Communicator" for his uncanny ability to convey his broad themes.

The Reagan administration approached its relationship with the media as "political jujitsu."[89] A jujitsu fighter tries to use the adversary's force to his or her own advantage through a clever maneuver. The administration knew the media would cover the president extensively to fill their news columns and newscasts. An aide explained the strategy: "The media, while they won't admit it, are not in the news business; they're in entertainment. We tried to create the most entertaining, visually attractive scene to fill that box, so that the networks would have to use it."[90]

Aides sent advance agents days or weeks ahead of the president to prepare the "stage" for media events—the specific location, backdrops, lighting, and sound equipment. A trip to Korea was designed to show "the commander in chief on the front line against communism." The advance man went to the demilitarized

President Reagan, staged to reflect "American strength and resolve" in Korea.
Corbis-Bettmann

zone separating North and South Korea and negotiated with the army and the Secret Service for the most photogenic setting. He demanded that the president be able to use the most exposed bunker, which meant that the army had to erect telephone poles and string thirty thousand yards of camouflage netting from them to hide Reagan from North Korean sharpshooters. The advance man also demanded that the army build camera platforms on a hill that remained exposed but offered the most dramatic angle to film Reagan surrounded by sandbags. Although the Secret Service wanted sandbags up to Reagan's neck, the advance man insisted that they be no more than four inches above his navel so viewers would get a clear picture of the president wearing his flak jacket and demonstrating "American strength and resolve."[91]

On a day-to-day basis, the administration planned its operations around its relationship with the media. In the morning aides met to plan public relations strategy for the day. They determined what "the line of the day"—the message—would be. They considered what questions the president would be asked and what answers he should give, and then they briefed him. Later in the day, after all his appearances, aides called each network to learn what stories about the president or his policies it was going to use on its evening newscast. If aides were not satisfied, they tried to convince the network to change its lineup. At night aides met to evaluate the success of their strategy and often called each network to praise or criticize its coverage.[92]

To set the agenda, and to prevent the media from setting it, the administration tried to control the president's appearances and restrict his comments. Aides especially worried that off-the-cuff comments would reveal Reagan's limited command of the facts and details behind his policies or would result in a blooper, such as the time he said that trees cause most air pollution. To keep such comments from damaging his image or at least overshadowing his message of the day, aides provided few opportunities for reporters to ask questions. When reporters asked questions inside a building, aides frequently demanded that the television lights be shut off so any answers could not be televised; outside they often ordered the helicopter's engines revved up so the questions would be drowned out. Aides scheduled few press conferences. Although conferences normally benefit presidents, they are subject to less control than media events and were considered too risky.

Paradoxically, Reagan was highly visible but not very accessible. By alternately using and avoiding the media, his administration succeeded in managing the news more than any other administration.

Bush Administration

Bush lacked Reagan's television appeal, so his administration deemphasized television appearances in favor of frequent press conferences and get-togethers with reporters. Occasionally, he telephoned reporters to talk or asked them to jog with him. In these settings his grasp of issues came across. He tried to impress reporters and, like Roosevelt, charm them, in the hope that he would receive favorable coverage. Journalists did consider Bush more accessible and open than Reagan.

For the invasion of Panama in 1989 and war with Iraq in 1991, however, the Bush administration insisted on strict control and censorship rather than accessibility and openness. When the United States invaded Panama to force General Manuel Noriega from office, reporters were delayed in arriving in Panama and then prevented from seeing most battles out of fear that they would witness civilian casualties.[93] When the United States fought Iraq, small pools of reporters were escorted to locations where American troops were living or fighting. Reporters were permitted to interview soldiers only when supervised by their officers, and they were allowed to send dispatches back to the United States only after they were cleared by military censors. The administration worried that pictures of American casualties or information about civilian casualties and property destruction would weaken support for the war.[94]

As a result of the administration's management of the news in the war against Iraq, television showed film of one precise bombing attack after another. Commentators lauded the "smart" bombs that were so accurate it was like having them "delivered by Federal Express." Yet after the war one official said only 7 percent of the bombs were "smart" bombs, and another said only 25 percent of the other bombs hit their targets. This means that at least sixty-one thousand tons of bombs landed where they were not supposed to.[95]

Polls showed that most Americans approved the military's control of the news, and a majority even thought the military should have more control of the news. Only 19 percent thought the military was "hiding bad news from the public."[96]

Clinton Administration

In his use of the media, Clinton emulated Roosevelt and Reagan. Like Roosevelt he tried to leapfrog reporters to reach citizens directly.[97] Like Reagan, he tried to focus on an issue and highlight a message of the day or week to influence public opinion on that issue.

Clinton was exceptionally knowledgeable about policies and very articulate when speaking. Unlike Roosevelt and Reagan, however, Clinton was not enthralling. He lacked discipline and, as a result, talked too long and gave too many details for most listeners. He strayed from his message of the day or week and thus blurred this message. Consequently, he did not effectively communicate his proposals, and many people did not really know what he stood for.

Clinton was impressive one on one, however, because of his knowledge and charm. According to a network correspondent, not a staunch supporter, "He is the most charming man I have ever met."[98]

But the media gave him negative coverage throughout his time in office. Some reporters felt they had "blown it" in covering the Reagan and Bush administrations and vowed not to be conned by the next administration.[99] In addition, many reporters thought Clinton did not tell the truth or at least did not leave an accurate impression. They considered him "a master of lawyerly evasion."[100] So they looked for manipulation, hypocrisy, or falsity behind every action or statement by the president.

As a result, Clinton faced a hostile press from the beginning.[101] According to a joke during his first term, he went on a fishing trip with reporters. After their boat left the shore, Clinton realized he had left his tackle on the dock. He stepped out of the boat, walked to the shore, picked up his tackle, and returned to the boat while staying on the surface of the water. The next day's headline read, "Clinton Can't Swim."[102]

As the investigations into the Whitewater land deal, the revelations about the president's personal life, and the concerns about his party's fund-raising raised ethical questions that swirled around his administration, they dominated the news and hindered his efforts to convey his messages and accomplish his goals. The Clintons became bitter toward the media, while reporters became more cynical toward the administration. The level of trust sank so low that during the 1996 campaign, after the president's opponent, Bob Dole, released his medical records because of concerns about his age, reporters asked why Clinton would not release his also. One asked the president's press secretary, "Does he have a sexually transmitted disease?"

Relationship between the Media and Congress

Members of Congress also use the media but have much less impact. Since 1970 nearly all have hired their own full-time press secretary who churns out press releases, distributes television tapes, and arranges interviews with reporters.[103] The Senate and House of Representatives have established recording studios for members, allowed television cameras into committee rooms, and supported creation of C-Span. Yet members still have trouble attracting the eye of the media. One president can be the subject of the media's focus, whereas 535 members of Congress cannot. Only a handful of powerful (or, occasionally, colorful) members receive much notice from the national media. Other members get attention from their home state or district media, but those from large urban areas with numerous representatives get little publicity or scrutiny even there.[104]

Congressional committees also try to use the media to influence public opinion. After Arizona and California voters supported initiatives on their state ballots in 1996 to allow sick people to use marijuana to control pain, the Senate Judiciary Committee held a hearing to discredit the initiatives and discourage people in other states from following their lead. The hearing, titled "A Prescription for Addiction? The Arizona and California Medical Drug Use Initiatives," included five opponents and just one proponent of marijuana use for sick people. The chair, Senator Orrin Hatch (R-Utah), opened the hearing by stating that the voters were fooled by millions of dollars spent on "stealth campaigns designed to conceal their real objective: the legalization of drugs." Hatch also asserted that marijuana has no medical value. One witness, representing the Federal Drug Enforcement Administration, charged that proponents of the initiatives "cynically used the suffering and illness of vulnerable people to further their own agenda." Witnesses predicted that allowing sick people to use marijuana would result in other people using the drug and then trying harder drugs as well. All the charges are debatable—for example, a federal judge concluded that medical evidence shows that smoking marijuana can ease the symptoms of some patients with AIDS, cancer, or glaucoma—but the committee was not trying to investigate the facts; it was trying to sway public opinion.[105]

Relationship between the Media and the Supreme Court

Unlike presidents and members of Congress, justices of the Supreme Court shun the media. They rarely talk to reporters, and they also forbid their law clerks from talking to them. The justices try to convey the impression that they are not engaged in politics; therefore, they insist they should not answer reporters' questions or concern themselves with public opinion.

As a result, the media do not cover the Supreme Court nearly as much as the presidency or Congress. Only a few newspapers have a full-time Court reporter; the newsmagazines and television networks do not. In one recent year, only 27 reporters had Court press credentials, while an estimated 1,700 reporters had White House press credentials.[106]

When the media do cover the Supreme Court, they focus on the rulings of the Court. They seldom run stories on the personalities of the justices, and they seldom investigate or peer behind the scenes of the Court. They often ignore even relevant concerns, such as the periodic questions about the justices' health. The correspondent for *USA Today* violated the norm when he dug up a story that only 29 of the 394 clerks who had been hired by the current justices were minorities (and that most of these were Asians). The story irritated other correspondents, some of whom refused to report it for their media.[107]

Most reporters on this beat, called "Washington's most deferential press corps,"[108] reject the role of watchdog. Consequently, the justices are shielded from both the legitimate investigation and the excessive scrutiny that officials in the other branches are subjected to. It is probably not a coincidence, then, that the public holds the Court in higher esteem than either of the other branches of government.

Bias of the Media

Every night Walter Cronkite, former anchor for "CBS Evening News," signed off, "And that's the way it is." His statement implied that the network reported the news exactly the way it happened, that the network held a huge mirror to the world and reflected an image of the world to the viewers—without any distortion. Yet the media do not hold a mirror. They hold a searchlight that seeks and illuminates some things instead of others.[109]

From all the events that occur in the world every day, the media can report only a handful as the news of the day. Even the fat *New York Times,* whose motto is "All the News That's Fit to Print," cannot include all the news. The media must decide what events are newsworthy. When the Wright brothers invited reporters to Kitty Hawk, North Carolina, to observe the first plane flight in 1903, none considered it newsworthy enough to cover. After the historic flight, only seven American newspapers reported it, and only two reported it on the front page.[110]

After the media decide what events to report, they must decide where to report them—on the front page or top of the newscast, or in a less prominent position. Then they must decide how to report them. Except for magazines, most media attempt to be "objective"; that is, they try to present facts rather than their opinions. Where the facts are in dispute, they try to present the positions of both sides. They are reluctant to evaluate these positions, although sometimes they do explain or interpret them.

In making these decisions, it would be natural for journalists' attitudes to affect their coverage. As one acknowledged, a reporter writes "from what he hears and sees and how he filters it through the lens of his own experience. No reporter is a robot."[111]

Political Bias

Historically, the press was politically biased. The first papers, which were established by political parties, parroted the party line. Even the independent papers, which succeeded them, advocated one side or the other. The attitudes of publishers, editors, and reporters seeped—sometimes flooded—into their prose. But papers gradually abandoned their ardor for editorializing and adopted the practice of objectivity to retain as many of their readers as possible.

Yet the public thinks the press is still biased. According to one survey, 41 percent think the press is "out to get" the groups they identify with: executives believe the press is out to get businesses, and laborers believe it is out to get unions. Liberals believe it is biased against liberals, and conservatives believe it is biased against conservatives. Republicans believe it is biased against Republicans, and Democrats believe it is biased against Democrats.[112]

Indeed, the public seems more critical today, when most media at least attempt to be objective, than in the past, when they did not even pretend to be. Then, citizens could subscribe to whichever local paper reflected their own biases (without ever recognizing that the paper reflected any biases). Now, as local newspapers, radio stations, and television stations have given way to national newspapers and networks, and as independently owned newspapers, radio stations, and television stations have given way to large chains and conglomerates, people have less opportunity to follow only those media that reflect their views. People who hold strong views inevitably are disappointed with more moderate coverage. So partisans on both sides simultaneously criticize the same media for being biased.

Bias for Established Institutions and Values

The media generally do reflect a bias for established institutions and values. This should not come as a surprise. Because the media are major businesses owned by large corporations, and because they need to retain their read-ers and viewers to make a profit, they consciously or unconsciously mirror the mainstream.

The media have a long history of bias against other ideologies, such as communism or even democratic socialism. The failures of noncapitalist economic systems are played up, the successes played down. In foreign policy matters, the U.S. government line usually is adopted. During the Cold War, this meant harsh attacks on the Soviet Union and leftist Latin American countries.[113] During the Persian Gulf War, this meant jingoistic coverage and unquestioning acceptance of the administration's claims.[114]

Correlated with the media's support for established institutions and values is their reliance on government officials for their news. A study of front-page stories from the *New York Times* and *Washington Post* over two decades found that 74 percent were based on statements by U.S. government officials.[115] This finding is striking considering that these papers have far more staffers and resources to do investigative journalism than other papers. Such heavy reliance on government officials means that the stories are likely to bear their strong imprint. Similarly, a study of ABC's "Nightline" found that 80 percent of the Americans interviewed on the program were from the government or corporate establishment (and 90 percent of these were white males). The watchdog group Fairness & Accuracy in Reporting (FAIR) found that representatives from peace, environmental, consumer, or labor groups were "hardly visible."[116]

Reporters turn to officials for news because it is easy and because, ironically, they want to avoid charges of bias. Reporters believe their peers, their superiors, and the public all consider officials newsworthy. Ignoring them or downplaying them might be interpreted as showing bias against them.[117]

Bias for Particular Candidates and Policies

Most debate about media bias revolves around charges that the media exhibit a preference for particular candidates and policies over others. Conservative groups, in particular, claim that the media are biased toward liberal candidates and policies.

In studying media bias, social scientists have examined the characteristics and behavior of journalists. They have found that journalists are not very representative of the public. They are disproportionately college-educated white males from the upper middle class. Further, they are disproportionately urban and secular, rather than rural and religious. They are disproportionately Democrats or independents leaning to the Democrats, rather than Republicans or independents leaning to the Republicans. Likewise, they identify themselves disproportionately as liberals rather than conservatives.[118]

For the congressional elections of 1992, Republicans campaigned against Democrats by linking them to President Clinton and by linking him to former President Carter. Both presidents, they charged, were failures. Time *magazine reinforced the Republicans' theme by running this series of computer-generated images showing Clinton becoming Carter.*

Cynthia Johnson/*Time* magazine

But journalists do differ among themselves. Those who work for the prominent, influential organizations—large newspapers, wire services, news magazines, and radio and television networks—are more likely to be Democrats and liberals than those who work for nonprominent organizations—small newspapers and radio and television stations.[119]

Journalists in prominent organizations are more likely than the public to support the liberal position on issues. At the same time, they support capitalism and do not think that our institutions "need overhaul."[120] Thus, they are not extremely liberal.

An increasing number of journalists are conservative. In the 1980s and 1990s, a vocal conservative media complex emerged, including such newspapers as the *Wall Street Journal* and the *Washington Times,* various magazines, and numerous radio and television talk shows. Conservatives dominate these media and also appear in other media as columnists, commentators, and cartoonists.

Examination of journalists' backgrounds and attitudes assumes that these color journalists coverage. But several factors mitigate the effect of these traits. For one thing, journalists do not seem to have intense opinions. Most did not become journalists because of a commitment to political ideology but because of the opportunity to rub elbows with powerful people and be close to exciting events. "Each day brings new stories, new dramas in which journalists participate vicariously."[121] As a result, most "care more about the politics of an issue than about the issue itself,"[122] which makes them less likely to voice their views about the issue.

In addition, media organizations pressure journalists to muffle their views, partly out of a conviction that it is more professional to do so and partly out of a desire to avoid the headaches that could arise otherwise—debates among their staffers; complaints from their local radio and television affiliates; complaints from their audience; perhaps even complaints from the White House, Congress, or the Federal Communications Commission (FCC), which licenses them.

Sometimes media executives or editors pressure reporters because they have contrary views. Reporters

learn not to explore certain subjects, not to ask certain questions. Reporters who pursue the stories regardless might find their copy edited, with the critical portions deleted. The *New York Times,* despite its liberal reputation, altered reporters' stories on foreign affairs to hew more closely to administrations' conservative policies.[123] CBS toned down correspondents' stories about Reagan's economic policies.[124] Reporters who pursue the stories might find themselves transferred to another beat. One who covered El Salvador for the *New York Times* wrote a series of reports about the government's massacre of nearly a thousand peasants. The reports contradicted Reagan's assertions that the nation was making great strides in human rights. Under pressure, the *Times* pulled the reporter off this beat.[125] Ultimately, reporters who pursue the stories could find themselves fired.[126]

For all of these reasons, the media do not exhibit nearly as much **political bias** as would be expected from journalists' backgrounds and attitudes. Although they do show a bias for established institutions and values, they do not show much bias for particular candidates in elections.

To measure bias, researchers use a technique called *content analysis.* They scrutinize newspaper and television stories to determine whether there was an unequal amount of coverage, unequal use of favorable or unfavorable statements, or unequal use of a positive or negative tone. They consider insinuating verbs ("he conceded" rather than "he said") and pejorative adjectives ("her weak response" rather than "her response"), and for television stories they evaluate the announcers' nonverbal communication—voice inflection, eye movement, and body language.

Studies of coverage of presidential campaigns found relatively little bias. The media typically gave the two major candidates equal attention, and they usually avoided any favorable or unfavorable statements in their news stories. They typically provided diverse views in editorials and columns, with some commentary slanting one way and other commentary slanting the opposite way. Thus, the authors of a major study examining forty-six newspapers concluded that American newspapers are "fairly neutral."[127] Some studies did find some bias

What Sells?

The most popular and least popular issues of *Time* magazine, measured by newsstand sales, show what kinds of news people are interested in. The most popular issues feature celebrities and disasters. The least popular issues often feature foreign affairs.

Hits			Misses		
Issue Date	**Cover Subject**	**Copies Sold**	**Issue Date**	**Cover Subject**	**Copies Sold**
Sept. 15, 1997	Princess Diana "Commemorative"	1,183,758	Oct. 10, 1994	Black Cultural Renaissance	100,827
Sept. 8, 1997	Death of Princess Diana	802,838	Aug. 22, 1994	Baseball Strike	101,125
Aug. 19, 1974	President Ford/ Nixon's resignation	564,723	May 17, 1993	"Anguish over Bosnia"	102,193
Dec. 22, 1980	Death of John Lennon	531,340	April 4, 1996	Nuclear Safety	108,900
Mar. 19, 1984	Michael Jackson	500,290	June 10, 1996	Benjamin Netanyahu	109,300
Aug. 2, 1982	Herpes	468,021	March 29, 1993	Boris Yeltsin	109,365
Feb. 10, 1986	*Challenger* Explosion	462,492	Dec. 21, 1992	Somalia: Restoring Hope	111,176
Jan. 28, 1991	War in the Gulf	433,625	June 3, 1996	Advocates for Children	111,700
Aug. 15, 1983	Babies: "What Do They Know?"	423,156	Nov. 20, 1996	GOP Front-Runner Bob Dole	112,310
June 2, 1980	Mount St. Helens	412,909	Oct. 24, 1994	America's Economy	113,041

SOURCE: *Time*, March 9, 1998, p. 177.

example, can mean a difference of $5 million in advertising for a station in a year.[143] The opportunity to make a profit is so enormous that CBS's "60 Minutes," the most watched program during some years, made more money in its first decade on the air than the entire Chrysler Corporation in the same decade.[144] (See also the box "What Sells?")

With chains and conglomerates taking over most media, the pressure to make a sizable profit has escalated. Where family owners used to be satisfied if their newspaper or radio station or television station made money, corporate executives now expect their media, like other big businesses on the stock market, to make the prevailing rate. They worry that financial analysts will rank them lower or that mutual fund managers will unload their stock if their earnings fall below those available "from investments anywhere else in the financial universe, from a shirt factory in Thailand to the latest Internet start-up."[145]

The pressure to make a profit and the need to attract an audience shape the media's presentation of the news and lead to a **commercial bias.** Sometimes this means that the media deliberately print or broadcast what advertisers want. At the request of the gas company sponsoring the drama *Judgment at Nuremberg,* one network bleeped the words "gas ovens" from descriptions of the Nazis' war crimes.[146] Other times the media censor themselves. When the auto industry was pressuring Congress to repeal seat belt and air bag regulations in the 1970s, the *New York Times* publisher urged the editors to present the industry position because it "would affect the advertising."[147] In articles on health, numerous magazines avoided references to the dangers of smoking for fear of losing advertising from tobacco companies. A poll of national and local reporters and news executives found that a third admitted to avoiding stories that would embarrass an advertiser or harm the financial interests of their own organization.[148]

Usually, though, commercial bias means that the media must print or broadcast what the public wants, which means that the media must offer what the public finds entertaining. This creates a "conflict between being an honest reporter and being a member of show business," network correspondent Roger Mudd confessed, "and that conflict is with me every day."[149] When CBS anchor Dan Rather was asked why he devoted time to the demolition of O. J. Simpson's house two years after his trial, Rather answered, "[F]ear ... the fear that if we don't do it, somebody else will, and when they do it, they will get a few more readers, a few more listeners, a few more viewers than we do. The result is the 'Hollywoodization of the news.'"[150]

The dilemma is most marked for television. Many people who watch television news are not interested in politics; a majority, in fact, say it covers too much politics.[151] Some watch the news because they were watching another program before the news and left the television on, others because they were going to watch another program after the news and turned the television on early. Networks feel pressure "to hook them and keep them."[152]

Therefore, networks try to make the everyday world of news seem as exciting as the make-believe world they depict in their other programs. One network instructed its staff: "Every news story should, without any sacrifice of probity or responsibility, display the attributes of fiction, of drama. It should have structure and conflict, problem and denouement, rising action and falling action, a beginning, a middle and an end."[153] As one executive says, television news is "**infotainment.**"[154]

So television anchors and newscasters, hired for their appearance and personality as well as their experience and ability, become show business stars. To enhance their appeal, networks and stations shape their image, ordering them to change their hairstyle and even, with tinted contact lenses, their eye color. They set up clothes calendars so newscasters will rotate their outfits.

Although appearance is important for both men and women newscasters, it is crucial for women. While viewers accept men aging on the screen, they do not seem to accept women aging. As one woman anchor commented, "The guys have got white hair, and the girls look like cheerleaders."[155] Indeed, according to one calculation, although a third of local anchors are women, only 3 percent are past forty; of the men, 50 percent are past forty and 16 percent are past fifty.[156]

The commercial bias of the media has a number of consequences. One is emphasis on human interest stories. In 1980 UPI and CBS carried seven times more stories about President Jimmy Carter's beer-drinking brother, Billy, than about the Strategic Arms Limitation Talks (SALT) between the United States and the Soviet Union.[157] By 1990, the networks had mentioned President Bush's dog, Millie, in more stories than they had mentioned three cabinet secretaries.[158]

The emphasis on human interest includes an em-

Bizzaro © by Dan Piraro. Reprinted with permission of Universal Press Syndicate. All rights reserved.

phasis on sex. In the past two decades, the media have examined the sexual affairs of numerous politicians. But this coverage pales in comparison with the treatment of the sexual escapades of President Clinton. When the allegations involving Monica Lewinsky became public, the pope was making a historic visit to Cuba. The networks, which had considered this visit so important that they had sent their anchors to broadcast from Havana, ordered them back to Washington to cover the racy allegations. At the same time, renewed violence in Northern Ireland threatened to scuttle the peace talks between Catholics and Protestants. Continued refusal from Iraq to cooperate with United Nations biological and chemical weapons inspectors threatened to escalate to military conflict. Yet reporters focused on what the president did with the former White House intern. The *Los Angeles Times* assigned twenty-six reporters to examine Lewinsky's life, interviewing baby-sitters and kindergarten classmates.[159] *Time* magazine e-mailed college classmates for personal information. The networks interviewed one person whose claim to fame was that he had lunch with her three years before. All along, one columnist laments, "We have ... leapt to conclusions, purveyed rumor as fact, offered banalities with the breathless excitement of discovery, and sheltered vile slanderers all in the name of the public's right to know."[160]

The emphasis on human interest also includes an emphasis on crime. Although the national media give crime extensive coverage (who could escape O. J. Simpson's case?), this emphasis is most apparent for the local media, where television news is a combination of mayhem and happy talk (or, in Ralph Nader's words, "something that jerks your head up every ten seconds, whether that is shootings, robberies, sports showdowns, or dramatic weather forecasts."[161]) The saying "If it bleeds, it leads," expresses, tongue in cheek, the programming philosophy of some stations. Studies show that crime coverage fills about a third of the local news in many cities.[162] One reporter put it bluntly, "It doesn't matter what kind of swill you set in front of the public. As long as it's got enough sex and violence in it, they'll slurp it up."[163]

The emphasis on human interest leads to another consequence of commercial bias—a **game orientation** in political reporting.[164] The underlying assumption is that politics is a game and politicians, whether candidates campaigning for election or officials performing in office, are the players. The corollary to the assumption is that the players are self-centered and self-interested. They are seeking victory for themselves and defeat for their opponents and are not concerned about the consequences of their proposals or of government's policies. With this orientation, reporters highlight politicians' strategies and tactics, and they present new developments according to how these developments help some politicians and hinder others. Reporters slight the substance and impact of politicians' proposals and policies.

After a candidates' debate, for example, the main thing correspondents discuss is who "won." They pay less attention to what was said and how it is significant for the country.

The game orientation appeals to journalists because it generates human interest. It offers new story lines as new information comes to light, much like a board game where "chance" cards inject unexpected scenarios and alter the players' moves and the game's outcomes. This orientation also appeals to journalists because it is easy and relatively free from charges of partisan or ideological bias. (Stories highlight which contestants are winning, not which ones should win or what consequences might result.) Analyzing policy lacks all of these advantages for journalists.

The game orientation attracts an audience, but it breeds more cynicism. It creates the impression that politics is just a game, not an essential activity for a democratic society; that politicians are just the players, not our representatives; that politicians act just in their self-interest, not in the public interest; and that politicians' goal is just to beat others, not to make good public policy.

The assumption that politics is a game and the corollary that the players are concerned solely with their own interests leads to the conclusion that their strategies and tactics are based mostly on manipulation and deception. Journalists, casting their wary eyes on politicians, look for manipulation and deception and interpret even sincere action in those ways.

For elections, the game orientation results in what is called "horse-race coverage," with "front-runners," "dark horses," and "also-rans." This coverage accounts for much of the total coverage of campaigns.[165] For example, in 1988 one-third of all network television stories about the presidential primaries referred to candidates' poll standings.[166] This is remarkable so early in the campaign, when most citizens know little about most candidates. It is likely that many viewers knew where the candidates were running in the race but not where they stood on the issues.

Horse-race coverage is not new and is not confined to television. An examination of presidential election coverage by metropolitan newspapers from 1888 on shows that the race was a staple of journalism long before the advent of broadcast media.[167] Yet other research suggests that the proportion of coverage focusing on the race has been increasing in recent decades (see Figure 3).

The quintessential reflection of horse-race coverage, reporting of candidates' poll standings, has increased greatly. Not only have the media reported more results of polls taken by commercial organizations, such as Gallup and Harris, but they have conducted more polls themselves. From 1976 to 1988, newspapers sponsored twice as many polls as before, and television stations sponsored three times as many. Since then, they have sponsored even more.[168] Now coverage of polls takes more space than coverage of candidates' speeches, and it usually appears as the lead or next-to-lead story.[169]

The emphasis on human interest stories and horse-race aspects of an election led one observer to summarize the 1976 presidential campaign as follows:

I saw President Ford bump his head leaving an airplane. . . . I saw Carter playing softball in Plains, Georgia. I saw Carter kissing [daughter] Amy, I saw Carter hugging [mother] Lillian. I saw Carter, in dungarees, walking hand in hand through the peanut farm with [wife] Rosalyn. I saw Carter going to church, coming out of church. . . . I saw Ford misstate the problems of Eastern Europe—and a week of people commenting about his misstatement. I saw Ford bump

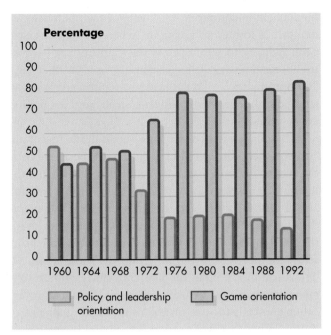

Percentage

FIGURE 3 ■ *Game Orientation in Presidential Campaigns Increases* In presidential campaigns in the 1960s, policy and leadership issues received approximately equal coverage with the strategies and tactics and the successes and failures that reflect the game orientation. In the 1970s, 1980s, and 1990s, however, policy and leadership issues have received a much smaller proportion of the coverage, according to an analysis of articles on the front page of the New York Times.

Note: Analysis is based on articles that can be categorized one way or the other.
SOURCE: Thomas E. Patterson, *Out of Order* (New York: Vintage, 1994), 74.

Legend: Policy and leadership orientation; Game orientation

his head again. I saw Ford in Ohio say how glad he was to be back in Iowa. I saw marching bands and hecklers, and I learned about the size of crowds and the significance of the size of crowds. . . .

But in all the hours of high anxiety that I spent watching the network news, never did I hear what the candidates had to say about the campaign issues. That was not news.[170]

Even after elections, the game orientation continues. During Reagan's first term, social programs were cut, income taxes were cut significantly, and military spending was increased sharply, but the main theme of media coverage was whether Reagan was "winning" or "losing" his battles with Congress and the bureaucracy. Similarly, when Clinton proposed a plan to overhaul the welfare system, all major newspapers focused on the political implications for his reelection; few even explained the plan, let alone its substantive implications. When he proposed more money for law enforcement, as a way to put "more cops on the beat," the media pointed out how this would sound in campaign ads but ignored where the extra officers would be, how

much they would cost, and whether they would have any effect on crime.[171]

The emphasis on human interest leads to another consequence of commercial bias—an emphasis on controversy rather than agreement. Stories about conflict provide drama. Reporters, one admits, are "fight promoters" rather than consensus builders.[172] Reporters frame disputes as struggles between opposite camps. Thus, some stories about survivors of the Holocaust include bizarre statements by deniers of the Holocaust, claiming that there was no plan to exterminate European Jews, or that Hitler was unaware of the effort, or that not nearly as many murders were committed as was generally claimed. The stories present these statements as though they constitute an opposing opinion that deserves a public platform.[173] With their focus on controversy, the media allow themselves to be manipulated by people who are unscrupulous or ignorant. And with the justification that there are two sides to every story, the media promote public confusion, too

Once the media frame an issue as a struggle between two sides, they depict attack and counterattack, using dueling sound bites from politicians and interjecting metaphors from wars. They talk about politicians who are "targets," who are "under fire," who receive "shots across their bow." They talk about politicians who engage in "search-and-destroy missions" and who "hold back no ammunition." Occasionally, they refer to a "cease-fire," but eventually they return to a "war of attrition" with "do-or-die" battles. Ultimately, they lament the politicians who "crashed in flames."[174]

A researcher studying the coverage of the debate over health care reform in 1994 sat with reporters listening to Hillary Clinton present the administration's plan. For two hours she discussed the plan, including its substance and the arguments raised against it. The reporters

found it completely uninteresting. They were talking to each other, passing notes around. But as soon as she made a brief attack on the Republicans, there was a physiological reaction, this surge of adrenaline, all around me. The pens moved. The reporters arched forward. They wrote everything down rapidly. As soon as this part was over, they clearly weren't paying attention any more.[175]

Not surprisingly, an experimental study later found that people who read fifteen newspaper articles on the health care debate knew no more about the proposals than people who read just one article.[176]

All this emphasis on human interest, including the attention to sex and crime, to the game, and to controversy, helps explain why the media spotlight scandals.

Since Watergate, which riveted the public, the media have played up other, lesser scandals. As one journalist himself has observed:

> When a scandal is breaking, talk show figures wring their hands about the "agony" of Watergate or Iran-Contra; but the truth is that journalists are happier at such moments than at any other time. The country's attention is turned toward Washington. People hang on disclosures of the latest "inside" news. Life is energizing and sweet for Washington journalists, even if the scandal of the moment is a big wheel-spinning exercise for the country as a whole.[177]

But the scandal must seem interesting to receive extensive coverage. When the savings and loan (S&L) scandal loomed in the 1980s, business reporters addressed it, but political reporters and editors ignored it for years. A banking reporter said, "You would relay this to your editors, but because it involved banking regulations, their eyes would glaze over."[178] The crisis was too complicated and too dull until it could be personalized and sensationalized. Finally, Charles Keating—the chair of a failed S&L and a highflier with three private jets, one with gold-plated bathroom fixtures—was linked to the scandal. Then "looted Rembrandts and party girls on yachts" were discovered, and the media and the public took notice.[179] But by this time the industry needed a $500 billion bailout from the taxpayers to prevent more insolvent S&Ls from collapsing (and taking depositors' savings with them).

By focusing on conflict and by framing most issues as though they have two—and only two—sides, the media polarize the public. After the rampage at Columbine High School in Littleton, Colorado, the public was subjected to a moronic debate about whether the incident was caused by the availability of guns in our society *or* by the glorification of violence in the media. The coverage prompted people to choose sides, as though one was correct while the other was incorrect and as though no other answer might also be correct. In contrast, Japanese television talk shows that address controversial issues typically have more than two guests, thus reducing the polarization while conveying the impression that the issues are complex and might have multiple answers.[180] American media prefer to focus on two opposing extremes. "The middle ground, the sensible center," one reporter acknowledges, "is dismissed as too squishy, too dull, too likely to send the audience channel surfing."[181]

These practices make it harder for people to accept compromises as solutions to problems and, therefore, harder for politicians to forge compromises. In fact, the media belittle compromises. They portray politicians on one side as losing or "giving in" when they should have been fighting to win. Even when Clinton faced a hostile Congress, they characterized him as a "waffler" and "compromiser."[182] Thus, the media reinforced some citizens' naive belief that politicians need not bargain and compromise.

The commercial bias of the media leads to certain consequences for television specifically. One is emphasis on events, or those parts of events, that have visual interest. The networks have people whose job is to evaluate all film for visual appeal. Producers seek the events that promise the most action; camera operators shoot the parts of the events with the most action; and editors select the portions of the film with the most action.[183] Television thus focuses on disasters, crimes, and protests far more than they actually occur, and when it covers other events, it focuses on the most exciting aspects of them. Sometimes it distorts reality to hold viewers' attention. In the summer of 1988, fires raged through Yellowstone National Park. Television showed a wall of flame night after night and called the park "a moonscape." As one lifeless scene followed another on the screen, NBC's Tom Brokaw intoned, "This is what's left of Yellowstone tonight." Yet three-fourths of the park, including its famed geysers and waterfalls, was nearly unscathed.[184]

The emphasis on visual interest often results in coverage of the interesting surface of events rather than the underlying substance—the protest but not the cause. When Iranians seized the American embassy and employees in 1980, the demonstrators discovered television's appetite for visual interest and teased it almost every night for more than a year. As the cameras arrived, they erupted with wild chants and threats, hung Jimmy Carter effigies, and shredded American flags. Yet the reasons for the seizure, rooted in Iranian problems, American policies, and superpower conflicts, were only briefly mentioned.[185]

Another consequence of commercial bias for television is that it covers the news very briefly. A half-hour newscast has only twenty-one minutes without commercials. In that time, the networks broadcast only about one-third as many words as the *New York Times* prints on its front page alone. Although television conveys visual impressions as well, the contrast in the amount of information these media transmit is striking.

The stories are short—about one minute each—because the time is short and because the networks think viewers' attention spans are short. Indeed, a survey found that a majority of eighteen- to thirty-four-year-olds who have remote controls typically watch more than one show at once.[186] Thus, networks do not allow leaders or experts to explain their thoughts about particular events or policies. Instead, networks take sound bites to illustrate what was said. Their correspondents usually do not have enough time to explain the events or policies or to provide background information about them.

A network correspondent was asked what went through his mind when he signed off each night. "Good night, dear viewer," he said. "I only hope you read the *New York Times* in the morning."[187]

When the chairman of the board of one network, in conversation with Reagan aide Michael Deaver, asked what the networks could do to provide more responsible reporting, Deaver answered, "Easy, . . . just eliminate ratings for news. You claim that news is not the same as entertainment. So why do you need ratings?" The chairman sighed, "Well, that's our big money-maker, the news."[188] The same is true for individual stations. One financial analyst estimated that 40 to 50 percent of their profits come from news programs.[189] A former network executive concluded, "Because television can make so much money doing its worst, it often can't afford to do its best."[190]

Overall, commercial bias of the media results in no coverage or superficial coverage of many important stories. This, more than any political bias, makes it difficult for citizens, particularly those who rely on television, to become well informed.

Impact of the Media on Politics

It is difficult to measure the impact of the media on politics. Because the many media provide varied though similar coverage and reach different though overlapping audiences, it is exceedingly difficult to isolate the impact of particular media on particular groups of people. Other factors also influence people's knowledge, attitudes, and behavior toward politics. But there is considerable agreement that the media have a substantial impact on the public agenda, political parties and elections, and public opinion.

Impact on the Public Agenda

The most important impact of the media is **setting the agenda**—influencing the process by which problems are considered important and alternative policies are proposed and debated.[191] The media publicize an issue, and people exposed to the media talk about the issue with their fellow citizens. Eventually, enough consider it important and expect officials to try to resolve it.[192]

The media's impact is most noticeable for dramatic events that occur suddenly, such as the dismantling of the Berlin Wall. The impact is less noticeable for issues that evolve gradually. Watergate required months of coverage before making it on the public agenda, and AIDS required the death of actor Rock Hudson before making it.[193]

Even for issues that evolve gradually, however, cumulative coverage by the media can have an impact. After years of extensive coverage, people told pollsters that drug use was the "most important problem" facing the country, and then they told pollsters that crime was. Studies comparing people's views with the media coverage of these problems and with the actual rates of these activities in the 1980s and 1990s show that people's views fluctuated more according to the media coverage than to the actual rates. When the media coverage increased, people considered the problems more serious, even when the actual rates of crime or drug use remained steady or decreased.[194]

The impact usually is greatest for stories that appear on the front page of the newspaper or top of the newscast rather than those buried in the back or at the end.[195] Many people who do not follow the news fully check the beginning of the newspaper or newscast for the "important" stories. Without being aware of it, they are accepting the media's role in identifying these stories as the important ones. Moreover, the impact usually is greatest on people who are most interested in politics, because they are most likely to follow the news and discuss it with others.[196] Yet the impact varies according to the personal experiences of the audience. For instance, people with recent unemployment in their family will be more sensitive to news about unemployment than other people.

The media's power to influence the agenda has important implications. The media play a key role in deciding which problems government addresses and which it ignores. They also play a key role in increasing or decreasing politicians' ability to govern and to get reelected. By publicizing some issues, the media create a golden opportunity for politicians with the authority and ability to resolve these issues. At the same time, the media create a pitfall for those who lack the power to resolve these issues. Thus, the Iranian seizure of the American embassy and hostages became the prominent issue in the country in 1980. Every night CBS's Walter Cronkite signed off, "And that's the way it is, the _____ day of American hostages in captivity," as if anyone needed reminding. President Carter's lack of success in persuading Iranian officials to release the hostages or in directing an American invasion to rescue them cost him dearly in his reelection bid that year.

Yet the role of the media in shaping the agenda should not be overstated. Individuals' knowledge and experience lead them to consider some things unimportant even when the media do cover them. And, of course, individuals' interests prompt the media to cover some things in the first place.[197]

Moreover, politicians play an important role in shaping the agenda. For much legislation, Congress initiates action and then the media publicize it.[198] For many issues, the president initiates action. In 1995 President Clinton launched a campaign to reduce smoking by teenagers. The media printed and broadcast many stories about this problem. They could have done so years before or after, of course, but they followed the president's lead. For elections candidates usually establish the agenda of policy issues. By emphasizing issues they think will resonate with the public and reflect favorably on themselves, candidates pressure the media to cover these rather than other issues. But the media usually establish the agenda of nonpolicy issues, involving the candidates' personality and behavior.[199] The media are able to set the agenda for nonpolicy issues because these are more likely to catch the public's fancy.

Impact on Political Parties and Elections

The media have had an important impact on political parties and elections. In particular they have furthered the decline of parties, encouraged new types of candidates, and influenced campaigns.

Political Parties

Political parties have declined in power on the national level in large part because of the influence of the media. In the young republic, political parties created and controlled most newspapers. Naturally, the papers echoed the parties' views and the journalists bowed to the parties' leaders. (The editor of one Democratic Party paper made sure a pail of fresh milk was left on the White House doorstep for President Andrew Jackson every morning, even if the editor had to deliver it himself.[200]) Yet people received much of their political information, however biased, from these papers.

When independent newspapers arose as profit-making businesses, the party papers declined and then disappeared. Eventually, people came to receive most of their political information from independent newspapers, magazines, radio stations, and television stations. Thus, people are no longer dependent on parties for their political information.

In other ways as well, the media, especially television, have contributed to the decline of parties. In place of selection by party bosses, television allows candidates to appeal directly to the people. If candidates succeed in the primaries, parties have little choice but to nominate them. In place of campaign management by party bosses, television requires new expertise, so candidates assemble their own campaign organization. Television advertising requires substantial amounts of money, so party funds are inadequate and candidates approach other donors. Television also gives voters information so they can make up their own minds about how to vote, rather than rely on the party organization to tell them. Thus, the media have supplanted parties as the principal link between people and their leaders.

Types of Candidates

Television has encouraged new types of candidates for national offices. No longer must candidates be experienced politicians who worked their way up over many years. Celebrities from other fields with name recognition can move into prominent positions without political experience. Jessie Ventura, who had been a professional wrestler, got elected governor of Minnesota. In recent years Congress has had an actor (Fred Grandy, R-Iowa—"Gopher" on "Love Boat"), a rock singer (Sonny Bono, R-Cal.), a professional baseball pitcher (Jim Bunning, R-Ky.), a professional football quarterback (Jack Kemp, R-N.Y.), a professional basketball player (Bill Bradley, D-N.J.), and two astronauts (John Glenn, D-Ohio, and Harrison Schmitt, R-N.M.).[201] Congress also has had a television commentator (Jesse Helms, R-N.C.) and a businessman who appeared in his company's commercials (Rudy Boschwitz, R-Minn.). Alternatively, unknowns with talent can achieve rapid name recognition and move into prominent positions. Jimmy Carter, who had served one term as governor of Georgia, was relatively unknown elsewhere in the country when he ran for the Democratic nomination for president in 1976. People kept asking "Jimmy who?" But through effective use of television, he won enough primaries so the party had to nominate him, even though the leaders were uncomfortable with him.

At the same time that television has allowed newcomers to run, it also has imposed new requirements on candidates for national office. They must demonstrate an appealing appearance and performance on camera; they must be telegenic. President Franklin Roosevelt's body, disabled from polio and usually in a wheelchair, would not be impressive on television. President Harry Truman's style—"Give 'em hell"—would not be impressive on television, either. Although effective in whistlestop speeches, it would be too "hot," too intense, to come into people's homes every day. A "cool," low-key style is more effective.

President Reagan was the quintessential politician for the television age. He was tall and trim with a handsome face and a smooth, reassuring voice. As a former actor, he could project his personality and convictions and deliver his lines and jokes better than any other politician. It is not an exaggeration to conclude, as one political scientist did,

> Without a chance to display his infectious smile, his grandfatherly demeanor, and his "nice guy" qualities to millions of Americans, Ronald Reagan, burdened by his image as a superannuated, intellectually lightweight movie actor with right-wing friends and ultraconservative leanings, might never have reached the presidency.[202]

Television has not created the public desire for politicians with an appealing personality. "When candidates shook hands firmly, kissed babies, and handed out cigars, the thrust was not on issues."[203] Yet television has exacerbated this emphasis on the right image.

The media in general have exacerbated other requirements on candidates for national office. In recent decades, the intense scrutiny and constant criticism screen out those who are unwilling to relinquish most of their personal privacy and individual dignity. Candidates, of course, must expect to sacrifice much privacy and be subject to much criticism, but now they are expected to endure even more. One columnist wonders whether public service will attract only those with the "most brazen, least sensitive personalities."[204]

Retired admiral Bobby Ray Inman, who had held positions in both Democratic and Republican administrations, was nominated to be secretary of defense by President Clinton. During the confirmation process, he came under attack by some senators and some newspapers. One editor told him, "Bobby, you just have to get a thicker skin. We have to write a bad story about you every day. That's our job." Although he was assured by members of both parties that he would be confirmed—the *New York Times* reported that his nomination was "unusually well received in Washington"—Inman withdrew his nomination, saying he did not want "the daily diet" of media criticism. Then, when he withdrew, the newspapers criticized him for being insecure.[205]

Franklin Roosevelt spent much of his life in a wheelchair, but journalists did not photograph him in it. A friend snapped this rare picture.
Courtesy Franklin D. Roosevelt Library 73-113:61

Campaigns

The media affect nomination and election campaigns through their news and commentary and candidates' advertisements. They help set the campaign agenda, as already explained. They also inform and persuade.

The media provide information about the candidates and the issues, and they also interpret this information.[206] The public learns about the candidates and the issues,[207] but in the process the public is influenced in making its choices.

Information about the candidates can have a major impact especially at the nomination stage. In presidential elections, a party without an incumbent president running for reelection might field a dozen candidates. The media cannot cover all adequately, so they narrow the field by considering some "serious" and giving them more coverage. Once the primaries begin, they label some "winners" and others "losers," and they give the "winners" more coverage.[208] In the Democratic race in 1992, even before a single primary, the press proclaimed Clinton the front-runner, and several magazines put his picture on their cover, although half of the public did not know who he was.[209]

Washington, Jefferson, and Lincoln in the Media Age

How would three of America's greatest presidents have fared in the media age? George Washington cut an impressive figure, but he had a speech impediment.

Thomas Jefferson was tall—six feet, two inches, when the average American man was about five feet, five inches—but he was shy, even awkward, with people. And apparently he never made a political speech.

Abraham Lincoln was also tall, but he was gangly. According to contemporaries, he was homely in different ways at different times. One newspaper called him "the ugliest man in the Union."[1] He had a "ploughed" face and a "doughnut" complexion, protruding ears, and "spider" legs.[2] He also had a high-pitched voice.

A modern observer speculated how television would cover the Gettysburg Address, which, though brief, would not be brief enough: The cameras would focus on the network correspondent describing the scene and recalling the battle, while in the background Lincoln would be speaking. Finally, the cameras would focus on Lincoln concluding, "government of the people, by the people, for the people, shall not perish from the earth."[3] But even this sound bite would be negated by the correspondent adding, "Lincoln campaign insiders said

THE FAR SIDE   By GARY LARSON

The Far Side © 1984 Farworks, Inc. All rights reserved.

the speech was an attempt to win support from veterans' groups."[4]

Are there contemporary Washingtons, Jeffersons, and Lincolns who might make effective leaders but who would not qualify because they are ineffective on television?

1. Thomas E. Patterson, *Out of Order* (New York: Vintage, 1994), 9.
2. Marcus Cunliffe, "What Did Abraham Lincoln Look Like?" *Washington Post National Weekly Edition,* February 27, 1984, p. 35.
3. Thomas Griffith, "Always Articulate on Sunday," *Time,* June 6, 1983, p. 55.
4. Political adviser Mike Murphy, quoted in Joe Klein, "Where's the Music?" *New Yorker* (September 1999): 42.

By making these judgments, the media strongly influence the election process at this stage.[210] Because few people have formed opinions about the candidates this early, they are open to impressions from the media. Therefore, when the media declare some candidates winners, they help create a bandwagon effect.[211] When they declare others losers, they make it hard for these candidates to attract contributors and volunteers and eventually supporters in the next primaries.

The media also can persuade voters directly. This influence can be seen in several ways.

Televised debates do not sway most viewers because people tend to engage in **selective perception,** which is a tendency to screen out information that contradicts their beliefs. Consequently, most people conclude that their candidate performed better.[212] However, the debates do sway some viewers, usually those who have moderate education and some interest in politics but who are not decided or at least not strongly committed to one candidate. In 1960 the debates might have caused enough voters to cast their ballots for Kennedy that he won the election.[213]

Media commentary about the debates also might sway some viewers. In 1976 Ford erroneously said there was "no Soviet domination of Eastern Europe." People surveyed within twelve hours after the debate said they thought Ford won. But the media zeroed in on this slip, and people surveyed later said they thought Carter won. In the first debate in 1984, Reagan appeared tired and confused. By a modest margin, people polled immediately after the debate said Mondale won. But the media focused on Reagan's age and abilities, and by increasingly large margins, people polled in the days after the debate said Mondale won. Perhaps viewers did not catch Ford's statement or, due to selective perception, notice Reagan's doddering, but the media called attention to them, which prompted many viewers to reconsider and reverse their verdict. Yet there is evidence that this effect does not last long. After the media frenzy wears off, the candidate bounces back.[214]

Newspaper endorsements of candidates apparently sway some readers, especially those with a ninth-through twelfth-grade education. People with less education are less likely to read editorials, while those with more education have more sources of information and more defined ideologies to guide their decisions.[215] Even if endorsements sway only a small percentage of voters, they could determine the outcome of tight races.[216] Endorsements have some effect on well-publicized races, such as those for president,[217] but they probably have greater effect on less publicized races, such as those for state legislator or local tax assessor, because voters have little other information to guide them.

Talk radio also influences listeners. People who tune in to talk radio are more likely to turn out to vote and even to participate in campaigns.[218]

Impact on Public Opinion

Social scientists long thought that the media influenced the things people thought about but not the opinions they held about these things. Some contemporary research, however, demonstrates that the media do have a substantial impact on public opinion. A comparison of the networks' newscasts with the public's policy preferences in a wide variety of foreign and domestic issues for fifteen years during the 1970s and 1980s shows that the media influence opinion about issues.[219] Other research shows that the media influ-

ence opinion about particular presidents.[220] They affect opinion indirectly, by providing the news and transmitting the views of various opinion leaders, as well as directly, through editorials and commentaries intended to sway opinion.

Many speculate that the media have contributed to the public's cynicism toward government in recent decades. The media have undermined the public's perception of the integrity of government and officials not just by reporting real shortcomings of programs and administrators, but by engaging in several practices already addressed in this chapter. The negative bias in coverage of all candidates and officials directly undermines them, while the game orientation more subtly undermines them. The emphasis on conflict leads to a focus on politicians' most extreme statements, which alienates the public and, at the same time, polarizes it. The practice of objectivity—reporting what he said versus what she said without evaluating the truth of either—passes along some false statements and some misleading ones and confuses the public.[221] Many people complain, "You can't believe any of them."

Some researchers have concluded that the result of these practices is to foster **media malaise** among the public.[222] This is a feeling of cynicism and distrust, perhaps even despair, toward government and officials. Indeed, according to a 1995 survey, the public is even more cynical than journalists themselves. Seventy-seven percent of the public gave government officials a low rating for honesty and ethics, while only 40 percent of the journalists did.[223] Most of the public believed that politicians could "never" be trusted to do the right thing. Yet the journalists saw the American political process as "a flawed but basically decent means of reconciling different points of view and solving collective problems."[224] They apparently report in a more cynical fashion than they actually feel because of the conventions of contemporary journalism. But the public, while deploring these practices, evidently sees them as reflections of reality. So cynical coverage by the press leads to even more cynical attitudes in the citizenry.[225]

The cynical attitudes have important implications for politics. They probably reduce satisfaction with candidates and officials and reduce turnout in elections. At the same time, they probably increase votes for "outsiders" who present themselves as "nonpoliticians."

Ironically, observes one writer, "The press, which in the long run cannot survive if people lose interest in politics, is acting as if its purpose was to guarantee that people are repelled by public life."[226]

The Media in Time

1690	First newspaper is published in the United States.	**1920s**	Radio and newsmagazines begin. Radio becomes popular, ushering in the era of the mass media.
1741	First magazines, including one by Benjamin Franklin, are published in the United States.	**1933**	President Franklin Roosevelt becomes the first president to cultivate public relations directly by giving "fireside chats." He becomes the most effective president using radio.
1791	The First Amendment, including freedom of the press, is adopted.		
1790s	Party papers begin, with Federalists printing a newspaper and then Jeffersonians printing another in opposition.	**1950s**	Television becomes popular, with most Americans getting their first TV.
1830s	Penny papers begin, with independent businesses printing nonpartisan papers, highlighting human interest, including crime news, and charging one cent.	**1960**	First televised debates between presidential candidates occur. Kennedy's success might have helped him win the race.
		1963	Television networks expand newscasts and emphasize visual interest. For the first time, people say they get more political information from television than any other source.
1840s	Invention of telegraph speeds transmission of news and supplants delivery by horseback. First wire service (AP) is established, providing independent news to papers.	**1968**	Media coverage of the Vietnam War shifts from a hopeful tone to a pessimistic one. Television makes the war the first "living room war" by bringing it into people's homes each night. Coverage highlights the "credibility gap" between what is occurring and what the government is telling citizens.
1861–65	Civil War. Reporters begin their role as eyewitnesses, going to battlefields and reporting what they see and hear rather than relying on what others write. After the war, reporters begin their role as interviewers, conducting the first interview of a president (Andrew Johnson).		
1886	Reporters expand their role as eyewitnesses, camping out on the lawn of President Cleveland's honeymoon hideaway.	**1972**	Watergate story breaks. In 1973 it dominates the news, and in 1974 it forces President Nixon from office. The story marks the high point in the media's investigative journalism.
1890s	Newspapers begin "yellow journalism"—sensationalizing news—to attract readers. Newspapers and magazines begin "muckraking"—exposing corruption by party machines and business monopolies—to crusade for causes. Some newspapers combine the two practices.	**1980**	CNN launches 24-hour news on cable television.
		1981	President Reagan becomes the most effective president using television.
		1990s	Concentration of the media and atomization of the media accelerate. The Internet becomes a major source of news and rumors.
1896	*New York Times* begins the practice of "objectivity" instead of deliberate slanting of news.	**1998**	All Monica, all the time. The saturation coverage marks the low point in the media's fixation on officials' personal conduct.
1901	President Theodore Roosevelt becomes the first president to cultivate press relations and hold press conferences.	**2000**	Largest media merger ever occurs, with AOL buying Time Warner.

Source of information about newspapers through the nineteenth century: Bernard Roshco, *Newsmaking* (Chicago: University of Chicago Press, 1975), 23–57.

Conclusion: Are the Media Responsive?

The media have to be responsive to the people to make a profit. They present the news they think the people want. Because they believe the majority desire entertainment, or at least diversion, rather than education,

they structure the news toward this end. According to a number of studies, they correctly assess their consumers.[227] For the majority who want entertainment, national television and radio networks and local television and radio stations provide it. For the minority who want education, the better newspapers and magazines provide it. Public radio, with its morning and evening newscasts, and public television, with its nightly news-

I KNOW MORE ABOUT THE PRIVATE LIVES OF CELEBRITIES THAN I DO ABOUT ANY GOVERNMENTAL POLICY THAT WILL ACTUALLY AFFECT ME.

I'M INTERESTED IN THINGS THAT ARE NONE OF MY BUSINESS, AND I'M BORED BY THINGS THAT ARE IMPORTANT TO KNOW.

THE MEDIA AIM TO PLEASE.

MAYBE THE ECONOMY SHOULD BE DISCUSSED IN CHEAP MOTEL ROOMS.

cast, also provide quality coverage. In addition, now numerous Web sites on the Internet provide news on demand. The media offer something for everyone.

When officials or citizens get upset with the media, they pointedly ask, "Who elected you?" Journalists reply that the people—their readers or listeners or viewers—"elected them" by paying attention to their news columns or newscasts.

To say the media are responsive, however, is not to say they perform well. Giving the people what they want most is not necessarily serving the country best. "This business of giving people what they want is a dope pusher's argument," says a former president of NBC News. "News is something people don't know they're interested in until they hear about it. The job of a journalist is to take what's important and make it interesting."[228] But people get what they want. As a result, they "seem to 'know' everything now—hearing the same news bulletins repeated around the clock—but they seem to understand precious little of what's really going on."[229] The media personalize and dramatize the news. The result is to simplify the news. Superficial coverage of complex events leaves the public unable to understand these events and, ultimately, unable to force the government to be responsive.

The media give us the big hype—"Hey, listen to this! Here's something new you can't miss!" They reflect a crisis *du jour* mentality in which everything is important but ultimately nothing is important. Almost any political development is important for a day or a week or occasionally a month. But almost no political development is important for long. So the media lurch from a supposed crisis to a real crisis, and back again. In the Clinton years, for example, the media flitted from the caning of a teenager in Singapore to the making of nuclear weapons in North Korea; from a civil war in the former Yugoslavia to the appropriate commemoration for the fiftieth anniversary of the end of World War II with Japan; from the president's haircut in an airplane, which cost $200, to his first budget bill, which reduced the deficit; from the Clintons' possible corruption in the Whitewater land deal to the effort by a friend of the Clintons to get a White House job in the "Travelgate" scandal; from the secrecy of the health care task force to the substance of health care reform; from the denial of a presidential appointment for Zoe Baird because she hired illegal aliens to the denial of a presidential appointment for Kimba Wood because—well, somebody must remember; it was considered important. The headlines and the stories clamoring for attention go by in such a blur that after a while they all become a jumble for many people. They leave no sense of what's actually a crisis, what's only a problem, what's merely an irritant, and what's truly trivial.[230]

Thus, most news coverage is episodic, presenting an event as a single, idiosyncratic occurrence, rather than thematic, presenting the event as an example of a larger pattern. For instance, a story might focus on one hungry person or group of persons rather than on malnutrition as a national problem. Episodic coverage is more common because it is more entertaining—dramatic, with human interest—than thematic coverage. But episodic coverage makes it hard for people to see the connection between problems in society and the actions of government and its officials. Then people do not hold their leaders accountable for addressing or resolving the problems.[231]

Although the media give people what they want, people criticize the media. Almost three-fourths tell pollsters the media get in the way of society's efforts to solve its problems. Only one-fourth say the media help solve the problems.[232]

People have gotten so critical that they rank reporters the lowest in public esteem of any profession (lower even than lawyers).[233] People also express less support for freedom of the press. In 1999 a majority said the press has too much freedom. In fact, a majority went so far as to say the media should not be allowed to endorse or criticize political candidates, and a third went further to say the media should not be allowed to publish a story without government approval.[234] Thus, at the same time the media are competing to give people what they want, their practices are alienating people.

The media's desperation is aggravated by a declining interest in politics and a decreasing number of people who read newspapers or watch newscasts. Although the public is better educated now than in the 1960s, it is less likely to follow the news and less able to answer questions about the government.[235] People under thirty-five especially reflect these trends. To keep these vanishing readers, many newspapers have revamped their formats. While some have improved their quality, more have emulated *USA Today* and reduced their substance to hold the attention spans of younger readers weaned on television. This has disturbing implications. Citizens who are not aware of the news or who do not understand it cannot fulfill their role in a democracy.

These trends come at a time when the media, despite their shortcomings, provide more news than ever and—with journalists better educated and better able to address complex topics—more effective news than ever. Because the media are somewhat responsive and effective, they have become powerful enough to serve as a check on government in many situations. This was evident during the major crises of recent decades. During the war in Vietnam, the media stood up to two presidents when Congress and the courts were relatively passive. During the Watergate scandal, the media led Congress and the courts in standing up to a president. The media serve as a check on the government in countless other situations. As a former government official noted, "Think how much chicanery dies on the drawing board when someone says, 'We'd better not do that; what if the press finds out?' "[236]

EPILOGUE

Evans Pursued the Story

You decided to meet with Admiral Boorda to confront him with your allegations and give him an opportunity to respond. But you did not want to give him much warning, so you did not tell his office why you wanted to meet other than that you were preparing a story about the admiral. Two hours before the meeting, an aide called for more information. Then, you revealed the purpose. Later, you explained, "If you go in too soon, the navy can counterattack, and the opposition gets the story."[237]

After Thomas revealed the purpose of the meeting, Boorda's aides checked with navy officials about the ribbons. A previous secretary of the navy had questioned why admirals wore so many ribbons. When the navy investigated the 257 admirals, it found that many wore ribbons, including the V, who technically should not have. Apparently the navy's practice of awarding ribbons deviated from its regulations. When Boorda was informed last year that he should not have worn the V, he took it off. "It was an honest mistake," he commented to an aide. He has not worn it since then.

After Boorda learned the purpose of the meeting, he went home for lunch. He typed a letter to his wife and another to the sailors. He said to the sailors:

What I am about to do is not very smart but it is right for me. You see, I have asked you to do the right thing, to care for and take care of each other and to stand up for what is good and correct. All of these things require honor, courage and commitment . . . our core values.

I am about to be accused of wearing combat devices on two ribbons I earned during sea tours in Viet Nam. It turns out I didn't really rate them. When I found out I was wrong I immediately took them off but it was really too late. I don't expect any reporters to believe I could make an honest mistake and you may or may not believe it yourselves. That is up to you and isn't all that important now anyway. I've made it not matter in the big scheme of things because I love our navy so much, and you who are the heart and soul of our navy, that I couldn't bear to bring dishonor to you. . . .

Finally, for those who want to tear our navy down, I guess I've given them plenty to write about for a while. But I will soon be forgotten. You, our great navy people, will live on. I am proud of you. I am proud to have led you if only for a short time. I wish I had done it better.

Then Boorda went out to his garden and shot himself in the chest.

At his funeral, Boorda was hailed as "the sailors' sailor." In Washington, however, he was criticized by some for having "thin skin." Yet, as one columnist observed, "Thin skin is the only kind of skin human beings come with."[238]

Newsweek's efforts to pursue the story did not reflect political bias against the navy or the admiral or the changes he was implementing. (Other critics of Boorda did have political motives—opposition to new policies that challenged navy traditions.) Its efforts instead reflected commercial bias. The magazine was trying to attract more readers by running provocative articles by prominent writers.

Of course, *Newsweek* had not even run the article when Boorda decided to kill himself. A columnist for *Newsweek* pointed out, "It is possible [Boorda] could have moved the story in a different direction, or talked the magazine out of publishing anything on the matter at all."[239] Evidently Boorda, who had considerable experience with the press, did not think this approach was possible.

No doubt *Newsweek*'s editors were as surprised as other people when Boorda killed himself. They were just trying to do their jobs. Yet their behavior reflects journalists' mind-set that public officials are not motivated by a desire to serve the public but to advance their career or enhance their power. Moreover, journalists see public officials as insincere. With this mind-set, journalists look for wrongdoing and seek to expose it. Essentially, journalists consider officials fair game for relentless attack.

Yet when journalists themselves come under rare attack from other media, they do not like it any more than officials do. In fact, they are just as thin-skinned as officials are.[240]

Key Terms

symbiotic relationship
adversarial relationship
leaks
scoop
presidential press conference
media events
sound bite
fireside chats

political bias
commercial bias
infotainment
game orientation
setting the agenda
selective perception
media malaise

Further Reading

Brill's Content, a magazine about the media for laypersons, is an interesting and observant watchdog.

Timothy Crouse, *The Boys on the Bus* (New York: Random House, 1972). An irreverent account of press coverage of elections by a writer who reported on the reporters rather than on the candidates along the presidential campaign trail in 1972.

Kathleen Hall Jamieson and David S. Birdsell, *Presidential Debates* (New York: Oxford University Press, 1988). A history of presidential debates and a set of proposals for their reform.

Howard Kurtz, *Spin Cycle: Inside the Clinton Propaganda Machine* (New York: Free Press, 1998). An examination of the Clinton administration's press operation.

John R. MacArthur, *Second Front: Censorship and Propaganda in the Gulf War* (New York: Hill & Wang, 1992). A searing critique of media coverage of the war.

Joe McGinniss, *The Selling of the President 1968* (New York: Simon & Schuster, 1969). An account of the often-comical efforts by Richard Nixon's advisers to transform him into a media candidate.

Electronic Resources

www.msnbc.com
For overall news.

www.nyt.com
The *New York Times,* for in-depth reports on international and national affairs.

www.washingtonpost.com
For political news from the capital.

www.sfgate.com
The *San Francisco Chronicle,* described as an "oasis of attitude" in the world of news.

www.alternet.org
Alternative journalism, for news and opinion not found in most media outlets.

www.slate.com
A "Webzine" with columns and wit and perhaps the best media analysis on the Web.

InfoTrac College Edition

"Kiwi Label"
"Emily's List"
"High-Tech's Link to Lawmaking"
"International Debate Over Transgenic Crops"

Notes

1. Source for information in this "You Are There" is Nick Kotz, "Breaking Point," *The Washingtonian* (December 1996): 94–121.

2. James David Barber, *The Pulse of Politics* (New York: Norton, 1980), 9.

3. Kevin Phillips, "A Matter of Privilege," *Harpers* (January 1977): 95–97.

4. Richard Harwood, "So Many Media, So Little Time," *Washington Post National Weekly Edition,* September 7–13, 1992, p. 28.

5. Thomas R. Dye and L. Hannon Zeigler, *American Politics in the Media Age* (Monterey, Calif.: Brooks/Cole, 1983), 123–124.

6. Edwin Diamond, *The Tin Kazoo* (Cambridge, Mass.: MIT Press, 1975), 13.

7. According to the first nationally representative study, conducted by the Henry J. Kaiser Family Foundation in 1999. "Media Use Almost a Full-time Job for American Youth, Study Finds," *Lincoln Journal-Star* (Knight Ridder Newspapers), November 18, 1999.

8. Doris A. Graber, *Mass Media and American Politics* (Washington, D.C.: Congressional Quarterly, 1980), 2.

9. William Lutz, *Doublespeak* (New York: Harper & Row, 1989), 73–74.

10. Shanto Iyengar, *Is Anyone Responsible? How Television Frames Political Issues* (Chicago: University of Chicago Press, 1991), 1.

11. "Ticker," *Brill's Content* (May 1999): 128.

12. Elizabeth Gleick, "Read All about It," *Time,* October 21, 1998, p. 66.

13. "Ticker," *Brill's Content* (May 1999): 128.

14. Thomas E. Patterson, *The Mass Media Election* (New York: Praeger, 1980), 58–60, 62–63.

15. Michael J. Wolf and Geoffrey Sands, "Fearless Predictions," *Brill's Content* (July/August 1999): 110.

16. Harwood, "So Many Media, So Little Time."

17. Donald Kaul, "Effects of Merger between AOL, Time Warner Will Be Inescapable," *Lincoln Journal-Star* (Tribune Media), January 18, 2000.

18. Howard Kurtz, "When the News Is All in the Family," *Washington Post National Weekly Edition,* January 17, 2000, p. 7.

19. Daniel Okrent, "Happily Ever After?" *Time,* January 24, 2000, p. 39.

20. Otto Friedrich, "Edging the Government out of TV," *Time,* August 17, 1987, p. 58; Edmund L. Andrews, "A New Tune for Radio: Hard Times," *New York Times,* March 1992; Sydney H. Schanberg, "The News You Don't Read," *Washington Post Weekly Edition,* September 6, 1999, p. 21.

21. Benjamin M. Compaine, *Who Owns the Media?* (White Plains, N.Y.: Knowledge Industry Publications, 1979), 11, 76–77; Michael Parenti, *Inventing Reality* (New York: St. Martin's, 1986), 27; Paul Farhi, "You Can't Tell a Book by Its Cover," *Washington Post National Weekly Edition,* December 5–11, 1988, p. 21; Andrews, "A New Tune for Radio."

22. Robert McChesney, "AOL–Time Warner Merger Is Dangerous and Undemocratic," *Lincoln Journal-Star* (Knight Ridder/ Tribune), January 17, 2000.

23. Elizabeth Lesly Stevens, "Mouse.Ke.Fear," *Brill's Content* (December 1998/January 1999): 95.

24. Rifka Rosenwein, "Why Media Mergers Matter," *Brill's Content* (December 1999/January 2000): 94.

25. Dean Alger, *Megamedia: How Giant Corporations Dominate Mass Media, Distort Competition, and Endanger Democracy* (Lanham, Md.: Rowman & Littlefield, 1998).

26. Neil Hickey, "Money Lust," *Columbia Journalism Review* (July/August 1998): 28.

27. Victor Navasky, "Is Big Really Bad? Well, Yes," *Time,* January 24, 2000.

28. Howard Kurtz, "Welcome to Spin City," *Washington Post National Weekly Edition,* March 16, 1998, p. 6.

29. Elizabeth Kolbert, "For Talk Shows, Less News Is Good News," *New York Times,* June 28, 1992, p. E–2.

30. Howard Fineman, "The Power of Talk," *Time,* February 8, 1993, p. 25.

31. "The Vocal Minority in American Politics," Times Mirror Center for the People and the Press, Washington, D.C., July 1993.

32. In addition, she received $50,000 for a book elaborating on her story, $250,000 for posing nude for *Penthouse* magazine, and about $20,000 for appearing on German and Spanish television shows. "Flowers Says She Made Half Million from Story," *Lincoln Journal-Star* (AP), March 21, 1998.

33. Eric Effron, "Sixties Minutes," *Brill's Content* (March 1999): 43.

34. Ernest Tollerson, "Politicians Try to Balance Risk against Rewards of Reaching Talk-Radio Audiences," *New York Times,* March 31, 1996, p. 12.

35. Richard Harwood, "The Growing Irrelevance of Journalists," *Washington Post National Weekly Edition,* November 2–8, 1992, p. 29.

36. Dan Balz, "A '90s Kind of Scandal," *Washington Post National Weekly Edition,* February 2, 1998, p. 8.

37. Tom Rosenstiel, *The Beat Goes On: President Clinton's First Year with the Media* (New York: Twentieth Century Fund, 1994), p. 35. For an extensive examination of this incident, see Dan E. Moldea, *A Washington Tragedy* (New York: Regnery, 1998).

38. Howard Kurtz, "The Story That Wouldn't Stay Buried," *Washington Post National Weekly Edition,* December 1, 1997, p. 12.

39. Kurtz, "Welcome to Spin City."

40. Richard Corliss, "Look Who's Talking," *Time,* January 23, 1995, p. 25.

41. Kurt Anderson, "The Age of Unreason," *New Yorker,* February 3, 1997, p. 42.

42. Dom Bonafede, "Press Paying More Heed to Substance in Covering 1984 Presidential Election," *National Journal,* October 13, 1984, p. 1923.

43. *All Things Considered,* National Public Radio, November 5, 1992.

44. "Comment: Take Five," *New Yorker,* November 23, 1992, p. 4.

45. Thomas M. DeFrank, "Playing the Media Game," *Newsweek,* April 17, 1989, p. 21.

46. Charles Peters, *How Washington Really Works* (Redding, Mass.: Addison-Wesley, 1980), 18.

47. William Greider, "Reporters and Their Sources," *Washington Monthly,* October 1982, pp. 13–15.

48. Elizabeth Drew, "Letter from Washington," *New Yorker,* September 12, 1988, p. 92.

49. Howard Kurtz, "Lying Down on This Job Was Just Fine," *Washington Post National Weekly Edition,* April 19, 1999, p. 13.

50. Ann Devroy, "The Republicans, It Turns Out, Are a Veritable Fount of Leaks," *Washington Post National Weekly Edition,* November 18–24, 1991, p. 23.

51. Daniel Schorr, "A Fact of Political Life," *Washington Post National Weekly Edition,* October 28–November 3, 1991, p. 32.

52. Howard Kurtz, "How Sources and Reporters Play the Game of Leaks," *Washington Post National Weekly Edition,* March 15–21, 1993, p. 25.

53. Steven Brill, "Pressgate," *Brill's Content* (July/August 1998): 123–151; Steven Brill, "At Last, a Leakless Investigation," *Brill's Content* (December 1998/January 1999): 31–34.

54. Brill, "Pressgate," 149.

55. Adam Cohen, "The Press and the Dress," *Time,* February 16, 1998, pp. 51–54.

56. Jonathan Alter, "When Sources Get Immunity," *Newsweek,* January 19, 1987, p. 54.

57. Samuel Kernell, *Going Public: New Strategies of Presidential Leadership* (Washington, D.C.: Congressional Quarterly, 1986), 59.

58. Woodrow Wilson also tried to cultivate correspondents and host frequent sessions, but he did not have the knack for this activity and he scaled back the sessions. Kernell, *Going Public,* 60–61. He did perceive that "[s]ome men of brilliant ability were in the

group, but I soon discovered that the interest of the majority was in the personal and the trivial rather than in principles and policies." James Bennet, "The Flack Pack," *Washington Monthly* (November 1991): 27.

59. Dwight Eisenhower was actually the first president to let the networks televise his press conferences, but he did not do so to reach the public. When he wanted to reach the public, he made a formal speech. The networks found his conferences so untelegenic that they stopped covering the entire session each time. Kernell, *Going Public,* 68.

60. Kernell, *Going Public,* 104.

61. Bennet, "The Flack Pack," 19.

62. Dom Bonafede, " 'Mr. President,' " *National Journal,* October 29, 1988, p. 2756.

63. Garry Wills, ". . . But Don't Treat It as a Game," *Lincoln Journal* (Universal Press Syndicate), March 26, 1993.

64. James Fallows, *Breaking the News: How the Media Undermine American Democracy* (New York: Pantheon, 1996), 196.

65. Charles Hagen, "The Photo Op: Making Icons or Playing Politics?" *New York Times,* February 9, 1992, p. H28.

66. Kiku Adatto, cited in Howard Kurtz, "Networks Adapt to Changed Campaign Role," *Washington Post,* June 21, 1992, p. A19.

67. Lance Morrow, "Time Essay," *Time,* August 18, 1980, p. 78.

68. David Halberstam, "How Television Failed the American Voter," *Parade,* January 11, 1981, p. 8.

69. George E. Reedy, *The Twilight of the Presidency* (New York: New American Library, 1970), 112.

70. Thomas Griffith, "Winging It on Television," *Time,* March 14, 1983, p. 71.

71. "Talking about the Media Circus," *New York Times Magazines,* June 26, 1994, p. 63.

72. W. Lance Bennett, *News: The Politics of Illusion,* 2d ed. (New York: Longman, 1988).

73. Larry J. Sabato, *Feeding Frenzy: How Attack Journalism Has Transformed American Politics* (New York: Free Press, 1991).

74. Deborah Tannen, *The Argument Culture* (New York: Ballantine, 1998), 81.

75. Ibid., 55.

76. Robert J. Bennett, "We Should Scuttle the Partisanship," *Washington Post National Weekly Edition,* March 24, 1997, p. 21.

77. Fallows, *Breaking the News,* pp. 62–63.

78. Joan Konner, "Diane 'Got' Gore. But What Did We Get?" *Brill's Content* (September 1999): 59–60.

79. Joseph N. Cappella and Kathleen Hall Jamieson, *Spiral of Cynicism* (New York: Oxford University Press, 1997), 31.

80. Mary Matalin and James Carville, *All's Fair* (New York: Random House, 1994), 184–185.

81. See Sabato, *Feeding Frenzy,* for additional reasons for this increase.

82. "Ticker," *Brill's Content* (July/August 1998): 152, citing the Project for Excellence in Journalism, "Changing Definitions of News: A Look at the Mainstream Press over 20 Years," March 6, 1998.

83. Fallows, *Breaking the News,* 196.

84. John David Rausch, Jr., "The Pathology of Politics: Government, Press, and Scandal," *Extensions* (University of Oklahoma), (Fall 1990): 11–12.

85. Tannen, *The Argument Culture,* 124.

86. Brill, "Pressgate," 134.

87. William Rivers, "The Correspondents after 25 Years," *Columbia Journalism Review* 1 (Spring 1962): 5.

88. James David Barber, *Presidential Character* (Englewood Cliffs, N.J.: Prentice Hall, 1992), 238.

89. Hedrick Smith, *The Power Game* (New York: Random House, 1988), 403.

90. Timothy J. Russert, "For '92, the Networks Have to Do Better," *New York Times,* March 4, 1990.

91. Smith, *Power Game,* p. 420.

92. Steven K. Weisman, "The President and the Press," *New York Times Magazine,* October 14, 1984, pp. 71–72; Dick Kirschten, "Communications Reshuffling Intended to Help Reagan Do What He Does Best," *National Journal,* January 28, 1984, p. 154.

93. When Reagan ordered the invasion of Grenada in 1983, the administration excluded reporters. For two days the only news that reached the public came from the administration, and it was uniformly positive about both the need for and the success of the invasion. However, in response to criticism from the media, the Pentagon established a pool system for future wars. Representative groups of reporters would be allowed to cover the action and share their information with other media. The military could transport and protect a few pools more easily than a huge number of individual reporters. But what the Pentagon did not admit was that the military, while appearing to cooperate, could control reporters' access to battles, individuals, and other sources of information more easily as well.

94. Howard Kurtz, "The Press Pool's Chilling Effect on Covering the War," *Washington Post National Weekly Edition,* February 18–24, 1991, p. 12; "Keeping It All Pretty Quiet on the Mideastern Front," *Washington Post National Weekly Edition,* February 4–10, 1991, pp. 34–35.

95. Calculated from David Sarasohn, "Not So Smart," *Lincoln Journal* (Newhouse News Service), April 2, 1991.

96. Richard Morin, "The New War Cry: Stop the Press," *Washington Post National Weekly Edition,* February 11–17, 1991, p. 38.

97. Sidney Blumenthal, "The Syndicated Presidency," *New Yorker,* April 5, 1993, p. 45.

98. Brit Hume (NBC News).

99. Howard Kurtz, "Rolling with the Punches from the Press Corps," *Washington Post National Weekly Edition,* January 24–30, 1994, p. 10; James Fallows, "The Media's Rush to Judgment," *Washington Monthly* (January/February 1994): 10–11.

100. Howard Kurtz, "Assessing—and Controlling—the Damage to the Presidency," *Washington Post National Weekly Edition,* February 2, 1998, p. 21.

101. For examination of coverage during Clinton's early time in office, see William Glaberson, "The Capitol Press vs. the President: Fair Coverage or Unreined Adversity?" *New York Times,* June 17, 1993, p. A11; Christopher Georges, "Bad News Bearers," *Washington Monthly,* July/August 1993, pp. 28–34.

102. Tannen, *The Argument Culture,* 54.

103. Stephen Hess, *Live from Capitol Hill!* (Washington, D.C.: Brookings Institution, 1991), 62; Timothy E. Cook, *Making Laws & Making News: Media Strategies in the U.S. House of Representatives* (Washington, D.C.: Brookings Institution, 1989), 2.

104. Hess, *Live from Capitol Hill!* 102.

105. Hendrik Hertzberg, "Comment: The Pot Perplex," *New Yorker,* January 6, 1997, pp. 4–5.

106. Robert Schmidt, "May It Please the Court," *Brill's Content* (October 1999): 74.

107. Ibid., p. 73.

108. Ibid.

109. Edward Jay Epstein, *News from Nowhere* (New York: Random House, 1973), 13.

110. Graber, *Mass Media and American Politics,* 62.

111. Milton Coleman, "When the Candidate Is Black Like Me," *Washington Post National Weekly Edition,* April 23, 1984, p. 9.

112. Roper Organization, "A Big Concern about the Media: Intruding on Grieving Families," *Washington Post National Weekly Edition,* June 6, 1984. Also, see Cappella and Jamieson, *Spiral of Cynicism,* 210. This phenomenon occurs even when individuals are judging the same newspaper, and the pattern holds regardless of the extent to which the paper is slanted in one direction. Russell J.

Dalton, Paul A. Beck, and Robert Huckfeldt, "Partisan Cues and the Media: Information Flows in the 1992 Election," *American Political Science Review* 92 (March 1998): 120–121.

113. Parenti, *Inventing Reality,* chaps. 7–11; Charles E. Lindblom, *Politics and Markets* (New York: Basic Books, 1977); MacDonald, *One Nation under Television;* Dan Nimmo and James E. Combs, *Mediated Political Realities* (New York: Longman, 1983), 135.

114. John R. MacArthur, *Second Front: Censorship and Propaganda in the Gulf War* (New York: Hill & Wang, 1992); James Bennet, "How They Missed That Story," *Washington Monthly,* December 1990, pp. 8–16; Christopher Dickey, "Not Their Finest Hour," *Newsweek,* June 8, 1992, p. 66.

115. Leon V. Sigal, *Reporters and Officials* (Lexington, Mass.: Heath, 1973), 120–121.

116. Lucy Howard, "Slanted 'Line'?" *Newsweek,* February 13, 1989, p. 6. See also Hess, *Live from Capitol Hill!* 50. This tendency is less typical of local news. Trivia buffs might ask who has been the subject of the most cover articles in *Time* magazine—Richard Nixon (fifty-five). "Numbers," *Time,* March 9, 1998, p. 189.

117. Cook, *Making Laws & Making News,* 8.

118. Lichter et al., *The Media Elite,* 21–25. See also Hess, *Live from Capitol Hill!* appendix A, 110–130.

119. John Johnstone, Edward Slawski, and William Bowman, *The Newspeople* (Urbana: University of Illinois Press, 1976), 225–226.

120. Stanley Rothman and S. Robert Lichter, "Media and Business Elites: Two Classes in Conflict?" *The Public Interest* 69 (1982): 111–125; S. Robert Lichter and Stanley Rothman, "Media and Business Elites," *Public Opinion* (October/November 1981): 44.

121. Stephen Hess, *The Washington Reporters* (Washington, D.C.: Brookings Institution, 1981), 89; Lichter et al., *The Media Elite,* 127–128.

122. James Fallows, "The Stoning of Donald Regan," *Washington Monthly* (June 1984): 57. Most individual reporters also probably care more about their career than ideology, but this could lead to bias. In 1976 one media analyst ran into an old friend, an NBC correspondent. When the analyst asked how she was doing, she answered, "Not so great. My candidate lost." That is, the candidate she had covered during the presidential primaries lost his bid for the nomination. Because reporters often follow "their" presidential candidate into office, she lost her chance to become NBC's White House correspondent. Graeme Browning, "Too Close for Comfort?" *National Journal,* October 3, 1992, p. 2243.

123. Parenti, *Inventing Reality,* 38, 56–57.

124. Mark Hertsgaard, "How Ronald Reagan Turned News Hounds into Lap Dogs," *Washington Post National Weekly Edition,* August 29–September 4, 1988, p. 25.

125. Joel Millman, "How the Press Distorts the News from Central America," *Progressive* (October 1984): 20.

126. Epstein, *News from Nowhere,* 206–207. This, however, is less of a problem than it used to be. Hess, *Washington Reporters.*

127. Russell J. Dalton, Paul A. Beck, and Robert Huckfeldt, "Partisan Cues and the Media: Information Flows in the 1992 Presidential Election," *American Political Science Review* 92 (March 1998): 118. Other studies reached similar conclusions. C. Richard Hofstetter, *Bias in the News* (Columbus: Ohio State University Press, 1976); Graber, *Mass Media and Politics,* 167–168; Michael J. Robinson, "Just How Liberal Is the News?" *Public Opinion* (February/March 1983): 55–60; Maura Clancy and Michael J. Robinson, "General Election Coverage: Part I," *Public Opinion* 7 (December/ January 1985): 49–54, 59; Michael J. Robinson, "The Media Campaign, '84; Part II," *Public Opinion* 8 (February/March 1985): 43–48.

128. Clancy and Robinson, "General Election Coverage"; Robinson, "The Media Campaign '84"; Michael J. Robinson, "Where's the Beef? Media and Media Elites in 1984," in *The American Elections of 1984,* ed. Austin Ranney (Durham, N.C.: Duke University Press, 1985), 184; Michael J. Robinson, "News Media Myths and Realities: What Network News Did and Didn't Do in the 1984 General Campaign," in *Elections in America,* ed. Kay Lehman Schlozman (Boston: Allen & Unwin, 1987), 143–170.

129. Ken Auletta, "Inside Story," *New Yorker,* November 18, 1996, p. 55. Most journalists—89 percent, according to one poll—voted for Clinton over Bush, but after the election, the media gave Clinton more negative coverage than they had given Bush in his first eighteen months. "Dealing with Bias in the Press," *Civilization* (February/March 1997): 24–27.

130. Thomas E. Patterson, *Out of Order* (New York: Vintage, 1994), 131.

131. Ibid., 100–107. Another reason was the slump in the economy, which resulted in coverage of the Bush administration trying to defend its economic policies against various critics of these policies. Another reason was the nature of Bush's campaign, which was sharply negative. Bush's attacks sparked a reaction from Clinton's campaign, and journalists included both in their effort to be balanced. The result, however, was more negative statements about Bush than about Clinton. Dalton et al., "Partisan Cues and the Media," 116.

132. "Clinton Gains More Support from Big Papers," *Lincoln Journal-Star* (*New York Times*), October 25, 1992. Contrary to assumptions, there is little relationship between newspapers' editorial endorsements and their news coverage or even their political columns. An endorsement for one candidate does not mean more positive coverage or columns for that candidate, because American media have established a tradition of autonomy in the newsroom. Dalton et al., "Partisan Cues and the Media," 118.

133. Stanley Rothman and S. Robert Lichter, "The Nuclear Energy Debate," *Public Opinion* 5 (August/September 1982): 47–48; Stanley Rothman and S. Robert Lichter, "Elite Ideology and Risk Perception in Nuclear Energy Policy," *American Political Science Review* 81 (June 1987): 383–404.

134. Lichter et al., *The Media Elite,* chap. 7.

135. Sabato, *Feeding Frenzy,* 87, and sources cited therein.

136. Robinson, "Just How Liberal Is the News?" 59.

137. Bruce Nussbaum, "The Myth of the Liberal Media," *Business Week,* November 11, 1996; Paul Starobin, "Bias Basics," *National Review,* October 28, 1996; Fallows, *Breaking the News,* 49.

138. Hofstetter, *Bias in the News;* Hess, *Live from Capitol Hill!* 12–13.

139. Robinson, "Just How Liberal Is the News?" 58; Arthur H. Miller, Edie N. Goldenberg, and Lutz Erbring, "Type-Set Politics," *American Political Science Review* 73 (1979): 69; Patterson, *Out of Order,* 6; Charles M. Tidmarch and John J. Pitney, Jr., "Covering Congress," *Polity* 17 (Spring 1985): 463–483.

140. Richard Morin, "The Big Picture Is Out of Focus," *Washington Post National Weekly Edition,* March 6, 2000, p. 21.

141. Steven Brill, "Quality Control," *Brill's Content* (July/August 1998): 19–20.

142. Patterson, *Out of Order,* 25, 245.

143. "Anchorwoman Verdict Raises Mixed Opinions," *New York Times,* August 9, 1983.

144. Theodore H. White, *America in Search of Itself* (New York: Harper & Row, 1982), 186.

145. James Fallows, "On That Chart," *Nation,* June 3, 1996, p. 15.

146. George F. Will, "Prisoners of TV," *Newsweek,* January 10, 1977, p. 76.

147. Parenti, *Inventing Reality,* 48.

148. "Poll: Reporters Avoid, Soften Stories," *Lincoln Journal Star* (AP), May 1, 2000; David Owen, "The Cigarette Companies: How They Get Away with Murder, Part II," *Washington Monthly* (March 1985): 48–54. Also see Daniel Hellinger and Dennis R. Judd, *The Democratic Facade,* 2d ed. (Belmont, Calif.: Wadsworth, 1994), 59. Through the 1920s, newspapers refrained from pointing out that popular "patent medicines" were usually useless and occasionally

dangerous, because the purveyors bought more advertising than any other business. Mark Crispin Miller, "Free the Media," *Nation,* June 3, 1996, p. 10.

149. Martin A. Linsky, ed., *Television and the Presidential Elections* (Lexington, Mass.: Heath, 1983).

150. "Q & A: Dan Rather on Fear, Money, and the News," *Brill's Content* (October 1998): 117.

151. Barry Sussman, "News on TV: Mixed Reviews," *Washington Post National Weekly Edition,* September 3, 1984, p. 37.

152. Bill Carter, "Networks Fight Public's Shrinking Attention Span," *Lincoln Sunday Journal-Star* (New York Times), September 30, 1990.

153. Epstein, *News from Nowhere,* 4.

154. William A. Henry III, "Requiem for TV's Gender Gap," *Time,* August 22, 1983, p. 57.

155. Tom Jory, "TV Anchorwoman's Suit Exposes Subtle Bias in Hiring," *Lincoln Journal,* July 31, 1983, p. 1A.

156. Marlene Sanders and Marcia Rock, *Waiting for Prime Time: The Women of Television News* (Urbana: University of Illinois Press, 1988), 147–148, cited in Hess, *Live from Capitol Hill!* 120.

157. Robinson, "Just How Liberal Is the News?" 60.

158. "Tidbits and Outrages," *Washington Monthly* (February 1990): 44.

159. Eric Pooley, "Monica's World," *Time,* March 2, 1998, p. 40.

160. Donald Kaul, "The Bad Guys Are Still Winning," *Lincoln Journal Star,* April 4, 1998.

161. Fallows, *Breaking the News,* 201.

162. Lawrie Mifflin, "Crime Falls, but Not on TV," *New York Times,* July 6, 1997, p. E3. According to one researcher, crime coverage is also "the easiest, cheapest, laziest news to cover" because stations just listen to the police radio and then send a camera crew to shoot the story.

163. Molly Ivins, "Don't Moan about the Media, Do Something," *Lincoln Journal-Star* (Fort Worth Star-Telegram), November 1999.

164. Patterson, *Out of Order,* 53–59 and generally.

165. For 1976 presidential campaign: Thomas E. Patterson, *The Mass Media Election* (New York: Praeger, 1980), 24. For 1984 presidential campaign: Henry E. Brady and Richard Johnson, "What's the Primary Message: Horse Race or Issue Journalism?" in *Media and Momentum,* ed. Gary R. Orren and Nelson W. Polsby (Chatham, N.J.: Chatham House, 1987), 127–186. For 1988 presidential campaign: Stephen Ansolabehere, Roy Behr, and Shanto Iyengar, "Mass Media and Elections: An Overview," *American Politics Quarterly* 19 (January 1991): 119. For 1992 presidential campaign and in general: Patterson, *Out of Order.* For 1992 congressional campaigns: Charles M. Tidmarch, Lisa J. Hyman, and Jill E. Sorkin, "Press Issue Agendas in the 1982 Congressional and Gubernatorial Election Campaigns," *Journal of Politics* 46 (November 1984): 1231.

166. S. Robert Lichter, Daniel Amundson, and Richard Noyes, "The Video Campaign: Network Coverage of the 1988 Primaries" (Washington, D.C.: American Enterprise Institute for Public Policy Research, 1988), 65.

167. Lee Sigelman and David Bullock, "Candidates, Issues, Horse Races, and Hoopla: Presidential Campaign Coverage, 1888–1988," *American Politics Quarterly* 19 (January 1991): 5–32. So was emphasis on human interest. In 1846 the *New York Tribune* described the culinary habits of Representative William "Sausage" Sawyer (D-Ohio), who ate a sausage on the floor of the House every afternoon: "What little grease is left on his hands he wipes on his almost bald head which saves any outlay for Pomatum. His mouth sometimes serves as a finger glass, his shirtsleeves and pantaloons being called into requisition as a napkin. He uses a jackknife for a toothpick, and then he goes on the floor again to abuse the Whigs as the British party." Cook, *Making Laws & Making News,* 18–19.

168. Richard Morin, "Toward the Millennium, by the Numbers," *Washington Post National Weekly Edition,* July 7, 1997, p. 35.

169. Patterson, *Out of Order,* 81–82.

170. Parenti, *Inventing Reality,* 15, quoting Malcolm Mac-Dougall, "The Barkers of Snake Oil Politics," *Politics Today* (January/February 1980): 35.

171. Fallows, *Breaking the News,* 162, 27.

172. David S. Broder, "Can We Govern?" *Washington Post National Weekly Edition,* January 31–February 6, 1994, p. 23.

173. Newspaper ads were placed in college papers by deniers, claiming that there is no proof that gas chambers actually existed. The editor of one paper justified accepting the ad by saying, "There are two sides to every issue and both have a place on the pages of any open-minded paper's editorial page." Tannen, *The Argument Culture,* 38. For examination of this phenomenon, see Deborah E. Lipstadt, *Denying the Holocaust: The Growing Assault on Truth and Memory* (New York: Plume, 1993).

174. Kathleen Hall Jamieson, *Dirty Politics: Deception, Distraction, Democracy* (New York: Oxford University Press, 1992), 184–185.

175. Kathleen Hall Jamieson, quoted in Fallows, *Breaking the News,* 224.

176. Cappella and Jamieson, *Spiral of Cynicism.*

177. Fallows, *Breaking the News,* 133.

178. Howard Kurtz, "Asleep at the Switch," *Washington Post National Weekly Edition,* December 21–27, 1992, p. 6.

179. Larry Martz, "For the Media, a Pyrrhic Victory," *Newsweek,* June 22, 1992, p. 32. See also Hobart Rowen, "Uncle Sam's Underwriter," *Washington Post National Weekly Edition,* May 15–21, 1989, p. 5.

180. Tannen, *The Argument Culture,* 286.

181. Howard Kurtz, quoted in Tannen, *The Argument Culture,* 29.

182. Serious observers did criticize Clinton for giving in too soon in some matters, but journalists' characterizations went beyond questions about tactics.

183. Epstein, *News from Nowhere,* 179, 195.

184. T. R. Reid, "Media Wrong about Yellowstone," *Lincoln Journal* (Washington Post), July 24, 1989.

185. David L. Altheide, "Format and Symbol in Television Coverage of Terrorism in the United States and Great Britain," *International Studies Quarterly* 31 (1987): 161–176.

186. John Horn, "Campaign Coverage Avoids Issues," *Lincoln Sunday Journal-Star,* September 25, 1988. Another survey found that 28 percent of women change channels every time during commercial breaks, while 40 percent of men do. "Ticker," *Brill's Content* (September 1999): 128.

187. John Eisendrath, "An Eyewitness Account of Local TV News," *Washington Monthly* (September 1986): 21.

188. Michael Deaver, "Sound-Bite Campaigning: TV Made Us Do It," *Washington Post National Weekly Edition,* November 7–13, 1988, p. 34.

189. Hess, *Live from Capitol Hill!,* 34.

190. Fred Friendly, quoted on *All Things Considered,* National Public Radio, March 4, 1998.

191. Donald L. Shaw and Maxwell E. McCombs, *The Emergence of American Political Issues: The Agenda-Setting Function of the Press* (St. Paul, Minn.: West, 1977). For a review of agenda-setting research, see Everett M. Rogers and James W. Dearing, "Agenda-Setting Research: Where Has It Been, Where Is It Going?" *Communication Yearbook* 11 (Newberry Park, Calif.: Sage, 1988), 555–594.

192. Lutz Erbring, Edie N. Goldenberg, and Arthur H. Miller, "Front-Page News and Real-World Clues: A New Look at Agenda-Setting by the Media," *American Journal of Political Science* 24 (February 1980): 16–49.

193. Michael Bruce MacKuen and Steven Lane Coombs, *More Than News* (Beverly Hills: Sage, 1981), 140; Rogers and Dearing, "Agenda-Setting Research," 572–576; G. E. Lang and K. Lang, *The*

Battle for Public Opinion (New York: Columbia University Press, 1983), 58–59.

194. Richard Morin, "Public Enemy No. 1: Crime," *Washington Post National Weekly Edition*, January 24–30, 1994, p. 37; Molly Ivins, "Hard Questions, Easy Answers," *Lincoln Journal* (Creators Syndicate), July 7, 1994; Richard Morin, "A Public Paradox on the Drug War," *Washington Post National Weekly Edition,* March 23, 1998, p. 35.

195. Shanto Iyengar and Donald R. Kinder, *News That Matters* (Chicago: University of Chicago Press, 1987), 42–45.

196. Erbring et al., "Front-Page News," 38; MacKuen and Coombs, *More Than News,* 128–137.

197. Rogers and Dearing, "Agenda-Setting Research," 569; MacKuen and Coombs, *More Than News,* 101; Erbring et al., "Front-Page News," 38.

198. Rogers and Dearing, "Agenda-Setting Research," 577, citing Jack L. Walker, "Setting the Agenda in the U.S. Senate," *British Journal of Political Science* 7 (October 1977): 423–445. See also Cook, *Making Laws & Making News,* 116, 130–131.

199. Michael J. Robinson and Margaret A. Sheehan, *Over the Wire and on TV* (New York: Russell Sage Foundation and Basic Books, 1983); Robinson, "The Media Campaign, '84," 45–47.

200. Thomas Griffith, "Leave Off the Label," *Time,* September 19, 1984, p. 63.

201. After one term, however, Schmitt was defeated by an opponent whose slogan was "What on Earth has he ever done?"

202. Doris A. Graber, "Kind Pictures and Harsh Words: How Television Presents the Candidates," in *Elections in America,* ed. Kay Lehman Schlozman (Boston: Allen & Unwin, 1987), 141.

203. Ibid., 116.

204. Anthony Lewis, quoted in Larry J. Sabato, "Open Season: How the News Media Cover Presidential Campaigns in the Age of Attack Journalism," in *Under the Watchful Eye,* ed. Mathew D. McCubbins (Washington, D.C.: CQ Press, 1992), 146.

205. Tannen, *The Argument Culture,* 79–83.

206. See the excellent summary found in Stephen Ansolabehere, Roy Behr, and Shanto Iyengar, "Mass Media and Elections," *American Politics Quarterly* 19 (January 1991): 109–139.

207. Bruce Buchanan, *Electing a President: The Markle Commission Report on Campaign '88* (Austin: University of Texas Press, 1990); Montague Kean, *30-Second Politics* (New York: Praeger, 1989). Marion Just, Lori Wallach, and Ann Crigler, "Thirty Seconds or Thirty Minutes: Political Learning in an Election," paper presented at the Midwest Political Science Association Meeting, April 1987, Chicago.

208. In the Democratic race in 1976, Carter finished second to "uncommitted" in the Iowa caucuses. This was enough to give him twenty-three times more coverage in *Time* and *Newsweek,* and five times more coverage on network television, than any of his rivals. Finishing first by just 4 percent in the New Hampshire primary landed him on the covers of *Time* and *Newsweek* and brought him twenty-five times more coverage on network television than the runner-up. David Paletz and Robert Entrum, *Media—Power—Politics* (New York: Macmillan, 1981), 35*ff.*

209. Patterson, *Out of Order,* 44.

210. Ansolabehere et al., "Mass Media and Elections," pp. 128–129; Christine F. Ridout, "The Role of Media Coverage of Iowa and New Hampshire in the 1988 Democratic Nomination," *American Politics Quarterly* 19 (January 1991): 45–46, 53–54; Marc Howard Ross, "Television News and Candidate Fortunes in Presidential Nomination Campaigns," *American Politics Quarterly* 20 (January 1992): 69–98.

211. Henry Brady, "Chances, Utilities, and Voting in Presidential Primaries," paper delivered at the Annual Meeting of the Public Choice Society, Phoenix, Arizona, cited in Ansolabehere et al., "Mass Media and Elections"; Bartels, *Presidential Primaries and the*

Dynamics of Public Choice (Princeton, N.J.: Princeton University Press, 1988).

212. Lee Sigelman and Carol K. Sigelman, "Judgments of the Carter-Reagan Debate," *Public Opinion Quarterly* 48 (1984): 624–628.

213. Theodore H. White, *The Making of the President 1960* (New York: Atheneum, 1961), 333.

214. John R. Zaller, "Monica Lewinsky's Contribution to Political Science," *PS: Political Science & Politics* (June 1998): 182–189.

215. MacKuen and Coombs, *More Than News,* 222.

216. For a review, see MacKuen and Coombs, *More Than News,* 147–161.

217. Robert S. Erickson, "The Influence of Newspaper Endorsements in Presidential Elections," *American Journal of Political Science* 20 (May 1976): 207–233; Dalton et al., "Partisan Cues and the Media."

218. David Barker, "The Talk Radio Community," *Social Science Quarterly* 79 (June 1998): 261–272; C. Richard Hofstetter, "Political Talk Radio, Situational Involvement, and Political Mobilization," *Social Science Quarterly* 79 (June 1998): 273–286.

219. Benjamin I. Page, Robert Y. Shapiro, and Glenn R. Dempsey, "What Moves Public Opinion?" *American Political Science Review* 81 (March 1987): 23–43. Critical news and commentaries about presidents seem to lower their popularity. Darrell M. West, "Television and Presidential Popularity in America," *British Journal of Political Science* 21 (April 1991): 199–214. Even television's "framing" of events, as isolated incidents or parts of patterns, affects viewers' opinions about these events. Shanto Iyengar, *Is Anyone Responsible? How Television Frames Political Issues* (Chicago: University of Chicago Press, 1991).

220. Iyengar, *Is Anyone Responsible?* chaps. 6, 8.

221. Kathleen Hall Jamieson, quoted in Howard Kurtz, "Tuning Out the News," *Washington Post National Weekly Edition,* May 29–June 4, 1995, p. 6; William Raspberry, "Blow-by-Blow Coverage," *Washington Post National Weekly Edition,* November 6–12, 1995, p. 29.

222. Michael J. Robinson, "Public Affairs Television and the Growth of Political Malaise," *American Political Science Review* 70 (1976): 409–432; Miller et al., "Type-Set Politics."

223. "Study: Public More Cynical Than Media," *Champaign-Urbana News Gazette (New York Times),* May 22, 1995.

224. Fallows, *Breaking the News,* 202–203.

225. Also, see Cappella and Jamieson, *Spiral of Cynicism.*

226. Fallows, *Breaking the News,* 247.

227. Graber, *Mass Media,* 244; Doris Graber, *Processing News: How People Tame the Information Tide* (New York: Longman, 1984). A 1993 survey concluded that almost half of Americans over sixteen have such limited reading and math skills that they are unfit for most jobs. One task the survey included was to paraphrase a newspaper story. Many people could scan the story but not paraphrase it when they finished it. Paul Gray, "Adding Up the Under-Skilled," *Time,* September 20, 1993, p. 75.

228. Reuven Frank, quoted in Neil Hickey, "Money Lust," *Columbia Journalism Review* (July/August 1998): 35.

229. Greider, "Reporters and Their Sources," p. 19.

230. Idea for this paragraph from James Fallows, "Did You Have a Good Week?" *Atlantic Monthly* (December 1994): 32, 34.

231. Iyengar, *Is Anyone Responsible?*

232. "The New Political Landscape," *Times Mirror Center for the People & the Press* (October 1994): 4.

233. Joe Klein, "Dizzy Days," *New Yorker,* October 5, 1998, p. 45.

234. Marta W. Aldrich, "Support for Media Freedoms Waning," *Lincoln Journal-Star* (AP), July 4, 1999.

235. Stephen Earl Bennett, "Trends in Americans' Political Information," *American Politics Quarterly* 17 (October 1989): 422–435;

Richard Zoglin, "The Tuned-Out Generation," *Time,* July 9, 1990, p. 64.

236. Peters, *How Washington Really Works,* 32.

237. Source for the epilogue, except where noted otherwise, is Kotz, "Breaking Point."

238. Tannen, *The Argument Culture,* 82.

239. Ibid., 74.

240. Regular reading of *Brill's Content* provides numerous examples. Another example comes from Jeffrey Toobin, *A Vast Conspiracy: The Real Story of the Sex Scandal That Nearly Brought Down a President* (New York: Random House, 1999), 248. After the 1992 election, Linda Bloodworth Thomason, a Hollywood supporter of Bill Clinton, produced a short film for the inauguration. The film included a series of sound bites from Washington journalists during the campaign, dismissing Clinton as "unelectable" and "dead meat." Although Thomason apparently regarded the film as "a harmless needle at some puffed up egos," some of the journalists regarded it as "an act of war." In Toobin's view, the controversy over the film, which poisoned the relationship between the president and the press from the beginning, reflected the thin skins of the press corps.

Interest Groups

YOU ARE THERE

Do You Make More Concessions, or Do You Fight?

You are Steven Goldstone, the CEO of RJR Nabisco. Your company owns RJ Reynolds, the nation's second largest tobacco company. It is June 1998, and you and the tobacco industry, historically one of the strongest and most powerful interests in Washington, are faced with paying billions of dollars in damages, strict regulation of tobacco advertising, regulation of nicotine as a drug, and heavy fines if youth smoking does not decrease over the next ten years. In the past, you might have been able to stave off such threats, but today you are willing to accept higher taxes and government restrictions, if they are coupled with protection from unending lawsuits with the potential to bankrupt the industry. But you are not in a position to make demands.

Public opinion has turned against you, and you have lost major allies in Congress. Recent polls show that more than 70 percent of Americans, many of them smokers, distrust tobacco companies and believe they are run by greedy executives who make a profit from marketing cigarettes to children and teens. Indeed, one news article labeled the tobacco industry "the Libya of American commerce."[1] This view is supported by research that shows that Joe Camel, an RJ Reynolds' creation, is as recognizable to six-year-olds as Mickey Mouse. Your industry's image has also been tarnished because you knew of the dangers of smoking long before warnings appeared on cigarettes. But the companies suppressed the evidence of health risks and publicly denied that there were any. Many Americans recall you and your fellow CEOs swearing before a congressional committee that cigarettes are not addictive. Recent disclosure of internal company documents confirms that your industry did indeed target teenagers with ads—and with some success. Three thousand teens and preteens begin smoking every day, a statistic the president has labeled "a national tragedy."

Republicans in Congress, once your staunch supporters, are also turning away. House Speaker Newt Gingrich recently told you and other CEOs that the party would not protect you against lawsuits. Gingrich, whose father and grandfather died of lung cancer, is fearful that protection for tobacco companies will lead to other industries descending on Washington seeking

Some interest groups are loosely organized and fleeting like this group of students who rallied in support of Clinton-Gore in the 1996 presidential election campaign.

Damian Dovarganes, AP/Wide World Photos

In 1773 a group of colonists organized to protest British taxes on tea by throwing tea into Boston Harbor. In 1989 groups organized to protest a congressional pay increase by sending teabags to their representatives in Washington.

© 1989 Ken Heinen

useful for those who wish to organize citizens but who lack financial resources for more sophisticated approaches.[13] For example, members and sympathizers of militia groups are able to use the Internet to keep each other informed about group activities.

The government is also important to group formation. Government efforts to deal with problems often prompt the organization of groups opposed to such efforts. In addition, government provides direct financial assistance to some groups, particularly nonprofit organization. Groups as diverse as the American Council of Education, the National Governors Association, and the National Council of Senior Citizens obtain a large percentage of their funds through federal grants and contracts.[14]

Group organizers also play a role in group formation.[15] These entrepreneurs often come from established groups. They gain experience and then strike out on their own. Many civil rights activists of the 1950s and early 1960s founded organizations in the late 1960s. Some used their skills to organize groups against the war in Vietnam and later to organize groups for women's rights and environmental causes.[16] Thus, the formation of one group often opens the door to the formation of others.

Why People Join

Some people join a group because of the group's political goals or cause. But many join for economic and social reasons.[17] Some groups offer monetary benefits to members such as discounted prices for goods and services. The large nonfarm membership of the Farm Bureau often is attributed to the cut-rate insurance policies offered through the organization.[18] The American Association of Retired Persons (AARP) provides health, home, and auto insurance; a motor club; a travel service; investment counseling; discount drugs and medicines; and a magazine. These services attract members and generate millions of dollars for the organization. Two-thirds of the AARP's revenue comes from business activities that provide discount services to members. Groups also provide social benefits. Some people join groups to make friends.

Because members pay dues, providing groups with resources to accomplish their goals and enhance their influence with government, most groups provide a mix of benefits in an effort to maximize their membership. The National Rifle Association (NRA) lobbies against gun regulation and control. Some people join for this reason. Others join to secure other NRA services: *The American Rifleman* (a monthly magazine), a hunter's information service, low-cost firearm insurance, membership in local gun clubs, and shooting competitions.[19] Still others join because they enjoy associating with fellow gun enthusiasts.

Some people join groups because they are coerced. For example, in many states lawyers must join the state bar association to practice law.

Who Joins?

Not all people are equally likely to join groups.[20] Those with higher incomes and education are more likely to belong. They can afford membership dues, have the leisure necessary to take part, and have the social and intellectual skills that facilitate group participation. They also appear more attractive to many groups and therefore are more apt to be recruited. Whites more often belong to groups than blacks, but mostly because of their higher average income and education.[21]

Have Americans Stopped Joining?

Americans still join organized groups but at a lower rate than previously.[22] Church membership and church-related activities have declined over the past twenty years. Membership in labor unions, once the most common organizational affiliation among American workers, has been declining for nearly four decades. Membership in the PTA has decreased during the past generation. In general, fewer people are joining and volunteering for a variety of civic and fraternal organizations. The declining impulse to join with others in common pursuits may even have influenced recreational activity. Although more Americans than ever bowl, league bowling is down by more than 40 percent. If the decline represented just a loss of revenue from the pizza and beer consumed by leagues, only bowling proprietors would care. However, the decline also means the loss of close personal relationships that foster discussion of public issues and trust among citizens, which are important to the success of government.

Some argue that the decline in membership in organized groups is not a serious problem, because informal social ties provide the same opportunity.[23] Yet people today claim that they are busier than ever before and that, between their work life and their family life, they have little time for other pursuits. Women's lives, in particular, have changed over the past generation, with most women now in the paid workforce. Women used to be the backbone of most local civic, religious, political, and educational groups, but working women now have less time to devote to such volunteer activity.

While formal membership in voluntary organizations is down, membership in mass organizations is increasing.[24] Many of these organizations are "checkbook organizations," in which members' only link to the organization is the occasional check they send to support it. They pay dues but do not interact with each other. Although these organizations can be successful politically, the benefits of social interaction are lost. Members do not discuss and share information that helps in discerning one's real stake in public affairs and politics.

Types of Interest Groups

Interest groups come in all sizes. Some have large memberships, such as the American Federation of Labor–Congress of Industrial Organizations (AFL-CIO) with thirteen million members. Others have small memberships, such as the Mushroom Growers Association with fourteen. Some have no members at all.

Corporations have no members at all but act as interest groups when they lobby government.[25] Some groups lobby on behalf of specific interests and are funded by the government, private foundations, other groups, or fees but have no members. The Children's Defense Fund (CDF) is one example. Founded in 1973, it is funded entirely from private funds and lobbies on behalf of children.[26]

Some groups have "checkbook" members, who send money but have no say in group decisions. Many **political action committees (PACs)** operate this way.

They raise money through direct mail and channel it to political candidates. How the money is spent is determined solely by the organization's leaders.

Some interest groups are formally organized, with appointed or elected leaders, regular meetings, and dues-paying members. Some are large corporations whose leaders are the corporate officers hired by boards of directors. Others have no leaders and few prescribed rules.

Thus, interest groups can be distinguished according to their membership and organizational structure. They also can be distinguished by their goals. Some groups pursue economic goals, primarily of benefit to their members. Others pursue political goals or causes that have consequences for all of us or, at least, are not limited to those who hold membership in the group.

Private Interest Groups

Private interest groups seek economic benefits for their members or clients. Three examples are business, labor, and agriculture.

Business

Business organizations are the most numerous and most powerful interest groups (see Figure 1). They spend huge amounts of money lobbying government. Some have argued that politics is essentially a confrontation between business and government.[27] Business seeks to maximize profit, whereas it is government's job to protect society from profit-seeking businesses.

Today, however, there is little confrontation between the two. While the Republican Party has traditionally favored business, in recent years the Democrats have also.[28] In spite of who occupies the White House or which party controls Congress, business has generally done well. The shift reflects business's increasing financial contribution to Democratic candidates; the election of moderate and conservative Democrats, like Clinton, sympathetic to business; and a general climate of opinion in the nation favorable to business and hostile to labor. With President Clinton's support, business won major international trade agreements, including "most favored nation" trading privileges for China. Labor and other groups protested serious human rights violations by China and the prospect the agreement will result in a loss of American jobs as firms transfer manufacturing to sites where labor costs are lower. While business has channeled increased campaign resources to Democrats, it continues to give more heavily to Republicans and is more committed to the Republican Party.

Labor

Organized labor is the principal competitor with business, but runs a distant second in influence. Although the United States has over one hundred labor unions, the AFL-CIO is the most important politically. It is a confederation of trade and industrial unions with a staff of five hundred and some of the most skillful lobbyists in Washington. Through its Committee on Political Education (COPE), it provides substantial sums of money as well as a pool of campaign workers to candidates for public office, typically Democrats. In the 2000 general election, the union spent nearly $40 million on campaign literature, phone banks to get out the vote, television issue aids, and voter registration.[29] The goal was to elect candidates sympathetic to labor.

The political influence of labor unions has waned considerably since the 1960s. One reason is that membership in unions, even though it has increased in recent years, continues to decline as a percentage of the workforce.[30] Only 14 percent of the nonagricultural workforce belongs to a union (see Figure 2). Another reason for the decline in membership is the loss to foreign countries of manufacturing jobs, in which unions have traditionally been strong, and an increase in service jobs, in which unions have been weak or nonexistent. Another reason is antiunion business practices. Many businesses are hostile to the prospect of their workers organizing and punish their employees who promote it. While illegal, such violations are seldom prosecuted. Court decisions have made it difficult, if not impossible,

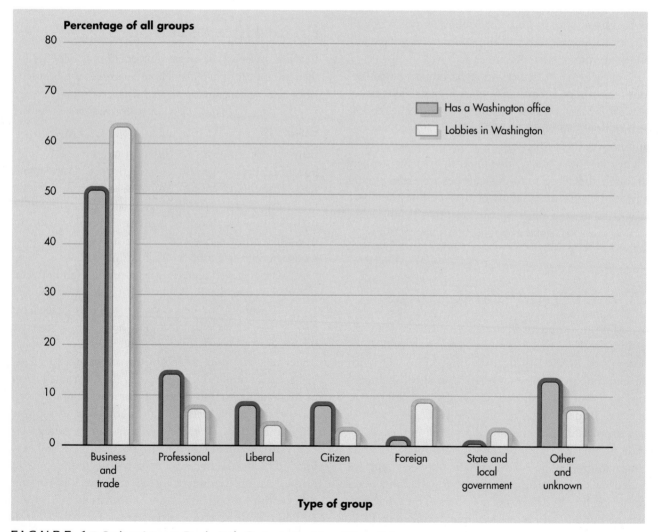

FIGURE 1 ■ *Business Interests Dominate the Contemporary Interest Group System*

Note: Groups with a Washington office number 2,810, and 6,601 groups lobby there. "Liberal" groups are those representing women, minorities, the poor, labor, and the elderly. "Citizen" includes public interest groups such as Common Cause.

SOURCE: K. L. Schlozman and J. T. Tierney, *Organized Interests and American Democracy* (New York: Harper & Row, 1986), p. 67.

IDA BRAYMAN
17 YEARS OLD

who was shot & killed by an Employer Feb. 5th 1913 during the great struggle of the Garment Workers of Rochester.

UNITED GARMENT AMERICA 60

Copyrigted 1913 by U. G. W. Local 14 Rochester N. Y.

This postcard commemorates the death of a seventeen-year-old woman striking for recognition of her union, an eight-hour day, and extra pay for overtime and holidays.
Gotham Book Mart, New York

for workers to organize.[31] Where employers play by the rules, such as those that employ teachers and government workers, union membership has increased. Business and the press have also convinced Americans that unions are something working men and women do not need.[32]

Labor's political influence has also declined as states in the South and Southwest, where the population is traditionally hostile to unions, have gained population and representation in Congress, while states in the North, with populations more sympathetic to unions, have lost representation. This trend is likely to continue. Global competition has also hurt unions, at least with respect to collective bargaining. Fearful of losing their jobs or putting their employer at a disadvantage in a competitive market, members are reluctant to strike. Without the threat of strikes, there is little reason to heed labor's demands or for employees to consider joining unions.

To expand their membership, unions have turned to the low-wage service sector. Labor won a major victory in 1999 when seventy-five thousand home nursing employees voted to be represented by the Service Employees International Union, making it the third largest union in the nation.[33] Unions are also expanding into the ranks of high-tech and professional workers. Efforts are under way to organize computer specialists where they are highly concentrated as in Silicon Valley.[34] Doctors employed by HMOs as well as those in private practice are organizing.[35] Even graduate teaching assistants at the nation's major universities are organizing for purposes of collective bargaining over wages and working conditions.

Agriculture

Agricultural interests are represented by a number of general and specialized groups. Some groups support government subsidies to help farmers, and others oppose such help.

The American Farm Bureau Federation, the largest of the general agriculture interest groups, began when the federal government established the agricultural extension service with agents in rural locations to help farmers. To encourage cooperation with agents, the government offered grants to states that organized county farm bureaus. By 1919 a national organization was formed.

Despite its roots, the Farm Bureau today is a conservative organization dominated by wealthy farmers with large land holdings and, as a result generally opposes big government. At the same time, many of its members benefit from government subsidies.

The National Farmers' Union, which is considerably smaller than the Farm Bureau, represents small farming interests. It strongly supports government subsidies to farmers. The American Agriculture Movement (AAM), which began as a protest movement by farmers who were badly hurt by falling prices in the mid-1970s, also speaks out primarily on issues that benefit small farmers and ranchers.[36]

Along with the general interest groups, hundreds of commodity organizations promote specific products and operate much like business trade associations. Examples include cattle, cotton, milk, tobacco, and wool producers. Large agribusiness firms such as Cargill also have powerful lobbies in Washington.

At the start of the twenty-first century, American agriculture is dominated by agribusiness and corporate farms. The individual small farmer is playing a smaller role and has relatively little political clout.

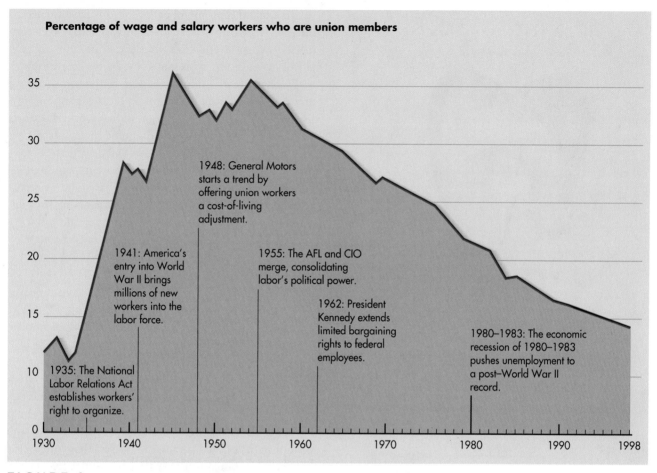

Percentage of wage and salary workers who are union members

35

30

25

1948: General Motors
starts a trend by
offering union workers
a cost-of-living
adjustment.

20

1941: America's
entry into World
War II brings
millions of new
workers into the
labor force.

1955: The AFL and CIO
merge, consolidating
labor's political power.

15

1962: President
Kennedy extends
limited bargaining
rights to federal
employees.

1980–1983: The economic
recession of 1980–1983
pushes unemployment to
a post–World War II
record.

10

1935: The National
Labor Relations Act
establishes workers'
right to organize.

0

1930   1940   1950   1960   1970   1980   1990   1998

FIGURE 2 ■ *Union Membership Has Decreased*

SOURCES: Christoph Blumrich, *Newsweek*, September 5, 1983, p. 51; *Statistical Abstract of the United States, 1990; Lincoln Journal,* March 1993.

Public Interest Groups

Public interest groups lobby for political and social causes. If they succeed, benefits are shared more widely than by just the members of the group. For example, the National Taxpayers Union lobbies for reduced taxes not only for its members but for everyone who pays taxes. Amnesty International lobbies for the rights of political prisoners around the world even though none of its members are prisoners. Although nearly all groups think of themselves as pursuing the public interest, the label applies only to those working for other than personal or corporate interests. However, "public interest" does not mean that a majority of the public necessarily favors the goals of these groups.

Public interest groups increased dramatically in number and size during the late 1960s and early 1970s.[37] Now they number more than 2,500, with forty million members.[38] Several factors account for this surge. Americans were becoming increasingly distrustful of government, which appeared to favor special interests over more general interests. The need for a balance between

the two led many to join public interest groups. Many middle-class Americans also had the financial means to support public interest groups. The new technology mentioned earlier also made it possible to reach and mobilize large numbers of them.

While many of the public interest groups that were established during the 1960s and 1970s were "shoestring" operations staffed by idealistic social reformers with few professional skills, the public interest organizations of today have larger budgets and memberships and a cadre of professionals—attorneys, management consultants, direct mail fund-raisers, and communications directors—handling day-to-day operations and seeking to influence government with a variety of strategies and tactics.[39]

Multiple-Issue Groups

Some public interest groups are multiple-issue groups, involved with a broad range of issues. Others have a narrower focus and are often referred to as single-issue groups. In this section, we provide some examples of well-known multiple-issue groups.

Women's Groups Groups advocating women's equality range from large, mass-based organizations with a broad agenda, such as the National Organization for Women (NOW), to much smaller groups with very specific interests such as electing women to public office.

NOW is the largest women's group with 250,000 total members and chapters in all fifty states.[40] It is well organized with field representatives and organizers, researchers, lobbyists, and specialists in various policy areas such as reproductive freedom and economic rights.

NOW is funded largely from membership dues but has actively solicited funds by mail. It also receives income from subscriptions and selling such things as T-shirts and posters. Private foundations interested in promoting women's rights also provide significant funding.

Although NOW began as a protest movement, today its focus is on lobbying at the national, state, and local levels. It provides leadership training and education for local and state groups and works with a shifting coalition of other women's rights groups.

In recent years the women's movement has divided between groups pushing an ideological agenda, such as NOW, which continues to see abortion as a major concern, and more pragmatic groups, such as the National Women's Political Caucus, which sees its task as electing women to public office regardless of their stands on the issues.

EMILY—short for "Early Money Is Like Yeast" (it makes the dough rise)—is an organization that recruits, trains, and endorses pro-choice Democratic women candidates and then works to fund and elect them to public office. The organization holds seminars for candidates, campaign managers, and press secretaries. It has helped elect five women to the Senate and thirty-four

The first wave of women's organizations campaigned for women's right to vote. Here, some of twenty thousand marchers parade for women's rights in New York City in 1917.

Corbis-Bettmann

to the House. In 1994 it contributed over $8 million to Democratic candidates, the largest contributor to the party. In 1996 it spent $10 million to get out the vote.[41]

Religious Groups Religious groups often lobby on political issues. The National Council of Churches, representing liberal Protestant denominations, has spoken out on civil rights, human rights, and other social issues. Catholic groups have been active in both antiabortion and antinuclear movements. Jewish groups have been involved in lobbying for liberal issues, such as the rights of workers and minorities.

Jewish groups have been particularly active in lobbying for Israel. Since its beginning in 1951, the pro-Israel lobby has lost on only three key decisions, all involving the sale of U.S. arms to Egypt and Saudi Arabia. The success of Jewish groups in lobbying for Israel reflects their commitment, organization, and political skill, and an opposition Arab lobby that is weak by comparison.[42]

Conservative Christian groups have had an especially big impact on American politics in recent years. Identified by a "born again" experience, a desire to win converts, and a literal interpretation of the Bible and spurred by what they saw as a decline in traditional values, members of the Christian right became active in politics in the 1970s.[43] The National Association of Evangelicals, representing conservative Protestant denominations, gained in visibility and prestige as the membership in conservative churches increased while membership in mainline churches declined.[44]

Opposed to abortion, divorce, homosexuality, and women's rights, conservative Christians were the major force behind the effort of television evangelist Pat Robertson to win the Republican presidential nomination in 1988. Following his loss of the nomination, Robertson converted a mailing list of two million names into the Christian Coalition. Unlike the religious right groups of the 1980s, which were primarily concerned with spreading their message through television and radio, the Coalition has sought to win control of the Republican Party. By 1992, the organization had gained dominance or leverage in twenty state parties.[45]

The Coalition recruits members and communicates its message through schools, newspapers, magazines, radio and television stations, and thousands of politically mobilized churches. The organization prides itself as a counterweight to what it describes as the "liberal establishment" controlled by "secular humanists who exert every effort to debase and eliminate Bible-based Christianity from society."[46] To achieve its goals, the Coalition

raises money for political candidates, registers voters, operates phone banks to get out the vote, and grades legislators.[47] Since 1994, it has distributed in churches on the Sunday before the election voter guides that rate Republican and Democratic candidates on key issues. The strategy became controversial in 1998 when many church pastors refused to allow the guides to be distributed. Claiming that the guides were biased in favor of Republicans, they were concerned about involvement in partisan political activity that could cause the loss of their tax-exempt status (although no churches have).[48] Robertson and the Coalition were outspokenly critical of President Clinton during the impeachment process, calling on him to resign and requesting Christians to send money to make sure that he did.[49]

The Coalition is not as uncompromising or singularly motivated by moral issues as it once was.[50] Its backing in 2000 of George W. Bush for the Republican presidential nomination over several other candidates more closely identified with the Christian right is one indication. The shift represents a desire to broaden its appeal. At the same time, it may weaken the organization because some members are agitated by efforts to merge the group's family values agenda with the traditional economic concerns of the Republican Party.[51] The group remains, however, the most powerful organization in the Republican Party.

The Interfaith Alliance began in 1994 to counter the message and political activity of the Christian Coalition and other conservative religious groups. Comprised of mainstream and minority religious and secular groups, it has chapters in seventeen states and represents hundreds of churches, faith, and civic organizations. The group holds rallies and public forums dealing with family values, poverty, and discrimination. It opposes prayer in schools but takes no position on abortion. Like the Christian Coalition, it produces voter guides and campaign literature. The organization elected members to local school boards and was active in a number of presidential primaries in 1996.[52]

Gays and Lesbians Gay rights organizations have a shorter history than most other major political groups. The first groups formed after World War II in an era when gays were labeled as deviates on the rare occasions when they came to public attention. For example, in 1954, after a raid of a bar where gay men congregated, a Miami newspaper headline read "Perverts Seized in Bar Raids." Early gay and lesbian groups focused largely on sharing information about how to survive and how to fight police repression.[53]

In the middle 1960s, a few gays followed the example of the civil rights movement and organized small public demonstrations. Other gays argued that such demonstrations undermined the safety and well-being of the homosexual subculture, which then existed underground in many large cities. Nonetheless, during the 1960s the gay rights movement became more radical and visible. Like Vietnam War protesters, women's rights advocates, and civil rights activists, many gays embarked upon active protests to challenge the status quo. News of a violent confrontation between gays and the police after a 1969 police raid of a gay bar in New York City helped fuel this new "gay liberation" movement. Street protests became common in large cities. Gays formed clubs on campuses. The issue of civil rights for gays was discussed in the 1972 presidential campaign, and in 1973 the American Psychiatric Association removed homosexuality from its lists of mental disorders.

While discrimination still exists, society has grown more tolerant of gays in the past twenty years. While gays are still barred from the military and often lose their jobs and are evicted if their sexual orientation becomes known, 80 percent of Americans think such discrimination is wrong (see Chapter 4). The AIDS epidemic, which began in 1981, opened a new chapter in the fight for gay rights. Media attention to the issue and its impact on the gay community raised the issue of discrimination against gays. It also revealed that many entertainers and celebrities are gay.

The election of Bill Clinton in 1992 also represented a turning point. While Clinton's public position on gay issues was mixed, he ended the federal policy treating gays as security risks and invited gay activists to the White House for the first time. The implicit message was that gays are part of the American community, have legitimate concerns, and are accepted as full participants in the game of politics. With Clinton's election, the radical and confrontational style of gay groups such as Queer Nation have taken a backseat to more mainstream gay rights groups such as the Human Rights Campaign (HRC) with a membership of 250,000. While HRC channels most of its campaign contributions to Democrats, it also supports Republicans. The hope is to elect supporters of gay rights in both parties. The strategy is paying off. Republicans in Congress have joined with Democrats in supporting a number of gay rights measures.[54] However, progress is likely to come slowly as the Christian right remains hostile to the gay rights agenda.

Today, gays and lesbians want to be free of discrimination and enjoy the rights of other Americans, including access to spousal health and death benefits provided by employers. This desire for economic equality is the justification for legitimizing same-sex marriage, although the economic issues could be resolved without taking this step. Same-sex marriage is the most controversial and emotional gay issue.

Elderly While the population of the nation as a whole has tripled since 1900, the number of elderly has increased eightfold. Today, persons over sixty-five constitute more than 12 percent of the population. Several groups, sometimes called the "gray lobby," represent their interests.

Founded in 1958 to provide insurance to the elderly, the American Association of Retired Persons (AARP), with thirty-three million members, is the nation's largest and one of its most powerful interest groups. Recruited by direct mail and word of mouth, the AARP attracts eight thousand new members a day. For $10, anyone over fifty can join and use the numerous benefits provided by the organization[55] (see Table 1).

With 1,800 employees and eighteen lobbyists, the AARP has become a potent political force. The AARP's lobbying efforts are directed primarily at preserving and expanding government benefits to the elderly, which total about $14 billion each month.[56] The Reagan administration quickly dropped the idea of cutting cost-of-living increases in Social Security to reduce the nation's deficit when the AARP and others protested. Reagan's budget director lamented, "These are people who have plenty of time on their hands, who are well organized, who vote regularly, and they are a massive political force."[57] Although programs for the elderly represent one-third of the budget, politicians are reluctant to touch them. Those who have suggested doing so have earned themselves the AARP label "granny-basher." Mindful of their political influence, Clinton got the AARP to support his effort to reform health care by including long-term nursing home care.

Table 1	The AARP Is a Big Business
Activity	**AARP's 1994 Revenue, in Millions of Dollars**
Health insurance	$120.0
Visa/MasterCard	8.7
Auto/home insurance	35.0
Car rental	4.5
Mutual funds	7.6
Pharmacy	4.3
Motor club	1.9

Seniors demonstrate against Medicare cuts.
Brad Markel/Gamma Liaison

Influence is exercised primarily by a flood of correspondence to members of Congress from AARP members. There is no congressional district where the AARP is not fifty thousand strong.[58]

To counterbalance the power of the gray lobby, a number of groups such as Americans for Generational Equity and the Children's Defense Fund have formed, but they are small by comparison.

Environmental Groups Environmental groups are another example of multiple-issue groups. Earth Day 1970 marked the beginning of the environmental movement in the United States. Spurred by an oil spill in California, what was to be a "teach-in" on college campuses mushroomed into a day of national environmental awareness with an estimated twenty million Americans taking part. A minority movement in the 1970s, the environmental lobby today is large and active and its values are supported by most Americans.[59]

Some environmental groups, such as the National Audubon Society, Sierra Club, and the Natural Resources Defense Council, have permanent offices in Washington with highly skilled professionals who carry out a full range of lobbying activities. All experienced substantial growth in membership and finances during the 1980s, when the Reagan administration threatened to undo the environmental gains of the 1970s.[60]

The so-called Greens are environmental groups that shun conventional lobbying approaches and are more confrontational. Groups such as Greenpeace, Earth First!, and the Sea Shepherds seek a "green cultural revolution." Local citizen groups have also organized in support of local environmental concerns such as the location of toxic or nuclear waste dumps. Citizens, skeptical of government and corporate claims that such facilities are safe, want them located elsewhere.[61]

Single-Issue Groups

Single-issue groups pursue public interest goals but are distinguished by their intense concern for a single issue and their reluctance to compromise. Members of the National Rifle Association (NRA) passionately oppose control of firearms. Although a majority of Americans have supported gun control for years, the NRA has successfully lobbied Congress to prevent it. The group has members in every congressional district and is well organized to mobilize them. It spent a great deal of money in a losing battle to defeat the Brady Act, which requires a five-day waiting period to purchase a gun. It also failed to prevent a ban on sales of assault weapons.

More recently, the gun lobby is working hard to fend off potential lawsuits filed by cities against gun manufacturers seeking compensation for police and health care expenses incurred as a result of gun violence. Local governments spurred on by the success of state governments in suing tobacco companies hope to win a similar kind of settlement. The NRA is working feverishly at the state level to outlaw such suits.[62]

Although the NRA remains a major political force, antigun sentiment is growing as more and more Americans respond to increasing gun violence that touches cities, suburbs, and small towns. The result is an increase in the political influence of antigun groups such as Handgun Control and politicians more willing to take on the NRA. Demonstrations such as the Mother's Day march in Washington in 2000, where nearly one million mothers gathered to hear speeches from celebrities and those victimized by gun violence, reflect the growing level of intensity among the population at large for what the marchers called sensible gun laws.

Demonstrations and expressions of antigun sentiment have energized the NRA and progun activists. Following a drop in membership, the organization now claims 3.6 million members. Fearful that the 2000 election of Democratic candidate Al Gore would mean gun control, the group waged an all-out effort to defeat him, pumping $15 million into the election campaign, making a major effort to register its members to vote, and training members in grassroots organizing. After George W. Bush secured the Republican nomination in the spring, a high-ranking official boasted at an NRA gathering, "if [Bush] wins the election, we will have a president where we work out of their office."[63]

Charlton Heston strikes a tough-guy pose as president of the NRA.
Art Streiber/Creative Photographers Inc.

The abortion controversy has generated a number of single-issue groups. The National Right to Life Committee seeks a constitutional amendment banning all abortions. The committee works to elect candidates who favor such an amendment and defeat those who do not. After the 1989 and 1992 Supreme Court decisions allowing more state regulation of abortion, pro-life groups turned their attention to state legislators. They pushed for laws requiring informed consent, waiting periods, and parental consent for minors. In 1996, the organization activated its eight million members and contributed heavily on behalf of Republican candidates.

Operation Rescue is a confrontational antiabortion group whose strategy has been to deny access to abortion clinics to women seeking abortions, as well as to disrupt abortion clinic operations and harass physicians who do abortions. Many "rescuers" have been jailed for their activities. The organization's direct action approach was dealt a blow when Congress passed the Freedom of Access to Clinic Entrances Act in 1994. The law made it a federal crime to hinder abortions by using threats, force, or obstruction. Although peaceful demonstrations that do not block clinic entrances are still legal, the law has discouraged some protesters as demonstrations at clinics have declined.

The movement was also dealt a setback in 1999 when pro-choice groups won a multimillion-dollar lawsuit against abortion foes who had posted the names, addresses, and license plate numbers of doctors who perform abortions and their family members on the Web.[64] Pro-choice advocates argued that the action, dubbed the "Nuremberg Files," was designed to threaten and intimidate them and likely to lead to violence, while the other side stated they were simply exercising their right to free speech. The movement was set farther back when the Food and Drug Administration approved RU-486, the so-called abortion pill, in 2000.

Historically, abortion has played a significant role in the Republican Party's presidential nomination process; it is a very important issue for social conservatives who typically back a strong pro-life candidate but less important for moderate Republicans who are primarily interested in economic issues and government spending. The conflict often surfaces in the party's platform as it did in 1996. Social conservatives prevented a pro-choice plank but avoided a major conflict by permitting pro-choice Republicans to register their opinion in an appendix to the platform.

Members of the national Abortion Rights Action League and Planned Parenthood are fervently committed to protecting women's right to abortion. Planned Parenthood is the oldest, largest, and best-financed advocate of reproductive freedom for women.

The right-to-life movement is considered a single-issue group.
Lynn Johnson/Aurora

Since 1988, the organization has mounted a major effort to win policymakers to the pro-choice point of view. Using the theme that Americans want abortion to be safe and legal, ads were placed in national newspapers. Testimony was provided by physicians who treated botched abortions in the days when abortion was illegal, by clergy involved in counseling, and by women who underwent illegal abortion because they had no choice. Three months before the 1989 Supreme Court decision allowing state regulation of abortion (for more on this issue, see Chapter 14), three hundred thousand pro-choice activists staged a march in Washington. Calling the event the "March for Women's Lives," the goal was to recast the issue in terms of freedom and choice rather than abortion. The three-day event received substantial publicity and demonstrated to members of Congress that the movement could mobilize a large number of supporters.[65]

Single-issue groups have increased in number since the mid-1960s. Some view this trend with alarm, because when groups clash over a highly emotional issue and are unwilling to compromise, government cannot resolve the issue.[66] The issue commands excessive time and energy of policymakers at the expense of broader issues that may be more important.

On the other hand, single-issue groups have always been part of politics.[67] These groups may even be beneficial because they represent interests that may not be well represented in Congress. Fears about single-issue groups may result from the groups' own exaggerated

claims of influence, their heavy media coverage, and, in the case of some antiabortion groups, their confrontational tactics.

Tactics of Interest Groups

Interest groups engage in a variety of tactics to secure their goals. Some try to influence policymakers directly, whereas others seek to mold public opinion and influence policymakers indirectly. Some do both. Some interest groups form broad coalitions to maximize their influence. Others that have little chance of succeeding using conventional techniques engage in protest activity. Both coalition formation and protest activity can involve direct and indirect techniques.

Direct Lobbying Techniques

Direct lobbying techniques involve personal encounters between lobbyists and public officials. Some lobbyists are volunteers; others are permanent, salaried employees of the groups they represent; and others are contract lobbyists, "hired guns" who represent any individual or group willing to pay for the service. Contract lobbyists include the numerous Washington lawyers affiliated with the city's most prestigious law firms. Many have worked for government, so they can boast of contacts in government and access to policymakers to plead their clients' cases. Most firms recruit from the ranks of both Republicans and Democrats to assure access regardless of which party controls government.

Making Personal Contacts

Making personal contacts, in an office or in a more informal setting, is the most effective lobbying technique. Compared to other forms of lobbying, direct personal contact is relatively inexpensive, and it minimizes problems of misinterpretation by allowing questions to be answered on the spot.

Lobbyists know that whereas contacting every legislator is unnecessary, contacting key legislators, those who sit on the committees having jurisdiction over matters of interest to the lobbyists, and staff serving those committees, is critical.[68] Conventional wisdom also suggests that only those legislators who support a group's position or who are known to be undecided should be contacted directly.[69] Putting undue pressure on known opponents may jeopardize prospects for working together in the future on other issues.

Providing Expertise

Although all groups provide information to public officials, some are known for providing information based on accurate and reliable research. Ralph Nader's organization, Public Citizen, which says that it lobbies for the average citizen, has such a reputation. In recent years, Public Citizen has lobbied against the erosion of government regulations dealing with clean air and water, safe drugs, food, and the workplace. It has also worked to limit corporate gifts, such as fancy vacations, to members of Congress and for campaign finance reform (see Chapter 9).

Lobbyists often have a great deal of knowledge and expertise that is useful in drafting legislation. A legislator may ask a lobbyist to draft a bill, or both may work together in drafting legislation. Sometimes interest groups themselves draft legislation and ask a sympathetic legislator to introduce it. General Electric drafted a tax reform measure that saved it millions in taxes. There is nothing illegal about this strategy.

Testifying at Hearings

Testifying at congressional hearings is designed to establish a group's credentials as a "player" in the policy area as well as to convince its own constituents that it is doing its job. A member of a prominent Washington law firm with responsibility at his firm for prepping witnesses to testify identified the Boy Scout motto "Be Prepared" as the most important principle to follow in getting ready for a hearing. Beyond that, he offers a few other tips: Keep it short. Time is at a premium in Washington. No one has an hour to listen to you. Don't read your statement. Good salespeople don't have prepared statements. They know the product and can talk to you about it. Don't be arrogant. Some witnesses are short with members because they believe committee members don't understand their business. Too bad. Most members of Congress don't care about your business; they are going to make a decision based on what they hear. Don't guess. If you don't know the answer to a question, say so and promise to supply the answer later. Don't be hokey, but illustrate whenever possible. It is easier to focus on a wrecked fender in a hearing room than to visualize a set of statistics.[71]

Another advantage of testifying is that it provides free publicity. Staging sometimes occurs. A lobbyist might ask a sympathetic legislator to raise certain questions that the lobbyist is prepared to answer or to indicate in advance what questions will be asked. Sometimes celebrities are invited to testify. In a not unprecedented

Pro-choice advocates form a human corridor to protect patients and workers entering a clinic in Buffalo.
Lynn Johnson/Aurora

To a large extent, lobbying is building relationships based on friendship. As a former chair of the House Budget Committee put it, "The most effective lobbyists here are the ones you don't think of as lobbyists." Referring to one prominent Washington lobbyist, he said, "I don't think of him as a lobbyist. He's almost a constituent, or a friend." Barbara Boxer, then a Democratic representative from California, referring to the same gentleman, described him as "a lovely, wonderful guy. In the whole time I've known him, he's never asked me to vote for anything." At a gathering she joked, he's almost "a member of the family."[70]

"Mr. Speaker, will the gentleman from Small Firearms yield the floor to the gentleman from Big Tobacco?"

but certainly rare move, Hillary Rodham Clinton, the principal player in developing the president's health care reform, testified before several congressional committees. This White House effort prompted a former Reagan aid to quip, they (the Clinton White House) "do PR the way [former chair of the Joint Chiefs] Colin Powell does war: maximum use of force."[72]

Giving Money

Lobbyists try to ensure access to legislators, and giving money is one way to guarantee this. A longtime financial backer of Ronald Reagan once said that having a dialogue with a politician is fine, "but with a little money they hear you better."[73] One Democrat commented in a similar vein, "Who do members of Congress see? They'll certainly see the one who gives the money. It's hard to say no to someone who gives you $5,000."[74]

The primary way groups channel money to legislators is through campaign contributions. Groups, including businesses and unions, may set up political action committees (PACs) to give money to campaigns of political candidates.

The number of PACs has grown dramatically since the mid-1970s as has the amount of money they have contributed. (We discuss PACs more fully in Chapter 9.)

Lobbying the Bureaucracy

For lobbyists, the battle is not over when a bill is passed. Lobbyists also must influence bureaucrats who implement policy. For example, regulations outlawing sex discrimination in educational institutions were drafted largely in the Department of Education with only broad guidelines from Congress. Although the legislation was passed in 1972, both women's rights groups and interests opposing them continue to lobby over the interpretation of the regulations (particularly with regard to equity in women's athletics).

In influencing bureaucrats, interest groups use most of the tactics already described (see also "The Ten Commandments of Lobbying"). They also try to influence who gets appointed to bureaucratic positions. For example, the auto industry opposed a number of Clinton's nominees to head the National Highway Traffic Safety Administration. While consumer groups want someone interested in promoting automobile safety, the industry is looking for someone more sympathetic to its interests and concerns. Senator Don Nickles from Oklahoma held up the nomination of Jane Henney, Clinton's nominee to head the Food and Drug Administration, until he was convinced she would not solicit a manufacturer for RU-486.[75] Nickles is antiabortion and a strong supporter of antiabortion groups. By influencing the appointments to an agency, an industry or group can improve their prospects for favorable treatment by the agency.

Lobbying the Courts

Like bureaucrats, judges also make policy. Some interest groups try to achieve their goals by getting involved in cases and persuading the courts to rule in their favor. Most groups do not litigate, but some use it as their primary tactic, particularly those that lack influence with Congress and the executive branch.

Litigation has been a favorite strategy of civil rights organizations. In 1999, five civil rights groups representing black, Hispanic, and Asian students sued the University of California.[76] At issue was an admissions policy giving students who took advanced placement courses an advantage. Such courses are rarely offered in poor, predominantly minority high schools; thus, the groups argued, minority students were being disadvantaged not on the basis of merit but wealth. Environmental groups and public interest lobbies such as Common Cause have also turned to the courts.

Groups can file civil suits, represent defendants in criminal cases, or file friend of the court briefs, which are written arguments asking the court to decide a case a particular way.[77]

Some groups use the courts to make their opponents negotiate with them. Environmental groups frequently challenge developers who threaten the environment in order to force them to bear the costs of defending themselves and to delay the project. The next time, developers may be more willing to make concessions beforehand to avoid lengthy and costly litigation.

Groups try to influence the courts indirectly by lobbying the Senate to support or oppose judicial nominees.

Indirect Lobbying Techniques

Traditionally, lobbyists employed tactics of direct persuasion almost exclusively—providing information, advice, and occasionally pressure. More recently, interest groups are going public, that is, mobilizing their activists and molding and activating public opinion. A study of 175 lobbying groups found that most were doing more of all kinds of lobbying activity, but the largest increases were in going public.[78] Talking with the media increased the most, and mobilizing the grassroots to send letters and telegrams and make telephone calls was second. (See also the box "Lobbying Goes High-Tech.")

Mobilizing the Grass Roots

The constituency of an interest group—a group's members, those whom the group serves, friends and allies of the group, or simply those who can be mobilized whether or not they have a connection to the group—can help in promoting the group's position to public officials. The National Rifle Association is effective in mobilizing its members. The NRA, like many mass membership organizations, can generate thousands of letters or calls to members of Congress in a short period of time. Calls from irate NRA members led one senator to remark, "I'd rather be a deer in hunting season than run afoul of the NRA crowd."[79]

Conservative Christian minister Jerry Falwell activated his "gospel grapevine" to flood the White House and Congress in opposition to President Clinton's plan to lift the ban on homosexuals in the military. Warning of a new radical homosexual rights agenda, he urged viewers of his "Old Time Gospel Hour" to call and register their opinions.

Senator John McCain (R-Ariz.), sponsor of antitobacco legislation, was swamped with letters opposing the bill sent by members of the National Smokers Alliance, an organization funded by the tobacco companies.[80] Senator Tom Harkin (D-Iowa) was surprised to receive hundreds of letters opposing his antitobacco position, strangely enough from only one small region in his state. The mystery was solved when Harkin learned that all the letters came from employees of a Kraft food plant, owned by R. J. Reynolds.[81]

Appeals to write or phone policymakers often exaggerate the severity of the concern and the strength of the opposition. To move members, it often takes the threat of a monstrous adversary or a catastrophic defeat.

The Ten Commandments of Lobbying

I Thou shalt speak only the truth, and speak it clearly and succinctly; on two pages and in 15-second sound bites.

II Thou shalt translate the rustle of thy grassroots into letters, phone calls, and personal visits.

III Thou shalt not underestimate thy opponent, for he surely packeth a rabbit punch.

IV Help thy friends with reelection; but in victory, dwelleth not on the power of thy PAC.

V Thou shalt know thy issue and believe in it, but be ready to compromise; half a loaf will feed some of thy people.

VI Runneth not out of patience. If thou can not harvest this year, the next session may be bountiful.

VII Love thy neighbor; thou wilst need him for a coalition.

VIII Study arithmetic, that thou may count noses. If thou can count 51, rejoice. Thou shalt win in the Senate.

IX Honor the hard-working staff, for they prepare the position papers for the members.

X Be humble in victory, for thy bill may yet be vetoed.

SOURCE: Ernest Wittenberg and Elisabeth Wittenberg, *How to Win in Washington* (Cambridge, Mass.: Blackwell, 1989), 16.

The so-called information superhighway is changing the way lobbyists, public officials, and the public communicate. As personal contact with members of Congress or their staffs becomes increasingly difficult, more lobbyists are turning to electronic mail to communicate with members of Congress. Although e-mail is not a substitute for a personal visit, only veteran lobbyists with strong personal relationships developed over the years are likely to be consistently able to gain personal access. For those new to the profession or those who lack personal relationships, e-mail may be the only alternative. Moreover, it is quick and cheap.

The information superhighway is aiding lobbyists in other ways, too. Web pages allow lobbyists (and the public) opportunities to find out easily the status of bills, schedules of hearings, and other relevant information (some of these sites are listed in the note). One site, *incongress,* is described as a "one stop shop of all the information that's floating around town." For a fee, lobbyists and interest groups can post issue-related information on the site. The information can be read by anyone who has access to the Internet.

Grassroots lobbying is also easier with the Internet. Interest groups have sites that not only provide information about an issue but also invite browsers to send e-mail messages to public officials. For example, *www.globalwarming-cost.org* concerns the United Nations' treaty to combat global warming. Sponsored by Western Fuels, an energy producer, the site encourages browsers to take a negative stand against the treaty and to register that negative opinion with the president and their member of Congress.

The site begins with "A United Nations Treaty regarding global warming will cost you! This website provides you with the free means to tell Washington to reject the UN treaty. Your views are important. An easily sent, free, E-mail message can help make a difference." The page asks readers to "learn" how global warming costs them by clicking on various icons for business, families, seniors, workers, and farmers. When the reader clicks on an icon, the next page provides information on how much families, for example, will pay. Readers can type in their own monthly energy costs for gasoline, electricity, and heating costs and be told how much the treaty

will cost them in additional charges for energy (as calculated by this antitreaty group). After readers indicate who they are and where they live, a letter is composed and sent to representatives in Congress, the president, and the vice president.

By using this technique, the group avoids the time and expense of recruiting citizens to write letters or following up to ensure that letters have been written. Moreover, because the letters come from constituents, members of Congress and their staff will pay at least some attention to them. Of course, these mass e-mail campaigns, with each message the same, may win some attention now because of their novelty, but we can expect that eventually they will be viewed as no more persuasive than mass postcard campaigns.

NOTE: The Web sites mentioned in the text are good places to start. Another useful site is http://congress.org/main.html, which will help you locate and send an e-mail to your member of Congress.
SOURCE: Ed Henry, "It's the '90s: Old Dogs, New Tricks," *Roll Call Monthly* (November 1997): 1.

To be effective, letters and phone calls must appear spontaneous and sincere. Groups often provide sample letters to aid constituents, but these are not as convincing as those written in a constituent's own words. Campaigns producing postcards with preprinted messages are seldom effective, unless there are tens of thousands and no opposition. While members of Congress often enlist organizations to mobilize constituents in support of legislation, many members are turned off by the flood of mail and calls they receive. As one lobbyist put it, "Members of Congress hate it when you call in the dogs."[82]

Grassroots lobbying was the hallmark of the successful effort to defeat President Clinton's health care reform proposal in 1994. Cigarette companies, drug manufacturers, health insurance agents, physicians, and hospital administrators mobilized their employees, clients, and friends to contact their representatives urging them to kill the measure.[83] Pressure or support of this kind can provide members of Congress in both parties with a reason to buck the president. As one lobbyist put it, "If done well, a member of Congress summoned to the Oval Office can turn to the president and say 'I can't go with you on this, Mr. President, because I promised the people in my district.'"[84]

The nature of grassroots lobbying has changed dramatically in the past decade. Today few groups, particularly those with resources, mount a lobbying campaign without it. Not only is it quite easy to communicate with citizens via e-mail, faxes, and electronic media informing them of a threat and what to do about it, dozens of public relations firms are willing to do the work of mobilizing a group's constituency, if there is one, or manufacturing the appearance of one, if there is not. Washington firms in the business of producing citizen movements on demand advertise specialties such as "development of third-party allies," "grassroots mobilization and recruitment," and "grasstops lobbying."[85] The latter involves identifying the person or persons that a member of Congress cannot say no to—a chief donor, campaign manager, political counselor or adviser—and let them do the heavy lifting of persuading the member of Congress to go along with the group. In many respects grassroots lobbying resembles a presidential election campaign, involving a number of specialists: a pollster to assess citizen opinion, a media consultant to produce and test market television ads, a communications adviser to enlist journalists to write stories and editorials, think tanks to provide supporting research, a recruiter to enlist local and community leaders, a Washington lobbyist to push the idea with members of Congress, and a legal expert to draft legislation. The grassroots industry spent upward of $800 million in 1998–1999 putting a "public look" on private interests.[86]

The strategy of massaging constituents and marshaling public opinion has become the method of choice for business lobbies and corporations. Relying on influential lobbyists with connections to party leaders and influential congressional committee chairs no longer works. Power is too dispersed. Today, you "send in the armies, ships, tanks, aircraft, infantry, Democrats and Republicans, grassroots specialists, and people with special relationships to members."[87]

Does grassroots lobbying enhance democracy or undermine it? Those in the business say their efforts mobilize real people with genuine and sincere interests in particular causes, whether they are members, employees, or simply isolated individuals identified by polling and research. Senator Carl Levin (D-Mich.) has a different view. "When public relations firms are paid to generate calls, it creates a distorted picture of public opinion. When a member gets 50 phone calls, what he doesn't know is that 950 other people were contacted and said no way."[88]

Groups also work hard to get their members to the polls on election day. Electing a sympathetic member to Congress is more effective in the long run than relying on the influence of constituents.

Molding Public and Elite Opinion

Groups use public relations techniques to shape public opinion as well as the opinions of policymakers (see, for example, the boxes "Deception or Just Politics?" and "Caps Off to the Beer Lobby"). Ads in newspapers and magazines and on radio and television supply information, foster an image, promote a particular policy, or some combination of these. The Health Insurance Association of America, for example, spent $17 million creating the now famous "Harry and Louise" commercials to defeat the Clinton health plan. Tobacco companies spent a record $40 million to defeat antitobacco legislation in 1998. Lockheed Martin, a defense contractor, tried to persuade Congress to purchase the company's F-22 fighter jet with an ad appearing in several publications widely read by members. The ad featured a postcard on a black background. On the card, which is dated June 18, 2007, a wife and mother writes home telling her husband and son not to worry because "those F-22s upstairs" are "ruling the sky." Across the bottom of the ad is the caption "One day in the future, someone you love may be depending on the F-22. . . . " According to the company, the ad was an attempt to give a human dimension to an issue that often is shrouded in Pentagon jargon and mind-numbing statistics. But Senator Dale Bumpers (D-Ark.) accused the firm of pandering to the emotions of lawmakers.[89]

Of course, by themselves ads are unlikely to move policymakers to action or shift public opinion dramatically in the short run. They are most effective in combination with other tactics, in particular grassroots mobilization.

Groups may stage events such as rallies or pickets to attract media coverage to their cause. For example, those opposing racial segregation in South Africa have won considerable attention picketing and protesting outside the South African embassy in Washington, D.C. They were especially effective because they enlisted members of Congress, community leaders, and other celebrities in their protests. Arrests of members of Congress and other celebrities for trespassing kept the issue in the limelight for months.

Framing the terms of the debate is crucial in winning public support. Those arguing in favor of tort reform (limiting damages courts will award to those injured in auto accidents, air disasters, unsuccessful surgeries, or other mishaps) focus on the few outrageously huge settlements for seemingly innocuous injuries. Those arguing against such changes focus on the poor widows left penniless after being permanently incapacitated by the rapacious behavior of a wealthy corporation.[90]

A tactic increasingly used by interest groups to influence public opinion is rating members of Congress. Groups may choose a number of votes crucial to their concerns such as abortion, conservation, or consumer affairs. Or they may select many votes reflecting a more general liberal or conservative outlook. They then publicize the votes to their members with the ultimate objective of trying to defeat candidates who vote against their positions. The impact of these ratings is probably minimal unless they are used in a concerted effort to target certain members for defeat.

Coalition Building

Coalitions, networks of groups with similar concerns, help individual groups press their demands. Coalitions can be large and focused on many issues or small and very specific. For example, 7-Eleven stores, Kingsford charcoal, amusement parks, and lawn and garden centers joined the Daylight Saving Time Coalition to lobby Congress to extend daylight saving time. All wanted additional daylight hours to snack, grill, play, or till the soil, which would mean more money in their pockets.

Deception or Just Politics?

Energy deregulation is a high-stakes game involving the $300 billion-a-year power industry. The struggle pits the nation's largest utility companies against smaller independent producers. If deregulation is approved, larger companies will be forced to share the market with smaller producers limiting profits and control. Organizations have formed on both the right and the left of the issue. On the right, there is the Citizens for State Power (CSP). On the left, there is the Electric Utilities Shareholders Alliance (EUSA). The first is run by two prominent conservative leaders and directs its appeals to Republicans in Congress; the second targets Democrats. But interestingly enough, both groups are creations of the same large electric companies who secretly funneled millions of dollars to both in an effort to derail deregulation.

The political consultants who run the "Project," as it is referred to by the handful of persons involved, call into action one or another of the two groups depending on the circumstances. When the need is to push a member of Congress from a conservative district, the right-leaning CSP swings into action, broadcasting ads critical of the member's position. When the target is a liberal district, it is the EUSA that broadcasts a critical message directing constituents to call 1-800-BAD-BILL. When lobbying pro-business members of Congress, the CPS emphasizes deregulation will cost money. When pro-environmentalist and liberal members need lobbying, the EUSA argues that the bill does not go far enough in protecting the environment or that it will cause layoffs and hurt small shareholders.

Why the deception? Appearing to have supporters on both the left and the right conveys that there is no opposition, that everyone is in agreement, and thus an easy call for Congress. It also allows Democrats and Republicans, liberals and conservatives to seemingly vote with their supporters, clients, and constituents. A liberal Democratic member can say he voted with the liberal EUSA. A conservative Republican can say she voted with the conservative CSP.

The tactic is one reason that energy deregulation is yet to pass Congress. For the past three and half years and at a cost of $17 million, the utilities have succeeded in bottlenecking legislation in the energy and power subcommittee.

A target of the CPS, Steve Largent, a conservative member of Congress from Oklahoma and proponent of deregulation, lamented that it is "bogus for the CPS to claim the conservative mantle and be protecting big utilities." The two front groups aired ads in fifty congressional districts, had trained operators arrange for residents to send telegrams and make phone calls to members' Washington offices, and recruited influential local citizens to spread the group's message, even the local dealers who sold members their cars. While most ads were not particularly negative, the one aired against Largent accused him of favoring "Boston, bureaucrats and biomass" because he cosponsored a bill with a House member from Massachusetts requiring utility companies to use alternative energy sources. Displeased with Largent, utility documents noted a willingness to "make his life uncomfortable."

A deception? No, just politics.

SOURCE: John Mintz, "The Utilities Secret Campaign," *Washington Post Nation Weekly Edition,* May 15, 2000, p. 13; "Pressure Surges to a New High to Legislate Electric Deregulation," *Congressional Quarterly Weekly,* April 22, 2000, pp. 949–950.

Caps Off to the Beer Lobby

Do you like to have a beer now and then? If so, perhaps membership in the Beer Drinkers of America is for you. But then again maybe it is not. While an organization for beer drinkers may seem slightly odd, an organization for beer producers and sellers seems quite likely.

A "fact sheet" put out by the organization says that the group has a membership of seven hundred thousand beer drinkers. Their mission is to mobilize members to fight things such as taxes on beer, restrictions on advertising, and deposit laws, ostensibly on behalf of beer drinkers.

How did the group get started? One version is that a few fellow beer drinkers decided to oppose a proposed tax on beer on the ballot in New Mexico. (We can visualize a couple of mad-as-hell couch potatoes sitting in a mobile home in the desert flinging empties at the TV and clamoring that they weren't going to take it anymore.) A more plausible version is that the group was the brain-child of a lobbyist trying to help a client beat back the beer tax. The lobbyist and a friend persuaded one beer company to put up some seed money and many beer retailers to spread the word. In less than a year, four thousand signed on. Today, money comes from two beer companies and from beer wholesalers who pressure their employees to join. Of the 700,000, only 150,000, most of whom are employed by the beer industry, actually pay dues; the rest support the group by signing petitions and writing letters.

Unfortunately for all the real beer drinkers in the country, the organization is a tool of the industry. Why all the deception? The industry hopes to use the group to scare members of Congress. Members might vote against the industry, but they do not want to go back to their districts having voted against "Joe Six-Pack." Increasingly, groups try to couch their real intent behind a name that they know will conjure up positive images on the part of the public and maybe policymakers.

SOURCE: Sean Holton, "Beer Biz Leaves 1 Drinker Foaming," *Orlando Sentinel,* September 12, 1993, pp. 1A, 7A.

Coalitions formed around the health care reform issue in 1995. The AFL-CIO, American Airlines, Chrysler Corporation, the American College of Physicians and the League of Women Voters supported health care reform, and the American Conservative Union, United Seniors Union, Citizens for a Sound Economy, and National Taxpayers joined a coalition of Citizens Against Health Rationing. Similarly, more than 2,700 companies and trade associations were members of USA★NAFTA, a coalition supporting the trade agreement.[91]

Coalitions demonstrate broad support for an issue and also take advantage of the different strengths of groups. One group may be adept at grassroots lobbying, another at public relations. One may have lots of money, another lots of members.

The growth of coalitions in recent years reflects a number of changes in the policy process.[92] Issues have become increasingly complex. Legislation often affects a variety of interests, which makes it easier to form coalitions among groups representing the interests. In addition, changes in technology make it easier for groups to communicate with each other and with constituents. And the number of interest groups is larger than it used to be, especially the number of public interest groups.

Many such groups have limited resources, and coalitions help them stretch their lobbying efforts. Some "black hat" business groups, with image problems, seek to associate themselves with "white hat" organizations ranging from labor unions to consumer groups.[93] The decentralization of Congress and the weakness of political parties also have led to coalition building to win needed majorities at the various stages of the policy process.

Coalitions vary in their duration—some are short term, whereas others are permanent. Coalitions involved with the health care issue remained only until the issue was resolved. Coalitions supporting and opposing NAFTA ceased to exist when Congress approved the measure.

On the other hand, the Leadership Conference on Civil Rights is a permanent coalition of 185 civil rights, ethnic, religious, and other groups (Elks, Actors Equity, YMCA, and the National Funeral Directors and Morticians Association). Unlike short-term coalitions, permanent ones need to be sensitive to how today's actions will affect future cooperation. Some issues may be avoided even though a majority of coalition members want to deal with them. When a coalition is unified, however, it can be formidable.

In elections, coordination among PACs in channeling money to political candidates is widespread. Business PACs, for example, take their lead from the Business Industry Political Action Committee (BI-PAC). Information is shared on candidates' issue positions, likelihood of winning, and need for funding.

Protest and Civil Disobedience

Groups that lack access or hold unpopular positions can protest. In the fall of 1999, for example, representatives from more than five hundred groups joined forces in protesting the World Trade Organization (WTO) at its meeting in Seattle.[94] The WTO represents 135 countries with authority to force countries to change their labor, environmental, and human rights laws that allegedly restrict trade among countries. In addition to high-profile labor unions and environmental groups, the demonstration drew less well-known organizations such as the Ruckus Society, a group that provides training in nonviolent protest, and the Raging Grannies, a human rights organization. The protestors charged the organization with responding more to the profit needs of international corporations than those of the environment, working men and women, the poor, women, and native people. The Sierra Club and Steelworkers held a Seattle tea party with the slogan "No Globalization without Representation." Following their Boston forebears, they ... el imported from China, hormone-treated

beef, and other goods they view as tainted by WTO decisions into the sea.[95] Taking a page from Vietnam War protests, the groups held a number of activities including teach-ins, concerts, and mock trials of corporations. Hundreds of protestors formed a human chain around Seattle's exhibition center, the site of the meeting, demanding the WTO cancel the debt owed by the world's poorest nations. The protest ended in violence as several hundred were arrested and jailed.

Peaceful but illegal protest activity, in which those involved allow themselves to be arrested and punished, is called *civil disobedience.* Greenpeace is an environmental and peace group that practices civil disobedience. It started in 1971 when a group of environmentalists and peace activists sent two boats to Amchitka Island near Alaska to protest a U.S. underground nuclear weapon test. The boats were named *Greenpeace,* linking the environment and peace. Although the boats failed to reach the island, the publicity generated by the affair led Washington to cancel the test.

Throughout the 1970s and 1980s, Greenpeace staged a number of such protests. To protest dumping of toxic wastes and sewage in the ocean, thirteen Greenpeace activists lowered themselves from a New York bridge and hung there for eight hours, preventing any sewage barges from carrying wastes out to sea. All were arrested. To protect endangered whales, members placed themselves in the path of a harpoon, narrowly missing being struck. Others parachuted over coal-powered power plants to protest acid rain. Their goal was to generate publicity and dramatic photographs that would activate the general population.

Greenpeace and several other protest organizations have moved away from the confrontational, "in your face" style of politics in recent years,[96] although four Greenpeace protesters chained themselves to a Canadian cargo ship in 1999 maintaining that it was loaded with paper made from rain forest trees.[97] Once organizations such as Greenpeace succeed in getting a hearing—that is, find someone in government who is willing to listen—they shift to an inside strategy, working with those in power rather than against them. Protest groups often drop the "yelling and screaming" for more conventional lobbying techniques once they have access to policymakers. It has also become increasingly difficult to draw media coverage to another story of a group of protesters willing to risk life and limb in the interest of preserving or preventing something, and it is publicity that makes such activities politically effective. The first time, these stories are front-page news. The second time, they are buried inside, if they get covered at all.

Protest can generate awareness of an issue, but to be successful, it must influence mass or elite opinion. Often it is the first step in a long struggle that takes years to resolve. Sometimes the first result is hostility toward the group using it. Antiwar protest by college students in the 1960s and 1970s angered not only government officials, who targeted the leaders for harassment, but also many citizens. In the early years of the women's movement, the media labeled many female protesters "bra burners" even though it is not clear that any woman ever burned a bra.

Extended protests are difficult because they demand more skill by the leaders and sacrifices from the participants. Continued participation, essential to success, robs participants of a normal life. It can mean jail, physical harm, or even death and requires discipline to refrain from violence, even when violence is used against the protesters.

The civil rights movement provides the best example of the successful use of extended protest and civil disobedience in twentieth-century America. By peacefully demonstrating against legalized segregation in the South, black and some white protesters drew the nation's attention to the discrepancy between the American values of equality and democracy and the southern laws that separated blacks from whites in every aspect of life. Protesters used tactics such as sit-ins, marches, and boycotts. Confrontations with authorities often won protesters national attention and public support, which eventually led to change. (See the box "Organizing Protest: The Montgomery Bus Boycott.")

All tactics can be effective, but some lend themselves better to some groups than others. For example, business groups with great financial resources can pay for skillful lobbyists and donate to political candidates. Labor unions have many members and can help candidates canvass and get out the vote. Public interest groups rely on activating public opinion and, where members are intensely committed to a cause, protest.

Greenpeace attempts to influence public opinion with dramatic events. Here, Greenpeace protests dumping of nuclear waste at sea, while dumpers prepare to drop a barrel of waste on the Greenpeace protesters.
Pierre Gleizes/Greenpeace

The 1955 Montgomery, Alabama, bus boycott was the first successful civil rights protest, and it brought its twenty-six-year-old leader, Dr. Martin Luther King, Jr., to national prominence. Montgomery, like most southern cities, required blacks to sit in the back of public buses while whites sat in the front. The dividing line between the two was a "no man's land" where blacks could sit if there were no whites. If whites needed the seats, blacks had to give them up and move to the back.

One afternoon, Rosa Parks, a seamstress at a local department store and a leader in the local chapter of the National Association for the Advancement of Colored People (NAACP), boarded the bus to go home. The bus was filled, and when a white man boarded, the driver called on the four blacks behind the whites to move to the back. Three got up and moved, but Mrs. Parks, tired from a long day and of the injustice of always having to move for white people, said she did not have to move because she was in "no man's land." Under a law that gave him the authority to enforce

segregation, the bus driver arrested her.

That evening a group of black women professors at the black state college in Montgomery, led by Jo Ann Robinson, drafted a letter of protest. They called on blacks to stay off the buses on Monday to protest the arrest. They worked through the night making thirty-five thousand copies of their letter to distribute to Montgomery's black residents. Fearful for their jobs and concerned that the state would cut funds to the black college if it became known they had used state facilities to produce the letter, they worked quickly and quietly.

The following day black leaders met and agreed to the boycott. More leaflets were drafted calling on blacks to stay off

Rosa Parks being fingerprinted after her arrest.
AP/Wide World Photos

the buses on Monday. On Sunday black ministers encouraged their members to support the boycott, and on Monday 90 percent of the blacks walked to work, rode in black-owned taxis, or shared rides in private cars.

The boycott inspired confidence and pride in the black community and signaled a subtle change in the opinions of blacks toward race relations. This

Success of Interest Groups

Although no interest group gets everything it wants from government, some are more successful than others. Politics is not a game of chance, where only luck determines winners and losers. Knowing what to do and how to do it—strategy and tactics—are important, as are resources, competition, and goals.

Resources

Although large size does not guarantee success, large groups have advantages. They can get the attention of ____ials by claiming to speak for more people or ____ing to mobilize members against them.

The geographical distribution of members of a group is also important. Because organized labor is concentrated in the Northeast, it has less influence in other parts of the country, particularly in lobbying Congress. The Chamber of Commerce, on the other hand, has members and influence throughout the country.

Other things being equal, a group with well-educated members has an advantage because highly educated people are more likely than others to communicate with public officials and contribute to lobbying efforts.

Group cohesion and intensity are also advantages. Public officials are unlikely to respond to a group if it cannot agree on what it wants or if it does not appear to feel very strongly about its position. For example, in recent years the NAACP has suffered from deep splits

was obvious when, as nervous white police looked on, hundreds of blacks jammed the courthouse to see that Rosa Parks was safely released after her formal conviction. And it was obvious later that evening at a mass rally when Martin Luther King cried out, "There comes a time when people get tired of being trampled over by the iron feet of oppression. There comes a time when people get tired of being pushed out of the glittering sunlight of life's July, and left standing amidst the piercing chill of an Alpine November." After noting that the glory of American democracy is the right to protest, King appealed to the strong religious faith of the crowd, "If we are wrong, God Almighty is wrong. . . . If we are wrong, Jesus of Nazareth was merely a utopian dreamer. . . . If we are wrong, justice is a lie." These words and this speech established King as a charismatic leader for the civil rights movement.

Each day of the boycott was a trial for blacks and their leaders. Thousands had to find a way to get to work and leaders struggled to keep a massive carpool going. However, each evening's rally built up morale for the next day's boycott. Later the rallies became prayer services, as the black community prayed for strength to keep on walking, for courage to remain nonviolent, and for guidance to those who oppressed them.

The city bus line was losing money. City leaders urged more whites to ride the bus to make up lost revenue, but few did. Recognizing that the boycott could not go on forever, black leaders agreed to end it if the rules regarding the seating of blacks in "no man's land" were relaxed. Thinking they were on the verge of breaking the boycott, the city leaders refused. Police began to harass carpoolers and issue bogus tickets for trumped-up violations. Then the city leaders issued an ultimatum: Settle or face arrest. A white grand jury indicted more than one hundred boycott leaders for the alleged crime of organizing the protest. In the spirit of nonviolence, the black leaders, including King, surrendered.

The decision to arrest the leaders proved to be the turning point of the boycott. The editor of the local white paper said it was "the dumbest act that has ever been done in Montgomery."[1] With the mass arrests, the boycott finally received national attention. Reporters from all over the world streamed into Montgomery to cover the story. The publicity brought public and financial support. The arrests caused the boycott to become a national event and its leader, Martin Luther King, a national figure. A year later, the U.S. Supreme Court declared Alabama's local and state laws requiring segregation in buses unconstitutional, and when the city complied with the Court's order, the boycott ended.

Rosa Parks became a hero of the civil rights movement. She has been honored many times since then, and millions saw her appearance at the 1988 Democratic National Convention.

1. Taylor Branch, *Parting the Waters, America in the King Years* (New York: Simon & Schuster, 1988), 83.
SOURCES: Taylor Branch, *Parting the Waters,* chapters 4 and 5; and Juan Williams, *Eyes on the Prize* (New York: Viking, 1987).

within its leadership. Some of these divisions are over tactics: Should the organization be more confrontational and aggressive or work cooperatively and passively within the system to achieve its goals? Some splits are over allies: Should the NAACP work with groups like Louis Farrakhan's Nation of Islam or restrict itself to more moderate and mainstream civil rights organizations? Such splits diminish the clout of a group.

A large **market share,** the number of members in a group compared to its potential membership, is another advantage. For years the AMA enrolled a large percentage (70 percent or more) of the nation's doctors as members. As its membership (as a percentage of the total number of doctors) declined, so did its influence.

The more money a group has, the more successful it probably will be. Not only does money buy skilled lobbyists and access to elected officials, it is also necessary for indirect lobbying efforts.

Knowledge is a major resource too. If leaders of a group are experts in a policy area, they are more apt to get the attention of public officials. Knowledge of how things get done in Washington is also helpful, which is why many groups employ former members of Congress and the executive branch as lobbyists.

When Bob Dole resigned from the Senate in 1995 to run for president, he indicated that if he lost the presidency, he would have no place to go but back to his hometown of Russell, Kansas. If he had done that, he would have been quite unusual. Few members of Congress return to their roots once their political

InfoTrac College Edition

"Curious Compassion"
"Will Pat Go?"
"Judicial Assault on Patronage"
"Putting People Last"

Notes

1. Jeffrey Goldberg, "Big Tobacco's Endgame," *New York Times Magazine,* June 21, 1998, p. 36. Information on Gingrich's father is also from this source. Other sources include Ceci Connolly and John Mintz, "How Big Tobacco Got Smoked," *Washington Post National Weekly Edition,* April 6, 1998, pp. 6–7; Ceci Connolly and John Mintz, "The Mississippi Connection," *Washington Post National Weekly Edition,* April 6, 1998, pp. 8–9; Saundra Tory and John Schwartz, "Making Nice to Make a Deal," *Washington Post National Weekly Edition,* March 9, 1998, p. 29; James Carney, "McCain's Big Deal," *Time,* April 13, 1998, pp. 62–64; John Bresnahan, "Tobacco Lobbyists Prepare for Fight," *Roll Call* (May 1998): 1 and 13; Alan Greenblatt, "Tobacco Debate Rages on, Keeping Bill Alive, If Unwieldy," *Congressional Quarterly Weekly Report* (June 13, 1998), pp. 1605–1607.

2. Ernest Wittenberg and Elisabeth Wittenberg, *How to Win in Washington* (Cambridge, Mass.: Blackwell, 1989), p. 24.

3. Jeffrey Birnbaum, *The Lobbyists* (New York: Times Books, 1992), p. 32.

4. M. A. Peterson and J. L. Walker, "Interest Group Responses to Partisan Change: The Impact of the Reagan Administration upon the National Interest Group System," in *Interest Group Politics,* 2d ed., eds. A. J. Cigler and B. A. Loomis (Washington, D.C.: CQ Press, 1987), 162.

5. A. de Tocqueville, *Democracy in America* (New York: Knopf, 1945), 191.

6. G. Almond and S. Verba, *Civil Culture* (Boston: Little, Brown, 1965), 266–306.

7. D. Truman, *The Governmental Process* (New York: Knopf, 1964), 25–26.

8. Ibid., 59.

9. Ibid., 26–33.

10. J. Q. Wilson, *Political Organization* (New York: Basic Books, 1973), 198.

11. G. K. Wilson, *Interest Groups in America* (Oxford: Oxford University Press, 1981), chapter 5; see also G. K. Wilson, "American Business and Politics," in *Interest Group Politics,* 2d ed., ed. Cigler and Loomis, 221–235.

12. K. L. Schlozman and J. T. Tierney, "More of the Same: Washington Pressure Group Activity in a Decade of Change," *Journal of Politics* 45 (May 1983): 335–356.

13. Christopher H. Foreman, Jr., "Grassroots Victim Organizations: Mobilizing for Personal and Public Health," in *Interest Group Politics,* 4th ed., ed. A. J. Cigler and B. A. Loomis (Washington, D.C.: CQ Press, 1994), 33–53.

14. J. L. Walker, "The Origins and Maintenance of Interest Groups in America," *American Political Science Review* 77 (June 1983): 398–400; see also *National Journal* (August 1981): 1376.

15. R. H. Salisbury, "An Exchange Theory of Interest Groups," *Midwest Journal of Political Science* 13 (February 1969): 1–32.

16. J. M. Berry, *The Interest Group Society* (Boston: Little Brown, 1984), 26–28.

17. Wilson, *Political Organization,* chapter 3.

18. C. Brown, "Explanations of Interest Group Membership over Time," *American Politics Quarterly* 17 (January 1989): 32–53.

19. C. Brown, "Explanations of Interest Group Membership." The National Rifle Association. Annual Meeting of Midwest Political Science Association, 1987.

20. National Opinion Research Center, General Social Surveys, 1987.

21. N. Babchuk and R. Thompson, "The Voluntary Associations of Negroes," *American Sociological Review* 27 (October 1962): 662–665; see also P. Klobus-Edwards, J. Edwards, and D. Klemmach, "Differences in Social Participation of Blacks and Whites," *Social Forces* 56 (1978): 1035–1052.

22. Robert D. Putnam, "Bowling Alone: America's Declining Social Capital," *Journal of Democracy* (January 1995): 65–78; see also Robert J. Samuelson, "Join the Club," *Washington Post National Weekly Edition,* April 15–21, 1996, p. 5.

23. Samuelson, "Join the Club."

24. Richard Stengel, "Bowling Together," *Time,* July 22, 1996, p. 35.

25. M. T. Hayes, "The New Group Universe," in *Interest Group Politics,* 2d ed., ed. Cigler and Loomis, 133–145.

26. C. Tomkins, "A Sense of Urgency," *New Yorker,* March 27, 1989, pp. 48–74.

27. Walker, "The Origins and Maintenance of Interest Groups in America"; E. E. Schattschneider, *Semi-Sovereign People* (New York: Holt, Rinehart, & Winston, 1960), 118.

28. David Broder and Michael Weisskopf, "Finding New Friends on the Hill," *Washington Post National Weekly Edition,* October 3–9, 1994, p. 11.

29. Steven Greenhouse, "AFL-CIO Plans $40 Million Political Drive," *New York Times,* February 18, 1999, p. A19.

30. Steven Greenhouse, "Union Membership Rose in '98, but Unions' Percentage of Workforce Fell," *New York Times,* January 20, 1999, p. A22; P. E. Johnson, "Organized Labor in an Era of Blue Collar Decline," in *Interest Group Politics,* 34th ed., ed. A. J. Cigler and B. A. Loomis (Washington, D.C.: CQ Press, 1991), 33–62.

31. "Labor's China Syndrome," *New Yorker,* June 5, 2000, p. 31.

32. Steven Greenhouse, "Union Membership Slides despite Increased Organizing," *New York Times,* March 22, 1998, p. 8a.

33. Frank Swoboda, "A Healthy Outcome for Organized Labor," *Washington Post National Weekly Edition,* March 8, 1999, p. 18; Steven Greenhouse, "In Biggest Drive since 1937, Union Gains a Victory," *New York Times,* February 26, 1999, p. A1.

34. Steven Greenhouse, "The Most Innovative Figure in Silicon Valley? Maybe This Labor Organizer, " *New York Times,* November 14, 1999, p. 26.

35. Steven Greenhouse, "Angered by HMO's Treatment, More Doctors Are Joining Unions," *New York Times,* February 4, 1999, pp. A1–A25.

36. A. J. Cigler and J. M. Hansen, "Group Formation through Protest: The American Agriculture Movement," in *Interest Group Politics,* 1st ed., ed. A. J. Cigler and B. A. Loomis (Washington, D.C.: CQ Press, 1983), chapter 4; A. J. Cigler, "Organizational Maintenance and Political Activity on the Cheap: The American Agriculture Movement," in *Interest Group Politics,* 1st ed., ed. Cigler and Loomis, 81–108.

37. A. S. McFarland, *Common Cause* (Chatham, N.J.: Chatham House, 1984); see also A. S. McFarland, *Public Interest Lobbies: Decision Making on Energy* (Washington, D.C.: American Enterprise Institute, 1976).

38. R. G. Shaiko, "More Bang for the Buck: The New Era of Full Service Public Interest Groups," in *Interest Group Politics,* 3d ed., ed. Cigler and Loomis, 109.

39. Ibid., 120.

40. For a discussion of the evolution of NOW and its success in lobbying Congress, see A. N. Costain and W. D. Costain, "The Women's Lobby: Impact of a Movement on Congress," in *Interest Group Politics,* 1st ed., ed. Cigler and Loomis.

41. Birnbaum and Pooley, "New Party Bosses."

42. E. M. Uslaner, "A Tower of Babel on Foreign Policy," in *Interest Group Politics,* 3d ed., ed. Cigler and Loomis, 309.

43. K. Wald, *Religion and Politics* (New York: St. Martin's, 1985), 182–212.

44. James L. Guth, John C. Green, Lyman A. Jellstedt, and Corwin E. Wmidt, "Onward Christian Soldiers: Religious Activist Groups in American Politics," in *Interest Group Politics,* 3d ed., ed. Cigler and Loomis, 57.

45. Sidney Blumental, "Christian Soldiers," *New Yorker,* July 18, 1994, p. 36.

46. Ibid., p. 37.

47. David Von Drehle and Thomas B. Edsall, "The Religious Right Returns," *Washington Post National Weekly Edition,* August 29–September 4, 1994, p. 6; "Prodding Voters to the Right," *Time,* November 21, 1994, p. 62.

48. Laura Goodstein, "Church Debate over Voter Guides," *New York Times,* October 29, 1998, p. A21.

49. "Citing 'Moral Crisis,' a Call to Oust Clinton," *New York Times,* October 23, 1998, p. A18.

50. Hanna Rosin, "Aiming at Mainstream," *Washington Post National Weekly Edition,* April 17, 2000, p. 17.

51. "Religious Right Returns," p. 6.

52. Charles Levendosky, "Alternative Religious Voice Finally Being Raised," *Lincoln Journal-Star* (March 3, 1996), p. 7b.

53. The source for most of the next paragraphs is Eric Marcus, *Making History: The Struggle for Gay and Lesbian Equal Rights 1945–1990* (New York: HarperCollins, 1992). Also see Jeffrey Schmalz, "Gay Politics Goes Mainstream," *New York Times Magazine,* October 11, 1992, pp. 18ff.

54. Richard Lacayo, "The New Gay Struggle," *Time,* October 26, 1998, pp. 33–36.

55. J. Tierney, "Old Money, New Power," *New York Times Magazine,* October 23, 1988, p. 69.

56. "Grays on the Go," *Time,* February 22, 1988, p. 69.

57. "Gray Power," *Time,* January 4, 1988, p. 36.

58. "Our Footloose Correspondents," *New Yorker,* August 8, 1988, p. 70.

59. C. J. Bosso, "Adaption and Change in the Environmental Movement" in *Interest Group Politics,* 3d ed., ed. Cigler and Loomis, 155–156.

60. Ibid., p. 162.

61. Ibid., p. 169.

62. "Echoes of Tobacco Battle in Gun Suits," *New York Times,* February 21, 1999, p. 18.

63. Thomas B. Edsall, "Targeting Al Gore with $10 Million," *Washington Post National Weekly Edition,* May 29, 2000, p. 11; John Mintx, "Would Bush Be the NRA's Point Man in the White House?" *Washington Post National Weekly Edition,* May 8, 2000, p. 14; Mike Dorning, "NRA Promises an All-out Assault on Al Gore's Presidential Campaign," *Lincoln Journal-Star,* May 21, 2000, p. 2a.

64. Sam Howe Verhovek, "Creators of Anti-abortion Web Site Told to Pay Millions," *New York Times,* February 3, 1999, p. A11.

65. A. Rubin, "Interest Groups and Abortion Politics in the Post-Webster Era," in *Interest Group Politics,* 3d ed., ed. Cigler and Loomis, 249–251; *Congressional Quarterly Weekly Report* (March 27, 1993), pp. 755–757.

66. D. Broder, "Let 100 Single-Issue Groups Bloom," *Washington Post,* January 7, 1979, pp. C1–C2; see also D. Broder, *The Party's Over: The Failure of Politics in America* (New York: Harper & Row, 1972).

67. Wilson, *Interest Groups,* chapter 4.

68. P. M. Evans, "Lobbying the Committee: Interest Groups and the House Public Works and Transportation Committee, in the Post-Webster Era," in *Interest Group Politics,* 3d ed., ed. Cigler and Loomis, 257–276.

69. Berry, *Interest Group Society,* 188.

70. Jeffrey Birnbaum, *The Lobbyists* (New York: Times Books, 1992), 40.

71. Wittenberg and Wittenberg, *How to Win in Washington,* 24.

72. David Broder and Spencer Rich, "The Health Care Battle Begins," *Washington Post National Weekly Edition,* September 27–October 3, 1993, p. 6.

73. E. Drew, *Politics and Money: The New Road to Corruption* (New York: Macmillan, 1983), 78.

74. Ibid.

75. Eric Schmitt, "Nomination for FDA Post Nears Approval in Senate," *New York Times,* October 21, 1998, p. A13.

76. Evelyn Nieves, "Civil Rights Groups Suing Berkeley over Admissions Policy," *New York Times,* February 3, 1999, p. A11.

77. For an article dealing with the success of interest group litigation at the district court level see L. Epstein and C. K. Rowland, "Debunking the Myth of Interest Group Invincibility in the Courts," *American Political Science Review* 85 (March 1991): 205–220.

78. S. Kernell, *Going Public* (Washington, D.C.: CQ Press, 1986), 34.

79. R. Harris, "If You Love Your Grass," *New Yorker,* April 20, 1968, p. 57.

80. Alison Mitchell, "A New Form of Lobbying Puts Public Face on Private Interest," *New York Times,* September 30, 1998, pp. A1, A14.

81. Ibid.

82. Evans, "Lobbying the Committee," p. 269.

83. Michael Weisskopf, "Letting No Grass Roots Grow under Their Feet," *Washington Post National Weekly Edition,* October 24, 1993, pp. 20–21.

84. Sandra Boodman, "Health Care's Power Player," *Washington Post National Weekly Edition,* February 14–20, 1994, pp. 6–7.

85. Ibid.

86. Ibid.

87. Ibid.

88. Ibid.

89. Michael Towle, "Ad for Fighter Plane Aimed at Congress," *Lincoln Journal-Star,* May 2, 1997, p. 7a.

90. Birnbaum, *The Lobbyists,* 40.

91. Dan Balz and David Broder, "Take Two Lobbyists and Call Me in the Morning," *Washington Post National Weekly Edition,* October 18–24, 1993, pp. 10–11.

92. Much of the information in this section is taken from B. A. Loomis, "Coalitions of Interests: Building Bridges in the Balkanized State," in *Interest Group Politics,* 2d ed., ed. Cigler and Loomis, 258–274.

93. Birnbaum, *The Lobbyists,* p. 83.

94. Steven Greenhouse, "Carnival of Derision to Greet the Princes of Global Trade," *New York Times,* November 11, 1999, p. A12.

95. Ibid.

96. Cary Goldberg, "How Political Theater Lost Its Audience," *New York Times,* September 21, 1997, p. 6.

97. "Greenpeace Protest Shipload of Newsprint," *Lincoln Journal-Star,* October 21, 1999, p. 3.

98. David Segal, "Bob Dole Leads the Cast of Rainmakers," *Washington Post National Weekly Edition,* September 22, 1997, p. 20.

99. Dan Clawson, Alan Neustadtl, and Denise Scott, *Money Talks* (New York: Basic Books, 1992), p. 91.

100. Schattschneider, *Semi-Sovereign People,* chapter 2.

101. Kevin Phillips, "Fat City," *Time,* September 26, 1995, p. 51.

102. Goldberg, "Big Tobacco's Endgame," p. 67.

103. Ibid.

104. Saundra Torry, "One for the Record," *Washington Post National Weekly Edition,* May 25, 1998, p. 10.

105. "Confidential Tobacco PR Memo," at www.citizen.org/tobacco/premo.htm.

Political Parties

YOU ARE THERE

Should You Endorse George W. Bush?

You are Senator John McCain, a Republican candidate for president. Having lost all of the big states in the March Super Tuesday primaries to opponent George W. Bush, you have just withdrawn from the race. You started off your nomination campaign strong, winning the Republican primaries in New Hampshire, Michigan, and your home state of Arizona, but you did so largely based on your appeal among independents and moderates, so-called swing voters. Where primary voting was limited to just Republicans, as in most of the Super Tuesday primaries, you lost.

You raised a number of issues that captured the attention of the voters, including campaign finance reform, which was at the center of your campaign. Your commitment to this and other issues is reflected in your concession address following your Super Tuesday defeat. "Our crusade continues tonight, tomorrow, the next day, the day after that and for as long as it takes to restore America's confidence and pride in the practice and institutions of our great democracy."[1]

After your unexpected win in New Hampshire, the nation's first primary, Bush faced a must-win situation in South Carolina. To defeat you, he waged a very negative campaign, spending $5 million to flood the airways with attacks against you. One ad derided the Straight Talk Express, the name you gave your campaign bus tour through New Hampshire, as the "Double-Talk Express." Some South Carolina voters revealed they were subjected to phone calls in which you were called a liar, a cheat, and a fraud. Christian conservatives made phone calls that described you as pushing for higher taxes and waffling on protecting human life. Push-polls planted negative information. Registered voters were called and told that as chairman of the Senate Commerce Committee, you raised money and traveled on the private jets of corporations that had legislation pending before your committee, then asked whether this would make them vote for or against you.[2] Perhaps more significant, Bush raised doubts in the minds of voters regarding the genuineness of your conservatism and the quality of your character. He falsely accused you of wanting to remove the pro-life plank from the GOP platform. He labeled you a hypocrite, accusing you of saying one thing and doing another. He equated your stand on campaign finance

Senator John McCain analogized his campaign to Luke Skywalker fighting his way out of the Death Star in Star Wars. Here McCain and his wife, Cindy, display light sabers from his supporters.
AP/Wide World Photos

reform and other issues as positions favored by Bill Clinton and Al Gore. Representatives of the Christian Coalition, National Right to Life Committee, and National Smokers Alliance drove home these messages in even harsher terms. A professor from Bob Jones University, the conservative Christian college where Bush opened his campaign in South Carolina, sent an e-mail falsely accusing you of fathering two children out of wedlock.[3]

Going negative paid off. Your negative rating among voters went from 5 to 30, and Bush won with 53 percent of the vote to your 41. You were put off by the tone of Bush's South Carolina effort and feel both your character and issue positions were slandered.

In Michigan, the assault continued. An ad implied that you were unfit to be president because of time spent as a POW.[4] Another assailed you for advocating a huge tax increase without mentioning that it was a tax on tobacco.[5] Illinois Representative Henry Hyde, a strong opponent of abortion, taped a phone message that was heard in ten thousand households criticizing you for wanting to change the Republican platform to approve of abortion in cases of rape or incest, a position that Bush himself endorses but that Hyde failed to mention.[6] In spite of the barrage, you managed a win.

But Super Tuesday's results make it clear that you will not get the nomination. So you withdraw. You are still smarting from the negative campaign waged against you. Yet Bush wants your support to unify the party. He is unwilling, however, to make concessions to you in terms of offering support for some of your positions. He wants to avoid the appearance of appeasing you, something that might alienate his conservative supporters. Indeed, when asked whether he planned to meet with you, he responded, "Why, I have nothing to learn from him."[7]

Despite that insult, you are undecided what you should do. Do you endorse Bush as your party's nominee and pledge to support him in the general election, even though he is unwilling to address the concerns you raised during the campaign? This would endear you to some in the party, perhaps win you a position on the ticket if you want it, and keep your prospects alive for a future run for the nomination. Do you withhold your endorsement and send a message that you will support him, if and when he addresses your concerns, recognizing that this might not happen? Doing so is likely to alienate you from other Republicans, including your party's members in Congress. That could also reduce any chance of you being the party's presidential nominee in the future. Other options include bolting the party and offering yourself as a third-party candidate and running against Bush and the Democratic nominee in November. That option would end any possibility for securing the Republican nomination in the future, further diminish your stock among Republican colleagues in the Senate, most of which do not care for you now, and likely condemn you to defeat at the polls (third-party candidates never win the presidency). It would, however, provide you a forum to bring your message to the American people.

George Washington warned against the "baneful" effects of parties and described them as the people's worst enemies. But, more recently, a respected political scientist, E. E. Schattschneider, argued that "political parties created democracy and that democracy was impossible without them."[8] The public echoes these contradictory views. Many believe that parties create conflict where none exists, yet most identify with one of our two major parties.[9]

These same feelings exist among candidates for office. They often avoid political parties by establishing their own personal campaign organizations and raising their own funds. If elected, they often do not follow the party line. At the same time, candidates for national and state offices are nominated in the name of political parties, they rely on parties for assistance, and they have little chance of winning unless they are Democrats or Republicans.

In this chapter, we examine American political parties to see why they are important and why many observers believe that if they become less important and effective, our system of government may not work as well as it does.

What Are Political Parties?

Political parties are a major link between people and government. They provide a way for the public to have some say about who serves in government and what policies are chosen. Political parties generally are defined as organizations that seek to control government by recruiting, nominating, and electing their members to public office. They consist of three interrelated components: the **party in the electorate,** those who identify with the party; the **party in government,** those who are appointed or elected to office as members of a political party; and the formal **party organization,** the party "professionals" who run the party at the national, state, and local levels (see Figure 1).[10]

In linking the public and government policymakers, parties serve several purposes. They help select public officials by recruiting and screening candidates and then providing campaign resources. They help empower citizens by activating and interesting them in politics. Individually, citizens have little power, but collectively, through parties, they can influence government.

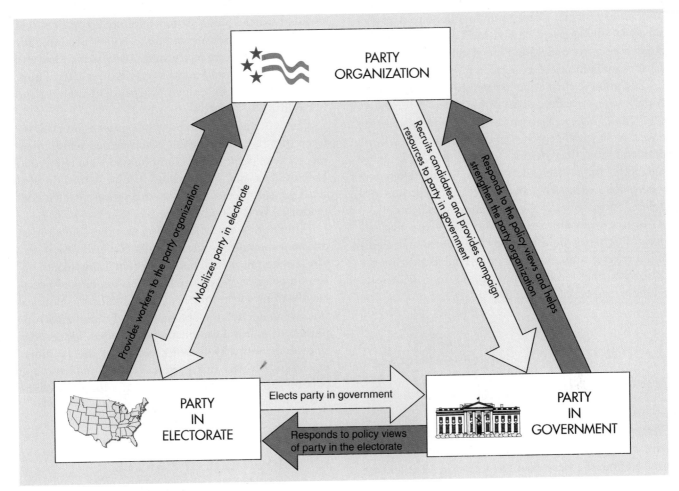

FIGURE 1 ■ *The Three Components of Political Parties*

Many voters feel an attachment to a political party, an affiliation they acquire early in life that aids them in deciding among competing candidates. Some voters simply vote their party identification, with little or no knowledge of candidates or issues. But a party vote is, in part, an issue vote. Political parties do have relatively consistent stances on issues, which is clear to most voters. Since the 1930s, the Democratic Party has favored an expanded role for the national government in dealing with the country's economic problems, while the Republican Party has favored minimizing this role, preferring to leave such issues to the marketplace to resolve—that is, the unregulated forces of supply and demand. Since the 1960s, the parties have also differed with respect to issues involving lifestyle and morality. Here Republicans favor government intervention to protect morality, while Democrats are less interventionist. This split is illustrated sharply on the abortion issue, with Republicans wishing government to ban abortions and Democrats supporting a woman's right to an abortion.

Most voters recognize these differences. Knowing a candidate belongs to a party is a clue to the candidate's general preference regarding the role of the national government in a number of areas such as health care, energy, the environment, abortion, and gay rights. Voters therefore do not need to study each candidate's position on such issues in great detail, a difficult and time-consuming task. The party label provides a general understanding of where the candidate stands. This is one reason why Schattschneider believed democracy was impossible without political parties. When citizens select a party, they have a clearer understanding of what their selection means in terms of the policy direction of the nation. Without the party label, citizens have no idea of how their vote for an individual candidate translates into public policy.

The party in government plays an important role in organizing and operating government; it formulates policy options and ultimately decides which to support or oppose. When political parties represent individuals from widely different backgrounds and interests, parties aid society by aggregating and mediating conflicts and contributing to political and social stability.

It is not fashionable to argue in favor of political parties and point to their contributions to democracy. Most Americans see parties as part of the "mess in Washington." Many believe that parties are responsible for the government's inability to act in dealing with the nation's problems and that partisan debates are meaningless squabbles. Many feel that parties create differences where none exist rather than reflect and represent real differences in how to solve the nation's problems.

In fact, without political parties, it is likely that our political system would be more fragmented and media and interest groups even more powerful. Parties are organizations that bind together people from all regions, religions, and economic groups.

Development and Change in the Party System

Most Americans think of the Democratic and Republican Parties as more or less permanent fixtures, and indeed they have been around a long time. The Democratic Party evolved from the Jacksonian Democrats in 1832, and the Republican Party was founded in 1854. Nevertheless, the current party system is only one of five distinct party systems that have existed in American history (see Figure 2).

In tracing the development of these systems, we need to keep two things in mind. First, parties developed after the nation's founding, grew to be very powerful in the late nineteenth century, and have declined in influence since then.

Second, there have been periods of stability in the party system when one party has dominated American politics and won most elections. There have also been periods of transition and instability when neither party has dominated, and control of government has been divided between the parties or has shifted back and forth. In transition periods, issues emerge that are difficult to resolve, and voters establish new party loyalties based on them. The transition from one stable party system to another is called a **realignment.**

Preparty Politics: The Founders' Views of Political Parties

Most of the Founders viewed political parties as dangerous to stable government. This antiparty feeling was rooted in three basic beliefs. First, the Founders

thought parties created and exploited conflicts that undermined consensus on public policy. Second, they thought parties were instruments by which a small and narrow interest could impose its will on society. Third, they believed parties stifled independent thought and behavior.[11]

James Madison feared political parties as much as interest groups because he felt both pursued selfish interests at the expense of the common good. He referred to both as "factions" in *Federalist* 10. John Adams dreaded what he considered the greatest political evil, the formation of rival political parties.

Therefore, it is not surprising that the Constitution does not mention political parties. Nevertheless, it created a system in which parties, or something like them, were inevitable. When the Founders established popular elections as the mechanism for selecting political leaders, an agency for organizing and mobilizing supporters of political candidates was needed. Indeed, despite their antiparty feelings, several of the Founders were active in the first parties. Thomas Jefferson and James Madison, for example, were the founders of the first political party.

First Party System: Development of Parties

With Washington's unanimous election to the presidency in 1788, it appeared the nation could be governed by consensus. But differences of opinion soon arose. Alexander Hamilton, Washington's secretary of the treasury, supported a strong national government. His following, the Federalists, were opposed by Thomas Jefferson, secretary of state, who feared a strong central government. The conflict led Jefferson to challenge Federalist John Adams for the presidency in 1796. Jefferson lost, but he then recruited able leaders in each state, founded newspapers, established political clubs, and in 1800 ran again and won. Jefferson's victory demonstrated the utility of political parties.

By Jefferson's second term, more than 90 percent of members of Congress were either Federalists or Jeffersonians (later called Jeffersonian Republicans) and consistently voted in support of their party.[12]

Second Party System: Rise of the Democrats

After a brief period of one-party rule ("the era of good feelings"), the Jeffersonian Republicans split into factions. One of these developed into the Democratic Party, led by Andrew Jackson, who won the presidency in 1828.

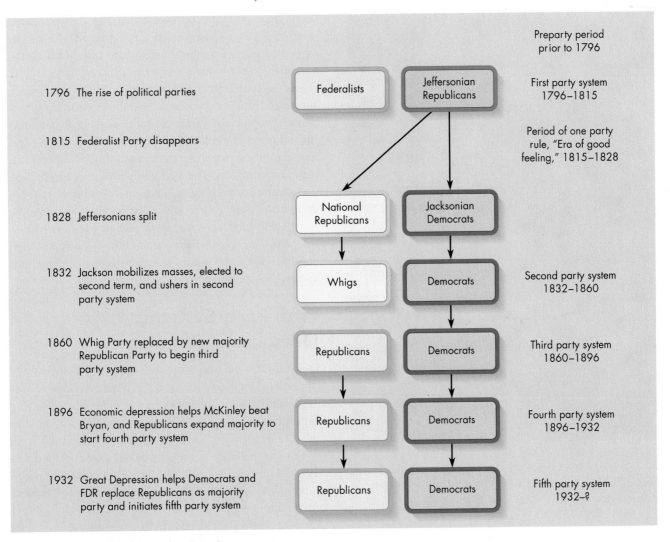

1796 The rise of political parties	Federalists	Jeffersonian Republicans	Preparty period prior to 1796
			First party system 1796–1815
1815 Federalist Party disappears			Period of one party rule, "Era of good feeling," 1815–1828
1828 Jeffersonians split	National Republicans	Jacksonian Democrats	
1832 Jackson mobilizes masses, elected to second term, and ushers in second party system	Whigs	Democrats	Second party system 1832–1860
1860 Whig Party replaced by new majority Republican Party to begin third party system	Republicans	Democrats	Third party system 1860–1896
1896 Economic depression helps McKinley beat Bryan, and Republicans expand majority to start fourth party system	Republicans	Democrats	Fourth party system 1896–1932
1932 Great Depression helps Democrats and FDR replace Republicans as majority party and initiates fifth party system	Republicans	Democrats	Fifth party system 1932–?

FIGURE 2 ■ *The Five American Party Systems*

The Jacksonian Democrats emphasized the common person and encouraged popular participation. As a result of their efforts, the vote was expanded to all white adult males. Presidential electors were selected in popular elections rather than by state legislatures, and the party convention became the instrument used to nominate presidential and other party candidates. No longer did members of the party in Congress select the party's presidential nominee. Instead, conventions opened up decisions to local as well as national party elites.

Many political leaders deplored Jackson's efforts to mobilize the masses. John Quincy Adams called Jackson a "barbarian." An Adams supporter referred to Jackson's victory as "the howl of raving Democracy."[13]

Jackson's popular appeal and the organizational effort of his party brought large numbers to the polls for the first time. By 1828, more than a million votes were cast for president. Building on the efforts of Jefferson, Jackson introduced a uniquely American idea, a mass-population-based party organization.

Third Party System: Rise of the Republicans

The conflict over slavery brought a new party alignment. Abolitionists and proslavery factions split the Whig Party, which had been the primary opposition to the Democrats. By 1860, the Whigs disappeared and a new party, the Republicans (not related to the Jeffersonian or National Republicans), emerged. The Republicans (also known as the GOP—Grand Old Party), reflecting abolitionist sentiment, nominated Abraham Lincoln for president. Northern Democrats who opposed slavery joined Republicans to form a new majority party.

After the Civil War, the Republicans usually won the presidency and controlled Congress. After 1876, however, elections were close and the parties evenly matched in Congress.

Parties were strong during this period. They controlled nominations for office and mobilized voters through extensive local organizations. Big-city political

The factions that developed into the first political parties were already vying with each other in Washington's administration. Thomas Jefferson (second from left) and Alexander Hamilton (fourth from left) are pictured here with Washington (right).
The Granger Collection, New York

machines provided employment and other help for many new immigrants in exchange for their allegiance. Corruption—vote buying and political payoffs—linked poor immigrants, big business, and party leaders in strong party machines.

Fourth Party System: Republican Dominance

The election of 1896 ushered in another party alignment. Democrat William Jennings Bryan appealed to southerners and farmers of the plains. He played to their hostility toward the Northeast, with its large corporations and growing ethnic working class. His was a religious appeal too, pitting fundamentalists against Catholics. But his appeal was too narrow, and the Democrats were soundly defeated.

During this period a third party, the Progressives, gained strength, chiefly among middle-class Americans concerned with the corruption of big-city machines. The movement championed a number of reforms designed to wrench political control from political parties and the lower-class immigrant groups they served. These included voter registration and the secret ballot, which reduced election fraud; the direct primary, which allowed voters rather than party bosses to nominate candidates for public office; and a merit system, which eliminated political patronage in the awarding of government jobs and contracts. The Progressives never captured the presidency, but their ideas did win favor with a larger audience and were enacted into law. In addition to checking corruption, the reforms weakened political parties, undermining their capacity to mobilize voters and their ability to use government to meet the needs of the citizens who support them.

Fifth Party System: Democratic Dominance

In the 1920s, the Republicans began to lose support in the cities. The party ignored the plight of poor immigrants and in Congress pushed through quotas limiting immigration from southern and eastern Europe. After the Depression hit in 1929, these immigrants, along with many women voting for the first time, joined traditional Democrats in the South to elect Franklin Roosevelt in 1932. This election reflected another party alignment.

The **New Deal coalition,** composed of city dwellers, blue-collar workers, Catholic and Jewish immigrants, blacks, and southerners, elected Roosevelt to an unprecedented four terms. The coalition was an odd alliance of northern liberals and southern conservatives. It stuck together in the 1930s and 1940s because of Roosevelt's personality and skill and because northerners did not seriously challenge southern racial policies.

But the coalition came unglued after Roosevelt's death. The Republicans, by nominating a popular war hero, General Dwight D. Eisenhower, won the presidency in 1952 and 1956. Although the Democrats regained the White House in 1960, the civil rights movement and the Vietnam War divided them sharply, and they lost again in 1968 and 1972.[14] They won in 1976 by nominating a southerner—Jimmy Carter—and because the Republicans suffered from the Watergate scandal. Even though the Democrats dominated Congress until 1994, they had much less success in winning the presidency. Democrats won the White House only three times after 1964, suggesting that the fifth party system may have ended.

In 1828, opponents of Andrew Jackson called him a jackass (left). Political cartoonists and journalists began to use the donkey to symbolize Jackson and the Democratic Party. In the 1870s, Thomas Nast popularized the donkey as a symbol of the party in his cartoons and originated the elephant as a symbol of the Republican Party. His 1874 cartoon (right) showed the Democratic donkey dressed as a lion frightening the other animals of the jungle, including the Republican elephant.

The Granger Collection, New York

Has the Fifth Party System Realigned?

The fifth party system has changed, but has a major realignment occurred? Many of the signs that preceded major realignments of the party system have been present for some time. **Ticket splitting**, voting for a member of one party for one office but a member of another party for a different one, reached an all-time high in 1992, owing in part to the strong showing of third party presidential candidate Ross Perot. In 1996, ticket splitting fell off a bit but was still twice as common as it was in the 1950s (see Figure 3).[15] At the national level, the Republicans have occupied the White House and the Democrats have controlled Congress most of the time since 1968.

Realigning periods also are characterized by compelling issues that fracture the unity of the major parties.[16] In the years before 1860, slavery was such an issue. It divided the Democrats and destroyed the Whigs. In 1932, economic issues led many Republicans away from their party to the Democrats. As memories of the Depression and influence of Depression-era economic issues fade, the potential exists for new issues to mobilize and realign voters.

The dominant Democratic coalition is less cohesive than in the heyday of the fifth party system. Blue-collar

ethnics and Catholics have found the Democrats much less attractive.[17] As New Deal policies succeeded, blue-collar workers became much less concerned with economic security and turned their attention to other issues. Many were upset with the party's promotion of civil rights. Divisions in the party over the Vietnam War pushed many who were in favor of the war, particularly blue-collar union members, to the Republicans. Some objected to the Democratic Party's positions on social issues such as opposition to capital punishment, prayer in schools, and support for abortion and the rights of criminal defendants.

In the 1980s, economic concerns returned. Blue-collar workers found their standard of living eroding and felt left behind.[18] This did not move them back to their Democratic roots, however. They resented what they believed to be the Democrats' favoritism toward minorities and policies that seemed to free citizens from personal responsibility for their actions (for example, crime policies that some saw as "coddling criminals"). The big-city machines that once mobilized workers to vote Democratic are gone, and the labor unions, which did the same, are dramatically weakened.

On the other hand, some changes drove some voters to the Democratic Party. Northern white Protestants and white-collar workers are somewhat less Republican

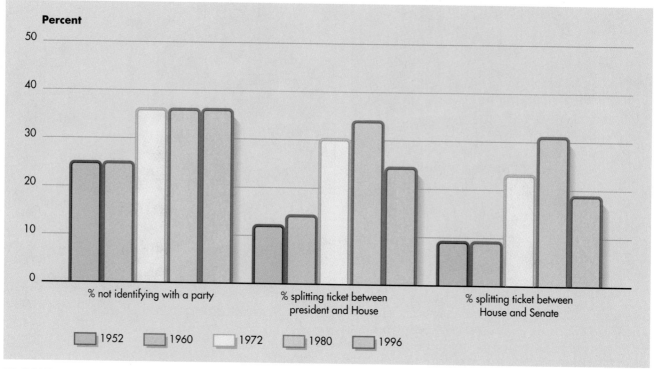

FIGURE 3 ■ *Is Partisanship Reemerging?*

SOURCE: CPS National Election Studies.

than they used to be. Many of them are employed by government and more sympathetic to government's role in solving societal problems. The Democrats also increasingly appeal to better-educated voters, who support Democratic initiatives such as health care reform, commitment to the environment, and abortion rights.[19]

In general, then, there has been some evidence of realignment focused on issues of government size and scope, with parties becoming more homogeneous.[20] Although only a modest realignment has occurred nationally, a regional one, confined to the South, has certainly occurred. Long a bastion of Democratic Party strength, the South began to drift away in the 1950s and showed major signs of change in 1964. For the first time in a century, the Republicans carried several southern states in the presidential election.

At the time he signed the 1964 civil rights bill, President Johnson confided that he believed the event would deliver the South to the Republicans for the next fifty years. And as predicted, in 1964 many white southerners voted for Barry Goldwater, the Republican nominee. Since 1968 Republicans have carried the South in all presidential elections, except for Jimmy Carter's election in 1976. Even then, a majority of white southerners voted for Ford. Clinton carried his home state,

Arkansas, and that of his running mate, Tennessee. He also picked up Louisiana and Georgia, but these states were recaptured by the Republicans in 2000.

White southerners increasingly vote for Republicans in congressional races, too. Since 1994, they have cast the majority of their votes for Republicans. The shift has led a few Democratic members of Congress to change their party in an effort to take advantage of the changing loyalties of white southerners. For the first time since Reconstruction, a majority of governors, U.S. house members, and senators from the eleven southern states are Republican.[21]

The change in party identification among white southerners is the main reason that polls have shown a decline in Democratic loyalties nationwide. The shift of white southerners to the Republican Party not only makes the South more Republican but also makes the Republicans more conservative. The change also gives the party system a somewhat more ideological look. The southern Democrats who changed tend to be conservatives and are more ideologically compatible with policies of the Republican Party.

The race issue, which spurred this realignment, continues to play a role. Where white southerners in the 1950s and 1960s claimed "betrayal" by the national

Democratic Party for its policies urging equality for blacks, they now say they object to its policies accepting affirmative action for minorities. The polarization between the races has sharpened the realignment. Defection of white southerners from the Democratic Party has left a southern Republican Party that is largely white and a Democratic Party that is largely black. Southern whites who are asked their party affiliation sometimes retort, "I'm white, aren't I?" meaning "I'm Republican."[22]

There also has been some **dealignment.**[23] More individuals have opted for independence as parties become less and less relevant. About one-third of all citizens do not choose to identify with a political party. Many voters who became eligible to vote for the first time during the 1980s and 1990s have not been attracted to either party, and some older voters lack firm attachments to their party. Many say that there is nothing that they like or dislike about parties. Similarly, the number who have something positive to say about one party and something negative to say about the other has declined; these trends suggest that parties are not as important to citizens as they were in the 1950s and 1960s.[24]

Candidates and the issues they choose to focus on have become more important. Citizen indifference to political parties and their decline in importance make it difficult for parties to link citizens to government and to enhance citizens' influence over government actions.

Dealignment also makes realignment less likely. Citizens who think parties are not important are unlikely to switch when their party fails to deal with the nation's problems. Nor are independents likely to be drawn to a political party in search of answers to national problems. Though some believe that the country is in the midst of a "rolling realignment," a movement of the nation to the right and the Republican Party in fits and starts since the early 1970s, the Democratic Party continues to be the party of choice for a plurality of Americans—a fact that is inconsistent with the idea of a rolling realignment.

In 2000, Republicans clung to their slim majority in Congress owing to incumbent advantage, superiority in raising campaign funds, and a reasonably satisfied electorate. However, this does not necessarily signal a realignment and permanent Republican majority. It is a reflection of continued volatility among voters as they respond to economic conditions and specific issues. The 2000 election revealed a closely divided nation. Both House and Senate are split almost evenly, and the presidential vote was the closest in modern history. Regional, race, and gender differences seem clear, yet the contours of a new party system are not.

Characteristics of the Party System

The American party system is characterized by some intriguing and even unique qualities.

Two Parties

First, the American party system is a **two-party system.** Only two parties win seats in Congress, and only two parties compete effectively for the presidency. The development and perpetuation of two parties is rare among the nations of the world.

In western Europe, for example, **multiparty systems** are the rule. Italy has nine national parties and several regional parties; Germany has five. Great Britain, although predominantly a two-party system, now has at least three significant minor parties. Multiparty systems also are found in Canada, which has three parties, and Israel, which has more than twenty.

Why do we have a two-party system? The most common explanation is the nature of our election system.[25] Public officials are elected from **single-member districts** under a **winner-take-all** arrangement. This means only one individual is elected from a district or state—the individual who receives the most votes. This contrasts with **proportional representation,** in which public officials are elected from multimember districts and the number of seats awarded to each party within each district is roughly equal to the percentage of the vote the party receives in the district. Thus, representation in the national legislature is approximately proportional to the popular vote each party receives nationwide.

In single-member district, winner-take-all systems, only the major parties have much chance of winning legislative seats. With little chance of winning office, minor parties tend to die or merge with one of the major parties. However, where seats are awarded in proportion to the vote, even a modest showing in the election—15 percent or less—may win a seat or two in the national assembly and provide a foundation upon which to build. Under such a scheme, a party, regardless of its electoral strength, has a presence in the legislature and someone to speak in support of its policy positions and issues.

While the election system influences the party system, the party system also influences the election system. Where only two parties exist, it is to their advantage to maintain an election system that undermines the development and growth of minor parties. For example, legislatures, controlled by the two parties, have tried to make it as difficult as possible for third parties to get on the ballot (though the courts have struck down many of these laws). Where several parties exist, it is to their advantage to establish an election system that benefits many parties.[26]

Fragmentation

The federal system, with its fragmentation of power between state and national levels, leads to fragmentation within parties. State and local parties have their own resources and power bases separate from those of the national parties.

Power also is fragmented at each level. At the national level, power is shared among the president and members of Congress. No one controls the party. Presidents often have a difficult time winning support for their policies among their party members in Congress. As parties have weakened, this problem has become more apparent. During the last year of President Bush's term, House Republicans supported him only 71 percent of the time, Senate Republicans 73 percent. In 1997 House Demo-crats supported President Clinton 71 percent of the time, Senate Democrats 85 percent. On a few major issues early in Clinton's term, congressional Democrats broke with him. For the North American Free Trade Agreement (NAFTA), two of the top three majority leaders in the House actually led the opposition, and two of the top three majority leaders in the Senate joined the opposition. Three Democratic committee chairs and seventeen subcommittee chairs in both the House and Senate joined with Republicans in defeating a Democratic-sponsored crime bill. To their dismay, these leaders later learned that the party's failure to pass legislation dealing with crime and other issues contributed to voters' disgust with the party and the Republican takeover in the 1994 elections.

These defections illustrate members' independence from their party. To be reelected, they need to satisfy only a plurality of the voters in their district or state, not the president. When Clinton considered a gas tax increase to reduce the deficit, Democratic Senator Herbert Kohl (Wisconsin) told him the increase would be no more than 4.3 cents per gallon. Clinton had to accept this figure because the bill's outcome was in doubt and the senator's vote was crucial. Kohl, a multimillionaire, paid for his initial election campaign and could pay for a reelection bid, so he felt no obligation to his party. Such independence makes it difficult to forge a unified party.

Moderation

American political parties are moderate; there are no extremely liberal or extremely conservative major parties. One reason for this is that the people themselves are moderate (see Figure 4). To attract the most voters, the parties try to appear moderate.

Because parties try to attract many voters, both have liberals as well as conservatives, though the Democratic Party has more liberals and fewer conservatives than the Republican Party. This combination prompts parties to moderate their appeals and nominate moderate candidates. When liberal or conservative candidates do get nominated, they usually move toward the middle on some issues or at least portray themselves as moderate. Ronald Reagan, when running for reelection, embraced a conciliatory stance toward the Soviet Union in contrast to his earlier "evil empire" posture. Bill Clinton became a "new kind" of Democrat. The implication was that, unlike those in the past who catered to minorities and special interests, he would deal with the problems of middle America. George W. Bush beat a hasty retreat from his conservative rhetoric in the South Carolina primary once the Republican nomination was secure. He avoided discussing issues such as abortion that would identify him with the right and focused on more centrist issues such as education, health care, and Social Security.[27]

Minor Parties in American Politics

Sometimes called "third parties," minor parties are as varied as the causes they represent. Some are one-issue parties, like the American Know-Nothing Party (1856), which ran on a platform opposing immigrants and Catholics, and the Prohibition Party (1869 to the present), which campaigns to ban the sale of liquor.

Other parties advocate radical change in the American political system. Economic protest parties, such as the Populist Party of 1892, sometimes appear when economic conditions are especially bad and disappear when times improve. Since the 1920s, the Communist Party has espoused the adoption of a communist system.

Some parties are simply candidates who failed to receive their party's nomination and decided to go it alone. In 1968, Alabama Governor George Wallace split from the Democratic Party to run for president as the candidate of the conservative American Independent Party. Failing to get the Republican nomination, John

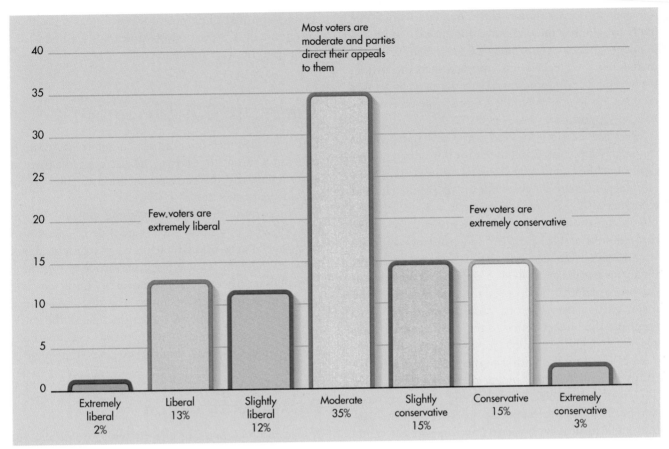

FIGURE 4 ■ *Parties Aim Their Campaigns to the Middle, Where the Voters Are*

SOURCE: Data from 1998 General Social Survey, National Opinion Research Center. The labels (such as "liberal") were self-descriptions.

Anderson launched a third-party campaign in 1980. Though both Wallace and Anderson had significant public support, neither won a large number of votes nor had much influence on the election outcome.

Ross Perot's third-party candidacy in 1992 had no association with either party. He simply decided to run. His willingness to use his personal fortune to fund his campaign, including buying large blocks of expensive television time, made him a highly visible alternative to the major-party candidates. Although he polled 19 percent of the vote, large for a minor party, his candidacy did not influence the election outcome. Ralph Nader, the consumer advocate, ran in 2000 for a second time as the nominee of the Green Party, an offshoot of the antinuclear and environmental movements. His campaign focused on checking the influence of big business on government, but he fell quite short.

Minor parties face many obstacles in trying to establish themselves. Some are structural barriers. State laws, for example, present obstacles to minor-party and inde-

pendent candidates seeking to get on the ballot. Federal laws make it difficult to secure public funding for campaigning.

There are also psychological barriers. Even though partisanship has weakened, minor-party and independent candidates confront the long-standing loyalty that most Americans have toward the major parties. Even when third-party or independent candidates are preferred to the major-party candidates, many voters are reluctant to cast a vote for them, believing that there is little chance they can win. Nearly one-third of those who expressed a first preference for Ross Perot in 1992 voted for one of the major-party candidates. Many did so because they felt Perot could not win. Often the major parties will encourage voters as a campaign tactic not to "waste their vote" by voting for a candidate who cannot win, as Gore did against Nader in 2000. Not only may voters waste their votes, but it may take away votes from their second choice and thus lead to the election of their least preferred candidate. Likewise, contributors are reluctant to donate money to a candidate who is unlikely to win. For these reasons, third parties and independent candidates are rarely taken seriously by the media and thus receive less coverage than the major-party candidates, adding further to the perception that they are less legitimate and less worthy of voter and financial support.

Practical barriers to third-party and independent candidates also exist. It is difficult for third parties to recruit qualified and experienced candidates. Most elected politicians are Republicans or Democrats and recognize that they are most likely to succeed in winning national office if they run as a major party candidate. Should a third-party or independent candidate have a marketable idea, one that is attractive to voters, the major parties are likely to co-opt it and present it as their own, eliminating the need for an alternative to the major parties. Perot's strong position on the need to eliminate the budget deficit in the 1992 campaign was at least partially responsible for the major parties' renewed efforts to deal with it in the 1996 campaign. Finally, third parties and independent candidates have done well only in elections when the nation has faced significant social and economic problems, and the parties failed to deal with them. Low support for third-party candidates in 2000 no doubt reflects a strong economy and a nation at peace.

Because third-party and independent candidates cannot win the presidency, their movements rarely extend beyond the defeat of their candidate. Perot was able to overcome this by again spending his own money. His "United We Stand America" movement from the 1992 campaign became the Reform Party in 1996. But Pat Buchanan, the party's nominee in 2000, received less than 1 percent of the popular vote. This dismal showing suggests that the party will go the way of most third or minor parties.

Many Americans want to see an alternative to the major parties. Over one-half have indicated that the nation needs a third party, although few actually vote for a minor party candidate. Verbal support is fueled by the perception that the Democrats and Republicans in Congress are unable to work together to solve the nation's problems, and thus, an independent or another party is likely to do a better job. Furthermore, the decline in importance of political parties and the increasing importance of media, particularly television, and political handlers is incentive for wealthy persons willing to spend their own resources to get in the race and challenge the major parties. Perot would have floundered quickly and with little notice if not for his capacity to buy hours of TV time. Most Americans learned about Perot from his TV "infomercials."

Party in the Electorate

Earlier we identified three distinct but interrelated aspects of political parties: the party in the electorate, the party in government, and the party organization (Figure 1). We can now examine each.

The party in the electorate—those individuals who identify with a political party—are a party's grassroots supporters. **Party identification** is a psychological link between individuals and a party; no formal or organization membership is necessary. In contrast, European parties do have members; members pay dues and sign a pledge that they accept the basic principles of the party. The percentage of voters who are members ranges from 1 or 2 percent in some countries to over 40 percent in others.

Party Identification

A majority of Americans identify with a political party (see Table 1). In 1996, 39 percent said they were Democrats, 28 percent Republicans, and 33 percent independent.

In Chapter 4, we discussed how political socialization leads to party identification early in childhood. While this is true, party identification can change and often does as a person's life situation changes, such as moving to a new job or community, or in response to changes in issue positions that conflict with one's party. As we have seen, for example, the national Democratic Party's increased support for civil rights and other liberal policies caused many white southerners to leave the party.

Table 1	Party Identification, 1996
Identifies self as:	**Percent**
Democrat	39
Independent	33
Republican	28

SOURCE: NES, 1996.

Characteristics of Democrats and Republicans

Generally, each party is more ideologically homogenous than it used to be, with most Republicans considering themselves conservative. In fact, the Republican Party represents an uneasy coalition of traditional conservatives, motivated primarily by a desire to minimize government intervention in the economy, and new conservatives, motivated primarily by a desire to institutionalize their religious and moral values. Called the *religious right,* the new conservatives want to increase government intervention in such areas as abortion, prayers in school, and pornography. In many states, the religious right controls the Republican Party. Since the 1992 Republican National Convention, the right has avoided open confrontations with moderate Republicans, and national party leaders have stressed issues such as lower taxes and smaller government, on which both agree. With white born-again Christians 17 percent of the electorate, winning elections may depend on keeping more divisive issues such as abortion in the background.

The two Republican factions were united in their hate for communism and their support for Reagan. But the disintegration of the Soviet Union and the communist bloc and the departure of Reagan leave them with less in common.[28]

The Democrats are also divided. Some want to return to their liberal roots by appealing to working men and women and denouncing Republican support for big business and wealthy taxpayers. Others want the party to appeal to moderates who want lower taxes, less government, and more local control. Clinton epitomized this thinking. A Clinton adviser says, "We can't define ourselves as the party of government."[29] The party is unlikely, however, to win back control of Congress unless it can appeal to both its liberal base and the moderate middle.

Although people from all walks of life are found in each party, there are differences in the social composition of the parties. Republicans are somewhat younger than Democrats and those calling themselves independent (see Table 2). Republicans are somewhat better educated than Democrats, but independents have the highest percentage of college graduates. Women are better represented among the ranks of Democrats, as are blacks. Although the activities of religious fundamentalists are much more influential in the Republican Party, an equal percentage of Democrats and Republicans claim to be fundamentalists. Religious fundamentalists are an even larger proportion of independents.

Table 2	Characteristics of Republicans, Democrats, and Independents		
Total	**Republican 28%**	**Democrat 39%**	**Independent 33%**
Age 18–25	12	7	7
26–50	56	51	52
51–65	17	20	21
Over 65	15	22	20
Less than high school education	18	20	9
High school graduate	36	42	35
Some college education	13	11	11
College graduate	34	27	46
Men	49	38	51
Women	51	62	49
White	86	77	96
Black	12	21	2
Native American	1	1	1
Asian	1	1	1
Protestant fundamentalist	35	34	47
Protestant mainstream	30	29	28
Catholic	30	32	24
Jewish	3	3	1
Other	1	2	0
Professional and business	39	42	48
Other white collar	15	13	20
Blue collar	46	44	32
Under $20,000	42	55	47
$20,000 to $50,000	39	36	39
Over $50,000	19	8	14
Conservative	77	22	39
Moderate	18	32	40
Liberal	5	47	22

SOURCE: NES, 1996.

There is little difference in the occupational breakdown of the party followings. Again the biggest difference is between partisans and independents. Republicans have a larger percentage than Democrats of those earning $50,000 or more, and fewer of those earning $20,000 or less. Independents fall in between the two, with less income than Democrats but more than Republicans. Conservatives clearly dominate in the Republican Party, with liberals most numerous in the Democratic Party. Here also, independents fall between the two party groups, having more liberals than the Republican Party but less than the Democrats, and more conservatives than the Democrats but fewer than the Republicans.

Party in Government

Nationally, the party in government is the party's elected members of Congress and, for the party that occupies the White House, the president. The party in government links the party in the electorate to their government. The job of the party in government is to enact policies that party voters favor. This seems like a simple idea, but political scientists have waged great debates over how close the link between the party in government and the party in the electorate should be.

Proponents of **responsible party government** believe that political parties should take clear and contrasting positions on political issues and require their elected members to support the party's positions. "Responsible" party government is responsible in that

- voters have a choice among parties advocating different positions;

- elected members of the party support and vote for their party's position; and

- the party with a majority in the legislature enacts its position into law.

Given these conditions, voting for one party rather than another has definite policy consequences. It increases the prospects for popular control of government because a voter knows exactly what a vote for one party means for public policy. For example, in a responsible party system, if the Republican Party's position is pro-life and the Democratic Party's position is pro-choice, a vote for a Republican candidate will mean a pro-life position. Should the Republicans win a majority, a pro-life position would be enacted into law.

Great Britain is an example of responsible party government. Political parties are heavily involved in developing, articulating, and implementing public policy. If elected party members defect too often from the party's position, party leaders can deny them the right to stand for reelection as the party's candidates.

American political parties are not as responsible in this way. They do not always offer clear and contrasting policy positions. When they do, party leaders have only limited authority to force their elected members to accept the party's position.

Although the United States is not a responsible party government, it has some elements of party responsibility. The party links presidents with the members of their party in Congress. Members of the president's party in Congress support his policies substantially more often than members of the opposition. Parties also have important organizational and leadership functions in Congress.

Party influence is also visible in congressional voting[30] and increased dramatically during the 1980s. This reflects the realignment of the South. In the days before blacks were allowed to vote and before the Republicans offered real challenges in most southern districts, the vast majority of southern members of Congress were white conservative Democrats who voted with the Republicans almost as often as with their own party.[31] As white conservatives have moved into the Republican Party, districts with conservative white majorities are much more likely to elect Republicans rather than conservative Democrats. Districts with large numbers of black voters are more likely than before to elect African Americans or moderate or liberal white Democrats. Thus, voting patterns of representatives from the South now divide along party lines as they do in the North.[32]

Republican control of both houses of Congress has increased the level of party unity. A number of conservative Republicans, committed to a very conservative agenda, were elected in 1994. Eager to retain control of Congress, moderate incumbent Republicans supported the program to show voters that the party could enact legislation and govern effectively.[33] Moderate Democrats, on the other hand, did not support the GOP's agenda so division between the parties reached record highs. Partisanship fell off a little in both the House and Senate after 1995 but is still much higher than in the 1970s and 1980s. Roll call votes on which majorities of the parties opposed each other ranged from 47 to 56 percent in the House and 50 to 63 percent in the Senate. On these votes, better than 86 percent of the Republicans voted with each other in opposition to the Democrats,

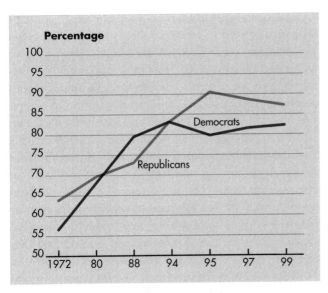

Percentage

FIGURE 5 ■ *Party Unity Increased in the 1980s and Has Remained High* The average percentage of times that Democrats and Republicans in Congress voted with their party on votes in which a majority of Democrats opposed a majority of Republicans

SOURCE: *Congressional Quarterly Weekly Report.*

and 80 percent of the Democrats voted with each other in opposition to the Republicans (Figure 5).[34] Party voting rivals the British Parliament, our example of responsible party government.

Party unity is likely to continue to remain high. Each party has a distinct vision of the best public policies and believes it can win public support for those policies.

To achieve higher levels of party unity in the United States would require major changes in government. Party leaders would have to be given more power to maintain party discipline in Congress. The president and congressional majority would have to have common party ties. This could be accomplished on a continuing basis only through a constitutional change providing for a parliamentary system similar to Britain's, in which Congress would elect the president. Such a change is highly unlikely.

Party Organization

The party organization is the third component of the political party. The major levels of party organization—national, state, and local—coincide with political units responsible for administering elections. Within the local parties there are further subdivisions. The smallest unit

is usually the precinct-level organization. Several precincts comprise a ward or district; several wards comprise the city or county organization.

Although party organization seems hierarchical (organized from the top down), it is not. Party organization is a layered structure with each layer linked to, but independent of, the others. Higher levels cannot dictate to or impose penalties on lower levels to ensure compliance.

Party organization is only loosely connected with the party in government. This contrasts with the British system, in which the party leaders in Parliament try to maintain a tight grip on the party organization.

National Party Organization

The **national party chair** heads the national party organization, called the national committee (discussed below). The president appoints the chair of his party; for the party not occupying the White House, the national committee selects the chair. The national chairs are not very visible to the public. They do not receive much media attention, and their names are unknown to most. Haley Barbour, chair of the Republican National Committee from 1993 to 1998, was an exception. He was a frequent guest on TV talk shows and, before 1994, was the party's leading spokesperson and constant critic of Bill Clinton. Barbour was also responsible for GOP-TV, the Republican National Committee's television network. This network, available via satellite, cable systems, the Internet, and TV stations nationwide, provides information on party activities, issues, and personalities. Barbour was also an effective fundraiser, wiping out the party's $4 million debt and raising $158 million with the aid of state parties in 1996.[35] Following his resignation in 1998, Barbour was implicated in a campaign funding scandal when information surfaced that he sought and accepted illegal contributions from foreign interests to fund a tax-exempt think tank used to develop Republican positions on issues.

Barbour's counterpart in the Democratic Party, Donald Fowler, who shared the position with Senator Chris Dodd of Connecticut, was much less visible, as is often the case with the president's party. Like Barbour, Fowler was implicated in campaign funding scandals in 1996 and resigned his position in 1998.

While the **national committees** are the primary governing institutions of the Democratic and Republican Parties, they seldom meet, and it is the national chair and the permanent staff who are the de facto national party organization. The national committees do choose

BECAUSE WE'VE **ALWAYS** REGISTERED REPUBLICAN, THAT'S WHY !

the site of their party's national convention and establish the formula for determining how many delegates each state receives.

National committee members are selected from each state using a variety of methods established by each state party. While states are represented equally on the Republican National Committee (RNC), the Democratic National Committee (DNC) awards states additional seats based on population and support for Democratic candidates in elections. The DNC also includes the party's leaders in Congress, the leaders of several state and local Democratic organizations, and representatives from elements of the party that are often underrepresented on the committee including blacks, Hispanics, and youth.

Both major parties also have **House and Senate campaign committees,** which have grown in influence owing to their ability to raise and distribute campaign funds to their party's candidates for Congress.[36] The National Republican Senatorial Committee raised $25 million in 1997, the National Republican Congressional Committee $20 million. The Democratic Senatorial and Congressional Campaign Committees raised $12 million and $10 million, respectively. Most of the money was used to fund House and Senate candidates in the 1998 elections.

Described as hollow shells in the 1950s and 1960s, the national party organizations are stronger today than they have been since the early twentieth century. Behind

their success is a steady flow of cash from large contributors that is used to assist candidates running for office and strengthen state and local party organizations. As we will see in Chapter 9, the parties can accept huge contributions from corporations, interest groups, and unions that individual candidates and campaigns cannot accept. The Republican Party has led the way in fund-raising, but Democrats are not far behind. Both parties actively recruit candidates to run for office, train them in various campaign technologies, and provide funds to mount an effective campaign. The RNC sponsors Nuts and Bolts seminars that are held throughout the country to provide training in fund-raising, developing a campaign strategy, using media, speech writing, polling, and getting out the vote. The party also has an array of how-to manuals for candidates and state and local party organizers. Both parties have facilities to produce their own radio and television ads.

The Web has become a new tool in the arsenal of political parties.[37] Here, too, the Republicans are ahead of the Democrats. The GOP hopes to put everything it does on-line. One reason is that more Republican than Democratic voters are on-line. Another is the desire to bypass the mainstream media, which it considers unfair, in getting the party's message out.

The box "Party Political Clicks" gives a sample of Web sites sponsored by the national parties and candidates. Citizens were also able to link to each party's 2000 presidential nominating convention via the Web. Each site was linked to the candidates' main themes, including Spanish-language versions, ways for citizens to volunteer, and well-produced position statements on issues. The most prominent feature at each site was a little box that popped up on the screen asking for donations. Democrats could even participate and register their opinions on the party convention platform. Each party also set up sites critical of the other party's presidential candidate.

In a no-holds-barred fight to win control of Congress, both parties constantly upgraded their congressional sites with better messages, better artwork, and more sophisticated technology. The new technology allows the parties to communicate with their activists. Overnight they can send millions of e-mails on a particular issue and do so at minimal cost. Fund-raising is also possible and is more effective than traditional mail solicitations.

The increasing capacity of the national party organizations to offer candidates assistance in their campaigns may contribute to the rising level of party voting in Congress. Members of Congress no doubt do feel beholden to the national party and perhaps a commitment to support party positions. At the same time, members are less beholden to state and local parties. Thus, national party organizations are growing in influence at the expense of state and local parties.[38] Today, the close link between the national party organizations and the parties in Congress moves us closer to the responsible party government model.

State and Local Party Organizations

Each state and local party has a chair and committee to direct the activities of their party activists. In some communities, parties may be so weak and unimportant that there is little party organization. Because of this, someone who wants to become active in the party organization only has to show up at party meetings and be willing to work.

Big-City Party Organizations

Unlike most local party organizations today, the **political machine,** which flourished in some of the nation's largest cities in the late nineteenth and early twentieth centuries, was strong and powerful. At the head of the machine was a boss, who often served as mayor and directed operations in such a way as to maintain control over the city and the organization. (See the box "A Day in the Life of a Machine Politician.")

The machine relied on the votes of the poor and working class, many of whom had only recently immigrated from Europe. Most accounts of machine politics are negative, dwelling on graft and corruption. However, the machine provided a number of valuable services. In a period when there were no welfare agencies, the machine provided jobs, food, and fuel for the thousands of immigrants who had no place else to turn. In return, party leaders expected individuals to vote for machine candidates.

Business also benefited from machines. The machine provided (for a fee) permits for business expansion, licenses, new roads, utilities, and police and fire protection.

The key to the machine's success was **patronage,** that is, giving jobs to party loyalists when the party controlled local government. An army of city employees, whose jobs depended on the political success of the machine, would dutifully bring family and friends to the polls on election day. One of the last of the big-city bosses, Mayor Richard J. Daley, head of the Chicago machine during the 1960s and 1970s, controlled thirty-five thousand public jobs and, indirectly through public contracts, ten thousand private ones.[39]

Reformers disturbed by corruption and by lower-class control of city politics eventually passed laws making it difficult for machines to operate. Merit examinations for city jobs, nonpartisan elections, secret ballots, and voter registration undercut the means that machines had to secure voter loyalty. Political machines were dealt another blow when the federal government assumed responsibility for welfare needs in the 1930s; individuals no longer had to rely on the machine. And with a more educated population and greater employment opportunities, patronage jobs were no longer as desirable.

voter. Because they believed that party leaders in their "smoke-filled rooms" were corrupt and not to be trusted, reformers established the **direct primary** to increase citizen participation and check the influence of party bosses in nominations. The primary allows the voters in an election to choose the party's candidates. Today all states use primary elections, sometimes in conjunction with caucuses and conventions, to nominate candidates. (See also the box "Why Not Return to the 'Smoke-Filled Rooms'?")

Primaries vary from state to state according to who is eligible to vote in them. A **closed primary** limits participation to those who are registered with a party or declare a preference for a party. Thus, only Democrats can vote in the Democratic Party's primary. An **open primary** imposes no such limits; regardless of party registration, one may vote in either party's primary.

Party leaders and others favoring strong parties oppose open primaries. They argue that only voters who are party supporters should be permitted to vote in the party's primary. They fear that independents and opposition partisans will vote for candidates who are less sympathetic to the party's position on issues or who are less likely to win.

A minority of states use runoff primaries, which pit the two highest vote getters in the primary against each other for the party's nomination. Over the years, the inability of the Republican Party to compete effectively for office in the South meant that the winner of the Democratic Party's primary was virtually assured of winning the general election. Due to the large number of Democratic candidates, sometimes the winner of the primary did not have a majority of the vote. In those cases, some southern states used a runoff election between the two highest vote getters in the primary.

Although primaries have increased citizen participation in nominations, turnout in primaries is quite low and unrepresentative. Turnout in presidential primaries averages at best 10 percent. While it is higher for primaries held early in the year, such as New Hampshire's, which is always first, for those that come later turnout falls off. In 2000, turnout was again high in New Hampshire and the states immediately following, but dropped dramatically when opponents to Bush and Gore withdrew from the race. Voters in primaries are unrepresentative of the public at large. Primary voters tend to have higher incomes and education and to be older, more interested in politics, and more partisan.[40]

In addition to attracting a small and unrepresentative group of voters to the ballot box, primaries have other

Why Not Return to the "Smoke-Filled Rooms"?

Some commentators have advocated returning to convention nominations. If we did so, the abuses that we associate with the smoke-filled rooms of a century ago would be less likely to occur today because of the greater likelihood of exposure by the media and hostile voter reaction. In states and localities where the parties are competitive, it is likely that conventions would produce strong candidates. This would give voters a real choice in the general election. However, in locales dominated by one party, the convention system would not necessarily produce stronger candidates than a primary. At the presidential level, smoke-filled rooms produced the likes of Franklin Roosevelt and John Kennedy.

Perhaps the greatest argument for smoke-filled rooms is Harry Truman. Although a product of machine politics, Truman was honest and incorruptible. Tapped to be FDR's vice president in 1944 by party bosses who knew Roosevelt would not live out his term, Truman became an excellent president.

Why haven't we returned to the convention system? Primaries are widely accepted. They *seem* more democratic because more people are involved than in conventions, where only party activists participate. But the sheer number of people involved is only one aspect of democracy and probably not the most important. Democracy also implies that those making the nominations are repre-

sentative of the public; primary electorates are not. Moreover, a democratic process must offer some choice, and primaries adversely affect competition.

Although it is unlikely that we will abolish primaries and return to conventions, in recent years party leaders have asserted more control in some states through preprimary endorsements. Parties endorse candidates for nomination. The endorsed candidates are listed first on the primary ballot or are simply publicized as the "official" party candidate. Although on occasion the preferred candidate is defeated, the voters usually go along with the party's choice. Such arrangements promote party strength and ultimately responsiveness to voters.

Political Parties in Time

1800 Thomas Jefferson builds the first American political party and with it defeats John Adams and the Federalists for the presidency. Jefferson's success marks the beginning of the first of several party systems in the United States.

1828 After dominating American politics for twenty-eight years, the Jeffersonians split into rival factions.

1832 Andrew Jackson builds a mass-population-based new Democratic Party, forerunner of the modern Democratic Party, wins a second term as president by defeating the Whigs, and ushers in a new party system. Jackson secures his nomination through the newly devised national nominating convention, which continues to play a role in party nominations today.

1860 Both the Democrats and Whigs split over slavery. Abolitionists form a new Republican Party to contest with the Democrats and elect Abraham Lincoln as president. Lincoln's victory marks the beginning of the third party system.

1880 Big-city political machines flourish, supported by patronage and corruption and a large immigrant population in need of the services they provide.

1890 The Progressive movement begins and directs its attention to ending corruption in political parties. Progressives advocate reforms, including nonpartisan elections in which the party affiliation of candidates are not listed on the ballot, awarding government jobs on the basis of merit, and using the direct primary as a method of nominating candidates for public office.

1896 Southern and Plains farmers back the Democratic Party nominee for president, William Jennings Bryan, against the Republican nominee, William McKinley. With the backing of eastern monied interests, McKinley wins, the Republican Party becomes the country's dominant party, and the election signals the beginning of the fourth party system.

1902 The direct primary, in which voters rather than party activists in conventions nominate party candidates, is introduced in Wisconsin and begins to spread rapidly from state to state.

1908 Oregon is the first state to nominate delegates to national party conventions in a presidential preference primary election.

1912 In spite of the dominance of the Republican Party, Woodrow Wilson defeats the Republican nominee Taft, as former Republican president Theodore Roosevelt runs as a candidate of the Progressive Party, dividing the Republican vote.

1932 Franklin D. Roosevelt, a Democrat, is elected to the first of four terms as president. His promise to deal with the Great Depression wins the votes of lower- and middle-class Americans, breaks Republican dominance in national politics, and begins the fifth party system.

1948 The Democrats nominate Harry Truman for president. The Southern wing of the party, so-called Dixiecrats, walk out of the nominating convention in protest over a pro–civil rights plank in the party platform.

1964 Democratic president Lyndon Johnson signs the 1964 Civil Rights Act passed by a Democratic majority in Congress, eroding the Democratic strength in the South. In 1968, Nixon carries every southern state.

1968 The Democratic Party is ravaged by divisions over civil rights and the Vietnam War. The divisions erupt in Chicago, site of the party's presidential nominating convention, where students and those seeking to reform the party clash with police outside the convention hall. Hubert Humphrey, Johnson's vice president, is nominated but is unable to bring the party together and loses to Republican Richard Nixon.

1970 The Democrats at a midterm convention vote to change the rules for selecting delegates to their presidential nominating conventions. The change sets in motion a move toward primary elections rather than caucuses as the principal means for selecting delegates in both parties and shifts power in the Democratic Party from party officeholders and activists to political outsiders supporting individuals candidates.

1980 The South completes a party realignment begun in 1948. Most white southerners shift loyalties to the Republican Party, most black southerners to the Democrats.

1988 Christian conservatives become a dominant force in the Republican Party.

1992 Bill Clinton breaks a three-term run of Republican success in winning the White House by moving the Democratic Party more toward the center. Clinton wins in a three-person race that sees minor-party candidate Ross Perot win 19 percent of the popular vote but no electoral college votes.

1994 The Republican Party wins control of both Houses of Congress for the first time since 1954.

1995 Party voting in Congress reaches a thirty-year high.

flaws. In some ways, the primary process is less responsive to voters than party conventions, where candidates were once selected by a small group of party leaders meeting in smoke-filled hotel rooms.

Primaries do not necessarily provide voters with much choice. Many primaries are uncontested. Often the presence of an incumbent deters challengers, or at least strong challengers. In either case, incumbents are almost always renominated.

Primaries also may make the general election less competitive. The minority party (that is, the party less likely to win the general election) often has no strong candidate who can mount an effective campaign in the general election. In preprimary days, party leaders generally made sure there were some candidates running in the general election regardless of election prospects.

Another problem with primaries is that the electorate may nominate a candidate known by his or her party peers to be incompetent, difficult to work with, or lacking in character and integrity. Although the convention system does not guarantee that such candidates will be avoided, party leaders are more likely to know the real strengths and weaknesses of potential candidates than are voters, who must rely on the media for information. Indeed, voters have so little information about primary candidates that success often turns on name recognition.

Primaries hurt the most, however, by freeing candidates from supporting the party's program. Candidates can bypass leaders and appeal to voters directly. It is nearly impossible for party leaders to withhold nominations from candidates who are party members in name only or who often vote with the other party. Thus, the party bonds are weakened, and members can feel free to vote and act however they want.

This outcome might seem desirable. But when candidates vote completely independent of their party, it is more difficult for voters to cast an informed vote. When parties offer a clear choice, voters know what they are voting for and can reward or punish the parties for what they do or plan to do in office. Thus, party voting can make government more responsive to the voters.

Conclusion: Do Political Parties Make Government More Responsive?

Although the Founders initially opposed the idea of political parties, some later turned to parties when they be-

gan to have serious differences of opinion about public policies. They recognized that their ideas could prevail if they aligned with others who agreed with them and together elected a majority in government. Then, as now, parties were a vehicle to organize a stable majority. For Jefferson and Madison, the important issue was the scope and power of national government. Jefferson's views prevailed, but only with the aid of the party he created.

While organizing a political party was a way for Jefferson, one of America's most influential leaders, to shape government, parties are also a way for average Americans to make government more responsive to them. Making government more accountable is the major contribution of political parties to democratic government. Democracy without political parties is difficult, and probably impossible, because there is no viable alternative to parties as a means of organizing a stable governing majority and making it accountable to the people.

Although in practice parties do not live up to this idea (what human institution does?), and we certainly might consider changes to make parties more responsible and responsive, Americans should be interested in strengthening parties. Without political parties that link candidates and voters on issues, voters are confronted with a hopelessly confusing array of candidates and have little idea of how a vote for any one of them will affect government. Without parties, the media, campaign consultants, lobbying groups, big donors, and self-financed wealthy candidates would play an even larger role in politics than they do now.

There is no doubt that parties are weaker than they were a century ago. But in the 1990s, parties experienced a resurgence in several key ways. In terms of the party in the electorate, the erosion of party strength has stopped. The proportion of voters claiming partisan allegiance has grown slightly after steady declines since the 1960s. Split-ticket voting, after reaching an all-time high in 1992, decreased dramatically in 1996 (see Figure 3).

The party in government is also stronger. Party cohesion in Congress has increased. With the demise of the southern Democratic conservatives, the Democratic Party is much more homogeneous. Many members of both parties are more dependent on the national party committees for campaign support than they were a decade ago. Both these trends have contributed to the increase in party voting and support for the president by his own party.[41]

Finally, as we have seen, national party organizations have become much more powerful. Their activities are fueled by their ability to raise and spend essentially unlimited amounts of money because of loopholes in campaign finance laws (for more on this, see Chapter 9). While parties still compete for influence with interest groups, pollsters, campaign consultants, and the media, it is often funds raised by the national parties that buy the polling, campaign consultation, and media time. Both presidential and congressional candidates need the national party organizations because of the parties' revenue-raising ability.

Each component of our political parties—party in the electorate, party in government, and party organization—has shown significant signs of revitalization. Where parties have made few recent gains, however, is in their lack of control over the nomination process. Political parties have little influence over who can run for party office. In spite of name recognition, endorsements, and a cache of money to throw at the 1996 nomination, the Republican Party could not prevent Steve Forbes, a multimillionaire magazine publisher, and Pat Buchanan, a television personality—neither of whom had ever been elected to anything—and a host of others from entering the race and challenging the party's choice, Bob Dole. These candidates were taken seriously. They got airtime, coverage by national newspapers and magazines,

and into presidential debates. They attacked Dole, undermining his chance of winning the presidency, and there was nothing he or the party could do about it. George W. Bush faced a similar although a less serious challenge in his quest for the Republican Party nomination in 2000. Today, anyone can claim to belong to a party and run for the party's nomination for president or any other office. In the past, the party organization could discourage candidates with little chance of winning an election, by withholding its support, or threatening sanctions if necessary.

Today, there are many indications of a resurgence in party strength. Yet, split-ticket voting and the divided government it produces make it unclear how one's vote will affect what government does. Citizens elect a president of one party and a majority in Congress of another and wonder why there is gridlock in Washington. Voters see parties as instruments of delay and deadlock, not realizing that it is often lack of party discipline, and not the reverse, that causes the deadlock. Citizens have a greater prospect of influencing the direction of government if they elect those who are loyal and committed to a party. This factor is what led E. E. Schattschneider to reflect on the inevitability and necessity of parties in our American democracy.

EPILOGUE

McCain Endorses

On the occasion of his withdrawal from the race, John McCain pledged to press his case for political reform and warned Republicans that they run the risk of disappearing if they do not get on board. He offered best wishes to George W. Bush but no endorsement. Bush acknowledged that both men needed time to think. McCain took a vacation and assessed his options. These, as described by an aide, included barnstorming the country to promote campaign finance reform, leading a fight at the Republican National Convention in an effort to include campaign finance reform in the party's platform, or making a third-party presidential bid. A third-party bid was unlikely. When questioned about this, McCain said, "I love my home."[42]

Following weeks of meetings between McCain's campaign staff and Bush's operatives, the two men met in Pittsburgh, two months after McCain's withdrawal from the race. At a news conference following the meeting, McCain initially seemed reluctant to utter his endorsement of Bush; however, pressed by reporters, he smiled and repeated several times, "I support Governor Bush." Bush responded, "I enthusiastically accept."[43] McCain went on to say that he and Bush agreed on Social Security, education, and the military and that he hoped Bush would win the presidency. It was an endorsement, but far from a wholehearted one. McCain also said that he will continue to push his reform agenda.

Whether the endorsement translated into votes for Bush in November is unclear. Most McCain voters did support Bush, but party loyalty played a big part in that.

Key Terms

New Deal coalition
ticket splitting
dealignment
two-party system
multiparty systems
single-member districts
winner-take-all
proportional
  representation
party in the electorate
party in government
party organization
realignment

party identification
responsible party government
national party chair
national committees
House and Senate campaign
  committees
political machine
patronage
caucus
direct primary
closed primary
open primary

Further Reading

David Brooks, ed., *Backward and Upward: The New Conservative Writing* (New York: Vintage, 1996). This is a collection of combative, often funny essays from the political right. The authors hold nothing sacred, and their lampooning of various liberal beliefs shows that conservatism is as much about personality as ideology.

James Carville, *We're Right, They're Wrong: A Handbook for Spirited Progressives* (New York: Random House, 1996). In this book, President Clinton's chief campaign adviser and one of Washington's most prominent Democratic strategists responds to the Republicans' platform during the 1994 and 1996 elections. Carville includes such features as the Republicans' "Biggest Lies" and "Most Expensive Boondoggles."

Congressional Quarterly, *National Party Conventions: 1831–1996* (Washington, D.C.: Congressional Quarterly Press, 1997). All you ever wanted to know about each party's national nominating convention, including lists of keynote speakers, platforms, delegate selection rules, nominees, and more.

David J. Gillespie, *Politics at the Periphery: Third Parties in Two-Party America.* (Columbia: University of South Carolina Press, 1993). This work provides both a historical review of the roles played by third parties in American politics and a look at the impact of recent third parties on election outcomes.

Stanley B. Greenberg, *Middle Class Dreams: The Politics and Power of the New American Majority* (New York: Times Books, 1995). President Clinton's adviser looks at the radical shape of American politics today and contends that both political parties have betrayed the middle class.

Edwin O'Connor, *The Last Hurrah* (New York: Bantam, 1957). A warm, intimate novel set in Boston in the 1950s that contrasts the old-style party election campaigns with new media-oriented ones.

William L. Riordon, *Plunkitt of Tammany Hall* (New York: Dutton, 1963). A series of witty talks by a ward boss of New York City's Democratic Party machine. A slice of Americana, this book discusses "honest graft" and other aspects of "practical politics" and in the process demonstrates why political machines flourished.

Mike Royko, *Boss: Richard J. Daley of Chicago* (New York: New American Library, 1971). An intriguing account of how the Chicago political machine operated under the late mayor Richard J. Daley.

Larry Sabato, *The Party's Just Begun* (Glenview, Ill.: Scott, Foresman, 1988). An overview of the American party system: why we need it, what it does, and how we can make it work better.

Electronic Resources

www.rnc.org/
The home page of the Republican National Committee. It provides many links to government institutions, important Republican office-holders, the national committee headquarters, and issue positions. See GOP-TV through the Web.

democrats.org/index/html
The home page of the Democratic National Committee. It provides similar links from a Democratic perspective, as well as links to information about Democratic Party history and past Democratic conventions.

www.reformparty.org/
The home page of the Reform Party, with information on plans for 2000 and beyond.

www.politicalindex.com/sect8.htm
This site gives you a flavor of many of the minor parties involved in U.S. politics. Check out the links to the U.S. Taxpayers Party, the Communists, the Libertarians, and many others.

www.greenparty.org
The site provides information on the Green Party, USA, including some information on Ralph Nader's run for the presidency.

InfoTrac College Edition

"How Gerrymandering Helped American Blacks"
"Voting Turnout"
"Leveling the Campaign Trail"
"Can Cheney Take Heat?"

Notes

1. Alison Mitchell, "McCain Seems Poised to End Campaign," *New York Times,* March 6, 2000, p. A20.
2. "Calling on Voters in a Fierce GOP Race," *New York Times,* February 14, 2000, p. A16.
3. Eric Pooley, "Read My Knuckles," *Time,* February 28, 2000, pp. 29–32.
4. Keith Bradshear, "After New Hampshire, a Push to Lift Up Bush," *New York Times,* February 22, 2000, p. A10.
5. Alison Mitchell and Frank Bruni, "Bush and McCain Swap Strategies for Next Battle," *New York Times,* February 21, 2000, p. A12.

6. Pooley, "Read My Knuckles."

7. Mitchell, "McCain Seems Poised to End Campaign."

8. E. E. Schattschneider, *Party Government* (New York: Holt, Rinehart & Winston, 1960), p. 1.

9. Jack Dennis, "Trends in Public Support for the American Party System," in *Parties and Elections in an Anti-Party Age,* ed. Jeff Fishel (Bloomington: Indiana University Press, 1978).

10. Frank Sorauf, *Political Parties in the American System,* 4th ed. (Boston: Little, Brown, 1980).

11. Richard Hofstadter, *The Idea of Party System: The Rise of Legitimate Opposition in the United States, 1780–1840* (Berkeley: University of California Press, 1969).

12. Theodore J. Lowi, *The Personal President: Power Invested, Promise Unfulfilled* (Ithaca, N.Y.: Cornell University Press, 1985).

13. James MacGregor Burns, *The Vineyard of Liberty* (New York: Knopf, 1982).

14. Kevin Phillips, *The Emerging Republican Majority* (New York: Doubleday, 1969).

15. Everett Carll Ladd, *Where Have All the Voters Gone?* (New York: Norton, 1982), 78; 1984 and 1988 data are from the 1984 and 1988 CPS National Election Study.

16. James L. Sundquist, *Dynamics of the Party System: Alignment and Realignment of Political Parties in the United States* (Washington, D.C.: Brookings Institution, 1973).

17. J. R. Petrocik and F. T. Steeper, "The Political Landscape in 1988," *Public Opinion Magazine* (September/October 1987): 41–44; H. Norpoth, "Party Realignment in the 1980s," *Public Opinion Quarterly* 51 (Fall 1987): 376–390.

18. Thomas Edsall, "The Democrats' Class and Gender Gap," *Washington Post National Weekly Edition,* June 6, 1994, p. 12.

19. Thomas Edsall, "The Fissure Running through the Democratic Party," *Washington Post National Weekly Edition,* June 6–12, 1994, p. 11.

20. Ibid.

21. Katharine Q. Seelye, "Democrats across U.S. Continue to Flee Party," *Lincoln Journal-Star,* October 7, 1995, p. 1A.

22. John Petrocik, "Realignment," *Journal of Politics* 49 (May 1987): 347–375; George Rabinowitz, Paul-Henri Gurian, and Stuart MacDonald, "The Structure of Presidential Elections and the Process of Realignment," *American Journal of Political Science* 28 (November 1984): 611–635; D. Broder, "The GOP Plays Dixie," *Washington Post National Weekly Edition,* September 12–18, 1988, p. 4; T. B. Edsall, "A Serious Case of White Flight," *Washington Post National Weekly Edition,* September 10–16, 1990, p. 13.

23. Walter Dean Burnham, *Critical Elections and the Mainstream of American Politics* (New York: Norton, 1970); Helmut Norpoth and Jerrold Rusk, "Partisan Dealignment in the American Electorate," *American Political Science Review* 76 (September 1982): 522–537; David W. Rhode, "The Fall Elections: Realignment and Dealignment," *Chronicle of Higher Education,* December 14, 1994, pp. B1–B2.

24. Martin P. Wallenberg, *The Rise of Candidate-Centered Politics* (Cambridge, Mass.: Harvard University Press, 1991).

25. Maurice Duverger, *Political Parties* (New York: Wiley, 1963). See also Edward R. Tune, "The Relationship between Seats and Votes in Two-Party Systems," *American Political Science Review* 67 (1973): 540–554.

26. See also Lowi, *Personal President.* He makes the point that two parties survived in the United States despite the use of multimember districts in elections for Congress in the nineteenth century.

27. Frank Bruni, "Bush Signaling Readiness to Go His Own Way," *New York Times,* April 3, 2000, pp. A1–A15.

28. D. Sarasohn, "Wall Falls on Reagan Coalition," *Lincoln Sunday Journal-Star,* February 18, 1990, p. 1C.

29. Steven Roberts, "Near Death Experience," *U.S. News and World Report,* November 6, 1996, p. 28.

30. William R. Shaffer, *Party and Ideology in the United States Congress* (Lanham, Md.: University Press of America, 1980).

31. Bruce I. Oppenheimer, "The Importance of Elections in a Strong Congressional Era," in *Do Elections Matter?* ed. Benjamin Ginsberg and Alan Stone (Armonck, N.Y.: Sharpe, 1996), 120–138.

32. David Broder, "Polarization Growing Force for Political Parties," *Lincoln Journal-Star,* January 22, 1995, p. 4B.

33. Dan Carney, "As Hostilities Rage on the Hill, Partisan-Vote Rate Soars," *Congressional Quarterly Weekly Report,* January 27, 1996, pp. 199–200.

34. *Congressional Quarterly Weekly Report,* December 11, 1999, pp. 2993–2994.

35. Lloyd Grove, "A Good Ol' Boy Going in for the Kill," *Washington Post National Weekly Edition,* August 22–28, 1994, pp. 13–14, 32.

36. Frank J. Sorauf, *Money in American Elections* (Glenview, Ill.: Scott, Foresman, 1988), 121–153; Paul Herrnson, *Party Campaigning in the 1980s* (Cambridge, Mass.: Harvard University Press, 1988).

37. Neil Munro, "The New Wired Politics," *National Journal,* April 22, 2000, pp. 1260–1263.

38. Xandra Kayden, "The Nationalization of the Party System," in *Parties, Interest Groups, and Campaign Finance Laws,* ed. Michael Malbin (Washington, D.C.: American Enterprise Institute, 1980).

39. Milton L. Rakove, *Don't Make No Waves, Don't Back No Losers* (Bloomington: Indiana University Press, 1975).

40. Austin Ranney, *Participation in American Presidential Nominations, 1976* (Washington, D.C.: American Enterprise Institute, 1977). See also Austin Ranney, "Parties in State Politics," in *Politics in the American States,* 3d ed., ed. Herbert Jacob and Kenneth Vines, (Boston: Little, Brown, 1980), pp. 61–99.

41. Oppenheimer, "The Importance of Elections."

42. Alexander Marko, "Bush, McCain Close Ranks, Do Maverick Voters Care?" *Christian Science Monitor,* May 10, 2000, p. 6.

43. Ibid.

Elections

To Package or Not?

You are Bill Clinton. It is May 1992, and you are sure you will win the Democratic nomination for president but unsure whether you can win the election. Your road to the nomination has been rocky; many people, including loyal Democrats, think you are a weak candidate. They fear you will drag the Democrats down to their fourth straight presidential election defeat. Now your campaign staff presents you with a plan that they think will lead to victory in November. But from your perspective the plan has significant problems.

You are one of six declared Democratic presidential candidates. None of you is well known; Paul Tsongas is a former U.S. senator from Massachusetts who dropped out of the Senate a decade earlier to battle cancer; Jerry Brown, a former governor of California; Tom Harkin, a U.S. senator from Iowa; Bob Kerrey, a U.S. senator and former governor of Nebraska; and Douglas Wilder, governor of Virginia, the first black ever to be elected governor. You and the others struggled for name recognition and votes in the snows of New Hampshire. Tsongas was predicted to win, since he had the advantage of being from neighboring Massachusetts.

Your candidacy started strong but soon floundered. Stories of your alleged womanizing flooded the media. The press gave extensive coverage to one woman, Gennifer Flowers, who claimed she had had a twelve-year affair with you. Fearing that your campaign would end soon after it began, you and your wife, Hillary, agreed to be on the television program *60 Minutes* to talk about these accusations and about your marriage. The show, which aired right after the Super Bowl, captured a huge audience. You denied having an affair with Flowers, admitted your marriage had had some hard times, but said you and Hillary had stuck together through good times and bad. The interview evoked sympathy for you. Polls showed that the scandal over Gennifer Flowers swayed only 11 percent of the voters, and 82 percent thought that enough had been said about your personal life.[1]

Just when you thought that crisis was over, the *Wall Street Journal* published a story on your draft record. Although many men your age had been drafted for the Vietnam War, many others avoided the draft, and you were one of them. The former ROTC head at the University of Arkansas claimed you had promised to

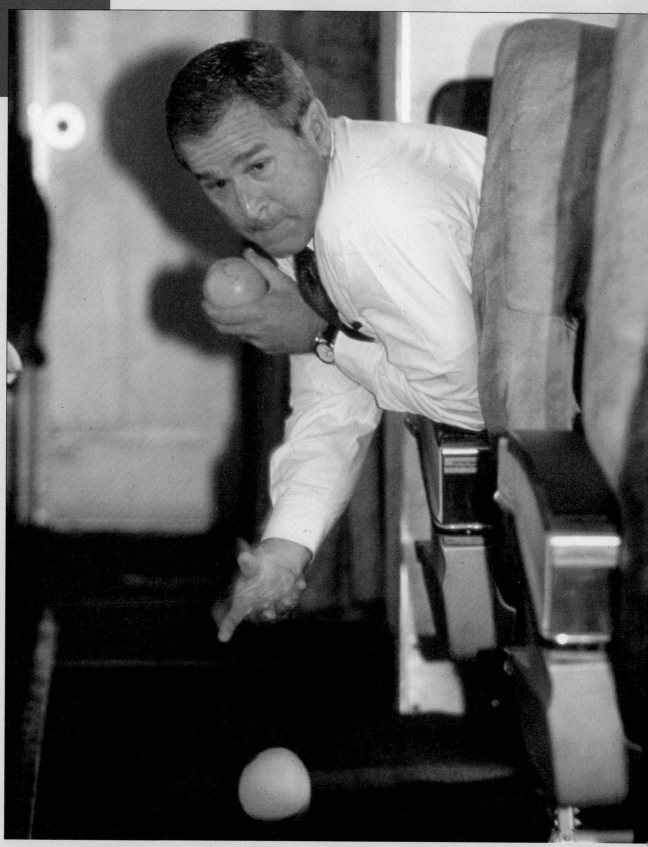

George W. Bush relaxes during a plane ride between primary campaign stops.
Brooks Kraft/Corbis-Sygma

join but then changed your mind when you were no longer threatened by the draft. Your letter to the head, thanking him for "saving me from the draft," was a follow-up story that made the media rounds. A week before the New Hampshire primary, support for you in the polls dropped seventeen points in forty-eight hours.[2] Polls indicated you could finish third behind both Tsongas and Kerrey.

Facing disaster, you spent the last week appearing on television night and day and meeting as many people as you could in malls and fast-food restaurants. New Hampshire had only 125,000 voters, and you must have met most of them. You finished second to Paul Tsongas and promptly labeled yourself the winner—"the comeback kid."

After New Hampshire, you became the front runner when Tsongas's campaign sputtered and died. Yet throughout the primary season, voters were never really very enthusiastic about you.[3] Before the primary season was over, your campaign team assembled focus groups of voters and then prepared a report. It concluded that most voters did not really know much about you, but many did not like you anyway. You are viewed unfavorably by a large minority of Democratic voters and by about 40 percent of all general election voters. The report states that voters have a general impression that "[Clinton] will say what is necessary and that he does not 'talk straight.' " Moreover, you are in large part responsible for this image, your con-

sultants inform you. They say that voters believe you are the ultimate politician: evasive, never gives a straight answer, always has handy lists and instant analysis. Moreover, voters say, "He's not real; he's privileged like the Kennedys; he can't stand up to special interests." The report concluded that people are discounting your messages because of their impression of you. And they do not like Hillary much, either, perceiving her as unaffectionate and not interested in her family.[4] Indeed, many voters do not even know you and Hillary have a daughter, because Hillary has tried to shield her from the media.

Your consultants outline a comprehensive strategy to try to remake your image, to "reposition" you, to reflect your human qualities, and to show that you can stand up to special interests. They call for creating an image of an "honest, plain-folks idealist and his warm and loving wife."[5] To create this image, the plan suggests specific tactics, such as your appearances on television talk shows, playing your saxophone, making fun of yourself, and saying unpopular things to powerful groups to prove your independence. It also suggests ideas for making your family more prominent. It calls for "events where Bill and Hillary can go on dates with the American people." Finally, it suggests broad strategies, such as a populist message that would appeal to the middle class, calling for change and pointing out failures of government to bring about a secure economic future.

Your advisers believe that these messages work. In focus groups, people become much more favorable about you when they are given information about your coming from a small town, surviving your childhood with an alcoholic stepfather, working your way through Yale, and now asking for change in American society.

It angers you that voters do not know much about you. At a staff meeting, you give vent to these feelings: "So far as I'm concerned, we're at zero. . . . We don't exist in the national consciousness. . . . I don't think you can minimize how horrible I feel, having worked all my life to stand for things, having busted my butt for seven months and the American people don't know crap about it."[6] You want to inform people about your real background and beliefs, and you see that this is a well-thought-out plan to do that.

Yet you realize there's a risk to this strategy. One risk is that it will seem too much like a strategy. People already think you are a slick politician, and this plan seems so programmed, so, well, political. Voters may believe that any new image is just that: an image, not reality. Moreover, there is a risk that some of the activities suggested will not seem very presidential: appearances on TV talk shows, playing your sax, and "dates with the American people." Perhaps these kinds of activities will make you seem less presidential than Bush.

What do you decide? Adopt the plan or not?

A mericans have fought and died in wars to preserve the rights of citizens to choose their leaders through democratic elections. Some have even died here at home, trying to exercise these rights. Despite this, most Americans take these important rights for granted; about half do not bother to vote even in presidential elections, and fewer still participate in other ways.

Moreover, the process by which we choose our leaders, especially the president, has been sharply criticized in recent years. Critics charge that election campaigns are meaningless and offer little information to the vot-

ers, that candidates pander to the most ill-informed and mean-spirited citizens, and that public relations and campaign spending, not positions on issues or strength of character, determine the winners.

In this chapter, we analyze why voting is important to a democracy and why, despite its importance, so few do it. We then examine political campaigns and elections to see how they affect the kinds of leaders and policies we have. We will see that the lack of participation by many reinforces the government's responsiveness to those who do participate, especially those who are well organized.

The American Electorate

During the more than two centuries since the Constitution was written, two important developments have altered the right to vote, termed **suffrage.** First, suffrage gradually has been extended to include almost all citizens aged eighteen or over. Second, deciding who may vote now lies largely in the hands of the federal government. The electorate has been widened mostly through constitutional amendments, congressional acts, and Supreme Court decisions.

Early Limits on Voting Rights

Although the Declaration of Independence stated that "all men are created equal," at the time of the Constitution and shortly thereafter, the central political right of voting was denied to most Americans. States decided who would be granted suffrage. In some only an estimated 10 percent of the white males could vote, whereas in others 80 percent could.[7]

Controversial property qualifications for voting existed in many states. Some argued that only those with an economic stake in society should have a say in political life. But critics of the property requirement repeated a story of Tom Paine's:

> You require that a man shall have $60 worth of property, or he shall not vote. Very well . . . here is a man who today owns a jackass, and the jackass is worth $60. Today the man is a voter and he goes to the polls and deposits his vote. Tomorrow the jackass dies. The next day the man comes to vote without his jackass and he cannot vote at all. Now tell me, which was the voter, the man or the jackass?[8]

Because the Constitution gave states the power to regulate suffrage, the elimination of property requirements was a gradual process. By the 1820s, most were gone, although some lingered to midcentury.

In some states, religious tests also were applied. A voter had to be a member of the "established" church or could not be a member of certain religions (such as Roman Catholic or Jewish). However, religious tests disappeared even more quickly than property qualifications.

By the time of the Civil War, state action had expanded the rights of white men. However, neither slaves, Indians, nor southern free blacks could vote, although northern blacks could in a few states.[9] Women's voting rights were confined to local elections in a few states.[10]

Blacks and the Right to Vote

The Civil War began the long, slow, and often violent process of expanding the rights of blacks to full citizenship. Between 1865 and 1870, three amendments were passed to give political rights to former slaves and other blacks. One, the Fifteenth Amendment, prohibited the denial of voting rights on the basis of race and thus gave the right to vote to black men.

For a short time following the ratification of this amendment, a northern military presence in the South and close monitoring of southern politics enabled blacks to vote and hold office in the South, where 90 percent of all blacks lived. During this **Reconstruction** period, two southern blacks were elected to the Senate and fourteen were elected to the House between 1869 and 1876.

Although blacks did not dominate politics or even receive a proportional share of offices, whites saw blacks' political activities as a threat to their own dominance. White southerners began to prevent blacks from voting through intimidation that ranged from mob violence and lynchings to economic sanctions against blacks who attempted to vote.

These methods, both violent and nonviolent, were tolerated by the North, where the public and political leaders had lost interest in the fate of blacks or had simply grown tired of the struggle. In 1876, a compromise ended Reconstruction. In the wake of the disputed 1876 presidential election, southern Democrats agreed to support Republican Rutherford B. Hayes for president in return for an end to the northern military presence in the South and a hands-off policy toward activities there.

By the end of the nineteenth century, blacks were effectively disfranchised in all of the South. The last black southern member of Congress served to 1901. Another would not be elected until 1972.

The loss of black voting rights was legitimized in southern constitutions and laws. **Literacy tests** were often required, supposedly to make sure voters could read and write and thus evaluate political information. Most blacks, who had been denied education, were illiterate. Many whites also were illiterate, but fewer were barred from voting. Local election registrars exercised nearly complete discretion in deciding who had to take the test and how to administer and evaluate it. Educated blacks often were asked for legal interpretations of obscure constitutional provisions, which few could provide.

Four of the men shown in this 1870 poster with Frederick Douglass (center) served in Congress: Hiram Revels in the Senate and Benjamin Turner, Josiah T. Walls, and Joseph Rainey in the House. Also pictured are writer William Wells Brown and Bishop Richard Allen, founder of the African Methodist Episcopal Church.
Library of Congress

Some laws had exemptions that whites were allowed to take advantage of. An "understanding clause" exempted those who could not read and write but who could explain sections of the federal or state constitution to the satisfaction of the examiner, and a "good moral character clause" exempted those with such character. Again, local election registrars exercised discretion in deciding who understood the Constitution and who had good character. Finally, the **grandfather clause** exempted those whose grandfathers had the right to vote before 1867—that is, before blacks could legally vote in the South.

The **poll tax** also deprived blacks of voting rights. The tax, though only a couple of dollars, was often a sizable proportion of one's monthly income. In some states individuals had to pay not only for the present election but for every past election in which they were eligible to vote but did not.

In the **white primary,** blacks were barred from vot-

ing in primary elections, where party nominees were chosen. Because the Democrats always won the general elections, the real contests were in the Democratic primaries. The states justified excluding blacks on the grounds that political parties were private, rather than governmental, organizations and thus could discriminate just as private clubs or individuals could.

Less formal means also were used to exclude blacks from voting. Registrars often closed their offices when blacks tried to register, or whites threatened blacks with the loss of jobs or housing if they tried to vote. Polling places were sometimes located far from black neighborhoods or were moved at the last minute without notifying potential voters. If these means failed, whites threatened or practiced violence. In one election in Mobile, whites wheeled a cannon to a polling place and aimed it at about one thousand blacks lined up to vote.

The treatment of blacks by the southern establishment was summarized on the floor of the Senate by South Carolina Senator Benjamin ("Pitchfork Ben") Tillman, who served from 1895 to 1918. As he put it, "We took the government away. We stuffed ballot boxes. We shot them. We are not ashamed of it."

Over time, the Supreme Court and Congress outlawed the "legal" barriers to black voting in the South. The Court invalidated the grandfather clause in 1915 and the white primary in 1944. Through the Twenty-fourth Amendment, Congress abolished the poll tax for federal elections in 1964, and the Court invalidated the tax for state elections in 1966.[11] But threats of physical violence and economic reprisals still kept most southern blacks from voting. Although many blacks in the urban areas of the rim South (such as Florida, North Carolina, Tennessee, and Texas) could and did vote, those in the rural South and most in the Deep South could not; in 1960, black registration ranged from 5 to 40 percent in southern states.[12] (See also the "American Diversity" box.)

The Voting Rights Act and the Redistricting Controversy

The **Voting Rights Act (VRA)** dramatically changed the face of the electorate in the South and then later in other parts of the nation (see the "What Government Does Right" box). Given the success of the VRA and faced with an expanded black electorate, some white officials in areas of large black populations used new means to diminish the political clout of African Americans. Their technique was *gerrymandering* (see box "Racial

Before the Voting Rights Act in 1965, few African Americans held major public office. Only a handful were members of Congress, and few were state legislators, mayors of major cities, or other important political officers. Following the Voting Rights Act, southern blacks began to have the political clout to elect members of their own race to office for the first time. Progress, slow to be sure, has occurred; in 1968, there were only twenty-three African American legislators in southern legislatures, but by 1997, there were over five hundred, including forty-five in Mississippi. Virginia, the heart of the Confederacy, elected the nation's first black governor, Douglas Wilder. And sixteen black members of Congress represent southern constituencies.

The number of northern black officeholders also has increased, reflecting heightened black political activity there too. Richard Hatcher, who became mayor of Gary, Indiana, in 1968, was the first black mayor of a major U.S. city. By 1993, there were thirty-eight black mayors in northern and southern cities of fifty thousand or more. This includes not only cities where blacks are a majority, such as New Orleans, Detroit, Baltimore, and Birmingham, but also cities where blacks are a minority, such as Seattle and Denver.

Nationally, the number of black officeholders has increased from an estimated 1,200 in 1969 to over 8,800 in 1998. Although this is far from proportional representation, it is a dramatic increase.

Hispanics, too, have improved their representation in political office. From a total of little more than 3,000 Hispanic public officials in 1985, their numbers have grown to nearly 5,500, including 200 state elected legislators and executives.

In sum, though progress seems slow, African Americans and Hispanics, like other ethnic groups, are beginning to achieve political clout through elections.

SOURCES: *Statistical Abstract of the U.S., 1999* (Washington, D.C.: Government Printing Office, 1999), Tables 481, 483, and 484; Joint Center for Political Studies, *National Roster of Black Elected Officials*, Web page.

Gerrymandering"). Through devices that political scientists call **"cracking, stacking, and packing,"** districts were drawn to minimize black representation depending on the size and configuration of the black and white populations. Cracking divides significant, concentrated black populations into two or more districts so that neither will be majority black; stacking combines a large black population with an even greater white population; and packing puts a huge black population into one district rather than two, where blacks might approach a majority in each.

Initially, the Supreme Court was reluctant to find these practices illegal without specific proof that their intent was to discriminate against black voters.[13] But in 1982, congressional revision of the VRA required states with large minority populations to draw boundaries in ways to increase the probabilities that minorities will win seats. The focus of the voting rights legislation, then, turned from protecting the right of suffrage to trying to ensure that voting rights result in the election of African American and other minority officeholders. With this new statute as an indication of congressional intent, the Court then did strike down districting in North Carolina as inappropriately diluting black voting power.[14]

After the 1990 census, eleven new **majority-minority** congressional districts were created for blacks and six for Hispanics. All but one were actually won by blacks and Hispanics in the 1992 election. Partly as a result of this redistricting, blacks were elected to Congress for the first time since Reconstruction in Alabama, Florida, North Carolina, South Carolina, and Virginia. Hispanics were elected for the first time ever in Illinois and New Jersey. In all, thirty-nine blacks and nineteen Hispanics were elected to Congress, a dramatic increase from the twenty-five blacks and ten Hispanics serving before the 1992 election.[15]

However, after this post-1990 redistricting, which used extensive gerrymandering to create the majority-minority districts, some white voters challenged their legality. In a series of cases, the Supreme Court then ruled that racial gerrymandering, the drawing of district lines specifically to concentrate racial minorities to try to ensure the election of minority representatives, is as constitutionally suspect as the drawing of district lines to diffuse minority electoral strength.[16] To the surprise of many, despite the consequent redrawing of several majority-minority districts after the 1994 election, the African American incumbents were still able to win reelection in 1996.

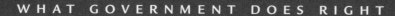
The Voting Rights Act Enfranchises Millions

Despite our shameful history of depriving African Americans of the right to vote, today black voting rates approach those of whites. In the Deep South, much of this dramatic change was brought about by the passage of the Voting Rights Act (VRA) in 1965, which made it illegal to interfere with anyone's right to vote. The act suspended the use of literacy tests, and, most important, it sent federal voter registrars into counties where less than 50 percent of the voting age population (black and white) was registered. The premise of this requirement was that if so few had registered, there must be serious barriers to registration. All of Alabama, Mississippi, South Carolina, and Louisiana, substantial parts of North Carolina, and scattered counties in five northern states were included in the area covered by registrars.

Any changes in election procedures had to be approved by the Department of Justice or the U.S. District Court for the District of Columbia. States or counties had to show a clean record of not discriminating for ten years before they could escape this supervision. Those who sought to deter blacks from voting through intimidation now had to face the force of the federal government.

Though black registration had been increasing in the rim South due to voter registration and education projects, the impact of the VRA in the Deep South was dramatic.[1] Within a year after federal registrars were sent, hundreds of thousands of southern blacks were registered, radically changing the nature of southern politics. In the most extreme case, Mississippi registration of blacks zoomed from 7 to 41 percent. In Alabama the black electorate doubled in four years.

Due to these increases, not only have dozens of blacks been elected, but white politicians must now court black voters to get elected. Even the late George Wallace, the segregationist Alabama governor who had opposed the civil rights movement in the 1960s, eagerly sought black votes in the 1970s and 1980s.

The VRA was renewed and expanded in 1970, 1975, and 1982. It now covers more states and other minorities, such as Hispanics, Asians, Native Americans, and Eskimos, and thus serves as a basic protection for minority voting rights. For example, states must provide bilingual ballots in counties in which 5 percent or more of the population does not speak English.

1. Richard Limpne, "Mass Mobilization or Government Intervention? The Growth of Black Registration in the South," *Journal of Politics* 57 (May 1995): 425–442.

Blacks line up to vote in Peachtree, Alabama, after enactment of the Voting Rights Act of 1965.
UPI/Corbis-Bettmann

This North Carolina district (12), shown on the maps, was drawn after the 1990 census to create a black majority district. It consists of parts of ten counties along the I-85 interstate and includes the predominantly black sections of Durham, Greensboro, Winston-Salem, and Charlotte. As one reporter noted, "In most electoral contests, candidates try to focus on finding out what the voters want. But in the 12th, the candidates face a challenge just *finding out who the voters are.*"[1]

The practice of drawing strangely shaped districts to fulfill political objectives, called *gerrymandering,* is hardly new in American politics. The name originated in 1812 when the Massachusetts legislature carved out a district that historian John Fiske said had a "dragon-like contour." When painter Gilbert Stuart saw the misshapen district, he drew in a head, wings, and claws and exclaimed, "That will do for a salamander!" Editor Benjamin Russell replied, "Better say Gerrymander," after Elbridge Gerry, then governor of Massachusetts.[2] Since then gerrymandering has been widely used by politicians to benefit their own political parties.

Supporters of racial gerrymandering believe it is the best way to increase minority representation. It provides a favorable setting for members of a minority racial group to elect members of their own race. But others argue that low numbers of racial and ethnic minorities in Congress cannot appropriately be changed by the use of deliberate

gerrymanders. Some also object to the creation of majority-minority districts because they see the dangers of thereby creating other districts with fewer minorities. These other districts will be more white than before, with representatives who are less sensitive to the interests of minorities.

One possible reform that meets the objectives of both groups is **cumulative voting.** Under that system, members of Congress would not be elected from single-member districts but from at-large districts in which several members of Congress would be elected at the same time. Voters would each have a number of votes equal to the number of seats in the district. They could apportion their votes among the candidates in any way that they preferred.

Members of any group, including racial, ethnic, religious, political, or economic groups, could target their votes on the candidates most likely to represent the group's interests. This election procedure could produce greater racial and ethnic diversity in representative bodies such as Congress without creating new districts on the basis of race or ethnicity.

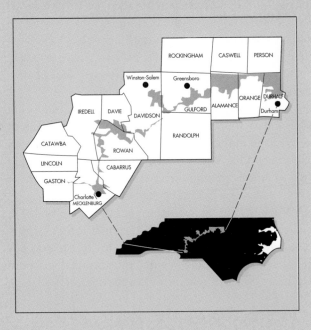

This procedure is not totally new to the United States; it was used for many years in Illinois to elect members of their state's House of Representatives. Still, acceptance of cumulative voting for congressional districts seems remote.

1. Charles Mahtesian, "Blacks' Political Hopes Boosted by Newly Redrawn Districts," *Congressional Quarterly Weekly Report,* April 25, 1992, p. 1087.
2. *Guide to Congress,* 2d ed. (Washington, D.C.: Congressional Quarterly, Inc., 1976), 563; *Congressional Quarterly, The Race to Capitol Hill,* February 29, 1992, pp. 103–105. OTHER SOURCES: Bruce E. Cain, "Voting Rights and Democratic Theory toward a Color-Blind Society?" *The Brookings Review,* Winter 1992, pp. 46–50; Carol M. Swain, "The Voting Rights Act: Some Unintended Consequences," *Brookings Review* (Winter 1992): 51; Douglas Amy, *Real Choices/New Voices: The Case for Proportional Representation Elections in the United States* (New York: Columbia University Press, 1993).

Women and the Right to Vote

When property ownership defined the right to vote, women property owners could vote in some places. When property requirements were removed, suffrage came to be seen as a male right only. Women's right to vote was reintroduced in the 1820s in Tennessee school board elections.[17] From that time on, women had the vote in some places, usually only at the local level or for particular kinds of elections.

The national movement for women's suffrage did not gain momentum until after the Civil War. Before and during that war, many women helped lead the campaign to abolish slavery and establish full political rights for blacks. When black men got the vote after the Civil War, some women saw the paradox in their working to enfranchise these men when they themselves lacked the right to vote. Led by Susan B. Anthony, Elizabeth Cady Stanton, and others, they lobbied Congress and the state legislatures for voting rights for women.

The first suffrage bill was introduced in Congress in 1868 and each year thereafter until 1893. Most members were strong in their condemnation of women as potential voters. One senator claimed that if women could hold political views different from their husbands it would make "every home a hell on earth."

When Wyoming applied to join the union in 1889, it already had granted women the right to vote. Congress initially tried to bar Wyoming for that reason but then relented when the Wyoming territorial legislature declared, "We will remain out of the Union 100 years rather than come in without the women." Still, by 1910 women had complete suffrage rights in only four states.

Powerful interests opposed suffrage for women. Liquor interests feared that women voters would press for prohibition because many women had been active in the temperance (antiliquor) movement. Other businesses feared that suffrage would lead to reforms to improve working conditions for women and children. Southern whites feared that it would lead to voting by black women and then by black men. Political bosses feared that women would favor political reform. The Catholic church opposed it as contrary to the proper role of women. According to some people, suffrage was a revolt against nature. Pregnant women might lose their babies, nursing mothers their milk, and women might grow beards or be raped at the polls (then frequently located in saloons or barber shops).[18] Others argued less hysterically that women should be protected from the unsavory practices of politics and should confine themselves to their traditional duties.

About 1910, however, the women's suffrage movement was reenergized, in part by ideas and tactics bor-

Women's contributions to the war effort during World War I helped lead to the ratification of the women's suffrage amendment in 1920. Here Broadway chorus women train as Home Guards during the war.
Brown Brothers

Women in Office

Even before women were given the right to vote nationally, they held political office. Women officeholders in colonial America were rare but not unknown. In 1715, for example, the Pennsylvania Assembly appointed a woman as tax collector.[1]

Elizabeth Cady Stanton, probably the first woman candidate for Congress, received twenty-four votes when she ran in 1866.[2] It was not until 1916 that the first woman member of Congress, Jeannette Rankin (R-Mont.), was actually elected. In 1872, Victoria Claflin Woodhull ran for president on the Equal Rights Party ticket teamed with abolitionist Frederick Douglass for vice president.

More than one hundred thousand women now hold elective office, but many of these offices are minor. Inroads by women into major national offices have been slow. Geraldine Ferraro's 1984 vice presidential candidacy was historic but not victorious. In recent years, women have only gradually increased their membership in Congress. But in the 1992 elections, women candidates won striking increases in national legislative office. Women have continued to gain seats and after 2000 numbered twelve in the Senate and fifty-nine in the House. About two-thirds of each group are Democrats.[3]

Real progress also has been made in state and local governments. Women hold 29 percent of all statewide elective offices, although only five women are governors

(interestingly, nineteen women are lieutenant governors). In 1969, only 4 percent of the state legislators were women; today 23 percent are. However, this progress slowed in the late 1990s. In eight states, women hold at least 30 percent of state legislative seats, although in Alabama they hold less than 10 percent, and the Arkansas state senate has no women members.[4]

More than 20 percent of the city council seats in medium and large cities are now occupied by women, and 16 percent are mayors of cities of America's one hundred largest cities. Women are twice as likely to be found on school boards, however, where they make up 40 percent of the members.

Does it make a difference in terms of policy to have women officeholders rather than men? Studies of the behavior of women members of Congress and other legislative bodies indicate that they are, on the whole, more liberal than men.[5] Women tend to give issues relating to women, children, and the family higher priority than male legislators do.[6] Women are also less likely to be involved in corrupt activities.

More and more women are getting graduate and professional education and working outside the home. These changes, coupled with increased public support for women taking an active role in politics, suggest that the trend toward more women in public office will continue.

"Nothing against Rudy. I just feel that a woman would be instinctively better on dairy issues."
© The New Yorker Collection 2000. Donald Reilly from cartoonbank.com. All rights reserved.

1. Joseph J. Kelley, *Pennsylvania: The Colonial Years* (Garden City, N.Y.: Doubleday, 1980), 143.
2. Elisabeth Griffin, *In Her Own Right* (New York: Oxford University Press, 1983).
3. One Senate election and one House election are too close to call. The possible female winner in each is not included in these counts.
4. Data are from Center for the American Woman and Politics, National Information Bank on Women in Public Office, Rutgers University. http://www.rci.rutgers.edu/~cawp/pdf/elective.pdf.
5. Susan Welch, "Are Women More Liberal Than Men in the U.S. Congress?" *Legislative Studies Quarterly* 10 (February 1985): 125–134.
6. Sue Thomas and Susan Welch, "The Impact of Gender on the Priorities and Activities of State Legislators," *Western Political Quarterly* (1991).

rowed from the British women's suffrage movement. A new generation of leaders, including Alice Paul and Carrie Chapman Catt, began to lobby more vigorously, reach out to the working class, and engage in protest marches and picketing, new features of American politics. In 1917, when the National Women's party organized around-the-clock picketing of the White House, their arrest and forced feeding during jail hunger strikes embarrassed the

administration and won the movement some support. These incidents, plus contributions by women to the war effort during World War I, led to adoption of the Nineteenth Amendment guaranteeing women the vote in 1920. Although only 37 percent of eligible women voted in the 1920 presidential election, as the habit of voting spread, women's rates of voting equaled those of men. (See also the box "Women in Office.")

Other Expansions of the Electorate

Federal constitutional and legislative changes extended the franchise to young adults. Before 1971, almost all states required a voting age of nineteen or more. The service of eighteen-year-olds in the Vietnam War brought protests that if these men were old enough to die for their country, they were old enough to vote. Yielding to these arguments and to the general recognition that young people were better educated than in the past, Congress adopted and the states ratified the Twenty-sixth Amendment giving eighteen-year-olds the right to vote.

Only convicted felons, the mentally incapable, noncitizens, and those not meeting minimal residence requirements are unable to vote now. Voting has come to be an essential right of citizenship rather than a privilege just for those qualified by birth or property.

Voter Turnout

Paradoxically, as the *right* to vote has expanded, the proportion of eligible citizens *actually* voting has contracted.

Political Activism in the Nineteenth Century

In 1896, an estimated 750,000 people—5 percent of all voters—took train excursions to visit presidential candidate William McKinley at his Ohio home during the campaign.[19] This amazing figure is but one indication of the high level of intense political interest and activity in the late nineteenth century.

In those days, politics was an active, not a spectator, sport. People voted at high rates, as much as 80 percent in the 1840 presidential election,[20] and they were very partisan. They thought independents were corrupt and ready to sell their votes to the highest bidder. In colonial America, voters usually voted by voice. By the mid–nineteenth century, most states used paper ballots. Elaborate and well-organized parties printed and distributed the ballots. Voters, after being coached by party leaders, simply dropped their party's ballot into the box. Split-ticket voting and secrecy in making one's choice were impossible.

Progressive Reforms

The **Progressive reforms** of the late nineteenth and early twentieth centuries brought radical changes to election politics. Progressive reformers, largely profes-

Until the turn of the twentieth century, there was no pretense of secrecy in voting. Each party's ballot was a different color. Voters chose their party's ballot, like this Republican ballot used in the 1888 Indiana elections. They then put that ballot in a clear glass-sided ballot box. Party ballots could make sure that "bought" voters stayed bought. The widespread vote buying in the 1888 election and the growing strength of party reform movements led to the secret ballot being adopted by thirty-eight states between the 1888 and 1892 elections and the remainder of states shortly thereafter. However, the 2000 election revealed that ballot format can still be both crucial and controversial.
Courtesy of Smithsonian Institute, neg. #98-4290

sional and upper middle class, sought to eliminate corruption from politics and voting. But they also meant to eliminate the influence of the lower classes, many of them recent immigrants. These two goals went hand in hand, because the lower classes were seen as the cause of corruption in politics.

The Progressive movement was responsible for several reforms: primary elections, voter registration laws, secret ballots, nonpartisan ballots (without party labels), and the denial of voting rights for aliens, which removed a major constituency of the urban party machines. The movement also introduced the merit system for public employment to reduce favoritism and payoffs in hiring.

The reforms, adopted by some states at the end of the nineteenth century, and by others much later, were largely effective in cleaning up politics. But the reformers also achieved, to a very large extent, their goal of eliminating the lower classes from politics. Taking away most of the reason for the existence of the political parties—choosing candidates and printing and distributing ballots—caused the party organization to decline, which in turn produced a decline in political interest and activity on the part of the electorate. Without strong parties to mobilize voters, only the most interested and motivated participated. The new restrictions on voting meant that voters had to invest more time, energy, and thought in voting. They had to think about the election months in advance and travel to city hall to register.

As a consequence, politics began to be a spectator activity. Voter turnout declined sharply after the turn of the century.

Turnout figures from the nineteenth century are not entirely reliable and not exactly comparable with today's. In the days before voter registration, many aliens could vote and some people voted twice. In some instances, more people voted in a state election than lived there! Nevertheless, it is generally agreed that turnout was very high in the nineteenth century and that it has diminished substantially; it dropped from more than 77 percent from 1840 to 1896 to 54 percent in the 1920–1932 era, when the Progressive reforms were largely in place. During the New Deal era, when the Democratic Party mobilized new groups of voters, turnout rose again, but it has never achieved anything close to the levels of the nineteenth century.

Recent Turnout

Between 1964 and 1996, turnout in presidential elections slowly declined, from 62 percent to 49 percent. That is, of all citizens who could have registered and voted, less than half voted. This means that only one-fourth of the potential voters actually vote for the winning candidate.

The turnout for off-year congressional elections is even lower. It has not exceeded 45 percent since World War II, and in 1998 it was 36 percent. Only in Minnesota did more than half of the voters turn out. Turnout in primary elections is far lower still, sometimes as low as 10 percent.

Although nations count their turnouts differently, it is clear that Americans vote in much lower proportions than citizens of other Western democracies (Figure 1). Only Switzerland, which relatively recently gave women the right to vote, approximates our low turnout levels.

Within the United States, turnout varies greatly among the states. In the 1996 presidential election, for example, 65 percent of Maine's citizens voted, but only 39 percent of Nevada's did. Turnout tends to be lower in the South and higher in the northern Plains and Mountain states.[21]

These differences suggest that not only are there certain kinds of people who are unwilling to vote, but there are also certain kinds of laws and political traditions that depress voting turnout.

Who Does Not Vote?

Before we can explain why some people do not vote, we need to see who the nonvoters are. The most important thing to remember is that voting is related to education, income, and occupation, that is, to socioeconomic class. For example, if you are a college graduate, the chances are about 80 percent that you will vote; if you have less than a high school education, the chances are only about half that.[22] Differences between higher- and lower-income people are also quite large. Two out of three nonvoters have incomes below the average.[23] This class gap in turnout is widening. Although voting among all groups of Americans has declined in the past thirty years, the proportion of college-educated persons who participated fell by less than 10 percent while that of high school–educated persons dropped by nearly 20 percent.

Though many people take it for granted that those in the working class vote at lower rates than those in the middle and upper classes, in the United States these differences are far wider than in other nations[24] and far greater than in nineteenth-century America. So there appears to be something unique about the contemporary American political system that inhibits voting participation of all citizens, but particularly those whose income and educational level are below the average.

Voting is also much more common among older than younger people. Ratification of the Twenty-sixth

In this chapter there are eight photos, each marked with a blue band along the top, that illustrate American campaign tactics throughout the years. In this photo from the 1828 campaign, Andrew Jackson's opponents accused him of executing soldiers he commanded (as symbolized by the coffins). Jackson won anyway.

Courtesy of Smithsonian Institute

Barriers to Registration

Most other democracies have nonpersonal systems of voter registration. That is, the state or parties are responsible for registering voters. Voter registrars go door to door to register voters, or voters are registered automatically when they pay taxes or receive public services. Consequently, almost everyone is registered to vote.

The United States puts the responsibility for registration on the individual, which has been a major impediment to voting. Only about 70 percent of U.S. citizens are registered.[35] About one-quarter of nonvoters surveyed in 1990 indicated they did not vote because it was too difficult. As one commentator put it, "The United States is the only major democracy where government assumes no responsibility for helping citizens cope with voter registration procedures."[36] Difficult registration procedures have a special impact on low-income Americans, who were 17 percent less likely to vote in states with difficult registration procedures than in other states.[37]

Some states make it more convenient to register by having registration periods lasting up to election day (most states require registration at least twenty-five days before the election), registration in precincts or neighborhoods instead of one county office, registration by mail, registration offices open in the evenings and Saturday, and a policy of not purging voters who fail to vote from the registration lists. (See the box "Same-Day Voter Registration" for another possible alternative.) In other jurisdictions, voter registrars not only do not provide these options but actually try to hinder groups working to increase registration. They may refuse to allow volunteers to register voters outside the registration office.[38] One estimate is that voting turnout would be 9 percent higher if all states' procedures were similar to those of states that try to facilitate voter registration.[39]

To try to increase registration, Congress passed a law allowing people to register at public offices such as welfare offices and drivers' license bureaus (for this reason it is called the **motor voter law**).[40] Similar plans have increased registration in the thirty or so states that had

Same-Day Voter Registration

Voting turnout in the United States is second from lowest among the nations of the industrialized world. There are a number of possible remedies to this problem. One popular proposal is to allow voters to register when they go to the polling place on election day. This would reduce the costs of voting by reducing the time spent in finding and going to the registration office and the foresight necessary to remember to do so weeks or months in advance of the election. Moreover, by allowing same-day registration, states would put less premium on permanence of residence. Since Americans are a mobile population, this would increase the number of citizens eligible to vote.

States that make registration difficult (closing registration long before the election, not allowing absentee registration, not having regular office hours at the registrar's office, and so forth) have voter turnout about 9 percent less than states that make registration easier.[1] Since same-day registration is another

way of making registration easier, we would expect it to improve turnout.

Three states (Maine, Minnesota, and Wisconsin) adopted same-day registration beginning in the 1970s, and that allows us to compare turnout between them and the other states. Since those three states have adopted same-day registration, their turnout in presidential elections has increased over 3 percent. The turnout rates in the other states, on average, have decreased almost 2 percent during that same time.[2] In other words, with everything else staying the same, same-day registration appears to improve voting turnout by about 5 percent. Other indicators of turnout change also suggest that same-day registration does lead to increased turnout.

Does the increase in turnout outweigh possible negative effects of this change? Opponents of the reform believe that it might lead to increased voter fraud; it might be easier for voters to vote multiple times, for example, if they do not have to register before the elec-

tion. However, the existing system does not protect very well against voter fraud for someone determined to vote more than once, either. With the expansion of sophisticated computer tools, we might expect that the means to combat voter fraud are increasingly at hand, same-day voting or not.

Ultimately, though, we have to decide whether the expansion of the electorate by 5 percent, or, in another estimate, eight million voters, is worth the additional risks that slightly more multiple voting might take place. And, whether or not we adopt same-day voting, we need to consider other means of increasing voter turnout, too.

1. Steven Rosenstone and Ray Wolfinger, "The Effect of Registration Laws on Voter Turnout," *American Political Science Review* 72 (March 1978): 22–45; G. Mitchell and C. Wlezien, "Voter Registration Laws and Turnout, 1972–1982," paper presented at the annual meeting of the Midwest Political Science Association, 1989.
2. Mark J. Fenster, "The Impact of Allowing Day of Registration Voting on Turnout in U.S. Elections from 1960 to 1992," *American Politics Quarterly* 22 (January 1994): 74–87.

---

these policies before the federal government did.[41] The law led to the greatest expansion of voter registration in American history; five million new voters registered. However, in the 1996 election, fewer voted than in 1992, indicating that the law did not have the desired effect of increasing turnout.[42]

A related proposal suggests that change-of-address cards filed with the post office be accompanied by cards that go to the voting registration offices in the voter's former residence and new residence. Registration in the new residence would be automatic. The proposal also would reduce election fraud by removing names of residents who move from voting rosters.[43]

As with every other aspect of American politics, race is a factor here, too. States with the highest proportion of black and other nonwhite populations have the highest barriers to registration.[44]

Failures of Parties to Mobilize Voters

Traditionally, political parties mobilized voters to turn out. Parties have become less effective in this role. They are spending more time raising funds than mobilizing voters.[45] The lack of effectiveness on the part of political parties in mobilizing millions of nonvoters, most of them working class or poor, is another reason for low voter turnout. Because of their low income, a majority of these nonvoters are Democrats. If mobilized, they would probably vote for Democrats, but not to the degree many Republicans fear. In many elections the preferences of nonvoters have simply reflected the preferences of voters.[46]

Republicans are most fearful of this potential electorate. One conservative analyst wrote that a national registration plan, by tapping the voting power of the poor, "has the potential for altering the American party system."[47]

From this 1840 Whig campaign gimmick came the phrase "keep the ball rolling."
Courtesy of Smithsonian Institute

Even some Democrats are wary. The party has embraced social and economic policies that attracted many middle-class and some business groups. The goals of these groups sometimes conflict with those of the working class and poor, and the party's leaders do not want to threaten these constituencies. They must be responsive to their funding sources as well as their potential voters. The party has thus muted its appeals to the working class. This further reduces the incentives of working-class people to vote and in turn decreases the incentive of Democrats to appeal to working-class voters.[48] However, increasing voter turnout has now become a partisan issue with most Democrats backing attempts to increase turnout (as they did with the motor voter plan), and most Republicans opposing them.

Voting as a Rational Calculation of Costs and Benefits

Nonvoting also may be the result of a rational calculation of the costs and benefits of voting. Economist Anthony Downs argues that people vote when they believe the perceived benefits of voting are greater than the costs.[49] If a voter sees a difference between the parties or candidates and favors one party's position over the other, that voter has a reason to vote and can expect some benefit from doing so. For that reason, people who are highly partisan vote more than those less attached to a party, and people with a strong sense of political efficacy, the belief they can influence government, vote more than others.

Voters who see no difference between the candidates or parties, however, may believe that voting is not worth the effort it takes and that it is more rational to abstain.

In fact, 40 percent of nonvoters in 1990 gave only the excuse that they were "too busy," suggesting a large degree of apathy.[50] Nevertheless, some people will vote even if they think there is no difference between the candidates because they have a sense of civic duty, a belief that their responsibilities as citizens include voting. Most voters feel gratified that they have done their duties as citizens. In fact, more voters give this as an explanation for voting than any other reason, including the opportunity to influence policy.[51]

Downs assumes that the costs of voting are minimal, but, in reality, for many people the time, expense, and possible embarrassment of trying to register are greater than the perceived benefits of voting. This is especially true for lower-income people who perceive that neither party is attentive to their interests. Moreover, it is possible that the frequency, length, and media orientation of campaigns lower the perceived benefits of voting for people of all incomes by trivializing the election and emphasizing the negative.

Other Campaign Participation

We have seen that only about half of all Americans vote in presidential elections, and even fewer vote in off-year congressional races. Still fewer participate actively in political campaigns. For example, in a recent year, about one-quarter of the population said that they worked for a party or candidate. About an equal proportion claimed that they contributed money to a party or candidate. Smaller proportions attended political meetings or actually belonged to a political club.

Unlike voting, rates of participation in campaigns have not declined over the past twenty years. This suggests not that people are less political than they used to be but that something about elections themselves has decreased voter turnout. Indeed, more people give money to candidates and parties than they used to, probably because, unlike twenty years ago, candidates and parties now use mass mailing techniques to solicit funds from supporters.[52] Hundreds of thousands of potential donors can be reached in a very short time.

Just as there is a strong class basis to voting, there is also a strong class basis to participation in campaign activities. Those with more education and income are more likely to participate. Those with only eight grades of education or less participate, on average, in only one of twelve types of political participation aside from voting, whereas those

Gay Power

In recent years, homosexuals have become more politically active. Spurred by the crisis of AIDS among the gay community and the initially slow response of the federal government to the disease, gays have organized to exercise political clout.

How much clout can gays have? Even the number of gays and lesbians in the United States is a politically sensitive question. Many gay activists argue that 10 percent of the population is gay. Various recent surveys of sexual activity indicate the number may be considerably lower, perhaps as low as 1 percent. Sexual orientation is not a question asked in standard national surveys, and if it were, it might not elicit truthful answers, so it is difficult to know the accuracy of the estimates. Whatever the numbers, homosexuals have been "coming out of the closet" in significant numbers in recent years.

Gay issues are now being openly considered in political campaigns. "Gay rights" includes a number of different things. Most discussed have been ending the ban on homosexuals in the military and giving gays and lesbians equal rights to jobs and housing. Some gay activists want legal recognition of same-sex marriages and a general acknowledgment of homosexuality as an acceptable lifestyle. The public overwhelmingly supports nondiscrimination in jobs and in the military but is not supportive of homosexual lifestyles and same-sex marriages. However, one state, Vermont, has legalized civil commitments of same-sex partners, thus granting them the economic and other rights of married couples.

Since the early 1990s, all the Democratic presidential candidates have

Barney Frank (D-Mass.), one of three openly gay members of Congress, at a fund-raiser.
Tracey Litt/Impact Visuals

courted the gay vote and sought financial support from the gay community. In some areas gays are a significant political force. In California, for example, perhaps as many as 10 percent of all voters are gay.

Most Republicans have been less supportive of homosexual rights. Such rights are anathema to many fundamentalist Christians, who consider homosexuality a sin and thus a totally unacceptable lifestyle. These fundamentalists, and other conservatives, are an important part of the Republican constituency. At the 1992 Republican convention, some speakers overtly attacked gays and gay rights. However, as one conservative political analyst remarked, "The gay-bashing turned people off."

In 1998, 69 percent of those who declared themselves gay, lesbian, or bisexual voted Democratic.

Several openly gay candidates have been elected to Congress and state leg-

islatures. Although the gay community has been weakened through the AIDS epidemic, which has already caused about 150,000 deaths, two-thirds of them gay men, AIDS has been important in encouraging gays to come out of the closet. It also possibly has been important in encouraging broader tolerance of gays. Twice as many people now say they know someone who is a homosexual than did so in the mid-1980s. Even though there is no consensus on homosexual issues, it seems clear that gays are gaining legitimacy in the political process.

SOURCES: Jeffrey Schmalz, "Gay Politics Goes Mainstream," *New York Times Magazine,* October 11, 1992, p. 18*ff.* Bill McAllister and Michael Weisskopf, "Breaking through the 'Lavender Ceiling,' " *Washington Post National Weekly Edition,* November 14–20, 1994, p. 14. Data on the 1998 election, *USA Today,* November 4, 1998, p. 17A.

with college education participate in three or four. Those with some college education actually increased their participation over the past twenty years, whereas those with less than a high school education decreased theirs. Thus, the class bias in participation, as in voting alone, has increased over time.[53]

Gender, race, age, and regional differences in participation also appear. Even taking education into account, men usually participate slightly more than women, whites somewhat more than blacks, older people more than younger people, and southerners more than northerners. But these differences change over time. Young people participated more than their elders, and blacks more than whites, during the late 1960s and early 1970s.[54] These were times of heightened interest in politics generally, and the civil rights and anti–Vietnam War movements drew many young and black people into political activity. (See also the box "Gay Power" for the role of gays and lesbians in U.S. politics.)

Presidential Nominating Campaigns

Many Americans believe in the Horatio Alger myth, that with hard work anyone can achieve great success. This myth has its parallel in politics, where it is sometimes said that any child can grow up to be president. In fact, only a few run for that office, and even fewer are elected.

Who Runs for President and Why?

In deciding whether to run for president, individuals consider such things as the costs and risks of running and the probabilities of winning.[55] Most people have little chance of being president: They are unknown to the public, they do not have the financial resources or contacts to raise the money needed for a national campaign, they have jobs they could not leave to run a serious campaign, and their friends would probably ridicule them for even thinking of such a thing.

But a few people are in a different position. Take, for instance, a hypothetical U.S. senator from Texas or a governor of California. By their vote-gathering ability in a large state, they have demonstrated some possibility that they could win. Their decision to run might hinge on such considerations as whether they think they could raise the money necessary to run a campaign, whether they are willing to sacrifice a good part of their private life and their privacy for a few years, and whether they would lose the office they currently hold if they run and lose.

These calculations are real. Most candidates for president are, in fact, senators or governors.[56] Vice presidents

In the nineteenth century, politics involved most people, and political parades and festivities were common. Here a torchlight parade honors Grover Cleveland in Buffalo in the late 1880s.
Corbis-Bettmann

also frequently run, but until George Bush's victory, they had not been successful in this century.

Why do candidates run? An obvious reason is to gain the power and prestige of the presidency. But they may have other goals as well, such as to gain support for a particular policy or set of ideas. Ronald Reagan, for example, clearly wanted to be president in part to spread his conservative ideology. Jesse Jackson wanted to be president in part to help those at the bottom of the social ladder (see the "American Diversity" box for views on electing an African American president one day). Eugene McCarthy ran in 1968 to challenge Lyndon Johnson's Vietnam policy.

Sometimes candidates run to gain name recognition and publicity for the next election. Most successful candidates in recent years have run before. George Bush lost the nomination in 1980 before being elected in 1988; Ronald Reagan lost in 1976 before his victory in 1980; Richard Nixon lost in 1960 before winning in 1968.

Sometimes candidates run for the presidency to be considered for the vice presidency, probably viewing it as an eventual stepping-stone to the presidency. But only occasionally, such as when Reagan chose Bush in 1980 or Kennedy chose Johnson in 1960, do presidential candidates choose one of their defeated opponents to run as a vice presidential candidate. In 1988 and 1992, nominees passed over their defeated rivals in choosing vice presidential running mates.

How a Candidate Wins the Nomination

Presidential candidates try to win a majority of delegates at their party's national nominating convention in the summer preceding the November election. Delegates to those conventions are elected in state caucuses, conventions, and primaries. Candidates must campaign to win the support of those who attend caucuses and conventions and of primary voters.

Normally, candidates formally announce their candidacies in the year preceding the presidential election year. Then their aim is to persist and survive the long primary and caucus season that begins in February of election year and continues until only one candidate is left. Candidates use a number of methods to try to maximize their chances of survival. They carefully choose the primaries they will enter and to which they will devote their resources. Candidates must enter enough primaries so they are seen as national, not regional, candidates, but they cannot possibly devote time and resources to every primary or caucus. Especially important are the early events—the Iowa caucus and the New Hampshire primary—and the larger state primaries.

Candidates try hard to raise substantial amounts of money early. A large war chest can mark a candidate as unbeatable. George W. Bush started strong in the 2000 primaries because he had raised millions more than all his opponents combined. Candidates also try to survive by establishing themselves as *the* candidate for a particular policy or other constituency. In 2000, Gary Bauer and Steve Forbes each tried to combat their better-known opponents by trying to win the loyalties of the new Christian Right within the Republican Party. They were unsuccessful in enlisting enough of these voters to offset Bush's head start.

To compete successfully, candidates also need considerable media coverage. They must convince reporters that they are serious candidates with a real chance of winning. Journalists and candidates establish expectations for how well each candidate should do based on the results of polls, the quality of a candidate's campaign organization, the amount of money and time spent in the campaign, and the political complexion of the state. If a candidate performs below expectations, even though garnering the most votes, it may be interpreted by the press as a weakness and hurt the campaign. On the other hand, a strong showing when expectations are low can mean a boost to a candidate's campaign.

Consequently, candidates try to lower media expectations. It is not enough to win a primary; you have to win by at least as much as the media claims you should, or you will be seen as a loser. In the Republican race in 1988, Pat Robertson's organizers tried to counter media predictions for the Iowa caucuses by urging supporters to tell pollsters that they were not going to attend the caucuses. Because pollsters do not count people who do not plan to vote, this tactic could result in an artificially low prediction—and then a surprisingly high vote.[57]

Sometimes even losers are portrayed as winners if they do better than expected. For example, in 1968 in the New Hampshire primary, antiwar candidate Senator Eugene McCarthy won 40 percent of the vote against President Johnson, who had become increasingly unpopular because of the Vietnam War. Although McCarthy did not win, he did much better than expected, and the press interpreted the vote as a repudiation of Johnson's leadership.

In sum, then, the primary season is a game among the media, the candidates, and the voters, with the candidates trying to raise voter enthusiasm and lower media expectations simultaneously.

Can an African American Be Elected President?

Will the American presidency continue to be held only by white, non-Jewish males? Can an African American or a woman ever be elected?

These questions sound familiar. In 1960, some doubted that a Catholic could ever be elected president. At that time, only 71 percent of all voters said they would vote for a Catholic for president.[1] The only previous major-party Catholic candidate, Alfred Smith, had been soundly defeated by Herbert Hoover in 1928. But then John F. Kennedy was elected. Since then, two Catholics, Geraldine Ferraro and Sargent Shriver, have run as vice presidential nominees without much attention paid to their religion. And the candidacy of Joseph Lieberman, an orthodox Jew, for vice president on the 2000 Democratic ticket was widely applauded.

But race has been a more pronounced cleavage in American society than religion. Racism persists, and race influences all kinds of political debates, from welfare reform to the all-volunteer military. The party realignment that has occurred in the South is shaped by racial

as well as class issues. A majority of white southerners, resentful of the Democratic Party's support of the civil rights struggle, has turned to the Republican Party.

Race was important in the 1988 campaign. It surfaced when the Republicans succeeded in tying Michael Dukakis to Willie Horton, an African American convict who raped a woman while on furlough from prison. It also came up when Jesse Jackson's prominence in the Democratic Party was highlighted and made to seem somehow illegitimate and frightening. A campaign letter from the California Republican Party asked, "Why is it so urgent you decide now? . . . Here are two [reasons]." Below were two photos, one of Bush and Reagan, the other of Jackson and Dukakis. "If [Dukakis] is elected to the White House," it continued, "Jesse Jackson is sure to be swept into power on his coattails."[2]

This is not to say that all of those who voted against Jackson in the primaries or against the Democrats in the general election were racists. Jackson had no experience holding office and is identified

with the most liberal wing of the Democratic Party.

Race seemed less important in 1996 when Colin Powell, an African American former chairman of the Joint Chiefs of Staff (the nation's highest military post), was considered a strong presidential candidate. Many from both parties were quite disappointed when he chose not to run.

As the figure shows, 7 to 8 percent of the public say they would not vote for a black or a woman who was their party's nominee, and a slightly lower proportion say they would not vote for a Jew. Although 7 to 8 percent is enough to make a difference in a close race, many more people today say they would vote for a black, Jew, or woman than said they would vote for a Catholic in 1960. John Kennedy's victory suggests that 7 or 8 percent is not an insurmountable barrier.

1. Barry Sussman, "A Black or Woman Does Better Today Than a Catholic in '60," *Washington Post National Weekly Edition,* November 21, 1983, p. 42.
2. "Though This Be Meanness, Yet There Is a Method in It," *Washington Post National Weekly Edition,* October 10–16, 1988, p. 26.

Declining Numbers Oppose Blacks, Women, and Jews for President

SOURCE: Gallup Polls. The question asked was "If your party nominated a generally well-qualified man for president and he happened to be a black [Jew], would you vote for him?" or "If your party nominated a woman for president, would you vote for her if she were qualified for the job?" No questions were asked about African Americans until 1958. The "1961" data for blacks are from 1963. The 1994 and 1996 data are from the NORC's General Social Surveys.

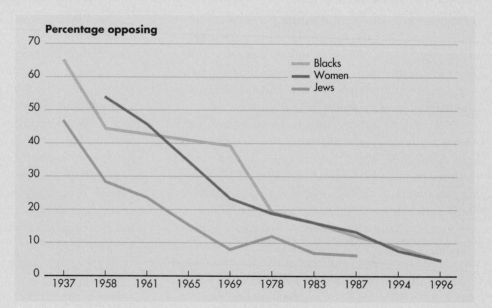

Soliciting votes by giving speeches and making appearances was once considered beneath the dignity of the presidential office. William Jennings Bryan was the first presidential candidate to break this tradition. In 1896 he traveled more than 18,000 miles and made more than 600 speeches in an effort to win voters. Although Bryan lost the election to William McKinley, his approach to campaigning became the standard. This photo illustrates how the term "stump speech" to refer to candidates' boilerplate campaign speeches may have developed.

Courtesy of Smithsonian Institute

The common wisdom about presidential primaries is that the key ingredient is "momentum." That is, a candidate needs to win early, or at least do better than expected, to gain momentum, then keep winning to maintain momentum. Jimmy Carter's 1976 victory in the Iowa caucuses, which attracted tremendous media attention, which in turn led to further primary wins, is an illustration.

Early in the primary season, candidates try to find the position, slogan, or idea that will appeal to the most voters. To take advantage of what appeared to be America's distrust of Washington, D.C., Jimmy Carter tried to create an image of an honest person who would never tell a lie. In 1984, Ronald Reagan presented himself as the candidate embodying traditional America. As one of his staff aides wrote in a campaign memo, "Paint RR as the personification of all that is right with, or heroized by, America."[58]

Candidates must avoid making a big mistake or, worse yet, being caught covering up a mistake or untruth. Edmund Muskie's front-running candidacy ground to a halt in 1972 when he cried at a public appearance while denouncing a newspaper attack on his wife. Gary Hart's 1988 candidacy collapsed when the media discovered that his marriage did not prevent him from having affairs with other women. He compounded the damage by lying. The Muskie incident was taken by the media and public to indicate that he could not handle the stress of a campaign or, by inference, the presidency. The Hart incident raised questions about his character and honesty.

Incumbent presidents seeking renomination do not have the same problems as their challengers. No incumbent who sought renomination has been denied it in this century.

In addition to these general strategies, candidates must deal specifically with the particular demands of caucuses, conventions, and primaries.

Presidential Caucuses and Conventions

Some states employ caucuses and conventions to select delegates to attend presidential nominating conventions. In 1992, one or both parties in sixteen states selected delegates in caucuses.

The Iowa caucuses, except for their timing and newsworthiness, are similar to those in other states. Normally, the campaign in Iowa starts months before the caucuses are actually held. In 1988, presidential candidates spent a total of 999 days campaigning in Iowa. Campaigning is, in large part, personal. Democrat Bruce Babbitt reported that one caucus attender, a tropical fish hobbyist, said he would deliver his vote to Babbitt if he could tell him the "pH and sediment density of the Congo River at its mouth." Babbitt assigned a staffer to look into the question.[59]

In early February, the caucuses are held in private homes, schools, and churches, and all who consider themselves party members can attend. They debate and vote on the candidates. The candidates receiving the most votes win delegates to later county and state conventions. The number of delegates is proportional to the vote that the candidate received at the caucuses (assuming the candidate got at least 15 percent).

Iowa, as the first state to hold its caucuses, normally gets the most attention. Thousands of representatives of the media cover these caucuses, which have gained importance beyond what one would normally expect for a small state. Although only a handful of delegates to the national convention are at stake, a win with the nation's political pros watching can establish a candidate as a serious contender and attract further media attention and financial donations important to continuing the campaign.

Wendell Willkie, Republican presidential candidate in 1940, rides into Elmwood, Indiana. In the days before television, motorcades allowed large numbers of people to see the candidates and were a way for the candidates to generate enthusiasm among the voters.
AP/Wide World Photos

Presidential Primaries

Delegates to presidential nominating conventions are also selected in direct primaries, sometimes called **presidential preference primaries.** In these elections, governed by state laws and national party rules, voters indicate a preference for a presidential candidate, delegates committed to a candidate, or both. Some states have preference primaries, but delegates are actually selected in conventions. These primaries are often called "beauty contests" because they are meaningless in terms of winning delegates, though they can be important in showing popular support. Like other primaries, presidential primaries can be open or closed.

Until 1968, presidential preference primaries usually played an insignificant role in presidential nominations. Only a handful of states employed primaries to select delegates. The conventional wisdom was that primary victories could not guarantee nomination but a loss would spell sure defeat.

The insignificance of most primaries was illustrated in 1968 by Vice President Hubert Humphrey's ability to win the party's nomination without winning a single primary. Humphrey was able to win the nomination be-

cause a majority of the delegates to the convention in 1968 were selected through party caucuses and conventions, where party leaders supportive of Humphrey had considerable influence.

Humphrey's nomination severely divided the Democratic Party. Many constituencies within the party, particularly those opposed to the Vietnam War, were hostile to Humphrey and believed that the nomination was controlled by party elites out of step with the preferences of rank-and-file Democrats.

Delegate Selection Reform

The response of the Democratic Party to these complaints was to change delegate selection procedures to make delegates more representative of Democratic voters. One change established quotas for blacks, women, and young people to reflect the groups' percentages in each state's population. These reforms significantly increased minority and female representation in the 1972 convention and, quite unexpectedly, made the primary the preferred method of nomination. Criteria of openness and representativeness could be more easily satisfied through primary selection. In recent years, more than 70 percent of the Democratic delegates were chosen in primaries.

The train "whistlestop" campaign was a staple of many presidential races. Here President Harry Truman gives a speech from the back of a train in 1948.
Corbis-Bettmann

The Democrats have replaced quotas for minorities with guidelines urging minority involvement in party affairs. However, the quota remains that half the delegates must be women.

The Democratic Party reforms diminished the participation of party and elected officials. Critics felt that this weakened the party and increased the probability of nominating a candidate who could not work with party leaders. Since 1984, 15 to 20 percent of the delegates have been "superdelegates" appointed from among members of Congress and other party and public officials. The change was to help ensure that the party's nominee would be someone who could work with other elected officials within the party.

The Republican Party has not felt as much pressure to reform its delegate selection procedures. Republicans have tried to eliminate discrimination and increase participation in the selection process.

Reforming the Nomination Process

Each election year political observers discuss changing the presidential nomination process. They correctly complain that primaries tend to weaken political parties and have very low, unrepresentative turnouts. Moreover, the current system gives disproportionate influence to two small states, Iowa and New Hampshire, that come first in the process. Voters in most other states do not get to see most candidates; they have already been weeded out by the time the April, May, and June primaries occur. Moreover, some charge that the current system is influenced too much by the media. The press exaggerates the victories of the winners and makes the losers seem weaker than they actually are.

Until recently, we could defend the primary system by pointing out two advantages of giving disproportionate influence to small states that select their delegates early. Only in these first small states do candidates come in contact with voters on a very personal basis. In large states, the primaries are strictly media events. For example, a survey showed that in the 1996 campaign, one of every five New Hampshire voters had met a presidential candidate. In large states, most voters go through their entire lives without ever meeting a presidential candidate.[60] Moreover, when small states came first, the candidates could test their popularity without spending millions of dollars. Those who were successful could then attract funds for the larger, more expensive races.

This system gave little-known candidates a better chance than most alternative arrangements would have.

But by 1996, large states such as California, New York, Texas, Florida, and Illinois moved their primaries earlier into the primary season to increase their influence on the nominating process. And, on **Super Tuesday,** most Southern states hold their primaries simultaneously. Now candidates can no longer bank on doing well in the early small-state primary elections and then having some momentum to help in raising large sums of money. The demands for fund-raising have grown, because candidates must have money in hand long before the first primary to book and run the massive television campaigns needed to reach primary voters in these large states and in the South. As a result, little-known candidates have a tougher battle now than in previous election years.

Some observers are glad that we no longer have the "smoke-filled rooms" where party bosses chose nominees. Nevertheless, the primary system has weakened political parties, and the small primary electorate is unrepresentative of the general public. Indeed, these voters might be less representative of the public than the party bosses who met in smoke-filled rooms. And they know less about the nominees than did the party bosses. But the days when party leaders could anoint the nominees are probably gone forever.

The National Conventions

Once selected, delegates attend their party's national nominating convention in the summer before the November election. Changes in party rules have reduced the convention's role from an arena where powerful party leaders came together and determined the party's nominee to a body that ratifies a choice based on the outcome of the primaries and caucuses.

In the "old" days, often many ballots were necessary before a winner emerged. In 1924, it took the Democrats 103 ballots to nominate John W. Davis. Now nominees are selected on the first ballot. In most election years, some experts predict a close nomination race, which would force the decision to be made at the convention. But in fact, the recent national party conventions served the purposes they have served for nearly forty years: to endorse the nominee and his choice for vice president, to construct a party platform, to whip up enthusiasm for the ticket among party loyalists, and to present the party favorably to the national viewing audience. Thus, even without the nomination job, national conventions give meaning to the notion of a national party.

Before 1972, delegates were predominantly white and male. After 1972, the percentage of delegates who were black, women, and under thirty increased substantially. In 1992, 52 percent of the Democratic and 45 percent of the Republican delegates were women; 17 percent of the Democratic and 4 percent of the Republican delegates were black. The latter figures are fairly close to the percentage of blacks among each party's supporters.

Convention delegates are still unrepresentative in terms of education and income. Compared to the population, delegates to national party conventions are well educated and well-off financially. To spend a week at a convention requires more money and free time than the average American has.

Delegates also tend to be more ideologically extreme than each party's rank and file. Democratic delegates are generally more liberal and Republican delegates more conservative than their party's supporters (see Figure 3).

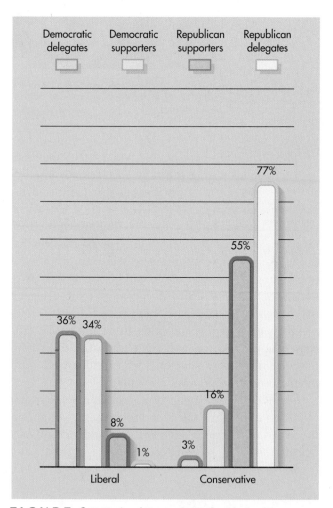

F I G U R E 3 ■ *National Convention Delegates Are More Ideologically Extreme Than Rank-and-File Members*

SOURCES: Data are from delegate and public surveys reported in *Washington Post National Weekly Edition*, August 26–September 1, 1996, p. A4, and August 12–18, 1996, p. A.

The Activities of the Convention

National party conventions are full of color and excitement. They are a montage of balloons, placards, and demonstrations. Candidates and their lieutenants scurry in search of uncommitted delegates. Behind-the-scenes negotiators try to work out differences among factions of the party. Journalists are everywhere covering everything from the trivial to the momentous. The keynote address reviews the party's glorious past and speaks to a promising future. Each candidate is placed in nomination by a party notable who reviews the candidate's background and experience. The roll call of the states ratifies the party's choice, and on the last night delegates cheer the acceptance speeches of the presidential and vice presidential nominees. Those who contested the nomination often join the nominees on the platform at the end in a display of party unity.

Aside from these very visible aspects, each convention has three important committees. The *credentials committee* reviews any challenges that may arise to the right of specific delegates to participate. The *rules committee* formulates convention and party rules, such as those governing delegate selection. The *platform committee* drafts the party's platform. The contents of the platform can generate conflict. For example, in 1968 the Democrats fought bitterly over a platform provision calling for an end to the Vietnam War. The failure of the party's nominee, Humphrey, to support the provision led many antiwar Democrats to sit out the election. After supporting the Equal Rights Amendment for years, the Republicans split over it and did not endorse it in their 1980s platforms. The abortion issue has spurred quarrels at more recent Republican conventions.

Apart from being important symbols of the direction the party wants to take, do platforms mean anything? Surprisingly, amidst the platitudes, more than half of the platforms contained pledges regarding proposed future actions, and most of those pledges were fulfilled.[61] Platforms do provide observant voters with information about what the party will do if elected.

The Media and the Convention

Before 1932, nominees did not attend the convention. Acceptance of the nomination took place sometime afterward in a special ceremony. Franklin Roosevelt broke with tradition in 1932 and presented his acceptance speech to the convention and to a nationwide radio audience; he did not want to lose an opportunity to deliver his message to the American people. The Republicans did not follow his example until 1944.

In the 1950s, at the dawn of the television age, Democratic Party leaders instruct their delegates how to behave on camera.
Courtesy of Smithsonian Institute

Since then, both parties' conventions have closed with the acceptance speeches of the presidential and vice presidential nominees.

With the beginning of radio coverage in 1924 and television coverage in 1940, the conventions have become media events. The parties try to put on a show they hope will attract voters to their candidates. Polls usually show the party's candidate doing better during and after the party's convention, called the "convention bounce," though the effect does not last long.[62]

Major addresses, such as the acceptance speech, are planned for peak viewing hours. Potentially disruptive credentials and platform proceedings often are scheduled for the early morning hours. Conventions have become tightly organized and highly orchestrated affairs in which little is left to chance. The stakes are too high.

Control, however, has its limits. If there are deep cleavages in the party, it may be impossible to prevent them from surfacing at the convention during prime

As a vice presidential candidate, Geraldine Ferraro drew large crowds and especially ignited the enthusiasm of many women.
Steve Leonard/Black Star

Selecting a Vice Presidential Nominee

Selection of a vice presidential candidate normally is done by the party's presidential nominee, then merely ratified at the convention, although in 1956, Democratic nominee Adlai Stevenson broke with tradition and left the decision to the convention.

Presidential candidates usually select a vice presidential nominee who can balance the ticket. What exactly does "balance" mean? A careful analysis of vice presidential choices of both parties since 1940 revealed that presidential candidates tend to balance the ticket in terms of age, choosing a running mate from a different age cohort.[63] Those with little Washington experience usually balance the ticket by choosing a Washington insider as a running mate (as in 1992 outsider Clinton did in choosing Gore and in 2000 outsider George W. Bush did in choosing Richard Cheney). However, Washington insiders tend to choose other insiders, as when Robert Dole chose insider Jack Kemp in 1996 and insider Al Gore chose insider Joseph Lieberman in 2000.

Although common wisdom also suggests that presidential candidates balance the ticket in terms of region (John F. Kennedy from Massachusetts chose Texan Lyndon Johnson in 1960) or ideology (the more liberal Michael Dukakis picked the more conservative Lloyd Bentsen in 1988), this happens only occasionally.[64] In 2000, both presidential candidates picked running mates whose ideologies were similar to their own.

Gender traditionally has not been part of a ticket balancing effort, but since Walter Mondale's historic choice of Geraldine Ferraro in 1984, women are sometimes among those given consideration.

The most important factor, however, is choosing a vice presidential running mate from a large state—the larger, the better.[65] Presidential candidates believe that choosing a vice presidential candidate from a large state will help win that state in the November election. In fact, this is not true; the added advantage of a vice presidential candidate in their home state is less than 1 percent, and the bigger the state, the less the advantage.[66]

Bush's 1988 selection of Indiana senator Dan Quayle illustrated the search for age balance and the tendencies for insiders to choose other insiders. Quayle was also from a different part of the country than Bush. Quayle, a conservative senator from Indiana, was youthful and charming but had little experience and was considered a lightweight. Though most of Bush's advisers seemed to think Quayle was a reasonably safe choice,[67] the media found that Quayle, though a hawk on the Vietnam issue, had spent his Vietnam years safely as a member of the Indiana National Guard. Debate raged over whether his

time. The 1968 Democratic Convention was filled with conflict—conflict inside the convention between the supporters of Hubert Humphrey and opponents of the Johnson policies on the Vietnam War and conflict outside the convention on the streets of Chicago between antiwar demonstrators and the Chicago police. Television covered both events, associating the division in the convention with the turmoil outside, and dimmed Humphrey's chances of winning the election.

In recent years, with the nomination settled well in advance of the convention and few vociferous floor fights over platforms, the conventions have been less dramatic and suspenseful. Consequently, the major networks are no longer showing them "gavel to gavel," leaving that coverage to specialty cable networks such as CNN and C-Span. Party leaders' control over the conventions backfired in terms of attracting and retaining a mass audience throughout.

family influence (his wealthy parents owned Indiana's largest newspapers) got him out of active service and into the guard. During the campaign, Bush's advisers would not let Quayle appear on network news shows or get close to metropolitan areas with major media markets.

Most observers believe Clinton's choice of Senator Albert Gore, Jr., was more astute. Though Gore did not, at first glance, fit the traditional image of a candidate chosen to balance the presidential candidate's characteristics (he was about the same age, of the same Baptist religion, from the same region, and of the same moderate Democratic ideology) or to bring with him a state with a large number of electoral college votes (Tennessee), he in fact did balance some of Clinton's weaknesses. Gore was a war veteran, while Clinton avoided service in Vietnam, and Gore's credentials as a family man had never been challenged. Gore had foreign policy expertise while Clinton did not. Perhaps more important, Gore's own moderate political philosophy strengthened Clinton's image as a moderate, Gore's youth strengthened Clinton's credibility as a candidate for change, and Gore's reputation as an environmentalist played well to many voters.

Do vice presidential choices affect the election outcome? In most cases probably not. As a cynical observer commented, "Pick anyone . . . if Quayle can't sink a ticket, nobody can."[68]

Independent and Third-Party Nominees

Independent and third-party candidates are part of every presidential campaign. Most of these candidates are invisible to all but the most avid political devotee. But sometimes strong independent candidates emerge, such as George Wallace in 1968, John Anderson in 1980, and Ross Perot in 1992 and 1996. The Perot candidacies were visible both because he had money to finance his campaign and because voters in recent years identify less strongly with parties and express more dissatisfaction with politics as usual. A strong independent candidate could influence the outcome of the election. Though many people thought Perot might have such an effect, his support was not strong enough.

It is not easy for independent candidates to get on the ballot. State laws control access to the ballot, and Democratic and Republican legislators and governors make those laws. Thus, the candidates of the Democratic and Republican Parties are automatically placed on the ballot in all fifty states, but independent candidates must demonstrate significant support to get on the ballot through petitions signed by voters.

The General Election Campaign

We take it for granted that the election campaign is what determines who wins. But consider this: Only once since 1952 has the candidate who was ahead in the polls in July, before the national conventions, lost. That year was 1988. Dukakis led in the preconvention period by six to ten points.[69] This suggests that although campaigns can make a difference, a lot of other factors determine who is elected.

Campaign Organization

Staffing the campaign organization is crucial, not only to get talented people but also to get those with considerable national campaign experience and a variety of perspectives. In 1984 and 1988, the Republicans had the advantage in national campaign experience, but in the 1990s, the advantage shifted to the Democrats. In 2000, Al Gore's team had more national experience than that of George W. Bush.

The candidate's own personal organization is only one part of the overall campaign organization. The national party organization and state parties also have some responsibilities, especially in registering potential party voters, getting them to the polls, and trying to make sure that the presidential candidate's local appearances will help the party's congressional and state candidates.

Images and Issues

Largely through the media, candidates try to create a favorable image and portray the opponent in an unfavorable way. The Bush campaign was remarkably successful at creating a negative image for Dukakis in 1988; Dukakis was unsuccessful in creating either a positive image for himself or reinforcing Bush's negative image.

In 1992, the Bush campaign struggled to create both a positive image for the president and a negative image for Clinton. But Bush could not find a focus for redefining himself, and his efforts to define a negative image for Clinton had limited success. The Clinton team had learned from the Dukakis debacle. They answered every attack Bush made, but at the same time they stayed focused on their own campaign message.

Issues also can be the basis for an appeal to voters. As they did in 1996 and 2000, Democrats traditionally have used the "pocketbook" issues, arguing that economic times are better when Democrats are in the White House. In 1984, however, Reagan was successful in focusing on economic issues and taking credit for a strong economic recovery.

Issue appeals are usually general, and often candidates do not offer a clear-cut choice even on the most important controversies of the time. For example, the 1968 presidential election offered voters little choice on Vietnam policy, because the positions of candidates Nixon and Humphrey appeared very similar.[70] Voters who wanted to end the war by withdrawing and others who wanted to escalate the war had no real choice of candidates.

Ideally, the major campaign themes and strategies have been put into place by the end of the summer, but these themes and strategies are revised and updated on a daily, sometimes hourly, basis as the campaign progresses. Decisions are made not just by the candidate and the campaign manager but by a staff of key advisers who include media experts and pollsters. Sophisticated polling techniques are used to produce daily reports on shifts in public opinion across the nation and in particular regions. Thus, media ads can be added and deleted as polls reflect their impact. Campaign trips are modified or scratched as the candidate's organization sees new opportunities. And media events can be planned to complement the paid advertising the candidate runs.

The Electoral College

All planning for the campaign has to take into account the peculiar American institution of the **Electoral College.** In the United States we do not have a direct election of the president, although this came as a shock to those who voted for Gore or Bush but saw the popular vote become meaningless in the post-election wrangling over who won Florida.

Voters choose electors of the Electoral College. These electors are party notables who gather in each state capitol in December after the presidential election to cast their votes for president and vice president. Each state has as many electors as its total representation in Congress (House plus Senate) (see Figure 4). The smallest states (and the District of Columbia) have three, whereas the largest state—California—has fifty-four.

With the exception of Maine and Nebraska, which divide some of their Electoral College votes according to who wins in each congressional district, all of each state's electoral votes go to the candidate winning the most votes in that state. If one candidate wins a majority of the electors voting across the United States, that candidate wins. If no candidate wins a majority, the election is decided in the House of Representatives, where each state has one vote and a majority is necessary to win. This has not happened since 1824, when John Quincy Adams was chosen. If voting in the Electoral College for the vice president does not yield a majority, the Senate chooses the vice president, with each senator having one vote.

The Founders assumed that the Electoral College would have considerable power, with each elector exercising independent judgment and choosing from among a large number of candidates. They did not foresee the development of political parties or the development of a political climate where the popular vote is seen as the source of legitimacy for a candidate. As state parties developed, the electors became part of the party process, pledged to party candidates. Thus, electors usually rubber stamp the choice of voters in each state rather than exercise their own judgment.

The Electoral College is based on states, so it encourages campaigns designed to win "states." In this sense, it reinforces the federal system and, because of the winner-take-all feature of the Electoral College, candidates concentrate their efforts in the larger states.

Campaign Strategies

Developing a strategy is an important element of a presidential campaign. But every strategy is surrounded by uncertainty, and even political pros cannot always predict the impact of a particular strategy.

Candidates seek to do three things: mobilize those who are already loyal to them and their party, persuade independent voters that they are the best candidate, and try to convert the opposition. Most candidates emphasize mobilizing their own voters. Democrats have to work harder at this than Republicans because Democratic voters often do not vote and are more likely to vote for the other party than are Republicans.

Both parties must try to persuade independent voters because independents are the swing voters; their votes determine the outcome. In 1964, when Johnson trounced Republican Goldwater, 80 percent of Republicans voted for Goldwater. In 1988, when Dukakis was soundly beaten by Bush, 75 percent of Democrats voted for Dukakis. It was the independent voters who determined the outcomes.

The crucial strategic question is where to allocate resources of time and money: where to campaign, where to buy media time and how much to buy, and where to spend money helping local organizations. Candidates must always remember that they have to

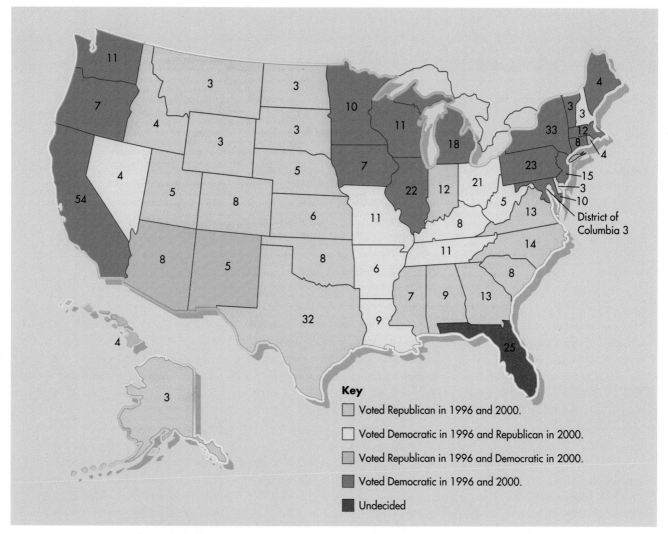

FIGURE 4 ■ *Party Strength Displays Geographic Patterns* The numbers inside the states indicate the electoral votes, out of a total of 538.

SOURCES: Richard Scammon and Alice McGilliaray, *American Votes 19* (Washington, D.C.: Congressional Quarterly, 1991), 9–13; *Congressional Quarterly Reports*, November 7, 1992, p. 3549.

win a majority of the Electoral College vote. The most populous states, with the largest number of electoral votes, are vital. Prime targets are those large states that could go to either party, such as Illinois, Texas, California, and New York.

Candidates also have to expand their existing bases of support. Most of the Rocky Mountain states have been solidly Republican in their presidential loyalties. Republicans must build on this base and their strength in the South by carrying some of the large eastern or midwestern industrial states to win.

Democrats have a strategic problem given the western Republican bloc. Between the end of Reconstruction and 1948, the South was solidly Democratic, but

there have been no solidly Democratic states in presidential elections since then (although Washington, D.C., has been solidly Democratic). Since 1976, the Democrats have consistently lost the South. During the 1980s, some strategists believed the Democrats should try to win back the South by choosing more conservative candidates. Others argued for a strategy to win without the South, aiming for the industrial states of the East and Midwest along with California and a few other states of the West. The nonsouthern strategy was used successfully by the Republicans between the 1870s and the 1920s, when they were able to capture the White House regularly without ever winning a southern state. This was Clinton's winning strategy (see Figure 4),

Butterfly Ballots and Pregnant Chads

The confusion surrounding the 2000 election outcome highlights an important but often ignored aspect of our electoral process: state law and local policies determine the mechanics of presidential elections. In this election, these mechanics also were important in determining the winner.

The Constitution gives the power to regulate elections to the states as part of the federal system. In some localities, votes are done on automatic voting machines, in other cases paper ballots are used. Still other jurisdictions use electronic devices that scan shading on small round circles the voters have marked, like the mark sense sheets on college exams. And yet others use the punch cards that were the focus of the controversies in Florida. Even in a single state, like Florida, some localities use paper ballots, others machines, and still others punch cards.

The butterfly ballot, the punch card that caused so much confusion for voters in Palm Beach County, Florida, was selected by the county, not by the state government or national parties. The odd format, which may not have met state standards, made it difficult for some voters to determine which punch hole corresponded to which presidential candidate. (It was labeled the butterfly ballot because candidate names appeared on both sides of a row of vertical punch holes rather than only on one side, the standard, less confusing, format.) Even though the problem was recognized early on election day by distraught voters leaving the polling places, there was no way that local election officials felt they could fix the problem then.

This butterfly ballot was used only in Palm Beach County. Probably as a result of that ballot, over three thousand votes were cast in the county for Patrick Buchanan, the right-wing candidate who

got only a few hundred votes in neighboring counties. The punch hole registering a vote for Buchanan was to the right of Gore's name on the ballot, leading some voters to punch it rather than the next hole below. This is particularly ironic because the areas of Palm Beach County casting the most votes for Buchanan were those inhabited by mostly elderly Jewish voters, the least likely group to support Buchanan, who is thought to be anti-semitic. And thousands of other votes in that county were invalidated because the presidential ballot was punched twice. While some spoiled ballots are normal in every election, many voters said they thought they voted for Gore, then discovered they had punched the Buchanan hole, then voted again for Gore. Of course, those ballots would be invalid.

One source of the litigation following the election focused on the butterfly ballot. Unfortunately, short of a new election in that county, it was not clear how these misvotes could be rectified.

Another legal dispute concerned the legality of recounts. The first recount, mandated by Florida law, simply counted the ballots the same way they were originally counted, so that in the punch card counties, the punch cards were run through the counting machine again. That recount registered several hundred more votes for Gore statewide. Democratic voters in several punch card counties then asked for a hand recount. The reason is that machine counts of punch cards do not count partially punched holes, that is, the holes where the tiny piece of paper, called a chad, is still hanging by one or more corners or is simply indented (the so-called "dimpled chads" or "pregnant chads").

These arcane details became the subject of fierce debates and even litigation. The election laws of some states,

including Texas' election law signed by Governor Bush, have standards for counting punch card ballots which allow hanging and indented chads to be counted. However, Florida had no law specifying how these were to be counted, and the Bush campaign sued in state and federal court to try to prevent the hand count. Though the Bush claim was that these counts were inaccurate and partisan, even the manufacturers of the punch card machines acknowledge that hand counts are the most accurate way to count punch card ballots. The real motive of the Bush campaign was the fear that a hand recount would produce more Democratic votes. In Democratic counties, recounts normally increase Democratic votes because the majority of hanging chads would be punched for the Democrats. This was why the demand for a recount was supported by the Gore campaign.

Voter anger and the need for labor-intensive hand recounts led a number of observers to call for election reform. One suggested the elimination of punch card ballot systems. Few disputed that this would be a step forward, though localities rightly wonder who would pay for the systems' replacement. Another suggested reform is to mandate a nationally formatted presidential ballot. And although this may sound sensible, such a ballot might threaten the rights of the states to determine which candidates are eligible to be on their own state's ballots.

The crowning indignity of the Florida election confusion was the joking comment of Cuba's Fidel Castro that he'd be glad to come over and straighten the system out.

1. Lawrence Longley and James Dana, Jr., "New Empirical Estimates of the Biases of the Electoral College for the 1980s," *Western Political Quarterly* 37 (March 1984): 157–175.

although he did win three southern states in each election.

The Media Campaign

The media campaign consists of paid advertising, personal appearances on talk shows, debates, and coverage on news broadcasts and in print media (see also the box "e-Campaigning"). Candidates have the most control over paid advertising and the least over news coverage; but even there, campaigns spend hundreds of hours devising strategies to show their candidates to best advantage.

Campaigns are expensive because they rely so heavily on the media to get the candidate's message to the voters. As one observer argued, "Today's presidential campaign is essentially a mass media campaign. It is not that the mass media entirely determine what happens.... But it is no exaggeration to say that, for the large majority of voters, the campaign has little reality apart from the media version."[71]

Impact of the Media

The media, through news coverage, personal appearances by candidates, and paid advertisements, help shape voters' opinions and choices in three ways. They inform, they help set the campaign agenda, and they help persuade voters.[72] In Chapter 5, we will discuss these effects.

Use of the Media

Media Events Candidates try to use the media to their advantage by staging media events that allow them to be photographed doing and saying noncontroversial things in front of enthusiastic crowds and patriotic symbols. As Bush campaign strategist Roger Ailes proclaimed twenty years ago, "This is the beginning of a whole new concept. This is the way they'll be elected forevermore. The next guys will have to be performers."[73]

Candidates and their advisers try to design settings that will encourage television reporters to focus their stories on the candidate and put his or her policies in the best light.[74] In 1988, George Bush almost literally wrapped himself in the flag, frequently "pledging allegiance," until negative media reaction led his advisers to decide that they were overdoing it.

Candidates spend most of their time going from media market to media market, hoping to get both national and local coverage.[75] Some candidates are much better than others at using the media. Gerald Ford was plagued by media coverage that seemed to emphasize his bumbling.

Advertising Paid advertisements allow candidates to focus on points most favorable to their case or to portray their opponents in the most negative light. Most political ads are quite short, thirty or sixty seconds in length.

e-Campaigning

Just as the ubiquitous Internet has affected business, education, and the media, so too has it changed politics. The contemporary candidacy would not be complete without an Internet address. These sites provide information on policies, report recent speeches, link to other relevant pages, offer opportunities to send messages to the candidates, and encourage Web browsers to volunteer. Some sites offer opportunities to register to vote. Candidates also use e-mail to communicate with supporters.

Sometimes, just as in business, e-campaigning provides more headaches. Steve Forbes's campaign manager, for example, sent out a message informing dozens of donors that they had "maxed out" on their federal campaign donations limits, so they could not send more money. After dozens of messages back from confused recipients, he confessed to a computer glitch.

Other candidates find that opponents or pranksters have purchased rival Internet addresses to parody their candidacies. So, www.gwbush.com is a parody on the Bush Web site, georgewbush.com, and www.Hillaryno.com is a response to www.hillary2000.org.

SOURCE: "Some Big Glitches in E-Campaigning," *New York Times,* November 7, 1999.

We write three weeks after the November 7, 2000, presidential election, and the winner is still in doubt. Democrat Al Gore led in the popular vote by about 200,000 of the more than 100 million votes cast. Gore is only three votes short, and Bush twenty-four votes away, from the two-hundred-eighty needed to win the Electoral College. Everything hangs on a vote recount in Florida, where Bush leads by less than six hundred of the nearly 6 million votes cast. Its twenty-five Electoral College votes will decide the outcome, once the courts can decide whether and how to recount the votes.

The discrepancy between the popular vote and the Electoral College vote highlights that what counts is the popular vote in each state, because that vote determines which candidate will receive the state's electoral votes. At the time the Constitution was written, the Founders neither wanted nor envisioned popular election of the president; selection of the president was placed in the hands of state elites. The Founders were less concerned with individual suffrage (states determined who could vote) than with the states' rights and with achieving a balance of power among the states.

A discrepancy between the electoral college and the popular vote outcome occurred three times in the nineteenth century (1824, 1876, and 1888).

However, after more than a century of presidential elections whose outcome was known once the popular vote was tallied, and since the principle of "one person one vote" has become enshrined in law and political culture, the American public has become used to thinking of elections as an expression of the will of the people.

When the 2000 election presented the possibility of an Electoral College winner who had not won the popular vote, there were immediate calls for the elimination or reform of the Electoral College system. One reform would be to abolish the Electoral College altogether, and leave the choice of president to the popular vote because direct election is a more understandable system. However, supporters of a popular vote system disagree over whether we should have a run-off election if no candidate wins a majority.

Even though one might think support for such a reform is assured, it is not. Small states might wish to preserve what they see as an advantage. Because the number of Electoral College votes equals the number of congressional districts plus two, the smallest states are overrepresented relative to their populations, just as they are in the United States Senate. On the other hand, many political and legal experts believe the Electoral College system gives greater weight to a vote cast in a large state; a one-vote margin in Pennsylvania, for example, yields twenty-three votes for the winning candidate compared to only three votes in North Dakota. So it is more important to get that extra vote in Pennsylvania. Therefore, candidates focus their campaigns in, and appeals to, the large states.

An even more undemocratic feature of the Electoral College is that not all states require their electors to cast their votes for the candidates who won the state vote. The **faithless elector** is one who casts his or her vote for a personal choice, even someone who was not on the ballot. Even though the intent of the Founders was to allow electors to cast their votes any way desired, today, most believe that in our more democratic era electors should be bound by the wishes of the voters in their states. However, no faithless elector has ever made a difference in the outcome of an election. But in the 2000 election, as few as three faithless electors could make a difference.

Yet another undemocratic feature of the current system is the contingency for the vote to be thrown into the House of Representatives. There is no expectation that each state's House delegation will vote as its state's voters did; rather, states will follow the majority party in their House delegation.

Television ads were first used in the 1952 campaign. One, linking the Democratic Truman administration to the unpopular Korean War, showed two soldiers in combat talking about the futility of war. Then one of the soldiers is hit and dies. The other one exposes himself to the enemy and is also killed. The announcer's voice says, "Vote Republican."[76] Today's ads are less melodramatic but still appeal to emotions. One classic example ad was the 1984 Reagan ad, depicting his policies as putting the country on the road to greatness again ("It's morning in America").[77]

Many ads are issue focused. Both Bush and Gore in 2000 sought to appeal to voters with ads on their stands on education and health care, for example.

Negative ads have become increasingly prominent because they are seen as more effective than positive ads. Media consultants tell candidates, "People won't pay any attention [to positive ads]. Better to knock your opponent's head off."[78] And polls show that negative ads can sometimes have a dramatic short-term effect on a candidate's standing.

Although the 1988 campaign probably set a modern record for negative campaigning, the phenomenon is as American as apple pie. When Thomas Jefferson faced John Adams in 1796, a Federalist editorial called Jefferson "mean spirited, low-lived . . . the son of a half-breed Indian squaw" and prophesized that if he were elected, "Murder, robbery, rape, adultery and incest will be openly taught and practiced."[79] When Andrew Jackson ran for president in 1832, his mother was called a prostitute, his father a mulatto (someone of mixed races, black and white), his wife a profligate woman, and himself a bigamist.[80] A British observer of American elections in 1888 described them as a "tempest of invective and calumny . . . imagine all the accusations brought against all the candidates for the 670 seats in the English Parliament concentrated on one man, and read . . . daily for three months.[81]

But why does negative advertising sometimes work when most people say they do not like it? People may say they like to hear about issues, but their actions belie their words. Politics is just not that important to most people, and indeed many are woefully ignorant about specific issues. If one out of seven Americans cannot find the United States on a world map, how interested are they going to be in a discussion of foreign policy?[82] Most people have a pretty good general picture of where the parties stand on a whole variety of general issues, but they are not particularly attuned to listening to debates on specifics, and the candidates realize this.

Negative ads have both virtues and drawbacks. On the positive side, such ads provide some helpful information about issues.[83] During a campaign, a candidate might produce ten or fifteen thirty-second ads, each providing new information, including information on issues. This material, though biased, is a valuable supplement to media news coverage, which focuses heavily on personalities, conflicts, and the "horse-race" aspect of campaigns.

Negative ads tend to reinforce previous inclinations. Thus, negative ads are more believable than positive ones at least to Republicans and independents, who are more cynical about politics and government to begin with. Some have found that negative ads decrease voter turnout by about 5 percent, chiefly among independents and moderates. However, a systematic analysis of all the studies of negative ads concluded that many negative effects have been exaggerated. There is little evidence, for example, that negative ads increase voter cynicism significantly.

Checks do exist on negative campaigns.[84] One check is the press, which could point out errors of fact. In recent campaigns, many in the press have tried to do this, but often end up simply giving more attention to the negative messages. The voters, who might become outraged, are another check. The third check is the candidate under attack, who in most cases will hit back. Both candidates were aggressive in countering negative ads in 2000.

Televised Debates Candidates also use televised debates as part of their media campaigns. In 1960 Kennedy challenged Nixon to debate during their presidential campaign. Nixon did not want to debate because as vice president he was already known and ahead in the polls. He remembered his first election to the House of Representatives when he challenged the incumbent to debate and, on the basis of his performance, won the election. Afterward he said the incumbent was a "damn fool" to debate. Nevertheless, Nixon did agree to debate, and when the two contenders squared off, presidential debates were televised to millions of homes across the country for the first time.

Nixon dutifully answered reporters' questions and rebutted Kennedy's assertions. But Kennedy came to project an image. He sought to demonstrate his vigor, to compensate for his youth and inexperience. He also sought to contrast his attractive appearance and personality with Nixon's. So he quickly answered reporters' specific questions and then directly addressed viewers about his general goals.

Kennedy's strategy worked. He appealed to people and convinced them that his youth and inexperience would not pose problems. While Kennedy remained calm, Nixon became very nervous. He smiled at inappropriate moments, his eyes darted back and forth, he had a five-o'clock shadow that gave him a somewhat sinister look, and beads of sweat rolled down his face.

According to public opinion polls, people who saw the debates thought that Kennedy performed better in three of the four. (The only debate in which they thought Nixon performed better was the one in which the candidates were not in the same studio side by side. They were in separate cities, and with this arrangement Nixon was less nervous.) Yet people who heard the debates on radio did not think Kennedy performed as well. They were not influenced by the visual contrast between the candidates. Clearly, television made the difference.

No more presidential debates were held for sixteen years. The candidates who were ahead did not want to risk their lead. But in 1976 President Ford decided to debate Carter, and in 1980 President Carter decided to debate Reagan. Both incumbents were in trouble, and they thought they needed to debate to win. Although

Families all across the country gathered in front of their TV to watch the first televised presidential debates in 1960, featuring Senator John F. Kennedy (D-Mass.) and Vice President Richard Nixon (R-Calif.).
UPI/Corbis-Bettmann

President Reagan was far ahead in 1984, he decided to debate Mondale because he did not want to seem afraid. By agreeing to debate, he solidified the precedent begun anew in 1976. In 2000, the low expectation by the media for Bush's performance, coupled with his congenial, personal style, helped him win the debates in the view of many, even though the debates revealed his limited grasp of issues.

Because candidates have different strengths, each campaign wants the other to agree to a debate format that builds on its candidate's strengths. The "debate about debates" is a typical campaign issue that frequently overshadows other, more important issues. It has become as predictable a part of campaigns as the debates themselves.

Campaign Funding

Success in raising money is one of the keys to a successful political campaign. Although some of the money for presidential campaigns comes from public funds, much

is raised privately. In Chapter 9 we will discuss campaign funding and its impact on politics.

The Permanent Campaign

The *permanent campaign* is a term coined by the current state of American electoral politics. During each election cycle, the time between the completion of one election and the beginning of the next gets shorter and shorter. By spring 1997, only a few months after Clinton's reelection, candidates of both parties were already busy visiting New Hampshire and other early primary states, assembling field operations, hiring consultants and fund-raisers, and commissioning polls. No longer does the election campaign start in the election year; now it is nearly a four-year process.

Several factors are responsible for this change, some political and some technological. The political process has changed a great deal during the past twenty years. In particular, primaries have become the chief means by which candidates get nominated, and parties have shrunk in importance in the nominating process. The necessity to win primaries in different regions of the nation means that potential candidates must start early to become known to key political figures, and ultimately to the voting public, in these states. In the "old days," candidates only had to woo party leaders, a process, which, though not easy, was much less public and much less expensive than campaigning for primary victories.

Technology has also contributed to the permanent campaign. Certainly, in comparison to the turn of the twentieth century, transportation and communication technology have revolutionized campaigns. Then, of course, travel was by rail, ship, or horse, and candidates could not simply dart about the country spending the morning in New York and the afternoon in Seattle. Telephone communication was primitive, and there were no radios or televisions. The idea of potential candidates spending four years publicly campaigning for office under these conditions would have been ludicrous.

But even in comparison with only thirty years ago, the media and information technology have revolutionized campaigning and thus have contributed to the permanent campaign. Modern computer and telephone technology enable the media and private organizations to take the pulse of the public through opinion polls almost continually. As polls have become more common, they have become a source of fascination by the media (and as pollsters have discovered that the media appetite for polls is nearly insatiable, polls have proliferated). Whereas in the 1950s polls were rarely done and poll results were rarely discussed in media coverage of elections, by the 1980s hundreds of stories about each election campaign focus on poll results. Indeed, much of the media coverage of the campaign focuses on exactly that (see Chapter 5 for more on this topic). Thus, candidates must pay attention to how well they do in the polls, which means they must begin campaigning early to earn name recognition by the public.

And, more generally, the fact that campaigns have become media events means that candidates must begin early to establish themselves as worthy of media attention. Until candidates have organizations, fund-raisers, and pollsters, they are not taken seriously by the media. Nor would it be very rational to do otherwise, because a modern campaign cannot succeed without these things.

All of these factors, then—the decline of the party organizations and the increased importance of primaries, the growth of polling, and the overwhelming role the media now play in campaigns—have contributed to the perpetual motion that modern elections have be-

come. These trends seem irreversible. Only the rolling back of the primary system would seem to make much difference, and that change is highly unlikely.

Voting

For fifty years, political scientists have argued about how voters make their choices. Are parties most important? Issues? Personalities? Political scientist Stanley Kelley has argued that voters go through a simple process in deciding how to vote. They add up the things they like about each candidate and party and they vote for the candidate with the highest number of "likes." If there is a tie, they vote on the basis of their party identification, if they have one. If they do not, they abstain. On the basis of this simple idea, Kelley explains more than 85 percent of the variation in voting choice.[85]

In making these calculations, then, voters consider three things:

- The party of the candidate, which has a great effect on how the voter views everything else about him or her
- The candidate's personality, style, and appearance
- The issue stands of the candidates and parties

Despite considerable disagreement as to exactly how each of these is weighted in the voter's mind, political scientists can offer some general conclusions.

Party Loyalties

One's party loyalty, called party identification, is probably the most important factor influencing a person's vote: Democrats tend to vote for Democrats and Republicans for Republicans. This is most true for lower-level contests such as state legislative elections, but it is also true for presidential races because party preference influences how a voter perceives a candidate's personality and issue stance. For some people, party identification is their only source of information about candidates, and they vote on the basis of it alone.

However, since the beginning of the twentieth century, and even since the 1950s, party has become less important to voters. There are more independents and more people who vote contrary to their partisan loyalties. Party loyalties seem to be in flux, and parties themselves have been weakened by competition from the media and interest groups. Nevertheless, if you are guessing how a person will vote, the best single bit of information

"This year I'm not getting involved in any complicated issues. I'm just voting my straight ethnic prejudices."

to have is the person's party identification.[86] In 2000, for example, among those who went to the polls, 86 percent of all Democrats voted for Gore, and 91 percent of all Republicans voted for Bush. These proportions were similar in the 1998 off-year election.[87]

How do people get to be Republicans and Democrats? Socioeconomic class is a very important predictor of the vote: the lower the income, the more likely to vote Democrat. But this general rule is cross-cut with distinctive ethnic and religious patterns (we use *ethnic* here to refer to differences of national origin and race).

For example, Jews are much more likely to vote Democratic than other whites of similar income. On the whole, they have a higher-than-average income, yet in both 1996 and 2000, over three-fourths of Jewish voters voted Democratic. As a group, they were exceeded in their Democratic allegiance only by blacks.[88]

Catholics used to be predominantly Democratic. They still are, but not as consistently. Though a majority of Catholics voted for Reagan in 1980 and 1984, they returned to the Democratic fold in the 1990s. They favored Clinton by significant margins but gave Gore only a small plurality.

Blacks are probably the most distinctive group politically. About 90 percent voted Democratic in 2000, a higher proportion than voted for Clinton.

Hispanics—who, like blacks, also have lower-than-average incomes—are not as universally Democratic as blacks and have voted Republican in significant numbers. Nevertheless, almost three-quarters voted Democratic in

recent congressional elections and two-thirds for recent Democratic presidential candidates. Among Hispanics, Cuban Americans are much more likely to be Republican than either Mexican Americans or Puerto Ricans. Many are refugees or descendants of refugees from Castro's Cuba and are intensely anticommunist.

The voting behavior of Asian Americans has been much less thoroughly studied than that of other groups (because until recently they were quite a small group). In 1992 and 1996, their voting patterns resembled those of whites, with a small plurality in favor of the Republican candidates, but in 1998 and 2000, a strong majority of Asian-Americans voted Democratic.

White Protestants generally give a majority of their vote to the Republicans and have done so for decades. Evangelical Protestants (such as Southern Baptist and Assembly of God) are much more likely to vote for Republicans than are mainline Protestants (such as Episcopalians or Presbyterians). However, as for other groups, income differences are important in determining the vote of Protestants.

Ethnicity and religion are important in determining the vote because they are shorthand terms for many other factors influencing political behavior—class, historical treatment within the society, and basic culture and values. Jews are predominantly Democratic, for example, because as a persecuted minority throughout much of their history, they have learned to identify with the underdog, even when their own economic circumstances move them into the middle or upper class. Catholics were sometimes discriminated against too; this discrimination plus their working-class status propelled them to the party of Roosevelt. As Catholics have moved into the middle class and as tolerance toward Catholics has grown, Catholics, like Protestants, have tended to vote their income.

Candidate Evaluations

Candidates' personalities and styles have had more impact as party influence has declined and as television has become voters' major source of information about elections. Reagan's popularity in 1984 is an example of the influence of a candidate and his personality. The perceived competence and integrity of candidates are other facets of candidate evaluation. Voters are less likely to support candidates who do not seem capable of handling the job, regardless of their issue positions. Jimmy Carter suffered in 1980 because of voter evaluations of his competence and leadership.

Clinton's popularity puzzled many observers. Many voters did not like his evasions and his public humiliation of his wife, but they voted for him anyway. During the impeachment debates, many journalists expressed amazement that Clinton's popularity remained high. The public, more than journalists, seemed to be able to separate his public and private roles. The public continued to support him because they felt he was doing a good job as president, not because they admired him personally.

Issues

Issues are a third factor influencing the vote. Although Americans are probably more likely to vote on issues now than they were in the 1950s, issues only influence some voters some of the time. In 1984 and 1988, for example, voters' issue positions overall were closer to the positions of Mondale and Dukakis than to winners Reagan or Bush. In 2000, voters saw themselves as much closer to Gore than Bush on the issues.[89]

Although other factors also influence voters, many do cast issue votes. To cast an issue vote, voters have to be informed about issues and have opinions. In recent elections, more than 80 percent of the public could take a position on issues such as government spending, military spending, women's rights, and relations with Russia.[90] Knowledge about these issues may have been vague, but individuals were able to understand the issues enough to define their own general positions.

Also, for voters to cast issue votes, candidates must have detectable policy differences. A substantial minority of voters are able to detect some differences among presidential candidates. In recent elections, the percentages able to identify correctly general differences between the major party candidates varied between 26 and 55 percent, the 55 percent being that in 1996.[91]

In every election since 1972, more than 70 percent of those who could correctly identify the positions of the candidates as well as their own position on an important issue cast a vote consistent with their own position.[92] We call this issue voting. Issues with the highest proportion of issue voting were those that typically divided Republicans and Democrats, such as government spending, military spending, and government aid to the unemployed and minorities. However, because only one-third to two-thirds of the electorate was able to define both their own and the candidates' positions on each issue, the proportion of the total electorate that can be said to cast an "issue vote" is usually less than 40 percent, and for some issues it is much less.[92]

Abortion is an issue on which voters cast issue-related votes. In 1996, for example, about 60 percent of the vot-

ers cast issue-related votes on abortion. Of those voters (who had a position and also knew where the candidates stood), 15 percent of those who opposed abortion under any conditions voted for Clinton compared with 81 percent of those who believed that abortion should be a matter of personal choice.[93]

Some scholars have suggested that issue voting is really more of an evaluation of the current incumbents. If voters like the way incumbents, or the incumbent's party, have handled the job in general or in certain areas—the economy or foreign policy, for example—they will vote accordingly, even without much knowledge about the specifics of the issues.

Voting on the basis of past performance is called **retrospective voting.** There is good evidence that many people do this, especially according to economic conditions.[94] Voters support incumbents if national income is growing in the months preceding the election. Since World War II, the incumbent party has won a presidential election only once when the growth rate was less than 3 percent (Eisenhower in 1956) and lost only once when it was more than 3 percent (Ford in 1976). Unemployment and inflation seem to have less consistent effects on voting, and economic conditions two or three years before the election have little impact on voting.[95]

Table 1 shows the relationship of the presidential vote to beliefs about whether federal policies have made the nation better or worse off. Those who believe the nation is better off are considerably more likely to vote for the incumbent presidential party than others. The same general pattern holds true if the question focuses on individual economic success rather than national.

President Bush was defeated in 1992 when the economy stagnated; on the other hand, Clinton's reelection in 1996 was surely assisted by the booming economy. In

Table 1	Voting Is Strongly Related to Views of the Economy		
Voters who believe that the policies of the federal government have made the nation's economy:	Percentage Who Voted for the Incumbent Party Nominee		
	1984	1992	1996
Better	84	79	82
Same	52	49	52
Worse	23	29	32

SOURCE: Paul Abramson, John Aldrich, and David Rohde, *Change and Continuity in the 1996 Election* (Washington, D.C.: Congressional Quarterly Press, 1998).

Elections in Time

Pre-1789 In colonial period, voting rights not clearly specified. In some areas, some women and free blacks were able to vote.

1789 New national constitution adopted. New state constitutions largely limit voting rights to white males and in many states to those with property. In a few states, religious tests also eliminate potential voters.

1790s–1820s Most states eliminate religious and property tests for voting.

1840 An estimated 80 percent of eligible voters vote in presidential election.

1865 The first post–Civil War constitutional amendment, the Thirteenth Amendment, abolishes slavery. Congress, through Reconstruction acts and a military occupation of the South, seeks to protect voting and other rights of southern black people.

1868 After their activism on behalf of abolition of slavery and voting rights for blacks, women turn to the issue of voting rights for women. In 1868, the first women's suffrage bill was introduced in Congress. It was introduced every year until 1893, and it failed every year.

1870 The third post–Civil War constitutional amendment, the Fifteenth Amendment, prohibits voting discrimination against men on the basis of color or "former condition of servitude" (i.e., slavery). Blacks vote and hold elected office at state level and in Congress. Women's voting rights are not protected by the Fifteenth Amendment, however.

1876 Reconstruction ends as southern Democrats agree to support the Republican presidential candidate in return for an end to northern military presence in the South. Process of disenfranchising black citizens begins through economic intimidation, violence, and legislation such as literacy tests, grandfather clauses, poll taxes, and white primaries.

1889 Wyoming applies to join the union. It is accepted and becomes the first state to grant women suffrage.

1890s–1920s Progressive reforms, ostensibly designed to remove corruption from politics, also work to remove working-class influence in politics. Progressive movement succeeds in getting a variety of electoral reforms approved in most states.

1901 Southern African American membership in Congress ends, not to begin again until 1972.

1910–1920 Women's suffrage movement becomes more activist in lobbying and protest tactics, and in 1917 begins picketing White House.

1920 Nineteenth Amendment to the U.S. Constitution guarantees women the right to vote.

1920–32 Voting turnout greatly declines, partly as a result of Progressive reforms.

1932–48 New Deal Democrats mobilize working-class voters and turnout increases, although not to the pre–Progressive era levels.

1940 For first time, party nomination conventions are covered by television. Parties begin to pay attention to staging and scripting these events, making them paradoxically less newsworthy to media.

1944 Supreme Court invalidates the white primary.

1964–66 Congress abolishes poll tax for federal elections (1964) and Supreme Court invalidates the poll tax for state elections (1966).

1965 Voting Rights Act, which makes it illegal to interfere with anyone's right to vote, becomes law. Federal registrars travel to South to register black voters, and the Department of Justice begins to monitor southern election laws for discriminatory intent or effect. Within a year, hundreds of thousands of southern blacks register for the first time.

1971 Passage of the Twenty-sixth Amendment to the U.S. Constitution makes voting a right for those eighteen and older.

1972 Primaries become major factor in nominating presidential candidates; national party nominating conventions become rubber stamps, with mostly a symbolic function of uniting the party.

1982 Revisions of Voting Rights Act requires states with large minority populations to draw boundaries in ways to increase probabilities minorities will be elected (minority-majority districts).

1992 After 1990 census, new majority-minority congressional districts were created, and blacks and Hispanics won election in most of those districts.

1993–96 In a series of cases, the Supreme Court invalidates the explicit use of race in drawing electoral districts. Despite the redrawing of many formerly majority-minority districts, African American incumbents win reelection in 1996.

1996 Though almost all adults are now eligible to vote, barely half do so, continuing a slow decline in turnout.

fact, political scientists believe that economic growth in the months before the election is one of the best predictors of election results and thus were perplexed by the close 2000 election.

Parties, Candidates, and Issues

All three factors—parties, candidates, and issues—clearly matter. Party loyalties are especially important because they help shape our views about issues and candidates. However, if issues and candidates did not matter, the Democrats would have won every presidential election since the New Deal. Republican victories suggest that they often have had more attractive candidates (as in 1952, 1956, 1980, and 1984) or issue positions (in 1972 and in some respects in 1980). However, the Democrats' partisan advantage shrank throughout the 1980s. Though there are still more Democrats than Republicans, the margin is modest and the number of independents is large.

Party loyalties have been even more important in congressional voting. The Democrats controlled the House continuously between 1954 and 1994 and controlled the Senate most of those years. However, the Democratic lock on the House was broken in the 1994 election, which found the Republicans winning control in a sweeping victory. Clearly, issues overcame traditional partisan habits in that election. Exactly which issues, however, were less than clear.

Conclusion: Do Elections Make Government Responsive?

Although election campaigns are far less successful in mobilizing voters and ensuring a high turnout today than they were in the past century, in a democracy, we expect elections to allow us to control government. Through them we can "throw the rascals out" and bring in new faces with better ideas, or so we think. But other than to change the party that controls government, do elections make a difference?

In the popular press, we hear a lot about "mandates." A president with a **mandate** is one who is clearly directed by the voters to take some particular course of action—reduce taxes or begin arms control talks, for example. George Bush had a substantial majority in his 1988 victory. But did he have a mandate? If so, what for? The campaign hardly talked about the budget deficit even though the election-day polls showed that this was the issue of concern to the largest group of voters. They, in turn, gave an overwhelming majority of *their* votes to Michael Dukakis. On other issues, such as protecting the environment, Bush portrayed himself as a liberal. On many issues, ranging from abortion to day care to defense policy, the two candidates clearly differed. But did Bush's victory mean that he was to limit abortions, leave it to the states to fund day care, or continue the Reagan defense policy? Did he have a mandate on any of these issues?

Like most things in politics, the answer is not simple. Sometimes elections have an effect on policy, but often their effects are not clear-cut. In 1996, some voters chose a candidate on the basis of the economy, others the budget deficit issue, others on health care, and so on. Only one issue (the economy) was the primary concern of even a quarter of the voters.

In 2000, voters favored the Democratic policy positions and did so in a time of peace and prosperity. Yet voters felt more comfortable with Bush's personality. The close race meant that neither party could claim a mandate.

It is primarily political parties that translate the mix of various issues into government action because voters' issue positions influence their party loyalties and their evaluations of candidates. Over time, a rough agreement usually develops between public attitudes and policies.[96] A vote for the candidate of one's own party is usually a reflection of agreement on at least some important issues.[97] Once in office, the party in government helps sort out the issues for which there is a broad public mandate from those for which there is not.

Elections that appear to be mandates can become "mandates for disaster." More than one observer has pointed out that every twentieth-century president who won election by 60 percent or more of the popular vote soon encountered serious political trouble. After his landslide in 1920, Warren Harding had his Teapot Dome scandal involving government corruption. Emboldened by his 1936 triumph, Franklin Roosevelt tried to pack the Supreme Court and was resoundingly defeated on that issue. Lyndon Johnson won by a landslide in 1964 and was soon mired in Vietnam. Richard Nixon smashed George McGovern in 1972 but then had to resign because of Watergate. Ronald Reagan's resounding victory in 1984 (a shade less than 60 percent) was followed by the blunders of the Iran-Contra affair. Of these presidents, only Roosevelt was able to recover fully from his political misfortune. Reagan regained his personal popularity but seemed to have little influence on policy after Iran-Contra. One recent observer has argued that these disasters come because "the euphoria induced by overwhelming support at the polls evidently loosens the president's grip on reality."[98]

Elections can point out new directions for government and allow citizens to make it responsive to their needs, but the fact that many individuals do not vote means that the new directions may not reflect either the needs or wishes of the public. If election turnout falls too far, the legitimacy of elections may be threatened. People may come to believe that election results do not reflect the wishes of the majority. For this reason, this slow and steady decline of turnout should concern all of us. If elections promote government responsiveness to those who participate in them, higher turnouts help increase responsiveness.

EPILOGUE

The Package Works

Clinton decided to follow the blueprint laid out in his campaign team's report. Between the end of the primaries and the convention, Clinton worked hard getting free media coverage and beginning the process of redefining his image. Avid TV viewers saw him on the *Today* show, MTV, *Good Morning America*, *Larry King Live,* and *Arsenio Hall,* where he put on his sunglasses and played "Heartbreak Hotel" on his sax. The print press quickly picked up on the new themes. *U.S. News and World Report* discussed "The Bill Clinton Nobody Knows," while readers of *People* magazine were treated to a cover story, "At Home with the Clinton Family."

From dead last in the three-way race in April, he began to gain strength in the polls. In a tie with his opponents before the Democratic convention, by the end of the convention, he was twenty-four points ahead.[99]

After the convention, instead of lowering his profile as candidates often do between the convention and Labor Day, the traditional beginning of the fall campaign, Clinton and Gore took to the heartland in a bus caravan. Clinton's team recalled the fate of Michael Dukakis in 1988. Dukakis had a lead over George Bush in midsummer and stayed out of the public eye until

The Clinton family became more prominent in Clinton's campaign after his campaign team discovered the public knew little about them.
Ira Wyman/Sygma

Labor Day. His lead evaporated. The Clinton and Gore bus tour, on the other hand, kept the campaign in the public eye, offered numerous photo opportunities of Bill and Hillary practically every day, got Clinton and Gore on local media throughout the Midwest, and helped solidify the image of Clinton as an average, likable guy.

It is probably true that Republican focus groups and surveys identified Clinton's weaknesses just as accurately

as did Clinton's own surveys. Indeed, a major part of President Bush's message was attacks on Clinton's family values, integrity, and trustworthiness. Bush and some of his campaign aides clearly thought this strategy would work in 1992, as it did in 1988 against Michael Dukakis. Though voters and analysts decried this negative strategy, it was successful in 1988. Because of the draft avoidance and womanizing charges,

Clinton seemed to be an even better target than Dukakis.

But the Bush strategy failed for several reasons. Voters were more concerned about the fate of the economy than about alleged character flaws. Indeed, in the second presidential debate, which included audience participation, one woman complained that "the amount of time the candidates have spent in this campaign trashing their opponents' character and their programs is depressingly large."[100] Second, the Clinton team learned from the Dukakis debacle. They answered every attack Bush made, but at the same time they stayed focused on their own campaign message. Third, the image modification brought about by the Clinton team had changed the basic impressions that the public had of Clinton, making him more impervious to attack. As one journalist reported, "By the time Mr. Clinton and Mr. Gore took to the highways on bus trips with their wives—double dates with the American people—the old Clinton image was so faded it hardly remained."[101]

Key Terms

suffrage
Reconstruction
literacy tests
grandfather clause
poll tax
white primary
Voting Rights Act (VRA)
cracking, stacking, and packing
majority-minority districts
cumulative voting
Progressive reforms
motor voter law
presidential preference primaries
Super Tuesday
Electoral College
faithless elector
permanent campaign
retrospective voting
mandate

Further Reading

Stephen Ansolabehere and Shanto Iyengar, *Going Negative* (New York: Free Press, 1996). Two political scientists report the results of their research on the impact of negative television ads on voters and voting.

Taylor Branch, *Parting the Waters: America in the King Years* (New York: Simon & Schuster, 1988). An excellent, readable account that illustrates the impact of political protest in changing America's race laws and to a considerable extent its attitudes about race.

Robert Darcy, Susan Welch, and Janet Clark, *Women, Elections, and Representation* (Lincoln: University of Nebraska Press, 1994). An examination of the potential barriers faced by women candidates.

Kathleen Hall Jamieson, *Packaging the Presidency* (New York: Oxford University Press, 1984). The history and impact of presidential campaign advertising.

Zachary Karabell, *The Last Campaign* (New York: Knopf, 2000). The story of the Truman-Dewey 1948 campaign that some campaign experts believe was the best in the second half of the twentieth century.

Frances Fox Piven and Richard Cloward, *Why Americans Don't Vote* (New York: Pantheon, 1988). The authors attribute nonvoting to restrictive registration laws and the disinterest of parties in mobilizing the working class.

Theodore H. White, *The Making of the President,* 4 vols. (New York: Atheneum, 1961, 1965, 1969, 1973). Journalistic accounts of presidential elections from 1960 to 1972. White was the first journalist to travel with the candidates and give an inside view of campaign strategy.

Electronic Resources

allpolitics.com.
Chat on-line with presidential candidates and keep up with the political news of the day.

democrats.org/party/ and www.rnc.org
Links to the Democratic National Committee and the Republican National Committee. Each of these pages contains information about the campaign organizations of the two national parties.

washingtonpost.com/wp-dyn/politics/
Go to a map of the United States and click on a state to get information about the politics and elected officials of that state.

odwin.ucsd.edu/idata/icpsr.html
This site, sponsored by the University of California at San Diego, provides access to information from national election studies done by political scientists since 1952. You can find out what voters thought on a broad variety of issues asked in each national election (presidential and most congressional) study.

politics.com.
Check who donates to which campaign, and keep current with the campaign stories of the day. See the results of the latest polls, and link to other sites.

InfoTrac College Edition

"Creating Static AOL"
"Monica Story Played Mid-America"
"Innocent Martyr"
"Horse Race Journalism"

Notes

1. "The Specter of Scandal," *Newsweek,* November/December 1992, p. 34.
2. *Newsweek,* July 20, 1992, p. 25.
3. Michael Kelly, "The Making of a First Family: A Blueprint," *New York Times,* November 14, 1992, p. 1ff.

4. Ibid. See also " 'Manhattan Project,' 1992," *Newsweek,* November 16, 1992, pp. 36–39.

5. Kelly, "The Making of a First Family."

6. "Manhattan Project," p. 38.

7. William Flanigan and Nancy H. Zingale, *Political Behavior of the American Electorate* (Boston: Allyn & Bacon, 1972), 13. See also Chilton Williamson, *American Suffrage from Property to Democracy* (Princeton, N.J.: Princeton University Press, 1960).

8. James MacGregor Burns, *Vineyard of Liberty* (New York: Knopf, 1982), p. 363.

9. August Meier and Elliot Rudwick, *From Plantation to Ghetto* (New York: Hill & Wang, 1966), 69.

10. Robert Darcy, Susan Welch, and Janet Clark, *Women, Elections, and Representation* (Lincoln: University of Nebraska Press, 1995).

11. Grandfather clause: *Guinn v. United States,* 238 U.S. 347, (1915); white primary: *Smith v. Allwright,* 321 U.S. 649 (1944).

12. Data on black and white voter registration in the southern states are from the *Statistical Abstract of the United States* (Washington, D.C.: U.S. Bureau of the Census, various years).

13. *City of Mobile v. Bolden,* 446 U.S. 55 (1980).

14. *Thornburg v. Gingles,* 478 U.S. 301 (1986).

15. Bob Benenson, "Arduous Ritual of Redistricting Ensures More Racial Diversity," *Congressional Quarterly Weekly Report,* October 24, 1992, p. 3385. For a very thorough review of the legal and behavioral impact of the Voting Rights Act, see Joseph P. Viteritti, "Unapportioned Justice: Local Elections Social Science and the Evolution of the Voting Rights Act," *Cornell Journal of Law and Public Policy* (Fall 1994): 210–270.

16. *Shaw v. Reno* 125 L.Ed.2d 511, 113 S.Ct. 2816 (1993); *Miller v. Johnson,* 132 L.Ed.2d 762, 115 S.Ct. 2475 (1995); *Bush v. Vera,* 135 L.Ed.2d 248, 116 S.Ct. 1941 (1996).

17. Darcy et al., *Women, Elections and Representation.*

18. The discussion in this paragraph is drawn largely from Lois Banner, *Women in Modern America* (New York: Harcourt Brace Jovanovich, 1974), 88–90; Glenn Firebaugh and Kevin Chen, "Vote Turnout of Nineteenth Amendment Women," *American Journal of Sociology* 100 (January 1995): 972–996.

19. Richard Jensen, "American Election Campaigns: A Theoretical and Historical Typology," paper delivered at the 1968 Midwest Political Science Association Meeting, quoted in Walter Dean Burnham, *Critical Elections and the Mainsprings of American Politics* (New York: Norton, 1970), 73.

20. Frances Fox Piven and Richard A. Cloward, *Why Americans Don't Vote* (New York: Pantheon, 1988), 30.

21. Daniel Elazar, *American Federalism: A View from the States* (New York: Crowell, 1972); *Statistical Abstract, 1997,* Table 465.

22. Piven and Cloward, *Why Americans Don't Vote,* 162. See also G. Bingham Powell, Jr., "American Voter Turnout in Comparative Perspective," *American Political Science Review* 80 (March 1986): 17–44.

23. Piven and Cloward, *Why Americans Don't Vote,* 17–18. Data are from 1980.

24. Powell, "American Voter Turnout," 30; Piven and Cloward, *Why Americans Don't Vote,* 119.

25. George Will, "In Defense of Nonvoting," *Newsweek,* October 10, 1983, p. 96.

26. Richard Morin, "The Dog Ate My Forms, and, Well, I Couldn't Find a Pen," *Washington Post National Weekly Edition,* November 5–11, 1990, p. 38.

27. Curtis Gans, quoted in Jack Germond and Jules Witcover, "Listen to the Voters—and Nonvoters," *Minneapolis Star Tribune,* November 26, 1988. This effect was foreshadowed by Michael J. Robinson, "American Political Legitimacy in an Era of Electronic Journalism," in *Television as a Social Force,* ed. Douglass Cater and Richard Adler (New York: Praeger, 1975).

28. Gans, quoted in Germond and Witcover, "Listen to the Voters."

29. Priscilla Southwell, "Voter Turnout in the 1986 Congressional Elections," *American Politics Quarterly* 19 (January 1991): 96–108;

30. Richard Lau, Lee Sigelman, Caroline Heldman, and Paul Babbitt, "The Effects of Negative Political Advertisments," *American Political Science Review* 93 (December 1999): 851–875. Research on turnout is found in Ansolabehere and Iyengar, *Going Negative.* In her book, *Packaging the Presidency* (New York: Oxford University Press, 1984), Kathleen Jamieson also argues that there are checks on misleading advertising, but later ("Is the Truth Now Irrelevant in Presidential Campaigns?") she argued that these checks did not work well in 1988. See Jamieson, *Dirty Politics: Deception, Distraction and Democracy* (New York: Oxford University Press, 1992).

31. Curtis B. Gans, "The Empty Ballot Box," *Public Opinion* 1 (September/October 1978): 54–57. See also Austin Ranney, *Channels of Power* (New York: Basic Books, 1983); and Richard Boyd, "The Effect of Election Calendars on Voter Turnout," paper presented at the Annual Meeting of the Midwest Political Science Association, April 1987, Chicago, Illinois.

32. Boyd, "The Effect of Election Calendars."

33. Ibid.

34. Ruy Texeira, *Why Americans Don't Vote: Turnout Decline in the United States 1960–1984* (Boulder, Colo.: Greenwood, 1987); Texeira, *The Disappearing American Voter* (Washington, D.C.: Brookings Institute, 1992); and Peverill Squire, Raymond Wolfinger, and David Glass, "Residential Mobility and Voter Turnout," *American Political Science Review* 81 (March 1987): 45–66.

35. For a review of these studies, see Bill Winders, "The Roller Coaster of Class Conflict: Class Segments, Mass Mobilization, and Voter Turnout in the U.S., 1840–1996," *Social Forces* 77 (1999): 833–860.

36. Piven and Cloward, *Why Americans Don't Vote,* 17.

37. Benjamin Ginsberg, *The Consequences of Consent: Elections, Citizen Control and Popular Acquiescence* (Reading, Mass.: Addison-Wesley, 1982), 37.

38. See Piven and Cloward, *Why Americans Don't Vote,* 196–197, for illustrations of these kinds of informal barriers.

39. Raymond Wolfinger and Steven Rosenstone, *Who Votes?* (New Haven, Conn.: Yale University Press, 1980), Table 6.1.

40. James A. Barnes, "In Person: Marsha Nye Adler," *National Journal,* February 18, 1989, p. 420.

41. Piven and Cloward, *Why Americans Don't Vote,* 230–231.

42. Michael Martinez and David Hill, "Did Motor Voter Work?" *American Political Quarterly* 27 (July 1999): 296–315.

43. Squire et al. See also Samuel C. Patterson and Gregory A. Caldeira, "Mailing in the Vote: Correlates and Consequences of Absentee Voting," *American Journal of Political Science* 29 (November 1985): 766–788.

44. Kim Quaile Hill and Jan E. Leighley, "Racial Diversity, Voter Turnout, and Mobilizing Institutions in the United States," *American Politics Quarterly* 27 (July 1999): 275–295.

45. Winders, "The Roller Coaster of Class Conflict."

46. For a review of this literature, see John Petrocik, "Voter Turnout and Electoral Preference," in Kay Schlozman, ed., *Elections in America* (Boston: Allen & Unwin, 1987). See also Bernard Grofman, Guillermo Owen, and Christian Collet, "Rethinking the Partison Effects of Higher Turnout," *Public Choice* 99 (1999): 357–376.

47. Kevin Phillips and Paul Blackman, *Electoral Reform and Voter Participation* (Stanford, Calif.: American Enterprise System, 1975).

48. Kim Quaile Hill, Jan Leighley, and Angela Hinton-Anderson, "Lower-Class Mobilization and Policy Linkage in the U.S. States," *American Journal of Political Science* 39 (February 1995): 75–86.

49. Anthony Downs, *An Economic Theory of Democracy* (New York: Harper & Row, 1957).

50. Morin, "The Dog Ate My Forms."

51. Kay Lehman Schlozman, Sidney Verba, and Henry Brady, "Participation's Not a Paradox: The View from American Activists," *British Journal of Political Science* 25 (January 1995): 1–36.

52. Norman H. Nie, Sidney Verba, Henry Brady, Kay Lehman Schlozman, and Jane Junn, "Participation in America: Continuity and

Change," paper presented at the Annual Meeting of the Midwest Political Science Association, Chicago, April 1988. The standard work on American political participation is Sidney Verba and Norman Nie, *Participation in America* (New York: Harper & Row, 1972).

53. Nie et al., "Participation in America"; Verba and Nie, *Participation in America.*

54. Paul Allen Beck and M. Kent Jennings, "Political Periods and Political Participation," *American Political Science Review* 73 (1979): 737–750; Nie et al., "Participation in America."

55. The following discussion draws heavily upon John Aldrich, *Before the Convention* (Chicago: University of Chicago Press, 1980).

56. Ibid. See also David Rohde, "Risk Bearing and Progressive Ambition: The Case of Members of the United States House of Representatives," *American Journal of Political Science* 23 (February 1979): 1–26.

57. "Political Grapevine," *Time,* February 8, 1988, p. 30.

58. "The Fall Campaign," *Newsweek,* Election Extra (November/December 1984), p. 88.

59. Bruce Babbitt, "Bruce Babbitt's View from the Wayside," *Washington Post National Weekly Edition,* February 24–March 6, 1988, p. 24. The 999 days figure is from the *Congressional Quarterly Weekly Report,* February 1, 1992, p. 257.

60. B. Drummond Ayres, Jr., "He's Taking Care of Political Business," *New York Times,* July 18, 1999, p. 12.

61. Gerald Pomper and Susan Lederman, *Elections in America* (New York: Longman, 1980), chap. 7.

62. Michael J. Robinson, "Where's the Beef?" in *The American Election of 1984,* ed. Austin Ranney (Durham, N.C.: Duke University Press, 1985).

63. Lee Sigelman and Paul Wahlbeck, "The Veepstakes: Strategic Choice in Presidential Running Mate Selection," *American Political Science Review* 94 (December 1997): 855–864.

64. Ibid.

65. Ibid.

66. Robert L. Dudley and Ronald B. Rapaport, "Vice-Presidential Candidates and the Home State Advantage: Playing Second Banana at Home and on the Road," *American Journal of Political Science* 33 (May 1989): 537–540.

67. "Squall in New Orleans," *Newsweek,* November 21, 1988, p. 103.

68. "Conventional Wisdom Watch," *Newsweek,* November 21, 1988, p. 18.

69. See *Congressional Quarterly,* July 23, 1988, p. 2015; Thomas Holbrook, "Campaigns, National Conventions and U.S. Presidential Elections," *American Journal of Political Science* 38 (November 1994): 973–998.

70. Benjamin Page and Richard Brody, "Policy Voting and the Electoral Process," *American Political Review* 66 (1972): 979–995.

71. Thomas F. Patterson, *Mass Media Elections* (New York: Praeger, 1980), 3.

72. The discussion of the functions of the media relies heavily on the excellent summary found in Stephen Ansolabehere, Roy Behr, and Shanto Iyengar, "Mass Media and Elections," *American Politics Quarterly* 19 (January 1991): 109–139.

73. *Congressional Quarterly Weekly Reports,* July 30, 1971, p. 1622, quoted in Ansolabehere, Behr, and Iyengar, "Mass Media and Elections," 109.

74. Martin Schram, *The Great American Video Game: Presidential Politics in the Television Age* (New York: Morrow, 1987).

75. Patterson, *Mass Media Election,* 4.

76. Robert McNeil, *The Influence of Television on American Politics* (New York: Harper & Row, 1968), 182.

77. Elisabeth Bumiller, "Selling Soup, Wine and Reagan," *Washington Post National Weekly Edition,* November 5, 1984, pp. 6–8.

78. Paul Taylor, "Pigsty Politics," *Washington Post National Weekly Edition,* February 13–19, 1989, p. 6.

79. Eileen Shields West, "Give 'em Hell These Days Is a Figure of Speech," *Smithsonian* (October 1988): 149–151. The editorial was from the *Connecticut Courant.*

80. Charles Paul Freund, "But Then, Truth Has Never Been Important," *Washington Post National Weekly Edition,* November 7–13, 1988, p. 29.

81. Quoted in Freund, "But Then, Truth Has Never Been Important," p. 29.

82. Freund, "But Then, Truth Has Never Been Important," p. 29.

83. Stephen Ansolabehere and Shanto Iyengar, *Going Negative* (New York: Free Press, 1996).

84. The study of negative advertising research was done by Richard Lau, Lee Sigelman, Caroline Heldman, and Paul Babbitt, "The Effects of Negative Political Advertisements," *American Political Science Review* 93 (December 1999) 851–875.

85. Stanley Kelley, Jr., *Interpreting Elections* (Princeton, N.J.: Princeton University Press, 1983); Stanley Kelley, Jr., Richard Ayres, and William G. Bower, "Registration and Voting: Putting First Things First," *American Political Science Review* 61 (June 1967): 359–379.

86. J. Merrill Shanks and Warren E. Miller, "Partisanship, Policy and Performance: The Reagan Legacy in the 1988 Election," *British Journal of Political Science* 21 (April 1991): 129–197; Eugene DeClerq, Thomas Hurley, and Norman Luttbeg, "Voting in American Presidential Elections," *American Political Quarterly* 3 (July 1975), updated and reported in David B. Hill and Norman Luttbeg, *Trends in American Electoral Behavior,* 2d ed. (Itasca, Ill.: F. E. Peacock, 1983), 50.

87. Marjorie Connelly, "Who Voted," *New York Times,* November 12, 2000, p. 4.

88. These data are from "Portrait of an Electorate," *New York Times,* November 10, 1996, p. 28. Lee Sigelman, "If You Prick Us, Do We Not Bleed? If You Tickle Us, Do We Not Laugh? Jews and Pocketbook Voting," paper prepared for presentation at the 1990 American Political Science Meeting: Susan Welch and Lee Sigelman, "The Politics of Hispanic Americans," *Social Science Quarterly,* 1991; *New York Times,* November 5, 1992, p. B9.

89. Paul Abramson, John H. Aldrich, and David Rohde, *Change and Continuity in the 1996 Elections,* revised ed. (Washington, D.C.: CQ Press, 1998), 121.

90. Ibid, 131.

91. Ibid., 135.

92. Ibid.

93. Ibid, 140.

94. Morris Fiorina, *Retrospective Voting in American National Elections* (New Haven, Conn.: Yale University Press, 1981).

95. Edward Tufte, *Political Control of the Economy* (Princeton, N.J.: Princeton University Press, 1978); Douglas Hibbs, "The Mass Public and Macroeconomic Performance," *American Journal of Political Science* 23 (November 1979): 705–731; John Hibbing and John Alford, "The Electoral Impact of Economic Conditions: Who Is Held Responsible," *American Journal of Political Science* 25 (1981): 423–439.

96. Benjamin I. Page and Robert Shapiro, "Effects of Public Opinion on Policy," *American Political Science Review* 77 (March 1983): 175–190.

97. Abramson, Aldrich, and Rohde, *Change and Continuity.* See also Benjamin Page and Calvin C. Jones, "Reciprocal Effects of Party Preferences, Party Loyalties and the Vote," in Richard Niemi and Herbert Weisberg, *Controversies in Voting Behavior,* 2d ed. (Washington, D.C.: CQ Press, 1984).

98. Arthur Schlesinger, Jr., *Wall Street Journal,* December 5, 1986.

99. This was the biggest convention bounce since polling began.

100. Maureen Dowd, "A No-Nonsense Sort of Talk Show," *New York Times* (October 16, 1992), p. 1.

101. Kelly, "The Making of a First Family." For scholarly works on the 1992 elections, see Robert Loevy, *The Flawed Path to the Presidency, 1992* (Albany: State University of New York Press, 1995); Robert Steed, Laurence Moreland, and Tod A. Baker, eds., *The 1992 Presidential Election in the South* (Westport, Conn.: Praeger, 1994); Abramson, Aldrich, and Rhode, *Change and Continuity.*

Money and Politics

YOU ARE THERE

To Accept or Not?

It is 1998, and you are Russ Feingold, a Democratic senator from Wisconsin.[1] First elected in 1992, you are running for reelection. A Rhodes scholar and Harvard law graduate, you have always wanted to be a United States senator. You have also always been something of a political maverick, not always toeing your party's positions on important issues (for example, you were the only Democrat to vote against the motion to dismiss the impeachment charges against Clinton, though you later voted against removing him from office).

You are best known, however, for your well-publicized fight to reform the system of campaign finance. You believe that big money has too much influence in American politics. In particular, you have consistently argued that we need to limit more stringently the donations that can be given to the political parties ostensibly for party-building activities (so-called unregulated "soft money"), provide more disclosure of donations, limit involvement of special interest groups (political action committees, or PACs) in campaign funding, and regulate campaign advertising, even that done by "independent" groups.

You have joined forces with Republican John McCain (Arizona) to sponsor the McCain-Feingold campaign finance bill that would accomplish many of those aims. Though you and McCain have won support for the bill from a majority of senators, you do not have enough votes to stop opponents from killing the bill through a filibuster (you need two-thirds of the votes to stop a filibuster; see Chapter 10). The bill has been filibustered to death three times in the last three years.

Back at home, in preelection polls, you are running about even with your opponent for the Senate seat, Mark Neumann, a Republican member of Congress. In this tight race, you are now faced with the question of whether to apply your principles to your election campaign. Having argued in Congress that too much money is spent in campaigns, that soft money has no legitimate role in campaigns, and that PACs have too great an influence, will you accept soft money and unlimited PAC donations for your campaign?

On the one hand, it would seem hypocritical to do so, given your consistent opposition to these money sources.

Patrick J. Kennedy (D-Mass.) and House Minority Leader Richard A. Gephardt (D-Mo.) work the phones to raise funds for Democrats running for the House.

Bill O'Leary/The *Washington Post*

Although you do not believe that special interest PAC money should be entirely outlawed, you have been strongly and consistently opposed to the practice of PAC monies from out of state providing the bulk of support for local or statewide campaigns. You believe that this practice drowns out the voices of a senator's constituents in favor of out-of-state special interests. You also believe that soft money contributions in the hundreds of thousands of dollars from large corporations and unions should not be the basis of financing for political party campaign advertisements.

On the other hand, this is a close race, and you could use the financial support from your party and sympathetic interest groups. Your opponent is hammering hard on you on a number of issues, including your opposition to partial birth abortions.

The National Republican Senatorial Committee is spending heavily on the race, and your opponent is a millionaire, with plenty of his own money to spend. Because the McCain-Feingold bill has not passed, spending an unlimited amount of soft money in your support is perfectly legal for your party to do, and it is also legal for you to accept donations from PACs.

What do you do and why?

Former Speaker of the House of Representatives Tip O'Neill once said, "There are four parts to any campaign. The candidate, the issues . . . , the campaign organization, and the money. Without money you can forget the other three."[2] Thus, conventional wisdom holds that "money is the mother's milk of politics." But we are not sure whether that milk is tainted or pure. On the one hand, without money, candidates or people with new political ideas could never become known in our massive and complex society. Television spreads names and ideas almost instantaneously, so having money to buy television time means your ideas will be heard. In that sense, money contributes to open political debate.

On the other hand, money can be a corrupting influence on politics. At the least, it can buy access to those making decisions. At the worst, it can buy decisions. Money allows some points of view to be trumpeted while others are forced to whisper. Some candidates or groups can afford to spend hundreds of thousands of dollars for each prime-time minute of national television or for prestigious Washington law firms to lobby; others can afford only Web pages and letters. Money increases inequities in political life.

Money, then, leads to a dilemma in politics. In our largely capitalist society, we expect substantial differences in wealth and income. In most cases, we see nothing wrong when those with great income buy goods and services that others cannot afford. But in politics, many people feel uneasy when those with great wealth are able to buy political favors. We feel so uneasy that we have outlawed certain kinds of buying of political favors, such as politicians paying voters for their votes or interest groups paying politicians and bureaucrats for their support.

But we are uneasy about other ways of limiting the influence of money. Many people feel that individuals or groups should be allowed to contribute as much money to candidates as they want, and that candidates should be permitted to buy as much media time to get their point of view across as they want and can afford. This view holds that contributing money and buying media time are forms of constitutionally guaranteed freedom of speech. The opposite view says that these practices distort the democratic process.

In this chapter, we first focus on the development of laws that regulate how money can influence politics, then we turn to the role and impact of money in elections, and finally we briefly examine conflict of interest on the part of decision makers in Congress and the executive branch.

The Development of Laws to Regulate Money and Politics

Concern about the illegitimate influence of money on politics is as old as the Republic. In his campaign for the Virginia House of Burgesses in 1757, George Washington was accused of vote buying. He had given out twenty-eight gallons of rum, fifty gallons of rum punch, thirty-four gallons of wine, forty-six gallons of beer, and two gallons of cider.[3] Because there were only 391 voters in his district, he had provided more than a quart and a half of beverages per voter![4]

Obviously, Washington survived these charges, and his constituents probably survived the effects of the rum and cider. But most discussions of the impact of money on politics were more sober. In his well-known analysis of controlling factions, James Madison, in *Federalist 10*, recognized that "the most common and durable source of factions has been the various and unequal distribution of property." Madison went on to say that although ide-

Money in Nineteenth-Century American Politics

The influence of money on politics has shaped several epochs of American history. For example, from the earliest westward expansion of the nation, charges of graft and corruption surrounded the government's sale and giveaway of land. Indeed, the West was developed by giving land to speculators and railroads, sometimes after bribes. When Congress was debating whether to give federal land to the railroads, the lobbyists "camped in brigades around the Capitol building."[6]

The impact of money on political life was probably at its peak in the late nineteenth century. The United States grew from a small agrarian society to a large industrialized one. Oil exploration and refining, the growth of the steel industry, the railroad companies that were spanning the nation, and other large corporations produced many millionaires. This was the era of "robber barons," when the owners of giant corporations (called "trusts") openly bought political favors.

Business contributions to campaigns and to politicians were routine. One railroad president justified bribery of political officials by noting, "If you have to pay money to have the right thing done, it is only just and fair to do so."[7] Mark Hanna, a Republican fundraiser in the presidential election of 1896, assessed banks at a fixed percentage of their capital and also collected substantial sums from most insurance companies and large corporations.[8] However, Cornelius Vanderbilt, one of the wealthiest men of his time, refused to contribute to election campaigns, believing that it was cheaper to buy legislators after they were elected!

Not only did lobbyists bribe politicians, but politicians bribed reporters. In the 1872 presidential campaign, the Republican Party gave money to about three hundred reporters in return for favorable coverage.[9] (See the box "Honest Graft" for more on money's role in nineteenth-century politics.)

Early Reforms

Around the turn of the century, the Progressive reformers and their allies in the press, called the **Muckrakers,** began to attack this overt corruption. They wanted to break the financial link between business and politicians. In 1907, a law prohibited corporations and banks from making contributions to political campaigns, and a few years later Congress mandated public reporting of campaign expenditures and set limits on campaign donations. Prohibitions against corporate giving to political

This Puck cartoon mocks President U. S. Grant's involvement in various corrupt activities. Grant (dressed in the flag suit) is shown supporting various political bosses and profiteers.
The Granger Collection, New York

ally no one should be allowed to make decisions affecting his or her own self-interest, almost any subject of legislation—taxes, tariffs, debts—involves self-interest. For those making laws, "every shilling with which they overburden the inferior number is a shilling saved to their own pockets."[5]

Madison hoped that the design of the new nation, with the power of the government divided among the branches of government and between the nation and the states, would mean that no one interest or faction would overwhelm the others. The interest of one person or group would check the interest of another.

This view of counterbalancing interests is an optimistic one and has not always worked. Over the decades, Americans have found it necessary to make additional rules to restrict the ways that those with money can try to influence policymakers.

campaigns were broadened over time to forbid utilities and labor unions from giving as well.

The **Teapot Dome scandal** of 1921 stimulated further attempts to limit the influence of money on electoral politics. The secretary of the interior in the Harding administration received almost $400,000 from two corporations that then were allowed to lease oil reserves in California and Wyoming (one of them was called the "Teapot Dome"). This led to the Federal Corrupt Practices Act (1925), which required the reporting of campaign contributions and expenditures.

Because none of these laws was enforced, each had only a momentary effect. Nevertheless, the reforms did seem to make open graft and bribery less acceptable and less common. Instead of outright bribes, political interests now sought to influence politicians through campaign contributions.

Labor unions, for example, set up **political action committees (PACs)** funded from dues. These committees then raised "voluntary" money from members to support candidates for elections. Then many businesses did the same.

The Role of Money in Election Campaigns

In 1971, changed conditions caused new laws to be passed.

Campaign Finance Laws

Prompted by the increasing use of television in campaigns, and the increasing cost of buying television time, Congress passed a law regulating spending on advertising in 1971. The law limited the amount that candidates could donate to their own campaigns and required candidates to disclose the names and addresses of donors of more than $100.

In the course of the Watergate investigations, it became clear that corporations were not abiding by these restrictions. Several corporations secretly funded President Nixon's reelection campaign. For example, Nixon's Justice Department negotiated a settlement favorable to the ITT Corporation in a pending legal dispute soon after an ITT subsidiary gave the Republican National

"Honest Graft"

The influence of money on local politics reached a high point in the late nineteenth century. Urban machines used money to cement a complex network of businesses, voters, and political party organizations. Business payoffs to government and party officials for licenses and contracts, and party payoffs to voters for their support, were the norm. Graft was tolerated and even expected.

As we saw in Chapter 7, George Washington Plunkitt was a famous leader of the New York City machine, Tammany Hall. Plunkitt, born in 1842, began life as a butcher's helper and ended up a millionaire through deals made in his role as a party leader and public official. He held a number of state and local public offices; at one point, he held four at the same time. He drew a salary for three of them simultaneously.

Plunkitt's view of graft illustrates the casual attitude about the influence of money on politics common among many of his time:

There's all the difference in the world between [honest graft and dishonest graft]. There's an honest graft, and I'm an example of how it works. I might sum up the whole thing by sayin': "I seen my opportunities and I took 'em."

Just let me explain. . . . My party's in power in the city, and it's goin' to undertake a lot of public improvements. Well, I'm tipped off, say, that they're going to lay out a new park at a certain place. I see my opportunity and take it. I go to that place and I buy up all the land I can in the neighborhood. Then the board of this or that makes its plan public, and there is a rush to get my land, which nobody cared particular for before. Ain't

it perfectly honest to charge a good price and make a profit on my investment and foresight? Of course, it is. Well, that's honest graft.

Tammany was beat in 1901 because the people were deceived into believin' that it worked dishonest graft. . . . [They supposed] Tammany men were robbin' the city treasury or levyin' blackmail on disorderly houses, or workin' in with the gamblers and lawbreakers. . . . Why should the Tammany leaders go into such dirty business when there is so much honest graft lyin' around?

. . . I don't own a dishonest dollar. If my worst enemy was given the job of writin' my epitaph . . . he couldn't do more than write: George W. Plunkitt. He Seen His Opportunities, and He Took 'Em.

SOURCE: William L. Riordon, *Plunkitt of Tammany Hall* (New York: Dutton, 1963).

Committee $400,000.[10] Altogether, twenty-one individuals and fourteen corporations were indicted for illegal campaign contributions, mostly but not entirely to the Nixon reelection campaign.

In response to these scandals, Congress again attempted to regulate campaign financing by passing the **Federal Election Campaign Act** in 1974. The following are key provisions of that law, the basics of which, along with individual state laws, regulate campaign finance today:

- Public financing of presidential campaigns. Each candidate is given tax dollars for his or her campaign, as we will see in more detail later.

- Limits on contributions of individuals and committees to campaigns for federal office

- Limits on overall expenditures by candidates' organizations in presidential campaigns

- Limits on overall expenditures by national party committees

- Limits on expenditures by PACs

- Limits on individual donations to PACs and to individual candidates

- Prohibitions on cash contributions of more than $100

- The establishment of a bipartisan Federal Election Commission to enforce the law

The 1974 act also imposed limits on spending by candidates' organizations in congressional races and limits on so-called **independent spending,** spending by groups not under the control of candidates. These limits were ruled unconstitutional and no longer obtain.

Because of the importance of money in campaigns, both elected officials and those who want something from the officials have found ways to get around the campaign finance laws.

Failures of the Campaign Finance Laws

The objectives of the 1974 law were to limit spending, to make the campaign finance system more open, and to force candidates to be less reliant on a few big donors. For many reasons, the law has not worked as it was intended. Indeed, the campaign finance laws no longer have any practical effect.

Spending Limits

In 1976, the Supreme Court knocked a hole in the law when it ruled that some portions of the act were unconstitutional.[11] In a case brought by an alliance of civil libertarians and conservatives, the Court struck down several spending limits for campaigns that were not publicly funded (in this case congressional campaigns). The

Court argued that spending restrictions violated individuals' rights of free speech because spending in a campaign enables candidates to get their message out. Giving money is a form of expression protected by the Constitution.

Spending limits still do obtain in presidential races, but these limits are more apparent than real. Presidential candidates who accept public financing, as most do, may not spend more than a fixed amount (in 1996, $56 million was spent on sixteen major party candidates) to get the nomination (the money comes from a voluntary checkoff of $3 on individuals' tax returns; the spending limit increases each year to take inflation into account). Candidates who do not accept public funding can spend as much as they can raise. Once candidates receive their parties' nominations, public funding pays them each about $62 million for the general election campaign (also adjusted each election for inflation), and they can accept several million more from their party's national committee. At this point, fundraising is supposed to be officially over for the candidates. However, because of lax interpretations of other parts of the 1974 law, the candidates do raise and spend money in other ways.

Independent Spending

Independent spending, another loophole in the law, is one of these ways. (*Loophole* is a common term for aspects of a law that intentionally or unintentionally limit its effectiveness or restrict its coverage.) The independent spending loophole was created by a little-noticed portion of the law reaffirming the right of unions and corporations to establish PACs using voluntary contributions. Now that there were limitations on the amount of money individuals could give to campaigns, PACs became the vehicle by which individuals could channel more money to their favorite candidates. Individuals could give a limited amount directly to candidates and then give $5,000 to each of several PACs, which in turn could give it to candidates.[12]

PACs quickly sprang up. Business and trade PACs multiplied especially quickly, from around 100 in 1974 to more than 4,700 today. Labor had dominated the PAC game before 1974; now, with fewer than four hundred PACs, it finds itself completely outnumbered.

Individuals and PACs avoid most rules and limitations by "independent spending." In 1985, the Supreme Court ruled that PACs can spend unlimited amounts working on behalf of issues or candidates, publicly funded or not, as long as they do not give funds directly to parties or candidates.[13]

The Court assumed this spending would be meaningfully independent. However, "independent spending" often is done by organized groups with indirect links to the candidate. Today, interest groups and political parties themselves also can spend as much as they want as long as they are not actually campaigning for a candidate. Instead, they can engage in "issues advocacy" even if it only helps candidates of one party. In 1996, for instance, the AFL-CIO spent as much as $35 million on an advertising campaign urging support for many of President Clinton's priorities. The union targeted its television ads at congressional districts with Republican incumbents.[14] Because contributions to groups engaged in "issues advocacy" are not limited by law, large donors can provide a great deal of indirect support to candidates for office without violating laws limiting campaign contributions.

The Court's rule to judge whether an ad is a campaign ad is whether it uses terms such as "vote for" or "vote against." However, this is a meaningless criterion because only a small proportion (4 percent) of ads sponsored by the candidates themselves use these phrases.[15] So this criterion has no teeth in discriminating between campaign ads and other ads sponsored by PACs or parties.

Inflation Erodes Contribution Limits

The 1974 law aimed to limit individual and group contributions to campaigns. But these parts of the law have also been negated.

The maximum individual contribution to candidates or parties (except for the soft money exception) remains $1,000, the same as in 1994. Thus, inflation has eroded the value of even this small amount, making the 1974 act ineffective in another way.

Soft Money

The largest loophole in the campaign funding regulation has been carved by those raising and spending **soft money.** *Soft money* is the term for donations given to political parties, ostensibly for uses other than campaigning. Donors who want to give more than their legal federal maximum can give to national party committees, which channel to state parties, which spend under less stringent state regulations.

Soft money was exempted from limitations of the 1974 act because it was not to be used for campaigns. Instead, it is supposed to be used for such "party-building" activities as national party conventions, voter registration drives, direct mailings, polling, issue ads, and advertisements for nonfederal party candidates.

In reality, most soft money is spent for national television advertisements for the parties' candidates. Even

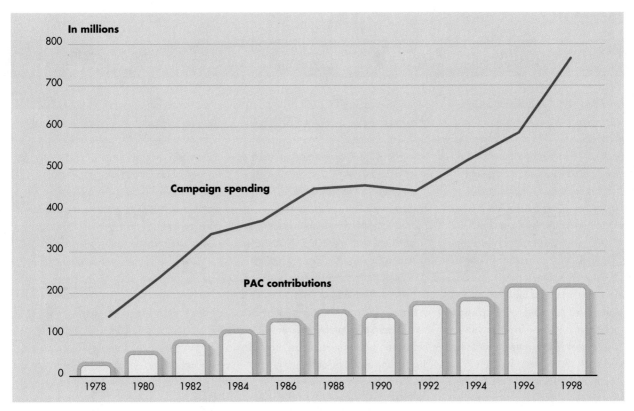

In millions

FIGURE 1 ■ *The Dough Rises: Congressional Campaign Spending ("Hard money" Only)*
Congressional campaign spending rose sharply in the 1990s after slow growth in the 1980s.

Note: These data include only "hard money" reported to the Federal Election Commission.
SOURCES: We borrowed the title from EMILY's List Newsletter (May 1988). Data are from the Federal Election Commission (www.fec.gov/press/releases.htm). Also see *Statistical Abstract of the United States 1999*, Tables 498 and 499.

though the parties claim they are running issue ads that contribute to party building, only 15 percent of the ads mention the party, while 99 percent mention a candidate.[16] As a spokesperson for the National Rifle Association commented, "It is foolish to believe there is any practical difference between issue advocacy and advocacy of a political candidate. What separates [them] is a line in the sand drawn on a windy day."[17]

In 1996 the Democrats' ads prominently featured Clinton. And the Republican National Committee made a sixty-second advertisement for the Dole campaign; fifty-six seconds dealt with Dole's life, four seconds with issues. The ad was not challenged. And as Dole explained, "It never says that I'm running for President. I hope that it's fairly obvious since I'm the only one in the picture."[18]

The soft money loophole allows people with money to spend as much as they want. For 1996, the Democrats received $120 million in soft money from special interests, the Republicans $140 million. Sometimes the parties resort to questionable tactics to raise money. In 1995, Republican National Committee chairman Haley Barbour sent letters to lobbyists offering incentives for contributing to the party. A contributor could be photographed with the GOP presidential candidates or have drinks in a private skybox at the Republican convention, depending on the size of the contribution. Dinner with President Clinton and Vice President Gore or visits to the White House were among the carrots the Democratic National Committee dangled in front of potential donors. (See the box "Selling Access to the White House.") As one observer commented, "Soft money is where rich people can play again."[19]

By 2000, the growth of soft money signaled to everyone not in solitary confinement that the campaign finance regulations dealing with contributions to candidates and parties were simply irrelevant. In May, George W. Bush held a fund-raiser for the Republicans where the take exceeded $21 million in large donations from individuals and corporations; a few weeks later President Clinton and Vice President Gore held one raising over $26 million from the same sorts of donors. By early June 2000, each party had raised over $200 million in soft money.

Who Gives? The Largest Soft Money Donors, 1999

To the Democrats		To the Republicans	
American Federation of State, County, and Municipal Employees	$2.7 million	Philip Morris (tobacco)	$2.9 million
Communication Workers of America	2.6	American Financial Group and Carl Lindner	1.6
Service Employees International	1.9	AT&T	1.6
Buttenweiser	1.5	Amway	1.5
Loral Space and Communications	1.4	RJR Nabisco (RJR Reynolds Tobacco)	1.1
National Education Association	1.3	Freddie Mac	1.1
Total soft money receipts	$124.5 million	Total soft money receipts	$159.3 million

This list of the largest soft money contributions to each of the parties in 1999 is a snapshot of the financial links between the political parties and big donors. The Democrats are strongly supported by big unions, which lobby for benefits for workers (such as minimum wages and workplace safety), trade legislation benefiting American workers, and social welfare legislation (family leave). Loral Space and Communications is a defense contractor selling satellites to the government.

The Republicans are supported by the tobacco industry, which sees Republicans as opposed to further regulation of tobacco. The American Financial group is trying to protect the interests of its major product, Chiquita bananas, the object of a trade war with Europe. Although their biggest gifts are to the Republicans, like many large corporations, AT&T supports both parties as insurance to get favorable legislation (in their case regarding access to high-speed cable lines in the changing world of high technology). Amway seeks influence over tax legislation and in 1997 got a special provision in the budget bill providing it with millions of dollars of benefits. Freddie Mac invests in housing construction and seeks federal insurance and favorable regulation.

SOURCE: Viveca Novek, "Dialing Back the Dollars," *Time*, September 6, 1999, and Common Cause (www.commoncause.org/landromat).

PACs

The funding activity of PACs differ greatly. Although there are 4,700 PACs, about one-third do not contribute to any candidates, while about 400 give over $100,000 in total. Less than 10 percent of the PACs account for three-fourths of all PAC donations. Thus, the number of key PACs is relatively small. Some of the biggest spenders include well-known groups such as the National Rifle Association, the Teamsters, and the American Medical Association. But they also include less well-known groups such as the Association of Trial Lawyers, the American Federal-State-County-and-Municipal Employees, and the American Institute of CPAs.[22]

PACs differ in the targets of their donations, but some patterns are clear. PACs show a distinct preference for Republicans in the presidential races and for incumbents—Republicans or Democrats—in congressional races (Figure 2). PACs usually want to give to the candidate they believe will win so they will have access to a policymaker.

If they guess wrong, PACs often give to the winner *after* the election, a practice called "catching the late train." After the surprise Republican victories in the 1994 congressional elections, PACs raced to help winning Republicans pay their campaign debts (Figure 2). As one noted, "We gave to Democrats because they were in control, and we're likely to do the same for Republicans. [T]hose who affect our company and our customers are in another party."[23] During the election campaign, Newt Gingrich (R-Ga.) warned PACs that if the Republicans took power, those not on board would "suffer the two coldest years in Washington."

Although the majority of PACs are business related and are ideologically much more sympathetic to the Republicans, before 1994 PACs gave predominantly to the Democrats because they were the majority party. When the Republicans gained control of both houses of Congress, they began receiving the majority of PAC donations (Figure 2). For most PACs, conservative ideological sentiment and the practical politics of supporting incumbents both point to the Republicans.[24]

What other criteria aside from incumbency guide PAC donations?[25] Most PACs give money to members in districts where the PACs have a substantial interest, such as a large number of union members for a union PAC or a large factory for a corporate PAC.

PACs also target contributions to members of key congressional committees. For example, PACs organized by defense contractors give disproportionately to members who serve on the Armed Services Committees, which have a big role in deciding what weapons to purchase. Unions and shipping companies involved in the maritime industry give large sums to those on the House Merchant Marine and Fisheries Committee and its Senate counterpart, Commerce, Science, and Transportation.[26] Members of congressional committees that specialize in tax law (Ways and Means, and Finance) and business regulations (Commerce) receive generous contributions from business PACs.

Women's PACs, including EMILY's List, one of 1992's biggest-spending PACs, are unusual in focusing most of their money on nonincumbents. Their goal is to get more women elected, which means supporting nonincumbents with strong chances of winning.

Special Interests as Victims? PAC, corporation, and union contributions to campaigns are products of mutual need. Special interests need access to and votes of members of Congress and the president, and elected officials need (or think they need) large sums of money to win elections. Thus, donations are useful to officials and to the donors. The question is whether they are useful to the public.

Although special interests try to buy access and sometimes votes, members of Congress are not simply victims of greedy PACs and corporations. Indeed, as one observer remarked, "There may be no question that the money flowing into campaign coffers is a crime. But there is a question whether the crime is bribery of public officials or extortion of private interests."[27]

Members themselves are increasingly aggressive in soliciting for donations. They fear defeat in the next election and think that raising a lot of money can protect them. Senators, for example, must raise more than $18,000 each week during all six years of their term to fund an average-cost winning reelection campaign. A senator from a high-cost state needs to raise $60,000 a week. On the other hand, many incumbents raise millions even when they face little-known opponents. Phil Gramm (R-Tex.), now retired, continued to solicit funds from lobbyists even after he had raised more than $6 million and his opponent had only $20,000.

Thirty years ago most fund-raising by members of Congress was done in their home districts. Members did not want their constituents to think they were influenced by Washington lobbyists. Today, half of the PAC funds raised are raised in Washington.[28] Members of Congress continually hold fund-raisers to which dozens of lobbyists for PACs are invited. Well-known lobbyists get hundreds of invitations to congressional fund-raisers every year.[29] Indeed, the number of these events is so large that a private company sells a special monthly newsletter listing all of them.

Some attempts to raise money are even more crass than fund-raisers. Some members keep lists of PACs that have given to them on their desks as an implicit indication that it is those groups that will have access. Others play one PAC off against another. Members might tell a representative of a bank PAC that they received contributions from savings and loan PACs and that the bank PAC should contribute or possibly miss out.[30] (See also the two "Who Gives?" boxes.)

Pressure on corporations and unions is unrelenting. Tom DeLay (R-Tex.), the majority whip in the House, is called "The Hammer" as a testament to his strong-arming potential donors. He offers lobbyists and corporate interests an open quid pro quo: they give and they get to help develop Republican strategy and interests and shape legislation that Republican leaders will support.[31]

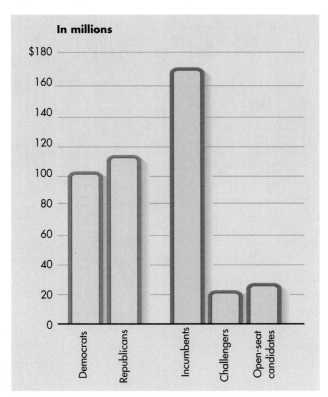

In millions

FIGURE 2 ■ *PACs Give Overwhelmingly to Incumbents*

SOURCE: 1997–1998 election cycle, *Statistical Abstract of the United States, 1999,* Table 499.

Who gives to campaigns? One writer labeled them the "donor class." The donor class is indeed different from a cross section of Americans. Defining the donor class as anyone who gives more than $200 to a congressional candidate, these individuals comprise only one-fourth of 1 percent of the population. They are whiter, richer, and more likely to be male than the public at large.

95 percent are white.

81 percent have family incomes more than $100,000.[1]

80 percent are men.

50 percent are over sixty.

20 percent have incomes over $500,000.

It is not surprising that these individuals are likely to have more access to their representatives than the average American. More than 50 percent had talked to their member of Congress since the last election and 30 percent had talked to their U.S. senator.

As a group, the donor class are more likely to be economically conservative, opposing the expansion of government's role in health care and welfare, for example. However, their social views (on issues such as gay rights and abortion) are no more conservative than the public as a whole.

1. In 1997, an income of $142,000 put a family into the top 5 percent of all incomes.
SOURCE: Bob Herbert, "The Donor Class," *New York Times,* July 19, 1998, p. 15.

"It says here that you gave a lot of money to both parties and neither expected nor received anything in return. Very nice, but we'll have to put you in the crazy section."

Regulation could provide a defense to that kind of pressure, of course. It puts a lid on spending and eliminates the "arms race" aspect of campaign funding in which candidates make ever bigger demands on potential donors. Now that campaign financing is essentially unregulated, those pressures are increasing. In reaction, in recent years, some corporations, including General Motors, Ameritech, and Monsanto, have said that they do not intend to give more political contributions. It is not clear that they will be able to stick to this resolution.

There is no question that the nature of raising money for campaigns has changed. Whatever the problems with the current system, however, we should be careful not to contrast it with an idealized version of the past. After all, almost one hundred years ago Mark Twain observed, "It could probably be shown by facts and figures that there is no distinctly native American criminal class except Congress." Big interests always have had influence and access in Washington. The ways in which they exercise that influence are different now. In some ways, this influence is more open because the campaign finance reforms have made public the organizations working for special interests and the money they spend doing it. Thirty years ago we would not have known how much each member of Congress received from each lobbying group; today we do.

The Impact of Campaign Money

We have discussed several aspects of money in elections: how much there is, who contributes it, and how they do so. Now we turn to the question of what difference campaign money makes. An obvious question is whether money influences the outcomes of elections. But we also will focus on three other kinds of potential effects of money and the way it is raised: the recruitment of good candidates, the policy decisions of elected leaders, and the cynicism of the public.

Does the Campaign Finance System Deter Good Candidates?

When John Glenn, an unsuccessful Democratic candidate in 1984, was asked whether running for president had been worth it despite his defeat, Glenn replied, "My family was humiliated. I got myself whipped. I gained 16 pounds. And I'm more than $2.5 million in debt. Except for that, it was wonderful."[32] In 1998, nearing the end of his career, Glenn remarked in a similar vein: "I'd rather wrestle a gorilla than ask anyone for another 50 cents."[33]

Other presidential candidates have lamented the difficulties and humiliations of having to raise money; Jack Kemp, Richard Cheney, and Dan Quayle, all potential 1996 presidential candidates, bowed out early in 1995 indicating that the magnitude of necessary fund-raising was one reason. In 2000, George W. Bush's huge campaign war chest deterred several potential candidates from entering the race. Others, such as Elizabeth Dole, dropped out after losing early primaries partly because of the impossibility of matching Bush's funding levels. Bush had raised and spent more money before the first primary than Bob Dole did in his entire 1996 election campaign.[34]

The necessity of raising a lot of money deters congressional candidates, too. As one leading congressional scholar noted, "Raising money is, by consensus, the most unpleasant part of a campaign. Many candidates find it demeaning to ask people for money and are uncomfortable with the implications of accepting it."[35] As one senator commented, "I never imagined how much of my personal time would be spent on fund raising. . . . I do not think a candidate for the U.S. Senate should have to sit in a motel room in Goldendale, Washington, at 6 in the morning and spend three hours on the phone talking to political action committees."[36] And, once elected, many new members of Congress are surprised and chagrined to find that they must begin raising funds for their next campaign almost before they are sworn into office.

Does Money Win Elections?

Money helps win elections, but other factors also determine the outcomes. The evidence is mixed as to the impact of money on winning presidential primaries. Some candidates are never considered serious because they do not have sufficient money to mount a large campaign. In that sense, money is crucial. But money alone cannot win. Sometimes the biggest spenders get nowhere. Beyond some point, money might not matter as much. Some analyses have shown that spending by the major

Oliphant© 1990 Universal Press Syndicate. Reprinted with permission. All rights reserved.

Democratic and Republican presidential primary candidates in each state bears little relationship to whether or not they won that state.[37]

By the time presidential candidates are nominated, they already have spent a great deal. The name recognition achieved during the primaries and at the national conventions carries into the general election campaign. Presidential candidates receive extensive free media coverage in news stories. The amount that they spend after the convention is less likely to be as crucial. This is just as well for the health of the two-party system, because if money determined elections, the Republicans would have won every presidential election since World War II. However, of the presidential elections lost by the Democrats during that time, probably only the election of 1968 between Richard Nixon and Hubert Humphrey was close enough that it might have turned out differently had the Democrats been able to spend more.[38] When the elections are close, as in 1968, the Republicans definitely have the advantage by having more money.[39]

In congressional races, incumbents usually start with a huge advantage. Their name is recognized by many of their constituents. Challengers must buy media to achieve similar recognition. Thus, the ability of the challenger to raise and spend money is crucial. As Figure 3 shows, challengers to incumbents have a very low probability of winning unless they raise $500,000 or more. Every $10,000 spent by a House challenger increases his or her vote total by more than 2 percent. The amount of money incumbents spend seems unrelated to whether they win or not. As challengers spend more, so do incumbents.[40]

In 1998, one in six congressional races had at least one candidate who spent at least $1 million. Nearly 80 percent of the $1 million spenders won. Overall, 94 percent of Senate and 95 percent of House races were won by the biggest spender.[41] Most of these were incumbents, and the link between spending and victory is also a link between incumbency and victory. Incumbents are able to raise more money than challengers. In 1998, for example, on average House incumbents raised $733,000, their challengers $184,000. Rarely is a challenger able to raise even half as much as the incumbent. Of course, sometimes the biggest spender loses, but the relative rarity of this occurrence only highlights the general link between spending and victory.

Does Money Buy Favorable Policies?

As we have seen, donors are not a random cross section of the public. Money seems to buy access, and that access is by the wealthiest segment of the population, whose views on public issues are not necessarily representative of the larger population.

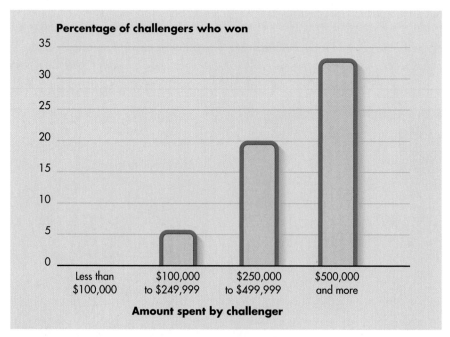

FIGURE 3 ■ *A Challenger's Success Is Related to Spending*

SOURCE: Larry Makinson and Joshua Goldstein, *Open Secrets: The Encyclopedia of Congressional Money and Politics* (Washington, D.C.: Congressional Quarterly, 1994).

"I appreciate your offer, but I'm afraid I'm already bought and paid for."

If money buys access, does it also buy votes? Both anecdotal and systematic evidence suggest that money does buy votes, although only under some conditions.

Money is not likely to buy votes on issues that are highly publicized, because legislators' constituents usually have strong views on these issues and legislators feel pressured to follow them.[42] For the same reason, money is less likely to buy roll-call votes on the floor of each house than votes in committees. The former are public and recorded; the latter are not as visible to the public. Compared to their activity on the floor, in committees, legislators with PAC support are more active in speaking and negotiating on behalf of the PAC's positions and offering amendments that reflect these positions.[43]

Money is also not likely to buy votes on moral issues, because legislators themselves often have firm views on these issues. These sorts of issues (abortion and school prayer, for example) also tend to be publicized.

But most matters that come to a vote are neither highly publicized nor moral issues. Most are relatively technical matters that constituents and legislators do not care as strongly about as do PACs. For these, members are susceptible. "You can't buy a Congressman for $50,000. But you can buy his vote," a member admitted. "It's done on a regular basis."[44]

One survey of members found that about one-fifth admit that political contributions have affected their votes on occasion, and another one-third are not sure.[45] Analysis of voting has revealed that contributions from the AFL-CIO affected voting on the minimum wage legislation, and contributions from the trucking interests led senators to vote against deregulation of trucking. Those senators facing reelection the year in which the vote was taken were most susceptible.[46] Voting is also related to donations in such disparate areas as minimum wage legislation, gun control, and regulation.[47]

One classic example concerns used-car legislation. Auto dealers spent $675,000 in the 1980 congressional elections. This investment seemed to pay off in 1982 when Congress voted against a rule requiring dealers to inform prospective buyers of any known defects in used cars. The senators who opposed the measure received twice as much money from the auto dealers' PAC as those who voted for it. In the House, those who opposed the measure received on average five times as much money as those who voted for it. Almost 85 percent of the representatives opposing the legislation had received PAC money.[48]

The relationship between PAC money and votes still existed even when the party and ideology of the

The Environmental Defense Fund once sent out a mass fund-raising mailing promising new members a copy of the book *50 Simple Things You Can Do to Save the Earth*. The book's number-one suggestion: stop junk mail. Ironically, environmental groups, like others, fill mailboxes with junk mail, which eventually amounts to 3 percent of the volume in our landfills.

PACs and political parties soliciting members and funds send out hundreds of millions of letters annually. For example, the National Rifle Association sends twelve million letters monthly, and the American Association of Retired People sends fifty million a year just prospecting for new members.[1]

Most people look forward to mail more than other daily activities such as watching television, eating, and pursuing hobbies.[2] Mail solicitations for money by PACs and other political groups provide an interesting diversion. Many read the letters, are convinced by the arguments, and write checks.

Getting a good response from mail solicitations appears to be both an art and a science. Here are some of the tricks of the trade used by successful PACs.

The *mailing list* is one key to success. Letters are not sent out randomly. Mailing lists of potential contributors are shared among like-minded groups, so you are likely to receive such mailings if you have already contributed to a candidate or cause or even if you buy goods from mail-order catalogs. One estimate is that average Americans in professional occupations spend eight months of their lives simply opening and sorting political and business junk mail.

The *envelope* should be personalized, with real stamps, not metered ones. Often the words URGENT or REPLY REQUIRED stimulate a better response. One PAC sent out a mailing with the words FEDERAL TAX REDUCTION INFORMATION ENCLOSED prominently displayed on the envelope (the PAC letter dealt with the activities of a PAC working to reduce taxes).

The *letter* often is written on expensive-looking paper. The text is written in short paragraphs at the sixth- to eighth-grade level to capture the reader's attention. On the other hand, the letter is often fairly long. Four pages are typical, but many are longer.

The *opening paragraph* is usually an attention grabber such as "I need your advice" or "This is the most urgent letter I have ever written."[3]

The *language* is usually emotional, overblown, and very negative. One 1995 Democratic fund-raising letter called Newt Gingrich a terrorist (the authors later apologized). The National Rifle Association's labeling of government agents as "jackbooted thugs" caused former President Bush to resign his membership. One NCPAC letter from Jesse Helms warned, "Your tax dollars are being used to pay for grade school courses that teach our children that cannibalism, wife swapping, and the murder of infants and the elderly are acceptable." Campaigning against PACs, an independent action PAC IAPAC warned that "money doesn't just talk, it leads many elected officials around on a leash."

Mailers use a personal approach, and their letters are sprinkled with *you*s.

---

members were taken into account. For conservatives, who might have voted against requiring auto dealers to list defects anyway, PAC contributions made only a marginal difference in their voting; but for liberals, PAC money substantially raised the probability that they would vote with the used-car dealers.[49] " 'Of course it was money,' one House member said. . . . 'Why else would they vote for used-car dealers?' "[50]

The relationship between PAC contributions and voting should not be exaggerated, however.[51] Even on these low-visibility votes, a member's party and ideology are important. The constituency interests of members are also key factors explaining votes. For example, members with many union workers in their districts are go-

ing to vote for those interests regardless of how much or little they get in PAC contributions.[52] Members without these constituents, though, may be more swayed by PAC contributions.

Money not only can help buy votes, it can buy influence with the executive branch, too. Presidential candidates tend to have widely publicized views, and their actions as president are subject to intense scrutiny and publicity. Once in office presidents need donors less than donors need them, thus making the leverage of a campaign donation uncertain. Contributors sometimes find, as did one contributor to the campaign of Teddy Roosevelt, "We bought the son of a bitch but he did not stay bought."[53]

A mailing from the National Taxpayers Union offered instructions as to how "you can save America from Washington." Well-heeled PACs sometimes use computers to intersperse your name throughout the letter.

Enclosures are common. Solicitors often promise you something for your membership or send along a small gift, such as a signed picture, stickers, or a pin. "While trying to appeal to you with flattery for your intelligence and compassion, direct mail packages are designed on the assumption you are a self-indulgent idiot," commented one observer of the direct-mail scene.

A *donor card* is crucial. Cards are enclosed to make it easy for recipients to give. This card can be pretty emotional, too. For example, one conservative PAC offered recipients two choices on the donor card. If they contributed to the PAC, they could stick a stars and stripes flag on the card. If they refused to contribute, they should stick on the white flag of surrender!

1. Jill Smolowe, "Read This!!!!!!!!" *Time,* November 26, 1990, p. 63.
2. Larry Sabato, "Mailing for Dollars," *Psychology Today* 18 (October 1984), pp. 38–43. This box draws heavily on the Sabato article.
3. Ibid. The remainder of the quotations are from this article, unless otherwise noted.

Calvin and Hobbes © Watterson. Reprinted with permission of Universal Press Syndicate. All rights reserved.

However, on actions not widely visible to the public, donors can help shape policy. In 1999, for example, the Clinton administration imposed a 100 percent tariff on several specialty goods imported from Europe (a 100 percent tariff, a tax, raises the cost of the goods to the importer and hence the customer by 100 percent). A number of U.S. businesses dependent on these imports were forced to take big losses and go out of business or stop selling the product.

The reason for this tariff was that a major contributor to both the Democratic and Republican campaigns, American Financial Group, owned the Chiquita banana firm. The European Union had placed barriers to the import of those bananas, thus potentially causing the owners a multimillion-dollar loss. In response to the pressure of the banana company owners, the United States retaliated, despite the fact that the banana company (in Latin America) employed no U.S. workers and that many U.S. small businesses were hurt by the retaliation of the U.S. government. But the contributor was a business partner of one of the Democrats' chief fund-raisers and had given the vast majority of his $5 million contributions to the Republicans. Many recipients of this largesse were among those pressuring the administration to take action on behalf of the banana company.[54]

Analyses of large donors to, and fund-raisers for, the 1992 Bush campaign reveal that many were given special favors or benefits from the federal government. The

Department of Labor reduced a proposed fine by nearly 90 percent against a large sugar farmer who gave $200,000 to the campaign.[55] The president proposed incentives for using corn-based ethanol in auto fuels, a proposal that would cost consumers three-tenths of a cent per gallon of gas purchased and yield a profit of $30 to $75 million. Archer-Daniels-Midland gave the Republican campaign more than $1 million.

While it is impossible to prove a cause-and-effect relationship in these cases, clearly large donors who expect favorable treatment have plenty of precedents to lead them to that conclusion. Thus, the leader of a watchdog group said, "The point is, we're not just electing politicians. . . . We're also electing their patrons and their priorities."[56]

The influence of big money in presidential campaigns probably makes both parties more conservative. The biggest contributors to the Republicans in the last few presidential elections have been some of the most conservative people within that party. The big money contributors to the Democrats are, on the whole, less liberal than the mainstream of the party.

Some Democratic House leaders were surprised when members said they could not vote against a capital gains tax cut (which would benefit the wealthy) because it would anger their business contributors. "I get elected by voters. I get financed by contributors. Voters don't care about this, contributors do."[57]

Large contributions to presidential campaigns often lead to appointments to public office, especially ambassadorships. The "spoils system," as it is called, has been with us since at least the time of Andrew Jackson, so it cannot be blamed on modern PACs and soft money.

Campaign Money and Public Cynicism

We have seen repeatedly that public confidence and trust in government have diminished greatly over time. Some of the reasons for this declining trust have nothing to do with money. But public trust was certainly affected by the Watergate scandal, and it is likely that revelations about big money lobbying activity since then have not improved the public's view of the honesty of public officials.

The current system appears to play a part in alienating voters and reducing voting turnouts. Even if we believe that no votes are actually bought, the appearance of conflicts of interest that permeates the existing system and clearly disturbs the public should give pause to those interested in the health of our political system.

Walter Lippman, a famous American journalist, once said that American communities govern themselves "by

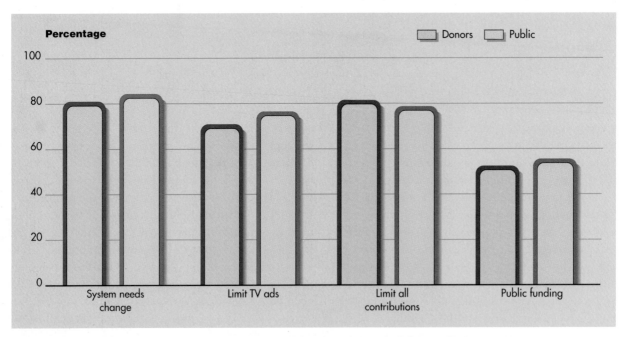

FIGURE 4 ■ *The Public and Donors Agree That the Campaign Finance System Needs to Be Fixed*

SOURCE: *Washington Post* national survey, reported in Ruth Marcus and Charles Babcock, "Feeding the Election Machine," *Washington Post National Weekly Edition*, February 17, 1997, p. 10.

fits and starts of unsuspecting complacency and violent suspicion." We think nothing is wrong, and then we think everything is wrong. So it is with our views of campaign money. For several years after the 1974 reforms, we thought things were going along pretty well. More recently, many have become convinced that the nation is in terrible jeopardy because of the influence of money.

Although the public seems overwhelmingly supportive of campaign finance reform (see Figure 4), it is not in the interests of many legislators to support it. The McCain–Feingold bill, discussed in the "You Are There" opening this chapter, had wide support from the Democrats and some support from Republicans, but it was killed in 1998 by the Republican leadership. Though this proposal or others are likely to continue to be on the agenda, it is clear that elected officials are more afraid of being without campaign donations than they are that voters will punish them for not supporting campaign reform.

And while it was the Republican leadership that killed the campaign finance bill in 1998, the commitment of many Democrats is also questionable. Ideologically, Democrats are more sympathetic to limiting the influence of big money, but practically, Democratic incumbents are heavily dependent on their PAC "fixes." When a Republican president was in office, Democratic members of Congress could vote their ideological inclinations for campaign finance reform, resting assured that the president would veto any serious reforms. When Clinton took office and indicated his support for reform, Democrats found innumerable ways to avoid passing a serious bill. Now that Republicans control Congress, Democrats rue their failure.

Nevertheless, as we begin the twenty-first century, it is not clear that either party has much incentive to support campaign finance reform. What does seem to be true is that the public is repelled by the existing system.

As Figure 4 shows, support for change is overwhelming in the general public. John McCain and Bill Bradley briefly mobilized voters in the 2000 primaries around the issue of campaign finance reform. With their defeat, few national leaders are strongly in favor of reform. Campaign finance reform continues to wait for its champion who can rally sustained public interest and support.

Conflicts of Interest

In addition to money's influence on political campaigns, it also leads to **conflicts of interest.** This term refers to officials making decisions that directly affect their own personal livelihoods or interests. The campaign contribution system we have just described is certainly a huge conflict of interest. Presidents and members of Congress make decisions about policies affecting those who give them campaign money. But conflicts of interest are not confined to decisions involving sources of campaign money. As Madison noted, almost every decision involves potential conflicts of interest. Decisions made by presidents, bureaucrats, and members of Congress can affect their personal financial interests (including stocks, bonds, or other investments).

Despite periodic attempts to limit conflicts of interest, violations of ethics codes still occur in Congress and in the executive branch. In 1981, six House members and one senator were convicted in an FBI undercover operation known as Abscam. Five were even videotaped accepting cash. Incidents of blatant bribery such as this are rare, but conflicts of interests are more common. They are harder to deal with, however, because the issues are less clear-cut.

It is difficult to untangle the effects of personal financial interests, constituency interests, and party loyalties. For example, people on the Agriculture Committee with agribusiness interests, as most have, often represent districts with large agricultural interests. If those members vote in favor of agricultural interests, they are voting both for their own interests and for their constituents' interests. And they are likely to think that they are advancing the national interest at the same time. It appears that the impact of these personal interests on

This secretly filmed picture shows the acceptance of money in the Abscam episode. As one of the implicated members said, "I'm gonna tell you something real simple and short. In this business, money talks and b _ _ _ s _ _ _ walks."
UPI/Corbis-Bettmann

voting is fairly small once constituency interests are taken into account.[58]

In the executive branch, decision makers operate under much less direct public and media scrutiny. Yet they, too, may be acting on matters that affect their personal economic position. Since the Carter administration, all high-level administrative officials have been required to file public financial disclosure statements to allow the public to see when they are making decisions that benefit their own financial interests. But the rules do not require officials to step aside on matters that would affect them financially.

It is also a conflict of interest to use one's government position to line up a job following a public service career. The Ethics in Government Act of 1978 tries to regulate this. The act bars former public servants from lobbying their former agencies for a year and on matters in which they "personally and substantially" participated as public officials, for life. Current employees also are prohibited from participating in decisions affecting in-

terests with which they are negotiating about future employment. But the act is not very stringently enforced. Because many companies that regularly deal with government think experience in government, especially in the agency that regulates the company's activities, is an asset, many officials take well-paying jobs in the industry they came to know while in government. Critics call this the "revolving door," referring to the movement of people from government service to the private sector and, sometimes, back again.

Using a government job to line up lucrative private employment also can involve **influence peddling,** using one's access to powerful people to make money. Former high government officials can and do use their access to former colleagues to win jobs representing clients in business or labor. A well-publicized case of influence peddling was that of Michael Deaver, the deputy chief of staff and one of President Reagan's closest advisers during his first term. Deaver left government, immediately set up a public relations and lobbying firm, and be-

Are There Democratic and Republican Kinds of Corruption?

Some observers have pointed out that while both Democrats and Republicans have ethical lapses, the kinds of ethics problems they have are quite different. Corrupt Democrats steal. They accept bribes and improper campaign donations, divert public funds to their own pockets, and, in general, engage in personal financial aggrandizement. This style of corruption is reminiscent of the "honest graft" of the big city political machines (see the box on Boss Plunkitt and "honest graft" earlier in the chapter). While some Republicans also steal—for example, former Vice President Spiro Agnew, who pleaded no contest to charges of kickbacks, bribery, and extortion, and former Representative Joseph McDade (R-Pa.), who has been indicted for bribery and racketeering (but not yet convicted)—most of these sorts of scandals involved Democrats. Examples in-

clude most of those involved in Abscam, four of the Keating 5, four Democratic members of Congress convicted of graft in the last five years, and most recently Daniel Rostenkowski (D-Ill.), former chair of the Ways and Means Committee, convicted of corrupt acts involving mail fraud.

Republican ethical failings tend to be related to the use of government for improper means. President Nixon's Watergate scandal involved trying to use the powers of government to punish his personal enemies and then lying about it. He also ordered Cambodia to be bombed and tried to keep it a secret. President Reagan tried to subvert the constitutional powers of Congress by secretly selling arms to Iran and supplying weapons to rebels in Nicaragua, both expressly against the law. While Democratic presidents have also been guilty of

misuse of government power (for example, President Johnson lying about alleged attacks by the North Vietnamese on an American ship to justify getting the United States more deeply involved in the Vietnam War and President Kennedy ordering the FBI to wiretap Reverend Martin Luther King), subverting government seems more a Republican style of corruption.

Why do these differences exist? They could be coincidental, of course. But one Democrat argued that these differences were tied to the class basis of the parties: "The lower classes steal, the upper classes defraud." A prominent Republican had a different view: "Most Republicans are contemptuous of government; few Democrats are." Whatever the reason, these examples suggest that partisanship extends to more than presidential preferences.

Money and Politics in Time

1787	Founders design Constitution of divided government power so that no one interest would dominate others.
Mid–19th century	Winning of the West built on land giveaways to speculators, who often bribed federal officials to obtain land.
Late 19th century	Era of overt graft. Businesses openly provide contributions to campaigns and candidates and often in direct return for favors. Urban political machines built on "honest" graft.
1907	Federal law prohibits corporations and businesses from making political contributions.
1921	Teapot Dome scandal leads to 1925 federal legislation requiring reporting of campaign contributions.
1972	Watergate scandal and cover-up reveal secret corporate funding of Nixon campaign.
1974	Congress passes Federal Election Campaign Act, designed to limit influence of money in campaigns through public disclosure of gifts, limits to size of gifts, and regulation of spending.
1975	Republicans establish "Eagle Club," exchanging invitations to White House for gifts of $10,000 or more.
1976	Supreme Court declares invalid parts of the 1974 campaign finance law, thus opening a large loophole in the law.
1970s–1990s	Growth of political action committees funneling private money to candidates. Further loopholes are created in the 1974 act.
1980s	Candidates discover that there are no limits on "soft" money donations to political parties, thus opening up avenues for donors to contribute unlimited amounts.
1996	Clinton's successful efforts to raise funds lead to invitations to White House in exchange for large donations. "Sleepovers" in Lincoln bedroom lead to ridicule and new calls to strengthen campaign finance laws.
2000	Final nail driven in coffin of 1974 act when PACs discover loopholes allowing them to accept gifts without disclosing names of donors.

gan soliciting clients largely on the basis of his close relationship with the president.[59]

Conflicts of interest and influence peddling are bipartisan phenomena. Such accusations swirled around the Clinton White House, although no high official has yet been convicted of illegal acts in office. But President Clinton and Hillary Clinton have been accused of conflicts of interest in the long-running investigation of the "Whitewater affair." A number of Clinton administration members, including a cabinet secretary, Mike Espy, left office under ethical clouds relating to conflicts of interest and interest peddling. Some of the allegations of improper behavior (such as Whitewater) took place before the accused persons assumed their current roles in the federal government. The large number of such instances led some commentators to point out that the ethical standards in the executive office are a good deal higher than in Congress or in some states, like Arkansas.

Conflicts of interest can never be completely eradicated from government, but presidents can make their expectations clear. Presidents Bush and Clinton have shown more concern about ethical issues than their predecessors, though conflicts of interest have been reg- ularly reported. Ironically, when such conflicts are made public instead of being ignored, public perceptions of lower ethical standards in government than elsewhere in society may be reinforced. There is little reason to think, however, that people in government are less ethical than those in business, labor, or other parts of the private sector. (See the box "Are There Democratic and Republican Kinds of Corruption?" also.)

Conclusion: Does the Influence of Money Make Government Less Responsive?

The influence of money in American politics is a perennial source of concern to those who want to live up to the democratic ideals of political equality and popular sovereignty. Our democratic values tell us that government should represent all, the poor as well as the rich, and that everyone should have an equal chance to influence government. We know that in the real world things do not work this way. We tolerate much inequality in access because that seems to be the way the world works in the private as well as in the public sphere, because everyone is not equally interested in influencing government, and because for most people the effort of changing this pattern would be greater than the benefits gained.

Nevertheless, our reaction to the influence of money seems to be cyclical. We tolerate it; then when stories of inside deals, influence peddling, and buying access and even votes become too frequent, we act to do something about it. We then slip back into apathy until the next cycle comes along.[60]

In recent history, the low point of the use of money to buy access was probably during the Watergate scandals associated with the 1972 election. We then reacted strongly to those scandals by passing new laws and in general cleaning up our campaign finance system. But as the years went by, we found ways to get around the laws until now they are nearly meaningless. Now it appears we are in another era of growing concern over ethical standards in government.

We should not think of our times as the low point in government morality. In political campaigns, big money is certainly less influential than it was a century ago. Campaign funding disclosure legislation means that the public can at least know who is buying influence.

Some commentators believe the standards of public conduct decreased during the 1980s and have remained low. But although conflicts of interest and influence peddling in government may shock some, they reflect the ethical standards of the larger society. Making money in any way possible seems to be the hallmark of modern times, the age of "pin-striped outlaws." Though several public officials during the 1980s and 1990s resigned after embarrassing revelations of conflicts of interests and sometimes illegal activities, many leaders of the business world have also seemed intent on making their fast buck, regardless of the ethics or legality of their actions. Numerous Wall Street bankers bought and sold illegal insider tips, savings and loan officers looted their institutions of millions of dollars, military contractors cheated government, and many other executives made millions in shady deals that were just this side of legality. One businessman lamented, "We are all embarrassed by events that make the *Wall Street Journal* read more like the *Police Gazette*."[61]

We should not exaggerate the amount of money involved in politics. Corporations spend much more to attract consumers than politicians spend to attract voters. In one month in 2000, a presidential election year, candidates spent nearly $8 million in advertising; car companies selling their wares spent over $1 billion.[62] It is not the amount of money in politics as much as its possible effects that concern us.

But the effects of money are hard to pin down. It is difficult to measure exactly the influence of money on political outcomes. Money sometimes influences votes and policies. Campaign contributions have some impact on voting in Congress. But at other times money appears to have little impact.

We do not know exactly how presidential candidates might be influenced by huge campaign donations or whether bureaucrats are using promises of future jobs as trade-offs for current favors. We think that good candidates are hindered or deterred from running by a shortage of money or even just by the knowledge that they need to raise big money, but it is difficult to measure exactly how many. Even though money is very tangible, its influence sometimes is quite intangible.

To the extent that money has an impact, it limits the responsiveness of government to the average citizen. It causes some policymakers to be more responsive to the big interests than to the average person. This does not mean, though, that those with the most money always win. Organization and a sense of the public interest can sometimes defeat even big money.

In designing laws to regulate the use of money in political life, perhaps the best that reformers can reasonably hope for is a system in which public officials who want to be honest will not feel under pressure to be influenced by money. Certainly, there will always be a few "bad apples," and no political system can protect us completely from them. It should be enough to design rules and structures that ensure that people of average honesty who serve in public office are rewarded for putting the public interest, rather than their private interests, first. Our current laws, especially our congressional campaign finance laws, do not always do that. The penalties we suffer are less in politicians stealing from the public till (the money does not amount to much). They are more in the loss of public trust, an increasing alienation from government, and an anger at politicians who seem to be putting their interests before the public interest. Perhaps, then, even a largely symbolic effort by our legislators to limit the influence of money on the political process is important, because it sends the signal that they are aware of and accountable to, public concerns.

Feingold Limits Campaign Donations

Senator Feingold chose to run what he labeled a "restrained" campaign.[63] Vowing to act in a manner consistent with the legislation he is trying to have enacted, he sought to limit the influence of money in the campaign. He refused to accept soft money contributions from the national party. He limited PAC contributions, accepting an amount that equaled only 10 percent of his overall campaign spending. He did not participate in raising soft money, and he raised most of his money from Wisconsinites rather than national constituencies. Finally, he limited his own personal donation to his campaign to $2,000. Of course, as he said, this was easy for him to do because he did not have great personal wealth. Overall, he spent only $1 per eligible voter.

Although his opponent agreed to limit his own campaign spending to $4.7 million, compared to Feingold's $3.8 million, the Republican National Committee spent heavily on the race, and overall Feingold estimated he was outspent about three to one. Despite

this, when the Democratic Senate Campaign Committee started running anti-Neumann ads, Feingold said "Get the hell out of my state with those things." As a consequence, his early lead shrank as the Republicans dominated the airwaves. Senator Feingold did win reelection, however, although his margin of victory was the closest of any Senate campaign in 1998: he won barely 50 percent to Neumann's 48 percent.

Despite the close call, Senator Feingold felt that he had made the right decision. By not having to focus on fund-raising, particularly out-of-state fund-raising, he believed he was able to spend more time actually talking to voters around the state. His campaign also strengthened his belief that, by not needing the help of the national party or special interest groups, he would be more free to vote his conscience and the interests of his Wisconsin constituents as he began his new term.

Of course, Wisconsin is a relatively small state. The kind of grassroots campaign that Senator Feingold ran successfully might not be workable in a

larger state. Moreover, despite the fact that he generally stuck to his guns, the dynamics of the race illustrate again why it is difficult to win support for campaign finance reform. When one party starts spending money in a close race, the impulse is for the other party to match or exceed it, a kind of campaign finance arms race. In a close contest, both sides want to do every-thing possible to win, and a few extra hundreds of thousands of dollars might indeed make the difference. So elected officials do not want to tie their own hands by limiting their abilities to raise funds from friendly interest groups.

But from a larger public perspective, of course, the dynamics of the campaign arms race are less benign. Friendly interest groups are not friendly out of a kind of charitable benevolence. Most interest groups, whether corporations, unions, or special interest groups, want access or more. Letting unlimited amounts of money flow into election campaigns no doubt means unlimited amounts of access for those who provide the money flow.

Key Terms

Muckrakers
Teapot Dome scandal
political action committees (PACs)
Federal Election Campaign Act

independent spending
soft money
conflicts of interest
influence peddling

Further Reading

Jeffrey Birnbaum, *The Money Men*. New York: Times Books, 2000. The real scandal in Washington isn't what's illegal, it's what's legal. This book follows the money in a very readable way.

Larry J. Sabato and Glenn Simpson, *Dirty Little Secrets: The Persistence of Corruption in American Politics* (New York: Times Books, 1996). An up-to-date look at corruption in politics.

Frank Sorauf, *Inside Campaign Finance: Myths and Realities* (New Haven, Conn.: Yale University Press, 1992). An overview that challenges conventional wisdom.

Electronic Resources

www.commoncause.org/issue_agenda/issues.htm
The home page of Common Cause, the public interest group whose major focus is reforming the campaign finance system. Linked to the page are the group's reports tracking relevant legis-lation, periodic reports on campaign spending, and reports on

financial ties of those voting against major regulatory legislation such as the tobacco bill.

www.pbs.org/wgbh/pages/frontline/president/

The home page for a PBS special "So You Want to Buy a President." Contains much useful data on how much is contributed and who the contributors are.

www.fec.gov/index.html

The Federal Election Commission does not have much regulatory power, but it does publish useful reports of campaign spending. This page describes election rules and links to FEC reports on campaign spending and on voter turnout.

www.politics.com

Links to news stories and polls, and allows you to see who in your neighborhood (or any other, by ZIP code) gave to which campaigns.

InfoTrac College Edition

"Big Oil Buys Senate, Says Feingold"
"Soft Money, Hardball Tactics"
"Hard Money. Soft Money. Lobbying Money"
"Clark's Date with Destiny"

Notes

1. Michael Barone and Grant Ujifusa, *The Almanac of American Politics 2000* (Washington, D.C.: National Journal, 1999), 1732–1734; Russ Feingold, "Running and Winning a Restrained Campaign," *Extensions* (Spring 1999): 4–8.

2. Jimmy Breslin, *How the Good Guys Finally Won: Notes from an Impeachment Summer* (New York: Ballantine, 1974), 14.

3. Congressional Quarterly, *Dollar Politics,* 3d ed. (Washington, D.C.: CQ Press, 1982), 3.

4. Ibid.

5. James Madison, *The Federalist Papers* 10.

6. Haynes Johnson, "Turning Government Jobs into Gold," *Washington Post National Weekly Edition,* May 12, 1986, pp. 6–7.

7. Quoted in Richard Hofstadter, *The American Political Tradition* (New York: Vintage, 1958), 165.

8. Congressional Quarterly, *Dollar Politics,* 3.

9. Larry J. Sabato, *Feeding Frenzy* (New York: Free Press, 1991).

10. Elizabeth Drew, *Politics and Money* (New York: Collier, 1983), 9.

11. *Buckley v. Valeo,* 424 U.S. 1 (1976).

12. See Marick Masters and Gerald Keim, "Determinants of PAC Participation among Large Corporations," *Journal of Politics* 47 (November 1985): 1158–1173; J. David Gopoian, "What Makes PACs Tick?" *American Journal of Political Science* 28 (May 1984): 259–281; Larry Sabato, *PAC Power* (New York: Norton, 1984), chap. 3; Theodore Eismeier and Philip H. Pollock, "Political Action Committees," in *Money and Politics in the United States,* ed. Michael Malbin (Chatham, N.J.: Chatham House, 1984).

13. *Federal Election Commission v. National Conservative PAC,* 470 U.S. 480 (1985).

14. Ruth Marcus, "Taking Issue with Advocacy," *Washington Post National Weekly Edition,* April 15–21, 1996, p. 13.

15. David Broder, "Both Major Parties Abuse Soft Money Loophole," *Centre Daily Times,* May 30, 2000, p. 6A.

16. Ibid.

17. Ruth Marcus, "Off the Ballot, but in the Contest," *Washington Post National Weekly Edition,* July 6, 1998, p. 13.

18. Alison Mitchell, "Time Passes, Money Flows," *New York Times,* June 16, 1996, p. E5.

19. Drew, *Politics and Money,* 105. See also "Please Hold for the President," *New York Times,* March 14, 1993, p. E16; Michael Wines, "Snapping at the Hand That Fed Clinton Well," *International Herald Tribune,* March 5, 1993, p. 3; Peter Stone, "Return of the Fat Cats," *National Journal,* October 17, 1992, p. 2352.

20. Carol Matlock, "Lobbying Focus," *National Journal,* November 5, 1988, p. 2868.

21. Alan C. Miller, Diaper Donors: Study Shows Children Giving to Candidates," *Lincoln Journal Star,* February 28, 1999; David Rosenbaum, "Soft Money and Some Not-So-Hard Promises," *New York Times,* April 11, 1999, p. 19.

22. Larry Makinson and Joshua Goldstein, *Open Secrets: The Encyclopedia of Congressional Money and Politics* (Washington, D.C.: Congressional Quarterly, 1994).

23. Michael Weisskopf, "To the Victors Belong the PAC Checks," *Washington Post National Weekly Edition,* January 2–5, 1995, p. 13. The remainder of the paragraph is also drawn from this source.

24. Jennifer Babson and Kelly St. John, "Momentum Helps GOP Collect Record Amounts from PACs," *Congressional Quarterly Weekly Report,* December 3, 1994, pp. 3456–3459.

25. See Kevin Grier and Michael Mangy, "Comparing Interest Group PAC Contributions to House and Senate Incumbents," *Journal of Politics* 55 (August 1993): 615–643.

26. J. David Gopoian, "Change and Continuity in Defense PAC Behavior," *American Politics Quarterly* 13 (July 1985): 297–322; Richard Morin and Charles Babcock, "Off Year, Schmoff Year," *Washington Post National Weekly Edition,* May 14–20, 1990, p. 15.

27. Gary Wasserman, "The Uses of Influence," *Washington Post National Weekly Edition,* January 11–17, 1993, p. 35.

28. Makinson and Goldstein, *Open Secrets,* 23.

29. Drew, *Politics and Money,* 68; Thomas B. Edsall, "More Than Enough Is Not Enough," *Washington Post National Weekly Edition,* February 9, 1987, p. 13. See also Edward Handler and John Mulkern, *Business in Politics* (Lexington, Mass.: Heath, 1982), 1–34.

30. Amy Dockser, "Nice PAC You've Got There . . . A Pity If Anything Should Happen to It," *Washington Monthly* (January 1984): 21.

31. Juliet Eilperin, " 'The Hammer' De Lay Whips Lobbyists into Shape," *Washington Post National Weekly Edition,* October 25, 1999, p. 8.

32. Meg Greenfield, "The Political Debt Bomb," *Newsweek,* April 1987, p. 76.

33. Quoted in *New York Times,* June 13, 1998, p. A7.

34. "Numbers," *Time,* February 28, 2000, p. 27.

35. Gary Jacobson, *Money in Congressional Elections* (New Haven, Conn.: Yale University Press, 1980), 61.

36. David Broder, "The High Road to Lower Finance?" *Washington Post National Weekly Edition,* June 29, 1987, p. 4; Diane Granat, "Parties' Schools for Politicians or Grooming Troops for Election," *Congressional Quarterly Weekly Report,* May 5, 1984, p. 1036.

37. Gary Orren, "The Nomination Process," in *The Elections of 1984,* ed. Michael Nelson (Washington, D.C.: CQ Press, 1986), chap. 2. See also Michael J. Robinson and Austin Ranney, eds. *The Mass Media in Campaign 1984* (Washington, D.C.: American Enterprise Institute, 1985); Michael Robinson, Clyde Wilcox, and Paul Marshall, "The Presidency: Not for Sale," *Public Opinion* (March/April 1989): 49–52.

38. Nelson Polsby and Aaron Wildavsky, *Presidential Elections* (New York: Scribner's, 1984), 56.

39. David Nice, "Campaign Spending and Presidential Election Results," *Polity* 19 (Spring 1987): 464–476, shows that presidential

campaign spending is more productive for Republicans than Democrats.

40. Gary Jacobson, *Money in Congressional Elections;* Jacobson, "Public Funds for Congressional Campaigns: Who Would Benefit?" in *Political Finance,* ed. Herbert E. Alexander (Beverly Hills, Calif.: Sage, 1979); Jacobson, "Parties and PACs in Congressional Elections," in *Congress Reconsidered,* 3d ed., ed. Lawrence C. Dodd and Bruce I. Oppenheimer (Washington, D.C.: CQ Press, 1985); Jacobson, *The Politics of Congressional Elections,* 2d ed. (Boston: Little, Brown, 1987), chap. 4; Jacobson, "The Effects of Campaign Spending in House Elections," *American Journal of Political Science* 34 (May 1990): 334–362; Christopher Kenny and Michael McBurnett, "A Dynamic Model of the Effect of Campaign Spending on Congressional Vote Choice," *American Journal of Political Science* 36 (November 1992): 923–937; Donald Green and Jonathan Krasno, "Salvation for the Spendthrift Incumbent," *American Journal of Political Science* 32 (November 1988): 884–907.

41. Leslie Wayne, "If No Guarantee of Victory, Money Sure Makes It Easier," *New York Times,* November 6, 1998, p. A23.

42. The survey of donors is reported in Bob Hebert, "The Donor Class," *New York Times,* July 19, 1998, p. 15; Woodrow Jones and K. Robert Keiser, "Issue Visibility and the Effects of PAC Money," *Social Science Quarterly* 68 (March 1987): 170–176; Janet Grenzke, "PACs and the Congressional Supermarket," *American Journal of Political Science* 33 (February 1989): 1–24, found little effect of PAC money on a series of votes that were not obscure. Laura Langbein, "Money and Access," *Journal of Politics* 48 (November 1986): 1052–1064, shows that those who received more PAC money spend more time with interest group representatives.

43. Jean Reith Schroedel, "Campaign Contributions and Legislative Outcomes," *Western Political Quarterly* 39 (September 1986): 371–389; Richard L. Hall and Frank Wayman, "Buying Time: Moneyed Interests and the Mobilization of Bias in Congressional Committees," *American Political Science Review* 84 (September 1990): 797–820.

44. "Running with the PACs," *Time,* October 25, 1982, p. 20. The quotation is from Representative Thomas Downey (D-N.Y.).

45. "Congress Study Links Funds and Votes," *New York Times,* December 30, 1987, p. 7.

46. John Frendreis and Richard Waterman, "PAC Contributions and Legislative Behavior: Senate Voting on Trucking Deregulation," *Social Science Quarterly* 66 (June 1985): 401–412. See also W. P. Welch, "Campaign Contributions and Legislative Voting," *Western Political Quarterly* 25 (December 1982): 478–495; Jonathan Silberman and Garey Durden, "Determining Legislative Preferences on the Minimum Wage," *Journal of Political Economy* 84 (April 1976): 317–329.

47. Laura Langbein, "PACs, Lobbies and Political Conflict: The Case of Gun Control," *Public Choice* 75 (1993): 254–271; Laura Langbein and Mark Lotwis, "The Political Efficacy of Lobbying and Money: Gun Control in the House, 1986," *Legislative Studies Quarterly* 15 (1990): 413–440; Jean Schroedel, "Campaign Contributions and Legislative Outcomes," *Western Political Quarterly* 39 (1986): 371–389.

48. Adam Clymer, "'84 PACs Gave More to Senate Winners," *New York Times,* January 6, 1985, p. 13.

49. Kirk Brown, "Campaign Contributions and Congressional Voting," paper prepared for the annual meeting of the American Political Science Association, 1983, cited in Malbin, *Money and Politics,* 134.

50. Drew, *Politics and Money,* 79.

51. See Grenzke, "PACs and the Congressional Supermarket"; also see Frank Sorauf, *Money in American Elections* (Glenview, Ill.: Scott, Foresman, 1988).

52. Janet Grenzke, "Political Action Committees and the Congressional Supermarket"; John Wright, "Contributions, Lobbying and Committee Voting in the US House of Representatives," *American Political Science Review* 84 (1990): 417–438; Henry Chappel, Jr., "Campaign Contributions and Voting on the Cargo Preference Bill," *Public Choice* 36, no. 2 (1981): 301–312.

53. Jasper Shannon, *Money and Politics* (New York: Random House, 1959).

54. "How to Be a Top Banana," *Time,* February 7, 2000, pp. 42*ff.*

55. "Study: Bush Donors Get Government Favors," *Lincoln Journal,* May 28, 1992 (a *Los Angeles Times* news release).

56. Charles Lewis quoted in "Book Details Candidates' Extensive Financial Alignments," *Lincoln Journal* (Tribune Media Sources), January 12, 1996, p. 5A.

57. Tom Kenworthy, "The Color of Money," *Washington Post National Weekly Edition,* November 6–12, 1989, p. 13.

58. Susan Welch and John Peters, "Private Interests in the U.S. Congress," *Legislative Studies Quarterly* 7 (November 1982): 547–555. See also John Peters and Susan Welch, "Private Interests and Public Interests," *Journal of Politics* 45 (May 1983): 378–396.

59. "Having It All, Then Throwing It Away," *Time,* May 25, 1987, p. 22.

60. Elizabeth Drew, "Letter from Washington," *New Yorker,* May 1, 1989, pp. 99–108; see also Dan Balz, "Tales of Power and Money," *Washington Post National Weekly Edition,* May 1–7, 1989, pp. 11–12.

61. "Having It All," p. 22.

62. Keith Bradsher, "How to Pooh-Pooh $70 Million War Chests," *New York Times,* April 30, 2000, p. 6.

63. Feingold, "Running and Winning a Restrained Campaign."

Congress

YOU ARE THERE

Should You Risk Your Career?

It is August 1993 and the House of Representatives is considering Bill Clinton's first budget bill. The bill, which includes a plan to substantially reduce the deficit, has been portrayed as a "make or break" moment in Clinton's presidential term. Failure to get the bill passed would reduce his persuasive power and stature at the outset of his administration, perhaps (the hyperbolic media pronounced) ruin his presidency. On the other hand, the media and the interested public will see passage of the bill as a huge victory, the first step in bringing the nation's deficit under control.

You are Marjorie Margolies-Mezvinsky, a freshman Democratic member of Congress from suburban Philadelphia. You are faced with a representative's worst nightmare: On an important, well-publicized vote, you must either stand with the president of your party against the wishes of the majority of your district's voters or vote with your district and contribute to your president's defeat.

You are not a typical member of Congress. A graduate of Columbia University, you are a television news reporter married to a former Iowa congressional represen-

tative. You have eleven children, including biological children, stepchildren, adopted children from Korea and Vietnam, and refugee foster children. After covering the Clarence Thomas–Anita Hill hearings as a journalist, you decided to run for Congress yourself. Your opponent, a former state representative and county commissioner, is well known for his constituency work (called a "zen master of constituency service" by the local paper), but you attacked him for feeding at the public trough and for waffling ("pro-choice, that's me; multiple choice, that's Jon Fox").[1] You supported abortion rights, improved health care programs, and a middle-class tax cut.

Just beginning your first term in office, you are already concerned about your reelection chances. Your district had been continuously represented by Republicans since 1916 (!) before you were elected. But in 1992, the voters of the district gave you a razor-thin majority (you won by only 1,300 votes out of 254,000 cast) and a plurality to Bill Clinton, largely because of economic concerns and partly because of an anti-incumbent mood. Since coming to Congress, you have positioned yourself well. You are

The Senate convenes to decide whether to remove President Clinton from office after he was impeached by the House of Representatives.
George Tolbert/Senate Photo Office

Representative Margolies-Mezvinsky with her aides moments before she must vote.

one of only five freshmen appointed to the powerful Energy and Commerce Committee. A position on that committee has given you access to important interests who have already contributed to your reelection campaign.

Clinton's budget bill calls for a combination of tax increases and spending cuts. It pleases no one entirely, but is the first significant move toward reducing the deficit since the 1990s. But the bill is in jeopardy for two reasons. First, the Republicans, the minority party in the House, are united in opposition. Many Republicans had supported similar budget measures when they were proposed by George Bush. But now that it is Clinton's budget bill,

they sense an opportunity to deal a major blow to his presidency by defeating this key economic package. The Republicans have traditionally positioned themselves as fiscally conservative (even though it was a Republican president, Ronald Reagan, who ran the largest deficits in U.S. history), and they do not wish to relinquish this advantage to the Democrats. But many conservative Democrats are defecting because they oppose the various tax increases, including a proposed tax on fuel as an energy-saving measure.

You initially voted against the bill because you have told your constituents you will not support the bill. You had mixed emotions when it passed by six votes. The bill has come back to the House after House and Senate representatives reached agreement in a conference committee (when the Senate and House versions of a particular bill are not identical, a committee is set up to negotiate a common version of the bill, which is then sent to each house for ratification). Now the House must ratify the results of that negotiation. You have already prepared a statement explaining your no vote on the budget bill. You think it does not go far enough to re-

duce the deficit. In particular, you believe that it does not pare enough away from entitlements, those programs like Medicare, welfare, and Social Security. As part of your justification for the no vote, you indicate that you believe the president should call a "summit" meeting to discuss entitlement spending.

But now the president has spoken to you at length, pleading for your support. He, and anyone who follows the news, knows the vote is extremely close. He needs every vote, including yours. Given the unanimous opposition of the Republicans, most Democrats must stand firm or the bill will be defeated. You know that a defeat on this bill could have serious repercussions for his entire presidency.

But you do not really favor the bill. It does not go as far as you want on spending cuts, and it contains too many tax increases. Moreover, you think your constituents are not in favor of it, either. You want to be reelected, and you fear that because you have told your constituents you will not support the bill, your constituents will think you have sold out. To vote for the bill could mean committing political suicide in your Republican district; even under the best of circumstances, you will have an uphill race. To waffle on this key issue could move your reelection chances from marginal to hopeless. What do you do?

The Founders clearly intended Congress to be the dominant branch of government. They laid out its role and powers in Article 1 and their discussion takes up almost half the document. By its formal powers, Madison believed, Congress would dominate the presidency because it alone had "access to the pockets of the people." But Congress has not always been first in the hearts of the people, nor has it always been the most respected or trusted branch of government. Americans continue to love the Congress the Founders created or

the idea of a Congress as described in Article 1, but they are not so thrilled about the actual behavior of its current members. On the other hand, most people like their own representatives and senators, at least well enough to return them to office at impressively high rates.

In this chapter, we look at the members of Congress, their backgrounds, elections, and what they do that makes them so popular back home that they are usually reelected. Then we look at Congress itself, how it works, and why it is a focus of public criticism.

Members and Constituencies

Alexis de Tocqueville was not impressed with the status of members of Congress, noting that they were "almost all obscure individuals, village lawyers, men in trades, or even persons belonging to the lower class." His view was shared by another European visitor, Charles Dickens, who was shocked in 1842 to find Congress full of tobacco spitters who committed "cowardly attacks upon opponents" and seemed to be guilty of "aiding and abetting every bad inclination in the popular mind."[2] However one views their behavior, members of Congress were not then, and are not now, a cross section of the American public. But the Congress of today is slowly beginning to look more like the people it represents, and it is more responsive to the public at large than the Congresses of the eighteenth and nineteenth centuries ever were or thought they should be.

Members

The Constitution places few formal restrictions on membership in Congress. One must be twenty-five years old to serve in the House and thirty in the Senate. One has to be a citizen for seven years to be elected to the House and nine to the Senate. Members must reside in the states from which they were elected, but House members need not reside in their own districts. As a practical matter however, it is highly unlikely that voters will elect a person to represent their district who is not from the district or who does not maintain a residence there.

Tenure

Every member of the House stands for election every two years, while each senator serves a six-year term, with one-third of the membership standing for election every two years. Although the Articles of Confederation set a limit on the number of terms a representative could serve, the Constitution places no cap on how many times an individual can be reelected. In the late eighteenth and early nineteenth centuries, leaving one's home to serve in Congress was considered by most a great sacrifice. Perhaps the Founders thought that no one would want to serve more than a few terms. In fact, during Congress's first forty years, 41 percent of House members, on average, dropped out every two years.

In the early nineteenth century, members of Congress made about $8 a day, which paid for boardinghouse

accommodations, firewood, candles, and their meals.[3] Washington was a muddy swamp, with debris-filled streets, farm animals running loose, and transportation so poor almost no one got home during a session.

But in the twentieth century, as Washington became a power center and a much more liveable city, and later as seats went uncontested in the one-party South, more legislators became career politicians, spending thirty and even forty years in Congress. These long-serving members began to dominate committee work and to control the legislative agenda. Although they by no means comprised a majority of Congress, they were probably in the minds of many Americans who began to see government as increasingly unresponsive to the public.

During the height of public anger with government in the 1990s, there was a nationwide move to limit the number of terms both state and national legislators could serve. By 1995, over 70 percent of the public said they favored term limits.[4] Though Congress narrowly defeated term limit legislation, in twenty-three of twenty-four states that allow ballot initiatives, voters adopted term limits for their members of Congress and state legislators.

But in 1995, in a 5–4 vote, the Supreme Court held term limits for members of Congress unconstitutional. The majority argued that permitting individual states to have diverse qualifications for Congress would "result in a patchwork of state qualifications, undermining the uniformity and national character that the Framers envisioned and sought to ensure."[5] By adding to the qualifications spelled out in the Constitution (age and citizenship), the states were in effect "amending" the Constitution. Only a constitutional amendment can amend the Constitution.

Some supporters cling to the mid–nineteenth century image of "citizen lawmakers," who set aside their personal business for a few years to attend to the public's business and then return home. Most supporters believe that by not having to worry constantly about getting reelected, legislators would be free to consider the "public interest," not "special interests," and would have no desire to build personal empires. Others also see term limits as a way to weaken the power of government by having a more rapid turnover of members of legislatures. By the late 1990s, the enthusiasm for term limits waned, with no new term limit legislation enacted.

Social Characteristics

For the first century of the Republic, the possibility of having citizen-legislators who were representative of the social characteristics of the general public was just a romantic notion. Only certain landed, business, or professional white men could even think about running for Congress. It was not until 1920 that a majority of Americans could vote or realistically stand for office. Today, though adults of all social classes can meet the minimum requirements needed to stand for office, the nomination and selection process limits the range of people who choose to run. Members tend to be very high in education, income, and occupational status compared to the rest of the population (see Table 1). Nearly all have college degrees, and a majority have graduate or professional degrees. Members are also quite well-off financially. Although blue-collar workers constitute nearly one-third of the working population, there are no blue-collar workers in Congress.

By far the most common occupation of both senators and representatives is the law. Over the past decade, about 40 percent of the members of the House and over 50 percent of the Senate were lawyers. But this pattern is beginning to change as legislative careers have become more demanding. Today it is difficult for lawyers to maintain their practices and also serve as legislators. Ethics laws requiring financial disclosure and information about client relations have also discouraged practicing attorneys from running. While the Senate is still dominated by lawyers, their numbers in the House are falling, and the numbers of people in agriculture, real estate, and education are increasing.[6] In addition, an increasing number of legislators view politics as their primary occupation.

Members of Congress always have been predominantly of white European descent and male. It is only slightly less so today, as Table 1 shows. White, non-Hispanic males, who make up about 35 percent of the total population, comprise about 75 percent of the House and 88 percent of the Senate. Seventy-two percent of all House members and 86 percent of all senators serving in 2000 had held prior elective office at the state or local level, and 124 members listed public service or politics as their only occupation.[7]

Another dent in the citizen-legislator ideal has been the presence of "dynasty" families (e.g., the Adamses, Harrisons, Lodges, and Kennedys). By one estimate, over the years sixteen "dynasty" families have produced thirty senators and fifty-six House members. In 2000, fifteen members of Congress held seats that had previously been filled by members of their families.[8]

Remuneration

Members of Congress receive an annual salary, plus money for office and staff. Under the Twenty-seventh Amendment pay raises cannot go into effect until a new Congress convenes, but in 1999, Congress passed a bill indexing their salaries to inflation, which qualifies them for automatic annual cost of living pay increases. In 2000 indexing increased salaries from $136,700 to $141,300. Seen in the context of professional salaries in the private sector, the cost of living in Washington, D.C., and the need for almost all members to maintain a residence in their home districts as well as in the capital, the salaries are not high. However, members do have generous benefits. In exchange for modest monthly premiums, they receive first-class health care, or, if they choose, free care at one of two military hospitals. Taxpayers spend about $2 million a year to keep a doctor and staff on site at the Capitol. If members do not like the treatment they receive, they can do something most of you cannot—they can sue their insurance companies because they are part of a federal rather than private program.[9]

Members are also participants in a generous federal pension program that is adjusted each year for inflation. The longest-serving members—those retiring with several decades of service—will receive about 75 percent of their salaries, or slightly less than $100,000 per year for those retiring in 2000.[10]

Party Identification

The party composition of Congress corresponds rather well with the party identification of the public. Just as Democrats have been more numerous than Republicans

Table 1	Members of 106th Congress Are Not Representative of the Public (1999–2001)		
	Population (%)	House* (%)	Senate* (%)
Lawyer	.3	39	57
Blue-collar	30	0	0
Race and ethnicity			
Black	12	8.5	0
Hispanic	11.4	4	0
Asian	3.7	0.7	2
American Indian	0.7	0	1
Women	51	12	9
Catholic	23	29	25
Jewish	2	5	11
Millionaires	3	12**	28**
Median age	35.2	52.6	58.3

*Does not include nonvoting members from Puerto Rico, Guam, Samoa, the Virgin Islands, or the District of Columbia.
SOURCES: *Congressional Quarterly Weekly Report,* January 9, 1999, pp. 60–63; *Statistical Abstract of the United States, 1999.*
**Data are for 1993–1994.

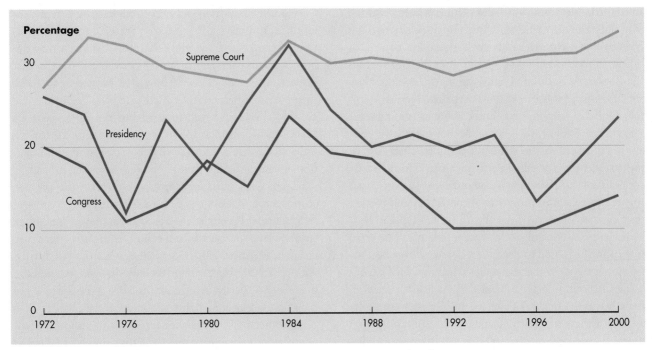

Percentage

30

20

10

0

1972   1976   1980   1984   1988   1992   1996   2000

Supreme Court

Presidency

Congress

FIGURE 1 ■ *Confidence in Political Institutions* *A higher percentage of the public has consistently said it has a "great deal of confidence" in the Supreme Court than in the presidency and Congress.*

SOURCE: Compiled from Harris Poll data by John R. Hibbing and James T. Smith for their article "What the American Public Wants Congress to Be" in *Congress Reconsidered,* 7th ed., ed. Lawrence Dodd and Bruce I. Oppenheimer (Washington, D.C.: Congressional Quarterly Press, 2001).

in the public, Democrats have held majorities in both houses of Congress most of the years since World War II (see endpapers). The Republican victory in 1994 corresponded with the increase in Republican partisans during the 1980s, though there are still more people who identify as Democrats than Republicans.

Members are more likely to share the issue position of constituents when the issue is important to constituents and when their opinions are strongly held.[11] However, there is evidence that members are more responsive to the opinions of independent voters than to their own partisans.[12] This is probably because members believe they can count on the support of their own partisans but need to appeal to voters not strongly committed to either party.

But in general, if districts are filled with farmers, the members must represent farmers, whether or not they know anything about farming. Representatives of districts with large universities must be sensitive to the reactions of students and professors even if they personally think academics have pointed heads.

Constituencies

The district a member of Congress represents is called a **constituency.** The term is used to refer to both the area within the electoral boundaries and its residents. There are two senators from each state. Each senator's constituency is the entire state and all its residents. Because every House district must have roughly the same number of residents, the number of districts in each state depends on total population. But six states have populations so small they are allotted a single seat in the House of Representatives; therefore, the states themselves constitute the House as well as the Senate district. In all other states, the geographic size of a constituency is determined by distribution of the population. In states with large urban populations, several districts may exist within a single city. The logistics of campaigning are thus very different for a representative from Manhattan, whose district can be measured in a few square miles, and one from Wyoming, who must cover the entire state.

Initially, the House of Representatives had fifty-nine members, but as the nation grew and more states joined the Union, the size of the House increased too. Since 1910, it has had 435 members except in the 1950s, when seats were temporarily added for Alaska and Hawaii. Every ten years, in a process called **reapportionment,** the 435 seats are distributed among the states based on population changes.

Within a constant 435-seat House, states with fast-growing populations gain seats, while those with slow-growing or declining populations lose seats. Since World War II, population movement in the United States has been toward the South, West, and Southwest and away from the Midwest and Northeast. This has been reflected in the allocation of house seats. Since 1950, California has gained twenty-two seats and New York has lost twelve, for example. This trend should continue after the 2000 census with Illinois, Wisconsin, Pennsylvania, Ohio, and New York all losing House seats and Arizona, Nevada, Colorado, Florida, Georgia, Texas, and California gaining seats.

States that gain or lose seats and other states with population shifts within the state must redraw their district boundaries, a process called **redistricting.** This is always a hot political issue. The precise boundaries of a district can influence the election prospects of candidates and parties. In fact, districts often are formed with weird shapes to benefit the party in control of the state legislature. The term **gerrymander** is used to describe a district where boundaries are set to maximize the political advantage of a party or a racial group (see also Chapter 8). Majority parties in state legislatures continue to secure political advantage by drawing districts of bizarre shapes, while still complying with the Supreme Court ruling that all congressional districts be approximately equal in population.

Before 1960, states were often reluctant to redistrict their state legislative and congressional boundaries to conform to population changes within the state for fear it would endanger incumbents and threaten rural areas whose populations were declining. After decades without reapportioning, some legislative districts in urban areas were as much as nineteen times the population of rural districts.

When state legislatures, frequently dominated by rural representatives, still refused to reapportion themselves, the Supreme Court in *Baker v. Carr* (1962) issued the first in a series of rulings forcing states to reapportion their legislative districts.[13] In 1964, the Court required congressional districts to be approximately equal in population, thus mandating the principle of "one person, one vote."[14] As a result, most states had to redraw district lines, some more than once, during the 1960s. These decisions fueled heated controversy, including a proposed constitutional amendment to overturn them. But after a while the principle of "one person, one vote" came to be widely accepted.

Because of the important role state legislatures play in the redistricting process, the 2000 state legislative elections were crucial for both parties. In the early 1980s, Democratic-controlled state legislatures were able to help Democratic candidates in states such as California by drawing lines that concentrated Republican strength in a few areas and created districts with small Democratic majorities.[15] After the 1990 state legislative elections, which gave Republicans more clout, many states drew boundaries favoring Republicans, a factor in the Republicans' victories in 1994.

Another important aspect of redistricting is representation of minorities. A significant increase in the proportion of blacks or Hispanics serving in Congress may depend on whether any more majority black or Hispanic districts are created. As we saw in Chapter 8, in 1992, eleven new districts were created with black majorities and six with Hispanic majorities; all but one were won by blacks and Hispanics. However, the Supreme Court has since ruled that while race may be taken into consideration, it cannot be the primary basis for creating districts.[16]

The racial redistricting issue also affects the partisan composition of Congress because more minorities are Democrats than Republicans. In some southern states, black voters were redistricted from solid Democratic districts to create new majority black districts, leaving the old districts with fewer Democrats and thereby creating Republican majorities.[17] Partly as a result, in 1994 Republicans got their first victories in eighteen congressional districts.

Another significant factor for increasing minority representation in Congress will be getting an accurate count in the 2000 census. The Census Bureau estimated a net undercount of 1.6 percent of the population in the 1990 census and said many of those not counted were urban or inner-city minorities.[18] Census response rates have been falling (from 83 percent in 1970, the first year the forms were sent by mail, to 65 percent in 1990), and in 2000 some members of Congress encouraged citizens who felt it an invasion of their privacy *not* to respond to the long census form. Because Congress has refused to authorize the use of sampling to estimate the size and racial breakdown of the uncounted portion of the population, it is possible that states with the most minorities might not gain as many seats in the reapportionment as population trends suggest.

Congressional Campaigns and Elections

To understand Congress, one must understand the process by which its members are elected.[19] Because reelection is an important objective for almost all members of Congress and *the* most important objective for many, members work at being reelected throughout their terms. Most are successful, though senators are not as secure as members of the House.

The Advantages of Incumbency

Before they even take the oath of office, newly elected representatives are given an introduction to the advantages of incumbency. At meetings arranged by the Democratic and Republican leadership and by the House Administrative Committee, new members learn about free mailing privileges, computers and software to help them target letters to specialized groups of constituents, facilities to make videotapes and audiotapes to send to hometown media, and other "perks" designed to keep members in touch with their constituencies and not coincidentally to help win reelection.

Incumbents win because they are better known than nonincumbents and voters evaluate them more positively. Almost all voters can recognize the name of their representatives; they have seen the representatives on television or received mail from them, and they can give a general rating of their performances (see Figure 1).[20] Although most voters can correctly identify their representatives as liberal or conservative, only a small minority know how their representatives voted on any issue.[21] Therefore, representatives have the advantage of name recognition without the disadvantage of having voters know how they really voted.

Representatives' high level of public recognition is not so surprising given that members of Congress spend most of their time and energy looking for and using opportunities to make themselves known to their constituents. Members visit their home districts or states an average of thirty-five times a year—at taxpayers' expense.[22] To accommodate these trips, the House usually operates on a three-day week, Tuesday through Thursday, allowing legislators four-day weekends in their districts. The Senate operates on a five-day week but takes off every fourth week to make longer home district visits possible.

Franking Privilege

The **franking privilege** is a great asset of incumbency because it allows members to write their constituents without using postage. Its main advantage is helping each member increase name recognition (and newly elected members can begin using the frank immediately, even before their swearing in). The frank cannot be used to send personal correspondence to constituents or to ask them for their vote or a campaign contribution. But members can send out newsletters that inform constituents of their work for the district or to survey constituents' issue positions. Much of the time, however, the frank is used to send constituents material they have requested, such as government forms or publications.

The frank is literally a facsimile of the member's signature and it works like metered mail, with the frank appearing where the stamp would be. It is not free; the Post Office records all franked mail and sends Congress a bill at the end of each year. That means the cost of the frank goes up with each postal increase. During the 1970s and 1980s, costs soared and Congress often spent more than it appropriated for mailings, sometimes for political advantage. For example, one senator sent seventeen million pieces of mail in a six-month period costing Congress and taxpayers $2.65 million. Congress then imposed restrictions on its use, and over the next decade, spending on mailings fell over $80 million. But even with the ban on mass mailings just before elections, use of the frank still increases by as much as 50 percent in election years.[23]

Through the 1990s, Congress apportioned the franking budget among its members according to size of their constituency, and it required public disclosure of how these allotments were spent. Evidence that public disclosure accounts for a good part of the decline in use of the franking privilege was found when spending more than quadrupled during a brief period of suspension of the disclosure requirement, and it immediately declined when disclosure was reinstated. However, heading into the 2000 election with a large budget surplus and control of Congress at stake, the House removed the spending cap and allowed members to use whatever portion of their office budgets they chose on the frank.[24] One political consultant estimates that the frank is worth at least $350,000 in campaign funds.[25]

The franking privilege becomes even more useful when combined with sophisticated word processing systems to target very specific constituency groups with "personalized" letters. Members can maintain incredibly specialized lists, not just of Republicans and Democrats but of those living near federal prisons, small-business owners, veterans, teachers, and government employees, for example. No group is too specialized or ostensibly apolitical to be targeted. Senator Charles Grassley (R-Iowa) even sent a letter to a thousand Iowans who had had intestinal surgery in honor of Ostomy Awareness Month.[26]

Media Advantage

In addition to "old-fashioned" mail, members use increasingly sophisticated production equipment and technology to make television and radio shows to send home. For example, one evening, on any of three local television news shows, residents of Boise, Idaho, might have seen their congressional representative, Larry Craig (R-Idaho), state in an interview that he was strongly opposed to a pay increase for Congress and would not take it if it were passed. The viewers were not told that the "interviewer" was one of Craig's congressional staffers and that the camera crew was that of the Republican Congressional Campaign Committee, which also paid for the taping.[27]

© 1994 Mark Alan Stamaty. Excerpted from "Washingtoon" with permission.

compared to senators from the smallest states. Senators from the smallest states do about as well in retaining their seats as House members from their states.[47]

Campaigns

In the nineteenth century, political campaigns were organized largely by political parties, and the candidates had relatively little to do. Today, however, congressional campaigns are candidate-centered. Most candidates hire the staff, raise the money, and organize their own campaigns. They may recruit campaign workers from local political parties; interest groups they belong to; unions;

church, civic, or other voluntary organizations; or they may simply turn to friends and acquaintances.[48]

Political parties do have a significant role, however. National and local parties also recruit potential candidates. Presidents make personal appeals to fellow party members who they think can run strong races, and national campaign committees also recruit aggressively. Said one Democratic congressional campaign chair, "I'm not looking for liberals or conservatives. That's not my bag. I'm looking for winners."[49] Parties redouble their efforts when, as in 1998 and 2000, control of Congress is at stake.[50] Besides, if candidates are not closely linked to parties then, once elected, they are not as indebted to their party nor as obligated to reflect party views.[51] Recognizing this, national parties have increasingly provided services to congressional candidates—helping them manage their campaigns, develop issues, advertise, raise money, and conduct opinion polls. National party organizations also give substantial sums of money to congressional candidates.[52]

The Media Campaign

To wage a serious campaign, the challenger or a contender for an open seat must wage a media campaign. Candidates hire media consultants and specialists in polling, advertising, and fund-raising.

Media campaigning has attracted a new type of congressional candidate and hence a new type of congressional incumbent. The old-style politician who might have been effective in small groups but who cannot appear poised and articulate on television has given way to one who can project an attractive television image. Candidates are elected on the basis of their media skills, which may not be the same skills as those needed to be a good lawmaker.

Campaign Money

The old adage says, "Half the money spent on campaigns is wasted. The trouble is, we don't know which half." This bromide helps explain why congressional campaigns are expensive. There is a kind of "campaign arms race" as each candidate tries to do what the other candidate does and a little more, escalating costs year by year.

In 1996, winners of House seats spent $680,000 on average. Million-dollar campaigns are no longer unusual. Because they are statewide, Senate races are much more expensive than House races. In 1996, winning Senate candidates spent more than $3.8 million, on average. In 1998, Senate incumbent Alfonse D'Amato spent $24 million in a losing race against House incumbent Charles Schumer, who spent $16.6 million on his victory. Fifteen other candidates spent over $5 million. In the 1998 House races, Newt Gingrich spent $7.5 million in a campaign for a safe seat.[53]

Voting for Congress

Party loyalty, candidate evaluations, and issues are important factors in congressional elections.[54]

Party loyalty is even more important for congressional than for presidential elections because congressional elections are less visible, so more people base their vote on party identification. Incumbency is also more important than in presidential races. The result is that increasingly, since about 1960, voters have split their tickets in voting for presidential and congressional candidates. Democrats especially are likely to desert their party when casting a vote for president. For example, one out of five Reagan voters in 1984 voted for a Democratic member of the House, leaving Reagan with only a 41 percent Republican House despite his commanding personal victory.

Normally, the party of a winning presidential candidate gains seats during a presidential election year and loses a number of seats in the midterm election. This maintains a sort of equilibrium in party control of Congress.[55] In most recent elections these losses have been modest. In 1998, however, the Democrats actually gained five seats in the House and lost no seats in the Senate. To some extent, midterm election results are a referendum on how well citizens think the president is doing. In 1998, Clinton was given credit for the economic good times the country was experiencing. The percentage of the total vote for congressional candidates that went to Democrats in 1996 and in 1998 was within a percentage point of the vote Clinton won in 1996.

The Representative on the Job

Informal Norms

First among the many lessons every new member must learn are the customary ways of interacting with colleagues both on and off the floor of Congress.[56] These **informal norms** help keep the institution running smoothly by attempting to minimize friction and allowing competition to occur within an atmosphere of civility. As in other American institutions, the norms of Congress are changing.

Throughout much of the twentieth century the most important norm was **institutional loyalty,** the expectation that members would respect their fellow members and the Congress itself, especially their own house. Personal criticism of one's colleagues was to be avoided, and mutual respect was fostered by such conventions as referring to colleagues by title, such as "The distinguished senator from New York," rather than by name. This norm has seriously eroded in the last two decades, leading some to call for a return to "civility."

Reciprocity, or "logrolling," is summarized in the statement, "you support my bill and I'll support yours." Sam Ervin, the late Democratic senator from tobacco-growing North Carolina, is reported to have told an audience from North Dakota, "I got to know Milt Young [then a senator from North Dakota] very well. And I told Milt, 'Milt, I would just like you to tell me how to vote about wheat and sugar beets and things like that, if you just help me out on tobacco.' "[57]

Tied to reciprocity is the norm of **specialization.** Given the scope of Congress's legislative authority members cannot be knowledgeable in all areas, so they specialize in subject areas related to their committee work. The Senate's smaller membership cannot support such an extensive division of labor. In any case, the Senate traditionally has been more individualistic than the House and less willing to give way to specialists. And some senators see themselves as potential presidential candidates who need to be well versed on a variety of issues.

Specialization and reciprocity increase the influence of individual members but also facilitate the smooth running of the institution. By specializing, a member can become an expert. Reciprocity helps each member get the votes needed to pass legislation favored in his or her district. This is another informal norm that is increasingly threatened.

Open meetings, media scrutiny, and a decentralized Congress have made it more difficult for members to "go along" on bills unpopular in their constituency.

Working Privately and "Going Public"

Twenty years ago the workaday routine in both House and Senate for resolving most issues involved bargaining with other members, lobbyists, and White House aides.

Working privately, one-on-one in small groups, or in committees, members and staff discussed and debated issues, exchanged information, and planned strategies. Even though many issues still are resolved through these private channels, much has changed in the way Congress operates.

Today leaders and individual members believe it is as important to "go public" to further their goals as it is to engage in private negotiation.[58] **Going public** means taking an issue debate to the public through the media as Congress does when it televises floor debates and important hearings.

C-Span

In the past, television networks only broadcast important Congressional proceedings such as the McCarthy hearings, and those for the Watergate scandal and for the Iran-Contra affair. In 1979, after considerable controversy and anxiety, the House began routinely to televise its proceedings. Fearful of being overshadowed by the House, in 1986 the Senate followed suit. But today exposure comes daily on C-Span with coverage available to 66 million households with cable television. Estimates are that more than one-third of C-Span subscribers watch their legislators at least one hour a month.[59] Even more see them in session when network and local news programs use footage of members making speeches.[60]

House Minority Leader Richard Gephart goes public, leading a walkout of Democratic members from a House session where the Republican leadership refused to consider their version of a prescription-drug-benefit bill. At the bottom of the steps are network television cameras that will take the Democrats' message directly to the public on the evening news. As insurance, the members have stamped a one-word message on umbrellas.
Dennis Cook/AP Wide World Photos

Other Use of the Media

During the 1980s, other use of the media by congressional leadership increased tremendously. Newt Gingrich's (R-Ga.) rise to power was attributed in part to his strategic use of television. He understood the potential of television and other technology. He used language that appealed to the public (as one reporter noted, he was "absolutist, aggressive, hyperbolic, informed, topical, unpredictable, and studied in his use of supercharged symbolic language").[61] His stated goal was to shape the entire nation through the news media.

Even before becoming a party leader, Gingrich illustrated strategic use of the media on the House floor denouncing Democrats regularly. Because the camera is stationary, on TV it looked as if he were speaking to an interested audience of members. In reality he was talking to an empty chamber.

The congressional leadership of both parties go public, too. Leaders regularly call producers of television talk shows to suggest guests. They meet with the press and often have prepared statements. Before important congressional votes on key issues, the leadership plans letters to the editors of important newspapers and floor speeches designed for maximum television coverage. For example, when the Republican leadership refused to allow the Democrats to bring their bill providing prescription drug benefits to a vote before the 2000 election, the Democratic leadership organized a walkout of party members while the vote on the Republicans' version of the bill was taking place. Striding down the Capitol steps to a battery of cameras, Minority Leader Gephardt excoriated both the Republicans' bill and their parliamentary tactics for the evening newscasts.

The more media-oriented among the rank-and-file members are also experts in providing short and interesting comments for the nightly network news, writing articles for major newspapers, and appearing on talk shows and as commentators on news programs.

Voting by Members

We have seen that members of Congress represent their constituents through service and by obtaining special benefits for their districts or states. A third major kind of representation is policy representation. In the eyes of most people, members are sent to Washington to make laws. By casting hundreds of votes each year, members try to represent the interests of their constituencies as they see them and in the process win support for reelection. Increasingly, constituents are becoming more active in communicating with their legislators. Members are flooded with faxes, e-mails, poll results, and mailgrams, often stimulated as a result of radio or television talk shows. These individuals, however, do not represent the entire constituency. Talk show callers and listeners, for example, are more likely than other voters to be conservative, Republican, and male.[62]

Constituency opinion is often uninformed, divided, or apathetic. Because most votes in Congress are on subjects the electorate knows little about, members cannot, and often do not want to, rely on a simple polling of constituents to tell them how to vote. The opinions of constituents do matter, but other influences are also important: the party, the president, the members' ideology, staffers, and caucus membership. Members look to these sources for cues as to how to vote.

Party and Constituency

Paradoxically, given the heated partisan rhetoric in Congress at the end of the Clinton administration, partisan voting was not increasing. Still, it was at a high level compared with previous eras. Partisan votes are those on bills on which the Republican and Democratic leadership have taken a position and the majority of one party opposes a majority of the other. In 1999, 63 percent of all recorded roll call votes in the Senate and 47 percent of those in the House were partisan. The small decline in partisan voting in the House balanced out a slight increase in the Senate.[63] Although tempers have run high, with heated exchanges in committee and conference negotiations, as well as in dealings between the White House and Republicans, the positions taken by congressional members on major issues are not as far apart as they were in 1995. It is a consequence of both parties trying to position themselves nearer the center where a large part of the electorate is clustered. Once a bill reaches the floor, some compromise has already been reached, and the vote on it may not reflect the intensity of the partisan haggling that produced it.

Another gauge of partisanship is that the parties are casting more unanimous votes. In 1999, of 235 partisan votes in the Senate, Democrats voted unanimously 100 times and Republicans 63 times, up from 33 for Democrats and 46 for the Republicans in the previous year. Unanimous voting in the House is much harder to achieve. House Republicans voted unanimously only 59 times on 288 party unity votes in 1999, and the Democrats a mere 11 times.[64]

There are several reasons for the continuing importance of party. All members of Congress are elected on

The GI Bill of Rights

It has been called the "greatest piece of legislation Congress ever passed," a "Marshall Plan for America," and "a magic carpet to the middle class." Virtually everyone has heard of the GI Bill of Rights, but few realize how broad its impact was on the country as a whole. When it was signed into law in 1944, just two weeks after D-Day, neither President Roosevelt nor Congress thought they were passing a transformative piece of legislation. They just wanted to provide the millions of veterans who would be returning from the war in Europe and Asia some help reintegrating into civilian life and the labor force.

Since the earliest days of the Republic, the national government has provided benefits to veterans for military service during wartime, but only after veterans organized to demand compensation for lost time and wages. Veterans of the Revolutionary and Civil Wars were promised a land bonus and eventually did receive a pension, but only after threatening revolt. Civil War veterans were extremely well connected in Congress, getting it to authorize pensions that by 1888 accounted for 20 percent of the federal budget. Partly in reaction to this excess, World War I veterans received a tiny cash payment on mustering out but were promised a small annuity to be paid near retirement age. This was too long a wait for those who fell on hard times in the early years of the Great Depression. But in 1932 when they marched on Washington to demand early payment of their "bonuses," their demonstration was violently suppressed by U.S. Army units un-

A federal law passed during World War II, the "GI Bill of Rights," transformed American society by granting each veteran educational benefits and loans to buy housing and start businesses. Though skeptics believed that veterans would not use the bill, returning World War II vets flooded America's universities by the millions, changing the face of higher education. As at other schools, Indiana University's facilities were soon overtaxed, forcing relocation of student registration to its field house.
Indiana University Photographic Services

der the command of General MacArthur. The spectacle of the military assaulting veterans may have been on the mind of Congress when it approved benefits for the twelve million men and women returning from service in World War II. No one was looking for another march on Washington.

A comprehensive assistance package was opposed by all the powerful leaders in Congress and by President Roosevelt. Some were opposed to providing cash assistance for fear it would encourage sol-

diers not to look for jobs, while others were against a bonus bill because it would single out for benefits only one group of people who contributed to the war effort. But some kind of bonus was supported by an overwhelming majority of the American public. In the end, the compromise bill—called the Bill of Rights for GI Joe and Jane—was written by a member of the American Legion. Its congressional sponsors were relatively unknown Republicans and conservative southern Democrats, some of whom supported the bill primarily

a partisan ballot, and Congress organizes itself on a partisan basis. Members tend to have policy views similar to others in their party, at least more similar than to those in the opposite party. Many members receive significant campaign support from the party, and party leaders try hard to influence party members to vote the "right" way, dispensing "perks" or exerting pressure. Party votes reflect constituency needs, too, because Democratic and Republican constituencies have different policy preferences.

as a way to prevent class warfare. Among the principal players was one woman, Edith Nourse Rogers, a liberal Republican from Massachusetts and the ranking minority member of the Veteran's Affair Committee, who had helped create the Women's Army Corps. She went on to become the first woman to chair a major House committee.

The Serviceman's Readjustment Act—or the GI Bill, as it was soon known—contained three major benefits: a living stipend and tuition vouchers for college, low-interest mortgages for purchase of a first home, and loans for starting new businesses. These measures set off a chain reaction that helped shape modern America. To understand how one bill could have such an impact, one has to keep in mind what the economic situation of the average GI was like when we entered World War II.

In 1940 the average soldier was twenty-six and had only one year of high school, and most came from families where college was financially impossible.[1] Had they not served in the war and received the GI benefit, most veterans could never have gone back to school. Many educators and college presidents opposed the voucher program, saying they would have to lower their standards and admit students with poor educational backgrounds. But veterans returned to school in record numbers, more than a million in 1946 alone, when they accounted for almost half of all college enrollments in the United States. In 1950 almost a quarter of all college students were still veterans.[2] This stimulated a tremendous growth in higher education, creating the need for many more faculty and new facilities, eventually giving rise in Wisconsin and other states to a new system of state colleges.

In the first years after the war, however, most veterans chose private schools since at the time vouchers provided enough to cover tuition in the Ivy League. By 1946 the influx of veterans almost doubled Harvard's enrollment, and they "hogg[ed] the honor rolls,"[3] there and throughout the Ivy League. With college educations many working-class families moved into the middle class, making it possible for them to afford to send their children to college and continue the families' upward mobility. With federally guaranteed mortgages many vets were also able to leave rental housing in the cities for homes in the outlying areas. So many new homeowners entered the market that it prompted the building of housing developments like Levittown and began the suburbanization of America. This in turn fostered the building of highways and schools, and the whole infrastructure necessary to support new towns.

The bill did not work equally well for everyone, in part because African Americans did not have the same choices as whites in using their benefits. With housing segregation in most new suburban areas, including Levittown, the route out of the city to affordable housing was less possible. Although black vets got the same educational benefits they did not have the range of choices in schools, given segregation in some universities and the use of a quota system in others. But thousands did get to college, among them many of those who would become leaders of the modern civil rights movement.

What was so significant about this legislation was that its purpose was not to grant minimum living stipends to retired people, but to provide financial help that made it possible for young men and women to become more productive citizens for the remainder of their lives. The GI bill provided education vouchers to eight million veterans. It increased home ownership from one in three before the war to two in three afterward. According to a 1986 government study, "each dollar invested in the bill yielded 5 to 12 dollars in tax revenues."[4] The GI Bill was such a success that it was renewed in 1956 with scaled-back benefits for those who served in Korea and Vietnam. Overall the bill's single most important contribution may have been in its extraordinary expansion of higher education because it "signaled the shift to the knowledge society"; for this reason, its passage may in the future be seen "as one of the most important events of the 20th century."[5]

1. Doris Kearns Goodwin, "Remembering the GI Bill," *The News Hour with Jim Lehrer* (PBS), July 4, 2000.
2. Michael J. Bennet, *When Dreams Come True: The GI Bill and the Making of Modern America* (Washington, D.C.: Brassey's, 1996), 18.
3. Ibid., 19.
4. Spencer Michaels, "Remembering the GI Bill."
5. Peter Drucker, *Post-Capitalist Society* (New York: Harper Business, 1993), 3.

Members must be responsive to their own constituents as well as to party members in general. Members must consider what benefits their district as a whole and also the needs of subgroups within the district, such as voters in their party, socioeconomic groups, and their own personal supporters.[65] Sometimes the interests of these groups may be in conflict. The representatives' personal constituency may be more liberal or conservative than the district as a whole. When members vote in conflict with what seems to be the sense of the majority of voters in the district, it may be that they are responding to their staunchest supporters. Of course, in those rare instances where most of the representative's constituents feel strongly about an issue, the member cannot buck an overwhelming majority and expect to win reelection (see "You Are There").

When neither the member or the member's constituents have strong feelings on an issue, it is certainly in the member's interest to go along with party leaders. Although their efforts are usually low-key, party leaders sometimes do turn on the heat. In a successful vote to override a Reagan veto, Democratic Senate leaders adopted a "baby-sitting" strategy to make sure that wavering Democrats did not get near anyone who might persuade them to uphold the president's veto. These Democrats were accompanied at all times by two other Democrats with the "right" views. For their part, Republicans called on Reagan to make personal appeals to wavering Republicans.

Ideology

On the whole, the member's ideology is usually not far from that of the party or constituency.[66]

In general, Democrats vote for more liberal measures than do Republicans. Historically, this has not always been true of southern Democrats, who often deserted the Democratic leadership and voted with Republicans because they shared their more conservative outlook. Thus, for about thirty of the years when the Democrats controlled Congress, they often did not have a "working majority."

Today, southern conservatives run as Republicans and have captured much of the formerly solid Democratic South. Southern Democrats are still more conservative than the Democratic Party in the North, but many districts are increasingly urban and contain voters who are more liberal than those of thirty years ago. Black voters are a substantial bloc in many southern districts and counterbalance the more conservative white vote.

Members within both parties still hold a sufficiently wide range of views for there to be issue-based or ideological alliances within each party. Among House Republicans, for example, there is a group of about fifty moderates, the New Republicans, who vote against the leadership on campaign finance, managed care, and other measures. There is also a forty-member Conservative Action Team who form voting alliances. Among the Democrats there is the Blue Dog Coalition, a group of cultural conservatives who vote as a block if two-thirds of their membership is in agreement. In 1999 the coalition split its vote only eight times. Defecting from their party, they have helped defeat bills on gun control and increased funding for the NEA.[67]

Special Interest Caucuses

An increasingly common influence on voting is membership in **special interest caucuses.** These organizations have been founded by members to further shared partisan, ideological, issue, regional, or identity interests. Caucus size ranges from a handful to more than a hundred. There are ninety caucuses in the House alone, and almost every member belongs to at least one. In some cases they are the source of a member's closest political allies. Prior to the 1995 Gingrich reforms, the most important caucuses had their own office space and budgets, but today they are run out of members' offices and are supported by their office staff and budgets, just as the smallest of the caucuses have always had to operate. Among the most significant of the caucuses are those designed to pool the strength of women and minorities (see the "American Diversity" boxes).

The President

The president is also a factor in congressional voting, due in part to his role as party leader.[68] The president appeals to fellow partisans to support a program and tries to persuade those in the other party to go along as well. Presidents can win support by granting or withholding favors, such as support for a member's proposed policy or pet project in his or her district.

Interest Groups

Interest group lobbyists are most effective when their interests overlap constituency interests or when the issue is technical or little publicized. They are also more likely to be effective when a bill is still in committee than when it is being debated on the floor of the House or the Senate.

Staffers

Staff can be a very important influence on a member's vote. Staff members are likely to have done the research and briefed the member on an issue. They probably have the greatest influence on technical issues or those the member does not care or know much about.

Other Members

Members also are influenced by other members of their party or their state's delegation, and by colleagues whose judgment or expertise they respect, or whose ideology or background they share. In fact, on most routine bills, cues from trusted fellow members are among the most important influences on members' votes. Sometimes strong relationships of trust develop across party lines, such as the close friendship between the liberal Democrat Edward Kennedy and the very conservative Orrin Hatch.

How Congress Is Organized

An institution of 535 members without a centralized leadership that must make decisions about thousands of proposed public policies each year is not an institution that can work quickly or efficiently. Each year in the past decade, from two thousand to ten thousand bills have been introduced in Congress, and two hundred fifty to two thousand have been passed.

Although many of these bills are trivial, such as those proclaiming "National Prom Graduation Kickoff Day" or naming local courthouses, others deal with crucial issues. In addition to making policy, Congress must oversee the performance of the federal bureaucracy in implementing bills previously passed.

Like all organizations, legislatures need some structure to be able to accomplish their purposes. Congress has a leadership system and a committee system, both organized along party lines. Alongside this partisan organization there exist many other organized groups—caucuses, coalitions, work and study groups, and task forces—whose membership cuts across party lines or reflects the division of interests within party caucuses. Some of this micro-organizing is a means of bypassing the committee system that dominates Congress's legislative and oversight functions.

How Congressional Organization Evolved

The Constitution calls for the members of the House of Representatives to select a **Speaker of the House** to act as its presiding officer and for the vice president of the United States to serve as president (or presiding officer) of the Senate. But the Constitution does not say anything about the powers of these officials, nor does it require any further internal organization. So little is said about the Speaker in the Constitution that it is not even specified that he need be a member of the House.

The first House, meeting in New York in 1789, had slow and cumbersome procedures. For its first several sessions, Congress's legislative work was accomplished by appointing ad hoc committees. By the Third Congress, there were about three hundred fifty, and the system had become too unwieldy. Soon permanent committees were created, each with continuing responsibilities in one area, such as taxes or trade.[69]

As parties developed, the selection of the Speaker became a partisan matter, and the Speaker became as much a party leader as a legislative manager. The seventh Speaker, Henry Clay (Ky.), who served ten of the years between 1811 and 1825, transformed the speakership from a ceremonial office to one of real leadership. To maintain party loyalty and discipline he used his powers to appoint committee members and chairs. Under Clay's leadership the House was the dominant branch, but its influence declined when it, like the rest of government, could not cope with the divisiveness of the slavery issue. By 1856 it took 133 ballots to elect a Speaker. In many instances there were physical fights on the House floor and duels outside.[70]

The Senate, a smaller body than the House, was less tangled in procedures, less rule-bound, and more effective in its operation. Its influence rose as visitors packed the Senate gallery to hear the great debates over slavery waged by Daniel Webster (Mass.), John C. Calhoun (S.C.), and Henry Clay (who had moved from the House). During this era, senators were elected by state legislatures, not directly by the people. Thus, they had strong local party ties and often used their influence to get presidential appointments for home state party members. But the Senate too became ineffective as the nation moved toward civil war. Senators carried arms to protect themselves as debates over slavery turned to violence.

After the Civil War with the presidency weakened by the impeachment of Andrew Johnson, strong party leadership reemerged in the House, and a period of congressional government began. Speaker Thomas Reed (Me.), nicknamed "The Czar" by his colleagues, assumed the authority to name members and chairs of committees and to chair the Rules Committee, which decided which bills were to come to the floor for debate. A major consequence of the Speaker's extensive powers was increased party discipline. Members who voted against their party might be punished by a loss of committee assignments or chairmanships.

At the same time, both the House and the Senate became more professional. The emergence of national problems and an aggressive Congress made a congressional career more prestigious. Prior to the Civil War, membership turnover was high; members of the House served an average of only one term, senators only four years. After the war, the strengthening of parties and the growth of the one-party South, when Democrats controlled virtually all elective offices, made reelection easier.

This desire for permanent careers in the House produced an interest in reform. Members wanted a chance at choice committee seats and did not want to be controlled by the Speaker. Resistance against the dictatorial practices of Reed and his successor Joseph Cannon (Ill.) grew. Cannon, more conservative than many of his fellow Republicans, used his powers to block legislation he disliked, to punish those who opposed him, and even to refuse to recognize members who wished to speak. In 1910 there was a revolt against "Cannonism," a synonym for the arbitrary use of the Speaker's powers.

The membership voted to remove the Speaker from the Rules Committee and to strip him of his authority to appoint committees and their chairs. The revolt weakened party influence because it meant party discipline could no longer be maintained by the Speaker punishing members through loss of committee assignments. And it gave committees and their chairs a great deal of independence from leadership influence.

The Senate also was undergoing a major reform. As part of the Progressive movement, pressure began to build for the direct popular election of senators. The election of senators by state legislatures had made many senators pawns of special interests—the big monopolistic corporations (called "trusts") and railroads. In a day when millionaires were not as common as now, the Senate was referred to as the "Millionaires Club."

Not surprisingly, the Senate first refused to consider a constitutional amendment providing for its direct election, although in some states popular balloting on senatorial candidates took place anyway. Finally, under the threat of a call for a constitutional convention, which many members of Congress feared might consider other changes in the Constitution, a direct election amendment was passed in the House and Senate in 1912 and ratified by the states a year later.

These reforms of the early twentieth century dispersed power in both the House and Senate and weakened leadership. House members no longer feared the kind of retribution levied by Speaker Cannon on members who deviated from party positions. In the Senate, popular elections made senators responsive to the diverse interests of the electorate rather than to party leaders.

Contemporary Leadership Positions

The modern leadership of Congress cannot be understood from reading the Constitution. Not only is the Speaker now a party leader, but none of the secondary leadership positions in the House nor any of the current top posts in the Senate are provided for in Article I. This is because they were not created as institutional offices but as party leadership positions, and there were no party organizations in Congress when it first met. The leaders in each party are selected by their full membership meeting in caucus. The full House must vote on the Speaker of course, but it is by a straight line party vote, so the real selection is made in the majority party's caucus. The Speaker is typically someone who has served in the House a long time and is usually a skilled parlia-

Vitriolic exchanges are not just a phenomenon of the contemporary Congress. Shown here is a fight in the House in 1798. After Representative Matthew Lyon (R-Vt.) spit on Representative Roger Griswold (Fed-Conn.), and the House refused to expel Lyon, Griswold attacked Lyon with a cane. Lyon defended himself with fire tongs as other members of Congress looked on (not without amusement, it seems).
Library of Congress

House Majority Whip Tom DeLay (R-Tex.) works the phones to determine how Republicans plan to vote on a pending issue. DeLay has exercised his powers more aggressively than his recent predecessors.
1997 David Burnett/Contact Press Images

mentarian and an ideological moderate. The institutional task of the Speaker is to see that legislation moves through the House. His (all speakers have been men so far) partisan task is to secure the passage of measures preferred by his party. By tradition the Speaker does not cast a vote on most bills before the House, participating only on "symbolic or party-defining issues."[71]

Trying to win partisan support is often difficult. The Speaker has some rewards and punishments to dispense for loyalty and disloyalty, but they are small compared to the power wielded by Reed and Cannon. The Speaker, however, does influence committee assignments, which committees will be given jurisdiction over complex bills, what bills will come to the House floor, and how campaign funds are allocated. He also has the sole power to decide who will be recognized to speak on the floor of the House and whether motions are relevant. He has the authority to appoint members to the Rules Committee and to certain special committees, and he controls some material benefits, such as the assignment of extra office space. Despite these formal powers, the Speaker must be persuasive to be effective. The few strong Speakers of the nineteenth and early twentieth century—Clay, Reed,

Cannon—have already been mentioned. In modern times the only Speaker to attempt the level of control of Reed and Cannon has been Newt Gingrich (R-Ga.). Although a sixteen-year veteran of the House, his only prior leadership service had been as a whip; he had never chaired a committee, or even a subcommittee, because the Republicans were in the minority during his pre-Speaker years. Like other Speakers who were too controlling, Gingrich met with rebellion in his own party and had to fight back a challenge to his leadership in his third year. Gingrich's demands for party discipline in support of a national legislative program (Contract with America) left many members with too little flexibility to respond to their constituencies and risked their chance for reelection. This is one reason that an ideological moderate with a conciliatory manner is often sought for the Speaker's position.

The current House Speaker, Dennis Hastert (R-Ill.), is more in the mold of a traditional Speaker. He is from the mainstream of the party and a mediator and persuader rather than an agenda-driven leader who uses a heavy hand to enforce party discipline. When he took over as Speaker, Hastert had only a five-vote margin to work with, the smallest any majority had had in fifty years. His approach to the Speakership is "not to throw his weight around" and to "do things in regular order." His low-key approach has its disadvantages with the public. Few people know anything about him, and those who do give him lower approval ratings than they give House Republicans.[72] But a Speaker does not need public approval to be successful, only to get his party's bills through to passage.

The party leadership in the House includes a **majority leader,** a **minority leader,** and majority and minority **whips.** The majority leader is second in command to the Speaker, and the minority leader is, as the name suggests, the leader of the minority party. Whips originated in the British House of Commons, where they were named after the "whipper in," the rider who keeps the hounds together in a fox hunt. This aptly describes the whips' role in Congress. Party whips try to maintain contact with party members, see which way they are leaning on votes, and attempt to gain their support. The current majority whip has numerous deputies and twenty-seven assistant whips who keep tabs on their assigned state delegations. The minority whip currently has four deputies.

The party apparatus in the House also includes committees to assign party members to standing committees, discuss policy issues, and allocate funds to party members running for reelection.

Senate majority leader Lyndon Johnson, persuading. LBJ "used physical persuasion in addition to intellectual and moral appeals. He was hard on other people's coat lapels. If one were shorter than Lyndon he was inclined to move up close and lean over the subject of his persuasive efforts." Here that subject is Senator Theodore Green (D-R.I.). "If a Senator were taller than [Johnson], he would come at him from below, somewhat like a badger." Senator Edmund Muskie (D-Me.), who was taller, "emerged from a meeting with Johnson with the observation that he had not known until this meeting why people had the hair in their nostrils trimmed." Quotes are from Eugene McCarthy, Up 'Til Now *(New York: Harcourt Brace, 1987).*

The Senate has no leader comparable to the Speaker of the House. The vice president is formally the presiding officer but in reality attends infrequently and has relatively little power. He is allowed to cast the tie-breaking vote in the rare instances in which the Senate is split evenly. The Senate has an elected president pro tempore, a mostly honorific post with few duties except to preside over the Senate when the vice president is absent. Because presiding over the Senate on a day-to-day basis is considered boring, junior members usually do it.

The position of Senate Majority Leader was not created until 1911 and has often been held by men of no particular distinction in their parties. The office has none of the Speakership's potential for control of chamber proceedings. Mike Mansfield, the longest-serving majority leader, argued that the function of the office was to be the servant, not the master of senators. A congressional watcher, putting it less elegantly, says, "Its holder is often more a coat-check attendant than a maitre'd or chef."[73] The instances of powerful majority leaders are few, the most notable being Lyndon Johnson, who happened to assume the office at a time when the Democrats had a slim hold on the Senate, giving him an opportunity to exercise his extraordinary powers of personal persuasion to keep party members in line on key votes. Johnson's reputation was made through a combination of personality and mastery of the legislative process (he had been an aide to the House Speaker and served in the House before election to the Senate). There is nothing inherent in the office to give a majority leader the power Johnson had, and no one has had it since.

The Senate Majority leader is a spokesperson for his party's legislative agenda and is supposed to help line up members' votes on key issues. But procedurally the Senate is a free-for-all compared to the House, with "every man and woman for him- or herself."[74] Unlike the Speaker, the Majority Leader cannot control the terms under which a bill is considered on the floor, since rules are assigned by unanimous consent in the Senate, and he has little power to stop a filibuster if a member wants to block legislation. This means a Majority Leader needs to do much more than keep his own party in line to keep legislation moving through the Senate.

The Leader can influence the general atmosphere of deliberation in the Senate by adopting a more conciliatory or more partisan approach to working the minority party. The current Majority Leader, Trent Lott (R-Miss.), has chosen a rather aggressively partisan approach, in contrast to his predecessor, Robert Dole, who worked very much in the conciliatory, clubby style common to the Senate. But Lott's partisanship is much less strident than Newt Gingrich's was in the House. Gingrich's style would never be accepted in the more equalitarian atmosphere of the Senate.

The Minority Leader's job is similar to that of the Majority Leader in trying to use a limited package of incentives and procedural ploys to enforce party discipline. Both parties also elect whips to assist in this task; the Republicans have five and the Democrats ten. These are important, if not essential, positions for working one's way into the top leadership.

Committees

Standing Committees

Most of the work of Congress is done in committees. Observers of American politics take this for granted; yet the power of legislative committees is rather rare among western democracies. In Britain, for example, committees cannot offer amendments that change the substance of a bill.

Today there are nineteen **standing committees** in the House and seventeen in the Senate. Each deals with a different subject matter, such as finance or education or agriculture. Each has a number of subcommittees, totaling eighty-seven in the House and sixty-eight in the Senate. Nearly all legislation introduced in Congress is referred to a standing committee and then to a subcommittee. Subcommittees hold public hearings to give interested parties a chance to speak for or against a bill. They also hold **markup** sessions to provide an opportunity for the committee to rewrite the bill. Following markup, the bill is sent to the full committee, which also may hold hearings. If approved there, it goes to the full House or Senate.

Standing committees vary in size from nine members to seventy-five in the House and from twelve to twenty-eight in the Senate. Trying to accommodate members' preferences for committee seats that allow them to help constituents has led to ever larger committees. Party ratios—that is, the number of Democrats relative to Republicans on each committee—are determined by the majority party. The ratios are generally set in rough proportion to party membership in the particular house, but the majority party gives itself a disproportionate number of seats on several key committees in order to ensure control.

Committee Membership

New members and those members seeking committee changes express their preferences to their party's selection committee. As a general rule, preferences will be granted, although there is a self-selection process whereby junior members usually do not ask for the most prestigious posts.

The committees dealing with budgets and appropriations are always sought after because the allocation of money gives members power and enhances their ability to help their districts. Most members want committee assignments that let them tell constituents that they are working on problems of the district. Members from agricultural districts, for example, strive to get on the agriculture committees.

The practice of filling committees with representatives whose districts have an especially strong economic interest in its work makes committees rather parochial in their outlook and fills them with members who have financial interests in the businesses they make policies for.[75] Most members who sit on the banking committees own bank stock, the many on agriculture committees own agribusiness stock, and those on the armed services committees hold stock in defense industries.[76]

Media coverage is another criterion important in deciding committee preference. The work of some committees is more likely to be covered by television. In a five-year period, the Senate Foreign Relations Committee had 522 network television cameras covering it, whereas the Indian Affairs Committee had 0.[77] Getting on the right committee is important to those who want to become nationally known. When a journalist once asked Senator Joseph Biden (D-Del.) why he was so newsworthy, Biden replied, "It's the committees, of course." Biden had served on the three committees with greatest media exposure.

Committee Chairs

The chair is usually the leader and most influential member of a committee. Chairs have the authority to call meetings, set agendas, and control committee staff and funds. In addition, chairs are usually very knowledgeable about matters that come before their committees, and this too is a source of influence. Some chairs have used their power to rule their committees with an "iron hand."

Usually, the member of the majority party with the longest service on a committee becomes its chair by the so-called **seniority rule.** The rule was adopted to protect committee members from powerful Speakers of the

House who often used their authority to award committee chairs to friends and allies. Under the ironclad seniority rule, chairs might have been senile, alcoholic, or personally disliked by every member of the committee, but if they had served the longest and their party had a majority in the House, they became chairs.

Many members believed the custom of seniority led to chairs who were out of step with the rest of the party and dictatorial. In response to those complaints, in the early 1970s both parties agreed that the seniority rule no longer had to be followed. A Committee on Committees in the Republican Party and a Steering and Policy Committee in the Democratic Party now recommend chairs. Then all members of each party caucus vote on these recommendations by secret ballot.

In 1975, in a striking break with precedent, the Democratic membership stripped three senior Democrats of their chairs. They did so again in 1985 and 1994. The Republicans also violated the seniority principle in their choice of chairs in 1995.[78] In the House, Speaker Gingrich elevated less senior members who were more conservative over other Republicans on the all-important Budget, Appropriations, and Banking committees. Still, the seniority principle applies most of the time because Congress assumes that members with long service on the committee will have the most expertise in its subject matter. That is usually true. Applying the seniority rule also eliminates potentially damaging intraparty fights over who will chair important committees. Some argue the seniority system is also the best protection for women and minorities as they gain seniority in the institution. This will be put to the test in 2001 when Marge Roukema (R–N.J.) will be in line to chair the Banking Committee.

Choosing chairs by means other than strict seniority has ended the days of the autocratic chair. And the reform has brought about an interesting change in the behavior of senior members. Before 1975, committee chairs were much lower in support for their party in roll-call votes than other party members.[79] Since 1975, committee chairs have been much more likely to vote with their party than other members. The same pattern holds true of those who are second, third, and fourth in seniority on each committee. Thus, removing seniority as a sole criterion for choosing committee chairs has meant that senior party members are much less likely to deviate from their party's position. In that sense, the reforms have strengthened party influence in Congress.

Facing vacancies in the chairs of several important committees in 2001, Hastert has indicated that, unlike Gingrich, he will look to the committees to submit nominations should the Republicans retain control of the House. His approach does not sit well with many House Republicans because they believe it fosters a spirit of competitiveness among those who want to chair committees. This illustrates the dilemma of the autocratic versus the conciliator approach to leadership. Gingrich created a great deal of tension and a splintering within the party because he tried for too much control. Now some claim Hastert is fostering division by *not* using the full powers of his office to control the assignment of committee chairs. An effective Speaker needs to find a balance between control and conciliation.

Subcommittees

Each committee is divided into subcommittees with jurisdiction over part of the committee's area. The House International Relations Committee, for example, has five subcommittees—one for Africa, one for Asia and the Pacific, and one for the Western Hemisphere, as well as one on trade and one on human rights.

Committee chairs traditionally dominated not only their committee but its subcommittees as well. Chairs chose the chairs of the subcommittees and controlled the subcommittees' jurisdiction, budget, and staff. Chairs thus could manipulate the subcommittees' action on proposed legislation as they saw fit.

In another rejection of domineering committee chairs, House Democrats made a number of rules changes in 1973 and 1974, sometimes called the **subcommittee bill of rights.** These measures reduced the control of the standing committee chairs by allowing each subcommittee to operate semi-independently of the parent committee. Similar changes took place in the Senate. These reforms allowed more members, especially newer members, to share in important decisions. In this way they made Congress more democratic.

But by diffusing power, they also made it less efficient because the very number of subcommittees contributed to government gridlock. Complex legislation might be sent to several subcommittees, each with its own interests and jurisdiction. For example, a clean air bill that passed the House and Senate in 1990 had been managed by seven different House committees. When the House had to meet in conference with the Senate to work out a unified version, the House ended up sending 140 members.[80] Rule changes under the new Republican majority cut the number of subcommittees significantly, streamlining the legislative process and leaving fewer chairs with independent authority. House standing committees are limited to five subcommittees (excluding oversight), and House members allowed no more than four subcommittee assignments. No restrictions were placed on subcommittee numbers in the Senate, but no Senator is supposed to sit on more than five.

One of the most significant rule changes was term limits for committee chairs, with most limited to three terms. This means that the younger men (and all were men) Gingrich nominated to chair key standing committees will have to relinquish their seats after the 2000 elections, unless there is another rule change. Two powerful chairs, Kasich of Budget and Archer of Ways and Means, decided to retire from the House when their terms were up, some say because of the impending loss of power.[81]

Even with the new limits, the average member is spread pretty thin. The typical senator sits on eleven committees and subcommittees; the average representative about seven. These multiple assignments mean that members have impossible schedules, and at times committees cannot obtain quorums because members are tied up in other committee work. This leaves it to the committee chair, a few colleagues, and staff to do much of the work and make many of the decisions.

Other Committees

There are a few other types of congressional committees. Select or special committees are typically investigative committees organized on a temporary basis to study a specific problem or to hold hearings and issue a report on special problems that arise, such as Watergate or the Iran-Contra scandal. These committees are disbanded when their work is completed. The exceptions are the House and the Senate Select Committees on Intelligence, which are in effect permanent committees. Joint committees include members from both houses with the chair rotating between a House and Senate member. There are four permanent joint committees, two of which study budgetary and tax policy. The other two administer institutions affiliated with Congress, such as the Library of Congress. Conference committees also are composed of members from both chambers. They are appointed whenever the Senate and the House pass different versions of the same bill. Members from the committees that managed the bill in their respective chambers work out a single version for the full membership to vote on. Conference committees are dissolved after the compromise version is agreed on.

Task Forces

The traffic jams and turf wars surrounding much committee work has led members of Congress with a sense of urgency about legislating in a particular area to look for ways to bypass the committee structure. This is a major reason for the use of a task force, or ad hoc committee, to study major issues and draft legislation.[82] Task forces have existed in the House for decades, used by Democratic and Republican leadership alike, usually to get around foot-dragging committees. Currently the House has a dozen task forces, about half working on issues as important as Medicare, AIDS, and drug policy. They achieved their greatest visibility when Gingrich was Speaker, when they became a vehicle for his "adhocracy" approach of aggressively pursuing a legislative agenda and moving it through the legislative process as fast as possible. To do that the Speaker sometimes bypassed committees, hand-picking members for a task force to draft bills such as a Republican version of Medicare reform. Democrats used the same strategy to bypass Ways and Means to write a welfare reform bill. But the most significant contribution of task forces has been writing bills that offer an alternative to what the relevant standing committees are likely to produce, and doing it more quickly.

A good example can be found in the attempt to pass legislation regulating tobacco. When the agreement between tobacco companies and the states reached Congress, the leadership, President Clinton, and key legislators such as Senator John McCain (R–Ariz.) worked outside the committee system to draft an acceptable bill. The tobacco bill did not pass, in large part because the tobacco industry "went public" with an advertising campaign against the bill, so it is doubtful that a committee-drafted bill would have fared better.

The use of a task force does have some advantages. It can overcome the paralysis that results from the divided partisan control of Congress and the presidency. Direct negotiations between the White House and congressional leaders can sometimes break long-standing deadlocks.

On the other hand, task forces bypass mechanisms for accountability to the public and to most rank-and-file members. Bills are written without formal hearings or the opportunity to point out potential pitfalls and problems of the legislation. Rank-and-file members often are faced with voting on a huge package of legislation about which they know only what they read in the newspaper.

The general impact of task forces under Gingrich was to weaken the power of standing committees and their chairs. However, with Hastert as Speaker, committee chairs receive much more deference, and task forces have declined in importance.

Evaluating Committee Government

The division of labor provided by committees and subcommittees enables Congress to consider a vast number of

In 1970, the thirteen African Americans then serving in Congress organized the Black Caucus, determined to gain some clout. This organization, which includes all but one African American member of Congress, now includes one-fifth of the entire Democratic Caucus.

Paradoxically, at a time when the caucus is at its all-time high in number of members, it is perhaps the weakest it has been in two decades. The reason is that all of its members are Democrats, and now they are the minority party in both houses. When the Democrats controlled the House, many black members had positions of power, chairing, in 1994, 26 percent of all House committees and many subcommittees too. In 2000 with the Democrats out of power, African Americans chair no committees or subcommittees.

One Black Caucus member serving as a deputy whip for the Democrats is in line for a top leadership position within the party organization, but this carries not nearly the clout of a committee chair. The House is currently the only venue for leadership positions since the only black member of the Senate lost her seat in 1998. But the caucus has little influence with the Republican majority because of its lack of Republican membership and because the black constituents of Republican

members of Congress tend to vote Democratic.

To be influential in these new circumstances, Black Caucus members will have to find new allies. Yet they must also continue speaking for their constituency. This is a difficult task because there are deep policy divisions between the Black Caucus and the Republican leadership. The only black Republican in Congress, J. C. Watts (who has refused to join the Black Caucus), is chair of the Republican Conference, a spokesman for Republican policy, and a member of its national campaign committee. Thus far the House leadership has made few black allies among ranking committee members or in the electorate in general, despite the fact that the Republicans have been actively courting African Americans.

Members of the Hispanic Caucus are probably better positioned to form alliances with the Republican leaders and chairs. The Caucus, formed in 1976, has only nineteen members (including two nonvoting delegates), but they are not nearly as unified on issues as are members of the Black Caucus. This is because Hispanic Caucus membership draws on a diverse group of Mexican, Puerto Rican, and Cuban Americans, whose constituencies split their votes among Republicans and Democrats. Also, like the Democrats, Re-

publicans are aggressively pursuing the votes of Hispanics, who are now the fastest-growing minority in the United States. With population trends showing that the main base of their electoral support—white men—is eroding, to hold their majority Republicans have little choice but to increase minority representation within the party.

Asian and Pacific Americans also have a caucus but publish no membership figures. The seven Asians in the House and Senate (including one nonvoting delegate) are a diverse group of Chinese, Japanese, and Pacific Islander descent, but all are Democrats. Like Hispanics, Asians are substantially underrepresented in the House and hold no top leadership positions.

If the significant increase in the Hispanic and Asian populations is reflected in the 2000 census, the representation of both groups in Congress should increase after reapportionment, especially given their concentration in a small number of states. Currently only seven states and Puerto Rico have Hispanic representation in the House (there are no Hispanic senators), and only three states and two territories have Asian representation, compared to twenty-two states and the District of Columbia who send black representatives to the House. This means African Americans have a say in far more

bills each year. If every member had to review every measure in detail it would be impossible to deal with the current workload. Instead, most bills are killed in committee, leaving many fewer for each member to evaluate before a floor vote. Committees also help members develop specializations. Members who remain on the same committee for some time gain expertise and are less dependent on professional staff and executive agencies for information.

But committee government also has disadvantages. By splitting off into subcommittees and developing expertise in a few areas, a House member runs the danger of being more responsive to narrow interests and constituencies and less responsive to national objectives when making national policy.

Over time, members of congressional subcommittees develop close relationships with lobbyists for the interest groups and staff in executive branch agencies af-

state delegations than do Hispanics and Asians. Despite the fact that Hispanics may soon outnumber African Americans as the largest minority in the United States, the issue of diversity within Hispanic constituencies means the Black Caucus will probably remain the most unified of the special interest caucuses and the best able to target its clout.

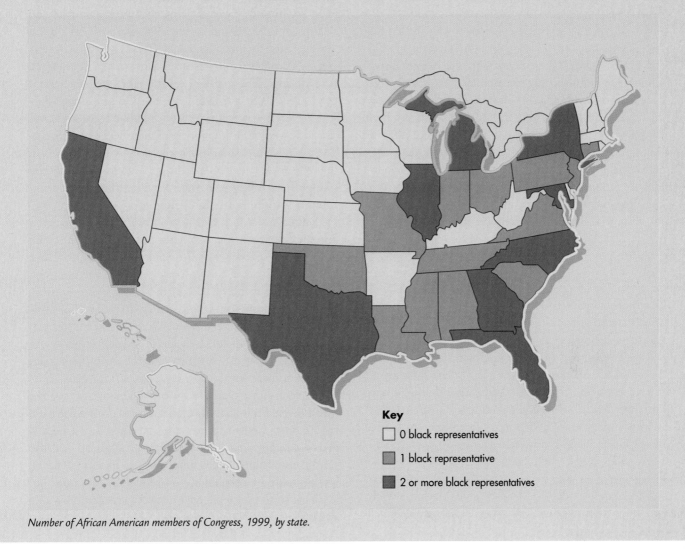

Key

□ 0 black representatives

▨ 1 black representative

■ 2 or more black representatives

Number of African American members of Congress, 1999, by state.

fected by their work. Over the years, these three groups—legislators, lobbyists, and bureaucrats—get to know each other, often come to like and respect one another, and seek to accommodate each other's interests. These personal relationships can result in favorable treatment of special interest groups.

The division of authority and specialization of individual members mean that Congress as a whole often cannot get things done because both energies and power are fragmented. Most members of the majority party in the Senate and about half of those in the House chair committees or subcommittees. With their own bases of power they are somewhat independent from party leaders. Thus, the opposition party in Congress often has difficulty mounting a coherent alternative to the president.

The fragmentation of power also means it is relatively easy for the president's own party to block his initiatives.

However, without powerful committees, if the majority leaders are not strong, bargaining over legislation can become a free-for-all, with dozens of legislators striking individual deals for their favorite program. Without strong committee chairs, individual members of Congress, often with no expertise or interest beyond a special interest, can hold a piece of legislation hostage in exchange for a tax loophole or bit of pork.

Many people believe that Congress is still ripe for reform. However, its burst of legislative energy early in 1995 suggests that when Congress fails to get things done, committee structure is only part of the reason. A cohesive House majority with strong leadership can pass legislation even with a complex committee structure. Conversely, if the public is divided and there is little strong leadership or incentive for members to carry out a legislative agenda, congressional structure only reinforces other impediments to action. As one member remarked, "How is a committee overhaul going to make me more courageous to do things I don't want to do now?"[83]

Staff

The term *Congress* encompasses not only our 535 elected representatives but also a staff of 17,700 people. This does not include the 7,000 Congress employs in support positions—security, maintenance, and so forth. The cost of running Congress is substantial at $2.6 billion per year.[84] As large as current numbers may seem, staff size has been falling since the early nineties, when Democrats made a 10 percent reduction. Much larger hits were sustained in 1995 when Republicans assumed control and reduced House staff size by 30 percent and made smaller cuts in the Senate.

Still Congress hires far more staff members than any other legislative body. The Canadian legislature, which is second in staff size, has only about 3,300 people.[85]

Types of Staff

Of the 17,700 aides, 2,500 are employed as committee staff, a number equal to the entire congressional staff in 1947. Another 11,700 serve as personal aides to members and are divided among the members' Washington and home district offices. Many are engaged in full-time constituency service; others are legislative aides, and one or two in each office do media work. Each House member receives a staff budget of about $600,000 and on average hires about twenty aides. Senators, who have no limit on staff size, are allotted from $1 to $2 million depending on state population. They employ anywhere

from thirty to forty aides and in addition receive roughly $400,000 to hire three legislative assistants.[86]

The remainder of the 17,700 serve as administrative personnel in congressional support agencies or work for the Senate and House leaders, who have much larger staffs than rank-and-file members.

One of the reasons for staff size is the heavy demand for constituency service. Another reason is that members of Congress try to develop their own expertise and sources of information so they will not have to rely on the executive branch. To this end, staff in support agencies carry out various research functions. The General Accounting Office checks on the efficiency and effectiveness of executive agencies; the Congressional Research Service conducts studies of public issues and does specific research at the request of members; the Office of Technology Assessment provides long-range analyses of the effects of new and existing technology; and the Congressional Budget Office provides the expertise and support for Congress's budgeting job.

Staffers do most of the background work on the complex foreign and domestic issues that cross the members' desks every day. To research difficult problems, they can call on the seven hundred full-time congressional research staff (CRS) in the Library of Congress. To illustrate how important their work is, we can consider the early days of the Gulf War when Congress was scrambling to keep up with the president's fast-moving policy. CRS was called on to research everything from Iraq's economic strengths and weaknesses, weapons programs, and culture, to the historical applications of the War Powers Resolution. All this information was pulled together in a briefing paper that "outlined the issues, analyzed the options, described legislation already on the books, listed applicable congressional hearing reports, and presented a chronology of events." Such reports are available to all members on-line and are periodically updated.[87]

Impact of Staff

The size and competence of staff have both positive and negative effects. By giving testimony at hearings and markup sessions, legislative and research staff can have great influence on the technical content of bills. The two top CRS social security experts have a combined fifty-five years of experience working on the issue and have contacts with experts in the academic world, in all the relevant federal agencies, and with the interest groups that lobby on behalf of social security recipients.[88] No member of Congress on his or her own would have the time to develop this kind of expertise, yet without it, competent legislation could not be written and Congress would not have the background it needs to challenge facts and figures presented in communications from the executive branch.

On the negative side, some scholars have argued that although large numbers of congressional aides may be necessary, they create paperwork and have a tendency to produce ever more research, committee work, and hearings. More information is collected than is possible for members to digest. Some argue that members have become office managers rather than legislators with time to think about policy. Congressional staffs have been accused of reducing the amount of discussion members have with one another over policy issues. As former Senator David Boren (D-Okla.) complained, "Very often, I will call on a senator on an issue, and he won't know anything about it. He'll ask me to get someone on my staff to call someone on his staff. It shuts off personal contact between senators."[89] This means the compromises and adjustments necessary to make policy are sometimes made by technicians rather than elected representatives.

What Congress Does

The importance of Congress is reflected in the major, explicit constitutional powers the Founders gave it: to lay and collect taxes, coin money, declare war and raise and support a military, and regulate commerce with foreign governments and among the states. Essentially, most of the powers the Constitution gives to the national government were given to Congress. These and other powers specifically mentioned in the Constitution are called the enumerated powers of Congress.

Congress also has implied powers; that is, it can make all the laws "necessary and proper" to carry out its enumerated powers. Although the Founders did not necessarily foresee it, this tremendous grant of power covers almost every conceivable area of human activity.

Lawmaking

Turning a bill into a law is like running an obstacle course. Approval must be obtained at each obstacle or the bill fails. The formal steps by which a bill becomes a law (see Figure 4) are important but do not reveal the compromises and trade-offs at every step in the process.

Those opposing a bill have an advantage because it is easier to defeat a bill than pass it. Because of the need to win a majority at each stage the end result is almost always a compromise.

Introduction

Bills may be introduced in either the House or the Senate, except for tax measures (which according to the Constitution must be initiated in the House) and appropriations bills (which by tradition are introduced in the House). This reflects the Founders' perceptions that on fiscal issues Congress would be more responsive to the people than the president and that the House would be more responsive than the Senate.

Although about half of all legislation passed is initiated by the president, only members of Congress can introduce bills. Interest groups or the president must find a congressional sponsor for a proposed bill.[90]

Referral and Committee Action

After a bill's introduction, it is referred to a standing committee by the Speaker of the House or the presiding officer in the Senate. The content of the bill largely determines where it will go, although the Speaker has some discretion, particularly over complex bills that cover more than one subject area. Many such bills are referred to more than one committee simultaneously.

Once the bill reaches a committee, it is assigned to a subcommittee. Bills receiving subcommittee approval go to full committee and if approved these go to the full House. Bills that get out of committee usually become law. Most bills, however, die in committee or subcommittee. Indeed, one of the main functions of committees is to screen bills with little chance of passage. (If a committee kills a bill, there are procedures that members can use to try to get the bill to the floor, but these are used infrequently.)

The markup stage in both committee and subcommittee is legally open to the public yet barely visible to it. Consequently, hearings are attended mainly by lobbyists. For critical meetings, lobbyists will hire messengers to stand in line for them, sometimes all night, and then pack the hearing room. Members who receive financial or other support from groups affected by the legislation often face intense and direct pressure to vote a particular way in committee. Sometimes they are mobbed by lobbyists when they leave the hearing room.

Scheduling and the Rules Committee

Once a bill is approved by committee, it is placed on one of five "calendars," each of which contains a particular type of bill (for example, all bills considered to be noncontroversial are placed on one calendar). Bills from each calendar are generally considered in the order that they are reported from committee. In the House, the **Rules Committee** sets the terms of the debate over the bill by issuing a rule on it. The rule either limits or does not limit debate and determines whether amendments will be permitted. A rule forbidding amendments means that members have to vote Yes or No on the bill; there is no chance to change it. If the committee refuses to issue a rule, the bill dies.

The Rules Committee is not as independent or powerful as it once was. In earlier years the committee was controlled by a coalition of conservative Democrats and Republicans who used the committee to block liberal legislative proposals including, for decades, meaningful civil rights proposals. It now functions as an arm of the majority leadership.[91] Members are nominated by the Speaker with the majority party receiving a disproportionately high number of the seats. The leadership uses its majority to fashion rules to control and expedite floor action.

Debate in the House

Debate on a bill is controlled by the bill managers, senior members of the committee that reported on the bill. The opposition too has its managers who schedule opposition speeches. "Debates" are not a series of fiery speeches of point and counterpoint. They are often boring, given to sparse audiences, some of whom are reading, conversing, or walking around. After the agreed-

	HOUSE	SENATE	PRESIDENT
Bill Introduction ↓	Given a number	Given a number	
	Referred to committee	Referred to committee	
In Committee ↓	Referred to subcommittee	Referred to subcommittee	
	Hearings held	Hearings held	
	Markup	Markup	
	Recommend passage or kill the bill	Recommend passage or kill the bill	
	Rules committee action (setting terms of debate)		
On the Floor ↓	Debate and amendment, if allowed under rule (usually one day)	Debate and amendment (days or weeks)	
	Vote on passage	Vote on passage	
In Conference ↓	Conference Committee reconciles different versions		
	Conference report adapted	Conference report adapted	
To President	Vote on veto override (if necessary)	Vote on veto override (if necessary)	Signs or vetoes

FIGURE 4 ■ *How a Bill Becomes a Law* These formal steps do not include the informal negotiations, discussions, and compromises that take place throughout the process. Neither do they include the efforts interest groups make to influence the decisions or the information legislators receive from their constituents.

Table 2	Important Differences between the House and Senate

House	Senate
Constitutional Differences	
Must initiate revenue bills.	Confirmation power over many major presidential appointments.
Initiates impeachment and votes on impeachment bills.	Tries impeached officials.
Apportioned by population.	Ratification power over treaties.
	Two members from each state.
Differences in Operation	
More centralized; procedures more formal:	Less centralized; procedures less formal:
Speaker's assignment of bills to committee hard to challenge.	Assignment of bills to committee appealable.
Rules Committee fairly powerful in controlling time and rules of debate.	No rules committee; limits on debate come through unanimous consent or cloture of filibuster.
Nongermane amendments forbidden.	Nongermane amendments permitted.
Majority party controls scheduling.	Schedule and rules negotiated between majority and minority leaders.
More impersonal.	More personal.
Power less evenly distributed.	Power more evenly distributed.
Members are highly specialized.	Members are generalists.
Emphasizes tax and revenue policy.	Has more foreign policy responsibilities.
Changes in the Institution	
Power of key committees and the leadership.	Senate workload and partisanship increasing; informality breaking down.
House procedures more efficient with less debate and fewer amendments.	Members are becoming more specialized; debate and deliberation are less frequent.
More organizing and bill writing outside committees.	

upon time for debate is over, usually no more than a day, the bill is reported for final action.

The Senate

Because the Senate is a smaller body, it can operate with fewer rules and formal procedures. (Table 2 summarizes House and Senate differences.) It does not have a rules committee. A lot of work is accomplished through the use of unanimous consent agreements, which allow the Senate to dispense with standard rules and limit debate and amendments. As the Senate's workload has increased and its sense of collegiality decreased, unanimous consent agreements are more difficult to gain from opponents of a bill. A few senators can delay or kill important bills.

Without unanimous consent, there is no rule limiting debate and there are no restrictions on adding amendments. Opponents can add all sorts of irrelevant amend-

ments to pending legislation. One senator held up an antibusing bill for eight months with 604 amendments.

The other major mechanism for delay in the Senate is the **filibuster.** This is a continuous speech made by one or more members to prevent the Senate from taking action on a bill. Before 1917, only unanimous consent could prevent an individual from talking. Today a **cloture** vote of three-fifths of the members limits delaying tactics to only thirty additional hours.

Like nongermane amendments, filibusters are used by both liberals and conservatives. The filibuster developed in the 1820s when the Senate was divided between slave and free states. Unlimited debate maintained the deadlock.[92] For over a century the filibuster was used primarily to defeat race and civil rights legislation. It took a cloture vote to end seventy-three days of debate and get the 1964 Civil Rights Act to the floor for a vote.

During Clinton's first year in office, Republicans used the filibuster quite frequently to block proposals from the Democratic Senate majority. After Republicans captured the Senate in 1994, the new majority leader, Trent Lott (R–Miss.), found himself frustrated by Democratic filibusters. "We are completely balled up and it's not my fault. I want us all to sober up here now and get on with the business of the Senate," he complained.[93]

Filibusters prevent domination by the majority and precipitous action, but by requiring sixty votes to end debate, they deny the majority the right to legislate and contribute to gridlock.[94] In 1991–1992 alone, the filibuster was used thirty-five times, compared with only sixteen times during the entire nineteenth century.

Conference Committee

The Constitution requires that the House and Senate pass an identical bill before it becomes law. Thus, the House and Senate versions of the bill must be reconciled. Sometimes the house that passed the bill last will simply send the bill to the other house for minor modifications. But if the differences between the two versions are not minor, a **Conference Committee** is set up to try to resolve them. The presiding officers of each house, in consultation with the chairs of the standing committees that considered the bill, choose the members of the committee. Both parties are represented.

To win approval, majorities of members from each house must agree to the Conference Committee version. Sometimes the bill is rewritten fairly substantially, and occasionally a bill is killed.

Once the Conference Committee reaches an agreement, the bill goes back to each house for ratification. It cannot be amended at that point so Congress must either "take it or leave it." This means the Conference Committee can be very influential.

Presidential Action and Congressional Response

The president may sign the bill, in which case it becomes law. The president may veto it, in which case it returns to Congress with the president's objections. The president also may do nothing, and the bill will become law after ten days unless Congress adjourns.

Most Presidents have not used the veto lightly, but when they do, they usually are not overridden by Congress. A two-thirds vote in each house is required to override a presidential veto. Congress voted to override only nine of former President Reagan's seventy-eight vetoes, only one of President Bush's forty-six, and two of the thirty-six Clinton cast during his first seven years.

Overseeing the Federal Bureaucracy

As part of the checks and balances principle, it is Congress's responsibility to make sure the bureaucracy is carrying out the intent of Congress in administering federal programs. This monitoring function is called **oversight** and has become more important as Congress continues to delegate authority to the executive branch. For a variety of reasons, Congress is not especially well equipped, motivated, or organized to carry out its oversight function. Nevertheless, it does have several tools for this purpose.

One tool is the General Accounting Office, created in 1921, which functions as Congress's watchdog in oversight and is mostly concerned with making sure that money is used properly.

Another tool is the **legislative veto,** a provision Congress adds to some legislation empowering it to block the way in which an executive branch agency implements some aspect of a law or regulation. Used since 1933, it allows one or both houses of Congress, or on occasion a congressional committee, to block executive action. In the 1970s especially, Congress was aggressive in restricting agency activities. For example, all Federal Trade Commission rulings were made subject to a legislative veto.

In 1983, the Supreme Court declared the legislative veto unconstitutional as a violation of the separation of powers principle. Legislation, the Court ruled, must be passed by both houses and signed by the president. Congress cannot take over executive functions. Even so, since that decision, more than one hundred bills have been passed with provisions for a legislative veto.[95] Though presumably they could not be enforced, legislative vetoes continue to be honored by federal agencies unwilling to risk congressional wrath.

Yet another, but not very effective, method of oversight is committee hearings. Members can quiz representatives from agencies on the operation of their agencies, but often the hearings go into great detail about some particular problem of minor importance and neglect broader policy questions. Poor attendance and the pressure of other business mean that members' attentions are usually not focused on congressional hearings. Nevertheless, officials in agencies view hearings as a possible source of embarrassment for their agency and spend a great deal of time preparing for them.

This is never more true than when Congress decides, for political reasons, to hold well-publicized hearings. In 1998, for example, Congress looked into alleged abuses at the Internal Revenue Service (IRS) with vivid

testimony from taxpayers about high-handed IRS tactics. Newscasts throughout the nation carried snippets of the most sensational allegations. Not surprisingly, these hearings were held in April, when many Americans were busy preparing their income tax returns.

Congress's control over the budget is the major way it exercises oversight. Congress can cut or add to agencies' budgets and thereby punish or reward them for their performance.

Informal oversight is a common tool.[96] One means is requiring reports on topics of interest to members or committees. In a given year the executive branch might prepare five thousand reports for Congress.[97] Moreover the chair and staff of the committee or subcommittee relevant to the agency's mission are consulted regularly by the agency. But one can question whether any serious oversight is exercised informally. Committee members with authority over an agency's budget get benefits for their constituents from that agency. By responding to congressional wishes, agencies get a favorable budget. There are few electoral or other incentives for members to become involved in the drudgery of more thorough oversight.[98]

Budget Making

An increasingly large part of the job of Congress is to produce a budget. The Constitution gives Congress the authority to control the federal purse by collecting taxes and spending money.

The topic of budget making may sound dull but without the money to implement them, laws would mean little.

There are two major features of congressional budgeting. First, the process is usually incremental; that is, budgets of one year are usually slightly more than budgets of the past year. Normally, Congress does not radically reallocate money from one year to the next; members assume agencies should get about what they received the previous year. This simplifies the work of all concerned. Agencies do not have to defend, or members scrutinize, all aspects of the budget.[99]

A second feature is that Congress tends to spend slightly more on federal agencies in election years.[100] This tendency increases in times of unemployment and moderates in times of inflation. Members are also more likely to vote for increasing federal payments to individuals (such as veterans' benefits or Social Security) in the years they are up for reelection.[101]

There are exceptions to this general rule, such as times of war or domestic crisis. There are also instances of ideological budgeting. Reagan's domestic budget cuts and increased military spending in 1981 were clearly an exception to incrementalism. The Contract with America approach to cutting programs wholesale is another example.

Budget legislation includes multiple separate bills, each focusing on a set of expenditures. In recent years, there has been a tendency to lump many parts of the budget together in omnibus bills. All budget legislation goes through a process similar to but more complicated than other bills.[102] To grasp the complexity, we have to understand the distinction between budget authorizations and budget appropriations. **Authorizations** provide agencies and departments with the legal authority

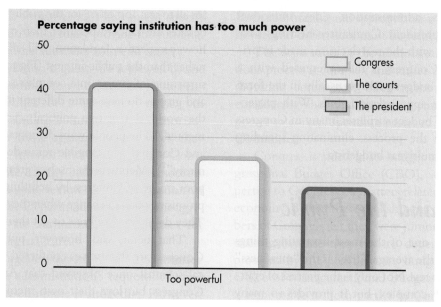

Percentage saying institution has too much power

Legend:
- Congress
- The courts
- The president

FIGURE 5 ■ *Public Perceives Congress as Most Powerful National Institution, and Likes It the Least*

SOURCE: John Hibbing and Elizabeth Theiss-Morse, *Congress as Public Enemy* (Cambridge: Cambridge University Press, 1995). Data are from 1993.

Despite all this, the idea of a Congress as enshrined in the Constitution is important and esteemed. It is the people *in* Congress and the way Congress works that the public dislikes. But most of the public is poorly informed about the work of Congress. They are much more likely to know about bounced checks and sexual improprieties of members of Congress than they are about legislation. For example, in 1994, although two-thirds were aware of new handgun regulations and family leave policy (granting most employees the right to take an unpaid leave for a new baby or family illness), less than one-third of the public knew that Congress had passed a budget bill cutting the deficit by billions, reduced taxes on the working poor and raised them on the very rich, made voting registration nearly automatic when individuals sign up for their driver's licenses, and given federal workers the right to get involved in politics.[108] Thus, the public evaluation of Congress as having accomplished "not much" or "nothing at all" was based on the public's lack of awareness of what Congress actually did. This pattern persists even with C-Span coverage, and even though most local papers each week print a congressional scorecard with the voting records on local legislators.

Congress in Time

1787	Constitutional convention delegates create a national legislature with two chambers, one based on population and chosen by direct popular vote, and the second with equal representation for every state and chosen by state legislators.
1800	Congress meets for first time in Washington.
1801	House decides its first presidential election, selecting Thomas Jefferson.
1803	Supreme Court gives federal courts the power to determine constitutionality of legislation passed by Congress.

1825	House resolves presidential election for second time, selecting John Quincy Adams from four candidates.
1828	Andrew Jackson assumes presidency and exerts power of office in dealing with Congress; first political use of veto power to check a congressional act.
1850	Slavery issue that has divided the House for decades comes to a head. Henry Clay, John C. Calhoun, and Daniel Webster make their final joint appearance in the Senate to find a compro-

mise on slavery that will prevent the South from seceding from the Union, but they fail.

1861–62 Congress expels fifteen senators for supporting secession; House expels three members for treasonable remarks.

1868 House impeaches President Andrew Johnson; Senate acquits by a single vote, but presidency gravely weakened. Period of "congressional government" begins.

1870s The Senate, dominated by lobbyists and professional politicians from state party organizations, is labeled a "millionaires club" and becomes the most unpopular branch of government.

1877 The House decides the presidential election when electoral votes are disputed and gives it to Rutherford B. Hayes in a compromise with southern states.

1890 Powerful Republican Speaker of the House forces adoption of "Reed rules" that enhance power of committee chairs and make it more difficult for members to obstruct legislative process.

1910 In a revolt against autocratic House Speaker Joe Cannon, members take away Speaker's authority to appoint committee members and chairs and reduce other powers, greatly weakening Speakership. Beginning of seniority system for selection of committee chairs.

1913 Seventeenth Amendment to the Constitution provides for direct election of senators; culmination of Progressive era reforms that reduce hold of big business interests on Congress.

1933 Special legislative session ("Hundred Days") called by FDR to deal with Great Depression; with little debate Congress passes major economic bills.

1946 Legislative Reorganization Act reforms procedures, restructures committees, and spreads workload more evenly across the membership. Beginning of "modern Congress."

1961 House votes to increase size of Rules Committee by three to override votes of conservatives who had a stranglehold on legislative agenda. Made possible introduction of 1960s civil rights legislation.

1964 For first time in its history Senate invokes cloture to end filibuster of a civil rights bill. End of a 175-year period in which antislavery and then civil rights bills were blocked from floor of House and Senate.

1964 Supreme Court establishes the one-person, one-vote rule that leads to redrawing of congressional districts.

1964 By passing Tonkin Gulf Resolution, Congress gives Presidents Johnson and Nixon a free hand in fighting Vietnam War.

1970 Congress reforms its procedures again: rolls back power of committee chairs, forces committees to release voting records to public, allows media coverage of committee hearings, and limits application of the seniority rule in assigning committee chairs. Begins short period of "subcommittee government."

1973 War Powers Resolution passed; Congress tries to recover war-making powers lost during years of the Vietnam War and the "imperial" presidency.

1974 House Judiciary Committee votes for Nixon's impeachment, but Nixon resigns before a full vote of the House.

1974 Congress passes Budget and Impoundment Act to recover budget powers lost to the executive branch; authorizes preparation of a congressional budget plan and limits president's ability to refuse to spend money congress has appropriated.

1977 Senate places limitations on use of the filibuster.

1979 First live coverage on radio and television of daily floor proceedings in House takes place on C-Span. Senate coverage follows in 1986.

1983 By Supreme Court ruling (separation of powers), Congress loses the legislative veto, the power to veto decisions made by agencies in the executive branch in implementing the laws it has passed.

1992 Public approval of Congress hits all-time low as members are accused of wrongdoing in use of House banking and postal system. Fifty-three representatives and eight senators decide not to stand for reelection.

1995 Republicans gain control of Congress for the first time in forty years, reorganize the House, cut committees, reduce staff by one-third, prohibit proxy voting, and privatize some House services. Term limits are set for committee chairs.

1995 Standoff on budget compromise between Congress and Clinton leads to two government shutdowns.

1995 Supreme Court rules state laws setting term limits for members of Congress are unconstitutional. Terms of membership can be changed by constitutional amendment only.

1997 Newt Gingrich fined and reprimanded for unethical behavior; first sitting House Speaker to be reprimanded.

1998 House holds hearings and impeaches President Clinton.

1999 Senate tries Clinton on two articles of impeachment and acquits.

Key Terms

constituency
reapportionment
redistricting
gerrymander
franking privilege
constituency service
casework
pork barrel
informal norms
institutional loyalty
reciprocity
specialization
going public
special interest caucuses
Speaker of the House

majority leader
minority leader
whips
standing committees
markup
seniority rule
subcommittee bill of rights
Rules Committee
filibuster
cloture
Conference Committee
oversight
legislative veto
authorizations
appropriations

Further Reading

Michael Barone et al., *The Almanac of American Politics* (Washington, D.C.: National Journal, since 1980). Offers a description of each member, his or her district, and voting record. Revised every two years since 1980. A volume similar in format and publication schedule is Alan Ehrenhalt's *Politics in America* (Washington, D.C.: CQ Press).

Congressional Quarterly Weekly Report. Published weekly, provides analyses of the workings of Congress and its members. The Congressional Quarterly also publishes a yearly summary of congressional action called the *Congressional Quarterly Almanac.*

Timothy Cook, *Making Laws and Making News* (Washington, D.C.: Brookings, 1989). A revealing account of how media coverage has affected the legislative process in the U.S. House.

Roger Davidson and Walter Oleszek, *Congress and Its Members,* 7th ed. (Washington, D.C.: Congressional Quarterly, 1999). Now a classic general work on Congress.

Richard Fenno, *Home Style* (Boston: Little, Brown, 1978). A readable book based on Fenno's travels with House members to their home districts). Fenno offers interesting and valuable insights into how members present themselves to the home folks. In *The United States Senate: A Bicameral Perspective* (Washington, D.C.: American Enterprise Institute, 1982), Fenno gives the same attention to senators.

Morris Fiorina, *Congress: Keystone of the Washington Establishment,* 2d ed. (New Haven, Conn.: Yale University Press, 1989). A small and significant book that argues that members of Congress love the big bureaucracy because it helps their constituents and thereby helps them win reelection.

Linda Fowler, *Candidates, Congress, and the American Democracy* (Ann Arbor: University of Michigan Press, 1993). How

the political system affects the recruitment of congressional candidates, and how the candidates affect the system.

Marjorie Margolies-Mezvinsky, *A Woman's Place: The Freshmen Women Who Changed the Face of Congress* (New York: Crown, 1994). Representative Margolies-Mezvinsky reflects on the changes brought about in Congress by the largest group of women representatives ever.

Timothy Phelps and Helen Winternitz, *Capitol Games: Clarence Thomas, Anita Hill and the Story of a Supreme Court Nomination* (New York: Hyperion, 1992). A close look at the Senate hearings on Clarence Thomas's nomination to the Supreme Court.

Pat Schroeder, *24 Years of House Work . . . and the Place Is Still a Mess* (Kansas City, Mo.: McMeel, 1998). One of the most outspoken women in Congress from 1973 to 1995, Schroeder tells how a woman politician succeeded in this male-dominated institution.

Steven Waldman, *The Bill: How the Adventures of Clinton's National Service Bill Reveal What Is Corrupt, Comic, Cynical—and Noble—about Washington* (New York: Viking, 1995). How a bill becomes a law in the 1990s, with a focus on Clinton's national service and student loan proposals.

Electronic Resources

www.whitehouse.gov/WH/html/legi.html
This link takes you to the official U.S. House and U.S. Senate pages. On them you can find information about the membership of each branch, roll-call votes, hearing schedules, historical information, and much more. The site contains links to individual members' pages too. The site also links to agencies of Congress, such as the General Accounting Office and the Library of Congress, and to other federal agencies.

www.washingtonpost.com/
This is the Web site of the Washington Post, *whose news coverage of Congress is unrivaled.*

thomas.loc.gov/home/thomas.html
Links to texts of bills, the congressional record (reporting the entire floor debates), and committee hearings and reports.

lcweb.loc.gov/global/legislative/congress.html
Want to know how many Asian Americans are in Congress and who they are? How much members of Congress make? Who the leadership is? This page links to all kinds of statistics about Congress, along with links to the home pages and e-mail addresses of members.

InfoTrac College Edition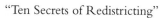

"Ten Secrets of Redistricting"
"True Undercount Experts"
"Unassuming Speaker Struggles"
"Caucus, White House Open Education"

Notes

1. These quotations, and much of this background information, are from Michael Barone and Grant Ujifusa, *The Almanac of American Politics* (Washington, D.C.: National Journal, 1994), 1108–1109; other sources include "Special Report," *Congressional Quarterly Weekly Report,* October 22, 1994, p. 3048; "The Last Stretch," *Congressional Quarterly Weekly Report,* August 7, 1993, pp. 2125, 2129. See also Marjorie Margolies-Mezvinsky, *A Woman's Place: The Freshmen Women Who Changed the Face of Congress* (New York: Crown, 1994).

2. James R. Chiles, "Congress Couldn't Have Been *This* Bad, or Could It?" *Smithsonian* (November, 1995): 70–80.

3. Ibid.

4. David Broder, "Dumbing Down Democracy," *Lincoln Journal,* April 5, 1995, p. 18.

5. Quoted in Kenneth J. Cooper and Helen Dewar, "No Limits on the Term Limits Crusade," *Washington Post National Weekly Edition,* May 29–June 4, 1995, p. 14.

6. Richard Pérez-Peña, "Lawyers Abandon Legislatures for Greener Pastures," *New York Times,* February 2, 1999, sect. 4, p. 3.

7. "New Congress Is Older, More Politically Seasoned," *Congressional Quarterly Weekly Report,* January 9, 1999, p. 63.

8. Jim Abrams, "The Son also Runs," *Champaign-Urbana News Gazette,* November 7, 1999, p. B1.

9. "Congress Enjoys Great Health Benefits," *Champaign-Urbana News-Gazette,* October 23, 1999, p. A-4.

10. "$100,000 Pension Set for Some Lawmakers," *Champaign-Urbana News-Gazette,* December 31, 1997, p. C-8.

11. Robert Erikson and Gerald Wright, Jr., "Policy Representation of Constituency Interests," *Political Behavior 2* (1980): 91–106; Erikson and Wright, "Voters, Candidates, and Issues in Congressional Elections," in *Congress Reconsidered,* 3d ed., ed. Lawrence Dodd and Bruce Oppenheimer (Washington, D.C.: CQ Press); Wright, "Policy Voting in the U.S. Senate: Who Is Represented?" *Legislative Studies Quarterly* 14 (November 1989): 465–486. See also Robert Erikson and Norman Luttbeg, *American Public Opinion* (New York: Wiley, 1973), 257; William Shaffer, "The Ideological and Partisan Linkages between U.S. Senators and Their Constituents," paper prepared at the Annual Meeting of the Midwest Political Science Association, Chicago, 1987; Warren Miller and Donald Stokes, "Constituency Influence in Congress," *American Political Science Review* 56 (March 1963): 45–56.

12. Wright, "Policy Voting in the U.S. Senate."

13. 369 U.S. 186 (1962).

14. *Wesberry v. Sanders,* 376 U.S. 1 (1964).

15. Bruce Cain and Janet Campagna, "Predicting Partisan Redistricting Disputes," *Legislative Studies Quarterly* 12 (1987): 265–274.

16. See report on *Miller v. Johnson,* 515 U.S. 900 (1995), in *New York Times,* July 2, 1995, pp. E1, E4.

17. Steven A. Holmes, "Did Racial Redistricting Undermine Democrats?" *New York Times,* November 13, 1994, p. 32.

18. "Debate over Sampling in Census 2000 Resurfaces," *Champaign-Urbana News-Gazette,* May 20, 2000.

19. See Thomas E. Mann, "Elections and Change in Congress," in *The New Congress,* ed. Thomas Mann and Norman Ornstein (Washington, D.C.: American Enterprise Institute, 1981), 32–54; David Mayhew, *The Electoral Connection* (New Haven, Conn.: Yale University Press, 1974); Glenn Parker and Roger Davidson, "Why Do Americans Love Their Congressmen So Much?" *Legislative Studies Quarterly* (February 1979): 53–62.

20. Thomas Mann and Raymond Wolfinger, "Candidates and Parties in Congressional Elections," *American Political Science Review* 74 (September 1980): 617–632; Patricia Hurley and Kim Q. Hill, "The Prospects for Issue Voting in Contemporary Congressional Elections," *American Politics Quarterly* 8 (October 1980): 446.

21. John Alford and John Hibbing, "The Disparate Electoral Security of House and Senate Incumbents," paper presented at the American Political Science meetings, Atlanta, Georgia, September 1989.

22. Richard Fenno, *Home Style* (Boston: Little, Brown, 1978).

23. For a brief history of the franking privilege, see *Congress from A to Z* (Washington, D.C.: Congressional Quarterly, 1999), 171–173.

24. "House Members Ready to Boost Office Funds," *Champaign-Urbana News-Gazette,* June 4, 1999, p. C-11.

25. Tim Miller, "Frankly Free Mail Seems to Help Incumbents," *Washington Post National Weekly Edition,* August 8, 1985, pp. 13–14. For an investigation of the impact of franked mail, see Albert Cover, "The Electoral Impact of Franked Congressional Mail," *Polity* 17 (Summer 1985): 649–663.

26. Miller, "Frankly Free Mail Seems to Help Incumbents." See Glenn Parker, "Sources of Change in Congressional District Attentiveness," *American Journal of Political Science* (February 1980): 115–124.

27. Carol Matlack, "Live from Capitol Hill," *National Journal,* February 18, 1989, p. 390.

28. *Congress from A to Z,* 466.

29. *Setting Course: A Congressional Management Guide* (Washington, D.C.: American University Congressional Management Program, 1984); Norman Ornstein, Thomas E. Mann, and Michael Malbin, *Vital Statistics on Congress, 1991–1992* (Washington, D.C.: American Enterprise Institute, 1992), p. 161.

30. Norman J. Ornstein, Thomas E. Mann, Michael J. Malbin, *Vital Statistics on Congress, 1997–1998* (Washington D.C.: Congressional Quarterly, 1998), 129.

31. Morris Fiorina, "Congressional Control of the Bureaucracy: A Mismatch of Incentives and Capabilities," in *Congress Reconsidered,* 2d ed., ed. Lawrence C. Dodd and Bruce I. Oppenheimer (Washington, D.C.: CQ Press, 1981), p. 341.

32. Morris Fiorina, *Congress: Keystone of the Washington Establishment* (New Haven, Conn.: Yale University Press, 1977), especially 48–49.

33. Robert Sherill, "Squealing on Porcine Politics," *Washington Post National Weekly Edition,* September 7–12, 1992, p. 35; the quote is by Alan Schick from Brian Kelly, "Pigging Out at the White House," *Washington Post National Weekly Edition,* September 14–20, 1992, p. 23.

34. "Highway Bill Larded with Hometown Projects," *Champaign-Urbana News-Gazette,* March 30, 1999, p. A5.

35. Lizette Alvarez, "Congress on Record Course for 'Pork,' with Alaska in a Class of Its Own," *New York Times,* November 19, 1999, p. A28.

36. Quoted in Kenneth Shepsle, "The Failures of Congressional Budgeting," *Social Science and Modern Society* 20 (1983): 4–10. See also Howard Kurtz, "Pork Barrel Politics," *Washington Post,* January 25, 1982, reported in Randall Ripley, *Congress,* 3d ed. (New York: Norton, 1983).

37. See Paul Feldman and James Jondrow, "Congressional Elections and Local Federal Spending," *American Journal of Political Science* 28 (1984): 152; Glenn R. Parker and Suzanne Parker, "The Correlates and Effects of Attention to District by U.S. House Members," *Legislative Studies Quarterly* 10 (1985): 239.

38. Christopher Buckley, "Hangin' with the Houseboyz," *Washington Monthly,* June 1992, p. 44.

39. Linda L. Fowler, *Who Decides to Run for Congress?* (New Haven, Conn.: Yale University Press, 1989); Linda L. Fowler, *Candidates, Congress and the American Democracy* (Ann Arbor: University of Michigan Press, 1993).

40. Thomas Mann, *Unsafe at Any Margin: Interpreting Congressional Elections* (Washington, D.C.: American Enterprise Institute, 1978).

41. "Women, Minorities Join Senate," *CQ Almanac,* 1992, pp. 8A–14A: "Wave of Diversity Spared Many Incumbents," *CQ*

Almanac, 1992, pp. 15A–21A, 24A; "The Elections" CQ, November 12, 1994, p. 3237.

42. Gary Jacobson, *The Politics of Congressional Elections,* 2d ed. (Boston: Little, Brown, 1987), p. 51.

43. Ibid.

44. Barbara Hinckley, "The American Voter in Congressional Elections," *American Political Science Review* 74 (September 1980): 641–650; Hinckley, "House Reelections and Senate Defeats: The Role of the Challenger," *British Journal of Political Science* 10 (October 1980): 441–460; Mann and Wolfinger, "Candidates and Parties"; Alan I. Abramowitz, "A Comparison of Voting of U.S. Senators and Representatives in 1978," *American Political Science Review* 74 (September 1980): 633–640.

45. Alford and Hibbing, "The Disparate Electoral Security of House and Senate Incumbents."

46. A good review of these arguments is found in John R. Hibbing and Sara L. Brandes, "State Population and the Electoral Success of U.S. Senators," *American Journal of Political Science* 27 (November 1983): 808–819. See also Eric Uslaner, "The Case of the Vanishing Liberal Senators: The House Did It," *British Journal of Political Science* 11 (January 1981), pp. 105–113; Abramowitz, "A Comparison."

47. Hibbing and Brandes, "State Population." See also Glenn Parker, "Stylistic Change in the U.S. Senate," *Journal of Politics* 47 (November 1985), pp. 1190–1202.

48. Edie Goldenberg and Michael Traugott, *Campaigning for Congress* (Washington, D.C.: CQ Press, 1984); Gary Jacobson and Samuel Kernell, *Strategy and Choice in Congressional Elections,* 2d ed. (New Haven, Conn.: Yale University Press, 1983).

49. Edward Walsh, "Wanted: Candidates for Congress," *Washington Post National Weekly Edition,* November 25, 1985, p. 9.

50. Ceci Connolly, "GOP Hold on House Hazier," *Washington Post,* June 8, 1998, p. A1.

51. Alan Ehrenhalt, "Technology, Strategy Bring New Campaign Era," *Congressional Quarterly Weekly Report,* December 7, 1985, p. 2561; Mann, "Elections and Change in Congress"; Jacobson, *The Politics of Congressional Elections.*

52. Paul Hernson, *Party Campaigning in the 1980s* (Cambridge, Mass.: Harvard University Press, 1988).

53. Michael Barone, Grant Ujifusa, and Charles E. Cook, Jr., *The Almanac of American Politics 2000* (Washington, D.C.: National Journal, 1999), 1813–1814.

54. See Gerald Wright, Jr., and Michael Berkman, "Candidates and Policy in United States Senate Elections," *American Political Science Review* 80 (June 1986): 567–588; Erikson and Wright, "Voters, Candidates, and Issues in Congressional Elections."

55. See James Campbell, "Explaining Presidential Losses in Midterm Elections," *Journal of Politics* 47 (November 1985): 1140–1157. See also Barbara Hinckley, "Interpreting House Midterm Elections," *American Political Science Review* 61 (1967): 694–700; Samuel Kernell, "Presidential Popularity and Negative Voting," *American Political Science Review* 71 (1977): 44–66; Edward Tufte, "Determinants of the Outcomes of Midterm Congressional Elections," *American Political Science Review* 69 (1975): 812–826; Alan Abramowitz, "Economic Conditions, Presidential Popularity and Voting Behavior in Midterm Elections," *Journal of Politics* 47 (February 1985): 31–43.

56. Herbert Asher, "Learning of Legislative Norms," *American Political Science Review* 67 (June 1973): 499–513. Michael Berkman points out that those freshmen who have had state legislative experience—now more than half of all House members—adapt to the job faster than other members. See "Former State Legislators in the U.S. House of Representatives: Institutional and Policy Mastery," *Legislative Studies Quarterly* 18 (February 1993): 77–104.

57. Minot (North Dakota) *Daily News,* June 17, 1976, quoted in Ripley, *Congress.*

58. Samuel Kernell, *Going Public* (Washington, D.C.: CQ Press, 1986).

59. R. E. Cohen, "The Congress Watchers," *National Journal,* January 26, 1985, p. 215.

60. Ronald Garay, *Congressional Television: A Legislative History* (Westport, Conn.: Greenwood, 1984), p. 143; Michael Robinson, "Three Faces of Congressional Media," in *The New Congress,* ed. Thomas Mann and Norman Ornstein (Washington, D.C.: American Enterprise Institute, 1981), 68.

61. Katharine Q. Seelye, "Gingrich Used TV Skills to Be King of the Hill," *New York Times,* December 14, 1994, p. A14.

62. Diane Duston, "They're Angry, Conservative, and They're Dialing Right Now," *Centre Daily Times* (AP Release), July 16, 1993, p. 1. The study was done by the Times-Mirror Center for the People and the Press.

63. Daniel J. Parks, "Partisan Voting Holds Steady," *Congressional Quarterly Weekly Report,* December 11, 1999, p. 2975.

64. Ibid., p. 2976.

65. Richard Fenno, "U.S. House Members and Their Constituencies: An Exploration," *American Political Science Review* 71 (1977): 883–917; and Fenno, *Home Style.*

66. Benjamin Page et al., "Constituency, Party and Representation in Congress," *Public Opinion Quarterly* 48 (Winter 1984), pp. 741–756; Jerrold E. Schneider, *Ideological Coalitions in Congress* (Westport, Conn.: Greenwood, 1979).

67. Mark Hankerson, "Participation Hits Record," *Congressional Quarterly Weekly Report,* December 11, 1999, p. 2979.

68. John Kingdon, *Congressmen's Voting Decisions* (New York: Harper & Row, 1973).

69. Congressional Quarterly, *The Origins and Development of Congress* (Washington, D.C.: CQ Press, 1976).

70. Neil McNeil, *Forge of Democracy* (New York: McKay, 1963), pp. 306–309.

71. Mark Hankerson, "Participation Hits Record," p. 2979.

72. Jackie Koszczuk, "Master of the Mechanics Has Kept the House Running," *Congressional Quarterly Weekly Report,* December 11, 1999, p. 2963.

73. Barone, *The Almanac of American Politics 2000,* p. 46.

74. Ibid.

75. Susan Welch and John G. Peters, "Private Interests in the U.S. Congress," *Legislative Studies Quarterly* 7 (November 1982): 547–555.

76. See Roger Davidson, "Subcommittee Government," in Mann and Ornstein, *The New Congress,* pp. 110–111. Some of this occurs because members of Congress tend to be wealthy, and the wealthy make investments in corporations. It also occurs because members' financial interests are often similar to the interests in their districts (e.g., representatives of farm districts are likely to be involved in farming or agribusiness).

77. Alan Ehrenhalt, "Media, Power Shifts to Dominate O'Neill's House," *Congressional Quarterly Weekly Report,* September 13, 1986, pp. 2131–2136; Stephen Hess, "Live from Capitol Hill, It's . . . ," *Washington Monthly* (June 1986): 41–43. The Biden quotation is from this article. See also Steven Smith and Christopher Deering, *Committees in Congress* (Washington, D.C.: CQ Press, 1984), 67.

78. Eric Planin, "David Obey Appropriates a New Fiefdom," *Washington Post National Weekly Edition,* May 9–15, 1994, p. 11.

79. John Hibbing and Sara Brandes-Crook, "Congressional Reform and Party Discipline: The Effects of Changes in the Seniority System on Party Loyalty in the U.S. House of Representatives," *British Journal of Political Science* 15 (April 1985).

80. *Congress from A to Z,* p. 378.

81. Richard E. Cohen, "Best Seats in the House," *National Journal,* March 4, 2000, p. 682.

82. For a review of how the task force has been used, see Walter Oleszek, "The Use of Task Forces in the House" (CRS Report for

Congress, # 96-843 GOV, 1996). The text can be found at www.house.gov/rules/96-843.htm.

83. John Fairhall, quoting Thomas Downey (D-N.Y.), "Bureaucratic Bloat Crippling Congress," *Lincoln Journal-Star,* June 7, 1992, p. 7B.

84. "House Members Ready to Boost Office Funds," p. C-11.

85. Michael J. Malbin, "Delegation, Deliberation, and the New Role of Congressional Staff," in Mann and Ornstein, *The New Congress,* p. 135.

86. Ibid.; *Congress A to Z,* 416.

87. Jeffrey Biggs, "Political Knowledge: Confessions of a Staffer," *Civilization* (April/May, 2000): 65. The author was an assistant to former House Speaker Tom Foley.

88. Ibid.

89. Alan Ehrenhalt, "In the Senate of the '80s, Team Spirit Has Given Way to the Rule of Individuals," *Congressional Quarterly Weekly Report,* September 4, 1982, p. 2175.

90. Ronald Moe and Steven Teel, "Congress as a Policy-Maker: A Necessary Reappraisal," *Political Science Quarterly* 85 (September 1970): 443–470.

91. Bruce Oppenheimer, "The Rules Committee," in *Congress Reconsidered,* ed. Lawrence Dodd and Bruce Oppenheimer (New York: Praeger, 1977), 96–116.

92. Thomas Geoghegan, "Bust the Filibuster," *Washington Post National Weekly Edition,* July 12–18, 1994, p. 25.

93. Quoted in Sarah A. Binder and Steven S. Smith, "The Politics and Principle of the Senate Filibuster," in *Extensions* (Norman: University of Oklahoma, Carl A. Albert Center, Fall 1997), 15–16.

94. Michael Malbin, "Leading a Filibustered Senate," in *Extensions* (Norman: University of Oklahoma, Carl A. Albert Center, Spring 1985), 3.

95. Louis Fisher, "A Washington Guidebook," *Public Administration Review* (January/February 1989): 86.

96. Morris Ogul, "Congressional Oversight: Structures and Incentives," in Dodd and Oppenheimer, *Congress Reconsidered.* See also Loch Johnson, "The U.S. Congress and the CIA: Monitoring the Dark Side of Government," *Legislative Studies Quarterly* 5 (November 1980): 477–501.

97. Joseph Califano, "Imperial Congress," *New York Times Magazine,* January 23, 1994, p. 41.

98. Morris Fiorina, "Congressional Control of the Bureaucracy: A Mismatch of Incentives and Capabilities," in Dodd and Oppenheimer, *Congress Reconsidered,* pp. 332–348.

99. Aaron Wildavsky, *The Politics of the Budgetary Process* (Boston: Little, Brown, 1964).

100. D. Roderick Kiewiet and Matthew McCubbins, "Congressional Appropriations and the Electoral Connection," *Journal of Politics* 47 (February 1985): 59–82.

101. John Hibbing, "The Liberal Hour: Electoral Pressures and Transfer Payment Voting in the United States Congress," *Journal of Politics* 46 (August 1984), pp. 846–865.

102. Allen Schick, *Congress and Money* (Washington, D.C.: Urban Institute, 1980).

103. Michael Wines, "Washington Really Is in Touch. We're the Problem," *New York Times* (October 16, 1994), section 4, p. 2.

104. John Hibbing and Elizabeth Theiss-Morse, *Congress as Public Enemy* (Cambridge, Mass.: Cambridge University Press, 1995). The next three paragraphs draw from this source.

105. Richard Fenno, "U.S. House Members and Their Constituencies: An Exploration," *American Political Science Review* 71 (September 1977): 883–917.

106. Ibid.

107. The information in this paragraph comes from Karen Foerstel, "Grass Greener After Congress," *Congressional Quarterly Weekly Report,* March 11, 2000, 515–519.

108. Richard Morin and Thomas Edsall, "Bumping Up against the Public Perception," *Washington Post National Weekly Edition,* April 17–23, 1995, p. 14. See also John Hibbing and Elizabeth Theiss-Morse," Civics Is Not Enough," *PS* 29 (March 1996), pp. 57–62.

109. David S. Broder, "Manpower Bill Shows Good Intentions Sometimes Survive," *Lincoln Journal-Star,* October 18, 1995, p. 9B.

110. Bill Turque, "Housebroken," *Newsweek,* November 29, 1993, p. 32.

111. Ibid. See also Margolies-Mezvinsky's story in "Freshman Rush—First You Run to Get Elected, Then You Just Keep Running," *Washingtonian Magazine* (April 1993): 76–80.

The Presidency

YOU ARE THERE

Stand by Your Man?

It is January 1998, and the *Washington Post* has broken another story about President Clinton's personal life. Now the special prosecutor is investigating the possibility that the president obstructed justice by encouraging a White House intern, Monica Lewinsky, to lie under oath about his relationship with her. Some people in the press and a few in Congress are actually talking about the possibility of impeachment hearings, and the president and White House staff are in a grim mood about having to devote time and resources to fight another attack on the administration.

You are the second in command, Albert A. Gore, Jr., vice president of the United States. The press is dogging the president's every move, but they have an eye on you, too. As the president maps out his strategy for handling the allegations and related legal problems, you also have to consider how to respond. Almost everyone believes you will be running for president in two years. You have already built the basis of a formidable campaign organization and have more than a leg up on any challenger in the Democratic primaries.

Despite these advantages, your election is far from guaranteed. Although six of the last nine vice presidents have been nominated for the presidency, George Bush was the first sitting vice president to win the presidency since 1836 when Martin Van Buren did it. Common wisdom says this is because vice presidents get saddled with the negatives of the presidents they have served without being able to take credit for the successes. How will you maintain your claim to a share in Clinton administration successes without being associated with the allegations of ethical and personal wrongdoing that have dogged the president? Will you stand by your man through this new crisis, or will you try to put some distance between yourself and the president so that, whatever happens, the damage to your future candidacy will be minimized?

The president is about to embark on his first trip outside Washington since the Lewinsky scandal hit the papers. As usual he is following up his State of the Union address by taking his message directly to the people, this year to Illinois and Wisconsin. You helped pick the sites for this year's visits, and the suggestion that you should accompany the president was meant to benefit you.[1] For the first time in your career you had been accused of serious—possibly criminal—wrongdoing,

Photograph for *Time* by Cynthia Johnson

violating campaign finance laws by accepting money from foreign nationals. When questioned by the press, you appeared completely flustered and answered the questions poorly. To boost your image, the president agrees that you should travel with him to the Midwest after his State of the Union address. The administration has been riding high on good economic news, including the lowest unemployment and inflation rates in a quarter century. Clinton's popularity ratings are unusually high for a minority president halfway through the second term of an administration that has been plagued by scandals. He hopes some of the ratings gloss will rub off on you.

But now, quickly, the tables are turned. The Justice Department has cleared you of any wrongdoing in fundraising, while the president is reeling from the new charges against him. Now it seems that your presence on the trip may be a boon to him. Is it time to lie low, even at the risk of appearing self-serving and disloyal, or is it time to go to the mat for a friend and political ally?

No president and vice president in the history of the country have had a closer working relationship than you and Clinton. You are both southerners, moderate Democrats, Ivy Leaguers, baby-boomers, and rock-and-rollers, and you have both spent most of your adult lives in electoral politics. You complement the president in many ways: your work on environmental issues shored up his mediocre record on environmental protection as governor of Arkansas; you have a special interest in the role of high technology in economic development, whereas he has been slow to adapt to the computer age; you served in Vietnam and he evaded the draft; you are a Washington insider while he is an outsider; you have a squeaky clean image in both your public and personal life, while the president has been seen as a deal maker and political compromiser and as someone with a rather undisciplined personal life.

In return, Clinton complements your many weaknesses as a campaigner. In contrast to your oft-described wooden demeanor and speaking style, he appears open and accessible and is a master of working the fence and extemporaneous speaking; and in his years of leading the Democratic Council, he gained a reputation as a policy wonk to match or surpass yours as an "eco-techno-nerd." You made a run for the presidency in 1988 and failed; running for vice president on the ticket with Clinton has revitalized your political career. You owe him.

On the other hand, Clinton owes you. You have been a loyal stand-in, friend, and adviser. He has been accused of zigzagging across the policy map, but you stayed right with him, never striking out an independent policy line or even hinting at it. Through all his troubled times, you have been at his side in public saying great things about him. But Clinton has not been ungrateful. Whereas many presidents have refused their vice presidents any significant policy or advising role, and sometimes even shut them out of the information loop completely, Clinton has made you a full partner in his administration. You are in on the big meetings and have become one of his closest advisers; his staff and yours work closely to coordinate activities of the two offices. During his first term, he put you in charge of some priority issues, such as downsizing government and environmental and high-tech policy. He has let you be out front with the press and has helped you make the vice presidency as visible as the office has ever been. Never appearing insecure about a possible contender within his own ranks, Clinton shows little reluctance to add to your political capital at every opportunity. He has let you use the vice presidency in an unprecedented way to prepare for your own run for the presidency in 2000.

But as a politician, Clinton knows that if scandal overtakes his administration it could ruin your chances in the primaries in 2000. As a friend and a political realist, he would certainly cut you some slack. So he would surely understand if you tried to carve out some space for yourself to ensure that your campaign is not taken out by flying debris before you even announce your candidacy. Do you accompany the president into untested waters, stand by his side, and reaffirm your faith in his leadership? Or do you have a scheduling conflict and stay in Washington?

Pharaohs, consuls, kings, queens, emperors, czars, prime ministers, and councils of various sizes served as executives in other governments before 1789. But no national government had a president, an elected executive with authority equal to and independent of a national legislature, until we elected George Washington.

The Founders viewed their creation as a chief executive officer, someone who would serve as both a check on bills passed by Congress and the administrator of those enacted into law. He would also be head of state, chief diplomat, and commander of the armed forces. At its inception the presidency was a not very powerful office of a fledgling country with few international ties and virtually no standing army. The office's first occupants were drawn from among the Founders; a few of them, Washington and Jefferson especially, served with some reluctance. Nevertheless, they were willing to lend their reputations and abilities to the cause of stabilizing the new government, and as a result, they had the opportunity to influence the direction of its development.

Throughout the nineteenth century, except for the Civil War period, real power at the national level resided in Congress, so much so that Woodrow Wilson characterized the federal arrangement in the 1880s as "congressional government." Thus, between Andrew Jackson and Franklin Roosevelt, many who sought the presidency were "ordinary people, with very ordinary reputations."[2] There were powerful exceptions, such as Abraham Lincoln, Theodore Roosevelt, and Woodrow Wilson, and a few, such as Civil War hero Ulysses S. Grant, who were able to convert military achievement into political victory.

Today the president of the United States is among the most powerful people in the world. By the 1970s, the scope of that power led one historian to write about an "imperial" presidency.[3] Yet most recent presidents have suffered reelection defeats and at times have seemed almost powerless to shape events affecting the national interest and their own reputations. A conservative Congress frustrated John Kennedy's policy initiatives before his assassination. Lyndon Johnson's bid for reelection was killed by a war that took Richard Nixon six years to end. And Nixon had to resign from office because of his Watergate cover-up. Ronald Reagan, one of our most popular presidents, was so frustrated when Congress thwarted his foreign policy initiatives that he condoned illegal activities, producing the Iran-Contra scandal and a tarnished personal reputation. Gerald Ford, Jimmy Carter, and George Bush failed to get reelected. At century's end, Bill Clinton discovered that instead of an imperial presidency, we may have an "impossible" or "imperiled" presidency.[4] Little wonder that a survey found that 52 percent of Americans would rather spend one week in jail than serve one term as president and that many Americans, instead of believing the president is too powerful, believe he is too weak to battle Congress and interest groups.[5]

In this chapter we will consider the paradox of presidential power and presidential weakness. After describing the growth of the modern presidency, we look at the constitutional provisions—the qualifications for the office and its responsibilities. We explain why a bureaucracy grew up around the presidency at the same time the president was becoming a more personal and accessible representative of the American people. Inevitably, the growth of the modern presidency has affected the balance of power between the executive and legislative branches, and that is another topic of this chapter.

The Growth of the Presidency

Someone once said that Americans were lucky because we always got presidential leadership when we needed it: during the birth of the nation, the Civil War, and foreign crises. This implies that our needs change, that we need more government and executive leadership during crises and less at other times. Presidential power was traditionally supposed to return to its "normal" low profile after we resolved special problems.

This expectation may have been realistic before the United States became a unified country that accepted Washington as the center of governmental power. But once the country stretched from Mexico to Canada and from the Atlantic to the Pacific, once it had a standing army and the ambition to control foreign intervention

Although political scientists rank Jefferson as a great president, he did not consider the office, or his performance in it, very important. His instructions for an epitaph listed what he thought were his three main accomplishments in life: authoring the Declaration of Independence and a Virginia law guaranteeing religious freedom and founding the University of Virginia. He did not include his two terms as president.
The Granger Collection, New York

in the hemisphere, and once it developed international trade aspirations, governmental power gravitated to Washington. The image of Thomas Jefferson sitting at his desk in isolation week after week conducting the presidency by personal correspondence was a quaint memory even twenty years later when Andrew Jackson was dubbed the "people's president."[6] Jackson was the first to act assertively to fulfill the popular mandate he saw in his election—the first to veto a bill because *he* did not like it. Thirty years later Lincoln boldly interpreted the Constitution to say individual states could not legally leave the Union, thereby setting the stage for the Civil War.

Teddy Roosevelt, who has been called the "preacher militant," used the presidency in an unprecedented way to challenge corporate power and to argue for labor reform and better living conditions for average Americans. He also saw an imperial role for the United States in world politics, especially through military expansion, and led the country toward those "entangling alliances" that Thomas Jefferson had warned against. Eight years after Roosevelt left office, Wilson became the first twentieth-century president to lead us into a major foreign involvement, World War I, and was the first president ever to travel to Europe while in office.

As we have already seen in Chapter 3, the Great Depression led to a large expansion in the role of the national government and tremendous growth in presidential power. Franklin Roosevelt was elected president in 1932 because people thought he would help them. His policies, which he called the New Deal, put the national government and the presidency in direct contact with many citizens for the first time. People saw presidential leadership as a way to deal with national needs. It was Roosevelt, not Congress, who provided the vision and legislative program to cope with the economic emergencies of the Great Depression. In his first inaugural address, he told Americans that he would ask Congress for "broad executive power" to fight the crisis, equivalent, he said, to what he might be granted if an enemy had invaded the country. The enactment of the New Deal programs led to an expansion of the executive branch because new agencies had to be created and new civil servants hired. This increased the president's power by making him more important as a manager and policymaker.

Radio and television also contributed to the expansion of presidential power. As an integral part of national life by the 1930s, broadcasting made the news seem more immediate and compelling. Along with the wire services, it gave people a way to follow presidents and a way for presidents to "sell" their policies and provide leadership. Because it is easier to follow one person than many (as in

Congress), the media helped make the presidency the focal point of national politics. With his radio broadcasts during the Great Depression, Roosevelt became a kind of national cheerleader, a one-man band of optimism, persuading the public that solutions were at hand.

Congress is not structured to provide this kind of national leadership. Its 535 members are divided into two houses and hundreds of committees and subcommittees and come from both major political parties. It is difficult for either the majority or minority leadership to develop, articulate, or keep its members faithful to national policy goals.

Even after the fifteen years of crisis receded, Roosevelt's successors had little opportunity to shrink the presidency. With the United States emerging from World War II as the preeminent world power, and with the onset of the Cold War, Congress was willing to cede even more leadership to the president to counter Soviet rivalry. Responsibilities as chief diplomat and commander in chief of the world's largest military establishment have made the president a principal actor in world politics, a platform not afforded to any other government official or institution.

Of his postwar administration, Harry Truman said, "Being president is like riding a tiger. You have to stay on or get swallowed." And thus we have today's presidency, with everyone looking to see if the man is riding the tiger or the tiger is swallowing the man.

Terms of Office

Qualifications

There are formal, constitutional qualifications to be president: one must be a "natural born citizen," at least thirty-five years old, and a resident of the United States for at least fourteen years before taking office.

Informally, it also helps to be a white male with roots in small-town America; a Protestant of English, German, or Scandinavian background; a resident of a state with a large population; and a good family man. In recent years, however, this profile has broadened considerably as society has become more tolerant of diversity. Nevertheless, some gender and racial barriers remain, although they are eroding.

Rewards

In return for services rendered, the Constitution authorized Congress to award the president "a Compensation," which could be neither increased nor de-

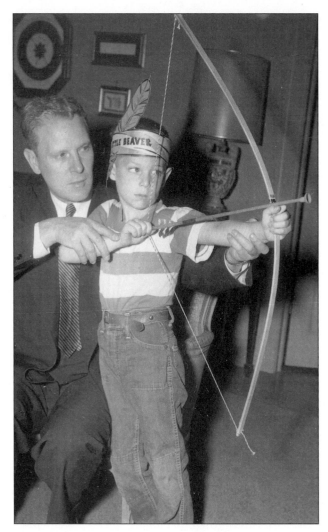

America does not have a monarchy, but it does have political dynasties. Both major party candidates in 2000 were sons of important American political leaders. Al Gore, on the left, is shown with his father, Albert Gore, Sr., Democratic senator from Tennessee, who was known for his support for civil rights and opposition to the Vietnam War. George W. Bush, shown with his father, former president, vice president, and Republican House member George Bush, is also the grandson of a U.S. senator.
Left: Corbis/Bettmann—United Press International. Right: George Bush Presidential Library

creased during a president's term of office. Our first seventeen presidents received an annual salary of $25,000. Grant got the first raise in 1873, a doubling to $50,000. The salary was $200,000 when Nixon took office. A majority of the public opposed a pay increase even as executive salaries skyrocketed in the 1990s.[7] By 1999 the president's salary ranked him 785 among the 800 highest paid CEOs, and under a cost-of-living allowance granted to Congress and to other executive branch officials, the vice president would be outearning him by 2005. Supporters of a pay increase argued that the president's low salary was holding down the base pay for all other top-level officials and interfering with government recruitment. Congress agreed, and effective 2001 the president will receive $400,000 per year and the vice president $181,400. Presidents also receive $50,000 for expenses and $100,000 for travel. In addition there are *substantial* fringe benefits. These include living quarters in one of the world's most famous mansions, a rural retreat in Maryland (Camp David), the best health care money can buy, and fleets of cars and aircraft. After leaving office, the president is entitled to a generous pension, as well as a security detail and money for an office and staff.

Tenure

Presidents serve four-year terms. The Twenty-second Amendment limits them to serving two terms, or ten years if they complete the term of an incumbent who dies or resigns. Four presidents have died in office from illness (Harrison, Taylor, Harding, and Franklin Roosevelt), and four were assassinated (Garfield, McKinley, Lincoln, and Kennedy).

Presidents can be removed from office for "Treason, Bribery, or other high Crimes and Misdemeanors" (Article II). The Founders established the impeachment option as part of the system of checks and balances, a final weapon against executive abuse of power. But, as retained, impeachment was intended to be a fundamentally legal procedure for removing a president whose offenses were "political," only in the sense, Hamilton wrote in *The Federalist* 65, that they are "injuries done immediately to society itself." Impeachment was adapted from British law, where it had served, according to Jefferson (who was not present at the writing of the Constitution), as "an engine more of passion than of justice."[8] (Britain last used impeachment in 1788, just as the United States was writing it into its Constitution.) Madison, who *was* present at the drafting, objected to the inclusion of the "and other high crimes and misdemeanors" phrase in the impeachment article precisely because he thought it was so vague it could be used for political purposes. Through a compromise brokered by George Mason it was retained.[9]

The procedure is cumbersome and meant to be; the Founders did not intend for the president, as head of state and the only nationally elected official in government, to be removed from office easily. Like the other major powers, the impeachment process is divided. The House has the power of **impeachment**—that is, the authority to bring formal charges against the president (similar to an indictment in criminal proceedings)—but the Senate has the power of removal. The Founders recognized that impeachment could become the partisan tool Jefferson feared because the process itself would "agitate the passions of the whole community." If trying the charges were left to the popularly elected House, Hamilton wrote in *Federalist* 65, "There will always be the greatest danger that the decision will be regulated more by the comparative strength of parties, than by the real demonstrations of innocence or guilt." What body, Hamilton asked, other than the (then unelected) Senate would be likely to feel *confidence enough in its own situation,* to preserve, unawed and uninfluenced, the necessary impartiality between an *individual* accused, and the *representatives of the people, his accuser?*" (Italics in original)

The House holds hearings to determine whether there is sufficient evidence to impeach, and if a majority votes yes, the president is impeached, and the process moves to the Senate, where a trial is held with the chief justice presiding. Conviction requires a two-thirds vote of members present in the Senate and results in removal from the presidency and, if the Senate so votes, loss of the right to hold other federal office. Under a 1958 law, conviction also results in the loss of all benefits, including pension, office and staff allowance, and Secret Service protection. The Senate can assign no additional punishment. Where applicable, however, a president removed from office can be subject to criminal charges and prosecuted through the court system.

Only three presidents have been targets of full impeachment proceedings. Andrew Johnson, who came to office on Lincoln's assassination, was a southerner who was unpopular in his own party; he was impeached by the House in a dispute over enforcement of Reconstruction policies in the post–Civil War South. The Senate failed to convict by a single vote. A century later the House Judiciary Committee voted to impeach Richard Nixon on obstruction of justice and other charges stemming from the Watergate scandal, but by resigning, Nixon prevented a vote by the full House and almost certain conviction in the Senate. Once out of office he avoided possible indictment on criminal charges through a full pardon granted by his successor, Gerald Ford. In 1998 Bill Clinton became the third target of the process when the House voted to open an unrestricted inquiry into possible grounds for his impeachment. After a $47 million investigation by Independent Counsel Kenneth Starr, the House held hearings and, in 1998, voted two articles of impeachment against President Clinton. All eleven charges of perjury and obstruction of justice stemmed from Clinton's testimony in the Paula Jones civil suit and from statements about his relationship with a White House intern. After a nationally televised trial, the Senate failed to convict, with neither article receiving even a majority of the vote.[10] Still, Clinton stands as the only elected president ever to be impeached. He was also cited for contempt and fined by a federal judge for misleading grand jury testimony and threatened with loss of his license to practice law. In addition, the independent counsel has held open the possibility that Clinton will face criminal charges after leaving office.

Succession

The original wording of the Constitution provided only that presidential powers "shall devolve on the Vice Pres-

ident" should the president die, resign, be removed, or become incapacitated. At the time the Constitution was written, it was assumed that the vice presidency would be occupied by the man who had been the runner-up in the presidential election. It was left to Congress to make provisions for a situation in which both the presidency and the vice presidency had been vacated. When Lincoln was assassinated, there were no provisions for replacing the vice president when the office was left vacant. Had Andrew Johnson been convicted in his impeachment trial, the presidency would have gone to the president pro tempore of the Senate who, according to rules in effect at the time, was the next in line of succession.

Not until 1947, two years after the death of Franklin Roosevelt had put the virtually unknown Harry Truman in the White House, did Congress pass the Presidential Succession Act. It establishes the order of succession of federal officeholders should both the president and the vice president be unable to serve. The list begins with the Speaker of the House, followed by the president pro tempore of the Senate, and then proceeds through the secretaries of the cabinet departments in the order in which the departments were created.

The Succession Act has never been used because we have always had a vice president when something happened to the president. The Twenty-fifth Amendment was ratified in 1967 to ensure, as much as possible, that this will always be the case. In the event that the vice presidency falls vacant, the amendment directs the president to name a new vice president acceptable to ma-

jorities in the House and Senate. The amendment has been used twice. Nixon chose Gerald Ford to replace Spiro Agnew, who resigned after pleading no contest to charges of taking bribes when he was a public official in Maryland. After Nixon resigned and Ford became president, Ford named Nelson Rockefeller, the former governor of New York, as his vice president.

The Twenty-fifth Amendment also charges the vice president and a majority of the cabinet—or some other body named by Congress—to determine, in instances where there is doubt, whether the president is mentally or physically incapable of carrying out his duties. This provision was meant to provide for situations in which it is unclear who is or should be acting as president, such as when James Garfield was shot in July 1881. He did not die until mid-September, and during this period he was completely unable to fulfill his duties. In 1919, Woodrow Wilson had a nervous collapse in the summer and a stroke in the fall and was partially incapacitated for seven months. No one was sure about his condition, however, because his wife restricted access to him.

Under the amendment's provisions, the vice president becomes "acting president" if the president is found mentally or physically unfit to fulfill his duties. As the title suggests, the conferral of power is temporary; the president can resume office by giving Congress written notice of his recovery. Reagan followed the spirit of this section in 1985. Before undergoing cancer surgery, he sent his vice president, George Bush, a letter authorizing him to act as president while Reagan was unconscious.

If the vice president and other officials who determined the president unfit do not concur in his judgment that he has recovered, they can challenge his return to office by notifying Congress in writing. Then it falls to Congress to decide whether the president is capable of resuming his duties.

Duties and Powers of Office

The original source of presidential power lies in the formal duties assigned by the Constitution. Additional authority stems from powers the federal courts have ruled are implied by the president's constitutional mandate, delegated authority from Congress, and informal powers acquired through the exercise of office.

Chief Executive

The enumeration of the president's formal duties begins with the simple statement that "Executive power shall be invested in a President. . . ." The Founders expected Congress to make policy and the president to administer it. The Constitution has few provisions that describe the president's administrative duties, but it does invest the president with the authority to demand written reports from his "principal officers." The Constitution also directs the president to nominate the most important officers of the executive branch.

The president was given power neither to create executive branch departments and agencies nor to fund them—this authority resides with Congress—so his means for controlling the bureaucracy over which he presides lies in his formal powers of appointment, his implied power to remove those he appoints, and his delegated authority to reorganize agencies and make budget recommendations.

Appointing Officials

The president nominates about 1,300 people to policy-making jobs in executive agencies and to positions as U.S. attorneys and marshals, ambassadors, and members of part-time boards and commissions. All appointments to these positions require Senate confirmation. Another 1,140 presidential appointments to senior civil service jobs do not need Senate approval.

In practice, the president's freedom to name people to some positions is limited by the custom of **senatorial courtesy.** This gives senators from the president's party

a virtual veto over appointments to positions, including judicial appointments, in their states. As the leader of his party, the president has a political (not governmental) obligation to help senators from his party get reelected. So he usually defers to their political needs and wishes when making federal appointments in their home states, even though doing so limits to some extent his freedom to choose.

Presidents have more latitude in nominating people to positions with national jurisdictions, such as cabinet posts and seats on regulatory boards and independent agencies. It has become customary to give preference in some appointments to people with politically useful backgrounds, such as naming a westerner secretary of the interior, a person with union ties to be labor secretary, or a close associate of the president to be attorney general. But these considerations were never confining and, as traditions, seem to be weakening.

It has also been customary for the Senate, no matter which party controls it, to approve the president's nominations to policymaking positions on the grounds that, having won the election, he is entitled to surround himself with people who can help put his policies in place. In the contentiousness of recent years, this practice also seems to be weakening. A Democrat-controlled Congress challenged several high-profile appointments made by Reagan and Bush, and under Republican control Congress has tabled or defeated many of Clinton's nominations.

Removing Officials

Although the power to remove appointees is not in the Constitution, presidents have it. Their power to name people they trust implies a power to remove those they find wanting, but because the power is not explicit, Congress has not always recognized it. The battle over removal powers was fought and largely won by Grover Cleveland, who on entering office in 1885 insisted on replacing many policymaking officials with his own appointees. Although the Senate challenged Cleveland, he persevered. His persistence is credited with helping revitalize a presidency still weakened by Johnson's impeachment.

In 1935, the Supreme Court refined this removal power by saying that presidents can remove appointees from purely administrative jobs but not from those with quasi-legislative and judicial responsibilities. Although this ruling protects many appointees, distinguishing quasi-legislative and judicial positions from those with no policymaking authority can be subjective.[11]

Of course, presidents can appoint and remove their political aides and advisers at will; none of these appointments require Senate approval. Presidents also have wide latitude in replacing cabinet heads and some agency directors—even though these positions do require Senate confirmation—because they are seen as agents of presidential policy. This does not keep the Senate from trying at times to badger a president into firing one of his appointees, as it did repeatedly with Clinton's attorney general, Janet Reno. A president may give in for political reasons, but the Senate cannot compel him to do so.

Presidents cannot remove the people they appoint to policymaking bodies on fixed-term appointments, as is the case with regulatory boards, the Federal Reserve Board, and the federal courts. To grant the president this power would interfere with the system of checks and balances among the executive, legislative, and judicial functions of government.

Reorganizing Executive Branch Agencies

When the president enters office, a huge bureaucracy is already in place. Each new president has to be able to reorganize offices and agencies to fit his administrative and working style and to be consistent with the issue priorities he has set.[12]

Since the 1930s, presidents have had the authority to submit plans to Congress to reorganize parts of the ex-

ecutive branch. This means redrawing agency boundaries to promote coordination when actions overlap or duplicate each other. It may involve merging or abolishing offices or creating new ones. If Congress approves the plan, the president issues a directive that puts the new organization, councils, or offices in place. Within the White House Office itself, the president has a fairly free hand to reshuffle staff and offices; see the discussion of the White House Office later. Nixon, for example, merged a number of offices to create the Domestic Policy Council to improve White House coordination of domestic programs. Clinton created the National Economic Council to coordinate departments and agencies that shape economic policy and to show that economic issues are a high priority for him.

Budget Making

The Founders gave Congress, and particularly the House of Representatives, the power of the purse. For many years the president had a negligible role in managing executive branch budgets. Agency funding requests went to the House unreviewed and unchanged by the White House. But by the end of World War I, a general awareness had developed that a larger government required better management. In the Budget and Accounting Act of 1921, Congress delegated important priority-setting and managerial responsibilities that have contributed to the president's dominance in budgetary politics.

The 1921 act requires the president to give Congress estimates of how much money will be needed to run the government during the next fiscal year. The president's annual budget message contains recommendations for how much money Congress should appropriate for every program funded by the national government. Formulating the message requires the White House to examine all agency budget requests and to decide which to support or reject. This exercise allows the president and his staff to initiate the annual budget debate on their own terms.

In addition, the act created the Bureau of the Budget (BOB). Originally a part of the Treasury Department, BOB was meant to be the president's primary tool in developing budget policy. It was made a part of the newly created Executive Office of the President in 1939. Nixon changed BOB's name to the Office of Management and Budget (OMB) to stress its function of helping the president manage the executive branch.

The process of writing and passing the annual budget resolutions is one of the greatest sources of friction in presidential-congressional relations. Without funding, little is possible. Having the OMB within the Executive Office of the President gives the president an edge in dealing with Congress on budget issues because its hundreds of experts work only for the president. Congress's nonpartisan budget office, the Congressional Budget Office (CBO), prepares budget reports that are regarded as substantially more reliable than those of the OMB, but the policy initiative lies with the OMB and the White House because they prepare the first budget draft. The annual budget is huge and hard to read and understand. Because the president presents it to Congress and the public, he has the opportunity to shape the debate over spending priorities. Presidents who are little interested in the details of domestic policy, such as Reagan and Bush, do not get maximum political leverage out of the budgetary powers Congress has delegated them. But a president whose strength lies in the mastery of detail may be able to use those powers, as Clinton did to dominate budgetary politics and the debate over deficit reduction.

The OMB not only proposes allocations for each department, agency, and program of the federal government, but it also monitors how and when executive branch agencies spend appropriated funds, their operating procedures, and the policies they develop. This gives the president another advantage over Congress, one that Reagan used to great advantage. By appointing agency and department heads who oppose policies he opposes but that Congress has funded, the president can issue directives that effectively bring policy implementation to a halt.

Other Executive Powers

In addition to the formal administrative powers granted under Article II and those delegated by Congress, federal courts have upheld additional powers that presidents have claimed are necessary to the administration of the executive branch.

Executive Privilege Since the 1970s, the courts have upheld the presidential claim to **executive privilege,** the right of a president to refuse to make public some internal documents and private conversations. The rulings have argued that executive privilege is a power inherent in the president's duty as chief executive because without it a president would not be able to get full and frank advice from his aides. Although ruling that the power is limited rather than absolute in scope, the courts have not defined its limits. In the landmark ruling ordering President Nixon to turn over tapes of Oval Office conversations to the Watergate special prosecutor

(see Chapter 2, "You Are There"), the Supreme Court did establish that executive privilege cannot be invoked to withhold evidence material to an investigation of criminal wrongdoing.

In the 1970s the federal courts requested that Congress specify the limits of the privilege, but it declined, leaving it to the courts to resolve each invocation of privilege that the president and Congress cannot resolve. President Clinton interpreted this power very broadly. He claimed that senior aides could not be required to answer certain questions put to them by a grand jury convened by the special prosecutor investigating possible obstruction of justice charges against the president. His reason was that their answers would make public the content of privileged conversations with the president. Clinton asked the federal courts to extend the cover of executive privilege to his conversations about political strategy with his aides and to those between his aides and the First Lady, whom he regards as a political adviser and whom the courts had already recognized as serving a quasi-official role. In 1998 the lower federal courts again confirmed the right to executive privilege and its application to conversations between the president, aides, and the First Lady. But it ruled against the president on the circumstances under which he invoked the privilege (withholding information from a grand jury hearing evidence about possible criminal wrongdoing), saying the aides' testimony might be relevant to the investigation. The administration did not appeal the ruling.

Executive Orders Because the Constitution charges the president with ensuring that "the laws be faithfully executed," the courts have ruled that the president has inherent power to take actions and issue orders to fulfill that duty. This gives the president the authority to issue directives or proclamations, called **executive orders,** that have the force of law and are therefore a form of legislative power residing in the executive branch. In arguing for these powers, presidents have claimed that "Article II of the Constitution grants them inherent power to take whatever actions they judge to be in the nation's best interests as long as those actions are not prohibited by the Constitution or by law." The rationale is that Congress often lacks the expertise and ability to act quickly when technological or other developments require fast action and flexibility.[13]

The recording and numbering of executive orders did not begin until 1907, and although an effort was made to identify and retroactively number orders issued back to the Lincoln administration, it is uncertain how many have been issued over the years. Since 1946, Congress has required all executive orders, except those dealing with classified national security issues, to be published in the *Federal Register*.[14] Many of these orders have had a significant impact. Truman, for example, used an executive order to integrate the armed forces, Kennedy to end racial discrimination in public housing, and Lyndon Johnson to require affirmative action hiring by firms with federal contracts.

Executive orders are used to implement the provisions of treaties and legislative statutes that are ambiguously stated (perhaps deliberately) by Congress. In fact, presidents have used executive orders to make policies opposed by congressional majorities. Reagan and Bush used this power to ban abortion counseling in federally financed clinics and financial aid to United Nations–sponsored family planning programs. Clinton canceled these orders in his first week in office. Thus, through the exercise of this inherent power of office the presidency has acquired significant legislative authority.

Executive orders are also commonly used by presidents to carry out more purely administrative duties in the form of directives issued to executive branch offices. These often deal with organizational problems and internal procedures, such as restructuring executive branch departments and agencies (discussed above). The contro-versial system used to classify government documents and withhold information from the public was established by executive order.

Head of State

As chief executive, the president is the presiding officer or head of government. But in our form of republic, the head of government is also the head of state; this arrangement is not common among Western democracies. A **head of state** is the official representative of a country, the person whose office symbolizes the collective unity and identity of the nation. When our president stands in public behind the Great Seal of the United States of America, he is not just a politician who was elected to govern but a nonpartisan representative of all the people, entrusted with the symbols, emblems, and traditions of the country. The unifying, nonpolitical nature of the role that the head of state is meant to serve is the reason why some countries separate this office (sometimes filled by a king or queen) from that of head of government. The latter is usually filled by the leader of a political party, who is by definition partisan. But the American president has to wear two hats, and members of Congress, the press, or the public who may attack him

As symbolic leaders, presidents often congratulate national sports heroes. Here, President Calvin Coolidge (a Republican, who served from 1923 to 1928 and was aptly known as "Silent Cal") presents a trophy to a Marine football team after its victory over Army. *New York Times*

freely in his partisan role as head of government usually show more deference when the president is acting in his capacity as head of state.

These duties include serving as official representative of the United States at a variety of state and ceremonial occasions both at home and abroad. It could be opening the Olympic Games; lighting the White House Christmas tree; attending the swearing in, coronation, or funeral of a foreign head of state; or serving as official greeter when a foreign head of state visits this country. The head of state is also empowered to take actions that symbolize national sentiment, such as issuing proclamations to commemorate events, or making gestures that express a humane national spirit, as in the granting of reprieves and pardons to people convicted of federal crimes.

In exercising the power of pardon, the president usually consults Justice Department lawyers and the relevant U.S. attorneys, but he is not required to do so. On his own authority he can erase guilt and restore the civil rights of anyone convicted of a federal crime, except an impeached president. One of Lincoln's last acts, signed the day he was assassinated, was to pardon a Union army deserter. Blanket pardons have been issued to Confederate Army veterans and Vietnam draft dodgers, but most presidents have used the power to clear the names of minor offenders who have served their sentences. Using it to absolve government officials or persons convicted of crimes with political overtones can evoke strong public reactions, as Bush found out when he pardoned Reagan's secretary of defense and five other officials charged with or convicted of crimes related to the Iran-Contra scandal. In all, Clinton used his pardon powers a rather paltry 146 times during his first seven years in office. This total compares to the 2,044 issued by Truman and well over a thousand each for Eisenhower and Lyndon Johnson.[15]

As head of state, the president is required by the Constitution to report to Congress "from time to time" about the "State of the Union." He notes the successes of the past year, addresses problems, and outlines his policy agenda for the coming year. Part of the report inevitably deals with the mood of the country and identifies goals for maintaining or increasing national unity.

Today these addresses are televised and delivered in the House of Representatives before a joint session of Congress at the start of each congressional session. The president is received as head of state, rather than as partisan head of government. Even when presidents are mired in political controversy at the time of the speech—Nixon during the Watergate investigation, or

Clinton in 1998, delivering the State of the Union address just weeks after the revelation of allegations of personal wrongdoing—congressional leaders usually caution the membership to show due respect to a person who is speaking in his constitutional role as head of state.

Chief Diplomat

As head of state, the president is given ceremonial powers "to receive Ambassadors and other public Ministers." In practice this means that when a country appoints a person to represent its interests to the United States, that ambassador must present his or her credentials to the president and have them accepted before taking up office. What appears to be a ceremonial duty has real potential for the making of foreign policy because the power to accept or reject foreign ambassadors, by extension, gives the president the power to decide which governments we will recognize and which we will shut out. Recognition is not automatic. We did not recognize the Soviet government until sixteen years after the Bolshevik Revolution of 1917 or that of the communist government of mainland China until over twenty-five years after it took power.

Article II also gives the president the power to make treaties with other countries, subject to Senate approval, and 'to appoint ambassadors and consuls to represent us abroad. In addition, the article contains implied powers, which were acknowledged by the Supreme Court in a 1936 decision.[16] Congress had authorized Franklin Roosevelt to ban arms sales to warring Bolivia and Paraguay, but a military aircraft manufacturer claimed that Congress lacked the constitutional authority to delegate such power. The Court ruled against the corporation, saying that the United States, like every nation, has implied powers to promote its interests in the world. The Court said there is a logic behind presidential power in foreign policy. A nation's government must be able to speak with one voice because having more than one voice can lead to confusion about what is official policy and therefore about what actions might be taken.

Commander in Chief

Using the military to achieve national goals is one way presidents conduct foreign policy. The Founders made the president "commander-in-chief." By this they meant that the president would be the "first general" and "first admiral," as Alexander Hamilton wrote in *Federalist* 69.

As the nation's foreign policy leader, President Franklin Roosevelt edited his own speech to Congress about the Japanese attack on Pearl Harbor. He added the word that made memorable his phrase "a date which will live in infamy."
Franklin D. Roosevelt Library

Almost all presidents have had military experience. Nine achieved the rank of general, and six were propelled to the presidency by virtue of military fame (Washington, Jackson, W. H. Harrison, Taylor, Grant, and Eisenhower). Both Theodore and Franklin Roosevelt served as secretary of the navy, and FDR played an active role in directing the naval war against Japan. No sitting president has ever led troops into battle, but modern weapons have led to more presidential involvement.

The decision to wage a limited war in Vietnam was based on presidential beliefs that defeating North Vietnam was not worth risking a nuclear holocaust. Since the end of World War II, all wars the United States has been involved in have had limited objectives that justified proportional rather than unrestricted commitments of weaponry and human resources. Under our Constitution, these decisions on goals and containing the costs and consequences of war are for elected civilian leaders to make, not the professional military.

Other technological developments have also given presidents more military leadership opportunities. Johnson and Nixon used sophisticated communications equipment to select targets in Vietnam. In the Persian Gulf War, Bush used modern transportation facilities to send large numbers of troops to the Gulf quickly with the latest "smart" weapons. His White House sent so many orders to General Norman Schwarzkopf in the Gulf (from how to stop a blockade-running Iraqi tanker to ending the ground war before Iraq's army was destroyed) that the general complained of "a total vacuum of guidance" when disagreements in Washington stopped the flow of instructions.[20]

Despite congressional oversight of military policy, presidential power is wide ranging and increasingly controversial as troops frequently are used without a declaration of war or even congressional approval. But presidents have historically assumed and exercised the most power during wars endangering our national survival. During the Civil War, Lincoln suspended the use of writs of habeas corpus, seized control of some eastern railroads, and blockaded southern ports. He took these actions as commander in chief and without congressional authorization. The war jeopardized national unity, and Lincoln believed he had to take extraordinary measures. Because most people in the North agreed with him, he was able to do what he thought necessary.

Acting under his self-defined authority as commander in chief, Franklin Roosevelt put one hundred thousand Americans of Japanese descent into camps during World War II. He had the government seize and operate more

But the Founders did not want to give the president the sole power to make war. In the words of Connecticut's Roger Sherman, they believed "the Executive should be able to repel and not to commence war." The Founders feared that presidents, like the British kings from whom they had recently freed themselves, would be too eager to go to war.[17] So they gave Congress the power to declare war. James Madison expressed the view of several of the Founders when he argued that "the executive is the branch of power most interested in war and most prone to it. [The Constitution] has, accordingly, with studied care, vested the question of war in the legislature."[18] Thus, the Founders created a system of checks and balances in military affairs; the president commands the troops, but Congress has the power to declare war and to decide whether to authorize funds to pay for it. Thomas Jefferson thought this arrangement would be an "effectual check to the dog of war, by transferring the power of letting him loose from the executive to the legislative body, from those who are to spend to those who are to pay."[19]

Ronald Reagan, a man not known to have close personal friends in politics, did not fill his top staff positions with longtime friends and close associates.

Among their most trusted advisers, presidents often count friends who do not hold official positions but whom they have come to trust for candid, unguarded conversation. The lawyer and former civil rights activist Vernon Jordan, for example, became well known as Clinton's "first friend." Richard Nixon had businessman Bebe Rebozo as a confidante, and Lyndon Johnson had lawyer and lobbyist Abe Fortas, whom he eventually appointed to the Supreme Court. Many presidents have counted their wives among their closest advisers (see "Who Elected Her?").

Members of the White House Office have greater influence than most advisers because the president appoints all of them, works daily with them, and tends to trust them more than others. They are often people who helped him get elected or worked for him when he held other offices.

Presidents have used different styles in running the White House Office. Roosevelt and Kennedy cared little for rigid lines of responsibility. They gave staffers different jobs over time and fostered a competitive spirit: Who could serve the president best?

Lyndon Johnson's style was the archetype of aggressive, hands-on management. Known for his commitment to using all resources at his disposal to find government solutions to virtually every problem, Johnson was often accused of overworking and bullying his staff. In an incident that captures this approach, Johnson once turned to an aide who was desperately trying to keep him from engaging in an unscheduled event and asked in a "low threatening tone, 'Are we gonna join the Can't Do It Club right here. . . .?' "[25]

In contrast, Eisenhower's administration has been characterized as "the hidden hand presidency," because his management style masked his involvement in decision making.[26] He did not want to risk his popularity by being out front on issues and often appeared diffident around his advisers and cabinet officers. Following military habits, he delegated authority yet closely monitored all decisions.

Like Eisenhower, Nixon valued formal lines of authority. Nixon's chief of staff, H. R. Haldeman, saw his job this way: "Every president needs a son of a bitch, and I'm Nixon's. I'm his buffer and his bastard. I get done what he wants done and I take the heat instead of him."[27] Part of Nixon's approach was to be reclusive and keep his cards close to his vest. He demanded at least two days a week when he would have to see no one so he could work in seclusion; even his closest staff often did not know what he was working on.[28]

The Watergate scandal led presidents Ford and Carter to avoid the appearance of strong staff chiefs. Reagan prided himself on delegating authority to the best people and letting them do their work without interference.[29] Serious problems developed, however, because no one had authority to make final decisions on more important matters, and Reagan was too removed from daily affairs to do so. This detached management style had its costs, most noticeably the Iran-Contra scandal.[30] Problems produced by his detached management style led Reagan to appoint a series of strong staff chiefs whose coordination of White House operations helped restore his image.

George Bush had more hands-on involvement in policy, but he spent more time on foreign policy and delegated domestic issues to his staff. Clinton's White House organization puts him in the center of decision making. He directed his first staff chief to channel all paperwork to him so his appointees would not repeat the frustration of a Bush cabinet member who had to mail his views to Bush because Bush's first staff chief, John Sununu, sat on them.

Thus, Clinton's choice of many staffers with little Washington experience and diverse views, and his choice of his wife, Hillary Rodham Clinton, to develop and help sell his health reform proposal, showed his determination to be in command and to immerse himself

President Kennedy's closest adviser was his brother Robert, whom he appointed Attorney General.
UPI/Corbis-Bettmann

in policy details. However, running the White House this way made it difficult for Clinton to keep his and the nation's focus on important issues. He got so bogged down in details that his wife complained that he had become the "mechanic-in-chief."[31] Under Clinton's second and third staff chiefs, lines of authority and communication were tightened. But his White House operation still reflected his love of policy details and an inability to stick to a few clear policy themes in communicating with the public and the media.

Office of the First Lady

A small number of special presidential assistants on the White House Office staff are assigned to work full-time for the First Lady.[32] The First Lady's role is ill-defined: there is no mention of a presidential spouse in the Constitution, and she has no official position, no title, and no salary. Yet she is definitely expected to serve, especially as what Martha Washington called "the hostess of the nation."[33]

The visibility of the First Lady increased enormously after the arrival of photography in the mid–nineteenth century; mass circulation newspapers and magazines provided new means for satisfying public curiosity about the president's private life. There was heightened interest in seeing presidents' wives in public, and early in the twentieth century First Ladies began accompanying their husbands at official functions.

A quantum leap in the conception of the First Lady's role occurred during the administration of Franklin Roosevelt. Eleanor Roosevelt held press conferences (for women journalists shut out of the president's briefings), wrote a syndicated newspaper column read by millions, and made regular radio broadcasts. She discussed policy with her husband, bombarded him with memos, and brought supporters of the causes she advocated into the White House. She served on countless committees and traveled around the world promoting racial equality, women's and social welfare issues, and the war effort.

Mrs. Roosevelt's stature was attained under the exceptional circumstances of her husband's long tenure in the White House during a period of national crisis (the Great Depression and World War II). Furthermore, after his incapacitation from polio years earlier, FDR had become dependent on Eleanor to keep his political career afloat by serving as his stand-in and surrogate campaigner. In combination with their strained marriage, this meant that Mrs. Roosevelt entered the White House as much FDR's political partner as his wife.

But the evolution of the role of First Lady is not just simple incremental growth of duties and staff over time.

The personality and orientation of the woman who fills the position and the relationship she has with her husband also affect the nature of the position. Eleanor Roosevelt's successor, Bess Truman, saw herself more as Harry Truman's wife than as First Lady. Uninterested in Washington politics or social life, she carried out as few functions as her title allowed and spent as much time as possible away from the capital.

With the era of television campaigns, the wives of presidential candidates began to figure much more prominently in campaign strategy. Even those not interested in electoral politics were used to great effect in getting votes. For example, Dwight Eisenhower considered his wife a better campaigner than he was, and Jacqueline Kennedy attained a level of popularity and celebrity that surpassed her husband's. First Ladies have been fixtures on the campaign trail ever since.

It has become the custom for First Ladies to identify causes, usually nonpartisan, on which they will focus special effort. Jacqueline Kennedy devoted herself to historic preservation; Lady Bird Johnson to environmental issues; Betty Ford to the creative arts and welfare of the elderly; Nancy Reagan to drug prevention; Barbara Bush to literacy; and Hillary Rodham Clinton to child welfare.

In addition, all First Ladies have the domestic staff of the White House residential quarters to oversee, as well as an intense schedule of state social functions. These traditional duties, combined with charity and issue-oriented work and the heavy demand for public appearances, have given the First Lady a formal, if not an institutionalized, role, complete with office, staff, and budget—but still no salary. For decades, funding her office presented legal problems since, officially, the First Lady is a private citizen and government funds could not be used to pay her staff. It was not until 1978 that Congress made formal budgetary provisions for the office.[34]

Nixon made a concerted attempt to modernize the office, located in the East Wing of the White House, and to integrate the activities of the First Lady's staff with those of the president's in the West Wing. Hillary Rodham Clinton moved into the West Wing. She had sixteen personal aides, including schedulers, publicity handlers, and a chief of staff, whose duties she described as equivalent to those of the president's chief of staff.

Office of the Vice President

The Office of the Vice President was made part of the EOP in 1972. Not long afterward, an official residence was established in the Admiral's House at the U.S. Naval

Does this sound familiar: a president's wife is accused of being a radical, more activist than her husband, and in danger of leading him in policy directions his opponents, and perhaps even his own party, do not support? Voters, pundits, and political columnists ask, "Who elected her?" The name of Hillary Rodham Clinton may come to mind or Eleanor Roosevelt. Yet the controversy over the First Lady and how her proximity to the president and the special confidence she shares with him might affect policy decisions has been with us since the administration of John Adams.

The president's wife has always had to walk a fine line, presiding over state social functions and being supportive of her husband without looking as though she is politically out in front of him. Martha Washington and Louisa Adams (wife of John Quincy Adams) were just two First Ladies who felt they were in a prison, hemmed in by the limits of acceptable behavior.[1] Barbara Bush's chief of staff described the position as "filled with banana peels and land mines."[2]

The first and second presidential wives—they did not yet have a formal title—Martha Washington and Abigail Adams, were preoccupied with the problems of keeping their families afloat economically while their husbands led public lives. Abigail Adams managed the family farm in Massachusetts, and Martha Washington ran the plantation at Mount Vernon. Although not always happy with it, neither rejected the role of manager of the domestic sphere and hostess for state social occasions. But whereas Martha Washington was basically unschooled and not much interested in public affairs, Abigail Adams was an accomplished writer with strong

'For gosh sakes, here comes Mrs. Roosevelt!'

political opinions and not afraid to express them (for example, that women would "foment a Rebellion" if they were made subject to laws without representation). Her views on women's rights and other issues, coupled with the fact that her long and happy marriage to John Adams made her his principal adviser, led both supporters and opponents of the president to believe she might have "undue" influence on policy decisions. When Adams's opponents referred to his wife as "Mrs. President," they meant something other than her marital status.

Abigail's daughter-in-law, Louisa Adams, and Dolley Madison are other nineteenth-century First Ladies who played crucial roles in their husbands' political careers. Dolley Madison was so highly regarded among Washington's influential that in 1844 Congress reserved

a seat for her whenever she chose to attend sessions.[3]

Influential First Ladies of the early twentieth century include Edith Wilson, who decoded classified diplomatic and military messages, encoded presidential responses, and served what she called a "stewardship" during a seven-month period when her husband was disabled by a stroke. Much of the work organizing and financing of Warren Harding's presidential campaign was done by Florence Harding, which explains her widely repeated query: "I got you the presidency; now what are you going to do with it?"

Although many First Ladies since have been political advisers to their husbands, no one did it quite so publicly, or from such an independent platform, as Eleanor Roosevelt. Her tenure as First Lady was unique in that she had a policy agenda that sometimes was at odds with the president's; she had her own coterie of supporters and direct access to the public through her news conferences, broadcasts, and newspaper column. In later years she served as a delegate to the United Nations and was a member of John Kennedy's Committee on the Status of Women. Her efforts for human rights and international cooperation earned her the title "First Lady of the World." More than any other First Lady, she can be said to have developed a reputation independent from her husband's legacy as president. Although some thought her too powerful, Mrs. Roosevelt always deferred to her husband in joint appearances, saying it was the job of a wife to offer no personal opinions, limit her appearances, and "lean back in an open car so voters [can] always see him."[4]

Mrs. Roosevelt's term may have been a type unto itself, but most First Ladies were not traditional wives who limited themselves to the domestic sphere. In modern times, Bess Truman, Mamie Eisenhower, Pat Nixon, and Barbara Bush come closest to the image of traditional wife. But these were hardly women without influence on their husbands. Despite her lack of interest in electoral politics, Bess Truman was called "The Boss" by Harry, who said he frequently consulted her on the content of his speeches and in making important decisions. Mamie ("Ike runs the country; I turn the pork chops") Eisenhower cut as traditional a figure as possible in the 1950s, but that did not keep her husband from listening to her opinion when she gave it or from wearing an "I Like Mamie" button when campaigning. Presidential husbands and wives who have led relatively separate lives, such as

John and Jacqueline Kennedy—she having no interest in electoral politics—are not that common among first couples. In most long and close marriages, it is natural for husbands and wives to become confidantes and to rely on one another's judgment.

A number of strong-willed women followed Jacqueline Kennedy into the White House. Lady Bird (Claudia) Johnson helped finance her husband's congressional campaigns and in his presidential race had her own campaign train to tour the South while her husband worked on in Washington. She is said to have greeted him in the evenings with the query, "Well, what did you do for women today?" Betty Ford was an outspoken supporter of the Equal Rights Amendment and abortion rights in defiance of her party's position, and she argued for a salary for her successors as First Lady. Her popularity often surpassed her husband's. Rosalynn Carter sat in on cabinet meetings, had weekly policy lunches with her husband, met with foreign heads of state to discuss policy, chaired the Commission on Mental Health Reform, and was at times derisively referred to as "copresident." Nancy Reagan's stepfather helped shape her husband's political philosophy, and she often controlled access to the Oval Office and weighed in on the hiring and firing of key advisers. The term *copresident* was revived for Hillary Clinton, a lawyer and lobbyist for child welfare causes, who has been one of her husband's closest advisers and strategists throughout his career in elective office, while also serving as the family's principal wage earner.

Although some political commentators and at least part of the public appear leery of activist First Ladies, it does

not seem to bother many of their husbands. FDR often disagreed with Eleanor's policy positions, but he depended on her to fill a public role he was physically unable to sustain, and the political circle that developed around her never appeared to threaten him. Reagan depended heavily on Nancy's advice. Carter called Rosalynn a "full partner" and his costrategist in the presidential campaign.[5] And Clinton clearly saw his wife's activist role as a natural continuation of the political partnership they had throughout their marriage. "It doesn't bother me for people to get excited and say she could be president. I always say she could be president, too."[6] An exception perhaps was Gerald Ford, who told his wife that her outspokenness cost him millions of votes in the 1976 election.[7]

Although Rosalynn Carter had more public hands-on involvement in policy, Hillary Clinton has prompted greater opposition to the activist conception of the office than anyone since Eleanor Roosevelt. In response to public criticism, she retreated into a more traditional role before the 1996 reelection campaign. But in 2000, Mrs. Clinton became the first presidential wife to run for elective office, moving out of the White House and taking up separate residence in the state of New York.

In some ways the concern over the influence and accountability of presidential spouses is moot. The First Lady is not subject to congressional approval, but neither are the members of the White House staff nor the president's close advisers outside government. But as Hillary Clinton has found, First Ladies are not immune from investigation of criminal wrongdoing, and when they serve by official appointment, as she did on the health care task force, they are subject to the same rules as other public officials.

How is issue advocacy of a presidential spouse different from that of any lobbyist? In cases in which wives have played active roles in getting their husbands nominated and elected, how realistic is it that they will expect that their advice will no be longer needed after the election? And how realistic is it to expect that their advice will no longer be offered when the decisions being made carry much higher stakes? Yet some seem to worry that the special nature of a marital relationship provides opportunities to influence—the kind Betty Ford called "pillow talk"—unavailable to oth-

ers. We frequently refer to lobbyists as "getting into bed" with politicians, but wives do not have to pay to get there, and if they are successful in changing their husband's views, it is not likely that money will have had anything to do with it.

Will the president's wife still be the "First Lady" in the next century? There probably will not be many more in the mold of Bess Truman or Mamie Eisenhower. Professional couples like the Clintons and Robert and Elizabeth Dole are more likely to occupy the White House. And inevitably there will be a First Gentleman. Will his influence be as feared as that of a presidential wife?

1. Edith P. Mayo, ed., *The Smithsonian Book of First Ladies* (Washington, D.C.: Smithsonian Institution, 1996), 11, 43.
2. Henry Louis Gates, Jr., "Hating Hillary," *The New Yorker*, February 26 and March 4, 1996, 121.
3. Mayo, *Smithsonian Book of First Ladies*, 31.
4. Carl Sferrazza Anthony, "The First Ladies: They've Come a Long Way, Martha," *Smithsonian Magazine* (October 1992): 150.
5. Gil Troy, *Affairs of State: The Rise and Rejection of the First Couple since World War II* (New York: Free Press, 1997), 236–272.
6. Mayo, *Smithsonian Book of First Ladies*, 277.
7. Troy, *Affairs of State*, 222.

OTHER SOURCES: Carol Chandler Waldrop, *Presidents' Wives: The Lives of 44 American Women of Strength* (Jefferson, N.C.: McFarland, 1989); *The Presidency A to Z: A Ready Reference Encyclopedia* (Washington, D.C.: Congressional Quarterly, 1992), 179–182; Lewis L. Gould, ed., *American First Ladies* (New York: Garland, 1996).

Observatory. Vice presidents also have their own budgets and a staff housed in the old Executive Office Building adjacent to the White House. In the Carter and Clinton administrations, when the president and vice president had close working relationships, Walter Mondale and Al Gore set up personal offices in the West Wing of the White House.

That vice presidents have succeeded to office unexpectedly nine times (eight presidential deaths and one resignation) may be responsible for the growing importance of the office.[35] Most recent vice presidents have been seasoned public servants with considerable experience and personal records of achievement. That they were willing to take the job suggests that it has become more than "standby equipment," as Nelson Rockefeller called it.

The only formal duties the vice president has are to preside over the Senate, cast tie-breaking votes, and succeed to the presidency should it be vacated. Presidents have traditionally given their vice presidents little information and few opportunities to prepare for succession. Harry Truman did not even know about the atom bomb until after Franklin Roosevelt's death, but within months he had to decide whether to use it against Japan. Woodrow Wilson's vice president, Thomas R. Marshall, said that holding the job was like being "a man in a

cataleptic fit. He cannot speak, he cannot move. He suffers no pain. He is perfectly conscious of all that goes on. But he has no part in it." Franklin Roosevelt's first vice president, John Nance Garner, was less elegant in observing that his job was not worth a "pitcher of warm piss."

Historically, presidents have had difficulty delegating important jobs to their vice presidents. One reason is that vice presidential candidates have often been chosen to balance a ticket geographically and ideologically, not because of closeness to the presidential candidate. (In the first elections, before the Twelfth Amendment, when the vice presidency was filled by the runner-up in votes to the president, the vice president was actually an electoral opponent of the president.) And once in office, some vice presidents have used the position to build an independent political base from which to run for the presidency. This has not always made them the most loyal supporters of the president's agenda.

Until the Carter administration, vice presidents were asked to deal mainly with partisan or ceremonial matters. Jimmy Carter was the first president to use his vice president for important work.[36] Carter had no national experience before his election and considered Mondale, a former U.S. senator, a major asset. Carter gave Mondale a White House office, scheduled weekly lunches with him, included him in all White House advisory groups and all important meetings, and asked him to lobby Congress and read the paperwork that crossed Carter's desk. Ronald Reagan, George Bush, and Bill Clinton added to this new tradition.

The relationship between Bill Clinton and Al Gore was surely one of the closest in the history of the presidency (see "You Are There" at the beginning of the chapter). Gore became so influential in the Clinton White House that he was referred to as a "shadow president" and his staff as a "shadow cabinet." There is no legal basis for institutionalizing such an expansion of the office because, beyond the few duties specified in the Constitution, whatever duties vice presidents assume, and whatever advising or policymaking authority they acquire, are at the president's discretion. Therefore, much depends on the personal relationship of the two people filling the positions and how needy the president is for assistance or how generous he is about sharing power.

The President and the People

Our earliest presidents had little contact with the general public and even communicated with Congress in writing. George Washington and Thomas Jefferson averaged only three speeches a year to the public, while John Adams averaged one. Adams in fact spent eight months of his presidency living in Quincy, Massachusetts, avoiding Congress and conflict over the War of 1812.[37]

Abraham Lincoln thought it prudent to avoid giving speeches. He told people gathered at Gettysburg the night before his famous address, "I have no speech to make. In my position it is somewhat important that I should not say foolish things. It very often happens that the only way to help it is to say nothing at all."[38] It has been many years since we have had such a diffident public speaker in the White House.

Until the advent of radio and television, presidents had to speak to the nation indirectly through newspapers. The development of new transportation and communication technologies has given presidents more opportunities to utilize the presidency as a "bully pulpit," as Teddy Roosevelt called it.

Franklin Roosevelt's fireside chats were the first presidential effort to use the media to speak directly and regularly to the nation. They helped make him, and his office, the most important link between people and government. In a personalized style he began, "My friends. . . ." People felt Roosevelt was talking to each of them in their own homes, and they gathered around their radios whenever he was on. Whereas President Herbert Hoover had received an average of forty letters a day, Roosevelt received four thousand letters a day after beginning his chats.[39] He even received some addressed not to "The President" but simply to "My Friend, Washington, D.C."

The Personal Presidency

Political scientist Theodore Lowi believes that we have had a **personal presidency** since the New Deal era.[40] He argues that, consciously or unconsciously, the American people have had a "new social contract" with the president since the 1930s. In return for getting more power and support from us than we give to other government officials, the president is supposed to make sure we get what we want from government.

The personal presidency ties government directly to the people and gives us someone to rally around during times of crisis. To the extent that it serves as a focal point for national unity, the personal presidency also contributes to our ability to achieve national goals.

Polls have consistently shown that Americans consider "leadership" very important in evaluating presidents.[41] Somewhat paradoxically in light of their fear of "big government," most people want a president who can get government to "do" things.

Franklin Roosevelt was the first president to use survey data to identify public needs and to use the media to tell people that he would give them what they wanted. Making himself the major link between public opinion and government often enabled him to overcome the inertia and divisions associated with a system of fragmented powers.

However, Roosevelt's actions also revealed a cost of the personal presidency: Presidents with great power often seek more. Roosevelt won reelection in 1936 by a landslide, confirming popular support for his New Deal. This led him to seek more power by trying to expand the size of an unfriendly Supreme Court so he could appoint judges who supported him. He also tried to get local and state parties to nominate congressional candidates he favored by using federal funds as a carrot. The defeat of pro-Roosevelt congressional candidates in 1938 ruined both his plans. People did not want to politicize the Court, and state and local parties wanted to pick their own nominees.

When President Franklin D. Roosevelt died, most Americans felt a personal loss. Here Chief Petty Officer Graham Jackson plays "Nearer My God to Thee" as the president's body is carried to the train that returned him to Washington.

Edward Clark/*Life* magazine © Time Inc.

Nixon and Reagan also tried to override constitutional limitations on their power after their landslide re-elections in 1972 and 1984, as evidenced in the Watergate and Iran-Contra scandals. The use of popular mandates to amass power in the Oval Office illustrates the relationship between the growth of the modern presidency and the rise of the personal presidency.

Practitioners of the personal presidency have sought more power because they promised more than they could deliver. To win approval for their programs, they needed more power to compete successfully with other parts of government and maintain their public support. Thus, they were caught in a cycle of making great promises, seeking more power to honor them, and making even greater promises to get more power. Inevitably, they promised more than they could deliver. Bush promised to send astronauts to Mars, protect the environment, be the "education president," and do many other things while cutting the budget deficit without raising taxes. Today promising *less* from government has become the tactic of the personal presidency. So while Clinton also began by making promises and saying he wanted "to do it all as quick as we can," he started his second term by announcing that "the day of big government is over."[42]

Yet Clinton had his own angle on the personal presidency, an approach that is said to "have changed the very nature of what the public expects of its Presidents." While deemphasizing big government, Clinton dwelt on "little initiatives," such as his proposal to adopt uni-

forms in public schools. These are what one of his top advisers called "kitchen table issues," problems that families deal with on a daily basis and may discuss around the kitchen table.[43] Not only was Clinton extremely adept at speaking directly to people in a conversational style, but he projected an intimate knowledge of domestic, school, and community problems that were of great concern in everyday life.

Lowi might have been right in calling the personal presidency the "victim" of democracy, but irresponsible leadership is not an inevitable consequence of the age of mass media. The separation of powers and the vote should check the short-term excesses of presidents. However, every president since the 1960s has needed and sought media exposure and in turn has had to submit to intense scrutiny by media that delve into every detail of his personal life, as well as his performance of official duties. Few people can withstand such prolonged exposure without losing public esteem. (For attitudes toward the presidency by its occupants, see the box "Match the Quote to the President.")

Persuading the Public

The relationship of the president to the people starts well before inauguration day. Changes in electoral laws have established a relationship with the public quite different from the one that the Founders saw for their head of state. The president is no longer just an elder statesman chosen by the Electoral College or a politician selected by party professionals to run for the presidency; he is a politician with a national constituency who convinced the rank-and-file voters in his party to choose him in the primaries and at least a plurality of the general population to vote for him in the general election. The modern president comes into office with extensive experience in persuading the public.

As presidential scholar Richard Neustadt pointed out long ago, presidents need more than their formal powers to achieve their goals. They need the **power to persuade**.[44] In addition to the public, presidents must be able to win over interest group leaders; newspaper and magazine publishers, reporters, and columnists; judges who hear challenges to their policies; and a majority in Congress. These policymakers and opinion elite, who Neustadt called Washingtonians, are, in short, the people the president needs to get his policies enacted. Because the Washingtonians also need him to get what they want, a president can bargain and persuade.

The effective president is "one who seizes the center of the Washington bazaar and actively barters . . . to build winning coalitions."[45] Presidents "remember" their friends by putting their pet projects in the budget, by campaigning for them, and by naming the people they want to public office.

In pursuit of his policy agenda, a president can use his powers to persuade the public as a means to bring pressure on reluctant Washingtonians, or when the public is disinterested or slow to accept, he can try to persuade Washingtonians to shape public opinion. In doing so he has much more to rely on than his rhetorical skills. A president's powers give him considerable favors and penalties to dispense. As the chief maker of foreign policy, he can seek support from Irish and Jewish Americans by supporting their objectives in Northern Ireland and the Middle East. As de facto leader of his party, he can use the symbolic resources of the presidency in campaigning for candidates he supports. And as chief budget maker, he has many favors to give and withhold, including support for hundreds of pork barrel projects.

Match the Quote to the President

Letters can be used more than once:

1. "I don't even remember that I ever was President."

2. "No man who ever held the office would congratulate another on attaining it."

3. "War and politics are so different."

4. "I still think it is the greatest job in the world."

5. His law partner said of him, "His ambition is a little engine that knows no rest."

6. He wanted to put a sign on the Oval Office that said, "Don't shoot; he's doing his damnedest."

7. Called having both home and office in the White House "an evil combination."

8. "This country is for white men and, by God, as long as I am President, it will be a government for white men."

9. "The Presidency is hell; there is no other word to describe it."

10. "I can use it [the presidency] for any damned thing I want to."

11. "Unpredictability is the greatest weapon a president can have."

12. "You are only fit to be president when you are not obsessed with it."

13. "Above all . . . try something."

14. "No man ever lived a really worthy life unless he possessed power."

15. "[The presidency] is the greatest sacrifice I ever made; I felt like I was facing my executioner."

SOURCES: 4, interview with Bill Clinton, *Lehrer News Hour*, March 2000; 7, Louis Achincloss, *Woodrow Wilson* (New York: Penguin, 2000), 55; all others from PBS "American Presidency" series (http//www.pbs.org).

A. Warren G. Harding

B. William J. Clinton

C. Ulysses S. Grant

D. John Quincy Adams

E. Woodrow Wilson

F. Abraham Lincoln

G. George Washington

H. Richard Nixon

I. Andrew Jackson

J. Franklin Delano Roosevelt

K. Andrew Johnson

L. William Howard Taft

M. Theodore Roosevelt

N. Benjamin Harrison

Answers

1, L; 2, D; 3, C; 4, B; 5, F; 6, E; 7, N; 8, K; 9, A; 10, I; 11, H; 12, B; 13, J; 14, M; 15, G.

The strategy of making a direct presidential appeal to the people to gain cooperation from Washingtonians is called *going public.*[46] The strategy includes giving prime-time television and radio addresses, holding press conferences, making speeches at events around the country, and using satellite technology to give interviews to local television stations, conventions, and other audiences.

Why have some presidents found going public attractive? One reason is that the weakness of party identification forces presidential candidates to appeal as widely as they can for support. They continue doing so after taking office because they have seen its value. In addition, national parties have been unable to represent the larger number of interests produced by government's larger role in society. This has helped disperse power

among alliances interest groups form with congressional committees, subcommittees, and executive agencies that write and administer the laws they lobby for and against. It is difficult for presidents to know, bargain with, and persuade all these Washingtonians. It is often easier to go public.

Finally, as outsiders, or presidential candidates without national political experience, Carter, Reagan, and Clinton have used the strategy of going public because they lacked ties with the Washingtonians they needed to govern.[47] In a 1981 television address to stimulate support for major tax cuts, Reagan asked viewers "to put aside any feelings of frustration . . . about our political institutions . . . [and] contact your senators and congressmen."[48] The public's reaction was swift and overwhelming. Many Democrats decided to support the president, and the cuts passed.

Going public has a number of important effects. It makes the workings of the presidency resemble an election campaign because presidents fly around the country to get their views in the media. Seeking coverage and support, they use the same simple, dramatic style to oversell their positions that they used as candidates. To identify public reactions, presidential staff regularly gather data just as they did on the campaign trail. A White House aide described the Reagan administration as "a P.R. outfit that became President and took over the country."[49]

Going public leads presidents to use "sound bites" to simplify their positions to build public support while working behind the scenes to build congressional and interest group support. This approach worked for Reagan, who publicly described his 1982 budget package as "a line drawn in the dirt" to stress his resolve. He traveled around the country to generate public support, and his staff used focus groups to identify popular reactions to his proposals. These analyses told his advisers where he could hold firm and where he should compromise. And he made the necessary changes in his package to build congressional support for it.

Clinton used Reagan's sound-bite and compromise strategy to gain congressional passage of the North American Free Trade Agreement and a ban on assault weapons. But Clinton's health care reform plan was too complex and difficult to understand, making it an easy target for interest groups to oppose by playing on fears of an unknown plan. His effort to build support for his position failed, and Congress defeated his bill.

Going public may sometimes lead presidents to emphasize public relations over results and to blame the

Although the public did not always agree with President Reagan's policies or views, he was popular in part because of his image as a rugged individualist.
Ronald Reagan Library

media rather than themselves for low poll scores. For example, Nixon claimed the media had hounded him from office, Reagan said they exaggerated the importance of the Iran-Contra scandal, and Clinton complained they did not give him credit for his first-year accomplishments. "I have fought more damn battles than any president has in 20 years with the possible exception of Reagan's first budget and not gotten one damn bit of credit from the knee-jerk liberal press," Clinton said. "I am sick and tired of it, and you can put that in the damn article."[50]

Bush's use of the going public strategy in garnering support for the Persian Gulf War was very skillful. He decided to use military force soon after Iraq invaded Kuwait in August 1990. Until January, when Congress approved this option, Bush made many speeches comparing Iraq's Saddam Hussein to Hitler, condemning his use of chemical and biological weapons on his own people, and warning that Iraq would soon have nuclear weapons. Bush's efforts won more public support for using force, which in turn made congressional support more likely.

Public Opinion and Effectiveness in Office

Americans pay more attention to the president than to other public officials, and we typically link government's success to the effectiveness of his leadership. Although many factors affect public opinion about presidential effectiveness, a positive image of a president's leadership skills helps protect his ratings after serious policy failures.

Many people are predisposed to support the president and to look at his overall record rather than his short-run successes.[51] Failure on specific issues does not always produce low scores on general performance. For example, majorities of respondents simultaneously disapproved of Reagan's handling of environmental and foreign policy issues, which the public thinks are important, *and* registered approval of his overall performance.

Crises called *rally events* affect presidential popularity.[52] President Clinton's approval ratings increased after the bombing of the federal building in Oklahoma City. Public support rises significantly at such times because people do not want to hurt the president, the symbol of national unity. However, the higher levels of support produced by rally events are rarely sustained.[53] The rise in support among those who were critical of a president before the event tends to be short-lived.

Support for Bush's policies toward Iraq after its invasion of Kuwait also demonstrates public readiness to rally around the president. In November 1990, the public was divided over Bush's decision to send more troops to the Persian Gulf, with 47 percent approving and 46 percent disapproving. By January 1991, after fighting began, almost 90 percent approved of the way he was handling the situation. As Figure 2 shows, this increasing support helped raise Bush's general approval ratings from 54 percent in October to 89 percent in February. The unexpectedly swift defeat of Iraq with surprisingly few American casualties kept Bush's poll scores high for some time.[54] However, the effect of the Gulf War faded as Americans began focusing on domestic concerns, especially economic problems. Bush's approval rating fell to 33 percent by mid-1992, leading to his defeat by Clinton in November.[55]

Clinton's up and down scores during his first term reflected public anxiety about his leadership skills. In 1995 polls 56 percent of Americans described Clinton as a weak president, and 80 percent expected the Republican Congress would have more influence than Clinton on the nation's direction.[56] But Clinton was far more adept at going public than the Republican leadership, and by the end of his first term, his approval rating was at 53 percent and Congress was in legislative retreat.

Winning consistently good ratings when public anger and frustration with government are widespread is difficult. Although short-term crises or rally events can help a president's ratings, long-term conditions will continue to influence them. Clinton's 67 percent approval rating during the impeachment investigation may have been sparked by a public backlash against the salaciousness of congressional and media commentary, but it is more likely that he got a positive bounce from public confidence in the overall state of the economy.

The more important issue is whether a president with high approval ratings can translate them into policy successes. Reagan had only qualified success in using his popularity to get Congress to enact his legislative proposals. He relied heavily on his own appointment and budgetary powers and the issuing of executive orders to accomplish much of his agenda. The problem with this approach is that it is easily reversible by a successor. Bush showed little inclination to use his high ratings to pursue any legislative agenda on domestic policy. Clinton, with higher sustained approval ratings than either Reagan or Bush late in their terms and a substantial legislative agenda, was not able to translate his popular support into victories in Congress.

The President and Congress

One thing the Founders did not anticipate is that the president would one day be dealing with Congress as the popularly elected leader of a national political party. Winning the nomination of a major political party is currently the only route to the White House (aside from succeeding a president who dies in office), and the victor does become the nominal head of the party and chief advocate for its policy agenda. This adds another dimension to the relationship between the executive and legislative branches: the president is never just the head of state or chief executive; he is also an electoral adversary of members of the House and Senate who do not belong to his party. He may use his reputation and the weight of his office to try to unseat them.

Party Leadership

To improve the electoral chances of their party, presidents try to help recruit good candidates for House and Senate races. In addition, presidents help raise money by being the headliner at fund-raising events and by staying on good terms with major contributors. They also send their aides around the country to help fellow Democrats or Republicans with their campaigns and sometimes even go themselves. Seeing a president in person—seeing a little history in the making—is exciting, and they almost always draw a

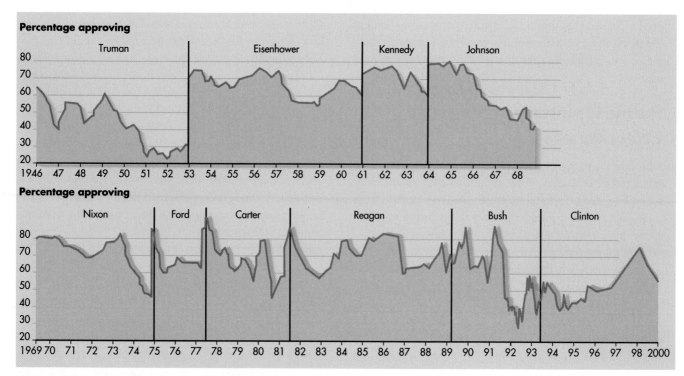

FIGURE 2 ■ Presidential Popularity Usually Declines over Time *Eisenhower and, to some extent, Reagan are exceptions to the post–World War II tendency for presidential popularity to fall during their tenures. Although Reagan's popularity plunged twenty points at the end of 1986 because of the Iran-Contra scandal, it partly rebounded by the end of his term. Most commentators thought this reflected popular fondness for Reagan as a person and Reagan's early successes rather than policy achievements late in his term. Bush began his term with high ratings typical of new presidents; after falling in 1990, his ratings rebounded to record heights during the Persian Gulf War, then began falling dramatically in 1991. Clinton's comparatively low first-year popularity reflects the minority share (43 percent) of the popular vote he received in 1992, reactions to his positions on controversial issues, and the first of the scandals to hit his administration. Despite his modest showing at the polls (49 percent) in 1996 and continuing scandals, Clinton's approval ratings soared to 67 percent in 1998 and were still in the mid to high-fifties when he left office.*

SOURCES: Caption: William Schneider, "Reagan Now Viewed as an Irrelevant President," *National Journal,* November 28, 1987, p. 3051. See also George Gallup, Jr., and Alec Gallup, "The Former President," *The Polling Report,* January 30, 1989, pp. 1 and 5. Figure data: Gallup Polls, reported in *Public Opinion* (January/February 1989), and updated. The question asked is "Do you approve or disapprove of the way [name of president] is handling his job as president?"

crowd and good media coverage. Candidates for any office are usually eager for a presidential visit, although in 1992 some Republican candidates avoided being photographed with Bush when he visited their districts, and in 1994 and 1998 some Democratic congressional candidates preferred to campaign without Clinton's support.

Presidential partisanship has a purpose: The more members of a president's party who sit in Congress, the more support he gets for his policies. However, a president's support, when he chooses to give it, is no guarantee of electoral success for congressional candidates, especially in off-year elections (see Table 1). Since 1932,

Table 1	Congressional Candidates Fall Off the President's Coattails in Off-Year Elections		
		Seats Gained or Lost by President's Party in	
Year	President	House	Senate
1934	Roosevelt (D)	+9	+10
1938	Roosevelt (D)	−71	−6
1942	Roosevelt (D)	−45	−9
1946	Truman (D)	−55	−12
1950	Truman (D)	−29	−6
1954	Eisenhower (R)	−18	−1
1958	Eisenhower (R)	−47	−13
1962	Kennedy (D)	−4	+4
1966	Johnson (D)	−47	−3
1970	Nixon (R)	−12	+2
1974	Ford (R)	−48	−3
1978	Carter (D)	−11	−3
1982	Reagan (R)	−26	0
1986	Reagan (R)	−6	−8
1990	Bush (R)	−8	−1
1994	Clinton (D)	−52	−9
1998	Clinton (D)	+5	0
Average, all off-year elections		−27	−4
Average, all presidential elections years		+21	+3

D = Democrat; R = Republican.

SOURCES: *Congressional Quarterly Guide to U.S. Elections, 1985* (Washington, D.C.: CQ Press, 1985), 1116; Harold W. Stanley and Richard G. Niemi, *Vital Statistics on American Politics,* 3d ed. (Washington, D.C.: CQ Press, 1992), Table 7–4; and *Congressional Quarterly Guide to Current American Government Spring 1991* (Washington, D.C.: CQ Press, 1991), 1. *Lincoln Star,* November 10, 1994, p. 1.

the president's party has lost an average of twenty-nine House and four Senate seats in off-year elections; in presidential election years, the average gains for the winning presidential candidate's party in Congress are almost a mirror image, twenty-one in the House and three in the Senate. The 1988 and 1992 elections were unusual. The Republicans lost three House seats and one Senate seat when Bush was elected, and the Democrats lost ten House seats with no change in the Senate when Clinton was elected. The off-year election of 1998 was also an anomaly. The Democrats actually gained House seats, the first time since 1934 that the president's party increased its seats in an off-year election.

The president usually tries to camouflage his actions as party leader when trying to persuade people to support him or to vote for his party's candidates. People are more likely to listen to a president when they see him in one of his other roles, such as head of state.

Divided Government

Presidents are normally active in support of House and Senate candidates not just because they are policy leaders, but also because one of the major factors influencing the working relationship between the president and Congress is whether the president's party controls the House and Senate. For all but two years since 1981, one party has controlled the White House and the other the Congress. This is called **divided government.** The Founders made divided government possible by dividing authority between the executive and legislative branches and providing that members of each would be elected in different ways and for different terms. This contrasts with parliamentary systems, in which voters elect members of the legislative branch and they in turn choose the executive leaders of the nation (see the box "Presidents and Prime Ministers").

In the first half of the twentieth century, divided government did not occur very often. From 1900 to 1950, only four of twenty-six presidential and midterm elections resulted in divided government. From 1952 to 1994, however, fourteen of twenty-two elections did.[57] Even with Reagan's overwhelming victory in 1980, the Republicans captured only the Senate. Their dominance lasted only until 1986, when the Democrats regained majority control. Bush faced both a House and a Senate controlled by the Democrats, and Clinton had a Republican Congress after 1994.

Some believe that divided government is partially responsible for our failure to solve many of our important problems. The term *gridlock* has often been used to

Presidents and Prime Ministers

Many Americans are frustrated by our system's fragmentation and by "gridlock," the inability of our elected officials to agree about how to solve our nation's problems. These differences can be exacerbated when different parties control the White House and Congress, as has been the case most years since World War II. Divided government makes it more likely that the president and congressional leaders will advocate different policies and priorities. It also makes it easier for elected officials to play the "blame game" and avoid taking responsibility for failed policies and inaction. We even have problems when the White House and Congress are controlled by the same party. The president and members of Congress often have different interests because they are elected by different constituencies at different times. And they can use the system's checks and balances to thwart each other's efforts.

In contrast, British heads of government, called prime ministers, seem to be better leaders and more accountable to the public. Like most democratic nations, Britain has a **parliamentary government**—that is, a system in which the executive is chosen by the legislature. The British government is marked by a unity of authority. The prime minister, or PM, is an elected member of the House of Commons, the lower house of Britain's national legisla-

ture called Parliament. (Parliament's other house, the House of Lords, is unelected and has limited power.) The PM is elected like other members of the Commons—by the voters of a constituency—and then is chosen by his or her party as its leader. The PM is always the leader of the majority or plurality party in the Commons and usually decides when elections to the Commons will occur. However, elections must take place within five years of the last election. As members of the Commons, the PM and the cabinet ministers appointed by the PM must argue for their policies and respond to criticism from minority party members in debate.

Rank-and-file members of the Commons have very little independent power and often do not live in the constituencies that elect them. National party organizations have a great deal of influence over who is selected to run for election to the Commons. Members who do not vote the party line sometimes lose their party's support for reelection. This helps explain why 97 percent of the bills sponsored by the PM and cabinet from 1945 to 1987 were enacted.[1]

Although this is an attractive picture in some respects, the Founders designed our system to represent the diverse interests of a large, heterogeneous population. While more effective leadership in government is appealing, greater centralization can mean less opportunity to

accommodate diverse local interests. Many Americans would not like a party organization to have the major influence on nominations for congressional office. Some would also be angry if representatives advocated positions contrary to local majority opinion on an important issue. America is a much more diverse society than Britain, perhaps making centralization less workable.

Diversity in America is also represented by powerful interest groups. Their close ties to congressional committees and subcommittees and executive branch officials give these interest groups considerable power to obstruct government. While these groups might be weakened by parliamentary-style arrangements, the interests they represent would still exist, as would their ability to lobby Congress and the executive branch.

Considering whether parliamentary forms would improve the workings of our government requires us to weigh some difficult trade-offs. Do we want to pay the costs of frequent gridlock and inefficiency to keep a system that is more responsive to diverse local and other interests?

1. Richard Rose, *Politics in England: Change and Persistence,* 5th ed. (London: Macmillan, 1989), 113.

suggest this policy stalemate. The president presents a program and Congress does not accept it. Or Congress passes a bill and the president vetoes it. The result can be a lot of squabbling and little action. The impeachment proceedings in 1998 were a period of especially bitter rivalry between the White House and Congress, and it brought legislative action to a halt.

But united government does not always eliminate gridlock. From 1946 to 1990, as many major laws passed during periods of divided government as in periods of united government. Adoption of policies that address major problems is usually the result of strong presidential leadership, national crisis, policy failure, or a change in public opinion rather than united government.[58]

Legislative Leadership

Because he is the head of a political party with an issue agenda, and because the public has come to expect policy leadership from the White House, a president usually takes office with legislative goals. This can mean a few key proposals such as for tax cuts, tax reforms, or downsizing government, or it can mean a comprehensive package of proposed legislation, such as Teddy Roosevelt's Square Deal, Wilson's New Freedom, Franklin Roosevelt's New Deal, and Johnson's Great Society. People often evaluate presidential leadership in terms of the content and impact of these programs.

All presidents have advisers who serve as congressional liaisons; they lobby for the president's agenda and facilitate exchange of information with members of Congress on pending legislation. How active the president's personal role is depends on his involvement in policy detail, knowledge of congressional operations, and powers of persuasion. In all, twenty-four presidents have served in Congress; among post–World War II presidents, only the three governors, Carter, Reagan, and Clinton, have not (Clinton ran for the House but lost). Truman, Kennedy, and Bush had short and undistinguished congressional careers, while Nixon used his short time in the House and Senate to build a national reputation. In their long years of congressional service, Johnson and Ford rose to leadership positions. As a former Senate majority leader of legendary persuasiveness, Johnson is the classic example of president as inside-dopester and congressional coalition builder. He knew how to approach members and was a masterful lobbyist. In working for a foreign aid bill, he invited key members to the White House for one-on-one talks described by an aide as "endless talking, ceaseless importuning, torrential laying on of the facts . . . for several days."[59]

Sometimes presidents are more heavy-handed in seeking support. A Reagan aide described how the White House changed one senator's vote: "We just beat his brains out. We stood him in front of an open grave and told him he could jump in if he wanted to [oppose Reagan]."[60] Such tactics can succeed but can also make a president look bad. In 1990, Bush was criticized for the way White House staff lobbied Congress for a budget plan. His chief of staff, John Sununu, called Trent Lott (R-Miss.), who was soon to become majority leader of the Senate, "insignificant" on television after Lott refused to support the plan. And Sununu alienated others with petty reprisals.

Presidents also use the prestige of their office as an instrument of persuasion. In 1975, Ford persuaded eighteen House members to change their votes to support one of his vetoes. He took them on his jet, Air Force One, and "lectured" them.[61] Because many members rarely, if ever, talk to a president, most consider these conversations memorable events and listen.

Reagan's leadership style in dealing with Congress involved going public to pressure it for support. In contrast, Bush used White House staff to negotiate policy matters directly with congressional leaders. Bush lacked Reagan's media skills and, as an insider, already had working relationships with Washington's influentials.

Clinton tried to generate congressional support for his policies by personally lobbying individual members and by trying to get backing in those parts of the country and from those interest groups most affected by the policies. One way he and his aides did this was to give interviews to journalists whose work reached those he wanted to influence. Clinton then tried to use popular support to build congressional backing by lobbying members both directly and indirectly, through intermediaries such as business and union leaders.

Presidents cannot always get the support they need, however. Members of Congress have their own constituencies and careers. And presidential persuasion does not always involve bargaining. Presidents also remind fellow Republicans or Democrats of the need to stick together to promote their party platform and achieve party goals. Bipartisan appeals can be effective, too, especially in foreign affairs.

Veto Power

No president has to rely solely on his persuasive powers to affect legislation. The Constitution has given the chief executive veto power over bills passed by Congress. The veto power is not listed among the president's formal powers in Article II but rather is included in Article I as a check on Congress's power to legislate.

When the president receives a bill passed by Congress, he has three options: he can sign it into law; he can veto it and send it back to Congress along with his objections; or he can take no action, in which case the bill becomes a law after ten congressional working days. An unsigned bill returned by the president can be passed into law if two-thirds of both houses vote to override the veto. But if Congress adjourns within ten working days after sending legislation to the White House, and the president chooses to pocket the bill, that is, not to act on it, the legislation dies. This option, called a *pocket veto*, is a means by which the president can kill a bill without facing an override attempt in Congress.

Given the presence of White House supporters in Congress and the president's ability to go public, mobilizing two-thirds majorities in both houses to override a veto is usually very hard. As a result, presidents can try to influence the content of bills by threatening to veto them if they do not conform to presidential wishes.

Only eight presidents never vetoed a bill. Franklin Roosevelt holds the record for most vetoes with 635 vetoes in fourteen years, only 9 of which were overridden. But Grover Cleveland used his veto 584 times in just eight years. Eisenhower vetoed 181 bills in eight years. Congress overrode only two, even though his party was in the minority for six of those years. Reagan vetoed seventy-eight bills with nine overridden, and Bush vetoed forty-six bills with one overridden. Clinton did not use the veto until his third year in office, casting only seventeen during his first full term. That was the lowest number for a full term since Woodrow Wilson's administration.

Presidents who use the veto too often may appear isolated or uncooperative or seem to be exercising negative leadership. But the fact that presidents are rarely overridden reminds us of their power when they decide they really want something.

Presidents since Chester Arthur have tried to persuade Congress to give them another form of veto power called the *line item veto.* With this authority, the president would be able to veto one or more portions of a bill while allowing the remaining provisions to pass into law. If Congress disagreed, it could override the veto by majority votes in both houses. A principal argument for delegating this authority would be that the president could make decisions that are politically difficult for members of Congress, such as killing pork barrel spending provisions in an appropriations bill. The counterargument is that for reasons of political cowardice Congress would be signing away part of its constitutional authority.

In 1997, after decades of lobbying by presidents, Congress gave the president the line item veto for appropriations bills. Clinton had the chance to exercise it eighty-two times before the Supreme Court struck it down as a violation of separation of powers. The ruling pointed to the constitutional provision that bills be accepted or rejected in their entirety by a president, implying that if Congress wants to change this requirement, it will have to be done by constitutional amendment rather than legislation.

Congressional Support

A president's reputation for effectiveness is based in part on how successful he is in getting congressional support. Franklin Roosevelt's ranking as one of our great presidents can be attributed in part to his legislative effectiveness. He was able to persuade Congress to enact much of his legislative program within the first one hundred days of his administration. Those were extraordinary times, and few presidents since have been able to match his success in Congress.

Reagan's effectiveness with Congress was greatest in his first year in office when he got Congress to approve a major tax cut and increase military spending. Economic problems produced in part by these changes and a growing public awareness that he was uninformed about White House activities led to a drop in his effectiveness with Congress during the remainder of his administration. As Figure 3 shows, Reagan's congressional support fell after 1981 and was low compared to other presidents.

Congressional support for Bush was weak throughout his term. Figure 3 shows that his first-year success with Congress was the lowest of any elected president since 1953, when scores were first computed. Bush had fewer congressional Republicans to work with than any GOP president in this century, but he also had low support among congressional Republicans. He lacked a well-articulated legislative program. He also failed to capture the public's attention with clear themes, what he once called the "vision thing." This prevented Bush from securing more congressional support, even after the Persian Gulf War when his popularity was very high.

Clinton tried to emulate Reagan's successful first-year strategy of asking Congress to vote on a few high-priority bills. This strategy lets presidents define their positions in relatively simple terms and seek congressional support when they are in their postelection honeymoon periods and before other influences on Congress have time to make mobilizing majorities more difficult. Enjoying early successes with Congress can help presidents build their professional reputations.

With both houses of Congress controlled by Democratic majorities, unlike Reagan and Bush, Clinton did not have to deal with a divided government. Despite substantial disagreements among congressional Democrats, Clinton succeeded in getting majority support for most of his early economic proposals. In fact, Clinton had the highest first-year success score with Congress (86 percent) since Eisenhower's 89 percent in 1953 and Johnson's 88 percent in 1964. Clinton's two-year record of congressional success exceeded that of every president since Johnson, a record that no doubt surprises many people.

Clinton's legislative record was impressive, but it did not give him a reputation for effectiveness. His success was overshadowed by the scandals that followed him into his second term and by his failure to articulate

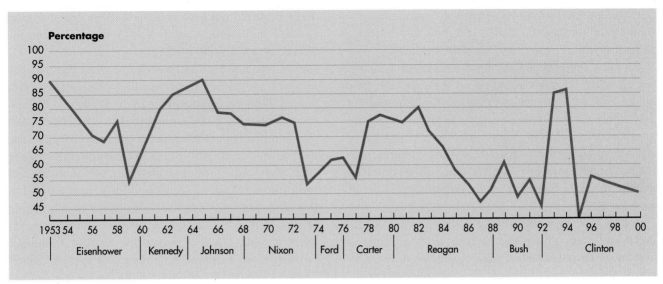

FIGURE 3 ■ *Presidential Success on Congressional Votes Often Declines over Time* Presidents usually have the most success with Congress early in their first terms. This figure shows the percentage of votes that presidents have won when they took a position. Clinton's 86.4 percent score ranks the highest of any president in his first year since Johnson's 88 percent in 1964 and Eisenhower's 89 percent in 1953, while his 1995 and 1999 scores of 36.2 percent and 37.8 percent are the two lowest in CQ's 47 years of record-keeping. Bush had the smallest first-year success of any of these presidents.

SOURCES: *Congressional Quarterly Weekly Report,* October 17, 1992, p. 3249; December 18, 1993, pp. 3427–3431; December 21, 1996; p. 3455; January 3, 1998, p. 27, and December 11, 1999, pp. 2971–2973.

larger goals so the American people knew where he wanted to lead them. In 1995 and 1998 he had the lowest success rates in Congress of any president in the second half of the century (see Figure 3).

Foreign Policy and Military Leadership

Over the years, the president has become more powerful than Congress in foreign policy, assuming powers that were not explicitly given to either the legislative or the executive branch. One reason for this dominance is that in foreign policy, more than in domestic, the president has more information than others do. He can often stifle debate by citing classified or secret information from the CIA, Defense Department, State Department, and other agencies and saying, "If you knew what I knew, you would agree with me." The president can also share certain information with Congress (and the public) while withholding other material. Members of Congress must often rely on the media and are at a distinct disadvantage in dealing with the president. In 1984, the Reagan administration mined harbors in Nicaragua after telling the Senate Intelligence Committee it was not doing so. When the facts became known, the chair of that committee, Barry Goldwater (R–Ariz.), wrote a

blistering public letter to the head of the CIA saying, not so formally, "I am pissed off."[62]

The administration also has a large role in shaping the agenda of debate. Alternatives acceptable to the administration are advanced through public statements, background briefings of the press and Congress, and "national" newspapers such as the *New York Times* or *Washington Post.* Many reasonable alternatives may never be suggested or receive support. Thus, media outlets did little to initiate discussions of our goals in the Persian Gulf, choosing instead to cover troop commitments largely as a logistical challenge and human interest story. Media acceptance of Pentagon restrictions on news gathering also helped Bush generate support for his policies by producing news of successful, not unsuccessful, attacks and by concealing information describing casualties on both sides.

Although different presidential advisers sometimes advocate conflicting views publicly, it is much easier for a president than for Congress to have a coherent policy. Thus, another advantage the president has over Congress is that he can act decisively, whereas Congress must reach agreement and vote in order to act and this takes time. President Bush ordered American troops to Somalia in December 1992, but the House Foreign Affairs Committee did not meet until May 1993 to authorize this action—the day after the United Nations had assumed responsibility in Somalia and most of our troops had come home.

Because the president is one and Congress is many, the president is usually more effective in appealing for public support. There is almost always a "rally 'round the flag" effect on both Congress and the public when the president takes a strong stance in foreign policy, especially if troops are involved. In these cases, Congress may hesitate to oppose the president because it fears doing so may be seen by other nations as a sign of United States weakness.

Vietnam is a good example of presidential dominance in foreign policy. Presidential policy dominated even with demonstrations, mass arrests, opposing editorials, negative opinion polls, and congressional criticism.

The Vietnam War raised major questions about presidential authority in foreign and military policy. Although Congress never declared war in Vietnam, it routinely appropriated money for it. Nonetheless, many members of Congress believed that Johnson and Nixon exceeded their authority in pursuing the war. This painful experience led Congress to try to supervise use of military force more closely.

In 1973, Congress passed the **War Powers Act** to limit the president's ability to commit troops to combat. It says the president can use troops abroad under three conditions: when Congress has declared war, when Congress has given him specific authority to do so, or when an attack on the United States or its military creates a national crisis. If a president commits troops under the third condition, he is supposed to consult with Congress beforehand, if possible, and notify it within forty-eight hours afterward. Unless Congress approves the use of troops, the president must withdraw them within sixty days, or ninety days if he needs more time to protect them. Congress can pass a concurrent resolution (not subject to presidential veto) at any time ordering the president to end the use of military force.

Congress passed the War Powers Act over Nixon's veto. He believed it violated his constitutional authority to protect the nation from military threats. Although presidents have not questioned Congress's constitutional authority to declare war, all have fought congressional involvement in the use of troops. As a result, enforcement of the act has proved difficult. For example, President Carter did not inform, let alone consult, Congress before using U.S. troops in an attempt to free the Iranian hostages in 1980. Congress did not protest. Neither did it protest after Bush sent troops to invade Panama in

1989. Bush did not even refer to the War Powers Act in the two-page letter he sent to Congress justifying the invasion sixty hours after it began.

On the whole, then, the War Powers Act has not stopped presidents from sending American troops abroad. This was certainly true in the Persian Gulf. President Bush sent 250,000 troops to the Gulf between August and November 1990 on his own authority. He also delayed announcing his decision to double this number until after the November elections, although he had made the decision in October. This kept the decision that changed our mission from defense (Operation Desert Shield) to offense (Operation Desert Storm) from coming to Congress until he had mobilized United States and world opinion and gained United Nations support. By the time Congress authorized using force in January 1991, the question of whether to do so was, practically speaking, already decided.

Congress has special need to be vigilant in election years because a president's public opinion scores, especially before national elections, can influence the use of military force abroad.[63] Presidents may be tempted to use rally events to increase their popularity and congressional support for their policies. A White House aide, acknowledging low presidential popularity in October 1983, said Reagan needed "a major victory somewhere to show that we can manage foreign policy." The United States invaded Grenada soon after. When Bush's scores were falling in 1990, his staff chief told associates that a short successful war against Iraq would guarantee Bush's reelection (he was wrong!).[64] In late 1998 and early 1999, when Clinton was the subject of impeachment hearings, he was accused of bombing Iraq and advocating NATO's bombing of Kosovo to detract attention from his political problems. But when NATO did bomb Kosovo in March 1999, Clinton's approval ratings fell five points in one week.[65]

Historically, a president's use of military force tends to raise his congressional support for about a month.[66] This led one observer to note that, based on U.S. experiences in Vietnam and Grenada, presidents who start military actions abroad must win them in a hurry if they want to stay popular.[67]

A president needs to be able to act decisively in international affairs. But we want to make sure the president does not act against our wishes. Congress has historically served as the most important check on the president, but its power to influence military policy is limited in emergency or crisis situations. An uneasy balance exists between presidential powers adequate to do the job and controls necessary to prevent abuse.

Although Congress has been reluctant to challenge presidential policies that were justified in terms of protecting national security, it has often refused to give its backing to presidential initiatives. Current studies suggest that even the widely held support for the "two presidencies" thesis—that presidents have substantially more success in winning support from Congress on foreign policy votes than on domestic policy—was largely unjustified if one looks at all the relevant votes cast by Congress.[68]

Since the end of the Vietnam War, Congress has sought to reassert its authority in foreign policy in a number of ways, including closer monitoring of intelligence operations, limiting the president's authority to enter into trade or other agreements with foreign countries, refusing to approve arms control and other treaties negotiated by presidents, and requiring congressional approval of major arms sales.

Perhaps the greatest threat to presidential foreign policy dominance, however, will turn out to be the end of the Cold War. Without the threat of a challenging external enemy of superpower status, Congress is unlikely to give the president the benefit of the doubt in major foreign policy initiatives, certainly not those involving a commitment of military forces. There is evidence of this with Clinton's administration. Clinton, the first post–Cold War president, has not been able to count on congressional support even when he has committed troops, as in Bosnia and Haiti. In 2000 the Senate tried, and narrowly failed, to use the War Powers Resolution to force Clinton to withdraw U.S. troops from the NATO contingent in Kosovo. Many of his trade and economic initiatives have met with similar resistance.

Limits on Presidential Power

As government grew during the first seventy-five years of the twentieth century, so did the office of the president. Some of these new powers came at the expense of Congress, but in large part they were delegated (such as, budget making), voluntarily ceded to the president (foreign policymaking during the Cold War), or assumed by default through congressional inaction. What the executive branch gained was not the simple sum of what the legislative branch lost, as if the president and Congress were contestants in a zero-sum game. Much of the power FDR assumed in dealing with the Great Depression and World War II had not been exercised by any branch of the national government before. Crises arose, presidential incumbents responded, and in the process they assumed powers of government not yet established at the federal level.

Today a person elected to the presidency becomes the recipient of the respect bestowed on the office itself: people stand when the president enters a room; "Hail to the Chief" is played when he appears on a dais or at ceremonial events; men and women in uniform salute him; he is surrounded by bodyguards and aides; the public and media scrutinize every detail of his personal life and public performance. He is almost universally regarded as the most powerful person in the world. Yet some presidents have become so frustrated by limitations on their power that they try to overcome those limitations by exceeding their constitutional authority.

There have been many extraordinary extensions of presidential authority, especially in wartime or crises, including Lincoln's suspension of habeas corpus, Franklin Roosevelt's attempts to pack the Supreme Court, and Nixon's and Lyndon Johnson's conduct of an undeclared war. The most famous example of illegal presidential action in the face of perceived frustration is Nixon's attempt to learn what his "enemies" were doing: invading individual privacy with phone taps, break-ins, and unauthorized reviews of income tax returns, and then obstructing justice by trying to cover up evidence of these acts.

Even the most persuasive presidents like FDR, Reagan, and Johnson do not get everything they want. There are many formal checks on their constitutional powers as well as many limitations inherent in the office or the men who have served there. Formal checks include the independence of the federal judiciary; the budgetary, confirmation, oversight, and removal powers of Congress; term limitations; and the power of the electorate to throw an incumbent out of office. When formal checks do not work, or do not work quickly enough, there is also the power of a free press. The abuses of office during the Nixon administration are instances where Congress and the public did not initially serve as a check on the president; illegalities might never have been revealed had it not been for investigative reporting by the *Washington Post*. Only after evidence was uncovered by the press did the Democratically controlled Congress deal seriously with accusations of wrongdoing.

Many idiosyncratic and situational factors also can impose restrictions on executive power, including the president's competence, personality, and attitude toward the exercise of power; the opportunity to exercise power presented by international or domestic crises, including warfare; the president's popularity and his reputation in Congress and with other Washingtonians; and the mood of Congress to use its powers fully to check the president.

In the last twenty-five years of the twentieth century, the power of the presidency appeared to wane. The decline began in reaction to the sometimes arrogant or imperial exercise of power during the Johnson and Nixon administrations, especially with respect to the conduct of the Vietnam War and abuses of the electoral process during Nixon's reelection campaign. Reagan's personal popularity and conception of the office of presidency—emphasizing the head of state and symbolic roles of the office over governance—restored some of the prestige or grandeur of the presidency, but the illegalities of the Iran-Contra affair and ethics scandals involving his appointees eroded public confidence again.

The end of the Cold War has also restricted the president's freedom to act unilaterally in international affairs and reduced his role as a rally figure to mobilize public opinion against foreign enemies. In domestic affairs, decades of budget deficits, the return of many responsibilities to the states, and a tendency toward downsizing national government limited how much the personal presidency can credibly promise or deliver to the American public. As the presidency grew with the expanding role of national government, so it may shrink if power continues to gravitate away from the center.

The Clinton presidency suggests that the personal presidency may be imploding and contributing to the shrinking of presidential power. Six years of ethics investigations, a record number of special prosecutors, sensational headlines, and constant scrutiny of the First Family's personal lives have contributed to the diminution of the office, although it can be argued that media attention might have been substantially less had the power of the office not already been receding.

Some historians and analysts have already claimed that Clinton's impeachment will be similar in impact to Andrew Johnson's, which weakened the presidency for the next half-century.[69] This argument is based in large part on precedents set by federal court decisions issued during the investigation. These rulings limit a president's ability to use executive privilege to deny Congress access to records of conversations he has with his advisers and to exercise attorney-client privilege to protect such records in cases in which the advice is provided by government lawyers. The court also allowed Secret Service agents to testify before grand juries about the president's activities, including his personal conduct. But perhaps most important was the court's ruling that a sitting president can be sued for private conduct that occurred before he took office. In the latter decision, judges reasoned it was unlikely that the need to defend himself in a civil suit would divert a president's time and energy from carrying out his duties. This was clearly not the case in the sexual harassment suit brought against Clinton, and critics of the decision wonder whether the filing of civil suits will become one more maneuver to hamstring the presidency.

Rating the Presidents

As children, we learned that George Washington, Abraham Lincoln, and Franklin Roosevelt were great presidents, but few of us think about most of the other presidents. How do they rate?

Presidential ratings surveys have been taken periodically since the historian Arthur Schlesinger, Sr., first polled fifty-five leading historians in 1948. In the many surveys since, some presidents have improved their showing remarkably, most notably Eisenhower, who rose from twenty-second place in a 1962 Schlesinger poll, to twelfth in a 1981 poll by David Porter, to ninth in a 1997 poll of 719 historians and political scientists shown here.[1]

While presidents ranked between the bottom and top tiers may move up and down the rankings over the years, almost all polls agree on Washington, Lincoln, and Franklin Roosevelt as the Greats and Jefferson, Jackson, Theodore Roosevelt, Wilson, and Truman as the Near Greats. The placement of Madison in the top ten in the ranking shown here differs sharply from a 1996 New York Times poll of thirty-two presidential scholars; they rated Madison average.[2] Some presidents—Taylor, Harding, and Ford—spent such short periods in office that they are hard to rank. In a survey of viewers and historians conducted by C-SPAN in 2000, the historians bumped John Kennedy and Lyndon Johnson into the top ten, while

dropping Madison back into the middle of the pack and leaving Clinton dead in the middle. Former presidents sometimes get a bounce in the poll ratings: Truman, Carter, and Reagan, for example, received much higher favorable ratings in retirement than they had at the end of their terms. But this does not necessarily lead to a higher ranking, as one can see in Clinton's case. You can review the survey results at http://americanpresidents.org/survey.

1. *Champaign-Urbana News-Gazette,* February 8, 1997, p. D-2, citing William J. Ridings Jr. and Stuart R. McIver, *Rating the Presidents* (Secaucus, N.J.: Citadel, 1997).
2. Arthur M. Schlesinger, Jr., "The Ultimate Approval Rating," *New York Times Magazine,* December 18, 1996, pp. 46–51.

Ranking U.S. Presidents

The Greats

U.S. President in Order of Overall Ranking	Leadership Qualities	Accomplishments and Crisis Management	Political Skill	Appointments	Character and Integrity
1 Lincoln	2	1	2	3	1
2 F. Roosevelt	1	2	1	2	15
3 Washington	3	3	7	1	2
4 Jefferson	6	5	5	4	7
5 T. Roosevelt	4	4	4	5	12
6 Wilson	7	7	13	6	8
7 Truman	9	6	8	9	9
8 Jackson	5	9	6	19	18
9 Eisenhower	10	10	14	16	10
10 Madison	14	14	15	11	6

The Failures (Listed Chronologically)

Pierce, Buchanan, A. Johnson, Grant, Harding, Hoover, Nixon

SOURCE: *Champaign-Urbana News-Gazette,* February 8, 1997, p. D-2.

Other observers see shorter-term consequences; they are more inclined to point to Clinton's personal conduct as having diminished the office and believe the main damage has been to Clinton's reputation and legacy.[70] Only time will reveal the long-term impact, but it seems unlikely that power has gravitated from the presidency to Congress as happened after Johnson's impeachment, in part because the presidency plays a far greater role in providing national leadership than it did in the mid-nineteenth century but also because, in exercising its formal powers on legally ambiguous grounds, Congress itself was weakened. While Clinton maintained throughout the impeachment process the highest sustained public approval ratings attained by any second term president, Congress's public approval ratings took a serious dip. The president's ability to carry out his legislative agenda was severely damaged, but congressional influence also suffered when leaders were cut out of the normal routine of consultation with the White House on foreign and domestic policy. Furthermore, the public backlash to the impeachment process and the continuous investigation of the Clintons' lives before and during their White House years contributed to Congress's decision in 1999 not to renew the independent counsel law, one of its own mandated checks on the abuses of executive power.

If the presidency *is* declining in power, there is no reason to believe that the decline will be permanent. Formal powers have remained fairly stable throughout the history of the office; it is how the inherent powers and the political role of the presidency are utilized by the incumbent, as well as the opportunities domestic and international political affairs afford him for the exercise of his office, that set the inner and outer limits of presidential power.

What Makes an Effective President?

Every president develops a track record of his effectiveness as a leader. Richard Neustadt calls it the president's professional reputation.[71] A president with an effective reputation has a record of getting what he wants, helping his allies, and penalizing the opposition. This reputation contributes to his continuing ability to persuade the public, Congress, and other Washingtonians. Few modern presidents were more adept at getting what they wanted from Congress than Lyndon Johnson, yet Johnson often is not ranked among the great presidents. A president's professional reputation is of great importance to him while he is in office and is a commentary on his political and administrative skills. But having the ability to get what he wants is not the same as being able to do what is best for the country, and therefore presidents seen as highly effective in office are not always judged by history to have been great presidents.

It is not always immediately clear how deep an impact a president's tenure has had on the direction of the country, and over time assessments of presidential performance do change. Truman exemplifies a president who was very unpopular during his tenure and in the immediate years afterward but who left a legacy of directness, personal integrity, and decisiveness on key decisions during an extremely difficult time (the national trauma of FDR's death while we were engaged in a world war).

Neustadt has called the presidency a "choice-making machine," and presidents who can act decisively are often well regarded. Truman epitomized the decisive style and has probably benefited from the contrast with the more waffling approaches of recent presidents who are often seen as driven by polls and focus groups. The "Buck Stops Here" sign that Truman kept on his desk illustrated both his sense of accountability and his nononsense rhetoric. In historical perspective his leadership skills have looked more impressive than they did while he was in office, and this view has helped move him to the ranks of near-great presidents.

Scholarly assessment of Eisenhower's administrations has also changed significantly. Early on after he left office, he was judged an average president, a good and honest man with strong administrative skills, but one who took few chances and lacked an overall vision for the country. In retrospect, analysts see as level-headed and prescient his leadership during an extremely volatile period in the nuclear arms race and his warnings about the dangers of the military-industrial complex to the economy and national purpose.

The Presidency in Time

1799 George Washington leaves presidency, declining to stand for third term. Sets precedent for limited term presidency.

1804 Ratification of Twelfth Amendment ends practice of the vice presidency going to the runner-up in presidential election. Lays ground for president and vice president to run as a team after party system develops.

1824 John Quincy Adams becomes president despite failure to win a majority in the Electoral College. First of three elections decided in the House of Representatives (also Hayes, 1876, and B. Harrison, 1888).

1829 Andrew Jackson wages campaign for mass support and enters office as first "people's president." First step in connecting presidency directly to national electorate.

1841 John Tyler first vice president to assume presidency on death of incumbent. Resolves constitutional question of whether vice president would assume full powers of office or serve in acting or interim role.

1861 Lincoln administration interprets Constitution to prohibit secession and goes to war to preserve Union. Power of presidency grows through broad interpretation of inherent powers of office.

1867 Senate refuses by single vote to convict the unelected and unpopular Andrew Johnson after impeachment by House. Prevents setting precedent for impeaching presidents over policy differences but cripples Johnson administration. Power of presidency recedes.

1898 McKinley becomes first foreign policy president since Monroe. Establishes first modern war room and involves United States in foreign wars.

1901 Teddy Roosevelt succeeds assassinated McKinley; establishes presidency as "bully pulpit" to advocate for the people. Expands foreign policy role. Uses family in campaign further personalizing the presidency. Power of office grows.

1910 Taft prepares first executive branch budget. Ten years later Congress delegates budget-making power to president. Initiative in fiscal matters moves to executive branch.

1918 Woodrow Wilson establishes U.S. role in world diplomacy. First president to travel to Europe while still in office.

1921 Coolidge and Hoover administrations deemphasize federal role; look to states and private sector to carry out social welfare functions. Power of office recedes.

1933 F. Roosevelt takes legislative initiative to end Great Depression. Begins fireside chats via national radio broadcasts. Strengthens personal presidency; power of presidency grows. Eleanor Roosevelt develops prominent public role for First Lady.

1951 Ratification of Twenty-second Amendment. Fearful FDR's four terms could reverse Washington's precedent of limited service, Congress amends Constitution to limit term of office.

1961 John F. Kennedy begins weekly televised press conferences. Speeds development of personal presidency and raises press expectations of access to president.

1964 Lyndon Johnson initiates Great Society program. Gets Congress to pass Gulf of Tonkin Resolution, giving him free hand as commander in chief in Vietnam without declaration of war. Begins era of "imperial presidency."

1972 Following criminal indictment, Spiro Agnew becomes first vice president to resign. Richard Nixon makes first use of Twenty-fifth Amendment (ratified 1967), naming Gerald Ford vice president.

1973 War Powers Resolution adopted to limit presidential war-making powers; congressional response to imperial presidencies of Johnson and Nixon.

1974 Nixon complies with Supreme Court order to surrender evidence in Watergate scandal that would make certain his impeachment by House and becomes first president to resign from office. Constitutional crisis averted and imperial presidency recedes.

1974 Gerald Ford first person to assume office without ever having run for presidency or vice presidency. Presides over period of stabilization.

1981 Ronald Reagan's personal popularity and initiative to end Cold War help restore public confidence in government. Power of office grows.

1986 Reagan's role in arms-for-hostages scandal increases public distrust of government and the presidency.

1998 Supreme Court reaffirms Nixon ruling by rejecting Bill Clinton's claim of executive privilege on records subpoenaed in impeachment hearings. Clinton becomes second American president to be impeached, but Senate declines to convict. Clinton's popularity reaches all-time high for second-term president, but power of presidency recedes.

1999 Congress declines to renew special prosecutor law used to investigate Nixon and Clinton presidencies.

How can presidential performance be measured? In characterizing the role of the president, the nineteenth-century historian Henry Adams wrote that he "resembles the commander of a ship at sea. He must have a helm to grasp, a course to steer, a port to seek."[72] That is, the incumbent must have a goal, a destination where he is leading the nation; he must have programs and a course of action to enable the nation to get there; and he must be a leader who is willing and able to use the instruments of office to achieve his goals.

Franklin Roosevelt characterized our great presidents as "leaders of thought at times when certain ideas in the life of the nation had to be clarified."[73] This reminds us that an opportunity factor is involved in rising to the highest ranks of performance. FDR's examples— "Washington embod[ying] the idea of the federal union, Jefferson and Jackson the idea of democracy, Lincoln union and freedom"—are of men who served at critical times in the country's development.[74] These are presidents whom almost all scholars rank among our greatest, and they are associated with ideas and policies that took root and affected the course of our country.

Any concept of presidential effectiveness inevitably involves the "vision thing." A president will likely be seen as effective only if he has a clear idea of where he wants to take the country. This is why Reagan is regarded by much of the public as a more effective president than Bush, even though scholars of the presidency give Reagan and Bush comparable rankings. To rank with the "greats," however, vision must be coupled with the political and administrative skills necessary to achieve it. In the scholarly consensus, Bush was willing and able to grab the helm but was steering to no port in particular; Reagan had a fixed destination but no firm hand on the helm and insufficient knowledge or interest to steer the ship. Like Bush, Reagan had a mediocre legislative record and an abysmal fiscal record, but in the public eye Reagan had a clear vision of what he wanted for the country. In contrast, Clinton had all the political and administrative skills to steer the ship but kept changing his destination. He was unsuccessful in projecting to the public a clear and consistent vision of where the country should be headed. In a recent survey, Reagan, Bush, and Clinton were all ranked as average presidents (see the box "Rating the Presidents").

Conclusion: Is the Presidency Responsive?

The presidency has become the most consistently visible office in government as well as one of the most personalized and responsive. Americans expect leadership from the president even in these days of "less" government.

Neustadt called twentieth-century public opinion about the presidency "monarchical." Johnson's and Nixon's "imperial" styles certainly were consistent with it. After a ceremony for Marines going to Vietnam, Johnson was directed to a helicopter by an airman who said, "That's your helicopter over there, sir." Johnson responded, "Son, they are all my helicopters." He once called the State of the Union speech the "State of My Union address."

Most recent presidents eventually learned hard lessons about the limits of presidential power. Indeed, the moral of the personal presidency suggests we have an "impossible" or "imperiled" presidency. Presidents who become popular by making exaggerated promises have trouble keeping them and their popularity in a system of fragmented power.

The presidency is responsive in that the president has an almost direct relationship with the public. Using the media, the president can tell us what he wants and attempt to shape our opinion. Through public opinion polls and the ballot box, we tell the president what we think. In this relationship there is a danger of overreponsiveness. To remain popular, a president may seek short-term solutions to the nation's problems and neglect long-term interests. Short-term responsiveness that caters to public opinion can siphon off the attention and resources a president should be devoting to the real needs of the nation.

EPILOGUE

"Every Step of the Way"

As Gore made the trip to Illinois and Wisconsin with the president, and he did not go quietly. At public assemblies, his introductions of Clinton were so rousing and emotion laden that they almost upstaged the president's talks. Evening news coverage focused on Gore's departure from his usual tepid delivery. Given his political situation, Clinton drew unusually receptive audiences, but Gore was not simply responding to vibrations from the audience. He and his staff had carefully considered their options before Gore decided on the tenor of his remarks.[75]

In many ways Gore's decision was a foregone conclusion given his political alliance with the president and friendship with both of the Clintons. When Clinton needed Gore, he was there, and when

John Russell/AP Wide World Photos

Gore needed Clinton, the president reciprocated. Aside from his personal feelings of loyalty, Gore had little to gain, and a lot to lose, in distancing himself from Clinton. Since everyone knew Gore wanted the presidency, stepping back from Clinton, who had been unprecedentally generous to his vice president, would only look crass and calculating. But did Gore have to go as far as he did, practically screaming his loyalty, emphasizing their personal friendship, and cajoling the public to "stand by his side"?

Gore's career had been built on personal character and credibility, as well as on devotion to policy detail. His reputation had taken some hard hits from the fund-raising allegations and his ties to the tobacco industry; he did not need any more questions about his character and credibility. After saying publicly that if he ran for the presidency, he would not try to separate himself from Clinton because he had been with him "every step of the way," Gore would have a lot of explaining to do. After the Lewinsky scandal broke, Tipper Gore had said, "I don't anticipate anybody being able to divide the Clintons and the Gores. Ever."[76] With this said, Gore was in a situation where half-measures or sitting on the fence might not have worked.

In addition, Gore had been through this before. The Lewinsky scandal may have had the feel of just one more partisan assault. Not for nothing was Clinton known as the "Comeback Kid." And in the unlikely event it did lead to a resignation, Gore would walk into the Oval Office as a man to whom personal and political loyalty meant something, as someone irrevocably tied to Clinton's policies, but whose personal life was never in danger of being confused with his predecessor's.

In reaffirming his support for the president, Gore was boosting confidence in someone from whom he probably could no longer be distanced, as well as in an administration on whose accomplishments he would run in 2000. And, unlike many vice presidents, Gore has every right to do this since he had a hand in shaping its major policies. This was both the advantage and the price of the partnership he developed with the president.

Gore finished out his term with lower approval ratings than Clinton but easily won the Democratic nomination for president. During the campaign, he did what he could to separate himself from the president while still claiming co-credit for the achievements of the Clinton years. He chose a running mate who was known for his stand on "moral issues" and who had been one of the strongest Democratic critics of Clinton during the Lewinsky scandal. Running with Lieberman on a "family values" platform, Gore was able to minimize the impact of the scandals and win the popular vote. But by distancing himself from Clinton he was unable to benefit fully from the administration's successes while at the same time leaving an impression of having changed issue positions and personality to fit his electoral needs.

Key Terms

impeachment
senatorial courtesy
executive privilege
executive orders
head of state

personal presidency
power to persuade
divided government
parliamentary government
War Powers Act

Further Reading

Michael R. Beschloss, ed., *Taking Charge: The Johnson White House Tapes, 1963–64* (New York: Simon & Schuster, 1997). Listen in on White House conversations President Johnson taped during his first year in office and see how one of the legendary exercisers of legislative and executive powers used his powers of persuasion in the conduct of office and hear his thoughts on the assassination of President Kennedy.

Thomas Blaisdell, Jr., and Peter Seltz, eds., *The American Presidency in Political Cartoons, 1776–1976,* rev. ed. (Salt Lake City: Peregrine Smith, 1976). A collection that gives a good idea of how presidents from Washington to Ford were treated by political cartoonists. Cartoons are accompanied by commentary on the political times in which they were drawn.

Colin Campbell and Margaret Jane Wyszomirski, eds., *Executive Leadership in Anglo-American Systems* (Pittsburgh:

University of Pittsburgh Press, 1991). Comparisons of presidential government in the United States and British and Canadian cabinet government with respect to domestic and foreign policymaking, the roles of political appointees and civil servants, and media relations.

Joseph J. Ellis, *American Sphinx: The Character of Thomas Jefferson* (New York: Knopf, 1997). A fascinating look at the mind and presidential style of one of America's greatest presidents.

Doris Kearns Goodwin, *No Ordinary Time* (New York: Simon & Schuster, 1994). An engaging study of life in the White House and the leadership of Franklin Roosevelt during World War II.

Charles O. Jones, *The Presidency in a Separated System* (Washington, D.C.: Brookings Institution, 1994). A book for post–Cold War times, it argues that constitutional limits make popular expectations of presidential leadership unrealistic and that responsibility for public policy must be shared by all branches of government.

Richard E. Neustadt, *Presidential Power and the Modern Presidents* (New York: Free Press, 1990). The most cited book on the presidency, it argues that presidential power is based on the ability to persuade.

Bradley H. Patterson, Jr., *The Ring of Power: The White House Staff and Its Expanding Role in Government* (New York: Basic Books, 1988). This book sees White House operations as so complex and involving so many officials that "the only decision a president carries out himself is to go to the bathroom."

Jeffrey Toobin, *A Vast Conspiracy: The Real Story of the Sex Scandal that Nearly Brought Down a President.* (New York: Random House, 1999). A former prosecutor with experience on an independent counsel staff traces the effort of Clinton's opponents to get him impeached. Contains history of the independent counsel law and its demise.

Electronic Resources

whitehouse.gov/
The White House home page has links to the Office of the Vice President, the First Lady, and all other EOP offices. You can tour the White House, read presidential speeches, and e-mail the president. The link to the First Lady's home page allows viewers to send e-mail, look at the work of the office, and link to biographies of each of America's First Ladies.

www.historyplace.com/specials/sounds.prez/ index.html
Contains sound bites from speeches made by all presidents since Franklin Roosevelt.

presidents.Swath.org
Contains outline biographies of all U.S. presidents, including education and work histories, and reviews major achievements of their administrations.

americanpresidents.org/
C-Span's Peabody Award–winning Web site for historical coverage of the American presidency.

w3.access.gpo.gov/usbudget/fy2001/guideto/html
A Citizen's Guide to the Federal Budget, Fiscal Year 2001. Reading the president's annual budget message is one way to find out the basic goals of any administration.

InfoTrac College Edition

"Clinton's Misuse of Executive Privilege"
"Bill Clinton's Staff"
"Hillary Makes Move"
"Life Cycle of Presidential Approval"

Notes

1. Richard L. Berke, "The Gore Guide to the Future," *New York Times Magazine,* February 22, 1998, pp. 30–35, 46–70. Other sources for this section include Richard L. Berke, "Gore Is No Typical Vice President in the Shadows, *New York Times,* February 19, 1995, pp. 1, 16; L. Edward Purcell, ed., *The Vice Presidents: A Biographical Dictionary* (New York: Facts on File, 1998), 401–407.

2. Theodore J. Lowi, *The Personal President* (Ithaca, N.Y.: Cornell University Press, 1985).

3. Arthur M. Schlesinger, Jr., *The Imperial Presidency* (Boston: Houghton Mifflin, 1973).

4. Harold M. Barger, *The Impossible Presidency* (Glenview, Ill.: Scott-Foresman, 1984).

5. Richard Morin, "A Pollster's Worst Nightmare: Declining Response Rates," *Washington Post National Weekly Edition,* July 5–11, 1993, p. 37; John Hibbing and Elizabeth Theiss-Morse, *Congress as Public Enemy* (Cambridge: Cambridge University Press, 1995).

6. Jefferson's management of the presidency is described in Joseph J. Ellis, *American Sphinx: The Character of Thomas Jefferson* (New York: Knopf, 1997), 186–228.

7. David Stout, "Presidential Candidates Seem Indifferent to a Salary Rise," *New York Times,* May 30, 1999, p. 16; Daniel J. Parks, "Prospective Presidential Pay Raise, First in 30 Years, Would Also Ease Other Officials' Salary 'Compression,' " *Congressional Quarterly Weekly Report,* May 29, 1999, p. 1264.

8. Quoted in Alen Cowell, "Impeachment: What a Royal Pain," *New York Times,* February 7, 1999, section 4, p. 5.

9. "George Mason: Forgotten Founder," *Smithsonian Magazine* (May 2000): 145.

10. The full text of Starr's report to Congress appeared in the *New York Times,* September 12, 1998, pp. B1–B18. The transcript of Clinton's grand jury testimony was reprinted in the *New York Times,* September 22, 1998, pp. B1–B8. You can review impeachment documents, hear sound bites from trial testimony, and look at the principal participants at www.pbs.org/newshour/ impeachment.

11. For discussion of the president's removal powers in light of a 1988 Supreme Court decision regarding independent counsels, see John A. Rohr, "Public Administration, Executive Power, and Constitutional Confusion," and Rosemary O'Leary, "Response to John Rohr," *Public Administrative Review* 49 (March/April 1989): 108–115.

12. Charles O. Jones, *The Presidency in a Separated System* (Washington, D.C.: Brookings Institution, 1994), 53.

13. *The Presidency A to Z: A Ready Reference Encyclopedia* (Washington, D.C.: Congressional Quarterly, 1992), 169.

14. Ibid., 170.

15. "The Power of the Pardon," *National Journal,* March 11, 2000, pp. 774–778.

16. *United States v. Curtiss-Wright Export Corporation,* 299 U.S. 304 (1936).

17. See the discussion in *Federalist Paper* 69, written by Alexander Hamilton.

18. Quoted in "Notes and Comment," *New Yorker,* June 1, 1987, p. 23.

19. Ibid.

20. John Barry, "What Schwarzkopf's Book Leaves Out," *Newsweek,* September 28, 1992, p. 68.

21. *Youngstown Sheet and Tube Co. v. Sawyer,* 343 U.S. 579 (1952).

22. Thomas F. Cronin, *The State of the Presidency* (Boston: Little, Brown, 1975), 118.

23. James Reston, "Cut the Public Relations Budget," *Lincoln Star,* February 7, 1989, p. 6.

24. Jones, *The Presidency,* 56–57.

25. "Hell from the Chief: Hot Tempers and Presidential Timber," *New York Times,* November 7, 1999, section 4, p. 7.

26. Fred I. Greenstein, *The Hidden-Hand Presidency* (New York: Basic Books, 1982).

27. Quoted in Richard Pious, *The American Presidency* (New York: Basic Books, 1979), 244.

28. *"American Presidents,"* episode 10 (PBS). Partial text can be found at www.pbs.org/ampres/.

29. Ann Reilly Dowd, "What Managers Can Learn from Manager Reagan," *Fortune,* September 15, 1986, pp. 32–41.

30. See John H. Kessel, "The Structures of the Reagan White House," *American Journal of Political Science 28* (May 1984): 231–258.

31. Hillary Rodham Clinton quoted in Carol Gelderman, *All the Presidents' Words: The Bully Pulpit and the Creation of the Virtual Presidency* (New York: Walker, 1997), 160.

32. "The White House Office," *U.S. Government Manual, 1997–1998,* 90–93.

33. Edith P. Mayo, ed., *The Smithsonian Book of First Ladies* (Washington, D.C.: Smithsonian Institution, 1996), 11.

34. Gil Troy, *Affairs of State: The Rise and Rejection of the First Couple since World War II* (New York: Free Press, 1997), 250. Troy also discusses attempts at reorganizing the first lady's office. See especially 178–188 and 248–258.

35. For a review of the backgrounds of men who have served in the vice presidency and the roles they have played, see Purcell, *The Vice Presidents;* Michael Nelson, *A Heartbeat Away* (New York: Priority, 1988); Paul C. Light, *Vice-Presidential Power: Advice and Influence in the White House* (Baltimore: Johns Hopkins University Press, 1984); and George Sirgiovanni, "The 'Van Buren Jinx': Vice Presidents Need Not Beware," *Presidential Studies Quarterly* 18 (Winter 1988): 61–76.

36. Purcell, *The Vice Presidents,* 380.

37. Jeffrey K. Tulis, *The Rhetorical Presidency* (Princeton, N.J.: Princeton University Press, 1987).

38. Garry Wills, *Lincoln at Gettysburg* (New York: Simon & Schuster, 1992), 31.

39. David Halberstam, *The Powers That Be* (New York: Dell, 1980), 30.

40. Lowi, *The Personal President.*

41. Associated Press, "Poll Shows Americans Want a Strong Leader," *Lincoln Journal,* June 16, 1992, p. 5.

42. "A Talk with Clinton," *Newsweek,* January 25, 1993, p. 37.

43. Carl M. Cannon, "Judging Clinton," *National Journal,* January 1, 2000, p. 23.

44. Richard E. Neustadt, *Presidential Power: The Politics of Leadership from FDR to Carter* (New York: Wiley, 1980).

45. Samuel Kernell, *Going Public: New Strategies of Presidential Leadership* (Washington, D.C.: CQ Press, 1986), 15.

46. Ibid.

47. Ibid., 38–42.

48. Ibid., 120.

49. "Notes and Comments," *New Yorker,* November 7, 1988, p. 29.

50. "The Presidency," *Newsweek,* December 20, 1993, p. 46.

51. George C. Edwards III, *The Public Presidency* (New York: St. Martin's, 1983), 253.

52. John Mueller, *War, Presidents and Public Opinion* (New York: Wiley, 1970).

53. For example, see Edwards, *The Public Presidency,* 239–247.

54. Poll scores reported here are from the following *National Journal* issues: December 8, 1990, p. 2993; January 19, 1991, p. 185; and February 16, 1991, p. 412.

55. For more on the Gulf War's impact on Bush's ratings, see John A. Krosnick and Laura A. Brannon, "The Impact of the Gulf War on the Ingredients of Presidential Evaluations: Multidimensional Effects of Political Involvement," *American Political Science Review* 87 (December 1993): 963–975.

56. These survey results are from "Opinion Outlook," *National Journal,* February 18, 1995, p. 452.

57. M. Fiorina, *Divided Government* (New York: Macmillan, 1992), 7.

58. D.R. Mayhew, "Divided Party Control: Does It Make a Difference?" *PS: Political Science and Politics* (December 1991): 637–640.

59. Reported in George C. Edwards III, *Presidential Influence in Congress* (San Francisco: Freeman, 1980), 125.

60. Quoted in Dick Kirschten, "Reagan Warms Up for Political Hardball," *National Journal,* February 9, 1985, p. 328.

61. Edwards, *Presidential Influence,* 127.

62. "A Furor over the Secret War," *Newsweek,* April 23, 1984, p. 22.

63. Charles W. Ostrom, Jr., and Brian I. Job, "The President and the Political Use of Force," *American Political Science Review* 80 (June 1986): 541–566.

64. Elizabeth Drew, "Letter From Washington," *The New Yorker,* February 4, 1991, p. 83.

65. Charlie Cook, "Why Kosovo Fails to Stir Public Passion," *National Journal,* April 3, 1999, p. 908.

66. Richard J. Stoll, "The Sound of the Guns," *American Politics Quarterly* 15 (April 1987): 223–237.

67. Richard J. Barnet, *The Rockets' Red Glare: When America Goes to War—The Presidents and the People* (New York: Simon & Schuster, 1990).

68. Karen Toombs Parsons, "Exploring the 'Two Presidents' Phenomenon: New Evidence from the Truman Administration," *Presidential Studies Quarterly* 24 (Summer 1994): 495–514.

69. See, for example, the comments of Arthur Schlesinger in "Judging Clinton," p. 22; Steven A. Holmes, "Losers in Clinton-Starr Bouts May Be Future U.S. Presidents," *New York Times,* August 23, 1998, p. 18; Adam Clymer, "The Presidency Is Still There, Not Quite the Same," *New York Times,* February 14, 1999, section 4, p. 1.

70. See, for example, David Broder and Dan Balz, "Who Wins?" *Washington Post National Weekly Edition,* January 15, 1999, pp. 6–7; "Judging Clinton," pp. 22–23.

71. Richard E. Neustadt, *Presidential Power: The Politics of Leadership from FDR to Carter* (New York: Wiley, 1980).

72. Quoted in Arthur M. Schlesinger, Jr., "The Ultimate Approval Rating," *New York Times Magazine,* December 18, 1996, p. 50.

73. Ibid.

74. Ibid.

75. Berke, "The Gore Guide to the Future," p. 32.

76. Quoted in ibid., p. 34.

The Bureaucracy

YOU ARE THERE

Attacking AIDS

Y ou are the government's top medical officer, the surgeon general of the United States, C. Everett Koop. It is 1986 and President Reagan has asked you to report to him on what has become a major problem: acquired immune deficiency syndrome (AIDS). AIDS involves a virus that weakens the body's immunity, making it vulnerable to deadly infections.

There have been more than 35,000 cases of AIDS so far in the United States, 493 of them children. Those who contract AIDS inevitably die, as 20,000 Americans have so far. You estimate that 1.5 million people have been exposed to the virus and that 270,000 will develop AIDS by 1991.[1] In the United States, people at most risk of getting it are intravenous drug users and homosexual men.[2] However, AIDS has begun to appear among heterosexual men and women through contact with intravenous drug users, prostitutes, bisexuals, and those who had multiple blood transfusions before the spring of 1985, when blood banks began testing for AIDS.

As long as almost all the victims came from the first two groups, most people did not worry about AIDS. As it began to spread, however, it became a major issue

arousing considerable public anxiety. For example, real estate agents trying to sell Rock Hudson's house found that clients would not enter it because they knew he had died of AIDS. And some parents have tried to bar child victims of AIDS from the schools their children attend.

Now the president has asked for a report advising him what to do. You do not expect an effective vaccine to be available until the mid-1990s at the earliest. A major issue that your report must deal with is whether we should require mandatory testing for AIDS. A blood test can reveal exposure to the AIDS virus, but it cannot predict who will get the disease because some who carry the virus will not contract the disease. Still, finding out who has been exposed to the virus can help limit the exposure of others to it.

Already, military recruits and Foreign Service officers must take a blood test to determine whether they have been exposed to AIDS. Proposals have been made to test many others, such as convicted prostitutes and intravenous drug users, hospital patients from fifteen to forty-nine years of age, venereal disease patients, and couples seeking marriage licenses. Secretary of Education William

Bureau of Engraving and Printing employees check the quality of $20 bills. The woman on the right is holding $8,000 of mistakes.
Ted Thai/*Time* magazine

Former Surgeon General Koop visits an AIDS patient.
© Rick Browne/Photoreporters

Few experts agree with Secretary Bennett, who argues that the key to stopping AIDS is to teach sexual abstinence to our children. Most experts recommend educating young people about "safe sex" and contraception. They say abstinence as a policy is unrealistic given the emphasis on sex in our society, as illustrated by studies showing that television programming refers to sexual intercourse at least once an hour. Their views reflect Senator Paul Simon's (D-Ill.) remark that, "It's been too long since [Bennett] was a teenager."

Many conservatives object strongly to sex education in schools. Referring to "safe sodomy" instead of "safe sex," they say "condomania" means we have given up trying to raise our children properly.

The president is comfortable with conservative views on AIDS. When he appointed you, you were a surgeon in Philadelphia, known for having pioneered techniques to separate Siamese twins and for being a born-again Christian with conservative views on abortion and birth control. You know your views were more important to the president than your surgical innovations. You agree with him on many issues and want to write a report he will like. Your political instincts push you this way.

On the other side of the coin, and in government there is always another side to the coin, you are a doctor who respects the views of health care professionals. You want to write a report that will help fight AIDS, without political interference. What should you do?

Bennett, whose views often echo the president's, also wants to include prison inmates and people planning to immigrate here. He says the government should notify spouses and past sexual partners if test results are positive—that is, if evidence of exposure to AIDS is found.

Many conservatives view AIDS as a moral issue. They think AIDS is a punishment for homosexuality and drug use. Some charge that public health officials are "intimidated by the homosexual lobby." One called AIDS the "first politically protected disease in the history of mankind."[3] They want you to recommend mandatory testing to identify who is infected so government can quarantine those who will not change their sexual or drug habits to protect society.

Most public health experts reject mandatory testing as unworkable. They argue that many people will go underground to avoid being tested. They also say mandatory testing of huge numbers of people will produce mistakes in test results. Furthermore, most experts oppose mandatory testing as a violation of doctor/patient confidentiality and doubt that most people will identify their sexual partners. They add that mandatory testing will only increase discrimination against homosexuals and others who have been exposed to AIDS and who may or may not contract it.

Americans expect their government to deliver billions of dollars worth of services to them, from highways for fast-moving cars to Social Security payments on time, from clean running water to safe neighborhoods, from protection from foreign enemies to cures for cancer. At the same time, most Americans denigrate their government and its bureaucracy, and some even express hatred toward it. In 1995, in Oklahoma City, scores of people were murdered because they were federal bureaucrats (or happened to be in the same building with bureaucrats).

Despite the strong emotions sometimes directed toward them, federal bureaucrats are ordinary people. But the jobs they are asked to do and the number of different groups to which they are responsible make them a target for public distress with society's problems.

The federal bureaucracy employs slightly more than three million civilians, who work in more than eight hundred different occupations in one hundred agencies, and slightly less than one million uniformed military personnel. The bureaucracy executes or enforces policies made by Congress and the president. Because policymakers have given government many different goals, the bureaucracy has many different jobs. It analyzes the soil, runs hospitals and utilities, fights drug abuse, checks manufacturers' claims about their products, to mention only a few bureaucratic responsibilities.

To some, the bureaucracy is the fourth branch of government—powerful, uncontrollable, and often seeming to have a life of its own. As the part of government that carries out the law, the bureaucracy is also political. People disagree about whether it does its job well, largely because they disagree about the goals policymakers set for it. One person's lazy, red tape–ridden, uncaring bureaucracy is another's responsive agency.

Bureaucracy

Around the turn of the century, the German social scientist Max Weber predicted that bureaucracy would someday dominate society. That future is now. Bureaucracy affects almost everything we do.

Nature of Bureaucracy

Although individual bureaucracies differ in many ways, all share some common features.[4] For example, all have hierarchies of authority; that is, everyone in a bureaucracy has a place in a pyramidal network of jobs with fewer near the top and more near the bottom. Almost everyone in a bureaucracy has a boss and, unless one is at the bottom of a hierarchy, some subordinates.

Individuals with more expertise and experience tend to have more authority. As a result, bureaucracy is not always consistent with democratic principles, which hold that everyone should have the same opportunity to influence events. Indeed, bureaucracy can endanger individual opportunities to express opinions, raise doubts about the value of individual opinions, and jeopardize the availability of information to individuals. In effect, bureaucratic tendencies, if unrestrained, can transform "citizens" into "subordinates."

Public and Private Bureaucracies

Many people associate public bureaucracies with monotony and inefficiency. A Virginia company sold a "Bureaucrat" doll, calling it "a product of no redeeming social value. Place the Bureaucrat on a stack of papers on your desk, and he will just sit on them."[5]

Although stereotyping the public service can produce some laughs, it misses the similarities shared by public and private bureaucracies. For example, both involve a good deal of routine. Auditing expense vouchers is as routine in a business firm as in a public agency. Both also have workers who are productive and efficient and others who are not. Executives in the Defense Department bought $600 toilet seats and spent more than $75 apiece for metal screws sold elsewhere for 57 cents. Their private counterparts at Chrysler, Lockheed, Penn Central, and hundreds of banks and savings and loans ran their businesses into the ground.

To some extent, the distinction between private and public bureaucracies has become blurred.[6] However, Americans typically distinguish public from private bureaucracies by looking at goals and openness.

Goals

Businesses are supposed to make a profit, while public agencies are supposed to promote the "public interest." Although people disagree over what the "public interest" is, they know public agencies do not exist to make a profit.

Public and private bureaucratic goals differ in another way too. It is usually easier to measure and put a value on efforts to achieve private goals than public ones. We can identify the value of a chair or a house by computing the cost of building them. Placing a value on such public goals as consumer safety or education is much harder. How many children must die from eating the contents of medicine bottles before government should require pharmaceutical manufacturers to use childproof caps on bottles? How many lives saved make it worthwhile for government to require auto manufacturers to install side-impact air bags, thereby raising auto prices?

Difficulties in measuring what government agencies do and disagreements over defining the public interest often produce charges that public bureaucracy is wasteful. Indeed, over two-thirds of the American public believes government programs are usually inefficient and wasteful.[7] Of course, private corporations may waste far more than government.[8] But government spending is so great that even if it wastes only proportionally as much money as a typical citizen does, the sums are vast.

Discussions of government "waste" are confusing because they refer to two quite different things. One involves inefficient or corrupt government agencies, those that, for example, do not get competitive bids and therefore pay more than they need to for supplies. This type

"I'm sorry, dear, but you knew I was a bureaucrat when you married me."

of waste also occurs when more employees are hired than are necessary to do a job, when consultants are paid to do little, or when errors are made in calculating welfare or farm subsidy payments so that recipients are overpaid.

A second kind of government "waste" is a program that some people find objectionable, no matter how well run it is. This meaning of waste has little to do with mismanagement or fraud. Waste in this sense may mean that a particular program serves relatively few people at a large cost. For example, a government commission labeled the operation of hundreds of very small post offices "wasteful." The commission did not allege fraud or mismanagement but said the post offices cost a lot for the small number of people served. However, residents of small communities argued that their post offices were not a waste but an important source of community pride.

The average citizen probably does not think much about waste, particularly this second kind, in private bureaucracies. If a business or industry makes a profit, we assume it is not being wasteful. We may not like chocolate-covered raisins, but we do not consider their manufacturer wasteful for making them as long as the product is profitable.

Openness

The openness of public bureaucracy is a second way of distinguishing it from private bureaucracy. Both often have internal disagreements about their goals, but differences about public agency goals are usually more visible. Private firms operate with much more secrecy than do public agencies, even when private actions have a significant impact on the public. For example, tobacco companies' lack of openness, while long assumed to be their right, cost the lives of many people. The courts ordered tobacco companies to open their files only after much scientific evidence on the dangers of tobacco had accumulated. In contrast, visibility, or openness, helps make public agencies responsive. Only by having knowledge of both the process and the content of public decisions can interested groups and individuals express their preferences effectively.

The question, of course, is openness to whom? Because the bureaucracy is doing the public's business, one answer is being open to the public. But being open to the public also means being open to the media who want to report significant conflicts and decisions made in the executive branch and open to interest groups who want to influence agencies' decisions.

In the Sunshine Act of 1977 and the Freedom of Information Act of 1966, as amended in 1974, Congress recognized the importance of keeping public bureaucracies open. The Sunshine Act requires regulatory agencies, such as the Food and Drug Administration, to give advance notice of the date, time, place, and agenda of their meetings and to follow certain rules to prevent unwarranted secrecy. The Freedom of Information Act lets people obtain information from agencies if it is not classified or concerned with sensitive matters.

The Freedom of Information Act was intended to make agencies more open to the public, but most requests for information come from businesses, interest groups, lawyers, and the media. Very few members of the general public take advantage of it. But groups that are directly affected by an agency's decisions have a strong incentive to use the act. Thus, in one year, 85 percent of the requests for information submitted to the Food and Drug Administration came from companies that it regulates. That information enables those companies to evaluate their strategies for influencing the agency's decisions that affect them. And media want to uncover disagreements and conflicts in the agency's internal decision-making process, something no agency would welcome.

Efforts to make government agencies more open often run up against a desire to limit the distribution of

critical or embarrassing information. It is the rare public or private bureaucracy that wants to reveal its failures. Thus, an evaluation of the Freedom of Information Act found that agencies used many tactics to discourage people from seeking information, such as delaying responses to requests, charging high fees for copies of records (the State Department once charged $10 a page for copying records), and requiring detailed descriptions of material in requests for information.[9] The Federal Bureau of Investigation (FBI) once refused to expedite the release of information to a prisoner on death row who was afraid he would be executed before the information was available. (The FBI's judgment that his situation did not show "exceptional need or urgency" was overruled by a federal court.)[10]

As the chief executive, a president's views on the openness of agencies have also been important. Recent presidents have had different views. Under Reagan and Bush, federal agencies adopted a narrow reading of the act, making it more difficult to get information.[11] Carter and Clinton attempted, somewhat unsuccessfully, to open the bureaucracy more and to classify fewer pieces of information. President Carter banned the classification of files lacking a clear relation to national security. In 1995, President Clinton issued an executive order that directed that most documents twenty-five years old or older be declassified and put a ten-year limit on how long documents can remain classified unless a review determines that they should remain so.[12]

Finally, problems with the Freedom of Information Act have surfaced because it was written with the expectation that all information would be on paper. But the federal government, like private businesses, stores an increasing amount of information electronically. The federal bureaucracy now has millions of computers. Retrieving the growing mass of information stored on computer can be easier than finding information on paper. However, the act neither defines when electronic information is in the public domain nor requires agencies to save and release it. Thus, the act does not say whether electronic messages used by officials to schedule meetings or exchange opinions are their private property or public records. Reagan, Bush, and Clinton aides used e-mail extensively. Bush took his aides' e-mail tapes with him when he left office and argued that the tapes were not public property. A federal appeals court ruled that these tapes are public records and must be preserved. The Clinton administration sided with Bush and argued that White House officials have a right to erase the e-mail messages they send to each other.[13] Defining such messages as public helps

---

The Under Secretary of Energy
Washington, D.C. 20585

December, 1992

MEMORANDUM FOR SECRETARIAL OFFICERS

SUBJECT: NE/NE-60 Concurrence

Recently, memoranda have been prepared for my signature or directed to departmental offices from other departmental offices which contain statements regarding whether the direction contained in the memorandum is applicable to Naval Reactors (NE-60). Several memoranda have been incorrect in their assumption regarding the effects on NE-60, resulting in unnecessary further correspondence to correct the misunderstanding.

Applicability to NE-60 of a contemplated action is not always obvious. In many cases, the impact is either indirect or the direct impact is not appreciated due to lack of understanding of the scope of NE-60 responsibility. To avoid misunderstandings in the future, you are requested to consult NE regarding applicability statements before they are made and before memoranda are presented to me, the Secretary, or Deputy Secretary for signature.

I appreciate your attention to this matter.

Hugo Pomrehn
Hugo Pomrehn

Sometimes real examples of bureaucratic thinking are stranger than ones we might imagine. Every issue, Washington Monthly *reprints a memo containing an especially striking example of bureaucratic language. Is it any wonder ordinary people do not trust—or understand—the bureaucracy?*

Some local post offices are economically inefficient, but residents of small towns lobby Congress to keep them open.
Ted Thai/*Time* magazine

Federal Bureaucracy

Growth of the Bureaucracy

The Founders did not discuss the federal "bureaucracy," but they did recognize the need for an administration to carry out laws and programs. They envisioned administrators with only a little power, charged with "executive details" and "mere execution" of the law. But the growing size and complexity of modern society and increasing demands that government do more have dramatically changed the nature of the federal bureaucracy.

George Washington's first cabinet included only three departments and the offices of attorney general and postmaster general, employing a few hundred people. More people worked at Mount Vernon, his plantation, than in the executive branch in the 1790s.[16] The Department of State had just nine employees. By 1800, the bureaucracy was still small, with only three thousand civil servants. Only the Treasury Department had much to do, collecting taxes and purchasing military supplies for an army of a few thousand. Since then, the bureaucracy has grown continuously, though not always at the same rate. Three eras of especially large growth have occurred.

The Civil War years (1861–1865) and the fifty years following the war were the first period of growth. Early in the twentieth century, reformers highlighted unsafe food and drugs and dangerous working conditions for millions of workers. Congress passed laws regulating food and drugs, and new agencies were born to apply the regulations. This era of industrialization, westward expansion, and population growth saw increasing demands for government to provide benefits to business, labor, and farmers. So Congress established the Departments of Commerce, Labor, and Agriculture. Worries about abuses by big business also led to the creation of new bureaucracies, such as the Interstate Commerce Commission, and expanded powers for others, such as antitrust law enforcement in the Justice Department.

A second surge of bureaucratic growth took place during the Great Depression in the 1930s. President Roosevelt changed Washington forever, from a sleepy southern city to an activist capital of a powerful nation. Roosevelt and Congress created a plethora of new agencies to combat the Depression, from the Social Security Administration and Civilian Conservation corps to the National Labor Relations Board and Federal Deposit Insurance Corporation. As one observer commented, he "didn't come alone, Roosevelt brought in people by the hundreds of thousands. . . . [They] came to help run the

hold officials accountable. The act also fails to address problems created by the loss of data over time because tapes and disks deteriorate or are incompatible with new generations of hardware and software. Congress has been trying to remedy computer-related problems for several years without success.

Some agencies are more open than others. Agencies that depend on public support and agreement with their goals are more likely to respond to media requests for information and news. The Food and Drug Administration, for instance, is much more accessible than the State Department.[14] Other agencies prefer less coverage. For them, no news is good news. The balance between openness and responsiveness to the public and undue access for interest groups and the media has been difficult to strike.

Despite the limitations of the Freedom of Information Act, it has enabled individuals and groups to gain important, useful, and even entertaining information. Citizens have used the Freedom of Information Act to gather injury and fatality information on defective cars, to assess dangerous infant formulas, to reveal a link between aspirin and a disease known as Reye's syndrome, to learn that J. Edgar Hoover and the FBI had planted a rumor that Jane Fonda proposed killing Richard Nixon, and to reveal that Elvis Presley volunteered to become an FBI informant but was not accepted.[15]

Wanted: Young Bureaucrats

The attractiveness of government service ebbs and flows over time, reflecting the ethos of the era, other job opportunities provided in the economy, and national needs. Many members of the World War II generation and the 1960s and 1970s generation of social change recognized the importance of public service and the potential for government to make positive changes in society. The World War II era presented crises to solve if the nation were to survive in a free world. The 1960s and 1970s offered other crises to overcome if the nation were to guarantee the rights of freedom to those in society not possessing those rights.

During the 1980s and 1990s, there were no national crises to draw people together in a common enterprise that could be expressed through government service. Those having grown up in the 1980s and 1990s seem less inclined to believe that government can make a positive difference. Indeed, young people heard a generation of politicians running against government. In the 1990s, given the alternative lure of the booming economy and the dot.coms, young people saw government service as

less attractive than the private sector. Public service took a back seat to "make as much as you can as quickly as you can." Even those who decided on a public service career had choices outside government, as the growth of nonprofit philanthropic organizations provided alternatives.

As the World War II generation passes from the workforce and the 1960s generation approaches retirement, will government service remain vital? The composition of the federal workforce gives some cause for concern. During the 1990s, the average age of government employees rose from forty-two to over forty-five, reflecting a real demographic change.[1] The average length of service rose similarly. Currently, about 20 percent of the federal workforce is under thirty-four compared with 38 percent in the entire civilian labor force, a rather dramatic difference.[2]

The dwindling recruitment of young people into the federal civil service has aroused concern.[3] One analyst of the workforce suggests that the government needs to change its recruiting practices. For example, it needs to recruit at the

middle and upper management level rather than always promoting from within. It also must become much more aggressive in recruiting at all levels, realizing that the competition for talented people is particularly stiff right now. He also suggests that many jobs could be made more challenging so that employees can feel like they are really making a difference.[4]

Of course, in harder economic times or periods of crises, government service will become more attractive. The challenge now is to improve its attractiveness in good times as well as bad.

1. Office of Workforce Information, Office of Personnel Management, "The Typical Federal Civilian Employee," *The Fact Book*, http://www.opm.gov/feddata/99factbk/pdf.
2. Bureau of Labor Statistics, *Current Population Survey, Employee Tenure in 1998*, Table 3, http://stats.bls.gov/news.release/tenure.t03.htm, for civilian labor force data; and Office of Workforce Information, Office of Personnel Management. *Demographic Profile of the Federal Workforce*, Table 11, http://www.opm.gov/feddata/demograp/tble11mw.pdf, for federal workforce data.
3. Paul C. Light, "The Empty Government Talent Pool: The New Public Service Arrives," *Brookings Review* (Winter 2000): 20.
4. Ibid., 23.

new idea of government that accounted for that expansion—brainy, self confident men and women who carried with them the belief in the capital as the nerve center of the nation." In Washington alone, the federal workforce rose from 63,000 in 1933 to 287,000 a decade later.[17]

A third era of bureaucratic growth came during the 1960s and 1970s as a response to public demands that government do more to fight poverty, protect the environment, promote civil rights, and ensure consumer and worker safety. During this time Congress created several new cabinet departments (Housing and Urban Development, Transportation, Energy, and Education) and agencies (Environmental Protection Agency [EPA], Occupa-

tional Safety and Health Administration [OSHA], and the Equal Employment Opportunity Commission [EEOC]). See the boxes on youth, women, and minorities for the roles of these groups in American bureaucracy.

Why the Bureaucracy Has Grown

President Reagan once expressed the popular dissatisfaction with big government by noting that he liked flying over Washington because being in the air made government look smaller (see the box "Are Bureaucrats the Enemy?" for more on such antibureaucracy views). Despite Reagan's pronounced feelings about the bureaucracy, it grew by over two hundred thousand employees

AMERICAN DIVERSITY

Women and Minorities in the Civil Service

Americans expect their public bureaucracies to be open and responsive. Andrew Jackson recognized this when he opened the civil service to frontiersmen of "common" origins. He hoped to make the bureaucracy more responsive and more representative by putting his frontier supporters in office. In the twentieth century, the expectation that public agencies should be open to all qualified applicants gave some groups, such as the Irish, Jews, and blacks, more job opportunities than in the more restricted private corporate world.

Although progress has been made, the federal bureaucracy does not yet fully reflect the diversity of the American people. The bureaucracy seems to have a "glass ceiling" that keeps women and minority men out of top management positions.[1] Most women work in lower civil service grades doing mostly clerical and service jobs. Women tend to earn several thousand dollars less and to be in jobs one to three grades lower than men with the same levels of education and federal job experience. Women are also less likely to be promoted in their first five years of federal employment than men with the same qualifications and background. And fewer women than men get to grade 13, the gateway to supervisory jobs. Thus, women are less likely than

men to be in grades from which they can be promoted to top-level jobs. Similarly, blacks, Hispanics, and other minorities hold relatively few top-level jobs in the federal government. Minority workers are also almost three times as likely to be fired as white workers.[2]

In the 1970s, both women and minorities made progress in filling high-level civil service jobs. In the 1980s, women made more progress than minorities, though in relation to their proportion of the population, minorities are better represented than women. In 1995, women comprised 51 percent of the total population, while African Americans totaled about 13 percent, Hispanics 10 percent, Native Americans 1 percent, and Asians

nearly 4 percent.[3] As the accompanying table indicates, the representation of women and minorities among top-level federal executives continued to improve during the 1990s but remains far from being proportional to their share of the total U.S. population.

Major discrepancies remain, in part, because those who enforced equal opportunity and nondiscrimination regulations were white men opposed to affirmative action policies. Indeed, the Justice Department backed white males who sued the government for reverse discrimination.

Problems also remain because performance evaluations in the bureaucracy favor employees who work overtime and who have worked in different offices as a

Percentage of Women and Minorities in High-Level Executive Jobs in the Federal Civil Service

	1985	1990	1998
Women	8	12	22
African Americans	4	5	7
Hispanics	1	2	3
Asians and Pacific Islanders	1	1	2

SOURCE: Data are for those at the executive/senior pay levels. Overall, about 7 percent of all federal employees are in this grade. Equal Employment Opportunity Commission, *Annual Report on the Employment of Minorities, Women and People with Disabilities in the Federal Government, for the Fiscal Year Ending 1994*, Table I-15. 1998 data from *Statistical Abstract of the United States, 1999*, Table 568. www.opm.gov/feddata/demograp/Table2mw.pdf

during his administration. Although many agencies lost personnel (the biggest loser was the Department of Housing and Urban Development), others such as the Defense, Justice, and Treasury Departments gained. The continued growth of the bureaucracy suggests that powerful forces in society view it as a source of benefits.

One scholar explained the bureaucracy's growth by pointing to Americans' discovery that "government can protect and assist as well as punish and repress."[18] Thus, at the same time we criticize government's growth, we

demand educational services, irrigation projects, roads, airports, job training, consumer protection, and many other benefits. Each of us might be willing to cut benefits for someone else, but most of us want government benefits for ourselves. As we have seen, over time, government responded to public wishes by creating federal agencies to assist and promote emerging economic interests of business, agriculture, and labor and, more recently, to provide health and economic benefits to workers, consumers, retirees, and other groups.[19]

women, including many Hispanic and black women. What is not inevitable is that more women and minorities will hold top-level jobs. For this to happen, policymakers must set clear goals, adopt effective recruitment and training programs, and treat complaints of discrimination sympathetically.

A shy woman who once said, "I hate politics," Eleanor Roosevelt became the most influential First Lady ever. In her role as wife and advisor to her husband, Franklin Delano Roosevelt, Mrs. Roosevelt prodded him to appoint women to high levels of the federal government.
UPI/Corbis-Bettmann

1. For summaries of the studies see Joanne Desky, "Women Bump into Glass Ceiling in Government," *PA Times,* December 1, 1992, pp. 1 and 16; Pan Suk Kim and Gregory B. Lewis, "Asian Americans in the Public Service: Success, Diversity, and Discrimination," *Public Administration Review* (May/June 1994): 285–290; Gregory B. Lewis, "Is It Time to Drop the Glass Ceiling Metaphor?" and Katherine C. Naff, "A Question of Equity in the Federal Government," both in *PA Times,* November 1, 1992, p. 8; Mary E. Guy, "Three Steps Forward, Two Steps Backward: The Status of Women's Integration into Public Management," *Public Administration Review* (July/August 1993) : 285–292.
2. Stephen Barr, "In the Line of Firings," *Washington Post National Weekly Edition,* February 21–27, 1994, p. 34; Craig Zwerling and Hilary Silver, "Race and Job Dismissals in a Federal Bureaucracy," *American Sociological Review* (October 1992): 651–660.
3. *Statistical Abstract of the United States, 1999,* Table 13. For a report on minority and especially African American progress, see Sylvester Murray et al., "The Role Demands and Dilemmas of Minority Public Administrators," *Public Administration Review* (September/October 1994): 409–416.
4. Katherine C. Naff, "Through the Glass Ceiling: Prospects for the Advancement of Women in the Federal Civil Service," *Public Administration Review* (November/December 1994): 513.

result of transfers. These criteria limit the careers of many women. For example, the government's poor record of providing job-site child care means that many women cannot work overtime because they, more than men, must juggle work and family commitments. Moreover, for many women the work environment is still hostile. They believe they are not as respected as men and have to meet higher standards to be promoted and rewarded.[4]

Some factors limit the ability of policymakers to diversify public service employment. For example, offices in parts of the country with small minority populations may have problems hiring minorities. However, other factors suggest that the diversification of the public service is inevitable. A large proportion of new entrants into the labor force are now

Sometimes bureaucracies grow in response to external threats. Though World War II was won over fifty years ago, our Department of Defense has never returned to its prewar size or scope. The Cold War gave us a new reason to support a massive military establishment. And, of course, from the war as well as later ones came demands for services for veterans, another area of government growth.

Because the bureaucracy has grown in response to demands for public services, its growth has not been un-controlled as some have charged. Every agency needs congressional and presidential approval of its programs, appropriations, staffing, and procedures. In fact, government also grows, ironically, because the president and Congress want it to be more accountable. This often results in hiring more managers, producing inefficiency and, ironically, more difficulty in holding agencies accountable.[20] Bureaucrats cannot produce growth on their own. Every agency exists because it is valuable to enough people with enough influence to sustain it.

The growth of the bureaucracy should be seen in the perspective of the overall growth of our economy and population. For example, the number of federal bureaucrats for every one thousand people in the United States decreased from sixteen in 1953 to ten in 1999.[21] This trend is likely to continue. Total personnel costs were only 7 percent of total federal spending in 1998.

The major growth in public employment has been at the state and local levels. Over 37 percent of all government workers were federal employees in 1953; in 1997 only 14 percent were. Only about 7 percent of these federal civil servants work in the Washington, D.C., metropolitan area.

Some of these trends are illustrated in Figure 1, which shows the growth in the size, cost, and regulatory activities of the executive branch. On a per-population basis, since 1960 the size of the bureaucracy has actually declined, but its expenditure of funds has doubled and its production of regulations has tripled. However, regulatory activity peaked in 1980 and is now much lower.

Types of Bureaucracy

Although the Constitution says little about the organization of the executive branch, the Founders probably expected all bureaucratic jobs to be included in only a few departments, each headed by one person. Yet the bureaucracy has become much more complex than this. There are several major types of federal bureaucracy.[22]

Departments

Fourteen departments are directly responsible to the president and headed by presidential appointees. Thirteen of these appointees, called secretaries, comprise the cabinet, along with the attorney general who runs the

Are Bureaucrats the Enemy?

When George Wallace ran as a third-party candidate for president in 1968, he campaigned against "pointy-headed bureaucrats" in Washington making decisions that regulated good people's lives. Bureaucrats, according to Wallace, were out of touch with everyday citizens and their concerns. Bureaucrats became symbols of big government and everything people dislike about big government.

Similar charges and criticisms abound today. Patrick Buchanan and Ross Perot are only the latest in a long line of politicians who run for office by criticizing government and the people who work for it. When they refer to "Washington," we all understand the reference: Big government using too much money to do things that are not needed. Why does big government do so many unneeded things? These critics would answer, "Because bureaucrats do not understand how people live. They are not like you and me." Instead, they are busybodies committed to expanding government's size, spending taxpayers' money, and designing regulations to make life more difficult for individuals and business.

Are government bureaucrats really like this? Are they different from other citizens? A comparison using a large national sample found that public employees are like everyone else in most ways. They are no more likely to favor raising taxes or government spending; they have about the same confidence in government and other institutions—such as organized religion, business, labor, and the press—as other citizens; and they are about as likely to favor busing and gun control.

When civil servants do differ from other citizens, they seem more open to diversity. For example, they are more likely to say they would vote for a black or woman as president and less likely to accept traditional gender roles. And they are somewhat *less* likely than other Americans to approve government intrusions into people's private lives. They are less likely to approve censoring people with unpopular views or laws banning pornography or interracial marriage. On only one issue are they more liable to favor "big government." They are somewhat more likely to favor wiretapping.

Not only do federal bureaucrats resemble us, they live around us, too. A small number—around 7 percent—work in Washington, D.C.,[1] but the rest work in branch offices scattered throughout the nation. Check the U.S. Government listing in your telephone book and see how many offices are located in or near your hometown. All the people who work there are bureaucrats in one sense or another. But they are your neighbors, pretty ordinary people you meet on the street every day.

1. U.S. Department of Commerce, Bureau of the Census, *Statistical Abstract of the United States, 1999,* Table 569.
SOURCE: Gregory B. Lewis, "In Search of the Machiavellian Milquetoasts: Comparing Attitudes of Bureaucrats and Ordinary People," *Public Administration Review* (May/June 1990): 220–227.

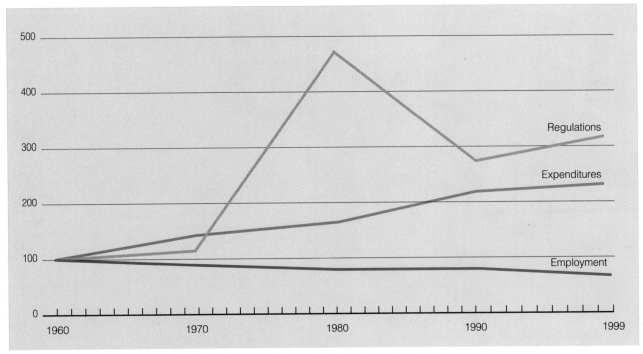

FIGURE 1 ■ *Federal Government Growth: Money, Rules, and People* The numbers listed vertically on the left are percentages, comparing each year with 1960. They indicate the growth of federal regulatory activity, federal spending, and the size of the civil service, each on a per-person basis.

SOURCES: Idea for chart from Hugh Heclo, "Issue Networks and the Executive Establishment," in Anthony King, ed., *The New American Political System* (Washington, D.C.: American Enterprise Institute, 1978), 90. Data are from the Budget of the United States Government and the *Statistical Abstract of the United States*. Data on numbers of regulations are drawn from Harold Stanly and Richard Niemi, *Vital Statistics of US Politics* (Washington, D.C.: Congressional Quarterly, 1998), 258.

Justice Department. Departments constitute the lion's share of the executive branch, with over 60 percent of all civilian workers. The largest employer is the Defense Department. The Department of Veterans Affairs is the newest department, created in 1989 from an independent agency (see Figure 2).

Independent Agencies

Independent agencies are independent only in that they are not parts of departments. Their heads are appointed by and responsible to the president. In this, independent agencies resemble departments. They differ from departments, however, in that they are often smaller and their heads do not sit in the cabinet. The largest of these agencies are the National Aeronautics and Space Administration and the General Services Administration.

Independent Regulatory Boards and Commissions

These boards and commissions regulate some aspect of the economy. Five to ten presidential appointees head every independent regulatory board and commission. By law, each board and commission must be balanced with members of both major political parties. Appointees serve staggered terms and cannot be removed by presidents who dislike their decisions. Examples of such boards include the Federal Communications Commission, which regulates the electronic media. The Securities and Exchange Commission makes and enforces rules regarding stocks, bonds, and securities. And the National Labor Relations Board regulates labor-management relations.

These and other regulatory agencies are "independent" because they are supposed to work free of partisan influences and presidential control. Many people believe regulatory problems are technical, not political, and should be removed from politics insofar as possible. Others point out that technical decisions may also be political. Just how strict or lax the regulations for nuclear power plants should be is a political as well as a technical question because it involves value judgments, weighing costs, health, and safety. Because the voice of the public is heard through elected officials, the immunity of regulators from "politics" means immunity from public, as well as presidential or congressional, control.

As a result, in recent years Congress has tended to place regulatory functions in the hands of agencies

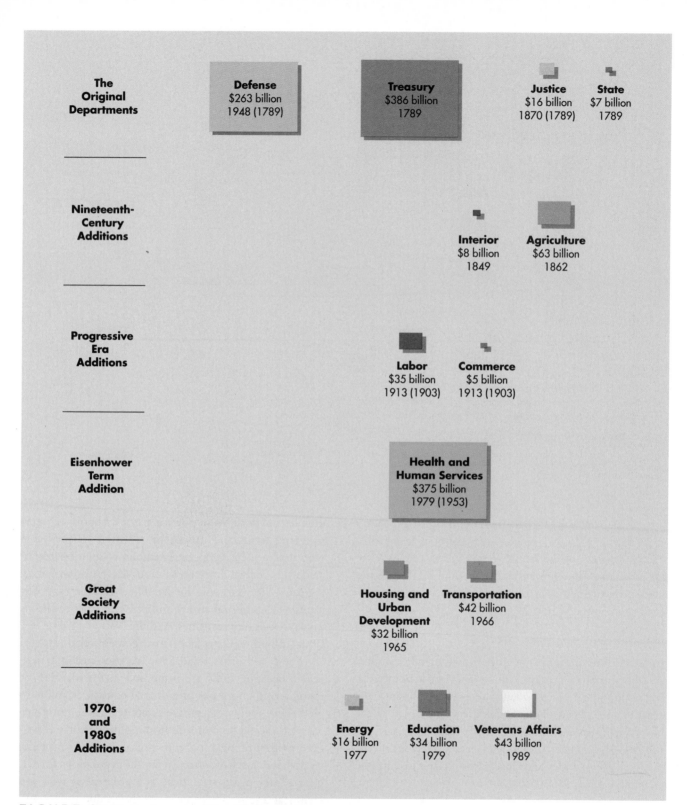

FIGURE 2 ■ *The Development and Size of Cabinet Departments*

Note: The figures in each box include 1999 budget estimates and year of founding. Some departments have undergone a name change or major reorganization. The date of their initial founding is in paren- theses. The modern Defense Department replaced the Departments of War (1789) and Navy (1798); the Justice Department replaced the Attorney General (1789); the Commerce and Labor Departments were first established in 1903 as a joint enterprise; and the Health and Human Services Department and the Education Department replaced the Department of Health, Education, and Welfare (1953).

SOURCE: *Statistical Abstract of the United States, 1999,* Table 547.

within the executive branch, which are more responsive to the president through his power of removal.

Government Corporations

Although government corporations charge for their services or products like private firms, their charges are not meant to make a profit. Historically, these corporations were created when government decided a service was important to the public interest but no private company could profit from providing it. The first government corporation, the Tennessee Valley Authority, still supplies electricity to its part of the country. COMSAT markets satellite communications capabilities to businesses and other governments. The Postal Service and AMTRAK (passenger railroad service) are other examples.

The operating costs and incomes of government corporations are not counted as expenditures and revenues in the annual budget. Thus, they have become an attractive device for elected officials who want to spend without enlarging the deficit. Real spending and deficits are put "off budget" to make the deficit look smaller. For example, when the Post Office showed a projected $2 billion deficit in 1990, it was taken out of the official budget.[23] Moving spending off the budget can be done with any government program, but officials find it easier to do with government corporations.

Bureaucratic Functions

After elected officials make a law, someone must carry it out. That is the job of the bureaucracy. Bureaucrats convert laws passed by Congress and signed by the president into rules and activities that have an actual impact on people and things. We call this process **policy implementation.**

For example, the Americans with Disabilities Act directs employers to make a "reasonable accommodation" for a competent worker with a disability that "substantially limits" a major life activity such as seeing or walking, except when this causes "undue hardship."[24] Although the act went into effect in 1992 and a bureaucracy, the Equal Employment Opportunity Commission (EEOC), is still trying to determine what the act means, much is unclear. What is the difference between a "reasonable accommodation" and an "undue hardship"? When voters want local governments to spend less, is the $2 million Des Plaines, Illinois, spent for sidewalks and curb cuts an "undue hardship" or not?[25] Will the EEOC let colleges and universities make only some classrooms accessible to students and staff in wheelchairs or must every classroom and faculty office be accessible to people with disabilities, by elevators, for example, at a cost of millions of dollars on older campuses?

In its early years Washington was described as "a miserable little swamp." When this photo was taken in 1882, the government was still comparatively small.
National Archives

After the answers to such questions are developed and formulated into rules, implementation involves carrying out the rules and negotiations over interpretations of the rules. State and local counterparts of the EEOC and their clients must be informed of the rules, assisted in their attempts to use the rules, and monitored in their progress. Bills must be paid, disputes resolved, and information collected as to how successful the program is.

As this example illustrates, the general process of policy implementation has two major components: making policies and administering them.

Making Policy

Over time, the policymaking functions of public bureaucracies have grown. Industrialization, population growth, urbanization, and profound changes in science, transportation, and communications have put problems of a more complex nature on government's agenda. The large number and technical nature of these problems, as well as policy differences among its members, have often limited Congress's ability to draft specific policy responses.

Congress often responds to this situation by enacting a general statement of goals and identifying actions that would help achieve them. Congress then has an agency with the relevant expertise draft specific rules that will achieve these goals. Thus, Congress gives agencies **delegated legislative authority,** the authority to draft, as well as execute, specific policies. The Tax Reform Act of 1986, for example, required thousands of rules to be written by the Internal Revenue Service (IRS) and the Treasury Department.

Agency-made policy is just as binding as acts of Congress because agencies make it on Congress's behalf. In strictly numerical terms, agencies make much more policy than Congress. On average, for example, executive agencies issue about seven thousand new rules and regulations a year compared to Congress's annual production of about three hundred new laws.

Many political scientists believe Congress abdicates its authority and acts in an irresponsible manner by refusing, because of political pressures and its heavy workload, to develop specific guidelines for agencies.[26] Thus, agencies sometimes are left to implement policies without much guidance from Congress beyond the bill itself. This congressional inaction has contributed to partisan conflicts. In the 1980s, intense policy differences divided Democratic congressional majorities and Republican executive branch officials. Committed to cutting domestic spending, the latter ignored or only partially implemented legislative directives they disliked. The

administration justified this by arguing that Congress's directions were unclear. This was sometimes true. For example, a section of a bill prohibiting discrimination against people with disabilities in federally subsidized programs had no congressional hearings, no mention in committee reports and floor debates, and no explanation elsewhere.[27]

Sometimes, however, these complaints about Congress were just an excuse not to implement disliked policies. In response, Congress began to adopt more detailed directives to agencies. Although this resulted in less agency-made policy (see Figure 1), executive officials still argued that congressional directives they disliked were too complex and unrealistic to follow.

In effect, the competition associated with legislative policymaking continued when Congress delegated legislative authority to agencies. This competition subsided when the Democrats won the White House in 1992 and reemerged after the Republicans won congressional majorities in 1994. The competition will likely continue regardless of who controls the White House and Congress because officials in both branches often have different priorities and policy positions. This puts agencies in the difficult position of having to satisfy diverse interests. To figure out what Congress, the president, and others want, agency officials read congressional debates and testimony and talk to members of Congress, committee staffers, White House aides, lobbyists, and others. While agencies also try to determine what the public wants, they are more likely to respond to well-organized and well-funded interests that closely monitor their actions. As a result, agency-made policy is often less responsive to the general public than to particular interests.

Regulation

A special kind of policymaking is called **regulation.** Though regulation is hard to define, in general, it is an action of a regulatory agency. Regulatory agencies have authority to establish standards or guidelines conferring benefits and imposing restrictions on business conduct, have heads or members appointed by the president, and have legal procedures generally governed by the Administrative Procedure Act (discussed later). Regulatory agencies include not only independent regulatory boards and commissions but also some independent agencies, such as the Environmental Protection Agency (EPA), and some agencies within cabinet departments, such as the Food and Drug Administration in Health and Human Services and OSHA within the Labor Department (see the box "Regulation and Ruptured

For Walt Frazier, working in chicken processing plants has definitely had pros and cons. He has earned a wage sufficient to feed his family. He has taken pride in his ability to work at great speed in the most dangerous place in the industry. Working in what is called "live hang," Frazier could snatch up a less-than-willing chicken off a conveyor belt and lift it over his head to a pair of hanging shackles at a rate of one bird every two seconds. His pain began in 1996. Later he learned that the repetitive stressful movement of his work ruptured the lining of his wrists and caused painful and dangerous cysts to form. At first, the nurse at the plant said that his developing cyst was nothing to worry about. Since then he has required three surgeries, but the pain remains.

Frazier's injuries are called "ergonomic" injuries because the work in live hang did not fit the worker. Other more common examples of such work include using computer equipment or a chair that does not fit the body of a worker. Resulting injuries include damage of many types, such as tendinitis, carpal tunnel syndrome, rotator cuff damage, and herniated disks.

The Occupational Safety and Health Administration (OSHA) bears responsibility for regulating conditions related to worker safety. OSHA has struggled throughout the 1990s to prevent ergonomic injuries. In 1995 it presented a draft of ergonomic standards. Business groups immediately lobbied Congress, resulting in a congressional prohibition against establishing ergonomic standards until 1998. A spokesperson for insurance companies complained that such a standard would be very subjective. Others complained about the costs. Since 1995, opponents of OSHA have three times forced it to back away from its efforts to establish an ergonomic standard.

Although business and industry protest the costs of compliance with the regulations, OSHA officials argue that ergonomic illnesses cost businesses about $20 billion in workers' compensation per year plus indirect costs of as much as $100 billion each year. They say that these costs are less than the costs of compliance.

The conflict continues. In 1999, OSHA issued an ergonomics standard telling employers to change the workplace to fit the physical limitations of the worker. Predictably business groups attacked the plan as intrusive, too costly, and based on inadequate research. Labor groups want OSHA to go further, requiring employers to address known problems rather than waiting for injuries to happen and covering more industries.

The case of ergonomic injuries illustrates well the competing pressures faced by regulatory agencies. Judgments based on neutral competence have economic and human impacts that quickly put them into the realm of politics.

SOURCES: Steve Bates, "When OSHA Calls," *Nation's Business* (September 1998): 20; Cindy Skrzycki, "Cracking Down on Workplace Injuries," *Washington Post National Weekly Edition*, November 29, 1999, p. 29; Susan G. Strother, "OSHA Finally Turns Attention to Ergonomics," *Lincoln Journal Star*, February 6, 2000, pp. 1D and 2D; Lena H. Sun and Gabriel Escobar, "The Price of Chicken," *Washington Post National Weekly Edition*, February 14, 2000, pp. 8–10.

Wrists" for more on OSHA and specifically its stand on ergonomics).

Some regulatory policies require businesses to meet standards, such as for clean air, safe disposal of toxic wastes, or safe workplaces. Failure to do so results in legal penalties. Federal regulators may set standards for certain types of products, particularly food and medical devices. The Food and Drug Administration, for example, sets a standard that allows only four condoms per one thousand manufactured to have defects. Lots with higher defect rates cannot be legally sold. The boxes "Your Hamburger: 41,000 Regulations" and "Anyone for Lunch?" describe other examples. Other regulations control who can own certain goods. For example, the Federal Communications Commission licenses people to own and operate radio and television stations. Regulations may require businesses to provide information, such as the cancer warnings on cigarette packages and the labels noting fat, sugar, salt, and vitamin content on packaged food.

Regulatory actions include two steps: making rules and adjudicating their enforcement. Rulemaking is the establishment of standards that apply to a class of individuals or businesses. For example, the Surface Transportation Board, formerly the Interstate Commerce Commission, sets standards that apply to interstate carriers such as railroads, trucking firms, and bus lines. Adjudication occurs when agencies try individuals or firms charged with violating standards. To do this, they use procedures that are very similar to those of courts.

Protesting "overregulation" is a popular pastime of Americans. The 41,000 regulations that accompany a hamburger may seem an obvious example of the absurdity of too much regulation. But the issue is more complicated than it seems at first glance. If government does not regulate pesticide use on crops, there is a significant risk of serious illness to consumers who eat the crops. If the government does not inspect to make sure livestock are free of tuberculosis, the incidence of TB bacteria in meat will be higher.

When examined closely, most of the regulations have a plausible rationale. But regulation is not free. The cost of regulating hamburger is about 8 to 11 cents per pound. Is this a high cost? It depends on the probability of contracting a serious disease and the value you as a consumer place on having some confidence in the quality of products you buy. Recently, after outbreaks of potentially deadly food poisoning from *E. coli* bacteria in ground beef, government officials have considered adopting additional regulations in response to consumers' concerns.

Then, of course, there are some regulations that are mystifying even to those not especially opposed to government regulation. What is the danger in eating a pickle sliced too thin? Only Uncle Sam knows!

SOURCES: *U.S. News & World Report*, February 11, 1980, p. 64. Copyright 1980, U.S. News & World Report, Inc.; Carole Sugarman, "A Beef with the Cattlemen," *Lincoln Journal-Star*, September 15, 1997, p. 32.

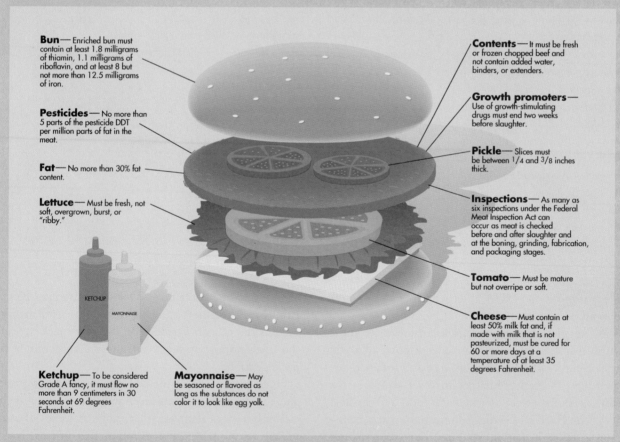

Bun— Enriched bun must contain at least 1.8 milligrams of thiamin, 1.1 milligrams of riboflavin, and at least 8 but not more than 12.5 milligrams of iron.

Pesticides— No more than 5 parts of the pesticide DDT per million parts of fat in the meat.

Fat— No more than 30% fat content.

Lettuce— Must be fresh, not soft, overgrown, burst, or "ribby."

KETCHUP

MAYONNAISE

Ketchup— To be considered Grade A fancy, it must flow no more than 9 centimeters in 30 seconds at 69 degrees Fahrenheit.

Mayonnaise— May be seasoned or flavored as long as the substances do not color it to look like egg yolk.

Contents— It must be fresh or frozen chopped beef and not contain added water, binders, or extenders.

Growth promoters— Use of growth-stimulating drugs must end two weeks before slaughter.

Pickle— Slices must be between 1/4 and 3/8 inches thick.

Inspections— As many as six inspections under the Federal Meat Inspection Act can occur as meat is checked before and after slaughter and at the boning, grinding, fabrication, and packaging stages.

Tomato— Must be mature but not overripe or soft.

Cheese— Must contain at least 50% milk fat and, if made with milk that is not pasteurized, must be cured for 60 or more days at a temperature of at least 35 degrees Fahrenheit.

The hamburger, staple of the quick, inexpensive meal, is the subject of 41,000 federal and state regulations, many of them stemming from 200 laws and 111,000 precedent-setting court cases. These rules, cited in a three-volume study by Colorado State University, touch on everything involved in meat production, including cattle-grazing practices, conditions in slaughterhouses, and methods used to process meat for sale to supermarkets, restaurants, and fast-food outlets. Here is just a sampling of the rules and regulations governing the burger.

Because of the dangers inherent in having one agency be the lawmaker, judge, and jury, in 1946 Congress passed the Administrative Procedure Act (APA) to establish fair and open procedures. For example, agencies must publish a description of their rulemaking procedures in the *Federal Register* and hold open hearings on proposed rules or provide for another means of public input. Those who believe they have been treated unfairly by an agency have the right to take their case to court.

Antiregulation feeling helps to fuel public distrust of government. Surveys report that the number of people who think government controls too much of our daily lives has risen from 57 percent to 69 percent since 1987.[28] As Figure 1 shows, regulation has increased since then. This is largely because of the passage of the Clean Air Act, the Civil Rights Act, and the Americans with Disabilities Act during the Bush years plus a reversal by Bush and Clinton appointees of the antiregulatory fervor of the Reagan years. Most Americans support the goals of these laws (for example, 78 percent of the public says government should do "whatever it takes to protect the environment").[29] But many also think that the regulations to implement these and other laws result in wasteful paperwork and more costs than benefits. For example, officials in Madison, Wisconsin, report that they spend 14 percent of their transit budget obeying regulations to ensure bus service to the disabled, who make up 1.5 percent of their users.[30]

Most regulations are based on laws that direct agencies to take certain actions to accomplish certain ends. Thus, Congress gave the EPA authority to tell business to use or not use certain processes to reduce pollution. This "command and control" strategy is expensive because agencies have to employ many experts to design rules to achieve the desired ends and then have to get those they regulate to obey the rules. The strategy also allows little flexibility for the agencies and the people they regulate.

Many people believe there may be better ways to achieve the goals of clean air, fairness to the disabled, and other desirable objectives.[31] Some argue that we should eliminate agency regulations and rely on lawsuits by private citizens to protect public health and safety by proving in court that they have been harmed by something, such as pollution. A problem with this idea is that it could pit individuals with limited means against industries with vast resources. It also moves problems to the courts more quickly. Other critics say we should entrust regulation to the states, which would finance their own efforts. Still others call for Washington to give block grants to states and allow them to set their own priori-

ties and devise solutions consistent with broad goals set at the federal level. And others argue we should make business and industry comply with goals and standards (for example, in environmental cleanups) but leave them more discretion on how to do it.

The Republican legislative majorities of the 1990s signaled their opposition to command-and-control regulation by threatening to pass bills that would stop the making of new regulations for one year and force agencies to give greater weight to the costs of new regulations (to kill those based on "minute or exaggerated risks").[32] And Clinton issued an executive order to cut paperwork, void many regulations, and create a pilot program to give business more flexibility to comply with clean air and water requirements. The Clinton administration's initiative on "reinventory government" also attempted to reduce and streamline regulatory activity. However, titanic political

At JFK International Airport in New York, a Department of Agriculture inspector searches for illegal immigrants—insects—in fruits and vegetables that travelers bring into the United States.
Charles Krebs

battles lie ahead because advocates of a cleaner environment, more rights for the disabled, and other interests protected by regulations point out that giving businesses more flexibility and weakening regulations is likely to erode progress toward goals they desire.

Administering Policy

Public bureaucracy's oldest job is to administer the law. To "administer" is to execute, enforce, and apply the rules that have been made either by Congress or the bureaucracy itself. Thus, if policymakers decide to go to war, they must empower an agency to acquire weapons, recruit and train soldiers, and lead them in battle with a winning strategy. Policymaking without administration is usually tantamount to having no policy at all.

Administration includes thousands of different kinds of activities. It involves writing checks to farmers who receive payments for growing—or not growing—crops, providing direct services to the public, evaluating how well programs are working, prosecuting those who try to defraud the government, and maintaining buildings and offices. For forest rangers, administration involves helping backpackers in the Grand Canyon or putting out a forest fire in northern Minnesota. For postal employees, it includes delivering the mail or repairing an automatic sorting machine.

Other Functions

In the course of policymaking and administration, the bureaucracy performs other functions. It collects data, such as in the census, and makes information available to us. Much of what we know about ourselves comes from the government's collection of data on births and deaths, occupations and income, housing and health, crime, and many other things. A cursory glance at the annual **Statistical Abstract** shows that the government reports to us everything from the incidence of abortions to the exports of zinc, and in between informs us how much celery we eat and how many VCRs we own.

The bureaucracy engages in research too. A prime example is the Department of Agriculture, which for nearly 140 years has conducted research on how to grow bigger and better crops, raise healthier animals, and transport and market products more effectively.

In addition, providing continuity is an important offshoot of the bureaucracy's activities. Presidents and members of Congress come and go, and political appointees in the bureaucracy stay an average of two years. Many barely learn their jobs by the time they leave. Career civil servants tend to know more about government's past and current efforts, which can make government more productive. At the same time, the presence of careerists can make the bureaucracy less responsive.

Bureaucracy also teaches citizens about government. First, it informs us about public policies and programs. For example, we contact the National Park Service if we want to know the rules governing camping in national parks. The bureaucracy also performs a socialization function. It helps us learn about government and our role as citizens.

Anyone for Lunch?

When Congress legislates food safety, federal regulatory agencies are charged with setting out specific criteria to determine what is safe and what is not. These examples of regulations about the maximum contamination allowed in food that meets federal standards for safety illustrate the detail and precision of some regulations. In all cases, food with this amount of contamination is considered safe for humans.

Chocolate: Up to sixty microscopic insect fragments per 100 grams or ninety insect fragments in one sample or one rodent hair per 100 grams

Frozen broccoli: Fewer than sixty aphids, thrips, and/or mites per 100 grams

Canned citrus juice: Fewer than five fly eggs or one maggot per 250 milliliters

Bay leaves: Up to 5 percent moldy or insect-infested pieces or 1 milligram of mammalian excretia per pound

SOURCE: From Judith Schiek Robinson, *Tapping the Government Grapevine* (Phoenix: Oryx, 1998), 118. She drew this example from Center for Food Safety and Applied Nutrition, *The Food Defect Action Levels* (Washington, D.C.: Food and Drug Administration, 1995).

Andrew Jackson opened the doors to the White House as well as to the government bureaucracy. The guests at a White House party open to the public consumed or carried away much of a 1,400-pound cheese.
The Granger Collection, New York

Expectations about the Federal Bureaucracy

Historically, Americans have had two sometimes contradictory expectations about public bureaucracy. They have wanted bureaucracies to be responsive to their needs, which often means responsive to majority views. But they have also wanted bureaucracies to be competent enough to do an effective job. They want fair, apolitical competence applied so that, for example, Social Security recipients who are Democrats do not receive favors when Democrats are in office and Republican recipients do not receive favors when Republicans are in office. For the bureaucracy to have both political responsiveness and neutral competence is often difficult.

Responsiveness

Responsiveness refers to a democratic desire that public agencies do what we want. We have shown how highly we value bureaucratic responsiveness in three major ways.

First, Americans elect more bureaucrats than citizens of other nations do. By the mid-1800s voters were electing numerous state and local executive officers from ballots (called *long ballots*) having hundreds of names. Many states and localities still have long ballots electing not only chief executives, such as governors and mayors, but also treasurers, clerks, sheriffs, surveyors, auditors, engineers, and other administrative officers. Electing rather

than appointing these officials is supposed to make them responsive, though in reality it may have the opposite effect by making it unclear who is really in charge.

The second way Americans have encouraged bureaucratic responsiveness is through **patronage.** Under the patronage system, elected officials appoint their supporters to administrative jobs in order to build their own political strength. Newly elected presidents and other executives replace everyone appointed by their predecessors with their own supporters: "To the victor belong the spoils." Andrew Jackson's presidential election in 1828 was a watershed in using the patronage system. Jackson and others believed that any white male citizen of average intelligence and goodwill could do a government job well. So he reversed the existing practice of naming mostly well-off people from the East Coast by appointing less well-off supporters from frontier areas.

A major problem with patronage is that it can lead to corruption, in particular to deal making between candidates and voters or, more unfortunately, individuals who control blocks of voters. Voters may support candidates who promise them jobs or other favors. Such corruption increasingly sullied city councils, state legislatures, and Congress during the 1800s.

Another problem with patronage is incompetence. People got bureaucratic jobs because they supported winning candidates, not because they knew how to do the jobs. This became a major problem as government jobs became more technical.

The third way Americans have sought bureaucratic responsiveness is by giving legislatures great authority over the bureaucracy. Before the Revolution and for a long time after, the bureaucracy performed a few relatively simple jobs and was relatively easy to control. Now the job of controlling the bureaucracy is much more difficult as government has become larger and more complex.

Neutral Competence

Neutral competence can be a contradictory objective to responsiveness. It holds that bureaucrats should be uninvolved or neutral in policymaking and chosen only for their expertise in executing policy. It assumes that there is no Republican or Democratic way to build a sewer, collect customs, or fight a war. In effect, it says politics has no place in bureaucracy. It also implies that bureaucrats should not profit personally from the decisions they make.

Woodrow Wilson, a major advocate of neutral competence, wrote that we can learn to execute policy both

Neutral Competence versus Politics in the U.S. Census

The Constitution directs that a count of all residents, called the *census,* be completed every ten years. The Census Bureau prepares for the next census far in advance in order to carry it out with the greatest accuracy. Conducting a census is neither easy nor inexpensive.

In the mid-1990s, a battle over the census arose that provides a classic example of the conflict between political responsiveness and neutral competence. The census is supposed to include all residents in the United States. Some residents, however, lacking a permanent address of their own, move from friend to friend or relative to relative. Others are homeless. Some fear disclosure of their whereabouts and any information they provide. Obtaining an accurate count of these people is nearly impossible. So the Census Bureau proposed to use a widely accepted form of scientific sampling to correct the census count in the year 2000. By using sampling, a more accurate count of these individuals, many of whom tend to be very poor or minorities, could be achieved.

Republicans, concerned with maintaining their majority in the House of Representatives, have strenuously objected. Knowing that undercounted persons tend to live in areas where Democratic candidates win elections, Republicans fear that adjusting the census through sampling will result in higher populations in Democratic areas and thus more congressional seats in those areas. As a consequence, the

Republicans might lose control of the House to the Democrats. To forestall this possibility, Republicans in the House attempted to amend several bills to require that the Census Bureau not utilize these methods of correcting the census. They also attempted to delay funding for the census. Democrats, of course, have an interest in improving the count of residents in areas that usually support them.

Earlier, Congress asked the National Academy of Sciences to find a method of reducing the undercount. The academy recommended statistical sampling. The Republican-appointed director of the 1990 census supported the plans of the Census Bureau to correct for the undercounting of many poor and minority residents. She wrote to the Republican leadership in Congress, expressing total support, but received no response from the House Republican leaders.

In early 1999, the U.S. Supreme Court ruled by a 5–4 vote that statistical sampling of the 2000 census could not be used to apportion seats in the House of Representatives among the states. But Justice O'Connor wrote the opinion, stating that sampling should be used "where feasible," for all other purposes. Republican leaders declared that they would insist on taking only the traditional count, without sampling. The director of the census stated that the bureau would undertake both counts. The head count would be used for the purpose of reapportionment, while the

Census workers in Alaska delivering census forms by dogsled.
Al Grillo/AP Wide World Photos

more accurate sampling system numbers would be used for remapping congressional districts and for distributing federal grants. With negative reactions from Republicans, clearly the conflict continues.

SOURCES: David S. Broder, "Census Sampling Issue May Have Huge Repercussions," *Lincoln Journal Star,* January 31, 1999, p. 6D; Art Pine, "Sampling to Augment Next Census," *Lincoln Journal Star (Los Angeles Times),* February 25, 1999, p. 1A.

expertly and responsively.[33] He believed that government jobs are either political or administrative in nature and that if we know which is which, we can create a bureaucracy that policymakers can control. Most current observers believe it is impossible to separate politics from administration completely, however.[34] The box on the

census illustrates the difficulties that can arise when we try to have full measures of both political responsiveness and neutral competence.

The first impact of the desire for neutral competence was the creation of the **Civil Service Commission** by the Pendleton Act in 1883. Patronage was a serious problem by the 1880s. Given the strength of political machines that had grown powerful through its use, Congress did not act until the 1881 assassination of President James Garfield by an unsuccessful job seeker.

The commission filled certain bureaucratic jobs with people who had proved their competence in competitive examinations and then protected these people from having to support or oppose particular candidates. Jobs under the commission's jurisdiction were part of the **merit system.**

The Pendleton Act authorized the president to extend merit system coverage to additional federal jobs by executive order. The merit system covered about 10 percent of the jobs in the federal bureaucracy in 1884. That figure is over 90 percent today; most of the remainder are covered by some other merit system such as that in the State Department's Foreign Service.

A merit system protects individuals from dismissal for partisan reasons. However, the system does not give "merit" a monopoly. The system favors veterans by adding a five-point bonus to their test scores (disabled veterans get ten points). People already in the system are also favored because they know about job openings first. Sometimes, job descriptions are written to fit particular individuals.

Another result of the push for neutral competence was the creation of independent regulatory boards and commissions. In 1887, Congress created the Interstate Commerce Commission to decide, on the basis of expert, not partisan, factors, such things as interstate freight rates, railroad ticket prices, conditions of service, and which companies could operate between different places. Some partisan influences remain: the president names and the Senate confirms board and commission members, and Congress and the president determine their funding. But partisanship is supposed to end there.

Limits on the partisan political activities of federal workers resulted from attempts to achieve neutral competence. The **Hatch Act** of 1939 says that federal employees can do very little in partisan campaigns, even in state and local ones. They can vote, attend rallies, and talk privately to others. But they cannot participate in party-sponsored voter registration drives, endorse party candidates, or work for or against them in any way. These prohibitions also apply to state and local government workers supported by federal funds.

The Hatch Act has been the subject of considerable controversy. Supporters argue that it protects the neutral competence of civil servants from partisan influences. Critics of the act say it makes civil servants second-class citizens by denying them the First Amendment guarantees of freedom of speech and association. In 1993, Con-

gress changed the law to allow most federal employees to run for office within political parties, to participate in political campaigns, and to raise funds for political action committees when they are off-duty. However, all employees of law enforcement and national security agencies remain under the earlier, more stringent prohibitions.[35]

The 1980s were troubled years for the entire civil service. Reagan's belief that "government isn't the solution, it's the problem" endorsed negative views of the public service and indicated a commitment to cut government activity. This and publicity glorifying private business made hiring and keeping good people in government difficult; the work of many agencies suffered. For example, the Food and Drug Administration (FDA) tests products that represent about a quarter of consumer spending. Yet in a decade that saw the onset of AIDS and the development of many new products, FDA staffing dropped 9 percent and food and drug inspections fell 40 percent. In 1990, the FDA took thirty-one months, not the six months required by law, to review new drug applications.[36]

Although Bush noted his "very high regard for the overall competence of career civil servants and for [their] vital role,"[37] he did little to overcome the trends of the 1980s. Clinton sent mixed signals to the bureaucracy. He described government, and by implication the bureaucracy, as a valuable tool for social change, but recommended freezing civil service salaries and vowed to cut one hundred thousand federal jobs. The number of new workers declined in the 1990s as the "baby bust" generation entered the job market and as one-quarter of the federal workforce reached retirement age. Government will have trouble competing with the private sector for workers because federal salaries lag behind comparable nongovernment jobs and this gap widens at higher levels.

Neutral competence also includes the idea that bureaucrats should not profit personally from their decisions. Civil servants should be experts in what they do but should not have a personal stake in it. For example, bureaucrats who are stockholders in chemical companies should not make policy about chemical waste. Even if policymakers could completely divorce themselves from their financial interests, their ties with a regulated firm would still produce an appearance of conflict of interest. Critics of policy could point to it, lowering public confidence in government.

Responding to concerns about conflicts of interest, Congress passed the Ethics in Government Act in 1978. The act sought to prevent ex-public officials with inside information about specific issues from using it and their contacts to give their private employers an unfair competitive advantage. The act barred ex-public servants

A disappointed office seeker assassinates President Garfield.
The Granger Collection, New York

from lobbying their former agencies for one year and, on matters in which they "personally and substantially" participated as public officials, for life. In 1989, news that ex-Reagan officials had used their government service for substantial financial gain led to the passage of a law designed to strengthen the 1978 act. It will have little impact if it is enforced as weakly as its predecessor.

To address these concerns, President Clinton signed an executive order requiring many of his political appointees to sign a pledge that they will not lobby the agencies in which they worked for five years and will never lobby for foreign political parties and governments. Analysts noted that the rules apply to only one-third of his appointees, that lobbying for foreign corporations is unaffected, and that Clinton said nothing about how he will enforce the rules. These rules had little more impact than the old ones.[38]

Although responsiveness and neutral competence contribute to an effective bureaucracy, each has problems and ultimately works against the other. The most

neutrally competent bureaucracy is not always the most responsive one and vice versa.

Controlling the Bureaucracy

To whom is the bureaucracy responsible? Although many bureaucratic decisions significantly affect our lives, most are not made in the public eye, and most citizens know little about them. No "Adm-Span" channel televises agency activities as C-Span covers Congress.[39] Nevertheless, many compete to influence public agencies: the president, parts of Congress, interest groups, and individual citizens. Whether they succeed depends on their resources, agency reactions, and agency ability to resist unwanted outside influence.[40]

President

The development of the bureaucracy led to demands for **executive leadership.** The president, constitutionally the "chief executive," has several tools to control the bureaucracy. One is budgeting. Presidents can try to limit agency appropriations to keep agencies from doing certain things, or they can tie conditions to appropriations to make them do things. Using these strategies effectively can be difficult, although President Reagan was able to weaken some regulatory agencies by significantly cutting their budgets.[41] President Bush's 1991 budget for the Internal Revenue Service proposed that the IRS target middle- and lower-income taxpayers for audits (to check the honesty of their tax returns) rather than wealthy individuals and companies. He cut the IRS's budget request to target rich tax cheats by over 90 percent.[42]

Second, presidents can try to control agencies by appointing people to them with views like their own. This is obvious in the case of cabinet departments. Reagan and Bush filled health care–related positions in the Department of Health and Human Services with people who were pro-life.[43] Clinton filled these jobs with people who are pro-choice. In appointments to regulatory agencies, Republican presidents tend to appoint pro-business people and Democratic presidents pro-consumer and pro-labor individuals.[44] Reagan's appointees to regulatory agencies such as OSHA, the Consumer Products Safety Commission, and the EPA agreed with his goal of reducing government regulation. Clinton's appointees to these agencies believe, with him, that government can be a valuable agent of social change.

Often, however, presidential appointees end up representing agency interests rather than presidential ones. This can happen because most appointees have less expertise and experience in agency operations than career civil servants and often come to rely on career officials for information about agency history, procedures, and policy questions.

Administrative reform is a third presidential opportunity to control the bureaucracy. Generally, the more sweeping a president's recommendation for change, the more he must anticipate congressional and interest group resistance. For example, Reagan wanted to abolish the Departments of Education and Energy and merge the Commerce and Labor Departments, but Congress would not support him.

Fourth, the White House can try to influence agencies not under presidential control by lobbying and mobilizing public opinion. For example, presidents try to influence Federal Reserve Board decisions on interest rates.

Despite these powers, there are many limits on the president's ability to control the bureaucracy. Given its size and complexity, the president cannot possibly control every important decision. Moreover, presidents have

found it increasingly difficult to lead an executive branch containing large numbers of merit system employees deliberately insulated from presidential control.

Presidential control problems became much more serious in the 1930s with the establishment of many new programs and agencies. In 1935, Franklin Roosevelt appointed the Brownlow Committee, named after its chair and composed of public administration specialists, which wrote an excellent statement of the principles of executive leadership in its 1937 report.

The report was very influential. At its suggestion, the Bureau of the Budget, created in 1921, was put into the new Executive Office of the President to help the president cope with the bureaucracy. Congress also passed legislation in 1939 permitting the president to create, merge, or dissolve agencies subject to Congress's disapproval.

In 1978, the Civil Service Reform Act replaced the Civil Service Commission with two agencies. One promotes executive leadership by working with the president in writing and administering civil service regulations. The other is supposed to protect civil servants from violations of these regulations. In addition, the act gave managers more opportunity to fire incompetent subordinates, authorized bonuses and a new pay scale for managers to encourage better performance, and created the Senior Executive Service (SES).

Despite this legislation, executive leadership is still thwarted by the difficulty of removing incompetents from the civil service. Although job security is not meant to shield public servants who do poor work, it does make firing incompetent workers difficult and time-consuming. The organization of public employees into unions contributes to this. The government's rate of discharging people for inefficiency is 0.01 percent a year. The 1978 reform has made little difference. As one public employee said, "We're all like headless nails down here—once you get us in you can't get us out."[45]

Agencies' connections to strong allies provide another limit to presidential leadership. Presidents have more success trying to control agencies that lack strong congressional allies and domestic clientele groups, such as the Treasury and State Departments, than agencies *with* such allies, such as the Agriculture and Health and Human Services Departments.

Congress

Creating and reorganizing agencies and enacting laws give Congress opportunities to tell agencies what to do and how to do it. In recent years, Congress took away some of the powers of the Federal Trade Commission to regulate used-car sales, practices of the insurance industry, and television advertising aimed at children. In doing so, Congress was responding to complaints (and campaign donations) from used-car dealers, the insurance industry, and other businesses that found their actions being circumscribed by the commission's new or proposed regulations. In 1995, congressional interest in cutting the bureaucracy and regulatory activity led Clinton to propose and later approve the elimination of the Interstate Commerce Commission, the original independent regulatory commission. Despite these examples, however, the existence of complex, technical issues and the tendency to state congressional goals in general terms often give agencies considerable leeway in doing their jobs.

Legislative oversight is another congressional tool of control, but it too has problems. Just as an agency's connections can work to thwart presidential control, they can also limit congressional oversight. Agencies frequently work closely with certain congressional committees and interest groups for mutual support; agencies adjust their actions to the preferences of the congressional committees that authorize their programs and appropriate their funds. For example, decisions by members of independent regulatory commissions are sensitive to the views of members of their congressional oversight committees. When the membership of the committees becomes more liberal, so, too, do the decisions regulators make.[46]

Constituent service is also a congressional tool for controlling the bureaucracy. Members of Congress often try to influence agencies on behalf of constituents. This becomes a problem when it leads to inefficiencies such as keeping unneeded military bases open to boost the economy of a member's district or when it impedes necessary government regulation, as it did when several prominent senators delayed investigation of corrupt and careless savings and loan operations.

Courts

The courts also influence the bureaucracy. Judicial decisions shape agency actions by directing agencies to follow legally correct procedures. Of course, the courts cannot intercede in an agency's decision making unless some aggrieved person or corporation files a suit against the agency. Nevertheless, in almost any controversial agency action, there will be aggrieved parties, and possibly some with sufficient resources to bring a court action.

The courts interpret lawmakers' intentions by deciding what congressional majorities and the president had in mind when they made a law. This can be difficult. Sometimes, in their haste, lawmakers may have left out parts of a law or, as a Supreme Court justice put it, "agreed to disagree."[47] Lawmakers may also have written a law so agencies can adapt it to unknown future conditions. How the courts read a law may add to or reduce the relative power of Congress and the president or expand the courts' own powers. We discuss these issues in Chapter 13.

Regulators as well as other agency policymakers appear to be quite sensitive to court decisions. For example, when the courts begin overturning the National Labor Relations Board's decisions in a pro-labor direction, NLRB decisions soon become more pro-labor. Similarly, decisions drift the other way when courts begin to overturn decisions in a pro-business direction.[48]

Interest Groups and Individuals

Interest groups want to make sure bureaucracies adopt rules and enforcement practices they favor. A law establishing new safeguards in toxic waste disposal may be applauded by environmental and citizen groups, but the job of these groups is not over until they make sure the Environmental Protection Agency writes strict rules to carry out the law and then enforces them. Thus, it is not enough to get a law passed that responds to your interests; the law must be implemented in a responsive way too.

How do groups seek to make sure this happens? One way is through relationships with Congress. If an agency seems to be sabotaging the intent of Congress, interest

"It's not mailmen per se. I'm just very anti-government these days."
© The New Yorker Collection 1995, Mischa Richter from cartoonbank.com. All rights reserved.

The Bureaucracy in Time

1789 The first federal departments, Treasury, State, and War, along with the Attorney General, are established to oversee basic governmental functions.

1800 The federal government employs three thousand people.

1849 The Department of Interior is created, the first new cabinet department. Shortly thereafter, in 1862, the Department of Agriculture is established.

1887 The first major federal regulatory body, the Interstate Commerce Commission (ICC), is created to regulate the burgeoning railroad industry.

1883 To reduce patronage and graft, the Pendleton Act establishes the Civil Service Commission and sets up a merit system within the federal bureaucracy.

1903–15 In the Progressive era, in response to concerns about big business and unsafe working and consumer conditions, Congress establishes several regulatory bodies, including the Food and Drug Administration and the Federal Trade Commission. In 1903, Congress also establishes a Department of Commerce and Labor to help stimulate economic activity, and a decade later they divide to become two departments.

1921 The Bureau of the Budget is created to rationalize the federal budget process.

1932–39 The New Deal stimulates the rapid growth of the federal bureaucracy as new agencies, including the Social Security Administration, are formed and others expand their mission.

1937 The Bureau of the Budget (later the Office of Management and Budget) is moved into the Executive Office of the President to give the president more control of the budget process.

1939 The Hatch Act prohibits federal employees (and state and local employees supported by federal funds) from participating in partisan electoral politics (except that they retain the right to vote).

1941–45 World War II stimulates a massive buildup of the Department of Defense. After the war, most soldiers are demobilized, but the Defense Department remains a large part of the federal bureaucracy.

1946 The Administrative Procedures Act establishes more fair and open procedures for rule making.

1953 The Department of Health, Education, and Welfare, now the largest domestic agency, is established. In 1979, it divides to form both the Department of Education and the Department of Health and Human Services.

1965 The Voting Rights Act is passed and the Justice Department is given a major role in the enforcement of voting rights for African Americans.

1965–70 The War on Poverty stimulates the launching of a Department of Housing and Urban Development and a Department of Transportation.

1966 The Freedom of Information Act lets people obtain nonclassified information from agencies.

1970s New public concern over the environment leads to the formation of the Environmental Protection Agency in 1970 and the Department of Energy in 1977.

1978 The Ethics in Government Act seeks to regulate conflicts of interests in the bureaucracy by prohibiting federal employees to go to work immediately for companies that they regulated.

1990s President Clinton pledges to decrease the size of the federal bureaucracy and to "reinvent" government, making it more efficient and responsive. The size of the bureaucracy decreases.

---

groups can work with friendly congressional committees to put pressure on the agency to mend its ways. Interest groups can also try to rally public opinion to their side and pressure Congress or the president to do something about the agency.

Interest groups try to influence agencies directly, too. For example, the broadcasting industry tries to shape Federal Communications Commission decisions to enable the industry to compete more effectively with cable television companies. Sometimes interest groups pressure an agency so effectively that the agency is said to be "captured."[49] This term is used most frequently in referring to regulatory agencies said to be controlled by the groups they are supposed to be regulating. Thus, the Nuclear Regulatory Commission looks out for the interests of the nuclear industry, which it is supposed to be regulating.

Studies of voting by regulatory commissioners also show an indirect influence of industry. Some commissioners come to their regulatory agencies from the industry they are regulating. These commissioners are more likely than others to take a pro-industry position in cases before the agency. Furthermore, commissioners leaving a regulatory agency to take jobs in a regulated industry become more pro-industry in their last year as regulators than others who are not leaving for such jobs.[50] They apparently anticipate a move to industry and, in a sacrifice of their neutral competence, try to make their decisions more acceptable to possible employers.

Can individual citizens influence the bureaucracy too? It is difficult for citizens acting as individuals to influence public agencies. Not surprisingly, as we have seen, few individuals take advantage of their right to information from the bureaucracy.

However, individual bureaucrats, called **whistle-blowers,** can sometimes open their agencies to public view. Their purpose is usually to expose mismanagement and abuse of discretion to make their agencies more responsive and productive. The most famous whistleblower is Ernest Fitzgerald. In 1968, as an Air Force cost accountant, he exposed bad management by revealing problems with the Lockheed C-5A transport plane. The plane vibrated so much in flight that its wings actually fell off if they were not replaced after only two hundred hours of flying time. Saying it wanted "to save expenses"—his $32,000 salary—the Air Force reacted by firing Fitzgerald. He sued to get his job back and won, but all he got was his title, office, and pay. The Air Force gave him nothing to do, and he had to wait for a court order in 1982 before the Air Force gave him responsibilities equal to his qualifications. The wings were repaired, and the C-5A operated successfully for many years.[51] In 1987, the Air Force was still trying to neutralize what one Pentagon veteran called "the most hated man in the Air Force" by juggling staff assignments.[52]

The 1978 Civil Service Reform Act created an agency to protect whistleblowers. During its first decade, the agency was ineffective because the act defined whistleblowers' rights narrowly and because of budget cuts and morale problems in the 1980s. In 1988, Reagan vetoed a bill designed to strengthen it. Congress passed the bill again in 1989 and Bush signed it into law. It gives whistleblowers more protection from agencies they accuse of mismanagement and harassment. A law passed in 1986 allows private citizens to be whistle-blowers too by suing companies with government contracts that defraud the government.[53]

Relying on brave people like Fitzgerald to get agencies to operate properly is a mistake. A 1993 study reported that over one-third of federal whistleblowers alleged they suffered some form of reprisal or threat of reprisal.[54] It is the rare person who will set aside ambition for promotion and cordial relations with colleagues to challenge the status quo. Most people, whether in the private or the public sector, find it difficult to expose the dirty laundry of the bureaucracy employing them.

Conclusion: Is the Bureaucracy Responsive?

Is the federal bureaucracy the uncontrollable fourth branch of government as some portray it? Our fragmented political system has created an environment of uncertainty and competition for public agencies. They have many bosses: a president, his appointees, Congress, and its many committees and subcommittees. In addition, numerous interest groups try to influence them. The often contradictory expectations of responsiveness and neutral competence contribute to the uncertainty of the bureaucracy's environment, too.

As a result, agencies try to protect themselves by cultivating the support of congressional committees and interest groups. Even presidents have trouble influencing agencies because of these alliances. Although some presidents, such as Franklin Roosevelt and Lyndon Johnson, have occasionally rearranged the status quo, their successes in representing a vision of national priorities are more the exception than the rule.

Well-organized interest groups and Congress can also influence agencies, often through the iron triangles that help stabilize agency environments. But interest groups do not represent everyone. Likewise, not everyone feels represented by members of Congress or can take advantage of the Sunshine and Freedom of Information Acts. As a result, agencies may not represent those who fall through the "safety net" of interest group and congressional representation.

Thus, diverse expectations of what government should do make the federal bureaucracy seem unresponsive. Even well-run agencies represent waste, and therefore a lack of responsiveness and executive leadership, to people unaware of, lacking need of, or opposed to their services.

Despite people's negative feelings about the bureaucracy, the mail is delivered, bridges get inspected, and passports are issued. As Charles Goodsell points out, "Unmistakably, . . . bureaucracy works most of the time."[55] It usually does what it is supposed to do. But when what the bureaucracy is supposed to do is unclear, it is harder for the bureaucracy to respond to our wishes.

The Surgeon General Chooses Neutral Competence

Surgeon General Koop issued a report in 1986 proposing expanded sex education and better education on the dangers of AIDS for schoolchildren. The thirty-six-page report ignored conservative views. It concluded that a lack of sex education impedes the effort to stop AIDS in the absence of a vaccine or cure. The report noted that testing all hospital patients is unnecessary because many of the thirty-seven million people hospitalized each year are children or the elderly, who face low risks of infection.

Later, in a radio broadcast, Koop called on the nation's networks to lift their self-imposed ban on condom advertising. He argued that "anyone who is sexually active should use a condom from start to finish. AIDS kills and sexually active people have to be told this." The networks indicated they would leave policy changes to their local affiliates.

The government's most visible response to AIDS was a brochure mailed to 107 million households in 1988 describing how AIDS is contracted and how to avoid it. That same year, a presidential commission and a National Academy of Sciences panel made recommendations about dealing with AIDS that echoed Koop's. Both criticized the government, and especially Reagan's White House, for a lack of leadership. At the same time, many conservatives were disappointed and angry, accusing Koop of not promoting chastity.

By 1995, AIDS had killed more than 204,000 people. And the demographics of the disease were changing. A majority of victims were still gay men, but there were signs that the spread of AIDS among gays had peaked. Increasingly, the new high-risk populations were intravenous drug users and poor inner city blacks and Hispanics. In 1993, over 40 percent of all Americans with the disease were minorities. It is now the second leading cause of death of men and the fourth leading killer of women aged twenty-five to forty-four. It is also the seventh leading cause of death of young children. Koop acknowledged that health workers have been "singularly unsuccessful in penetrating the drug-addicted culture" with educational messages.[56] An observer noted that heterosexual AIDS is becoming a "poor people's disease."[57]

Civil servants are supposed to be responsive to public opinion and their

Courtesy of New York City Department of Health

superiors, in Koop's case the president. At the same time, they are supposed to do their jobs in a neutrally competent way. As surgeon general, Koop said, "I'm not afforded the luxury of bringing ideology or morals into my job, especially with the sort of threat we have with AIDS."[58] He could not respond to presidential expectations because his professional expertise led him to different conclusions.

Key Terms

independent agencies
policy implementation
delegated legislative authority
regulation
Statistical Abstract
patronage

neutral competence
Civil Service Commission
merit system
Hatch Act
executive leadership
whistleblowers

Further Reading

David Burnham, *A Law unto Itself: Power, Politics and the IRS* (New York: Random House, 1990). An analysis of the enforcement of the federal tax code, a code so complex it seems to invite bureaucratic inefficiency and abuses.

Irving L. Janis, *Victims of Groupthink* (Boston: Houghton Mifflin, 1972). Explaining why people often prefer getting along to making hard decisions, he helps us see why whistleblowers are rare souls.

James H. Jones, *Bad Blood* (New York: Free Press, 1981). Award-winning account of the Public Health Service's experiment in which black men with syphilis were left untreated so doctors could see the effects of the disease. The book is revealing about the nature of both bureaucratic behavior and racial discrimination.

Robert N. Kharasch, *The Institutional Imperative: How to Understand the United States Government and Other Bulky Objects* (New York: Charterhouse Books, 1973). A witty and insightful study of such topics as the "irrelevance" of bureaucratic morality and purpose, Pentagon "busyness," and the "Sweet Uses of Stupidity."

Jonathan Kwitny, *Acceptable Risks* (New York: Poseidon Books, 1992). A fast-paced and well-written story of two men who prodded and fought the Food and Drug Administration to make potentially helpful medicines available to AIDS patients. A good illustration of both agency rigidity and, ultimately, responsiveness.

Electronic Resources

www.whitehouse.gov
www.gao.gov
www.state.gov
Each federal agency has its own Web page. These are the ones for the White House, the General Accounting Office, and the Department of State.

www.opm.gov/feddata/index.htm
Review tables that reveal the composition of the federal workforce, demographics, occupation, pay, and many other facts.

www.fedstats.gov/
Federal agencies collect many statistics about the American population, the economy, housing, employment, and many other areas of life. This Web site provides a guide to finding and using those statistics, whether they involve the mean household income of American families or last year's export trade data.

www.usajobs.opm.gov/
At this site, you can see what jobs are open in the federal government and make an online application.

InfoTrac College Edition

"Racial Inequalities in Vocational Funding"
"Excessive Government Regulation Hammers Taxpayers"
"Funding Ergonomics Rule Blocked"
"Turkey Farm"

Notes

1. "AIDS:" Who Should Be Tested?" *Newsweek*, May 11, 1987, pp. 64–65.

2. Stephen Jay Gould, "The Exponential Spread of AIDS Underscores the Tragedy of Our Delay in Fighting One of Nature's Plagues," *New York Times Magazine*, April 19, 1987, p. 33.

3. "AIDS Becomes a Political Issue," *Time*, March 23, 1987, p. 24.

4. For a description of Weber's view of bureaucracy, see H. H. Gerth and C. Wright Mills, trans., *From Max Weber: Essays on Sociology* (New York: Oxford University Press, 1946), 196–239.

5. Taken from Bruce Adams, "The Frustrations of Government Service," *Public Administration Review* 44 (January/February 1984): 5. For more discussion of public attitudes about the civil service,

see Herbert Kaufman, "Fear of Bureaucracy: A Raging Pandemic," *Public Administration Review* 41 (January/February 1981): 1.

6. Barry Bozeman, *All Organizations Are Public: Bridging Public and Private Organizational Theories* (San Francisco: Jossey-Bass, 1987).

7. Donald S. Kellermann, Andrew Kohut, and Carol Bowman, *The People, The Press and Politics on the Eve of '92: Fault Lines in the Electorate* (Washington, D.C.: Times Mirror Center for The People & The Press, December 4, 1991), p. 39.

8. Mark Green and John Berry, *The Challenge of Hidden Profits: Reducing Corporate Bureaucracy and Waste* (New York: Morrow, 1985).

9. Reported in Sam Archibald, "The Early Years of the Freedom of Information Act—1955–1974," *PS: Political Science & Politics* (December 1993): 730.

10. Debra Gersh Hernandez, "Many Promises, Little Action," *Editor & Publisher*, March 26, 1994, p. 15.

11. General Accounting Office, *Freedom of Information Act: State Department Request Processing* (Washington, D.C.: U.S. Government Printing Office, January 23, 1989).

12. "President Declassifies Old Papers," *Omaha World-Herald*, April 18, 1995, p. 1.

13. Hernandez, "Many Promises, Little Action," p. 12; and George Lardner Jr., "Hit That 'Save' Button," *Washington Post National Weekly Edition*, August 23–29, 1993, p. 32.

14. Stephen Hess, *The Government/Press Connection: Press Officers and Their Offices* (Washington, D.C.: Brookings Institution, 1984), p. 101.

15. Evan Hendricks, *Former Secrets: Government Records Made Public through the Freedom of Information Act* (Washington, D.C.: Campaign for Political Rights, 1982).

16. Joyce Appleby, "That's General Washington to You," *New York Times Book Review*, February 14, 1993, p. 11. This is a review of Richard Norton Smith, *Patriarch* (Boston: Houghton Mifflin, 1993). See also James Q. Wilson, "The Rise of the Bureaucratic State," *The Public Interest* 41 (Fall 1975): 77–103.

17. Karl Vick, "The President Who Woke Up Washington," *Washington Post National Weekly Edition*, April 28, 1997, 8.

18. Leonard D. White, *Introduction to the Study of Public Administration*, 4th ed. (New York: Macmillan, 1955), p. 4.

19. James Q. Wilson, "The Rise of the Bureaucratic State."

20. Paul C. Light, *Thickening Government: Federal Hierarchy and the Diffusion of Accountability* (Washington, D.C.: Brookings Institution, 1995).

21. Office of Management and Budget, *Special Analyses: Budget of the United States: Fiscal Year 1990* (Washington, D.C.: U.S. Government Printing Office, 1989), 1–13; *Historical Tables: Budget of the United States: Fiscal Year 1996* (Washington, D.C.: U.S. Government Printing Office, 1995), 245.

22. Harold Seidman and Robert Gilmour, *Politics, Position and Power: The Dynamics of Federal Organization*, 4th ed. (New York: Oxford University Press, 1986), 249–292. See also Herbert Kaufman, "Emerging Conflicts in the Doctrines of Public Administration," *American Political Science Review* 50 (December 1956): 1057–1073, for a study of the growth of American public bureaucracy focusing on the conflicting expectations people have of it.

23. See Lawrence J. Haas, "Dodging the Budget Bullet," *National Journal*, October 1, 1988, pp. 2465–2469; Donald F. Kettl, "Expansion and Protection in the Budgetary Process," *Public Administration Review* 49 (May/June 1989): 231–239; Seidman and Gilmour, *Politics, Position, and Power*, 281–292.

24. For a discussion of these issues see Peter T. Kilborn, "Big Change Likely as Law Bans Bias toward Disabled," *New York Times*, July 19, 1992, pp. 1 and 16.

25. Jill Smolows, "Noble Aims, Mixed Results," *Time*, July 31, 1995, p. 54.

26. Theodore Lowi, *The End of Liberalism* (New York: Norton, 1969).

27. Thomas J. Anton, *American Federalism and Public Policy* (Philadelphia: Temple University Press, 1989).

28. Virginia I. Postrel, "Red (Tape) Alert," *Washington Post National Weekly Edition,* February 20–26, 1995, p. 23.

29. Ibid.

30. John M. Goshko, "The Big-Ticket Costs of the Disabilities Act," *Washington Post National Weekly Edition,* March 20–26, 1995, p. 31.

31. For more, see Margaret Kriz, "A New Shade of Green," *National Journal,* March 18, 1995, pp. 661–665.

32. Gary Lee, "Deregulating Regulations," *Washington Post National Weekly Edition,* February 20–26, 1995, pp. 6–7.

33. Woodrow Wilson, "The Study of Administration," *Political Science Quarterly 56* (December 1941), pp. 481–506. This was reprinted from the article's original publication in *The Academy of Political Science* in 1887.

34. See David H. Rosenbloom, "Editorial: Have An Administrative Rx? Don't Forget the Politics!" *Public Administration Review* (November/December 1993): 503–507.

35. "Hatch Act Revamped," *PA Times,* November 1, 1993, p. 3; "Hatch Act Political Curbs Retained for Some Workers," *Lincoln Star,* July 16, 1993, p. 3.

36. Walter Williams, "So, You Like Government on Cheap?" *Lincoln Sunday Journal-Star,* October 21, 1990, p. 6B. See also E. J. Dionne, Jr., "Are We Getting the Kind of Public Servants We Deserve?" *Washington Post National Weekly Edition,* August 13–19, 1990, p. 31; Gregory B. Lewis, "Turnover and the Quiet Crisis in the Federal Civil Service," *Public Administration Review* (March/April 1991): 145–155.

37. Reported in "Bush Commits to Support the Public Service," *PA Times,* November 25, 1988, p. 1. See also Judith Havemann, "Panel Seeks Raises for Civil Service," *Washington Post,* March 30, 1989, p. A20.

38. Information about conflict-of-interest matters is in Ronald Brownstein, "Agency Ethics Officers Fear Meese Ruling Could Weaken Conflict Laws," *National Journal,* March 23, 1985, pp. 639–642; W. John Moore, " Ethics Plan: Too Stingy or Humbug?" *National Journal,* December 19, 1992, p. 2898.

39. Steven Maynard-Moody, "Beyond Implementation: Developing an Institutional Theory of Administrative Policy Making," *Public Administration Review* 49 (March/April 1989):, 139.

40. B. Dan Wood, "Principals, Bureaucrats, and Responsiveness in Clean Air Enforcements," *American Political Science Review* 82 (March 1988): 213–234.

41. George C. Eads and Michael Fix, *Relief or Reform?* (Washington, D.C.: Urban Institute Press, 1984), chap. 7.

42. David Ellis, "White House to IRS: Hands Off the Rich," *Time,* April 1, 1991, p. 15.

43. Richard Lacayo, "Pro-Choice? Get Lost," *Time,* December 4, 1989, pp. 43–44.

44. Jeffrey Cohen, "The Dynamics of the Revolving Door," *American Journal of Political Science* 30 (November 1986): 689–708.

45. Charles Peters, *How Washington Really Works* (Reading, Mass.: Addison-Wesley, 1980), 46–47.

46. Terry Moe, "Regulators' Performance and Presidential Administrations," *American Journal of Political Science* 26 (May 1982): 197–224; Terry Moe, "Control and Feedback in Economic Regulation," *American Political Science Review* 79 (December 1985): 1094–1116.

47. Joan Biskupic, "Asking the Court to Read between the Lines," *Washington Post National Weekly Edition,* May 9–15, 1994, p. 32.

48. Moe, "Control and Feedback."

49. The term *capture* is widely used, but its use by political scientists studying regulation seems to have originated with Samuel Huntington, "The Marasmus of the ICC," *Yale Law Journal* 61 (April 1952): 467–509; it was later popularized by Marver Bernstein, *Regulating Business by Independent Commission* (Princeton, N.J.: Princeton University Press, 1955).

50. Bernstein, *Regulating Business;* William Gormley, "A Test of the Revolving Door Hypothesis in the FCC," *American Journal of Political Science* 23 (November 1979): 665–683; Jeffrey Cohen, "The Dynamics of the Revolving Door," *American Journal of Political Science* 30 (November 1986): 689–708.

51. See "C-5As with Wing Modifications Planned for September Delivery," *Aviation Week & Space Technology,* December 22, 1969, p. 13; "Whatever Happened to the C-5A 'White Elephant'?" *U.S. News and World Report,* June 19, 1972, p. 63.

52. David C. Morrison, "Extracting a Thorn, Air Force–Style," *National Journal,* March 7, 1987, p. 567. For more on Fitzgerald's experiences, see A. Ernest Fitzgerald, *The Pentagonists: An Insider's View of Waste, Mismanagement, and Fraud in Defense Spending* (Boston: Houghton Mifflin, 1989).

53. W. John Moore, "Citizen Prosecutors," *National Journal,* August 18, 1990, pp. 2006–2010.

54. Merit Systems Protection Board, Office of Policy and Evaluation, "Whistleblowing in the Federal Government: An Update" (Washington, D.C., 1993).

55. Charles T. Goodsell, *The Case for Bureaucracy: A Public Administration Polemic,* 2d ed. (Chatham, N.J.: Chatham House, 1985), 140.

56. Lawrence K. Altman, "Who's Stricken and How: AIDS Pattern Is Shifting," *New York Times,* February 5, 1989, pp. 1 and 16. See also Sandra Panem, *The AIDS Bureaucracy* (Cambridge, Mass.: Harvard University Press, 1988).

57. Ibid.

58. Koop's 1987 remark is quoted in Julie Kosterlitz, "Health Focus," *National Journal,* January 28, 1989, p. 259.

The Judiciary

YOU ARE THERE

Is the President Immune?

You are Justice John Paul Stevens, and you must decide how to vote on a sensitive constitutional issue facing the U.S. Supreme Court in 1997: Is a president, during his term in office, immune from a lawsuit based on alleged actions he took before becoming president?

Paula Jones, a clerical worker in an Arkansas state agency, claims that Bill Clinton, as governor of Arkansas in 1991, made a sexual advance toward her—"He exposed himself"—at a conference in a hotel where she staffed the registration desk and he delivered a speech. After she refused his overture, Jones claims that she suffered hostility from her superiors and a change in her duties. Essentially, Jones argues that Clinton sexually harassed her.[1] She is suing for $700,000.

President Clinton denies that the incident or the treatment after the conference ever occurred. Regardless, he maintains that as president he is immune—that is, he cannot be sued—during his term in office. He acknowledges that as a private citizen he could be sued after he leaves the White House.[2]

This case is unique. Only three prior presidents have been sued for incidents occurring before taking office. The suits against Theodore Roosevelt and Harry Truman were dismissed before these men were inaugurated. Two suits against John Kennedy, arising from an automobile accident involving staff members in the campaign, were settled out of court after Kennedy took office.

Some presidents have been sued for incidents occurring during their term, but there are few court rulings to guide you. The primary precedent is a Supreme Court ruling in 1982 involving President Richard Nixon.[3] During his term, Nixon had ordered the firing of a Pentagon accountant who had told Congress that an Air Force cargo plane was costing more, and performing worse, than it was supposed to. (Its wings were falling off after 200 hours of flight time.) The firing was unlawful, so the accountant sued the president. The Court ruled that although the Constitution does not mention **presidential immunity,** the concept of separation of powers entails such immunity. Presidents must be free to make decisions without worrying about lawsuits or spending time defending themselves against lawsuits. Otherwise, presidents might be weaker than our constitutional framework envisions.

More specifically, the Court ruled that presidents have immunity, forever,

Lynn Johnson/Aurora

for acts that occur while in office and that relate to their official responsibilities. This precedent does not determine whether immunity exists for decisions made before taking office or for decisions unrelated to a president's official responsibilities.

The president's lawyer has argued that a key rationale for immunity—to shield presidents from diverting their attention and energy from governmental matters in the process of defending themselves against private suits—would apply to Clinton's situation just as it did to Nixon's. The lawyer has cited additional reasons that seem plausible in the 1990s: that Jones's suit, if allowed to continue, might inspire copycat suits; that it might prompt others to seek the fame that it has brought

her; and that it might tempt interest groups to tie up and possibly bring down presidents they oppose. Presidents would feel pressure to defend themselves against politically motivated suits rather than attend to the country's business.

Jones's lawyers have countered that nobody, not even a president, is above the law. Moreover, his alleged tawdry behavior was not related to his official responsibilities and did not occur during his presidential term. Although Jones could sue after Clinton left office, even if the Court rules against her now, her lawyers have noted that a suit would be harder to win if key evidence is lost or an important witness dies in the intervening years.[4]

You have several options. You could grant or deny the president's request for

temporary immunity. Or, like the federal trial court, you could grant partial temporary immunity. This judge ruled that the president was immune from trial but not from "discovery"—the process of disclosing information and establishing facts to be used at trial. This compromise would allow Jones to preserve a record of crucial evidence and testimony but allow Clinton to avoid a trial while in office.

You are a Republican, appointed by President Gerald Ford, but you have become a liberal on the bench. And, like other Americans, you have your own opinions about Bill Clinton. Yet you realize that your partisan ties or ideological views or personal feelings about him should not determine your decision in this important case. How do you decide? And why?

The public expresses more support for the Supreme Court than for the president or Congress.[5] The public dislikes the disagreements and debates and the negotiations and compromises among officials, and it deplores the efforts of interest groups to influence policies. These messy features of democratic government, which are so visible in the executive and legislative branches, are not very visible in the judicial branch. Many people conclude that they do not occur.

Indeed, many people assume that courts are nonpolitical and that judges are objective. People say we have "a government of laws, not of men." But this view is a myth. At any time in our history, "It is individuals who make, enforce, and interpret the law."[6] When judges interpret the law, they are political actors and courts are political institutions.

Thus, public support for the Supreme Court and for the lower courts rests partly on false assumptions about the absence of politics in this branch. There is plenty of politics, as will be seen in all of the topics covered in this chapter—the history, structure, jurisdiction, composition, operation, and impact of the courts.

Development of the Courts' Role in Government

The Founders expected the judiciary to be the weakest branch of government. In the *Federalist Papers,* Alexander Hamilton wrote that Congress would have power to pass

the laws and appropriate the money; the president would have power to execute the laws; but the courts would have "merely judgment"—that is, only power to resolve disputes in cases brought to them. In doing so, they would exercise "neither force nor will." They would not have any means to enforce decisions, and they would not use their own values to decide cases. Rather, they would simply apply the Constitution and laws as written. Consequently, the judiciary would be the "least dangerous" branch.[7]

This prediction was accurate for the early years of the Republic. The Supreme Court was held in such low esteem that some distinguished men refused to accept appointment, or they accepted appointment but refused to attend sessions. The first chief justice thought the Court was "inauspicious,"[8] without enough "weight and dignity"[9] to play an important role. So he resigned to be governor of New York. The second chief justice resigned to be envoy to France.

When the capital was moved to Washington in 1801, new homes were built for Congress and the president but not for the Supreme Court. Planners considered the Court too insignificant for more than a small room in the Capitol. But the Court could not even keep this room. For decades it would be shunted from one location to another, from the marshal's office to the clerk's office, from the clerk's home to the Capitol's cellar—a dark and damp chamber in which visitors joked that Lady Justice would not need to wear a blindfold because she could not see anyway—and from the District of

Columbia Committee Room to the Judiciary Committee Room.[10] It would not get its own building until 1935.

However, the status of the Court began to change after the appointment of the fourth chief justice—John Marshall. Under the leadership of Marshall, the Court began to develop "weight and dignity" and to play an important role in government. The lower courts eventually would as well.

The development of the courts' role in government can be shown by dividing the courts' history into three eras—from the founding to the Civil War, from the Civil War to the Great Depression, and from the Great Depression to the present.

Founding to the Civil War

The primary issue for the courts in the era from the country's founding to the Civil War was the relationship between nation and state. In addressing this issue, the Supreme Court established judicial review and national dominance.

Judicial Review

Judicial review is the authority to declare laws or actions of government officials unconstitutional. The Constitution does not mention judicial review, but the Founders apparently expected the courts to exercise it. In the *Federalist Papers,* Hamilton said the courts would have authority to void laws contrary to the Constitution,[11] and at the time some state courts did have such authority. Yet the Founders did not expect the courts to exercise it vigorously.

The Supreme Court articulated the power of judicial review in the case of ***Marbury v. Madison*** in 1803.[12] The case had its origins in 1800, when the Federalist president John Adams was defeated in his bid for reelection by Thomas Jefferson and Federalist members of Congress were defeated by Jeffersonians. With both the presidency and Congress lost, the Federalists tried to ensure continued control of the judiciary. The lame duck president and Congress added more judgeships, most of which were not needed. (Forty-two were for justices of the peace for the District of Columbia, which was sparsely populated.) They hoped to fill these judgeships with loyal Federalists before the new president and Congress took over. In addition, Adams named his secretary of state, John Marshall, to be chief justice. At the time, though, Marshall was still secretary of state and was responsible for delivering the commissions to the new appointees. But he ran out of time and failed to deliver four commissions for District of Columbia justices of the peace. He assumed that his successor would deliver

This portrait of William Marbury reflects the importance of Marbury v. Madison. *It is the only portrait of a litigant owned by the Supreme Court Historical Society.*
Supreme Court Historical Society

them. But Jefferson, angry at the Federalists' efforts to pack the judiciary, told his secretary of state, James Madison, not to deliver the commissions.[13] Without the signed commissions, the appointees could not prove that they had in fact been appointed.[14]

William Marbury and the three other appointees petitioned the Supreme Court for a writ of mandamus (Latin for "we command"), a writ that orders government officials to do something they have a duty to do. In this case it would order Madison to deliver the commissions.

As chief justice, Marshall was in a position to rule on his administration's efforts to appoint these judges. Today this would be considered a conflict of interest, and he would be expected to disqualify himself. But at the time people were not as troubled by such conflicts.

Marshall could issue the writ, but Jefferson would tell Madison to disobey it and the Court would be powerless to enforce it. Or he could not issue the writ, and the Court would appear powerless to issue it. Either way the Court would demonstrate weakness rather than strength. But Marshall shrewdly found a way out of the dilemma.

Marshall interpreted a provision of a congressional statute in a questionable way and then a provision of the Constitution in a questionable way as well. Marbury had petitioned the Court for a writ of mandamus under the authority of a provision of the Judiciary Act of 1789 that permitted the Court to issue such a writ. Marshall maintained that this provision broadened the Court's original jurisdiction and thus violated the Constitution. (The Constitution allows the Court to hear cases on appeal, and it gives the Court original jurisdiction—that is, the authority to hear cases that have not been heard by any other court before—in cases involving a state or foreign ambassador. Marbury's involved neither.) Yet it was quite clear that the provision did not broaden the Court's original jurisdiction—so clear, in fact, that Marshall did not even quote the language he was declaring unconstitutional. Further, even if the provision did broaden the Court's original jurisdiction, it is not certain that this would violate the Constitution. (The Constitution does not say the Court shall have original jurisdiction *only* in cases involving a state or foreign ambassador.) Many members of Congress who had drafted and voted for the Judiciary Act had been delegates to the Constitutional Convention, and it is unlikely that they would have initiated a law that contradicted the Constitution. (One, Oliver Ellsworth, had been coauthor of the bill and then chief justice of the Supreme Court before Marshall.) But these interpretations allowed Marshall a way out of the dilemma.

Marshall concluded that the Court could not order the administration to give the commission because the provision of the act was unconstitutional. Thus, Marshall exercised judicial review. He wrote, in a statement that would be repeated by courts for years to come, "It is emphatically the province and duty of the judicial department to say what the law is."

Marshall justified judicial review this way: The Constitution is the supreme law of the land. If other laws contradict it, they are unconstitutional. So far, few of his contemporaries would quarrel with his reasoning. Marshall continued: Judges decide cases, and to decide cases they have to apply the Constitution. To apply it, they have to say what it means. They can be trusted to say what it means because they take an oath to uphold it. Here many would quarrel with his reasoning. Other officials have to follow the Constitution and take an oath to uphold it, and they could interpret it as appropriately as judges could.

Chief Justice Marshall (right) swears in President Andrew Jackson in 1829. Although Marshall's party, the Federalists, had dissolved, Marshall remained as chief justice, serving for thirty-four years.
Granger Collection

The Quintessential American?

Thomas Jefferson is well known among Americans, with his face on nickels and a beautiful monument in Washington. His adversary, John Marshall, is relatively unknown despite the chief justice's historic accomplishments in strengthening the Supreme Court and the national government.

Though distant cousins and Virginia natives, these two great Americans detested each other, perhaps because they were so different from one another. Jefferson was an aristocrat, broadly educated, with an interest in science and a flair for inventing things, and also with an interest in architecture and real talent for practicing it, as evidenced by Monticello, his home. He owned slaves, yet he lived beyond his means and usually was over his head in debt. Marshall, the oldest of fifteen children from a frontier family, was a self-made man. He worked hard to establish himself as a lawyer. He also tried to increase his wealth as a land speculator. By combining law and business, Marshall reflected the American fascination with these two professions.

During the Revolutionary War, Marshall served with General George Washington through the long winter at Valley Forge. He witnessed American farmers selling their food to British troops rather than to American troops who desperately needed it, because the American army paid with worthless money. The American government under the Continental Congress was too weak to tax, so it lacked the resources to back up the money it printed. This experience would contribute to Marshall's belief in a strong government.

After the war, Marshall gained extensive political experience. He served in the Virginia legislature, the Virginia convention for ratification of the Constitution, and the United States House of Representatives, and he served as a United States minister to France. He led a delegation to France in 1797 to negotiate a treaty between the two countries. But when the French foreign minister demanded money in exchange for an agreement, Marshall rebuffed him and returned home a hero. Outraged Americans threatened war, but Jefferson, who admired French society and fancied French finery, upbraided Marshall for antagonizing French officials.

President John Adams appointed Marshall secretary of state and, at the end of his administration, chief justice of the Supreme Court. By the time Marshall reached the Court, his political experience certainly had sharpened his political acumen to the point where he could lead his brethren and write persuasive opinions for the Court over the opposition of other officials and opposing parties.

Throughout his career, Marshall dressed slovenly and got along well with people from all classes. He seemed as comfortable in rowdy taverns as in genteel homes. (They say that as a candidate for Congress he provided the best whiskey on election day.) Even as chief justice, he often shopped for his sick wife. At market one day a young dandy who did not recognize him said, "Here, my man. Just take this turkey to my house," and tossed a coin. Marshall took the coin and delivered the turkey.[1]

The aristocratic Jefferson envisioned an agrarian country and championed the poor farmers who seemed at the mercy of the commercial interests of the northern cities. He spoke against efforts to strengthen the national government, which, he believed, would be controlled by these powerful interests. The self-made Marshall, however, envisioned a commercial empire and advocated a strong government that could provide a stable economy in which business could flourish. Over the years Americans would talk like Jefferson—"That government is best which governs least" would become a perennial quotation—but they would act like Marshall, and the country would develop as Marshall envisioned far more than as Jefferson did.

In other ways Marshall was more advanced for his times, though less successful in furthering his views. He opposed slavery and favored equality for women. He was unsympathetic to efforts to drive Indian tribes off their lands. When Georgia tried to force the Cherokees from the state, the Supreme Court held the laws unconstitutional.[2] But Georgia ignored the ruling, and former Indian fighter President Andrew Jackson reportedly said, "John Marshall has made his decision. Now let him enforce it."

1. Robert Wernick, "Chief Justice Marshall Takes the Law in Hand," *Smithsonian* (November 1998): 159.
2. *Worcester v. Georgia,* 31 U.S. 515 (1832).
SOURCE: Robert Wernick, "Chief Justice Marshall Takes the Law in Hand," *Smithsonian* (November 1998): 157–173.

But Marshall was persuasive enough to convince many people. A sly fox, he sacrificed the commissions—he could not have gotten them anyway—and established the power of judicial review instead. In doing so, with one hand he gave the Jeffersonians what they wanted, while with the other he gave the Federalists something much greater. And all along he claimed he did what the Constitution required him to do.

Jefferson saw through this. He said the Constitution, in Marshall's hands, was "a thing of putty."[15] But the decision did not require Jefferson to do anything, so he could not do anything but protest. Most of Jefferson's followers were satisfied with the result. They were not upset that the Court had invalidated a Federalist law or especially concerned with the means used to do so.

Of course, they were shortsighted because this decision laid the cornerstone for a strong judiciary. Thus, the case that began as a "trivial squabble over a few petty political plums"[16] became perhaps the most important case the Court has ever decided. (See also the box "The Quintessential American?")

National Dominance

After *Marbury* the Court did not declare any other congressional laws unconstitutional during Marshall's tenure, although it did declare numerous state laws unconstitutional.[17]

The Court also furthered national dominance by broadly construing Congress's power. In *McCulloch v. Maryland*, explained in Chapter 3, the Court interpreted the "necessary and proper clause" to allow Congress to legislate in many matters not mentioned in the Constitution. The Court also furthered national dominance by narrowly construing states' power to regulate commerce.[18]

When President Andrew Jackson named Roger Taney to replace Marshall, proponents of a strong national government worried that Taney would undo what Marshall had done. But, although Taney did not further expand national power, he upheld national supremacy and thus solidified most of Marshall's doctrine.

Yet in one case Taney severely undermined the Court's reputation. In the Dred Scott case,[19] the Court jumped into the thick of the slavery conflict and declared the Missouri Compromise of 1820, which controlled slavery in the territories, unconstitutional. This was only the second time the Court had declared a congressional law unconstitutional, and it could not have come in a more controversial area or at a less opportune time. The slavery issue had polarized the nation, and the ruling polarized it further. Southerners had been disenchanted with the Court

Although many children worked long days in unhealthy conditions, the Supreme Court declared initial laws prohibiting child labor unconstitutional. This boy worked in the coal mines in the early 1900s.
Utah State Historical Society

because of its emphasis on a strong national government. Now northerners became disenchanted too. The Court's prestige dropped so precipitously that it could play only a weak role for two decades. President Abraham Lincoln refused to enforce one of its rulings,[20] and Congress withdrew part of its jurisdiction.[21] As a result, the Court shied away from important issues.

The Taney Court naively thought it could resolve the clash over slavery and thereby resolve the conflict between nation and state. But no court could achieve this. It would take the Civil War to do so.[22]

Civil War to the Depression

With the controversy between nation and state muted, the next primary issue for the courts was the relationship between government and business in cases involving regulation of business.

After the war, industrialization proceeded at a breakneck pace, bringing not only benefits but many problems. Some corporations abused their power over their employees, their competitors, and their customers. Although legislatures passed laws to regulate these abuses, the corporations challenged the laws in court. The Supreme Court, dominated by justices who had been lawyers for corporations, reflected the views of corporations and struck down the regulations on them.

Beginning in the 1870s, intensifying in the 1890s, and continuing in the 1900s, the Court invalidated laws that regulated child labor,[23] maximum hours of work,[24] and minimum wages for work.[25] It also discouraged employees from joining unions and unions from striking employers,[26] and it limited antitrust laws.[27] In just one decade, the Court invalidated forty-one state laws regulating railroads.[28]

In 1935 and 1936, the Court struck down twelve congressional laws,[29] nearly nullifying President Franklin Roosevelt's New Deal program to help the country recover from the Great Depression.

The Court's action precipitated another major crisis. Roosevelt was reelected resoundingly in 1936. Heady from his victory and frustrated by his lack of opportunities to appoint new justices in his first term, he retaliated against the Court by proposing what was soon labeled a **court-packing plan.** The plan would have authorized the president to nominate and the Senate to confirm a new justice for every justice over seventy who did not retire, up to a total of fifteen. At the time, there were six justices over seventy, so Roosevelt could have appointed six new justices and assured himself a friendly Court. Roosevelt claimed the plan was to help the Court cope with its increasing caseload, but virtually everyone could see through this. Even many of his supporters criticized him for tampering with the Court.

Before Congress could vote on the plan, two justices who often sided with four conservative justices against New Deal legislation switched positions to side with three liberal justices for similar legislation. Chief Justice Charles Evans Hughes and Justice Owen Roberts apparently thought the Court would suffer if it continued to oppose the popular president and his popular programs. Their "conversion" tipped the scales from votes of six to three against New Deal legislation to five to four for similar legislation. As a result, Roosevelt's plan became unnecessary, and Congress scuttled it. Hughes's and Roberts's switch was dubbed "the switch in time that saved nine."

Thus, the Court resolved this issue in favor of government over business. Since then it has permitted most efforts to regulate business.

Depression to the Present

With the controversy between government and business subdued, the next primary issue for the courts was the relationship between government and the individual in cases involving civil liberties and rights. Often this issue featured a conflict between the majority, whose views were reflected in government policy toward civil liberties and rights, and a minority who challenged the policy.

Historically, the Supreme Court had shown limited concern for civil liberties and rights. But this attitude began to broaden when President Dwight Eisenhower, fulfilling a campaign pledge to a presidential rival, Earl Warren, appointed him chief justice. From 1953 through the 1960s, Warren led the Court more effectively than any chief justice since Marshall. The **Warren Court** completely overhauled doctrine involving racial segregation, criminal defendants' rights, and reapportionment. It also significantly altered doctrine involving libel, obscenity, and religion. In the process it held many laws unconstitutional. It was more activist in civil liberties and rights cases than the Court had ever been (see Figure 1).

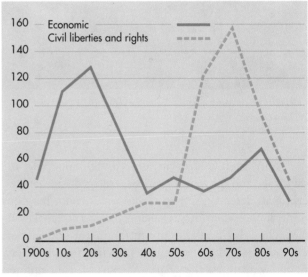

F I G U R E 1 ■ *Laws Regulating Economic Activity and Restricting Civil Liberties and Rights Declared Unconstitutional by the Supreme Court since 1900 The Supreme Court was nearly as activist in striking down laws in the 1910s, 1920s, and 1930s as it was in the 1950s, 1960s, and 1970s. But in the former years it was activist in economic cases (usually ones involving governmental regulation of business), while in the latter years it was activist in civil liberties and rights cases.*

SOURCES: Congressional Research Service, *The Constitution of the United States: Analysis and Interpretation and 1990 Supplement* (Washington, D.C.: U.S. Government Printing Office, 1987 and 1991); Lawrence Baum, *The Supreme Court*, 6th ed. (Washington, D.C.: CQ Press, 1998), 213. Data are through 1996 and were multiplied by 1.43 to create a ten-year rate for the decade.

Chief Justice Earl Warren, flanked by Justices Hugo Black (left) and William Douglas.
Dennis Brack, Black Star

The Warren Court sympathized with unpopular individuals and powerless groups—alleged subversives, criminal defendants, racial minorities, and religious minorities—when they challenged governmental policies. Thus, the most elite institution in our government used its power to benefit many nonelites in our society. In its sympathies, the Warren Court sharply differed from previous Courts, which historically favored the haves over the have-nots and efforts to preserve the status quo over struggles to change it.

The Warren Court's decisions brought about a backlash in the late 1960s. President Richard Nixon vowed to change the direction of the Court, and in 1969 he appointed Warren Burger to be chief justice after Warren retired. Then Nixon and his former vice president, President Gerald Ford, appointed four more justices when vacancies occurred. They wanted to slow, halt, or even reverse the Warren Court's actions. They expected the **Burger Court** to make a "constitutional counter-revolution."

But the Court did not. Although it eroded some of the Warren Court's doctrine, particularly in the area of criminal defendants' rights, it left most of the doctrine intact. Further, it advanced doctrine in two areas where the Warren Court was silent—sexual discrimination and abortion. Although it was not as committed to civil liberties and rights as the Warren Court, the Burger Court was more committed to them than any earlier Court.

Presidents Reagan and Bush also wanted to reverse the Court's liberal doctrine. When Burger retired, Reagan elevated William Rehnquist, the most conservative associate justice, to be chief justice in 1986. Then Reagan appointed three more conservatives, and Bush appointed two more conservatives. By this time, Republican presidents had named ten straight justices.

The election of President Clinton led to the appointment of the first Democratic justices since 1967. Although these two moderates have slowed any further swing to the right, the conservatives control the **Rehnquist Court.** But conflicts among the conservatives have splintered the bloc. Some are bold, anxious to sweep away liberal precedents and substitute conservative principles. Others are cautious, willing to uphold liberal precedents they would not have agreed to set in the first place, and inclined to decide cases on narrow bases rather than on broad principles. In some terms, the former group has dominated, but in other terms the latter group has dominated. Overall, the Rehnquist Court, though markedly more conservative than the Burger Court, has not overturned most of the previous Courts' doctrine.

Yet the Rehnquist Court has altered some of the previous Courts' doctrine. The conservative justices have continued to erode criminal defendants' rights. They have also made it harder for racial minorities to use affirmative action and for religious minorities to follow the tenets of their religion. At the same time, they have made it somewhat easier for Christian denominations to play a prominent role in public settings. In two less obvious areas, the Rehnquist Court has altered doctrine in more fundamental ways. It has tightened access to the courts for individuals and groups trying to challenge government policies. And it has limited efforts by the federal government to impose new regulations on the states. In these ways the Republican justices have mirrored the views of the Republican presidents and members of Congress in the 1980s and 1990s.

In sum, throughout its history the Court's role in government has been that of a policymaker—in relationships between nation and state, government and business, and government and the individual. In the first and second eras, the Court was a solidly conservative policymaker, protecting private property rights and limiting government regulation of business; in the third era, the Court was a generally liberal policymaker, permitting government regulation of business and supporting civil liberties and rights for the individual.

It now appears that the third era is over. Although the Rehnquist Court has not overturned most of the previous Courts' doctrine, it has deemphasized individual rights,[30] refusing to expand them and even cutting back on them in some areas.

The Next Era

If the third era is over, what controversy will the fourth era address? We probably will not know for many years, until we can look back with more perspective than we have now, but it is interesting to speculate.

Might the fourth era focus on information technology, including computers, the software they use, and the data they store? And might it resolve disputes about which people have access to this technology, when people have access to it, how people can use it—in short, in what ways and to what extent the government and the private sector can impose restrictions on the new technology? These questions would be similar to ones the Court answered about freedom of speech, freedom of the press, libel, and obscenity in the third era. Or perhaps the emphasis will be on privacy from all the intrusions of this new technology. The Court has barely addressed invasion of privacy in the third era. (Chapter 14 explains the Court's doctrine in this area.)

Or might the fourth era focus on biotechnology? Advances in genetics herald a revolution promising the opportunity for people to live longer and for parents to choose various characteristics of their children, such as gender and eye color, and alter other characteristics, such as intelligence, personality, and athletic ability. Research even offers the possibility of cloning. Initial legal issues might involve restrictions on experiments and techniques. Once the techniques are developed, the legal issues might involve access to these procedures.

Courts

Most countries with a federal system have one national court over a system of regional courts. In contrast, the United States has a complete system of national courts side by side with complete systems of state courts, for a total of fifty-one separate systems. This setup makes litigation far more complicated than in other countries.

Structure of the Courts

The Constitution mentions only one court—a supreme court—although it allows Congress to set up additional, lower courts, which it did in the Judiciary Act of 1789. The act was a compromise between Federalists, who wanted a full system of lower courts with extensive jurisdiction—authority to hear and decide cases—in order to strengthen the national government, and Jeffersonians, who wanted only a partial system of lower courts with limited jurisdiction in order to avoid strengthening the national government. The compromise established a full system of lower courts with limited jurisdiction. These courts were authorized to hear disputes involving citizens of more than one state but not disputes relating to the U.S. Constitution and laws. The state courts were permitted to hear all these cases.

In 1875, Congress granted the federal courts extensive jurisdiction. Sixteen years later Congress created another level of courts, between the Supreme Court and the original lower courts, to complete the basic structure of the federal judiciary.

The **district courts** are trial courts. There are ninety-four, based on population but with at least one in each state. They have multiple judges, although a single judge or jury decides each case.

The **courts of appeals** are intermediate appellate courts. They hear cases that have been decided by the district courts but are appealed by the losers. There are twelve, based on regions—"circuits"—of the country. They have numerous judges, although a panel of three judges decides each case.

The Supreme Court is the ultimate appellate court. It hears cases that have been decided by the

"And don't go whining to some higher court."

courts of appeals, district courts, or state supreme courts. (Although it can hear some cases—those involving a state or diplomat—that have not proceeded through the lower courts first, in practice it hears nearly all of its cases on appeal.) The group of nine justices decides its cases.

The district courts conduct trials. The courts of appeals and Supreme Court do not; they do not have juries or witnesses to testify and present evidence—just lawyers for the opposing litigants. Rather than determine guilt or innocence, these courts evaluate arguments about legal questions arising in the cases.

The state judiciaries have a structure similar to the federal judiciary. In most states, though, there are two tiers of trial courts. Normally, the lower tier is for criminal cases involving minor crimes, and the upper tier is for criminal cases involving major crimes and for civil cases. In about three-fourths of the states, there are intermediate appellate courts, and in all of the states there is a supreme court (although in a few it is called another name).

Jurisdiction of the Courts

Jurisdiction is the authority to hear and decide cases. The federal courts can exercise jurisdiction over cases in which the subject involves either the U.S. Constitution, statutes, or treaties; maritime law; or cases in which the litigants include either the U.S. government, more than one state government, one state government and a citizen of another state, citizens of more than one state,[31] or a foreign government or citizen. The state courts exercise jurisdiction over the remaining cases. These include most criminal cases because the states have authority over most criminal matters and pass most criminal laws. The state courts hear far more cases than the federal courts.

Despite this dividing line, some cases begin in the state courts and end in the federal courts. These involve state law and federal law, frequently a state statute and a federal constitutional right. For these cases there are two paths from the state judiciary to the federal judiciary. One is for the litigant who lost at the state supreme court to appeal to the U.S. Supreme Court.

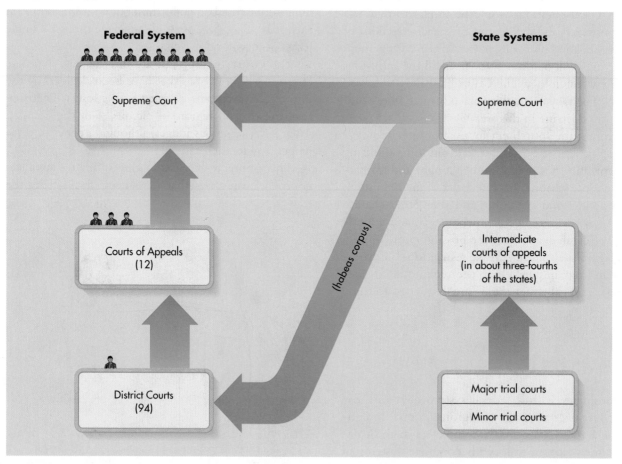

FIGURE 2 ■ *Federal and State Court Systems* The arrows indicate the primary avenues of appeal, and the heads indicate the usual number of judges who hear cases in the federal system.

The other path, available only in a criminal case, is for the defendant who has exhausted possible appeals in the state courts to appeal to the local federal district court through a writ of **habeas corpus.** Latin for "Have ye the body!" this writ demands that the state figuratively produce the defendant and justify his or her incarceration. If the district court decides that the state courts did not grant the defendant's constitutional rights, it will reverse the conviction. After the district court's decision, the losing side can try to appeal to the courts of appeals and Supreme Court (see Figure 2).

Judges

Selection of Judges

Benjamin Franklin proposed that judges be selected by lawyers because lawyers would pick "the ablest of the profession in order to get rid of him, and share his practice among themselves."[32] The Founders rejected this unique idea in favor of a plan whereby the president nominates judges and the Senate confirms them. There are no other requirements in the Constitution, although there is an unwritten requirement that judges be lawyers and an expectation that they be members of the president's political party. Most have been active party members who have served in office or contributed to candidates. In the twentieth century, presidents nominated members of their party from 82 percent of the time (William Howard Taft) to 99 percent of the time (Woodrow Wilson).[33] Thus, the process of selecting federal judges is highly political.

Mechanics of Selection

For the lower courts, lawyers who want to become a judge try to become politically active in their party. When vacancies arise, they lobby political officials, bar association leaders, or interest group leaders in the hope that these people will recommend them to the administration. They especially focus on their senators, who play a key role through the practice of senatorial courtesy. This tradition allows senators of the president's party to recommend and to veto candidates from their state. This practice applies not only to district courts, which lie within individual states, but sometimes to courts of appeals, which span several states. For courts of appeals, senators informally divide the seats among the states. (But this practice does not apply to the Supreme Court because it has too few seats.)

Senatorial courtesy can tie the president's hands. In deference to southern senators, President John Kennedy, who advocated civil rights, appointed southern judges who advocated segregation. One characterized the Supreme Court's desegregation ruling as "one of the truly regrettable decisions of all time," and another called blacks "niggers" and "chimpanzees" in court.[34] However, senatorial courtesy is not as ironclad now as it was then. There is more give and take between the senators and the president.

For the Supreme Court, lawyers who want to become a justice try to become politically active in their party and also prominent in the legal profession. They write articles or give speeches designed to attract officials' attention. When vacancies arise, political officials, bar association leaders, and interest group leaders urge consideration of certain candidates. The administration also conducts a search for acceptable candidates. Sometimes even sitting justices make a recommendation. Chief Justice Burger recommended Harry Blackmun, a childhood pal and the best man at his wedding, and Justice Rehnquist recommended Sandra Day O'Connor, a law school classmate whom he had dated occasionally.

Once the president has chosen a candidate, he submits the nomination to the Senate, where it goes to the Judiciary Committee for hearings. Senators question the nominee about his or her judicial philosophy, and interest groups voice their concerns. If a majority of the committee consents, the nomination goes to the whole Senate. If a majority of the Senate consents, the nomination is confirmed.

The mechanics of selection for all federal courts are similar, but the process of selection for the Supreme Court is more politicized at every stage because the Court is more powerful and visible. Its seats are fought over more intensely.

Criteria Used in Selection

The Founders expected judges to be selected by merit; they did not foresee the policymaking role of the courts or the development of political parties and senatorial courtesy, which have thrust political criteria into the process of selection.

Criteria Used by Presidents Although presidents want judges who have merit, they select them primarily on the basis of politics. They look for members of their party, usually those who have some political experience, either in office or with the party behind the scenes, and often those who have certain ideological views. President Theodore Roosevelt sought judges who opposed monopolies and supported the rights of labor unions, and President Franklin Roosevelt sought judges who supported his New Deal policies. President Richard Nixon vowed to appoint judges who would change the direction of the Warren Court. But Presidents Ronald Reagan and George H. Bush made the most concerted efforts to appoint conservatives. They, in fact, made the most concerted efforts since Franklin Roosevelt to appoint judges on the basis of ideological views. They had candidates fill out lengthy questionnaires and then submit to day-long interviews probing their positions. They expected candidates, for example, to oppose the right to abortion, the Supreme Court's ruling establishing the right, and the Supreme Court's reasoning in the case.

Sometimes presidents, under pressure from groups, look for judges who would provide more diversity on the courts. In the past, presidents chose Catholics and Jews to balance the Protestants who dominated the bench. In 1967 President Lyndon Johnson chose the first black justice, Thurgood Marshall, and in 1981 President Reagan chose the first woman justice, Sandra Day O'Connor. Presidents have bowed to the pressure from various groups to solidify their support from these groups. Reagan, who was not a staunch advocate of women's rights, nonetheless made a campaign pledge to appoint a woman to the Supreme Court to shore up his support among female voters. (Then, after fulfilling this pledge, he felt no need to appoint many women to the lower federal courts.)

Presidents Carter and Clinton made the most concerted efforts to appoint women and minorities to the federal courts. Before Carter took office, only eight women had ever served on the federal bench.[35] Sixteen percent of Carter's appointees were women, and 21 percent were racial minorities.[36] Twenty-six percent of Clinton's appointees were women, and 17 percent were blacks.[37]

Demands for diversity can limit presidents' choices, but presidents can acquiesce to these demands and still find candidates from their party with the desired political experience and ideological views. When Thurgood Marshall retired in 1991, President Bush felt obligated to nominate another black for this seat, but he wanted to nominate a conservative. He chose Clarence Thomas, a black conservative court of appeals judge. Whereas Marshall had been an ardent champion of civil rights, Thomas had opposed affirmative action and drawn the ire of most black leaders.

Individual justices do not always reflect their group's views. Justice O'Connor has voted against the feminist groups' position in some cases, while Justice Thomas has voted against the civil rights groups' position in many cases. Sometimes groups have to satisfy themselves with the symbolic benefits of having a "member" on the Court. (See also the box "Do Women Judges Make a Difference?")

Criteria Used by Senators Senators usually have been willing to confirm nominations to the lower courts but occasionally have been reluctant to confirm nominations to the Supreme Court. Because the high court is more important and appointments to it are more visible, these nominations are more likely to become embroiled in controversy. Since the late 1960s senators have rejected six nominations to the Court—two by President Lyndon Johnson, two by President Nixon, and two by President Reagan.[38]

Senators decide whether to confirm a nomination primarily on the basis of the qualifications and ideology of the nominee.[39] If the qualifications are good, they usually approve, regardless of the ideology. But if the qualifications are questionable, they often consider how closely the nominee's ideology matches theirs. (However, they are reluctant to admit this because doing so would reveal the politics involved, and most of the public thinks politics should not be involved.)

When Nixon chose court of appeals judge G. Harold Carswell, law scholars familiar with his record were dismayed. At Senate hearings they testified that he was undistinguished and opposed to civil rights. Nixon's floor manager for the nomination, Senator Roman Hruska (R–Neb.), blurted out in exasperation, "Even if he is mediocre there are a lot of mediocre judges and people and lawyers. They are entitled to a little representation, aren't they, and a little chance? We can't have all Brandeises, Cardozos, and Frankfurters, and stuff like that there."[40] This was the kiss of death. Once Carswell's supporters acknowledged his mediocrity, senators who objected to his views on civil rights could vote against him freely, and his nomination was doomed.

Yet when presidents nominated justices with unquestioned qualifications, they rarely faced a problem. One exception was Reagan's nomination of Robert Bork in 1987. Bork had criticized Court doctrine in his writings and speeches, and the debate focused on his ideology. In addition to rejecting a right to privacy, which is the basis of Court decisions allowing birth control and abortion, he had criticized Court decisions and congressional laws advancing racial equality. Bork's positions struck many Americans as extreme, and his nomination was voted down.

Do Women Judges Make a Difference?

Some argue that there should be more women judges because women are entitled to their "fair share" of all governmental offices, including judgeships. Others argue that there should be more so women as well as men will feel that courts represent them. Still others argue that there should be more because women, compared to men, have different views and would make different decisions.

A study of Justice Sandra Day O'Connor, the first woman on the Supreme Court, shows that although she generally votes as a conservative, she usually votes as a liberal in sex discrimination cases. Moreover, her presence on the Court apparently sensitized her male colleagues to gender issues. Most of them voted against sex discrimination more frequently after she joined the Court.[1]

Some studies find similar results for women justices on state supreme courts. Even women justices from opposite political parties support a broad array of women's rights in cases ranging from sex discrimination to child support and property settlement.[2]

But studies that compare voting patterns on issues less directly related to gender have less clear findings. Women judges appear more liberal than men in cases involving employment discrimination and racial discrimination. Perhaps the treatment they have experienced as women has made them more sympathetic to the discrimination others have faced. On the other hand, women judges do not appear more liberal or conservative than

men in cases involving obscenity or criminal rights.[3]

Studies that compare sentencing of criminal defendants in state courts find small differences between men and women judges.[4] However, women judges do tend to sentence convicted defendants somewhat more harshly, especially black men who are repeat offenders. Apparently women judges consider these defendants more dangerous or more prone to commit new crimes after prison. Possibly women judges are influenced by the fact that these defendants are less often contrite or by the fact that they are less often married and employed than other defendants.[5]

But the studies comparing men and women judges find more similarities than differences. This should not be surprising, because the two sexes were subject to the same training in law school and the same socialization in the legal profession, and they became judges in the same ways as others in their jurisdiction.

Perhaps the most significant difference women judges have made has been to protect the credibility of women lawyers and witnesses. In court, occasionally men judges have made disparaging remarks about women lawyers, suggesting that they should not be in the profession—for example, calling them "lawyerettes" and chastising them either for not wearing a tie like men or, alternatively, for wearing pants like men. More frequently men judges or lawyers have made paternalistic or personal remarks to women lawyers or witnesses, referring

to them by their first name or by such terms as "young lady," "sweetie," or "honey." Or the men, in the midst of the proceedings, have commented about their perfume, clothing, or appearance. "How does an attorney establish her authority when the judge has just described her to the entire courtroom as 'a pretty little thing'?"[6] Even if the men consider their remarks harmless compliments rather than intentional tactics, their effect is to undermine the credibility of women lawyers and witnesses in the eyes of jurors. Women judges have attempted to squelch such remarks.

1. Karen O'Connor and Jeffrey A. Segal, "Justice Sandra Day O'Connor and the Supreme Court's Reaction to Its First Female Member," in Naomi B. Lynn, ed., Women, Politics and the Constitution (New York: Haworth Press, 1990), pp. 95–104.
2. David W. Allen and Diane E. Wall, "Role Orientations and Women State Supreme Court Justices," Judicature 77 (November/December 1993), pp. 156–165.
3. Sue Davis, Susan Haire, and Donald R. Songer, "Voting Behavior and Gender on the U.S. Courts of Appeals," Judicature 77 (November/December 1993), pp. 129–133; Thomas G. Walker and Deborah J. Barrow, "The Diversification of the Federal Bench," Journal of Politics 47 (1985), pp. 596–617.
4. John Gruhl, Cassia Spohn, and Susan Welch, "Women as Policymakers: The Case of Trial Judges," American Journal of Political Science 25 (May 1981), pp. 308–322.
5. Darrell Steffensmeier and Chris Hebert, "Women and Men Policymakers: Does the Judge's Gender Affect the Sentencing of Criminal Defendants?" Social Forces 77 (March 1999): 1163–1196.
6. William Eich, "Gender Bias in the Courtroom: Some Participants Are More Equal Than Others," Judicature 69 (April/May 1986), pp. 339–343.

This battle prompted some observers to ask whether anyone with a record could be nominated again. Indeed, when Bush had his first vacancy, he chose a man who had left no trail of controversial writings and speeches. David Souter, though a former New Hampshire attor-

ney general and then state supreme court justice, was called the "Stealth candidate" (after the bomber designed to elude radar). Souter was a private person, living alone in a house at the end of a dirt road and not answering his neighbors' phone calls some nights. He had expressed few positions and made few decisions reflecting his views on federal constitutional doctrine. Even in his confirmation hearings he refused to reveal his views. It was assumed that he was another conservative, because of his lifestyle and because of his support from conservative aides to the president, yet he offered a small target and won confirmation easily.

When Bush had his second vacancy and chose Thomas, he realized that the nomination could be controversial (even before the charges of sexual harassment surfaced) but saw that it would split the Democratic coalition: some Democrats would be sympathetic because of Thomas's race, while others would be critical because of his views. For insurance the administration instructed Thomas to soft-pedal his views.

Both Souter and Thomas said they could not reveal their views because they would have to decide these issues and so would need to preserve their impartiality. Yet both stated their support for capital punishment, although they would also have to decide these cases. The difference is that their view on capital punishment coincided with that of three-fourths of the public, whereas their views on other issues probably did not.

When Clinton had his first vacancy, he was wary because the Senate had forced him to withdraw several nominations to other positions and because Republicans had vowed to avenge Bork's defeat. The president chose Ruth Bader Ginsburg, a court of appeals judge for thirteen years. The nomination satisfied Republicans because Ginsburg had often voted with Republicans on the bench, yet it also pleased some Democratic constituencies. Women's groups, of course, expected more seats, and Jews, who had not had a representative on the Court since 1969, also wanted a seat.

Ginsburg refused to discuss doctrine at her hearings, but her record showed a commitment to abortion rights and sexual equality. Although she had tied for first in her graduating class from Columbia Law School in 1959, she was turned down for a clerkship by Justice Felix Frankfurter and for a job by New York City law firms. The firms, just beginning to hire Jews, were not ready to hire mothers with young children. She taught law and then served as an attorney for the American Civil Liberties Union (ACLU). In the 1970s, she argued six sex discrimination cases before the Supreme Court and, with an innovative approach, won five.

When Clinton had his second vacancy, he was still wary of a confirmation fight. Instead of the people he most desired, he chose Stephen Breyer, a court of appeals judge with a reputation as a moderate.

Nominations to the Court, which were contentious during the nineteenth century but not during the first half of the twentieth century, have become contentious again partly because of the Court's activism—both liberals and conservatives have seen what the Court can do—and partly because of the struggle for control of the divided government since the late 1960s. In most years, Republicans have dominated the presidency while Democrats have dominated Congress (though in the 1990s, the situation has been just the reverse), so both have fought over the judiciary to tip the balance. Republicans, especially, have been frustrated by their inability to push their civil liberties and rights policies through Congress, so they have hoped that their appointees to the Court would do what their members in Congress have not been able to do.

Even nominations to the lower courts have become contentious in recent decades. The Senate has confirmed fewer nominations to the lower courts in the fourth year of a president's term, especially when the Senate has been controlled by the other party.[41] Senators in the other party hope their candidate will capture the White House in the next election. They delay confirmation so there will be numerous vacancies for the new president and, through senatorial courtesy, for themselves to fill as well.

Efforts to delay confirmation have become more pronounced since the Republicans won control of the Senate in 1994. They dragged their feet even at the beginning of President Clinton's second term, following a pace that kept about one hundred seats vacant.[42] These vacancies contributed to backlogs in the courts' dockets, prompting Chief Justice Rehnquist to complain about the Senate's inaction. The Republicans responded that the president was slow to submit nominations and that the Judiciary Committee needed to scrutinize nominees to make sure they were not "liberal activists." In reality, Clinton, who was unwilling to risk a confirmation fight over any judicial nominee, nominated moderates almost exclusively, disappointing liberals by not trying to balance the conservatives still on the bench from the Reagan and Bush years.[43]

The Republicans' tactics served several goals. Their efforts to delay confirmation and their complaints about liberal activists were like brushback pitches in baseball: they warned the president, as he stepped up to the plate to choose his candidates, not to be aggressive and not to get close in selecting the ones he might prefer. They also warned sitting judges not to decide cases as they might prefer. One Republican leader, who called for impeaching judges, said, "The judges need to be intimidated."[44]

| Table 1 | Appointees of Democrats and Republicans Vote Differently |

A study of the votes of federal district court judges appointed by President Nixon through President Clinton shows differences according to the political party of the president. The study also shows some differences, in criminal justice and in civil rights and liberties cases, among appointees of Republicans. Compare the appointees of Bush and Reagan with those of earlier Republicans. These results reflect the effort that the Bush and Reagan administrations made to nominate candidates who held conservative views on these issues.

Issue	Percentage of Liberal* Votes by Appointees of					
	Nixon (R)	Ford (R)	Carter (D)	Reagan (R)	Bush (R)	Clinton (D)
Criminal justice	30	32	38	23	29	34
Civil rights and civil liberties	37	39	52	33	33	39
Labor and economic regulation	48	55	62	49	51	62

*Liberal votes were defined as ones in favor of criminal defendants' or prisoners' rights in criminal justice cases; individuals' rights, involving freedom of expression or religion and equality between the races or sexes, in civil rights and liberties cases; and workers' or economic underdogs' interests, rather than businesses' or economic upper dogs' interests, in labor and economic regulation cases. Cases from 1992 to 1996 are included.
SOURCE: Ronald Stidham, Robert A. Carp, and Donald R. Songer, "The Voting Behavior of President Clinton's Judicial Appointees," *Judicature* 80 (July/August 1996): 16–20.

Republican strategists told Republican officials that complaining about liberal activists is a winning political issue. One said, "You can both channel populist anger at the notion of elitist judges with a general sense of resentment that the federal government is controlling people's lives too much."[45] In addition, complaining about liberal activists helps raise money for conservative organizations. One conservative group circulated a videotape attacking federal judges and asked for donations to block Clinton's nominations.[46]

The immediate result of these tactics, according to a political scientist who studies the nomination and confirmation process, is a polarization and a delay "unprecedented in its scope." He analogizes the Republicans' efforts to President Roosevelt's court-packing plan.[47]

Results of Selection

Judges are drawn primarily from the lower federal and state courts, the federal government, or large law firms. These established legal circles are dominated by white men so, not surprisingly, most judges have been white men. Although recent presidents have appointed more minorities and women, the composition of the bench changes slowly because of life tenure for the judges.

Most judges have been wealthy. A third of Bush's appointees to the lower courts were millionaires. Five or six of the justices on the Supreme Court are millionaires.[48]

Despite some efforts to provide diversity, no effort has been made to represent various groups according to their proportion of the population. Throughout history, judges have come from a narrow, elite slice of society. Most have been born into families of Western European stock (especially English, Welsh, Scotch, and Irish), profess the Protestant religion (especially Episcopalian, Presbyterian, Congregational, and Unitarian), and are upper middle or upper class. Moreover, they have been born into families with traditions of political or even judicial service, families with prestige and connections as well as expectations for achievement.[49]

With the power to nominate judges, presidents have a tremendous opportunity to shape the courts and their decisions (see Table 1). By the time Carter finished his term, he had appointed about 40 percent of the lower court judges, although he had no opportunity to appoint Supreme Court justices. By the time Bush finished his term, he and Reagan had appointed about 65 percent of the lower court judges and five Supreme Court justices (in addition to elevating Rehnquist from associate to chief justice).

Tenure of Judges

Once appointed, judges can serve for "good behavior." This means for life, unless they commit "high crimes and misdemeanors." These are not defined in the Constitution but are considered serious crimes or, possibly, political abuses. Congress can impeach and remove judges as it can presidents, but it has impeached only thirteen and removed only six. The standard of guilt—"high crimes and misdemeanors"—is vague, the punishment drastic, and the process time consuming, so Congress has been reluctant to impeach judges.

As an alternative, in 1980 Congress established other procedures to discipline lower federal court judges. Councils made up of district and appellate court judges can ask judges to resign or can prevent them from hearing cases, but cannot actually remove them. The procedures have been used infrequently, although their existence has prompted some judges to resign before being disciplined.

Qualifications of Judges

Given the use of political criteria in selecting judges, are judges well qualified?

Political scientists who study the judiciary consider federal judges generally well qualified. This is especially true of Supreme Court justices, apparently because presidents think they will be held responsible for the justices they nominate and do not want to be embarrassed by them. Also, because presidents have so few vacancies to fill, they can confine themselves to persons of their party and political views, and even to persons of a particular region, religion, race, and sex, and still locate good candidates. This is less true of lower court judges. Presidents and senators jointly appoint them, so both can avoid full responsibility for them. These judges are also less visible, so a lack of merit is not as noticeable.

Presidents do appoint some losers. President Truman put a longtime supporter on a court of appeals who was "drunk half the time" and "no damn good." When asked why he appointed the man, Truman candidly replied, "I . . . felt I owed him a favor; that's why, and I thought as a judge he couldn't do too much harm, and he didn't . . . he wasn't the worst court appointment I ever made. By no means the worst."[50]

Sometimes presidents appoint qualified persons who later become incompetent. After serving for many years they incur the illnesses and infirmities of old age, and perhaps one-tenth become unable to perform their job well.[51] Yet they hang on because they are allowed to serve for "good behavior." The situation has prompted proposals for a constitutional amendment setting a mandatory retirement age of seventy. This change would have a substantial impact because fully one-third of all Supreme Court justices, for example, have served past seventy-five. But constitutional amendments are difficult to pass, and mandatory retirement ages are out of favor now. Further, some of the best judges have done some of their finest work after seventy.

Independence of Judges

Given the use of political criteria in selecting judges, can judges be independent on the bench? Can they decide cases as they think the law requires? Or do they feel pressure to decide cases as presidents or senators want them to?

Because judges are not dependent on presidents for renomination or senators for reconfirmation, they can be independent to a great extent. In the Watergate tapes case, three Nixon appointees joined the decision against President Nixon. In a case involving a law authorizing a special prosecutor to investigate and prosecute misconduct by governmental officials, Chief Justice Rehnquist wrote the majority opinion and another Reagan appointee joined the decision upholding the law against a challenge by President Reagan (whose aides had been prosecuted under the law).[52]

After surveying Warren and Burger Court decisions involving desegregation, obscenity, abortion, and criminal defendants' rights, one scholar observed, "Few American politicians even today would care to run on a platform of desegregation, pornography, abortion, and the 'coddling' of criminals."[53]

Presidents have scoffed at the notion that their appointees become their pawns. A study concluded that one-fourth of the justices deviated from their president's expectations.[54] Theodore Roosevelt placed Oliver Wendell Holmes on the Court because he thought Holmes shared his views on trusts. But in an early antitrust case, Holmes voted against Roosevelt's position, which prompted Roosevelt to declare, "I could carve out of a banana a judge with more backbone than that!"[55] Holmes had plenty of backbone; he just did not agree with Roosevelt's position in this case. Likewise, President Eisenhower placed Earl Warren on the Court, in part because he thought Warren was a moderate. But Warren turned out to be a liberal. Later Eisenhower said his appointment of Warren was "the biggest damn fool thing I ever did."[56] President Truman concluded that "packing the Supreme Court simply can't be done . . . I've tried it and it won't work. . . . Whenever you put a man on the Supreme Court he ceases to be your friend."[57]

Truman exaggerated, although some presidents have had trouble "packing" the courts. They have not been able to foresee the issues their appointees would have to rule on or predict the ways their appointees would change on the bench. Nevertheless, presidents who have made a serious effort to find candidates with similar views usually have not been disappointed.

Access to the Courts

In this litigation-prone society, many individuals and groups want courts to resolve their disputes. Whether these individuals and groups get their "day in court" depends on their case, their wealth, and the level of court involved.

Both sides in Paula Jones's suit against President Clinton used the media to influence public opinion. They expected the jurors to reflect the public's views. Jones's team, financed by conservative interest groups, had her made over (from left to right) to appear more appealing.
Left: Michael Tighe/Outline. Right: AP/Wide World Photos

Courts hear two kinds of cases. **Criminal cases** are those in which governments prosecute persons for violating laws. **Civil cases** are those in which persons sue others for denying their rights and causing them harm. Criminal defendants, of course, must appear in court. Potential civil litigants, however, often cannot get to court.

Wealth Discrimination in Access

Although the courts are supposed to be open to all, most individuals do not have enough money to hire an attorney and pay the costs necessary to pursue a case. Only corporations, wealthy individuals, or seriously injured victims suing corporations or wealthy individuals do. (Seriously injured victims with a strong case can obtain an attorney by agreeing to pay him or her a sizable portion of what they win in their suit.) In addition, a small number of poor individuals supported by legal aid programs can pursue a case.

The primary expense is paying an attorney. In 1996 new lawyers in law firms charged an average of $95 per hour, while established partners charged an average of $183 per hour.[58] Other expenses include various fees for filing the case, summoning jurors, paying witnesses, and also lost income from the individual's job due to numerous meetings with the attorney and hearings in court.

Even if individuals have enough money to initiate a suit, the disparity continues in court. Those with more money can develop a full case, whereas others must proceed with a skeletal case that is far less likely to persuade judges or jurors. Our legal system, according to one judge, "is divided into two separate and unequal systems of justice: one for the rich, in which the courts take limitless time to examine, ponder, consider, and deliberate over hundreds of thousands of bits of evidence and days of testimony, and hear elaborate, endless appeals and write countless learned opinions" and one for the nonrich, in which the courts provide "turnstile justice."[59] (During the week that one judge spent conducting the preliminary hearing to determine whether there was sufficient evidence to require O. J. Simpson to stand trial for murdering his ex-wife and her friend, other judges in Los Angeles disposed of 474 preliminary hearings for less wealthy defendants.) Consequently, many individuals are discouraged from pursuing a case in the first place.

Interest Group Help in Access

Interest groups, with more resources than most individuals, help some individuals gain access. The groups sponsor and finance these individuals' cases. Of course, the groups do not act purely out of altruism. They choose selected cases they hope will advance their goals. An attorney for the ACLU, which takes cases as a way to prod judges to protect constitutional rights, admitted that the criminal defendants the ACLU represents "sometimes are pretty scurvy little creatures, but what they are doesn't matter a whole hell of a lot. It's the principle that we're going to be able to use these people for that's important."

Some liberal groups, especially civil liberties organizations such as the ACLU, civil rights organizations such as the National Association for the Advancement of Colored People (NAACP), environmental groups such as the Sierra Club, and consumer and safety groups such as Ralph Nader's organizations, use litigation as a primary tactic. Other groups use it as an occasional tactic. In the 1980s and 1990s, some conservative groups began to use litigation as aggressively as these liberal groups. The Rutherford Institute, for example, arose to help persons who claimed their religious rights were infringed, representing children who were forbidden from reading the Bible on the school bus or praying in the school cafeteria. The institute then took on Paula Jones's suit after her previous attorneys quit when she rejected a settlement offered by President Clinton. The institute steered her to other lawyers (a Dallas firm that had fought to reinstate the Texas sodomy statute after it had been found unconstitutional) and funded her case.

Interest groups have become ubiquitous in the judicial process. About half of all Supreme Court cases involve a liberal or conservative interest group,[60] and many lower court cases do as well. Even so, interest groups can help only a handful of the individuals who lack the resources to finance their cases.

Restrictions on Access

Even if litigants have enough wealth or interest group help, they must overcome various restrictions on access imposed by the courts. According to the Constitution, litigants can get access only for a "case" or "controversy." Courts interpret this to mean a real dispute—one in which the litigants themselves have lost rights and suffered harm. This major restriction is called **standing to sue.**

This principle is illustrated by a series of cases challenging Connecticut's birth control law. Passed in 1879, the law prohibited giving advice about, or using, birth control devices. Actually, the law was not enforced much; women with a private doctor could get advice and a prescription. But the law effectively prevented opening birth control clinics that would help poor women without a private doctor or young women who did not want to go to their family doctor.

In the 1940s a doctor challenged the law, arguing that it prevented him from advising patients whose health might be endangered by childbearing. The courts said he did not have standing because he could not point to any injury he had suffered.[61] In the 1960s a doctor and two patients, who had experienced dangerous pregnancies in the past, challenged the law, claiming that it forced them to choose between stopping sexual activity or risking dangerous pregnancies. Again the courts said they did not have standing because they could not point to any injury they had suffered, or would suffer, because the law was rarely enforced.[62] Finally, the head of Connecticut's Planned Parenthood League and the head of Yale's obstetrics and gynecology department opened a birth control clinic. Within days they were arrested. Although they could not get access in a civil suit, they could in the criminal case. In the process of defending themselves, they claimed the law was unconstitutional, and the Supreme Court agreed.[63]

Although this doctrine is technical, its implications are highly political. Without access, of course, individuals and groups have no chance to get courts to rule in their favor. And whether they get access depends, to a considerable extent, on the ideology of the judge presiding. According to one study, Reagan's appointees to the district courts denied access to underdogs (individuals, groups representing individuals, or unions) in 78 percent of the cases in which they sued but denied access to upperdogs (governments or corporations) in only 41 percent of the cases in which they sued. These rulings contrast with those of Carter's and Nixon's appointees, who were both less strict in denying access and more even-handed in treating underdogs and upperdogs.[64]

Proceeding through the Courts

Cases normally start in a district court. Individuals who lose have a right to have their case decided by one higher court to determine if there was a miscarriage of justice. They normally appeal to a court of appeals. Individuals who lose at this level have no further right to have their case decided by another court, but they can appeal to the Supreme Court. However, the Court can exercise almost unlimited discretion in choosing cases to review. No matter how important or urgent an issue seems, the Court does not have to hear it.

Litigants who appeal to the Supreme Court normally file a petition for a **writ of certiorari** (Latin for "made more certain"). The Court grants the writ—that is, the Court agrees to hear the case—if four of the nine justices vote to do so. The rationale for this "rule of four" is that a substantial number, but not necessarily a majority, of the justices should think the case is important enough to review. Generally, the Court agrees to review a case when the justices think an issue has not been resolved satisfactorily or consistently by the lower courts.

From more than seven thousand petitions each year, the Court selects less than one hundred to hear, thus exercising considerable discretion (see Figure 3). The oft-spoken threat "We're going to appeal all the way to the Supreme Court" is usually just bluster. Likewise, the notion that the Court is "the court of last resort" is misleading. Most cases never get beyond the district courts or courts of appeals.

That the Supreme Court grants so few writs means the Court has tremendous power to control its docket and therefore to determine which policies to review. It also means the lower courts have considerable power because they serve as the court of last resort for most cases.

Deciding Cases

In deciding cases judges need to interpret statutes and the Constitution and determine whether to follow precedents. In the process they make law.

Interpreting Statutes

In deciding cases judges start with statutes—laws passed by legislatures. If the statutes are ambiguous, judges need to interpret them in order to apply them to their cases.

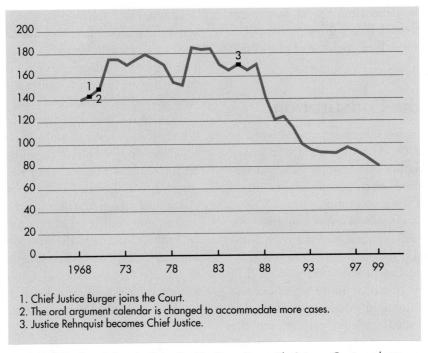

1. Chief Justice Burger joins the Court.
2. The oral argument calendar is changed to accommodate more cases.
3. Justice Rehnquist becomes Chief Justice.

FIGURE 3 ■ *Rehnquist Court Decides Fewer Cases* *The Supreme Court now hears fewer than half as many cases per term as it heard in the 1970s and 1980s. Have Chief Justice Rehnquist and other conservative justices intentionally shrunk the Court's docket in their effort to have the courts play a reduced role in government?*

SOURCE: Adapted from David M. O'Brien, *Storm Center*, 5th ed. (New York: Norton, 2000).

Sometimes statutes are ambiguous because of their nature. To be broad enough to cover many situations, their words and phrases must be so general that they might not be clear. Other times statutes are ambiguous because of the nature of the legislative process. To satisfy public demand for action on problems, legislators are urged to move quickly, even if they are not prepared. They are encouraged to act symbolically, even if they cannot alleviate the problems this way. They are pressed to compromise, even if they must include fuzzy provisions in statutes to avoid upsetting fragile agreements negotiated among themselves. Thus, a member of Congress, tongue in cheek, told one justice that they purposely use "unintelligible language" in statutes so the courts will "tell us what we mean."[65]

When statutes are ambiguous, judges try to ascertain the legislators' intent in passing them. They scrutinize the legislators' remarks and debates. But they often find that different members said different things, even contradictory things, and most members said nothing about the provisions in question. This gives judges considerable leeway in construing statutes.

Congress passed a statute that imposes a minimum sentence of five years in prison for anyone convicted of a violent crime or a drug trafficking crime in which he or she "uses" a gun. The question arose: What does "uses" mean? The Supreme Court had to interpret this provision in 1995. After police arrested a man for possession of cocaine, they found a gun in a bag in the trunk of his car. Although the man had not directly employed the gun when he had obtained the cocaine, lower courts concluded that he had used it by having it accessible to himself and near the cocaine, and they imposed the sentence under the statute. The Supreme Court unanimously reversed.[66] Justice O'Connor illustrated the problem by posing this statement: "I use a gun to protect my house, but I've never had to use it." That is, people mean different things by the word *use*. The lower courts interpreted the word essentially as a synonym for *possess*. But Justice O'Connor observed that the same statute has another provision that refers to a person who "carries" a gun and another statute has a provision that refers to a person who "possesses" a gun. Therefore, Congress must have intended *use* to mean something different than *carry* or *possess*. So the Supreme Court ruled that "use" means active use, whether brandishing, striking, or firing the gun or even making reference to having a gun.

In the process of interpreting statutes, judges can make law. In a recent term the Supreme Court essentially rewrote the law delineating sexual harassment at work and the law providing civil immunity to police officers who engage in reckless high-speed chases that injure others.[67]

Interpreting the Constitution

After interpreting statutes, judges determine whether they are constitutional. Or, if the cases involve actions of government officials rather than statutes, judges determine whether the actions are constitutional. For either, they need to interpret the Constitution.

Compared to constitutions of other countries, our Constitution is short and therefore necessarily ambiguous. It speaks in broad principles rather than in narrow details. The Fifth Amendment states that persons shall not be "deprived of life, liberty, or property without due process of law." The Fourteenth Amendment states that persons shall not be denied "the equal protection of the laws." What is "due process of law"? "Equal protection of the laws"? Generally, the former means that people should be treated fairly and the latter means that they should be treated equally. But what is fairly? Equally? These are broad principles that need to be interpreted in specific cases.

Sometimes the Constitution uses relative terms. The Fourth Amendment provides that persons shall be "secure . . . against unreasonable searches and seizures." What are "unreasonable searches and seizures"? Other times the Constitution uses absolute terms. These appear more clear-cut but are deceptive. The First Amendment provides that there shall be "no law . . . abridging the freedom of speech." Does "no law" mean literally no law? Then what about the proverbial example of the person who falsely shouts "Fire!" in a crowded theater? Whether relative or absolute, the language needs to be interpreted in specific cases.

Occasionally, politicians assert that judges ought to be "strict constructionists"; that is, they ought to interpret the Constitution "strictly." This is nonsense. Judges cannot possibly interpret ambiguous language strictly.

When the language does not give sufficient guidance, some judges believe they should follow the intentions of the framers.[68] Yet these intentions are difficult to ascertain. James Madison's notes of the Constitutional Convention or the *Federalist Papers* are considered the most authoritative sources, but relying upon them is fraught with problems. Because Madison edited his notes many years after the convention, his experiences in government or lapses of memory might have colored his version of the intentions of the delegates. Because

Madison, Hamilton, and Jay published the *Federalist Papers* to persuade New York to ratify the Constitution, their motive might have affected their account of the intentions of the delegates. Furthermore, there were fifty-five delegates to the Constitutional Convention and many more to the state ratifying conventions, and the sources do not indicate what most thought about any of the provisions. Undoubtedly, all did not think the same.

Other judges believe they need not follow the intentions of the framers. They maintain that the Constitution was designed to be flexible and adaptable to changes in society.[69] These judges try to distill the general meaning of the provisions of the Constitution and apply this meaning to the contemporary situations facing them. The Fourteenth Amendment's equal protection clause does not refer to schools, and its framers did not intend it to relate to schools. However, they did intend it to grant blacks greater equality than before, and

Chief Justice William Rehnquist dons his robe in the Supreme Court's robing room.
Ken Regan/Camera 5

therefore the Court applied this meaning to segregated schools. Then the Court applied it to other segregated facilities, then to other racial minorities, and then to women. In short, the Court extracted the general meaning of equality and extended it to prohibit discrimination in many situations. In this way the Court put into practice Chief Justice John Marshall's statement that the Constitution is "intended to endure for ages to come."[70]

When judges interpret the Constitution, they exercise discretion. As former Chief Justice Hughes candidly acknowledged, "We are under a constitution, but the Constitution is what the Supreme Court says it is."[71]

Restraint and Activism

All judges exercise discretion, but not all engage in policymaking to the same extent. Some, classified as restrained, are less willing to declare statutes or actions of government officials unconstitutional, whereas others, classified as activist, are more willing to do so.

Restrained judges argue that the judiciary is the least democratic branch because judges are appointed for life rather than elected and reelected. Consequently, they should be reluctant to overrule the other branches. They should be wary of "government by judiciary." "Courts are not the only agency of government that must be presumed to have the capacity to govern," Justice Harlan Stone said. "For the removal of unwise laws from the statute books appeal lies not to the courts, but to the ballot and the processes of democratic government."[72] Restrained judges also contend that the judiciary is the branch least capable of making policy because judges are generalists. They lack the expertise and resources that many bureaucrats and legislators use to help make policy. Restrained judges further maintain that the power to declare laws unconstitutional is more effective if it is used sparingly. Justice Louis Brandeis concluded that "the most important thing we do is not doing."[73] That is, the most important thing judges do is declare laws constitutional and thereby build up political capital for the occasional times that they declare laws unconstitutional.

Activist judges do not share these qualms. Instead, they seem more outraged at injustice. Court of appeals judge David Bazelon, of the District of Columbia, said the test should be "Does it make you sick?" If so, the law or action should be struck down.[74] Activist judges also seem more concerned about obtaining results than following technical procedures.

Chief Justice Warren asked lawyers who emphasized technical procedures during oral arguments, "Yes, yes, yes, but is it right? Is it good?"[75] In addition, activist judges seem more pragmatic. District court judge Frank Johnson, who issued sweeping orders for Alabama's prisons and mental hospitals, replied to critics, "I didn't ask for any of these cases. In an ideal society, all of these . . . decisions should be made by those to whom we have entrusted these responsibilities. But when governmental institutions fail to make these . . . decisions in a manner which comports with the Constitution, the federal courts have a duty to remedy the violation."[76]

The distinction between restrained and activist judges does not necessarily parallel that between conservative and liberal judges. In the 1950s and 1960s, it did; the Supreme Court was both activist and liberal. But in the early 1930s, the Court was activist and conservative; it struck down regulations on business. In the late 1930s, it was restrained and liberal; it upheld similar regulations on business.

But we should not make too much of the distinction between restraint and activism. It is usually more important to know whether a judge is conservative or liberal. Although a restrained conservative might vote differently than an activist conservative in some cases, the two conservatives are likely to vote the same in most cases. A study of the justices appointed to the Supreme Court from 1953 through 1987 found that their conservative or liberal attitudes accounted for most of their individual votes, regardless of their restraint or activism (and regardless of the existence of relevant precedents or unique facts in the cases).[77] Some researchers conclude that "judicial restraint" is little more than "a cloak for the justices' policy preferences."[78] That is, it enables them to proclaim their "restraint" while actually voting on the basis of their ideology—without ever admitting this to the public. For example, the conservative justices on the Rehnquist Court, many of whom profess their "restraint" and all of whom were appointed by presidents who touted their "restraint," have been conservative activists at times. They have struck down laws implementing affirmative action programs, laws establishing legislative districts to benefit racial minorities, and laws regulating gun registration and possession. Thus, although restraint and activism are useful concepts—they help us understand the roles judges can play—we should be skeptical when we hear these terms used, especially by judges or politicians trying to pacify or inflame the public.

Following Precedents

In interpreting statutes and the Constitution, judges are expected to follow precedents established by their court or higher courts in previous cases. This is the rule of **stare decisis** (Latin for "stand by what has been decided").

When in 1962 the Supreme Court held unconstitutional a New York law that required public school students to recite a nondenominational prayer every day, the ruling became a precedent.[79] Then in 1963 the Court held unconstitutional a Baltimore school board policy that required students to recite Bible verses.[80] The Court followed the precedent it had set the year before. Then in 1980 the Court held unconstitutional a Tennessee law that forced public schools to post the Ten Commandments in all classrooms.[81] Although this law differed from the previous ones in that it did not require recitation, the majority concluded that it reflected the same goal—to use the public schools to promote the Christian religion—so it violated the same principle, separation of church and state. Then in 1992 the Court ruled that clergy cannot offer prayers at graduation ceremonies for public schools.[82] Although this situation, too, differed from the previous ones in that it did not occur every day at school, the majority reasoned that it, too, reflected the same goal and violated the same principle. Finally, in 2000 the Court ruled that schools cannot use, or allow clergy or students to use, the public address system to offer prayers before high school football games.[82a] Thus, for almost four decades the Court followed the precedent it originally set when it initially addressed this issue.

The primary advantage of stare decisis is that it provides stability in the law. If different judges were to decide similar cases in different ways, the law would be unpredictable, even chaotic. "Stare decisis," Justice Brandeis said, "is usually the wise policy; because in most matters it is more important that the applicable rule of law be settled than that it be settled right."[83] Another advantage of this practice is that it promotes equality in the law, ensuring that judges treat comparable cases similarly. Otherwise, judges might appear to be arbitrary and discriminatory.

The primary disadvantage of stare decisis is that it produces excessive stability—inflexibility—in the law when it is adhered to strictly. Times change and demand new law, but precedents of past generations bind present and future generations. Justice Holmes declared, "It is revolting to have no better reason for a rule of law than that it was laid down in the time of Henry IV. It is still more revolting if the grounds upon which it was laid down have vanished long since, and the rule simply persists from blind imitation of the past."[84]

Even when judges agree to follow precedents, sometimes they have discretion to decide which ones to follow. There might not be any that are controlling but several that are relevant, and these might point in contrary directions. This situation often arises when courts face technological changes in society. In 1996 the justices weighed government regulation of indecent programming on cable television. They had precedents that governed broadcast television, telephones, and bookstores. But, as Justice Breyer observed, none of these really paralleled cable television, which looks like broadcast television but uses telephone lines rather than airwaves to transmit its signals. Thus, he was uncertain which precedents to use. Apparently, the others were uncertain also, as the nine justices split three ways and wrote six opinions while upholding one section and striking down two other sections of the law.[85]

Making Law

Many judges deny that they make law. They say that it is already there, that they merely "find" it or, occasionally, "interpret" it with their education and experience. They imply that they use a mechanical process. Justice Roberts wrote for the majority that struck down a New Deal act in 1936:

> It is sometimes said that the Court assumes a power to overrule . . . the people's representatives. This is a misconception. The Constitution is the supreme law of the land. . . . All legislation must conform to the principles it lays down. When an act of Congress is appropriately challenged in the courts as not conforming to the constitutional mandate, the judicial branch of government has only one duty—to lay . . . the Constitution . . . beside the statute . . . and to decide whether the latter squares with the former.[86]

In other words, the Constitution itself dictates the decision.

However, by now it should be apparent that judges do not use a mechanical process—that they do exercise discretion. They *do* make law—when they interpret statutes, when they interpret the Constitution, and when they determine which precedents to follow or disregard.

In doing so, they reflect their own political preferences. As Justice Benjamin Cardozo said, "We may try to see things as objectively as we please. Nonetheless, we can never see them with any eyes except our own."[87] That is, judges too are human beings with their own perceptions and attitudes and even prejudices. They do not, and cannot, shed these the moment they put on their robes.

But to say that judges make law is not to say that they make law as legislators do. Judges make law less directly. They make it in the process of resolving disputes brought to them. They usually make it by telling governments what they cannot do, rather than what they must do and how they must do it. And judges make law less freely. They start not with clean slates but with established principles embodied in statutes, the Constitution, and precedents. They are expected to follow these principles. If they deviate from them, they are expected to explain their reasons.

Deciding Cases at the Supreme Court

The Supreme Court's term runs from October through June. Early in the term the justices decide which cases to hear, and by the end of the term they decide how to resolve these cases.

After the Supreme Court agrees to hear a case, litigants submit written arguments. These "briefs" identify the issues and marshal the evidence—statutes, constitutional provisions, precedents—for their side. (The word *briefs* is a misnomer, as some are hundreds of pages long.) Often interest groups and governments submit briefs to support one side. These "friend-of-the-court" briefs present additional evidence or perspectives not included in the litigants' briefs. Major cases can prompt many briefs. An abortion case in 1989 prompted a record seventy-eight briefs.

Several weeks after receiving the briefs, the Court holds oral arguments. For these the justices gather in the robing room behind the courtroom. They put on their black robes and, as the curtains part, file into the courtroom and take their places at the raised half-hexagon bench. The chief justice sits in the center, and the associate justices extend out in order of seniority. The crier gavels the courtroom to attention and announces:

> *The Honorable, the Chief Justice and Associate Justices of the Supreme Court of the United States! Oyez, oyez, oyez! [Give ear, give ear, give ear!] All persons having business before the Honorable, the Supreme Court of the United States are admonished to draw near and give attention, for the Court is now sitting. God save the United States and this Honorable Court.*

The chief justice calls the case. The lawyers present their arguments, although the justices interrupt with questions whenever they want. When Thurgood Marshall, as counsel for the NAACP before becoming a justice, argued one school desegregation case, he was interrupted 127 times. The justices ask about the facts of the case. "What happened when the defendant . . . ?" They ask about relevant precedents that appear to support or rebut the lawyers' arguments. "Can you distinguish this case from . . . ?" They ask about hypothetical scenarios. "What if the police officer . . . ?" With these questions the justices want to know what is at stake, how a ruling would relate to existing doctrine, and how a ruling might govern future situations. They are experienced at pinning lawyers down. Chief Justice Rehnquist, who is affable toward his colleagues, is tough on the lawyers appearing before him. When asked if the lawyers were nervous, he replied, "I assume they're all nervous—they should be."[88] Occasionally, a lawyer becomes unnerved and faints on the spot.

The chief justice allots half an hour per side. When time expires, a red light flashes on the lectern, and the chief justice halts any lawyer who continues. Rehnquist, who values efficiency and punctuality, cuts lawyers off in midsentence when their time expires.

The oral arguments identify and clarify the major points of the case for any justices who did not read the briefs, and they assess the potential impact of possible rulings. The oral arguments also serve as a symbol: They give litigants a chance to be heard in open court, which encourages litigants to feel that the eventual ruling is legitimate. However, the oral arguments rarely sway the

The job of a justice is unlike that of other political officials. Even after three decades of experience, Justice William Brennan often ate at his desk so he could finish his work.

Lynn Johnson/Aurora

justices, except occasionally when the lawyer for one side is especially ineffective.

The Court holds Friday conferences to make a tentative decision and assign the opinion. The decision affirms or reverses the lower court decision; it indicates who wins and who loses. The opinion explains why. It expresses principles of law and establishes a precedent for the future. It tells judges on lower courts how to resolve similar cases.

A portrait of Chief Justice Marshall presides over the conference. To ensure secrecy, no one is present but the justices. They begin with handshakes. (During his tenure Chief Justice Marshall suggested that they begin with a drink whenever the weather was bad. But even when it was sunny, Marshall sometimes announced, "Our jurisdiction extends over so large a territory that the doctrine of chances makes it certain that it must be raining somewhere."[89] Perhaps this accounts for his extraordinary success in persuading his colleagues to adopt his views.) Then the justices get down to business. The chief justice initiates the discussion of the case. He asserts what he thinks the issues are and how they ought to be decided, and he casts a vote. The associate justices follow in order of seniority. Although the conference traditionally featured give and take among the justices, under Rehnquist discussion has been perfunctory as the conference has become a series of quick votes.[90]

The Court reaches a tentative decision based on these votes. If the chief justice is in the majority, he assigns himself or another justice to write the opinion of the Court. If not, the most senior associate justice in the majority assigns one to write it. This custom reveals the chief justice's power. Although his vote counts the same as each associate justice's vote, his authority to assign the opinion can determine what the opinion says. If he assigns it to some colleagues, he knows it will lay down broad principles and use strong language; if to others, he knows it will hew more closely to the facts of the case and use more guarded language.

Before Marshall became chief justice, each justice wrote his own opinion. But Marshall realized that one opinion from the Court would hold more weight. He often convinced the other justices to forsake their opinion for his. As a result, he authored almost half of the Court's 1,100-some opinions in his thirty-four years. Recent chief justices have assigned most opinions—from 82 to 86 percent—but have authored just slightly more than their share—from 12 to 14 percent.[91] Some Court watchers believe Rehnquist has downplayed his conservative views after becoming chief justice, perhaps

to join a majority of his colleagues and thereby retain control of the opinion.[92]

After the conference, the Court produces the opinion. This is the most time-consuming stage in the process. After Justice Louis Brandeis died, researchers found in his files the thirty-seventh draft of an opinion he had written but still had not been satisfied with.

Because the justices are free to change their vote anytime until the decision is announced, there is much maneuvering and politicking. The justice assigned the opinion tries to write it to command support of the justices in the original majority and possibly even some in the original minority. The writer circulates the draft among the others, who suggest revisions. The writer circulates more drafts. These go back and forth, as the justices attempt to persuade or cajole, nudge or push their colleagues toward their position.

These inner workings underscore the politicking among the justices. Justice William Brennan, a liberal activist on the Warren and Burger Courts, was a gregarious and charming Irish American who was well liked by his colleagues. After drafting an opinion, he sent his clerks to other justices' clerks to learn whether the other justices had any objections. Then he tried to redraft it to satisfy them. If they still had qualms, he went to their offices and tried to persuade them. If necessary, he compromised. "He [didn't] want to be 100% principled and lose by one vote," a law professor observed.[93] Brennan was so adept at persuasion that some scholars consider him "the best coalition builder ever to sit on the Supreme Court."[94] In fact, some say the Warren and Burger Courts should have been called the Brennan Court.

Justice Antonin Scalia, a conservative activist on the Rehnquist Court, is a brilliant and gregarious Italian American who, when appointed by President Reagan, was expected to dominate his colleagues and become the leader of the Court. Yet he has not fulfilled this expectation. He has been brash and imprudent, appearing to take more pleasure in insulting his colleagues than in persuading them.[95] In a case in which Justice O'Connor, also conservative but more cautious, did not want to go as far in limiting abortion rights as he did, Scalia wrote that her arguments "cannot be taken seriously."[96] In another case in which Chief Justice Rehnquist, who usually votes with Scalia, voted opposite him, Scalia wrote that his arguments were "implausible" and suggested that any lawyer who advised his client as Rehnquist urged should be "disbarred."[97] As a result, Scalia has not been as effective in forging a consensus among conservatives as Brennan was among liberals.

My dissenting opinion will be brief. "You're all full of crap."
Reproduced by special permission of *Playboy* magazine. Copyright © 1972 by *Playboy*.

As a result of the maneuvering and politicking, opinions often are compromises among justices in the majority. As Justice Harlan Stone explained to a law professor who criticized one of his opinions:

> *I should have preferred to have written your opinion than the one which will actually appear in the books. Had I done so, I should have been in a minority of two or three, instead of a majority of six. Someone else would have written the opinion [of the Court]. . . . I proceed upon the theory . . . that the large objectives should be kept constantly in mind and reached by whatever road is open, provided only that untenable distinctions are not taken, and that I am not in the process, committed incidentally to the doctrine of which I disapprove or which would hinder the Court's coming out ultimately in the right place.*[98]

If the opinion does not command the support of some of the justices in the original majority, they write a concurring opinion. This indicates that they agree with the decision but not the reasons for it. Meanwhile, the justices in the minority write a dissenting opinion. This indicates that they do not agree even with the decision. Both concurring and dissenting opinions weaken the force of the majority opinion. They question the validity of it, and they suggest that at a different time with different justices there might be a different ruling. Chief Justice Hughes used to say that a dissenting opinion is "an appeal to the brooding spirit of the law, to the intelligence of a future day."

Finally, the Court's print shop in its basement prints the opinions. Then the Court announces its decisions and distributes the opinions in public session. (The box "The Justices Do Their Own Work" describes more of the Court's job.)

The Power of the Courts

Alexis de Tocqueville observed that unlike in other countries, "Scarcely any political question arises in the United States that is not resolved, sooner or later, into a judicial question."[99] Because Americans are more inclined than other people to bring suits, courts have many opportunities to try to wield power.

This inclination does not in itself guarantee that the courts can wield power, but they have been able to because the public venerates the Constitution and the courts interpret it, and because the courts enjoy relative, though not absolute, independence from the political pressures on the other branches.

The use of judicial review and the use of political checks against the courts reveal the extent of the power of the courts.

Use of Judicial Review

Judicial review—the authority to declare laws or actions of government officials unconstitutional—is the tool that courts use to wield power. When courts declare a law or action unconstitutional, they not only void that particular law or action, but they also might put the issue on the public agenda, and they might speed up or slow down the pace of change in government policies.

When the Supreme Court declared a Texas abortion law unconstitutional in *Roe v. Wade* in 1973, the Court put abortion on the public agenda.[100] The issue had not been a national controversy before the decision.

The Court used judicial review as a catalyst to speed up change in the desegregation cases in the 1950s. At the time, President Eisenhower was not inclined to act, and although many members of Congress were, they were unable to act because the houses were dominated by southerners who, as committee chairs, blocked civil rights legislation. The Court broke the logjam.

The Court used judicial review as a brake to slow down change in the business regulation cases in the first third of the twentieth century. The Court delayed some policies for several decades.

The process of deciding cases shows that the Supreme Court operates very differently than the presidency or Congress. The justices take responsibility for their decisions. As Justice Brandeis observed decades ago, "the reason the public thinks so much of the justices of the Supreme Court is that they are almost the only people in Washington who do their own work."

Presidents have numerous aides and a large White House staff. Although presidents are responsible for their policies, aides do much of their work for them, deciding what subjects they will address at which times, what answers they will give to reporters' questions, what speeches they will give to which audiences, and, of course, what language they will use in these speeches. Presidents even turn to their pollsters to determine what positions they should take in light of the opinions the public holds. Members of Congress, who also are pulled in many directions at once, rely upon their aides and committee staffers when deciding how to interact with constituents, lobbyists, and colleagues throughout the day, as well as how to position them-

selves on issues and how to vote on legislation.

Justices do have their clerks, who are recent graduates of law schools, usually the most elite students from the most prestigious institutions. Each year each justice can hire four clerks to help read petitions asking the Court to hear new cases, research statutes and precedents for pending cases, and draft opinions in these cases. Periodically, a fuss is made about the clerks' role and influence. Sometimes critics of decisions suspect that the clerks manipulated the justices.[1] But most observers discount such assertions. A law professor who was a clerk to Justice Blackmun said, "They are like the students of Michelangelo. They may put the ink on paper, but it is according to the justices' design."[2] A former clerk who was also a congressional committee staffer and a vice presidential aide thinks that clerks, who are young and inexperienced, have less impact than staffers and aides in the other two branches.[3]

Much of the business of the Supreme Court is conducted in public, unlike that of Congress, whose chambers are nearly deserted even when its houses are in

session. The justices are on public display in open court, listening to the arguments and asking questions of the attorneys. They are expected to be knowledgeable about the case and about past rulings and current doctrine in the area. No aides whisper in their ear to cue them and feed them questions.

When the justices decide their cases, they not only cast a clear vote, but they state their reasons. They consider, very carefully, whether to join the majority opinion or a concurring or dissenting opinion. Even then, they make fine distinctions. In one case, Justice O'Connor joined a concurring opinion except for one sentence. In another case, Justice Thomas joined the majority opinion except for one footnote.[4] Each justice, then, is open to scrutiny and criticism of his or her reasoning. Although justices exercise discretion when they interpret statutes, constitutional provisions, and precedents, the expectation that they justify their conclusions makes them accountable. They realize that lower court judges, lawyers, law professors, law students, and sometimes the general public will evaluate their work.[5]

Judicial review, an American contribution to government, was for years unique to this country. It is now used in numerous other countries but not as extensively or as effectively as in the United States.

The Supreme Court alone has struck down more than one hundred provisions of federal laws and more than one thousand provisions of state and local laws (see Figure 4). The Court has struck down more of the latter for several reasons: State and local legislatures enact more laws; these legislatures reflect parochial, rather than national, interests, so they enact more laws that the national Court considers in conflict with the national Constitution; and these legislatures are less risky to confront than Congress.

The number of laws struck down, however, is not the true measure of the importance of judicial review. In-

stead, the ever present threat of review has undoubtedly prevented legislatures from enacting many laws they feared would be struck down.

By using judicial review to play a strong role in government, the Court has contradicted the Founders' expectation that the judiciary would be the weakest branch. Although it has been the weakest at times, it has been the strongest at other times. Arguably, these include some years during the early nineteenth century, when the Court established national dominance; the late nineteenth century and early twentieth century, when the Court thwarted efforts to regulate business; and the 1950s and early 1960s, when the Court extended civil liberties and rights.

Nevertheless, the extent to which the Court has played a strong role in government should not be exag-

Two clerks meet with Justice Stevens.
© 1986 Ken Heinen

program but later vote against appropriating money for the program.

It is easier for the justices to do their own work because they are not pulled in as many directions as presidents and members of Congress. It is easier for the justices to take responsibility for their own work because they have judicial independence. They do not need to be as responsive to the public as presidents and members of Congress do. Although the justices do not always make wise decisions, at least the process of making judicial decisions allows the legal profession and sometimes the public to hold them accountable.

Then they make public all the materials from the case—the record from the lower court, briefs from the litigants, and transcripts of the oral arguments.

Contrast this accountability with the difficulty of determining responsibility in Congress. Even when votes are recorded in Congress, it is often unclear how particular members acted on the issues.

Many bills are so complex and so loaded with diverse provisions that it is hard to know what a vote "for" or "against" them means. When amendments to bills are proposed, it is hard to know whether members' votes reflect their views on the amendment or represent their efforts to bolster or torpedo the overall bill. Sometimes members vote to authorize a

1. The machinations of conservative clerks in the 1980s are revealed by Edward Lazarus, *Closed Chambers* (New York: Times Books, 1998), while the possible influence of liberal clerks in the 1970s is examined by Bob Woodward and Scott Armstrong, *The Brethren* (New York: Simon & Schuster, 1979).
2. Harold Koh, quoted in Tony Mauro, "Justices Give Pivotal Role to Novice Lawyers," *USA Today,* March 13–15, 1998, p. 2A.
3. Ibid.
4. Ronald Suresh Roberts, *Clarence Thomas and the Tough Love Crowd* (New York: New York University Press, 1995), 84.
5. Even when a justice sits out a case due to illness or possible conflict of interest, his or her absence is announced and then recorded with the justices' opinions.

gerated. The Court has not exercised judicial review over a wide range of issues; in each of the three eras of its history, it has exercised review over one dominant issue and paid relatively little attention to other issues. Moreover, the one dominant issue always has involved domestic policy. Traditionally the Court has been reluctant to intervene in foreign policy.[101] Even when the war in Vietnam was the most contentious issue in the country, with many people questioning its constitutionality and numerous men challenging the draft, the Court refused to review the issue.

When the Court has tackled an issue, it has been cautious. Of the provisions of congressional laws held unconstitutional, more than half were voided more than four years after they had been passed, and more than one-fourth were voided more than twelve years after they had been passed.[102] These laws were voided after many members of Congress who had initiated and voted for them had left Congress. The Court confronted Congress when it was safer to do so.

Use of Political Checks against the Courts

Although the courts enjoy relative independence from the political pressures on the other branches, they certainly do not enjoy absolute independence. Because they are part of the political process, they are subject to political checks, which limit the extent to which they can wield judicial review.

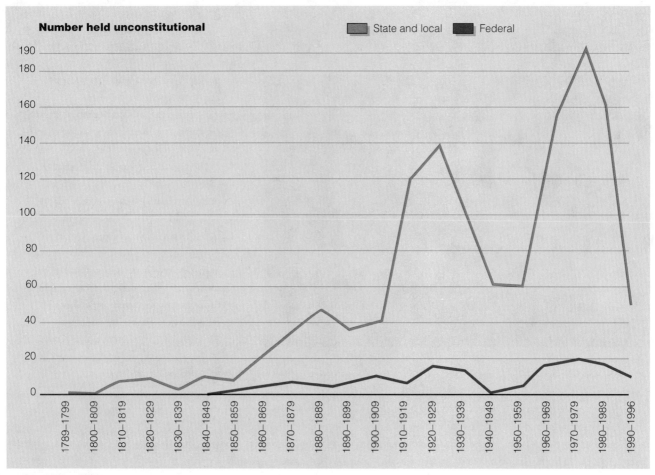

Number held unconstitutional

State and local   Federal

FIGURE 4 ■ *The Supreme Court Has Declared Unconstitutional More State and Local Laws Than Federal Laws*

SOURCES: Harold W. Stanley and Richard G. Niemi, *Vital Statistics on American Politics,* 4th ed. (Washington, D.C.: CQ Press, 1994), 308; Lawrence Baum, *The Supreme Court,* 6th ed. (Washington, D.C.: CQ Press, 1998), 201, 203.

Checks by the Executive

Presidents can impose the most effective check. If they dislike judges' rulings, they can appoint new judges when vacancies occur. A sizable proportion of these appointees remain on the bench even two decades after presidents leave the White House.[103] Even so, it can be difficult to get judges to reverse precedents or to make decisions beyond the existing political consensus, as Presidents Reagan and Bush discovered.

Presidents and state and local executives, such as governors and mayors and even school·officials and police officers, can refuse to enforce courts' rulings. School officials have disobeyed decisions requiring desegregation and invalidating class prayers. Police officers have ignored decisions invalidating some kinds of searches and interrogations.

Yet executives who refuse to enforce courts' rulings risk losing public support, unless the public also opposes the rulings. Even President Nixon complied when the Court ordered him to turn over the incriminating Watergate tapes.

Checks by the Legislature

Congress and the state legislatures can overturn courts' rulings by adopting constitutional amendments. They have done so four times (Eleventh, Fourteenth, Sixteenth, and Twenty-sixth Amendments).[104] They can also overturn courts' rulings by passing new statutes. When courts base decisions on their interpretations of statutes, or when they make decisions in the absence of statutes, legislatures can pass new statutes to negate the decisions. In 1986 the Supreme Court ruled that the Air Force did not have to allow an ordained rabbi to wear his yarmulke with his uniform.[105] The next year Congress passed a statute permitting military personnel to wear some religious apparel while in uniform. From

The Judiciary in Time

FIRST ERA: NATION VERSUS STATE

1789 Congress establishes federal trial courts (district courts).

1803 *Marbury v. Madison.* Chief Justice Marshall articulates judicial review.

1819 *McCulloch v. Maryland.* Marshall interprets necessary and proper clause to give Congress and national government more power.

1857 Dred Scott Case. Supreme Court, under Chief Justice Taney, strikes down law limiting slavery in the territories and inflames northerners opposed to slavery.

1865 Civil War resolves nation-state controversy in favor of nation.

SECOND ERA: GOVERNMENT VERSUS BUSINESS

1871 Congress grants federal courts full federal jurisdiction.

1873 Although Industrial Revolution leads to demands for government to regulate business, Supreme Court begins to strike down these laws. Court would continue to do so through 1936.

1891 Congress establishes federal appellate courts (courts of appeal) to complete the basic structure of the federal judiciary.

1935 Supreme Court finally gets its own building.

1935–36 Supreme Court invalidates twelve congressional laws encompassing much of President Franklin Roosevelt's New Deal program to cope with Depression.

1937 Roosevelt proposes court-packing plan.

1937 "Switch in time that saves nine." Supreme Court reverses course, upholds New Deal legislation.

Switch resolves government-business controversy in favor of government regulation.

THIRD ERA: GOVERNMENT VERSUS INDIVIDUALS

1953 Earl Warren becomes Chief Justice, beginning Warren Court period.

1962 Fifth liberal appointed to Supreme Court, providing solid liberal bloc for Warren Court, which overhauls doctrine to favor individual rights over government interests and minority rights over majority desires in many areas.

1967 First black justice, Thurgood Marshall, appointed to Supreme Court.

1968 Supreme Court appointments become contentious, with two nominees of President Johnson not confirmed. In coming years, two of President Nixon's appointments and two of President Reagan's also would not be confirmed.

1968 Warren Court becomes campaign issue, with Richard Nixon promising to change direction of the Court.

1969 Warren Burger becomes Chief Justice, beginning Burger Court period.

1981 First woman justice, Sandra Day O'Connor, appointed to Supreme Court.

1986 William Rehnquist becomes Chief Justice, beginning Rehnquist Court period.

1991 Tenth straight Republican appointed to Supreme Court. Rehnquist Court veers to the right. Individual rights and minority rights lose favor; third era apparently ends.

1967 through 1990, Congress passed statutes to negate 121 Supreme Court rulings.[106]

Legislatures can refuse to implement courts' rulings, especially when money is needed to implement them. The legislators simply do not appropriate the money.

Although these checks are the most common, Congress has invoked others, although only rarely: it can alter the structure of the lower federal courts; it can limit the appellate jurisdiction of the Supreme Court; and it can impeach and remove judges.

As a result of occasional checks or threatened checks, the courts have developed a strong sense of self-restraint to ensure self-preservation. This, more than the checks themselves, limits their use of judicial review.

Conclusion: Are the Courts Responsive?

Courts tend to reflect the views of the public. A study comparing 110 Supreme Court rulings from 1936 through 1986 with public opinion polls on the same issues found that the rulings mirrored the polls in 62 percent of the cases.[107] Thus, the justices either responded to the public or, having been appointed by officials elected by the public, simply reflected the public's views.

Research shows that citizens know little about the cases (and less about the judges; more adults can identify the character names of the Three Stooges than a single justice on the Supreme Court[108]), but they do remember controversial decisions, and they do recognize broad trends. A study of public opinion toward the Supreme Court from 1966 to 1984 found that the public became more negative when the Court upheld more criminal rights and struck down more congressional statutes.[109] This opinion pressured presidents and members of Congress to appoint justices with different views. Thus, these officials responded to the public, and ultimately they got the Court to respond to the public.

Although the courts are directly or indirectly responsive to the public, the Founders did not intend for them to be very responsive. The Founders gave judges life tenure so courts would be relatively independent of officials and the public.

Indeed, the courts are more independent of political pressures than the other branches are. This enables them, in the words of appellate court judge Learned Hand, to stand as a bulwark against the "pressure of public panic." It provides a "sober second thought."[110]

The courts can even protect the rights of various minorities—racial minorities, religious minorities, criminal defendants, and alleged subversives—against the demands and the wrath of the majority. Chapters 14 and 15 will show how courts extended civil liberties and rights to unpopular individuals and groups who lacked clout with the executive and legislative branches and support from the public. Yet protecting the rights of these individuals and groups historically has been the exception rather than the rule. It was typical of the Warren Court era and to some extent the Burger Court era, but it was not typical of most years before and has not been typical of most years since.

The courts are part of the political process and are sensitive to others in the process, especially to the president, Congress, and public. Although they enjoy relative independence, they do not have absolute independence from political pressure. Thus, they have "learned to be a political institution and to behave accordingly." They have "seldom lagged far behind or forged far ahead" of public opinion.[111]

EPILOGUE

The Court Allows the President to Be Sued and the Government to Be Disrupted

During oral arguments for *Clinton v. Jones*, the justices signaled their decision in the case. Their questions reflected their skepticism that a lawsuit would occupy much of a president's time or absorb much of his energies. Justice O'Connor suggested that the only aspect of a trial that would take very long would be "the concern about damage control." Justice Scalia snickered that "we see presidents riding horseback, chopping firewood, fishing, playing golf and so forth and so on."[112]

The justices rejected the trial court's careful compromise, that Jones could establish a record of facts now but could not sue Clinton until he left office, and ruled against the president unanimously.[113] They held that presidents do not have immunity for actions that occur before their term in office or that involve personal matters rather than presidential responsibilities. Justice Stevens wrote the opinion, expressing doubt that a trial would take "any substantial amount" of time or prompt other suits that would "engulf the Presidency." Stevens did say that the trial judge could schedule the trial and the president's testimony around his other obligations. Only Justice Breyer, who authored a concurring opinion, expressed concern that the ruling understated the potential for lawsuits to undermine the presidency.

The justices concluded that providing immunity for presidents would disregard the interests of litigants. But the justices ignored the interests of the public in having unfettered presidents who could exercise effective leadership. On the day the Court issued its ruling, President Clinton and Russian president Boris Yeltsin were in Paris to sign an agreement that would allow the NATO alliance to expand into Eastern Europe. That night American television networks highlighted the Court ruling and downplayed the NATO agreement. The next morning American newspapers did the same.

In preparation for the trial, the process of discovery began, with the attorneys asking questions of the two litigants and potential witnesses. When Clinton's attorney questioned Jones in Arkansas, the president, who as a litigant normally would be present to advise his attorney, was in Washington preparing the United States' response to Iraq's expulsion of United Nations weapons inspectors, a response that envisioned military retaliation and, possibly, another Middle Eastern war. Also during these days, the president was conferring with the president of Mexico, negotiating with Congress over its refusal to provide the United States' contribution to the International Monetary Fund for a loan to prop up the sagging Asian economies, and defending against congressional critics his nominee to head the Justice Department's civil rights division.[114] When Jones's attorneys questioned Clinton, the president was in the midst of preparing his State of the Union address. Regardless, he became the first sitting president to be a defendant and to be questioned under oath.[115]

Jones's attorneys leaked rumors and information from discovery to reporters. The result was a titillating sideshow, with talk about "distinguishing characteristics" of the president's genitals and speculation as to what these might be and how they might be confirmed in court.

To bolster Jones's claims about Clinton's behavior, her attorneys investigated reports about other women who allegedly had sexual relationships with him. Although consensual relationships might have been irrelevant and inadmissible in Jones's suit, her attorneys passed along this information, encouraging the media to report it and the special prosecutor to expand his investigation to encompass it. Without Jones's suit, the public would probably not have had knowledge of allegations of a relationship with Monica Lewinsky or an encounter with Kathleen Willey, nor would the media have paid attention to such allegations.

In short, the suit took considerable time and energy to defend against, and it undermined the president's effectiveness. It also distracted the media and the public—when they were not cracking jokes, people were scolding him as immoral or sympathizing with him as a victim. They seemed only dimly aware of his performance in office.

In the meantime, the two sides tried to negotiate a settlement before trial, as happens in most civil suits. Clinton ultimately offered $700,000—the entire sum Jones originally sued for—but Jones rejected the money, apparently on the advice of her husband or that of a political activist who had become her confidante and adviser. They wanted a trial to humiliate the president.[116]

As the trial date neared, however, the trial judge, Susan Webber Wright, a Republican appointed by President Bush, dismissed Jones's suit. Although Wright did not exonerate Clinton, she concluded that Jones had too little evidence to prove her contentions—too little even for a jury to weigh.[117] Moreover, the incident, if it happened, was "boorish and offensive," she wrote, but it did not constitute sexual harassment. (Chapter 15 will discuss sexual harassment in more detail.)

But Jones appealed the ruling. Soon after, the president's affair with Monica Lewinsky became public, and the lawyers for both Jones and the president realized that although this affair did not involve sexual harassment this news might influence the appellate court. Jones demanded money to settle the case, and the president agreed to pay $850,000. Although this settlement extricated the president from any further proceedings in this case, his effectiveness was diminished for the rest of his term, and his reputation will be besmirched in history. The suit inflicted much damage.

The Supreme Court's reputation might be tarnished as well. The justices' ruling proved to be shortsighted, even naive about the nature of our political system. To think that such a suit could go to trial today without disrupting the president and the rest of the political process was wishful thinking.

The Supreme Court's ruling, of course, serves as a precedent, despite Judge Wright's decision to dismiss Jones's suit. Other persons can sue future presidents—whether for real or imagined injuries, and whether out of personal or political motives. The ruling, then, could weaken the presidency.

Yet the Court's ruling does illustrate a desirable feature of our constitutional system. The judiciary has so much independence that the justices felt free to challenge the most powerful official in the government. Even Clinton's two appointees felt free to rule against him. And then the trial judge, a member of the opposite party and an appointee of the president whom Clinton beat, felt free to rule in his favor.

Key Terms

presidential immunity
judicial review
Marbury v. Madison
court-packing plan
Warren Court
Burger Court
Rehnquist Court
district courts
courts of appeals

jurisdiction
habeas corpus
criminal cases
civil cases
standing to sue
writ of certiorari
restrained judges
activist judges
stare decisis

Further Reading

Robert Chrisman and Robert L. Allen, eds., *Court of Appeal: The Black Community Speaks Out on the Racial and Sexual Politics of Thomas vs. Hill* (New York: Ballentine, 1992). Passionate and provocative essays by black writers reflecting on the nomination and confirmation of Justice Thomas.

Richard D. Kahlenberg, *Broken Contract* (Boston: Faber & Faber, 1992). A memoir by a student at Harvard Law School that tells you a lot about law schools, the legal profession, and the nature of American law.

David M. O'Brien, *Storm Center,* 3d ed. (New York: Norton, 1993). A lively account of the Supreme Court and its very human justices.

LeRoy Phillips and Mark Curriden, *Contempt of Court* (New York: Faber & Faber, 1999). The story of the Supreme Court's only criminal trial—of the Chattanooga sheriff for allowing a lynch mob to murder a defendant whose appeal was pending before the Supreme Court in 1906.

Bob Woodward and Scott Armstrong, *The Brethren* (New York: Simon & Schuster, 1979). A behind-the-scenes look at the politicking among Supreme Court justices for major cases during the 1970s.

Electronic Resources

supremecourtus.gov
The Supreme Court's official site, with decisions and opinions posted the day they are announced.

oyez.nwu.edu/
This excellent site has biographies of all the Supreme Court justices, current and previous. It is a multimedia site, where you can hear the marshal cry "Oyez, oyez," listen to oral arguments in important cases, take a virtual tour of the Court, and search for Court decisions by subject, date, or citation.

www.courttv.com/library/supreme/
This site, developed by a private company, contains biographies of all the Supreme Court justices. It provides links to summaries of recent key decisions and the text of actual decisions. A similar site operated by Cornell University is supct.law.cornell.edu/supct/justices/fullcourt.html

InfoTrac College Edition

"Real Stakes in November"
"Workaholic"
"Peer Sexual Harassment Outlawed"
"Textualist Jurisprudence, Justice Scalia"

Notes

1. Technically, Jones could not sue on the basis of sexual harassment, however, because the statute of limitations had expired. Instead, she sued on the basis of denial of civil rights, intentional infliction of emotional distress, and defamation. (The latter stemmed from assertions by presidential aides that the incident had not occurred and the resulting implication that she had lied.) Yet the evidence relevant to these claims would be nearly the same as for a sexual harassment suit.

2. This conclusion would parallel the conclusion of many legal scholars about immunity from criminal prosecution. Although presidents, of course, can be impeached for criminal (or noncriminal) behavior, they might have immunity from prosecution while remaining in office. Thus, the special prosecutor told the grand jury that it could not indict President Nixon for Watergate crimes. (Instead, the grand jury cited the president as an "unindicted co-conspirator.") The Supreme Court initially agreed to address this question in the Watergate tapes case but ultimately avoided it. At

least it is clear that presidents can be prosecuted after leaving office. Hence, President Nixon's effort to arrange a pardon for himself before agreeing to step down.

3. *Nixon v. Fitzgerald,* 457 U.S. 731.

4. The federal appellate court cited these possibilities when it ruled against the president.

5. John Hibbing and Elizabeth Theiss-Morse, *Congress as Public Enemy: Public Attitudes toward American Political Institutions* (New York: Cambridge University Press, 1995), chaps. 2 and 3.

6. John R. Schmidhauser, *Justices and Judges* (Boston: Little, Brown, 1979), 11.

7. *Federalist Paper #78.*

8. Henry J. Abraham, *Justices and Presidents* (New York: Oxford University Press, 1974), 74.

9. Henry J. Abraham, *The Judicial Process,* 3d ed. (New York: Oxford University Press, 1975), 309.

10. Drew Pearson and Robert S. Allen, *The Nine Old Men* (New York: Doubleday, Doren, 1937), 7; Barbara A. Perry, *The Priestly Tribe: The Supreme Court's Image in the American Mind* (Westport, Conn.: Praeger, 1999): 8–9.

11. *Federalist Paper #78.*

12. 1 Cranch 137 (1803). Technically, *Marbury* was not the first use of judicial review, but it was the first clear articulation of judicial review by the Court.

13. Jefferson was also angry at the nature of the appointees. One had led troops loyal to England during the Revolutionary War. Eric Black, *Our Constitution: The Myth That Binds Us* (Boulder, Colo.: Westview, 1988), 66.

14. Debate arose over whether the four should be considered appointed. Their commissions had been signed by the president, and the seal of the U.S. had been affixed by Marshall, as secretary of state. Yet it was customary to require commissions to be delivered, perhaps because of less reliable record keeping by government or less reliable communications at the time.

15. Walter F. Murphy and C. Herman Pritchett, *Courts, Judges, and Politics,* 3d ed. (New York: Random House, 1979), 4.

16. John A. Garraty, "The Case of the Missing Commissions," in John A. Garraty, ed., *Quarrels That Have Shaped the Constitution* (New York: Harper & Row, 1962), 13.

17. *Fletcher v. Peck,* 6 Cranch 87 (1810); *Martin v. Hunter's Lessee,* 1 Wheaton 304 (1816); *Cohens v. Virginia,* 6 Wheaton 264 (1821).

18. *Gibbons v. Ogden,* 9 Wheaton 1 (1824).

19. *Scott v. Sandford,* 19 Howard 393 (1857).

20. *Ex parte Merryman,* 17 Federal Cases 9487 (1861).

21. *Ex parte McCardle,* 7 Wallace 506 (1869).

22. For examination of the ways in which the Civil War and Reconstruction fomented a constitutional "revolution," see Bruce Ackerman, *We the People: Transformations* (Cambridge, Mass.: Harvard University Press, 1998). Ackerman offers a similar examination of the significance of the New Deal period.

23. *Hammer v. Dagenhart,* 247 U.S. 251 (1918).

24. *Lochner v. New York,* 198 U.S. 45 (1905).

25. *Adkins v. Children's Hospital,* 261 U.S. 525 (1923).

26. *Adair v. United States,* 208 U.S. 161 (1908). *In re Delis,* 158 U.S. 564 (1895).

27. *United States v. E. C. Knight Co.,* 156 U.S. 1 (1895).

28. Lawrence Baum, *The Supreme Court,* 2d ed. (Washington, D.C.: CQ Press, 1985), 177.

29. C. Herman Pritchett, *The American Constitution,* 2d ed. (New York: McGraw-Hill, 1968), 166.

30. With the possible exception of freedom of speech, which will be addressed in Chapter 14.

31. If at least $75,000 is at stake, according to congressional law.

32. Henry Abraham, "A Bench Happily Filled," *Judicature* 66 (February 1983): 284.

33. Harry P. Stumpf, *American Judicial Politics,* 2d ed. (Upper Saddle River, N.J.: Prentice Hall, 1998), 175. After Taft nominated a Catholic to be chief justice, the Speaker of the House cracked, "If Taft were Pope, he'd want to appoint some Protestants to the College of Cardinals." Henry J. Abraham, *Justices and Presidents: A Political History of Appointments to the Supreme Court,* 2nd ed. (New York: Oxford University Press, 1985), 168.

34. Victor Navasky, *Kennedy Justice* (New York: Atheneum, 1971), 245–246.

35. M. Nejelski, *Women in the Judiciary: A Status Report* (Washington, D.C.: National Women's Political Caucus, June 1984).

36. Sheldon Goldman, "Reagan's Second Term Judicial Appointments," *Judicature* 70 (April/May 1987): 324–339.

37. David Byrd, "Clinton's Untilting Federal Bench," *National Journal* (February 19, 2000), 555–557.

38. One of President Reagan's nominees, Douglas Ginsburg, withdrew his nomination due to widespread opposition in the Senate, so officially his nomination was not denied.

39. Qualifications include conflicts of interest or the appearance of conflicts of interest as well as other indicators of merit. Charles M. Cameron, Albert D. Cover, and Jeffrey A. Segal, "Senate Voting on Supreme Court Nominees: A Neoinstitutional Model," *American Political Science Review* 84 (June 1990): 525–534.

40. Abraham, *Justices and Presidents,* 6–7.

41. Jeffrey Segal and Harold Spaeth, "If a Supreme Court Vacancy Occurs, Will the Senate Confirm a Reagan Nominee?" *Judicature* 69 (1986): 188–189.

42. Al Kamen, "Switching Sides to Court Victory," *Washington Post National Weekly Edition,* July 14, 1997, p. 15.

43. Neil A. Lewis, "Impeach Those Liberal Judges! Where Are They?" *New York Times,* May 18, 1997, p. E5.

44. House Majority Whip Tom DeLay (Tex.). Joan Biskupic, "Objecting to Judicial Activism," *Washington Post National Weekly Edition,* September 22, 1997, p. 6.

45. Lewis, "Impeach Those Federal Judges!"

46. Neil A. Lewis, "Stalled Judicial Nominee Feels the Personal Pain of Politics," *New York Times,* November 16, 1997, p. 22. One nonpartisan research center—the Miller Center of Public Affairs at the University of Virginia—has attributed these tactics, in general, to the Republicans' reliance on conservative interest groups that focus primarily on the judiciary. Garland W. Allison, "Delay in Senate Confirmation of Federal Judicial Nominees," *Judicature,* 80 (July/August 1996): 14.

47. Sheldon Goldman. Biskupic, "Objecting to Judicial Activism."

48. Breyer, Ginsburg, O'Connor, Souter, Stevens, and possibly Scalia.

49. Schmidhauser, *Justice and Judges,* 55–57.

50. Merle Miller, *Plain Speaking* (New York: Berkeley/Putnam's, 1974), 121.

51. Harold W. Chase, *Federal Judges* (Minneapolis: University of Minnesota Press, 1972), 189.

52. *Morrison v. Olson,* 487 U.S. 654 (1988).

53. Martin Shapiro, "The Supreme Court: From Warren to Burger," in *The New American Political System,* ed. Anthony King, (Washington, D.C.: American Enterprise Institute, 1978), 180–181.

54. Robert Seigliano, *The Supreme Court and the Presidency* (New York: Free Press, 1971), 147–148.

55. Abraham, *Justices and Presidents,* 62.

56. Earl Warren, *The Memoirs of Earl Warren* (Garden City, N.Y.: Doubleday, 1977), 5.

57. Abraham, *Justices and Presidents,* 63.

58. "How Much Do Lawyers Charge?" *Parade,* March 23, 1997, p. 14.

59. Lois G. Forer, *Money and Justice* (New York: Norton, 1984), 9, 15, 102.

60. Karen O'Connor and Lee Epstein, "The Rise of Conservative Interest Group Litigation," *Journal of Politics* 45 (May 1983): 481. See also Richard C. Cortner, *The Supreme Court and the Second Bill of Rights* (Madison: University of Wisconsin Press, 1981), 282.

61. *Tileston v. Ullman,* 318 U.S. 44 (1943).

62. *Poe v. Ullman,* 367 U.S. 497 (1961).

63. *Griswold v. Connecticut,* 381 U.S. 479 (1965).

64. C. K. Rowland and Bridget Jeffery Todd, "Where You Stand Depends on Who Sits," *Journal of Politics* 53 (February 1991): 175–185.

65. Fred Barbash and Al Kamen, "Supreme Court, 'A Rotten Way to Earn a Living,'" *Washington Post National Weekly Edition,* October 1, 1984, p. 33.

66. *Bailey v. U.S.,* 133 L.Ed.2d 472 (1995).

67. Linda Greenhouse, "Sure Justices Legislate. They Have To," *New York Times* (July 5, 1998), section 4, p. 1.

68. Robert Bork, *The Tempting of America* (New York: Touchstone/Simon & Schuster, 1990).

69. Lawrence Tribe, *On Reading the Constitution* (Cambridge, Mass.: Harvard University Press, 1992).

70. *Osborn v. U.S. Bank,* 9 Wheaton 738 (1824), at 866.

71. Abraham, *Judicial Process,* p. 324.

72. *U.S. v. Butler,* 297 U.S. 1, at 94.

73. Murphy and Pritchett, *Courts, Judges, and Politics,* p. 586.

74. "Judicial Authority Moves Growing Issue," *Lincoln Journal,* April 24, 1977.

75. Alexander Bickel, *The Morality of Consent* (New Haven, Conn.: Yale University Press, 1975), p. 120.

76. "Judicial Authority Moves Growing Issue."

77. Jeffrey A. Segal and Albert D. Cover, "Ideological Values and the Votes of U.S. Supreme Court Justices," *American Political Science Review* 83 (June 1989): 557–564. For different findings for state supreme court justices, see John M. Scheb II, Terry Bowen, and Gary Anderson, "Ideology, Role Orientations, and Behavior in the State Courts of Last Resort," *American Politics Quarterly* 19 (July 1991): 324–335.

78. Harold Spaeth and Stuart Teger, "Activism and Restraint: A Cloak for the Justices' Policy Preferences," in *Supreme Court Activism and Restraint,* ed. Stephen P. Halpern and Clark M. Lamb, (Lexington, Mass.: Lexington, 1982), 277.

79. *Engel v. Vitale,* 370 U.S. 421 (1962).

80. *Abington School District v. Schempp,* 374 U.S. 203 (1963).

81. *Stone v. Graham,* 449 U.S. 39 (1980).

82. *Lee v. Weisman,* 120 L.Ed.2d 467 (1992).

82a. *Santa Fe Independent School District v. Doe* (2000).

83. *Burnet v. Coronado Oil and Gas,* 285 U.S. 293 (1932), at 406.

84. Abraham, *Judicial Process,* 13.

85. *Denver Area Educational Telecommunications Consortium v. Federal Communications Commission,* 116 S.Ct. 2374 (1996).

86. *U.S. v. Butler,* 297 U.S. 1 (1936), at 79.

87. Murphy and Pritchett, *Courts, Judges and Politics,* 25.

88. David J. Garrow, "The Rehnquist Reins," *New York Times Magazine,* October 6, 1996, p. 70.

89. Robert Wernick, "Chief Justice Marshall Takes the Law in Hand," *Smithsonian* (November 1998): 162.

90. Joan Biskupic, "Here Comes the Judge? Maybe Not," *Washington Post National Weekly Edition,* February 14, 2000, p. 30.

91. Jeffrey A. Segal and Harold J. Spaeth, *The Supreme Court and the Attitudinal Model* (New York: Cambridge University Press, 1993), 262–264.

92. Jeffrey Rosen, "Rehnquist's Choice," *New Yorker,* January 11, 1999, p. 31.

93. Michael S. Serrill, "The Power of William Brennan," *Time,* July 22, 1985, p. 62.

94. Ibid.

95. David J. Garrow, "One Angry Man," *New York Times Magazine,* October 6, 1996, pp. 68–69.

96. *Webster v. Reproductive Health Services,* 492 U.S. 445 (1989).

97. *U.S. v. Virginia,* 135 L.Ed.2d 735, 787–789 (1996).

98. Alpheus T. Mason, *Harlan Fiske Stone* (New York: Viking, 1956), 308.

99. Baum, *The Supreme Court,* 4.

100. 410 U.S. 113.

101. Craig R. Ducat and Robert L. Dudley, "Federal Appellate Judges and Presidential Power," paper presented at the Midwest Political Science Association Meeting, April 1987.

102. Baum, *The Supreme Court,* 158.

103. Sheldon Goldman, "How Long the Legacy?" *Judicature,* 76 (April/May 1993): 295.

104. The Eleventh Amendment overturned *Chisholm v. Georgia* (1793), which had permitted the federal courts to hear suits against a state by citizens of another state. The Fourteenth overturned the Dred Scott case, *Scott v. Sandford* (1857), which had held that blacks were not citizens. The Sixteenth overturned *Pollock v. Farmers' Loan and Trust* (1895), which had negated a congressional law authorizing a federal income tax. The Twenty-sixth overturned *Oregon v. Mitchell* (1970), which had negated a congressional law allowing eighteen-year-olds to vote in state elections.

105. *Goldman v. Weinberger,* 475 U.S. 503 (1986).

106. William N. Eskridge, Jr., "Overriding Supreme Court Statutory Interpretation Decisions," *Yale Law Journal* 101 (1991): 338.

107. Thomas R. Marshall, "Public Opinion, Representation, and the Modern Supreme Court," *American Politics Quarterly* 16 (July 1988): 296–316.

108. Richard Morin, "A Nation of Stooges," *Washington Post,* October 8, 1995, p. C5.

109. Gregory A. Caldeira, "Neither the Purse nor the Sword," paper presented at the American Political Science Association Meeting, August 1987.

110. Abraham, *Justices and Presidents,* 342–343.

111. Robert G. McCloskey, *The American Supreme Court* (Chicago: University of Chicago Press, 1960), 225.

112. Excerpts of oral arguments are from "The Ruling That Entangled the President," *New York Times,* March 15, 1998, Week in Review, p. 7.

113. 137 L.Ed.2d 945 (1997).

114. Vincent Bugliosi, *No Island of Sanity: Paula Jones v. Bill Clinton* (New York: Ballantine, 1998). This book is an extended critique of the Supreme Court's ruling in this case.

115. Richard Lacayo, "The Big Face-off," *Time,* January 26, 1998, p. 46.

116. Jeffrey Toobin, "Casting Stones," *New Yorker,* November 3, 1997, pp. 55–57.

117. Jones's lawyers seemed so obsessed with the possible affairs of the president that they paid little attention to the purported employment discrimination that Jones claimed. This charge—that she suffered at work because she rebuffed the president—would, if proved, establish her harassment claim. Yet during her deposition, she said that her lawyers had not reviewed her employment records with her. During the president's deposition, her lawyers made little effort to probe this possibility. Jeffrey Toobin, "How Paula Jones's Defenders Left Her Defenseless," *New Yorker,* April 13, 1998, p. 27.

Civil Liberties

Does Religious Liberty Include Animal Sacrifice?

You are Justice Anthony Kennedy of the U.S. Supreme Court facing an unusual case from Hialeah, Florida. The Church of the Lukumi Babalu Aye has brought suit against the city because of ordinances that restrict the church's practices.

The church follows the Santeria religion, which originated in Nigeria four thousand years ago. The religion spread to Cuba when Nigerians were brought as slaves and eventually to Florida when Cubans fled their communist government. Santeria now blends ancient African rites and Roman Catholic rituals, but its distinguishing and most provocative practice is animal sacrifice. Adherents believe animal sacrifice is necessary to win the favor of the gods, and they practice it at births, marriages, and deaths, and at initiations of new members and priests. Chickens, ducks, doves, pigeons, sheep, goats, and turtles are killed by knife; their blood is drained into pots; and their meat is prepared for eating.

Santeria long existed underground, but the church decided to bring it into the open in 1987, leasing a used-car lot and announcing plans for a church building, cultural center, museum, and school in the Miami suburb. Then "the

neighborhood went ape," according to one resident.[1] The city council held an emergency session, at which one council member stated that devotees "are in violation of everything this country stands for," while another quoted the Bible in opposition. The council president asked, "What can we do to prevent the church from opening?"

The city attorney's office drafted a series of ordinances, which the city council passed, that essentially deny adherents the opportunity to practice their religion. Although the ordinances do not explicitly refer to Santeria, they prohibit ritualistic animal sacrifice. They make exception for kosher slaughter for persons who follow Jewish dietary laws.

The church filed suit, claiming that the ordinances impinge on members' free exercise of their religion guaranteed by the First Amendment of the Constitution. The free exercise clause allows individuals to practice their religion as they see fit. Governments cannot restrict a particular religion or practice, unless there is a compelling reason to do so. The city countered that there were compelling reasons: First, animal sacrifice presents a health risk to the adherents, because the animals are uninspected and might be un-

Ernesto Pichardo, priest of the Church of the Lukumi Babalu Aye.
Tom Salyer

sanitary, and to the public, because the carcasses sometimes are found rotting in the streets and floating in the canals. (The church responded that it properly disposes of the remains but that adherents of Santeria who are not members of the church might not.) Second, animal sacrifice entails cruelty to animals. (The church responded that it humanely kills the animals by slicing their carotid artery, as kosher slaughter does.) Third, animal sacrifice results in emotional injury to children who witness it.

The church's priest, Ernesto Pichardo, suggested that town officials were hypocrites. "You can kill a turkey in your backyard, put it on the table, say a prayer, and serve it for Thanksgiving. But if we pray over the turkey, kill it, then eat it, we violated the law."[2]

But the federal district court ruled for the city, and the federal court of appeals affirmed. Now it is 1993, and the Supreme Court is deciding the case.

You were appointed by President Reagan because you were a conservative judge on a lower court. As a justice, you have usually voted for government authority over individual rights. (Even now you are relatively unknown. A group of tourists of the Court, thinking you were also sightseeing, asked you to take their picture.)

You are a Roman Catholic, a former altar boy, and you seem inclined to accommodate people's religious desires or demands, yet your views appear uncertain. A year ago, for instance, you wrote the majority opinion that invalidated prayers at graduation ceremonies for public elementary, middle, and high schools.[3] In cases involving minority religious practices, you voted to allow Hare Krishnas the right to distribute literature at public airports, yet you voted to deny members of the Native American church the right to use peyote, a hallucinogen, in worship ceremonies.[4] In that case you joined an opinion that could make it difficult for members of minority religions to adhere to their practices.

So how do you decide this case?

Americans value their "rights." Eighteenth-century Americans believed that people had "natural rights" by virtue of being human. Given by God, not by government, the rights could not be taken away by government. Contemporary Americans do not use this term, but they do think about rights much as their forebears did.

Yet Americans have a split personality about their rights. As Chapter 4 described, most people tell pollsters they believe in various constitutional rights in the abstract, but many do not accept these rights when applied to concrete situations. For example, most people say they believe in free speech, but many would not allow communists, socialists, or atheists to speak in public or teach in schools.

Surveys in recent years show that Americans remain divided over their support for civil liberties. Thirty-one percent say freedom of expression should not apply to network television; 28 percent say it should not apply to newspapers; and 26 percent say it should not apply to art, film, or music. Fifty-five percent think songs with sexually explicit lyrics should be barred from radio and television, and 50 percent think books with "dangerous ideas" should be banned from school libraries.[5] Forty percent believe police should be able to search homes of suspected drug dealers without search warrants.[6] At the same time, most people acknowledge that it is dangerous to restrict some people or some activities because this could lead to restricting others as well.

Conflicts over civil liberties and rights have dominated the courts since the Great Depression. This chapter, covering civil liberties, and the next, covering civil rights, describe how the courts have interpreted these rights and tried to resolve these conflicts. We will explain the most important rights and recount the struggles by individuals and groups to achieve them. We will see how judges act as referees between litigants, brokers among competing groups, and policymakers in the process of deciding these cases.

The Constitution and the Bill of Rights

Individual Rights in the Constitution

Although the term *civil liberties* usually refers to the rights in the Bill of Rights, a few rights are granted in the body of the Constitution. The Constitution bans religious qualifications for federal office and guarantees jury trials in federal criminal cases. It bans **bills of attainder,** which are legislative acts rather than judicial trials pronouncing specific persons guilty of crimes, and **ex post facto laws,** which are legislative acts making some behavior illegal that was not illegal when it was done. The Constitution also prohibits suspension of the writ of habeas corpus, except during rebellion or invasion of the country. These rights are significant, but they by no means exhaust the rights people believed they had at the time the Constitution was written.

The Bill of Rights

Origin and Meaning

The Constitution originally did not include a bill of rights; the Founders did not think traditional liberties needed specific protections because federalism, separation of powers, and checks and balances would prevent the national government from becoming too powerful. But to win support for ratification, the Founders promised to adopt amendments to provide such rights. James Madison proposed twelve, Congress passed them, and in 1791 the states ratified ten, which came to be known as the Bill of Rights.[7] Of these, the first eight grant specific rights (see the box "Civil Liberties in the Bill of Rights"). (The Ninth says the listing of these rights does not mean they are the only ones the people have, and the Tenth says the powers not granted to the federal government are reserved for the state governments.)

The Bill of Rights provides rights against the government. According to Justice Hugo Black, it is "a collection of Thou shalt nots" directed at the government.[8] Essentially, the Bill of Rights provides rights for minorities against the majority, because government policy concerning civil liberties tends to reflect the views of the majority.

As Chapter 2 explained, the Founders set up a government to protect property rights for the well-to-do minority against the presumably jealous majority. Separation of powers, checks and balances, and various specific provisions of the Constitution were intended to limit the ability of the masses to curtail the rights of the elites. However, as Americans became more egalitarian and as the masses got more opportunity to participate in politics, the importance of property rights has declined while the importance of other rights has increased. At the same time, the role of the Bill of Rights has increased to protect the have-nots of society—the unpopular, powerless minorities in conflict with the majority.

Responsibility for interpreting the Bill of Rights generally falls on the federal courts. Because their judges are appointed for life, they are more independent from majority pressure than elected officials are.

Application

For many years the Supreme Court applied the Bill of Rights only to the federal government—not to state governments (or local governments, which are under the authority of state governments). The Court ruled that the Bill of Rights restricted only what the federal government could do.[9]

The Founders thought that states, being closer to the people, would be less likely to violate their liberties. Also, they knew that many states had their own bills of rights, and they expected the rest to follow.

The Court applied the Bill of Rights this way because the Founders did not realize that states would come to violate people's liberties more frequently than the federal government. The state governments, representing smaller, more homogeneous populations, tended to reflect majority sentiment more closely than the federal government, and they often rode rough-shod over criminal defendants or racial, religious, or political minorities. When disputes arose, state courts tended to interpret their bills of rights narrowly.

However, starting in 1925[10] and continuing through 1972,[11] the Supreme Court gradually applied most provisions of the Bill of Rights to the states, using the Fourteenth Amendment's due process clause as justification. This clause, adopted after the Civil War to protect blacks from southern governments, reads, "Nor shall any state deprive any person of life, liberty, or property, without due process of law." The clause refers to states and "liberty." It is ambiguous, but the Court interpreted it to mean that states also have to provide the liberties in the Bill of Rights.

The Court has applied all but two provisions of the First and the Fourth through the Eighth Amendments to the states: guarantee of a grand jury in criminal cases and guarantee of a jury trial in civil cases. In addition, the Court has established some rights not in the Bill of Rights, and it has applied these to the states, too: presumption of innocence in criminal cases, right to travel within the country, and right to privacy. Thus, most provisions in the Bill of Rights, and even some not in it, now restrict what both the federal and state governments can do.

To see how the Court has interpreted these provisions, we will look at three major areas—freedom of expression, rights of criminal defendants, and right to privacy.

Freedom of Expression

The **First Amendment** provides freedom of expression, which includes freedom of speech, assembly, and association;[12] freedom of the press; and freedom of religion.

The amendment states that "Congress shall make no law" abridging these liberties. The language is absolute, but few justices interpret it literally. They cite the example of the person who falsely shouts "Fire!" in a

- **First Amendment**
  freedom of religion
  freedom of speech, assembly, and association
  freedom of the press
- **Second Amendment**
  right to keep and bear arms
- **Third Amendment**
  forbids quartering soldiers in houses during peacetime
- **Fourth Amendment**
  forbids unreasonable searches and seizures

- **Fifth Amendment**
  right to grand jury hearing in criminal cases
  forbids double jeopardy (more than one trial for the same offense)
  forbids compulsory self-incrimination
  right to due process
  forbids taking private property without just compensation
- **Sixth Amendment**
  right to speedy trial
  right to public trial
  right to jury trial in criminal cases

  right to cross-examine adverse witnesses
  right to present favorable witnesses
  right to counsel
- **Seventh Amendment**
  right to jury trial in civil cases
- **Eighth Amendment**
  forbids excessive bail and fines
  forbids cruel and unusual punishment

crowded theater and causes a stampede that injures someone. Surely, they say, the amendment does not protect this expression. So the Court needs to draw a line between expression the amendment protects and that which it does not.

Freedom of Speech

Freedom of speech, Justice Black asserted, "is the heart of our government."[13] First, by allowing an open atmosphere, it maximizes the opportunities for every individual to develop his or her personality and potential to the fullest. Second, by encouraging a variety of opinions, it furthers the advancement of knowledge and discovery of truth. Unpopular opinions could be true or partially true. Even if completely false, they could prompt a reevaluation of accepted opinions. Third, by permitting citizens to form opinions and express them to others, it helps them participate in government. It especially helps them check inefficient or corrupt government. Fourth, by channeling conflict toward persuasion, it promotes a stable society. Governments that deny freedom of speech become inflexible; they force conflict toward violence.[14]

Seditious Speech

The first controversies to test the scope of freedom of speech involved **seditious speech,** speech that encourages rebellion against the government. The government

historically prosecuted individuals for seditious speech during or shortly after war, when society was most sensitive about loyalty.

Numerous prosecutions came with World War I and the Russian Revolution, which brought the Communists to power in the Soviet Union in 1917. The Russian Revolution prompted a "Red Scare," in which people feared conspiracies to overthrow the U.S. government. Congress passed the Espionage Act of 1917, which prohibited interfering with military recruitment, inciting insubordination in military forces, and mailing material advocating rebellion; and the Sedition Act of 1918, which prohibited "disloyal, profane, scurrilous, or abusive language about the form of government, Constitution, soldiers and sailors, flag or uniform of the armed forces." Many states passed similar laws. In short, government prohibited a wide range of speech.

During the war the federal government prosecuted almost two thousand and convicted almost nine hundred persons under these acts, and the states prosecuted and convicted many others. They prosecuted individuals for saying that war is contrary to the teachings of Jesus, that World War I should not have been declared until after a referendum was held, and that the draft was unconstitutional. Officials even prosecuted an individual for remarking to women knitting clothes for the troops, "No soldier ever sees those socks."[15]

These cases gave the Supreme Court numerous opportunities to rule on seditious speech. In six major cases, the Court upheld the federal and state laws and affirmed the convictions of all the defendants.[16] The defendants advocated socialism or communism, and some advocated the overthrow of the government to achieve it. Except for one—Eugene Debs, the Socialist Party's candidate for president—the defendants did not command a large audience. Even so, the Court concluded that these defendants' speech constituted a "clear and present danger" to the government. Justice Edward Sanford wrote, "A single revolutionary spark may kindle a fire that, smouldering for a time, may burst into a sweeping and destructive conflagration."[17] In reality, there was nothing clear or present about the danger; the defendants' speech had little effect.

More prosecutions came after World War II. In 1940, Congress passed the Smith Act, which was not as broad as the World War I acts because it did not forbid criticizing the government. But it did forbid advocating overthrow of the government by force and organizing or joining individuals who advocated overthrow.

The act was used against members of the American Communist Party after the war. The uneasy alliance be-

Eugene Debs, the Socialist Party's candidate for president, criticized American involvement in World War I and the draft. He was convicted for violating the Espionage Act and sentenced to ten years in prison. When President Harding pardoned him early, Debs commented, "It is the government that should ask me for a pardon."
UPI/Corbis-Bettmann

tween the United States and the Soviet Union had given way to the Cold War between the countries. Politicians, especially Senator Joseph McCarthy (R-Wis.), exploited the tensions. McCarthy charged various government officials with being communists. He had little evidence, and his tactics were called "witch-hunts" and, eventually, **McCarthyism.** Other Republicans also accused the Democratic administration of covering up communists. They goaded it into prosecuting members of the communist Party so it would not appear "soft on communism."

In 1951, the Court upheld the Smith Act and affirmed the convictions of eleven top-echelon leaders of the Communist Party.[18] These leaders organized the party and the party advocated overthrowing the government by force, but the leaders had not attempted overthrowing it. (If they had, they clearly would have been guilty of crimes.) Even so, the Court majority concluded that they constituted a clear and present danger, and Chief Justice Fred Vinson wrote that the government does not have to "wait until the putsch is about to be executed, the plans have been laid and the signal is awaited" before it can act against the party. The minority argued that the Communist Party was not a danger. Justice William Douglas said that the party was "of little consequence. . . . Communism has been so thoroughly exposed in this country that it has been crippled as a political force. Free speech has destroyed it as an effective political party." Following the Court's decision, the government prosecuted and convicted almost one hundred other communists.

But the Cold War thawed slightly, the Senate voted to condemn McCarthy, and two new members, including Chief Justice Earl Warren, joined the Court. In a series of cases in the 1950s, the Court made it more difficult to convict Communists,[19] thereby incurring the wrath of the public, Congress, and President Eisenhower. In a private conversation, Warren asked Eisenhower what he thought the Court should do with the communists. Eisenhower replied, "I would kill the S.O.B.s."[20]

The government took other action against communists. The federal government ordered communists to register, and then some state governments banned them from public jobs such as teaching, or private jobs such as practicing law or serving as union officers. Legislative committees held hearings to expose and humiliate them. The Court heard numerous cases involving these actions and usually ruled against the government.

The Vietnam War did not prompt the same fears that World Wars I and II did. Congress did not pass

At congressional hearings, Senator Joseph McCarthy identified locations of alleged communists and "fellow travelers."
UPI/Corbis-Bettmann

comparable laws, perhaps because many "respectable" people opposed this war and also because the Court in the 1950s and 1960s increasingly allowed seditious speech.

The Court developed new doctrine for seditious speech in 1969. A Ku Klux Klan leader said at a rally in Ohio that the Klan might take "revengeance" on the president, Congress, and Supreme Court if they continued "to suppress the white, Caucasian race." The leader was convicted under a statute similar to those upheld after World War I, but this time the statute was unanimously struck down by the Court.[21] The justices said people can advocate—enthusiastically, even heatedly—as long as they do not incite illegal action. This broad protection for seditious speech remains in effect today.

Thus, after many years and many cases, the Court concluded that the First Amendment protects seditious speech as much as other speech. Justice Douglas noted that "the threats were often loud but always puny."[22] Even the attorney general who prosecuted the major Communist cases later admitted that the cases were "squeezed oranges. I didn't think there was much to them."[23] Nevertheless, the Court had permitted a climate of fear to overwhelm the First Amendment for many years.

Although the country is at peace today, these precedents will be important again. Already they have had some effect on government action against right-wing militia groups. Since the Oklahoma City bombing in 1995, government surveillance of these groups and enforcement of gun laws have stepped up, but prosecution of the members, under terrorism laws, has been limited because most of the "evidence" is fiery rhetoric, which is protected speech (unless it reflects concrete plans to violate any laws).

Now we will turn to other speech—nonseditious speech—to see how the Court has interpreted the First Amendment in these situations.

Public Forum

People usually communicate with each other in private. But sometimes speakers want more listeners and they use public places where people congregate. This means speakers will be heard by some listeners who do not like their message or their use of public places to disseminate it, and it also means speakers might disrupt the normal purposes of these places.

The Court holds that individuals have a right to use public places, such as streets, sidewalks, and parks, to express their views on public issues. These places constitute the **public forum** and serve as "the poor person's printing press."

When speakers seek to use other public facilities, the Court has to determine which ones are also part of the public forum. It decided that federal and state capitol grounds,[24] Supreme Court grounds,[25] and public school grounds[26] are part of the forum. It decided that blacks could protest library segregation at a public library[27] and promoters could show the rock musical *Hair* at a public theater[28] because these, too, are part of the forum.

On the other hand, the Court decided that civil rights activists could not demonstrate against jail segregation outside a jail because of the need for security[29] and that Dr. Benjamin Spock—the baby doctor—and other antiwar activists could not encourage opposition to the Vietnam War at an army base because of the need for discipline in the army.[30]

Normally, only publicly owned facilities are considered part of the public forum, but the proliferation of shopping centers and malls prompted speakers to use these privately owned facilities to reach crowds of shoppers. The Warren Court permitted them to do so, saying that shopping centers and malls are similar to downtown shopping districts where streets and sidewalks are part of the public forum.[31] But the Burger Court overruled the Warren Court; it allowed the shopping centers and malls to prohibit speech. Thus, the Burger Court emphasized property rights over First Amendment rights in this situation.[32]

Even in public forums people cannot speak whenever and however they want. The Court has divided speech into three kinds—pure speech, speech plus conduct, and symbolic speech—and established doctrine for each.

Pure Speech

Pure speech is speech without any conduct (besides the speech itself). Individuals can say what they want as long as they do not cause a breach of the peace or a riot, or hurl "fighting words" at specific persons, except at police officers, who are supposed to be trained and disciplined to take abuse.[33]

Before the Court's ruling in 1972, arrests for swearing were common. In the District of Columbia, for example, more than half of the fifteen thousand to twenty thousand arrests for "disorderly conduct" each year involved swearing, usually at police.[34]

Individuals can use offensive language in many situations.[35] During the Vietnam War, a man walked through the corridors of the Los Angeles County courthouse wearing a jacket with the words "Fuck the Draft" emblazoned on the back. Police arrested him. The Court reversed his conviction, and seventy two–year-old Justice John Harlan remarked that "one man's vulgarity is another's lyric."[36] (See also the box on hate speech.)

The media, however, cannot broadcast some offensive language. A California radio station broadcast a monologue by comedian George Carlin. Titled "Filthy Words," it lampooned society's sensitivity to seven words that "you couldn't say on the public airwaves . . . the ones you definitely wouldn't say, ever." The seven words, according to the Federal Communications Commission report, included "a four-letter word for excrement" repeated seventy times in twelve minutes. In a close vote, the Court ruled that although the monologue was part of a serious program on contemporary attitudes toward language, it was not protected under the First Amendment because people, including children, tuning the radio could be subjected to the language in their home.[37]

Yet the Court struck down a Utah law restricting "indecent material" on cable television. The difference apparently is that people choose to subscribe and pay for cable television.[38]

Speech Plus Conduct

Speech plus conduct is speech combined with conduct that is intended to convey ideas—for example, a demonstration in which protesters chant slogans or carry signs with slogans (the speech) and march, picket, or sit in (the conduct).

Individuals can demonstrate, but they are subject to some restrictions. Places in the public forum are used for other purposes besides demonstrating, and individuals cannot disrupt these activities. They cannot, Justice Arthur Goldberg remarked, hold "a street meeting in

the middle of Times Square at the rush hour."[39] Thus, abortion protesters can demonstrate on public streets and public sidewalks by abortion clinics, and they can approach staffers and patients who come and go. But protesters cannot block access (and, to ensure this, judges can order them not to come within a certain distance—for example, fifteen feet—of driveways and doorways).[40]

To help enforce the restrictions, governments can require groups to obtain a permit, which can specify the place, time, and manner of the demonstration. However, officials cannot allow one group to demonstrate but forbid another, no matter how much they dislike the group or its message. They cannot forbid the group even if they say they fear violence, unless the group actually threatens violence. In short, officials may establish restrictions to avoid disruption, but they may not use these restrictions to censor speech.

Accordingly, lower federal courts required the Chicago suburb of Skokie to permit the American Nazi Party to demonstrate in front of the town hall in 1978.[41] About forty thousand of Skokie's population of seventy thousand were Jews. Of these, hundreds had survived the German Nazi concentration camps during World War II, and thousands had lost relatives who died in the camps. The city, edgy about the announced demonstration, passed ordinances that prohibited wearing "military-style" uniforms and distributing material that "promotes and incites hatred against persons by reason of their race, national origin, or religion." These ordinances were thinly disguised attempts to bar the

Hate Speech on Campus and the First Amendment

A student puts a sign on her dorm room door that announces, "People who will be shot on sight—preppies, bimbos, men without chest hair, and homos."

A fraternity holds a "slave auction" as a fund-raiser. White pledges in blackface and Afro wigs perform skits. Afterward, audience members bid on the performers.

Two black students find the letters *KKK* carved into their dorm room door and a note saying, "African monkeys, why don't you go back to the jungle."

After a class discussion of media treatment of African Americans, a black woman receives a card asking her to have "a very bad Christmas" and calling her a "nigger."

Such incidents have forced members of college and university communities—students, faculty, and administrators—to consider in a real and personal way the meaning of the First Amendment. Many conclude that hate speech should be prohibited and that students who engage in it should be punished. They argue that students who hurl epithets or slurs at others, especially anonymously, are more interested in intimidating than in initiating a dialogue about issues. They also argue that civility and tolerance must be maintained. Otherwise, victims of such speech are made to feel unwelcome on campus

and in some cases are kept from concentrating on their studies. A student who was jeered nightly by students taunting, "Faggot!" said, "When you are told you are not worth anything, it is difficult to function."[1]

Some legal scholars believe hate speech could be a violation of the Fourteenth Amendment's equal protection clause—which guarantees "equal protection of the laws" and restricts discrimination in society—if it creates a hostile and intimidating environment for minority students.[2]

Other scholars, however, believe such speech is protected by the First Amendment. Precedents described in this chapter emphasize that even repulsive speech is allowed. Indeed, the First Amendment would be meaningless if only speech acceptable to everybody were protected.

Critics of speech codes point to history: The First Amendment has helped minorities make their case against discrimination. By thwarting southern law enforcement officials' efforts to censor and intimidate the media, the amendment helped the civil rights movement gain national support. On the other hand, censorship has been used against minorities. It is short-sighted to expect new censorship to be used primarily for minorities against

majorities. New censorship could be directed at students and speakers who say the sorts of things Malcolm X once said. During the year and a half that the University of Michigan's speech code was in effect, more than twenty black students were charged with violations by white students, and no white students were charged with violations.[3]

Critics also say the codes could be directed at students who make relatively innocuous comments. A Brown University student was the first casualty. He was expelled for shouting "nigger" and "faggot" to no one in particular while drunk. A University of Pennsylvania student faced disciplinary action for yelling, "Shut up, you water buffalo. If you're looking for a party, there's a zoo a mile from here," to a dozen sorority sisters singing loudly outside his dorm window while he was writing a paper one night. It turns out that the women were black and considered the remark a racial slur.[4] (The women who filed the grievance later dropped it.)

Critics observe that more than any other institutions, colleges and universities traditionally have fostered free inquiry and free expression. They have allowed, even encouraged, a variety of views so the views could be debated.

The answer to the problem, these critics contend, is more, not less,

demonstration, and the courts threw them out. One quoted Justice Oliver Wendell Holmes's statement that "if there is any principle of the Constitution that more imperatively calls for attachment than any other it is the principle of free thought—not free thought for those who agree with us but freedom for the thought we hate."[42]

The Rehnquist Court, however, did uphold a Mil-

waukee suburb's ordinance that prohibited picketing at a residence.[43] The city passed the ordinance after antiabortionists had picketed, six times in one month, the home of a doctor who performed abortions. Although protesters can march through residential neighborhoods, the Court said, a city can prohibit them from focusing on a particular home. Thus, the Court emphasized the right to privacy at home over the right to demonstrate in this situation.

speech. According to the theory of free expression, the remedy for bad ideas is more speech to demonstrate why the ideas are wrong. Four black women at Arizona State University passed a dorm room door with a "job application form" for minority applicants. The form asked for:

- Sources of income: (1) theft, (2) welfare, (3) unemployment;
- Marital status: (1) common law, (2) shacked up, (3) other;
- Number of legitimate children (if any).

Although ASU had a speech code, the women did not try to invoke it or even approach the administration. First they knocked on the door and told one of the occupants what they thought of the form. Then they organized an open meeting in the dorm. Eventually, a news conference and a rally were held, and a program on African American history was instituted in the dorm. All along there was a lively exchange in the campus newspaper. The women accomplished more and, in the process, kept the focus on racism rather than on a speech code.[5]

Supporters of speech codes are not convinced that more speech is the answer. They think that minorities who talk back will be perceived as making a direct challenge and that a verbal confrontation could escalate into a violent one. They argue that codes are necessary to dampen such potential conflict.[6]

Many schools have enacted speech codes, but federal district courts struck down codes at the Universities of Michigan and Wisconsin on grounds that they were overly broad and inherently vague.[7] The Supreme Court has not ruled on the constitutionality of these codes, but it struck down a St. Paul, Minnesota, ordinance that prohibited people from writing graffiti and displaying objects such as a Nazi swastika or a burning cross on public or private property.[8] This ruling probably means that the Court would invalidate campus speech codes as well.

Now some schools are reinventing their speech codes and applying them to computers. George Mason University has a policy prohibiting students from using computers to "harass, threaten, or abuse others." Virginia Tech has a policy also prohibiting students from using computers to "annoy another person." Although this policy probably would be struck down, the school used it to discipline a student for posting a message on the Internet home page of a gay men's group calling for gays to be castrated and to "die a slow death."[9]

The Supreme Court has said that illegal *conduct* associated with hate speech can be punished. A person who erects a burning cross on private property can be prosecuted for trespassing, starting an open fire, and littering, or for such major crimes as arson and making terroristic threats. Similarly, students who engage in hate speech in some situations might be punished for defacing public property or making terroristic threats.

1. Mary Jordan, "Free Speech Starts to Have Its Say," *Washington Post National Weekly Edition,* September 21–27, 1992, p. 31.
2. Mary Ellen Gale, "On Curbing Racial Speech," *The Responsive Community* (Winter 1990–91): 53, 57.
3. Nadine Strossen, *Defending Pornography: Free Speech, Sex, and the Fight for Women's Rights* (New York: Scribner's, 1995).
4. Mike Littwin, "Penn's Water Buffalo Debate," *Lincoln Journal* (Baltimore Sun), May 13, 1993.
5. Nat Hentoff, "The Right Thing at ASU," *Washington Post National Weekly Edition,* July 1–7, 1991, p. 28.
6. Richard Delgado and David H. Yun, "Pressure Valves and Bloodied Chickens: An Analysis of Paternalistic Objections to Hate Speech Regulation," *University of California Law Review* 82 (1994): 716.
7. *Doe v. University of Michigan,* 721 F.Supp. 852 (E.D. Mich., 1989); Jordan, "Free Speech Starts to Have Its Say." A California court also struck down Stanford University's antiharassment code, which was similar to a speech code.
8. *R.A.V. v. St. Paul,* 120 L.Ed.2d 305 (1992). Yet the Court has upheld state laws that provide longer sentences for violent crimes motivated by bias than for the same crimes without evidence of bias. *Wisconsin v. Mitchell,* 124 L.Ed.2d 436 (1993).
9. Michael D. Shear, "A Tangled World Wide Web," *Washington Post National Weekly Edition,* October 30–November 5, 1995, p. 36.

Symbolic Speech

Symbolic speech is the use of symbols, rather than words, to convey ideas.

During the Vietnam War, men burned their draft cards to protest the draft and the war. This was powerful expression, and Congress tried to stifle it by passing a law prohibiting destruction of draft cards. The Supreme Court was uncomfortable with symbolic speech and reluctant to protect it. Even Chief Justice Warren worried that this would mean that "an apparently limitless variety of conduct can be labeled 'speech.' " The Court upheld the law.[44]

One year later, however, the Court was willing to protect symbolic speech. A junior high and two senior high school students in Des Moines, Iowa, including Mary Beth Tinker, wore black armbands to protest the

Mary Beth Tinker, here with her mother and brother, wore a black armband at school to protest the Vietnam War.
UPI/Corbis-Bettmann

war. They were suspended, and they sued school officials. Public schools, Justice Abe Fortas said, "may not be enclaves of totalitarianism." They must allow students freedom of speech, providing students do not disrupt the schools.[45]

In the 1960s and 1970s, many students wore long hair or beards in violation of school policy. Some claimed they did so to protest "establishment culture." Blacks and Indians claimed they wore Afros and braids to show racial pride. Federal courts of appeals split evenly as to whether this was symbolic speech. The Supreme Court refused to hear any of these cases, so there was no uniform law across the country.

Some individuals treated the American flag disrespectfully to protest the Vietnam War. A Massachusetts man wore a flag patch on the seat of his pants and was sentenced to six months in jail. A Washington student taped a peace symbol on a flag and then hung the flag, upside down, outside his apartment. The Court reversed both convictions.[46]

When a member of the Revolutionary Communist Youth Brigade burned an American flag outside the Republican National Convention in Dallas in 1984, the justices faced the issue of actual desecration of the flag. The Rehnquist Court surprisingly permitted this symbolic speech.[47] Two Reagan-appointed conservatives joined the three most liberal members of the Court to forge a bare majority. The foremost free speech advocate on the bench, Justice William Brennan, wrote that the First Amendment cannot be limited just because this form of expression offends some people. "We do not

consecrate the flag by punishing its desecration, for in doing so we dilute the freedom that this cherished emblem represents." The ruling invalidated laws of forty-eight states and the federal government.

Chief Justice Rehnquist emotionally criticized the decision. He said the First Amendment should not apply because the flag is a unique national symbol. He recounted the history of the "Star-Spangled Banner" and the music of John Philip Sousa's "Stars and Stripes Forever," he quoted poems by Ralph Waldo Emerson and John Greenleaf Whittier that refer to the flag, and he discussed the role of the "Pledge of Allegiance."

Civil liberties advocates praised the decision. One lawyer for the defendant said, "If free expression is to exist in this country, people must be as free to burn the flag as they are to wave it." Another said veterans should cheer the decision because it shows that the values in the Bill of Rights that they fought for are intact. Yet veterans groups were outraged.

After administration officials assessed public opinion by monitoring talk shows, President Bush stood in front of the Iwo Jima Memorial and proposed a constitutional amendment to override the decision.[48] Members of Congress, always anxious to appear patriotic, lined up in support. But some, especially Democrats, later came out in opposition. They criticized the proposal for creating an unprecedented exception to the First Amendment. Instead of the proposed amendment, Congress passed a statute prohibiting flag desecration. Apparently, a majority felt that this less permanent substitute would be an adequate shield against the public's wrath. Yet in 1990, the justices, dividing the same way, declared the statute unconstitutional for the same reasons they reversed the Dallas conviction.[49] President Bush, this time waving a model of the Iwo Jima Memorial, proposed another constitutional amendment, and Senate Republican leader Robert Dole (Kan.) warned Democrats that their opposition to the amendment "would make a good 30-second spot" for the upcoming elections, but Congress rejected the amendment. Members sensed less pressure from the public. By the second year of debate on this issue, the initial emotional reaction of the public had ebbed. More voices had spoken out against dilution of the First Amendment. Then in 1995, after Republicans became the majority in Congress, they renewed efforts to adopt a constitutional amendment but fell three votes short in one house.

Protesters torch flags in Chicago.
Bob Kusel/Sipa Press

Freedom of the Press

Unlike most civil liberties cases, which pit a relatively powerless individual or group against the government, freedom of press cases usually feature a more powerful publisher or broadcaster against the government. Even so, these cases still involve rights against the government.

Prior Restraint

The core of freedom of the press is freedom from **prior restraint**—censorship. If the press violates laws prohibiting, for example, libelous or obscene material, it can be punished after publishing such materials. But freedom from prior restraint means the press at least has the opportunity to publish what it thinks is appropriate.

Freedom from prior restraint is not absolute. At the height of the Vietnam War, the secretary of defense in the Johnson administration, Robert McNamara, became disenchanted with the war and ordered a thorough study of our involvement. The study, called "The Pentagon Papers," laid bare the reasons the country was embroiled—reasons not as honorable as the ones officials had been giving the public—and it questioned the effectiveness of military policy. The study was so revealing that McNamara remarked to a friend, "They could hang people for what's in there."[50] He printed only fifteen copies and classified them "Top Secret" so few persons could see them. One of the thirty-six authors, Daniel Ellsberg, originally supported the war but later turned against it. To prod the government into stopping it, he photocopied the papers and gave them to the *New York Times* and *Washington Post,* which published excerpts.

Although the papers embarrassed the Kennedy and Johnson administrations, President Nixon, who was in office at the time, was continuing to fight the war, so the excerpts infuriated him. Meeting with his chief of staff and his national security adviser, he demanded:

> I have a project I want somebody to take. . . . This takes 18 hours a day. It takes devotion and loyalty and diligence such as you've never seen. . . . I really need a son of a bitch . . . who will work his butt off and do it dishonorably. . . . And I'll direct him myself. I know how to play this game and we're going to start playing it. . . . I want somebody just as tough as I am for a change. . . . We're up against an enemy, a conspiracy. They're using any means. We're going to use any means.[51]

This tirade set in motion the developments that eventually would culminate in the Watergate scandal.

But immediately Nixon sought injunctions to restrain the newspapers from publishing more excerpts. However, the Supreme Court refused to grant them.[52] Most justices said they would grant injunctions if publishing the papers

The chief of the presses of the Washington Post *hails the Supreme Court's decision allowing publication of the Pentagon Papers.*
AP/Wide World Photos

clearly jeopardized national security. But information in the papers was historical; it did not directly hinder the war effort. Thus, the rule remained—no prior restraint—but exceptions were possible.

The Rehnquist Court did approve prior restraint in a situation far removed from national security. When journalism students at a St. Louis high school wrote articles for their newspaper about the impact of pregnancy and of parents' divorce on teenagers, the principal deleted the articles and three of the students sued. The Court, noting that students below the college level have fewer rights than adults, decided that officials can censor school publications.[53]

Principals typically have exercised their authority over articles covering school policies or social issues. A Colorado principal blocked an editorial criticizing his study hall policy while allowing another editorial praising it. A Texas principal banned an article about the class valedictorian who succeeded despite the death of her mother, the desertion of her father, and her own pregnancy. An editorial urging students to be more responsible about sex was censored by a Kentucky principal, who feared it could be interpreted as condoning sex, while a survey on AIDS was censored by a Maryland principal, who prohibited students from defining the term "safe sex." A North Carolina high school newspaper was shut down and its adviser was fired because of three articles, including a satirical story about the "death" of the writer after eating a cheeseburger from the school cafeteria.

High school newspaper advisers say that principals have tightened their control in recent years. Over a third of the advisers report that principals have rejected articles or required changes in articles for their paper.[54]

Some principals have disciplined students who have used the Internet to criticize school officials or policies. But, like underground newspapers of the 1960s and 1970s, Web pages created off campus (rather than in computer class) cannot be censored by administrators. Web pages cannot be used to make terroristic threats, however. A Georgia student was arrested for suggesting that the principal be shot, his daughter kidnapped, his car scratched with keys, and its locks clogged with superglue.

Despite these exceptions to freedom from prior restraint, the press in the United States is freer than that in Great Britain, where freedom from prior restraint began. Britain has no First Amendment and tolerates more secrecy. In 1987, the government barred publication of controversial and embarrassing memoirs by a former security service agent, even though they were being pub-

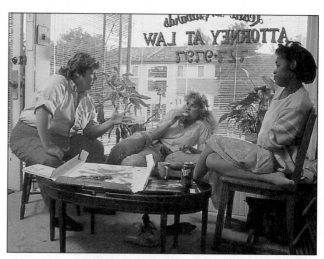

Leanne Tippell and Leslie Smart, two of the St. Louis high school students who sued their school for suppressing their student newspaper story, meet with their attorney, Leslie Edwards (left).
© 1994 Bob Sacha

lished in the United States at the time. A year later the government banned radio and television interviews with all members of the outlawed Irish Republican Army (IRA) and its political party, including its one representative in Parliament.[55] The government even banned broadcast of a song by a popular folk group because the lyrics supported people convicted of IRA bombings. During the Persian Gulf War, the French government banned sale of a song—"Go for It, Saddam"—that criticized the West. After neo-Nazi violence in 1992, the German government banned the sale of music by skinhead groups.

Restrictions on Gathering News

Although prior restraint is an obvious limitation on freedom of the press, restrictions on gathering news in the first place are less obvious but no less serious. They also keep news from the public.

The Burger Court was not vigilant in guarding the press from these restrictions. Most important, it denied reporters a right to keep the names of their sources confidential. In investigative reporting, reporters frequently rely on sources who demand anonymity in exchange for information. The sources might have sensitive positions in government or relations with criminals that would be jeopardized if their names were publicized. A Louisville reporter was allowed to watch persons make hashish from marijuana if he kept their names confidential. But after publication of the story, a grand jury demanded their names. When the reporter refused to reveal them, he was cited for contempt of court, and his conviction was upheld by the Supreme Court.[56] The majority said reporters' need for confidentiality is not as great as the judicial system's need for information about crimes. So either reporters cannot guarantee a potential source anonymity, or they may have to choose between breaking their promise or being cited for contempt and jailed for an indefinite period of time.

Invasion of Privacy

The right to a free press can conflict with an individual's right to privacy when the press publishes personal information. The Supreme Court has permitted the press to publish factual information. For example, although a Georgia law prohibited the press from releasing names of crime victims to spare them embarrassment, an Atlanta television station announced the name of a high school girl who was raped by six classmates and left unconscious on a neighbor's lawn to die. The girl's father sued the station, but the Court said the press needs freedom to publish information that is a matter of public record so citizens can scrutinize the workings of the judicial system.[57]

In 1975, a man in a crowd of people watching President Gerald Ford noticed a woman pull out a gun. He grabbed the gun and prevented the assassination. Reporters wrote stories about this hero, including the fact that he was a homosexual. This caused the man embarrassment and some practical problems, and he sued. The courts sided with the press again. The man's good deed made him newsworthy, whether he wanted to be or not.[58] Persons who become newsworthy are permitted little privacy. Justice Brennan said this is a necessary evil "in a society which places a primary value on freedom of speech and of press."[59]

Libel and Obscenity

Despite broad protection for the press overall, courts grant much less protection for libelous and obscene material. Traditionally, they considered such material irrelevant to the exposition of ideas and search for truth envisioned by the framers of the First Amendment. Whatever benefit such material might have was outweighed by the need to protect persons' reputations and morals. Courts thus allowed states to adopt and implement libel and obscenity laws as they saw fit.

Libel

Libel consists of printed or broadcast statements that are false and that tarnish someone's reputation. Victims are entitled to sue for money to compensate them for the damage.

The Warren Court decided that traditional state libel laws infringed on freedom of the press too much and forced radical changes in these laws. Its landmark decision came in *New York Times v. Sullivan* in 1964.[60]

The *Times* ran an ad by black clergymen who criticized Montgomery, Alabama, officials for their handling of racial protests. The ad contained some trivial inaccuracies. It did not mention any officials by name, but the commissioner of police claimed it referred to him implicitly, and he sued. The local jury ordered the *Times* to pay him a half million dollars! The Court could see that the law was used to punish a detested northern newspaper for an ad that criticized the handling of controversial civil rights protests. And the Court could not ignore the size of the award or the fact that another jury had ordered the *Times* to pay another commissioner a half million dollars for the same ad. It was apparent that libel laws could be used to wreak vengeance on a critical press.

The Court ruled against the police commissioner and made it harder for public officials to win libel suits. It said officials must show not only that the statements about them were false but also that the statements were made with "reckless disregard for the truth." This provides the press some leeway to make mistakes and print false statements, as long as the press is not careless to the point of recklessness.

This protection for the press is necessary, according to Justice Brennan, because "the central meaning of the First Amendment" is that individuals should have the right to criticize officials' conduct. This statement prompted one legal scholar to herald the decision as "an occasion for dancing in the streets."[61]

In later cases the Court extended this ruling to public figures—persons other than public officials who have public prominence or who thrust themselves into public controversies. The court held several persons to be public figures: candidates for public office,[62] a retired general who spoke for right-wing causes,[63] a real estate developer,[64] and a university athletic director.[65] The Court justified making it harder for public figures to win libel suits by saying that they sometimes influence public policy as much as public officials do. They also are newsworthy enough to get coverage to rebut any false charges against them.

The Burger Court was less inclined to consider various persons public figures,[66] but it maintained the core of the Warren Court's doctrine, which shifted the emphasis from protection of personal reputation to protection of press freedom.

This shift in emphasis has aided the press tremendously at a time when its coverage of controversial

The Internet enables people to get pornography in the privacy of their home, without having to go to a seedy adult bookstore or movie theater and without risking the embarrassment that might occur. Users can type in key words, such as *sex*, and easily find their way to "Bianca's Smut Shack." Perusing pornography is one of the most common, if not the most common, recreational uses of computers. (At one university, thirteen of the forty most visited sites had names like "rec.arts.erotica.")[1] Much of this pornography depicts sex with children or animals or other deviant practices such as bondage or sadomasochism.

Shocked by the amount and the nature of online pornography, and worried about its availability to children, Congress passed the Communications Decency Act in 1996. The law prohibited people from knowingly circulating "obscene" or "indecent" material online "in a manner available" to those under eighteen. Thus, the law banned sexual material that would be defined, under existing law, as "obscene" and additional material that would be considered "indecent." However, the latter was not clearly defined.[2]

A coalition of forty-seven groups filed suit to have the law declared unconstitutional. These included the ACLU, the American Library Association, and the computer companies Microsoft and America Online. The U.S. Chamber of Commerce filed a supplementary brief arguing that the law threatened corporations' ability to compete globally in an age of new communications.

The new technology of the Internet has made the old laws under the First Amendment difficult to apply. A commentator observed that "it's one thing to support the free speech rights of bookstore owners, quite another to have an 'XXX' store open at the end of the block, and still another to have its contents available in your rumpus room."[3]

So what precedents should apply? Is the Internet like the print media, which have substantial freedom so long as they do not publish the narrow category of sexual material defined as obscenity? Or is the Internet more like the broadcast media, which have less freedom because they are pervasive and reach into people's homes? Or, because the goal is to protect children, is the law more analogous to child pornography laws that prohibit a broader range of material than regular obscenity laws?

A lower federal court recognized that the Internet is a different medium and is, in fact, the most participatory speech medium yet developed. As such, the judges concluded, it should be nurtured, not stifled. In 1997 the Supreme Court, in its initial effort to apply the First Amendment to cyberspace, agreed.[4] It did not want the Internet censored more than other media. Thus, the Internet would receive as much protection as books, magazines, and newspapers (and more than radio and television). As a result, the portion of the law banning "obscene" material was upheld, while the portion banning additional "indecent" material was struck down. This portion was too broad and too ambiguous. It might lead to prosecution of people for discussing homosexuality or prison rape. It could even lead to prosecution of parents for sending their child information about birth control. Or the stiff penalties, two years in prison and a $250,000 fine, might cause people to avoid subjects they should feel free to address. Then the law would have a chilling effect on speech, which the First Amendment is supposed to guard against.

Although the goal of protecting children was worthy, the justices said, the result would be to prevent adults from communicating with each other, because the nature of the Internet made it impossible to know who might receive the material. Adults might be prosecuted if children obtained the material even though the adults were unaware that the children were doing so.

The Court took a bold step. But, of course, this was just a first step. Evolving technology will force the Court to take more steps in coming years.

1. Philip Elmer-DeWitt, "On a Screen near You: Cyberporn," *Time*, July 3, 1995.
2. In one section, the law vaguely referred to images of "sexual or excretory activities."
3. John Schwartz, "The New Cultural Battleground Comes with a Mouse," *Washington Post National Weekly Edition*, February 23, 1998, p. 22.
4. *Reno v. American Civil Liberties Union*, 138 L.Ed.2d 874 (1997).

Free Exercise of Religion

The **free exercise clause** allows individuals to practice their religion without government coercion. Government occasionally has restricted free exercise of religion directly. Early in the country's history, some states prohibited Catholics or Jews from voting or holding office, and as late as 1961 Maryland prohibited nonbelievers from holding office.[79] In the 1920s, Oregon prohibited students from attending parochial schools.[80] More recently, prisons in Illinois and Texas prohibited Black

Muslims and Buddhists from receiving religious publications and using the prison chapel.[81] The Supreme Court invalidated each of these restrictions.

Government also has restricted free exercise of religion indirectly. As society has become more complex, some laws inevitably have interfered with religion, even when not designed to. The laws usually have interfered with minority religions, which do not have many members in legislatures looking out for their interests.

At first the Court distinguished between belief and action: individuals could believe what they wanted, but they could not act accordingly if such action was against the law. In 1878, male Mormons who believed their religion required polygamy could not marry more than one woman.[82] The Court rhetorically asked, "Suppose one believed that human sacrifices were a necessary part of religious worship?" Of course, belief without action gave little protection and scant satisfaction to the individuals involved.

In the 1960s the Warren Court realized this and began to broaden protection by granting exemptions to laws. A Seventh-Day Adventist who worked in a textile mill in South Carolina quit when the mill shifted from a five- to six-day workweek that included Saturday—her Sabbath. Unable to find another job, she applied for unemployment benefits, but the state refused to provide them. To receive them she had to be "available" for work, and the state said she was not available because she would not accept jobs that required Saturday work. The Court ordered the state to grant an exemption to its law.[83] The Burger Court ruled that employers need to make a reasonable effort to accommodate employees' request to fit work schedules around their Sabbath.[84]

Amish in Wisconsin withheld their children from high school, although the law required attendance until age sixteen. The parents sent their children to elementary and junior high school to learn basic reading, writing, and arithmetic, but they complained that high school would subject their children to worldly influences that would interfere with their semi-isolated agricultural life. The Warren Court ruled that the Amish could be exempt from the additional one to two years the law required beyond junior high school.[85]

Congress, too, has granted some exemptions. It excused the Amish from participating in the Social Security program, because the Amish support their own elderly. And in every draft law it excused conscientious objectors from participating in war.

The Court has been most reluctant to exempt individuals from paying taxes. It did not excuse either the Amish[86] or Quakers, who as pacifists tried to withhold the portion of their income taxes that would go to the military.[87] The Court worried that many other persons would try to avoid paying taxes, too.

The Rehnquist Court has been especially reluctant to grant exemptions.[88] The Native American church uses peyote, a hallucinogen from a cactus, in worship ceremonies. Members believe the plant embodies their deity and eating it is an act of communion. Although peyote is a controlled substance, Congress has authorized its use on Indian reservations, and almost half the states have authorized its use off reservations by members of the church. But when two members in Oregon, a state that did not allow its use off reservations, were fired from their jobs and denied unemployment benefits for using the substance, the Court refused to grant them an exemption.[89] A five-justice majority rejected the doctrine and precedents of the Warren and Burger Courts. Justice Scalia, a Catholic, admitted that denying exemptions will put minority religions at a disadvantage but said that this is an "unavoidable consequence of democratic government." That is, denying minority rights is acceptable because of majority rule. This rationale, of course, could be used to emasculate not only the free exercise clause but other provisions of the Bill of Rights as well.

Alfred Smith, fired for using peyote in religious ceremonies, challenged Oregon's law.
© Phil Schofield

Although Congress overturned the narrow focus of the decision, involving Indians' use of peyote,[90] the broad implications of the decision remained. Some adherents of minority religions were not allowed to practice the tenets of those religions. Families of deceased Jews and Laotian immigrants who reject autopsies on religious grounds were overruled. Muslim prisoners whose religion forbids them from eating pork were refused other meat instead. Members of the Sikh religion, who wear turbans, had been exempted from the federal law requiring construction workers to wear hard hats, but the Occupational Safety and Health Administration (OSHA) rescinded the exemption in the wake of the ruling.[91]

Even mainstream churches worried about the implications of the ruling, and a coalition of religious groups lobbied Congress to overturn it. Congress passed and President Clinton signed an act that reversed the ruling and substituted the previous doctrine. But in 1997 the Rehnquist Court invalidated the act because it challenged their authority and altered their interpretation of the First Amendment without going through the process required to amend the Constitution.[92]

Establishment of Religion

Two competing traditions regarding the role of government have led to conflict over the **establishment clause.** Many early settlers in America wanted government to reinforce their religion, yet the framers of the Constitution were products of the Enlightenment, which emphasized the importance of reason and de-emphasized the role of organized religion. The two individuals most responsible for the religious guarantees in the First Amendment, Jefferson and Madison, feared the divisiveness of religion. They wanted strict separation of church and state, advocating not only freedom *of* religion for believers but freedom *from* religion for others.[93]

Early decisions by the Supreme Court usually reflected the first of these traditions. In 1892, Justice David Brewer smugly declared that "this is a Christian nation."[94] But as the country became more pluralistic, the Court moved toward the second of these traditions. Since the early 1960s, the Court generally has interpreted the establishment clause not only to forbid government from designating an official church, like the Church of England in England, but also to forbid government from aiding one religion over another or even from aiding religion over nonreligion.

Courts have used the clause to resolve disputes about prayer in public schools. In 1962 and 1963, the Supreme Court issued its famous (or infamous) prayer rulings. New York had students recite a nondenominational prayer at the start of every day, and Pennsylvania and Baltimore had students recite the "Lord's Prayer" or Bible verses. The Court, with only one justice dissenting, ruled that these practices violated the establishment clause.[95] The prayers technically were voluntary; students could leave the room. But the Court doubted that the prayers really were voluntary. It noted that nonconforming students would face tremendous pressure from

The country's religious diversity has led to demands for some exotic exemptions. Inspired by the Bible's statement that Jesus' followers "shall take up serpents" and "if they drink any deadly thing, it shall not hurt them," members of the Holiness Church of God in Jesus' Name handle snakes and drink strychnine. Some become enraptured and entranced to the point of hysteria, and occasionally some die. In 1975 the Tennessee Supreme Court forbade such practices, saying that the state has "the right to guard against the unnecessary creation of widows and orphans." However, the practices continue in some places.
Courtesy of National Archives

A mosque in an Ohio cornfield reflects our religious pluralism.
Peter Yates/SABA

teachers and peers, and that leaving the room usually connotes punishment for bad behavior. Thus, the Court said the prayers fostered religion. According to Justice Black, "Government in this country should stay out of the business of writing and sanctioning official prayers and leave that purely religious function to the people themselves and to those the people choose to look to for religious guidance." Schools could teach about religion, but they could not promote it.

For similar reasons the Court ruled that Kentucky could not require public schools to post the Ten Commandments in classrooms.[96]

Many people sharply criticized the rulings. A representative from Alabama lamented, "They put the Negroes in the schools, and now they've driven God out."[97] Actually, the justices had not driven God out because students could pray on their own anytime they felt the need.

A survey of teachers two years after the rulings found that prayers and Bible readings had decreased but by no means disappeared. Schools in the West, East, and, to a lesser extent, the Midwest generally complied with the rulings, but schools in the South overwhelmingly refused to.[98] For example, just 1 of 121 districts in Tennessee fully complied. A local official said, "I saw no reason to create controversy," and another asserted, "I am of the opinion that 99% of the people in the United States feel as I do about the Supreme Court's decision—that it was an outrage. . . . The remaining 1% do not belong in this free world."[99]

Despite the passage of time, periodic news reports indicate that many schools, especially in the rural South, still use prayers or Bible readings in violation of the Court's rulings. These practices are reinforced by social pressure. In 1993 a woman whose family had moved to Pontotoc, Mississippi, to be near relatives discovered that Christian prayers were being broadcast on the intercom and the Bible was being taught in a class. When she objected, rumors circulated that she was an outside agitator paid by the ACLU to force the town to change. One of her children said his teacher told the class that he did not believe in God, while another of her children said he kept "getting jumped" in the bathroom. Then the woman lost her job in a convenience store after customers threatened to boycott the store.[100]

Congress considered a constitutional amendment to overturn the rulings but did not pass one for several reasons. Some people support the rulings. Others support the Court and do not want to challenge its authority and thereby set a precedent for other groups on other matters. Some religious leaders doubt that groups would ever agree about specific prayers. America's religious diversity means that the prayers would offend some students or parents. Prayers that suit Christians might not suit Jews; those that suit Jews might not suit persons of other faiths. Recent immigrants from Asia and the Middle East, practicing Buddhism, Shintoism, Taoism, and Islam, have made the country even more pluralistic. Now, according to one researcher, America's religious diversity is greater than that of any country in recorded history.[101] Thus, asking students in this country to say a prayer would be like "asking the members of the United Nations to stand and sing the national anthem of one country."[102] Other religious leaders expect that officials anxious to avoid controversy would adopt the religious equivalent of canned peas—bland and watered-down prayers. They also expect that prayers would become rote exercises while students were daydreaming or checking out their classmates. In either event, the prayers would trivialize religious faith.

In lieu of an amendment, about half the states have passed laws providing for a "moment of silence" to begin each school day. Although the laws ostensibly are for meditation, some legislators admit they really are for prayer. The Supreme Court invalidated Alabama's law that authorized a moment of silence "for meditation or voluntary prayer" because the wording of the law endorsed and promoted prayer.[103] Yet a majority of justices indicated that they would approve a moment of silence if students were not encouraged to pray.

Although the Rehnquist Court's support for the prayer rulings was uncertain, the Court did reaffirm them and even extend them. It held that clergy cannot offer prayers at graduation ceremonies for public elementary, middle, and high schools.[104] The prayers in question were brief and nonsectarian, but the majority reasoned, "What to most believers may seem nothing more than a reasonable request that the nonbeliever respect their religious practices, in a school context may appear to the nonbeliever or dissenter to be an attempt to employ the machinery of the state to enforce a religious orthodoxy." Although attendance at the ceremony was voluntary, like participation in school prayers, the majority did not consider it truly voluntary. Justice Kennedy wrote, "Everyone knows that in our society and in our culture high school graduation is one of life's most significant occasions. . . . Graduation is a time for family and those closest to the student to celebrate success and express mutual wishes of gratitude and respect. . . ." The Court's decision was by a bare majority, but the opinion's wording was emphatic.

The Court's stance on student-led prayers at graduation, however, is ambiguous. In 1992, the Court refused to review a federal court of appeals ruling that allowed student-led prayers at graduation ceremonies.[105] A Texas school board permitted the senior class to decide whether to have a prayer and, if so, which student to give it. The appellate court held that this policy was not precluded by the Supreme Court's ruling, because the decision was not made by officials and the prayer was not given by a clergy member, so there would not be any official coercion. But in 1996 the Court also refused to review a federal court of appeals ruling from a different circuit that would prohibit student-led prayers at various school events.[106] The Court's reluctance to resolve this controversy means that the ruling of each court of appeals remains but applies only to schools in its circuit, and that no appellate ruling governs schools in the rest of the country.

The first appellate court's holding encouraged opponents of the Supreme Court's school prayer rulings to use the same approach to circumvent these rulings as well. Several southern states passed laws allowing student-led prayers. Some school officials, who selected the students, let them give the prayers over the intercom. Federal courts in Alabama and Mississippi invalidated these laws, because school officials were involved and because all students were required or at least pressured to listen to the prayers.

In 2000, the Rehnquist Court invalidated the use of schools' public address systems by clergy or students to give prayers at high school football games.[106a] Although student attendance is voluntary, the games are official school events.

The public demand is fueled by the symbolism of school prayer and a nostalgia for the less troubling times before the 1960s. As one writer perceived, the demand "doesn't have much to do with prayer anyway, but with a time, a place, an ethos that praying and pledging allegiance at the beginning of school each day represent."[107] Many people echo the feelings of a Pennsylvania school board member who said, "The country has certainly gone downhill since they took it out."[108] For these people, reinstitutionalization of school prayer would be a symbol that our society stands for appropriate values. For some religious leaders, however, calls for school prayer are "a cynical exploitation" of the public by politicians who imply that "two-minute pieties" will make up for the decline of values in society.[109]

The public demand is also aggravated by occasional reports of school officials who mistakenly believe that court rulings require them to forbid all forms of religious expression. Thus, some confused administrators have prohibited a few students from wearing religious jewelry, reading the Bible while riding the bus, and praying before eating their lunch.[110]

In another case, the Supreme Court said that the University of Missouri at Kansas City had to make its meeting rooms available to students' religious organizations on an equal basis with other organizations, even if the religious organizations used the rooms for prayer or worship.[111] Otherwise, the university would be discriminating against religion. After this decision, Congress passed a law that requires public high schools as well to allow meetings of students' religious, philosophical, or political groups outside class hours. The Court accepted this law in 1990.[112] Justice O'Connor said high school students "are likely to understand that a school does not endorse or support student speech that it merely permits on a nondiscriminatory basis." Students have established Bible clubs in a quarter of the public schools, according to one estimate.[113] (As a result of this act, students have also established gay-straight clubs—organizations of gay and straight students who support the rights of gays, lesbians, and bisexuals—in more than seven hundred high schools.[114]) Yet students' desires for Bible clubs have not always been the driving force. Adults who are anxious to put prayers back into the schools have often taken the initiative. Organized networks encourage the clubs and provide advice, workshops, and handbooks for them.

The Rehnquist Court also said that the University of Virginia had to provide funding, from students' fees, to students' religious organizations on an equal basis with other campus organizations, even if a religious organization sought the money to print a religious newspaper.[115] On the basis of this precedent, a federal court of appeals ruled that the University of South Alabama had to provide funding to a gay organization.

Despite its prayer rulings, the Court has been reluctant to invalidate traditional religious symbols. It has not questioned the motto "In God We Trust," on our money since 1865, or the phrase "One nation under God" in the Pledge of Allegiance since 1954.

The Burger Court upheld the display of a nativity scene on government property, at least if it is part of a broader display for the holiday season.[116] Pawtucket, Rhode Island, had a crèche, Santa Claus, sleigh with reindeer, Christmas tree, and talking wishing well. Although the nativity scene was an obvious symbol of Christianity, the Court said it was a traditional symbol of a holiday that has become secular as well as religious. Moreover, the presence of the secular decorations diluted any religious impact the nativity scene would have. A crèche by itself, however, would be impermissible.[117]

Courts have also used the establishment clause to resolve disputes about teaching evolution in schools. In 1968, the Supreme Court invalidated Arkansas's forty-year-old law forbidding schools from teaching evolution.[118] Arkansas and Louisiana then passed laws requiring schools that teach evolution to also teach "creationism"—the biblical version of creation.[119] In 1987, the Court invalidated these laws, because their purpose was to promote the fundamentalist Christian view.[120] Yet teaching evolution remains controversial.

A Christian Bible club meets in a Minneapolis school.
Steve Liss/*Time* magazine

What about the Second Amendment?

Individuals and interest groups opposed to gun control cite the **Second Amendment,** which provides "the right of the people to keep and bear arms." But these opponents seldom quote the rest of the amendment, which reads in its entirety, "A well regulated militia, being necessary to the security of a free state, the right of the people to keep and bear arms, shall not be infringed." The amendment was adopted at a time when there was no standing army to protect people from foreign invasions, Indian uprisings, or mob riots. The language links the right to bear arms with the security of the state. The language suggests that the right belongs to each state or, if to individuals, only to individuals when they are protecting their state—that is, when they are serving in the militia of their state. Today the militia is the National Guard in each state. The National Guard does not require members to furnish their own weapons. Therefore, the amendment might be a useless anachronism.

"You know, if she weren't part of a well-regulated militia I'd be a little nervous."

Accordingly, the federal courts routinely uphold gun control laws when they are challenged as violations of the Second Amendment. The Supreme Court rarely reviews these decisions, even one in which an appellate court allowed a Chicago suburb to ban possession of handguns.[1]

Many science teachers skip it to avoid confrontations with conservative parents or religious groups.[121]

Courts have also used the establishment clause to resolve disputes about aid to parochial schools. Historically most parochial schools were Catholic schools. Protestants opposed aid to these schools because they feared growth of the Catholic church. But changes in society, beginning with the desegregation of public schools, prompted more Protestants to form their own schools.[122] Now millions of students attend either Catholic or Protestant schools, and their parents pay tuition and other expenses. Schools have asked legislatures to provide money to defray part of the costs of their nonreligious activities. Courts have had to decide whether providing the money helps religion or whether denying it hinders religion. In addition, courts have had to determine if providing the money leads to excessive entanglement of church and state because of the monitoring required to ensure that the money is not spent for religious purposes.

The Court has upheld some types of aid[123] but has rejected most types.[124] Yet the Court, reflecting shifting coalitions of justices, has not drawn a clear line separating permissible from impermissible forms of assistance.[125]

Despite frequent tensions and periodic conflicts, the effort to separate church and state over the years has enabled the United States to manage, and even nourish, its religious pluralism. The effort has kept much religious debate and potential religious fights out of the political arena. But this practical arrangement is opposed primarily by religious conservatives, whether Protestant, Catholic, or Jewish, who most fear the changes in modern society. They believe that their religion is so important that it should be reinforced by the government.

Conservative Chief Justice Warren Burger criticized the National Rifle Association for misleading people by insisting that the Second Amendment right should prevent gun control legislation. He said the amendment "has been the subject of one of the greatest pieces of fraud—I repeat the word 'fraud'—on the American public."[2]

Yet the persistent views of the American public have prompted legal scholars to take a closer look at the adoption of the Second Amendment. Some have concluded that there might be a right for individuals, separate from the right for states and National Guards, to own and use guns. Their rationale is that the original notion of a militia encompassed all individuals who had political rights, such as the right to vote in elections and serve on juries—that is, all white males who owned property. Today individuals who have political rights include all adult citizens (except

felons in most states). Thus, the word *militia* in 1791 might mean all adult citizens today. However, this expanded view of the Second Amendment would provide a right only for individuals to own and use guns to defend their state or, possibly, their homes or themselves.[3] It would not provide a right to own and use guns for hunting or other recreational purposes because the language—"the security of a free state"—indicates that the justification for the right is just protection.

Even if this expanded view of the Second Amendment becomes more common, it would not bar most gun control proposals. The amendment refers to a "well regulated militia," making clear that arms can be regulated (as they were even in colonial times). As Justice Stevens observed, arms have "long been subject to pervasive governmental regulation because of the dangerous nature of the product

and the public interest in having that danger controlled."[4]

So a huge gap remains between what many people think and what most judges and legal scholars have concluded.

1. *Quilici v. Morton Grove*, 695 F.2d 261 (7th Cir., 1982). A federal district court did make headlines in 1999 when it ruled unconstitutional a federal law that prohibits a person under a restraining order from owning a gun. This apparently was the first time a court struck down a law because it infringed on the Second Amendment.
2. Joan Biskupic, "A Second (Amendment) Look at Bearing Arms," *Washington Post National Weekly Edition,* May 15–21, 1995, p. 33.
3. In the original debate over the proposed amendment, the framers apparently never discussed the use of firearms for personal protection. Garry Wills, *A Necessary Evil: A History of American Distrust* (New York: Simon & Schuster, 1999).
4. *U.S. v. Thompson/Center Arms Co.,* 504 U.S. 505, 526 (1992).
SOURCE: Except where noted, Laurence H. Tribe, *American Constitutional Law,* 3d ed., vol. 1 (New York: Foundation Press, 2000), 894–903.

Rights of Criminal Defendants

The Fourth, Fifth, Sixth, and Eighth Amendments provide numerous **due process** rights for criminal defendants. When the government prosecutes defendants, it must give them the process—that is, the procedures—they are due; it must be fair and "respect certain decencies of civilized conduct,"[126] even toward uncivilized people.

One defense attorney said many of his clients "had been monsters—nothing less—who had done monstrous things. Although occasionally not guilty of the crime charged, nearly all my clients have been guilty of something."[127] Then why do we give them rights? The reason is that we give all individuals rights. As Justice Douglas observed, "respecting the dignity even of the least worthy citizen . . . raises the stature of all of us."[128]

But why do we give all individuals rights? We do so because we have established the **presumption of innocence.** This presumption is "not . . . a naive belief that most or even many defendants are innocent, or a cavalier attitude toward crime. It reflects mistrust of the state. Requiring the state to prove guilt is a way of saying, 'We won't take your word for it.' "[129] Of course, when the crime rate is high or a crime is particularly heinous, many people fear the state less than the criminals. Then they want to give officials more authority and defendants fewer rights. But this is the way people eventually lose rights.

Search and Seizure

England fostered the notion that a family's home is its castle, but Parliament made exceptions for the American colonies. It authorized writs of assistance, which allowed customs officials to conduct general searches for goods imported by colonists without paying taxes to the crown. The English tradition combined with the colonists' resentment of the writs of assistance led to adoption of the Fourth Amendment, which forbids **unreasonable searches and seizures.**

One type of seizure is the arrest of a person. Police must have evidence to believe that a person committed a crime. Another type of seizure is the confiscation of illegal contraband. The general requirement is that police should get a search warrant from a judge by showing evidence that a particular thing is in a particular place.

However, the Supreme Court has made exceptions to this requirement that complicate the law. These exceptions account for the vast majority of searches. If persons consent to a search, police can conduct one without a warrant. If police see contraband in plain view, they can seize it; they do not need to close their eyes to it. If police have suspicion that a person is committing a crime but lack evidence to arrest him, they can "stop and frisk" the person—give him a pat-down search. If police have evidence to arrest someone, they can search her and the area within her control. If police face an emergency situation, they can search for weapons. If police want to search motor vehicles in some situations, they can do so because vehicles are mobile and could be gone by the time police get a warrant.

Customs and border patrol officials can search persons and things coming into the country to enforce customs and immigration laws. Airport guards can search passengers and luggage to prevent hijackings. And prison guards can search prisoners to ensure security.

These are all general principles that need to be interpreted in specific cases. The law is so complex that it is difficult to determine the legality of many searches and seizures.

In defining reasonable and unreasonable searches and seizures, the Court has tried to walk a fine line between acknowledging officials' need for evidence and persons' need for privacy.

Exclusionary Rule

To enforce search and seizure law, the Court has established the **exclusionary rule,** which bars from court any evidence obtained in violation of the Fourth Amendment. The rule's goal is to deter police from illegal conduct.

Although the Court issued the rule for federal courts in 1914,[130] it did not impose the rule on state courts until 1961. Even so, the Warren Court's decision, in the case of *Mapp v. Ohio,*[131] was one of its most controversial. Until this time, police in many states had ignored search and seizure law.

The decision still has not been widely accepted. The Burger Court created an exception to it. In a pair of cases, the justices allowed evidence obtained illegally to be used in court because the police had acted in "good faith."[132]

Electronic Surveillance

The Fourth Amendment traditionally applied to searches involving a physical trespass and seizures producing a tangible object. Electronic surveillance, however, does not require a physical trespass or result in a tangible object.

This posed a problem for the Supreme Court when it heard its first wiretapping case in 1928. Federal prohibition agents tapped the telephone of bootleggers by installing equipment on wires in the basement of the bootleggers' apartment building. The majority of the Court rigidly adhered to its traditional doctrine, saying this was not a search and seizure so the agents did not need a warrant.[133]

In a classic example of keeping the Constitution up to date, the Warren Court overruled this precedent in 1967.[134] Because electronic eavesdropping might threaten privacy as much as traditional searching, officials must get judicial authorization, similar to a warrant, to engage in such eavesdropping.

Yet judicial authorization is easy to get. In a recent four-year period, the FBI requested 2,686 wiretaps, and the courts granted all but one.[135]

Self-Incrimination

The Fifth Amendment provides that persons shall not be compelled to be witnesses against themselves, that is, to incriminate themselves. Because defendants are presumed innocent, the government must prove their guilt.

This right means that defendants on trial do not have to take the witness stand and answer questions, and neither prosecutor nor judge can call attention to their failure to do so. Neither can suggest that defendants must have something to hide and thereby imply that they must be guilty. (But if defendants do take the stand and testify, this constitutes a waiver of their right, so the prosecutor can cross-examine them and they must answer.)

This right also means that prosecutors cannot introduce into evidence any statements or confessions from defendants that were not voluntary. However, the meaning of "voluntary" has changed over time.

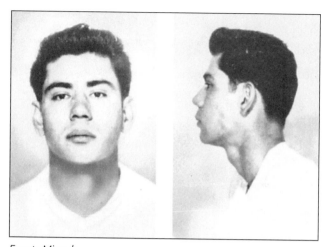

Ernesto Miranda.
Mark Solomon/*Time* magazine

- You have the right to remain silent.
- If you talk, anything you say can be used against you.
- You have the right to be represented by an attorney.
- If you cannot afford an attorney, one will be appointed for you.

The Burger and Rehnquist courts have not required police and prosecutors to follow *Miranda* as strictly as the Warren Court did but, contrary to expectations, have not abandoned *Miranda*. In 2000, the Rehnquist Court reaffirmed *Miranda* by a 7–2 vote.[141]

Even with the warnings, many suspects talk anyway. Some do not understand the warnings. Others think police, who rattle off the warnings fast or in a monotone, give them only because they are required to, not because they actually mean them. Also, all suspects in an interrogation are in a coercive atmosphere and face tactics designed to exploit their weaknesses.

Counsel

The Sixth Amendment provides the **right to counsel** in criminal cases. Initially, it permitted defendants to hire an attorney to help them prepare a defense, and later it permitted defendants to have the attorney represent them at trial. But it was no help to most defendants because they were too poor to hire an attorney.

Consequently, the Supreme Court required federal courts to furnish an attorney to all indigent defendants as long ago as 1938.[142] But most criminal cases are state cases, and although the Court required state courts to furnish an attorney in some cases, it was reluctant to impose a broad requirement on these courts.[143]

In 1963, the Warren Court accepted the appeal of Clarence Earl Gideon. Charged with breaking into a pool hall and stealing beer, wine, and change from a vending machine, Gideon asked the judge for a lawyer. The judge refused to appoint one, leaving Gideon to defend himself. The prosecutor did not have a strong case, but Gideon was not able to point out its weaknesses. He was convicted and sentenced to five years. On appeal, the Warren Court unanimously declared that Gideon was entitled to be represented by counsel.[144] Justice Black explained that "lawyers in criminal courts are necessities, not luxuries." The Court finally established a broad rule: State courts must provide an attorney to indigent defendants in felony cases.

Gideon proved the Court's point. Given a lawyer and retried, he was not convicted. The lawyer did the effective

For years law enforcement officials used physical brutality—"the third degree"—to get confessions. After 1936, when the Supreme Court ruled that confessions obtained this way were invalid,[136] officials resorted to more subtle techniques. They held suspects incommunicado, so the suspects could not notify anyone about their arrest, and delayed bringing them to court, so the judge could not inform them of their rights.[137] Officials interrogated suspects for long periods of time without food or rest, in one case with alternating teams of interrogators for thirty-six hours.[138] They tricked suspects. In one case, police told a man they would jail his wife if he did not talk, although they knew she was not involved, and in another they told a woman they would take away her welfare benefits and even her children if she did not talk, although they did not have authority to do either.[139] The Court ruled that these techniques, designed to break the suspects' will, were psychological coercion, so the confessions were invalid.

The Warren Court still worried that many confessions were not truly voluntary, so it issued a landmark decision in 1966. Arizona police arrested a poor, mentally disturbed man, Ernesto Miranda, for kidnapping and raping a woman. After the woman identified him in a lineup, police interrogated him for two hours, prompting him to confess. He had not been told that he could remain silent or be represented by an attorney. In *Miranda v. Arizona,* the Court decided that his confession was not truly voluntary.[140] Chief Justice Warren, himself a former district attorney, noted the tremendous advantage police have in interrogation and said suspects needed more protection. The Court ruled that officials must advise suspects of their rights before interrogation. These came to be known as the **Miranda rights:**

When a Court Reverses a Conviction . . .

. . . the defendant does not necessarily go free. An appellate court normally only evaluates the legality of the procedures used by officials; it does not determine guilt or innocence. Therefore, when it reverses a conviction, it only indicates that officials used some illegal proce- dure in convicting the defendant—for example, they may have used evidence from an improper search and seizure. Then the prosecutor can retry the defendant, without this evidence, if the prosecutor thinks there is enough other evidence. Often prosecutors do retry the defendants, and in about half the cases judges or juries reconvict them.[1]

1. Robert T. Roper and Albert P. Malone, "Does Procedural Due Process Make a Difference? A Study of Second Trials," *Judicature* 65 (1981): 136–141.

job defending him that he had not been able to do himself. (See also "When a Court Reverses a Conviction . . . .")

In 1972, the Burger Court expanded the rule: State courts must provide an attorney to indigent defendants in misdemeanor cases too, except those that result in no incarceration at all,[145] because even misdemeanor cases are too complex for defendants to defend themselves. In addition, the Court decided that courts must provide an attorney for one appeal.[146]

Receiving counsel does not necessarily mean receiving effective counsel, however. Some assigned attorneys are inexperienced, some are incompetent, and most are overworked and have little time to prepare the best possible defense.

Some places make little effort to provide effective counsel, even in murder cases where capital punishment looms. In Illinois, at least thirty-three convicts on death row had been represented at trial by attorneys who later were disbarred or suspended.[147] In Louisiana, a defendant was represented by an attorney who was living with the prosecutor in the case. In Florida, a defendant was represented by an attorney who was a deputy sheriff at the time. In Georgia, a black defendant was represented by a white attorney who had been the Imperial Wizard of the local Ku Klux Klan for fifty years.[148] In another case from Georgia, the attorney was so unversed in criminal law that when he was asked to name criminal rulings he was familiar with, he could think of only one (*Miranda*).[149] In three murder cases in one recent year in Texas, defense attorneys slept through the trials. When one of these defendants appealed his conviction on the ground that he did not receive his constitutional right to counsel, the appellate court announced that "the Constitution doesn't say the lawyer has to be awake."[150] At least he was present. In Alabama, a defendant was represented by an attorney who failed to appear when his case was argued before the state supreme court. The defendant lost and was executed.[151]

There is so little effort to provide effective counsel because no powerful constituency urges adequate representation. Criminal defendants have no political power in our system, and the public has little sympathy for their rights. Government responds to the public by increasing the funding for prosecutors while ignoring the quality of representation for defendants.[152]

Jury Trial

The Sixth Amendment also provides the **right to a jury trial** in "serious" criminal cases. The Supreme Court has defined "serious" cases as those that could result in more than six months' incarceration.[153]

The right was adopted to prevent oppression by a "corrupt or overzealous prosecutor" or a "biased . . . or eccentric judge."[154] It also has served to limit governmental use of unpopular laws or enforcement practices. Regardless of the extent of evidence against a defendant, a jury can refuse to convict if it feels the government has overstepped its bounds.

The jury is to be "impartial," so persons who have made up their minds before trial should be dismissed. It also is to be "a fair cross section" of the community, so no group should be systematically excluded.[155] But the jury need not be a perfect cross section and, in fact, need not have a single member of a particular group.[156] Most courts use voter registration lists to obtain names of potential jurors. These lists are not truly representative because poor people do not register at the same rate as others, but courts have decided that the lists are sufficiently representative. And Congress passed and President Clinton signed the "motor voter bill," which requires drivers' license and welfare offices to offer voter registration forms. Presumably, more poor people will register and be eligible to serve on juries.

Cruel and Unusual Punishment

The Eighth Amendment forbids **cruel and unusual punishment** but does not define it. The Supreme Court had defined it as torture or any punishment grossly disproportionate to the offense, but the Court had seldom used the provision until applying it to capital punishment in the 1970s.

Because the death penalty was used at the time the amendment was adopted and had been used ever since, it was assumed to be constitutional.[157] But the Burger Court, albeit with Chief Justice Burger and the other three Nixon appointees in dissent, held that capital punishment as it was then being administered was cruel and unusual.[158] The Court said the laws and procedures allowed too much discretion for those who administered

the punishment and too much arbitrariness and discrimination for those who received it. It was imposed so seldom, according to Justice Potter Stewart, that it was "cruel and unusual in the same way that being struck by lightning is cruel and unusual." Yet when imposed, it was given to blacks disproportionately to their convictions for murder.

The decision invalidated the laws of forty states and commuted the death sentences of 629 inmates. But because the Court did not hold capital punishment cruel and unusual in principle, about three-fourths of the states adopted new laws that permitted less discretion in an effort to be less arbitrary and discriminatory.

These changes satisfied a majority of the Court, which ruled that capital punishment is not cruel and unusual for murder if administered fairly.[159] But the death penalty cannot be imposed automatically for everyone convicted of murder, for the judge or jury must consider any mitigating factors that would call for a lesser punishment.[160]

Clarence Earl Gideon, convinced he was denied a fair trial because he was not given an attorney, read law books in prison so he could petition the Supreme Court for a writ of certiorari. Although he had spent much of his life in prison, he was optimistic. "I believe that each era finds an improvement in law each year brings something new for the benefit of mankind [sic]. Maybe this will be one of those small steps forward."

Both courtesy of the National Archives.

Also, capital punishment cannot be imposed for rape, because it is disproportionate to that offense.[161]

The new laws apparently have reduced but not eliminated discrimination. Although past studies showed discrimination against black defendants, recent studies show discrimination against black or white defendants who murder whites. People who affect the decision to impose the death penalty—prosecutors, defense attorneys, judges, and jurors—appear to value white lives more. Despite evidence that in Georgia those who kill whites are more than four times as likely to be given the death penalty as those who kill blacks, the Rehnquist Court, by a five to four vote, upheld capital punishment in the state.[162]

The new laws have not addressed an equally serious problem: the inadequate representation provided for poor defendants who face the death penalty.

In recent decades, the primary criticism against capital punishment was that it discriminated against racial minorities and the poor. Although the punishment is irrevocable, most people dismissed any suggestions that innocent defendants might be put to death. They assumed that criminal justice systems used careful procedures and made no mistakes in these cases at least. However, since capital punishment was reinstated in the 1970s (with stricter procedures), eighty-five inmates awaiting execution have been released because new evidence, sometimes DNA tests, revealed their innocence.[163] Some were the victims of sloppy or biased police or overzealous prosecutors; others were the victims of emotional or prejudiced jurors. Many were the victims of inadequate representation.

Due to the patterns of racial discrimination and inadequate representation, the American Bar Association called for a moratorium on the use of capital punishment in 1997. After Illinois released its thirteenth innocent inmate from death row, most after investigations by Northwestern University journalism students, its governor announced a moratorium in 2000. Other states are considering similar moratoriums.

Rights in Theory and in Practice

Overall the Supreme Court has interpreted the Bill of Rights to provide an impressive list of rights for criminal defendants (although one of the greatest changes from the Warren Court to the Burger and Rehnquist Courts has been a decline in support for criminal defendants—see Figure 1). Yet not all rights are available for all defendants in all places. Some trial court judges,

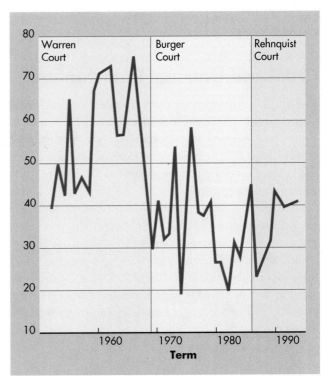

F I G U R E 1 ■ *Support for Rights of Criminal Defendants Has Declined* Percentage of Supreme Court criminal rights cases decided in favor of the defendant.

SOURCE: Lee Epstein, Jeffrey A. Segal, Harold J. Spaeth, and Thomas G. Walker, *The Supreme Court Compendium: Data, Decisions, and Developments,* 2d ed. (Washington, D.C.: Congressional Quarterly, 1996), Table 3-8.

prosecutors, and police do not comply with Supreme Court rulings. If defendants appeal to a high enough court, they probably will get their rights, but most defendants do not have the knowledge, the resources, or the perseverance to do this.

When rights are available, most defendants do not take advantage of them. About 90 percent of all criminal defendants plead guilty, and many of them do so as part of a **plea bargain.** This is an agreement between the prosecutor, the defense attorney, and the defendant, with the explicit or implicit approval of the judge, to reduce the charge or the sentence in exchange for a plea of guilty. A plea bargain is a compromise. For officials it saves the time, trouble, and uncertainty of a trial. For defendants it eliminates the fear of a harsher sentence. However, it also reduces due process rights. A plea of guilty waives defendants' rights to a trial by a jury of their peers, in which defendants can present their own witnesses and cross-examine the government's witnesses, and in which they cannot be forced to incriminate themselves. A plea of guilty also waives the right to counsel to some extent because most attorneys appointed to represent defendants are overworked and inclined to pressure defendants to plead guilty so they do not have to prepare a defense. Despite these disadvantages for due process rights, the Court allows plea bargaining because of its practical advantages.[164]

Right to Privacy

Neither the Constitution nor the Bill of Rights mentions "privacy." Nevertheless, the right to privacy, Justice Douglas noted, is "older than the Bill of Rights,"[165] and the framers undoubtedly assumed that people would have such a right. In fact, the framers did include amendments that reflect a concern for privacy: the First Amendment protects privacy of association; the Third, privacy of homes from quartering soldiers; the Fourth, privacy of persons and places where they live from searches and seizures; and the Fifth, privacy of knowledge or thoughts from compulsory self-incrimination. The Supreme Court would use these to establish an explicit **right to privacy.**

So far the Court's right-to-privacy doctrine reflects a right to autonomy—what Justice Louis Brandeis called "the right to be left alone"—more than a right to keep things confidential. As noted earlier in the chapter, the Court has been reluctant to punish the press for invasion of privacy.[166]

Birth Control

The Warren Court explicitly established a right to privacy in 1965 when it struck down a Connecticut law that prohibited distributing or using contraceptives.[167] To enforce the law the state would have had to police people's bedrooms, and the Court said the very idea of policing married couples' bedrooms was absurd. Then the Court struck down Massachusetts and New York laws that prohibited distributing contraceptives to unmarried persons.[168] "If the right of privacy means anything," Justice Brennan said, "it is the right of the individual, married or single, to be free from unwarranted governmental intrusion into matters so fundamentally affecting a person as the decision whether to bear or beget a child."[169]

Abortion

When twenty-one-year-old Norma McCorvey became pregnant in 1969, she was divorced and already had a five-

Norma McCorvey arrives at the U.S. Supreme Court April 26, 1989, before the justices heard a key abortion case from Missouri seeking to limit the landmark 1973 Roe v. Wade *decision. McCorvey was the Jane Roe in the case.*
AP/Wide World Photos

year-old daughter, and she sought an abortion. But Texas, where she lived, prohibited abortions unless the mother's life was in danger. She discovered, "No legitimate doctor in Dallas would touch me. . . . I found one doctor who offered to abort me for $500. Only he didn't have a license, and I was scared to turn my body over to him. So there I was—pregnant, unmarried, unemployed, alone, and stuck."[170]

Too poor to go to a state that permitted abortions, McCorvey decided to put her baby up for adoption. But the state law still rankled her. With the help of two women attorneys recently out of law school, she used her case to challenge Texas's law. She adopted the name Jane Roe to conceal her identity.

In *Roe v. Wade* in 1973, the Burger Court extended the right to privacy from birth control to abortion.[171] The majority concluded that because doctors, theologians, and philosophers cannot agree when life begins, judges should not assert that life begins at conception, thus deeming a fetus a person and abortion murder. Given the uncertainty as to when life begins, the majority decided that a woman's right to privacy of her body is paramount.

enough to make the decision herself. If she is not mature enough, she must become a mother. These laws, Justice Marshall wrote in dissent, force "a young woman in an already dire situation to choose between two fundamentally unacceptable alternatives: notifying a possibly dictatorial or even abusive parent or justifying her profoundly personal decision in an intimidating judicial proceeding to a black-robed stranger."

Pro-life groups advocated these laws with the expectation that they would result in fewer abortions. They believed that many teenagers would go to their parents rather than face the forbidding atmosphere of a court hearing and that their parents would persuade or pressure them not to have the abortion. Some evidence indicates that the laws have had this effect.[183]

When teenagers do go to court, they routinely get waivers in some states but not in others. The Nebraska Supreme Court ruled that a fifteen-year-old was too immature to decide to have an abortion, because although she could discuss the consequences of keeping the baby or giving it up for adoption, discuss her philosophy of abortion, and explain the procedures involved, she was unable to explain the risks involved.[184]

Then pro-life groups focused on one abortion procedure called "intact dilation and extraction" in medicine but referred to as "partial-birth abortion" in politics. In this procedure, a doctor delivers the fetus except for the head, punctures the skull and drains the contents, and then removes the fetus from the woman. The procedure is used occasionally for late-term abortions when other methods might be more dangerous for the woman. But because the procedure is more gruesome than other methods, pro-life groups used it to try to sway people who are undecided in the abortion debate. Numerous states passed laws banning the procedure, but the Supreme Court struck down Nebraska's law in 2000.[185] The five-justice majority said the law was too broad—the language might ban other methods as well—and this procedure might be the safest one sometimes.

Frustrated by the Court's refusal to overturn *Roe*, the pro-life movement adopted more militant tactics. Organizations such as Operation Rescue engage in civil disobedience, blockading clinics and harassing workers and patients as they come and go. Some organizations spray chemicals inside clinics, ruining carpets and fabrics and leaving a stench that makes the clinics unusable. Such incidents occurred fifty times in one year alone.[186]

Protesters in Charleston, South Carolina, distributed fliers in the city's poorest neighborhood encouraging residents to rob an abortion clinic: "The killers accept only cash! They kill about 60 babies each week. That is $16,500 of CASH taken to the bank each week. That means that an average of $5,500 is waiting there each day of business in cash before closing hours."[187]

Organizations also target doctors, nurses, and other workers of the clinics. Operation Rescue runs a training camp in Florida that instructs members how to use public records to locate personal information about employees, how to tail them to their homes, and how to organize demonstrations at their homes. Organizations put up "Wanted" posters, with a doctor's picture, name, address, and phone number. They encourage others to harass the doctor, his or her spouse, and even their children. (One thirteen-year-old was confronted in a restaurant and was told that he was going to burn in hell.)[188] Some activists have come out in favor of killing abortion doctors. One organization released a "deadly dozen" list of abortion doctors—practically a hit list. One minister wrote a book—*A Time to Kill*—and markets a bumper sticker—"EXECUTE ABORTION-ISTS-MURDERERS."[189]

In this climate, three doctors, two clinic receptionists, and one clinic volunteer have been killed, and seven other doctors, employees, and volunteers have been wounded.[190] Numerous clinics have been fire-bombed.

The tactics have had their intended effect on doctors.[191] They have made the practice of providing abortions seem dangerous and even undesirable. Fewer medical schools offer abortion classes, fewer hospitals provide abortion training, fewer doctors study abortion procedures, and fewer gynecologists and obstetricians, despite most being pro-choice, perform abortion operations.[192]

One pro-life leader proclaimed, "We've found the weak link is the doctor." Another observed, "When you get the doctors out, you can have all the laws on the books you want and it doesn't mean a thing."[193]

Abortions remain available in most metropolitan centers but not in most rural areas. Eighty-three percent of U.S. counties have no doctor who performs abortions. Some states have only one or two cities where women can obtain abortions.[194]

Despite the dissatisfaction of activists on both sides, it is worth noting that the unelected, nonmajoritarian Supreme Court has come closer to forging a policy reflective of public opinion than have most politicians. Polls show the majority of the people want to keep the right to abortion but would like to discourage it somewhat.[195] The Court's doctrine now essentially articulates this view.

Homosexuality

The Court has not extended the right to privacy to protect homosexual acts. Almost half the states have laws prohibiting sodomy—oral and anal sex.[196] Although these laws are primarily symbolic and rarely enforced, they can be invoked against either homosexuals or heterosexuals.[197] For example, when police delivered a summons to residents of a house and discovered them violating the law of Georgia, police arrested them. Although prosecutors did not file charges, one of the men sued to have the courts declare the law unconstitutional. In 1986, the Supreme Court, by a one-vote margin, refused to do so.[198]

Justice Powell believed the law was unconstitutional, but after voting against it in conference, he switched before the decision was announced in court because the man had not been prosecuted. After public reaction to the *Roe* ruling, Powell was leery of potential reaction to another controversial ruling, especially when the law might never be enforced. When he retired, however, he admitted he made a mistake.[199]

Although the Court has not extended the right to privacy to homosexual acts, it has struck down laws directed against homosexual individuals. Colorado voters adopted a constitutional amendment prohibiting laws that bar discrimination against homosexuals, but in 1996 the Court invalidated the amendment.[200] The majority said it was based on animus toward homosexuals. They were singled out and denied the opportunity, enjoyed by everyone else, to seek protection from discrimination. The ruling put the brakes on the movement to adopt similar provisions in other states.

© Los Angeles Times. Reprinted by permission.

Although some state and local legislatures have passed laws barring discrimination in employment, housing, credit, insurance, and public accommodations, in 1996 Congress, by one vote, rejected a bill barring discrimination in employment. At the same time, it passed the Defense of Marriage Act, which forbids federal recognition of same-sex marriages and thus denies federal benefits, such as Social Security, for same-sex couples. The act also allows states to disregard same-sex marriages performed in other states.[201] Thirty states have passed laws to do so.[202] (Under the full faith and credit clause of the Constitution, states normally must recognize the public records and judicial proceedings of other states.) The act was prompted by speculation that some states might approve same-sex marriages, thus allowing homosexual couples to get married in one of these states and then return to their home state as married couples.

Courts in Alaska and Hawaii did rule in favor of same-sex marriages, but their decisions were negated by voters in initiatives to restrict marriages to unions between men and women. However, the Vermont Supreme Court ruled that the state must either legalize same-sex marriages or equalize the benefits received by same-sex couples and traditional married couples. The legislature decided to equalize the benefits, such as family leave, bereavement leave, health insurance, pension benefits, and inheritance rights. To implement this policy, the legislature established "civil unions," with procedures for couples to become official partners (similar to marriage) and procedures for them to dissolve their relationship (similar to divorce). These civil unions provide most of what regular marriages would provide, except the unions do not apply to federal benefits and, for couples who move from Vermont, the unions do not apply in other states. Also, of course, the unions do not provide the same symbolism that the marriages would. Thus, homosexuals see them as a long stride but not the final step.

Congress also blocked President Clinton's pledge to issue an executive order barring discrimination against homosexuals in the military.[203] Since World War II, the military has rejected recruits who admit to being homosexual and discharged troops who are found to be homosexual. According to the military, having homosexuals in the trenches or on ships undermines the discipline and morale essential for combat.[204] However, when more troops were needed during the Korean, Vietnam, and Persian Gulf Wars, the military did not find this to be such a problem, as it relaxed its policy.[205] And most other democracies do not find this such a problem either. Western European countries, Canada, Japan, and Israel, which has a battle-tested military, tolerate homosexuals in their services.[206]

But strident opposition from military officials and members of Congress forced President Clinton to accept a compromise, a policy called "don't ask—don't tell." The military (including the Reserves and National Guard) is not allowed to ask questions about sexual orientation on enlistment or security questionnaires but is allowed to discharge members for statements admitting homosexuality or conduct reflecting homosexuality (or bisexuality). Such conduct is defined broadly to encompass not only sexual actions, but also holding hands, dancing, or trying to marry someone of the same sex. The restrictions apply off-base as well as on. They do not encompass reading gay publications, associating with gay people, frequenting gay bars or churches, or marching in gay rights parades.

The policy has not helped much. Many commanders have seemed confused, and some have been unwilling to accept the policy; they continue to ask and pursue. And the debate about the policy called attention to homosexuality, so "everyone from private to general openly speculated about who in their unit might be gay, and as a result there are some people who've had a bull's eye on their back."[207] In fact, more homosexuals have been discharged since the policy went into effect. Female homosexuals have been discharged at a disproportionate rate, perhaps because women in general have not been fully accepted in the services.[208]

Right to Die

The Court has broadened the right to privacy to provide a limited right to die. When Nancy Cruzan's car skidded off an icy road and flipped into a ditch in 1983, doctors were able to save her life but not her brain. She never regained consciousness. She lived in a vegetative state, similar to a coma, and was fed through a tube. Twenty-five at the time of the accident, she was expected to live another thirty years. When her parents asked doctors to remove the tube, the hospital objected and the state of Missouri, despite paying $130,000 a year to support her, also objected. This issue, complicated enough in itself, became entangled in other controversial issues. Pro-life groups said denying life support was analogous to abortion; disability groups said that her condition was merely a disability and that withholding food and water from her would lead to withholding treatment from other people with disabilities.[209]

In this case the Rehnquist Court established a limited right to die.[210] The justices ruled that individuals can refuse medical treatment, including food and water, even if this means they will die. But states can require individuals to make their decision while competent and alert. (Presumably, individuals can also prepare a "living will" or designate another person as a proxy to make the decision in the event that they are unable to.)

Several months after the Court's decision, Cruzan's parents returned to a Missouri court with evidence that their daughter would prefer death to being kept alive by medical machines. Three of Cruzan's former coworkers testified that they recalled conversations in which she said she never would want to live "like a vegetable." Her parents asked for permission to remove her feeding tube and the court agreed. She died twelve days later.

Although the legal doctrine seems clear, practical problems persist. Many people do not indicate their decision. Approximately ten thousand people in irreversible comas now did not indicate their decision beforehand.[211] Some people who do indicate their decision beforehand waver when they face death. Some doctors, who are in the habit of prolonging life even when their patients have little chance of recovering or of enjoying life, resist their decision. The doctors try to persuade the patients or their families not to "pull the plug."[212]

The Rehnquist Court has resisted patients' pleas to extend the limited right to die to encompass a broader right to obtain assistance in committing suicide.[213] Thus, the Court has drawn a distinction between stopping treatment and assisting suicide; individuals have a right to demand the former but not the latter. The justices seemed tentative, as is typical with an issue new to the courts. Chief Justice Rehnquist emphasized, "Our holding permits this debate to continue, as it should in a democratic society." Under the Court's doctrine, states can prohibit assisted suicide, as the majority have done, or they can allow it, as Oregon has done.

A majority of the public favors a right to assisted suicide,[214] but conservative religious groups oppose one. They insist that people should not take a life. Some ethicists worry that patients will be pressured to give up their life because of the costs, to their family or health care provider, of continuing it. Thus, they fear that a right will become a duty.

Meanwhile, the practice, even where officially illegal, is widely condoned, much as abortion was before *Roe*. Almost a fifth of doctors who treat cancer patients in Michigan admitted in a survey that they have assisted suicide, and over half of two thousand doctors who treat AIDS patients in San Francisco also admitted that they have done so.[215]

Civil Liberties in Time

1791 The Bill of Rights is adopted.

1917 A decade of congressional and state laws and governmental prosecutions against seditious speech begins. The Supreme Court upholds these acts on the grounds that the protesters' speech constitutes a "clear and present danger." The government's behavior reflects sensitivity about loyalty during World War I and the "Red Scare" after the communist revolution in the Soviet Union. The Court's attention to this issue marks the beginning of its conspicuous interest in civil liberties.

1925 The Court applies a provision of the Bill of Rights to the states, initiating a trend that would continue through 1972.

1940 Congress passes the Smith Act, which forbids advocating overthrow of the government by force or joining others who advocate overthrow.

1950 Senator McCarthy charges government officials with harboring communists. His accusations, asserted forcefully but supported by no evidence, would capture public attention but ultimately lead to the term *McCarthyism*.

1951 The government uses the Smith Act to prosecute communists, and the Court approves. The government's behavior reflects the Cold War and the public's fear of the American Communist Party.

WARREN COURT

1957 The Court begins to liberalize obscenity doctrine to allow publication of more sexual material under the First Amendment.

1961 *Mapp v. Ohio.* The Court applies the exclusionary rule to the states as a means to enforce search and seizure law of the Fourth Amendment.

1962 The Court issues its first ruling prohibiting official prayers in public schools, as a violation of the establishment clause of the First Amendment.

1963 The Court grants exemptions for religious minorities from secular laws that restrict the practice of their religion, under the free exercise clause of the First Amendment.

1963 *Gideon* case. The Court requires states to furnish an attorney for indigent defendants in felony cases, under the Sixth Amendment.

1963 The Court begins a series of decisions expanding the rights of protesters to express themselves under the First Amendment.

1964 *New York Times v. Sullivan.* The Court begins to overhaul libel doctrine to provide more protection for the press under the First Amendment.

1965 The Court articulates an explicit right to privacy in a birth control case.

1966 *Miranda v. Arizona.* The Court requires police to give warnings before interrogating suspects, to prevent compulsory self-incrimination under the Fifth Amendment.

1967 The Court expands search and seizure law to cover electronic surveillance under the Fourth Amendment.

1969 The Court decides to protect seditious speech as much as other speech under the First Amendment.

1969 The Court agrees to protect some symbolic speech under the First Amendment.

BURGER COURT

1971 The Court rejects the Nixon administration's attempt to prohibit newspapers from publishing the "Pentagon Papers," as a violation of freedom of the press under the First Amendment.

1972 The Court requires states to furnish an attorney to indigent defendants in misdemeanor cases, thus expanding the Warren Court's ruling for felony cases.

1972 The Court invalidates capital punishment as it is being administered now, as a violation of the cruel and unusual punishment provision of the Eighth Amendment.

1973 *Roe v. Wade.* The Court extends the right to privacy to abortion. The ruling galvanizes religious conservatives, who would become a major force in American politics in the 1980s and 1990s.

1976 The Court upholds new laws providing less discretion in sentencing defendants to capital punishment.

1986 The Court refuses to extend the right to privacy to homosexual acts.

REHNQUIST COURT

1989 The Court permits flag burning, thus expanding the Warren and Burger Courts' doctrine allowing symbolic speech.

1990 The Court establishes a limited right to die, authorizing individuals to refuse medical treatment.

1990 The Court denies exemptions for religious minorities from secular laws, thus overturning the Warren Court's doctrine allowing these exemptions.

1991 The Court prohibits official prayers at graduation ceremonies, thus expanding the Warren Court's doctrine prohibiting school prayers.

1997 The Court decides to protect expression on the Internet as much as expression in newspapers, magazines, and books, under the First Amendment.

Conclusion: Are the Courts Responsive in Interpreting Civil Liberties?

The Supreme Court has interpreted the Constitution to provide many important civil liberties. The Warren Court in the 1950s and 1960s expanded civil liberties more than any other Court in history. It applied many provisions of the Bill of Rights to the states. It substantially broadened rights in the areas of speech, libel, obscenity, and religion. It enormously broadened rights of criminal defendants in the areas of search and seizure, self-incrimination, counsel, and jury trial. And it established a right to privacy.

Observers predicted the Burger Court would lead to a constitutional counterrevolution. However, it did not. The Burger Court in the 1970s and 1980s narrowed rights in the areas of freedom of the press, libel, and obscenity. It narrowed rights of criminal defendants in the areas of search and seizure, self-incrimination, and jury trial. It also narrowed opportunities for convicted defendants to appeal on the basis that their rights were violated.[216] But the Court accepted the core of the Warren Court's doctrine and, in fact, even extended it in two areas—right to counsel and right to privacy.

Nor has the Rehnquist Court produced a constitutional counterrevolution. It has narrowed rights further in some areas, but it also has accepted most of the Warren Court's doctrine.

The decisions of these Courts show the extent to which the Supreme Court is responsive to the people in civil liberties cases. The majority of the people support civil liberties in general but not necessarily in specific situations. Elites support civil liberties more than the masses. As the Court has expanded civil liberties, it has not been very responsive to the majority. But it has been more responsive to elites, and it has been very responsive to minorities.

The Court, given relative independence from the rest of the political process, was not intended to be very responsive to the majority. Therefore, it does not have to mirror public opinion, although it cannot ignore this opinion either. It must stay within the broad limits of this opinion, or it will be pulled back. Thus, the Warren Court went too far too fast for too many people. It produced a backlash that led to the Burger and Rehnquist Courts, which have been more responsive to majority opinion. At the same time, they have been less vigilant in protecting civil liberties.

EPILOGUE

The First Amendment Protects Animal Sacrifice

Although the case of *Church of the Lukumi Babalu Aye v. Hialeah* might seem bizarre, it did not prove difficult for the justices to decide. The justices unanimously struck down the ordinances.[217] Justice Kennedy wrote the opinion, concluding that the ordinances restricted the Santeria religion without compelling reasons.

Although the ordinances did not mention the Santeria religion, they were written in such a way that they restricted this religion and its practices but virtually no others. The ordinances exempted Jewish kosher slaughter and also a variety of other animal killings—hunting, fishing, euthanasia, and eradication of insects. State law even allowed the use of live rabbits to train greyhound dogs for racing. Thus, the argument that restriction of animal sacrifice was necessary to prevent cruelty to animals rang hollow.

The ordinances also made no effort to regulate the disposal of carcasses from hunting and fishing or the disposal of garbage from restaurants, which would be more voluminous than the carcasses from Santeria ceremonies. Thus, the argument that restriction of animal sacrifice was necessary to prevent a public health risk also rang hollow.

In short, the Court concluded that Hialeah had targeted the Santeria religion because officials and citizens disapproved of it. "Although the practice of animal sacrifice may seem abhorrent to some," Kennedy wrote, "religious beliefs need not be acceptable, logical, consistent, or comprehensible to others in order to merit First Amendment protection." And, he reminded, "it was historical instances of religious persecution and intolerance that gave concern to those who drafted the free exercise clause."

Key Terms

bills of attainder
ex post facto laws
First Amendment
freedom of speech
seditious speech
McCarthyism
public forum
pure speech
speech plus conduct
symbolic speech
prior restraint
libel
obscenity
separation of church and
state

free exercise clause
establishment clause
Second Amendment
due process
presumption of innocence
unreasonable searches and
seizures
exclusionary rule
Miranda rights
right to counsel
right to a jury trial
cruel and unusual punish-
ment
plea bargain
right to privacy

Further Reading

Dan T. Carter, *Scottsboro: A Tragedy of the American South* (Baton Rouge: Louisiana State University Press, 1979). An examination of the infamous Scottsboro, Alabama, rape case that prompted the Supreme Court to begin to provide counsel to poor defendants.

Fred W. Friendly, *Minnesota Rag* (New York: Random House, 1981). A lively chronicle of the Court's first important freedom of the press case—*Near v. Minnesota* in 1927.

David J. Garrow, *Liberty and Sexuality: The Right to Privacy and the Making of* Roe v. Wade (New York: Macmillan, 1994). An exhaustive account of the hard road to *Roe*.

Franz Kafka, *The Trial* (numerous editions, 1937). One of the great novels of the twentieth century, which shows, perhaps more dramatically than anything else written, what life without due process rights would be like.

James Kirby, *Fumble: Bear Bryant, Wally Butts, and the Great College Football Scandal* (New York: Dell, 1986). Law for football fans—the story of the libel suit against a national magazine for writing that the coach of Alabama and athletic director of Georgia fixed a football game between the two schools. The author, a lawyer, was hired by the Southeastern Conference to determine what really happened in the dispute.

Anthony Lewis, *Gideon's Trumpet* (New York: Vintage, 1964). A wonderful account of Clarence Earl Gideon's suit and the Court's landmark decision.

Patricia G. Miller, *The Worst of Times* (New York: Harper-Collins, 1992). Recollections of women who had abortions before *Roe* made them legal and interviews with abortionists, doctors, and police who witnessed the effects.

Electronic Resources

w3.trib.com/FACT/
A home page for the First Amendment, sponsored by the Casper, Wyoming, Star-Tribune, and winner of a national award for best on-line newspaper services. Links to many resources on different issues involving the First Amendment, including freedom of the press, Internet censorship, state freedom of information laws, and others. Links to Supreme Court decisions and original documents.

www.clas.ufl.edu/users/gthursby/rollfreedom.htm
A link to a variety of sources on freedom of religion, historical and contemporary, from the Christian Research Institute to the American Secular Union.

www.aclu.org/index.html
The home page of the American Civil Liberties Union, a group organized to protect civil liberties through legal and political action. Links to information and position papers on many issues covered in this chapter, including church and state, reproductive rights, flag burning, free speech, gay rights, and many others.

www.naral.org and www.prolife.org/ultimate/
The first site is the home page of the National Abortion Rights Action League, a pro-choice group, and the second site is a link to pro-life groups. Each provides perspectives on the conflict over abortion rights.

InfoTrac College Edition

"'Net Endangers a Basic American Liberty"
"Press Freedom Your Freedom"
"Miranda Morass"
"Abortion Fumble"

Notes

1. Bob Cohn and David A. Kaplan, "A Chicken on Every Altar?" *Newsweek,* November 9, 1992, p. 79. Previously, Santeria had been practiced semi-openly in parts of New York City and Puerto Rico.

2. Ibid.

3. *Lee v. Weisman,* 112 S.Ct. 2649 (1992).

4. *International Society for Krishna Consciousness v. Lee,* 120 L.Ed.2d 541 (1992); *Employment Division v. Smith,* 494 U.S. 872 (1990).

5. Richard Morin, "Is There a Constitutional Right to Rap Rambunctiously?" *Washington Post National Weekly Edition,* September 24–30, 1990, p. 37.

6. "Poll: 33% of Americans Can Identify Bill of Rights," *Lincoln Journal-Star* (AP), December 15, 1991.

7. The states did not ratify a proposed amendment that would have required at least one representative in Congress for every fifty thousand people. That amendment would have put about five thousand members in today's Congress. The states did not ratify, until 1992, another proposed amendment that would have prohibited a salary raise for members of Congress from taking effect until after the next election to Congress.

8. *Reid v. Covert,* 354 U.S. 1 (1957).

9. *Barron v. Baltimore,* 32 U.S. 243 (1833).

10. *Gitlow v. New York,* 268 U.S. 652 (1925). *Gitlow* is usually cited as the first, because it initiated the twentieth-century trend. However, *Chicago, Burlington and Quincy R. Co. v. Chicago,* 166 U.S. 266 (1897), actually was the first. It applied the Fifth Amendment's just compensation clause, requiring government to pay owners "just compensation" for taking their property.

11. *Argersinger v. Hamlin,* 407 U.S. 25 (1972).

141. *Dickerson v. U.S.* (2000).

142. *Johnson v. Zerbst*, 304 U.S. 458 (1938).

143. *Powell v. Alabama*, 287 U.S. 45 (1932).

144. *Gideon v. Wainwright*, 372 U.S. 335 (1963).

145. *Argersinger v. Hamlin*, 407 U.S. 25 (1972); *Scott v. Illinois*, 440 U.S. 367 (1974).

146. *Douglas v. California*, 372 U.S. 353 (1953).

147. Wendy Cole, "Death Takes a Holiday," *Time*, February 14, 2000, p. 68.

148. *Time*, April 29, 1991.

149. Peter Applebome, "Indigent Defendants, Overworked Lawyers," *New York Times*, May 17, 1992, p. E18.

150. Alan Berlow, "Texas, Take Heed," *Washington Post National Weekly Edition*, February 21, 2000, p. 22.

151. Richard Carelli, "Death Rows Grow, Legal Help Shrinks," *Lincoln Journal-Star* (AP), October 7, 1995.

152. The Burger Court did rule that the right to counsel entails the right to "effective" counsel, but the Court set such stringent standards for establishing the existence of ineffective counsel that few defendants can take advantage of this right. See *Strickland v. Washington*, 466 U.S. 668 (1984); *U.S. v. Cronic*, 466 U.S. 640 (1984).

153. *Baldwin v. New York*, 339 U.S. 66 (1970); *Blanton v. North Las Vegas*, 489 U.S. 538 (1989).

154. *Duncan v. Louisiana*, 391 U.S. 145 (1968).

155. *Taylor v. Louisiana*, 419 U.S. 522 (1975).

156. *Swain v. Alabama*, 380 U.S. 202 (1965).

157. The Court implicitly upheld the death penalty in *Wilkerson v. Utah*, 99 U.S. 130 (1878); *In re Kemmler*, 136 U.S. 436 (1890).

158. *Furman v. Georgia*, 408 U.S. 238 (1972).

159. *Gregg v. Georgia*, 428 U.S. 153 (1976).

160. *Woodson v. North Carolina*, 428 U.S. 289 (1976).

161. *Coker v. Georgia*, 433 U.S. 584 (1977).

162. *McCleskey v. Kemp*, 95 L.Ed.2d 262 (1987). Studies of Florida, Illinois, Mississippi, and North Carolina have found similar results. Fox Butterfield, "Blacks More Likely to Get Death Penalty, Study Says," *New York Times*, June 7, 1998, p. 16.

163. As of February 2000.

164. *Brady v. United States*, 397 U.S. 742 (1970).

165. *Griswold v. Connecticut*, 38 U.S. 479 (1965).

166. For a rare exception, see *Time v. Hill*, 385 U.S. 374 (1967).

167. *Griswold v. Connecticut*.

168. *Eisenstadt v. Baird*, 405 U.S. 438 (1972); *Carey v. Population Services International*, 431 U.S. 678 (1977).

169. *Eisenstadt v. Baird*.

170. Lloyd Shearer, "This Woman and This Man Made History," *Parade* (1983).

171. 410 U.S. 113 (1973).

172. Bob Woodward, "The Abortion Papers," *Washington Post National Weekly Edition*, January 30–February 5, 1989, pp. 24–25.

173. All but New York's. Three other states allowed abortion on demand though not quite as extensively as *Roe*, so the ruling also invalidated their laws. Jeffrey A. Segal and Harold J. Spaeth, *The Supreme Court and the Attitudinal Model* (New York: Cambridge University Press, 1993), 333.

174. *Akron v. Akron Center for Reproductive Health*, 76 L.Ed.2d 687 (1983).

175. "The Supreme Court Ignites a Fiery Abortion Debate," *Time*, July 4, 1977, pp. 6–8.

176. *Beal v. Doe*, 432 U.S. 438 (1977); *Maher v. Roe*, 432 U.S. 464 (1977); *Poelker v. Doe*, 432 U.S. 519 (1977); *Harris v. McRae* 448 U.S. 297 (1980).

177. Benjamin Weiser, "The Abortion Dilemma Come to Life," *Washington Post National Weekly Edition*, December 25–31, 1989, pp. 10–11.

178. "Facts in Brief: Abortion in the United States" (New York: Alan Guttmacher Institute, 1992); Stephanie Meneimer, "Ending

179. *Webster v. Reproductive Health Services*, 106 L.Ed.2d 410 (1989).

180. *Planned Parenthood of Southeastern Pennsylvania v. Casey*, 120 L.Ed.2d 674 (1992).

181. William Booth, "The Difference a Day Makes," *Washington Post National Weekly Edition*, November 23–29, 1992, p. 31.

182. *Hodgson v. Minnesota*, 111 L.Ed.2d 344 (1990); *Ohio v. Akron Center for Reproductive Health*, 111 L.Ed.2d 405 (1990); *Planned Parenthood Association of Kansas City v. Ashcroft*, 462 U.S. 476 (1983).

183. Carlson, "Abortion's Hardest Cases," p. 24.

184. Butch Mabin, "Supreme Court Says Teen Seeking Abortion Too Immature," *Lincoln Journal-Star*, December 13, 1997.

185. *Stenberg v. Carhart* (2000).

186. Alissa Rubin, "The Abortion Wars Are Far from Over," *Washington Post National Weekly Edition*, December 21–27, 1992, p. 25.

187. Sandra G. Boodman, "Bringing Abortion Home," *Washington Post National Weekly Edition*, April 19–25, 1993, p. 7.

188. Richard Lacayo, "One Doctor Down, How Many More?" *Time*, March 22, 1993, p. 47.

189. Douglas Frantz, "The Rhetoric of Terror," *Time*, March 27, 1995, pp. 48–51.

190. Dan Sewell, "Abortion War Requires Guns, Bulletproof Vests," *Lincoln Journal-Star* (AP), January 8, 1995.

191. "Blasts Reawaken Fear of Domestic Terrorism," *Lincoln Journal-Star* (Cox News Service), January 17, 1997.

192. Richard Lacayo, "Abortion: The Future Is Already Here," *Time*, May 4, 1992, p. 29; Jack Hitt, "Who Will Do Abortions Here?" *New York Times Magazine*, January 18, 1998, p. 20.

193. Randall Terry, quoted in Anthony Lewis, "Pro-Life Zealots 'Outside the Bargain,'" *Lincoln Journal-Star* (*New York Times*), March 14, 1993; Joseph Scheidler, quoted in Boodman, "Bringing Abortion Home," p. 6.

194. Cynthia Gorney, "Getting an Abortion in the Heartland," *Washington Post National Weekly Edition*, October 15–21, 1990, pp. 10–11.

195. Joe Klein, "The Senator's Dilemma," *New Yorker*, January 5, 1998, p. 32.

196. The majority of states abolished their laws prohibiting sodomy in the 1970s, due to the "sexual revolution" rather than a desire to protect homosexual acts.

197. The laws of five states—Arkansas, Kansas, Missouri, Oklahoma, and Texas—target homosexuals. "Two Men Fined for Sodomy Appeal to Challenge Texas Law." *Lincoln Journal-Star* (AP), November 21, 1998. The laws are also criticized by advocates for people with disabilities, who say the laws forbid the only kind of sex that people who must use wheelchairs can have.

198. *Bowers v. Hardwick*, 92 L.Ed.2d 140 (1986); see also *Doe v. Commonwealth's Attorney*, 425 U.S. 901 (1976).

199. "Ex-Justice's Second Thoughts to Make Heated Debate Hotter," *Lincoln Sunday Journal-Star*, October 28, 1990. The Texas law has been enforced against homosexuals as recently as 1998. "Two Men Fined for Sodomy Appeal to Challenge Texas Law."

200. *Romer v. Evans*, 134 L.Ed.2d 855 (1996).

201. The House sponsor of the act, Robert Barr (R-Ga.), said the act was necessary because "The flames of hedonism, the flames of narcissism, the flames of self-centered morality are licking at the very foundation of our society, the family unit." At the time he was protecting the family unit, he was in his third marriage. Margaret Carlson, "The Marrying Kind," *Time*, September 16, 1996, p. 26.

202. As of March 2000. "Californians Approve Proposition Rejecting Gay Marriage," *Lincoln Journal-Star* (AP), March 8, 2000.

203. President Clinton also ordered the FBI to end its policy that made it difficult for homosexuals to be hired.

204. The policy originally was based on psychoanalytic theory, which considered homosexuality a mental illness. This conclusion was rejected by the American Psychiatric Association some years later.

205. Randy Shilts, "What's Fair in Love and War," *Newsweek,* February 1, 1993, pp. 58–59.

206. Israel drafts every eighteen-year-old man and woman. It does consider homosexuality in the assignment of jobs. Gays who admit their orientation to their superiors confidentially are restricted from security-sensitive jobs for fear they are susceptible to blackmail. But gays who acknowledge their orientation openly could not be blackmailed, so they are treated the same as straights. Shilts, "What's Fair in Love and War," pp. 58–59; Eric Konigsberg, "Gays in Arms," *Washington Monthly,* November 1992, pp. 10–13; "Canada Had No Problems Lifting Its Military Gay Ban," *Lincoln Journal-Star* (AP), January 31, 1993. See also Randy Shilts, *Conduct Unbecoming: Gays and Lesbians in the U.S. Military* (New York: St. Martin's, 1993).

207. Philip Shenon, "New Study Faults Pentagon's Gay Policy," *New York Times,* February 26, 1997, p. A8.

208. "Group Says Gays Worse Off in Military since New Policy," *Lincoln Journal-Star,* (AP), February 28, 1996; Shenon, "New Study Faults Pentagon's Gay Policy." Pentagon officials say many discharges result from recruits who decide that they do not like the military and who then volunteer that they are homosexual as a way of getting discharged. Dana Priest, "The Impact of the 'Don't Ask, Don't Tell' Policy," *Washington Post National Weekly Edition,* February 1, 1999, p. 35. As a result of the increase in discharges, the Clinton administration tried to bolster the policy by having the services discourage harassment, from threats to derogatory jokes aimed at gays, and by requiring low-ranking officers to consult with senior legal advisers before beginning an investigation into alleged homosexual conduct.

209. Al Kamen, "When Exactly Does Life End?" *Washington Post National Weekly Edition,* September 18–24, 1989, p. 31; Alain L. Sanders, "Whose Right to Die?" *Time,* December 11, 1989, p. 80.

210. *Cruzan v. Missouri Health Department,* 111 L.Ed.2d 224 (1990).

211. Otto Friedrich, "A Limited Right to Die," *Time,* July 9, 1990, p. 59.

212. Tamar Lewin, "Ignoring 'Right to Die' Directives, Medical Community Is Being Sued," *New York Times,* June 2, 1996, p. 1.

213. *Washington v. Glucksberg,* 138 L.Ed.2d 772 (1997); *Vacco v. Quill,* 138 L.Ed.2d 834 (1997).

214. David E. Rosenbaum, "Americans Want a Right to Die. Or So They Think," *New York Times,* June 8, 1997, p. E3.

215. Ibid.

216. *Stone v. Powell,* 428 U.S. 465 (1976).

217. 124 L.Ed. 2d 472 (1993).

Civil Rights

Compromise or Continue to Fight?

You are Fannie Lou Hamer, a leader of the Mississippi Freedom Democratic Party (MFDP), a group of mostly African Americans challenging the seating of the regular state Democratic Party delegates at the national Democratic Party Convention in 1964. You have to decide whether to accept a compromise offered by national party officials.

You have come a long way.[1] You were born the youngest in a family of twenty children in the small town of Ruleville, located in the heart of the Mississippi Delta. Like many other African Americans, your parents were sharecroppers, picking cotton on a white family's plantation in exchange for housing and a little money for food.[2] At the age of six, after the owner enticed you with treats from the plantation store, you began picking cotton, too.

You were not satisfied with your life because you had little control over it. For instance, the owner of your house refused to fix the toilet, saying you did not need one indoors. (Yet his house had a separate bathroom for the dog.) And when you entered the hospital to have a small tumor removed, you were sterilized without your knowledge or permission.

So when the civil rights movement reached Ruleville in 1962, you were ready. You were forty-four years old, yet you could not vote. At a meeting at church, a leader of the Student Non-Violent Coordinating Committee (SNCC) and a minister with Martin Luther King's Southern Christian Leadership Conference (SCLC) spoke. When they asked who would try to register to vote, you raised your hand. Two weeks later you and seventeen others were driven to the county seat. You were confronted by many people, you recalled, "and some of them looked like the Beverly Hillbillies . . . but they wasn't kidding down there; they had on, you know, cowboy hats and they had guns; they had dogs."[3] The registrar pulled out a copy of the state constitution and asked you to explain one section. You could not, so he would not register you.

On the way back to Ruleville, the civil rights workers' bus was stopped and the driver was arrested. The charge? The bus was too yellow. (Police said it looked like a school bus.) Once home, the owner of the plantation where you had toiled for eighteen years told you to go back and take your name off the registration forms or leave the plantation. You told him, "I didn't go down there to register for you. I

The civil rights movement led to the integration of some communities, such as this suburb in New Jersey.
Justine Parsons

Fannie Lou Hamer leads marchers in song.
© Charmian Reading, 1966

went down to register for myself."[4] You left your house on the plantation and moved in with friends in town (and after the cotton season, your husband also was evicted from the plantation).

It became clear that getting your rights would not be easy. But you are deeply religious, and you told people, "Whether I want to do it or not, I got to. This is my calling. This is my mission."[5]

With help from the SNCC workers, you studied the state constitution and several months later returned to register again. This time you passed the "test." At the next election, however, you were not allowed to vote because you had not paid poll taxes in the previous years when you were not allowed to vote.

You were determined to get your right to vote and to help others get theirs. You attended an SCLC training course. While returning on the bus, you and others in the group sat at a whites-only lunch counter in the station and then complained when a white girl was moved ahead of you in the line. The driver explained that "niggers are not to be in front of the line."[6] When the bus reached the next town, the members of your group were arrested and severely beaten. For the rest of your life, you would be plagued by ailments from this beating.[7]

Yet you continued. You organized throughout the Delta, inspiring your neighbors to be strong and mocking those, such

as the "chicken-eating preachers," who were less courageous. You traveled throughout the country to help raise funds for civil rights organizations. Although you are short and overweight and you have little education, you are a charismatic figure in the movement—a rousing speaker, perhaps more than anyone except King, and a beautiful singer. After your speeches, you lead the audience in religious hymns and movement songs, breaking down the barriers among strangers.

"We're tired of all this beatin', we're tired of takin' this," you say to anyone who will listen. "All my life I've been sick and tired. Now I'm sick and tired of being sick and tired."[8]

Now, in 1964 you were permitted to vote for the first time in your life, but most blacks still are prevented from voting, and all are prevented from participating in the regular Democratic Party in Mississippi. The state party, whose platform endorsed segregation, controls the state legislature, whose laws make voting by blacks nearly impossible. So you and a few others decided to organize your own party.[9]

The Mississippi Freedom Democrats' immediate goal is to challenge the regular Democrats chosen as delegates to the national convention this year. The Freedom Democrats claim that the delegates are unlawful representatives of the state because they were chosen by unlawful means.

The MFDP held its own precinct, county, and state conventions and allowed whites as well as blacks to participate. You were elected as one of the delegates. But when you and the other members of the upstart delegation arrived in Atlantic City, New Jersey, for the Democratic National Convention, you learned that national party officials, though sympathetic to your cause, did not want you to challenge the regular delegation.

President Johnson, who took office after President Kennedy was assassinated, is

running for his own term. Although a southerner—a Texan—he favors civil rights. He plans to tap Minnesota Senator Hubert Humphrey as his running mate. At the 1948 convention Humphrey gained attention by calling for government to open the door to people of all races. His speech caused many white southerners to walk out in protest.

Johnson will face the Republican, Arizona Senator Barry Goldwater, whose positions are closer to many white southerners' views. The Democrats are worried that, with the civil rights movement and the combination of Humphrey's liberalism and Goldwater's conservatism, southerners will not vote solidly Democratic this year as they have historically. Now Johnson and other officials are vexed that a challenge by the MFDP, even if unsuccessful, would attract publicity that would upset southerners still more.

So Johnson sent word that he might not pick Humphrey if the Freedom Democrats persisted. Clearly, you would prefer Humphrey to anyone else mentioned as a possible vice presidential candidate.

If you gave up your challenge, officials said you could sit as honored guests in the balcony. You rejected this offer; it sounded like the segregated seating in the movie theaters back home. Then officials made their final proposal: You could have two seats as at-large delegates. The regular delegates could keep their seats but would have to pledge loyalty to the national ticket. (It was likely that many would refuse and would leave.) Further, officials promised that in the future delegates would not be seated if their state party did not allow full participation by blacks.

Do you accept this compromise? Some national civil rights leaders urge you to. They stress that you are now involved in politics, not protest, and that politics is the art of compromise.[10]

Civil rights refer to equality of rights for persons regardless of their race, sex, or ethnic background. The Declaration of Independence proclaimed that "all men are created equal." The author, Thomas Jefferson, knew that all men were not created equal in many respects, but he sought to emphasize that they should be considered equal in rights and equal before the law. This represented a break with Great Britain where rigid classes with unequal rights existed; nobles had more rights than commoners. The Declaration's promise did not include nonwhites or women, however. Thus, although colonial Americans advocated equality, they envisioned it only for white men. Others gradually gained more equality, but the Declaration's promise remains unfulfilled for some.

Race Discrimination

African Americans, Hispanics, and Native Americans all have endured and continue to face much discrimination.

Discrimination against African Americans

Slavery

The first blacks came to America in 1619, just twelve years after the first whites. The blacks, like many whites, initially came as indentured servants. In exchange for passage across the ocean, they were bound to an employer, usually for four to seven years, and then freed. But later in the seventeenth century, the colonies passed laws requiring blacks and their children to be slaves for life. Once slavery was established, the slave trade flourished, especially in the South.

As a result of compromises between northern and southern states, the Constitution accepted slavery. It allowed the importation of slaves until 1808, when Congress could bar further importation, and it required the return of escaped slaves to their owners.

Shortly after ratification of the Constitution, northern states abolished slavery. In 1808 Congress barred the importation of slaves but did not halt the practice of slavery in the South. Slavery became increasingly controversial, and abolitionists called for its end.

Southerners began to question the Declaration of Independence and to repudiate its notion of natural rights. They attributed this idea to Jefferson's "radicalism."[11]

Dred Scott.
The Granger Collection, New York

The Supreme Court tried to quell the antislavery sentiment in the **Dred Scott case** in 1857.[12] Dred Scott, a slave who lived in Missouri, was taken by his owner to the free state of Illinois and the free territory of Wisconsin and, after five years, was returned to Missouri. The owner died and passed title to his wife, who moved but left Scott in the care of people in Missouri. They opposed slavery and arranged to have Scott sue his owner for his freedom. They argued that Scott's time in a free state and a free territory made him a free man even though he was brought back to a slave state. The owner, who also opposed slavery, had the authority to free Scott, so the purpose of the suit was not to win his freedom. Rather, she and others sought a major court decision to keep slavery out of the territories.

In this infamous case, Chief Justice Roger Taney stated that no blacks, whether slave or free, were citizens, and that they were "so far inferior that they had no rights which the white man was bound to respect." Taney could have stopped here—if Scott was not a citizen, he could not sue in federal court—but Taney continued. He declared that Congress had no power to control slavery in the territories. This meant that slavery could extend into the territories Congress already had declared free. It also raised the possibility that states could not control slavery within their borders.[13]

Although most slaveowners were white, some were black. William Ellison of South Carolina was one. Born a slave, he bought his freedom and then his family's by building and repairing cotton gins. Over time he earned enough to buy slaves and operate a plantation. With sixty slaves, Ellison ranked in the top 1 percent of all slaveholders, black or white.

Ellison was unusual, but he was not unique. In Charleston, South Carolina, alone, more than one hundred African Americans owned slaves in 1860. Most, however, owned fewer than four.

Although part of the slave-owning class, black slaveholders were not much more acceptable to whites. Ellison's family was granted a pew on the main floor of the local Episcopal church, but they had to be on guard at all times. Failure to maintain the norms of black-white relations—acting deferentially—could mean instant punishment. And as the Civil War approached, whites trying to preserve the established order increasingly viewed free blacks, even slaveholders, as a threat. Harsher legislation regulated their lives. For example, they had to have a white "guardian" to vouch

for their character, and they had to carry special papers to show their free status. Without these papers, they could be sold back into slavery.

Some black slaveholders showed little sign that they shared the concerns of black slaves. Indeed, Ellison freed none of his slaves.

SOURCE: Michael P. Johnson and James L. Roark, *Black Masters* (New York: Norton, 1984).

By this time, slavery had become the hottest controversy in American politics, and this decision fanned the flames. It provoked vehement opposition in the North and prompted further polarization, which eventually led to the Civil War. Meanwhile, Scott got his freedom from his owner.

The North's victory in the Civil War gave force to President Lincoln's Emancipation Proclamation ending slavery.[14] But blacks would find short-lived solace.

Civil War Amendments and Reconstruction

After the war, Congress passed and the states ratified three constitutional amendments. The Thirteenth prohibited slavery. (Mississippi became the last state to ratify the amendment—in 1995.) The Fourteenth granted citizenship to blacks, thus overruling the Dred Scott decision, and also granted "equal protection of the laws" and "due process of law." The **equal protection clause** eventually would become the primary guarantee that government would treat people equally. The Fifteenth provided the right to vote for black men.

These amendments not only provided specific rights for blacks, but they also transformed the relationship between the federal and state governments. Each amendment included a stipulation that "Congress shall have power to enforce" the provisions of the amendment. This stipulation granted the federal government new power—whatever power was necessary to guarantee these rights. This new power stands in marked contrast with the original understanding of the Founders that the

federal government would have limited power. The Civil War and these amendments together thus constituted a constitutional revolution, in the eyes of some legal scholars.[15] This transformation was intentional; Congress did not trust southern states to enforce constitutional provisions they had just fought a war against.

Congress also passed a series of Civil Rights Acts to reverse the "Black Codes" that southern states had enacted to deny the newly freed slaves legal rights. These Civil Rights Acts allowed blacks to buy, own, and sell property; to make contracts; to sue; and to be witnesses and jurors in court. They also allowed blacks to use public transportation, such as railroads and steamboats, and to patronize hotels and theaters.[16]

Even so, most freed blacks faced bleak conditions. Congress rejected proposals to break up plantations and give former slaves "forty acres and a mule" or to provide aid to establish schools. Without land or education, they had to work for their former masters as hired hands or sharecroppers. Their status was not much better than it had been. Landowners designed a system to keep the former slaves dependent. They allowed sharecroppers to sell half their crop and keep the proceeds, but paid so little, regardless of how hard the farmers worked, that the families had to borrow to tide them over the winter. The next year they had to work for the landowner to pay off their debt. The following year the cycle continued. And, lacking education, most sharecroppers did not keep records of how much they owed and how much the landowner owed them, and many were cheated.

During the period of Reconstruction, the Union army enforced the new amendments and acts. While the army occupied the South, military commanders established procedures to register voters, including the newly freed slaves; hold elections; and ratify the Fourteenth Amendment. The commanders also started schools for children of the newly freed slaves. But in state after state, the South resisted, and eventually the North capitulated. After a decade, the two regions struck a deal to end what was left of Reconstruction. The 1876 presidential election between Republican Rutherford Hayes and Democrat Samuel Tilden was disputed in some states. To resolve the dispute, Republicans, most of whom were northerners, and Democrats, many of whom were southerners, agreed to a compromise: Hayes would be named president, and the remaining Union troops would be removed from the South.

In hindsight, it should not be a surprise that Reconstruction did not accomplish more. It was not easy to integrate four million former slaves into a southern society that was bitter in its defeat and weak in its economy. Northern citizens who expected progress to come smoothly were naive. When it did not come quickly, they became disillusioned.

Public attitudes during Reconstruction thus began a recurring cycle that continues to this day: The public gets upset about the treatment of African Americans and supports some efforts to improve conditions. But the public is naive, and when the efforts do not immediately produce the expected results, the public becomes disillusioned and dissatisfied with the costs. The public's lack of patience then forces officials to put the race problem on the back burner for some future generation to handle.[17]

Segregation

In both the South and the North, blacks came to be segregated from whites.

Segregation in the South The reconciliation between Republicans and Democrats—northerners and southerners—was effected at the expense of blacks. Removing the troops enabled the South to govern itself again, and this enabled the South to reduce blacks to near-slave status.

Before the Civil War, slavery itself had kept blacks down, and segregation would have been inconvenient when blacks and whites needed to live and work near each other. There was no residential segregation—not in rural areas, where former slaves' shacks were intermixed with plantation houses, and not in urban areas, where few blocks were solidly black. But after slavery, southerners established segregation as another way to keep blacks down. Initially, they did so haphazardly—one law here, another there. By the early 1900s, however, there was a pervasive pattern of **Jim Crow laws.**

Jim Crow laws segregated just about everything. Some segregated blocks within neighborhoods, others neighborhoods within cities. Laws in some small towns excluded blacks altogether. Some did so explicitly; others simply established curfews that required blacks to be off the streets by 10 P.M. Laws also segregated schools, which blacks had been allowed to attend during Reconstruction, and even textbooks (black schools' texts had to be stored separately from white schools' books). Many laws segregated public accommodations, such as hotels, restaurants, bars, and transportation. At first the laws required the races to sit in separate sections of streetcars; eventually, they required them to sit in separate cars; finally, they also forced them to sit in separate sections of waiting rooms. Other laws segregated parks, sporting events, and circuses. Laws segregated black and white checkers players in Birmingham and established districts for black and white prostitutes in New Orleans. They segregated drinking fountains, restrooms, ticket windows, entrances, and exits. They segregated the races in prisons, hospitals, and homes for the blind. They even segregated the races in death—in morgues, funeral homes, and cemeteries.

Blacks were forced to defer to whites in all informal settings as well, and failure to do so could mean punishment or even death. Blacks were "humiliated by a thousand daily reminders of their subordination."[18]

Meanwhile, northern leaders, who had championed the cause of the slaves before and during the Civil War, abandoned blacks a decade after the war; Congress did not pass new laws, presidents did not enforce existing laws, and the Supreme Court gutted the constitutional amendments and Civil Rights Acts. All acquiesced in "the southern way."

The Supreme Court struck down the Civil Rights Act allowing blacks to use public accommodations, including transportation, hotels, and theaters.[19] Where the Fourteenth Amendment said that "no state" shall deny equal protection, the Court interpreted this to mean that "no government" shall, but private individuals—owners of transportation, hotels, and theaters—could. The Court's interpretation might seem plausible, but it was clearly contrary to Congress's intent.[20]

Then the Court upheld segregation itself. Louisiana passed "an Act to promote the comfort of passengers," which mandated separate accommodations in trains. New Orleans black leaders sponsored a case to test the act's constitutionality. Homer Adolph Plessy bought a ticket and sat in the white car. When the conductor

Tulsa's black neighborhood after whites burned it down in 1921.
Tulsa Historical Society

ordered him to move to the black car, Plessy refused. He maintained that the act was unconstitutional under the Fourteenth Amendment. In ***Plessy v. Ferguson*** in 1896, the Court disagreed, claiming that the act was not a denial of equal protection because it provided equal accommodations.[21] Thus the Court established the **separate-but-equal doctrine,** which allowed separate facilities if they were equal. Of course, government required separate facilities only because it thought the races were not equal, but the Court brazenly commented that the act did not stamp "the colored race with a badge of inferiority" unless "the colored race chooses to put that construction on it." Only Justice John Harlan, a former Kentucky slaveholder, dissented: "Our Constitution is color-blind, and neither knows nor tolerates classes among citizens."

Three years later the Court accepted segregation in schools.[22] A Georgia school board turned a black high school into a black elementary school. Although the board did not establish a new high school for blacks or allow them to attend the ones for whites, the Court did not object. This set a pattern in which separate but equal meant separation but not equality.

Segregation in the North Although Jim Crow laws were not as pervasive in the North as in the South, northerners imitated southerners to the point where one writer proclaimed, "The North has surrendered!"[23]

Job opportunities were better in the North. Southern blacks were sharecropping—by 1930 80 percent of those who farmed were still working somebody else's land[24]—and northern factories were offering jobs. Between 1915 and 1940, more than a million southern blacks headed north in the "Great Migration." But they were forced to live in black ghettos because they could not afford better housing and because they could not escape discrimination in the North, either.

Denial of the Right to Vote

With the adoption of the Fifteenth Amendment, many blacks voted and even elected fellow blacks to office during Reconstruction, but southern states began to disfranchise them in the 1890s (as explained in Chapter 8). Thus, they were unable to elect black representatives or even pressure white officials to oppose segregation.

Violence

To solidify their control, whites engaged in sporadic violence against African Americans. In the 1880s and 1890s, whites lynched about one hundred blacks a year. In the 1900s vigilante "justice" continued (Table 1). For example, a mob in Livermore, Kentucky, dragged a black man accused of murdering a white man into a theater. The ringleaders charged admission and hanged the man. Then they permitted the audience to shoot at the swinging body—those in the balcony could fire once; those in the better seats could empty their revolvers.[25] In 1919 there were twenty-five race riots in six months. White mobs took over cities in the North and South, burning black neighborhoods and terrorizing black residents for days on end.[26]

In 1921, ten thousand whites burned down thirty-five blocks of Tulsa's black neighborhood. The incident that precipitated the riot was typical—a report of an assault by a black man on a white woman. The report was false, fabricated by the woman, but residents were inflamed by a racist newspaper and encouraged by the city's officials. Up to three hundred people were shot, burned alive, or tied to cars and dragged to death. Survivors reported corpses stacked like firewood on street corners and piled high in dump trucks.[27]

The Ku Klux Klan, which began during Reconstruction and started up again in 1915, played a major role in inflaming prejudice and terrorizing blacks. It was strong enough to dominate many southern towns and even the state governments of Oklahoma and Texas. It also made inroads into some northern states.

Federal officials said such violence was a state problem—presidents refused to speak out, and Congress re-

Table 1	Why Whites Lynched Blacks in 1907
Whites gave the following reasons for lynching blacks, who may or may not have committed these acts.	

Reason	Number
Murder	5
Attempted murder	5
Manslaughter	10
Rape	9
Attempted rape	11
Burglary	3
Harboring a fugitive	1
Theft of 75¢	1
Having a debt of $3	2
Being victor over white man in fight	1
Insulting white man	1
Talking to white girls on telephone	1
Being wife or son of rapist	2
Being father of boy who "jostled" white women	1
Expressing sympathy for victim of mob	3
	56

SOURCE: Adapted from Ray Stannard Baker, *Following the Color Line* (New York: Harper & Row, 1964), 176–177.

fused to pass legislation making lynching a federal offense—yet state officials did nothing.

For at least the first third of the twentieth century, white supremacy reigned—in the southern states, the border states, and many of the northern states. It also pervaded the nation's capital, where President Woodrow Wilson instituted segregation in the federal government.[28] (See also the box "Passing the 'Paper Bag Test.' ")

Overcoming Discrimination against African Americans

African Americans fought white supremacy primarily in three arenas: the courts, the streets, and Congress. In general, they fought in the courts first and Congress last, although as they gained momentum they increasingly fought in all three arenas at once.

The Movement in the Courts

The first strategy was to convince the Supreme Court to overturn the separate-but-equal doctrine of *Plessy v. Ferguson.*

The NAACP In response to white violence, a group of blacks and whites founded the **NAACP,** the National Association for the Advancement of Colored People, in 1909. In its first two decades, it was led by W. E. B. DuBois, a black sociologist. In time it became the major organization fighting for blacks' civil rights.

Frustrated by presidential and congressional inaction and its own lack of power to force action, the NAACP decided to converge on the federal courts, which were less subject to pressures from the majority. The association assembled a cadre of lawyers, mainly from Howard University Law School, a black university in Washington, D.C., to bring lawsuits attacking segregation and the denial of the right to vote. In 1915 they persuaded the Supreme Court to strike down the grandfather clause (which exempted persons whose ancestors could vote from the literacy test),[29] and two years later they convinced the Court to invalidate laws prescribing residential segregation.[30] But the Court continued to allow most devices to disfranchise blacks and most efforts to segregate.

In 1938 the NAACP chose a thirty-year-old attorney, Thurgood Marshall, to head its litigation arm.[31] Marshall, whose mother had to pawn her engagement and wedding rings so he could go to an out-of-state law school because his in-state school—the University of Maryland—did not admit blacks, would become a tireless and courageous advocate for equal rights. (In 1946, after defending four blacks charged with attempted murder during a riot in rural Tennessee, he would narrowly escape a lynch mob.)[32]

position and popularity, the president could have speeded implementation by speaking out in support of the decision, yet he did not do so for more than three years. When nine black students tried to attend a white high school under a desegregation plan in Little Rock, Arkansas, the governor's and state legislature's inflammatory rhetoric against desegregation encouraged local citizens to take the law into their own hands. Finally, Eisenhower acted; he sent federal troops and federalized the state's national guard to quell the riot.

A few years later President Kennedy used federal marshals and paratroopers to quell violence after the governor of Mississippi blocked the door to keep James Meredith from registering at the University of Mississippi. Kennedy again sent troops when the governor of Alabama, George Wallace, proclaiming "segregation now, segregation tomorrow, segregation forever," blocked the door to keep blacks from enrolling at the University of Alabama.

After outright defiance, some states attempted to circumvent the ruling by shutting down their public schools and providing tuition grants for students to use at private schools, which at the time could segregate. They also provided other forms of aid, such as textbooks and public recreation facilities, for private schools. These efforts hindered desegregation and hurt black education because the black communities seldom had the resources to establish their own schools.

The states also tried less blatant schemes, such as "freedom of choice" plans, that allowed students to choose the school they wanted to attend. Of course, virtually no whites chose a black school, and due to strong pressure, few blacks chose a white school. The idea was to achieve desegregation on paper, or token desegregation in practice, in order to avoid real desegregation. But the Court rebuffed these schemes and even forbade discrimination by private schools.[42]

The Court's firm support gave blacks hope. Thurgood Marshall said, "Chief Justice Warren became the image [of the Court] that allowed the poor Negro sharecropper to say, 'Kick me around Mr. Sheriff, kick me around Mr. County Judge, kick me around Supreme Court of my state, but there's one person I can rely on.'"[43]

Nevertheless, progress was excruciatingly slow. If a school district was segregated, a group like the NAACP had to run the risks and spend the time and money to bring a suit in a federal district court. Judges in these courts reflected the views of the state or local political establishment they came from, so the suit might not be successful. If it was, the school board had to prepare a desegregation plan. Members of the school board reflected

Outside the Supreme Court, NAACP attorneys George E. C. Hayes, Thurgood Marshall, and James M. Nabrit celebrate the Brown v. Board of Education decision.
AP/Wide World Photos

the views of the community and the pressures from the segregationists, so the plan might not be adequate. If it was, segregationists would challenge it in a federal district court. If the court upheld the plan, segregationists would appeal to a federal court of appeals. Judges in these courts came from the South, and they sat in Richmond and New Orleans. However, they were not as tied to the state or local political establishment, and they usually decided against the segregationists. But then segregationists could appeal to the Supreme Court. Segregationists knew they would lose sooner or later. But the process took several years, so they were able to delay the inevitable.

Thus, segregationists tried to resist, then to evade, and finally to delay. In this they succeeded. In 1964, a decade after *Brown,* 98 percent of all black children in the South still attended all-black schools.[44]

By this time, the mood in Congress had changed. Congress passed the Civil Rights Act of 1964, which, among other things, cut off federal aid to school districts that continued to segregate. The following year it passed the first major program providing federal aid to education. This was the carrot at the end of the stick: School districts began to comply to get the federal money.

Finally, by 1970 only 14 percent of all black children in the South still attended all-black schools. Of course,

Two years after the Supreme Court's *Brown* decision, the Mississippi legislature created a secretive agency to "protect the sovereignty of the State of Mississippi and her sister states." The Sovereignty Commission lasted until 1973. Little information about its practices came to light, however, until 1998, when a twenty-one-year legal battle ended and a federal court required disclosure of the commission's records.

This tax-supported secret police force acted to preserve segregation. The Sovereignty Commission hired a public relations officer, established a speakers' bureau, and produced propaganda films to portray race relations in the segregated state in a positive light. It persuaded newspapers to kill stories it disapproved of and run stories it submitted. (For example, "Mississippi authorities have learned that the apparently endless 'freedom' rides into Mississippi and the South were planned in Havana, Cuba, last winter by officials of the Soviet Union.")

It also set up a network of spies—"eyes and ears" in each of the state's eighty-two counties—to collect information on everyone who posed a threat to segregation, from civil rights workers to ordinary white folks who made an improper comment at an inopportune time. The commission estimated that it had files on ten thousand people, tracing their whereabouts and detailing such personal information as their financial transactions and sexual practices.

The commission dispatched an investigator to the University of Southern Mississippi to determine whether a white woman was dating a young man who was "said to be part Negro"; another investigator was sent out to determine whether an out-of-wedlock baby was the offspring of an interracial liaison.

The commission fed its information to the individuals' employers and to the Ku Klux Klan. Individuals were fired, and some apparently were beaten and killed as a result. (The commission circulated the license plate number of the car driven by three civil rights workers murdered in Neshoba County.) The commission also disseminated misinformation, smearing individuals and causing one early black applicant to the University of Southern Mississippi to be convicted and imprisoned on false charges.

Although the commission was an extreme incarnation of attitudes typical at the time, it was not alone. Commissioners shared information with officials in the FBI and members of Congress. Both of these institutions were investigating communists and other "subversives" and were skeptical about the patriotism of civil rights leaders and fearful of the changes sought by the civil rights movement.

Even in 1998, a former commissioner defended the commission's practices: "It was all-out warfare to keep the communists and the agitators from taking over Mississippi," he said. "We did what we had to do."

SOURCES: Calvin Trillin, "State Secret," *New Yorker,* May 29, 1995, pp. 54–64; John Cloud, "The KGB of Mississippi," *Time,* March 30, 1998, p. 30; "Files Provide Look at Infamous Panel," *Champaign-Urbana News-Gazette* (AP), March 15, 1998.

---

some went to mostly black schools. Even so, the change was dramatic. Since then, though, many white students have left the public schools for private schools, causing creeping resegregation of the public schools.

Busing *Brown* and related rulings addressed **de jure segregation**—segregation enforced by law. This segregation can be attacked by striking down the law. *Brown* did not address **de facto segregation**—segregation based on residential patterns—typical of northern cities and large southern cities, where most blacks live in black neighborhoods and most whites live in white neighborhoods. Students attend their neighborhood schools, which are mostly black or mostly white. This segregation is much more intractable because it does not stem primarily from a law, so it cannot be eliminated by striking down a law.

Civil rights groups proposed busing some black children to schools in white neighborhoods and some white children to schools in black neighborhoods. They hoped to improve black children's education, their self-confidence and aspirations, and, eventually, their college and career opportunities. They also hoped to improve black and white children's ability to get along together.

The Burger Court authorized busing within school districts—ordinarily cities—including southern cities where there was a history of de jure segregation and northern cities where there was a pattern of de facto segregation but evidence that school officials had located schools or assigned students in ways that perpetuated this segregation.[45]

But even extensive busing within cities could not desegregate most large cities, where blacks and other minorities together became more numerous than whites. After World War II, affluent whites began to leave central cities for their suburbs, and after the courts upheld busing, more did so. Then the birthrates of whites fell and the immigration rates of whites from foreign countries fell, relative to those of nonwhites. Due to these factors, there were not enough whites to desegregate the schools in most large cities. Consequently, civil rights groups proposed busing some white children from the suburbs to the cities and some black children from the cities to the suburbs. This approach would provide enough of both races to achieve balance in both places.

The Burger Court rejected this proposal by a five to four vote in 1974.[46] It said busing is not appropriate between school districts unless there is evidence of intentional segregation in both the city and its suburbs. Otherwise, such extensive busing would require too long rides for students and too much coordination by administrators. Although there was intentional segregation by many cities and their suburbs,[47] the evidence is not as clear as that of the segregation by southern states at

the time of *Brown,* so it is difficult to demonstrate a pattern by the cities and their multiple suburbs to the extent expected by the judges. Consequently, the Court's ruling made busing between cities and suburbs very rare.

Thurgood Marshall, by then on the Court, dissented and predicted that the ruling would allow "our great metropolitan areas to be divided up each into two cities—one white, the other black." Indeed, the ruling did contribute to this result.

During these years relatively few students were bused for desegregation—4 percent in one typical year. These students were far fewer than those bused, at public expense, to segregated public and private schools.[48]

Nevertheless, busing ran up against a wall of public opinion. White parents criticized the courts sharply. Their reaction stemmed from prejudice against blacks; bias against poor persons; fear of the crime in inner city schools; worry about the quality of inner city schools; and desire for the convenience of neighborhood schools. They also resented the courts for telling local governments what to do. In addition, some black parents opposed busing because it disrupted their children's lives and exposed them to the hostility of white students in their new schools. Black parents also resented the implication that their children could learn only if sitting next to white children. But other black parents favored bus-

Busing led to rioting in some cities, such as Boston. Here protesters assault a black man in 1976.
Stanley J. Forman, Pulitzer Prize, 1977

ing because of the opportunity for their children to go to better schools.

Due to the opposition of white parents, busing prompted an increase in white flight, so there were fewer white students to balance enrollments and fewer middle-class students to provide stability in the cities' schools. It also furthered the deterioration of minority communities, because it diminished the neighborhood schools that had helped define these communities and hold them together.[49]

Busing could not accomplish all that civil rights groups and federal judges expected—or at least hoped—it could. Busing could not compensate for massive residential segregation. It could not overcome students' poverty or their parents' lack of involvement in their education. Thus, studies of the performance of minority children bused to white schools showed disappointing, mixed results.

In 1991 the Rehnquist Court decided that school districts have no obligation to reduce de facto segregation and, in fact, limited obligation to reduce the vestiges of de jure segregation.[50] This ruling relieved the pressure on school districts, and by the mid-1990s most had stopped mandatory busing. When some tried other programs to balance enrollments, the Court looked askance at these programs.[51] In the 1990s the rulings reflected none of "the moral urgency of *Brown*."[52] Instead, the justices decided that desegregation is less important than minimizing judicial involvement in education and judicial authority over local governments. In these ways the majority of the justices mirrored the views of the Republican presidents who had appointed them.

The Movement in the Streets

After the NAACP's early successes in the courts, other blacks, and some whites, took the fight to the streets. Their bold efforts gave birth to the modern civil rights movement.

The movement began in Montgomery, Alabama, in 1955, when Rosa Parks refused to move to the back of the bus. Her refusal and arrest prompted blacks to boycott city buses. For their leader they chose a young Baptist minister, Dr. Martin Luther King, Jr. The boycott catapulted the movement and King to national attention (as explained in Chapter 6).

King was the first charismatic leader of the movement. He formed the Southern Christian Leadership Conference (SCLC) of black clergy and adopted the tactics of Mahatma Gandhi, who had led the movement to free India from the British. The tactics included direct action, such as demonstrations and marches, and civil disobedience—intentional and public disobedience of laws considered unjust. The tactics were based on nonviolence, even when confronted with violence. This strategy was designed to draw support from whites by contrasting the morality of the movement's position with the immorality of discrimination and violence against blacks.

For a long time some whites, focusing on civil rights leaders such as King and even fearing foreign "communists," deluded themselves into thinking that "outside agitators" were responsible for the turmoil in their communities.[53] But the movement grew from the grass roots, and it eventually shattered this delusion.

The movement spread, especially among black students. In 1960, four black students of North Carolina A&T College sat at the lunch counter in Woolworth's and asked for a cup of coffee. The waitress refused to serve them, but they stayed and were arrested. On following days, as whites waved the Confederate flag and jeered, more students sat at the lunch counter. Within a year such sit-ins occurred in more than one hundred cities.

When blacks asserted their rights, whites often reacted with violence. In 1963, King led demonstrators in Birmingham, Alabama, for desegregation of public facilities. Public Safety Commissioner Eugene "Bull" Connor had

Martin Luther King, under arrest in 1958.
Charles Moore/Black Star

police unleash their dogs to attack the marchers. In 1964, King led demonstrators in Selma, Alabama, for voting rights. State troopers clubbed many of the marchers, and vigilantes beat and shot marchers.

In the summer of 1964, black and white college students mounted a voter registration drive in Mississippi. By the end of the summer, one thousand had been arrested, eighty beaten, thirty-five shot, and six killed.[54] These included one southern black and two northern whites who were murdered by Klansmen, allegedly with aid from a sheriff and deputy sheriff, in Neshoba County. (This incident was fictionalized in the movie *Mississippi Burning.*)

Perpetrators of the violence usually were not caught. When they were, they usually were not punished. Law enforcement was frequently in the hands of bigots, and juries generally were all white. The Supreme Court had struck down discrimination in choosing juries,[55] but discrimination continued through informal means.

During these years, most whites told pollsters they disliked the civil rights movement's speed and tactics: "They're pushing too fast and too hard." At the same time, most said they favored integration more than ever. And they seemed repelled by the violence. The brutality against blacks generated more support for them.

Although the movement's tactics worked well against southern de jure segregation, they did not work as well against northern de facto segregation or against both regions' job discrimination. By the mid-1960s, a decade after the *Brown* decision, progress had stalled and dissatisfaction was growing. Young blacks from the inner city,

who had not been involved in the movement, questioned two of its principles—interracialism and nonviolence. As James Farmer, head of the Congress of Racial Equality (CORE), later explained, these blacks began to say, "What is this we-shall-overcome, black-and-white together stuff? I don't know of any white folks except the guy who runs that store on 125th Street in Harlem and garnishes wages and repossesses things you buy. I'd like to go upside his head. [Or] the rent collector, who bangs on the door demanding rent that we ain't got. I'd like to go upside his head."[56] These blacks criticized King and his tactics. In place of the integration advocated by King, some leaders began to call for "black power." This phrase meant different things to different people. To some it meant political power through the ballot box; to others, economic power through boycotts of segregated businesses or ownership of their own businesses. At least it implied black pride and self-reliance. And in place of the nonviolence practiced by King, some leaders began to urge violence in retaliation for the violence of whites. The movement splintered further.

The Movement in Congress

As the civil rights movement expanded, it pressured presidents and members of Congress to act. Presidents Kennedy and Johnson supported civil rights but felt hamstrung by southerners in Congress who, through the seniority system, had risen to chair key committees and dominate both houses. As a result, the presidents considered civil rights leaders unreasonable and the move-

When three civil rights workers were murdered in Neshoba County, Mississippi, no one was ever indicted by the state. After an investigation, eighteen persons, including the sheriff (right) and deputy sherriff (left), here in court, were indicted by the federal government for the lesser charge of conspiracy. (There was no applicable federal law for murder.) Ultimately, seven persons, including the deputy, were convicted by the federal court.
AP/Wide World Photos

ment a nuisance that alienated the southerners upon whom the presidents had to rely. But once the movement demonstrated its strength, it was able to prod officials to act. After two hundred thousand blacks and whites marched in Washington in 1963, President Kennedy introduced civil rights legislation, and President Johnson, with his consummate legislative skills, forged a coalition of northern Democrats and northern Republicans to overcome southern Democrats and pass the Civil Rights Act of 1964. After one thousand blacks and whites had been arrested and many had been attacked in Selma, the public outcry led Johnson to introduce and Congress to pass the Voting Rights Act of 1965. Three years later Johnson introduced and Congress passed the Civil Rights Act of 1968.

Within a span of four years, Congress passed legislation prohibiting discrimination in public accommodations, employment, housing, and voting.

Although President Johnson believed he was doing the right thing, he realized the political ramifications. Upon signing the first of these acts, he commented that he was handing the South to the Republican Party "for the next 50 years."[57] He was perceptive. In the next election, he became the first Democrat since the Civil War to lose the white vote in the southern states. In less than a decade, the South, which had been solidly Democratic since the Civil War, would go from the most Democratic region of the country to the least.[58]

Desegregation of Public Accommodations The **Civil Rights Act of 1964** prohibits discrimination on the basis of race, color, religion, or national origin in public accommodations. This time, unlike after the Civil War, the Court unanimously upheld the act.[59]

The act does not cover private clubs, such as country clubs, social clubs, or fraternities and sororities, on the principle that the government should not tell people with whom they must associate in private. (The Court has made private schools an exception to this principle to help enforce *Brown*.)

Desegregation of Employment The Civil Rights Act of 1964 also prohibits employment discrimination on the basis of race, color, religion, national origin, or sex and (as amended) physical handicap, age, or Vietnam-era veteran status. The act covers employers with fifteen or more employees and unions.[60]

In addition to practicing blatant discrimination, some employers practiced more subtle discrimination. They required applicants to meet standards unneces-

Civil rights demonstrators were pounded by fire hoses in some southern cities.
© 1963 Charles Moore/Black Star

sary for their jobs, a practice that hindered blacks more than whites. A high school degree for a manual job was a common example. The Court held that standards must relate to the jobs.[61] However, standards that hindered blacks more than whites are not necessarily unlawful. Washington, D.C., required applicants for police officer to pass an exam. Although a higher percentage of blacks failed to pass, the Court said the exam related to the job.[62]

The Court has allowed employers to reduce their workforce by laying off workers with less seniority, even if these workers are disproportionately black.[63] The principle of "last hired, first fired" thwarts desegregation of employment when an employer hires more blacks to compensate for past discrimination but then lays off the newer workers when the economy slows.

Desegregation of Housing Although the Supreme Court had struck down laws that prescribed segregation in residential areas, whites maintained segregation by making **restrictive covenants**—agreements among neighbors not to sell their houses to blacks. In 1948, the Court ruled that courts could not enforce these covenants because doing so would involve the government in discrimination.[64]

Realtors also played a role in segregation by practicing **steering**—showing blacks houses in black neighborhoods and whites houses in white neighborhoods. Unscrupulous realtors practiced **blockbusting.** After a black family bought a house in a white neighborhood, realtors would warn white families that more blacks would move in. Because of prejudice and fear that their houses' values would decline, whites would panic and sell to the realtors at low prices. Then the realtors would re-sell to blacks at higher prices. In this way neighborhoods that might have been desegregated were instead resegre-gated—from all white to all black.

Banks and savings and loans also played a role. They were reluctant to lend money to blacks who wanted to buy a house in a white neighborhood. Some engaged in **redlining**—refusing to lend money to those who wanted to buy a house in a racially changing neighbor-hood. The lenders worried that if the buyer could not keep up with the payments, the lender would be left with a house whose value had declined.

The government also played an important role. The Veterans Administration and the Federal Housing Au-thority, which guaranteed loans to some buyers, were reluctant to authorize loans to blacks who sought to buy a house in a white neighborhood. And the federal government, which funded low-income housing, al-lowed local governments to locate such housing in ghettos. In these ways the governments helped perpet-uate segregation.[65]

But the **Civil Rights Act of 1968** bans discrimi-nation in the sale or rental of housing on the basis of race, color, religion, national origin, and (as amended) on the basis of sex, having children, or having a disabil-ity. The act covers about 80 percent of the available housing and prohibits steering, blockbusting, and redlining.

Restoration of the Right to Vote After years of skirmishing with the states, the Supreme Court and Congress barred measures designed to keep blacks from voting. The Voting Rights Act of 1965 permitted large numbers of blacks to vote for the first time (as explained in Chapter 8).

Continuing Discrimination against African Americans

African Americans have overcome much discrimination but still face continuing discrimination. Overt laws and blatant practices have been struck down, but subtle man-ifestations of old attitudes and habits persist—and in ways far more numerous and with effects far more seri-ous than this one chapter can convey.[66] Moreover, African Americans must cope with the legacy of gener-ations of slavery, segregation, and discrimination and, for many of them, the effects of generations of poverty. And

they must cope with the attitudes of whites. Although few people say they want to return to the days of legal segregation, about half reject the dream of an integrated society.[67] (See the box "How Much Is White Skin Worth?" for a hypothetical but telling response to cop-ing with discrimination.)

Discrimination in Education

For blacks who can afford it, a great deal of desegrega-tion has occurred in education. Affluent parents who can pay for private schools or live in expensive neigh-borhoods with good public schools can send their chil-dren to integrated schools. However, for most blacks in big cities, medium cities, or areas where private schools predominate, there has been much less desegregation.

Although de jure segregation of schools has been eliminated, de facto segregation remains. In fact, this segregation is getting worse. After progress in the mid-1960s and 1970s, the trend toward desegregation re-versed itself in the 1980s and got worse in the 1990s. "For the first time since the *Brown v. Board* decision," ac-cording to one study, "we are going backwards."[68]

The reversal is due to white flight to the suburbs, leaving fewer white children, and higher nonwhite birthrates and immigration rates, producing more non-white children. In our forty-seven largest cities, only one of four students in public schools is white.[69] To a lesser extent, the reversal is due to the Burger and Rehnquist Courts' limited acceptance of busing or alternatives to balance enrollments and to the Reagan and Bush ad-ministrations' lax enforcement of desegregation orders. School districts got the message that school desegrega-tion was no longer an important national goal.[70]

As a result of these trends, there is more segregation today in northern cities, where the segregation has been mostly de facto, than in southern cities, where the seg-regation was mostly de jure.[71] Yet both regions are ex-periencing increasing segregation.

The persistence of de facto segregation and the wan-ing of commitment to integration have led national, state, and local officials to adopt the attitude, "We still agree with the goal of school desegregation, but it's too hard, and we're tired of it, and we give up."[72]

Reforms proposed for urban schools rarely in-clude desegregation. Officials speak of a ghetto school that is more "efficient" or one that gets more "input" from ghetto parents or offers more "choices" for ghetto children. But the existence of segregated edu-cation as "a permanent American reality" appears to be accepted.[73]

How Much Is White Skin Worth?

"You will be visited tonight by an official you have never met. He begins by telling you he is extremely embarrassed. The organization he represents has made a mistake, something that hardly ever happens.

According to their records, he goes on, you were to have been born black—to another set of parents, far from where you were raised.

However, the rules being what they are, this error must be rectified, and as soon as possible. So at midnight tonight, you will become black. And this will mean not simply a darker skin, but the bodily and facial features associated with African ancestry. However, inside, you will be the person you always were. Your knowledge and ideas will remain intact.

But outwardly you will not be recognizable to anyone you now know.

Your visitor emphasizes that being born to the wrong parents was in no way your fault. Consequently, his organization is prepared to offer you some reasonable recompense. Would you, he asks, care to name a sum of money you might consider appropriate? He adds that his group is by no means poor. It can be quite generous when the circumstances warrant, as they seem to in your case. He finishes by saying that their records show you are scheduled to live another fifty years—as a black man or woman in America.

How much financial recompense would you request?

A professor who puts this parable to white college students finds that most feel $1 million per year—$50 million total—would be appropriate. This much would protect them from, and reimburse them for, the danger and discrimination they would face if they were perceived as black. In acknowledging that white skin is worth this much, the students also are admitting that treatment of the races, even today, is not nearly equal.

SOURCE: Andrew Hacker, *Two Nations: Black and White, Separate, Hostile, Unequal* (New York: Scribner's, 1992), 31–32.

A writer who visited many central city classrooms and talked with students, teachers, and administrators observed that Martin Luther King was treated as

an icon, but his vision of a nation in which black and white kids went to school together seemed to be effaced almost entirely. Dutiful references to "The Dream" were often seen in school brochures and on wall posters in February, when "Black History" was celebrated in the public schools, but the content of the dream was treated as a closed box that could not be opened without ruining the celebration.[74]

Indeed, many cities have a school named after King—a segregated school in a segregated neighborhood—"like a terrible joke on history," a fourteen-year-old, wise beyond her years, remarked.[75]

Many minorities have gotten so frustrated that they themselves have questioned the goal of school desegregation. Instead, they have voiced greater concern about improving the quality and safety of their schools and neighborhoods.[76]

Unequal Funding In areas where schools are segregated, the quality varies enormously—from "the golden to the godawful," in the words of a Missouri judge.[77] And, of course, minorities are more likely to be in the "godawful."

Schools are financed largely by property taxes paid by homeowners and businesses. Wealthy cities get more in property taxes than poor ones. In modern America, this means suburban school districts get more to spend per pupil than central city school districts. Moreover, although many suburbs tax their residents at a lower rate than cities do, suburbs still bring in more revenue because their property is valued at a higher level. Thus, these suburbs ask their residents to sacrifice less but still provide their children with an education that costs more.[78] It is common, therefore, for a city such as Detroit to spend $3,600 per pupil while a suburb spends $6,400 per pupil per year, or for Camden, New Jersey, to spend $3,500 per pupil while Princeton spends $7,700.[79]

Spending-per-pupil figures do not take into account that the needs of poor children, after years of neglect and with scores of problems at home and in the neighborhood, are greater than the needs of other children. Schools for poor children would require *more* funding to provide their students an equal education.

So, many inner city schools are bleak institutions, reflecting disrepair and filth. A Camden school has a fire alarm system that has not worked in twenty years. An East St. Louis, Illinois, school has, a visitor discovered, a boys' bathroom in which "[f]our of the six toilets do not work. The toilet stalls, which are eaten away by red and brown corrosion, have no doors. The toilets have no seats. One has a rotted wooden stump. There are no paper towels and no soap. Near the door is a loop of wire with an empty toilet-paper roll." Yet the visitor was told, "This is the best school we have in East St. Louis." At another school in the city, sewage repeatedly backed up into the bathrooms and kitchen and flooded the gym and parking lot.[80]

Many inner city schools are overcrowded. Classes routinely are held in former coatrooms and closets. At one school two classes are held in converted coal bins while another is held in the current bathroom. Some cities in New Jersey literally ran out of classrooms and tried to rent space in vacant schools in the suburbs. But the cities were turned down because the suburbs did not want the mostly nonwhite children using the empty buildings.[81]

Many inner city schools do not have texts for all their students, texts that are at the appropriate grade levels, or texts that are up-to-date. A Chicago school has not had a library for twenty-one years. Some schools cannot afford to hire science, art, music, or physical education teachers. Almost all cannot afford to offer competitive salaries to hire good teachers in the subjects the schools do offer. A New York City principal says he is forced to take the "tenth-best" teachers. "I thank God they're still breathing."[82]

To save money, the Chicago school system relies on substitutes for a fourth of its teaching force. It cannot attract and hold enough substitutes, so on an average morning 5,700 students in 190 classrooms show up to find they have no teacher.[83]

A Chicago alderman, reflecting the prevailing middle-class view about local education, said, "Nobody in his right mind would send [his] kids to public school."[84]

Despite the pervasive pattern of unequal funding, cash alone would not solve all the problems. Cultural and economic factors in inner cities also restrict the quality of education available. But cash would help. According to one calculation, if New York City schools had been funded at the same level as the highest spending suburban schools on Long Island, a typical fourth grade class of thirty-six children would have had $200,000 more invested in their education in one year. The difference would have been enough to divide the class in half, hire two excellent teachers, and provide the classrooms with computers, new texts, reference books, learning games, carpets, air conditioning, and new counselors to help the children cope with problems in their environment outside school.[85]

Some states have equalized funding, but moves to do so in other states have encountered fierce opposition. After the New Jersey Supreme Court in 1990 ordered the state to reduce disparities between districts, the Democratic governor and legislature increased some taxes and cut some spending in other areas. The governor also redirected a portion of state aid from suburban schools to inner city schools to comply with the order. Suburbanites were furious; the next year they elected veto-proof majorities of Republicans to both houses of the state legislature in an attempt to block the program, and in the next election they ousted the governor.

An alternative to equalized funding would be for states to provide supplementary funding for schools in inner cities. But peoples' priorities run in other directions. In 1999 the Pennsylvania legislature approved $160 million of public financing for new stadiums for the Eagles and Phillies and another $160 million of public financing for new stadiums for the Steelers and Pirates, while the schools in Philadelphia and Pittsburgh languished.[86]

Second-Generation Discrimination Even where desegregation of schools has been achieved, segregation within schools exists. This "second-generation discrimination" isolates many minority students by placing them in separate programs or classes from white students. Black children are more likely to be put in "special education" classes for slow learners and less likely to be put in programs for gifted students. They are more likely to be put in classes for the educable mentally retarded (EMR).[87]

These facts by themselves are not necessarily evidence of second-generation discrimination, because the long legacy of discrimination and the dismal living conditions of many blacks make it harder for them to succeed in school. However, in school districts where more minorities are school board members or are administrators or teachers, less disparate treatment occurs.[88] The presence of minorities in authoritative positions apparently sensitizes white administrators or teachers to this discrimination.

Discrimination in Public Accommodations

Black newlyweds no longer have to spend their wedding nights in a funeral parlor, as Martin Luther and Coretta Scott King did. Most businesses comply with the Civil Rights Act of 1964 prohibiting discrimination in public accommodations.[89]

However, Jim Crow still lives in some places. For example, numerous blue-collar bars and lounges in New Orleans operate as though the act is not on the books. One serves blacks through a side window while it allows whites to drink inside. Others keep separate rooms for

A Philadelphia teacher tries to teach English in a hallway of an elementary school.
David Fields Photography

blacks and whites. Others use separate entrances—blacks through a back or side door, whites through the front door. "I can go to the front door, now," a black patron says. "But no one is going to let me in. All I'll do is get my feelings hurt. If you want service, you go around to the back room—that's for blacks."[90] Although illegal, these practices persist if no one files a complaint or brings a lawsuit.

In recent years a Denny's restaurant in Maryland refused to serve a group of blacks—unbeknownst to the restaurant, Secret Service agents—and the Denny's chain in California faced a lawsuit for discriminating against blacks. The plaintiffs said Denny's refused to honor offers for free birthday meals, assessed them a $2 cover on top of the cost of their meals, and asked them to pay in advance for their meals.[91] An Avis franchise in North Carolina refused to rent cars to blacks.

Some businesses try to circumvent the act. For instance, some restaurants give blacks poor service so they will not return. A suburban mall refused to allow city buses from Buffalo in its parking lot, although it allowed Canadian buses to bring their shoppers from across the border. Mall executives assured shopkeepers that "you'll never see an inner-city bus on the mall premises."[92]

Even some businesses that try to comply with the act have employees who treat blacks differently and embarrassingly. As one writer notes, "You stroll into a shop to look at the merchandise, and it soon becomes clear that the clerks are keeping a watchful eye on you. Too quickly, one of them comes over to inquire what it is you might want, and then remains conspicuously close as you continue your search. It also seems that they take an unusually long time verifying your credit card. Then you and a black friend enter a restaurant, and find yourselves greeted warily, with what is obviously a more anxious reception than that given to white guests. Yes, you will be served, and your table will not necessarily be next to the kitchen. Still, you sense that they would rather you had chosen some other eating place."[93]

Because the Civil Rights Act does not apply to private clubs, many country clubs and golf clubs discriminate against blacks. One estimate is that three-fourths of these clubs have no black members, and many of the remainder have only one or a few token members.[94] Thus, the business, professional, and political elites who form the membership perpetuate inequality in their circles and also send a message that discrimination is acceptable for others in society.

Discrimination in Employment

Although the Civil Rights Act of 1964 and affirmative action (discussed later in the chapter) have prompted more employers to hire and promote African Americans, discrimination remains.

A 1991 study of Chicago and Washington, D.C., used pairs of white and black male college students who were matched in education, experience, age, speech, demeanor, and physical build. The men applied for nearly five hundred advertised jobs involving retail, service, clerical, or physical labor. The whites advanced farther in the hiring process 20 percent of the time, while the blacks did 7 percent of the time. (They were equal in the remainder.) The blacks found the most discrimination

A Grand Rapids artist put up this billboard to prompt white motorists to think about how they would feel if discrimination were directed at them instead. By the next day the word NIGER [sic]had been scrawled on the billboard, and the mayor had gotten so many complaints that the artist had to take the billboard down.
© Mark Heckman

in white-collar jobs—one who had applied for a job as a hotel desk clerk was offered a job as a bellboy—and those requiring contact with customers.[95] These results not only reflect discrimination against blacks but also contradict the perception that there is widespread reverse discrimination against whites.

A 1992 investigation by the Equal Employment Opportunity Commission (EEOC) uncovered discriminatory practices by employment agencies that hire workers for many companies. The agencies devised code phrases the companies could use to screen out applicants of a particular race or sex or age as a way to violate the law without being caught. If, for example, a business did not want any blacks, it was instructed to specify, "No Z." If it simply preferred whites, it was instructed to say, "Talk to Mary." Through these phrases, one Los Angeles agency alone discriminated against 3,900 applicants.[96]

Many blacks who are hired are passed over when they believe they should be promoted.[97] But discrimination at this point is more subtle and more difficult to prove. Black employees at Texaco filed suit but felt stymied until a white executive, who was being forced to retire early, disclosed secret tape recordings of a meeting at which top executives discussed the suit and admitted shredding documents and hiding others that had been subpoenaed by aggrieved employees. In the wake of the publicity, the company quickly settled the suit.

Many blacks are also subjected to racial slurs—in comments, notes, and graffiti—on the job. They face an unfriendly or hostile environment.

Upper-level executives realize that it is economically advantageous to have a diverse workforce, but some middle-level white managers and lower-level white workers interact poorly with the black employees.

Discrimination in Housing

The Civil Rights Act of 1968 prohibiting discrimination in housing has fostered some desegregation of housing, especially big apartment complexes, which are more visible and therefore more susceptible to pressure from civil rights groups and the government. And the act has resulted in large penalties on individuals found guilty of violations. Lawyers for fair-housing organizations say white jurors think discrimination has been eliminated—until they hear the testimony, which jars them into granting large awards.[98]

But the act is working at a snail's pace to change housing patterns. One reason is economic. Most blacks do not have enough money to buy homes in white neighborhoods. This problem is aggravated by local zoning laws designed to establish a certain type of community. Often these laws require large lots and large houses, which command high prices.

Another reason is continuing discrimination. Occasional violence and considerable social pressure discourage blacks who try to move into white neighborhoods. Actual discrimination by homeowners, realtors, lenders, and insurers also stymies them. A study of forty metropolitan areas found that blacks who try to buy a house face discrimination 75 percent of the time, and those who try to rent do so 62 percent of the time.[99]

Some realtors still practice steering. Many lenders apparently require extra proof that blacks will repay their home loans. A study by the Federal Reserve Board examined 5.3 million mortgage applications to 9,300 financial institutions in nineteen major cities in 1990. It found that applications from blacks were denied more than twice as often as those from whites with comparable income. As a result, applications from high-income blacks were rejected about as often as those from low-income whites.[100] Some insurers evidently practice a version of redlining. A 1993 study of five large midwestern cities concluded that insurance companies charged blacks in inner cities twice the rate for homeowners' insurance that they charged whites with similar income.[101] Because lenders normally require borrowers to get homeowners' insurance to qualify for a home loan, higher-priced insurance makes it harder to buy the home.

The Clinton administration proposed that the government phase out its public housing projects and give residents vouchers—government coupons—to use for any housing unit they locate on their own. The goal was to let them escape the dreary environment of the huge projects, but one consequence would be to desegregate more neighborhoods, as the minorities in the projects fanned out through the city or, possibly, adjacent suburbs. Congressional Republicans blocked the proposal. Although they support the concept of vouchers—allowing individuals to choose a service rather than having the government determine what particular service is best for them—and the use of vouchers to enable children to attend religious schools, many oppose the use of vouchers to enable minorities to move into white neighborhoods.[102]

For all of these reasons, residential segregation remains pervasive in metropolitan areas. However, it is declining slowly. The percentage of blacks living in non-black neighborhoods, defined as areas with less than 10 percent blacks, has inched from about 10 percent to 12 percent.[103] Still, Asians and Hispanics with third grade educations are more likely to live in integrated neighborhoods than blacks with Ph.D.s.[104]

Segregation does not continue because blacks "want to live by their own kind," as some whites insist. Surveys show that only about 15 percent want to live in segregated neighborhoods, while 85 percent would prefer mixed neighborhoods. (Many say the optimal level would be about half blacks and half whites.) Yet whites tend to move out, and new ones do not move in, when blacks reach 8 to 10 percent.[105] These very different views make integration an elusive goal, particularly because blacks make up 12 to 13 percent of the American population and a much larger percentage of some cities.

These patterns and attitudes are all the more troublesome because residential segregation, of course, leads to further school segregation.

To add potential injury to the insult for blacks, a study of the Environmental Protection Agency's enforcement of air, water, and hazardous waste pollution laws from 1985 to 1991 concluded that the government took longer to act in minority communities, imposed smaller fines against polluters in those communities, and required less stringent solutions in those communities.[106]

Discrimination in Other Ways

African Americans face discrimination from police officers. The practice of **racial profiling,** which is based on the assumption that minorities, especially males, are more likely to commit crimes, especially ones involving drugs, targets minorities for stops and searches. So officers stop minority drivers without any evidence and often search them and their car.[107] Racial profiling sometimes is directed toward pedestrians and toward passengers in airports as well. Although police departments deny following this practice, statistics show clear evidence that disproportionate numbers of minorities are stopped and searched. Interstate 95 from Florida to New York is notorious. On I-95 through Maryland, while 18 percent of the speeders were black, 29 percent of those stopped and 71 percent of those searched were black. On the New Jersey Turnpike, while 15 percent of the speeders were black, 35 percent of those pulled over were black.[108] The practice of racial profiling contributes to the tensions between minorities and police.

Now African Americans speak of the moving violation "DWB"—Driving While Black. A Chicago journalist who was stopped at least every other time he traveled through the Midwest learned not to rent flashy Mustangs or wear his beret. Others avoid tinted windshields or expensive sunglasses—any flamboyance—to avoid the cops.[109]

New York residents protest the not guilty verdict given to four police officers who killed an unarmed man in the doorway of his apartment building. They wave their wallets to mock the officers' claims that they thought the victim's wallet was actually a gun.
Bebato Matthews/AP Wide World Photos

Other discrimination from police officers is less common but more serious. Sometimes officers arrest black citizens without legal cause, and occasionally they use excessive force against them. Numerous examples attest to improper beatings.[110] Sometimes officers lie while testifying against black suspects in court. As a result, even prominent African Americans say their "worst fear is to have to go before the criminal justice system."[111] It is little wonder, then, that black jurors hearing the O. J. Simpson trial and black citizens following it put less faith in the police testimony than white observers did.

Cautious parents feel obligated to teach their children how to avoid sending the wrong signals to police. Some parents urge their children not to wear street fashions and not to use cell phones, which from a distance might be mistaken as weapons. Some schools offer survival workshops for police encounters. Minority officers instruct the students what to do when they get stopped: don't reach for an ID unless the officer asks for one; don't mumble or talk loudly; don't antagonize by asking for a badge number or threatening to file a complaint.[112]

Most blacks, even those in the upper and middle classes and those in professional occupations, face insults because of their race. Black women tell of being mistaken for hotel chambermaids. One family therapist, invited to speak at a conference, was stopped in the hallway by a white attendee who asked where the restrooms were. When the therapist appeared taken aback, the attendee said she thought the woman worked at the hotel. Although the therapist was wearing her official name tag

and presenter's ribbon, the attendee did not look past her black face.[113] Black women also tell of waiting for friends in hotel lobbies and being mistaken for prostitutes by white men and police officers. A distinguished black political scientist tells of people who assume he is a butler, in his own home. Black doctors tell of dressing up when they go shopping to avoid being regarded as shoplifters. But even dressing up is no guarantee. A black lawyer, a senior partner in a large law firm, arrived at work early one morning, before the doors were unlocked. As he reached for his key, a young white lawyer, a junior associate in the firm, arrived, blocked his entrance, and asked, repeatedly and demandingly, "May I help you?" The white associate had taken the black partner for an intruder.[114] Although in these encounters the insults were unintentional, the stings hurt just the same.

Overall, discrimination against African Americans continues. Whites speak of "past discrimination"—sometimes referring to slavery, sometimes to official segregation—but this phrase is misleading. Of course, there is a lot less discrimination now due to the civil rights movement, Supreme Court decisions, and congressional acts. However, there is nothing "past" about much "past discrimination."[115] The effects linger and, indeed, the discrimination itself persists.

Even when blacks point out the discrimination, some whites insist there is little discrimination left. These whites apparently assume they know more than blacks do about what it is like to be black.

As African Americans have become frustrated with the slow pace of progress, some have been attracted to the black separatist movement. These blacks, seeing themselves as realistic, consider integration a naive ideal from the 1950s and 1960s—an impossibility even in the future. They want to direct their energy toward building up the black community.[116] (Supreme Court Justice Clarence Thomas seems to hold this view.) But most blacks, remaining hopeful, consider separatism premature and risky; they fear it will play into the hands of the most prejudiced whites trying to perpetuate discrimination.

Improving Conditions for African Americans?

Despite continuing discrimination, African Americans have taken great strides toward achieving equal rights. These strides should have led to much better living conditions for them and to a healthier racial climate in society. If we look at the actual conditions and the actual climate today, we see that many African Americans are indeed better off, but others are no better off and some might be worse off than before the civil rights movement.

Since the 1960s, blacks' lives have improved in most ways that can be measured.[117] Blacks have a longer life expectancy and a lower poverty rate than before. They have completed more years of education, with larger numbers attending college and graduate school. They have attained higher occupational levels—for example, tripling their proportion of the country's professionals[118]—and income levels. (Yet their average income is only about half of whites' average income.) Many more have reached the middle class. About half of all blacks consider themselves middle class, and even more are classified as middle class or higher—fully 59 percent are "middle class" and another 11 percent are "affluent," according to one calculation.[119] A third have moved to the suburbs,[120] and many have bought their own homes.

The integration of African Americans into sports, music, and other forms of entertainment has been dramatic. In all these areas, they have become highly visible. In the mid-1980s, a Louisville sportswriter cracked that a Martian would sit in the White House before a black man would coach basketball at the University of Kentucky. But in 1998 the university hired a black man, Tubby Smith, who guided the team to a national championship in his first season.

During the same years that blacks' lives have improved, whites' racial attitudes have also improved. Although answers to pollsters' questions cannot be accepted as perfect reflections of people's views, especially on emotional matters such as racial attitudes, the answers can be considered general indicators of these views. Polls

encompassing a wide variety of racial questions show that whites' views have changed significantly (even assuming that some whites gave more socially acceptable answers than they really felt).[121] Whites and blacks both report more social contact with members of the other race since the 1960s (see Table 2), and both report more approval of interracial dating and marriage (see Table 3). The acceptance of interracial dating and marriage is especially significant, because these practices were the ultimate taboos in segregated society. Interracial couples represented the clearest breach and their potential offspring the greatest threat to continued segregation.

Some whites, of course, remain blatant racists (perhaps from 2 to 24 percent, according to various estimates by social scientists).[122] But blatant racist behavior occurs less frequently and is condemned more quickly than before.

Even so, blacks have pessimistic views of whites' attitudes. In 1989, one-fourth of blacks believed that at least a quarter of whites were in the Ku Klux Klan; one-fourth

Table 2	Blacks and Whites Have Had More Social Contact since the 1960s

The percentages of respondents who say that members of the other race do the following:

	Blacks	Whites
Live in their neighborhood		
1964	66	20
1976	70	38
1994	83	61
Are friends of theirs		
1964	62	18
1976	87	50
1989	82	66
Are "good friends" of theirs		
1975	21	9
1994	78	73
Have been dinner guests in their home		
1973	39	20
1994	53	34
Attend their church		
1978	37	34
1994	61	44

SOURCE: Stephan Thernstrom and Abigail Thernstrom, *America in Black and White* (New York: Simon & Schuster, 1997), 521.

Table 3 — Approval of Interracial Dating and Marriage Has Increased since the 1960s

The following percentages say it is all right for blacks and whites to date each other.

	Blacks	Whites
1963	NA	10
1987	72	43
1994	88	65
Ages 18–24	NA	85
Age 65 or over	NA	36

The following percentages say it is all right for blacks and whites to marry each other.

	Blacks	Whites
1958	NA	4
1968	48	17
1978	66	32
1983	76	38
1994	68	45

SOURCE: Stephan Thernstrom and Abigail Thernstrom, *America in Black and White* (New York: Simon & Schuster, 1997), 524–525.

of blacks also believed that most whites shared the views of the KKK. In 1992, two-thirds of blacks believed that about half of whites were "basically prejudiced." (Whites also believed this about whites.)[123] One sociologist estimates that, despite the improvement in whites' attitudes, there are still two white racists for every African American. For socioeconomic reasons, blacks are more likely to come into contact with prejudiced whites, who live and work in closer proximity to blacks, than they are to come into contact with tolerant whites, who are more educated, prosperous, and suburban.[124] Furthermore, some blacks have not experienced the overall improvements. It would be more surprising if they were not pessimistic.

When the push for civil rights opened doors, some blacks were not in a position to pass through. About a third of the black population lives in poverty—three times the rate among the white population—and about a tenth, the poorest of the poor, exists in a state of economic and social "disintegration."[125] This "underclass" is trapped in a cycle of self-perpetuating problems from which it is extremely difficult to escape. These people are isolated from the rest of society and demoralized about their prospects for improvement.

The problems of the lower class and underclass were exacerbated by economic changes that began in the 1970s and hit the poor the hardest. Good-paying manufacturing jobs in the cities—the traditional path out of poverty for immigrant groups—disappeared. Chicago lost over three hundred thousand jobs, New York over five hundred thousand.[126] Many jobs were eliminated by automation, while many others were moved to foreign countries or to the suburbs. Although service jobs increased, most were outside the cities also. And most either required more education or paid lower wages than the manufacturing jobs had.

As a result, black men, especially, lost their jobs and lost their ability to support a family. This led not only to pressure on intact families but to a decrease in the number of "marriageable" black men and an increase in the number of households headed by black women.[127] The percentage of such households rose from about 20 percent in 1960 to nearly 50 percent in 1994.[128] And 60 percent of black children live in such households. These families are among the poorest in the country.

Meanwhile, the black middle class fled the inner cities to the suburbs. Their migration left the ghettos with fewer healthy businesses, strong schools, or other institutions to provide stability and fewer role models to portray mainstream behavior.[129] By 1996 one Chicago ghetto with sixty-six thousand people had just one supermarket and one bank but forty-eight state-licensed lottery agents and ninety-nine state-licensed liquor stores and bars.[130] The combination of chronic unemployment in the inner cities and middle-class migration from the inner cities created an environment that offers ample opportunity and some incentive to use drugs, commit crimes, and engage in other types of antisocial behavior.

The development of crack, a cheap form of cocaine, in the mid-1980s aggravated these conditions. It led to more drug use and drug trafficking that overwhelmed whole neighborhoods. Crack ravaged the lives of users in ways that other drugs did not, and by producing steady demand by users and huge profits for dealers, it stimulated more violence. As drug gangs multiplied and tangled with each other for control of turf, drug executions and drive-by shootings became commonplace.[131]

The spread of AIDS, rampant among intravenous drug users, further aggravated these conditions.

Half of the victims of murder and more than half of those charged with murder are black, although the population is only 12 percent black.[132] Two-thirds of the defendants sent to state prisons for drug offenses are black. According to one study in Washington, D.C., one-fourth of black males born in the 1960s were charged with drug dealing between the ages of eighteen and twenty-four.[133] (Of course, part of this is due to harsher treatment of black drug offenders than of white.)

The plight of young black men is worse than that of any other group in society. In 1990, almost one of every four black men between the ages of twenty and twenty-nine was serving a criminal sentence in prison or was on probation or parole; by 1995 almost one of every three was.[134] Also, a black man in Harlem has less chance of living past forty than a man in Bangladesh.[135]

After the riots in the 1960s, the Kerner Commission, appointed by President Johnson to examine the cause of the riots, concluded, "What white Americans have never fully understood—but what the Negro can never forget—is that white society is deeply implicated in the ghetto. White institutions created it, white institutions maintain it, and white society condones it." After the riots, however, governments did little to improve the conditions that precipitated the riots. Now the conditions in the ghettos are worse.

After the 1992 riots in Los Angeles that followed the trial of the police officers who beat Rodney King, there was more talk about improving conditions in the ghetto. But a columnist who had heard such talk before commented, "My guess is that when all is said and done, a great deal more will be said than done. The truth is we don't know any quick fixes for our urban ills and we lack the patience and resources for slow fixes."[136]

These problems are all the more difficult to resolve, because the cities have lost political power as they have lost population due to white flight and black migration. In 1992, for the first time, more voters lived in the suburbs than in the cities. These voters do not urge action on urban problems. Sometimes, in fact, they resist action if it means an increase in their taxes or a decrease in their services.

For the black lower class, and especially for the black underclass, it is apparent that civil rights are not enough. As one black leader said, "What good is a seat in the front of the bus if you don't have the money for the fare?"[137] But the lower class and underclass do not define most blacks, and the poverty-stricken inner city does not typify the environment for most blacks today.

Discrimination against Hispanics

Hispanics, increasingly called Latinos, are people with Spanish-speaking backgrounds. The first Latinos came to America from Spain in the 1500s. They settled in the Southwest, and when the United States took this land from Mexico in 1848, they became U.S. citizens. Other Latinos came to America more recently.

Latinos include groups with different cultural traditions. About 61 percent trace their ancestry to Mexico and live mainly in the Southwest, though some live in large cities in the Midwest. About 15 percent are from Puerto Rico, which is a commonwealth—a self-governing territory—of the United States. As members of the commonwealth, they are U.S. citizens. Most live in New York, Boston, Chicago, and other cities in the North. Another 6 percent are from Cuba. Following the establishment of a communist government in Cuba in 1959, many fled to the United States and settled in south Florida. In recent years, Latinos from other Caribbean or Central American countries have immigrated to the United States to escape turmoil and oppression.

Despite the diversity of their origins, Latinos are heavily concentrated. More than half live in California and Texas.

Latinos represent about 12 percent of the U.S. population. Already the United States has the seventh largest Latino population in the world, and within the United States this group is the second fastest growing minority (after Asians). Due to a high birthrate, they are predicted to overtake blacks within a decade.[138]

Latinos never endured slavery, but they have suffered discrimination. Many Latinos are Caucasian. However, many Puerto Ricans and Cubans have African ancestry, and many Mexicans have some Indian ancestry, so they have darker skin than non-Hispanic whites. Like blacks, Hispanics have faced discrimination in education, employment, housing, and voting.[139]

Latinos also encounter discrimination due to continuing immigration. The illegal immigrants pouring in from Mexico exacerbate hostility and discrimination against Latinos, especially in the Southwest. U.S. Border Patrol and local law enforcement officials, who cannot tell the difference between Latinos who are citizens or legal residents and those who are not, often stop them for questioning not only at the border but inland as well. (Agents stopped the mayor of Pomona, California, more than one hundred miles from the border, and ordered him to produce papers to prove that he is a legal resident.) Even if officials are well intentioned, their conduct is considered harassment by law-abiding legal residents.

Latinos also encounter discrimination from police, as African Americans do. Police use racial profiling, suspecting them of crimes involving drugs as well as illegal immigration. In Illinois, Latinos constitute 8 percent of the population but 30 percent of those stopped by police.[140]

Discrimination in Education

For years Latino children in some areas were not allowed to attend schools at all. In other areas they were segregated into "Mexican" schools whose quality was not comparable with Anglo schools.[141]

In the 1940s, Mexican American organizations asked the courts to find that Mexican Americans were "white" so that they could not be segregated. The federal courts agreed.

This strategy backfired, however, after the Supreme Court declared segregation by race illegal. Many school districts accomplished "integration" by combining blacks with Latinos, leaving non-Hispanic whites in separate schools.[142]

Even when admitted to schools, Latinos faced discrimination due to their language. Traditionally, teachers and administrators forbade students from speaking their native Spanish to each other in school. They reprimanded, spanked, or expelled those who did. Some even anglicized students' names in class and in school records so that "Jesus" became "Jesse" and "Miguel" became "Michael."[143]

Although de jure segregation has been struck down,[144] de facto segregation exists in northern and southwestern cities where Latinos are concentrated, due to residential segregation and white flight to the suburbs. Many Latinos attend schools with more than 90 percent minorities, and most attend schools with more than half minorities.[145] As a result, Latinos in Los Angeles, for example, are more likely to attend segregated schools than blacks in Alabama or Georgia.[146]

Even where Latinos go to desegregated schools, they are often segregated within the schools. They face "second-generation discrimination," though not as much as blacks.[147]

Predominantly Latino schools, like predominantly black schools, are not as well funded as other schools. Because minority schools are frequently in poor communities, they do not receive as much revenue from property taxes. In San Antonio, Mexican American families were concentrated in the poorest districts, while wealthy families were concentrated in a section that was incorporated as a separate district, though it was surrounded on four sides by the rest of the city. Its property taxes financed its schools only. When Mexican American parents sued, the Burger Court ruled that the Fourteenth Amendment's equal protection clause does not require states to equalize funding between school districts.[148] Although some states proceeded to equalize funding, other states have not.

Latinos' primary problem in education, however, is the language barrier. Many are unable to speak English, causing them to fail in school and drop out of school at higher rates than other students, even African Americans. One-third of Latinos leave school at some point; one-fourth drop out in high school.[149]

Bilingual education was established to help such students. These classes use the students' native language to teach them English and also substantive subjects such as math. The goal is to transition from their native language to English within three years. In 1968, Congress encouraged bilingual education by providing funding, and in 1974 the Supreme Court, in a case brought by Chinese parents, held that schools must teach students in a language they can understand.[150] This can be their native language, or it can be English if they have been taught English. These federal actions prompted many states to establish bilingual education programs.

More than 150 languages, from Chinese to Yapese, have been offered nationwide. Because almost three-fourths of the students who do not speak English are Hispanic, Spanish is the most common.[151]

Bilingual education programs have been controversial. Latino parents want their children to learn English, and to learn it well. A survey of Latinos in forty cities found that more than 90 percent thought U.S. citizens and residents should learn English.[152] A survey of Cuban Americans in south Florida found that 98 percent thought it was important for their children to read and write "perfect English."[153] And their children apparently agree. More than four-fifths of immigrant children in south Florida and more than two-thirds of those in San Diego prefer English to their familial language.[154] Latino parents and children worry that bilingual programs will delay the mastery of English. Seventy-five percent of recent immigrants, including 56 percent of Mexican immigrants, oppose these programs.[155]

In fact, bilingual programs have not worked as well in practice as they have promised in theory. Although their results are difficult to measure because the programs vary, being staffed at different levels and for different lengths of time, they have been disappointing. Perhaps these results should not be surprising, given that the programs grew partly out of political as well as pedagogical needs. Latino groups in the Southwest saw them as a way to tap into federal antipoverty funds.[156]

Indeed, the debate revolves around politics as much as education. Some Latino groups see bilingual education as a way to preserve their native language and culture. They consider it to be a component of multiculturalism. So they want it not as a temporary bridge until students learn English but as a permanent fixture through high school. Many Anglo citizens, especially those who fear the influx of immigrants, also see bilingual education as a way to preserve Latinos' native language and culture. But these Anglos discount the need for multiculturalism. Instead, they want the students to be exposed only to English so that they will be more likely to assimilate into society. Some Latino leaders accuse these Anglo citizens of "cultural genocide."[157]

For both sides, then, bilingual education has become a symbolic issue. It prompts concerns, even fears, about the relative dominance of Anglo culture and Hispanic culture and about the extent to which Anglo Americans will make room for Hispanic Americans in society.

The debate is complicated by economic and bureaucratic problems in bilingual programs. Because they require more teachers and smaller classes, the programs are expensive and impractical. Many schools cannot find enough teachers in the necessary languages. California, where half of all students in bilingual programs lived, fell twenty-one thousand teachers short in 1998.[158] Schools

Latinos are gradually improving their status. This woman toils as a migrant farm worker, but her son graduated from college and now runs personnel management programs for farmers.
© Mario Pignata-Monti

were unable to offer bilingual education to two-thirds of the students who were eligible.[159]

For all of these reasons, California citizens voted to abolish bilingual programs in 1998. Now non-English-speaking students receive intensive immersion in English for one year and then move into regular classes. Initial research indicates that Spanish-speaking students are improving rapidly in their ability to read English and to understand other subjects taught in English.[159a]

Despite the disappointing results of bilingual programs and the common perceptions of many Americans, current immigrants throughout the country are learning English. Among Spanish speakers in the United States, over 90 percent speak English.[160] Although about half of those who arrived as teenagers or adults do not speak English proficiently, almost all of those who arrived as younger children or who are in the second generation do speak English proficiently.[161] Cuban Americans are learning it as fast or faster than any group in history.[162] Mexican Americans are learning it as they live longer in the United States. Although many of those who come for work and plan to return to Mexico do not speak English, most of those who plan to remain in the United States learn to speak more English, and almost all of their children learn to speak fluent English.[163]

It is true that some immigrant communities, especially Cubans in south Florida and Mexicans in parts of the Southwest, are so large that people can survive without learning English. But most feel pressure to learn English to function in the broader society and for their children to succeed in school.

Combating Discrimination against Hispanics

In the 1960s Latino advocacy groups tried to imitate African American groups by using protests and other forms of direct action. The Chicano movement attempted to forge a powerful bloc from the diverse population of the Hispanic people. Cesar Chavez successfully led a coalition of labor, civil rights, and religious groups to obtain better working conditions for migrant farm workers in California. But few visible national leaders or organizations emerged.

In 1977, when the first Hispanic member of Congress from California approached the Speaker of the House about the possibility of establishing an Hispanic caucus, as other groups had established various caucuses, the Speaker teased, "Where are you going to hold the meetings—in a telephone booth?"[164]

Latinos are more diverse and less cohesive than blacks. Most do not even consider themselves part of a large group of Hispanics.[165] They profess strong loyalty to people of their national origin and have little contact with Hispanics with other ancestry. Thus, most do not call themselves "Hispanics" or "Latinos," but "Mexican Americans," "Puerto Ricans," or "Cuban Americans."[166] Also, they have different legal statuses. Puerto Ricans have American citizenship by birth, but many Latinos do not have it at all. And they lack a common defining experience in their background, such as slavery for blacks, to unite them.

But where they are highly concentrated, they are increasingly powerful at the local and state levels of government (and even at the national level—the congressional Hispanic caucus grew to seventeen members in 2000). Rather than portraying themselves as a victimized group, they are moving into the mainstream. Rather than focusing primarily on immigration issues, bilingual education, and affirmative action, they are addressing broader concerns, such as health care and school class-size reduction. Yet Latino politicians have not shaped a common agenda, perhaps because Latino people, of diverse origins, do not share a common agenda.[167]

Nevertheless, the people are moving up the ladder. More attend college and become managers and professionals. At least those who speak educated English appear to be following the pattern of Southern and Eastern European immigrants—arriving poor, facing discrimination, but eventually working their way up. They are also assimilating through high rates of marriage to non-Latinos.

Discrimination against Native Americans

More than two million Native Americans live in the United States. Although some are Eskimos and Aleuts from Alaska, most are Indians, representing more than 550 tribes with different histories, customs, and languages. Most are proud of their tribal heritage and prefer to be known by their tribal name, such as Cheyenne or Sioux, than by the collective terms, Native Americans and Indians. About half live on reservations.

Although Native Americans have faced some discrimination similar to that against blacks and Hispanics, they have endured much discrimination of a different nature.

Government Policy Toward Native Americans

The government's policy toward Native Americans has varied over the years, ranging from forced separation at one extreme to forced assimilation at the other.

Separation Initially, the policy was separation. For many years people believed the continent was so vast that most of its interior would remain wilderness, populated by Indians who would have ample room to live and hunt. The Constitution reflects this belief. It grants Congress authority to "regulate commerce with foreign nations,

"I love the way you make those yams. You'll have to give me the recipe before your culture is obliterated from the face of the earth."

and among the several states, and with the Indian tribes." In early cases Chief Justice John Marshall described the tribes as "dependent domestic nations."[168] They were within U.S. borders but outside its political process.

Early treaties reinforced separation by establishing boundaries between Indians and non-Indians. The government thought these boundaries were necessary for its growth, the Indians for their survival. The boundaries were intended to minimize conflict. White hunters or settlers who ventured across the boundaries could be punished as the Indians saw fit.

But as the country grew, it became increasingly difficult to contain settlers within the boundaries. Mounting pressure to push Native Americans further west led to the Indian Removal Act of 1830, which authorized removal of tribes east of the Mississippi River and relocation on reservations west of the river. At the time people considered the Great Plains to be the great American desert, unfit for habitation by whites but suitable for Indians. At first, removal was voluntary, but eventually it became mandatory for most and was supervised by the U.S. cavalry.

Assimilation and Citizenship As more settlers moved west, the vision of separate Indian country far enough beyond white civilization to prevent conflict faded. In the 1880s, the government switched its policy to assimilation. Prompted by Christian churches, officials sought to "civilize" the Indians, that is, to incorporate them into the larger society, whether they wanted to be incorporated or not. In place of their traditional means of subsistence, rendered useless once the tribes were re-

moved from their homeland, the government subdivided reservation land into small tracts and allotted these tracts to tribe members in hopes that they would turn to farming as white and black settlers had. (In the process, the government reclaimed "surplus" land and sold it to white settlers. Ultimately, the Indians lost about two-thirds of their reservation land.)[169] Bureau of Indian Affairs agents, who supervised the reservations, tried to root out Native American ways and replace them with white dress and hairstyles, the English language, and the Christian religion. Government boarding schools separated Native American children from their families to instill these new practices.

Early in the history of the United States, Native Americans were not considered citizens but members of separate nations. Treaties made exceptions for those who married whites and for those who left their tribes and abandoned their tribal customs. But in 1890, after government policy switched to assimilation, Congress permitted some who remained with their tribes on reservations to become citizens by applying to the U.S. government. Citizenship was sometimes marked by a formal ceremony. In one the Indian shot his last arrow and then took hold of the handles of a plow to demonstrate his assimilation.[170] After World War I, Congress granted citizenship to those who served in the military during the war, and finally in 1924, Congress extended it to all those born in the United States.

Citizenship enabled Indians to vote and hold office, though some states effectively barred them from the polls for decades. Arizona denied them the right to vote until 1948, Utah until 1956.[171]

Tribal Restoration By the 1930s, the government recognized the negative consequences of coerced assimilation. Most Indians could speak English, but they were poorly educated in other respects. And with their traditional means of earning a living gone, most were poverty stricken. The policy led to destruction of Native American ways without much assimilation into white society. Consequently, in 1934 Congress implemented a new policy of tribal restoration that recognized Indians as distinct persons and tribes as autonomous entities that were encouraged to govern themselves once again. Traditional cultural and religious practices were accepted, and children, no longer forced to attend boarding schools, were taught some Indian languages.

Native Americans feel renewed cultural pride but also the lure of modern American technology.
© TSM, Mug Shots, 1977

The government even made an effort to settle claims for wrongful taking of tribal land. For several decades the Indian Claims Commission authorized the payment of money—not the return of property—to tribes whose land was illegally taken by the government anytime since 1776. But the commission faced an impossible task. Most tribes had a hazy conception of land ownership and did not keep written records. How would disputed land be valued—according to the earlier subsistence living of the Indians or the later market value to farmers, ranchers, and miners? And how would religious land be valued? (Native religions focused on particular parcels of land or prominent features of the landscape, rather than on buildings such as churches.) Ultimately, the commission authorized as much money as it thought was politically feasible, but this amounted to less than $1,000 for every Native American.[172]

Reflecting the policy of tribal restoration and the efforts of other minorities in the 1960s and 1970s, Indian interest groups became active. Indian law firms pursued cases in court, seeking to protect not only tribal independence and traditional ways, but also land, mineral, and water resources. The diversity of the tribes—they are divided by geography and culture and located in many of the remotest and poorest parts of the country—makes it difficult for them to present a united front. Nevertheless, they have been able to wrest some autonomy from the government. In particular, they have gotten more authority over the educational and social programs administered by the Bureau of Indian Affairs for the tribes.[173]

In recent years Indians have fought for an end to digging up old gravesites and for a return of bones and artifacts unearthed from them. With little regard for Native American culture, "pothunters" have searched for artifacts to sell to collectors. Such looting raises the ire of archaeologists who say, "We'll never know what's

been taken or how it relates to what remains in the ground. Everything has been scrambled." But digging for scientific purposes itself enrages some Indians, who say that archaeologists are "hardly any better than grave robbers themselves; only difference is they've got a state permit." Until recent years, in fact, many laws about exhumation of bones applied only to those of whites.[174]

Some tribes are enjoying renewed vitality with the income they receive from mineral rights or gambling casinos. After a Supreme Court ruling and a congressional law in the 1980s underscored tribal sovereignty on tribal land, tribes could establish gambling casinos on reservations, even if their state did not allow casinos.[175] Almost three hundred tribes have done so, although less than a dozen have found a bonanza.[176] Even so, they have heard complaints about "rich Indians" (a very inaccurate description of most Indians). With their new revenues, the tribes have begun to buy into the political process, as other groups have done. Threatened by gambling interests in Las Vegas and Atlantic City, which fear that tribal casinos will lure away potential customers, the tribes have formed their own lobby, the National Indian Gaming Association, and made their own contributions to politicians.

Overall, Native Americans enjoy renewed pride. From 1970 to 1990, according to birth and death records, the Indian population increased by 760,000. Yet, according to people's self-identification for the census, this population rose by 1.4 million.[177] Evidently, many people, including those with only distant Indian ancestry, who did not wish to identify themselves as Indians in 1970, did by 1990.

Now more Indians share the views of one activist who says, "You have a federal government, state governments, and tribal governments—three sovereigns in one country. This is . . . the civil rights movement of Native Americans."[178]

Nevertheless, Indians remain at the bottom of America's racial and ethnic totem pole. They are the least educated and most unemployed group, the poorest and sickest group, with the highest rates of alcoholism and the lowest life expectancy, of any people in the country.

Sex Discrimination

Discrimination against Women

For many generations, people believed that natural differences between the sexes required them to occupy separate spheres of life. Men would dominate the public domain of work and government, while women would dominate the private domain of the home. Both domains were important, and men were considered superior in one while women were considered superior in the other. Unlike racial minorities, women were not held in disdain in every aspect of life.

Thomas Jefferson, the most egalitarian of the Founders, reflected this widespread view when he said, "Were our state a pure democracy there would still be excluded from our deliberations women, who, to prevent deprivation of morals and ambiguity of issues, should not mix promiscuously in gatherings of men."[179] That is, women are more moral than men, so they would be corrupted by politics, but also more irrational, so they would confuse the issues. For both reasons, they should not be involved in politics.

Women were denied the right to vote in most places, and married women were denied other rights. They did not have the right to manage property they owned before marriage, to manage wages they received from jobs, to enter into contracts, or to sue. Although some states eventually enacted laws granting women these rights, when disputes arose within families, male judges hesitated to tell other men how to treat their wives. Often, then, these rights did not exist in practice until well into the twentieth century.

Even women's citizenship was tied to their husbands'. If a foreign woman married an American man, she automatically became a United States citizen. But if an American woman married a foreign man, she automatically lost her United States citizenship. (Women's citizenship would not become independent of their husbands' until 1922, shortly after women gained the right to vote.)

Women were also barred from schools and jobs. Before the Civil War, they were not admitted to public high schools. Because they were being prepared for motherhood, education was considered unnecessary, even dangerous. According to the *Encyclopaedia Britannica* in 1800, women had smaller brains than men.[180] Education would fatigue them and possibly ruin their reproductive organs. Similarly, before the Civil War, women were not encouraged to hold jobs. Those who sought employment were shunted into jobs that were seen as extensions of the domestic domain, such as producing textiles, clothes, and shoes in sex-segregated factories.[181]

This traditional conception of gender roles created problems for women who did not fit the mold. Myra Bradwell ran a private school, founded a weekly newspaper, and worked for civic organizations. She was active in the women's suffrage movement and instrumental in persuading the Illinois legislature to expand women's legal rights. But after studying law, she was denied a license to practice law solely because she was a woman. The U.S. Supreme Court upheld the Illinois policy in 1873.[182] Justice Joseph Bradley declared:

> [L]aw as well as nature itself, has always recognized a wide difference in the respective spheres and destinies of man and woman. Man is, or should be the woman's protector and defender. The natural and proper timidity and delicacy which belongs to the female sex evidently unfits it for many of the occupations of civil life. . . . The constitution of the family organization . . . indicates the domestic sphere as that which properly belongs to the domain and functions of womanhood. The harmony . . . of interests and views which belong, or should belong, to the family institution is repugnant to the idea of a woman adopting a distinct and independent career from that of her husband. . . . The paramount destiny and mission of woman are to fulfill the noble and benign offices of wife and mother. This is the law of the Creator. And the rules of civil society must be adapted to the general constitution of things, and cannot be based upon exceptional cases.

Sometimes it was difficult to distinguish between this separate-but-equal view and discriminatory treatment. In the 1860s and 1870s, the doctors who practiced scientific medicine formed the American Medical Association (AMA) to drive out other people who offered medical services. These people included not only hucksters and quacks, but also women who served as midwives or abortionists. Although abortions had been widely available, the AMA, drawing upon popular fears about the women's suffrage movement, convinced male state legislators that abortions were "a threat to social order and to male authority."

The woman who seeks an abortion, the AMA explained, "becomes unmindful of the course marked out for her by Providence, she overlooks the duties imposed on her by the marriage contract. She yields to the pleasure—but shrinks from the pains and responsibilities of maternity. . . . Let not the husband of such a wife flatter himself that he possesses her affection."[183]

Sometimes the discriminatory treatment was even more blatant. The Mississippi Supreme Court acknowledged a husband's right to beat his wife.[184] According to the "rule of thumb," a husband could not beat his wife with a weapon thicker than his thumb.

The Women's Movement

Early feminists were determined to remedy these inequities. Many had gained political and organizational experience in the abolitionist movement. It was not considered "unladylike" for women to campaign for the end of slavery, because the movement was associated with religious groups. Yet women were barely tolerated by the male leaders of the movement and not allowed to participate fully in the major antislavery society. They formed their own antislavery society, but when they attended a convention of antislavery societies, they were not allowed to sit with the male delegates.

Angry at such treatment, the women held a meeting to discuss the "social, civil and religious rights of women." This first Women's Rights Convention in 1848 adopted a declaration of rights based on the Declaration of Independence. It said, "We hold these truths to be self-evident: that all men and women are created equal." The convention also passed a resolution in favor of women's suffrage.

Following the Civil War, women who had worked in the abolitionist movement expected that women, as well as blacks, would get legal rights and voting rights. When the Fourteenth and Fifteenth Amendments did not include women, they felt betrayed and disassociated themselves from the black movement. They formed

During World War II, women were urged into the labor force to replace men called to war. "Rosie the Riveter" became a symbol of women working in the war effort. Following the war, they were told that it was patriotic to go home and give their jobs to returning veterans. The 1955 magazine cover on the right depicts the stereotypical women's role in this postwar era before the beginning of the modern women's movement.

their own organizations to campaign for women's suffrage. This movement, led by Susan B. Anthony and Elizabeth Cady Stanton, succeeded in 1920, when the Nineteenth Amendment gave women the right to vote.

Then dissension developed within the women's movement. Many groups felt the passage of the Nineteenth Amendment was but a first step in the struggle for equal rights. They proposed the Equal Rights Amendment to remedy remaining inequities. Other groups felt the battle had been won. They opposed the Equal Rights Amendment, arguing that it would overturn labor laws recently enacted to protect women. Because of this dissension and the conservatism in the country, the movement became relatively dormant.[185]

The movement reemerged in the 1960s. As a result of the civil rights movement, many women recognized their own inferior status. Numerous writers sensitized more women to this. Betty Friedan published *The Feminine Mystique,* which grew out of a questionnaire she circulated at her fifteenth college reunion. The book addressed the malaise that afflicted college-educated women who had been socialized into the feminine role but who were finding it unsatisfying.[186] In 1964 Friedan's manifesto became the bestselling nonfiction paperback. In 1966 Friedan and other upper-middle-class, professional women formed the National Organization for Women (NOW). They resolved "to bring women into full participation in the mainstream of American society now."

Other women, also middle class but veterans of the civil rights and antiwar movements, had developed a taste for political action and gained political experience. They formed other organizations. Where NOW fought primarily for women's political and economic rights, the other organizations fought more broadly for women's liberation in all spheres of life. Together these organizations pushed the issue of discrimination against women back onto the public agenda.

Nevertheless, they were not taken seriously for some years. In 1970, *Time* magazine reported, "No one knows how many shirts lay wrinkling in laundry baskets last week as thousands of women across the country turned out for the first big demonstration of the women's liberation movement. They took over [New York City's Fifth Avenue], providing not only protest but some of the best sidewalk ogling in years."[187]

Although the movement tried to broaden its base beyond upper-middle-class and college-educated women, it was unable to do so. The movement generated an image of privileged women who looked with disdain on other women. *Housewife* became a derisive term. Traditional women viewed the movement as being antimotherhood and antifamily and, as it became more radical in the 1970s, prolesbian. This image gave "women's liberation" a bad name, even while most women agreed with most goals of the movement.[188]

The Movement in Congress and the Courts

Congress initially did not take the modern women's movement seriously either. When civil rights proponents sponsored a bill to forbid racial discrimination in employment, eighty-one-year-old Representative Howard Smith (D-Va.) proposed an amendment to add sex discrimination to the bill. A foe of equal rights for blacks, Smith thought his proposal so ludicrous and radical that it would help defeat the entire bill. Indeed, during debate on the amendment, members of Congress laughed so hard that they could barely hear each other speak.[189] But the joke was on them, because the amendment, and then the entire bill, passed.

Congress later adopted legislation to forbid sex discrimination in credit and education. Congress also passed the Equal Rights Amendment.

The **Equal Rights Amendment (ERA)** simply declared, "Equality of rights under the law shall not be denied or abridged by the United States or by any state on account of sex." Introduced in 1923 and every year thereafter, Congress passed the amendment in 1972.

It appeared the amendment would zip through the states. Both parties endorsed it, and the majority of the public supported it. But after about half the states ratified it, the amendment bogged down. Observers noted that it would make women subject to the draft and, possibly, combat duty. Opponents charged that it would result in unisex restrooms and homosexual rights. Legal scholars denied that it would lead to these latter consequences, but after the judicial activism of the 1950s, 1960s, and 1970s, some people distrusted the courts to interpret the amendment.

The main problem, however, proved to be the symbolism of the amendment. For many women the ERA represented an attack on the traditional values of motherhood, the family, and the home. Early feminists emphasized equality in employment so much that they gave some women the impression that they were against these values. Traditional women sensed implicit criticism for being housewives.[190] To underscore the symbolism, women in anti-ERA groups baked bread for state legislators about to vote on ratification. Because of the symbolism, even some women who favored equality opposed the amendment itself. Although many young women supported it, fewer of their mothers and

Although the Supreme Court had ruled that sexual harassment was a form of job discrimination prohibited by the Civil Rights Act of 1964,[1] and Congress had passed a law allowing victims to collect monetary damages from employers for distress, illness, or loss of their job due to harassment, there was little public awareness of the law until Clarence Thomas's confirmation hearings for appointment to the Supreme Court in 1991.

The hearings propelled sexual harassment to the forefront of societal debate. For seven days the public was riveted to the televised hearings. Anita Hill's charges—that Thomas, as her supervisor at the Equal Employment Opportunity Commission, made lewd comments about her, about sex, about finding pubic hairs on Coke cans and watching animals have sex in films—led to many discussions around workplace water coolers.

After the hearings, more women recognized that behavior they had dismissed as merely annoying was actually harassment. The number of complaints filed with the EEOC doubled (though in recent years it has leveled off).

Courts recognize two types of sexual harassment. The most obvious is quid pro quo, in which a supervisor makes unwanted sexual advances and either promises good consequences (for example, a promotion) if the employee goes along or threatens bad consequences (for example, an undesirable reassign-

ment) if the employee refuses. Less obvious is creating a hostile environment that interferes with the employee's ability to do the job. To prove a hostile environment, the employee must demonstrate that the conduct was severe or persistent.

Paula Jones's suit against President Clinton was dismissed because the alleged sexual advance was considered neither severe enough nor, as a single incident, persistent enough to constitute a hostile environment. If it happened, the judge said, it was "boorish and offensive" but not technically harassment.

Although many men seem to worry that innocuous comments will be classified as sexual harassment, Justice Antonin Scalia emphasized that the law did not create "a general civility code."[2]

Yet there is considerable confusion, because the law is relatively recent and different courts have issued varying interpretations. In addition, employers, who can be held responsible for sexual harassment by their employees (even if the employers are unaware of the harassment), can defend themselves by having policies to prevent such conduct.[3] Some have adopted "zero tolerance" policies to insulate them from employee lawsuits. These policies are stricter than the law, and they have led to the firing of a few men who would not have been convicted under the law. For example, an executive told a woman coworker about the plot of the "Seinfeld" show he had seen the night before.

Seinfeld was telling his friends about a woman he met but whose name he could not remember except that it rhymed with a female body part. The coworker complained of sexual harassment, and Miller Brewing Company fired the executive, despite his nineteen years of service to the company. (When the executive sued the company, however, a mostly female jury awarded him millions of dollars for being wrongfully dismissed.)

Consultants who advise employers have observed that women in traditional female jobs, such as secretary, are more likely to be subjected to quid pro quo harassment from supervisors, whereas women in traditional male jobs, especially blue-collar jobs, are more likely to be subjected to hostile environment harassment from coworkers. Hundreds of women in the Mitsubishi auto plant in Normal, Illinois, experienced incidents ranging from finding plastic penises in tool buckets to being asked their sexual habits and preferences, being called "bitches," "sluts," and "whores," rather than their names, and being grabbed by their breasts, buttocks, and genitals. Some women had their work sabotaged to make their performance seem slow and shoddy.[4]

The dynamics of sexual harassment do not revolve around sex as much as they reflect abuse of power. A supervisor or coworker makes a woman feel vulnerable and thus exercises psychological dominance over her.

grandmothers did; and although many working women supported it, fewer housewives did. Women's organizations had not created an effective grassroots campaign to sway traditional women. Ultimately, the disaffection of many women allowed male legislators to vote according to their traditional attitudes. They did not need to worry that a strong majority of their female constituents would object.[191]

In 1980 the Republican Party became the first party not to endorse the ERA since 1940, and President Reagan became the first president not to support the amendment since Truman.

Consultants have also observed that a very small percentage of men harass women but these men do it a lot. One consultant has found that perhaps three to five men out of one hundred create problems, but these men might affect fifty women in the same workplace. The harassers typically feel bitter toward women or threatened by them. Some have long been bullies toward men as well as women.[5]

Surveys show that a third of female workers say they have been sexually harassed on the job.[6] After twenty-three women acknowledged in 1992 and 1993 that they had to fend off sexual advances by Senator Bob Packwood (R.-Ore.), the *Washington Post* conducted a survey of women who worked as aides to members of Congress or staffers for congressional committees. It found the same results: A third of the women had been sexually harassed in the hallowed halls of Congress, and a third of these had been harassed by a member of Congress. (The others had been harassed by supervisors, coworkers, or lobbyists.)[7]

Yet few victims file formal complaints, let alone bring lawsuits, because they need their jobs. According to several studies, only 3 percent of women who have been harassed have filed formal complaints.[8] On Capitol Hill, 80 percent of the women surveyed said they would lose their job if they did, 80 percent said they would never find another job there if they did, and 70 percent said nothing would be done to the harasser anyway.[9]

Sexual harassment can be directed toward men as well.[10] About 15 percent of male workers say they have been sexually harassed by men or women on the job.[11]

Recently, a backlash has set in, apparently because of the legal confusion in the courts and zero tolerance policies of some employers. A majority—57 percent of men and 52 percent of women—say that "we have gone too far in making common interactions between employees into cases of sexual harassment."[12]

Defining sexual harassment too broadly jeopardizes free speech. One library employee filed a complaint against another because the other had posted an innocuous *New Yorker* cartoon in his own cubicle.[13] One graduate teaching assistant filed a complaint against another because the other had placed a photograph of his wife, wearing a bikini, on his desk in their office at the University of Nebraska.

While companies and courts have been sensitive, sometimes overly sensitive, to sexual behavior, they have been callous toward the discrimination that sexual harassment law originally was intended to prevent. When women have coworkers who will not train them and will not work with them, coworkers who repeatedly subject them to verbal abuse and obscene gestures, the women face discrimination, but the courts usually rule against them because the coworkers' behavior was not sexual. Yet these women face more discrimination than

women whose sensibilities are offended by a sexual remark or off-color joke. Some judges have interpreted the law to be puritanical toward sex but indifferent toward discrimination.[14]

1. *Meritor Savings Bank v. Vinson,* 91 L.Ed.2d 49 (1986).
2. *Oncale v. Sundowner Offshore Services,* 140 L.Ed.2d 201 (1998).
3. *Faragher v. Boca Raton,* 141 L.Ed.2d 662 (1998); *Burlington Industries v. Ellerth,* 141 L.Ed.2d 633 (1998).
4. Kirsten Downey Grimsley, Frank Swoboda, and Warren Brown, "Trouble on the Line," *Washington Post National Weekly Edition,* May 6–12, 1996, pp. 6–7.
5. Kirsten Downey Grimsley, "Confronting Hard-Core Harassers," *Washington Post National Weekly Edition,* January 27, 1997, p. 6.
6. Richard Morin, "Think Twice Before You Say Another Word," *Washington Post National Weekly Edition,* December 28, 1992–January 3, 1993, p. 37.
7. Richard Morin, "Jack and Jill Went Up the Hill," *Washington Post National Weekly Edition,* March 1–7, 1993, p. 37.
8. Daniel Goleman, "Sexual Harassment: About Power, Not Sex," *New York Times,* October 22, 1991, p. B8.
9. Morin, "Jack and Jill Went Up the Hill."
10. *Oncale v. Sundowner Offshore Services.*
11. Janice Castro, "Sexual Harassment: A Guide," *Time,* January 20, 1992, p. 37.
12. John Cloud, "Sex and the Law," *Time,* March 23, 1998, p. 49.
13. Henry Louis Gates, Jr., "Men Behaving Badly," *New Yorker,* August 18, 1997, p. 5.
14. For further analysis and a critique, see Jeffrey Toobin, "The Trouble with Sex," *New Yorker,* February 9, 1998, pp. 48–55.

When the deadline set by Congress expired in 1982, the ERA fell three states short of ratification by the necessary three-fourths—thirty-eight—of the states. Like the Nineteenth Amendment, it was not ratified primarily by southern states.

Courts traditionally upheld laws that limited women's participation in the public domain and occasionally even laws that diminished their standing in the private domain. As late as 1970, the Ohio Supreme Court held that a wife is a husband's servant with "no legally recognized feelings or rights."[192]

The Burger Court finally reversed this pattern of

decisions. In 1971, for the first time, the Court struck down a law that discriminated against women,[193] heralding a long series of rulings that invalidated a variety of such laws. In these rulings the Court used the congressional statutes and also broadened the Fourteenth Amendment's equal protection clause to apply to women as well as to racial minorities.

The change was especially apparent in a pair of cases involving the selection of jurors. For the pool of potential jurors, some states drew the names of men, but not women, from voter registration or other lists. These states allowed women to serve only if they voluntarily signed up at the courthouse. Consequently, few women served. In 1961, the Court let Florida use these procedures because the "woman is still regarded as the center of home and family life."[194] In 1975, however, the Court forbade Louisiana from using similar procedures,[195] thus overturning a precedent only fourteen years old.

The Court's rulings rejected the traditional stereotypes that men are the breadwinners and women the childrearers in society. The Court invalidated Utah's law that required divorced fathers to support their daughters until age eighteen but their sons until twenty-one.[196] The state assumed that the daughters would get married and be supported by their husbands, whereas the sons would need to get educated for their careers. But the Court noted, "No longer is the female destined solely for the home."

Employment The Civil Rights Act of 1964 forbids discrimination on the basis of sex as well as race in hiring, promoting, and firing. It prohibits discrimination on the basis of sex, except where sex is a "bona fide occupational qualification" for the job. The Equal Employment Opportunity Commission (EEOC), which enforces the act, interprets it broadly and accepts sex as a legitimate qualification for very few jobs. For example, employers can seek a man or woman to be a restroom attendant, lingerie salesclerk, model, actor, or performer in the entertainment business where sex appeal is considered necessary. On the other hand, employers cannot seek a male for jobs men traditionally held, such as those that entail heavy physical labor, unpleasant working conditions, late-night hours, overtime, or travel.

Some employers are reluctant to comply. For matched pairs of men and women, résumés were sent to sixty-five Philadelphia restaurants in 1995. The men were more than twice as likely to get an interview and more than five times as likely to get the job at the higher-priced restaurants than the equally qualified women were.[197]

The **Equal Pay Act** of 1963 requires that women

and men receive equal pay for equal work. The act makes exceptions for merit, productivity, and seniority.

Yet working women earn only $0.76 for every $1.00 working men earn (although young women, from sixteen through twenty-four, earn more than $0.90 for every $1.00 young men earn).

Women make less partly because they have less education and experience than men in the same jobs; many stopped their schooling or working to marry and have children. Women who have equal education and experience as men in the same jobs and who have not interrupted their working for child rearing do make almost the same as men–$0.95 for every $1.00.[198]

Women make less primarily because they have different jobs than men, and these jobs pay much less. Traditionally, women have been shunted into a small number of jobs. These "pink-collar" jobs include secretaries (98 percent are women), household workers (97 percent), child care workers (97 percent), nurses (93 percent), bank tellers (90 percent), librarians (83 percent), elementary school teachers (83 percent), and health technicians (81 percent). In contrast, few women are carpenters (1 percent), firefighters (2 percent), mechanics (4 percent), or truck drivers (5 percent).[199]

Although the Equal Pay Act mandates equal pay for essentially equal work, it does not require equal pay for comparable work—usually called **comparable worth.** According to a personnel study in Washington State, maintenance carpenters and secretaries performed comparable jobs, but the carpenters, mostly men, made about $600 a month more than the secretaries, mostly women. Overall, the study found that "men's jobs" paid about 20

"Some kids at school called you a feminist, Mom, but I punched them out."

percent more than comparable "women's jobs." These findings prompted unions representing government employees in the state to file a suit and demand an increase in pay for jobs held mostly by women. The federal court of appeals, in an opinion by Judge Anthony Kennedy, now on the Supreme Court, rejected comparable worth. Nevertheless, some state and city governments have begun to implement comparable worth plans for their employees after prodding by unions and women's groups. Most private companies, however, have not adopted comparable worth because it would require them to pay most of their women employees more.

Although formal barriers against women have been lifted, informal ones remain. Many women get hired, but some women do not get promoted as fast or as high as comparable men. They hit a "glass ceiling."

Many women in masculine workplaces feel pressure to submerge feminist beliefs. "You're not a feminist, are you?" is a familiar query. Women who seek career advancement say they would commit "professional suicide" if they spoke up for their rights or beliefs as women.[200]

Some women also face sexual harassment (see the box "Sexual Harassment at Work").

Mothers with young children confront more obstacles. Their male employers and coworkers think women should be responsible for child rearing, but these men do little to accommodate the demands of child rearing. Most companies do not provide paid maternity leaves, flexible schedules, or on-site day care. The United States lags far behind many other countries, ninety-eight of which grant partly paid maternity leaves for at least three months.[201]

Congress passed and President Clinton signed a bill requiring employers to grant unpaid maternity and paternity leaves. Companies must allow unpaid leaves for up to three months for workers with newborn or recently adopted children or with seriously ill family members. The act applies to companies that have fifty employees and to workers who work twenty-five hours a week for a year.[202] This covers about half of American workers.

So far, however, relatively few workers have taken advantage of family leaves or flexible schedules where they are available. Most workers cannot afford to take unpaid leave. Moreover, managers often do not support such measures, and coworkers resent the additional burdens, so employees are reluctant to take advantage of them. At a time when many companies have laid off workers to cut costs, "If you look like you are not career-oriented, you can lose your job."[203]

Mothers and fathers with young children often face unreasonable time demands from employers accustomed to hiring married men who have a wife at home to rear the children, maintain the house, and run the errands. Now employers are putting the same demands on married women. Nobody is left to do the jobs of the housewife. Although women often continue to perform most of them, both spouses frequently feel stretched thin and stressed out.

Not surprisingly, among men with children, those who have a wife at home rise up the career ladder faster than those who have a wife working outside the home. (The latter men apparently put in less "face time" at work.) And executives who reach the higher rungs "almost always" are men who have a wife at home.[204] An executive of a Fortune 500 company, in a conversation with business professors at a southwestern university in a recent year, admitted that his company still prefers to hire men married to women who remain at home.[205]

Thus, women have gained some acceptance in the workplace, but they, and their spouses, have not yet overcome the expectations that developed long before they were ever allowed in the workplace.

Credit The Equal Credit Opportunity Act of 1974 forbids discrimination on the basis of sex or marital status in credit transactions. Historically, banks, savings and loans, credit card companies, and retail stores discriminated against women. Typically, these businesses determine how much money people can borrow according to how much they earn. Yet the lenders refused loans to single women, regardless of income, because they assumed that the women would work only until they got married and became pregnant. Likewise, the lenders did not count a wife's income as part of a couple's total income, again because they assumed the wife would work temporarily. Only if women were professionals or in their forties would lenders count their income the same as men's. When businesses lent money to a married couple, they put the transactions in just the husband's name. Upon divorce or widowhood, women had no credit record and little chance to obtain credit.

The Equal Credit Opportunity Act requires lenders to lend to single women and to count the wife's income as part of a couple's total income. It restricts lenders from asking women whether they intend to bear children. The act also requires lenders to put accounts in the names of both spouses if they request.

Education The Education Amendments of 1972 (to the Civil Rights Act of 1964) forbid discrimination on the basis of sex in schools and colleges that receive federal aid. The amendments were prompted by discrimination against women by undergraduate and graduate colleges, especially in admissions and financial aid.

The language of the amendments, often referred to as "Title IX," is so broad that the Department of Education, which administers them, has established rules that cover more aspects of education than their congressional supporters expected.[206] The department has used the amendments to prod institutions into employing and promoting more female teachers and administrators, opening vocational training classes to women and home economics classes to men, and offering equal athletic programs to women. If institutions do not comply, the government can cut off their federal aid.

The amendments have affected athletic programs especially. Before the amendments, schools provided fewer sports for females than for males, and they spent far fewer dollars—for scholarships, coaches, and facilities—on women's sports. Now the department interprets the amendments to require a school either to have about the same percentage of female athletes as female undergraduates, to continually expand opportunities for female athletes, or to fully accommodate the interests and abilities of female students. (The latter would occur if a school's female students were satisfied that it offered sufficient opportunities for them, given their interests and abilities, even if the opportunities were not equal to those for men.)

Very few colleges meet the first requirement. To comply, most are trying to meet the second requirement by expanding the number of women's sports. But they worry that they will have to fulfill the first requirement eventually. And they fear that they will have to cap the squad size of their football team, which has the most players and costs the most money, to do so. This would lessen the imbalance in the numbers of male and female athletes, and it would free more money for women's teams.

Thus, some colleges have resisted enforcement of Title IX, partly because it comes at a time when athletic departments are struggling to stay out of "the red" and partly because it threatens deeply ingrained cultural values that are reflected in men's athletics. Administrators and boosters fear that women's sports will take money from men's sports and thereby weaken the primacy of men's athletics.

When Brown University tried to eliminate women's volleyball and gymnastics (at the same time it dropped men's golf and water polo), members of the women's teams sued. More than sixty schools filed briefs supporting Brown's decisions and criticizing the department's interpretations of Title IX. Lower courts ruled against Brown, and in 1997 the Supreme Court refused to hear the case, which left the lower courts' rulings intact. The Supreme Court's refusal signaled that the department's interpretations would remain and the schools would have to comply.

Already Title IX has had a major impact. Colleges have increased their women's teams, from an average of six to an average of eight.[207] The number of schools that offer women's soccer, for example, has more than tripled.[208] On the other hand, many colleges have eliminated some men's teams, especially wrestling, gymnastics, and swimming, to reduce the imbalance. Now women make up 42 percent of all college athletes and receive 42 percent of the scholarship money (though their teams have lower coaches' salaries and operating expenses).[209]

Colleges with a successful football or basketball program have increased their women's teams the most because these sports generate revenue that funds women's sports. Colleges with no football program have also increased their women's teams. Colleges with a football program but who are not members of a major conference lag behind. They pour money into football but lack revenue from television or bowl contracts to fund women's sports.[210] Title IX has also had a major impact on high schools, which have increased their girls' teams, and on American Olympic teams, which have benefited from the women's training in college.

Men resisted the expansion of women's athletics. The Boston Marathon traditionally was for men only, and when the first woman tried to participate in 1967, a marathon official assaulted her.
UPI/Corbis-Bettmann

But supporters have a broader goal in mind as well. "If girls are socialized the way boys are to take part in sports," the editor of a women's sports magazine says, and "if boys and girls grow up with the idea that girls are strong and capable, it will change the way girls and women are viewed—by themselves and by society."[211]

Discrimination against Men

Although most sex discrimination has been directed at women, some has been directed at men. The traditional conception of gender roles has created problems for men who did not fit the mold either.

When the Burger Court rejected stereotypes that led to discrimination against women, it also rejected some that led to discrimination against men. It invalidated Mississippi's law that barred men from one of the state's university nursing schools.[212] It also invalidated Alabama's law that allowed just women to seek alimony upon divorce.[213] Thus, the Court rejected stereotypes that only women become nurses and only women are dependent upon their spouses.

On the other hand, the Burger Court upheld some laws that were designed to protect women but that discriminate against men. It affirmed laws that prohibit statutory rape—intercourse with a minor, with consent—by males but not by females.[214] It also affirmed draft registration, required for males but not for females.[215] In 1980, President Carter asked Congress to reinstate draft registration, though not the draft itself, to show our "toughness" to the Soviet Union and other communist countries. Carter urged Congress to include women in the program. Although Congress had admitted women to the military academies in 1975, it was not ready to include them here. The Court upheld the law, rationalizing that registration eventually could lead to the draft and the draft eventually could lead to combat. And it insisted that most women are not capable of combat. Thus, the Court accepted the stereotypes that only men initiate sex with underage partners and only men can fight in war.

In the absence of war, the most significant discrimination against men may occur in divorce cases, where the norm is to grant custody of children to mothers and require payment of support by fathers. Although courts give fathers visitation rights, they permit mothers to move miles away, making visitation difficult and sporadic. And although governments have taken steps to enforce support payments, they have done little to enforce visitation rights. This practice reflects the stereotype that fathers are capable of financing their children's

Commander Kathleen McGrath became the first woman to captain a navy warship in 2000.
© Ed Kashi

upbringing but not of bringing them up themselves. The Supreme Court has ignored this problem.

Overall, however, Congress and the courts have moved steadily toward legal equality for the sexes. Women, and men, have accomplished through congressional and judicial action much of what they would have accomplished with the ERA. It is an indication of the success of the movement that young women today take their equality for granted, that they focus on their personal life rather than see the need for further reform.

Affirmative Action

Assume there is a track meet. A black runner and a white runner start together. But the officials force the black runner to carry heavy weights, and he falls behind. Eventually, the officials realize this is unfair, and they take the weights off. Of course the black runner is still behind. Would this be fair? Assume, instead, the officials not only take the weights off but allow him to catch up. Would this be more fair? Or would it be unfair to the white runner who was not responsible for the weights and who might have run faster than the black even without the weights?[216]

This scenario captures the dilemma of civil rights policy today. Although most race and sex discrimination has been repudiated by the courts and legislatures, the effects of past discrimination survive. Now the question is whether civil rights policy should ignore race and sex or take race and sex into account to compensate for the effects of past discrimination. That is, should the policy require nondiscrimination only or **affirmative action** as well?

Affirmative action applies to employers in hiring and promoting minorities and women, governments in reserving a portion of their contracts for businesses owned by minorities and women, and colleges and universities in admitting minorities and women.

The Civil Rights Act of 1964, which bars discrimination in employment, does not mention affirmative action, but it does authorize the bureaucracy to make rules to help end discrimination. In 1969, the Department of Labor called for affirmative action by companies doing business with the federal government. Later the Equal Employment Opportunities Commission called for affirmative action by governments and the Office of Education by colleges as well. Presidents from Nixon through Carter supported it with executive orders, and the Supreme Court sanctioned it in a series of cases.[217] Many state and local governments also adopted it.

Affirmative action applies most extensively to employment. It requires positive steps to ensure that qualified minorities and women receive a fair share of jobs at all levels. Just what the positive steps and the fair share should be are the subject of much controversy.

If the number of minorities and women in a company or government agency, at any level, is less than the number in the local labor force, the company or agency must agree to recruit more or, in serious cases, draw up an affirmative action plan. The plan must include goals to hire or promote more minorities or women and a timetable to reach these goals. If the company or agency does not reach them, it must show that it made an effort to reach them. If the company or agency cannot satisfy the government, it can be denied future contracts or aid, but employers rarely are penalized.

Some government pressure evidently is necessary. White men dominate public and private institutions, and as the personnel director of a Fortune 500 company observed, "People tend to hire people like themselves."[218]

Although the requirements for affirmative action plans speak of "goals," some people say they really mean quotas. Critics charge that quotas would result in both lower standards and reverse discrimination.[219] But affirmative action usually does not require actual quotas. Admittedly, the terms blur; if employers are pressured to meet "goals," they might interpret them to be quotas. But only occasionally, and only after a finding of deliberate and systematic discrimination, does affirmative action entail actual quotas.

The Supreme Court has issued mixed rulings on the legality of quotas. In *University of California Regents v. Bakke* in 1978, the Court upheld the policy of the medical school at the University of California at Davis to consider race as a factor in admissions, but it struck down the policy to establish a quota of sixteen spaces for minorities out of one hundred spaces in the class. On the other hand, the Court upheld quotas for skilled workers, firefighters, and state police.[220] The primary factor in determining the legality of quotas is whether the employer or union discriminated in the past. The University of California at Davis had no history of discrimination, but the other employers did.

In reviewing an affirmative action plan, the Court also looks at two crucial elements: the plan must not prevent all white men from being hired and promoted, and it must be temporary (usually until the percentage of black employees approaches the percentage of black workers in the community).

Because of concern that affirmative action should not pose too great a burden on innocent individuals, the Court has struck down affirmative action in laying off workers—that is, struck down protection for minorities and women when employers pare their workforce for economic reasons. Instead, the Court has accepted the traditional practice, based on seniority, that the last hired is the first fired.[221]

The Rehnquist Court, however, has signaled a change of direction in affirmative action doctrine. Although the Court has not barred affirmative action programs, a slim majority has made it more difficult for governments to adopt some programs.[222] Governments must have clear evidence of specific discrimination, rather than cite the general pattern of historical discrimination, and they must show how particular programs would ameliorate the problems.

Affirmative action programs have helped minorities and women. Companies that do business with the federal government, and therefore are subject to affirmative action, have shown more improvement in hiring minorities and women than other companies. And state and local governments, also subject to affirmative action, have shown more improvement in hiring than private companies. Organizations subject to affirmative action have shown even more progress in promoting minorities and women previously kept in low-level positions.[223]

The state of Alabama, for example, made dramatic gains. After a court found that the state troopers had never employed any blacks, it ordered them to hire one new black for every new white until the force reached 25 percent black. The force became the most integrated force in the country. Faced with the threat of a similar order, other departments of the state government quickly hired more blacks at all levels.

Affirmative action has helped middle-class and some lower-class blacks get jobs in government and business.[224] It has noticeably increased the number of blacks in government agencies, police departments, fire departments, construction trades, and textile companies. Affirmative action has also helped women get jobs in government and business that traditionally went only to men.

But affirmative action has not pulled blacks out of the "underclass." Many, from families that have suffered long-term poverty, experience continual unemployment because they lack the education and the skills necessary to compete for available jobs.[225]

And affirmative action, of course, cannot create new jobs or better jobs. Thus, it is not as helpful to minorities or women as a flourishing economy is.

In short, affirmative action should not be credited by proponents for more benefits nor blamed by opponents for more harms than it actually causes. It has boosted some minorities and women, but it cannot help many others. It has displaced some white men, but it has not affected many others.

Thirteen percent of white men think they lost a job or promotion because of their race, and 10 percent think they did because of their sex.[226] Many others claim they "heard about" another white man who did. Yet affirmative action is not as pervasive as many people assume.[227]

Similarly, some students think they lost a seat at a college they applied to because of their race. But 60 percent of colleges admit nearly all students who apply; only 20 percent are selective enough to use affirmative action much.[228] Students who apply to elite schools are more likely to lose a seat because other applicants' parents are alums of these schools. Typically, a fifth of Harvard's students have had preferential treatment because their parents attended the school. Harvard's "legacies" are more than twice as likely to be admitted as blacks or Latinos. A similar advantage exists at other selective schools, including public schools such as the Universities of California and Virginia.[229] Affirmative action may be more widespread in graduate schools, however.[230]

Many people subconsciously view affirmative action as they do handicapped parking. When looking for a parking space in a crowded lot, numerous drivers see the handicapped space and think, "If it weren't for that reserved space, I could park here." In reality, if the space wasn't reserved, only one other driver could park there.[231] So it is with affirmative action. Many white men think they would get a particular job or school seat if it weren't for affirmative action, but only one would. Meanwhile, the rest feel victimized by the policy.

For both sides in the controversy, affirmative action has become a symbol. For civil rights leaders, it represents fairness and real progress toward equality. For critics, it represents unfairness and an attack on individuality and meritocracy. It is important to debate these values, but it is also important to recognize that affirmative action is neither the key public policy for racial and sexual equality nor the biggest stumbling block for individual achievement as supporters and detractors seem to assume.

Public opposition to affirmative action has been festering for years. According to opinion polls, a majority of whites agree with the statement "We have gone too far in pushing equal rights in this country."[232] More specifically, 75 percent of Americans oppose giving a "preference" for blacks and other minorities in hiring, promoting, and admitting to college "to make up for past discrimination." Seventy-three percent oppose a "preference" for women. Although large majorities of whites and males think affirmative action programs have increased opportunities for minorities and women, only 34 percent of whites and 37 percent of males think this is "a price worth paying" if these programs result in less opportunity for white men.[233]

Despite the public opposition, the public debate over affirmative action had been muted until recently. In the late 1960s and 1970s, when affirmative action was introduced, government policy was initiated by executive orders, implemented by bureaucratic agencies, and sanctioned by judicial rulings. The legislative branch, controlled by Democrats sympathetic to civil rights, acquiesced, so Congress never staged a sharp debate on affirmative action as it has done for other controversial policies.

Republican candidates realized the volatility of this issue and reopened—some might say, reignited—the debate. When the Republicans wrested control of Congress from the Democrats in 1994, affirmative action was no longer protected. Republicans in Congress called for a review of affirmative action programs, with an eye toward shrinking or dismantling them.

There is a widespread expectation that the Rehnquist Court, with its majority of Republican appointees, will invalidate affirmative action. Already the U.S. Court of Appeals for the Fifth Circuit, which covers Texas, Louisiana, and Mississippi, ignored the *Bakke* precedent and ruled that public universities in these states cannot use

Notes

1. The information for this section is from Kay Mills, *This Little Light of Mine: The Life of Fannie Lou Hamer* (New York: Plume, 1994).

2. In the Delta, as in much of Mississippi, most blacks picked cotton or cleaned or cooked for white people. Black teachers had some status, but they were hired and usually controlled by the white officials of the segregated school systems. Only black preachers and funeral directors had any independence.

3. Mills, *This Little Light,* 36.

4. Ibid., 38.

5. Ibid., 18.

6. Ibid., 57.

7. This incident received little media coverage because no reporters were present. This result prompted civil rights leaders to seek help from white college students, assuming, correctly, that if any of them were harmed there would be more coverage of the repression blacks encountered. Thus began the recruitment of northern college students for voter registration drives during the summer.

8. Mills, *This Little Light,* p. 93.

9. The Republican Party was not a viable party in the state at the time. There was a black wing of the party, called the "Black and Tans," but its only role was to help dispense patronage when there was a Republican president. In fact, the head of the Mississippi Black and Tans was an attorney who lived in Washington, D.C. Mills, *This Little Light,* 109.

10. Ibid., 128.

11. Russell Nye, *Fettered Freedom* (Lansing: Michigan State University Press, 1963), 187, 227–229.

12. *Scott v. Sandford,* 19 How. 393 (1857).

13. Despite the ruling, Taney considered slavery "a blot on our national character." Three decades before the case, he had freed his own slaves, whom he had inherited from his parents. When the South seceded, Taney remained with the Union. Richard Shenkman, *I Love Paul Revere, Whether He Rode or Not* (New York: HarperCollins, 1991), 168.

14. The Emancipation Proclamation apparently was a tactical move to discourage European countries from aiding the Confederacy. It gave the Civil War a moral purpose, making foreign intervention less likely. The proclamation could not free southern slaves at the time because the Union did not control southern states then.

15. Bruce Ackerman, *We the People: Transformations* (Cambridge, Mass.: Harvard University Press, 1998); George P. Fletcher, "Unsound Constitution: Oklahoma City and the Founding Fathers," *New Republic,* June 23, 1997, pp. 14–18. These conclusions make dubious the arguments that judges should be guided only by the intentions of the original Founders as they resolve contemporary cases. Ignoring the transformation that occurred as a result of the Civil War and these amendments amounts to using a highly selective and self-serving version of history.

16. Civil Rights Act of 1866; Civil Rights Act of 1871; Civil Rights Act of 1875.

17. See generally Eric Foner, *Reconstruction: America's Unfinished Revolution* (New York: Harper & Row, 1988).

18. C. Vann Woodward, *The Strange Career of Jim Crow,* 2d ed. (London: Oxford University Press, 1966), 44. As another scholar observes, "When a city segregates the races on a public beach, the chief harm to the . . . minority is not that those people are denied access to a few hundred yards of surf" but that they are degraded. Jim Crow laws constituted "an officially organized degradation ceremony, repeated day after day." The degradation was heightened because it was specified by the law, which people view as a reflection of community values. Through the law, the majority told the minority that they did not belong to the community where they lived. Kenneth Karst, "Equality, Law, and Belonging: An Introduction," in *Before the Law,* 5th ed., ed. John J. Bonsignore, Ethan Katsh, Peter d'Errico, Ronald M. Pipkin, Stephen Arons, and Janet Rifkin (Geneva, Ill.: Houghton Mifflin, 1994), 429.

19. *Civil Rights Cases,* 109 U.S. 3 (1883).

20. C. Herman Pritchett, *The American Constitution,* 3d ed. (New York: McGraw-Hill, 1977), 486.

21. *Plessy v. Ferguson,* 163 U.S. 537 (1896). The Court's ruling prompted states to expand their Jim Crow laws. Before *Plessy* states segregated just trains and schools.

22. *Cumming v. Richmond County Board of Education,* 175 U.S. 528 (1899). Then the Court enforced segregation in colleges. It upheld a criminal conviction against a private college for teaching blacks together with whites. *Berea College v. Kentucky,* 211 U.S. 45 (1908).

23. Woodward, *Strange Career of Jim Crow,* 113. Before the Civil War northern states had passed some Jim Crow laws, which foreshadowed the more pervasive laws in southern states after the war. Leon F. Litwack, *Trouble in Mind: Black Southerners in the Age of Jim Crow* (New York: Knopf, 1998).

24. Jacqueline Jones, *The Dispossessed: America's Underclasses from the Civil War to the Present* (Basic Books, 1992), 83. And they were still being cheated. One sharecropper went to the landowner at the end of the season to settle up but was told he would not receive any money that year because the landowner needed it to send his son to college. The sharecropper moved North. Interview with sharecropper's son, "The Best of Discovery," Discovery Television Channel, June 11, 1995.

25. Richard Kluger, *Simple Justice* (New York: Knopf, 1976), 89–90.

26. Woodward, *Strange Career of Jim Crow,* 114.

27. Yet talk of the riot was banished from newspapers, textbooks, and everyday conversations. After some years, most Oklahomans were unaware of it, except those who lived through it. In the 1990s, newspaper articles prompted the state to establish a commission to investigate the riot, leading to more awareness. Jonathan Z. Larsen, "Tulsa Burning," *Civilization* (February/March 1997): 46–55; Brent Staples, "Unearthing a Riot," *New York Times Magazine,* December 19, 1999, pp. 64–69.

28. Wilson apparently opposed segregation in government but still allowed it to appease southerners who were a major portion of his Democratic Party and whose support was essential for his economic reforms.

29. *Guinn v. United States,* 238 U.S. 347 (1915).

30. *Buchanan v. Warley,* 245 U.S. 60 (1917).

31. In 1939 the NAACP established the NAACP Legal Defense and Educational Fund as its litigation arm. In 1957 the IRS, pressured by southern members of Congress, ordered the two branches of the NAACP to break their connection or lose their tax-exempt status. Since then they have been separate organizations, and chapter references to the "NAACP" are to the NAACP Legal Defense and Educational Fund.

32. Juan Williams, "The Case for Thurgood Marshall," *Washington Post,* February 15, 1999.

33. Kluger, *Simple Justice,* 134.

34. *Missouri ex rel. Gaines v. Canada,* 305 U.S. 337 (1938).

35. *Sweatt v. Painter,* 339 U.S. 629 (1950).

36. *McLaurin v. Oklahoma State Regents,* 339 U.S. 637 (1950).

37. Earl Warren, *The Memoirs of Earl Warren* (Garden City, N.Y.: Doubleday, 1977), 291.

38. 347 U.S. 483 (1954).

39. *Holmes v. Atlanta,* 350 U.S. 879 (1955); *Baltimore v. Dawson,* 350 U.S. 877 (1955); *Schiro v. Bynum,* 375 U.S. 395 (1964); *Johnson v. Virginia,* 373 U.S. 61 (1963); *Lee v. Washington,* 390 U.S. 333 (1968).

40. *Brown v. Board of Education II,* 349 U.S. 294 (1955).

41. Justice Tom Clark later told a political science conference that one justice had proposed desegregating one grade a year, beginning with kindergarten or first grade, but this concrete standard was rejected because the other justices felt it would take too long. In retrospect, it might have been quicker, and easier, than the vague standard used.

42. *Griffin v. Prince Edward County School Board,* 377 U.S. 218 (1964); *Norwood v. Harrison,* 413 U.S. 455 (1973); *Gilmore v. Montgomery,* 417 U.S. 556 (1974); *Green v. New Kent County School Board,* 391 U.S. 430 (1968).

43. James F. Simon, *In His Own Image* (New York: McKay, 1974), 70.

44. William Cohen and John Kaplan, *Bill of Rights* (Mineola, N.Y.: Foundation Press, 1976), 622.

45. *Swann v. Charlotte-Mecklenburg Board of Education,* 402 U.S. 1 (1971); *Columbus Board of Education v. Penick,* 443 U.S. 449 (1979); *Dayton Board of Education v. Brinkman,* 443 U.S. 526 (1979); *Keyes v. School District 1, Denver,* 413 U.S. 921 (1973).

46. *Milliken v. Bradley,* 418 U.S. 717 (1974).

47. For example, some suburbs of Kansas City, Missouri, did not allow black students to attend high schools. Some black families, then, moved back to the city, aggravating both school segregation and residential segregation. James S. Kunen, "The End of Integration," *Time,* April 29, 1996, p. 41.

48. Lee A. Daniels, "In Defense of Busing," *New York Times Magazine,* April 17, 1983, pp. 36–37.

49. Rob Gurwitt, "Getting Off the Bus," *Governing* (May 1992): 30–36.

50. *Board of Education of Oklahoma City v. Dowell,* 112 L.Ed.2d 715 (1991). The Court said school districts could stop busing when "the vestiges of past discrimination had been eliminated to the extent practicable." See also *Freeman v. Pitts,* 118 L.Ed 2d 108 (1992).

51. *Missouri v. Jenkins,* 132 L.Ed.2d 63 (1995).

52. Anjetta McQueen, "Desegregation Waning," *Lincoln Journal Star* (AP), May 16, 1999.

53. FBI director J. Edgar Hoover ordered wiretaps that he hoped would link King with communists. When the taps failed to reveal any connection, Hoover had agents bug a hotel room, where they heard King having extramarital sex. Taylor Branch, *Pillar of Fire: America in the King Years 1963–65* (New York: Simon & Schuster, 1998).

54. Woodward, *Strange Career of Jim Crow,* p. 186.

55. *Norris v. Alabama,* 294 U.S. 587 (1935); *Smith v. Texas,* 311 U.S. 128 (1940); *Avery v. Georgia,* 345 U.S. 559 (1952).

56. Henry Louis Gates, Jr., "After the Revolution," *New Yorker,* April 29 and May 6, 1996, p. 60.

57. Patrick Reddy, "Why It's Got to Be Al or Nothing," *Washington Post National Weekly Edition,* October 18, 1999, p. 23.

58. For national elections. The transformation took longer for state and local elections.

59. *Heart of Atlanta Motel v. United States,* 379 U.S. 421 (1964).

60. For discussion of organized labor's ambivalence toward enactment and enforcement of the employment provisions of the act, see Herbert Hill, "Black Workers, Organized Labor, and Title VII of the 1964 Civil Rights Act: Legislative History and Litigation Record," in Herbert Hill and James E. Jones, *Race in America* (Madison: University of Wisconsin Press, 1993), 263–341.

61. *Griggs v. Duke Power,* 401 U.S. 424 (1971).

62. *Washington v. Davis,* 426 U.S. 229 (1976). When the Burger Court held that standards must relate to the job, it placed the burden of proof on employers. (They had to show that their requirements were necessary.) In *Wards Cove Packing v. Atonio,* 490 U.S. 642 (1989), the Rehnquist Court shifted the burden of proof to workers. This technical change had a substantial impact; it made it hard for victims to win in court. In 1991, Congress passed new legislation to override the ruling and clarify its intent that employers should bear the burden of proof.

63. *Firefighters Local Union v. Stotts,* 81 L.Ed.2d 483 (1984).

64. *Shelley v. Kraemer,* 334 U.S. 1 (1948).

65. Less directly, the numerous national and state policies that encouraged urban sprawl provided the opportunity for middle-class whites to flock to the suburbs—and leave the cities disproportionately black.

66. For more extensive examination, see Andrew Hacker, *Two Nations: Black and White, Separate, Hostile, Unequal* (New York: Scribner's, 1992).

67. Richard Morin, "Southern Discomfort," *Washington Post National Weekly Edition,* July 15–21, 1996, p. 35.

68. Gary Orfield, quoted in Mary Jordan, "Separating the Country from the *Brown* Decision," *Washington Post National Weekly Edition,* December 20–26, 1993, p. 33.

69. Mary Jordan, "On Track Toward Two-Tier Schools," *Washington Post National Weekly Edition,* May 31–June 6, 1993, p. 31.

70. Jordan, "Separating the Country from the *Brown* Decision."

71. J. Harvie Wilkinson, *From Brown to Bakke* (New York: Oxford University Press, 1979), 118–125; "School Segregation Worsens, Study Says," *Lincoln Journal (Los Angeles Times),* December 14, 1993; William Celis 3d, "Forty Years after *Brown,* Segregation Persists," *New York Times,* May 18, 1994, p. A1.

72. Kunen, "The End of Integration," p. 39.

73. Jonathan Kozol, *Savage Inequalities: Children in America's Schools* (New York: HarperPerennial, 1992), 4.

74. Kozol, *Savage Inequalities,* 3.

75. Ibid., 35. However, only three public schools in Alabama are named after King, a native of the state. "Numbers," *Time,* January 24, 2000, p. 23.

76. Gurwitt, "Getting Off the Bus," Jervis Anderson, "Black and Blue," *New Yorker,* April 29 and May 6, 1996, p. 64.

77. "That's Quite a Range," *Lincoln Journal,* January 21, 1993.

78. In addition, cities have numerous nonprofit institutions—colleges, museums, hospitals—that benefit the entire urban area but do not pay property taxes. According to one estimate, 30 percent of the cities' potential tax base is tax exempt, compared with 3 percent of the suburbs'. Kozol, *Savage Inequalities,* 55.

79. Ibid., 198, 137, 236, 57. (There are a few exceptions, such as Newark, New Jersey, which spent more than $9,000 per pupil in recent years. Jordan, "On Track toward Two-Tier Schools," p. 31.)

80. Kozol, *Savage Inequalities,* 140, 36, 23–24.

81. Ibid., 155–156.

82. Ibid., 53, 84.

83. Ibid., 52.

84. Ibid., 53.

85. Ibid., 123–124. Researchers debate the extent to which more resources lead to more learning. The results are mixed, though most show that resources do improve learning. Larry V. Hedges, Richard D. Laine, and Rob Greenwald, "Does Money Matter? A Metaanalysis of Studies of the Effects of Differential School Inputs on Student Outcomes," *Educational Researcher* 23 (1994): 5–14; Kevin B. Smith and Kenneth J. Meier, "Politics, Bureaucrats, and Schools," *Public Administration Review* 54 (1994): 551–558; David Card and Alan B. Krueger, "Does School Quality Matter?" *Journal of Political Economy* 100 (1992): 1–40; Ronald F. Ferguson, "Paying for Public Education: New Evidence on How and Why Money Matters," *Harvard Journal of Legislation* 28 (1991): 465–498; Keith Baker, "Yes, Throw Money at the Schools," *Phi Delta Kappan* 72, no. 8 (1991): 628–631. For an earlier, contrary view, see Eric A. Hanushek, "The Economics of Public Schooling: Production and Efficiency in Public Schools," *Journal of Economic Literature* 24, no. 3 (1986): 1141–1177.

86. Steve Lopez, "Money for Stadiums but Not for Schools," *Time,* June 14, 1999, p. 54.

87. Robert England and Kenneth Meier, "From Desegregation to Integration: Second Generation School Discrimination as

an Institutional Impediment," *American Politics Quarterly* 13 (April 1985): 227–247; Charles Bullock and Joseph Stewart, "Incidence and Correlates of Second-Generation Discrimination," *Race, Sex, and Policy Problems,* ed. Marian Palley and Michael Preston (Lexington, Mass: Lexington Books, 1979); Stephen Wainscott and J. David Woodard, "Second Thoughts on Second Generation Discrimination," *American Politics Quarterly* 16 (April 1988): 171–192.

88. Kenneth Meier and Robert England, "Black Representation and Educational Policy," *American Political Science Review* 78 (June 1984): 392–403; Kenneth Meier, Joseph Stewart, and Robert England, *Race, Class, and Education: The Politics of Second-Generation Discrimination* (Madison: University of Wisconsin Press, 1989).

89. Suits claiming discrimination fell 51% from 1975 to 1984. Marc Galanter, "Beyond the Litigation Panic," in *New Directions in Liability Law, Proceedings of the Academy of Political Science* 37 (New York: Academy of Political Science, 1988): 21, 23.

90. Gary Boulard, "Jim Crow Said Alive in the South," *Lincoln Journal* (*Los Angeles Times*), October 3, 1991.

91. Colleen Barry, "Denny's Accused of Discrimination," *San Diego Union-Tribune,* March 25, 1993, p. A–3.

92. Edward Barnes, "Can't Get There from Here," *Time,* February 19, 1996, p. 33.

93. Hacker, *Two Nations,* 48–49.

94. William A. Henry III, "The Last Bastions of Bigotry," *Time,* July 22, 1991, pp. 66–67.

95. "Study Demonstrates Hiring Discrimination against Blacks," *Lincoln Star* (*Washington Post*), May 15, 1991.

96. "Deciphering a Racist Business Code," *Time,* October 19, 1992, pp. 21–22.

97. Earl G. Graves, *How to Succeed in Business without Being White* (New York: HarperBusiness, 1997).

98. Jerry DeMuth, "Fair-Housing Suits: Color Them Gold," *Washington Post National Weekly Edition,* August 11, 1986, p. 34.

99. Jonathan Kaufman, "In Big-City Ghettos, Life Is Often Worse Than in '60s Tumult," *Wall Street Journal,* May 23, 1980.

100. Jerry Knight, "Coloring the Chances of Getting a Mortgage," *Washington Post National Weekly Edition,* October 28–November 3, 1991, p. 26; "Racial Disparities Seen in Home Lending," *Lincoln Journal* (AP), October 22, 1991.

101. "Possible Redlining Investigated," *Champaign-Urbana News-Gazette* (AP), February 15, 1993.

102. Nina Burleigh, "The Suburbs Won't Vouch for This," *Time,* May 13, 1996, p. 43. Yet Presidents Nixon and Ford instituted a small-scale program for housing vouchers, and President Reagan also supported the idea.

103. Barbara Vobejda, "Neighborhood Integration, Inch by Inch," *Washington Post National Weekly Edition,* March 23–29, 1992, p. 37.

104. Nancy Denton and Douglas Massey, "Residential Segregation of Blacks, Hispanics, and Asians by Socioeconomic Status and Generation," *Social Science Quarterly* 69 (December 1988), 259.

105. Hacker, *Two Nations,* 35–38.

106. "Study Says EPA Penalties Smaller in Minority Areas," *Lincoln Journal* (*Newsday*), September 14, 1992. President Clinton issued an executive order intended to prevent minority neighborhoods from being burdened with an unfair share of dumps, incinerators, and other sources of pollution, but state governments and industrial groups challenged the order.

107. According to Supreme Court interpretation of Fourth Amendment search and seizure law, police can stop and frisk individuals who officers have "reasonable suspicion" to believe are committing a crime. But officers must have more than a hunch to meet the standard of "reasonable suspicion" (though less than the "probable cause" required to obtain a search warrant). A person's race is not a valid criterion, except when the person's race and physical description match those of the suspect being sought.

108. John Lamberth, "DWB Is Not a Crime," *Washington Post National Weekly Edition,* August 24, 1998, p. 23.

109. Michael A. Fletcher, "May the Driver Beware," *Washington Post National Weekly Edition,* April 8–14, 1996, p. 29.

110. Pierre Thomas, "Bias and the Badge," *Washington Post National Weekly Edition,* December 18–24, 1995, pp. 6–9.

111. Henry Louis Gates, Jr., "Thirteen Ways of Looking at a Black Man," *New Yorker,* October 23, 1995, p. 59; Anderson, "Black and Blue," p. 64.

112. Tammerlin Drummond, "Coping with Cops," *Time,* April 3, 2000, pp. 72–73.

113. Laura M. Markowitz, "Walking the Walk," *Networker* (July/August 1993): 22.

114. William Raspberry, "The Little Things That Hurt," *Washington Post National Weekly Edition,* April 18–24, 1994, p. 29. And see Ellis Cose, *The Rage of a Privileged Class* (New York: HarperCollins, 1993).

115. Kozol, *Savage Inequalities,* 179–180.

116. Juan Williams, "Why Segregation Seems So Seductive," *Washington Post National Weekly Edition,* January 24–30, 1994, p. 24. For an extended examination, see Derrick Bell, *Faces at the Bottom of the Well: The Permanence of Racism* (New York: Basic Books, 1992).

117. Stephan Thernstrom and Abigail Thernstrom, *America in Black and White: One Nation, Indivisible* (New York: Simon & Schuster, 1997), especially part 3. Some improvement began before the civil rights movement—when southern blacks migrated to northern cities in the 1940s.

118. Andrew Tobias, "Now the Good News about Your Money," *Parade,* April 4, 1993, p. 5.

119. James P. Smith and Finis Welch, "Race and Poverty: A 40-Year Record," *American Economic Review* 77 (1987): 152–158.

120. Joel Garreau, "Candidates Take Note: It's a Mall World After All," *Washington Post National Weekly Edition,* August 10–16, 1992, p. 25.

121. Thernstrom and Thernstrom, *America in Black and White,* 500.

122. Ibid., 507.

123. Ibid., 506.

124. Orlando Patterson, quoted in ibid., 507.

125. Orlando Patterson, quoted in Anderson, "Black and Blue," p. 62.

126. From 1967 to 1987, according to calculations by William Julius Wilson. David Remnick, "Dr. Wilson's Neighborhood," *New Yorker,* April 29 and May 6, 1996, p. 98.

127. Sociologist William Julius Wilson develops this idea extensively in *The Truly Disadvantaged* (Chicago: University of Chicago Press, 1987).

128. U.S. Department of Commerce, *Statistical Abstract of the United States 1995* (Washington, D.C.: U.S. Government Printing Office, 1995), Table 70.

129. Wilson, *The Truly Disadvantaged.*

130. Remnick, "Dr. Wilson's Neighborhood," p. 98.

131. Samuel Walker, *Sense and Nonsense about Crime and Drugs,* 3d ed. (Belmont, Calif.: Wadsworth, 1994), xviii, 3.

132. Thernstrom and Thernstrom, *America in Black and White,* p. 533.

133. Peter Reuter, "Why Can't We Make Prohibition Work Better: Some Consequences of Ignoring the Unattractive," in *Perspectives on Crime and Justice: 1996–1997 Lecture Series* (Washington, D.C.: National Institute of Justice, 1997), 30–31.

134. Connie Cass, "More Young Black Men in Trouble with Law," *Lincoln Journal-Star* (AP), October 5, 1995.

135. "Doctor: Harlem's Death Rate Worse Than Bangladesh's," *Lincoln Journal* (AP), January 18, 1990.

136. Donald Kaul, "Only Surprise Is That Riots Didn't Happen Sooner," *Lincoln Journal* (Tribune Media Services), May 19, 1992.

137. *New York Times,* April 2, 1978.

138. Michael A. Fletcher, "Latinos at the Back of the Class," *Washington Post National Weekly Edition,* August 10, 1998, p. 33.

139. Although Hispanics commonly are spoken of as though they are a separate race, they really are not. Most are an amalgam of European, African, and/or Indian ancestry that makes it impossible to identify a race. On the 1990 census forms, where individuals indicate their own race, half of the Hispanics left this line blank. Hacker, *Two Nations,* 6.

140. Tammerlin Drummond, "It's Not Just in New Jersey," *Time,* June 14, 1999, p. 61.

141. Guadaloupe San Miguel, "Mexican American Organizations and the Changing Politics of School Desegregation in Texas, 1945–1980," *Social Science Quarterly* 63 (1982): 701–715. See also Luis R. Fraga, Kenneth J. Meier, and Robert E. England, "Hispanic Americans and Educational Policy: Structural Limits to Equal Access and Opportunities for Upward Mobility," unpublished paper, University of Oklahoma, 1985.

142. San Miguel, "Mexican American Organizations," 710.

143. Leo Grebler, Joan W. Moore, and Ralph C. Guzman, *The Mexican-American People* (New York: Free Press, 1970), 157.

144. Even children of illegal aliens have been given the right to attend public schools by the Supreme Court. The majority assumed that most of these children, although subject to deportation, would remain in the United States, given the large number of illegal aliens who do remain here. Denying them an education would deprive them of the opportunity to fulfill their potential and would deprive society of the benefit of their contribution. *Plyler v. Doe* 457 U.S. 202 (1982).

145. Fraga et al., "Hispanic Americans," 6.

146. Karen De Witt, "The Nation's Schools Learn a 4th R: Resegregation," *New York Times,* January 19, 1992, p. E5.

147. Luis Ricardo Fraga, Kenneth Meier, and Robert England, "Hispanic Americans and Educational Policy: Limits to Equal Access," *Journal of Politics* 48 (November 1986): 850–873.

148. *San Antonio Independent School District v. Rodriguez,* 411 U.S. 1 (1973).

149. Anjetta McQueen, "Dual-Language Schools Sought," *Lincoln Journal-Star* (AP), March 16, 2000.

150. *Lau v. Nichols,* 414 U.S. 563 (1974).

151. McQueen, "Dual-Language Schools Sought."

152. Lynne Duke, "English Spoken Here," *Washington Post National Weekly Edition,* December 21–27, 1992, p. 37.

153. Eloise Salholz, "Say It in English," *Newsweek,* February 20, 1989, p. 23.

154. Joel Kotkin, "Can the Melting Pot Be Reheated?" *Washington Post National Weekly Edition,* July 11–17, 1994, p. 23.

155. James Traub, "The Bilingual Barrier," *New York Times Magazine,* January 31, 1999, pp. 34–35.

156. Ibid., pp. 33–34.

157. Margot Hornblower, "No Habla Espanol," *Time,* January 26, 1998, p. 63.

158. "Bilingualism's End Means a Different Kind of Change," *Champaign-Urbana News-Gazette* (Knight Ridder), June 7, 1998.

159. Hornblower, "No Habla Espanol."

159a. Jacques Steinberg, "Test Scores Rise, Surprising Critics of Bilingual Ban," *New York Times,* August 20, 2000, p. Y1.

160. 1990 Census of the Population, Social and Economic Characteristics, Part I, Table 13; Less than 5 percent of Asian-language speakers and less than 2 percent of other-language speakers do not speak English.

161. Nancy Landale and R. S. Oropesa, "Schooling, Work and Idleness among Mexican and Non-Latino White Adolescents," Pennsylvania State University, Population Research Institute, working paper, 1997.

162. Thomas Boswell and James Curtis, *The Cuban American Experience* (Totowa, N.J.: Rowman & Allanheld, 1983), 191.

163. Kevin F. McCarthy and R. Burciaga Valdez, *Current and Future Effects of Mexican Immigration in California—Executive Summary* (Santa Monica: Rand Corporation, 1985), 27.

164. Gregory Rodriguez, "Finding a Political Voice," *Washington Post National Weekly Edition,* February 1, 1999, p. 23.

165. "Survey: Hispanics Reject Cohesive Group Identity," *Lincoln Journal* (AP), December 15, 1992.

166. Lynne Duke, "English Spoken Here," *Washington Post National Weekly Edition,* December 21–27, 1992, p. 37.

167. Rodriguez, "Finding a Political Voice," pp. 22–23.

168. *Cherokee Nation v. Georgia,* 5 Peters 1 (1831); *Worcester v. Georgia,* 6 Peters 515 (1832).

169. Alfonso Ortiz, *The Pueblo* (New York: Chelsea House, 1994), 10.

170. Vine Deloria, Jr. and Clifford M. Lytle, *American Indians, American Justice* (Austin: University of Texas Press, 1983), 221.

171. Ibid., 222–225.

172. Michael Lieder and Jake Page, *Wild Justice* (New York: Random House, 1997).

173. Indian Self-determination Act (1975).

174. Harvey Arden, "Who Owns Our Past?" *National Geographic* (March 1989): 383, 388, 393.

175. According to the Indian Gaming Regulatory Act (1988), tribes can establish casinos if their reservation lies in a state that allows virtually any gambling, including charitable "Las Vegas nights."

176. Kathleen Schmidt, "Gambling a Bonanza for Indians," *Lincoln Journal-Star* (Medill News Service), March 23, 1998.

177. Felicity Barringer, "Ethnic Pride Confounds the Census," *New York Times,* May 9, 1993, p. E3.

178. W. John Moore, "Tribal Imperatives," *National Journal,* June 9, 1990, p. 1396.

179. Ruth B. Ginsburg, *Constitutional Aspects of Sex-Based Discrimination* (St. Paul, Minn.: West, 1974), 2.

180. Karen DeCrow, *Sexist Justice* (New York: Vintage, 1975), 72.

181. Nadine Taub and Elizabeth M. Schneider, "Women's Subordination and the Role of Law," in *The Politics of Law: A Progressive Critique,* revised ed., ed. David Kairys (New York: Pantheon, 1990), 160–162.

182. *Bradwell v. Illinois,* 16 Wall. 130 (1873).

183. From an amicus curiae (friend of the court) brief by 281 historians filed in the Supreme Court case, *Webster v. Reproductive Health Services,* 106 L.Ed.2d 410 (1989).

184. Donna M. Moore, "Editor's Introduction" in Moore, *Battered Women* (Beverly Hills: Sage, 1979), 8.

185. Barbara Sinclair Deckard, *The Women's Movement,* 2d ed. (New York: Harper & Row, 1979), 303.

186. In the early 1960s, a board game for girls—"What Shall I Be?"—offered these options: teacher, nurse, stewardess, actress, ballerina, and beauty queen. David Owen, "The Sultan of Stuff," *New Yorker,* July 19, 1999, 60.

187. Reprinted in "Regrets, We Have a Few," *Time,* Special Issue: 75 Years of *Time,* 1998, p. 192.

188. For an examination of Betty Friedan's role in the movement and the political dynamics among the various factions in the movement, see Judith Hennessee, *Betty Friedan: Her Life* (New York: Random House, 1999). For an examination of women's views toward feminism, see Elinor Burkett, *The Right Women* (New York: Scribner, 1998).

189. DeCrow, *Sexist Justice,* 119.

190. Thus, Betty Friedan later felt compelled to write a book espousing the concept of motherhood: *The Second Stage* (New York: Summit, 1981).

191. For a discussion of these points, see Jane Mansbridge, *Why We Lost the ERA* (Chicago: University of Chicago Press, 1986); Mary Frances Berry, *Why ERA Failed* (Bloomington: Indiana University Press, 1986); Janet Boles, "Building Support for the ERA: A Case of 'Too Much, Too Late,' " *PS* 15 (Fall 1982): 575–592.

192. Shenkman, *I Love Paul Revere,* 136–137.

193. *Reed v. Reed,* 404 U.S. 71 (1971).

194. *Hoyt v. Florida,* 368 U.S. 57 (1961).

195. *Taylor v. Louisiana,* 419 U.S. 522 (1975).

196. *Stanton v. Stanton,* 421 U.S. 7 (1975).

197. "White Men Still First," *Lincoln Journal-Star,* April 1, 1995.

198. Diana Furchtgott-Roth, "Same Pay for Same Job Is Law; Same Pay for Different Job Is Wrong," *Lincoln Journal-Star* (*Washington Post*), February 2, 2000.

199. U.S. Department of Commerce, *Statistical Abstract of the United States, 1997* (Washington, D.C.: U.S. Government Printing Office, 1997), Table 645.

200. Naomi Wolf, "Stirring the Women's Movement from Its Dormant Decade," *Washington Post National Weekly Edition,* October 21–27, 1991, p. 23.

201. Susan Benesch, "The Birth of a Nation," *Washington Post National Weekly Edition,* August 4, 1986, p. 12.

202. The act also requires employers to continue health insurance coverage during the leave and to give the employee the same job or a comparable one upon her or his return.

203. Lisa Genasci, "Many Workers Resist Family Benefit Offers," *Lincoln Journal* (AP), June 28, 1995.

204. *Time,* June 28, 1993, pp. 55–56.

205. From a personal conversation with a business professor in attendance at a conference.

206. Joyce Gelb and Marian Lief Palley, *Women and Public Policies* (Princeton, N.J.: Princeton University Press, 1982), 102. The author of Title IX, Rep. Patsy Mink (D.-Haw.), had applied to medical schools but was not considered because she was a woman. Mink intended Title IX to open the doors. She said it was "never intended to mean equal numbers or equal money" in athletics. Susan Reimer, "Title IX Has Unintended Consequences," *Lincoln Journal Star* (*Baltimore Sun*), April 9, 2000.

207. Steve Wulf, "A Level Playing Field for Women," *Time,* May 5, 1997, p. 80.

208. Jeremy L. Milk, "Women's Soccer on a Roll," *Chronicle of Higher Education,* November 3, 1993, p. A39.

209. Suggs, "Uneven Progress for Women's Sports," pp. A52–A56.

210. Welch Suggs, "Uneven Progress for Women's Sports," *Chronicle of Higher Education,* April 7, 2000, p. A52.

211. Mary Duffy, quoted in E. J. Dionne, Jr., "Nothing Wacky about Title IX," *Washington Post National Weekly Edition,* May 19, 1997, p. 26.

212. *Mississippi University for Women v. Hogan,* 458 U.S. 718 (1982).

213. *Orr v. Orr,* 440 U.S. 268 (1979).

214. *Michael M. v. Sonoma County,* 450 U.S. 464 (1981).

215. *Rostker v. Goldberg,* 453 U.S. 57 (1981).

216. A simplified version of this scenario was used by President Johnson in support of affirmative action.

217. Early decisions include *University of California Regents v. Bakke,* 438 U.S. 265 (1978); *United Steelworkers v. Weber,* 443 U.S. 193 (1979); *Fullilove v. Klutznick,* 448 U.S. 448 (1980).

218. Robert J. Samuelson, "End Affirmative Action," *Washington Post National Weekly Edition,* March 6–12, 1995, p. 5.

219. Two critics include Thomas Sowell, *Preferential Policies: An International Perspective* (New York: Morrow, 1990), and Dinesh D'Souza, *Illiberal Education* (New York: Free Press, 1991).

220. *United Steelworkers v. Weber; Sheet Metal Workers v. EEOC,* 92 L.Ed.2d 344 (1986); *Firefighters v. Cleveland,* 92 L.Ed.2d 405 (1986); *United States v. Paradise Local Union,* 94 L.Ed.2d 203 (1987).

221. *Firefighters v. Stotts,* 467 U.S. 561 (1985); *Wygant v. Jackson Board of Education,* 90 L.Ed.2d 260 (1986).

222. *Richmond v. Croson,* 102 L.Ed.2d 854 (1989); *Adarand Constructors v. Pena,* 132 L.Ed.2d 158 (1995). The perception that minorities are taking over is also reflected in a peculiar poll finding: The average American estimated that 32 percent of the U.S. population was black and 21 percent was Hispanic at a time when they were just 12 percent and 9 percent. Richard Nadeau, Richard G. Niemi, and Jeffrey Levine, "Innumeracy about Minority Populations," *Public Opinion Quarterly* 57 (1993): 332–347.

223. James E. Jones, "The Genesis and Present Status of Affirmative Action in Employment" paper presented at the American Political Science Association Annual Meeting, 1984: Robert Pear, *New York Times,* June 19, 1983; Nelson C. Dometrius and Lee Sigelman, "Assessing Progress Toward Affirmative Action Goals in State and Local Government," *Public Administration Review* 44 (May/June 1984) 241–247; Peter Eisinger, *Black Employment in City Government* (Washington, D.C.: Joint Center for Political Studies, 1983); Milton Coleman, "Uncle Sam Has Stopped Running Interference for Blacks," *Washington Post National Weekly Edition,* December 19, 1983.

224. Gertrude Ezorsky, *Racism and Justice: The Case for Affirmative Action* (Ithaca, N.Y.: Cornell University Press, 1991), 48–49, 63–65.

225. Wilson, *The Truly Disadvantaged.*

226. Donald Kaul, "Privilege in Workplace Invisible to White Men Who Enjoy It," *Lincoln Journal-Star,* April 9, 1995; Richard Morin and Lynne Duke, "A Look at the Bigger Picture," *Washington Post National Weekly Edition,* March 16–22, 1992, p. 9.

227. Eisinger, *Black Employment in City Government.*

228. James Traub, "The Class of Prop. 209," *New York Times Magazine,* May 2, 1999, p. 51.

229. John Larew, "Why Are Droves of Unqualified, Unprepared Kids Getting into Our Top Colleges?" *Washington Monthly,* June 1991, pp. 10–14; Theodore Cross, "Suppose There Was No Affirmative Action at the Most Prestigious Colleges and Graduate Schools," *Journal of Blacks in Higher Education* (Spring 1994): 47, 50.

230. For an examination of the *Bakke* ruling and its impact on graduate schools, see Susan Welch and John Gruhl, *Affirmative Action and Minority Enrollments in Medical and Law Schools* (Ann Arbor: University of Michigan, 1998).

231. Thomas J. Kane, "Racial and Ethnic Preference in College Admissions," paper presented at Ohio State University College of Law Conference, "Twenty Years after *Bakke,*" April 1998.

232. Richard Lacayo, "A New Push for Blind Justice," *Time,* February 20, 1995, p. 39.

233. Richard Morin and Sharon Warden, "Poll Says Americans Angry about Affirmative Action," *Washington Post,* March 24, 1995, p. A4. There appears to be majority support for the vague concept of "affirmative action," undefined, but the support evaporates when the questions use language indicating or implying any preference for minorities or women. Richard Morin, "No Place for Calm and Quiet Opinions," *Washington Post National Weekly Edition,* April 24–30, 1995, p. 34. Public opinion about affirmative action divides largely along racial lines. Although 81 percent of whites oppose affirmative action for minorities, 46 percent of blacks do.

234. *Hopwood v. Texas,* 78 F.3d 932 (1996).

235. So far the primary effect on the University of California system has been "cascading," with minority enrollments dropping at the most competitive UC campuses but increasing at the less

competitive ones. Minorities have been cascading from the top tier to the next tiers, where their academic records more closely match other students' records. Traub, "The Class of Prop. 209."

236. This "is one of the better kept secrets of the debate." Alan Wolfe, "Affirmative Action, Inc.," *New Yorker,* November 25, 1996, p. 107. See also numerous sources cited therein.

237. Kluger, *Simple Justice,* 90.

238. Neal R. Peirce, "It's Later in the Day for a Nation Fashioned by European Immigrants," *Lincoln Sunday Journal-Star,* May 19, 1991.

239. Dick Kirschten, "Not Black-and-White," *National Journal,* March 2, 1991, pp. 496–500.

240. Mills, *This Little Light,* 132.

241. Ibid., 114, citing Lyndon Johnson, *The Vantage Point* (New York: Holt, Rinehart & Winston, 1971), 101.

242. Mills, *This Little Light,* xiii.

Economic Policy

YOU ARE THERE

Should a Moderate Democrat Support Regressive Tax Legislation?

You are Patty Murray, junior senator from Washington and the Democrat's deputy whip. It is June 2000, and Congress is trying to wind up its work for the summer recess. A close presidential race is shaping up, and everyone is eager to get out on the campaign trail. With a budget surplus, this is turning into a bumper year for benefits and tax breaks; the smell of pork is in the air. Among the many measures Congress is bringing to a vote before the recess is a repeal of the tax levied against inherited wealth, called the estate or "death" tax. Some Republican members of Congress have been trying for several years to pass similar bills, and now with money to spend and voters to woo, the timing is perfect. The House has already passed a version of the bill that would lower the top tax rate immediately and completely eliminate the tax on all estates by 2010. If passed, loss of revenue from the tax would cost the federal government an estimated $105 billion during the phaseout period and $50 billion per year in the decade after the repeal.[1]

Currently the tax is levied only against individuals who leave estates of $675,000 or more, or $1.3 million if the estate includes a family farm or small business.

A 1997 bill you supported has already provided incremental increases in the threshold so that by 2006 no estate worth less than $1 million will be subject to the tax. Even today only 2 percent of all adults who die each year leave estates worth enough to be subject to the tax, and of those just the 6 percent valued at $5 million or more account for over half of all revenue generated by the tax.[2] Although Republicans say the repeal of the tax is meant to make it financially possible for owners of small farms and businesses to leave them to their spouses and children, only a very small portion of these farms and businesses are worth enough to be subject to the tax.

President Clinton and Al Gore, the presumptive Democratic nominee for president, and almost all other Democrats are adamantly opposed to repealing the estate tax because they believe it will benefit only the wealthiest Americans, widen the income gap, and substantially reduce federal and state revenues (most states with inheritance tax get a percentage of the federal tax). They believe the best use of the surplus is to pay down nearly $6 trillion of national debt and bolster Social Security reserves so that when the economy slows or takes a downturn, as it always does

The Internet has spawned many new businesses, including on-line retailers—"e-tailers." Some economists now believe we are finally realizing productivity gains from technology.

© Rich Frishman/frishphoto.com

Although family farmers comprise a tiny percentage of those who would benefit from abolishing the estate tax, Republicans focused on them to win support for repeal. Hammering on this theme, the House leadership had the bill delivered to the president by tractor.
AP/Wide World Photos

after a boom period, the federal treasury will be prepared.

In general, you are a supporter of the Democrats' argument that any new tax cuts must target low- and middle-income families, not the wealthy, and help reduce the widening income gap between the poor and well-off. For this reason you have announced your opposition to the Republicans' "marriage penalty" tax cut because you said it will help only a small number of well-off married couples and do nothing to fix the overall tax penalties that affect couples in all income groups. You also have

criticized the Republicans for offering so many new benefits without "debate on how tax cuts fit in with our long-term budget goals . . . , reducing the national debt . . . and extending the long-term solvency of Social Security and Medicare."[3]

But you have the specific needs of your constituents to consider. You ran for Senate as "the mom in sneakers." The daughter of a disabled veteran, you were a stay-at-home mom after college, only later returning to the labor force as a teacher. You served on the local school board and have made increased funding for education

one of your major issues. You see the problems of women and children, and low- and middle-income families, especially rural families, as your special concern. In fact, you have started your own "Rural Initiative" to benefit Washington's rural residents.[4] Your state still has a number of family farms and orchards, as well as many small high-tech firms trying to get off the ground. You think there is something to the Republicans' argument that the estate tax has ruined some family farms and mom-and-pop businesses by forcing children who inherit to sell them off to pay estate taxes.[5]

In your first Senate race in 1992, you ran as well as Clinton; in 1998, you did eight percentage points better than Clinton's 1996 totals, winning Seattle with 63 percent of the vote. Thus, you have shown you can win without national coattails. Now Clinton is a lame duck and you are not up for reelection until 2004, so you do not need to worry about coordinating issues with the Gore campaign. Although your state leans Democratic, the party split is close, and you can use crossover votes. But the Democrats have treated you well. You got good committee assignments, including a seat on the Appropriations Committee, and although a junior member of the Senate with only a few years' prior legislative experience in the state senate, you were given a role in the Senate's minority leadership. After your big 1998 win, you were named vice chair of the Democratic Senatorial Campaign committee. You think that the confidence the party has shown in you might deserve, even require, loyalty on a partisan vote.

Should you follow the party leadership and your own commitment to progressive tax reform and to using the budget surplus to pay down debt, shore up Social Security, and increase funding for education? Or do you put first those family farmers and small business owners among your constituents? How do you vote on repeal of the estate tax?

Americans pride themselves on their free market economy. Yet when economic problems occur, they want government to do something. The degree to which government should be involved in the economy is a perennial source of conflict.

Only a few people believe government should not be involved at all. Most agree, for example, on the following:

1. Government, not volunteer efforts, must pay for a military force. Thus, government must tax. We cannot individually decide whether to contribute to maintaining our nation's defense. If we did, some citizens would become "free riders."[6] Without paying, they would benefit from the voluntary contributions of others.

2. The market cannot determine which television or radio company should have the right to broadcast at a specific frequency. If broadcasting companies competed on the same frequency, none would be intelligible to listeners.

3. Market forces alone cannot regulate supply and cost of food and lifesaving medicine. Deaths from malnutrition and treatable illnesses would be much more frequent than they already are without government aid to the poor, disabled, and elderly.

Despite broad consensus on points such as these, there is much honest disagreement about how far government should go in regulating the economy and altering the distribution of wealth.

Types of Economic Systems

Capitalism

The role of government in the economy largely determines the kind of economic system we have. An economy in which individuals own businesses, factories, and farms is called a free market, free enterprise, or **capitalist economy.**

In a pure capitalist economy, prices, profits, working conditions, and wages would be totally determined by the market. Manufacturers would sell goods at what the market could bear, pay workers as little as possible, and manufacture products as cheaply as possible, concerned with health and safety only to the extent dictated by individual morality and the necessity to maintain consumer loyalty.

The idea that a capitalist economy would promote prosperity was popularized in 1776 by the British economist Adam Smith in *The Wealth of Nations.*[7] In his view, as each person seeks to maximize his or her own economic well-being, the collective well-being is enhanced. Businesses become more efficient, sell more at lower cost, hire more workers, and hence promote the economic well-being of the workers as well as the owners.

Socialism and Communism

Socialism is another kind of economic system. In theory it refers to collective ownership and control by the people of a country's productive capacity: its factories, farms, land, and capital. But in practice it commonly refers to a system in which government owns the businesses and farms and has the power to control wages and the supply of and demand for goods.

There have been many well-known theorists of socialism, but none so famous as Karl Marx. He was even better known for his writings on communism; perhaps this is why socialism is often used interchangeably with communism. But in theory communism is a more advanced form of economic organization than socialism. Collectively owned economic units would also become self-governing, and the need for formal government or "the state" would disappear. No country that called itself communist ever came close to achieving this utopian goal. In fact, in those countries labeled communist, the state grew in size and became increasingly more invasive in the economy and private lives.

The core of the debate between capitalists and socialists is an intense disagreement about how much control government should have over the economy and the consumption and work habits of its citizens. Sometimes in American public debate one candidate will accuse another of supporting "socialism"; in this context, socialism is often just a synonym for something a person does not like, especially bigger government.

Mixed Economies

In practice, there are no pure capitalist systems in the world and no pure socialist ones. In the United States, for example, government owns power-generating dams, some railroads, and much land. It loaned money to the Chrysler Corporation to save it from bankruptcy and has bailed out several large banks in danger of failing. In other modern societies, such as Britain, France, Sweden, Germany, and the former communist nations of eastern Europe, government owns airlines, television networks, and telephone systems.

Adam Smith believed that a free, but not completely unregulated, market would best promote efficiency and individual economic well-being.
Corbis-Bettmann

Just as all capitalist nations have socialist components, socialist nations have capitalist aspects. Even before the reforms of the late 1980s, which led to communist governments being swept away across Eastern Europe, most of these nations found it useful to tolerate or even encourage some private enterprises, and some, such as Hungary, had quite large private economies.

Most countries, then, have a **mixed economy.** Some are more capitalist, others more socialist, but all have elements of both.

Government plays a large role in the economies of most mixed systems. For example, government directly influences the behavior of business and industry through regulation and taxation. Even Adam Smith believed there was always some role for government in a capitalist system, such as to stop one business from dominating the market and to protect the nation against external threats.

Our own system is a mixture of private enterprise and government ownership combined with considerable government intervention through taxation and regulation (see Chapter 18).

In nineteenth-century America, government involvement in the economy was much less than it is today. Initially, we moved toward a more active economic

role for government because of abuses by big business in the late nineteenth century: child labor was widely used; workers were paid a pittance; filthy and unsafe working conditions (as suggested by the term *sweatshop*) led to thousands of workers' deaths from industrial accidents; foods and drugs were often unsafe; and the markets for some products came to be dominated by a few large producers who controlled prices and wages. Public anger led to increased government regulation of wages, working conditions, content of foods and drugs, and more.

Government also intervenes in the economy by taxing and spending. Budget policies can make the rich richer and the poor poorer, or it can make the poor better off at the expense of the rich. Most Western democracies have fairly elaborate social welfare systems that redistribute some wealth from the rich to the poor in order to provide them with a minimal standard of living. In the United States, we do less of this than do most other industrialized nations.

Despite our mixed economy, we have a very individualistic, capitalistic ethic. The idea that individuals, not government, should provide services and that government should be small influences a wide range of public policies. The belief that individuals are poor because of their own failings limits our sense of responsibility to provide support for low-income families. The idea that private business is inherently self-regulating makes it difficult to enact higher standards for worker health and safety. The belief that private profit is not only the most important goal of business, but perhaps the only one, means that those fighting to protect the environment from abuse by industry must either defeat or find compromise with a powerful lobby.

Economic Systems and Political Systems

Our Constitution specifies only a little about the nature of our economic system. It emphasizes private property rights and gives government taxation and regulatory powers. By contrast the governments of most other mixed and socialist economies, whether democracies or dictatorships, have constitutions that link their political system to a form of economic organization and give government major responsibilities for achieving economic goals.

Economic distinctions between capitalism and socialism are not necessarily linked to gradations in democracy. Capitalist systems are not inevitably democratic. The most democratic systems in the world are mixed economies with strong elements of capitalism (such as Sweden, Britain, and Denmark), but many capitalist systems are undemocratic (the most blatant example being South Africa under white rule). Indeed, there is an inevitable tension between capitalism and democracy. The capitalist marketplace rewards and encourages inequities that, if unchecked, threaten democratic beliefs about individual equality.

For example, capitalist systems place no upper limits on the accumulation of wealth, even though wealth can be used to buy greater access to decision makers. The potential for greater exercise of influence by the wealthy weakens the concept of one person, one vote.

Socialist systems promote equality in wages, but in practice most socialist systems have tolerated significant disparity in overall standard of living. Socialist theory also advocates democratic control by workers, but in countries such as the former Soviet Union and China, the Communist Party has used its dictatorial powers to deny individual freedom. Today, in eastern Europe and the independent republics formed from the old Soviet Union, many of the political parties working to establish democratic governments hope to retain some elements of socialism in their economies.

Regulating the Economy

Economic cycles of boom and bust have been one of the constants of human history. Good times with rising living standards are followed by bad times when harvests are poor, people go hungry, unemployment is rife, and living standards decline. Until modern times, governments did little to regulate these cycles, although some tried to ease the consequences of the bad times by distributing grain to people who were starving or by providing temporary shelters for the homeless. Only recently have governments tried, through economic policies, to prevent these cycles from occurring.

The idea that government intervention could ease the boom and bust cycle of the economy was revolutionary. Classical economists had argued that the market would adjust itself without government action. But in democratic societies, as government became larger and more powerful, people expected government to "do something" to alleviate economic problems.

Economic Problems

One of the familiar economic problems that modern government is expected to "do something" about is unemployment. Even in a "full employment" economy

several percent of the labor force will be out of work—people who quit their jobs to look for others, those just entering the workforce, those unable to work, and those who do not want to work for one reason or another. But most Western countries experience periods when there are many people unemployed because the economy does not create enough new jobs.

A **depression** is a period of prolonged high unemployment. During the Great Depression (1929–1935), over one-quarter of the American working population were without jobs.

A second recurring economic problem is **inflation**—a condition of increasing prices during which wages and salaries do not keep pace with the price of goods. As a dollar becomes worth less, there is little incentive to save and great incentive to borrow. In the late 1950s and early 1960s, inflation in the United States was quite low, as little as 2 or 3 percent a year, but the Vietnam War and the high cost of imported oil during the early 1970s stimulated a sharp rise. It was not until the 1990s that inflation returned to pre–Vietnam War levels.

Though some economists believe moderate inflation is not a bad thing,[8] many people feel threatened by it. It erodes the value of savings and gives people an incentive to consume rather than save. Bankers hate inflation because the dollar paid back to them in the future is going to be worth a lot less than the dollar they lend today. Inflation drives interest rates up as banks charge higher and higher interest to compensate for the declining value of the dollar. Credit becomes more expensive, which makes it difficult for businesses and industries to expand. And, of course, inflation is bad because people think it is bad—they worry about it getting out of control.

A third economic problem is stagnant production, that is, the failure of the economy as a whole to produce increasing amounts of goods and services. Two or more consecutive quarters (a quarter is three months) of falling production are termed a **recession.** During the peak of the recession in 1981–1982, over 10 percent of the American workforce was unemployed, and many others had only part-time work or had simply quit looking for work.

Productivity, one measure of the country's economic health, is the ratio of the total hours worked by everyone in the labor force to the dollar value of goods and services they produce (that is the gross domestic product, or GDP). When businesses and industries discover new ways to produce goods and services using less labor, productivity rises. To achieve improvement in the overall standard of living without increasing inflation, productivity must steadily rise. Productivity is also

In Germany in 1923, inflation was so high that a basket of money barely sufficed to buy a few groceries. This hyperinflation was caused by the German government's printing ever more money to repay the victors of World War I the penalties they had assessed. The government finally ended the inflation by issuing new currency, one unit of which was equal to one trillion of the old. This made the lifetime savings of many people worthless.
Corbis-Bettmann

a measure of competitiveness; businesses must become increasingly more efficient to be competitive at home and abroad.

For decades the United States had the highest productivity rates in the world. Although Japan and Germany began to close the gap in the 1980s, the American labor force, when measured by worker output per hour, is still the most efficient in the world. As businesses began streamlining and cutting back their labor forces in the early 1990s, the U.S. economy registered sharp increases in productivity.

The sum of inflation and unemployment, known as the "misery index," is an economic indicator that is especially important for anyone holding or running for office. As the number of people looking for work and the prices people have to pay for basic goods and services rise, the misery index goes up; the higher the index, the more likely people will be thinking about the economy when they enter polling booths. Because de-

pression, inflation, and recession all affect people's standard of living, most people expect government to take action to stimulate or slow the economy. But they do not agree on which are the most appropriate or effective responses.

The ultimate goal in any economy is to have low unemployment, low inflation, and increasing productivity while total economic output grows steadily. Achieving all of this simultaneously is rare, however. There has long been a consensus among economists that unemployment and inflation are inversely related and that if unemployment falls below about 6 percent, wages and prices will begin to rise. Inflation is usually at its lowest when unemployment is high and production sags. Conversely, increasing employment often brings high levels of inflation. This means usually some trade-off occurs among these three goals. At least that was the assumption before 1995, when the U.S. economy entered a period of economic growth with rising productivity, the lowest unemployment (4.3 percent) in a quarter century, and a low, stable inflation rate between 2 and 2.6 percent.

Government's Economic Tools

Government has two primary tools to help achieve its economic goals: fiscal policy and monetary policy.

Fiscal Policy

Government decisions on how much money it will spend and how much tax it will levy determine **fiscal policy.** Increased spending stimulates the economy and increases employment; lower government spending helps slow the economy and decreases inflation. How great an impact government has depends on how much it spends in relation to the size of the economy.

Tax policy can also help regulate economic cycles. Tax cuts can be used to leave more money in the hands of the consumer, thus stimulating private spending and reducing unemployment. Increased taxes take more money out of the hands of the consumer, slow the economy, and thus reduce inflation.

Government's ability to regulate economic activity through spending and taxation is limited, however. Sometimes the economy responds to government changes too quickly, other times not quickly enough. International trends also affect our economy, as we shall see in the last section.

Who makes fiscal policy? In the United States, laws regarding taxation and spending require approval by Congress and the president. In making his recommendations to Congress about taxes, spending, and other economic matters, the president is advised primarily by three people: the secretary of the treasury; the head of the Office of Management and Budget (OMB), who is responsible for preparing the annual budget message; and the chair of the Council of Economic Advisers, a group of economists who are specialists in fiscal policy matters. Sometimes, of course, these three advisers to the president are at odds with each other or uncertain their advice is sound. Indeed, Harry Truman once said he was in search of a one-armed economist so that the person could never make a recommendation and then say "on the other hand, . . ."[9] Economics, like political science, is an inexact science!

To improve communication and policy coordination among his economic advisers in the cabinet and the Executive Office of the President (EOP), President Clinton created the National Economic Council, a new office within the EOP's Office of Policy Development. Its members include the vice president and the heads of Labor, Commerce, Treasury, the OMB, and the Council of Economic Advisers. The Council's chair briefs the president daily and helps translate the needs and demands of executive branch agencies into workable policies. Its primary responsibility is to monitor the implementation of economic policies to ensure they are consistent with the achievement of the administration's overall goals.

Congress has its own fiscal specialists on committees such as Appropriations and Budget and relies heavily on the director of the Congressional Budget Office.

Approaches to Fiscal Policy

That government can have a substantial impact on the economy through its fiscal policy has been accepted wisdom since the British economist John Maynard Keynes published *A General Theory of Employment, Interest and Money*.[10] In 1935, Keynes argued that government could stimulate the economy by increasing spending in a time of high unemployment. This would put more money into the economy, thus stimulating the demand for goods and services and, in turn, causing factories to produce more and hire more workers. Therefore, even if government had to borrow to increase spending,

John Maynard Keynes's ideas revolutionized economics.
UPI/Corbis-Bettmann

the deficit could be justified because eventually higher employment rates would increase tax revenue.

Keynesian economics ran counter to the conventional wisdom of the time. During the Great Depression, President Hoover believed that if the government went into debt it would make the Depression worse, not better. His opponent in the 1932 election, Franklin Roosevelt, also ran on a pledge of a balanced federal budget. It was only after he was elected that Roosevelt adopted the Keynesian idea that government itself could help the nation get out of the Depression by borrowing and spending money.

Keynesian thinking dominated fiscal policy for several decades. Well into the 1960s economists were optimistic that government could successfully regulate the economy to maintain high levels of employment and reasonable inflation. But by the 1970s this confidence disappeared because of simultaneous high unemployment and high inflation. No government policies coped well with **stagflation,** the word coined to describe this combination of economic stagnation and inflation. Stagflation dealt a blow to Keynesian economics, which predicts that high unemployment and inflation cannot exist simultaneously (because, historically, higher levels of unemployment had driven prices down). The arrival of stagflation signaled a new era in the development of the American economy and led to increasing dissatisfaction with existing fiscal policy.

In 1981, the Reagan administration came to the White House with a new policy, **supply-side economics,** that promised to reduce inflation, lower taxes, increase military spending, and balance the budget simultaneously. The basic premise of this theory is that as government taxes less, more money is freed for private investment. Therefore, when the economy is sluggish, supply-siders advocate tax cuts to stimulate growth. They believe people will save some of the money they would have paid in taxes, thus making more money available to lend to businesses for expansion and modernization. Taxpayers would also be left with more money to spend on consumption; and to satisfy the increased demand, businesses would hire more workers. With increased employment, fewer people collect unemployment compensation and more pay taxes. So, according to supply-side economics, even though the tax rate is lower, government revenue increases.

These ideas appealed to conservatives because they offered an economic rationale for smaller government. They also have broad appeal to Republicans who, since the Great Depression, have drawn substantial electoral support from the wealthiest Americans. Whereas Keynesian economics has been used to endorse across-the-board tax cuts to stimulate consumer spending, the supply-side approach puts more emphasis on tax cuts for the highest income groups as a means of encouraging private investment.

The extent to which government should regulate the economy is one key to understanding differences between Keynesians and supply-siders over fiscal policy. Keynesians believe that government intervention can be effective both in steering the economy and in cushioning the blow to consumers of a sluggish or overheated economy. Supply-siders believe that taxing and spending for these purposes are inappropriate and inefficient uses of governmental powers. They believe it is better to leave as much money and as many decisions on spending and investing as possible in the hands of consumers.

Supply-side economics, as implemented by Reagan's economic team and continued by the Bush administration (even though Bush had once labeled it "voodoo economics"), led to disillusionment with the policy. Dramatically increased spending for the military combined with small cuts in spending for social programs and the loss of billions of dollars in tax revenues left the country with $2.5 trillion of new debt.

The fiscal policies of the Republican leadership that assumed control of Congress in 1995 had much in common with supply-side thinking, especially its emphasis on tax cuts for the wealthy and the belief that government attempts to redistribute wealth through tax and spending policies are a misuse of power. However, post-Reagan leaders of the Republican Party had no patience with deficits and assumed an aggressive posture toward coupling tax and spending cuts.

Monetary Policy

Whereas fiscal policy affects the economy through spending and taxation decisions, **monetary policy** attempts to regulate the economy through control of short-term interest rates and the supply of money. Monetary policy is made by the Federal Reserve Board (Fed), which is comprised of a Board of Governors, twelve Federal Reserve Banks located in major cities around the country, and the Federal Open Market Committee (FOMC). The FOMC is made up of the seven-member Board of Governors and five of the twelve Federal Reserve Bank heads, who serve on a rotating basis (except the head of the New York Bank, who is a permanent member). The FOMC meets eight times a year to determine monetary policy. Since

Many people credit Chairman of the Federal Reserve Board Alan Greenspan with a large share of the responsibility for the economic boom of the 1990s.
Michael O'Neill/Corbis

The role of the Fed as governing body of the nation's central banking system is crucial. As Will Rogers once said, "There have been three great inventions since the beginning of time: fire, the wheel, and central banking!" The Fed is *the* bank for the federal government; it distributes our currency, supervises and regulates some national banks, and acts as clearinghouse for many of the checks written on those banks. But from the standpoint of the overall health of the economy, its most important work is using its monetary powers to maintain a balance between demand and supply.[12]

The Fed controls the supply of money in several ways. It can buy and sell hundreds of millions of dollars of treasury notes and bonds. When it buys, it pumps money into other banks; when it sells, it depletes the money reserves of the banks and thus takes money out of the economy. The Fed also changes the interest rates it charges banks to borrow its money. Low interest rates stimulate borrowing and put more money into the economy. As a last resort, the Fed can increase or decrease the amount of reserves (cash on hand) it requires banks to have. If the reserve requirement is increased, banks take money out of circulation to build up their reserves. If the reserve requirement is decreased, banks take money out of reserves and lend it to customers, thus increasing the money supply.

When the Fed makes money scarce, interest rates go up and businesses and industries find it harder to borrow money for plant expansion. As a result, production and inflation may slow. When the Fed allows more money into the economy, interest rates go down, making it easier for businesses to borrow for expansion.

Monetary policy is a dry subject, but its effects can be dramatic. In the nineteenth century when fiscal policy was not yet a major factor in the economy, "tight" money was often the main issue in elections. In 1982, when the Fed tightened the money supply, forcing interest rates, unemployment, and bankruptcies up, one man entered the offices of the Fed and tried to kill its chair.[13] Other groups drew up "wanted" posters for the board members. And still others, thrown out of work or off their farms, killed themselves.

Today, the chair of the Federal Reserve Board is one of the most powerful people in the country. His comments on the state of the economy can cause the stock market to soar or plummet. His influence grew in the 1980s as huge budget deficits limited the options available to the president and Congress to stimulate or slow the economy through taxing and spending. By the 1990s with little flexibility left in fiscal policy, some economic

1978, its primary mandate from Congress has been to achieve price stability and full employment (remember that full employment is considered achieved when the unemployment rate falls somewhere between 5 and 6.5 percent).

Fed members are appointed by the president, with the consent of the Senate, to fourteen-year terms. The terms are staggered in such a way that, barring resignations, the maximum number any president could appoint in a four-year term is two. Another factor that helps to maintain the independence of the Fed is that it does not depend on Congress for funding; its operating costs come out of the interest earned on its holdings of U.S. government securities. The chair, however, serves only a four-year term (although reappointment is possible), opening the door to influence by Congress and the president. The head of the Fed is required by law to give testimony to Congress twice a year on monetary policy, but he is usually called before congressional committees at other times as well. The current Fed chair, Alan Greenspan, is an adept Washingtonian now in his fourth term and known for his ability to cultivate members of Congress and the cabinet.[11]

observers looked to monetary policy as the principal means for fine-tuning the economy. Today, with fiscal policy under much tighter control, Wall Street and business continue to look on monetary policy as the primary means for stimulating growth and productivity as well as for slowing the economy when it becomes overheated. This development is seen as favorable by monetarists, who have always believed that if government has to tinker with economic cycles it should be done through monetary and not fiscal policy.

Monetary policy is made primarily to protect the value of currency and ultimately to protect investors. Fiscal policy is geared much more toward protecting the average consumer against unemployment and the effects of inflation (rather than toward *preventing* inflation). While many people are both investors and consumers, and while fiscal and monetary policy should be complementary and not at odds, at times they may seem to be at cross-purposes.

To see how this works, we can look at the fiscal policy of the Clinton administration and the monetary policy of the Fed under the chairmanship of Alan Greenspan. Clinton came into office with the goal of "growing" the economy and increasing the real wages of workers. Primarily a politician, his eye was on the earning and buying power of the average voter. As protector of the currency, Greenspan did not want to see Clinton achieve his goals through a too-rapid expansion of the money supply or by wage increases that were too quick or precipitous. Primarily a banker, his eye was on investors.

During Clinton's first two years in office, the growth rate soared, five and a half million new jobs were created, and inflation stayed at or below 3 percent. But as the unemployment rate fell toward 6 percent and then below it, the Fed began imposing a series of interest rate hikes. Greenspan also started jawboning (see the next section), trying to slow the economy and offset a rise in inflation. Although it is arguable whether the impact of monetary policy can be felt so quickly, by early 1995, the rate of growth did slow and unemployment rose for the first time in two years.

To a large extent, the concerns of the Fed and the Clinton administration should have overlapped. In an era of flat wages, workers did not want higher prices, and Clinton certainly would not have wanted to take the rap for high inflation and a devalued dollar. On the other hand (remember that expression?), most workers would rather have a job and higher prices than have no job and stable prices, especially in an era of decreased spending

for welfare. And while no politician may claim to favor it, the devalued dollar can lead to more exports, and more exports can mean more jobs.

In addition to the difference in the priorities of fiscal and monetary policymakers, accountability is also an issue. If greater power to regulate the economy *has* gravitated toward monetary policymakers, it has passed into the hands of men and women who are not directly accountable to voters and whom most Americans cannot identify. This is especially significant because of the value we place on equality of opportunity. The Fed cannot determine which sectors of the economy will grow or who will reap the benefits of growth, just as it has no authority to make policy on how wealth is distributed across the population. To the extent government can influence this aspect of the economy, the responsibility falls to the elected officials who set fiscal policy.

Jawboning, or Persuasion

The government, and the president in particular, has an informal means for affecting the economy—trying to persuade businesses or individual consumers to behave in a certain way. *Jawboning,* or persuasion, can make a difference because psychological factors affect economic behavior. For example, economists recognize the importance of consumer confidence, that is, the degree of optimism individuals have about the economy. Confidence is rooted in the real performance of the economy, but sometimes there is a lag between the economy's performance and consumers' perception of its health. A president can try to persuade businesses to expand or consumers to spend, for example, by expressing his confidence in the country's economic direction. Lyndon Johnson was extremely skillful in persuading business and labor leaders to accept his economic policies, and Kennedy and Reagan were remarkably adept at persuading both business and the public. In contrast, Carter's calls for sacrifice to meet economic problems seemed to decrease consumer confidence, and Bush was unsuccessful in trying to convince the public that the country was coming out of recession in 1992.

Perhaps the most impressive feats of jawboning in recent years have come from Fed chairs. Their comments can have dramatic effects on the stock market. However, when the economy is in a prolonged period of expansion, as it presently is, and consumer confidence is very high, the Fed chair's persuasive powers are not as strong. When Greenspan tried in 1999 to cool what he saw as a dangerously overheated economy by accusing investors in the stock market of "irrational exuberance"

Ed Stein reprinted by permission of Newspaper Enterprise Assn., Inc.

and threatening new interest rate hikes, his comments produced only a short-term flurry of activity, and the stock market continued to climb.[14]

Managing the Economy for Political Purposes

Partisan differences exist in the management of the economy. Conservatives and Republicans tolerate higher unemployment more easily than do liberals and Democrats, whereas liberals and Democrats are more tolerant of inflation.[15] The business and middle-class supporters of the Republican Party are more concerned about inflation, whereas the working class has more to fear from unemployment and other attempts to "cure" inflation. Thus, Republicans first try to bring down inflation, while Democrats first try to stimulate the economy.[16]

Policymakers use knowledge of fiscal and monetary policy to improve the economy in election years by trying to increase the income of individual citizens and reduce inflation and unemployment. There is an observable relationship between trying to win elections and the kind of economic policy a president pursues.[17] Real changes in disposable income available to voters tend to be larger in election years than in other years. Unemployment tends to decrease in presidential election years, although not in off-year election years.

This suggests that presidents consciously work to manipulate the economy in ways that will benefit them

at the polls. The timing of policies therefore is crucial. Cuts in government spending and increases in taxes reduce real personal income, so presidents usually do not recommend budget cuts or tax increases in election years. Congress, too, responds to an electoral cycle. Prior to the 1998 midterm election, Congress passed, and the president signed, a $200 billion mass transit and highway bill containing at least $9 billion worth of pork barrel projects. Spending on selected benefit programs also tends to increase somewhat in election years.[18]

The 2000 election year was especially lucrative for constituent interests for two reasons. Control of Congress was up for grabs, with the Republicans holding only a five-seat majority and twenty-one of its members retiring. Second, a much higher than expected budget surplus made it possible to fund a cornucopia of benefits. Among them were new subsidies for farmers, tax breaks for married couples, removal of caps on the earnings of Social Security recipients, higher deductibles for individual retirement accounts, and over $1 billion in new research and development funds requested by senators for universities in their home states. There was even something for the dead as Congress voted to repeal estate taxes (later vetoed by Clinton). Furthermore, many candidates were promising a cut in the personal income tax. In all, Congress approved more than $700 billion in tax cuts and deductions in the year before the 2000 election.

Making no adjustments in fiscal policy can also have an electoral impact, as President Bush found out in 1992. Believing that the economy was on the road to recovery and that he had already interfered too much, Bush took no action. He also apologized to voters throughout the campaign for raising taxes early in his term. Although he presented the outlines of a new fiscal plan two months before the election, when it was clear Clinton's lead in the polls was related to the state of the economy, by then it was too late. In November 1992, 43 percent of all voters said the economy and jobs were the issues that most affected their vote, and 53 percent of them voted for Clinton.[19]

The Federal Reserve Board, although not under the president's direct control, is capable of acting in a partisan way in dealing with inflation and unemployment. During an election campaign when the economy is the central issue, there is enormous potential for politicization of the Fed. In the summer before the 1992 election, following a jump in the unemployment rate, the Fed lowered its prime lending rate (in an attempt to increase borrowing and thus consumer and business spending). President Bush had publicly demanded such a reduction just several days earlier. Although Bush denied it, his secretary of the treasury was accused of pressuring the Fed's chair to lower rates even further as a condition of his renomination for another term.[20] The Fed chair does not have to listen to the president, even when there is a good working relationship, as there has been between Clinton and Alan Greenspan. In 1994, when Clinton was hoping to benefit in the midterm elections from a period of strong economic growth, Greenspan was arguing that the economy was growing too rapidly and warning of an inflationary spiral.

The economy has an impact on the vote, although it is not as simple as we might suspect. Those who have studied the impact of economic hard times on individual vote choices have reported that how people feel they are doing compared to a year or two before does have some mild influence on their presidential and congressional voting choice. If they feel things are improving, they are somewhat more likely to favor the incumbent; if they believe their financial situation is eroding, they are somewhat more likely to vote against the incumbent. Evidence indicates that voters respond to changes in real per capita income in the few months before the election.[21] Voters are more concerned, however, with the state of the overall economy than with their own family's situation. But they do not seem to respond decisively to changes in unemployment or inflation levels. There was evidence for this in the 1994 election. With

the economy strong and unemployment low, voters were strongly anti–status quo, expressing deep pessimism over the country's future.[22] But in 1998, after four years of economic boom, the president's party gained seats in Congress for only the second time in this century.

Some observers believe the current run of prosperity has changed, if only temporarily, the economy's impact at the polls. Whereas in the past, a prolonged period of low unemployment, low inflation, and rising wages would have helped incumbents, it did not help Vice President Gore early in his presidential campaign. He had to emphasize other issues such as "family values," income inequality, and health care to catch up to Bush in the polls. The reason, some argue, is that people were doing so well that they took continued growth and near full employment for granted when expressing a preference for Gore or Bush.

But there were other factors limiting the economy's impact on the 2000 election. In prolonged good times, people take the economy for granted. It is in bad times that the economy becomes a campaign issue. In bad economic times, the incumbents are scapegoats, deserved or not. In good times, other factors are given credit, such as individual hard work. The stock market is also a factor. Half of all Americans now own stock, and many of those who have profited most in the nineties boom did so from stock market investments. Business innovation is another factor: one economist argues that it would have made little difference whether a Republican or a Democrat occupied the White House during the nineties because almost all of our economic growth has been technology driven.[23] If voters adopt the view that most of the credit for economic good times lies outside the White House and Congress, then incumbents can gain little at the polls from nine years of prosperity.

The Budget in the Economy

The size of the annual federal budget tells us government's share of the domestic economy and indicates the potential for fiscal policy to affect the nation's economy. The federal budget also reflects the country's political goals and values, because who is taxed, at what rates, and what government spends the money on tell us a lot about national priorities. Government spending is often discussed within the larger debate over fundamental political values, and disagreements on taxation have always been linked to the debate over the proper size and role of government in both a democracy and a free market economy.

The United States spends a smaller percentage of its GDP on government than other Western industrial countries or Japan. For the past forty years, federal government spending has hovered near 20 percent of GDP, while state and local government spending has been growing, now adding another 9 percent to the cost of government. Nearly 70 percent of our $9 trillion economy is accounted for by private spending.

Our Tax Burden

We often believe our tax rates are high, yet our tax burden is the smallest in the industrial world (Figure 1). Reasons for this include our aversion to taxes and big government, our less than comprehensive social welfare system, and the low percentage of government ownership of economic enterprises.

The income tax burden for most Americans has been falling. In 1999, on average, families paid less than 9 percent of their income in tax. One-third of all eligible taxpayers paid no income tax in 1999.[24] A four-person household with median income of $54,900 paid 7.46 percent, the lowest amount since 1965. Even those in the top 1 percent of earnings ($719,000 and more) paid only 22.2 percent.

Offsetting the lightened income tax burden are the payroll taxes withheld for Social Security and Medicare; they now take, on average, another 9 percent of income. However, on retirement, the majority of workers get benefits well in excess of what they have had withheld in payroll taxes. Together, then, personal income and payroll taxes take an average of 17.8 percent of household income, and most households pay state and local taxes in addition.

The distribution of this tax burden across the population differs from that in other industrial democracies, in part because the United States taxes its wealthiest citizens at a much lower rate. Japan and Western European countries rely more heavily on taxing goods and services, which means that, relative to the United States, a larger share of the tax burden falls on consumption than on income. By placing greater emphasis on Social Security and personal income taxes, our tax policy allows the average worker to keep a smaller part of a paycheck than his or her counterpart in Europe or Japan. At the same time, the wealthiest Americans have a double advantage over their counterparts in that both their incomes and their consumption are taxed at substantially lower levels than in other developed countries. This helps to explain why the United States now has the most unequal distribution of wealth of all the industrial democracies.

As Figure 2 shows, the government does raise small amounts of revenue by taxing consumption through the levies it places on the sale or manufacture of some luxury and nonessential items such as liquor and cigarettes, as well as on a few essential products such as gasoline. These excise taxes are designed not only to raise revenue but to limit or discourage use of scarce or dangerous products, which is why they are sometimes called "sin taxes." On average, they take another 1 percent of household income.

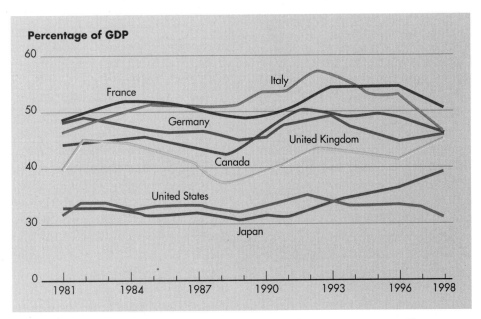

FIGURE 1 ■ *United States Allocates a Smaller Portion of Its GDP to Government Than Any Other Industrialized Nation*

SOURCE: Organization for Economic Cooperation and Development.

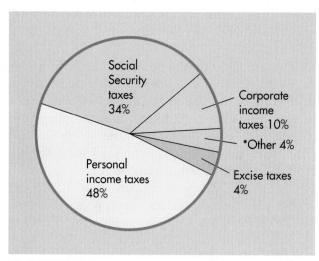

FIGURE 2 ■ *Estimated Federal Revenue Sources, 2001†*

*Customs duties; fines; penalties, Federal Reserve earnings.
†Does not include $215 billion from business activities such as park fees. This is subtracted from spending.
SOURCE: *Budget of the United States Government, Fiscal Year 2001,* p. 2.

In 2001, personal and corporate income taxes will account for 58 percent of all federal revenue, and Social Security taxes paid by workers and their employers for another 34 percent. The proportion of revenue coming from corporate income tax continues to fall and is dramatically below the level of the 1950s and 1960s, when it accounted for about 25 percent of all federal revenue. Social insurance payroll taxes, in contrast, are the fastest-growing source of federal revenue and account for all of the budget surplus.

Income Tax Policy

Our tax code is complex. President Franklin Roosevelt once stated that the tax code "might as well have been written in a foreign language," and the laws are dozens of times more complex now.[25] The complexity occurs because Congress and the president have designed a tax code to achieve a variety of social goals. Congress wants to encourage families where both parents work to have adequate care for their children, so it allows credits for child care; it wants to encourage business growth, so it gives credits and deductions for investment. (A *deduction* is the amount taxpayers have spent for some item, such as mortgage interest or business equipment, that they are allowed by law to subtract from their income before figuring their tax liability.) Congress believes that voluntary giving to charitable organizations is good, so it creates deductions for that too. Congress wants to help people buy homes and stimulate new housing construction, so deductions are allowed for interest on mortgage

payments. Though these and hundreds of other exemptions and deductions may individually be desirable, together they create a tax code that is difficult to understand and favors wealthier Americans who are able to take advantage of more loopholes. Every taxpayer, however, receives one standard deduction of at least $4,300, plus the personal exemption ($2,750), for a total cost in lost revenue of $7,050 per taxpayer each year.

In 1986, Congress passed major income tax reform in an effort to make the tax structure fairer, simpler, and more efficient. The code's definition of fairness is spreading the tax burden among households according to their ability to pay. A tax structure based on the principle of wealthy and middle-income households paying higher percentages of their income in taxes than poorer households is called **progressive.** A tax that requires the poor to pay proportionately more than those in middle- and upper-income brackets is a **regressive tax.**

The 1986 tax law tried to achieve greater fairness by reducing deductions and exemptions, and lowering the number of tax rates from fifteen to four (counting the zero rate for low-income households). These simplifications in turn were to make the system more efficient. Taxes should have been easier to calculate and the forms less time-consuming to complete. However, in a test of the new code's simplicity and efficiency, a mythical family's income and expenses for 1989 were sent to fifty tax experts to calculate their tax liability. They arrived at fifty different answers ranging from a tax bill of $12,500 to nearly $36,000.[26]

One of the reasons the tax code remains so complex is that the reform did not go far enough in reducing deductions and loopholes. That so many exemptions and special provisions were retained is testimony to the power of a variety of interests. For example, middle-income Americans along with housing construction and real estate lobbies ensured that mortgage interest on first and some second homes would remain deductible. Part of the cost of travel, meals, and entertaining for business purposes is still deductible, as is interest on business loans. In addition, loopholes in the tax code have made it possible for a majority of foreign corporations to pay few or no taxes.[27] (The cost of some of the major deductions is shown in Figure 3.)

Current Tax Issues

With sharp rises in Social Security taxes and hikes in state and local taxes to compensate for reduced federal funding for social services, most Americans felt no tax relief from the 1980s tax cuts. And because the benefits of the Reagan tax cuts and the 1986 tax reform went

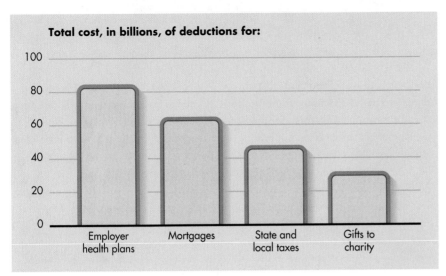

FIGURE 3 ■ *Tax Deductions Mostly Benefit Middle- and Higher-Income Families* *Billions of dollars of tax revenue are lost through deductions, largely benefiting middle- and upper-class families.*

SOURCE: Table 5-3. "Major Tax Expenditures in the Income Tax." *Analytic Perspectives on FY 2000 Budget.*

Total cost, in billions, of deductions for:

lopsidedly to the wealthy, the income tax was somewhat more regressive after the 1986 reform than before it. Therefore, when faced with the problem of how to increase revenue to help balance the budget, the Clinton administration submitted legislation designed to make the income tax more progressive by forcing the wealthiest Americans to carry a larger share of the burden. In 1993, Congress increased the highest tax rate on ordinary income from 31 to 36 percent. When income exceeds $250,000, a 10 percent tax surcharge applies, making the effective rate 39.6 percent for those in the highest income group. The top corporate tax rate rose from 34 to 35 percent. The law eliminated some business deductions and reduced the deduction for business meals and entertainment, but overall tax breaks to business still cost the Treasury $100 billion annually.[28] The purpose of the Clinton bill was to raise more revenue by making the tax structure more progressive; it did little to make it simpler or more efficient.

Achieving a tax policy that is both fair and simple is difficult given our complex occupational and income structure, and perhaps impossible without a total overhaul of the system of deductions. One solution to some of these problems is to abolish our present tax code and replace it with a **flat tax,** that is, a single rate for all income groups.

A flat tax advocated by many Republicans calls for a flat rate of 16 to 17 percent for all Americans and the elimination of all deductions other than a personal exemption of $33,800 for a family of four. It would greatly simplify the present 9,400-page tax code, cut millions for administering the IRS from the federal budget, and

reduce the present U.S. 1040 to a single page or a post-card-sized form. Opponents of the bill argue that a flat tax promotes simplicity and efficiency over fairness. The tax code historically has defined fairness as requiring a multirate structure, so tax burdens would increase in proportion to one's ability to pay. Although most agree that this principle has been deeply compromised by a system of deductions favoring wealthier Americans, supporters of progressive taxation would rather reform and simplify the present code.

Flat tax advocates believe that a progressive tax policy punishes people for earning more and creating wealth. They argue that fairness can be better achieved by requiring all Americans to pay the same proportion of their income to the government. Supporters also claim that with the large personal exemption, lower-income individuals would pay a smaller percentage of their income in taxes than under the present system, and that there would be a de facto zero tax rate for an estimated ten million of the poorest Americans.

Others advocate a move toward taxing consumption by eliminating the personal income tax in favor of a 15 percent national sales tax. To reduce the regressivity of the tax, it would exempt basic necessities such as food and clothing, on which the lowest-income groups spend a high proportion of their earnings. With a national sales tax, there would be no need to file a return because taxes would be paid as one spends. But Social Security and Medicare taxes would still be withheld from paychecks.

Many people find the prospect of a simplified procedure for filing taxes very attractive, but critics argue that the rates assessed by both proposals are far too low

Tax Credits to Build Low-Income Housing

For years both local and federal authorities have looked for solutions to urban blight in residential areas of major cities like Detroit, Los Angeles, and New York City. Already in a state of deterioration from local government neglect, some of the neighborhoods were virtually razed during the riots that followed the assassination of Martin Luther King in the summer of 1968. Some of the hardest hit areas were never rebuilt and became hangouts for drug users and sellers. Although a steady parade of American presidents visited these sites during the 1970s and 1980s promising to do something, little was accomplished.

In the South Bronx, one of the worst areas, community activists finally organized in the 1980s to raise funds to rebuild their neighborhood. The city turned over abandoned buildings it had seized for nonpayment of taxes and made loans for rehabilitation. With funding from the Ford Foundation, the activists set up their own nonprofit corporation. But rebuilding was a job requiring hundreds of millions of dollars—beyond the reach of a private foundation—and attracting investors to a low-income, high-crime neighborhood was difficult. To get private contractors to bid on rebuilding projects, government support and funding were needed. With federal tax credits for low-income housing and additional support from city government, the activists were able to get private contractors to commit to building affordable private housing for low- and middle-income families. Between 1986 and 1994, $1 billion in public money helped build 4,500 homes and refurbish 19,000 apartments for working-class families.

For years the federal government has wanted to find a new approach to providing housing for poor and low-income Americans. It has earned mixed reviews at best for the public housing projects it commissioned, funded, and owns. Most are densely populated high-rises that have become run-down and crime-ridden. Encouraging private contractors to build affordable single-family houses and low-rise apartments in residential areas of major cities is one way for the government to withdraw from its role as landlord, support local initiatives, give taxpayers the kind of housing they prefer, and reduce crime and urban blight.

SOURCES: Matthew Purdy, "Left to Die, the South Bronx Rises from Decades of Decay," *New York Times,* November 13, 1994, pp. 1, 47; Patrick Breslin, "On these Sidewalks of New York, the Sun Is Shining Again," *Smithsonian Magazine,* October 1995, pp. 100–111.

Federal tax credits stimulated private and community investment in this burned-out section of the South Bronx. These photos were taken before (1981) and after (1994) this investment, in what was one of the most bleak central city areas in the United States.
Both by Camilo Jose Vergara

to recover the revenues that would be lost by eliminating the multirate personal income tax. Although not yet in agreement on how to do it, Congress has committed to overhauling the present tax code by 2002.

In the meantime, Congress has resorted to passing ever more deductions as a means of undercutting existing tax rates. The number of new deductions, such as an additional tax credit for children under seventeen, and life-long-learning and other education credits, is the main reason the income tax burden fell for many families in 1999 and 2000. Although elected officials continue to tout a tax cut, respondents to a 1999 poll placed tax cuts eighth of fifteen on a list of priorities.[29] The main grievances are with the complexity of the code, threatening notices from the IRS, the time it takes to file (an average of 35.8 hours for a 1040 form), and the difficulty getting clear answers to questions.[30]

In 1998, Congress approved, and Clinton signed, a major reorganization of the IRS designed to strengthen taxpayer rights and make the agency more accountable to the public. In response to the shakeup, the IRS changed its mission from "collecting the proper amount of tax due" to providing "quality service" and "applying the tax law with integrity and fairness for all." But for all the talk of simplifying the massive and complex tax code, tax laws grew 10 percent faster after the Republicans took control of Congress than in the five previous years, adding another 6,400 pages to the code. In addition, while giving the agency 1,200 more laws to comply with (many resulting from the new deductions), Congress cut the number of IRS agents by 16,000.[31] Staff reductions came at a time when the number of income tax reports was increasing due to rising employment and when the number of complex returns being filed increased due to the growing number of high earners. Under the new system, the collection of delinquent taxes has declined, and the tax report of a person making less than $25,000 is more likely to be audited than that of a person earning $100,000 or more.[32]

Where the Money Goes

In 1999, for the first time in 30 years, the federal government proposed spending approximately the same amount it raised in revenues. Under an agreement reached with Congress in 1997, the president was committed to balancing the budget by 2002. But continued economic growth and low unemployment produced greater than anticipated federal revenues, leading to a surplus in 1998 and the passage of a balanced budget three years ahead of schedule. In 2001 the government

proposes to spend 9 percent *less* than it expects to receive in revenues.

Discretionary and Mandatory Spending

Legislation passed in 1990 to bring the budget deficit under control divided federal spending into two categories: discretionary, and direct or mandatory (Figure 4). **Discretionary spending** is set by annual appropriations bills passed by Congress, and as the label suggests, amounts are established at the discretion of members of Congress in any given year. Included in this category of spending are such items as government operating expenses and salaries for many federal employees. Spending on an item is limited by the dollar ceilings, or caps, that Congress authorizes for the year.

Mandatory spending, in contrast, is mandated by permanent laws. Even though some of these outlays are provided for by annual appropriation bills, Congress *must* spend the money because there are laws that order it to do so. Examples of mandatory spending are payments made for Medicare and Medicaid, various government subsidies such as farm price supports, and unemployment insurance. In 2001, discretionary

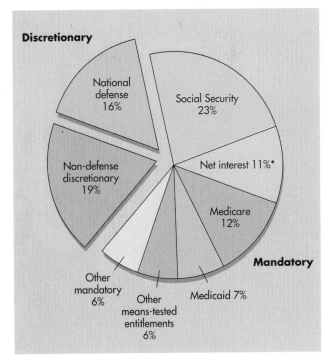

FIGURE 4 ■ *Estimated Federal Spending, 2001*

*Does not include interest paid on government securities held by the Social Security Trust Fund.
SOURCE: *A Citizens' Guide to the Federal Budget: Budget of the United States Government, Fiscal Year 2001* (Washington, D.C.: U.S. Government Printing Office, 2000).

spending is expected to account for about one-third of all budgetary outlays, and mandatory spending for two-thirds.

As its name implies, mandatory spending is harder than discretionary spending for Congress to control. Yet mandatory spending is not uncontrollable in every instance. In considering the president's budget, Congress cannot simply refuse to fund Medicaid, for example, nor can it decide to drastically lower its funding level. But it can amend the law to change eligibility, or it can repeal the law and remove any need for appropriations. Since 1990, Congress has been barred by law from passing any bill that increased mandatory spending without offsetting spending cuts or increased revenue to support it. This provision of the budget law is called pay-as-you-go, or simply "pay-go."

Most direct spending then, while not controllable through the budgetary process alone, can be altered by legislation. An expenditure such as interest on the national debt, however, is truly mandatory and can be reduced only by paying down the debt.

Clearly, any serious effort to reduce budget deficits required reductions in mandatory spending or substantial tax increases. That is why, when Republicans committed both to tax cuts and to balancing the budget assumed leadership of Congress in 1995, they immediately introduced legislation to alter the permanent laws that created, and order spending for, welfare, farm subsidies, and other programs.

Budget Forecasting

Deciding how large the budget should be and how much should go to each government activity are part of the political process. Because the amount the government can spend is supposed to be a function of the revenue it collects, revenue projection is crucial to budget making.

Predicting revenue is not a science, as much as we would like to think otherwise; it is rooted in political as well as economic considerations. To estimate accurately what revenues are likely to be and what outlays will be needed, budget writers have to estimate future rates of economic growth, inflation, unemployment, and productivity. With economic growth comes greater revenue. If factories are idle, workers are laid off and more money will be needed for unemployment insurance, welfare support, crime control, and even mental health care.

Small errors in predictions make an astoundingly large difference. For example, underestimating unemployment by 1 percent can mean a multibillion-dollar error in budgeting because unemployment reduces revenue and increases expenditures.

Presidents usually rely on estimates of economic growth, inflation, and unemployment that are most fa-

"Why, Yes, I am an economic forecaster. How did you guess?"
© 1982, John Trever/Albuquerque Journal

vorable to their own economic program. President Reagan's projections were especially far off the mark. David Stockman, Reagan's first budget director, described how such estimates were made for his first budget. To justify a huge tax reduction and show a balanced budget, significant economic growth and low inflation had to be projected. The administration's initial figures included a 2 percent projected inflation rate, a figure far below the existing rate. The chair of the Council of Economic Advisers, Murray Weidenbaum, said, "Nobody is going to predict 2% inflation on my watch. We'll be the laughingstock of the world."[33] So Stockman and Weidenbaum bargained over what the forecasts would be; Weidenbaum selected an inflation figure he could live with, and Stockman raised the economic growth projections. Of course, both were horribly wrong, and that is why the real deficit was 100 times bigger than projected.

For several years during the Clinton administration, the OMB's predictions of economic growth were too low and of unemployment too high. Consequently, the OMB underestimated revenues from personal income taxes, overstated budget deficits, and was unable to project the possibility of balancing the budget by 1999. In addition, the unexpected increase in revenue from Social Security withholding (due to the high rate of employment) moved predictions of a shortfall in the Social Security Trust Fund from 2001 to 2037.

The projections made by the Congressional Budget Office (CBO) are usually more reliable than those of the White House. The CBO, because it serves both parties and the political agenda of neither, is not compelled to accept the most or the least rosy estimates of economic performance. But, accepting projections that the rate of growth could not be sustained, both the OMB and the CBO again underestimated the size of the budget surplus in 2000.

Deficits and Debt

Politically driven economic forecasting, tax cuts unmatched by spending cuts, dramatically increased health care costs for the poor and elderly, and huge outlays for unforeseen events such as the savings and loan bailout all contributed to past deficits in the federal budget. A budget deficit occurs when federal spending exceeds federal revenues. This happened in all but eight years. The accumulation of money owed by the government from all budget deficits is the **national debt.** Between 1980 and 1995, our national debt quadrupled to more than $4.6 trillion and in 2000 stood at $5.6 trillion.

Our spending was largely for the military, social insurance programs for the middle class, and interest on the debt rather than for investments that lay the basis for future economic growth.

Despite the widespread conviction that moderate deficits are sometimes needed to stimulate the economy, most experts agree that the huge recurring deficits of the 1980s and 1990s impaired the country's long-term health. When government borrowing reaches a high level it crowds out private borrowing and therefore private investment. And the intense competition for investment dollars drives up interest rates. Budget deficits, coupled with private debts, left too little money in the United States to finance this mass borrowing, and we had to borrow from foreign as well as domestic sources. The outflow of interest and other payments made by our government to foreign investors in the 1980s and 1990s also contributed to our trade deficit and made us increasingly vulnerable to the uncertainties of international markets.

The economy also suffered from government's reduced flexibility in fiscal policy when as much as $0.15 of every tax dollar was designated for interest payments. There was less money for spending to meet urgent needs in education, health care, research, and infrastructure improvements necessary to economic growth.

A continuing problem is the huge amount of the national debt owned by government agencies. Although the public (domestic and foreign institutions and individual investors) holds $3.6 trillion of the debt, state, local, and federal government agencies hold nearly $2 trillion. The Social Security Trust Fund, for example, is required by law to invest its surplus (money paid in each year by workers and employers in excess of what is needed to meet outlays to Social Security recipients) in government securities. Just as you, a private investor, might loan the government money by buying a Treasury bond, so does the Social Security Trust Fund. The interest paid on these securities stays in the Trust Fund along with the bonds. The government uses the cash received from the Trust Fund purchase of securities, just as it uses the cash you spend to buy a bond, to offset the budget deficit. It means less money has to be borrowed from banks and other institutions. The question is whether the government will have the money to pay off the securities held by the Trust Fund when they mature, and if not, who will pay the benefits due retiring workers (see Chapter 17).

For some the solution to recurring deficits is amending the Constitution to require a balanced budget. The most recent call for a constitutional convention had won support in thirty-two states by 1990, just two short of the minimum needed, before the time limitation on ratification expired. But changing the constitution is usually regarded as a last-ditch alternative, and shepherding an amendment through to ratification can take years. Therefore many in Congress look to legislative action as a quicker and surer route to deficit reduction.

Because the Treasury Department cannot borrow beyond limits set by Congress, one obvious option is for Congress to refuse to approve an increase in the debt ceiling and force the Treasury Department to stop borrowing money. Congress has done this a few times, but when the government runs out of operating funds, it must shut down, just as it did in 1996, when Congress failed to pass appropriations bills.

Hypothetically, the government could print more money or stop making interest payments when budget shortfalls occur. Defaulting would destroy the government's financial credibility at home and abroad with the banks and corporations who help finance the debt, and it would betray millions of private citizens who invest in government bonds individually or through their pension plans. If the Treasury Department simply printed more money, the market would be flooded with dollars, setting off an inflationary spiral.

In 1985, Congress tried to force spending reductions by passing the Balanced Budget and Emergency Deficit Control Act, more commonly referred to by its cosponsors' names—Gramm-Rudman-Hollings (GRH). This act was supposed to trigger automatic cuts in most programs if annual goals for deficit reduction were not met.

The experience of GRH frightened the budget balancers in Congress because it led to even more playacting about the budget than usual. The deficit was artificially reduced by selling off public land and public enterprises, a one-shot infusion of money that does nothing to solve any long-range spending problems (it is like selling your house to pay off a vacation) and by gimmicks such as delaying military pay raises for a day. Spending items were put into an "off-budget category" and not counted in the estimate of the deficit. Had the items been included in the budget, the deficit would have doubled.

The surplus in the Social Security Trust Fund was used to offset part of the deficit while interest paid on Trust Fund debt holdings was put off-budget. More dangerously, to make the budget look more balanced, balances in accounts created to maintain and improve roads and air traffic were not spent even though the funds were desperately needed. Senator Warren Rudman, a cosponsor of the budget bill, got so sick of these games, he decided not to run for reelection.

FIGURE 5 ■ *The Deficit Disappears*

*Congressional Budget Office estimate
SOURCE: *Statistical Abstract of the United States, 2000,* Table 542. After a peak in 1992, the deficit began shrinking after passage of key deficit reduction legislation in 1993 (see "You Are There," Chapter 10).

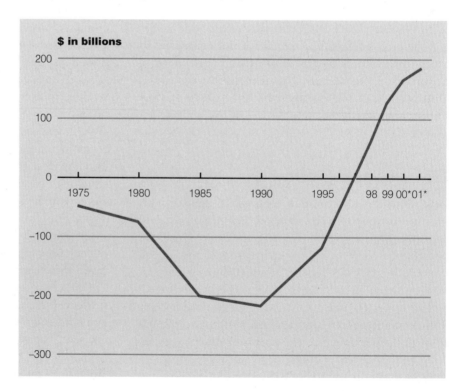

After the failure of GRH, no serious effort to deal with the deficit through budgetary reform came until 1990, when President Bush and the Democratic majority in Congress reached an agreement to set caps on discretionary spending for three years and to require that tax cuts and increases for entitlement programs had to be offset by new revenue or offsetting spending cuts (the pay-go system). This was the first serious measure to bring spending in line with revenue. In 1993, against the wishes of many Democrats, Clinton proposed a renewal of the spending caps. His offer was one part of a larger package designed to bring mandatory spending under control through sweeping reforms in the permanent laws governing spending for health care and welfare.

The size of the deficit fell each year of Clinton's first term (Figure 5), and midway through his second term, the budget went into surplus. At that point any major fiscal impact of revamping entitlement programs was yet to be felt; despite budget politicking, the deficit disappeared in large part due to increased revenues generated by economic growth and low unemployment.

With the budget balanced, there is still the matter of paying off more than $5.6 trillion of accrued debt. The figure sounds staggering, but the picture is not all gloom and doom. In 1790, the fledgling U.S. government had run up a national debt of $75.4 million, mainly from the costs of the Revolutionary War. This figure was fifteen times greater than the new government's annual revenues, whereas in 2000 our national debt was "only" three times larger than the $1.9 trillion in revenues. It took almost fifty years to pay off that first debt, but by 1835 the United States was virtually debt-free.[34] During that period of steady debt reduction, the country continued to grow and prosper. A small part of the current publicly held debt has already been paid off, and Clinton's fiscal 2001 budget contained a plan for paying off all of the public debt by 2013.

If existing growth, employment, and tax rates continue as they are, and there are no major treasury-draining crises, surpluses are projected to total about $2 trillion over the next decade. The unexpected size of the surplus has triggered a debate over how to use it. Almost everyone agrees that a substantial part of it must be used to shore up Social Security and Medicare. But there is disagreement over whether the economy would benefit more from a cut in income taxes or from paying down the debt. Those who support reducing debt level point to the amount of money tied up in annual interest payments. In the single year between 1998 and 1999 as the budget went into surplus, money spent on net interest payments on the debt dropped by $13 billion; if the budget stays in surplus in the decade from 1998 to 2009, as projected, annual interest payments will decline from $243 billion to $71 billion. Even to Bill Gates $172 billion is a lot of money.

Opponents of rushing to pay off debt fall into two general categories: those who believe a cut in the income tax is important for continued economic growth, and those who believe it is more important to invest in education, train future workers, and improve infrastructure important to industrial growth and increased productivity. But since virtually all of the surplus is from payroll taxes withheld for Social Security and Medicare benefits and needed for future retirees, experts do not even agree whether the surplus is real or just an accounting device.

Postwar Boom and Bust

The health of any economy depends on many factors, only some of which government can influence and none of which it can completely control. But the role of government has to change over time if it is to be responsive to public needs and to structural changes in the economy. As we enter the twenty-first century, the relationships between governments and economies are everywhere in flux.

In the United States after the Great Depression, the Keynesian-influenced activist role of the government was not seriously challenged until the Reagan years, and even then without great impact. But the collapse of one-party socialist systems in Eastern Europe and a relative decline in U.S. economic strength revived the debate over government's role in a free market economy. Before looking to the future, we look back briefly at the U.S. economy since World War II and government's contributions to current problems and successes.

The American Quarter Century

In the late 1940s, following World War II, we were the undisputed economic power of the world. Optimistic (and perhaps jingoistic) Americans talked of the "American century," in which America would dominate the world much as Britain had done in the nineteenth century and other powers had done in earlier eras. The economies of World War II allies (Britain, France, the Soviet Union) and enemies (Germany, Italy, and Japan) alike, were shattered by the expense and human loss of

The American postwar economy lifted millions of families into middle-class status and comfort. At left is a poverty-stricken family in 1936. Victims of the drought and depression, they had left Oklahoma, where they were homeless with little to eat, to find a better future in California. At right is the same family forty-three years later in front of one daughter's home in Modesto. Is such dramatic improvement in family fortunes probable today?

Left: Library of Congress. Right: Bill Ganzel, University of Nebraska Press

the war, the dislocation of populations in some nations, and the destruction of factories, businesses, and public facilities such as highways and railroads in others. In these circumstances our economy boomed, and we produced goods for the entire world.

The economic good times continued, fueled in part by our growing population, for twenty-five years. Slowdowns in economic growth and increases in unemployment were temporary, inflation was not serious, and productivity marched steadily upward. Our standard of living zoomed as Americans bought cars, new homes, household appliances, and luxury items in quantities unheard of before. Most people could anticipate being better off in the future than in the present and felt sure that their children would be even better off. Economic improvement seemed inevitable, not for everyone, of course, but for most people.

The late 1960s brought the first obvious signs of trouble as inflation rose along with spending on the Vietnam War. Then in 1973 the bottom fell out of our

economic machine. A group of oil-producing nations (called OPEC), which controls much of the world's known reserves, forced a large price increase in oil. Dependent on foreign oil, Americans found prices skyrocketing, not only for gas for their cars but for almost everything else. Petroleum products ran our factories and our farm machinery and were essential ingredients in the manufacture of goods ranging from plastics to pesticides, petrochemicals to Chapstick. The United States was not alone in its distress. All of the industrialized and much of the developing world also experienced rampant inflation. But the United States, used to being "on top of the world," may have been shaken more deeply.

The oil price shock was not the only blow to our economy. During the 1970s, the baby boom generation—those born in the late 1940s and early 1950s—entered the workforce in record numbers. As a consequence, unemployment increased because the economy was not growing fast enough to absorb millions of new workers. To add to our woes, other industrial nations of the world had long since recovered from the devastation of World War II and were giving us stiff competition in the international marketplace. Developing nations of Asia were also beginning to industrialize and, with low wage rates for their workers, were underselling us in international markets. Many of our heavy industries shriveled as U.S. and foreign manufacturers discovered they could buy steel and machinery cheaper in Japan, Korea, or Germany, and consumers at home and abroad decided they preferred energy-efficient, foreign-made cars to those produced by the American auto industry. These developments increased unemployment as workers in declining industries were laid off.[35]

Despite these woes and the fact that inflation made the dollar worth less in 1979 than in 1970, real income in the 1970s increased by over one-fourth, and the distribution of income between the rich and poor changed little.[36] The average person was better off but felt worse off because of the specter of rising inflation, which reached double-digit figures during some months of the late 1970s. During the decade, inflation totaled 112 percent, compared to only 31 percent in the 1960s and 20 percent in the 1950s. Economists could not agree on any solution to inflation that would not increase unemployment. Pessimists, looking at the shattered U.S. economy, noted that the "American century" had lasted only twenty-five years.

When gas prices increased and supplies ran low, some areas, including California, had gas rationing. Here motorists push their car to a gas pump.
Korody/Sygma

The Reagan-Bush Years

During his eight years in the White House, Ronald Reagan succeeded in reviving public confidence in the economy. As promised, he reduced income taxes, increased military spending, and lowered inflation. Inflation rates after 1982 were the lowest since the early 1970s, due in part to a big drop in oil prices. However, most of the decrease in inflation was due to the Federal Reserve Board's policies of taking money out of the economy by raising prime interest rates and making it very expensive for businesses to borrow money. This tight money policy slowed growth, and with it inflation, but it also contributed to a severe recession in 1981 and 1982. High unemployment drove down wages as workers threatened with layoffs agreed to forgo pay increases and in some cases even to accept pay cuts and reduced fringe benefits.

With the Fed's tight money policy and the sharp drop in inflation, farmland plummeted in value, deflating even more than wages. Having borrowed amounts for expansion far in excess of the new value of their land, farmers were unable to sell the land at prices equal to their debt when banks called in their loans. Thousands of farmers lost their land and homes and were thrown into an uncertain job market.

In 1982, unemployment reached 11 percent—its highest level since the Great Depression—but then began to fall as an economic recovery took hold. Higher levels of consumer spending, stimulated by the tax cut, and record levels of government spending increased the demand for goods, which in turn fueled more production and employment. Moreover, the economy had grown in response to the baby boom generation; but then in the latter part of the 1980s, the smaller number of children born during the "baby bust" era (the mid- to late 1960s) entered the workforce, leaving many parts of the country with labor shortages. By the time Reagan left office, the unemployment rate was around 5 percent.

Unfortunately, the boom in our economy was built in large part on a foundation of debt. Supply-side economics did not work; though production increased, new business did not generate enough tax revenue to make up for the lower rates. Individuals borrowed heavily, too. Buying on credit became such a way of life for Americans that, in 1990, 90 percent of all bankruptcies were filed by individual consumers unable to pay their debts.[37]

During the Reagan years, we did not save or invest for the future. We consumed about as much as we earned. Indeed, if it were not for pension funds and the

Social Security Trust Fund, collectively as consumers we would have spent all we earned. Most public borrowing paid for consumption rather than modernization of our nation's industries or improvement of our rapidly deteriorating infrastructure of roads, bridges, and water treatment plants. By the time President Bush took office, 42 percent of America's highway bridges were closed or restricted to light traffic; a bridge failed every two days.[38]

President Bush rode into office on the Reagan administration's successes in reducing inflation and unemployment and building up the military. Due to the growing deficit, Bush did agree to new taxes but otherwise veered little from the Reagan economic path, despite his earlier rejection of supply-side policies.

As Bush turned his attention to foreign policy and the end of the Cold War, economic conditions at home deteriorated. Inflation rose and more than one million private sector jobs were lost in 1990–1991. Corporate profits fell by almost 6 percent, and economic growth slowed almost to a halt. The nation was declared to be in recession as unemployment rose to 7.5 percent. With the budget and trade deficits soaring, Bush could not turn to the supply-side cure of further tax reductions to stimulate the economy. Yet government continued to spend. By the time Bush left office, another trillion dollars had been added to the national debt.

Age of Diminished Expectations

By the time Clinton entered the White House, Americans were pessimistic about the country's economic future. They were living in an era of diminished expectations with declining real wages and living standards.[39] In real dollars (that is, dollars adjusted for inflation), the average family in 1995 earned only about as much as it did in 1975, even though by 1995 most families had two wage earners, rather than one.

From the post–World War II decades into the 1970s, family income grew over 3 percent a year.[40] Indeed, in 1966, a fifty-year-old man could look back over a ten-year period in the workforce and see that his income had risen over 30 percent. At the end of the 1980s, he could look back over the same number of years and find his income had risen only 10 percent.[41] In real terms, workers were earning less than their parents did at a comparable age, and growth in living standards had nearly stopped.

Opportunities knocked for most college-educated young adults, but getting a college education became increasingly difficult for students from poor families. The

"The poor are getting poorer, but with the rich getting richer it all averages out in the long run."

proportion of students from poor families attending college dropped by 4 percent between 1976 and 1986.[42] There were fewer well-paying jobs for blue-collar workers than there had been twenty years earlier. Heavy industries that traditionally paid high wages to unionized workers fell on hard times. Many lost their highly paid jobs (sometimes upward of $14 per hour) for positions that barely paid minimum wage. By 1995, of all men between the ages of 25 and 34, 32 percent earned "less than the amount necessary to keep a family of four above the poverty line." Mothers had to work longer hours to maintain the old standard of living.[43]

Real wage rates in many nonservice jobs decreased too. Wage concessions made by workers worried about job security meant that even a unionized job in industry did not provide protection against declining income. However, unionized workers in almost all job categories still fared better than nonunionized workers, especially in fringe benefits.[44]

The 1990s were a time of taking stock of what the 1980s' private and public spending binge wrought. The president and Congress reined in spending, and businesses that had overexpanded in the 1980s began cutting back their labor forces, eliminating unnecessary jobs and computerizing clerical work. Even when economists pronounced the recession over in 1993, factories relied on temporary employees or on overtime work to meet increasing demand rather than bear the expense of recruiting, training, and picking up fringe benefits for new workers. By one estimate money spent on overtime pay rather than on wages for new workers cost the economy 1.3 million jobs and accounted for most of the lost jobs in the manufacturing sector in the late 1980s.[45] With fewer employees turning out more goods and services, productivity began to increase sharply in 1992–1993.

The 1990s Recovery

It should be evident now that our country passes through cycles of economic boom and bust. As we write in late 2000, the record period of economic expansion continues. The United States has experienced a remarkable nine years of low unemployment, economic growth, and low inflation. It appears that the country has completed a difficult transition from an economy based on manufacturing to one where jobs are generated primarily by high-tech and service industries, just as we earlier made the difficult transition from agriculture to manufacturing. At century's end, Americans' confidence in the economy was at its highest point in fifty years.

The recovery has been a song in two keys. From the standpoint of a job hunter, the economy looked good; jobs were plentiful, and real income moved upward for almost all workers except farmers. But, the Bureau of Labor Statistics predicted of the fifty-one million new jobs that would be created by 2006, twenty-two million would be low-skill service jobs paying low wages.[46] Although in 1997 unskilled workers were beginning to earn more for the first time in two decades, they were losing benefits at an alarming rate.[47] In 1999, 35 percent of all parents had no medical insurance, up from 31 percent in 1997.[48] Poor parents who left welfare and took jobs often lost their coverage, either because they earned too much to qualify for Medicaid and their jobs provided no coverage, or because states did not tell them they were still eligible for Medicaid. Eighteen percent of all children live in households with incomes below the poverty line.[49] To the millions of uninsured Americans in low-paying jobs, a million immigrants, many of them poorly educated, were being added each year (see the American Diversity box).

The booming economy of the late 1990s has given the illusion that money grows on trees for many people, but others have been left in the dirt.

"The economy's never been better. Here's another potato!"

AMERICAN DIVERSITY

Does Immigration Benefit the Economy?

Concerns about the number and national origins of immigrants have been with us almost since settlers began colonizing North America. But during the 1980s and early 1990s, as the arrival of millions of new Americans coincided with slow economic growth, serious unemployment, and huge budget deficits, another round of anti-immigration sentiment surfaced. It led to new state and federal laws restricting benefits and services available to both legal and illegal immigrants, calls for suspending immigration, and even for the elimination of the Immigration and Naturalization Service (INS). Concern over immigration policy continued to mount in the 1990s even as unemployment and inflation dropped to record lows, the deficit declined, and the economy grew. As we enter the twenty-first century, is immigration benefiting the economy or hurting it? Experts disagree. (We ignore noneconomic benefits and costs of immigration in this discussion.)

Without doubt, the population growth brought by immigration stimulates the economy by increasing the demand for goods and services. A certain portion of immigrants come with very high or even unique job skills, adding to economic growth and productivity. People who receive residency visas within the quota reserved for priority job skills are likely to be well educated, as are those who come on nonimmigrant student visas and stay on. (Immigrants are disproportionately represented among university professors.)

A 1997 study by the National Academy of Sciences (NAS) concluded that immigration produces a small net gain of $1 billion to $10 billion a year for our $8 trillion economy, while having a very small negative impact on the wages and job opportunities of native workers.[1] While the majority of immigrants need more services than native residents and have fewer resources to pay for them, the study concluded that, on average, adult immigrants pay more in taxes over a lifetime than they receive in benefits. Most of these revenues, however, go to the federal government, while states and localities pick up much of the cost for education, health care, and other social services.

But there is another side. Most illegal immigrants and the majority of immigrants who come in under one of the family preference programs have lower educational levels than native workers. By one estimate, during the 1980s immigration "contributed to an increase of 15% in the number of high school dropouts in the U.S. workforce—causing a 5% decline in wages for native workers who had dropped out of high school."[2] In California, where competition for low-wage laborers is fierce, businesses have turned to nonunionized immigrants, driving native workers out of unskilled positions and slashing the going wage rates.[3] In Pittsburgh the asbestos workers union saw the going wage drop from $31 to $19 per hour and safety conditions deteriorate, under competition from nonunionized immigrants willing to work for as little as $11 or $12 an hour.[4]

Moreover, the calculation of economic benefits depends on whether the study includes both parents and children in immigrant households. The national net gain figures cited earlier hold true only if one looks at the cost incurred per adult worker. When the costs of benefits for children are factored in, each immigrant produces a net loss in revenue.[5] One independent study concluded that over his or her lifetime an immigrant never repaid in taxes an amount equivalent to benefits received, unless one counted in the tax contributions of grown children. And even then the immigrant would remain "a fiscal burden for twenty-two years."[6]

In fact, the same NAS study that concluded immigration produced a small net gain for the country as a whole also estimated that states and localities lose $25,000 a year per immigrant. And, since most immigrants cluster in six states and several major cities, these costs are not evenly distributed. In California, which absorbs a very disproportionate share of both legal and nonlegal immigrants, the

---

While the federal government was eliminating its budget deficits, Americans were increasing theirs. In 2000, total consumer debt, at $6.8 trillion, or $20,000 per capita, surpassed the national debt in size. Americans devoted more of their disposable income to servicing their debts than the federal government spent paying interest on the national debt).[50]

Why are wages, benefits, and spending habits problems for government? Why not let the market take its course? One reason has to do with the cost of government, and the second has to do with how a democracy functions. In any society with a well-established political system, people have expectations of government, and in democracies, officials try to meet some of those expectations if they want to be reelected. But meeting those expectations incurs costs.

We have come to expect that government will shoulder part of the risk of living in a market economy.

total cost of immigration per year for each nonimmigrant household was estimated to be $1,778 in 1994–1995.[7] Because states have little control over the level of new arrivals each year and therefore over how to budget for them, governors of high-impact states like California and Florida have sued the federal government for reimbursement of the cost of providing education, health care, and social services.

On the surface these problems do not seem radically different from the problems of economic integration this country has always faced. But there are some reasons to think that they could be:

■ Older economies cannot grow at the same rate as young economies.

■ The current level of immigration has added pressure on some of the institutions, such as schools and the health care and welfare systems, about whose adequacy Americans are most concerned. Six percent of immigrants receive some form of welfare on arrival in the country, double the rate for U.S. citizens.[8] In addition, the public school system is in disarray and perhaps not capable of continuing to absorb so many children with no knowledge of English and in need of remedial instruction. A parallel point could be made about the health care system and its skyrocketing costs.

■ The economic benefits of immigration go disproportionately to the well-off (such as employers of low-paid unskilled labor), while the costs fall disproportionately on the poor (competition for low-wage labor and for social services), a fact that could worsen the growing income gap between rich and poor.

■ Although the goods produced and consumed by immigrants undeniably add to GDP, not all earnings are spent in the United States. A substantial portion of household income of some immigrants is sent abroad to help relatives. Mexican Americans are estimated to send $6 billion annually to their families in Mexico, making it the third-largest source of foreign revenue for that country.[9] Many other immigrants from Central America, China, India, Africa, and elsewhere do the same, adding to the trade deficit.

■ Immigration now accounts for most of the population growth in the United States and leads to rapid development in those areas where settlement is concentrated. This in turn has an impact on environmental and quality of life issues, especially on urban congestion and land and resource conservation. If legal and illegal immigration continue at current rates, U.S. population will surpass 500 million by 2050 according to Census Bureau estimates.

There are more factors to consider in deciding what immigration policy you support than the economic costs and benefits to the country, principal among them that immigration is at the core of American identity. Yet even looking only at the economics of immigration it is clear that this issue is more complex than its most vocal supporters and opponents suggest.

1. Robert Pear, "Academy's Report Says Immigration Benefits the U.S.," *New York Times,* May 18, 1997, pp. 1, 12.
2. Dick Kirschten, "American Dreamers," *National Journal,* July 5, 1997, p. 1367.
3. Roy Beck, "The Wages of Immigration," *Washington Post National Weekly Edition,* April 29–May 5, 1996, p. 24. Also see Beck's *The Case against Immigration: The Moral, Economic, Social and Environmental Reasons for Reducing U.S. Immigration Back to Traditional Levels* (New York: Norton, 1996).
4. Peter Passell, "Benefits Dwindle along with Wages for the Unskilled," *New York Times,* June 14, 1998, p. 23.
5. Pear, "Academy's Report," p. 12.
6. John Cassidy, "The Melting-Pot Myth," *The New Yorker,* July 14, 1997, p. 42, citing a study by Berkeley economist Ronald Lee.
7. Kirschten, "American Dreamers," p. 1366.
8. William Booth, "Diversity and Division," *Washington Post National Weekly Edition,* March 2, 1998, p. 7.
9. *New York Times,* June 18, 2000, p. 18.

Everyone is familiar with Social Security and Medicare for older Americans and welfare and Medicaid for the poor. But government also assumes risks for millions of middle-class Americans through flood and crop insurance, pension fund and credit union insurance, life insurance for veterans and federal employees, bank deposit insurance, and a variety of risk insurance programs for businesses involved in defense-related work or overseas investing. All of these risks assumed by government programs are liabilities that in bad economic times can cost billions, potentially trillions, of dollars, yet they do not figure in budget proposals beyond cash outlays in a fiscal year.[51] Of course, no one expects all banks, pension funds, and credit unions to fail, but when just one program had to make massive payouts (insurance on deposits in failed savings and loans) in the 1980s, the toll on the budget was severe. So it is easy to see why a healthy economy is important to government.

Second, there is some evidence that the gap between rich and poor is widening. Although overall earnings rose between the 1970s and 1990s, once adjusted for inflation, the average income of the poorest fifth fell by 5 percent.[52] By the end of the century, the average corporate executive, paid $11.9 million per year, earned more in one day than the average American worker earned in a year.[53] Yet the difference in total wealth is far greater than earnings alone suggest, because those in the highest income brackets have had money to save, invest in the stock market, and buy homes, which made it possible for them to increase their wealth substantially during the real estate and stock booms of the 1990s. The concentration of wealth and privilege (especially access to higher education in elite institutions) has become so pronounced that one observer refers to the formation of an "overclass."[54]

The United States is now the most economically stratified country in the modern industrial world. One percent of the population controls almost 40 percent of the country's wealth, and America's children are among the poorest in the industrialized world (ranking sixteenth out of eighteen).[55] Reduced spending for social programs, including worker training, college loans, and welfare, and proposed new tax cuts for the wealthy are likely to add to the maldistribution of income. Aid for lower-income students is also declining in the private sector. In the competition for students, many universities no longer consider need as the primary factor in awarding grants and scholarships. Three-quarters of all grants awarded by colleges and universities between 1989 and 1995 went to middle- and upper-income students, with the fastest rate of increase among students from upper-income homes.[56] If the middle class is declining, this is clearly a danger sign because democratic stability rests in part on a large middle class. A society of haves and have-nots with relatively few in the middle is not likely to be very stable.[57]

The prosperity we enjoy and the economic problems we face have never been totally the direct result of government policy. Private spending accounts for 70 percent of our economy, so economic policies of the private sector and the consumption and saving habits of Americans play an enormous role in the state of the economy at any time. But government's role in protecting us from recession and depression, creating jobs, and guaranteeing minimum wages and safety conditions has been altered by global economic change.

Japan, the European Union, China, Taiwan, Hong Kong, South Korea, Singapore, and several Latin American countries are now major rivals in world trade. We cannot dominate markets with our manufactured or agricultural products, and we cannot keep jobs within our borders when it is more profitable for businesses to operate elsewhere. The competition is good in that it forces us to become more efficient and brings greater prosperity to the citizens of other countries (who are potential consumers of goods and services we produce). But it has had an impact on the kinds of jobs available to Americans and the wages paid: 20 to 25 percent of the growth in wage inequality in the United States has been attributed to labor competition in a global market.[58]

The American Economy in the Twenty-First Century

According to UN statistics, at least one-third of world production is controlled by multinational corporations. This international dispersion of economic activity—investment, research and development, production, and distribution—through the networking of companies across national borders is called **globalization.** By definition globalization means that business is not as nation-centered today as it was in the mid-twentieth century. Because business exists primarily to make a profit, loyalty to a particular place is less important than favorable economic conditions for production and distribution. Thus corporations are continuously scouting for those locations where, for example, labor costs are cheapest and regulation least burdensome. To trade unions and environmental and consumer groups it means that U.S. corporations are becoming less dependent on and less responsive to American workers and consumers. It also means that they may be moving beyond the reach of government regulation that was adopted to safeguard workers' and consumers' rights and to protect the public against environmental abuses or other negative consequences of business activity.

As the U.S. economy's position in the global economy has changed, so has the government's ability to effect economic change. The days when the board chairman of General Motors could say "What is good for GM is good for the country and what is good for the country is good for GM" are over. The American economy is now a region of the global economy, and both business and labor must compete in an international market. We may still jealously guard our territorial

boundaries but today no border can contain financial and intellectual activities.

A revolution in technology—computers, telecommunications, and transportation—brought us to this new era. Money can be transferred to foreign banks instantaneously through computerized accounts, making competition for investment international. The most highly paid workers—scientists, systems planners and analysts, lawyers, and artists, for example—are very mobile; modern transportation makes it feasible to travel to employment opportunities anywhere in the world, and telecommunications makes it easy to transmit their ideas. They are part of an international labor pool.

Blue-collar workers, too, compete in an international market, not just against available labor in the United States. Manufacturers relocate where low overhead and wages ensure higher profits, and highly paid North Americans lose jobs to poorly paid Latin Americans and Asians.

Businesses do not make decisions on relocating to another city or country based on how their departure will affect the local economy. Workers do not worry

(unless restricted by national security laws) about whether the company they sell their invention, new software, or design idea to is an American-based or a foreign company as long as they get the highest possible price for their services or product.

Some say that we need to stop thinking about how to maintain an "American" economy and prepare the American labor force to compete in the global economy.[59]

In today's world, national competitiveness no longer depends on the amount of money the nation's citizens save and invest in building more factories on American soil. It depends instead on the skills and insights workers can contribute to the global economy. Given our great university system and leadership in high technology, the United States has a greater potential than almost any other country to train workers for the economy of the twenty-first century. But doing this will mean upgrading the educational system so that it does an equally good job for people in all income groups. In the global economy of the twenty-first century, our economic well-being will depend on it.

The question is how to make available to all Ameri-

Economic Policy in Time

1790 The newly created United States government begins operations with a war debt fifteen times its annual revenues.

1791 The First Bank of the United States is established.

1792 New York Stock Exchange opens.

1819 A four-year period of economic growth and speculation is followed by economic bust and a run on banks (a panic). The Panic of 1819, the first in a cycle of boom-and-bust periods in U.S. history, was followed by the Panics of 1837, 1857, 1873, 1893 (also called a depression), 1907, and the Great Depression of 1933.

1832 President Jackson vetoes Congress's attempt to recharter the Second National Bank.

1834 The national debt is paid off.

1901 President Theodore Roosevelt endorses federal regulation of big business and the breakup of large trusts (monopolies). Government promoted as defender of the average citizen against big business.

1913 Establishment of the Federal Reserve System (Fed) and the Federal Open Market Committee (FOMC) to set monetary policy independently from Congress and the president. The Fed, with its twelve regional banks, was designed as an alternative to one national bank.

1913 Ratification of the Sixteenth Amendment allowing Congress to lay and collect a tax on personal income.

1921 Bureau of the Budget (later the Office of Management and Budget) created by act of Congress as it transfers primary responsibility for writing the annual budget to the executive branch.

1929 Stock market crash sets in motion a run on banks and the Great Depression, which leaves one-quarter of the population unemployed.

1933 Fearing political instability, President Roosevelt uses government resources to stimulate the economy and provide social insurance programs for the unemployed and elderly; government regulation of banking and the stock market begins.

1933 First federal minimum-wage law sets hourly wage at 25¢.

1935 Passage of the National Labor Relations Act, the "Magna Carta" of American workers. Gave govern-

ment power to enforce workers' right to bargain collectively and led to the growth of the trade union movement.

1945 World War II ends and, combined with the costs of fighting the Great Depression, leaves the U.S. with a $242 billion debt. As the least damaged country to emerge from the war, the U.S. becomes the world's preeminent economic power.

1946 First impact of the 1944 G.I. Bill of Rights is felt as returning veterans cause college enrollments to explode and stimulate a vast expansion of the higher education system.

1971 President Nixon floats U.S. currency, cutting all remaining ties to the gold standard.

1977 Energy crises stimulate recession and U.S. enters a fifteen-year period of transition from a manufacturing and agricultural economy to one based on high technology and service industries.

1983 President Reagan adopts a budget policy of increased military spending and tax cuts. U.S. enters worst recession since the Great Depression: over the next decade the national debt doubles, and U.S. becomes the world's largest debtor nation.

1987 Alan Greenspan appointed head of the Fed; declining fiscal flexibility of Congress and the president contributes to enhanced power of Greenspan and the FOMC.

1990 President Bush and the Democratic Congress set mandatory caps on spending to rein in runaway budget deficits.

1993 President Clinton goes against many in his party to support renewal of spending caps as part of a larger deficit-reduction plan.

1997 First balanced budget since 1969. Unemployment rate at record low, but trade deficit at record high, and U.S. continues to have the most unequal distribution of wealth in the industrialized world.

1998 Period of budget surpluses begins, and government begins to pay down the national debt of more than $5 trillion.

2000 U.S. sets a record for the longest period of economic expansion in its history.

cans the technology necessary to close what some call a "digital divide." This is a term for the gap in access to computers and Internet hookups that exists between the well-off and the poor, whites and minorities, the well educated and the less educated, and between urban and rural residents. Half of all households have computers,

and 40 percent have Internet connections, but those with incomes of $75,000 and higher are nine times more likely to have a home computer and twenty times as likely to have Internet access.[60] For this reason, some argue the key contributing factors are—just as with political participation rates—income and education. However, some studies show that a significant gap in home computers and Internet access exists between white and black households with the same income.[61] Whatever causes the gap, it is certain that it increases exponentially because those with training and access are able to keep pace with the almost daily changes in technology and software, while those without do not just stand still but lose ground rapidly.

The economic significance of the digital divide is that opportunities for both job seekers and consumers are increasingly tied to computer training and Internet access. In 1998, for example, the Internet created 1.2 million jobs in the United States, and jobs in the information technology sector "pay almost 80 percent more than the average private sector wage."[62] Many new businesses are home start-ups in which all transactions are conducted via the Internet; similarly, much of the day trading on the stock market, which has made small fortunes for thousands of Americans, has been conducted from home computers with Internet hookups. To compete on an equal footing in today's job market, computer training and Internet access are essential. In addition, for consumers, the Web is becoming increasingly important to search for low-cost goods and services: $8 billion worth of consumer goods were sold off the Web in 1998 alone. With income disparity in the United States already a serious problem, many in government want to do something to level this playing field. But as with all other aspects of government intervention in the economy, the question is what is it appropriate for the government to do.

In the twenty-first century, the American economy is moving faster than the ability of many of its citizens to keep pace in education and training, leaving them without the chance to participate in the new prosperity. The government continues to allow businesses to bring in a few hundred thousand highly trained computer programmers and software developers from other countries each year because we are not training or retraining our own citizens fast enough to keep up with the growth in the technology sector. If the gap in opportunity and income is not to get increasingly wider, all Americans will have to have access to the essential tools to participate in the new economy. As one senator told a group of school children, "Not everyone can be a Michael Jordan, but if you have technology, all of you can play this game."[63]

Even if an "American economy" no longer exists, there is not much evidence that Americans, except perhaps those in the highest-income groups, have stopped thinking that there is an economy contiguous with the country's borders and that their government is responsible in some way for its performance. This creates a set of expectations that government officials may be increasingly less able to meet.

While our government cannot control developments in the global economy or dictate to corporations where they will do business or how many or what kind of jobs they will create, the government can take actions to encourage economic growth. For example, it can adopt fiscal policies that avoid another cycle of huge budget deficits, thus freeing more money for private borrowing and investment, and it can support programs for retraining workers who have lost their jobs and in upgrading their technology skills.

The federal government can also monitor trade practices to see that foreign markets are open to American products, encourage reform of the educational system, fund repair and upgrading of the country's infrastructure; and target new technologies and industries for government support. Government can also do nothing and allow the market to set the terms of competition and the distribution of wealth, but this option has not been chosen by any modern industrial country.

Conclusion: Is Our Economic Policy Responsive?

If we can draw one lesson from the performance of the American economy during the 1970s and 1980s, it is that economic policymakers, both government and private, were living for the short term. In the 1980s, corporate America improved its profit margin at the expense not only of investment but also of workers, many of whose real wages fell significantly. Government policymakers preferred politically popular tax cuts to either balancing the budget or investing in programs to improve our nation's infrastructure, promote research, or upgrade human capital through education and training. Moreover, government was content to let income inequalities grow and even exacerbated them by cutbacks in social programs.

The mid-1990s saw a movement away from policy geared toward short-term electoral results and toward longer-term solutions to the problem of maintaining the country's economic vitality, in part because the electorate in 1992 and 1994 signaled its support for a change in fiscal policy. Coming out of the transition to a high-tech, service economy, the United States began a period of economic growth and deficit reduction and entered the twenty-first century as the largest and most productive economy on earth. It also had the greatest income disparity of all the industrial democracies, fostered in part by public policy (a tax structure that placed the heaviest burdens on middle- and lower-income groups) and in part by private policies (market changes in the job and wage structure) that government was less and less willing to ameliorate.

Congress and the White House were divided over how government should respond to this disparity. The Clinton administration argued that a responsive government is one that uses fiscal policy both to foster economic growth and to regulate the distribution of income generated by that growth. Congress under Republican leadership argued that the country's economic difficulties stemmed precisely from this overresponsive, interventionist, Keynesian approach. In their view the most responsive government is that which leaves an unfettered market to "grow" the economy and distribute its wealth. This is the essence of the long-standing debate in American political life over the proper relationship of government to the economy.

Murray Votes to Repeal Tax on Wealthy

Murray joined eight other Democrats in the Senate in crossing over to vote yes on repeal of the estate tax. The vote was short of the two-thirds that would be needed to override the presidential veto that Clinton has said he will use "without hesitation."[64] That means some senators, especially the Democrats, may have voted for the bill to please constituents in an election year, believing it would never become law.

Before the vote was taken, Murray issued a statement calling on Democrats to enter the debate with a plan of their own to end the tax in the most progressive way possible. She said she supported the repeal "in the context of a modest, targeted tax cut benefitting working families."[65] Murray maintained the Senate version of the bill *was* progressive because, unlike the House version, it retained the requirement that those who inherit still have to pay a capital gains tax on property or assets if they sell them. (The House had exempted up to $4.3 million from capital gains tax in addition to repealing the estate tax). The Senate version, Murray argued, would allow those who want to run their parents' farms and businesses

to retain them while taxing those who sold wealth accumulated by their parents. She did not address the fact that the overwhelming majority of estates that would become exempt from tax are *not* small farms or businesses.

It is clear that Murray believed the president's opposition would prevent the bill from becoming law. But by helping pass the bill, she also helped force the issue into a reconciliation process with House members and Clinton aides. Any bill that emerged with the possibility of getting a presidential signature was likely to target tax reductions for small business owners and family farmers and smaller estates. Some—although not Murray—even hoped Clinton would veto the bill so retention of the estate tax could be blamed on the Democrats in the election. Of course, Murray did not mention that her Microsoft multimillionaire constituents would be as free to transfer their wealth untaxed to the next generation as those small farmers and business owners whose needs purportedly were the motivation for her vote.

Murray's vote suggests why balancing the budget is usually so difficult. Members cast votes to please their constituencies, and what could be more

popular than a tax cut? Her vote, like many cast each year by members of all political stripes, serve the short-term electoral interests of the members more than the long-term interests of the country. Thus, conservative Republicans who decry big government vote for massive pork barrel projects for their districts, including the development of weapons systems that military leaders say they do not need, and liberal Democrats, who believe in progressive taxes, vote for tax breaks for the wealthy. During a time of budget surpluses such as we had at the end of the 1990s and into 2000, it may seem only fair to give some of those dollars back to taxpayers. But while the deficits are gone for now, we still have a national debt of more than $5 trillion that has to be paid. In repealing the estate tax Congress not only gave up a substantial portion of current and projected surpluses that might be used to pay down the debt but reduced the permanent tax base by hundreds of billions of dollars—all to benefit 2 percent of the population. Those dollars may not be needed now, but down the line when the good times pass—and they always do—Congress could find it difficult once again to balance the budget.

Key Terms

capitalist economy	supply-side economics
socialism	monetary policy
mixed economy	progressive tax
depression	regressive tax
inflation	flat tax
recession	discretionary spending
productivity	mandatory spending
fiscal policy	national debt
Keynesian economics	globalization
stagflation	

Further Reading

William Grieder, *Secrets of the Temple* (New York: Simon & Schuster, 1988). It is hard to imagine a book about the Federal Reserve Board being interesting, but this one is. Reveals the human face behind this most technical institution.

Robert Heilbroner, *The Worldly Philosophers,* 6th ed. (New York: Simon & Schuster, 1986). A readable account of the lives and ideas of famous economists throughout history.

Robert Heilbroner and Lester Thurow, *Economics Explained* (New York: Random House, 1982). A readable discussion of major economic concepts and issues.

Paul Krugman, *Peddling Prosperity in the Age of Diminished Expectations: U.S. Economic Policy in the 1990s* (New York: Norton, 1995). An economist from MIT writing for a general reading audience explains the trade and budget deficits, inflation, unemployment, Fed policies, devaluation, and the S&L scandal in terms of their costs to the nation's overall economic health.

Michael Lind, *The Next American Nation: The New Nationalism and the Fourth American Revolution* (New York: Free Press, 1995). This study of American identity by an editor of *The New Republic* includes two chapters (4 and 5) on the social and political consequences of the growing concentration of wealth and privilege in the United States.

Robert Reich, *The Work of Nations* (New York: Vintage, 1992). Argues that we must see ourselves as part of a world economy and be prepared to compete internationally.

Amartya Sen, *Development as Freedom* (New York: Knopf, 1999). A Nobel laureate in economics and one of the world's leading authorities on development explains the relationship between income and well-being and between economic development and democracy.

David Stockman, *The Triumph of Politics: Why the Reagan Revolution Failed* (New York: Harper & Row, 1986). Reagan's budget director tells all.

Edward Tufte, *Political Control of the Economy* (Princeton, N.J.: Princeton University Press, 1978). An interesting, sophisti-

cated, but readable account of the relationship between trying to win elections and economic policymaking.

Electronic Resources

interactive.wsj.com/std_regchoice.html
The Wall Street Journal *probably has the best coverage of economic news of any U.S. newspaper. However, if you want to see the Web edition, you must subscribe.*

www.whitehouse.gov/fsbr/esbr.html
The link to federal economic statistics including GDP, income, wealth, unemployment, prices, and interest rates and a variety of international statistics.

www.louisville.edu/library/ekstrom/govpubs/ federal/agencies/council/council.html
Even the Council of Economic Advisers has its own Web page, with numerous links to economic statistics, budgets of the United States, and other useful information.

www.bog.frb.fed.us/
This is the Web site of the Federal Reserve Bank with links to the regional banks. This site offers a history of the Fed, a description of the work of its constituent parts, testimony and reports to Congress, consumer information, and publications free to the public (including a comic book version of "The Story of Monetary Policy").

www.gpo.gov/usbudget/fy2001/guidetoc.html
At this U.S. Government Printing Office site, you will find A Citizen's Guide to the Federal Budget for fiscal year 2001. Revenue sources and government spending by category are explained with a minimum of jargon. The site also contains a glossary of budget terminology.

www.irs.ustreas.gov/
The Web site of the Internal Revenue Service provides help with personal income taxes; users can download forms and publications and get information on the reform of the IRS passed by Congress in 1998.

InfoTrac College Edition

"American Dream Tax"
"Greenspan Gipper Gates"
"Flat-Tax Prophet"
"Debt We Do Part"

Notes

1. Richard W. Stevenson, "House Approves a Bill to Repeal the Estate Tax," *The New York Times,* June 10, 2000, p. A12.
2. Ibid.
3. Statement by Senator Patty Murray on Marriage Penalty Tax Relief. The text can be found at Murray's Senate Web site (www.senate.gov/-murray/releases/00/07/2000720833.html)
4. Michael Barone, Grant Ujifusa, and Charles E. Cook, Jr., *The Almanac of American Politics 2000* (Washington D.C.: National Journal, 1999).

5. Statement by Senator Patty Murray in Favor of the Estate Tax Elimination Act (S. 1128). The text can be found at www.senate.gov/-murray/releases/00/06/2000620515.html.

6. Mancur Olson, *The Logic of Collective Action* (New York: Schocken, 1971).

7. Adam Smith, *An Inquiry into the Wealth of Nations* (1776; reprinted in several editions, including Indianapolis: Bobbs Merrill, 1961).

8. James Galbraith, *Balancing Acts* (New York: Basic Books, 1988); Robert Heilbroner and Lester Thurow, *Five Economic Challenges* (Englewood Cliffs, N.J.: Prentice Hall, 1981), p. 62.

9. Quoted in *Time,* January 30, 1989, p. 46.

10. John Maynard Keynes, *The General Theory of Employment, Interest and Money* (1936).

11. Ben Wildavsky, "Atlas Schmoozes," *National Journal,* May 17, 1997, pp. 974–977.

12. For a brief review of the Fed's work, see James L. Rowe, Jr., "Holding the Purse Strings," *Washington Post National Weekly Edition,* June 28, 1999, pp. 6–8.

13. William Grieder, *Secrets of the Temple* (New York: Simon & Schuster, 1988), 461. Grieder's analyses of the Reserve Board's anti-inflation policies in the early 1980s are revealing and compelling.

14. Louis Uchitelle, "He Didn't Say It. But He Knew It," *New York Times,* April 30, 2000, sect. 3, p. 1.

15. Douglas Hibbs, "Political Parties and Macroeconomic Policy," *American Political Science Review* 71 (December 1977); Paul Peretz, *The Political Economy of Inflation* (Chicago: University of Chicago, 1983).

16. Henry Chappell and William Keech, "The Economic Conservations of the Reagan Administration," paper presented at the conference on the Resurgence of Conservatism in the Anglo-American Democracies, May 1986; Douglas Hibbs, *The American Political Economy: Macroeconomics and Electoral Politics* (Cambridge, Mass.: Harvard University Press, 1987).

17. Edward Tufte, *Political Control of the Economy* (Princeton, N.J.: Princeton University Press, 1978).

18. William Keech and Kyoungsan Pak, "Electoral Cycles and Budgetary Growth in Veterans Benefit Programs," paper presented at the Midwest Political Science Association Meeting, April 1988; John Hibbing, "The Liberal Hour," *Journal of Politics* 46 (August 1984): 846–865.

19. *National Journal,* November 7, 1992, p. 2544.

20. Steven Greenhouse, "Brady Sought Greenspan Policy Pledge," *International Herald Tribune* (NYT), September 25, 1992, p. 13.

21. There is a huge literature, well summarized in Peretz, *Political Economy of Inflation.* For a sampling, see James Kuklinski and Darrell West, "Economic Expectations and Voting Behavior in U.S. House and Senate Elections," *American Political Science Review* 75 (June 1981): 436–447; John Owens and Edward Olson, "Economic Fluctuations and Congressional Elections," *American Journal of Political Science* 24 (August 1980): 469–493; John Hibbing and John Alford, "The Electoral Impact of Economic Conditions," *American Journal of Political Science* 25 (August 1981): 423–439; Douglas Hibbs, "The Dynamics of Political Support for American Presidents among Occupational and Partisan Groups," *American Journal of Political Science* 26 (May 1982): 312–332; Robert Erikson, "Economic Conditions and the Presidential Vote," *American Political Science Review* 83 (June 1989): 567–573.

22. "Poll: Citizens OK About Money, Glum on Future," *Champaign-Urbana News-Gazette,* April 12, 1995, p. B8.

23. Paul Krugman, "Dynamo and Microchip," *New York Times,* February 20, 2000, sect. 4, p. 13.

24. Glenn Kessler, "The Lightened Federal Tax Load," *Washington Post National Weekly Edition,* April 3, 2000, p. 18.

25. Robert J. Samuelson, "The True Tax Burden," *Newsweek,* April 21, 1986, p. 68. To get a good idea of just how complex our tax system is, go to the IRS Web site (http://www.irs.ustreas.gov/); click on forms and publications and scroll through the vast array of forms that must be filed when claiming deductions.

26. "Don't Feel Alone if Tax Confusing: 50 Experts Differ over Family Return," *Lincoln Star* (AP Report), February 18, 1989, p. 2.

27. Donald L. Barlett and James B. Steele, *America: What Went Wrong?* Kansas City, Mo.: Andrews & McMeel, 1992, p. 41; Robert D. Hershey Jr., "A Hard Look at Corporate 'Welfare,' " *New York Times,* March 7, 1995, pp. C1–C2.

28. Michael Wines, "Using Taxation in a Good Cause Often Backfires," *New York Times,* June 6, 1993, p. E3.

29. Lori Nitschke, "Has the Tax Cut Crusade Lost Its Appeal?" *Congressional Quarterly Weekly Report,* April 10, 1999, p. 82.

30. David Cay Johnston, "The Tax Maze Begins Here. No Here. No . . . ," *New York Times,* February 27, 2000, sect. 3, p. 1.

31. David Cay Johnston, "I.R.S. Is Bolstering Efforts to Make Cheaters Pay Up," *New York Times,* February 13, 2000, p. 28.

32. David Cay Johnston, "I.R.S. More Likely to Audit the Poor and Not the Rich," *New York Times,* April 16, 2000, p. 28.

33. David Stockman, *Triumph of Politics* (New York: Harper & Row, 1986).

34. Thomas K. McCraw, "Deficit Lessons: Hamilton the Hero," *New York Times,* February 21, 1995, p. C1.

35. See John Schwartz, *America's Hidden Success,* rev. ed. (New York: Norton, 1988), and Bennett Harrison and Barry Bluestone, *The Great U-Turn* (New York: Basic Books, 1988), for analyses of the economy in the 1970s.

36. Paul Peretz and Raymond Ring, "Variability of Inflation and Income across Income Classes," *Social Science Quarterly* 66 (March 1985): 203–209.

37. *New York Times,* April 18, 1991, p. C18.

38. George Will, "Good Roads, Robust Economy Linked," *Lincoln Star,* March 12, 1990.

39. Paul Krugman, *Age of Diminished Expectations: U.S. Economic Policy in the 1990s* (Cambridge, Mass.: MIT Press, 1992), x.

40. John Berry, "The Legacy of Reaganomics," *Washington Post National Weekly Edition,* December 19–25, 1988; Spencer Rich, "Are You Really Better Off Than You Were Thirteen Years Ago?" *Washington Post National Weekly,* September 8, 1986, p. 20; Levy, "We're Running Out of Gimmicks to Sustain Our Prosperity," *Washington Post National Weekly Edition,* December 29, 1986, pp. 18–19.

41. "Two Trillion Dollars Is Missing," *New York Times,* January 8, 1989, p. E28.

42. Barbara Vobejda, "Class, Color, and College," *Washington Post National Weekly Edition,* May 15–21, 1989, p. 6.

43. Lester C. Thurow, "Companies Merge; Families Break Up," *New York Times,* September 3, 1995, p. E11.

44. Louis Uchitelle, "For Employee Benefits, It Pays to Wear Union Label," *New York Times,* July 16, 1995, p. 10.

45. Louis Uchitelle, "Fewer Jobs Filled as Factories Rely on Overtime Pay," *New York Times,* May 16, 1993, p. 15.

46. "Money on the Mind" issue of *New York Times Magazine,* June, 7, 1998, p. 75.

47. In 1982, 49 percent of low-wage employees had health insurance, but only 26 percent did in 1996. Peter Passell, "Benefits Dwindle along with Wages for the Unskilled," *New York Times,* June 14, 1998, p. 23.

48. "Study Finds Uninsured Poor Parents on Rise," *Champaign-Urbana News Gazette,* April 25, 2000, p. 1.

49. "Report: U.S. Kids Faring Well; Still Too Much Drinking," *Champaign-Urbana News Gazette,* July 13, 2000, p. A8.

50. Clyde Prestowitz, Jr., "The 'New Economy' Has Not Abolished the Business Cycle," *Champaign-Urbana News Gazette,* February 2, 2000, p. B5.

51. Ben Wildavsky, "Looming Liabilities," *National Journal,* January 17, 1998, pp. 102–105.

52. "American Income Gap Widens with Booming Stock Market," *Champaign-Urbana News Gazette,* January 18, 2000, p. A8; Richard W. Stevenson, "In a Time of Plenty, the Poor Are Still Poor," *New York Times,* January 23, 2000, sect. 4, p. 3; Louis Uchitelle, "How Slow Can Your Paycheck Grow?" *New York Times,* February 20, 2000, sect. 3, p. 2.

53. David Leonhardt, "Executive Pay Drops Off the Political Radar," *New York Times,* April 6, 2000, sect. 4, p. 5. For a survey of executive salaries, see "Will Today's Huge Rewards Devour Tomorrow's Earnings?" April 2, 2000, sect. 3, pp. 1, 14–17.

54. Michael Lind, *The Next American Nation: The New Nationalism and the Fourth American Revolution* (New York: The Free Press, 1995), pp. 139–216.

55. Keith Bradsher, "Gap in Wealth in U.S. Called Widest in West," *New York Times,* April 17, 1995, p. C4.

56. "College Grants Found Increasingly Going to Wealthier," *Champaign-Urbana News Gazette,* February 18, 2000, p. A3.

57. See, for example, Charles F. Cnudde and Deane E. Neubauer, eds. *Empirical Democratic Theory* (Chicago: Markham, 1969).

58. David E. Sanger, "Look Who's Carping about Capitalism," *New York Times,* April 6, 1997, p. E5. This estimate has been accepted by the former chair of the Council of Economic Advisers, Laura D. Tyson.

59. One proponent of this view is former Labor Secretary Robert Reich. See his *Work of Nations: Preparing Ourselves for the Twenty-first Century* (New York: Vintage, 1992).

60. Molly Peterson, "Net Dreams," *National Journal,* March 11, 2000, p. 767.

61. Katie Hafner, "A Credibility Gap in the Digital Divide," *New York Times,* March 5, 2000, sect. 4, p. 4.

62. "A National Call to Action to Close the Digital Divide," White House press release, April 4, 2000 (www.whitehouse.gov/WH/New/html/20000404.htm).

63. Peterson, "Net Dreams," p. 767.

64. "House Approves a Bill to Repeal the Estate Tax," p. A12.

65. Murray statement in favor of the Estate Tax Elimination Act.

Social Welfare and Health Policy

YOU ARE THERE

Can This Bill Be Saved?

You are President Bill Clinton. It is January 1994, and you are drafting your State of the Union speech. You are trying to decide what to say about the pending legislation to reform American health care. Making sure that no American is without adequate health care was one of your campaign themes. One of the first actions you took after being elected was to appoint Hillary Rodham Clinton, your wife, to head a large task force to study and recommend changes in the nation's health care system. Their report recommended far-reaching and complex changes in the way Americans pay for health insurance, changes that are being fought by those who benefit from the current system, especially insurance and drug companies. Congress is deeply split over the issue, and even many Democrats do not support your proposals. You are now faced with the decision of whether to stick with your original plan or to offer compromises to those who do not want as far-reaching reform as you do.

Everyone agrees that the problems facing America's health care system are daunting. Most people think the health care system is in a crisis, perhaps even in its death throes. Most agree that the crisis is produced by two factors: rocketing costs and diminishing access to quality health care. But opinions differ wildly as to the right prescription for the problem.

Health care costs have increased an average of 10 percent per year for three decades, far outpacing inflation. We spend more on health care, whether measured per person or as a proportion of our national income, than any other country in the world. Over 14 percent of our entire economy goes toward health care, twice the rate in most nations. The soaring costs are a major drain on the economy. Half of the projected increase in budget deficits in the next few years reflect the growth of health care costs. You have stated, "If we don't do something on health care, it's going to bankrupt the country."[1] Another observer commented, "We are offering the health industry each year an unlimited budget and they are exceeding it."[2]

The spiraling costs of health care are dragging down businesses, too. In one recent year, General Motors paid more for health care benefits than for the steel to make its products.[3] During the Bush presidency, 1.2 million new jobs were created in the American economy, but *all* of that growth was accounted for by the health care system. In the rest of the

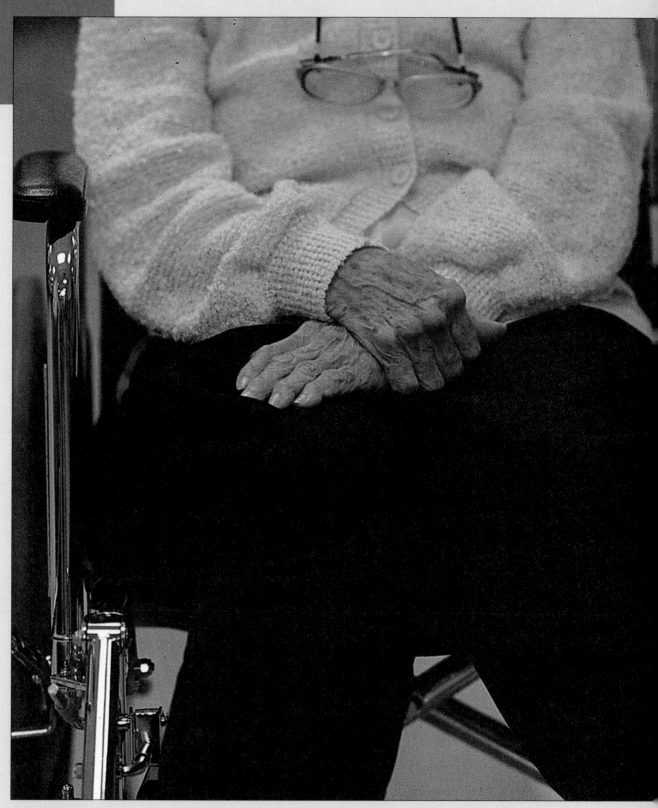

Bill Luster/Matrix International

economy, new jobs were canceled out by jobs lost. Businesses pay increasing amounts for health care packages for their workers and retirees. Keeping up with ever higher medical insurance costs leaves little for wage increases for workers. If businesses drop these benefits, as many have, their workers are left without insurance coverage. Many major corporations, including many with relatively generous health care benefits, have been cutting jobs to reduce their costs. During the first three months of 1994, the U.S. economy lost more than three thousand jobs daily on average. Many of the newly unemployed workers then found themselves without health care coverage.[4]

While government and business are suffering from escalating health care costs, individuals suffer the most. About twenty million people covered by private insurance lack sufficient coverage and should be considered "underinsured." Between forty-eight and fifty-eight million Americans can no longer afford health insurance and thus can no longer afford most health care.[5] Most of the uninsured in the United States have full-time jobs.[6] The medically uninsured include farmers and others who are self-employed, employees of small businesses offering no fringe benefits, those whose insurance companies no longer will insure them because they are too sick, the unemployed, and, of course, the children of all these adults. Even the employees in one-third of doctors' offices lack health insurance.[7] Eight million of the uninsured are middle class. The rest are working class or poor.

As a result, nearly 20 percent of Americans with diseases such as diabetes or high blood pressure do not get treatment because they cannot afford it. Fifty percent of the children in the inner city are not immunized against common diseases. Even those who are insured fear catastrophic illnesses that require expensive, prolonged treatment. Such illness puts them at risk of losing their insurance and draining their family's savings.

Increasing costs, then, lead to decreasing access to good health care or, indeed, any health care. A paradox is that, despite the huge amounts we spend on health care, we are the only industrial democracy in the world that does not provide health insurance coverage or state-supported medical care for all citizens.

Hillary Clinton's task force has recommended, and you have backed, a bill supporting **managed competition**, a new concept that, as one observer joked, "no real *person* has ever heard of."[8] Managed competition would join employers and individuals into large groups or cooperatives to purchase health insurance. Each large group could, in theory, bargain with health providers and insurers for the best rates and the highest quality. To make sure everyone is covered by the plan, each employer would be mandated to provide insurance benefits. Those not employed or self-employed would be covered either through taxes or by other means and would become part of one of the cooperatives, all of which would have to offer a minimum package of benefits. In other words, all Americans would be covered.

Though many people whose employers have sought alternative bids from health care providers are already part of managed competition plans, such a plan mandated throughout the economy has never been tried. Moreover, you have promised that except for taxes on cigarettes and liquor, taxes would not increase.

This plan has been attacked by conservatives, who believe it goes too far, and by liberals, who do not believe it goes far enough. Conservatives do not like forcing employers to provide health insurance coverage and creating mechanisms so that everyone has insurance. Though most liberal Democrats are supporting your plan, many of them believe that you should have recommended a more thorough single-payer plan, where the government collects a tax and provides health insurance to everyone (Canada has such a system). Insurance companies are adamantly opposed to your plan because they believe it would limit their freedom and their profits. They attack the plan with a clever set of television advertisements featuring the fictional "Harry" and "Louise" who raise questions about what the reform would mean to them and other Americans. The American Medical Association, the nation's largest group of doctors, first supported the idea of universal health insurance but has backed away from supporting your plan because doctors believe it will increase red tape, paperwork, and other administrative burdens on doctors and hospitals.[9] Most Republicans have attacked the plan, and you will not be able to count on much support from them.

Last year over 80 percent of the public agreed that health care in America was in a crisis state, but now fewer appear to be supportive of reform. Many interest groups have bought television ads to raise questions about the plan. And doctors' and hospital groups are even leaving literature in doctors' offices to scare patients about the proposed changes. In fact, interest groups have spent $46 million in ads and contributions to fight the plan.[10] You find it hard to allay the public's fears; your plan is complicated (the proposed legislation is 1,300 pages long) and deals with abstract provisions, rules, and concepts, such as "managed competition," that few people understand. It is not easy to explain or sell in a few simple sound bites.

What do you do? You are deeply committed to making sure that everyone, rich or poor, has access to quality health care. You have made health care a top priority on your presidential agenda. Therefore, you know you will need to compromise to get some health bill. Being inflexible in the face of this opposition might mean losing any chance of health care reform this year or in the immediate future. On the other hand, to propose a compromise now might be taken as a sign of weakness, and you might get nothing. Besides, you feel strongly that you should not compromise on key aspects of the plan such as making sure it covers everyone. You do not want to disappoint those millions of Americans who currently have no health care because they cannot afford health insurance or payments for health services. So what do you do?

The term *social welfare policies* generally brings to mind programs for the poor: welfare mothers, indigents receiving free cheese from government surplus, or people living in public housing. Yet government social welfare programs aid almost all groups—the rich as well as the poor and many in between. Indeed, most social welfare spending in the United States is not for the poor but for those of middle and upper income. Government aid provides $10 of every $100 in income Americans receive. Only $0.90 of that is welfare for the poor; most of the rest is Social Security and pensions for government employees.

You are undoubtedly a beneficiary of federal social welfare programs yourself—programs that support students, aid farmers, help pay mortgages on homes, aid veterans, provide funds for the unemployed and elderly, or supply school lunches (Figure 1). Most of these go to middle- or lower-middle-income people since poor people generally cannot buy homes, go to college, or get federal farm sup-

port, and they are less likely to have jobs entitling them to Social Security and unemployment compensation.

In the United States, we do not have what is sometimes termed "a welfare state," where a coordinated set of income support programs provides help in a uniform way for those who need it. Instead, our social welfare programs are largely uncoordinated efforts designed to solve the particular problems of specific groups (e.g., college students, the poor, farmers, the elderly) by means that vary from program to program. The programs often have multiple goals. For example, the government provides cheese and other surplus commodities to the poor partly to ease the problem of food surpluses.

In this chapter, we will describe welfare programs for the rich, poor, and middle class. We will then discuss health policies, a set of programs that consumes a considerable proportion of our national resources.

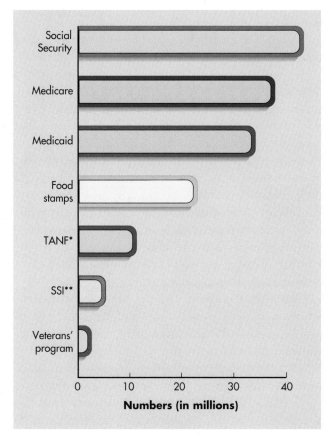

FIGURE 1 ■ *One-Third of All Americans Receive Direct Federal Aid* More than sixty-six million Americans receive direct federal aid. This does not include indirect subsidies or tax subsidies.

*TANF is Temporary Assistance for Needy Families, the replacement for the old AFDC "welfare" program.
**SSI is Supplemental Security Income, the aid program for the needy elderly and disabled.
SOURCE: *Statistical Abstract of the United States, 1999,* Tables 173, 179, 604, 617, 631, 633, and 636.

What Are Social Welfare Policies?

We use the term *social welfare policy* to refer broadly to direct or indirect government financial subsidies for individuals. People receive direct subsidies individually from the government by means of a check or other financial benefit. Social Security payments, surplus food, and subsidized student loans are direct subsidies. Indirect subsidies are not paid individually to beneficiaries. Instead, the government provides goods or services that are used collectively—for example, government support for education. Students receive a government service at only a fraction of its true cost because taxpayers in the school district, state, and nation pay the difference.

A third kind of subsidy is one provided through tax benefits. A tax break subsidy permits some people and corporations to pay less in taxes than others of the same income. Most tax subsidies go directly to middle- and upper-income people or indirectly to them through corporate tax breaks. Since shareholders of corporations are usually upper-income people, they benefit the most from these tax subsidies.

Evolution of Social Welfare Policies

At the time the Constitution was written, no level of government was deeply involved in social welfare policies. Colonial local governments were responsible for the poor but gave little aid. Orphaned or destitute children were apprenticed to better-off families, where they worked as servants. Workhouses were established for the able-bodied poor, and some minimal aid was given to the old or sick.[11] Churches and other private charities helped the "deserving" poor and unfortunate. Those thought to be undeserving were treated harshly. These attitudes reflected the belief that individuals were mostly responsible for their own fate. Government had little role in making life better.

As Chapter 6 shows, the political parties provided informal welfare for many immigrants in the late nineteenth and early twentieth centuries. But these efforts occurred mostly in big cities with political machines.

The idea that government should provide extensive common public services such as education, hospitals, and asylums developed in the nineteenth century. The concept of paying individuals benefits is mostly a twentieth-century one. Gradually, the belief grew that government has a responsibility to help at least some of those at the bottom of the ladder. These changed attitudes led to state laws, beginning in 1911, establishing aid programs for poor children and their mothers. Fifteen years later, most of the states had such laws, replacing apprenticeships and poorhouses. Most of our major national social welfare programs were first developed in the 1930s as part of the New Deal and have expanded since then. Other major social welfare innovations, such as Medicare, began in the 1960s.

Social Welfare for Everyone

Social Security is a social welfare program for all classes of Americans who have worked or are dependents of workers. Nearly one of every six individuals now receives a Social Security payment, and seven of ten can expect to be covered now or in the future. Social Security payments account for 22 percent of federal spending, and Social Security taxes produce 34 percent of all federal revenues.

How Social Security Works

Social Security is not paid out of general revenues but is financed through a payroll tax on employees and employers paid into a special trust fund. The tax is slightly over 7.7 percent of the first $72,600 of an employee's wages. Although employers contribute to the program, their cost is generally assumed to be passed on to the employee in the form of lower wages.[12]

One of the success stories of American public policy, Social Security gives most elderly the freedom to swim in society's mainstream. However, some changes are needed to maintain its benefits for the next generation.
Mary Ellen Mark

Individuals collect their Social Security benefits upon reaching retirement age. Partial benefits can be collected before age sixty-five, full benefits after (although this minimum age is being raised a month or so each year). Survivors (spouse and dependent children) of contributors to the program can also collect benefits.

Since only those who have paid into the program (and their survivors) can collect benefits, the program is regarded as a social insurance program. Those receiving payments believe they are not receiving "welfare" but only getting back what they paid into the program through payroll deductions. Unlike private insurance programs, however, Social Security pays its recipients far more than they paid it. Social Security recipients receive back their contributions, with interest, in six years, while they typically receive Social Security for fourteen years.[13] The program has stayed afloat because of ever increasing numbers of people paying in at steadily rising rates. Thus, workers today are supporting retirees of yesterday.

President Roosevelt and the other New Dealers who initiated the Social Security program would probably be astounded at its current magnitude. It was originally designed to ensure that the elderly would not live in poverty after retirement. Over the years, the disabled and survivors of those covered by Social Security have become eligible. Health benefits (Medicare) were also added. The program has therefore grown in size from about 220,000 recipients in 1940 to almost forty-four million today. Over one-quarter of all households receive Social Security. The average benefit to a retired worker, a mere $18 per month in 1940, increased to $765 in 1997.[14] Even taking inflation into account, real benefits have tripled.

In 1950, Social Security accounted for only 3 percent of all retirement income. It is now around 40 percent. Without Social Security, almost half of our senior citizens would be poor; with it only about 10 percent are.[15] Social Security payments to surviving dependents also lift nearly one million children out of poverty.

Problems with the Program

Social Security is a great public policy success story. Each year it lifts out of poverty about fifteen million retirees, people with disabilities, and families with dependent children whose working parent has died. It is a major source of retirement income for many millions and a valuable supplement for millions more. Largely because of increased Social Security benefits, the poverty rate among the elderly is less than half what it was in 1965. Still, there are problems with the program.

The first is that Social Security pays benefits to those who do not need them, thus wasting resources. Sixty percent of Social Security payments go to those above the poverty line.[16] This problem is also an asset, however; since people do not have to show a financial need to receive Social Security, millions can accept it without the public stigma of being on welfare. This aspect of the program increases its political popularity. Moreover,

middle- and upper-income beneficiaries now pay taxes on 85 percent of their Social Security income at the same rate at which the rest of their income is taxed.

A second problem is that retirement benefits are inadequate for poorly paid workers. Workers who earned very low wages during their careers—and who probably do not have private pensions—receive low payments. Three-quarters of the elderly earning less than $10,000 a year have no income other than Social Security. Social Security provides over 90 percent of the income for about one-quarter of the elderly.[17]

Some elderly are poor enough to qualify for Supplemental Security Income (SSI), but many poor elderly "fall through the cracks" and are not eligible for these payments *or* for an adequate Social Security income. One survey of workers revealed that 58 percent of those earning under $20,000 and 71 percent of those earning $20,000 to $29,999 worried that they will not be able to afford to retire at a reasonable age.[18]

A third problem is that lower-income workers are hardest hit by Social Security taxes. Workers pay taxes on only the first $72,600 they earn; this means lower- and middle-income earners pay the tax on all they earn, while higher-income workers have income not subject to Social Security taxes. Although low-income workers receive more benefits relative to their earnings than

wealthier ones do, Social Security has been called the poor person's welfare payment to the middle class.

A final problem with Social Security is that the president and Congress are using today's surpluses to offset the nation's budget deficit. In recent years, the Social Security Trust Fund has had huge and growing surpluses. These surpluses are necessary in order to be prepared for the drain on Social Security that will occur in the next twenty or thirty years as the baby boom generation (born in the late 1940s and early 1950s) reaches retirement age. Yet, to make the budget seem more balanced than it really is, policymakers are using trust funds to pay current bills (as many state officials are doing with state pension funds). It is unlikely that Congress and the president would allow the system to go bankrupt. However, our political leaders have not had the courage to confront the Social Security issue squarely. Most young people believe that Social Security will not be there when they retire (more believe in UFOs than believe Social Security will be around).[19]

The idea of "privatizing" Social Security has won some support, and was part of the Republican platform in 2000. The proposal is that individuals could invest some of their Social Security funds in the private market and thus gain a bigger return than they get from the government trust fund. This idea has some plausibility, especially in an era when the stock market appears to be increasing. However, the idea is a risky one. What happens when the market drops? Will government provide an insurance for failed investments? If not, what happens to those people who make imprudent or simply unfortunate investments? It would seem that there would be an inevitable pressure to make losses good, which then undermines the rationale for privatization.

The Future of Social Security

Social Security costs are increasing, largely because our population is getting older. People sixty-five and older were only 13 percent of the population in 1998, but they are projected to be 17 percent in 2020. In the United States, as in most other industrial nations, the entry of women into the workforce, marriage at later ages, and contraception and abortion have lowered the fertility rate to less than the natural population replacement level.[20] Even though immigration is replacing some population, the population is aging and will do so at an even more rapid pace after 2000. By 2030, there may be only slightly over two active workers to support each Social Security retiree, compared to almost four in 1990.[21] This will put more of a strain on the system.

As a welfare program for everyone, Social Security continues to be politically popular among all groups.

When former Speaker of the House Tip O'Neill spoke of the Third Rail of Politics, "Touch it and you die," he was referring to Social Security. Everyone believes he or she will live to old age, and, as Senator Daniel Moynihan (D-N.Y.) has pointed out, "Social Security has removed much of the fear of growing old."[22] Still, the program periodically comes under attack. Its very success at reducing poverty among the elderly prompts some people to question whether we should be devoting so many of our resources to the no-longer-poor elderly and so few to the younger generation. Moreover, its popularity makes it difficult to change. Everyone agrees we need to put the program on a sounder financial basis for the future by raising the retirement age, reducing the automatic cost of living increases that recipients get, taxing more income, or all of these. But politicians shy away from any of these changes because they are afraid of the political clout of the elderly.

The elderly's concerns are hardly irrational. Many of those who criticize Social Security aim not just at improving it but at dramatically changing its nature, from a quasi–social insurance model to a means-tested "welfare" program. Given the political unpopularity of welfare programs, it is no wonder that interest groups representing the elderly oppose that change. Such a program would likely wither from lack of political support, suffer from greatly increased administrative costs (to determine eligibility), and diminish the personal dignity afforded the elderly who must rely on it.

Given the wealth of our society, a reasonable question is whether we can devise a program as successful at raising children out of poverty as Social Security has been for the elderly. (See Figure 2 for the relative poverty rates of the elderly and children.) As one mem-

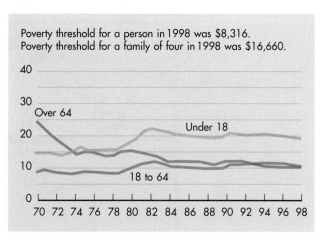

Poverty threshold for a person in 1998 was $8,316.
Poverty threshold for a family of four in 1998 was $16,660.

FIGURE 2 ■ *Children Are Most Likely to Be Poor* While *poverty rates for the elderly have declined in the last three decades, poverty rates of children have increased markedly.*

SOURCES: U.S. Bureau of the Census, from www.census.gov/hhes/poverty/histpov/hstpov3.html and www.census.gov/hhes/poverty/histpov/hstpov1.html.

ber of Congress commented, "We should be proud of what we have done for the elderly and horrified at what we're doing to our children."[23] But we should not blame the elderly for the plight of our children; we should blame our own reluctance to support meaningful programs to lift children out of poverty while providing their parents with opportunities to work.

Social Welfare for the Poor

How Many Are Poor?

We think of the United States as a rather egalitarian society, but in fact income is more unevenly distributed between the rich and the poor here than in any other industrialized country in the world. In countries such as Germany, Belgium, Portugal, Austria, and Japan, income inequality is half or less that in the United States. In addition, in the United States income inequality is growing and the gap between rich and poor increasing (Table 1). The poorest 20 percent of families earn less than 4 percent of all income, and the richest 20 percent earn almost half of the income.

Distribution of wealth, which includes homes, land, savings, and stocks and bonds, as well as cash, is even more skewed. One percent of Americans own 40 percent of all wealth and over half of all income-producing wealth, such as business investments, farms, and so forth. The bottom half of Americans own only 4 percent of the nation's wealth.[24]

The Census Bureau defines as poor anyone beneath a certain income. In 1998, the poor included those with an income below $16,660 for a family of four. Due to the booming economy and the Great Society programs of the 1960s, the proportion of families in poverty dropped from 21 percent in 1959 to 10 percent in 1973, the lowest point ever achieved in the United States. It then increased rather steadily, reaching a high of 14 percent in 1993. In 1998, 11 percent of families remained below the poverty level.[25]

Not everyone agrees with the Census Bureau's estimates. Some conservatives argue that the estimates overstate the number of poor because they do not take into account many "in-kind" benefits poor people receive, such as food stamps, housing, and medical care. If we considered this income, about 4 percent fewer would be considered poor. Others argue that the Census Bureau understates the amount of poverty by using estimated costs for food, housing, and fuel that are too low.[26]

Not surprisingly, those who believe government should do relatively little to increase income equality tend to minimize the extent of the poverty problem; those who favor a more activist government usually have a higher estimate. What is beyond dispute, however, is that a sizable minority of the American population—anywhere from 10 to 25 percent—does not have enough money to live at a decent standard. By all measures, the number living in poverty increased in the 1980s.

Many observers are quite concerned about the growing gap between rich and poor in America. Until 1979, that gap had stayed fairly steady since World War II. Between the war and the late 1970s, the rich grew richer, but so did the middle class. The numbers living in poverty shrank. But during the 1980s, the gap widened. Table 1 demonstrates this trend of increasing income inequality. Imagine that all households in the United States are lined up in a row, with the household with the lowest income at one end and the household with the highest income at the other. Then examine the share of total income received by each fifth (20 percent) of the households in this lineup. In 1980, the lowest fifth received 4.3 percent of the total income, and the highest fifth received 43.7 percent. During the 1980s and 1990s, the share of the richest fifth increased markedly, and the share of total income received by the highest 5 percent increased even more markedly. Put another way, in 1999, the 2.7 million Americans with the largest incomes received as much after-tax income as the 100 million Americans with the lowest incomes.[27] Reasons for the widening gap include the loss of manufacturing jobs, unemployment, and declining real wages for workers; the lack of child support paid by fathers to divorced and unwed mothers; and the Reagan tax and spending policies, which redistributed the wealth upward by reducing taxes for the better-off and reducing spending for the poor.

Table 1	Income Distribution Is Becoming More Lopsided		
Percentage of Households	Percentage of Income Earned		
	1980	1990	1998
Lowest fifth*	4.3	3.9	3.6
Next lowest	10.3	9.6	9.0
Middle fifth	16.9	15.9	15.0
Next highest	24.9	24.0	23.2
Highest fifth	43.7	46.6	49.2
Top 5%	15.8	18.6	21.4

*The fifth of households receiving the least income per household.
SOURCE: U.S. Bureau of the Census at www.census.gov/hhes/income/histinc/h02.html.

Who Is Poor?

The *Wall Street Journal* commented on the growing gulf between rich and poor: "At the top is a growing over-class of well-educated two-income families. At the bottom is a growing underclass of single mothers, Baby Boomers stuck in low paying jobs, and children who inherited poverty from their parents."[28] With the important omission of race, the *Journal* description accurately depicts those most vulnerable to poverty.

Race, Education, Family Status, and Sex

Race, education, family status, and sex are important predictors of poverty. Whites are less likely to be poor than blacks and Hispanics. In 1997, about 24 percent of all blacks and 25 percent of Hispanics, but only 8 percent of all whites were poor.[29]

Years of education have a powerful impact on poverty levels for all races. As Figure 3 shows, both education and race strongly influence the likelihood of a family living in poverty. Whites who have not completed their high school education are two and a half times more likely to be poor than whites who have a high school diploma and ten times more likely to be poor than those with a college degree. Blacks with little advanced education are almost eight times as likely to be poor as black college graduates. Among those

with little education, blacks and Latinos are far more likely to live in poverty than whites; the gap narrows but is still discernible among the best educated. Education, then, is important in explaining differences in poverty level among races, but even when education is taken into account, African Americans and Latinos are more likely to be poor, especially if they are not college graduates.

Families headed by a married couple are much less likely to be poor than are single-parent families, especially those headed by a woman (see Table 2). Individuals living alone or with other nonfamily members are also more likely to be poor.

Single women and their dependent children are the largest group of poor people in the United States. Female-headed families make up 22 percent of families with children. Yet they comprise 61 percent of these families that are in poverty. This has been called the **feminization of poverty.**

The number of poor, female-headed families with children grew in the 1970s, 1980s, and early 1990s, but tumbled in the last half of the decade. Compared with 1960, before the Great Society programs, the *rate* of poverty in female-headed families has decreased from 56 to 30 percent. But the *number* of female-headed families with children has more than doubled since 1960, increasing from 10 to 24 percent.

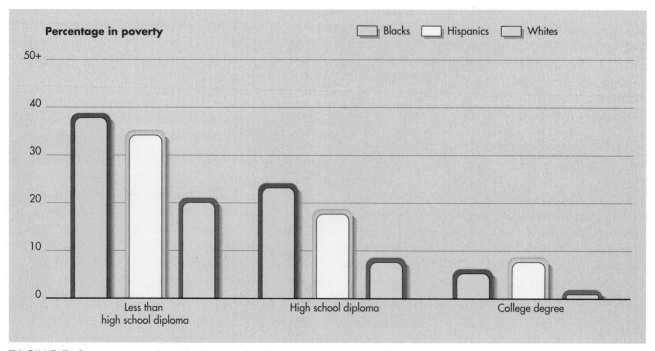

F I G U R E   3 ■ *Percentage of Families in Poverty by Education Level of Householder*

SOURCE: *Statistical Abstract of the United States, 1999*, Table 769.

Table 2	Poverty Is Much More Common in Female-Headed and Minority Families	
		Percentage in Poverty
All families		10
White		6
Black		23
Hispanic		23
Married-couple families		5
White		4
Black		7
Hispanic		16
Female-headed families, no husband present		30
White		21
Black		41
Hispanic		44

SOURCE: U.S. Census Bureau at www. census.gov/hhes/poverty/poverty98/pv98est1.html.

Over 40 percent of black and Hispanic female-headed families fall beneath the poverty line, and 21 percent of white female-headed families do so. For whites, the primary reason for poor female-headed families is divorce. When divorce occurs, even between a middle-class couple, often the women and children fall into poverty. The woman cannot earn enough to support a family, and child support from the man is typically erratic and inadequate. Less than half the children of divorced white women receive support payments. Children of black women who are divorced are even less likely than white women to receive support.[30]

However, among blacks the chief reason for poor, female-headed families is not divorce but the number of mothers who have never been married. Unwed teenage mothers are likely to stay in poverty the rest of their lives; the younger a woman is when a child is born, the more children she is likely to have and the less likely she is to complete her education and thus be able to command a decent wage. Only a tiny proportion of children of unwed mothers receive support from the fathers.

Among blacks the feminization of poverty is especially acute. On average, black two-parent families have middle-class incomes; only 9 percent are poor. Two-parent black families are much less likely to be in poverty than one-parent white families. But since large proportions of black families are headed by women (47 percent in 1998), large proportions of black children are born in poverty—today, nearly half of all black children are born into poverty.

Age

Due to Social Security, poverty among the aged has dramatically decreased, and only the very elderly (over age eighty-five) who live alone have exceptionally high poverty rates compared to other groups.[31] On the other hand, 20 percent of all children live in poverty, the highest rate of any age group.

Geography

Despite the economic boom in the South in recent years, it has proportionally more poor than the North. And, of course, inner city poverty rates are much higher than those in the suburbs. Rural poverty is also serious, but 70 percent of all poor people live in cities.

The Causes of Poverty

Finding remedies for poverty depends primarily on diagnoses of what causes it. But individuals of different political ideologies disagree vehemently on the causes of poverty. In the following discussion we use the terms "conservative explanations" and "liberal explanations" broadly; not all conservatives agree with each other, nor do all liberals have the same views.

Conservative Explanations

Conservatives emphasize that people are poor because of their own failures. As one conservative argued, "The only dependable route from poverty is always work, family and faith."[32] He believes the poor are poor because they do not work as hard as others, they are more likely to live in broken homes, and they lack faith in God, capitalism, and the future. Other conservatives argue that the poor do not rise out of poverty because they are too oriented to the present, rather than saving and working toward the future.[33] Having children before a couple is prepared to support them is an example of a present orientation.

Most conservatives are, of course, willing to admit that some people are poor through no fault of their own—the ill, the aged, children, and the handicapped—but their discussions of how to reduce poverty do not focus on these groups. In general, conservatives believe the free market economy can provide jobs and adequate incomes for all who want them.

As a consequence, conservatives tend to oppose government programs for the able-bodied poor because they believe such programs weaken individuals' incentives to work. Conservatives also believe government intervention into the economy—through minimum wages and mandatory social insurance programs like Social Security, for example—aggravates poverty by interfering with the natural workings of the market system.

Liberal Explanations

Liberals place less of the blame on the poor for their problems. As Michael Harrington notes:

> The real explanation of why the poor are where they are is that they made the mistake of being born to the wrong parents, in the wrong section of the country, in the wrong industry, or in the wrong racial or ethnic group. Once that mistake has been made, they could have been paragons of will and morality, but most of them would never have had a chance to get out of poverty.[34]

Liberals are more likely than conservatives to believe that at the heart of many poor people's problems is the lack of jobs paying wages adequate to support a family. Although millions of Americans have relatively secure and high-paying jobs in management, professional occupations, and unionized blue-collar jobs, other Americans do not. They have little job security, few hopes of advancement, and low-paying jobs like car washing, farm labor, private household work, unskilled hospital work, many clerical jobs, retail store sales, and nonunionized labor in rural and southern areas. Even with steady work, employees in these and similar occupations can hardly earn enough to keep a family above the poverty line. Indeed, about half of family heads of poor families work, but even working full-time at a minimum wage job yields an income little more than $10,000, far below the poverty line for a family (Figure 4).[35] Employment is, unfortunately, not a cure-all for poverty.

Liberals believe government should ensure those who have menial jobs a decent standard of living. Thus, they favor minimum wage laws and mandatory fringe benefit programs such as health insurance. They also believe government should help people obtain the education and training necessary to advance beyond these menial jobs, so they favor education and job-training programs. Liberals also usually believe that racial and

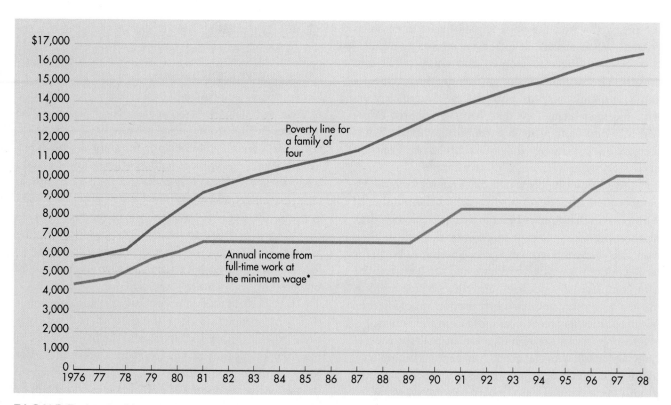

FIGURE 4 ■ *Working at a Minimum Wage Job No Longer Is Enough to Support a Family*
Although the minimum wage was increased in 1996, even working full-time at minimum wage provides for less than a minimum standard of living.

*Assumes minimum wage for 40 hours per week, 50 weeks per year.
SOURCES: U.S. Census Bureau at www.census.gov/hhes/poverty/histpov/ hstpov1.html and *Statistical Abstract of the United States, 1999*, Table 705, footnote 1, plus calculations from this data.

sexual discrimination are partially responsible for the fact that women and minority males are the ones most frequently mired in poverty. ⌐

Public opinion on the causes of poverty reflects these basic divisions. About one-third adopt the more conservative view and believe people are poor primarily due to lack of effort. Another third have a stance more common among liberals and believe people are poor largely because of conditions beyond their control. The other one-third of the public believes both are reasons for poverty.[36]

Basic Programs for the Poor

We have government programs to help the poor, just as we do to help the middle class and rich. But programs for the poor seem to be the target of substantially more criticism than programs for others. Liberals, for example, believe the programs provide inadequate support and are ineffective in moving people into the mainstream economy. Conservatives criticize the programs as an actual roadblock to self-sufficiency.

We have seen no scientific study of this attitude, but the average citizen appears to think that programs for the poor are huge parts of the federal budget. In fact, while programs for the poor are not small change, they pale in comparison to spending on the middle class through Social Security and Medicare.

We will now examine four traditional programs for the poor: Earned income tax credit; aid for families, formerly **Aid to Families with Dependent Children (AFDC)** and now **Temporary Aid to Needy Families (TANF); Supplemental Security Income (SSI);** and food stamps. We will describe Medicaid in our later discussion of health policy.

A nearly invisible program for the poor is the **earned income tax credit (EITC),** which has been in place since 1975. This is a negative income tax, giving eighteen million working poor families an income tax break. Families whose income is extremely low receive a check from the government rather than paying taxes, while other workers with families receive a credit but still pay taxes. This approach to poverty avoids a bureaucracy (it is all done through income tax filing) and rewards work. Though the EITC has had bipartisan support (President Reagan noted it was the "best anti-poverty, best pro-family, best job-creation measure to come out of Congress"), the program continues to be attacked by conservative budget cutters.

AFDC originated in New Deal Social Security legislation providing income support for dependent children. Coverage was later added for mothers with de-

Wasserman © 2000, *Los Angeles Times.* Reprinted by permission.

pendent children and still later for both fathers and mothers with dependent children. Programs for the blind, elderly, and disabled, called SSI, also originated in the New Deal.

AFDC and SSI have been **means test** programs; participants must periodically demonstrate eligibility by showing they are poor—they must have both limited income and few assets. For SSI, a program for the elderly and disabled only, a couple may have up to $2,250 in liquid assets of cash or stocks—in other words, scarcely enough for a decent funeral. SSI recipients are automatically eligible for food stamps and Medicaid. But most SSI recipients still remain in poverty in almost all states.

The SSI program is relatively uncontroversial because few people believe that the elderly, blind, or disabled should be forced to work to earn their government subsidy. However, though SSI costs about the same as AFDC, the latter program has been much more a focus of criticism because it assisted able-bodied women and their children. But after decades of criticisms of AFDC, the structure of welfare was fundamentally changed when TANF was adopted.

Reforming Welfare for the Poor

Assessments of Welfare Programs Prior to 1996

Scholars and politicians have waged a spirited debate over how successful our welfare programs have been. Supporters assert that several programs have been successful. The program for health care for low-income pregnant women, for example, reduced infant mortality by twenty thousand to thirty-five thousand deaths per year.[37] Medicare and Medicaid have improved health care for the poor and elderly.[38]

Those who argue that programs for the poor work point out that hardly any program for the poor actually has enough funds to allow all the poor to participate. For example, only about 20 percent of children eligible for Head Start can be accommodated in the program, even though study after study shows that preschoolers with Head Start experience do much better in school than other poor children. Similarly, less than 60 percent of poor pregnant women can receive food supplements and pre-natal care, even though it is clear that the relatively cheap food supplements and prenatal care would save thousands of dollars in treatment for each child born with problems because of the mother's poor health and nutrition.

Despite these successes, critics argue that these pro-grams, particularly AFDC, have fostered dependency rather than encouraging independence and hard work. For example, though the number of AFDC recipients was fairly stable from the mid-1970s to the late 1980s, it zoomed up in the recession of the late 1980s and early 1990s. In contrast to the common stereotype, however, the increase in welfare recipients is not tied to the growth in welfare benefits, which have dropped steadily since the 1970s in real terms (taking inflation into account).

The number of recipients increases fastest when eco-nomic times are hard; but when the economy is good,

the rolls have not always fallen back to their previous level. Part of the reason is that, even in years when the economy was growing, job growth has not been in high-paying blue-collar jobs. Job prospects for people without college degrees have deteriorated during the late 1970s and 1980s.

Another reason for the continued growth in welfare rolls has been that the proportion of births to unmarried women has continued to be high, nearly 70 percent of births in the black community, and has risen to over 25 percent among whites (Figure 5). Nearly one-third of all births are to women without husbands, many of them teenagers. Over 80 percent of unwed mothers go on the welfare rolls for at least some time.

Most of the recipients of AFDC were recipients for a relatively short time.[39] They found a job, married some-one who earned more than a poverty income, or both. However, nearly one-quarter of women going on AFDC stayed for ten years or more, and another 20 percent stayed for six to nine years. Those who stayed on welfare have been more likely to be teenage mothers with no high school diploma, have no husband, and to be black or His-panic. As one commentator remarked, "An eighteen-year-old girl from a broken family with two babies, no high school degree, no work experience, and no husband is going to have serious trouble supporting herself."[40]

There is no evidence that welfare causes fathers to leave their homes or unwed mothers to have babies; nei-

In the 1930s, homelessness was largely caused by the Great Depression. Here is photographer Dorothea Lange's historic photo of a homeless Oklahoma family during that era. Today the homeless population is increasing despite overall economic prosperity. Some live on the streets, and other live in cars or shelters.
Left: Library of Congress. Right: Rober Ferrone.

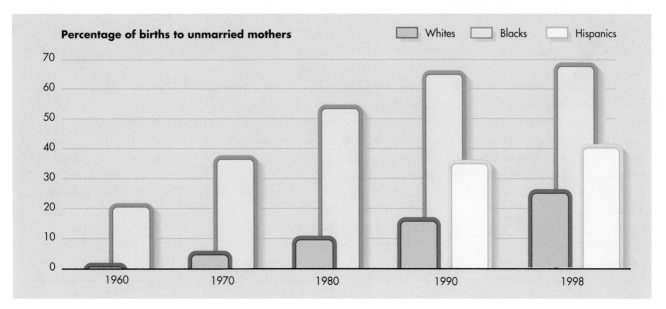

FIGURE 5 ■ *Births to Unmarried Mothers Are Increasing*

SOURCES: National Center for Health Statistics, reported in the *New York Times,* July 26, 1992, p. 12; *Statistical Abstract of the United States, 1999,* Table 92; and "Births: Final Data for 1998," *National Vital Statistics Reports,* Centers for Disease Control and Prevention, March 28, 2000.

ther did AFDC provide any incentive to do otherwise.[41] Moreover, the system has discouraged work. Women who chose low-paid work over welfare have been economically worse off because they needed to pay for child care and they usually lost their medical benefits. Thus, for the last twenty-five years, almost everyone agreed that the welfare system needed to be reformed. But, serious reform attempts bogged down in debates over what causes poverty and whether the system should maximize the carrot or the stick in getting people off welfare.

There is no simple answer for explaining patterns of welfare dependence. Clearly, racism is an important contributor. Racism perpetuates housing segregation patterns that make it very difficult for blacks with working-class incomes to escape neighborhoods with high levels of crime and poor school systems. Racism also limits the ability of working-class blacks to get decent jobs. But other factors are also at work: the changing economy resulting in the loss of tens of thousands of factory jobs held by unskilled and semiskilled workers, the altered societal norms of sexual behavior that have led to acceptance of unwed motherhood (and fatherhood), and the decay of the social institutions and norms within lower-class black communities that tied them to the larger society.

A New Welfare Structure

In 1993, President Clinton took office promising to end welfare "as we know it." In the 1994 elections, the Republican "Contract with America" promised even more dramatic reform. After heated debate, in 1996

Congress passed, and the president signed, a welfare reform bill that abolished the previous AFDC system whereby welfare was an entitlement to all those who met federal guidelines. Instead, in the new TANF program, states were mandated to set up their own welfare systems under loose federal guidelines. The federal government now gives block grants to states to run these programs.

TANF is designed to assist needy families to care for children in their own homes. In that sense, it is similar to AFDC. However, unlike AFDC, rhetorically TANF makes keeping two-parent families intact a goal of the program. Also unlike AFDC, federal rules for TANF require recipients to work after two years on assistance. "Work" can include job training, community service, or even education. Working families can receive assistance for a lifetime maximum of five years, though states have discretion to reduce this, and some have.[42]

Initially, those who feared the impact of TANF on children and on people who were unable to find employment severely criticized the program. In response, some modifications were made to allow recipients to receive child care, transportation, and other noncash assistance beyond the two-year cutoff. These modifications were designed to help those who took low-paying jobs and who needed such additional assistance to keep their families intact.[43] However, states have the authority to enact more stringent limits.

Federal regulations set limits, requirements, and penalties but allow states great flexibility in designing

Food Stamps and Hunger in America

In 1991, one out of every eight American children went hungry each day because their families could not afford to buy enough food. An equal number did not get enough to eat some of the time. Such children, not surprisingly, tend to be sick, have trouble learning and paying attention, and miss school often. Poverty takes its toll on America's children. But what can be done about it?

The major federal programs to combat hunger are federally supported, free and reduced-price school lunches for poor children and the **food stamp program.** The food stamp program, for families and individuals, has given poor people coupons redeemable in grocery stores for food. The stamps may be used only to purchase unprepared food and cannot be used for eating out or for bathroom or kitchen items, liquor, or tobacco.

The food stamp program grew from smaller origins, expanding most noticeably in the early 1970s in response to an investigation of hunger in America that found conditions previously thought to occur only in the poorest countries of

Africa, Asia, and Latin America. This study of hunger in the United States revealed that tens of thousands of Americans suffered from malnourishment, resulting in retarded growth, anemia, protein deficiencies, high rates of infant mortality, scurvy and rickets (from insufficient vitamin C, vitamin D, and milk), and an impaired ability to learn.

There is little doubt that food stamps helped raise the level of health and nutrition among the very poor. In the first years of the program, malnutrition among the poor decreased, and they had far fewer diseases caused by poor nutrition. One physician, part of a team returning to poverty-stricken areas where severe cases of malnutrition had been found earlier, reported that "It is not possible any more to find very easily the bloated bellies, the shriveled infants, the gross evidence of vitamin and protein deficiencies that we identified in the late 1960s."

Alleviating hunger through the food stamp program can thus be counted as an example of government doing something right, of government acting effectively to address a serious problem. Unfortunately,

we would have to judge it to be a limited success, largely due to reductions in the program and its funding. After growing in the 1970s, the food stamp program, like the school breakfast and lunch programs, was cut back during the 1980s. In 1996, welfare reform imposed further cuts.

Previously, the only eligibility requirement for food stamps was to be poor. In the years just before 1996, one of every ten Americans received food stamps. With welfare reform, food stamps are no longer available to everyone who is poor. Now able-bodied poor people without dependents must meet work requirements or be limited to receiving food stamps for only three months of each thirty-six-month period. People who would earlier have received food stamps may become ineligible when they are unable to find work. They may have limited education and few job skills and may thus be unemployed for lengthy periods of time even when the economy is strong. Their situation will become even more bleak when the economy weakens.

their own TANF programs. Ideally, in a few years, we can compare the successes and failures of a variety of state approaches. This arrangement may work as an example of the states "as laboratories of democracy," discussed in Chapter 3.

The Effects of Reform

Early evaluations of TANF were mixed.[44] On the positive side, by 1999, almost seven million fewer people received welfare than in 1993, a 50 percent decline. Between 60 and 90 percent of those leaving found jobs. Both parties hailed this as a success of the legislation. Although much of the decline reflected the economic boom of the late 1990s (employers needed workers and often hired relatively low-skilled and inexperienced ones), welfare reform was estimated to account for

one-third of the welfare rolls reduction.[45] Many states became more oriented toward helping clients develop job and life skills rather than focusing on regulating and control.

The negative effects were less obvious but no less real. Some people left the rolls without necessarily finding jobs.[46] Of those who did find jobs, many are low-wage jobs with no benefits. The average hourly wage for former recipients is $6.61. Although some former recipients remain eligible for food stamps, often they do not receive them. Thus, fully one-third of the families leaving welfare report that food is in short supply and that they have trouble paying rent or utility bills.[47]

It is not surprising that the jobs awaiting many former welfare recipients are not always good ones. Many

A jobless breadwinner in Texas.
Dan Ford Connolly/Mercury

aid from local food banks increased by an average of 16 percent in 1997. The same study reported that 19 percent of the people requesting food aid had to be turned away because these private food programs lacked sufficient resources to meet the demand.

Hunger is a problem that government can address with some considerable success. The only problem that appears to stand in the way is our lack of a commitment to do so.

SOURCES: "How Hungry Is America?" *Newsweek,* March 14, 1994, pp. 58–59; "10% Rely on Food Aid," *Lincoln Star,* March 9, 1994, pp. 1, 9; Guy Gugliotta, "Bare Cupboards in the Golden Years," *Washington Post National Weekly Edition,* November 19–December 5, 1993, p. 37; U.S. Bureau of the Census, Current Population Reports, pp. 10–41 (Washington, D.C.: 1995); "Food-Stamp Cuts Mean More in U.S. Going Hungry," *Lincoln Journal-Star,* January 5, 1998, pp. 1A, 5A; David Super, "Overview of the Food Stamp Time Limits for People between Ages 18 and 50," Center on Budget and Policy Priorities, March 24, 1997, from www.cbpp.org/fs1850ov.htm; *The Decline in Food Stamp Participation in the 1990's* (Washington, D.C.: U.S. Department of Agriculture, Economic Research Service, June 2000). Quotation is from the Field Foundation study, reported in Michael B. Katz, *In the Shadow of the Poorhouse* (New York: Basis Books, 1986).

Clearly fewer people participated in the food stamp program from 1994 to 1999. During this period, average monthly participation declined sharply, from 27.5 million people in 1994 to 18.2 million in 1999. A sizeable portion of those who became nonparticipants have incomes below 50 percent of the poverty line. Fully six out of ten of those who would be eligible according to their income receive no food stamps.

Further evidence is accumulating that people are going hungrier than they did when food stamps were available to more people and in larger amounts. One recent study found that requests for emergency

of those on welfare have a skimpy employment history, may not have even a high school diploma, lack job skills, and are single parents. Some of these conditions arise from racial discrimination in housing, education, and other areas; these problems are compounded in our largest cities. Urban counties contain 33 percent of the total population, but by 1999, they had a nearly 60 percent share of the welfare caseload, an increase from slightly less than half before welfare reform.[48]

Moreover, TANF has done little to address the problem of unemployed fathers of children on welfare. Even in 1998, with the growing economy, 17 percent of black men between twenty and twenty-four were unemployed.[49] With these men not considered "marriageable" the problem of out-of-wedlock births continues to increase (Figure 5), adding to the problem of

poverty. A remedy for this problem requires jobs, not only welfare reform.[50]

Other problems add to the job-seeking difficulties of welfare recipients. Sizeable proportions suffer from disabilities, either mental or physical, learning disabilities, and substance abuse problems. Any one of these conditions make finding and keeping a job difficult, and many unemployed have more than one of these problems.[51]

The condition of children in welfare families is a serious concern in evaluating the effect of welfare reform. Because the adults who left or were forced off the rolls were parents, there is evidence that those children who remained poor fell deeper into poverty after the reform.[52] Many of the services that welfare families received that enabled them to provide minimal support for their children—food stamps, Head Start, parenting assistance for families—were either dropped or limited.[53] Some states have also found that TANF is not saving them much, if any, money.

The desire to reduce costs for the federal government was one of the forces driving welfare reform. For example, Wisconsin, one of the first states to push for substantial welfare reform, has found that efforts to create true self-sufficiency for former welfare recipients have *increased* costs, not cut them. Wisconsin's governor Tommy Thompson, a Republican, declared that saving money is a false hope. For example, while cutting the number of welfare recipients by 65 percent over a decade, his state moved from spending $12 million on child care in 1987 to estimated spending of $180 million in 1998.[54] If former welfare recipients must work, someone must care for their children.

By leaving the states great discretion, the federal changes in 1996 and later modifications fail to provide assurance that child care will be affordable, that jobs will be available, that job training will be sufficient, and that wages will be high enough to ensure economic self-sufficiency. These responsibilities are largely entrusted to the states. Critics worry that over time the states will engage in a competition to incur as little cost as possible.

The 1996 welfare legislation reflects conservative thinking that government is helping poor people too much and thus eroding personal responsibility. It also reflects conservative thinking that states should be responsible for social welfare policies. It largely ignores liberal solutions, which are based on the idea that poor people are poor largely through lack of opportunity.

Despite the problems we have enumerated, TANF has worked for many. At least in good economic times, welfare rolls can be reduced and more people employed.

The most compelling reasons for a better welfare system are probably not financial. We need to stop the loss of human potential for the benefit of the poor themselves and for the larger society, which is denied the benefits of their productivity. In America, we like to think everyone can have a chance to achieve to the best of his or her ability, and that parents can have a reasonable hope that their children's lives will be better than their own. Moreover, democracies function better when there are no permanent classes of "haves" and of "have-nots." People who must worry about how to feed and house themselves are not going to be full participants in politics. And having too many such people could undermine the political system itself. Only time will tell whether the welfare reform of 1996 and the subsequent actions by the states have helped our nation resolve these problems.

Social Welfare for the Well-Off

Programs for the poor often produce outrage; even Medicare and Social Security and other largely middle-class programs are often subject to scrutiny. But programs for the well-off are subjected to public debate less frequently, perhaps because benefits for the wealthy are less obvious and more diverse than benefits for the poor. Despite this, the more than $150 billion in subsidies and tax breaks for businesses exceeds spending on the poor.

Tax Breaks

The biggest subsidies for the better-off often appear as tax benefits rather than as payment programs. The tax benefits for people who buy homes cost the U.S. Treasury more than three times as much as TANF payments did.

The tax write-off for business for machinery and building depreciation costs the taxpayer far more than SSI, and tax write-offs for charitable deductions are almost 50 percent higher than the cost of food stamps (see Figure 6). Tax breaks for corporations cost the Treasury billions of dollars more.[55]

Farm Subsidies

Payments to the better-off segment of society are not just through tax breaks.

A comment that "the biggest welfare queens wear overalls and have hairy arms" highlights the role of agriculture subsidies as a form of welfare.[56] Farming is undoubtedly the most heavily subsidized occupation in America. At a cost of nearly $30 billion each year, farm

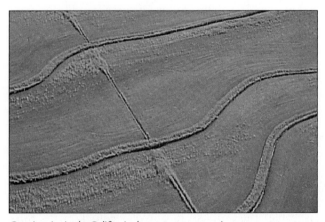

Growing rice in the California desert—at taxpayers' expense.
Richard Ross

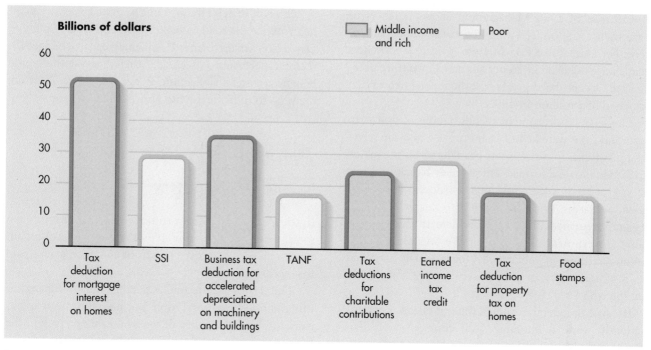

Billions of dollars

Middle income and rich | Poor

Tax deduction for mortgage interest on homes	SSI	Business tax deduction for accelerated depreciation on machinery and buildings	TANF	Tax deductions for charitable contributions	Earned income tax credit	Tax deduction for property tax on homes	Food stamps

F I G U R E   6 ■ *A Comparison of the Cost of Federal Programs for the Poor and Selected Tax Breaks for the Middle-Income and Rich*

SOURCES: *Statistical Abstract of the United States, 1999,* Tables 549, 613, 631, 635; Administration for Children and Families, Department of Health and Human Services, Fact Sheet on TANF, February 17, 2000 at www.acf.dhhs. gov/programs/opa/facts/tanfpr.htm.

subsidies total more than the earned income tax credit, yet there are only about 1 million farmers (who have sales of $10,000 or more).

Farm subsidies occur because government pays producers of a particular commodity (e.g., corn, wheat, or rice) more than the market commands. Since the government pays more than the market price, farmers sell their crops to the government in return for the higher price. Farmers are also paid for not producing. For example, after accumulating thousands of tons of cheese, butter, and dried milk, Congress decided to pay dairy farmers to get out of business and stay out for five years. Thousands accepted at a cost of $1.8 billion to the federal government. We pay cotton farmers nearly $1 billion a year. Indeed, in some years during the 1980s, the federal government was contributing over half of all farmers' income, as high as 70 percent in some farm states. In theory, farm subsidies are not subsidies for the rich. But more subsidies go to wealthy farmers than to small or middle-income farmers. In 1987, farmers with sales over $500,000 averaged more than $60,000 in payments and more than $100,000 in loans from Uncle Sam.[57] Payments over $1,000,000 are not unusual, leading former farm state senator James Exon (D-Neb.) to call this "a major national dis-

grace."[58] In 1996, Congress succeeded in passing a farm bill that phases out many crop supports over a seven-year period. If these reductions escape revision, subsidy payments to farmers will be reduced. Some observers suggest that most farmers will initially receive more dollars under this new legislation than under the former system.[59]

Another type of subsidy to farmers comes in the form of loans from the Farmers Home Administration (FmHA). A former secretary of agriculture noted that some of these loans might more accurately be called grants. One southern California dentist has been in default on his $3.5 million loan for his cattle ranch for thirteen years. Since his account first became delinquent, he has purchased an oceanfront house valued at $817,000 and an office building worth $1.7 million. Between 1988 and 1992, the FmHA wrote off $11.5 billion in bad loans and still carries about $5.2 billion in delinquent loans.[60]

Other Subsidies

Though the people of the western United States like to think of themselves as self-reliant, many occupations are heavily subsidized. Mining and logging companies and ranchers lease federal land at bargain-basement prices.

The Bureau of Land Management allows ranchers to graze their cattle on 270 million acres of public land at a cost per animal of $1.35 in 1996 (private landowners charge an average of $9.26 per animal). Permitting grazing at these subsidized prices cost the federal treasury an estimated $55 million in 1992.[61]

The federal government spends billions of dollars to move and store water. Most water project costs are never repaid. For example, the water brought to California by the $8.8 billion California Central Valley Irrigation Project has created wealth for huge corporate as well as individual farms. But of the $36,000 cost per acre, the irrigators returned only $527 per acre to the government. Government charges mining companies little or nothing to mine on public land. One company extracted $8.75 billion worth of gold in seven years. It now will buy the land for $15,000.[62]

Because of federal subsidies, water is cheap and, consequently, waste is endemic. Golf courses water their greens, suburbanites their lawns, and most important, farmers grow water-intensive crops, sometimes to be bought by the federal government through subsidies. Ironically, the most water used by California farmers is by those growing crops that can be grown more economically elsewhere, such as alfalfa, cotton, pasture for cows and sheep, and rice, which normally is grown only in very wet climates. These crops use far more water than the grapes, nuts, oranges, strawberries, and tomatoes we associate with California farming.[63]

At a cost of $29 billion annually, military pensions cost nearly twice the total federal cost of TANF ($17 billion). David Stockman, former President Reagan's budget director, called them a "scandal," partly because the typical beneficiary starts collecting at age forty-one. Most of them go to individuals with above-average incomes.[64]

Federal Health Care Programs

In the United States, government aid for health care is a social benefit for some people of all income groups, but not for all people. Forty percent of all health care is paid for by the government.

The health care system is paradoxical. Compared to other nations, we spend more but help fewer. Partly because of this, the quality of medical care received in the United States can be the best in the world for those who can pay for it, but overall it lags behind much of the industrial world and some of the less-developed world too. A study done in 2000 showed that the United States spends more per person for health care than any other nation but ranks thirty-seventh in quality of care.[65] Our infant mortality rates are higher than in seventeen other nations, and our life expectancy is lower than Cuba's—and many other nations. On some criteria of health care, black Americans are little better off than people in the

Keeping Kids Healthy

For a two-year-old child, an asthma attack is very serious. But if that child has no health insurance, the situation can indeed be dire. Luckily for Tyler Stovall, his mother had heard a radio commercial about available public insurance. Just three days before a serious asthma attack that required medical attention, she signed him up under a new federal program called the Children's Health Insurance Program (CHIP).

This program, created in 1997 and working through state programs, seeks to insure the 15 percent of all children who are not enrolled in Medicaid, whose parents do not qualify for Medicaid, or who cannot afford private insurance. A recent survey found that seven million children qualify for coverage under the program, although only two million are enrolled. (Many families with two workers or those with incomes around $25,000 do not know of their eligibility for this insurance program.)

Advocates of these changes hope to mend one hole in the social safety net, the one through which many children continue to fall when their medical needs are not cared for.

SOURCES: *State Children's Health Insurance Program Now Reaching Two Million* (Washington, D.C.: Health Care Financing Administration, January 11, 2000); David Ho, "7m Kids Eligible for Health Program," *Washington Post* (Associated Press), August 9, 2000; *Report to the President on School-based Outreach for Children's Health Insurance*, (Washington, D.C.: Department of Health and Human Services, July 2000); *Additional Comments: Proposed Rule, State Children's Health Insurance Program*, National Conference of State Legislatures, January 7, 2000; *The State Children's Health Insurance Program: Preliminary Highlights of Implementation and Expansion* (Washington, D.C.: Health Care Financing Administration, July 2000).

United States Lags behind in Infant Mortality, and African Americans Lag Farther Behind

The **infant mortality rate,** the number of deaths per one thousand live births, is one measure of the quality and availability of health care. If either the mother or the child fails to receive adequate care, the child may suffer and, in the worst case, die within the first year. Measured by infant mortality rates, as on other measures, the United States lags behind all other western democracies and several other nations too. At the same time, the United States spends more money on health care than any other nation. The table provides a sampling of comparisons. One might reasonably expect that the more a country invested in health care spending, the fewer infants would die. But this does not always appear to be the case. Japan spends only 7.2 percent of its gross domestic product (GDP) on health care, yet it has only 4.1 infant deaths per 1,000 live births. Canada spends 9.2 percent of its GDP on health care and has an infant mortality rate of 5.5. In contrast, the United States spends 13.9 percent of GDP on health but has a considerably higher in-

Country	Deaths per 1,000 Live Births	Percentage of GDP Spent on Health
Japan	4.1	7.2
Canada	5.5	9.2
France	5.6	9.6
United Kingdom	5.8	6.8
United States (whites)	6.0	
United States (total)	6.3	13.9
Hungary	9.5	6.5
Chile	10.0	—
United States (blacks)	13.7	
Mexico	24.6	4.7
China	43.3	—
Nigeria	69.5	—

SOURCE: *Statistical Abstract of the United States, 1999,* Tables 133, 1352, 1355.

fant mortality rate than either Japan or Canada. Furthermore, despite this high level of health care spending, the infant mortality rate for U.S. blacks is higher than the rate in many countries and well over double that for U.S. whites. In this area at least, health care spending overall has not produced the desired results.

poor nations of Latin America, Asia, and Africa. In some central city neighborhoods, blacks are *worse* off than if they lived in those countries. Analysts have concluded that neither income nor educational differences explain the poorer health of African Americans compared with people in the United States overall; instead, they conclude that racial discrimination plays a large part in explaining why blacks receive less and poorer-quality health care than others.[66]

Despite our large expenditures on health care, our public hospitals in big cities are overflowing with people suffering from diseases we thought we had conquered, such as tuberculosis, and AIDS. Our rural hospitals are closing daily, unable to make ends meet. Our

great university teaching hospitals are going deeply into debt and fighting for survival. To understand these problems, we need to understand government's role in the health care system.

The federal government has been involved in some aspects of health care for decades, but before 1965 there was no general federal support for individual health care. In 1965, after years of debate over government's responsibility to fund health care, concern about the problems of millions of Americans who could not afford adequate health care prompted President Johnson to propose and Congress to pass two programs, Medicare (for the elderly) and Medicaid (for low-income persons).

Medicare

Medicare is a public health insurance program that funds many medical expenses for the elderly and disabled. It includes hospital insurance and additional, voluntary coverage that helps pay for physicians' services, outpatient hospital services, and some other costs.

The hospital insurance part is paid for by Social Security taxes, while the other part is financed through general revenues and through the monthly premiums paid by participants. Those eligible for Social Security benefits are eligible for Medicare, and over 90 percent of Social Security recipients buy the optional insurance. The program covers about 40 million people at a cost of $250 billion.

Although many factors affect our health, it is clear that Medicare has benefited the health of the elderly. Compared to the period before 1965, more people see doctors now, and the elderly have more but shorter hospital stays. There have been declines in death rates from diseases affecting the elderly, such as heart attacks and strokes, and decreases in the number of days of restricted activity that older people experience.[67]

In spite of these substantial accomplishments, Medicare has not been a complete success. It is expensive, and many of those who need it have trouble paying for it. Experts of both political parties estimate that the Medicare program will go broke in the next few years unless changes are made in the program or some new national health care system is put in place. A similar cost problem afflicts the other major federal health care program, Medicaid.

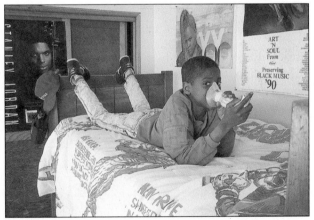

Like most individuals in middle-class families, this young man gets good medical treatment for chronic illnesses, such as asthma. However, poverty-stricken Americans are much more likely to die from lack of treatment of such diseases.

Medicaid

Medicaid is primarily a federal-state program to help poor and disabled people pay their medical bills. States set their own Medicaid eligibility standards, within certain federal guidelines. In some states, almost all the poor are covered by Medicaid, but in others relatively few are.

Medicaid, which covers about thirty-five million people and costs $175 billion, covers health care costs for one in four children, pays for one in three births, and funds more than half of all the nursing home care in the country.[68] When a family's resources run dry in paying an aging relative's nursing home care, Medicaid takes over.

Health Care Reforms

Our health care system suffers from both high costs and inadequate coverage for all Americans.

Why Costs Increase

One major problem with health care in the United States is cost. Related to that is the problem of access to good health care by poor and working-class citizens.

One reason for higher costs is that the number of elderly is increasing, and the number of very elderly (those over eighty) is increasing even faster. The elderly have more health problems than others, so as their numbers increase, the demand for medical services rises.

A second reason is the growing use of high technology in medicine. CAT scanners, dialysis equipment, intensive care units, and other sophisticated medical tools cost millions of dollars. High technology has made possible organ transplants and other procedures unheard of a few years ago, but at a huge cost.

Hospitals all want the most sophisticated equipment, which multiplies the overall cost of the system and results in duplication and underutilization. If one hospital has a sophisticated machine, others nearby also want it, even if there are not enough patients in the city to use the extra machines. The resulting competition for patients encourages marketing to persuade doctors to use the equipment so that it can be paid for. The American Hospital Association advises hospitals to spend about $8,000 per month "marketing" MRI (very sophisticated three-dimensional X rays) services to doctors.[69] The public—as patients, insurance buyers, and taxpayers—picks up the bill.

High-technology medicine also creates new demands for medical procedures. When better procedures become available, more people want them, so even if the new procedures are cheaper than the old, the total cost

© 1995 Mark Alan Stamaty. Excerpted from "Washington" with permission.

is higher. Surgery for cataracts, an eye disease affecting many elderly, is an example. Until a decade ago, surgery was painful and often ineffective. Now new techniques and materials allow plastic lenses to be inserted into the eye surgically, greatly improving vision. As a consequence, many more people receive the surgery, yielding a greatly increased total cost.[70]

A third reason for increasing costs is that many unnecessary procedures are done. One study estimated that one-quarter to one-third of all medical procedures are unneeded or are actually harmful.[71] For example, delivery of babies by caesarean (c-section) is the most common surgical procedure in America; doctors can charge more for caesareans than for a "normal" delivery, and a c-section can be done at the doctor's and patient's convenience. The proportion of births by caesarean is increasing, and experts estimate that twice as many are done as are necessary. The incidence of caesareans done on women with commercial insurance is far higher than the incidence on women without insurance, suggesting that c-sections are done more frequently when doctors think they can get the additional fees for performing them.[72]

A final cause of rising health care costs is poverty and social disorder. The decay of our inner cities has led to an epidemic of crime and disease that ultimately strains the health care system. Hospital emergency rooms must take care of victims of knife and gunshot wounds, whether the victims are insured or not. "Crack babies," victims of their mothers' drug addiction, cost $2,000 per day to treat in intensive care. AIDS victims, now found disproportionately among drug addicts and their offspring, multiply each year. Babies born prematurely and underweight (who cost up to $2,500 per day to treat) increase in number because poverty-stricken, often teenage mothers cannot get adequate prenatal care and sometimes even adequate food. High poverty rates and the millions of uninsured also mean that people with "ordinary" diseases such as heart problems and diabetes do not get adequate early treatment, making their conditions harder, and often more expensive, to treat.

Access

Given the aging population and the increasing expense of medical care, all people in the United States cannot have all the medical care they want. Though we pretend otherwise, in reality we have a rationing system for medical care; it is a rationing through ability to pay. If you can afford it, or if you have private or government insurance, then you can have the most expensive treatment, even if it will prolong your life only a few days or make you only marginally better off or not better off at all. If you do not have funds or insurance, then you may die at an early age even though you have a condition that could be controlled fairly easily.

In the United States 16 percent of the population does not have health insurance (see Figure 7). Even 16 percent of full-time workers do not have insurance. In seven states, over 20 percent do not have it. When uninsured people do go to the hospital, they receive fewer tests and less frequent surgery and are more likely to die.[73] One interpretation is that many unnecessary tests and operations are being done on insured patients, but the other interpretation is that needed tests and surgery are not being done on poor patients. Neither interpretation speaks well for the way we ration medical care.

As a consequence, we spend a very large proportion of health care resources on people in the last year of their lives. Thirty percent of all Medicare costs are incurred for just that, much of it for the last month of treatment. One doctor has called this the practice of "$100,000 funerals."[74] According to one U.S. health policy expert:

We want the very best care, and we want it now. We are obsessed with state-of-the-art technology and do not want to drive 100 miles to have access to it. We are not accustomed, as are the British, French, Germans, Canadians and Japanese, to thinking that maybe, if you are 85 years old, you shouldn't have triple bypass surgery.[75]

At the same time we are putting terminally ill patients on expensive equipment, we deny basic preventive medicine to millions of uninsured children.

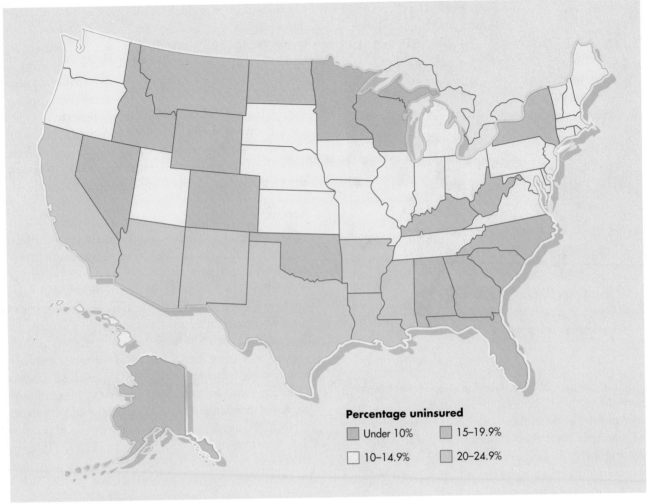

Percentage uninsured

- Under 10%
- 15–19.9%
- 10–14.9%
- 20–24.9%

FIGURE 7 ■ *Significant Numbers Are Uninsured*

SOURCE: *Statistical Abstract of the United States, 1999,* Table 190.

Other nations also ration medical care, but they do it in a different way. In Canada, for example, one focus is on preventive medicine. Expensive tests are reserved for those with a high probability of benefiting from them. People sometimes have to wait for elective surgery, ensuring that facilities will be used more efficiently. In several European countries, rationing is done by making decisions about who gets first priority for expensive procedures. For example, priority for an elective hip replacement would be given to a middle-aged working person over an elderly person (such choices would normally not be made if surgery were needed for life-threatening conditions).

Responding to Crisis

The health care market has changed dramatically over the past decade because of the pressures of cost and access. The traditional "fee for service" method of health care now involves less than half of the privately insured public.[76] Em-

ployers shop around for the best "deal" for insurance for their employees, a process already leading to a managed competition plan for more than half of all Americans (compared to only 10 percent in 1988). Most employees have a limited choice of doctors and hospitals if they want insurance to cover their bills. Medicare sets limits on what it will pay for each procedure. New health care organizations that have sprung up to challenge the old fee-for-service practice account for about 25 percent of all health care.[77] Called **health maintenance organizations (HMOs),** these groups of doctors agree to provide full health care for a fixed monthly charge. This system provides direct incentives for doctors to keep costs low, avoid unnecessary hospitalization and procedures, and emphasize preventive medicine. Private insurers try to limit unnecessary operations and provide incentives for outpatient care rather than hospital stays. Critics claim that these incentives result in doctors undertreating patients.

The Canadian Way

The quality of and access to health care in the United States are often compared unfavorably to that in Canada. In fact, one noted British publication joked that "a Canadian is an American without a gun and with health care."[1] The **Canadian health care plan** provides free health care to everyone—rich and poor without costs such as copayments, deductions, or dollar limits on medical coverage.[2] A tax supports the system, and government pays doctors for the services they perform. It is called a *single-payer system.* Individuals choose their own doctors, but the provincial (what are called "states" in the United States are called "provinces" in Canada) governments pay doctors for services performed. Fees are strictly regulated. Consequently, doctors' incomes are about one-third lower than in the United States, but in exchange doctors are free from most of the burdensome red tape that is making the practice of medicine so unpleasant for many U.S. doctors.

The administrative costs of the Canadian system are much lower than in our system. Here, hospitals and doctors must cope with both government regulation and oversight by insurance companies. For example, Johns Hopkins Medical Center is required to keep track of 18,000 different charge categories for 500 different insurance plans. At this one hospital alone, billing insurance companies, government, and patients costs $13 million.[3] It is not surprising that, in the United States, administrative costs are almost 25 percent of all health costs, compared to administrative costs of only 9 percent in Canada, due mainly to the economies of

a single-payer system.[4] Overall, costs are about 22 percent less in Canada. Where studies have been done, it appears that the quality of medical care is overall somewhat better in Canada (they ranked 30th to our 37th in the study cited earlier), though Canadians may have to wait longer for surgery that is not urgent.[5]

When Canadians and Americans are asked in surveys to compare the two systems, almost all Canadians (91 percent) and a plurality (43 percent) of Americans say Canada has a better health system. Barely one-quarter of Americans and almost no Canadians think the U.S. system is better.[6] Many Canadians point to life expectancy differences with the United States as evidence of the quality of their system. In Canada, life expectancy in 1997 for men was 75.8 years and for women was 81.4 years. In the United States in the same year, life expectancy was 73.6 for men and 79.4 for women.[7]

But powerful interest groups in the United States are opposed to the Canadian system. In general, Americans dislike "socialized medicine," fearing they will lose their ability to choose their own physician (in the Canadian system patients do choose their physicians, however). Some doctors are opposed to the Canadian system, though others think it might be the best alternative to meet the crisis. Insurance companies are strongly against the Canadian system because it would remove them as major parts of the health care system.

Because of the complexity of the health care issue and the volatility of public opinion on it, one newspaper spon-

sored a "Citizens Jury" to weigh the evidence to find the best health care program. In contrast with opinion polling, which asks for views based on whatever information the public has, the Citizens Jury takes a different approach. The jury, chosen to be representative of the country on all aspects of race, age, gender, geography, and so forth, studied various health care reform proposals, heard presentations of varying perspectives, asked their own questions, and, at the end of their study and deliberation, chose a single-payer plan, which is similar to the Canadian system. This plan, according to one of the jurors, "offers just one bureaucracy, the federal government. Tax it, pay it, and get it over with."[8] Many observers think that the Clinton health care proposals would have been more successful if they had adopted this Canadian, single-payer approach.

1. *The Economist,* quoted in the *Lincoln Journal,* October 25, 1993.
2. *Canada's Health Care System,* Health Canada, Health System and Policy Division, 1999 at www.hc-sc.gc.ca/datapcb/datahesa/E-sys.htm.
3. Spencer Rich, "Trimming Waste Will Help, But It's Not a Cure-all," *Washington Post National Weekly Edition,* May 17–23, 1993, pp. 8–9.
4. James Brooke, "A Crossroads in Canadian Health Care," *New York Times on the Web,* May 9, 2000.
5. "Study: Canadian Care Cost Efficient," *Champaign-Urbana News Gazette,* March 18, 1993, p. D1.
6. Larry Hugick, "American Unhappiness with Health Care Contrasts with Canadian Contentment," *Gallup Poll Monthly* 311 (August 1991), pp. 2–3.
7. Brooke, Ibid.
8. William Raspberry, "The Single-Payer Plan," *Washington Post National Weekly Edition,* October 25–31, 1993, p. 29.

States are trying their own reforms. Maryland is attempting to standardize health insurance billing forms. Oregon decided it will not use Medicaid funds to pay for certain expensive procedures and will target more funds to preventive medicine, such as prenatal care. Hawaii requires employers to provide insurance benefits for all workers and regulates insurance costs (consequently, only 8 percent of Hawaiians do not have health insurance). Several other states considered such legislation but backed off.

The federal government has tried to cut costs by tightening access to Medicaid and by limiting the amount it pays on bills doctors and hospitals submit to Medicare and Medicaid. But these are stopgap solutions, as Medicare and Medicaid costs spiral at the same time that increasing numbers of Americans cannot afford private health care and are not eligible for either Medicare or Medicaid. Private enterprise insures those at least risk—the young, the well, and the well-off. Government, and ultimately the taxpayers, pay for many of those most likely to be sick—the elderly and the poor.

There seem to be two main alternatives. One is to adopt some type of national health insurance system as all other industrial democracies have done. Another alternative is to force private insurance companies to share the risk of insuring those most likely to be ill. Managed competition incorporates this idea.

Social Welfare and Health Policy in Time

18th and 19th century	Local governments and churches treat poverty by establishing poorhouses and work farms for indigent.
Late 19th century	Political parties provide aid to needy residents in many cities in return for partisan support.
1890	Jacob A. Riis, in *How the Other Half Lives*, exposes appalling living conditions in working-class tenement houses in New York.
1911	Massachusetts enacts the first minimum wage law.
1916	President Woodrow Wilson signs legislation providing workers with compensation for on-the-job injuries.
1935	President Franklin Roosevelt signs the Social Security Act, creating a social insurance program designed to pay retired workers age sixty-five or older a continuing income after retirement. This legislation also includes unemployment insurance, aid for needy families (later AFDC) and old-age assistance (later SSI). Other legislation adopted in 1935 established the National Labor Relations Board, protecting workers' rights to collective organization and bargaining.
1938	Congress passes a law creating the Farm Security Administration, providing financial aid to farm laborers, and also the Fair Labor Standards Act, requiring overtime pay and establishing a minimum wage.
1939	Amendments to Social Security add coverage for the spouse and minor children of a retired worker and survivors benefits paid to the family if the covered worker dies.
1950	Further amendments to Social Security raise benefit levels. These had not changed since recipients first received them.
1964	President Johnson, in his inaugural address, calls for a "War on Poverty."
1964	The Office of Economic Opportunity (OEO) is created to provide a comprehensive approach to problems of poverty. Setting out with little funding but raising high expectations, the office worked for ten years but was understandably unable to "win" the war.
1965	Medicare bill is signed, extending health coverage to Americans aged sixty-five or older. Nearly twenty million beneficiaries are enrolled in Medicare in the first three years of the program.
1965	Medicaid is established
1969	President Nixon proposes a Family Assistance Plan to guarantee a minimum income level for all families with dependent children. His proposal proved to be unacceptable to members of Congress, who defeated it.
1971	Supplemental Security Income (SSI) program is established, incorporating state and local programs that had received partial federal funding into the federal social security system.
1972	First annual cost-of-living allowances (COLAs) provided to social security beneficiaries, based on increases in consumer prices.
1981	Omnibus Budget Reconciliation Act and its amendments broaden eligibility for food stamps and limited eligibility for AFDC while allowing AFDC recipients to keep less of their earnings. This legislation also authorized states to operate work relief programs known as "workfare."
1990	President Bush signs the Americans with Disabilities Act.
1996	Welfare reform legislation passes, limiting welfare benefits to no more than five years.

"Kids, your mother and I have spent so much money on health insurance this year that instead of vacation we're all going to go in for elective surgery."

The public is unsure what it wants.[78] While over two-thirds believe the system needs significant change and almost everyone believes it needs *some* change, there is little consensus on the kind of change. The public is divided on whether government or private insurers should cover costs. People are split over whether government regulation should limit choice if cost savings could be found. Most want to regulate doctors' salaries, but that is only a small part of the cost problem. Other versions of health policy reform would make smaller changes in the present system.

This ambivalence, coupled with unhappiness about the expense of the current system, suggests the possibility that support for a coherent, well-explained program could be found.

Conclusion: Are Social Welfare Programs Responsive?

Our social welfare system is extremely complex. The major beneficiaries of direct income support programs are the elderly of all classes, while programs for the poor are a much smaller part of all social welfare payments. Many programs also provide support for middle- and upper-income groups, including direct income supplements, tax breaks, and support for services largely used by the nonpoor.

These programs reflect the responsiveness of government to different groups. Most taxpayers define themselves as middle income, and they support services for themselves and others like them. Benefits to the upper classes are tolerated to a large extent because many of them go unnoticed or because the groups receiving them are powerful and respected in society. Those that do not go unnoticed, such as tax breaks, are resented, however.

Programs for the poor are both obvious and unpopular. The poor, although a sizeable proportion of the population, do not have the status or organization to win public support for programs benefiting them. In hard times, when support is most needed, programs for the poor often take the brunt of budget cuts as they did during the Reagan years.

Not all Americans view politics only in terms of what they get. In the past, many religious, labor, civic, and business groups have rallied to the side of the poor. Now, some of these groups and others of the nonpoor are working to solve current problems. The nonpoor are finding out that the growth of the urban underclass harms not only those in it but also other citizens, who must pay for new jails, who are increasingly unable to buy reasonably priced health insurance, whose children are exposed to drug sellers, who see homeless on their way to work and in their neighborhoods, and who, in many cities, have become afraid to walk in their own neighborhoods or take public transportation. Businesses are discovering that the decay of public services, particularly schools, increases their costs when workers are ill educated and trained. Extreme inequality is exacerbating our racial problems too. Some blacks believe the failure of government to deal with drugs and crime in inner city ghettoes is part of a genocidal plot, while some whites see these same problems and use them to denounce civil rights and welfare. Increasing economic inequality seems to undermine our ability to deal with either poverty or racial issues.

But can we generate the will to act to save a generation of millions of children whose environments now provide them with little chance of developing into productive citizens? So far, we have not. We act sluggishly in confronting domestic problems. The problem is not money. We spent more in the first twenty-eight hours of the Persian Gulf War than the federal government spends in a year for maternal and child health; we spent more in four days of that war than for Head Start in an entire year.[79] We cut welfare and Medicare while we provide increased tax breaks for the wealthy. The money is there for programs we think are important. Thus, our social welfare policies illustrate the popular, if ungrammatical, saying: "Them that has, gets." Social welfare policies illustrate again that government is most responsive to those who are most organized and have the most resources.

Health Care Reform Dies

President Clinton announced in his State of the Union speech that he would veto any bill that did not include universal coverage. Although he said that he was willing to compromise on other parts of the plan, he was not willing to compromise on making sure that all Americans have some minimal level of health insurance.

Despite his expressed willingness to compromise, the original Clinton bill continued to wend its way through the five House and two Senate committees that had jurisdiction over it. When the committees were finished and no consensus was reached, the congressional leadership tried to patch a compromise together. By the fall, the bill was dead. And, in the 1994 elections, Republicans swept to victories, winning majorities in both houses and dooming serious health care reform for at least two years.

Meanwhile, though politicians are not talking about the problems of the health care system, the number of uninsured continues to rise as does the cost of the American health care system. At the same time, even without government, the system is radically changing itself into the kind of system that many of the Clinton bill's opponents feared: big organizations (in this case private corporations) are taking over the medical "industry," while most people no longer have a choice of doctors or treatments. Three-fourths of all doctors are under contract to cut fees and accept oversight of their medical decisions; in other words, they have joined managed care plans of the kind the president had proposed. The market is putting a crimp on fees, and where managed care has grown fastest, "Incomes of specialists are dropping like stones . . . and doctors who are not well ensconced in H.M.O.s

© 1994 Mark Alan Stamaty. Reprinted with permission.

are in a state of near panic."[80] Mergers of hospitals, laboratories, and clinics are making the health care field a major industry. Economics dictates nearly every aspect of medical care, including dismissing mothers and their newborns from hospitals sometimes only hours after delivery.

Meanwhile, costs of Medicare and Medicaid soar, and millions of people are not covered by any insurance, private or public. In an interesting turn of events, in 1995 Republicans were calling the health care system a "crisis," because of the predictions that Medicare will run short of money in a few years. By 1998, public attention was focusing on the deficiencies in the increasing numbers of HMOs.

Was Clinton's decision not to compromise a mistake? If he had vigorously pursued a compromise, a weaker bill might have resulted, but even that was no guarantee. It would probably have been a long way from his original idea of universal coverage. Many health care experts believe, however, that Clinton's mistake was not his refusal to compromise in January 1994, but his insistence on compromise at the beginning of the whole process. A Canadian single-payer plan might have been sold to the American public instead of the Clinton plan because it is simpler to explain, more accountable, and more plausible to argue that it would reduce administrative costs. It would have put him in a better position to compromise later and get part of what he wanted.

Key Terms

managed competition
Social Security
feminization of poverty
Aid to Families with Dependent Children (AFDC)
Temporary Aid to Needy Families (TANF)
Supplemental Security Income (SSI)
earned income tax credit (EITC)

means test
food stamp program
farm subsidies
infant mortality rate
Medicare
Medicaid
Canadian health care plan
health maintenance organizations (HMOs)

Further Reading

Laurie Kaye Abraham, *Mama Might Be Better Off Dead: The Failure of Health Care in Urban America* (Chicago: University of Chicago Press, 1993). The chronicle of a poor family's attempts to obtain health care.

Walt Bogdanich, *The Great White Lie* (New York: Simon & Schuster, 1992). This description of the health crisis in America's hospitals probably should not be read if there is a hospital stay in your future!

Robert Coles, *The Youngest Parents: Teenage Pregnancy as It Shapes Lives* (New York: Norton, 1997). Based on several years of intensive interviews with a diverse group of teenage parents, this book illumines their lives, largely by letting them speak for themselves.

Nicholas Lemann, *The Promised Land* (New York: Knopf, 1991). A readable account of the black urban underclass, told through the story of individuals who moved north to escape brutal conditions in Mississippi.

Frank Levy, *The New Dollars and Dreams: American Incomes and Economic Change* (Russell Sage, 1998). Examines changes in the U.S. economy bringing further inequality to the distribution of income.

Clifton Luttrell, *The High Cost of Farm Welfare* (Washington, D.C.: Cato Institute, 1989). Taxing the poor to pay the rich through farm subsidies.

Charles Murray, *Losing Ground: American Social Policy, 1950–1980* (New York: Basic Books, 1984). Argues that social welfare programs for the poor have made things worse, not better.

John E. Schwarz, *America's Hidden Success: A Reassessment of Twenty Years of Public Policy,* 2d ed. (New York: Norton, 1988). Argues that the Great Society programs of the 1960s and 1970s were largely successful in reducing poverty and achieving other goals.

William J. Williams, *The Truly Disadvantaged: The Inner-City, the Underclass and Public Policy* (Chicago: University of Chicago Press, 1987). Argues that the worsening plight of the black underclass is due to the changing structure of the national economy, which is increasing the number of poor-paying jobs, and to the success of the black middle class, who when they leave the ghetto leave an ever more concentrated underclass behind.

Electronic Resources

www.aphsa.org/
This page of the American Public Human Services Association has information about and analysis of all welfare programs. It is a useful site for tracking the progress of welfare reform.

www.ncsl.org/statefed/welfare/
As part of its responsibility to state legislative bodies, the National Conference of State Legislatures provides assessments of changes in federal welfare law. In addition, this is a source of information on what individual states are deciding to do.

www.ssa.gov/
Like all other government agencies, the Social Security Administration has its own Web site, providing a broad array of information. Here employers can find out how to comply with laws governing

Social Security taxation, and parents of disabled children can learn how to avoid losing SSI benefits.

www.hhs.gov/agencies/
This page links to the agencies of the Department of Health and Human Services, including the Food and Drug Administration, the Administration for Children and Families, and the Centers for Disease Control and Prevention.

InfoTrac College Edition

"Forget Electioneering Blather"
"Poverty: Well Done"
"Ignored Component Welfare Reform"
"Direct Access Doesn't Necessarily Raise Costs"

Notes

1. "Issue One: Health Care," *Newsweek,* December 28, 1992, p. 32.
2. "Issue One: Health Care."
3. Janice Castro, "Condition: Critical," *Time,* November 25, 1991.
4. Frank Swoboda, "A Gold Watch and No Health Care Coverage," *Washington Post National Weekly Edition,* June 6–12, 1994, p. 21.
5. Spencer Rich, "Getting a Count on Those Who Lack Coverage," *Washington Post National Weekly Edition,* September 27–October 3, 1993, p. 9.
6. Michelle A. Clark, "Health Insurance in America," *Regional Economist,* January 1993, pp. 5–9.
7. "One-Third of Doctors' Offices Don't Provide Health Insurance," *Lincoln Star,* April 30, 1994, p. 23; Dana Priest and Amy Goldstein, "Uninsured: Even Middle Class," *International Herald Tribune,* December 23, 1992, p. 3.
8. Robin Toner, "Hillary Clinton's Potent Brain Trust for Health Reform," *New York Times,* February 28, 1993, sect. 3, p. 1.
9. Michael Weinstein, "The Freedom to Choose Doctors: What Freedom?" *New York Times Magazine,* March 27, 1994, pp. 64–65.
10. "Lobbyist Blitzkrieg Criticized," *Lincoln Journal,* September 23, 1994 (*Los Angeles Times* release).
11. Patricia Dunn, "The Reagan Solution for Aiding Families with Dependent Children: Reflections of an Earlier Era," in Anthony Champagne and Edward Harpham, eds., *The Attack on the Welfare State* (Prospect Heights, Ill.: Waveland, 1984), 87–110.
12. Harrell Rodgers, *The Cost of Human Neglect* (Armonk, N.Y.: Sharpe, 1982). The full name of Social Security is the Old Age Survivors Disability and Health Insurance Program; *Statistical Abstract of the United States, 1999,* Table 614.
13. Charles Peters, "Tilting at Windmills," *Washington Monthly* (June 1986), p. 10.
14. Peter Kilborn, "The Temptation of the Social Security Surplus," *New York Times,* December 27, 1988, p. 5; *Statistical Abstract of the United States, 1999,* Table 617.
15. Robert Pear, "U.S. Pensions to Lift Many of the Poor," *New York Times,* December 28, 1988, p. 1; John Kearney, Herman Grundmann, and Salvatore Gallicchio, "The Influence of Social Security Benefits and SSI Payments on the Poverty Status of Children," *Social Security Bulletin* 57 (Summer 1994): 27–31; Laurence H. Thompson, "The Advantages and Disadvantages of Different Social Welfare Strategies," *Social Security Bulletin* 57 (Fall 1994): 3–10.
16. Melinda Upp, "Relative Importance of Various Income Sources of the Aged, 1980," *Social Security Bulletin* 46 (January 1983): 5.

17. Ibid.
18. David W. Moore and Leslie McAneny, "Workers Concerned They Can't Afford to Retire," *Gallup Poll Monthly,* May 1993, pp. 16–23.
19. George Church and Richard Lacayo, "Social Security," *Time,* March 20, 1995, pp. 24–32.
20. Jonathan Rauch, "Growing Old," *National Journal,* December 31, 1988, p. 3235.
21. Ibid.
22. Paul Taylor, "Remember the Generation Gap?" *Washington Post National Weekly Edition,* January 20, 1986, p. 24.
23. Paul Taylor, "Like Taking Money from a Baby," *Washington Post National Weekly Edition,* March 4–10, 1991, p. 31.
24. David Gordon, "To Have and to Have Not," *Washington Post National Weekly Edition,* November 10, 1986, p. 23; and "Rich Are Richer, Poor Poorer, and Middle Class Is Vanishing," *Lincoln Star,* November 22, 1986; Daniel Patrick Moynihan, "Half the Nation's Children Born without a Fair Chance," *New York Times,* September 25, 1988.
25. Richard B. Freeman, "Labor Market Institutions and Earnings Inequality," *New England Economic Review* (May/June 1996): 158.
26. Martin Anderson, *Welfare: The Political Economy of Welfare Reform in the U.S.* (Stanford, Calif.: Hoover Institution, 1978); Richard Margolis, "The Arithmetic of Poverty," *The New Leader,* April 16, 1990, pp. 14–15; Julie Kosterlitz, "Measuring Misery," *National Journal,* August 4, 1990, pp. 1892–1896; Jason De Parle, "In Debate over Who Is Poor, Fairness Becomes the Issue," *New York Times,* September 3, 1990, pp. 1, 10.
27. U.S. Bureau of the Census at www.census.gov/hhes/income/histinc/h02.html and www.census.gov/hhes/income98/in98dis.html (and calculations from these data); an analysis of Congressional Budget Office data by Isaac Shapiro and Robert Greenstein, *The Widening Income Gulf,* September 4, 1999, Center on Budget and Policy Priorities.
28. David Wessel, "U.S. Rich and Poor Increase in Numbers; Middle Loses Ground," *Wall Street Journal,* September 22, 1986, p. 1.
29. *Statistical Abstract of the United States, 1999,* Table 768.
30. Data on feminization of poverty from Harrell Rodgers, *Poor Women, Poor Families* (Armonk, N.Y.: Sharpe, 1986), and Bureau of the Census, Current Population Reports, *Characteristics of the Population below the Poverty Level 1984,* Series P–60, no. 152, 1986.
31. Bureau of the Census, *Demographic and Socioeconomic Aspects of Aging in the United States,* Series P–23, no. 138.
32. George Gilder, *Wealth and Poverty* (New York: Basic Books, 1981), 68.
33. Edward Banfield, *The Unheavenly City Revisited* (Boston: Little, Brown, 1974). See also Charles Murray, *Losing Ground* (New York: Basic Books, 1984).
34. Michael Harrington, *The Other America: Poverty in the United States* (New York: Macmillan, 1962); *Statistical Abstract of the United States, 1999,* Table 705, fn. 1; conversation with Department of Labor official.
35. Isabel Sawhill, "Poverty and the Underclass," *American Agenda: A Report to the Forty-First President of the U.S.A.* (Washington, D.C.: Urban Institute Press, 1988).
36. Gallup polls, March 1985.
37. Gary Copeland and Kenneth Meier, "Gaining Ground," *American Politics Quarterly* 15 (April 1987): 254–273.
38. Schwartz, *America's Hidden Success.*
39. Duncan, *Years of Poverty;* Spencer Rich, "Who Gets Help and How," *Washington Post National Weekly Edition,* May 15–19, 1989, p. 37.
40. Erik Eckholm "Solutions on Welfare: They All Cost Money," *New York Times,* July 26, 1992, p. 1ff.

41. Reported in the *Lincoln Star*, March 21, 1987, p. 2.

42. *Fact Sheet on TANF*, Administration for Children and Families, Department of Health and Human Services, February 17, 2000 at www.acf.dhhs.gov/programs/opa/facts/tanfpr.htm.

43. *Temporary Assistance for Needy Families (TANF) Program*, Administration for Children and Families, Department of Health and Human Services, final rule summary at www.acf.dhhs.gov/programs/ofa/exsumcl.htm; Liz Schott, Ed Lazere, Heidi Goldberg, and Eileen Sweeney, *Highlights of the Final TANF Regulations*, Center on Budget and Policy Priorities, April 29, 1999.

44. Jack Tweedie, "Eight Questions to Ask about Welfare Reforms," *State Legislatures*, January 1999, at www.ncsl.org/statefed/welfare/8quest.htm.

45. Pamela Loprest, "Long Ride from Welfare to Work," *Washington Post*, August 30, 1999, at www.urban.org/news/press/loprest083099.html.

46. "Rule Violations Force Thousands off Welfare Rolls," *Lincoln Journal Star* (Associated Press), March 29, 1999, pp. 1A and 8A; Barbara Vobejda and Judith Havemann, "Sanctions Fuel Drop in Welfare Rolls," *Washington Post*, March 23, 1998, p. A01 at www.washingtonpost.com/wp-srv/politics/special/welfare/stories/wf032398.htm.

47. Loprest, "Long Ride from Welfare to Work."

48. "Unfinished Business: Why Cities Matter to Welfare Reform" (Center on Urban & Metropolitan Policy, Brookings Institution, July 2000); Dan Froomkin, "Welfare's Changing Face," *Washington Post*, July 23, 1998, at www.washingtonpost.com/wp-srv/politics/special/welfare/welfare.htm.

49. *Statistical Abstract of the United States, 1999* (Washington, DC: Government Printing Office, 2000), Table 680.

50. From William Julius Wilson quoted in Thompson, "The Way Off Welfare." See also Katharine L. Bradbury, "The Growing Inequality of Family Incomes: Changing Families and Changing Wages," *New England Economic Review* (July/August 1996), pp. 55–82; Pamela Loprest, *Families Who Left Welfare: Who Are They and How Are They Doing?* Urban Institute, February 1999.

51. Eileen P. Sweeney, *Recent Studies Indicate That Many Parents Who Are Current or Former Welfare Recipients Have Disabilities* (Center on Budget and Policy Priorities, February 29, 2000); Erica Goode, "Childhood Abuse and Adult Stress," *New York Times*, August 2, 2000, at www.nytimes.com/library/national/science/health/080200hth-stress-women.html.

52. *Changes since 1995 in the Safety Net's Impact on Child Poverty*, December 23, 1999, Center on Budget and Policy Priorities at www.cbpp.org/12-23-99wel-es.htm.

53. Nancy K. Cauthen and Jane Knitzer, "Beyond Work: Strategies to Promote the Well-Being of Young Children and Families in the Context of Welfare Reform," National Center for Children in Poverty, November 1999, at www.acf.dhhs.gov/programs/opre/director.htm.

54. E. J. Dionne, Jr., "Welfare Reform's Clues Are in Wisconsin," *Washington Post National Weekly Edition*, September 29, 1997, p. 26.

55. "Many of Wealthy Either Escape Taxes or Pay Low Percentage," *Lincoln Star*, June 30, 1993, p. 38.

56. "The Anatomy of Pork," *Newsweek*, April 13, 1992, p. 26.

57. William Robbins, "Costly Farm Price Supports Are under Sharper Scrutiny," *New York Times*, December 5, 1983, pp. 1ff., Ward Sinclair, "Big California Farms Harvest Federal Cash," *Washington Post National Weekly Edition*, January 2, 1984, p. 30; data from *Statistical Abstract of the United States, 1991*, Table 1127, p. 1.

58. Ward Sinclair, "The High Price of American Rice," *Washington Post National Weekly Edition*, July 21, 1986, p. 21; "Urban Solons Want Farm Policy Reforms," *Lincoln Star*, September 8, 1986, p. 1.

59. "Hiding from the Farm Bill," *Washington Post*, April 7, 1996, at http://legiweb.legislate.com/d/hr2854/251930.htm.

60. Sharon LaFraniere, "Though They Owe, Still They Reap," *Washington Post National Weekly Edition*, February 28–March 6, 1994, pp. 10–11.

61. James P. Donahue, "The Corporate Welfare Kings," *Washington Post National Weekly Edition*, March 21–27, 1994, p. 24; "Government Lowers Grazing Fees," *Lincoln Journal Star*, January 24, 1996, p. 6B.

62. Molly McGregor, "Irrigation Farming: Subsidizing Mother Nature," *Journal of Freshwater* 6 (1982), pp. 518–521; Donahue, "Corporate Welfare Kings."

63. "Nature Humbles a State of Mind," *New York Times*, February 10, 1991, p. E3; Marc Reisner, "The Emerald Desert," *Greenpeace* (July/August 1989): 7.

64. John Beckerman, "Stockman Is Right: Military Pensions Are a Scandal," *Washington Post National Weekly Edition*, April 1985, p. 25; *Statistical Abstract of the United States, 1999*, Table 618; *Fact Sheet on TANF*, Administration for Children and Families, Department of Health and Human Services, February 17, 2000 at www.acf.dhhs.gov/programs/opa/facts/tanfpr.htm.

65. Lauren Neergaard, "U.S. Health Care Costs Rank High," *Centre Daily Times* (Associated Press), June 21, 2000, p. 11A.

66. Rodgers, *Cost of Human Neglect*, p. 91. Recent studies show that this continues to be true. See Peter Kilborn, "Racial Health Gap Remaining a Reality," *Lincoln Journal Star* (from *New York Times*), January 26, 1998, p. 3A.

67. Clarke E. Cochran et al., *American Public Policy* (New York: St. Martins, 1982), 262. See also Spencer Rich, "Look Again: The Anti-Poverty Programs Do Work," *Washington Post National Weekly Edition*, May 21, 1984, p. 24.

68. Matthew Miller, "Where It May Really Hurt," *Time*, December 18, 1995, p. 29.

69. Nancy Watzman, "Socialized Medicine Now, without the Wait," *Washington Monthly* (October 1991): 43–50.

70. Robert Samuelson, "Why Medical Costs Keep Soaring," *Washington Post National Weekly Edition*, December 5–11, 1988.

71. Erik Eckholm, "Those Who Pay Health Costs Think of Drawing Lines," *New York Times*, March 28, 1993, p. 1.

72. Watzman, "Socialized Medicine." In Canada, doctors cannot collect as much per caesarean if the frequency with which they do the procedure exceeds the ratio considered reasonable. Thus, the economic incentive to do caesareans disappears.

73. *Statistical Abstract of the United States, 1999*, Table 190. Malcolm Gladwell, "Health Insurance Warning Signs," *Washington Post National Weekly Edition*, January 28–February 3, 1991, p. 38.

74. Charles Peters, "Tilting at Windmills," *Washington Monthly* (March 1985): 11.

75. Richard Rich, quoted in "Access vs. Equity: The Real Health Care Reform Issue," *The LAS Newsletter* (University of Illinois) (Winter 1994): 6.

76. "While Congress Remains Silent, Health Care Reforms Itself," *New York Times*, December 18, 1994, p. 1.

77. *Statistical Abstract of the United States, 1999*, Table 191. Tables 185 to 190 provide other information about medical care coverage and spending.

78. Robert Shapiro, Lawrence Jacobs, and Lynn Harvey, "Influences on Public Opinion toward Health Policy," paper prepared for the 1995 Midwest Political Science Association, Chicago, Illinois.

79. Marc Kranowsky, "Military Costs Dwarf Domestic Programs," *Lincoln Star*, February 6, 1991, p. 28. This is based on an estimate of the cost of war at $500 million per day.

80. Erik Eckholm, "While Congress Remains Silent, Health Care Transforms Itself," *New York Times*, December 18, 1994, p. 1.

Regulation and Environmental Policy

YOU ARE THERE

Endangered Species or Endangered Jobs?

You are Bruce Babbitt, President Clinton's newly appointed secretary of the interior. In office only a month, you are already facing a decision that you have labeled a "test case" for the new administration's enforcement of the Endangered Species Act. You must make a recommendation to the president on how to resolve the conflict between environmentalists demanding protection of virgin, or natural-growth, forests in Oregon, Washington, and California and a timber industry fighting for increased access to government land.[1]

You are a former governor of Arizona, another state with large parts of its land under federal control. You have experience in negotiating land use with the federal government and are considered knowledgeable on natural resource management issues. You grew up near the Grand Canyon, hiking and camping on protected lands, and see yourself as a committed environmentalist.

Clinton said he wanted to be the environmental president that Bush only promised to be, but his record as governor was widely criticized during the campaign. You were appointed to Interior to beef up his image and to provide, along with Vice President Gore, an expertise the president does not have.

You share with the president the view that environmental and other interest group politics have been too adversarial and that an attempt must be made to find a middle ground. And like him, you know what it is like to be a governor facing a business slowdown, rising unemployment, and the increasing costs of complying with federal regulations.

You have been handed a very difficult situation, one in which the differences between militant environmentalists and angry loggers have led to violence. The issue came to a head when environmentalists sued the U.S. Forest Service to stop what they claimed was excess logging in the old-growth forests of the Northwest. They said it violated the Endangered Species Act by threatening to destroy the habitat of the spotted owl. A federal judge agreed and ordered the Forest Service to stop the logging until an acceptable plan for protecting the owl's habitat was drawn up.

It is not only the owl that is at stake; an estimated six hundred additional plants and animals depend on the particular habitat provided by old-growth forests. Their preservation is seen as

Oakland Museum of California, Oakland Museum Association purchase

essential to maintaining biodiversity and the planet's ecological balance. Ninety percent of our virgin timberland has already been destroyed. Even though loggers plant trees where they cut, new trees on timber farms cannot replace the old-growth forests as wildlife habitats. Environmental activists want a permanent ban on logging on seven million acres in the three states and want the old-growth forests left to take their natural course.

The thirty thousand loggers whose jobs are on the line want to know why protecting a rare owl is more important than safeguarding their ability to support their families. Many believe there is no proof that the endangered species could not adapt to life in newly planted forests. They say that the timber is there to be used and that if they are not allowed to cut it, they will lose their homes and jobs.

Conservationists argue that if we do not protect our ecosystem, eventually no one will have a job. They are worried not just about endangered species but about air and water pollution, soil erosion, and long-term damage to the fishing and timber industries from bad land manage-

ment practices. They criticize the timber industry for complaining that it does not have enough logs to keep mills open while it exports 20 percent of its cut overseas and receives a tax break from the government for doing so. They say it is better to save jobs by halting timber exports and diverting logs to domestic saw mills. As new studies are done and logging is suspended without any final resolution in sight, positions on both sides harden.

During his campaign for the White House, President Clinton promised if elected to hold a conference in the Northwest to hear all sides in the debate. He committed himself to finding a permanent answer to the conflict between logging and preservation, one that would both protect the owl's habitat and revitalize the timber industry. You are sent to tour the area, meet with all parties to the dispute, and make a policy recommendation to the president before he holds his promised conference on timberland use.

Your visit reinforces your belief that a middle ground must be found. You are awed by the timberland and understand the environmentalists' drive to preserve it.

But you are also deeply affected by saw mills without timber to process and logging families in danger of losing their homes. You tour an experimental forest where loggers are allowed to cut but required to leave some of the trees standing on each acre. When you offer this as an example of a middle road, it is rejected by environmentalists who say the method cannot preserve habitat and by loggers who say their profits are significantly reduced when they leave trees standing in cut areas.

Environmentalists think our very existence is at stake, but whatever the scale of some future ecological disaster, the loggers view it as less threatening than the present-day loss of their jobs. How do you weigh the interest of the environment against the demands of the loggers? You have two main options: allowing logging to proceed or banning it in all old-growth forests. Or you could recommend banning logging in some but not all forests. You could also recommend more study, but this just postpones a decision that must be made. What do you recommend?

Americans have paradoxical attitudes about regulation. We call on government to protect us from unsafe workplaces, unclean air and water, fraudulent advertising, hazardous highways and drunk drivers, dangerous drugs, and many of life's other perils. But then we want government "off our backs"; we resent regulations, rules, and red tape. We want government involved in protecting us, but we are uncertain about how, when, and how much.

The extensive rulemaking authority of the executive branch (Chapter 12), Congress's oversight functions, and its power to regulate foreign and interstate commerce have an enormous influence on the behavior of both business and consumers.

In a true free market economy, there would be no forced saving for retirement, no minimum wage or child labor laws, no bankruptcy protection for businesses and individuals, no farm subsidies or tariffs on imports that compete with domestic goods, no regulated public utility rates, no government-run corporations like Amtrak, the post office, and the TVA, no laws protecting work-

ers' safety or the quality of the air and water, and no redistribution of wealth through progressive taxation and welfare programs. None of these would exist because a basic principle of capitalism is that unrestricted competition in the marketplace gives us the best chance to obtain the economic goals we desire.

Adam Smith believed the "invisible hand" of the marketplace works to increase production and make individual firms more efficient.[2] Although each individual firm does not intend to work toward the greater good of society, the greater good is in fact achieved as each firm tries to maximize its own profit. If the economy did work this way, we would have little regulation. But unfortunately the economy goes awry in ways that threaten the public good because individuals and businesses do not always behave honestly, cautiously, and considerately. So government regulates to limit or correct these effects.

But how much risk should government protect us from? How should the benefits of regulation be weighed against the costs of those regulations to business and industry?

"There, there it is again—the invisible hand of the marketplace giving us the finger."

The public gives no clear-cut answer to these questions. Regulation that is seen as beneficial by one group is regarded by another as wasteful and unnecessary red tape. This is why there is continuing controversy over what should be regulated, how much regulation is needed, and the regulatory mechanisms that should be used.

Development of Regulation

Reasons for Regulation

Damage to Common Property

One reason for regulation has been called the **tragedy of the commons**.[3] The "commons" refers to the air we breathe and the water we drink, which belong to us all. The "tragedy" is that some individuals may seek to exploit them for their own uses to the detriment of the common good. To maximize their profits, farmers pump as much irrigation water as they need from rivers or aquifers, even in water-short areas, and industries spew toxic chemicals into the air or bury them in the soil. They are acting in accord with the profit motive. Indeed, most individuals who exploit the commons gain economically and so have no incentive not to do so. But when many people exploit the commons, the community as a whole suffers.

Consider the case of Los Angeles and General Motors (GM). Los Angeles once had a low-pollution electric railway system. In the 1930s, GM bought the system and then destroyed it, because GM wanted to sell cars, trucks, and buses. The company replaced the electric system with noisy, polluting diesel buses, so uncomfortable and unreliable that Los Angelenos were given a great incentive to rely on private autos.

In 1949, after buying and destroying electric railway systems in more than one hundred cities, GM was fined a paltry $5,000 by the government for illegally conspiring to replace municipal services with its own. Meanwhile, the company made millions of dollars. Due in large part to reliance on cars, smog in Los Angeles became a major health hazard. Some studies claimed that children who grew up in Los Angeles lost up to 50 percent of their lung capacity from breathing in the polluted air.[4] Obviously, it is absurd to charge GM with creating the entire automobile culture of Los Angeles, but clearly its drive for private profits did not contribute to the common good.

When GM or any other entity, such as a chemical company that disposes of its toxic wastes in an unsafe way, imposes a cost on the public, it has created an **externality.** Externalities are costs or benefits that are not reflected in market prices. Environmental degradation is a negative externality because the social costs, the burdens imposed on society, are not reflected in the cost of the goods whose production caused the damage. When a coal-burning utility emits sulfur dioxide into the air, for example, the company is essentially disposing of a by-product at no cost by simply burning it off and releasing it into the air. This places an unfair burden on the public, both in terms of the health risks and the costs of environmental cleanup. It also leads to inefficiency in the marketplace because the utility is not made to bear the true cost of generating electricity. If companies are allowed to externalize costs in this way, they will produce more of a product than is "socially beneficial." But if they have to absorb or internalize the costs of emitting pollutants, instead of foisting them off on the public, they will have "an incentive to reduce production to acceptable levels or to develop alternative technologies."[5]

To make the market more efficient and to get companies to stop making products whose real cost is not reflected in the price charged for that product—to get polluters to stop polluting, for example—the government can set standards for how much of the pollutant can be emitted (and recover costs through penalties and fines from violators), or it can impose taxes on emissions or discharges and charge for pollution up front (more on this later in the chapter).

Inefficient Competition

In a capitalist system, government intervention is also justifiable when competition is inefficient. Adam Smith believed that in an open market goods and labor would be used in a way that would maximize profit and limit cost. Because of competition among firms desiring to sell their products to consumers, manufacturers would

In 2000 Houston, a center of the petro-chemical industry, surpassed Los Angeles as the smog capital of the United States.
Phillippe Diederich, Houston, TX

make goods as cheaply as possible. But sometimes competition is not efficient. For example, because it is not cost-effective (due to large capital outlays) for each community to have more than one company laying gas pipelines or generating electric power, competition cannot work to drive down prices or increase efficiency. Thus, utilities (such as gas and electric producers) are controlled monopolies in most countries, including, until recently, the United States, where regulating is done largely by state governments. The government allows a utility to be the only provider of a service in a given geographic area, but it regulates prices because people do not have a choice of sellers of electricity or gas. Smith himself agreed that this form of government intervention was appropriate. (The deregulation of electric utilities by some states in the late 1990s is discussed later in the chapter.)

Lack of Necessary Coordination

Another reason for regulation is that sometimes the free market produces an unacceptable lack of coordination. An obvious example is regulation of airline flights. The free market is not well suited to determine which planes shall have priority to take off at 2:00 P.M. on a certain runway at Kennedy International Airport in New York. Competition could lead to disaster. Thus, the Federal Aviation Administration (FAA) has been empowered to coordinate air traffic patterns.

We could let the market make decisions about takeoff and landing priorities by selling takeoff rights for a fee. But regulation would still be needed to make sure that all the planes authorized to take off at a given time did so in a way to maximize safety.

Unacceptable Inequities

Another reason for regulation is to promote equity. Equity in this context does not refer to equality in outcome but to ensuring fair conditions for participation in the marketplace. Sometimes individuals or groups are severely disadvantaged by the private marketplace. For example, legislation setting minimum wages, banning child labor, protecting workers' rights to organize, and defining minimum standards for workplace health and safety is intended to redress the inequity in power between individual workers and employers.

Regulations forbidding race and gender discrimination are also designed to enhance equity. Consumer protection laws, such as those forbidding false advertising, and laws licensing pharmacists, physicians, lawyers, and public accountants are based on the assumption that consumers will often not have sufficient information to evaluate the competence of those selling the service or product. Government seeks to remedy an inequity in information between the buyer and the seller of a product or service.

Antitrust regulation reduces inequity by prohibiting monopolies. A **monopoly** is one or a few firms that control the sale of a product or service in a particular market. Where a monopoly exists, the producer(s) can fix prices, setting them well above the cost of production, or they can sell below cost to drive small businesses out of the market. Under the Sherman Antitrust Act of 1890 and the Clayton Act of 1914, uncontrolled monopolies and price rigging are illegal. One firm may use antitrust laws to sue others, or the government itself may initiate antitrust actions. The enforcement of antitrust legislation has waxed and waned over the years.

Mergers can lead to monopolies as competitors combine forces to control a larger share of the market. Therefore, when large companies want to merge or acquire their competitors, they are required to submit their proposals for review to the Justice Department or the Federal Trade Commission so that government regulators can determine whether their combination would adversely affect competition and prices. Our economy has experienced five major waves of business mergers, or "corporate consolidations," as Fed Chair Alan Greenspan calls them: at the turn of the twentieth century, in the 1920s, the 1960s, the 1980s, and the 1990s. The number of merger proposals tripled during the nineties, with more than seventy thousand deals worth nearly $6 trillion during the Clinton years alone.[6] Some see this trend as a repeat of the corporate mergers that swept the American economy at the turn of the century, when General Motors was created from more than two dozen car companies, and U.S. Steel was formed by combining many small steel companies. In these situations government regulators have to decide whether the mergers will make the economy more efficient and competitive or whether they will create monopolies and lead to unfair pricing.

Ninety-five percent of the merger proposals made during the Clinton years went unchallenged by the Justice Department, but it was joined by many state governments in taking antitrust action against Microsoft, accusing the company of trying to corner the market in computer software. Although the case revealed that Microsoft made a 90 percent pretax profit on its Windows operating system and the Justice Department did convince a federal judge to order the division of Microsoft into two separate companies, the government's case did not rest on the price-fixing standard. Instead, government lawyers established a new basis for challenging monopolies—constraint of innovation or technological change.[7]

Correcting inequities in the marketplace is one of the most controversial types of regulation. Conservatives often argue that this type of regulation is unnecessary because they believe the free market is self-regulating. Unsafe or ineffective products will sooner or later end up unwanted; pizza eaters can stop buying pizza with artificial cheese; unions can protect workers from unreasonable demands of corporations. (But some oppose unions too, believing unions interfere with the free market for labor.)

Defenders of equity-based regulations point out that the market works too slowly in providing vital information. People have been killed and injured before infor-

Children working in a vegetable cannery. At the turn of the century, many young children worked twelve-hour days in unhealthy conditions. New Deal–era regulations outlawed most child labor, but abuse of child labor laws is increasing in some urban areas.
The Granger Collection, New York

mation about defective products became widely known. In the mid-1960s, many children were born with serious deformities because of the prescription drug thalidomide, which their mothers took during pregnancy. This incident caused Congress to set higher standards for drug safety and the Food and Drug Administration (FDA) to tighten its drug-testing rules. And before 1972, twenty million consumers were injured each year by unsafe products, and of those thirty thousand were killed and more than one hundred thousand permanently disabled. This prompted Congress to establish the Consumer Product Safety Commission (CPSC), an independent regulatory agency mandated to establish safety standards for consumer products.

Some people have a good deal of faith in "educating" the public about risks. They believe education campaigns, not regulation, are the best way to protect people. But education campaigns are not cheap, especially over a long period of time, and not always effective either. The government's campaign to educate the pubic about the health hazards of smoking has had a significant impact, but fifty million Americans still smoke, and the campaign has cost tens of millions of dollars.

Steve Kelley/Copley News Service

Congress does not regulate to remedy the effects of every inequity. Sometimes the costs are seen as greater than the gains; in other cases, resistance by politically powerful groups—the tobacco and telecommunications industries, for instance—is stronger than lobbying by potential beneficiaries of regulation.

Kinds of Regulation

There are several types of regulation:

1. *Requiring information.* Government may regulate by requiring that an employer, lender, or other entity provide certain kinds of information to employees or consumers. For example, credit card companies must provide cardholders with information about interest rates and how to appeal charges they think are not really theirs. Manufacturers of many food products must list ingredients on the label and give their nutritional content. This allows consumers to see whether their peppermint ice cream, for example, is colored with beet juice or red dye number 2, a potentially dangerous additive, and how many calories come from fat and sugar. This requirement is called **truth in labeling.** Manufacturers sometimes oppose labeling the contents of their goods because, as one said, "If you label, you're telling consumers there is something wrong with this product."[8]

The FDA also requires that when information *is* provided, it should be accurate. Many manufacturers have taken advantage of a new public awareness of the relationship between health and nutrition by labeling their products as "health" foods. The FDA has forced manufacturers to remove words such as "fresh" from processed juices and "no cholesterol" from food products that are high in vegetable fats that could contribute to heart disease. It is also demanding that manufacturers remove false claims that their products are "organic," "biodegradable," or in other ways "environmentally safe." Such consumer come-ons are called "green fraud."

2. *Licensing.* Government may regulate by requiring people to obtain licenses to practice certain trades, or professions, or to operate certain businesses. For example, the federal government licenses radio and television stations, and states license doctors, beauticians, dentists, and many others. This reassures clients and patients that those providing the services have met minimum qualifications for their professions. Licensing is also valuable for those receiving a license because it allows them to make money while keeping others out.

3. *Setting standards.* Manufacturers must meet certain standards for content, quality, environmental cleanliness, workplace safety, and employee wages

and working conditions. A product called chicken soup must have a minimum of chicken in it, and hot dogs cannot include more than a certain proportion of bone, hair, insects, and other extraneous material. The FDA requires manufacturers of condoms to test them for leaks and to destroy an entire batch of one thousand if more than four are defective. Failure to maintain the standards can result in fines or other legal penalties if convicted.

4. *Providing economic incentives.* Higher taxes may be imposed on goods or activities viewed as less beneficial than on those deemed more beneficial. Examples are a tax on cars that use fuel inefficiently or on an industry that emits toxic chemicals into the air. Some people, particularly conservatives, believe taxation is a better way to achieve regulatory goals than setting mandatory standards because it gives individuals or businesses an incentive to comply and the choice not to.

5. *Limiting liability.* Some regulations are designed to discourage legal actions against individuals or firms. Congress has passed laws limiting the ability of patients to sue their HMOs and the liability of nuclear power plants in case of a nuclear accident. In the latter case, taxpayers, not the industry, pick up the cost of claims above a certain amount.

The Regulatory Process

Many Americans blame federal bureaucrats when they are stymied by byzantine rules or endless paperwork to get government approval for some activity. But rule writing, implementation, and enforcement is a many-layered process, with at least five different aspects: passing the legislation that defines regulatory goals, writing rules to achieve those goals, overseeing the rule writers, implementing and enforcing the rules, and keeping pace with change after the standards are set and rules are written.

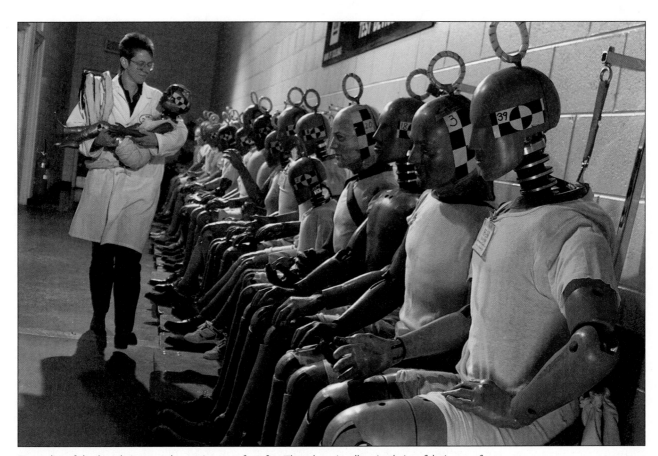

To save lives, federal regulations mandate testing autos for safety. These dummies allow simulation of the impact of crashes on humans. No doubt these crash test dummies were the inspiration for the rock group of the same name.
Brad Trent

Here we discuss rule writing, oversight, and implementation, leaving to the next section the discussion of reforming rules to keep pace with change.

Writing Regulations

Most regulatory activity stems from very general, even vaguely stated mandates because passing legislation, especially in a divided government, requires compromise. If bill writers were too specific, legislation would probably never get passed. When a bill is passed establishing some regulatory goal, such as driver safety, child labor, safe food, or clean air, its content rarely includes specifics on how the goals are to be achieved. Instead, as discussed in Chapter 12, after a bill becomes law it is up to executive branch specialists to write the rules necessary to achieve these goals. Because most regulations are implemented at the state level, federal regulators often work with their state counterparts in writing these rules.

Laws granting regulatory authority often require public input, so citizens and interest groups also get involved in rule writing. This has been true since the beginning of the twentieth century for areas of regulatory policy such as food safety and fair labor practices. But historically much of the public's input came from the interest groups and industries that would be affected by the rules being written. In fact, interest groups and industry lobbyists work so closely with regulators in writing rules that there is always concern, as discussed in Chapter 12, that agencies can be "captured" by those they are supposed to be regulating. In the 1960s when the participation and procedural "revolutions" swept through government, Congress began placing more emphasis on citizen participation in rule writing. The Consumer Product Safety Act law even authorized nongovernmental groups and organizations to submit their own versions of rules to agencies.[9] This movement to democratize the process by providing more public hearings and extended periods for public comment on regulations had advocates among both pro- and antiregulatory groups in Congress. On the one hand, it was a way to open up the process and make it more accountable, but it was also a way of slowing down the issuance of new rules by allowing many opportunities for rule opponents to impede the process. Where citizens see an immediate impact of rules, such as those on handling toxic waste in their communities, ensuring clean drinking water, defining safe foods, or placing restrictions on the use of public lands, a surprising number of people attend hearings or submit written comments. Using the Web sites of regulatory agencies to solicit comments has also greatly increased the public's role in writing rules.

No matter how many individuals and groups get involved in the process, writing effective regulations requires guidelines beyond the policies and goals stated in the authorizing legislation.

One of the standards by which the effectiveness of any regulation is judged is whether it results in a net benefit for society. It is easy for both the average citizen and the bureaucrat to see that it is not cost-effective to enforce a rule requiring all workplace toilet seats to be horseshoe shaped. No one fought to prevent the rule's abolition. But in most cases it is far more difficult to decide if a rule has more negative than positive effects. How do we decide whether the risk involved in using a particular chemical or product, or working in a hazardous environment is great enough to regulate? There is no agreement on this.

In authorizing new regulations, Congress uses different standards of risk. One is the "no-risk" standard: if a substance is found to cause cancer, it cannot be used—even in amounts well below the danger level. Sometimes called the better-safe-than-sorry rule, it is often applied to regulations on food and drug safety.

In other cases the "margin of safety" criterion is used. The regulatory agency establishes a reasonable standard and then allows an extra margin of safety. For example, standards for clean air mandate the Environmental Protection Agency to declare how much lead, sulfur, and other materials can be in the air before it is unsafe. Then the agency is supposed to set the standards a little higher to allow the extra margin of safety.[10]

Sometimes Congress mandates a standard whereby cost of the regulation is to be weighed against the risk. The process of making this evaluation is called **cost-benefit analysis.** Many consumer product safety regulations apply this risk standard. A product is not to be regulated unless the benefits outweigh the costs. Generally, proregulation groups prefer the no-risk or extra margin standards, while antiregulation forces prefer cost-benefit analysis.

Deciding which standard to apply and assigning values to these standards inevitably involve both science and politics. For example, critics of cost-benefit analyses have charged that these analyses are not done fairly or competently.[11] They believe that costs are concrete and easily calculated, while benefits are often more difficult to put in dollar terms. How do you quantify saving human lives? If a particular rule is likely to save five lives per year at a cost of $5 million, does the regulation offer a net cost or a net benefit? It ultimately depends on a value judgment, which, critics charge, can be obscured by a cost-accountant mentality (see Table 1).

Table 1	How Much Is a Saved Life Worth?	

Here are estimates of the value of life that are built into some government regulations. Figures do not include benefits of the regulations, other than lives saved, such as prevention of property damage and injuries that do not result in death.

		Estimated Cost of Regulation Per Life Saved
Automobiles	Reduce lead content of gasoline from 1.1 to 0.1 grams per gallon	No net cost
	Child restraints in cars	$1.3 million
	Dual master cylinders for car brakes	$7.8 million
Ejection system	for the B-58 bomber	$22 million
Flashing lights	at railroad crossings	$730,000
Asbestos	Banned in brake linings	$230,000
	. . . in automatic transmission parts	$1.2 billion
Radiation	Safety standards for X-ray equipment	$400,000
	. . . for uranium mine tailings	$190 million

SOURCE: Harvard Center for Risk Analysis. Cited in Peter Passell, "How Much for a Life?" *New York Times*, January 29, 1995, p. F3.

For example, in its cost analyses, the Occupational Safety and Health Administration (OSHA) figures a human life is worth $2 million, the CPSC $1 million, and the FAA $650,000.[12] Thus, using the $1 million estimate, the CPSC told manufacturers of reclining chairs they need not fix a problem with the chairs that had resulted in several children being strangled unless fixing it cost less than 25¢ per chair. The CPSC's economists figured out that at more than 25¢ for each of forty million chairs manufactured, the cost of fixing the problem would be more than the lives of the children were worth.[13]

Once in final form, rules are published in the Code of Federal Regulations and updated each year. Divided into more than three hundred categories or titles, each representing a regulatory area, they total tens of thou-sands of pages; Title 40 alone—environmental protection rules—required twenty-four volumes by 1999. But rule writing is just the beginning of the process.

Regulatory Oversight

Rule writing is overseen primarily by Congress and the president. Federal courts also have a role when the legality of rules is challenged by an aggrieved party. Ultimately it is Congress that has the broadest powers of oversight because at the beginning of the process, it can influence the ways rules are written by the clarity of direction it writes into the enabling legislation. Congress can also amend the original law, change budget authorization for agencies, or attach riders to appropriations bills that effectively kill agency-written rules. And, until 1983, Congress had the legislative veto that allowed one or both houses of Congress, or sometimes even committees, to approve or kill rules.

The president has several ways to exercise oversight. Since the Carter administration, a principal means has been to issue executive orders that identify an overall rationale for rule writing that is in keeping with the political philosophy and goals of the administration. With Carter it was rational management and public participation; with Reagan and Bush, cost-benefit analysis, or, more specifically, eliminating rules whose implementation were costly to business. Clinton's executive orders stressed public participation and openness as well as cost-effectiveness.

Presidents also exercise oversight through their appointment powers since all agency heads are presidential appointees. Those on fixed-term appointments are not under the same pressure to follow presidential preferences as the head of the EPA, for example, but most have been preselected on the basis of policy agreement with the president. In addition, the Office of Management and Budget (OMB), which is the principal oversight agency for the executive branch and which must approve agency budget requests, is also headed by a presidential appointee.

The OMB authority to review agency rules derives from an executive order issued by President Reagan as part of his efforts in administrative deregulation. This innovation was designed to give the OMB the authority to identify and eliminate duplicate rules and to develop procedures for cost-benefit analyses.

Many argued that giving this power to the OMB would erode the independence of regulatory agencies. Regulations developed by agencies under formal rules and according to due process could be killed by the

Most Americans share the belief that the private sector can do many things better than government and have a general distaste for red tape and in-your-face government. But it was the federal government, not industry, that took the initiative on environmental protection and workplace health and safety. Federal regulations have resulted in a multitude of benefits for the American public. Workers are safer on the job, endangered species have been saved, large-scale reforestation has taken place, and recycling has become commonplace.

Although to some Americans there is no such thing as a good regulation, most would agree that the following federal regulations, many administered by state governments, are examples of "what government does right." The benefits have not come cheap, but all have been realized through regulatory activity.

Because of government regulations mandating unleaded and lower leaded gasoline, the lead content of the air has dramatically decreased. Fewer children have brain damage and fewer adults have high blood pressure from airborne lead.[1]

Crib safety standards have reduced infant crib deaths by 44 percent since 1974, and standards for fire-resistant children's sleepwear have reduced serious burns and deaths by 20 percent. A regulation requiring collapsible steering columns on cars and trucks is estimated to have saved twenty-six thousand lives over a twenty-five-year period.[2] Requiring baby seats in cars has saved thousands more.

Industrial accidents and deaths decreased because of OSHA's rules on workplace safety. In one two-year period, these rules prevented an estimated 350 deaths and saved $15 billion in lost time and employee compensation for accidents. In 1999 workplace injuries and illnesses fell to the lowest rate on record.[3]

In 1965 more than 50 percent of men and about 35 percent of women smoked; smoking is linked to one in seven deaths in the United States and costs billions in health care.[4] Restrictions on tobacco use and advertising, and an aggressive public education campaign, have helped reduce the number of Americans who smoke to about a quarter of the adult population.

FDA testing of over-the-counter and prescription drugs has saved an untold number of lives. Although the testing process lengthens the time it takes to get products on the market, American drugs have been safer than those produced in Europe where the regulatory process is less stringent. Of all the drugs removed from the market as unsafe between 1990 and 1992, only nine were U.S.-made and three involved criminal withholding of evidence of risk by the manufacturers.[5]

Despite the problems in regulating the environment, there have been significant successes. In 1972 the Great Lakes were near cesspools, and Lake Erie was in such a bad state that it caught on fire. Today, the Great Lakes and 60 percent of all rivers and lakes are safe for swimming and fishing and 89 percent of Americans have safe drinking water.[6] Toxic emissions into the air by industry are 50 percent

lower than in 1990, and smog has decreased by a third, even though more cars are being driven than ever before. Los Angeles has the cleanest air in the forty years air quality has been monitored; it had no smog alerts in 1999, compared to 122 in 1977.[7] While the Superfund program is cleaning up the worst toxic waste sites around the country, the EPA's Brownfields program is helping reclaim abandoned industrial and commercial sites in inner cities (brownfields) by providing tax incentives to private investors to clean them up and start new business. As dangerous waste sites are being reclaimed and neighborhoods made safer for children to play in, new industries and jobs are being brought into neglected urban areas.

If the federal government had not regulated these activities, who would have? Would it have been done better or cheaper?

1. David Bollier and Joan Claybrook, *Freedom from Harm* (Washington, D.C.: Public Citizen and Democracy Project, 1986).
2. *Lincoln Journal,* April 19, 1987, p. 7.
3. *Budget of the U.S. Government, Fiscal Year 2001.*
4. "Cigarette Makers Reach $368 Billion Accord to Curb Lawsuits and Curtail Marketing," *New York Times,* June 21, 1997, p. 8.
5. Peter H. Stone, "Ganging up on the FDA," *National Journal,* February 18, 1995, pp. 412–413.
6. Gregg Easterbrook, "Here Comes the Sun," *New Yorker,* April 10, 1995, pp. 39–40; Budget of the U.S. Government, Fiscal Year 2001, p. 86.
7. Easterbrook, "Here Comes the Sun," p. 39; "Hey! I Can See L.A.!" *New York Times,* April 26, 1998, Section 4, p. 2; Barbara Whitaker, "Los Angeles Loses Distinction: Worst Summer Smog Day," *New York Times,* September 5, 1999, p. 15.

They can lobby bureaucrats who write the rules mandated by legislation, agency heads responsible for implementation of rules, or members of congressional committees with oversight functions. Rules, and the way they are or are not enforced, can be appealed to the agencies issuing them, and in some cases challenged in federal courts. For powerful interest groups there are opportunities to pressure the White House on the appointment of agency heads and the content of specific rules.

Because regulation does incur costs as it bestows benefits, it is inevitable that those who sustain the costs will compete with those seeking benefits to influence the process of writing and implementing rules. All of this competition between pro- and antiregulation forces, between regulators and the regulated, and among the regulators themselves, slows implementation and enforcement of rules designed to achieve regulatory goals established by Congress. Effective implementation is also slowed by weak enforcement powers. Although agencies are authorized to assess penalties for noncompliance, these punishments are usually negligible. In the face of these obstacles it is amazing how much federal and state regulators have been able to achieve in protecting lives, safeguarding the environment, and promoting equity and competitiveness in the marketplace (see the "What Government Does Right" box).

Cycles of Regulation

Like other government activity, the push for government regulation comes in fits and starts. The first spurt came in the late 1800s, when a poor economy led to charges, especially by farmers, that the large corporations of the day were exploiting the public. In 1890 with the Sherman Antitrust Act, Congress prohibited firms

The Electreat, a device first sold in 1918, could (so its manufacturers claimed) cure everything from headaches to tonsillitis and get rid of dandruff as a bonus. It was the first device outlawed by the FDA.
O'Lindan Collection, FDA History Room

from conspiring to set prices or in other ways to restrain trade. It also declared monopolies illegal and established the Interstate Commerce Commission to regulate the railroads.

The next burst of regulatory activity came after the turn of the century, in the Progressive Era. Demands for consumer protection arose largely because industrialization and railroad transportation created national markets for goods formerly produced and consumed locally. In these new national markets, consumers had little recourse if the products they bought from distant companies were not safe or reliable. Consumer fraud became endemic. Business engaged in deceptive advertising, food products often contained harmful substances (Coca-Cola contained cocaine; formaldehyde was used to preserve milk), and popular patent medicine usually contained alcohol or addictive drugs, such as opium.[19] Reformers also pointed to unsafe and unsanitary conditions in the meat-packing industry. After the media and so-called muckrakers highlighted these scandals, Congress banned certain food additives, prohibited false claims about products, and gave the Department of Agriculture power to inspect meat sold in interstate commerce.

The New Deal era spurred further regulatory activity. After one hundred people died from an unsafe drug, Congress passed an act mandating that the FDA declare a drug safe before it could be marketed.

In the activist 1960s and 1970s, reformers were again influential in pressuring Congress to undertake new regulatory activity. New agencies were established to regulate consumer product safety (the CPSC), the environment (the EPA), and industrial safety (OSHA). The powers of older agencies, such as the Federal Trade Commission (FTC), were strengthened.

Deregulation

As long as there has been regulation, there have been demands for **deregulation**—that is, ending regulation in a particular area. Although deregulation has had broad bipartisan support since the 1970s, some partisan differences in the nature of this support have been expressed. The Carter administration and Democrats in general tend to support deregulation to the extent that it makes business activity more efficient and less cumbersome. Many Republicans have gone further by opposing in principle some kinds of regulation as interference with market competition.

Deregulation can be carried out legislatively, that is, by act of Congress, or administratively, by executive orders, new appointments, and the oversight function of the

I've deregulated Arthur, but he still doesn't run very efficiently."

OMB. The Carter administration relied mainly on legislation. Reagan, the president most ideologically committed to deregulation, tried to enact many of his reforms through administrative action. One method was to strip regulatory agencies of personnel and budgets. Agency budgets decreased 8 percent during Reagan's first term, with some agencies taking much larger cuts. On the whole, agencies regulating consumer and environmental interests were hardest hit; those regulating health and safety were cut less.[20] Not until 1988 did regulatory agencies recover to the level of funding they had in 1980.

Another deregulation technique used by President Reagan was to appoint people to regulatory posts who favored either little regulation or self-regulation by industry. This meant that the number of regulations proposed and enacted decreased, and enforcement slowed too.

Critics point out that these attacks on regulation made worse the very problems that antiregulation forces complain about: understaffed agencies meant longer delays, larger backlogs, and inadequately researched decisions.

Types of Deregulation

Legislative and administrative deregulators may cast a narrow net, targeting individual rules, industries, or specific agencies, or a broad net, targeting the entire regulatory apparatus.

Eliminating Rules Both Presidents Carter and Reagan promoted regulatory reform through the elimina-

tion of unnecessary rules. During the Carter administration, OSHA abolished more than 1,100 of its 10,000 rules; many, such as the horseshoe-shaped toilet seat rule, had been severely criticized as nitpicking. OSHA paperwork requirements, particularly for small businesses, were reduced, and safety inspections were concentrated on the industries with the worst safety records. The Reagan administration continued this pattern.

But at the outset of the Clinton administration, federal statutes and formal rules still totaled about one hundred million words. OSHA's remaining four thousand major regulations specified "everything from the height of railings to how much a plank can stick out from a temporary scaffold," although most of its one hundred and forty regulations on wooden ladders were eliminated.[21] It is easy to see why rule elimination is a logical target for a deregulator; it is not only costly and inefficient to monitor and enforce rules on the grain of wood in ladders, it is also impossible. In 1994, there were only two thousand safety inspectors to cover six million workplaces. OSHA administrators estimated that if meeting every rule was the measure of compliance, then about 80 percent of all workplaces would be in violation of the law.[22] There are two ways to look at this situation: either OSHA does not have enough inspectors to ensure compliance, or many rules still exist whose enforcement Congress does not see as crucial to worker safety.

Deregulating by Industry Many proponents of deregulation argue that it is not enough to streamline, eliminate the more trivial rules, and make regulators more accountable; in some areas regulators simply should not be regulating at all.

The Carter administration, which was primarily committed to rule elimination, also moved to deregulate entire industries, beginning with trucking and the airlines. The advantage to industry of less regulation is transparent, but it is also meant to benefit consumers by providing greater choice and lower prices and fares due to increased competition and greater efficiency in the marketplace. Not everyone agrees that these goals have been achieved by wholesale deregulation of industries. Here we look at the example of airline deregulation.

Before 1978, commercial airlines were heavily regulated. Under a 1938 law, an airline had to gain the approval of the Civil Aeronautics Board (CAB) to fly any particular route and to set its fares. Originally, this procedure was designed to help the struggling airline industry by protecting it from competition.

In the years after the 1938 law was passed, the airline industry grew in size and economic strength. By the mid-1970s, the oil crisis had caused fares to skyrocket and put many airlines in economic difficulties. Many felt that the time was right for deregulation although the airlines were wary. Forty years of federal rule making protected existing carriers by making it almost impossible for new airlines to enter the industry.

One reason for deregulation was to make the industry more competitive. By opening up competition among the airlines, proponents of deregulation hoped the airlines would seek ways to become more efficient and then lower fares. In 1978, President Carter signed a bill phasing in deregulation. Airlines were allowed to fly new routes without CAB approval and were permitted flexibility in setting their fares. However, airlines serving certain routes between small communities were given subsidies to ensure that these communities would be served for at least ten years. The CAB itself was abolished, and regulation of airlines was left to the Federal Aviation Administration (FAA), which oversees safety matters.

At first deregulation increased competition. The number of airlines nearly tripled between 1978 and 1983. But in the following decade, many airlines folded or were bought out by larger carriers. By 1990, the eight largest airlines controlled about 90 percent of all commercial air travel in the United States. Even so, in the first five years of the 1990s, the industry lost almost $13 billion before beginning to show modest profits in 1996.

In the economic recovery of the late 1990s, airlines' business boomed, but their profit margins remained below those of other major industries. To cut costs, airlines began forming strategic alliances; Continental and Northwest, Delta and United, and American and US Airways proposed forming alliances with their major international competitors that, if consolidated, could give them control over 82 percent of domestic air travel. Although national security policies prohibit U.S. carriers from merging with foreign airlines, these "proxy mergers" allow them to share flight codes, coordinate schedules and baggage handling, and honor one another's frequent flyer programs.[23] The major carriers also plan further domestic consolidation, with United Airlines bidding for US Airways, the country's sixth largest carrier. If approved, United would carry about 25 percent of the country's air passengers.[24]

Competition has been further diminished because the airlines have divided up the nation into regional turfs. In ten major cities, two-thirds of the air traffic is controlled by one airline, such as TWA in St. Louis and Northwest in Minneapolis and Detroit. Even in huge airports such as Chicago and Atlanta, two airlines, United and American, control three-fourths of the traffic. A 1999 Government Accounting Office study showed that at concentrated or "fortress" hubs, the fares of the dominant airlines were consistently higher than the fares at other airports, costing travelers $1 billion annually.[25]

Domination by the major carriers contributes to congestion at major airports. These carriers have special twenty- to thirty-year leasing arrangements with large airports where they control much of the traffic. At over half of the largest airports, these long-term leases give a single airline a veto over airport expansion. Thus, the dominant airline can stop an expansion project that would provide new gates for potential competitors.[26] Denver's International is the first new airport to have been built since 1976.

The busiest airports have been plagued by flight delays, with July 2000 the worst month on record. At these airports the daily number of allowable landings and takeoffs is set by the federal government. Prior to 1986, the Department of Transportation allocated those slots among all carriers, but since then, carriers have been allowed to buy, sell, lease, or trade their landing and takeoff slots. The rule change has increased the major carriers' control of airport slots from 78 to 98 percent.[27]

While travelers do have more flights to choose from, planes are more crowded, flying at 70 to 80 percent of capacity compared to 50 percent in the decade before deregulation. Passenger complaints and lost baggage claims have skyrocketed. Even though average airfares have dropped 36 percent since deregulation, passengers now have to contend with a byzantine system for setting fares. On one 1997 United Airlines domestic flight, twenty-nine passengers with identical coach accommodations paid twenty-three different fares, ranging from $87 to $728.[28]

Still, the average urban traveler is better off than residents of small and midsize cities who have been left with a single carrier and monopoly prices. While deregulation has been called "an unmitigated disaster for rural areas," it has not been especially good for business travel, either; fares are 50 percent higher than in 1996.[29]

In the struggle to be competitive and profitable, some airlines may have shortchanged passenger safety. Due to the higher volume of air traffic, jets built in the 1960s have been kept in service beyond their planned life span, and today American carriers have the oldest jet fleet in service in the industrialized world.[30] In addition, the number of experienced mechanics available to service them has declined. According to government reports, Valujet had an accident rate fourteen times higher than that of the major airlines before its

Copyright 1987, *Boston Globe*. Distributed by Los Angeles Times Syndicate. Reprinted by permission.

poor safety record put it out of business.[31] The former inspector general of the Department of Transportation was so alarmed by the FAA's failure to enforce air safety regulations that she resigned and wrote a book about it.[32]

President Reagan may have contributed to safety problems by getting rid of thousands of experienced air traffic controllers (whose job it is to monitor air traffic and communicate with pilots, telling them when it is safe to take off and land and what traffic pattern they must follow). In 1981, to break their strike, he fired about two-thirds of the nation's sixteen-thousand air controllers. While passenger volume has more than doubled, with twenty thousand flights carrying two million passengers a day, the FAA employs about the same number of air traffic controllers today as it did in 1981.[33] However, the FAA has under way a $13 billion software and hardware upgrade for the air traffic control system and major expansions for busy airports such as Chicago's O'Hare. In 1997, in response to the increasing number of accidents and incidents (near-misses, for example), the government ordered the nation's air traffic controllers to take refresher courses.[34] But with the exception of 1996 (the deadliest year since 1985), air traffic fatalities have fallen so dramatically that today the only safer mode of transportation is a city bus.[35]

When deregulation of the airline industry was approved, the government thought it was encouraging more competition, greater efficiency, and lower fares. But in spring 1999, fed up with growing consolidation in the industry, an explosion of consumer complaints, and heavy lobbying by business travelers for price relief,

Congress introduced thirteen passenger bills of rights. After airlines executives promised to adopt their own bill of rights, Congress tabled legislation and gave the airlines a year to show improvement.[36]

Reregulation

In politics as in physics, actions usually produce reactions. Actions to deregulate bring cries for some **reregulation,** a resumption of regulatory activity. Airline deregulation is an example of this cycle of action and reaction. Many in Congress believe the airlines have failed in their promise to reform themselves and are ready to open debate on reregulation. If the country were to be reduced to three mega-airlines, all the consumer benefits of deregulation could disappear. "With only three carriers, we'd have to treat them as a utility," one member of Congress said. "Nobody wants to talk about the nasty-R word, but the reality is it may have to happen."[37]

Banking provides a good example of how industry deregulation that began in the Reagan administration led to reregulation in the Bush years.[38] Traditionally, banks and savings and loan (S&L) institutions were heavily regulated and protected from competition. But during the 1970s and early 1980s, interest rates rose rapidly, and banks and S&Ls competed fiercely to retain their depositors and attract new ones. They were also in competition with the federal government for investors' money as interest rates on treasury notes continued to rise. In the bipartisan deregulatory mood of the time Congress adopted a series of measures, beginning in 1980, to deregulate many aspects of the banking industry. To help S&Ls be more competitive, the cap was lifted on the interest they could pay depositors; at the same time Congress raised the maximum level of federal deposit insurance allowable on each account. Both banks and S&Ls were given more freedom to decide what financial services to offer. Within days, interest was being paid on checking accounts; credit card companies raised their interest rates; brokerage, insurance firms, and even department stores got into the banking business; and S&Ls offered a new range of services and made new types of investments formerly prohibited.

With the cap removed on interest rates, some S&Ls attracted new depositors by paying interest rates that were more than double the interest rates their mortgage holders were paying. With these policies it was only a matter of time before the S&Ls would go broke, unless they made windfall profits from their investments. As a result, many S&Ls, big and small, made increasingly risky

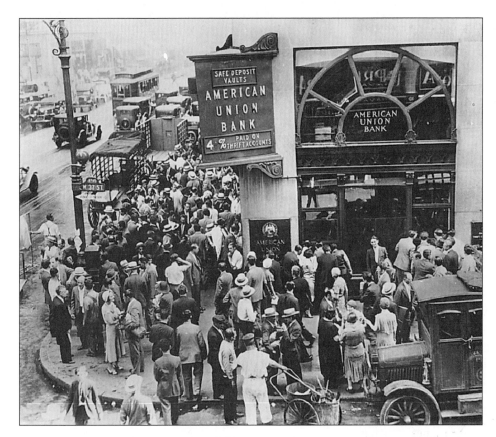

The bank failures of the 1930s, which wiped out the life savings of ordinary and wealthy citizens alike, led the government to provide insurance for depositors at banks and savings and loans. This program meant that the taxpayers in general, and not individual depositors, paid the bill when reckless and sometimes illegal actions of banks and savings and loans caused a new round of failures after deregulation in the 1970s.
Paula Nelson/Dallas Morning News

investments to survive and profit in the now highly competitive atmosphere. Banks, too, made high-risk loans to foreign governments and domestic farmers, while some S&Ls made shaky real estate investments, then saw the bottom drop out of their investments when real estate prices plummeted.

During this period, federal scrutiny of bank and S&L activities fell off drastically, even though the government, through its deposit insurance program, guaranteed each deposit (of up to $100,000) that the banks and S&Ls used for their risky investments. Charles E. Schumer (D-N.Y.) has said the government "behaved like a fire insurance company that said to its customers: 'Go ahead, play with matches. We'll cover you if anything goes wrong.'"

The Federal Home Loan Bank Board, which regulates S&Ls, was repeatedly denied its requests for more examiners and auditors. In the last half of the 1980s, one thousand banks failed, including the nation's eighth largest, Continental Illinois. Thanks to the federal deposit insurance program, few individuals lost their savings, but it took an additional $4 billion loan from the government to restore Continental Illinois to solvency.

The S&L crisis proved much more costly; 27 percent of all thrifts failed. Covering the losses, the federal insur-ance company for S&Ls, the Federal Savings and Loan Insurance Corporation (FSLIC), went broke. As a consequence, the Federal Deposit Insurance Corporation (FDIC), the institution that insures bank deposits, took control of more than two hundred S&Ls, trying to put them on a sounder financial base. By 1996, more than $132 billion of taxpayer money had been committed to the bailout.

In short, deregulation in the financial industry led to disaster. Proponents of deregulation argue that a truly free market would be more efficient because consistently bad business decisions would bring failure without benefit of a taxpayer rescue. But in the case of Continental Illinois and the hundreds of insolvent S&Ls, the government believed the nation could not afford to let them go under. Huge banks defaulting and millions of people losing their savings would send shock waves throughout the nation, so the federal government stepped in to save them. Thus, critics of banking deregulation argue that since banks have the luxury of Uncle Sam's pocketbook when things go wrong, they should be forced by Uncle Sam to conduct themselves in a prudent manner. The S&L bailout reflected this view by imposing tougher new regulations that S&Ls must now meet.

Deregulation: Here We Go Again

At the end of the Bush administration, as the country faced huge budget and trade deficits and an economy that was barely growing, most officials were looking for ways to cut spending and encourage economic growth. In this atmosphere there was near unanimous support for reducing the regulatory burden on both private and public entities to see whether it would help speed the economic recovery. During the long period of economic expansion that followed, sentiment for deregulation did not decrease but continued to gain momentum.

At least four factors contributed to the deregulatory zeal of the past eight years. The first stems from the general policy approach of the Clinton administration, which was to find the middle ground in every policy dispute. Although Clinton favored health-based regulations, he opposed overconcentration of rule making in the federal government and was sympathetic to the complaints of both business and state government about the cost of implementing regulations.

A second factor was the divided government of the 1990s and the strong deregulatory policy of the Republican leadership that took control of both houses of Congress in 1995. Rather than trying to repeal existing regulation, the Republicans' approach was to suggest replacing existing health-based regulatory standards with "risk assessment." This is a more stringent calculation of cost against benefits based on rigid standards of scientific proof that a particular product or act being regulated is harmful to the public.

Republicans also wanted to open the process of rule writing even further to peer and judicial review, processes that could kill proposed regulations by tying them up in administrative and court challenges.

Critics called it a paralysis approach to deregulation: "Its cleverness lies not in streamlining the regulatory process but in adding 31 new steps, two additional years of review, and $700,000 in additional cost to every rule issued by the [EPA] and other federal agencies. . . . In case that doesn't work, [the bill] also creates 267 new opportunities to sue at every step of agency rule-making." The process was likened to injecting Arnold Schwarzenegger with steroids, "in hopes he soon will be so muscle-bound he can't move at all."[39]

A third factor sustaining deregulatory momentum has been structural change in the global economy. Advances in transportation and telecommunications have changed the "balance between government and international markets" and the terms of business competition.[40] Global competition for market share has allowed business, including the heavily regulated banking and utilities industries, to argue that to have the freedom to reorganize on a scale necessary to maintain competitiveness in international markets, they must be deregulated. This argument found broad bipartisan support in Congress and the Clinton administration.

In 1999, for example, Congress essentially dismantled the Glass-Steagall Act that had separated the banking, insurance, and securities industries since the Great Depression. Commercial banks, already the second most profitable of all industries, are now free to engage in securities trading and to handle the title insurance of your new home as well as to give you a home mortgage and handle your checking account. Congress has even sanctioned the creation of banks for large depositors where accounts will not be protected by deposit insurance.

Within the new bigger-companies-for-bigger-markets rationale, the number of mergers has mushroomed, with only token opposition from Justice's antitrust division or from the FTC, even though they have included the twenty largest mergers in U.S. history.[41] Warner-Lambert and Pfizer, two of the country's largest pharmaceuticals, merged; the Seven Sister oil companies became five (the merger of Exxon and Mobil was the largest industrial merger in history); and the seven Baby Bells became four. Proposed mergers would reduce major airlines to three; give five cable companies control of forty of fifty-nine cable networks; and, if the Worldcom-Sprint merger—which the government has challenged—wins approval, reduce long-distance providers to two.[42] The freight and shipping industries have also undergone similar consolidations.

While the number of merger proposals more than tripled between 1991 and 1999, staff size at the FTC, decimated during the Reagan years, grew by only several dozen and has yet to catch up to where it was in 1980. To cut the caseload Congress, with the support of FTC and Justice, may exempt mergers of smaller companies from regulatory review. Many in government see the current wave of mergers as inevitable, necessitated by global competition. One antitrust expert said there is no going back to the Brandeis ideal of human-sized institutions because of the price we would pay in efficiency, technological innovation, and global competitiveness. "The trick is to take account of the modern needs for efficiency but still use antitrust to give us workably competitive markets."[43] But critics of "merger mania" believe too little thought has been given to its consequences—namely, that the greater the assets companies acquire through mergers, the more resources they have to buy still other companies. One member of Congress has warned that the "explosion in capitalization means that some companies have [a] capacity for acquisition that is unimaginable. . . . We've got to have the [antitrust] resources that prevent this society from turning from a capitalist society into an oligarchy."[44]

A fourth stimulus to deregulation is the power of large corporations in the political process. Through their key role in campaign finance for candidates of both major parties (see Chapter 9), they are guaranteed at least a symbolic hearing of their arguments for deregulation.

Keeping Pace with Change

A former EPA director once said that the EPA's mission is like trying to give someone an appendectomy while the person is running the hundred-yard dash.[45] The agency is always shooting at a moving target: just as regulators establish rules for dealing with a pollutant, research reveals new dimensions to the problem or identifies other toxins from new sources.

Today many other regulators must share this sentiment as rapid advances in technology over the past decade have challenged government's regulatory powers. One of the most difficult issues has emerged from advances in biotechnology: Should government or the marketplace decide whether science should engineer, and business market, human life?

Some argue that cloning, for example, could save thousands of lives by providing healthy tissue, bone mar-

row, or organs needed by people with illnesses that require grafts or transplants from a genetically matched person. Some make a straightforward argument for genetic engineering; they see nothing wrong with procedures that could eliminate the risk of disabling diseases or birth deformities in unborn children. Cloning might also allow infertile couples to have children. In fact, some see cloning as a reproductive freedom issue, and just as they do not want government to regulate whether a woman can terminate a pregnancy, they do not believe government should prevent the cloning of offspring.

Typically, government regulates to promote public health and safety and equal access in the marketplace. To what standard does it look to determine whether cloning is good or bad for the public, and what is the legal basis for this regulatory authority? Should the decisions be made by committees of scientists, doctors, clergy, and ethicists? If so, who would choose the committee members, and how would they be accountable to the public?

Consumer concern about the safety of genetically engineered foods has also brought demands for new regulation. Lawsuits have been filed against the federal government and biotech companies demanding that the foods grown from genetically altered seeds (called "frankenfoods" by their critics) be more carefully studied before being declared safe. In some cases, opponents have demanded the removal of food already on the market. While the FDA insists that genetically altered foods

New scientific developments that affect ecological balances prompt calls for regulation, in this case of genetically altered food.
AP/Wide World Photos

are safe, it has written new rules requiring manufacturers to inform the FDA of their intent to market such products and has drawn up guidelines for those who want to label contents voluntarily. But food safety is not the only issue. About half the soybeans and a third of the corn planted in the United States are grown from genetically altered seed stocks, creating the potential for emergence of pesticide-resistant insects.[46] In this area, too, government has begun to act, ordering farmers to grow at least 20 percent of their corn and soybeans from nongenetically altered seed.

Communications technology is another area where changes are occurring more rapidly than regulators can keep pace. In 2000 42 percent of Americans had access to the Internet, and online commerce was booming. Many of its supporters see the Internet as the model of a free market, open to all and completely unregulated, and they believe it should stay that way. Supporters of government oversight say an unregulated Internet has resulted in consumer and credit card fraud, illegal online securities trading, criminal solicitation, access of children to pornography, and public dissemination of personal credit and medical histories and other invasions of personal privacy. Congress has yet to adopt measures to regulate in most of these areas, but more than seventy-five bills dealing with issues of privacy, access, and content on the Internet were under consideration in 2000.[47]

Advocates of greater government oversight believe that excitement over the development of e-commerce, the new ease in rapid global communication, and the emergence of global markets have contributed to the "general ideological drift toward greater respect for the market [and] unwarranted deregulatory zeal."[48] Regulating high tech requires scientific study and time for assessment and also that members of Congress familiarize themselves with the intricacies of a multitude of new technologies and their applications before they write legislation. But changes are occurring with such rapidity it seems impossible that government regulation will be able to keep pace with their application in the market.

Regulatory Politics and Environmental Protection

Government action to safeguard public health through protection of the environment has had more bipartisan legislative, and broader public, support than almost any area of regulation. For a quarter-century, the importance of this type of regulatory activity has been proclaimed by leaders from Richard Nixon—who called a clean environment the "birthright" of every American—to Al Gore, who wrote a best-selling book based on the notion that safeguarding the environment should be "the central organizing principle for civilization."[49]

A majority of the public supports spending for environmental protection, even when agreeing with the statement that government should regulate less. For example, a 1995 poll in which a majority of respondents agreed that "government regulation of business usually does more harm than good" showed 78 percent of the same respondents also agreeing with the statement that "this country should do whatever it takes to protect the environment."[50] In 1999 more than two-thirds of Americans surveyed were still worried a "great deal" about safe drinking water, toxic waste contamination, pollution of rivers, lakes and reservoirs, and air pollution.[51] Nevertheless, neither widespread support for regulatory activity nor its real achievements were able to prevent a strong backlash from developing against the environmental activism of federal agencies and interest groups. This is reflected in federal funding, which peaked in 1980, fell sharply during Reagan's deregulatory push, and has grown only by modest increments since (Figure 1).

Another sign of the backlash is that few new environmental proposals have become law since the Republicans gained control of Congress in 1995. There has been so much opposition in Congress to new initiatives on air quality and global warming that Clinton did not even submit an international agreement on global warming to the Senate for consideration. Moreover, Congress has tried to kill new White House and EPA initiatives on air and water quality and wilderness preservation by attaching riders to appropriations bills to cut off funding for implementation. Why, when there is so much bipartisan support for environmental protection, is there such strong opposition from a minority?

The crucial question in the debate over government's role can be stated simply, but it cannot be answered simply. How can we define standards that protect society's interest in having a clean and healthy environment and at the same time not unreasonably handicap business and individual producers of pollution? Historical and current debates over environmental policy revolve around this issue.

In this section we use the example of environmental protection to illustrate how legislators, regulators, and interest groups have contributed to the politicization of the regulatory process.

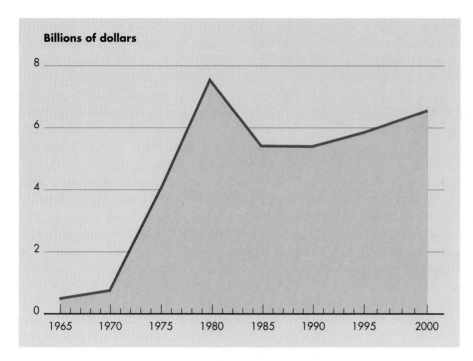

Billions of dollars

FIGURE 1 ■ *Spending for Environmental Protection in the Regulatory-Deregulatory Cycle* From almost nothing, federal spending for environmental protection rose dramatically after 1973 as Congress passed legislation to control air, water, and hazardous waste pollution. Deregulation brought a sharp drop in spending during Reagan's first term (1981–1985), but after that spending grew slowly until 1996, when the Republican leadership called for cutting the EPA's budget by one-third. Although that effort failed, spending for environmental protection has never returned to its 1980 peak level. (Amounts shown are in 1992 constant dollars.)

SOURCE: Budget of the United States 1999, Historical Tables, Table 3.2.

Evolution of Government's Role

Eighteenth-century Americans did not worry about harming the environment. The continent, largely unsettled, was graced with resources that seemed almost infinite: "A fertile, widespreading country . . . blessed with a variety of soils . . . and watered . . . with innumerable streams, for the delight and accommodation of its inhabitants."[52]

The Constitution contains no hint of concern about preserving and protecting the environment. Indeed, the Founders' and our own orientation to the environment is rooted in the Western, Judeo-Christian tradition that the physical world exists to serve human needs.[53] This sentiment was reinforced during the eighteenth-century period known as the Enlightenment, which led people to believe that through science and learning, we could conquer almost any obstacle to human progress.[54] The possible negative consequences of science and technology for the environment were a long way away.

But in the nineteenth century, concern grew about the effect that the industrial revolution, coupled with rapid population growth, might have on the environment. Late in that century, a conservationist movement to preserve some of the natural environment from farmers and loggers who were clearing the land resulted in the creation of the national forests and a national park system.[55]

Along with concern about saving some forests and other areas of scenic beauty came an awareness of pollu-

tion. The first effort to combat water pollution was an 1899 law requiring that individuals dumping waste into navigable waters get a permit from the Army Corps of Engineers. In 1924, Congress banned oceangoing ships from dumping oil in coastal waters. Neither of these acts was enforced very well, but the legislation did indicate an embryonic concern with pollution.

The modern environmental movement probably stems from a book, *Silent Spring,* published in 1962 by Rachel Carson. Carson showed that pesticides used in agriculture find their way into the air and water and harm crops, animals, and people. Moreover, she demonstrated that scientists and engineers did not know the extent of these harmful effects, nor did they seem particularly concerned. The chemical industry immediately attacked Carson, accusing her of hysteria and misstatement of facts. The industry's attacks created widespread publicity for her views and raised the environmental consciousness of millions of Americans.

The decade and a half following the publicity over Carson's book was characterized by a burst of new regulatory activity. Beginning in 1964 and continuing through 1977, Congress passed a series of laws designed to protect the air and water from pollution and to deal with hazardous waste.

Public concern peaked too. Huge oil spills, rivers catching fire, and the growing impact of the automobile on air quality lent substance to these concerns. By 1970, opinion polls showed that the most frequently cited public problem was protecting the environment, surprising in light of the continuing protest against the Vietnam War.[56] In April 1970, Earth Day was inaugurated, and hundreds of thousands of citizens across the nation demonstrated to show their concern about the environment. Every year since, one day in April has been set aside to celebrate the planet's resources and to heighten environmental awareness.

In 1970, Congress gave citizens a more formal way to affect environmental policy. New legislation, the National Environmental Policy Act, mandated government agencies to prepare **environmental impact statements** for internal projects or projects they fund. These analyses were to detail the effect, including any negative consequences, a project or other activity would have on the environment. No new buildings, dams, sewers, pipelines, or highways were to be built, nor any research or other government projects initiated, until this statement had been filed.

Not only did the law give federal agencies the power to comment on each other's environmental impact statements, but it also gave citizens access. Early environmental legislation was the first to incorporate the 1960s ethic of public involvement and "full disclosure of the information on which government bases its decisions."[57] These provisions became an important device for organizations interested in protecting the environment, giving them real opportunity to influence environmental policies. Within a few years, more than four hundred legal suits were filed to force the government

to comply with the act's provisions; by 1980, thousands had been filed.[58] Strictly enforced by the courts, the act affected the activities of dozens of federal agencies.

Another landmark move marking the growing federal involvement in environmental protection was the 1970 creation of the **Environmental Protection Agency (EPA)** by President Nixon.[59] Recognizing that responsibilities for pollution control were spread throughout the executive branch, Nixon, with congressional approval, brought them together in one regulatory agency with a single head who reported to the president.

During the EPA's first years, three foundational pieces of environmental protection legislation were passed by Congress: the Clean Air Act (1970), the Clean Water Act (1972), and the Endangered Species Act (1973). During the 1970s, the EPA received extensive new mandates to regulate hazardous waste, pesticides, and noise pollution. Today, under the watch of seventy congressional committees and subcommittees, the EPA administers sixteen major environmental statutes and more than ten thousand pages of regulations.[60]

Implementing Environmental Regulations

Passing laws is one thing, enforcing them another. Congress mandated the EPA to achieve certain goals, but the EPA had to write the rules for reaching them and then monitor their implementation by the states. For example, under the Clean Air Act the EPA was ordered to establish air quality standards for major pollutants, a task the EPA estimated would require writing three hundred to four hundred rules. States were mandated to draw up plans that would bring local air quality into compliance with these new federal standards. In keeping with the commitment to public involvement in the regulatory process, the Clean Air Act also permitted citizens to sue to enforce its provisions.[61] Of course, the industries and public utilities subject to the new rules also had the right to challenge them. Because the process is vulnerable at all stages to influence by affected parties, enforcing air quality standards for industries has been difficult.

Auto manufacturers, which had to reduce auto emissions or face fines, immediately asked for more time to reduce emissions, claiming they could not meet the standards. After the price hike in oil in 1973 brought financial difficulties to auto manufacturers in the mid-1970s, several extensions were granted. However, it became apparent that, counter to U.S. auto manufacturers'

An Earth Day celebrant illustrating a possible future scenario if air pollution is not curbed.
AP/Wide World Photos

claims, the standards *were* technologically feasible since foreign manufacturers were able to meet them. Consequently, by the end of the 1970s, the standards had been restored, only to be partly rolled back during Reagan's deregulation campaign.

Though in theory the EPA can have a noncomplying company closed down, this is simply not politically feasible or particularly wise. Generally, the agency is reluctant to enforce standards against large companies with political clout or small profit margins, especially industries crucial to the nation's economic health. To take action against a large industry requires significant political will all the way to the White House. That kind of commitment has not been evident.

The standards approach to rule writing provides few incentives for industry to comply. Penalties are often not assessed, and when they are, the fines are usually far less than the cost of complying with the standards. Also, the practice of specifying methods of compliance for entire industries does not make sense in every instance; a company might achieve compliance more cheaply using methods other than those the regulation specifies.

To deal with these objections, the Carter administration adopted the policy of allowing compliance in some industries to be based on the **bubble concept.** This policy allows companies to meet an overall standard for emission of pollutants. Imagine that a bubble has been placed over a factory with ten smokestacks, each emitting pollutants. Under the old rules, each smokestack would have to meet EPA standards. Under the bubble concept, one or more smokestacks might exceed the limits on emissions as long as the total emissions within the bubble met the standard. Rather than bringing all ten smokestacks into compliance, the company might find it cheaper to install equipment on five smokestacks if doing so would reduce total emissions to the required level. The bubble concept permits flexibility in determining how the standard will be met and greatly reduces the cost of compliance to business.

A more flexible system allows for a multifactory bubble. The standard is set for a geographic area, and factories within that area are allowed to buy and sell pollution rights. For example, the EPA sets a limit on how much sulfur dioxide (the chemical that causes acid rain) can be emitted into the air in a particular area; then state environmental agencies sell permits to pollute. Each permit is good for one ton of emissions per year. Utility companies, which emit a great deal of sulfur dioxide, can then decide whether it is cheaper for them to buy and install scrubbers to reduce plant emissions or to buy permits that allow them to pollute the air. This approach allows industries some flexibility in meeting pollution standards, but if they do pollute, they must pay in advance.

The bubble concept was hardly a panacea, however. It still required the EPA to set standards for each particular type of pollutant. This process can take years for each pollutant; thus, of the 320 toxic chemicals released into the environment, the EPA set standards for only 7 in its first twenty years. Believing it would be impossible to set standards for each separate chemical, the EPA replaced the pollutant-by-pollutant approach with a more comprehensive industry-by-industry approach.[62] Now limits are set on all toxic emissions combined, and industries with emission levels below allowable limits earn credits that they can "bank" or sell to other industries whose emission levels are above the standard. This is called emissions trading.

Regulation of air quality is a good illustration of how industry and public responses to the implementation of rules can influence reassessment and revision. The goals of the original Clean Air Act have not been weakened; in fact, they have been strengthened by subsequent amendments and reauthorizing legislation. But the rules to reach those goals have been revised in ways that make them less cumbersome and more cost-effective to administer. The emissions trading approach has since been adopted by international environmental agencies as a means for achieving worldwide reductions in the emission of carbon dioxide and other gases linked to global warming, with nations, rather than U.S. states, buying and selling permits to pollute.

Water Quality

Before 1972, at least eighteen thousand communities regularly dumped their untreated raw sewage into rivers and lakes. Food, textile, paper, chemical, metal, and other industries discharged twenty-five trillion gallons of waste water each year.

These activities occurred despite federal attempts to improve water quality. A 1948 law authorized the federal government to give funds to local governments to build sewage treatment plants. Thousands of communities used the grants for this purpose, and the program was seen as a welcome pork barrel project as much as a regulatory one. In 1965, Congress mandated that states establish clean water standards in order to get these sewage treatment grants. But the law was not effective. States did not want to establish stringent quality standards because they were afraid industries would leave.

In 1972, the federal government tried again. It set as goals "fishable and swimmable" waters by 1983 and zero

Despite enforcement problems, federal regulation has resulted in cleaner water.
©Kevin Schafer/kevinshafer.com

discharges into water by 1985. Industries were to have permits to discharge wastes; they were to use the "best practicable" technology by 1977 and the "best available" technology by 1983 to make sure the pollutants discharged were the smallest amounts possible. The EPA set uniform national standards for discharge control for each type of industry so states did not have to compete to get industries or to keep them from moving away by setting the laxest standards.

It took years to implement water quality standards effectively for many of the same reasons that confounded air quality enforcement: rules not correctly written, inadequate monitoring, industry resistance, and foot dragging in Congress. A substantial number of industries and municipalities did not meet the standard of technology necessary to clean up waste.[63] Some sewage treatment facilities were built inadequately, and others were operated improperly because they lacked trained technicians. The EPA and state environmental agencies did not have the personnel to monitor carefully how lo-

cal governments spent their sewage grants. Local governments also resisted the standards set by the Clean Water Act because of the cost to municipal budgets. Most towns and cities, especially during the bad economic times of the 1970s, did not have the resources to pay for what was essentially an unfunded mandate.

Congress yielded to political pressure from local governments and industry. In 1977, it weakened some of the provisions of the 1972 act, and granted exemptions and extensions. Thus, polluters had reason to believe they need not comply with standards or deadlines because Congress would come to their rescue.

Congress also dragged its feet on enforcement of the 1974 Safe Drinking Water Act, waiting a dozen years before imposing a timetable on the EPA for issuing safety standards. Finally, in 1991, Congress did pass new and more stringent safety standards for tap water, requiring more frequent testing for lead levels in municipal water supplies, only to see them threatened by a new round of deregulation. But the problem in achieving the goals of clean water legislation were not all due to resistance to regulation and its costs. Part of the problem was with the rules themselves: when the first rules were written, not enough was known about the sources of water pollution to determine which sources to target first. Industries and municipal sewage plants account for only part of the water pollution problem. Other contributors were not being regulated. For example, what are called "nonpoint" sources (that is, discharges that do not come from a specific pipe) account for as much as half of all water pollution. Runoff of fertilizer from farmlands is a big source of nonpoint pollution and is difficult to control. So are the sewers connecting drains and grates in city streets. Storm sewers collect gas, oil, fertilizers, pesticides, animal excrement, and other unpleasant substances and then deposit them directly into the nearest waterway.

New rules being written to achieve clean water goals stress pollution from these nonpoint sources. For example, the EPA has told states that they have to develop plans for controlling pesticide runoff from farms and for limiting urban sprawl. This will create a new set of enforcement problems. Cracking down on farmers and construction firms or local land developers is much more difficult politically than attacking huge corporations that dump toxic waste in public waterways. In the Grain Belt states, local politicians may find it hard to tell cash-strapped family farmers that if they do not alter their use of pesticides (changes that could lower production) they may have to help pay for pesticide cleanup.

Despite all of these problems, today's drinking water is much safer than it was before the clean water laws were enacted, and 60 percent of all rivers and lakes are now safe for swimming and fishing.

Hazardous Waste

In the mid-1970s, residents living near Niagara Falls, New York, began to complain about pungent fumes, dead bushes and trees, holes opening in the ground, thick oils fouling their basement pumps, children and pets developing sores and blisters, and high rates of birth defects and miscarriages. Eventually, they realized they were living nearly on top of twenty-one thousand tons of dangerous chemicals dumped in the abandoned Love Canal more than two decades earlier. In the old days, people dumped wastes anywhere, without much thought for the hazards they might create. There was no clear understanding about whose responsibility it was to clean up the sites. After many months of negotiation, the canal was declared a disaster area, the state bought the residents' homes, and the residents were evacuated.[64] But who was responsible for the mess in Love Canal was still unclear.

In 1982, the EPA declared the town of Times Beach, Missouri, a hazardous area because of the dioxin that had been added to the paving mixture used to build the town's roads. A decade later none of the town's 2,200 inhabitants were suffering side effects of dioxin. The federal official who ordered the evacuation said it had been a mistake.
UPI/Corbis-Bettmann

The Love Canal incident occurred while the EPA was writing new regulations for handling hazardous waste. The rules require hazardous substances to be tracked from generation through disposal. This is called a manifest system or a **"cradle-to-grave"** procedure.[65] When toxic wastes are produced, treated, transported, or disposed of, the handlers must file a one-page form (a manifest) identifying the type and quantity of waste, where it was produced, who transported it, and to what storage or waste site it was shipped. Copies are filed with all participants in the process.

The Love Canal incident not only put the spotlight on the current regulations the EPA was writing to implement a 1976 law, it also revealed that the law had a large loophole: it only dealt with current waste sites, not long since abandoned ones like Love Canal.

In 1980, Congress attempted to remedy the problem with new legislation designed to find and clean up existing hazardous waste sites. The bill ordered owners of hazardous waste sites to report them and placed liability for cleaning up the sites with their owners, but it authorized the EPA to clean up leaking sites if the responsible parties could not be located. The bill also imposed a tax on industry to help pay for the cleanup. This revenue, along with federal funds for the cleanup, is referred to as the **Superfund.**

To carry out these laws, the EPA began to develop regulations for storage and treatment facilities for hazardous waste and for landfills. It also began to evaluate

While the EPA struggles to collect restitution from private businesses and industries for environmental cleanup, who will hold the nation's worst polluters—the Departments of Defense and Energy (DOD and DOE)—responsible for unsafe activities? The problems of accountability are even more formidable than for the private sector. The Department of Justice does not want to sue other federal agencies; the EPA can impose fines but has no power to collect them; and citizens' right to sue the federal government has been restricted where national security activities are at issue. Charges can be brought against the private industries that pollute while fulfilling DOD or DOE contracts, but they can claim they were just following orders from federal agencies. States left with huge toxic waste problems by weapons or energy plants have been told by the Supreme Court that they cannot collect civil penalties from a federal agency. How can government be made accountable for damage to the environment and the health of its citizens? Who will regulate the regulators?

Much of the government's polluting is tied to the development of nuclear weapons and nuclear power. These projects have already exacted enormous health costs. In the 1940s, when government engineers recruited Navajo men and boys living near Cove, Arizona, to mine the uranium necessary for new atomic weapons programs, no one mentioned the dangers of radon exposure. And no one warned the citizens of Nevada about radioactivity, even though the government exploded more than one thousand bombs in their state. Atomic Energy Commission documents refer to people living in the fallout area as "a

low-use segment of the population."[1] In one government study of how irradiated nutrients are metabolized (paid for by the Quaker Oats Company), boys in a state home were fed oatmeal laced with radioactive isotopes. In other experiments, terminal cancer patients were radiated to toxic levels; hospital patients were injected with plutonium, and at least two hundred thousand military personnel were exposed to radioactive materials to test consequences of exposure to atomic weapons and bomb blasts.

Not until the 1990s did Congress hold hearings on the "human radiation experiments" and appropriate money to compensate for injuries and deaths to uranium miners, participants in nuclear testing, and victims of radioactive fallout.[2] By that time Congress was also facing the massive cost of cleaning up toxic waste and other pollution at the nation's military bases and nuclear weapons plants.[3] Plants that built nuclear bombs focused on national security and gave little attention to safety procedures or to the effects their actions might have on surrounding communities. Leaking earthen pits were used as dumps for industrial chemicals and radioactive wastes. Sewage systems, some built when the plants opened, leaked pollutants into the ground. Inadequate or nonexistent air pollution control devices allowed toxic and sometimes radioactive emissions into the air. Other radioactive waste was discharged into streams and rivers.

The nuclear weapons plant in Hanford, Washington, knowingly released into the air massive amounts of radioactive materials, including iodine, for test purposes. Downwind, near Mesa, Wash-

ington, in an area known as the "death mile," 14 of 108 residents became ill with or died of cancer, and several children died or were born with disabilities.[4] Researchers from the Centers for Disease Control believe that twenty thousand children in eastern Washington may have been exposed to unhealthy levels of this iodine by drinking milk from cows grazing in contaminated pastures.[5]

In Fernald, Ohio, a red-and-white checkerboard design on a water tower and the name "Feed Materials Production Center" led some residents to believe a local firm produced animal feed. Instead it made uranium rods and components for warheads. Residents were stunned to find out that, for thirty-five years, the plant had dumped radioactive refuse into pits in the ground that regularly overflowed when it rained. The plant also discharged 167,000 pounds of wastes into a local river and released about twice that much into the air. Though these actions were taken by the private company that ran the plant, they were approved and even encouraged by the supposed regulators, the Atomic Energy Commission. As Senator John Glenn (D-Ohio) commented ironically, "We are poisoning our people in the name of national security."[6]

After federal courts ruled that the EPA has the authority to regulate waste disposal at federal weapons plants, the agency fined the DOE $300,000 for delays in implementing a cleanup plan for the Fernald plant. But it had no way to collect the fine, any more than it could force the DOE to carry through on plans to clean up the Hanford Nuclear Reservation. However, after receiving some bad press coverage, the DOE agreed to pay a much smaller fine and

unexploded artillery and mortar shells. The OMB estimates that by 2001 two-thirds of the "worst" toxic waste dumps will be cleaned up, but that would still leave hundreds more.[7] During the 1980s, these sites were labeled "national sacrifice zones," because they could not be returned to normal use without some danger to human life. A recent study commissioned by the DOE gave the term new meaning when it concluded that 109 of the 144 sites used for nuclear weapons development, including Hanford, cannot—for reasons of technology, money, and political will—be fully cleaned up and will remain polluted in perpetuity.[8] The bill for decades of carelessness and neglect has come due.

1. Carole Gallagher, *American Ground Zero: The Secret Nuclear War* (Cambridge, Mass.: MIT Press, 1993), p. xxiii.
2. Hearings on *The Human Radiation Experiments* (S.hrg. 103–1060; s.hrg. 104–588).
3. Cass Peterson, "A Monumental Cleanup Job," *Washington Post National Weekly Edition,* December 12–18, 1988, p. 11.
4. "Nuclear Danger and Deceit," *Newsweek,* October 31, 1988, pp. 20–30.
5. "They Lied to Us," *Time,* October 31, 1988, p. 64.
6. Ibid., p. 61.
7. *Budget of the U.S. Government, Fiscal Year 2001,* 82.
8. "Nuclear Sites May Be Toxic in Perpetuity, Report Finds," *New York Times,* August 8, 2000, p. A12. The study was carried out by the National Academy of Science.

OTHER SOURCES: John Hanrahan, "Testing Ground," *Common Cause,* January/February 1989; Mathew Wald, "When the Government Runs Afoul of Its Own Regulators," *New York Times,* March 10, 1991, p. E16; Keith Schneider, "A Valley of Death for the Navajo Uranium Miners," *New York Times,* May 3, 1993, p. A18; Bill Turque and John McCormick, "The Military's Toxic Legacy," *Newsweek,* August 6, 1990, p. 20; Bruce van Voorst, "A Thousand Points of Blight," *Time,* November 9, 1992, pp. 62–69; "Nuclear Waste Cleanups," *National Journal,* December 14, 1996, pp. 2678-2679.

Cheerleaders at Hanford, Washington, High School, whose teams are named the "Bombers," illustrate the civic pride in the nuclear weapons plant located nearby.
Doug Menuez, Reportage

negotiated a new thirty-year cleanup schedule with local regulators. DOE estimates of the cost of cleaning up after the nuclear weapons program continue to rise and now stands somewhere between $168 and $212 billion.

Like the DOE, the DOD is also facing huge cleanup problems. Its domestic military installations produce more hazardous waste each year than the top U.S. chemical companies. This includes many bases that have been closed to reduce military spending. None can be sold or converted to any civilian use until they are detoxified and made safe from such hazards as

each of the nation's known hazardous waste sites and to target some for cleanup with the Superfund.

In 1986, Congress amended the Superfund Act to give communities the right to know about chemicals made, used, and stored by local businesses. Citizens themselves now put pressure on industry to clean up unsafe dumps. But they are not always strong enough to face up to large industries.

Almost every stage of the waste regulation process is open to "technical controversy, litigation, and other challenges."[66] The complexity of the problems inherent in defining hazardous waste, setting standards for disposal, and identifying existing dumps are mind-boggling. As a simple example, chemical manufacturers were reluctant to release to the EPA information about new chemical compounds for fear of giving away trade secrets. Of forty-eight thousand chemicals listed by the EPA, practically nothing is known about thirty-eight thousand, and only five hundred have been tested for cancer-causing effects.[67]

The EPA was assigned these new duties without a substantial increase in staff or budget. Moreover, the EPA has lacked the clout necessary to enforce hazardous waste laws against two of the nation's worst polluters— the government's own Departments of Defense and Energy (see the box "Who Will Regulate Government?").

The EPA has also had difficulty establishing industry liability for cleanup on sites where several or more companies have dumped wastes. The insurance companies against which claims are made for cleanup of such sites challenge the liability of the industries they cover. A Rand study of Superfund spending claimed that only 10 percent of the money from insurance company settlements went to site cleanup, while 90 percent was spent on legal costs.[68] Still, by 2003 the government expects to have cleaned up nine hundred sites, about two-thirds of those on the priority list.[69]

Reforming Environmental Regulations

At the outset of the Clinton administration, Congress held hearings to consider renewing several major pieces of environmental legislation and to evaluate the whole process by which environmental policy is made and implemented. A few months after taking office, Carole Browner, head of the EPA and a former environmental activist and aide to Al Gore, told a House subcommittee that she was "appalled" by the EPA's "total lack of management, accountability and discipline." The subcommittee chair concurred, calling the EPA "one of the worst cesspools" he had ever seen.[70]

But the agency itself was not solely responsible for the mess. The public's fear of exposure to toxic substances has pressured government to regulate on the basis of inadequate scientific evidence, accepting worst-case scenarios and setting low- or no-risk standards where they are not necessary.

Everyone breathes the air and drinks the water, and one in four Americans lives or works in proximity to a

Dug from an ancient salt deposit located a half mile beneath the New Mexico desert, this storage site is scheduled to receive plutonium and other nuclear waste from weapons plants for the next thirty-five years. Since 1979, the Department of Energy has spent $2 billion on preparations and legal costs and will spend $100 million annually to maintain the site.
Michael Medford

hazardous waste site.[71] Therefore, environmental protection has a huge constituency. With the information explosion on how exposure to toxic substances in our food, water, land, and air may be linked to cancer and other illnesses, Americans have become increasingly health conscious. Heightened awareness of environmentally related diseases has led to increased pressure on government to protect us from toxic substances.

Critics say this fact has at times made government too responsive to public pressure and created a politics of panic.[72] For example, Congress passed the Ocean Dumping Act in the wake of a public outcry over the littering of East Coast beaches with medical and human waste and dead sea life in the summer of 1989. After cities spent billions to comply with the law, some experts said the beaches were contaminated by overtaxed storm sewer systems, not from toxic waste dumped in the ocean. While limiting the use of oceans as dumping grounds is a good thing in itself, it is extremely expensive to regulate, and the danger it presents is far less than that from inadequate sewage systems.

Policies on toxic waste and hazardous substances are singled out by critics as the worst examples of wasteful spending and misguided priorities. They point to studies by the National Cancer Institute that claim that only 1 to 3 percent of the nation's half-million yearly cancer deaths resulted from exposure to environmental pollutants.[73] Yet regulations to control these pollutants often force businesses and government to spend billions of dollars to restore contaminated sites to a pristine state.

Reformers cite the unsafe standard for dioxin presence in water, which is equivalent to one drop in Lake Michigan, and the so-called dirt-eating rules, or standards of safety determined by how much chemical-contaminated soil a child could consume without becoming ill.[74] Opponents of the no-risk standard ask whether it is cost-effective to clean up all toxic waste sites to the point that dirt is safe to eat, or the water safe to drink, especially if the amount of chemical contained in that soil or water presents no significant risk through normal exposure.

In too many cases, critics argue, the evidence used to support policy decisions has been unsound. Laws are made and standards mandated, only to have researchers revise the findings on which the laws were based. Scientists studying dioxin and DDT toxicity, for example, have said that early estimates of the danger level for human exposure were faulty. Much of the research on toxicity has been based on animal studies using the method of administering a "maximum tolerance dose" of the substance being studied. Researchers say that two-thirds of the chemicals such studies showed to be carcinogenic

would be benign if ingested at lower levels. In addition, there is not a direct correspondence between rodent and human body chemistry, so we cannot be certain that humans will be affected in the same way rats are when exposed to the same chemicals. Arsenic, for example, is highly toxic to humans but not to rats.[75]

Environmentalists ask whether we really want to risk people's lives by waiting until we get better evidence. They support low- and no-risk standards and believe it is better to err on the side of safety and not wait to regulate until people start dying. They take issue with the National Cancer Institute findings and claim environmental pollutants are responsible for up to 15 percent of all cancer deaths.

The jobs Congress has asked the EPA to do are huge compared to the resources the agency has, and some say while billions are spent to achieve unrealistic and unnecessary goals, more threatening hazards are ignored. The National Cancer Institute, for example, thinks priority should be given to public education on diet and other behavior that puts people at greater risk for cancer than exposure to environmental pollutants. City governments would rather spend federal grants on repairing sewer systems than on trying to restore contaminated sites to the safety thresholds prescribed by Congress.

Some believe environmental interest groups are partially responsible for for a high-pressure approach to regulation by playing on public fears and making unreasonable demands for safety standards. This creates obstacles to the EPA's planning. Environmentalists have also been criticized for being unwilling to admit their successes for fear of losing financial support for their organizations and momentum for the movement. These successes, coupled with what has been characterized as "compassion fatigue" among the American public, has led to an intense competition among environmental groups for membership and financial support.[76] This in turn, the groups' critics argue, has led them to make "apocalyptic prophecies to further their political objectives." One fund-raising letter from the National Audubon Society, for example, claimed that it could "project with some accuracy the eventual end of the natural world as we know it."[77]

Many people have also criticized the command and control approach to regulatory policy that lays down rules and orders people to comply.[78] To force compliance with rules requires monitoring by a large, expensive, and unwanted bureaucracy. When rule breakers are caught, they are assigned penalties that realistically cannot be enforced, even after huge sums are spent on legal fees to force compliance. The new reforms stress the need to make greater use of economic incentives to encourage desired behavior and to reduce the cost of enforcing regulations. Instead of trying to control their behavior after the fact individuals and businesses "face up to the full costs and consequences" of harmful actions at the time they make their decisions."[79]

The objective of this reform is to discourage environmentally or other socially harmful behavior by driving up its cost and thereby putting the individual or business engaging in it at a competitive disadvantage in the marketplace. This approach tries to eliminate a negative externality by bringing the polluter's incentives in line with the social costs imposed on the public. Disincentives could take the form of high-cost pollution permits for companies that decide to pollute and taxes on manufacturing or purchasing environmentally harmful products, waste disposal processes, and energy use. Environmental groups support heavy "green" taxes on "products and activities that pollute, deplete or otherwise degrade natural systems."[80] Such taxes would help pay for mounting cleanup costs and at the same time would provide a market incentive to avoid actions that endangered the public.

Such alternatives have been proposed by those deregulation advocates who, in almost every instance, place individual and private property rights above those of common property (that is, mineral resources, waterways, and parklands) and the public good. They assume that the marketplace is the only arena for resolving what is rational and appropriate economic behavior. But the marketplace is no more nor less than the people who operate within it, precisely because it is a place where individuals and businesses pursue private gain. There is no guarantee that the cumulative effect of these actions will benefit the common good.

Other supporters of regulatory reform believe it is possible for the government to set standards for health and safety and environmental protection while limiting its role in rule writing. This view was expressed in a best-selling book by Philip Howard on regulatory law much cited by both Republicans and Democrats (see "Further Reading"). Howard argues that the federal government has gone too far in its belief that science and technology make it possible to protect against every public danger. This has led to an excessive number of rules that try to anticipate every eventuality and in the process produced a country suffocating under the weight of law.

Howard's solution is to decentralize the rule-writing process while leaving federal standards in place. This would allow businesses and localities more flexi-bility in finding ways to meet the mandated standards, greatly reduce the oversight bureaucracy, and result in more cost-effective rules. This was generally in line with the form of deregulation advocated by the Clinton administration.

Clinton, a critic of the confrontational politics of the more militant environmental interest groups, but a supporter of their general goals, gave high priority to achieving consensus between the various parties affected by environmental regulation (see the "You Are There" section). In accordance with the Clinton-Gore "reinventing government" policy, EPA administrator Browner advocated a "Common Sense Initiative" to revise unrealistic, costly standards and to eliminate unnecessary rules.[81] She said the issues of risk assessment, property rights, and unfunded mandates "cast a shadow over environmental legislation" and had to be "addressed head-on" before any new regulations could be written.[82]

The EPA's attempts to control pollution and hazardous substances are undermined by fast-changing technology, inconsistent goals of political leaders, and of course, resistance by regulated groups. Deregulators particularly targeted landmark environmental legislation such as the Clean Water Act, which is extremely costly to implement, and the Endangered Species Act, which many western farmers and ranchers believe interferes with their property rights. Defending environmental protection in principle has remained good politics, but forcing *implementation* of EPA rules has not been seen as good politics by the Republican-controlled Congress. While it did not revoke the major clean air and water statutes, it did little to compel state governments, which have responsibility for 85 percent of all enforcement cases, to comply with them.

One observer said that the Republican tactic of bringing regulatory activity to a halt without actually repealing the legislation was "the equivalent of a neutron bomb: a tactical weapon that leaves the legal edifice of environmental laws standing but kills all the bureaucrats."[83]

Environmental protection has also been frustrated by the public. We want clean air and water, but we do not want to give up gas-guzzling cars and SUVs, plastic containers, energy-consuming conveniences, and other pollution-causing aspects of our lifestyles. We use far more energy per person than do the people of any other nation except Canada, and with energy use comes pollution. Part of this heavy consumption is due to our wealth, but part is due to our wastefulness. High oil prices in the 1970s curbed energy use for a while, but we have returned to our more wasteful ways. To ask the EPA to control pollution, then, is to ask it to protect us from ourselves.

Changing human behavior is at the center of the current debate over how much progress has been made in environmental protection and how much remains to be done. The optimists point to real achievements in improving air and water quality, reforestation, and cleaning up toxic waste and believe it is possible to control or limit ecological damage through adjustments in human behavior. The realists rely on science to provide the technology needed to combat the environmental damage that is an inevitable by-product of economic development, and remind us of the importance to our economic security of continued growth. The pessimists also recognize the achievements made in rolling back damage from pollution and other consequences of our current lifestyles. But they argue that the major ecological threats cannot be addressed without fundamental change in human behavior. Representative of this pessimistic outlook, Al Gore has said, "The maximum that is politically feasible, even the maximum that is politically *imaginable* right now, still falls short of the minimum that is scientifically and ecologically necessary."[84]

Benefits and Costs of Regulation

There have been many acknowledged successes of regulation.[85] But the benefits of regulation are produced at a cost. Some are trivial, such as depriving hunters of the satisfaction of shooting eagles. But some are significant. Businesses and environmentalists differ wildly about what the net cost of these improvements has been. The EPA estimated the cost of meeting air quality standards approved in 1999 at $3.5 billion annually, while the Chamber of Commerce, which joined the trucking and manufacturing industries in appealing the new rules to the Supreme Court, set the annual cost to industry at $46 billion.[86] These and all other estimates are controversial, although it is indisputable that regulation requires industry to increase its costs to relieve the larger community of the burden of pollution, unsafe products, hazards to workers, or other negative aspects of business activity.

Estimates vary depending on what monetary value is put on intangibles such as human health, comfort, appreciation of clean air, or loss of individual liberties.

But the best estimates show that air pollution control, for example, has been a large net benefit not only to the nation's air quality but to its economy. Although industries must pay employees to deal with federal regulations, and some pollution control equipment costs millions, pollution devices improve health and ultimately mean fewer days lost from sickness, reduced medical costs, and longer life for materials less damaged by corrosion.[87] Cleaning up the air also increases agricultural output. Some people are laid off when factories choose to close rather than install pollution control devices, but even more people are employed making, distributing, and educating people about air pollution devices.

In addition, in 1998, nearly sixty thousand public and private companies were engaged in environmental activities, employing 1,348,000 people and generating annual revenues of $59 billion.[88] Ecotourism is also developing as a major industry, helping revive small towns and rural areas bypassed by development. Today the number of birdwatchers is greater than that of hunters and fishermen combined, and birders spend an estimated $20 billion a year on travel to festivals and on gear and seeds.[89]

Yet, regulation remains controversial because some believe that its cost is too high and can be counted in decreased productivity, lost jobs, crushing paperwork, endless litigation, and loss of liberties to businesses and individual property owners. It is how these calculations are made that brings values, and therefore politics, into the regulatory process. There is no way for science or accounting alone to place a value on a human life that all will agree on, any more than regulators can put a dollar value on preservation of the bald eagle or of wilderness areas within national parks that will be acceptable to everyone. Many do not even accept the idea that quantitative values can be placed on human life or on the intrinsic satisfactions that exist above and beyond the economic value of protecting endangered species and their habitats.

This argument is increasingly made by environmentalists in legal battles to stop offshore oil drilling and logging in wilderness areas. The basic premise of this approach to cost-benefit analysis is that the cost of preserving a wilderness area must be offset by its "existence value" or "contingent value," the price the public is willing to pay just for the sake of keeping a pristine area in existence. But even those who concede that it is valid to factor existence value into the equation are uncertain how to determine the dollar value people will place on a wilderness area, and some environmentalists worry that setting a dollar value on nature is a bad precedent. Interior Secretary Bruce Babbitt, for example, has said we have reached the

Regulation and Environmental Policy in Time

1849 Interior Department created to help manage the opening of the West; administered nearly half of all U.S. land in the 1880s.

1872 Designation of Yellowstone as the first national park; beginning of National Park System.

1890 First antitrust legislation is passed to break up monopolies and end price fixing. First cycle of regulation begins. Interstate Commerce Commission created.

1899 First water pollution law passed, poorly enforced.

1901 Theodore Roosevelt succeeds to presidency and calls for worker safety and child labor laws and other business regulation. Develops reputation as "trustbuster."

1910 Progressive movement activists lobby throughout next decade for greater regulation of business, child labor laws, and worker safety.

1909–13 President Taft becomes bigger trustbuster than Roosevelt.

1918 Food and Drug Administration created.

1962 Rachel Carson's *Silent Spring* exposes dangers of pesticides like DDT and stimulates the modern environmental movement; new activism leads to creation of Consumer Product Safety Commission and OSHA.

1970 Richard Nixon creates the Environmental Protection Agency; the first Earth Day is celebrated.

1971 The EPA bans DDT.

1972–76 Federal government enters an era of environmental activism, as Congress passes the Clean Water Act, the Endangered Species Act, the Safe Drinking Water Act, and the Toxic Substances Control Act.

1978 President Carter leads a bipartisan effort to deregulate the trucking and airline industries and to eliminate unnecessary rules; begins modern era of deregulation.

1979 President Carter declares 54 million acres of Alaska a wilderness area, protecting it for eternity—the largest land set-aside in the history of the country.

1979 An accident at the Three Mile Island nuclear power plant reverses the trend toward greater dependency on nuclear power as source of electricity.

1980 Congress creates a Superfund for cleaning up the country's worst toxic waste sites.

1980 Congress begins partial deregulation of banking; over the next decade more than a quarter of all savings and loan associations in the United States fail due to fraudulent lending and invest-

ment practices. Deposit insurance reserves are exhausted. Depositors are bailed out by U.S. taxpayers at cost of $150 billion, leading to reregulation of S&Ls.

1981 President Reagan steps up deregulation process by appointing agency heads opposed to enforcement of existing regulation. Drastically reduces size of Federal Trade Commission and antitrust division of the Justice Department.

1985 First scientific reports on existence of a hole in the ozone layer; global warming becomes a public issue.

1986 Congress establishes a public "right to know" about toxic emissions; leads to greater citizen participation in monitoring of polluting agencies and industries.

1989 The *Exxon Valdez* oil tanker spills 11 million gallons of crude oil in Prince William Sound; the subsequent court fight ends in the largest criminal environmental settlement in U.S. history.

1993 President Clinton adopts a "reinventing government" program to eliminate rules and to streamline and downsize government; renews emphasis on deregulation to rationalize government.

1993–99 Period of large-scale mergers in communications, transportation, and energy industries begins; includes the largest mergers in U.S. history.

1994 In collaboration with private business, the EPA begins the Brownfield program to clean up abandoned industrial and toxic waste sites in inner cities and convert them to productive use. Part of EPA's "environmental justice" pledge to prevent poor neighborhoods from bearing the brunt of polluting industries.

1999 Interior Department celebrates it 150th year, managing 378 national parks, 514 refuges and wilderness areas, and millions of acres of rangeland.

1999 Recognizing that rapid expansion of the Internet has overtaken the government's ability to protect patient and consumer privacy, online stock trading, and E-commerce, members of Congress introduce seventy-five bills to regulate the Internet.

1999 Banking industry deregulated, negating the Glass-Steagall Act, which had regulated banks since the Great Depression.

2000 Major airlines propose merging to create three large carriers, and Congress threatens to reregulate the industry.

point where "We know the cost of everything and the value of nothing . . . you can't just cost this stuff out." He argues that it is dangerous to use contingent value because it may lead to an underestimation of the value of wilderness areas and furthermore that economics should not drive a debate that is about something much deeper.[90]

Americans want government to anticipate problems and to proscribe behavior by businesses and individuals that endangers public health. But we do not want to force unnecessary, costly regulations on business that will drive up prices for consumers, slow the economy, and increase unemployment. Is our national economic condition such that we must pick our poisons and regulate to protect public health and safety only when it is "cost-effective"?

Conclusion: Is Regulation Responsive?

Government regulates economic activities largely to protect the health and safety of Americans, to maintain the purity of the natural environment, and to protect business. Businesses often favor regulation because it protects them against competition from domestic or foreign competi-tors, but often they complain that regulation hurts them by decreasing their autonomy and increasing their costs of operation. These complaints have been met with legislative attempts to deregulate and by budget cuts for, and lax enforcement by, both federal and state regulatory agencies. Though the public approves of cutting red tape, efforts to get government completely out of the business of protecting health, safety, and the environment have been opposed by a majority of the public.

In forming our opinions about government regulations and regulators, it is sometimes easy to forget that regulators are carrying out congressional acts. While bureaucrats may be overly zealous or overly lax in enforcing those laws they are mandated to enforce, ultimately it is Congress that decides what is to be regulated and calls the agency or state governments to heel when they are overregulating or neglecting to regulate.

Regulation is a good example of fluctuations in government responsiveness to the public. At times, regulatory effort is directed primarily toward protecting business. At times of heightened public awareness of finite natural resources and the health risks of environmental degradation, consumer and environmental groups have succeeded in getting government to better regulate business and itself. In general, regulation exists because influential groups—sometimes representing a majority, other times not—desire government action to protect their interests.

At Loggerheads

Despite the dissatisfaction of both loggers and environmentalists with his compromise approach, Babbitt stuck to the middle ground.[91] After his review of the spotted owl controversy, Babbitt decided it was time for the Interior Department to develop a new policy for handling the environment-versus-jobs issues facing the Clinton administration. In particular, he wanted to prevent bitter conflicts over enforcement of the Endangered Species Act in which the opposing sides hunker down into confrontational stances and fight it out in federal courts.

Babbitt announced a plan to make a biological survey of the country's ecosystems that will enable the government to see emerging problems and deal with them while there is still an opportunity to be flexible. The government could bring together all parties potentially affected by actions it might take to preserve a threatened habitat, and then negotiate a solution that considered everyone's needs.

Eventually, this developed into a new policy, Habitat Conservation initiatives, but not soon enough to resolve the dispute in the Northwest. President Clinton, announcing a solution that followed the Babbitt approach of finding a middle ground between the demands for job protection and old-growth forest preservation, said the decision was more difficult than he ever thought it could be, but that we have "to play the hand we were dealt." Clinton allowed the loggers to clear dead timber in the spotted owl's habitat and to cut in old-growth forests. But he set a much lower limit on harvests than existed before the temporary court ban. He authorized funding for retraining of loggers and set aside some acreage to experiment with the new forestry Babbitt advocated. But he also banned logging on large tracts, closed off some

". . . Following up on that rumor that the spotted owl was bought off by the lumber interests. . ."

watershed areas, and ended subsidies for the export of logs.

The compromise solution angered both environmentalists and loggers. The timber industry said up to eighty-five thousand jobs would be lost. Environmentalists, who got more of what they wanted than the loggers, said an 80 percent effort was not enough; only a 100 percent ban on logging would preserve the ecosystem. Logging interests filed suit over the plan's legality, claiming the government could not enforce the Endangered Species Act on privately owned land. In 1995, the Supreme Court upheld the Clinton-Babbitt plan.

The Clinton administration could do little to stop the spotted owl controversy from playing itself out in the courts. But it hoped Babbitt's plan for ecosystem management would prevent similar controversies over enforcement of the Endangered Species Act from degenerating into all-or-nothing disputes in which no one's demands can be satisfied.

Key Terms

tragedy of the commons
externality
antitrust regulation
monopoly
truth in labeling
cost-benefit analysis
deregulation
reregulation

environmental impact
 statement
Environmental Protection
 Agency (EPA)
bubble concept
cradle-to-grave
Superfund

Further Reading

Rachael Carson, *Silent Spring* (New York: Fawcett, 1962). This book, and industry's reaction to it, spurred the development of the modern environmental movement.

Mark Dowie, *Losing Ground: American Environmentalism at the Close of the Twentieth Century* (Cambridge, Mass: MIT Press, 1995). A former publisher of *Mother Jones* argues that the environmental movement has become weak and irrelevant by catering to Washington and losing touch with its grassroots supporters.

Gregg Easterbrook, *A Moment on the Earth: The Coming Age of Environmental Optimism* (New York: Viking, 1995). An environmental reporter gives an upbeat assessment of the achievements of environmentalism and argues that the movement needs to acknowledge its successes and redefine its priorities and tactics.

Carole Gallagher, *American Ground Zero: The Secret Nuclear War* (Cambridge, Mass.: MIT Press, 1993). A photojournalistic study of the victims of radioactive fallout from nuclear testing in Nevada.

Richard Harris and Sidney Milkis, *The Politics of Regulatory Change* (New York: Oxford University Press, 1989). An evenhanded account of the rise and fall of deregulation during the Reagan administration.

Philip K. Howard, *The Death of Common Sense: How Law Is Suffocating America* (New York: Random House, 1994). A best-selling look at regulation (described earlier in the chapter).

Shepard Krech III, *The Ecological Indian: Myth and History* (New York: Norton, 1999). An environmental anthropologist examines the stereotype of the ecologically correct American Indian and shatters some myths about the relationship between Indian cultures and the environment.

Jonathan D. Moreno, *Undue Risk: Secret State Experiments on Humans* (New York: Freeman, 1999). A biomedical ethicist describes U.S. Department of Defense, Atomic Energy Commission, Public Health Service, and CIA experiments on Americans during World War II and the 1950s and concludes human rights should never be subordinated to national defense.

Walter Rosenbaum, *Environmental Politics and Policy,* 3d ed. (Washington, D.C.: CQ Press, 1995). Probably the best overview of environmental policy.

Electronic Resources

www.epa.gov/
The home page of the EPA includes information on issues, organization, regulations, and even graduate fellowships offered by the agency. You can also find a guide to all major environmental protection projects in your state.

www.ftc.gov/
The home page of the Federal Trade Commission. It provides links similar to those at the EPA site.

www.sierraclub.org/
The home page of the Sierra Club, one of the largest and most influential environmental interest groups. From this page, you can check on the environmental voting records of your members of Congress and see where they got their campaign contributions.

www.fda.gov/
The Web site of the Food and Drug Administration contains information on all major areas of the agency's work in food and drug safety, reports on current research, and pending regulations and legislation.

InfoTrac College Edition

"Regulatory Reform: More Work Needed"
"Tragedy Walkerton"
"New Standards Proposed for Radon in Drinking Water"
"Flow Control Shields Hauler"

Notes

1. This "You Are There" segment is drawn from the following sources: *McNeil-Lehrer Newshour,* "Focus—Forest Forum," April 1, 1993 (transcript #4597, pp. 7–10); Philip Shabecoff, *A Fierce Green Fire* (New York: Hill & Wang, 1993), chap. 7; Timothy Egan, "The Things That Get Left Out in the Fight for the Wild Northwest," *New York Times,* May 30, 1993, p. E1; "Babbitt: Spotted Owl 'Test Case' for Clinton," *Champaign-Urbana News Gazette* (AP), February 9, 1993, p. A6; "2-Year Logging Delay Forecast in Owl Habitat," *New York Times,* August 2, 1992, p. 17.

2. Adam Smith, *An Inquiry into the Wealth of Nations* (1776; several editions; a recent one is Indianapolis: Bobbs-Merrill, 1961).

3. See discussion in William Ophuls, *Ecology and the Politics of Scarcity* (San Francisco: Freeman, 1977).

4. NBC News Special Report on the 20th Anniversary of Earth Day, April 22, 1991.

5. *Environmental Encyclopedia* (Detroit: Gale Research, 1993), 320–321; Ruth A. Eblen and William R. Eblen, eds., *The Encyclopedia of the Environment* (New York: Houghton Mifflin, 1994), 243.

6. Kirk Victor and Michael Posner, "Merger Mania," *National Journal,* July 15, 2000, pp. 2282; Stephan Labaton, "Oligopoly," *New York Times,* June 11, 2000, sect. 4, p. 1.

7. Steve Lohr, "The New Math of Monopoly," *New York Times,* April 9, 2000, sect. 4, p. 1. Excerpts from the federal court ruling against Microsoft appeared in *New York Times,* April 4, 2000, pp. C14–C15.

8. Margaret Kriz, "Global Food Fight," *National Journal,* March 4, 2000, p. 689.

9. Cornelius M. Kerwin, *Rulemaking: How Government Agencies Write Law and Make Policy* (Washington, D.C.: CQ Press, 1994), 171.

10. See discussion in Walter A. Rosenbaum, *Environmental Politics and Policy* (Washington, D.C.: CQ Press, 1985), 90–95.

11. See Susan Tolchin and Martin Tolchin, *Dismantling America* (Boston: Houghton Mifflin, 1983), especially Chap. 4. See George C. Eads and Michael Fix, *Relief or Reform?* (Washington, D.C.: Urban Institute Press, 1984), 241–245, for an assessment of cost savings under Reagan's regulatory policies.

12. *Fortune,* February 3, 1986; Michael Reagan, *Regulation* (Boston: Little, Brown, 1987), 126.

13. Bill McAllister, "If a Human Life Is Worth $1 Million, What's a Recliner Worth?" *Washington Post National Weekly Edition,* June 8, 1987, p. 33.

14. Tolchin and Tolchin, *Dismantling America.*

15. "A New Rule Clouds the Clean Air Act," *New York Times,* June 28, 1992, p. E6.

16. John H. Cushman, Jr. "Republicans Plan Sweeping Barriers to New U.S. Rules," *New York Times,* December 25, 1994, pp. 1, 12.

17. Kerwin, *Rulemaking,* 264.

18. Margaret Kriz, "Electric Power Play," *National Journal,* June 3, 2000, pp. 1744–1748.

19. Kenneth J. Meier, *Regulation* (New York: St. Martin's, 1985) 78–80.

20. Eads and Fix, *Relief or Reform?* 153. See also Reagan, *Regulation,* 105–106.

21. Philip K. Howard, *The Death of Common Sense: How Law Is Suffocating America* (New York: Random House, 1994), 26, 12.

22. Ibid., 32.

23. "Demise of 'Regs' Threw Airlines into Tailspin," *Congressional Quarterly Outlook,* October 16, 1999, p. 14.

24. Laurence Zuckerman, "Rising Tide of Passengers Fume over Delays at Nation's Airports," *New York Times,* July 16, 2000, p. 1.

25. Kathy Koch, "Can Congress Prevent Aviation Gridlock?" *Congressional Quarterly Outlook,* October 16, 1999, p. 7.

26. Kirk Victor, "Hub Cap," *National Journal,* May 12, 1990, p. 1145.

27. "Demise of 'Regs' Threw Airlines into Tailspin," p. 15.

28. Matthew L. Wald, "So, How Much Did You Pay for Your Ticket?" *New York Times,* April 12, 1998, sect. 4, p. 1.

29. Koch, "Can Congress Prevent Aviation Gridlock?" p. 7; Jeff Plungis, "Lawmakers Wary of Unfriendly Skies Weigh Revisiting Airline Regulation," *Congressional Quarterly Weekly Report,* July 8, 2000, p. 1675.

30. Koch, "Can Congress Prevent Aviation Gridlock?" p. 9.

31. Figure cited on PBS series, "Surviving the Bottom Line," Part 1 (broadcast January 16, 1998).

32. Mary Schiavo, with Sabra Chartrand, *Flying Blind, Flying Safe* (New York: Avon, 1997), excerpted in *Time,* March 31, 1997, pp. 52–62.

33. Matthew L. Wald, "Getting There: A Reality Check," *New York Times,* June 25, 2000, sect. 5, p. 12.

34. "U.S. Airline Deaths Down during 1997," *Champaign-Urbana News-Gazette,* February 25, 1998, p. C6.

35. Wald, "Getting There: A Reality Check," sect. 5, p. 14.

36. Plungis, "Lawmakers Wary of Unfriendly Skies," pp. 1671–1675; David Leonhardt, "Promises in the Sky," *New York Times,* June 25, 2000, sect. 5, pp. 13, 26.

37. Plungis, "Lawmakers Wary of Unfriendly Skies," p. 1671.

38. For an evaluation of the impact of Reagan's deregulation efforts, see Richard Harris and Sidney Milkis, *The Politics of Regulatory Change* (New York: Oxford University Press, 1989).

39. Denis Hayes, "Earth Day Plus 25 Years: Things Are Looking Up for the Earth," *Champaign-Urbana News-Gazette,* April 23, 1995, p. B1.

40. Daniel Yergin and Joseph Stanislaw, *Commanding Heights: The New Relationship between Government and the Marketplace* (New York: Simon & Schuster, 1998), 11.

41. Victor and Posner, "Merger Mania," p. 2281.

42. Labaton, "Oligopoly," pp. 1, 4.

43. Ibid., p. 1.

44. Victor and Posner, "Merger Mania," p. 2289.

45. Quoted in David Bollier and Joan Claybrook, *Freedom from Harm* (Washington, D.C.: Public Citizen and Democracy Project, 1986), 95.

46. Kriz, "Global Food Fight," p. 688.

47. "Internet Bills Multiply," *Congressional Quarterly Weekly Report,* September 4, 1999, p. 2033.

48. Richard W. Stevenson, "Playing Catch-up with Monopolies," *New York Times,* November 14, 1999, sect. 4, p. 16.

49. Albert Gore, Jr., *Earth in the Balance* (Boston: Houghton Mifflin Company, 1992), 294.

50. Gregg Easterbrook, "Here Comes the Sun," *New Yorker,* April 10, 1995, p. 42.

51. Mary H. Cooper, "Setting Priorities and Paying the Tab," *Congressional Quarterly Outlook,* June 5, 1999, p. 9.

52. John Jay, "The Federalist #2," in *The Federalist: A Commentary on the Constitution of the United States* (New York: Modern Library), 8–9.

53. Lynn White, Jr., "The Historical Roots of Our Ecological Crisis," *Science* 155 (March 10, 1967).

54. See Robert Nisbet, *The History of the Idea of Progress* (New York: Basic Books, 1980), for an interesting examination of the idea of progress from antiquity to the present.

55. See Meier, *Regulation,* chap. 6, for an overview of early attempts by the federal government to protect the environment.

56. James Anderson, David Brady, and Charles Bullock, *Public Policy and Politics in America* (North Scituate, Mass.: Duxbury, 1977), 74.

57. Kerwin, *Rulemaking,* 171.

58. Meier, *Regulation,* 145; Norman Vig and Michael Kraft, "Environmental Policy from the Seventies to the Eighties," in *Environmental Policy in the 1980s,* ed. Vig and Kraft (Washington, D.C.: CQ Press, 1984), 16.

59. Information about the founding of the EPA is drawn from Steven A. Cohen, "EPA: A Qualified Success," in *Controversies in Environmental Policy,* ed. Sheldon Kamieniecki, Robert O'Brien, and Michael Clarke (Albany: State University of New York Press, 1986), 174–199; Meier, *Regulation,* 142–146.

60. Easterbrook, "Here Comes the Sun," pp. 38–42; Margaret Kriz, "A New Shade of Green," *National Journal,* March 18, 1995, p. 662; Howard, *The Death of Common Sense,* 26.

61. Meier, *Regulation,* 147.

62. Quoted from the EPA's long-term mission statement, "Preparing for a New Era of Environmental Protection," at http://www.epa.gov/.

63. Helen Ingram and Dean Mann, "Preserving the Clean Water Act," in *Environmental Policy in the 1980s,* ed. Vig and Kraft, 260.

64. See Lois Gibbs, *Love Canal* (Albany: State University of New York Press, 1983), for the Love Canal story from the perspective of the woman who organized the neighborhood to demand that government do something. Andrew Danzo, "The Big Sleazy," *Washington Monthly,* September 1988, pp. 11–17, describes bureaucratic delay in helping the residents of Love Canal. See also Adeline Gordon Levine, *Love Canal: Science, Politics, and People* (Lexington, Mass.: Heath, 1982).

65. The Resource Conservation and Recovery Act of 1976 and the Toxic Substances Control Act of 1976; also see the EPA's dictionary of terms at http://www.epa.gov/.

66. Rosenbaum, *Environmental Politics,* 215.

67. *Time,* January 2, 1989, p. 47.

68. "Little of Superfund Settlements Go to Cleanup," *New York Times,* April 26, 1992, p. 16.

69. *Budget of the U.S. Government, Fiscal Year 1999,* 178.

70. "E.P.A. Chief Is Harsh about Her Agency," *New York Times,* March 11, 1993.

71. Albert Gore, Jr., "Earth Days Have Become Earth Years," *New York Times,* April 23, 1995, p. E16.

72. Much of the discussion in this section is based on a series of articles on environmental policy written by Keith Schneider, Michael Spector, and Joel Brinkley that ran in the *New York Times* from March 21 to March 26, 1993.

73. Keith Schneider, "Second Chance on Environment," *New York Times,* March 26, 1993, p. A17.

74. Keith Schneider, "New View Calls Environmental Policy Misguided," *New York Times,* March 21, 1993, p. 16.

75. Joel Brinkley, "Many Say Lab-Animal Tests Fail to Measure Human Risk," *New York Times,* March 23, 1993, p. A16.

76. Keith Schneider, "For the Environment, Compassion Fatigue," *New York Times,* November 6, 1994, p. E3.

77. National Audubon Society fund-raising letter cited by Keith Schneider, "Big Environment Hits a Recession," *New York Times,* January 1, 1995. p. F4. Other critical assessments of the environmental movement's pessimistic outlook can be found in Martin W. Lewis, *Green Delusions* (Durham, N.C.: Duke University Press, 1992); Bill McKibben, "An Explosion of Green," *Atlantic Monthly,* April 1995, pp. 61–83; Evan J. Ringquist, "Is 'Effective Regulation' Always Oxymoronic? The States and Ambient Air Quality," *Social Science Quarterly* 76, no. 1 (March 1995): 69–87.

78. David Osborne and Ted Gaebler, *Reinventing Government: How the Entrepreneurial Spirit Is Transforming the Public Sector* (New York: Penguin Books [Plume], 1992), pp. 299–305.

79. Ibid., 302.

80. Philip Shabecoff, "Tax Proposed on Products and Activities That Harm Environment," *New York Times,* February 10, 1991, p. 1.

81. *Budget of the U.S. Government, Fiscal Year 1996,* 81–90.

82. Carol Browner, quoted by Margaret Kriz, "The Conquered Coalition," *National Journal,* December 3, 1994, p. 2827.

83. John H. Cushman, Jr., "Republicans Clear-Cut Regulatory Timberland," *New York Times,* March 5, 1995, p. E16.

84. Quoted by Bill McKibben, "Not So Fast," *New York Times Magazine,* July 23, 1995, p. 25.

85. See research by Nicholas Ashford reported in U.S. Senate Governmental Affairs Committee, 96th Congress, March 25, 1980, "Benefits of Environmental, Health, and Safety Regulation" (Washington, D.C.: U.S. Government Printing Office); Gregg Easterbrook, *A Moment on the Earth: The Coming Age of Environmental Optimism* (New York: Viking, 1995).

86. Eads and Fix, *Relief or Reform?;* Keith Bradsher, "Auto Pollution Plan is Drawn Into a Vortex," *New York Times,* May 16, 1999, p. 22; "Clean Air Act Challenged in Supreme Court," *The Champaign-Urbana News-Gazette,* September 17, 2000, p. A-10.

87. See Rosenbaum, *Environmental Politics,* 126–127; Bollier and Claybrook, *Freedom from Harm,* 116.

89. *Statistical Abstract of the United States, 1999,* Table 415.

89. Jonathan Rosen, "Birding at the End of Nature," *New York Times Magazine,* May 21, 2000, p. 66.

90. Sam Howe Verhovek, "They Exist: Therefore They Are. But, Do You Care?" *New York Times,* October 17, 1999, sect. 4, p. 5.

91. The epilogue is based on the following sources: *McNeil-Lehrer Newshour,* "Nurturing Nature," July 1, 1993 (transcript #4662, pp. 2–10); "Clinton's Forest Compromise Is Assailed from All Sides," *Congressional Quarterly,* July 3, 1993, pp. 1726–1727; Louis Jacobson, "Babbitt's Got a Plan," *National Journal,* March 3, 1993, pp. 635–638; William K. Stevens, "Babbitt to Map Ecosystems under Policy Shift," *New York Times,* March 14, 1993; Margaret Kriz, "Aiming for the Green," *National Journal,* October 4, 1997, pp. 1958–1965.

Foreign Policy

YOU ARE THERE

State's Rights or Human Rights?

You are Madeleine Albright, the first woman and only the second naturalized American to serve as secretary of state. Born in Yugoslavia, where your father was serving with the Czech diplomatic corps, your family fled to England when the Nazis invaded your homeland. Your parents returned at war's end only to see Czechoslovakia fall under Soviet domination. This time they fled to the United States, where you grew up and became a citizen and later a professor of international relations. You became an activist in the Democratic Party, serving as foreign policy adviser to presidential candidate Michael Dukakis, and you got to know many in the party leadership, including then Governor Bill Clinton. Even though you are not a career diplomat and had not held public office before, years later Clinton named you U.S. ambassador to the United Nations and then secretary of state. You have an easy rapport with the president and share his view that in the post–Cold War world, a new order of threats to global security demands a new kind of diplomacy.

Now it is the winter of 1999, and the president has to make a decision on how the U.S. will respond to another outbreak of violence in the former Yugoslavia. Yu-goslavia was a country made up of six federated republics, most of which had populations divided among ethnic and religious groups with a history of tense, if not violent, relationships: Serbs, Croats, Albanians, Orthodox Catholics, and Muslims. At the end of the Cold War, as many formerly communist countries were breaking up and reorganizing, war broke out between some of Yugoslavia's ethnic groups. The United States hesitated for three years before joining European allies in helping negotiate and enforce a cease-fire among Bosnian Serbs, Croats, and Muslims. As the rest of the world stood by, there were almost weekly revelations of rapes, dispossessions, concentration camp atrocities, and murder, including the largest mass murder in Europe since World War II (the 1995 killing of seven to ten thousand Muslims by Serbs in a UN "safe" area). By the time we got around to joining an intervention force with our allies, thousands were dead and Yugoslavia was broken up and partitioned.

This time it is ethnic Albanians in the province of Kosovo who are engaged in hostilities with the Serbs, the dominant ethnic group of Serbia. Predominantly Muslim and from a different linguistic

Signaling the growing importance of Asia in United States foreign policy, Clinton became the first president since John Kennedy to visit India, the world's second most populous country and an emerging nuclear power.

Chris Usher/*Newsweek*

A Kosovar Albanian buries the remains of twenty-two relatives killed by the Serbs.
Ron Haviv/Saba

group than the Christian Serbs, the Kosovar Albanians want to break away and establish their own country. They have already formed a liberation army. Army units sent by the government in Belgrade, the capital of Serbia, are marching toward Kosovo to put down the independence movement. As their Serbian neighbors attack them and burn their homes, Kosovar Albanians are fleeing to the mountains on foot, with little food or clothing during the dead of winter.

Should the United States stand on the sidelines again and let Yugoslavs fight their own battles, even if thousands more civilians die? The president is getting arguments from all sides. Some say the United States should stay out because it is a civil war and we have no national interests at stake—or, as former Secretary of State James Baker once put it, "We don't have a dog in that fight." Others argue that it is our moral obligation to prevent the slaughter of civilians and that we are better prepared than any other country to do it. But even those favoring intervention are not in agreement about whether the United States should send in ground troops as part of a multilateral force, act alone or with our allies to bomb Serb forces, or perhaps limit our involvement to providing humanitarian support to

keep fleeing Albanians from starving or freezing.

As secretary of state, and as someone very familiar with this region, your policy recommendation will carry real weight. One thing you are certain of is that you want to avoid another Rwanda. In 1994, while you were still at the UN, the United States faced a decision on whether to intervene in Rwanda when the majority Hutus drove the minority Tutsis into neighboring countries, leaving more than a half million dead, many hacked to death in their homes. We had opportunities to intervene through UN auspices to prevent the worst of the killing, but we chose to do nothing. You took intense international criticism for your role in this decision and reportedly emerged sadder and wiser.

Now, as you face the decision on Serbia, reporters come at you from a personal angle, too, revealing that although you were raised a Catholic, your family were converts from Judaism and your grandparents and other relatives left behind in Czechoslovakia had been killed in the Holocaust.[1] American Jews had been among the first to call on Clinton to stop the Serbian attack on Kosovar Muslims. After learning about your background,

some people ask how you can think twice about intervening to stop ethnic slaughter.

Furthermore, you took office in full agreement with Clinton that ethnic and religious persecution, the oppression of women, the poverty of children, the spread of disease, and the degradation of the environment are among the most serious threats to national security and global stability in the post–Cold War world. When you singled out violence toward women as an object of U.S. foreign policy, you criticized those who say it can't be stopped because it is cultural; you said, "It's criminal, and we each have a responsibility to stop it."[2] You believe the same thing is true of ethnic warfare. It has taken a real effort to get the State Department bureaucracy to accept this new priority of global concerns. But now on record as placing a priority on human rights in U.S. foreign policy, can you advise the president to do nothing when every time the news is turned on viewers see unspeakable abuses?

You are certain that, from a moral standpoint, intervention is the right choice. But from the standpoint of international law it is more tricky. Serbia is a sovereign nation, and Kosovo is threatening to secede. We fought our own civil war over that issue. Do we want to send the message to other countries that we are willing to intervene in the internal affairs of sovereign nations?

And how practical is it, really? Our intervention in Haiti to restore constitutional government and help the economy get back on track has done almost nothing to improve the situation for the ordinary Haitian. Years after the fighting stopped, UN troops are still policing Bosnia and Rwanda, with little progress toward resolution of the differences among rival ethnic groups. And clearly we do not intervene everywhere human rights are abused. For example, our Chinese policy, which you support, overlooks political and religious oppression and assumes that only economic development can improve the situation.

Moreover, every time we intervene militarily, it adds to international expectations that the United States is willing to risk American lives to police conflicts around the world. The American public won't be quick to see a national security interest in Kosovo, and there is no time to make the case,

with people dying every day. On the other hand, you warned the American people at the outset of your term that what the history of the twentieth century taught us was that "problems abroad, if left unattended, will all too often come home to America."[3]

What do you advise: go in alone with ground troops, take limited action as part of a multilateral force with our European allies, or stay out and leave it to European nations to assume responsibility for a conflict that is in their backyards?

The foreign policy of the United States has a substantial impact on the world; yet we are not all-powerful. We are one of many players; decisions about war and peace and about trade are made by people in all nations. In this sense public expectations about what we can achieve have often been unrealistically high. Throughout the 1960s, 1970s, and 1980s, many Americans saw only our international failures: defeat in Vietnam; the 1979 capture of our Iranian embassy; Soviet influence in Cuba; the loss of American troops in Lebanon; the humiliation of the arms-for-hostages deal with Iran in 1986; and the shrinking American share in world markets for many goods, including steel and autos.

But we have had notable foreign policy successes: limitations in the arms race and, in conjunction with other nuclear powers, avoiding the catastrophe of nuclear war; peace settlements in the Middle East in 1979 and 1993–1994; normalization of our relations with the People's Republic of China, the world's most populous nation; a cease-fire in Northern Ireland in 1999; and helping to prevent hundreds of thousands of deaths from starvation in Africa. Even though it may have had much more to do with internal problems than with U.S. actions, the defeat of communism in Europe realized another major objective of American foreign policy.

In this post–Cold War era, many of the resources that had been devoted to competition with the former Soviet Union have been redirected toward pursuit of other goals. At the same time, the nature of international cooperation and competition is changing, and we are forced to rethink the means we use to pursue our foreign policy objectives. We are more preoccupied with internal problems and less willing to devote as much of our energies and resources to foreign policy as we have in the past. Yet we are increasingly aware of the relationship between foreign and domestic policy, especially the impact of trade relations on American business, agriculture, and labor.

In this chapter we examine past and present foreign policy goals, how foreign policy decisions are made, and the challenges policymakers face in the post–Cold War era.

Foreign Policy Goals

The goals any nation has and the means it uses to pursue them are influenced by its traditions, core values, ideology, and geopolitical situation (that is, the advantages and limitations imposed by geographic location, size, and wealth relative to other nations). Foreign policies are the strategies adopted and actions taken by a government to achieve its goals in its relationships with other nations. These actions range from informal negotiations to waging war, from writing position papers to initiating trade boycotts. They may require economic, political, cultural, or military resources.

The art of foreign policymaking includes choosing means suitable to the objective sought. Due to our size and great wealth, huge diplomatic corps, military forces, and intelligence establishment, we have the fullest possible range of foreign policy instruments at our disposal. Sometimes the mere possession of so many means of pursuing foreign policy objectives affects the setting of the objectives themselves; that is, the more a country is able to do, the more it may try to do.

Our primary foreign policy goal is, as is every nation's, to protect our physical security. The United States has been successful in achieving this goal: no foreign armies have been on continental U.S. soil since the British in the War of 1812. In contrast, Germany, France, the former Soviet Union, and other nations of continental Europe have been militarily occupied both in this century and the last. Our success is due largely to our separation from the other major powers by two oceans and being bounded on the north and south by two friendly countries. Although less important in today's era of missiles and bioterrorism, this separation was vital in ensuring our security in earlier eras. In the State Department's year 2000 mission statement, protection of our physical borders is fourth on a list of seven broad national interests. Today more emphasis is placed on the threat to American security presented by the proliferation of weapons of mass destruction than from an actual invasion of United States territory. As we will discuss later, how we provide for our physical security in an age of high technology and globalization is undergoing serious rethinking.

A second goal is to protect the physical security of our neighbors and major democratic allies. Since World War II we have committed ourselves, through the North Atlantic Treaty Organization (NATO), to join in the defense of Canada and western, southern, and, now, some eastern European nations. We also have treaty commitments to Japan, South Korea, and the nations of South and Central America.

A third goal is to protect our economic security. Although the United States is blessed with many natural resources, we must purchase abroad such essential resources as oil, manganese, and tin. Safeguarding our access to these resources may include stabilizing the governments of producing nations or protecting the sea-lanes in which the goods are shipped. Today, ensuring the privacy of information transfers, including financial transactions, and securing computer systems against hackers are becoming as important to national security as protecting sea-lanes.

Our economic well-being is equally dependent on selling our goods abroad, which in turn depends on how cheaply we can manufacture or grow products desired in other parts of the world and how willing our trading partners are to buy them. Economic self-interest is almost always a factor in foreign policy, including dealings with our close allies, because they do not always want to import U.S. goods that will compete with their own. Thus, trade missions and international conferences on trade and tariffs are crucial to achieving our foreign policy goals, even though until very recently the public paid scant attention to them.

A fourth overlapping goal is to extend our sphere of influence. Historically, this has meant keeping foreign powers out of the Caribbean and Latin America. In the 1780s, Thomas Jefferson said he hoped Spain would hold onto its territory in South America until "our population can be sufficiently advanced to gain it from them piece by piece."[4] Since then we have said that Latin America is our "turf."

In modern times our sphere of interest extends around the world. We have sought to influence security arrangements on all continents. We have more military bases and more troops outside our borders than has any other country in the world. We also try to spread our influence by promoting democracy, capitalism, and Western cultural values. Our State Department maintains a system of public libraries around the world to dissemi-

nate information on our government, economy, and popular culture and also funds thousands of cultural and academic exchanges between American and foreign artists and scholars each year. At most, we offer our political and economic systems as models of development, and, at least, we try to foster a favorable attitude toward the United States that will make it easier for us to achieve our foreign policy goals.

Our specific foreign policy objectives, such as protecting access to oil in the Middle East, removing barriers to trade with Japan and China, or the economic restructuring of Russia, are almost always related to achieving one or more of these four general goals.

Making Foreign Policy in a Democracy

Alexis de Tocqueville was one of the first to remark that it is difficult to have a coherent foreign policy in a democracy. His sentiments have been echoed thousands of times since. Why, when there has been basic agreement on the broad goals of our foreign policy, has the United States had such difficulty articulating a coherent and consistent set of objectives?

Some of the confusion in foreign policymaking is because we elect new leaders every four or eight years. Inconsistencies within a single administration can partially be explained by the sheer number of organizations and individuals who in some way influence the process of making and implementing foreign policy: the president, members of Congress, heads of relevant cabinet departments and independent agencies, chiefs of the armed services, White House staff and other political advisers, interest groups, lobbyists, the media, and the public. Leaders and citizens from other countries may also have some influence when they are crucial to the successful pursuit of an objective. Which of these groups and individuals will actually have some impact on policy varies greatly with the issue and the decision-making style of the president.

Historically, inconsistencies in our foreign policy were rarely caused by differences among policymakers over fundamental goals but rather over whether action was necessary in a specific situation and what that action should be. For example, most Americans supported the goal of containing Soviet influence. But they did not agree on how much intervention in the internal affairs of another country was justifiable or on what form that intervention should take.

Since the end of the Cold War, however, there has been disagreement even over the fundamentals. Of course, policymakers still believe that physical and economic security are primary goals, but there is more confusion than at any time in the past over what are the primary threats to national security and exactly who and what we should be protecting ourselves from.

In this section we will look at some of the groups and individuals who influence the foreign policymaking process and how division and conflict among them can affect the content and execution of U.S. policy.

The Inner Circle

As head of state and commander in chief of the armed forces, the president is in control of the nation's entire diplomatic and military establishments. In addition, as the nexus of the vast diplomatic and military communications and intelligence networks, he has the most complete and privileged access to information of anyone in the policymaking network. In times of crisis, without immediately available alternative sources of reliable information, members of Congress and the public historically have almost always relied on the president's sources. However, in this age of a weakened presidency, a contentious Congress, and an information explosion, the president's policy is much more likely to be challenged.

Given the central role of the president in foreign policymaking, and the fact that most presidents enter the office with very little foreign policy expertise—George Bush was an exception—it is important to know who advises him.

No firm rules dictate whom the president must consult on foreign policy, but usually he gives at least a perfunctory hearing to those people who head departments and agencies involved with making or implementing policy. The government officials best positioned to advise the president on foreign policy include the secretaries of defense and state, the national security adviser, and the head of the CIA. The Joint Chiefs of Staff, the U.S. ambassador to the United Nations, the secretary of the treasury, the director of the Arms Control Agency, and influential members of Congress are also frequently consulted.

These individuals represent a wide range of experience and bring different perspectives to the analysis of foreign policy issues. The secretary of state is usually concerned with the nation's diplomatic relations and the use of diplomatic channels to implement the president's policies. The secretary of defense (a civilian) is primarily concerned with military and security issues and the use of the military to pursue foreign policy goals. Members

of the Joint Chiefs of Staff are military professionals who give advice to the president on both the readiness of their service arms and the appropriateness of their use in specific situations. Members of Congress may be consulted because they are political allies of the president, because they are in leadership positions crucial for mobilizing support on an issue, or because they have developed expertise in military or foreign policy issues through their committee assignments.

The president may also consult his wife or friends and advisers outside government, not because of their expertise in foreign or military policy but because he trusts in their good judgment and wants the perspective of people close to him who may have no organizational interests or policy agenda to further. In recent years it has become common for presidents to call on private citizens to negotiate disputes, a practice that has been dubbed the franchising or subcontracting of foreign policy. These freelancers are often retired diplomats, but individuals with little foreign policy experience, such as former presidential candidate Jesse Jackson, have also been used.

The most noted of these private diplomats is former president Jimmy Carter, who heads a center, affiliated with the Carter presidential library, devoted to international mediation. Carter has gone, sometimes at his own initiative, to many trouble spots, including Bosnia, where he helped negotiate a short-lived truce, and North Korea. His mission to Haiti with General Colin Powell in 1994 successfully negotiated the departure from Haiti of the military junta, allowing U.S. troops to come ashore unopposed. Some of these high-profile visits, and Carter's public comments about them, made the former president appear at times to be conducting an independent policy line.

Who the president draws into his inner circle of advisers depends in large part on his experience and decision-making style. President Kennedy, who had almost no foreign policy experience, assembled a committee of cabinet heads and close advisers to help him construct his response to the Soviets during the Cuban missile crisis. But during the Persian Gulf crisis, President Bush reportedly made the decision to send troops to Saudi Arabia relying almost exclusively on his own judgment and that of a few close advisers.

President Bush preferred foreign to domestic policy and allotted his attention and energies accordingly. To a lesser extent this was also true for Richard Nixon. If a president comes to office with a foreign policy agenda and expects to make his political reputation and leave his mark on history in this policy area, he will likely surround himself with like-minded people and will replace those who disagree with him or ignore their advice. Bush appointed both members of the foreign policy establishment who had held high positions in previous administrations and several associates from his tenure as CIA director, an organizational tie that made many in Congress uncomfortable.

Ex-governors like Carter, Reagan, and Clinton can compensate for their lack of foreign policy experience when they become president by surrounding themselves with experts. Nevertheless, Carter and Reagan chose foreign policy advisers with limited experience and had difficulty maintaining unity among them.

In contrast, Clinton appointed an experienced team of advisers, including a number from the Carter administration, but was himself undecided on policy direction early in his presidency.

Specialists

The process of formulating long-term policy usually involves more people than the number involved in decision making in crisis situations. The 26,000-member State Department has experts on every region of the globe and on substantive policy issues such as economic assistance, trade, political affairs, and arms control.

Political officers in Washington and in our embassies and consulates abroad write daily summaries of important political and economic events in the countries to which they are assigned. This information is used to provide daily briefings for higher-level officials, but almost none of it ever reaches the president's desk and only a small portion of it can be read even by the secretary of state.

Specialists in other cabinet departments and independent agencies, such as Defense, Treasury, Commerce, Agriculture, Justice, the Arms Control and Disarmament Agency, and the CIA, also do important background work. Their work can be crucial to the negotiation of arms control and law of the sea treaties, trade agreements, and immigration policy, for example.

We should not assume that these experts present neutral information that is somehow mechanically cranked out as public policy. Even if the experts do their best to provide the most accurate information and comprehensive policy alternatives possible, top policymakers see the information through their own perceptual and ideological lenses. So, for example, information on human rights violations in Argentina received by President Reagan, who was concerned primarily with U.S.-Soviet rivalry, led to very different policy recommendations than the same information presented to President Carter, who made human rights the cornerstone of his

foreign policy. Nevertheless, issue and area specialists are crucially important in providing accurate information and the historical context for current policies.

Our Vietnam policies failed in part because many of our best Asian experts had been purged from the State Department during the McCarthy era. The Reagan administration ignored advisers who cautioned against its covert policies in Nicaragua and Iran and replaced State Department experts who disagreed with its Central America policies. More than most presidents, Reagan made appointments to key positions in the State Department based on political considerations rather than on career expertise.

High turnover in specialist positions has, at times, put us at a disadvantage relative to our adversaries and allies. Almost all of the policymaking positions within the foreign policy establishment are held by political appointees who usually stay only a few years. This turnover compounds the loss of expertise that comes from maneuvering specialists out of career positions when their recommendations do not support the preferred policies of a particular administration. During the Cold War, for example, the former Soviet Union had much the same team of arms control negotiators for many years. Our negotiating teams changed, on average, every three to four years. Since arms control is an extremely complex field, our negotiators were continually in the process of learning.

Experts outside government who are associated with various think tanks are also sometimes influential in foreign policymaking. Primarily located in Washington, close to decision makers and the national media, these institutions—including the Institute for Policy Studies on the left of the political spectrum; the Cato, Hudson, and Heritage Foundations on the right; and the Brookings Institute, the American Enterprise Institute, the Center for Strategic and International Studies, and the Council on Foreign Relations in the middle—conduct and publish research on policy issues. These think tanks offer a home for foreign policy experts whose party is out of office and a place for academic foreign policy experts to get Washington experience and become more visible. By writing articles for national newspapers and journals and being interviewed on news and public affairs programs, experts in these institutions "wage perpetual war against each other" trying to determine the course of American foreign policy.[5]

Congress

The leading members of congressional committees on foreign affairs and armed services and of the oversight committees for intelligence agencies play a larger role in

Figuring Out How U.S. Foreign Policy Is Made

One insight into U.S. foreign policy-making was offered by Nizar Hamdoon, Iraq's ambassador to the United States from 1983 to 1987, years when we supported Iraq in its war with Iran and before the Persian Gulf War. Hamdoon lived through what he calls "every ambassador's nightmare" when, during his term, the Iraqi Air Force mistakenly attacked a U.S. ship. Dealing with this tragedy, he believed, confirmed several lessons he had learned about how Americans make foreign policy. Though these observations were written in the late 1980s, they are equally true today.

1. Washington is driven by crises and expectations of crises. To influence policy, one needs to seize opportunities that arise during these crises.

2. Make contact with media and give them access. Don't be afraid of them. They shape public opinion, and public opinion is what matters, especially during a crisis. Be honest with the media, and when they call, be available.

3. Don't ignore the bureaucracy. A diplomat watches the internal debates of, and listens to gossip about, the middle-level bureaucracy. By the time policy pronouncements are made from the top, it may be too late to influence them.

4. Cultivate good relations with the "desk officer" at the State Department, that is, the official who is in charge of policymaking and information about your particular country. Also cultivate congressional staff. Hamdoon reported that the Iraqi Embassy held a lunch or dinner for congressional staff every few weeks.

5. Never feel secure about any issue. Things can happen quickly in Congress, the executive branch, or the media, and you had better be ready.

6. Take the long-range view of issues.

7. Reach out to all Americans, no matter what their position on issues. Be prepared to debate rationally and refute stereotypes of your country.

8. Get away from Washington. As Hamdoon said, "If you stick too long in the capital, you begin to think that America is a nation of opportunists, and that nobody cares about you unless you are a power broker in a business suit." But, he concluded, people outside Washington are not so influenced by the media and not so caught up in what's happening today.

9. Watch out for checks and balances. Washington is different from other capitals because in Paris, London, or Moscow there is a central government in charge of foreign policy. In the United States, you may deal with a State Department official today, only to find that the policy has been reversed by Congress tomorrow. The positive side of this, however, is that you can affect policy because it is so changeable. "Nothing is ever final in Washington. . . . Everything and everyone is workable."

SOURCE: This box is summarized from Nizar Hamdoon, "The Washington Education of an Arab Diplomat," *Washington Post National Weekly Edition*, September 14, 1987, p. 24.

---

foreign policy than the average member. But Congress as a whole has specific constitutional authority to act as a check on the president's policies through its power to declare and fund wars and the requirement for Senate ratification of treaties and confirmation of ambassadorial and high-level State Department officials. Because Congress appropriates all money for carrying out foreign policy, the president is limited in the actions he can take without congressional approval.

Rivalry between the White House and Congress in foreign policymaking intensifies or diminishes with the issue in question. Nowhere is conflict greater than over the use of the military to achieve foreign policy goals. (This subject is discussed in greater detail in Chapter 11.)

Politicians and scholars have been arguing for more than two hundred years about how Congress's constitu-

tional authority to "declare war" limits the president's authority as commander in chief. The Founders, believing it too dangerous to give war powers to the president alone, were also unwilling to accept wording that would have given Congress the power to "make war." Instead they gave Congress the power to "declare war," leaving the president, according to James Madison's notes on the debate, "the power to repel sudden attacks."[6] This left Congress and the president to struggle over what constitutes an attack on the United States and when a military intervention is a war.

In 1973, during the congressional debate over whether to enact the War Powers Act restricting the president's authority to commit U.S. troops to combat in emergency situations, Senator Jacob Javits (R–N.Y.) compiled a list of more than two hundred occasions when the president had sent troops into combat situations without congressional approval. In fact, Congress has exercised its power to declare war only five times, and on only one of those occasions, the War of 1812, did it conduct a debate before issuing the declaration. Yet the two undeclared wars in Korea and Vietnam alone produced almost one hundred thousand American deaths, more than the combined losses of all of our declared wars, except World War II.[7]

The War Powers Act, which was intended to curb what Congress believes is presidential usurpation of its authority, has been opposed by every president since Johnson. No prior approval was sought for sending troops to Lebanon, Grenada, or Panama. President Bush asked for a congressional resolution of support for use of force in the Persian Gulf only after fifty-four members of Congress sued him for breach of the War Powers Act. Even then Bush said he was not legally required to get such support. During the Clinton administration, at different times Democrats have tried to strengthen the act and Republicans to repeal it; neither's efforts were successful. As one supporter of the act commented, "Every president finds Congress inconvenient, but we're a democracy, not a monarchy."[8]

Whatever their differences with Congress, presidents in the postwar era have usually proclaimed their desire to have a "bipartisan" foreign policy; that is, they want support from both parties so as not to make our foreign policy a subject of divisive squabbling. Presidents need that support when treaties are to be ratified, because it is rare for one party to have the necessary two-thirds majority in the Senate or for members to be united in their ranks. Carter, for example, had to woo and win Republican support to secure ratification of the hotly contested Panama Canal treaties, which returned control of the U.S.-built canal and the Canal Zone to the government of Panama.

Presidents like to say that in facing the rest of the world, Americans are all on the same side. But this is too simplistic. Policies shaping how we deal with the rest of the world are controversial and complex. Party positions do differ on these as on most other issues. For example, the roll-call votes of members of Congress on foreign policy differ according to party affiliation.[9] Democrats are more likely than Republicans to favor cuts in military spending, to agree that the United States was partially responsible for the Cold War, and to support military intervention to stop human rights abuses. Republicans are more likely to support unrestricted trade, military intervention to protect U.S. economic interests, and military aid to poor countries rather than aid for development, health, and family planning. They are also more likely than Democrats to oppose placing U.S. troops under foreign command as part of multilateral forces.[10]

Differences between the two major parties on foreign policy are usually apparent in the national platform each party issues in presidential election years. Even so, it often seems that the opposition party has no coherent alternative to the president's policy. This is probably because under normal circumstances members of Congress spend most of their time on the domestic issues that are so important to their constituents (especially at election time). In times of crises, as when U.S. troops are committed to combat, the opposition party usually rallies in support of administration policy so that the country can present a united front to the world. Once these troops are actually engaged in battle, those who continue to oppose the president's actions can find themselves in the position of appearing to give higher priority to their policy preferences than to the safety of U.S. troops. At this point it is very difficult for the opposition party to oppose the president's policy effectively.

President Bush won congressional support for the use of force in the Persian Gulf by a fairly narrow margin, but once the air war began, there was virtually no criticism of administration policies by members of Congress. There was substantial bipartisan criticism of Johnson's and Nixon's Vietnam policies, but this dissent came late in the course of the fighting, when public opinion was turning against the war and administration policies did not seem to be working. Even then, Congress approved virtually all expenditures requested to wage the war.

Perhaps one of the reasons our major parties do not present clear policy alternatives is that they do not have the tradition of forming shadow cabinets, as is done in Great Britain, for example. In a shadow cabinet, leading members of an opposition party are given the responsibility of formulating policies that can serve as alternatives to those of the party in power.

In Congress, members of the opposition party are more likely to state policy alternatives on an ad hoc basis acting as individuals, not for the party. The public may be confused when it hears a half dozen or more policy alternatives presented by members of the same party, and it may even conclude that they are "lone rangers" trying to gain political advantage in a situation that seems to call for national unity.

Interest Groups and Lobbyists

A multiplicity of interest groups are concerned with foreign policy issues: international businesses; public interest groups, such as those that lobby on environmental and human rights issues; veterans' organizations; farmers who grow crops for export; labor unions; and ethnic groups interested in their ancestral lands, such as African, Jewish, Arab, Irish, Cuban, and Polish Americans.

In general, it is harder for interest groups to affect foreign policy than domestic policy. Part of the reason for this is that the president and the executive branch have greater weight than Congress in day-to-day foreign policy decision making. But interest group activity has always been effective in some policy areas, especially those related to trade and foreign investment. For example, farm and business organizations lobby on behalf of import quotas to protect their domestically produced goods and against embargoes that prevent them from selling their products abroad. Electronics industries lobby against national security restrictions that keep them from exporting computer equipment and software that have defense applications. When Congress placed sanctions on India and Pakistan for conducting nuclear tests, it exempted what could have been the biggest penalty—food exports. Wheat farmers in the Northwest argued that sanctions on food exports would have prevented them from bidding on a $37 million wheat order from Pakistan, their biggest customer.[11] In 1997, when Congress approved far less than the State Department requested to pay dues to nearly fifty international organizations, interest groups lobbied heavily for their reinstatement. Congress may not like appropriating money for the Cotton Advisory Committee and the International Natural Rubber Organization, but American farmers and businesses think it is in their economic interest to belong and thus to have a say in decision making. Similarly, when Congress failed to appropriate money for the UN-affiliated Food and Agriculture Organization (FAO), the American Grocers lobby fought back. The FAO sets international standards for processed foods, and American grocers want to participate in setting guidelines they will have to meet.[12]

Americans have a long history of trying to win favorable U.S. policy for their countries of birth or ancestry. Some have even undertaken private action in support of home countries: Irish Americans have run guns to the Irish Republican Army and Jewish Americans to Jews in Palestine trying to establish an independent Israel, while Cuban Americans have trained a military force on U.S. soil to overthrow the Castro government in Cuba.

Perhaps no other nationality group has had as much success in setting the foreign policy agenda for their homeland as Cuban Americans. This is in part because there was a predisposition in Congress for their policy preference, and in part because their population is concentrated in one state with a large number of electoral votes. One of Cuban Americans' rare lobbying failures was their attempt to get the government to grant asylum to a six-year old boy whom the U.S. Coast Guard had found floating in the sea after having survived an escape attempt that took the life of his mother. Even though the boy's father wanted his son returned to Cuba, Cuban Americans were able, with a well-organized, high-pressure media campaign, to tie the case up in the court for months and force many top policymakers to take a position on the issue. The boy, Elian Gonzalez, became a staple of TV news channels and consequently a familiar figure for most American. But the Cuban American tactic backfired because many Americans saw the main issue as one of parental custody and disagreed with Cuban Americans using the issue of a young child's refugee status as a tool in their opposition to the Castro government. Within months after the incident, Congress voted to ease economic sanctions against Cuba, in large part because the U.S. farm and business lobbies, afraid of losing export and investment opportunities on the island to Canada and Europe, have become more influential than the Cuban American lobby.

In recent years three factors have opened up the foreign policy decision-making process to greater influence by interest groups. The first is the growing importance of campaign spending and the rise of PACs. Both the president and members of Congress depend on large campaign contributions from interest groups and are thus more vulnerable to a wide range of their demands.

Second, the personal presidency in combination with the rise of identity politics has increased the need of presidents to serve a multitude of constituencies and interests. Under pressure from African American interest groups, Clinton gave U.S. policy toward Africa a prominence it never had previously. His twelve-day trip to six African nations in 1998 was the first by a U.S. president since Carter visited two African nations twenty years earlier, and Clinton followed with a second African visit near the end of his term. Women's and religious interest groups have also become important lobbies, affecting policies on foreign aid, family planning, abortion, immigration, and women's rights. Women's groups found an advocate in Secretary of State Madeleine Albright, who identified international

Madeleine Albright, the first woman to serve as secretary of state, promised to use her tenure to advocate for women's rights around the world. Here she reads Girls Can Be Anything *to Washington, D.C., schoolchildren.*
AFP/Joyce Naltchayan

women's rights as one of the Clinton administration's priority issues.

Third, the globalization of economic activity has intensified interest groups' efforts to influence trade policy because of their concern about its impact on wages, job opportunities, child labor, worker safety, and the environment. This has led to new and very vocal alliances among trade unions and environmental and human rights groups to oppose current trade policy. During a conference of the world's top trade officials in Seattle in 1999, thousands of protestors took to the streets and managed to shut down parts of the city and interrupt the proceedings.

Private citizens who are part of Washington's elite also play a role in foreign policy.[13] For example, Henry Kissinger, former secretary of state, Brent Scowcroft, former national security adviser, and Lawrence Eagleburger, former undersecretary of state, formed a consulting business. They advised some of the world's largest corporations about foreign affairs and how international developments might affect the world economic climate in general and their corporations in particular. At the same time, Kissinger and his associates provided advice to government through their service on various advisory boards. Kissinger, for example, served on the president's Foreign Intelligence Advisory Board, where he had access to sensitive information. After Bush was elected, Scowcroft once again became national security adviser and Eagleburger returned to the State Department, thus providing examples of Washington's revolving door.

Some former members of Congress and high-level political appointees have become registered agents (lobbyists) for foreign governments after leaving office. Those who are public officials one day are private citizens the next and public officials again a few years later.[14] Rules about what constitutes a conflict of interest in such cases are unclear.

Public Opinion

Overall, the views of the public on foreign policy are not that different from those of policymakers. When they do vary, public opinion has little direct effect on foreign policy most of the time. One reason is that only a minority of Americans know much about important foreign policy issues, and many have no opinion about them. The public has always been more interested in domestic issues that impinge directly on daily life, such as the availability of jobs and the cost of consumer goods. Although there is growing awareness of the impact of foreign policy, especially trade issues, on daily life, it is difficult for the public to be well informed on the technical problems involved in trade and tariff negotiations.

The public often has no effective way to influence foreign policy decisions because much of our foreign policy is made incrementally over a long period of time and out of public view. Some of the most important decisions are made in "crisis" situations or in secrecy for national security reasons. On issues like the invasion of Grenada, for example, there was public opinion only after the fact; even Congress did not receive advance notice.

In general, the public is more likely to concede its ignorance on a wider range of issues in foreign policy than in domestic policy and accept the judgments of decision makers. Therefore, on most issues, it is easier for the president to influence public opinion through use of the media than it is for public opinion to change the president's policy.

Sometimes, however, public opinion resists attempts to change it. It is more likely to remain firm when the public holds the administration in low repute or when the government is divided, as it was on Vietnam. Deeply held opinions are also more resistant to administration pressure.

In the long term, the public always has the option of voting out of office those who disagree with majority views on foreign policy issues. However, it is difficult to use the vote to mandate that a president take a specific action, since, as we saw in Chapter 8, people vote on the basis of many different issues, most of them involving domestic policy.

Trade policy provides a good illustration of the limits on the ability of public opinion to change the president's position on a foreign policy issue. The many interest groups who have allied to oppose U.S. trade policy constitute a substantial segment of the general public; their opposition to the North American Free Trade Association (NAFTA), which eliminated trade barriers among Mexico, Canada, and the United States, was so strong that it led most Democrats, who were then the majority in Congress, to openly oppose the position of a president from their own party. With the vote coming just a year before the 1994 election, the House Speaker refused to take a position, while the majority leader and whip set up a phone lobby to persuade other Democrats to vote against the bill. One member said, "All of the traditional groups we count on to reelect us [Democrats] are against NAFTA."[15] The only person in his district willing to help get the bill passed was a Republican from the Chamber of Commerce. Despite this, and similar opposition to the U.S. granting permanent normal trading relations (PNTR) for China from his own party's leadership and from traditional Democratic constituencies, Clinton never wavered in his support for either NAFTA or PNTR for China.

Despite limitations on the public's influence in foreign policymaking, in some dramatic instances it does have an impact. Public opinion was quite sharply against Reagan in his Iran arms deals. Iran was among Americans' least popular nation, and the public was not persuaded that we should be sending weapons to it. This was a case of the public pressuring the president to enforce his own stated foreign policy, which was not to trade arms for hostages, nor even to negotiate with hostage takers. This opinion then stimulated the press and Congress to continue their investigation of the sale of arms to Iran. The results of those investigations in turn fueled negative public opinion.

Ultimately, without some public support, foreign policy objectives that require substantial commitments of time and resources will prove unsuccessful. The necessity of public support for large-scale undertakings is evident in attempts to manipulate public access to information. This is most common during wartime, when the government can justify press censorship on national security grounds. Withholding negative information (for example, high casualty rates, slow progress, civilian losses) can help keep public support high. The Persian Gulf War was fought with keen attention to public opinion. The short air war preceding the ground attack was calculated not only to minimize military casualties and the length of the ground war but also to maintain public support for the president's policies. Moreover, the restricted press coverage, which did not allow casualties to be shown, enhanced that support.

Sometimes the withholding or manipulating of information can backfire, as it certainly did during the Vietnam War. And Reagan's use of covert action in channeling money from Iran arms' sales to Nicaraguan guerrillas to skirt congressional and public opposition to his policy eventually increased that opposition.

In general, it is getting harder for the president, or the president and Congress together, to appeal for public support based on a claim of privileged information. This is another way in which the information revolution is affecting the conduct of foreign policy. Even though the president and Congress may have more reliable information, and better analysis of it, the press, interest groups, and the general public now have many more sources of information on foreign policy issues than they had a decade ago. More Americans are in e-mail contact with people in other countries and have access to the Web sites of foreign newspapers, governments, and think tanks, as well as to declassified documents in electronic archives. An ordinary citizen with a little money can even purchase some of the same satellite surveillance data collected by our most sophisticated intelligence gatherer, the National Reconnaissance Office. Private firms here and abroad, including former Soviet intelligence operatives, sell satellite reconnaissance photography to order.[16]

Changing Approaches to U.S. Foreign Policy

Isolationism

Historically, noninvolvement with other nations outside the Americas was a principal goal of our foreign policy. This policy is called **isolationism.** In the nineteenth and early twentieth centuries, Americans generally stayed aloof from European conflicts and turned inward, busy with domestic expansion and development.

One important exception was our continuing military and political involvement in Latin America, which was justified by the **Monroe Doctrine** of 1823. In articulating this doctrine, President James Monroe warned European powers that were not already in Latin America to stay out. This was a brazen move because we were a minor power challenging the major powers of the time.

As European powers withdrew from the region in the late nineteenth and early twentieth centuries, the United States began to play an increasingly active, and at times interventionist, role. With little regard for national sovereignty, we sent troops to protect U.S. citizens or business interests and to replace existing governments with those more sympathetic to our wishes. Paradoxically, the Monroe Doctrine derived from isolationist, not interventionist, sentiment. By keeping foreign powers on their side of the ocean and out of our hemisphere, we believed we would be less likely to be drawn into their conflicts abroad.

During this time, Americans did not think it appropriate to intervene in the problems of Europe or to keep a large standing army at home. This attitude was an offshoot of the predominant mood in domestic affairs: preoccupation with economic growth and a fear of strong central government. Isolationism was also a realistic position in the sense that the United States was not yet a world power. Yet another source of isolationist sentiment were those who believed that the United States was unique and that the more entangling alliances it entered into with foreign countries, the more likely it would "be corrupted and its unique nature . . . subverted."[17]

This isolationist sentiment lapsed briefly in 1917–1919, when America entered World War I on the side of the British and French against Germany, but rapidly revived afterward. Despite the wishes of President Woodrow Wilson, the United States refused to join the League of Nations, the ill-fated precursor to the United Nations. Although we have no public opinion polls from these early years, with hindsight, 70 percent of Americans in 1937 thought it had been a mistake to enter World War I.

Yet the United States was never truly isolationist. Throughout the whole early "isolationist" era, we frequently intervened diplomatically and militarily in the Caribbean and Central America and consistently sought to expand U.S. commercial and cultural influence throughout the world. Even President McKinley, who was labeled an "imperialist" by Democrats for his military adventures in the Caribbean and the Philippines, was easily reelected. Polls from the post–World War I era show that Americans overwhelmingly favored joining an international peacekeeping body like the League of Nations. And historians have pointed out there were enough votes in the Senate to ratify participation in the League had President Wilson been willing to accept amendments to the treaty agreement.[18]

Americans have almost always been willing to participate in world affairs when our interests were clearly at stake. But we are often reluctant to recognize what is at stake. In 1939, we refused to join Britain in its war to stop Nazi Germany's attempted conquest of Europe. It was not until the December 1941 Japanese attack on Pearl Harbor, Hawaii, that the public was willing to support entry into World War II. When Germany and Italy then declared war on the United States, we fought in Europe alongside Britain, the Soviet Union, and remnant armies from the occupied nations of Europe.

Containment

The Allied victory in 1945 brought a split between the Soviet Union and its Western allies. The Soviet Union lost twenty million people in the war (the United States lost four hundred thousand). Given these losses in a German invasion that was only one of many invasions of Russian territory over the centuries, the Soviet government was determined, especially as a protection against Germany, to have friendly neighbors in Europe, just as we wanted them in Latin America. To ensure this, the Soviet Union was willing to use any means, including intervention, to secure communist governments in the ring of nations surrounding it—Poland, Czechoslovakia, Romania, Hungary, and Bulgaria. Our wish for free elections in these nations was seen by the Soviet Union as an attempt to isolate it. The Russians believed we wanted to surround them with anti-Soviet governments, thus making their sacrifices in World War II futile. Many of our policymakers saw the subversion of eastern European governments as the beginning of a Soviet effort to conquer Europe.

As the only major power not decimated by the war, the United States was unable to return to its isolationist pre-war stance. In 1947, the Truman administration formulated a policy to limit the spread of communism by meeting any action taken by the Soviet Union to spread its influence with counterforce or a countermove by the United States. Known as **containment** (or the Truman Doctrine), this policy led U.S. decision makers to see most of the world's conflicts in terms of rivalry between the Soviet Union and the United States. The Soviet coup d'état in Czechoslovakia in 1948 and the rise to power of the Chinese communist government of Mao Zedong in 1949 fueled U.S. fears that the communists would try to expand the area under their control as far as possible. Thus, when communist North Korea attacked South Korea in 1950, we intervened as the nucleus of a United Nations force, believing we had to stop the spread of communism in Korea before the Soviets undertook further expansion.

Just as isolationism began as a defensive posture to keep European conflicts out of the Americas, so containment was aimed at limiting the Russians to their post–World War II reach and out of our sphere of influence. Instead of

trying to roll back Soviet power, containment was designed to keep it from expanding to a point that changed the global power balance or dragged the United States into unwanted conflicts. The chief instruments of containment policy were economic and military aid to developing countries, cultural exchanges, covert activity, alliance building, nuclear deterrence, and, as in Korea and Vietnam, limited war fought with conventional weaponry.

Containment philosophy was at work in the Marshall Plan, which provided economic relief to the nations of western Europe in 1947 (aid was offered to some eastern European governments but refused). In addition, the United States entered into military alliances with friendly nations in Europe and Asia to stop the spread of, or to roll back, Soviet influence. The most important of these was **NATO,** the **North Atlantic Treaty Organization,** which in 1949 joined the United States, Canada, and their western European allies in a mutual defense pact against Soviet aggression in Europe. Building these military alliances to compete with the Soviet Union and its eastern European allies reflected the **Cold War** era that we had now entered. We were not in military battle with the Russians, but the deep hostility between the two nations threatened to turn any conflict into a major armed confrontation.

Nuclear Deterrence

The nuclear era began in 1945, when the United States dropped atomic bombs on the Japanese cities of Hiroshima and Nagasaki. Although the debate on the necessity and ethics of dropping these bombs still contin-

ues, Japan quickly surrendered, bringing the war in the Pacific to an end.

At the close of the war, the United States was the only nuclear power. The Soviet Union exploded its first bomb in 1949, but it did not have an operational warhead until the mid-1950s and for a while thereafter had no intercontinental bombers or missiles to deliver the bombs. Despite our nuclear superiority, we found our power limited. Nuclear weapons were of little use in the pursuit of most foreign policy objectives because the threat of inflicting mass destruction to achieve a nonvital objective was not credible to opponents. Thus, during the period of nuclear superiority the United States saw its Nationalist allies lose to communists in China, its French allies lose to Ho Chi Minh in Indochina, and an anticommunist uprising in Hungary in 1956 crushed by Soviet tanks.

In 1955, the Soviet Union and its East European satellites formed the Warsaw Pact, a military alliance to counter NATO. People began to see international relations as a bipolar competition between a Western bloc of countries united under the U.S. nuclear umbrella and an Eastern bloc of nations operating under the protection of the Soviet nuclear umbrella.

American nuclear dominance began to erode in the late 1950s. *Sputnik* (the Soviet satellite that was the first to orbit the earth) showed that the Soviet Union had successfully built large rockets capable of firing missiles that could reach the United States. The fear of Soviet rocketry advances led to a program to build and deploy nuclear-tipped intercontinental ballistic missiles (ICBMs) to supplement our bomber force.

Fifty years after the bombing of Hiroshima, the city appears fully restored, but the U.S. decision to use atomic weapons is still so controversial that the Smithsonian Institution had to withdraw a planned fiftieth anniversary exhibit that presented arguments against as well as for the bomb's use. Other assaults on cities, such as the firebombing of Tokyo and Japan's "Rape of Nanjing," caused as many or more deaths, but the use of the atomic bomb stands out in public memory because it opened the door to a new kind of warfare.
Both photos from Sygma

Even with Soviet advances, American nuclear superiority was maintained for another decade. Yet everyone agreed that neither side could attack the other without the certain knowledge that the attacker as well as the attacked would suffer enormous damage. No sane leader would risk so much damage by striking first.[19] This capability, with the appropriate acronym of **MAD,** is called **mutual assured destruction.**

Despite public frustration with the Cold War—being neither totally at war or at peace—successive administrations found that "rolling back" communism in

the nuclear age was not possible without the kind of risk and commitment of resources most Americans were unwilling to assume. While the Kennedy administration did risk nuclear war over Soviet placement of nuclear weapons in Cuba, ninety miles from our shores, such risks were not taken when the Soviet Union invaded Hungary in 1956, Czechoslovakia in 1968, or Afghanistan in 1979. And the Soviet Union never directly confronted the United States in Vietnam.

One of the basic premises of containment was that all communist nations were controlled by the Soviet

Union. But as the 1950s progressed, it became clear that this was not true. Both Albania and Yugoslavia spurned Moscow's control. The Chinese became increasingly independent and in the early 1960s broke with the Soviet Union, declaring "there are many paths to socialism." Despite this, we continued to define most international events in terms of communists versus anticommunists no matter how poorly such a characterization fit. This conviction formed the basis for the **domino theory,** the proposition that if one country fell to communist rule, it would set off a chain reaction in neighboring countries, just as a long line of dominoes standing on end will fall in sequence when the first one is toppled. If U.S. intervention could prevent the first country to come under attack from falling, others would stand firm. This rationale led us into Vietnam, our longest war.

In a march on Washington, antiwar protesters put flowers in guns of military police to symbolize peace.
Paul S. Conklin

Vietnam

Early Period If one were ranking the landmark events of the twentieth century, surely World War II would rank at the top. We live in a completely different world than would have existed had Hitler not been defeated. Fighting alongside Britain and the Soviet Union, the United States achieved its greatest military victory and forged the alliance with western Europe that led to our most important treaty relationship. Yet the Vietnam War has had a far greater impact on U.S. foreign and military policy in the last quarter of the century. In this section we try to explain why.

When we became involved in Vietnam, it was still part of the French colonial territory of Indochina. After the defeat of the Japanese occupying forces in World War II, the Indochinese Communist Party, led by Ho Chi Minh, engaged the returning French forces in a war for independence. Ho appealed several times to the United States—a critic of both British and French colonial policies—for support in this effort but was rebuffed. As the war in Indochina dragged on, the Cold War settled in, and containment became the organizing concept in American foreign policy. By 1954, when Ho's troops defeated the French in a major battle, the United States was underwriting 80 percent of the cost of the French effort in Vietnam. But after considerable deliberation, the Eisenhower administration refused to provide troops or air support to save the French because Eisenhower believed this could bog us down in a long war requiring many troops.

At a conference in Geneva in 1954, a temporary boundary was established separating the territory of Ho's government in the North from that of the French-and U.S.-backed government in the South until elections could be held to choose leaders for all of Vietnam.

The new prime minister in the South, Ngo Dinh Diem, was a staunch anticommunist Catholic with influential friends in the U.S. Catholic community and Congress. With U.S. backing, Diem's government refused to participate in the elections scheduled for 1956. We believed Ho's government would win the election. The temporary partition between the North and South continued, and after the assassination of Diem in 1963, it soon became clear that the South Vietnamese government would collapse without more U.S. intervention.

Armed Intervention In 1964, President Johnson won congressional approval for massive intervention in Vietnam. In an August television address to the American public, Johnson claimed that two U.S. destroyers had been attacked by North Vietnamese torpedo boats while on routine patrol in international waters near the Gulf of Tonkin. He announced his intention to retaliate by bombing sites in North Vietnam. The next day, after presenting misleading information about the role of the U.S. destroyers in initiating the attack, he asked Congress to endorse the Gulf of Tonkin Resolution authorizing him "to take all necessary measures to repel any armed attack against the forces of the U.S. and to prevent further aggression."

Presidents Johnson and Nixon used the Tonkin Resolution to justify each act of escalation of the war. This deception laid the groundwork for the gradual erosion of congressional support for the war effort.

In early 1965, Johnson sent in U.S. troops in the belief that the war would be over "in a matter of months."

After all, the United States had sophisticated equipment and training and complete air superiority. But three years later, after half a million U.S. troops had been committed to combat, the Vietcong—North Vietnam's southern allies—were able to launch a major offensive that demonstrated that all our military efforts had not made one square foot of Vietnam truly secure. When the Joint Chiefs of Staff requested more than two-hundred thousand additional troops, a stunned President Johnson decided to undertake a review of Vietnam policy. Even the Joint Chiefs were not sure how many years and troops it might take to win. As public opposition to the war grew, Johnson called for peace talks and announced that he would not run for reelection. The talks began in May 1968 and dragged on through the administration of Johnson's successor Richard Nixon.

President Nixon wanted to leave Vietnam without appearing to have lost the war. To accomplish this, he tried "Vietnamizing" the war by forcing the South Vietnamese government to give more responsibility to its own army. He authorized the massive bombing of Hanoi and began withdrawing U.S. troops.

President Johnson listens in anguish to a tape sent by his son-in-law (Charles Robb, then an officer in Vietnam, later a U.S. senator from Virginia), talking about the men lost in battle in Vietnam.
Jack Kightlinger/Lyndon Baines Johnson Library

Nixon's most controversial war policy was his decision to expand the war into neighboring Cambodia, supposedly to destroy a huge underground headquarters of the North Vietnamese army near the Vietnamese border. In addition to igniting the largest public protests of the war, the invasion finally led to significant congressional opposition. The Tonkin Gulf Resolution was repealed, and a resolution passed prohibiting the president from using budgeted funds to wage a ground war in Cambodia. Nixon had planned to withdraw the troops from Cambodia anyway and did so quickly. But bombing in Cambodia continued until 1973, when Congress forbade the use of funds for this purpose. This was the only time Congress actually blocked presidential policies in the war.

In 1973, the United States and North Vietnam signed a peace agreement. We might have reached the same agreement in 1969, but President Nixon believed this would jeopardize his reelection chances in 1972 and perhaps other foreign policy goals, too.[20] The victory of the Vietcong and North Vietnamese finally occurred in 1975 as the South Vietnamese army disintegrated in the face of a communist attack.

Lessons from Vietnam Much of our thinking about the use of the military today is informed by the lessons of policy failures in Vietnam.[21] Even though at its peak in 1968–1969 our military force in Vietnam exceeded half a million, had sophisticated equipment and training, and had complete air superiority, we were eventually defeated. Why did we fail?

- *We did not have clear goals.* Policymakers never agreed on whether we were fighting China, the Soviet Union, North Vietnam, or rebels in the South (the Vietcong). It was not clear what or whom we were trying to defend or what Vietnam was supposed to look like after the North was defeated.

- *We did not understand the political aspects of the war.* Supporting a series of unpopular South Vietnamese governments, we were at first oblivious to the vast indigenous opposition to the South Vietnamese government from communists, other nationalists, and Buddhists. Our inability to construct an effective policy for "winning the hearts and minds" of the domestic opposition to the South Vietnamese government appears to have been a fatal weakness of policymakers from Eisenhower through Nixon.

In 1995, on the twentieth anniversary of the war's end, Robert McNamara, secretary of defense in the Kennedy and Johnson administrations and a

This photo of a naked South Vietnamese girl screaming after a napalm attack by "friendly" forces was one of the most famous photographs of the war and one that fueled antiwar protest. The girl, Kim Phue, survived although in pain and under long-term treatment for her wounds. Now living in Canada, she is pictured here with her son, Huan, meaning "prospects." She notes, "I know my picture did something to help stop the war. I have to show [my son] what happened to his mom, to her country, and that there should never be war again."
Left: AP/Wide World Photos. Right: Joe McNally/*Life* magazine © Time Inc.

principal architect of early Vietnam policy, wrote a book publicly stating for the first time that by 1967 he had come to the conclusion that the war was a mistake and could not be won. Principal among his eleven reasons for the loss were the incompetence of the South Vietnamese government and armed forces and American underestimation of the North Vietnamese.[22] (President Johnson's refusal to accept this conclusion led McNamara to leave—or be made to leave—the cabinet in 1968.)

■ *We did not understand the nature of guerrilla warfare.* For much of the war, we did not fight against a standing army dressed in the uniform of an enemy force. It was often impossible for our troops to tell soldier from civilian or enemy from ally. Although we inflicted heavy casualties on the Vietcong and North Vietnamese forces, we killed thousands of civilians in the process. Our opponents were able to demonstrate to the people of the South that their government and its ally, the United States, could not protect them or their villages. In fact, the Vietcong were able to dominate much of the rural South. Our policies—to "destroy villages in order to save them" and to take people from their own villages to "strategic hamlets," where presumably they were safe from the Vietcong—were bitterly resented by many South Vietnamese.

■ *We were impatient with the war and were unwilling to devote unending resources to winning it.* We knew from the British experience in defeating communist guerrillas in Malaysia that we would need at least ten soldiers to the guerrillas' one and that we might need ten years to win the war, but no leader dared tell the public that we must commit ourselves for that long. We were unwilling to invest the resources or time needed to defeat a guerrilla enemy. Since the goals were unclear, few wanted to risk use of the ultimate weaponry that could have destroyed the North. Although this stance was rational, it did not seem to lead to the obvious question of whether our objectives were worth the effort we were making.

■ *We did not have public support.* Although public opinion was generally supportive during the first years of the war, support eroded as it appeared we were bogged down in an interminable and indecisive conflict. Only about 20 percent of the public favored an immediate withdrawal in 1965, but by mid-1969, support for withdrawal began to increase and by 1970 reached 50 percent. By 1971 public support for withdrawal grew to overwhelming proportions.[23]

The United States persisted in Vietnam for nearly eleven years because most policymakers believed in standing firm against what they saw as communist aggression. But Vietnam shattered the belief in containment and U.S. illusions that it could serve as the world's police force. Many Americans believed both our aims and tactics in Vietnam were immoral. Others believed our aims were just but unachievable. Still others believed we should have stayed until we won. All these sentiments led to a good deal of public self-examination about the war.

The failure of our Vietnam policy led to an attitude among the public and officials of uncertainty about our foreign policy goals and our ability to achieve them through military means. This has been called the **Vietnam syndrome.** Decision makers became more reluctant to commit troops to combat situations or to threaten military action to pursue containment goals. Some people believed this new caution was a positive development that would keep us from becoming involved in new military entanglements we could not win. But many others believed this national self-doubt tied the hands of decision makers and prevented them from using the full range of our capabilities to pursue national interests abroad.

Detente

Richard Nixon came to office after public opinion had begun to turn against the war. Perhaps partly for this reason and partly because his central interest was in foreign and not domestic policy, he immediately began looking for ways to shape international relations in the post–Vietnam War era.

As a man whose career was built on making political hay out of his staunch anticommunism, President Nixon was well placed to make diplomatic overtures to the Soviet Union without fear of being attacked by any but the most diehard Cold Warriors. Thus, Nixon and his national security adviser and later secretary of state, Henry Kissinger, developed a policy called **detente,** which was designed to deescalate Cold War rhetoric and to promote the notion that relations with the Soviet Union could be conducted in ways other than confrontation. We could reward the Soviet Union for "good behavior" on the international scene and at the same time reduce our own military expenditures, slow the arms race, and perhaps step back from the brink of war. The detente doctrine recognized that although the Soviet Union

Mobs of South Vietnamese civilians scale the walls of the U.S. embassy in Saigon, trying to hitch a ride on the evacuation helicopters as the North Vietnamese enter the city and the last Americans leave in 1975.
AP/Wide World Photos

would remain our adversary, it too had legitimate interests in the world. Detente also recognized the growing military strength of the Soviet Union and that it was in our interests to pursue bilateral agreements, such as on arms control, that would try to limit this strength.

Among the most notable achievements of the policy of detente were the Strategic Arms Limitation Talks, which produced a treaty (SALT I), signed by President Nixon and Soviet leader Leonid Brezhnev in 1972. SALT I limited the number of ABM (antiballistic missile—a defensive missile) launchers that each side could possess and put a five-year freeze on the number of offensive missiles in each side's stockpile.

During this era of new diplomacy with the Soviet Union, President Nixon also sent out feelers to see if China was interested in reestablishing diplomatic ties. Even though it was home to one-fifth of the world's population, China had been shut out of the mainstream diplomatic community, largely due to U.S. pressure, since the communist victory in 1949. After two years of negotiations through third parties, the first cultural exchange (a visit by the U.S. Ping-Pong team) was arranged in 1971. By the time of President Nixon's visit in 1972, many nations had resumed diplomatic relations with China, and it had regained its seat in the United Nations Security Council. (Full diplomatic recognition by the United States did not come until the Carter administration.)

The resumption of diplomatic relations between China and the United States was one of the most remarkable achievements of the Nixon-Kissinger attempts to make a breakthrough in the Cold War stalemate. Nonetheless, it was consistent with their balance-of-power approach to foreign policy. By making this effort during a period of hostility in relations between the Soviet Union and China, Nixon was probably hoping to gain leverage in dealings with the Soviet Union (what some referred to as "playing the China card").

The Nixon-Kissinger visits to China were all the more remarkable because they occurred while U.S. troops were still fighting in Vietnam. It had been the specter of a Sino-Soviet-led communist bloc and a near paranoid fear of "yellow hordes" advancing throughout Asia that led us to fight in Korea and Vietnam. Within a few short years, China's image was recast from dreaded enemy to friendly ally, and Cold War fears of world communist domination were greatly diminished.

The doctrine of detente complemented the mood of isolationism and weariness that grew in the wake of the Vietnam War. Public and elite opinion after the war was

One of the first major achievements of the Nixon-Kissinger policy of detente was to reestablish normal relationships with the People's Republic of China, governed by the Communist Party since 1949. Here Nixon attends a state banquet in Beijing with then premier Zhou Enlai.
Courtesy of National Archives

divided. Isolationist, go-it-alone sentiment peaked immediately after the war but then declined.

A new spirit of cooperative internationalism characterized the early Carter administration.[24] Carter and his advisers saw the world as far more complex than Cold War rhetoric suggested. They believed problems of global poverty, inequitable distribution of wealth, abuse of human rights, and regional competitiveness were substantial threats to world order and that the United States should work with other nations to solve these problems.

Carter continued the negotiations begun during the Ford administration on a follow-up treaty to SALT I, and in 1979 he and President Brezhnev signed SALT II, which placed limitations on offensive missiles. But the stunning invasion of Afghanistan by the Soviets in 1979 ended the chance of gaining Senate approval for the treaty. Public and elite opinion shifted; Cold War views, never completely dead, became much more respectable again.

Cold War Revival

The Reagan administration took office in 1981 determined to challenge the Soviet Union in every way possible. During his first term, Reagan totally renounced the Nixon-Kissinger principle of detente and labeled the Soviet Union an "evil empire." He and his advisers continued to view the world largely in light of a U.S.-Soviet competition. They painted a simple picture of an aggressive and reckless Soviet Union and a peace-loving and virtuous United States. Despite the rhetoric, however, the administration did not risk direct confrontation. But Reagan's approach differed from containment because it was more ideologically than strategically driven; he sought not just to contain the Soviets but to undo the status quo. One method Reagan endorsed was stepping up the arms race and, by forcing them to keep pace, drive the Soviets into economic ruin. The centerpiece of this policy was his plan to build an antimissile defense system, the Strategic Defense Initiative (SDI) or Star Wars program. The plan was based on a laser technology that did not yet exist but that was supposed to intercept and destroy nuclear-tipped ballistic missiles before they reached their targets in the United States. Its projected cost was tens of billions of dollars. Reagan's SDI and military buildup programs increased defense spending to record peacetime levels.

Though the election of Reagan put a Cold Warrior in the White House, the public was not willing to buy Cold War arguments wholeheartedly. Vietnam had increased public fears of U.S. involvement in long wars with fuzzy objectives. By Reagan's second term, a dramatic drop in public support for increased military spending and growing public pressure for progress on arms control helped push the administration toward a less belligerent stance. Violent rhetoric was toned down and conciliatory gestures multiplied.[25] Washingtonians believed President Reagan wanted to reach some agreement with the Soviets in order to be remembered as a peacemaking president.

To comply with the SALT treaty, the air force chopped up B-52 airplanes. Each plane got four chops from a huge guillotine blade, and the pieces were sold as scrap for 16¢ a pound. The planes were left in their dismembered state for ninety days so that Russia could confirm their destruction with a satellite photo.
Alex MacLean

Ending the Cold War

The moderation in Reagan's rhetoric was also a response to changes in the Soviet Union. In 1985, Mikhail Gorbachev, the new general secretary of the Communist Party of the Soviet Union, called for "new thinking" and began to shake up Soviet society as it had not been shaken since the Russian Revolution in 1917.[26] Faced with a stagnating economy and an antireform Soviet leadership, Gorbachev encouraged competition in the economy, criticism of corruption and inefficiencies by government agencies, and free elections of some government legislative bodies.

In addition to shaking up Soviet society, Gorbachev challenged the status quo in the international community with his policy of *glasnost,* or opening to the outside world. He encouraged foreign investment and requested foreign aid to help rebuild the Soviet economy; he made it easier for Soviet citizens to emigrate, pulled Soviet troops out of Afghanistan, and reduced aid to Soviet-

backed governments in Nicaragua and Cuba. In 1988, Gorbachev announced to the United Nations that the Communist Party had no monopoly on the truth and backed up this statement by accepting multiparty elections in eastern Europe.

Gorbachev also took the initiative in resuming arms control negotiations with President Reagan. In 1987, the two men reached an agreement on intermediate-range nuclear forces (INF). Under this agreement, the United States and the Soviet Union would remove from Europe all missiles with a range of 300 to 3,100 miles. To ensure compliance, the United States sent inspectors or monitors to the Soviet Union, and the Soviets sent them to western Europe and the United States to observe production facilities and the dismantling and removal of the missiles.

During the first two years of the Bush administration, the Soviet empire in eastern Europe disintegrated with such rapidity that all policymakers were caught off guard. The Soviet-dominated governments were dismantled, Communist Parties changed their names, opposition parties formed, and free multiparty elections were held.

In late 1989, demonstrators assaulted the most visible symbol of the Cold War, the Berlin Wall (built by the Soviets in 1961 to divide Soviet-occupied East Berlin from NATO-occupied West Berlin), and began tearing it down. A year later the reunification of Germany marked the end of the post–World War II power alliance in Europe.

In 1991, while Gorbachev vacationed, a handful of party hard-liners and key people in the KGB and Defense Ministry joined forces to take over the Soviet government. Poorly planned and without organizational depth or popular support, the coup lasted only three days. Held indirectly responsible for the coup by many for having put in power those who led it, Gorbachev resigned as head of the Communist Party and stripped the party of its role in government. Faced with massive restructuring problems and the possibility of food shortages, he made major foreign policy concessions to Western governments in order to obtain economic aid. Among them was an agreement to remove Soviet military forces from Cuba, the last vestige of Cold War competition in the western hemisphere.

With no strong center left in Moscow, the Baltic states immediately declared their independence. Soon other republics followed suit or announced their intent to redefine their relationship with the national government inside a reformulated federal structure. Gorbachev was left with no country to lead, his power supplanted by the presidents of the independent republics. As the Soviet Union passed from the scene, replaced by new republics, all nations were groping to figure out what the new alignment of the world order would be.

Early in the 1990s, President Bush referred to a "new world order," although no one was quite certain what it meant in terms of concrete foreign policies, other than the absence of U.S.-Soviet military competition. In the new order, foreign policies would presumably be less dependent on military capabilities. Still, some feared that, as the world's sole remaining military superpower, the United States would feel freer to use its military advantage in pursuit of its foreign policy goals; however, without the Soviet threat to justify expenditures, the United States began to shrink its military. There was also strong public pressure to avoid new foreign entanglements. With the Cold War over, Americans seemed weary of trying to understand and change the world. They were more impressed by the failures of foreign aid, military intervention, and diplomacy than by foreign policy successes, more weighed down by problems at home than by those in other countries. Bush found he could justify intervention in the Gulf, and later in the civil war in Somalia, only through cost sharing and participation in an international force under UN auspices.

Merchant Diplomacy and Multilateralism

Bill Clinton took office as the first president born after World War II and one of the few never to have served in the military. He was a self-described child of the Cold War, an opponent of the Vietnam War, and more shaped by the skepticism of that era than by memories of the Allied victory in World War II. In his campaign he reminded

Before anticoup demonstrators in Moscow, a Soviet soldier displays the flag with a large hole where the hammer and sickle had been.
Andy Hernandez/SIPA

AMERICANS REACT TO THE CRISIS IN KOSOVO...

WONDER HOW MY MUTUAL FUNDS DOING?

HAVE TO TAKE THE KIDS TO PRACTICE.

IF I LEAVE NOW, I CAN STILL BEAT THE TRAFFIC.

I'M GONNA HAVE TO UPGRADE THE WHOLE SYSTEM.

CUTE JACKET. BET IT COSTS A FORTUNE.

Reprinted with special permission of North American Syndicate.

voters that we had not defeated the Soviet Union in battle but that it had collapsed from within due to "economic, political and spiritual failure." The lesson, Clinton said, was, "Given the problems we face at home, we must first take care of our own people and their needs." In this sense "foreign and domestic policy are inseparable," and the best foreign policy is to have a strong economy.[27]

With this as his theme, Clinton signaled a change in approach to foreign policy. Befitting the end of the Cold War, greater emphasis would be given to economic than to military instruments of foreign policy, and more attention would be paid to using our economic strength to achieve political goals, such as promotion of democracy and human rights, which Clinton said we had neglected in our pursuit of strategic interests.

Predictably, Clinton's foreign policy was rooted in the pursuit of national economic interests, so much so that almost all issues were discussed in terms of their value to U.S. trade relations. (Clinton's second-term national security adviser was an international trade lawyer.) This led some observers to label his foreign policy "merchant diplomacy."[28] Deemphasizing military in favor of economic diplomacy suited Clinton's approach to foreign policy, according to one presidential aide, because the president saw force as a zero-sum (winner-take-all) game. "He is not a zero-sum kind of guy—he is a positive-sum guy; he likes situations in which everyone can come out a winner."[29] This approach was also compatible with the public mood, which, although not one of withdrawal from world affairs, was leery of new political entanglements.

While maintaining a commitment to high levels of military spending, Clinton's foreign policy has relied lit-

tle on the independent use of military force. Clinton sent troops to Haiti in 1994 to oust a military dictatorship and restore the elected president only after gaining UN backing. It marked the first time an American president had sought prior international approval for a military intervention in the Caribbean. To some it was a radical departure from, or even an end to, the Monroe Doctrine.[30] If not an aberration, it could signal a major shift in American foreign policy and an adjustment to new realities of the post–Cold War world. The United States, like other industrial democracies, is reluctant to go it alone in any military venture, preferring multilateral cooperation to unilateral action. The difficulty with this approach is that the national interests (and therefore the motivation for intervening) that each country has at stake in any international dispute vary. This can paralyze the policy process and make military cooperation to resolve a conflict impossible to achieve.

Military Instruments of Foreign Policy

For more than forty years we thought our military strength was our most important asset in our effort to keep the world "free." Relying on the strategy of mutually assured destruction, we built up an arsenal of nuclear-tipped missiles and bombers capable of delivering nuclear warheads.

But the effectiveness of nuclear weapons as an instrument of foreign policy depended on their *not* being used. The nuclear arsenal helped to achieve the ultimate goal of avoiding defeat or destruction by a foreign power, but it was not a flexible instrument of policy. Even though we built a wide range of smaller *tactical* nuclear weapons, they too were of little use because their introduction on a battlefield risks an escalation to more powerful weapons and might endanger our own troops.

In the first decades of the Cold War, we relied so heavily on nuclear deterrence that we neglected other aspects of our military capability, including the capacity to fight limited wars with conventional weaponry. Yet conventional fighting forces have always been more important than nuclear weapons in pursuing containment and other foreign policy goals.

In the 1960s our military planners thought we should be strong enough to fight two and a half wars at the same time: major wars against big powers such as the Soviet Union and China, in which nuclear weapons would presumably play a role, and regional or guerrilla wars in Asia, Africa, or Latin America, waged with conventional weaponry. As the Vietnam War demonstrated what a drain on our economic and military resources a limited war could be, the Nixon administration lowered our goal to waging one major and one smaller war. Our defeat in Vietnam, combined with the growing likelihood that containment would be pursued through military intervention and limited wars, led the Carter and Reagan administrations to place greater emphasis on improving combat readiness and building a new arsenal of high-tech weaponry.

Spending on nuclear preparedness itself became an instrument of foreign policy in the 1980s, as Reagan vowed to crush the Soviets economically by forcing them into a spending war in a race to acquire an antiballistic missile system. The arms race added to the Soviets' economic woes but also endangered our own economic security by contributing to huge budget deficits and robbing the civilian economy of many of our best scientists and engineers. In total an estimated $5.1 trillion (not counting cleanup costs) was spent on nuclear preparedness, consuming from one-fourth to one-third of all military spending and producing about seventy thousand warheads and weapons.[31]

During the Bush administration, the military was assigned the mission of preparing to fight two major regional conflicts simultaneously, with emphasis on conventional warfare. This is known as the "two major theater war" policy, or 2MTW. The end of the Cold War had removed the need to prepare for a major nuclear conflagration with the Soviet Union. The arsenal of warheads, ICBMs, and nuclear bombers was drastically cut, and many domestic and foreign bases closed. (The United States had about 10,400 operable nuclear weapons in 2000 and, under existing arms agreements with Russia, plans to reduce this number to 3,000 by 2002.)

Although the 2MTW policy remains in place, since the Gulf War, the size of the military has been cut by a third, a hundred bases have been closed, and mandatory spending caps have limited annual increases in the defense budget. At the turn of the century military spending was slightly below its 1997 level of 3.2 percent of GDP, the lowest comparative level since before World War II.[32]

In its 1996 appropriations request, the Clinton administration said, "The U.S. today is the only nation with the logistical, mobility, intelligence, and communications capabilities which allow it to conduct large-scale, effective military operations on a global scale."[33] This has led some to characterize the United States at this point in history as the "essential nation."[34] But

defining an appropriate use for the military has been complicated by the increasing tension between civilian and military leadership. Part of this tension stems from the Vietnam experience, and some undoubtedly comes from the end of the draft and the conversion to an all-volunteer armed services more than twenty-five years ago. Today, even though it is required by law that young men register for the draft when they reach age eighteen, one in five fail to do so.[35] Few politicians under the age of fifty have served in any branch of the armed forces. As a veteran, Al Gore was an exception among the highest-ranking civilian decision makers in the Clinton administration; the president, the secretaries and deputy secretaries of defense and state, the national security adviser, and the CIA director had no military experience. Since the end of the Vietnam War, the proportion of members of Congress who have had military training has fallen from 77 to 33 percent.[36] Retired officers have commented warily on the increasing defiance of the president and civilian authority by high-ranking officers. One observer says "the day is coming when military and civilian leaders will stare at one another across a nearly unbridgeable cultural divide."[37] Even if this prediction is unduly pessimistic, there do appear to be substantial differences in civilian and military views on the appropriate use of the armed forces in the post–Cold War era.[38]

The use of the military to pursue foreign policy objectives is also constrained by budgetary pressures and the still strong lessons of Vietnam: Do not commit U.S. troops where no clear objectives or time table can be established. However, due to the size and capabilities of our military establishment, our desire to play a world leadership role, and the expectations of other world leaders about our role in world peacekeeping, it is impossible for any American president to ignore the uses of the military in the pursuit of foreign policy goals.

Military Intervention

Over the course of American history, the military has been used less often to wage total or limited warfare than to intervene in small countries whose affairs have been seen as linked to U.S. economic or security interests. During the Cold War, we were somewhat more reluctant to intervene with U.S. troops, preferring where possible to give military aid and training to indigenous forces in order to avoid confrontation with the Soviet Union. But even then, we maintained several hundred military installations and hundreds of thousands of troops abroad.

Protecting American industries sounds patriotic. Supporters of protectionism argue that these policies protect new industries until they can get established and support old industries essential to our defense and basic self-sufficiency. They also say that protectionist policies can save American jobs and maintain our standard of living by placing tariffs on imported goods manufactured by foreign workers paid subsistence wages. They even claim protection can help make domestic industries more efficient and competitive. They point to Harley-Davidson, which, with tariff protection, raised its product quality, productivity, and profits.

Protectionist policies usually mean higher consumer prices, however. Auto quotas added about $1,300 to the price of each new Japanese car and $650 to each new American car sold here. Each job saved by the import quotas on Japanese cars cost American consumers more than $100,000.[47] It would have been much cheaper to compensate the auto workers thrown out of work and retrain them for other jobs. Quotas imposed on some clothing raised prices by an estimated 20 percent.[48] And the tariffs on computer chips doubled the price of chips within a year, increasing prices charged to U.S. computer firms that bought chips from Japan. Thus, the tariff ended up helping the Japanese computer industry more than our own.

Higher prices for consumer products are just one of the criticisms of protectionism made by advocates of **free trade.** Free trade is a policy of minimum intervention by governments in trade relations. Its advocates, or

A Barbie doll and a G.I. Joe fighter plane from China. A baseball mitt from South Korea and another from the Philippines. Adidas running shoes from South Korea and Nikes from Taiwan. Teapots and china from England, cognac and crystal from France. A suburban Los Angeles family of five was asked to identify all of their possessions made in foreign countries or in the United States by foreign companies. The family also located products from Colombia, Denmark, Germany, Hong Kong, Italy, Malaysia, Mexico, Singapore, Sweden, and Switzerland. By far the most, however, were from Japan—two cars, three motorcycles, and one bicycle; cameras, binoculars, and a telescope; a TV, VCR, Nintendo, stereo, and tape player; a clock, watch, and calculator; a microwave; and a lawn mower.
Henry Groskinsky

free traders, believe government regulation of trade, for economic or political reasons, reduces the efficiency of the world economy, thus preventing countries from maximizing their income.[49] Free trade, like capitalism, is a relative term; all countries place some restrictions on trade to protect domestic labor and business interests. In fact, historically forms of protection applied to 30 to 40 percent of all trade.

Free traders claim that, in addition to increasing prices, protectionism also discourages industry efficiency and competitiveness. They say the success of a Harley-Davidson is an exception and point to the benefits to the U.S. auto industry of international competition. Opening U.S. markets to Japanese cars gave Americans the choice of a superior product, and they deserted self-satisfied U.S. manufacturers in droves. The American auto industry was forced to improve its efficiency and its cars. Today American auto workers can turn out a car for significantly less money than Japanese workers, and they have a product much superior to their 1970s models. By 1993, almost half of all Americans thought U.S. cars were a better value than Japanese-made cars.[50]

Finally, critics of protectionism say that it invites other nations to aim their own protectionist policies at goods we want to export to them. Retaliatory measures can spiral into a trade war, and trade wars have the potential to expand into military competition to protect market access.

Despite these dangers, pressure for protectionist legislation continues to grow because job retention and creation are major issues in all industrialized countries. But the ability of the U.S. government to adopt protectionist measures is limited by membership in the World Trade Organization (WTO). The WTO, headquartered in Geneva, Switzerland, was founded in 1995 to remove barriers to free trade and to mediate trade disputes between member countries. It has 136 members, and others participate in the organization while awaiting full membership. WTO policies are set primarily by consensus of member countries, represented by their trade ministers. All members belong to the general council, which is empowered to resolve trade disputes. However, there is an appellate body, and countries can be sanctioned for not abiding by WTO decisions.[51]

The near universal membership of the WTO includes many smaller and poorer countries who do not have the legal infrastructure or the political freedoms that exist in the United States. This has created fear among U.S. interest groups that membership in WTO will roll back regulatory standards to those of the lowest level among the membership. Unions fear they will lose well-paying jobs with benefits to nonunionized workers in poorer countries who will work for low wages, no benefits or safety protections, and who perhaps lack the freedom to unionize. Environmental activists fear that none of the regulations applied to food production and distribution in the United States will be enforced for foodstuffs imported from countries without a commitment to environmental protection. They claim that globalization and free trade are hastening the relocation of industry to countries where there are no limitations on toxic emissions into the air and water or regulation of the dumping and storing of hazardous waste. Human rights groups claim free trade is adding to the already widespread abuse of child labor, unequal pay for women, and the exploitation of prison labor. They oppose the removal of barriers to trade and investment in countries controlled by dictatorships, fearing that by helping build up their economies, we will strengthen the governments and contribute to even greater human rights abuses.

When free trade advocates in developing countries hear attacks on "environmental" or "human rights" abuses by their governments, they often take them as code words for protectionism and dismiss the substance of the complaints. But free trade opponents point to the impact of the North American Free Trade Agreement (NAFTA). This agreement among the United States, Canada (our leading trade partner), and Mexico phases out tariffs, duties, and other trade barriers and creates near total market access for agricultural products. Since NAFTA was passed, trade between Mexico and the United States increased from $82 billion to more than $200 billion in 1999. But more than two-thirds of Mexicans still live in poverty, according to UN statistics.[52]

NAFTA created the world's second largest and richest trading bloc. There is no doubt that it was a response to the **European Union (EU).** The very countries that have served as our staunchest military allies are at the same time among our strongest economic competitors. In 1992, the EU removed all internal economic barriers and customs posts for member nations. Formerly called the European Economic Community, or Common Market, the EU was formed in 1957 to foster political and economic integration in Europe. The membership of the EU has expanded to fifteen from its original six members (Table 1). Although its economic output is smaller than that of the United States, the EU, with a single trade policy, a single agricultural policy, and a single market of 340 million people, is the world's single biggest importer and

Reprinted with permission of North America Syndicate

exporter. The EU took another step toward the economic integration of Europe when twelve of its fifteen members agreed to phase in a common currency (the euro) by 2002.

The United States is particularly concerned about EU competition in the export of agricultural goods. Although much is made of U.S. farm subsidies, European farmers are among the most highly subsidized in the world. The removal of import quotas and fees within the EU and a unified policy on price supports for European farmers will make it even harder for us to export our agricultural products to Europe. In the late 1990s, the food war escalated as U.S. farmers fought to ban imports of European beef after the outbreak of "mad cow" disease in England, and European farmers waged a campaign to ban the import of genetically altered foods ("frankenfoods") and hormone-fed beef and poultry into European markets. The EU has also successfully appealed to the WTO to force an end to U.S. government subsidies (in the form of a tax break) for American exporters. With American farm exports and income falling and record numbers of farmers leaving the land, competing with EU agricultural exports will be one of our most serious trade problems as we enter the next century.

Trade problems in East Asia also loom large in our foreign policy. Until 1997 this region had some of the fastest growing economies in the world, including Japan, China, Taiwan, South Korea, Indonesia, and Singapore. In 1997, when major recessions hit South Korea and In-

donesia, we faced one of those paradoxical problems in foreign policy—providing aid to our trade competitors (see "Foreign Aid" later in the chapter).

Developing export and investment opportunities in the massive Chinese market will continue to receive priority in our relations with the People's Republic, as is evidenced by the token actions taken against that government for its brutal repression of the prodemocracy movement in 1989 and Clinton's decision in 2000 to grant China permanent normal trade relations. Our relations with China demonstrate how difficult it is in a world of powerful trading nations to use trade to achieve political goals such as promotion of human rights or internal reform. We have pressured China far more on the issue of protecting the copyrights of American artists, musicians, and writers than on human rights. China's consumer market of 1.3 billion people that the U.S. business community has long coveted is each day more accessible. Jeopardizing access to this market in a period of high trade deficits in order to defend a principle was a bigger risk than Clinton was willing to take, even though imports from China account for much of our trade deficit.

It takes great skill, clear goals, and substantial leverage to promote human rights through foreign policy, and it is almost impossible to do so without antagonizing other governments for interfering in their domestic affairs. If trade can be used to pressure another government to take some action we favor, it will most likely be in situations where we have a distinct advantage over the trading partner as, for example, when it has no other export markets for its products, or when it cannot find another supplier for goods it needs to import. In today's world, where we are in stiff competition for export markets with China, Japan, and the countries of Europe and Latin America, our trade leverage has diminished.

Economic Sanctions

Economic sanctions are policies designed to get a state to change its behavior, or to take some action or set of actions, by refusing to engage with it in the conventional range of international economic relations (for example, trade, aid, loans) or by denying it access to specific economic goods or services. Economic sanctions are generally regarded as middle-of-the-road measures.[53] They are stronger than talking diplomacy but weaker than military confrontation. The United States has used sanctions to try to force internal political reforms, improve human rights, end trade barriers, change military and

Ronald McDonald is flattened by protesters in Cavaillon, France. Europeans are increasingly upset by the importation of American genetically altered food, while the French in particular are angry about the increasing popularity of American fast foods.
Reuters/STR/Archive Photos

weapons policies, and destabilize governments. In fact, between 1917 and 1998 Congress passed ten separate laws authorizing the president to impose various kinds of sanctions. No country in the world has imposed them as often as the U.S.; in 1998 we had sanctions in place against twenty-six countries that held half of the world's population.[54]

When the United Nations voted to place economic sanctions on Iraq for its invasion of Kuwait in August 1990, it set off another round in an old debate on the usefulness of such measures. There is a widespread belief that economic sanctions are not effective in getting governments to change their behavior. Opponents argue that sanctions require unrealistic amounts of time and international cooperation to bring about the desired results. The longer the sanctions are in effect, the argument continues, the greater the temptation for nations to pursue their own economic interests by trading or selling prohibited goods to the targeted nation.

Those who believe that under the right circumstances economic sanctions can work point to their use against the government of South Africa. South Africa, one of the largest countries in Africa, was governed by a white minority of five million in a nation of about thirty million. Due to the system of apartheid, the huge black majority had no say in government and lacked basic civil rights, including the right to vote, the right to marry a person of another race, equal opportunities for good jobs and pay, and the right to live in most areas of the country. All black adults had to carry identification cards, and thousands were arrested each year for not having proper identification. Most public facilities were segregated. Both black and white critics of the regime were subject to arbitrary arrest and indefinite imprisonment.

The Reagan administration, a supporter of the white government of South Africa, developed a policy called "constructive engagement." The idea of constructive engagement was to keep good relations with South Africa and try to persuade its government to move slowly toward democracy, a policy similar to that now pursued toward China.

In 1985, however, increased black protest and demonstrations in South Africa focused world attention on apartheid. In the United States, college students and others also staged demonstrations in cities and on campuses. Public opinion and protests pressured corporations to remove their businesses from South Africa and colleges, churches, cities, and foundations to "divest," sell stocks in companies that had investments in South Africa, and to refuse to do business with companies that operated in South Africa.

In 1985, in the face of public opinion and a Congress threatening to impose severe restrictions on U.S. economic involvement with South Africa, Reagan dropped the policy of constructive engagement and imposed mild economic sanctions. In this case it might be said that government policy was coopted by the private sector. The actions taken by corporations, under shareholder and public pressure, to divest their holdings in the South African economy had a greater impact than the limited action taken by the U.S. government. Divestiture occurred on an international scale, with corporations from all parts of the world pulling out of South Africa. These actions, coupled with sanctions placed on South Africa by the United Nations, undoubtedly played a role in the elimination of all remaining apartheid laws and the end of white minority rule.

In situations where the international community cannot achieve such widespread consensus as on South Africa, economic sanctions have not been as effective in attaining their objectives. One study of 103 instances of economic sanctions dating from World War I found a success rate of 36 percent. Sanctions were most effective when the goals were modest or when the sanctions were used to destabilize a government; they were least effective in damaging a country's military capacity or in effecting some major change in a state's behavior.[55] Sanctions are much more likely to be successful when a large state targets a much smaller, weaker state, but even then there is not a high likelihood of success if the goals are too ambitious. Only four of sixteen U.S.-backed sanctions during the Reagan administration were considered successful. During the first three years of the Clinton administration, sanctions were imposed or threatened sixty times against thirty-five countries, with twenty-two new cases in 1996 alone.[56] Countries targeted included Cuba, Libya, Iran, Burma, Colombia, Iraq, Russia, Syria, Vietnam, China, Azerbaijan, and Yugoslavia. Opponents say sanctions accomplish little and cost the United States $15 billion a year in lost exports.

Rarely does the United States target a large or powerful country, unless it is to achieve a very limited objective, such as by using trade sanctions to force the former Soviet Union to allow the emigration of Jews. The United States elects not to impose an embargo on China, even though democracy and human rights are at the very least as scarce as in Cuba, against whom we have had a trade embargo for 40 years. China is a large and economically powerful country, and the last two administrations decided that sanctions would achieve nothing while hurting the United States economically.

The Cuba example shows that even against a much smaller country, which was once quite dependent on the United States as a trading partner, sanctions will not necessarily be effective. Even the most severe form of sanction, a trade embargo, has not achieved its goal of effecting significant political and economic reform or destabilizing the Castro government. Sanctions likely contributed to a lower standard of living for Cubans, but they did little to change the leadership's policies or lifestyle. Many other countries are willing to trade with Cuba, and meanwhile the Cuban government was able to use the U.S. embargo to deflect criticism from its own economic failures.

The international sanctions imposed on Iraq after it invaded Kuwait are the toughest imposed on any nation in modern times and are estimated to have cost Iraq more than $120 billion. Yet they did virtually nothing to change the behavior of the Iraqi government. UN arms inspectors were not even able to carry out their weapons-monitoring program. An estimated seven hundred thousand Iraqi children have died from malnutrition or disease since the sanctions have been in place, even though con-

Moments before being photographed signing peace accords between Israel and the Palestinians, the leaders adjust their ties—Israel's Rabin, Egypt's Mubarak, Jordan's Hussein, and President Clinton—with the Palestinians' tieless Arafat looking on.
Barbara Kinney/The White House

cessions were made allowing Iraq to sell oil to buy food and medicine for children. These deaths and the malnourishment of a million other Iraqi children are attributed in large part to the sanctions.[57] Meanwhile, Iraq is once again one of our largest suppliers of oil.

Congress has been questioning the long-term value of embargoes, as evidenced in its approval of an easing of sanctions against Cuba in 2000. Under pressure from farmers who were suffering one of their worst economic crises since the 1970s and eagerly looking for new markets for their crops, Congress attached a measure to an Agriculture Department appropriation bill prohibiting the president from including food and medicine in future embargoes of other countries unless approved by Congress.

Sanctions may be continued despite evidence of their ineffectiveness simply as a way to exact punishment for behavior other states cannot change. A senior Clinton aide has said, "Sanctions are not a precision-guided instrument. . . . But they are effective at . . . exacting a cost for behavior that's repugnant, dangerous, and destabilizing."[58]

More graphically, a congressional aide compared sanctions to chicken soup: "We all know they don't work. But they make us feel good." The downside has been painted by a business lobbyist: "Chicken soup keeps you from going to the doctor and taking the corrective measures you really need. Worse yet it really does a job on the chicken."[59]

Foreign Aid

Extending economic assistance to other countries is another tool of American foreign policy. Aid can take the form of grants, technical assistance, or guaranteed loans, for example. The primary object of the aid is to promote development and stability, but indirectly it is a means for influencing the direction of other countries' development, expanding export markets for U.S. goods, and in general spreading our sphere of influence. The grants and loans are often used to purchase American goods, or to repay loans from American banks or public agencies.

In the fifty-five years since the end of World War II, the United States has spent more than a half trillion dollars on foreign aid, about two-thirds of which was given in military assistance. Most of the money earmarked for economic assistance has been channeled through USAID. Whereas economic sanctions operate by *denying* a state goods or services until it changes its behavior, foreign aid is used as an *incentive* to change behavior or as a reward for actions taken. In recent years, for example, the United States has paid millions of dollars in aid to the Ukraine and Russian Republics to destroy nuclear weapons inherited from the Soviet arsenal and promised $4.6 billion to North Korea to pay for denuclearization and the development of alternative energy sources. And in each year since 1976, when they signed the U.S.-brokered peace treaty, Israel and Egypt have received at least 40 percent of our annual aid budget.

The greatest success ever achieved with foreign aid was the rebuilding of Europe after World War II under the Marshall Plan. Since that time major successes have been rare, and in recent years there has been great disillusionment with economic aid as an effective means for achieving our goals. Too often the money ended up in the bank accounts of corrupt leaders, as in Haiti, Zaire, and Panama, for example, or was spent on showy construction projects that did little to further development.

Such failures have led to congressional and public disillusionment with the effectiveness of foreign aid, both as a tool of foreign policy and as a spur to economic development. In response to criticism, USAID closed its missions in twenty-three countries, and in 1995 Congress cut its budget and threatened to eliminate it before moving it to the State Department. The attack on foreign aid was rationalized as budget cutting, but the program accounts for a tiny proportion of the federal budget and costs the average taxpaying family just $32 per year.[60] Our aid to the world's poorest countries costs about $6 per U.S. citizen annually.[61]

Loans and credits to help bail out countries suffering from recession or financial collapse are an increasingly common form of foreign aid. When recession hit South Korea (the world's eleventh largest economy) and Indonesia (the world's fourth most populous country), the Clinton administration moved quickly to help broker aid from the International Monetary Fund (IMF). Our share, which Congress was reluctant to approve, was $18 billion.

The American public also has been reluctant to help pay for the financial failings of other countries, especially when they are strong trade competitors. But it is a reality of the global economy that we are all swimming in the same financial sea and that a regional economic crisis can quickly become a world crisis. If it foments political instability, such an economic crisis may even lead to larger security crises. The technology that has allowed money to move almost instantaneously from one country to another has also, Fed Chair Alan Greenspan warns, "enhanced the ability of the system to rapidly transmit problems in one part of the globe to another."[62] To prevent or minimize the impact on our economy, we have to help pay for other governments' mistakes.

Aid from America and other industrialized nations helps keep these Sudanese children alive, but some experts also believe that such aid can prolong these civil wars.

Brennan Linsley/Associated Press

One of our most perplexing foreign policy problems is how to use aid to help the world's poorest countries. Our relations with developing countries are important, yet in most cases military aid, military intervention, and economic aid have not worked very well in promoting economic progress, democratic government, or positive attitudes toward the United States.

One major reason is that in the 1980s the four largest recipients of U.S. aid in Africa other than Egypt—the Sudan, Somalia, Liberia, and Ethiopia—were targeted because of their geopolitical importance, not for their ability to use aid wisely. Moreover, in sub-Saharan Africa, which has twenty-two of the world's thirty poorest countries but where the United States has few strong strategic interests, we spread $700 million in development aid among forty-eight countries in 1998[63] (compared to $5 billion for Israel and Egypt alone).

In constant dollars, U.S. aid money declined by nearly 20 percent over the past twenty years, from an all-time high in 1949 when over 3 percent of GDP was devoted to foreign assistance, to today when it is less than 0.5 percent of GDP.[64] But how much can aid help? Some argue that the world's poor do not need an infusion of cash as much as they need a transfer of knowledge because most of the progress in developing countries has come from science—health care, seed breeding, improved farming—rather than from economic and social development programs.[65]

The fear is that globalization will exacerbate an already lopsided division of the world's wealth, as anyone without educational or technological resources will be left behind. World Bank figures show that in 1998 about 1.3 billion people, a quarter of the world's population, were living in "extreme poverty" (defined as living on less than $1 per day), barely improving over the previous decade. The highest poverty rates are in South Asia, now the home of two nuclear powers, and sub-Saharan Africa. The only significant gain in living standards in this period has been for East Asians. Today the richest 20 percent have 86 percent of world GDP, while the poorest 20 percent have just over 1 percent. The world's richest three billionaires own more of the world's wealth than the poorest six hundred million people combined.[66]

Some may ask why we should come to the aid of governments with poor human rights records that are sometimes militantly anti-American in their foreign policy rhetoric or of corrupt governments that have made little effort to improve the lot of the average person. Putting aside the humanitarian issues and looking at these problems in terms of our national interests, the fact remains that it is not in our interest that half of the world's population is unable to buy the agricultural and industrial goods we export. Supporters of aid say it is a good investment that will pay off in stability and friendly governments, which will translate into more exports and reduced defense spending for us. For many years the world's largest economies have been one another's principal trading partners. With the populations of these countries stabilizing, can their economies continue to grow without parallel growth in developing economies? The countries of Africa, for example, have a combined market of 700 million people but accounted for only 1 percent of all U.S. trade in 1997.[67]

The Clinton administration, not surprisingly, has put most of its effort into trade policy: "We've got to reaffirm unambiguously that open markets and rules-based trade are the best engine we know to lift living standards, reduce environmental destruction and build shared prosperity. This is true whether you're in Detroit, Davos, Dacca, or Dakar."[68] This is another example of the Clinton win-win strategy transposed from domestic to foreign policy: Increasing trade with Africa creates jobs in the United States and raises living standards in Africa, while costing the American taxpayer virtually nothing in aid.

Defining Security in the Global Age

We began this chapter by stating that the first and most transparent foreign policy goal of any country is protecting its security. The end of the Cold War and globalization have required a redefinition of national security and a reassessment of how prepared we are to meet the new challenges. With the end of the Cold War one immediate problem became clear. Many simmering conflicts that had been contained by the threat of their spilling over into the U.S.-Soviet rivalry were unleashed; at the end of the century, one-third of the world's 193 nations were waging war. In addition new threats have arisen from independent or state-sponsored terrorism. This has made the threat from weapons of mass destruction much more uncertain.

Today, the most difficult security challenge is preventing terrorist groups, acting alone or in concert with a state hostile to the United States, from gaining access to missile technology and to the materials needed to make biological, chemical, or nuclear weapons. During the Cold War, only five nations (the United States, the Soviet Union, Britain, France, and China) produced and stockpiled nuclear weapons. Two of those powers were our allies in NATO, and with the Soviet Union we at least had diplomatic relations and the capacity to negotiate treaties on testing, stockpiling, and even use (as in the no-first-strike agreements). The MAD (mutual assured destruction) strategy was rooted in, and dependent upon, the conviction that the fairly small number of people who were in a position to make decisions about the use of nuclear weapons were sane and rational and that the threat of mutual destruction would keep any leader from launching a first strike.

As the number of states that have or are trying to gain nuclear capability has increased, the materials and technology to make nuclear weapons have proliferated across the globe. When India and Pakistan conducted tests in 1998, the number of nuclear-ready countries increased to seven. Another thirteen nations probably have the capacity to produce warheads: Israel, Iraq, Iran, North Korea, Algeria, Libya, Romania, Argentina, Brazil, South Africa, and three states created out of the former Soviet Union—Belarus, Kazakhstan, and Ukraine. The latter three states, with American technical and financial assistance, are transferring their war-

heads to Russia and have no independent capability to use the weapons that remain deployed in their territories. Argentina, Brazil, Algeria, and South Africa have renounced nuclear weapons and put their programs under the supervision of the International Atomic Energy Commission. After its defeat in the Gulf War, Iraq was forced to renounce its weapons program and submit to United Nations monitoring, but this process broke down before it could dismantle Iraq's chemical and biological weapons programs.

The largest stores of the enriched uranium and plutonium needed to make nuclear weapons are in the United States and the successor states of the Soviet Union, mainly Russia. In addition to the amounts produced for research and continuing weapons production, large reservoirs are accumulating from the dismantling of thousands of warheads as required by disarmament agreements between the United States and Russia. All of this material has to be disposed of or stored, and Russian storage sites are scattered and poorly secured. A major aspect of the U.S. response to the new security threat has been to assist Russia and its neighbors with transporting, storing, and safeguarding these materials.

The production and storage of enriched uranium and plutonium are supposed to be carefully recorded and monitored, but record keeping has been so inadequate, especially at Russian sites, that no one is sure exactly how much material is missing. Substantial black market trafficking in these materials is well documented.[69] Enriched uranium is relatively easy to smuggle because it has no smell and emits so little radioactivity that, if shielded, it cannot be located by the detectors in use in the majority of the world's airports. (The most lethal substances used to make chemical or biological weapons are more dangerous to handle and transport, although only very small quantities are needed to wreak great damage.) Once the material is acquired, the assembly is not especially difficult; the technology necessary to build a simple uranium bomb like the one dropped on Hiroshima in 1945 is available to "anyone with a personal computer."[70]

The black market activity in weapons-grade material encourages the proliferation of missile technology and increases the likelihood that governments that acquire nuclear warheads will be able to develop short- or medium-range delivery capabilities much faster than would be expected through the normal research and development process. The breakup of the Soviet Union and the downsizing of its rocketry and weapons programs have left many scientists looking for work. The intense competition for export markets, including foreign customers for

Foreign Policy in Time

1797 George Washington gives farewell address warning U.S. against becoming involved in affairs of foreign countries; sets isolationist tone of foreign policy for the next century.

1801 Thomas Jefferson assumes presidency and reduces size of military; tries to close U.S. embassies and shut down U.S. ports to foreign trade to prevent U.S. from being drawn into war in Europe.

1812 Congress declares war for first time; defeats Britain, effectively ending its presence in North America outside Canada.

1820 President Monroe issues policy statement (the Monroe Doctrine) warning European powers off new settlements or foreign ventures in the Americas, declaring the area within the U.S. sphere of influence; 175-year period of U.S. intervention in Central America and the Caribbean begins.

1848 Congress declares war against Mexico and seizes territory now comprising Texas, Arizona, New Mexico, California, and Colorado.

1898 U.S. enters the Cuban and Philippine wars for independence from Spain, seizes Puerto Rico and the Philippines, makes them U.S. territories, crushes Philippine independence movement. Cuba becomes independent but under U.S. influence.

1917 U.S. declares war against Germany and the Central Powers, three years after World War I began in Europe.

1919 President Wilson attends peace negotiations in Paris and lobbies for creation of a League of Nations to end war for all time. Senate refuses to ratify U.S. entry into the League.

1941 Two years after Britain went to war against Nazi Germany, U.S. enters the war against Axis powers after Japan bombs U.S. naval base in Pearl Harbor.

1944 At Bretton Woods conference to rebuild postwar international organizations, the U.S. and its West European allies create new international monetary organizations, including the World Bank and International Monetary Fund, which they dominate for the next fifty years.

1945 U.S. drops the only two atomic weapons ever used in battle on Hiroshima and Nagasaki, leading to Japanese surrender and end of World War II; U.S. emerges as preeminent world power.

1947 U.S. proposes the Marshall Plan of economic aid to rebuild European countries destroyed by World War II; the Soviet Union refuses to participate.

1947 The Cold War begins. President Truman outlines a containment policy (Truman Doctrine) for dealing with Soviet aggression and occupation of other countries. Containment remains the central concept in U.S. foreign policy for the next forty years.

1948–49 West Berlin, occupied by Allied forces, is blockaded by the Soviet Union; U.S. airlifts in supplies to keep Berliners from starving.

1949 United Nations is created: U.S. joins World War II allies as permanent members of Security Council.

1949 The North Atlantic Treaty Organization is created by the U.S., Canada, and ten European countries to prevent Soviet aggression in western Europe.

1949 The Communist Party wins control of China, but the United States refuses to recognize it, and continues to accept the Nationalist Party in exile on Taiwan as the official government of China.

1950 Truman authorizes U.S. troops to lead a UN force to repel a North Korean invasion of South Korea, drawing the U.S. into combat with the Chinese.

1955 In response to NATO and U.S. troops stationed in Europe, the Soviets create the Warsaw Pact with membership drawn from the eastern European countries it occupied after the war.

1955 The Soviet Union obtains intercontinental ballistic missiles and the nuclear era begins; U.S. pursues nuclear-weapons-building program as part of its mutually assured destruction (MAD) strategy.

1962 The discovery of Soviet missiles in Cuba leads to ten-day world crisis and the threat of a nuclear war before President Kennedy and Soviet Premier Khrushchev work out a compromise for the missiles' removal.

1964 Congress passes the Tonkin Gulf Resolution and Presidents Johnson and Nixon use it to legitimize turning the Vietnamese civil war into a U.S. war of containment in Southeast Asia.

1972 President Nixon visits China, the first official contact since the U.S. refusal in 1949 to recognize the Communist-led government of Mao Zedong.

1973 End of Vietnam War after five years of negotiation in Paris; labeled the only war the U.S. ever lost. North Vietnam assumes control of all of Vietnam. The Vietnam syndrome restrains U.S. use of military force in other potential combat situations.

1987 President Mikhail Gorbachev begins a period of restructuring the government of the Soviet Union and opening the country to the West (*glasnost*).

1990 Berlin Wall is torn down.

1990 President Bush organizes a UN force to repel Hussein's invasion of Kuwait in the Persian Gulf War.

1991 A failed coup attempt in the Soviet Union leads to the breakup of the union and the end of Communist one-party rule in Russia. End of Cold War and the emergence of the U.S. as the world's only military superpower.

1992 The emergence of the Internet as a common mode for international communications and financial transactions speeds the process of globalization.

1992 The breakup of the Republic of Yugoslavia leads to civil war and the subsequent involvement of the U.S. military in NATO efforts to contain ethnic warfare in Bosnia and in 1999 in Kosovo.

1995 World Trade Organization (WTO) established to replace the General Agreement on Tariffs and Trade (GATT); removes barriers between world trading partners and regulates disputes.

1998 Three former Warsaw Pact members join NATO.

high-tech equipment, has led business lobbies to pressure government to remove restrictions on the export of products and services that may have military applications. Joint business ventures on high-tech projects in foreign countries can also lead to the transfer of technology. With technology and expertise moving across borders and available in books or on the Internet, the breakdown of security measures in Russia, and the deliberate dissemination of restricted technology by states interested in increasing the number of nuclear powers, the likelihood that nuclear weapons will fall into the hands of "rogue" states or terrorist groups continues to grow.

It is hard to imagine that we might look back at the Cold War as a simpler time, yet today's world is more complex than it was in the days of MAD. Nuclear proliferation makes defense against nuclear strikes exceedingly difficult because it is no longer sufficient just to monitor national defense establishments. It is less certain from where or from whom a strike might come. Iraq's ability to block the work of the UN inspection team and the CIA's failure to predict India's nuclear tests despite years of surveillance of its arms program is not reassuring about our ability to determine when independent actors have gained access to nuclear, chemical, and biological weapons or missile technology.

Virtually everyone agrees on the seriousness of the new threats if not on how to protect against them. One response has been to revive the antimissile defense system begun in the Reagan administration, preparing not to defend against a massive nuclear attack but to intercept and destroy a single or several missiles launched by a rogue state or a terrorist group. Opposition to this defense strategy has been vehement on two points: the technology does not work, and the strategy itself has a dangerous premise. "The old line in the sand was between two ideologies, each held by people the other believed to be capable of acting sensibly," but the new line is "between people who can be counted on to behave like us and people who can't. Under the old thinking the best defense was the threat of an overwhelming offense. But in the new world . . . the best defense in some cases is actually a defense."[71] The assumption, antimissile defense system critics say, is that nuclear weapons *will* be used and we will be able to defend ourselves against them. This premise, they argue, is both misleading and destabilizing and "represents a fundamental shift in how the nation thinks about nuclear war."[72] In addition, many defense experts believe there is far greater danger that terrorists would use biological rather than nuclear weapons, in part because dangerous germs are cheap and easy to come by and do not require expensive missile delivery systems.

Globalization has intensified the threat from terrorist attack simply because of the level of exchange between countries and because of the many points of vulnerability, including the computer systems on which international business and finance, as well as national security systems, are now completely dependent. Globalization gives added weight to the old caveat about foreign problems left unattended finding their way to our door because today this does not just refer to armed conflicts but to financial and environmental crises and epidemic diseases that can spread rapidly from one country to another.

For this reason, the Clinton administration declared health, education, and environmental protection in developing countries as primary U.S. foreign policy goals, linking them to U.S. national security. Almost everyone can see the worldwide AIDS epidemic as an urgent humanitarian and health issue, but many in Congress were stunned by Clinton's characterization of the AIDS epidemic in Africa as a national security issue. However, given international health organizations' death projections for some African countries where as many as a third of the population may be infected, it is not difficult to see the epidemic as a potentially destabilizing force. This is the new meaning of security in a very interdependent world.

Conclusion: Is Our Foreign Policy Responsive?

Our foreign policy reflects our conflicting values and goals. We pride ourselves on our strength and power and have spent billions of dollars to build a strong military, yet since Vietnam we have been uncertain how to use that power. We desire a strong alliance system and have entered into treaties with many nations around the world, but are reluctant to get involved in "their affairs."

The Persian Gulf War clearly boosted American morale and caused a rush of patriotic fervor, so much so that some claim it laid to rest the so-called Vietnam syndrome. Some even thought that this renewed belief in America's ability "to get the job done" would lead us to look for new jobs for our armed forces to take on. But domestic problems and lack of public support for new foreign ventures constrained policymakers.

Is the direction of our foreign policy responsive to the public? Public attitudes can constrain the general policy directions of the president and Congress, but presidents can do a lot to shape these attitudes. Over the long term, as in Vietnam, the administration must be somewhat responsive to public sentiment that intensely opposes administration policy. In most specific foreign policy decisions, the public has little influence because it is not well-informed. Ordinarily, the public will support a president, at least in the short run, especially if he can convince them that our national security is threatened. But the 1990s were not ordinary times, and the public today is more aware of the convergence of domestic and foreign policy issues and feels more threatened by economic uncertainties than by military threats from foreign powers. Americans continue to be interested in international issues directly affecting their lives: immigration, trade, contagious diseases, environmental protection, and cross-border drug trafficking and crime. 1997 polls showed they favored a strong multilateral response to crossnational health problems, like the spread of mad cow disease and AIDS, and to world environmental problems like global warming, even if it would lead to consumption limits and higher gasoline prices in the United States.

While Congress was withholding UN dues and threatening to withdraw from many affiliated agencies, 64 percent of Americans polled said they held the UN in high regard, and only 13 percent thought the United States should act alone in tackling international crises. The poll showed an unusual divergence of views between the opinion leaders and members of the general public who participated in the survey. While only 27 percent of opinion leaders wanted to see the United States share power equally with other major countries, 50 percent of the general public favored the idea.[73]

Americans today are more connected to all parts of the globe through cultural, financial, and communications links than at any time in our history. Our style and standard of living are inextricably linked to our success as a world trading partner, and there has been substantial popular support for the constant expansion of markets and for removal of barriers to the export of American goods. The latter is virtually impossible to achieve without intervening in the domestic affairs of other countries. Furthermore, given the multiethnic immigrant background of our population, cultural and political ties to the rest of the world—with all their ramifications for foreign policy—are unavoidable. It is reasonable to expect, given the reconfiguration of the international system, that U.S. foreign policy would undergo major change. But withdrawal is not realistic.

It is possible that Americans now have a better understanding of the limitations of superpower status and are unwilling to see resources committed to unwinnable goals. They may well have lowered their sights on what it is possible to achieve through foreign policy. This is less neo-isolationism than realism, or what has been called the "new humility" in American foreign policy.[74]

As the head of the world's largest military and economic power and a partner in major military and trade alliances, the president has a constituency larger than the American public. He is often called upon to be responsive to the needs of other people or countries: victims of famines, civil wars, natural disasters, and human rights abuses, or countries in need of military and economic assistance. In such cases the president and Congress have to weigh external demands against the needs and wishes of the American people. But if the United States is to continue to act in a leadership role in international politics, as the American public has long wanted it to, it must demonstrate some measure of responsiveness to the needs of other countries.

EPILOGUE

Albright Supports Intervention

Albright joined other members of the Clinton foreign policy team in advising the president that he must take action to bring an end to a humanitarian crisis. She said we have an obligation to stop ethnic warfare and to reassure our allies that stability in Europe is still a central foreign policy goal for the United States.

The State Department issued a statement saying, "No one should forget that World War I began in this tinderbox. If actions are not taken to stop conflict now, it will spread and both the cost and risk will be substantially greater."[75] Albright, a self-described "aggressive multilateralist," agreed that the most limited and acceptable way of

intervening would be to join our European allies in conducting air strikes against Serb targets. If intervention were limited to an air war, U.S. casualties could be minimized, perhaps making U.S. involvement more acceptable to the public. Also, if we conducted the strikes as part of a multilateral force, it would reduce the load on the American military, spread responsibility, reduce expectations that we would act alone, while demonstrating to our closest allies our commitment to European security. We also would show the world that human rights is a principle on which the United States would act—at least in some cases.

Clinton ordered U.S. forces to join a NATO air strike against the Serbian armed forces. After seventy-eight days of bombing, the Serbs advancing on Kosovo were stopped, and almost eight hundred thousand Kosovars returned to what was left of their homes. The action did not claim a single U.S. life, but Kosovar refugees mistaken by NATO pilots for Serbian troops were killed, as were Chinese civilians in the Chinese Embassy in Belgrade when it was accidentally bombed. The air war created a huge international flap, straining our relations with China and Russia. The Serbian army suffered few losses, and no real military objectives were achieved.

Although the refugee problem was alleviated, the air strike did not achieve the stated objectives of achieving a durable peace and providing for democratic self-government of the Kosovar people. UN peacekeeping forces moved in to partition the province, keep out the Serbian army, disarm the Kosovar liberation army, and form a barrier between Serbia and Albanian residential areas. This is how the situation stood in 2000, with no resolution in sight and with UN peacekeepers, including 5,900 Americans, as the only force preventing war from resuming. Not much could be done to solve the political problems that gave rise to the conflict because this is not the job of the military. Until elections drove the Serbian president from power in the fall of 2000, there were no domestic leaders toward whom the United States could direct diplomatic efforts at resolving the underlying problems. But the new president is also a strong Serbian nationalist and opponent of Kosovar independ-

ence, and Serbs in general remain hostile to the United States and NATO for bombing civilians and destroying much of the nation's infrastructure. Some see this kind of limited intervention as the main use for U.S. military forces in the future and that perhaps the world already assumes that the U.S. is willing to intervene in ethnic conflicts and civil wars. When asked why the administration decided to make such a commitment to Kosovo when it had not acted in Rwanda, Albright said that the administration has consistent principles and flexible tactics and that we can't have a "cookie-cutter" foreign policy. "We get involved when the crime is huge, where it's a region that affects our stability . . . or where there is no organization capable of dealing with it. Just because you can't be everywhere doesn't mean that you don't act anywhere. We're evolving these rules. There's not a doctrine that really sets this forth in an organized way yet."[76]

Key Terms

isolationism
Monroe Doctrine
containment
North Atlantic Treaty
    Organization (NATO)
Cold War
mutual assured destruction (MAD)

domino theory
Vietnam syndrome
detente
glasnost
protectionism
free trade
European Union (EU)

Further Reading

Louis Fisher, *Presidential War Power* (Lawrence: University of Kansas Press, 1995). A staff member of the Congressional Research Service reviews presidential use of the military from the first days of the republic to the present and concludes that congressional war-making powers have been usurped by the executive branch.

Thomas L. Friedman, *The Lexus and the Olive Tree: Understanding Globalization* (New York: Farrar, Strauss & Giroux, 1999). A *New York Times* foreign correspondent explains in everyday language why involvement in the global economy turns countries into the equivalent of public companies; makes national governments more, not less, important; and shrinks your political clout while broadening your economic choices.

Walter Isaacson and Evan Thomas, *The Wise Men: Six Friends and the World They Made* (New York: Simon & Schuster, 1986). An insight into the foreign policymaking establishment that dominated the postwar era into the early 1960s.

Robert S. McNamara, *In Retrospect: The Tragedy and Lessons of Vietnam* (New York: Times Books, 1995). A former secretary of defense and principal architect of Vietnam War policy gives eleven reasons why he thinks the Vietnam War was a mistake, rejecting the domino theory and placing a preponderance of blame on the incompetence of South Vietnamese forces and U.S. underestimation of the North Vietnamese.

David Remnick, *Lenin's Tomb: The Last Days of the Soviet Empire* (New York: Random House, 1993). A chronicle of the demise of the Soviet Union.

Barry Rubin, *Secrets of State: The State Department and the Struggle over U.S. Foreign Policy* (New York: Oxford University Press, 1985). After learning about conflicts among those charged with making foreign policy, readers will finish the book surprised we have a foreign policy at all.

Neil Sheehan, *A Bright Shining Lie* (New York: Random House, 1988). The Vietnam War as seen through its effect on a young American officer.

Gaddis Smith, *The Last Years of the Monroe Doctrine, 1945–1993* (New York: Hill & Wang, 1994). A distinguished scholar of American foreign policy argues that the goals of the

Monroe Doctrine were a fantasy and that U.S. policy-makers and the American public finally have come to accept them as unachievable.

Kenneth Timmerman, *The Death Lobby: How the West Armed Iraq* (New York: Houghton Mifflin Co., 1992). An account of how the United States and its allies built up the war machine of Saddam Hussein during the Iran-Iraq War. The author accuses intelligence agencies of being so focused on preventing an Iranian victory that they overlooked or ignored Iraq's nuclear weapons program.

Electronic Resources

usinfo.state.gov
This site has the United States Information Agency's daily briefings and news on a variety of international issues from the official U.S. government perspective. Includes links to several foreign language sources and a searchable database from archived material.

www.state.gov/
The home page of the State Department. Links to information on the department itself and on a variety of international issues, organized by region and by issue.

www.nytimes.com/
The home page of the New York Times. The Times provides the most thorough coverage of international news by any U.S. newspaper.

www.economist.com/
The home page of the international magazine The Economist. The Economist specializes in in-depth articles on important international and political issues and provides a foreign perspective on the news.

www.amnesty.org/
The home page of Amnesty International, an international human rights interest group. Provides extensive links to other human rights groups here and abroad.

www.heritage.org/
The home page of the Heritage Foundation, which provides a conservative perspective on international and domestic issues.

www.pbs.org/wgbh/amex/vietnam/index/html
PBS's Web site on the history of the Vietnam War.

www.pbs.org/wgbh/pages/frontline/shows/future/etc/transcript.html
This site contains the transcript of Frontline's program "The Future of War." Military experts discuss the meaning of readiness in the post–Cold War era.

InfoTrac College Edition

"Kosovo Class Half Full"
"Cuban-American Dialogues"
"Paying Attenshun"
"Inside Saddam's Iraq"

Notes

1. Thomas W. Lippman, "Madame Secretary," *National Journal,* June 3, 2000, pp. 1740–1743. Excerpts from his forthcoming book, *Madeleine Albright and the New American Diplomacy* (Boulder Colo.: Westview, 2000).

2. Madeleine K. Albright, speech to California Women's Conference; the text of the speech can be found at secretary.state.gov/www/picw/trafficking/mkaca.html.

3. Graduation speech delivered at Harvard University, reprinted in *New York Times,* June 6, 1997, p. A8.

4. Walter LaFeber, *New York Times,* July 3, 1983. "Diplomatic Subcontracting's Fine If You Get Good Help," *New York Times,* September 25, 1994, p. E6.

5. I. M. Destler, Leslie H. Gelb, and Anthony Lake, *Our Own Worst Enemy: The Unmaking of American Foreign Policy* (New York: Simon & Schuster, 1984), 115–116.

6. Joan Biskupic, "Constitution's Conflicting Clauses Underscored by Iraqi Crisis," *Congressional Quarterly Weekly,* January 5, 1991, p. 34; Madison's notes from *Documents Illustrative of the Formation of the Union of the American States,* quoted in "Framers Were Wary of War Powers," the same source.

7. Ronald D. Elving, "America's Most Frequent Fight Has Been the Undeclared War," *Congressional Quarterly,* January 5, 1991, p. 37.

8. Rep. Toby Roth (R-Wis.), quoted in Katharine Q. Seelye, "House Defeats Bid to Repeal 'War Powers,' " *New York Times,* June 11, 1995, p. A7.

9. Barry B. Hughes, *The Domestic Context of American Foreign Policy* (San Francisco: Freeman, 1978), chap. 5.

10. Robert Weissberg, *Public Opinion and Popular Government* (New York: Prentice Hall, 1976).

11. Eric Schmitt, "How to Bypass Sanctions and Do Business," *New York Times,* August 9, 1998, sect. 4, p. 4.

12. Eric Schmitt, "Let's Hear It for the World," *New York Times,* April 5, 1995, sect. 4, p. 16.

13. Information in this paragraph is based on Jeff Gerth with Sarah Bartlett, "Kissinger and Friends and Revolving Doors," *New York Times,* April 30, 1989, p. 1ff.

14. For a discussion of the foreign policy establishment, see Walter Isaacson and Evan Thomas, *The Wise Men: Six Friends and the World They Made* (New York: Simon & Schuster, 1986).

15. Carl M. Cannon, "Judging Clinton," *National Journal,* January 1, 2000, p. 21.

16. Robert Wright, "Private Eyes," *New York Times Magazine,* September 5, 1999, pp. 50–54; William J. Broad, "Snooping's Not Just for Spies Any More," *New York Times,* April 23, 2000, sect. 4, p. 6.

17. Historian Michael Hogan quoted in John M. Broder, "Gentler Look at the U.S. World Role," *New York Times,* October 31, 1999, p. 14.

18. Paul Johnson, "The Myth of American Isolationism," *Foreign Affairs* 74, no. 3 (May/June 1995): 162.

19. Bruce Russett, *The Prisoners of Insecurity* (San Francisco: Freeman, 1983).

20. See James Nathan and James Oliver, *United States Foreign Policy and World Order,* 2d ed. (Boston: Little, Brown, 1981), 359–361.

21. For one view of the impact of Vietnam on the thinking of today's high-ranking officers, see (Major) H. R. McMaster, *Dereliction of Duty* (New York: HarperCollins, 1997).

22. Robert S. McNamara, *In Retrospect: The Tragedy and Lessons of Vietnam* (New York: Times Books, 1995).

23. Weissberg, *Public Opinion and Popular Government,* 144–148.

24. Ole Holsti, "The Three-Headed Eagle," *International Studies Quarterly* 23 (September 1979): 339–359; Michael Mandelbaum and William Schneider, "The New Internationalisms," in *The Eagle Entangled: U.S. Foreign Policy in a Complex World,* ed. Kenneth Oye, Donald Rothchild, and Robert J. Lieber (New York: Longman, 1979), 34–88.

25. For an analysis of U.S.-Soviet relations in the Reagan era, see Alexander Dallin and Gail Lapidus, "Reagan and the Russians," and Kenneth Oye, "Constrained Confidence and the Evolution of Reagan Foreign Policy," in *Eagle Resurgent?,* ed. Kenneth Oye, Robert Lieber, and Donald Rothchild (Boston: Little Brown,

1987); John Newhouse, "The Abolitionist," Parts 1 and 2, *New Yorker,* January 2 and 9, 1989.

26. See George F. Kennan, "After the Cold War," *New York Times Magazine,* February 5, 1989, pp. 32*ff.*

27. Bill Clinton, "A Democrat Lays Out His Plan," *Harvard International Review* (Summer 1992).

28. Quoted in Thomas Friedman, "What Big Stick? Just Sell," *New York Times,* October 2, 1995, p. E3.

29. Ibid.

30. Elaine Sciolino, "Monroe's Doctrine Takes Another Knock," *New York Times,* August 7, 1994, p. E6. For a discussion of the U.S. turn to multilateralism see Stanley Hoffmann, "The Crisis of Liberal Internationalism," *Foreign Policy* 98 (Spring 1995): 159–177.

31. Brookings Institute estimate, cited in Tom Cohen, "The NATO Connection," *Champaign-Urbana New Gazette,* March 14, 1999, p. B5; A lower estimate of the costs of nuclear preparedness can be found in David C. Morrison, "Putting a Price Tag on the Arms Race," *National Journal,* May 13, 1995, p. 1171.

32. James Kitfield, "Strategic Muddle," *National Journal,* November 22, 1997, p. 2358.

33. *U.S. Budget for Fiscal 1996* (Washington, D.C.: U.S. Government Printing Office, 1995), 121.

34. Kitfield, "Strategic Muddle."

35. "Nearly 1 in 5 Failing to Register for Draft," *Champaign-Urbana News Gazette,* May 8, 2000, p. 1.

36. James Kitfield, "Standing Apart," *National Journal,* June 13, 1998, p. 1351; Charles Pope, "New Congress is Older, More Politically Seasoned," *Congressional Quarterly Report,* January 9, 1999, p. 60.

37. Ibid., p. 1352.

38. The Clinton administration's new guidelines for the use of nuclear weapons, for example, established a different policy than that recommended in the Pentagon's 1997 Quadrennial Defense Review. Kitfield, "Strategic Muddle," pp. 2357–2358.

39. Eric Schmitt, "Aid Dresses Up in a Uniform," *New York Times,* May 10, 1998, Section 4, p. 5; Christine Spolar, "Not Everyone Is Hot to Trot for NATO," *Washington Post National Weekly Edition,* June 30, 1997, p. 8.

40. Quoted in David E. Sanger, "Corrosion at the Core of Pax Pacifica," *New York Times,* May 14, 1995, sect. 4, p. 1; Nicholas D. Kristof, "Drawing a Line in the Pacific," *New York Times,* July 16, 1995, p. E4; James Sterngold, "Some Leaders in Japan Begin to Question U.S. Bases," *New York Times,* August 28, 1994, p. 7.

41. Cited in "Still No Policy on Arms Sales," *New York Times,* April 3, 1994, op-ed page. The world's primary arms suppliers are the five permanent members of the UN Security Council: the United States, Russia, the United Kingdom, France, and China; Michael R. Gordon, "Russia Is Pushing to Increase Share in Weapons Trade," *New York Times,* July 16, 2000, p. 4.

42. Jim Hoagland, "What Goes Around . . . ," *Washington Post National Weekly Edition,* January 24, 2000, p. 5.

43. Joan Spero, an undersecretary of state, quoted in David E. Sanger, "How Washington Inc. Makes a Sale," *New York Times,* February 19, 1995, sect. 3, p. 1.

44. David E. Sanger, "Foreign Relations: Money Talks, Policy Walks," *New York Times,* January 15, 1995, sect. 4, p. 1.

45. "Diplomacy's New Hit Man: The Free-market Dollar," *New York Times,* May 24, 1998, sect. 4, p. 5.

46. Julie Kosterlitz, "Trade Crusade," *National Journal,* May 9, 1998, pp. 1054–1055.

47. Alan Blinder, *Hard Heads, Soft Hearts* (New York: Addison-Wesley, 1988), 118–119.

48. "What Am I Bid for This Fine Quota?" *Time,* March 16, 1987, p. 59; "The Battle over Barriers," *Time,* October 7, 1985, pp. 22–35.

49. For a concise summary of the advantages and disadvantages of protectionism and free trade, see Paul Krugman, *The Age of Di-minished Expectations* (Cambridge, Mass.: MIT Press, 1992), 101–113.

50. David E. Sanger, "64% of Japanese Say U.S. Relations Are 'Unfriendly,' " *New York Times,* July 6, 1993, pp. 1, 6.

51. For a description of WTO structure, membership, and activities, see "WTO: Special Report," *Congressional Quarterly Weekly Report,* November 27, 1999, pp. 2826–2838.

52. Mark Schapiro, "Revenge on the Nerds," *Civilization* (June/July 2000): 59.

53. Gary Clyde Hufbauer and Jeffrey J. Schott, with Kimberly Ann Elliot, *Economic Sanctions Reconsidered: History and Current Policy* (Washington, D.C.: Institute for International Economics, 1985), 10.

54. Gary Hufbauer, "Foreign Policy on the Cheap," *Washington Post National Weekly Edition,* July 20–27, 1998, p. 22.

55. Ibid., p. 80.

56. Steven Lee Myers, "Converting the Dollar into a Bludgeon," *New York Times,* April 20, 1997, p. E5.

57. Philip Shenon, "Washington and Bagdad Agree on One Point: Sanctions Hurt," *New York Times,* November 22, 1998.

58. Quoted by Steven Greenhouse, "U.S. View of Sanctions: Turn Up Heat Half Way," *New York Times,* July 3, 1994.

59. Dick Kirschten, "Chicken Soup Diplomacy," *National Journal,* January 4, 1997, p. 13.

60. Joseph Kahn, "The World's Bankers Try Giving Money, Not Lessons," *New York Times,* October 1, 2000, sect. 4, p. 5.

61. Missy Ryan, "Arrested Development," *National Journal,* June 10, 2000, p. 1822.

62. David E. Sanger, "Strategies in a Market Era," *New York Times,* January 4, 1998, sect. 4, p. 4.

63. James Bennet, "Africa Gets the Clinton Treatment," *New York Times,* March 29, 1998, sect. 4, p. 4.

64. Ryan, "Arrested Development," p. 1822.

65. Ibid.

66. Tom Walker, "Planet of Riches Still Blighted by Poverty," *Sunday Times* (London), January 2, 2000, p. 16.

67. "Clinton: Will Aid Africa Trade, Democracy," *Champaign-Urbana News-Gazette,* March 23, 1998, p. 1.

68. Clinton quoted in Jane Perlez, "At Conference on Trade, Clinton Makes Pitch for Poor," *New York Times,* January 30, 2000, p. 6.

69. Material in this section is drawn from Michael Gordon, "A Whole New World of Arms Races to Contain," *New York Times,* May 3, 1998, sect. 4, p. 1; John Kifner and Jo Thomas, "Singular Difficulty in Stopping Terrorism," *New York Times,* January 18, 1998, p. 16; Keith Easthouse, "The Stewardship Debate," *Champaign-Urbana News Gazette,* June 14, 1998, pp. B1, B4–B5; Michael R. Gordon, "Russian Thwarting U.S. Bid to Secure a Nuclear Cache," *New York Times,* January 5, 1997, pp. 1, 4.

70. Quoted from PBS's *Frontline* Web site at www.pbs.org/wgbh/pages/frontline.

71. Michael Oreskes, "Troubling the Waters of Nuclear Deterrence," *New York Times,* June 4, 2000, sect. 4, p. 3.

72. Ibid.

73. A poll conducted by Maryland's Program on International Policy Attitudes and the Pew Research Center for People and the Press, reported by Barbara Crossette, "U.S. Public Likes Its Foreign Affairs in Nontraditional Terms, Poll Says," *New York Times,* December 28, p. 8, and commented on in *New York Times* editorial, January 4, 1998, sect. 4, p. 10.

74. Stanley Hoffman, quoted by Thomas L. Friedman, "A Diplomatic Question: Embargo or Embrace?" *New York Times,* September 4, 1994, p. E4.

75. "U.S. and NATO Objectives and Interests in Kosovo," U.S. State Department Fact Sheet, March 26, 1999, www.state.gov/www/region/eur/fs_990326_ksvobjectives.html.

76. Lippman, "Madame Secretary," pp. 1742–1743.

The Declaration of Independence *

In Congress, July 4, 1776.

A Declaration by the Representatives of the United States of America, in General Congress assembled.

When in the Course of human Events, it becomes necessary for one People to dissolve the Political Bonds which have connected them with another, and to assume among the Powers of the Earth, the separate and equal Station to which the Laws of Nature and of Nature's God entitle them, a decent Respect to the Opinions of Mankind requires that they should declare the causes which impel them to the Separation.

We hold these Truths to be self-evident, that all Men are created equal, that they are endowed by their Creator with certain unalienable Rights, that among these are Life, Liberty, and the Pursuit of Happiness—That to secure these Rights, Governments are instituted among Men, deriving their just Powers from the Consent of the Governed, that whenever any Form of Government becomes destructive of these Ends, it is the Right of the People to alter or to abolish it, and to institute new Government, laying its Foundation on such Principles, and organizing its Powers in such Forms, as to them shall seem most likely to effect their Safety and Happiness. Prudence, indeed, will dictate that Governments long established should not be changed for light and transient Causes; and accordingly all Experience hath shewn, that Mankind are more disposed to suffer, while Evils are sufferable, than to right themselves by abolishing the Forms to which they are accustomed. But when a long Train of Abuses and Usurpations, pursuing invariably the same Object, evinces a Design to reduce them under absolute Despotism, it is their Right, it is their Duty, to throw off such Government, and to provide new Guards for their future Security. Such has been the patient Sufferance of these Colonies; and such is now the Necessity which constrains them to alter their former Systems of Government. The History of the present King of Great Britain is a History of repeated Injuries and Usurpations, all having in direct Object the Establishment of an absolute Tyranny over these States. To prove this, let facts be submitted to a candid World.

He has refused his Assent to Laws, the most wholesome and necessary for the public Good.

He has forbidden his Governors to pass Laws of immediate and pressing Importance, unless suspended in their Oper-ation till his Assent should be obtained; and when so suspended, he has utterly neglected to attend to them.

He has refused to pass other Laws for the Accommodation of large Districts of People, unless those People would relinquish the Right of Representation in the Legislature, a Right inestimable to them, and formidable to Tyrants only.

He has called together Legislative Bodies at Places unusual, uncomfortable, and distant from the Depository of their Public Records, for the sole Purpose of fatiguing them into Compliance with his Measures.

He has dissolved Representative Houses repeatedly, for opposing with manly Firmness his Invasions on the Rights of the People.

He has refused for a long Time, after such Dissolutions, to cause others to be elected; whereby the Legislative Powers, incapable of Annihilation, have returned to the People at large for their exercise; the State remaining in the mean time exposed to all the Dangers of Invasion from without, and Convulsions within.

He has endeavoured to prevent the Population of these States; for that Purpose obstructing the Laws for Naturalization of Foreigners; refusing to pass others to encourage their Migration hither, and raising the Conditions of new Appropriations of Lands.

He has obstructed the Administration of Justice, by refusing his Assent to Laws for establishing Judiciary Powers.

He has made Judges dependent on his Will alone, for the Tenure of their offices, and the Amount and payments of their Salaries.

He has erected a Multitude of new Offices, and sent hither Swarms of Officers to harass our People, and eat out their Substance.

He has kept among us, in times of Peace, Standing Armies, without the consent of our Legislatures.

He has affected to render the Military independent of, and superior to the Civil Power.

He has combined with others to subject us to a Jurisdiction foreign to our Constitution, and unacknowledged by our Laws; giving his Assent to their Acts of pretended Legislation:

For quartering large Bodies of Armed Troops among us:

---

*The spelling, capitalization, and punctuation of the original have been retained here.

For protecting them, by a mock Trial, from Punishment for any Murders which they should commit on the Inhabitants of these States:

For cutting off our Trade with all Parts of the World:

For imposing Taxes on us without our Consent:

For depriving us, in many cases, of the Benefits of Trial by Jury:

For transporting us beyond Seas to be tried for pretended Offences:

For abolishing the free System of English Laws in a neighbouring Province, establishing therein an arbitrary Government, and enlarging its Boundaries, so as to render it at once an Example and fit Instrument for introducing the same absolute Rule into these Colonies:

For taking away our Charters, abolishing our most valuable Laws, and altering fundamentally the Forms of our Governments:

For suspending our own Legislatures, and declaring themselves invested with Power to legislate for us in all Cases whatsoever.

He has abdicated Government here, by declaring us out of his Protection and waging War against us.

He has plundered our Seas, ravaged our Coasts, burnt our towns, and destroyed the Lives of our People.

He is, at this Time, transporting large Armies of foreign Mercenaries to compleat the works of Death, Desolation, and Tyranny, already begun with circumstances of Cruelty and Perfidy, scarcely parallelled in the most barbarous Ages, and totally unworthy the Head of a civilized Nation.

He has constrained our fellow Citizens taken Captive on the high Seas to bear Arms against their Country, to become the Executioners of their Friends and Brethren, or to fall themselves by their Hands.

He has excited domestic Insurrections amongst us, and has endeavoured to bring on the Inhabitants of our Frontiers, the merciless Indian Savages, whose known Rule of Warfare is an undistinguished Destruction, of all Ages, Sexes and Conditions.

In every state of these Oppressions we have Petitioned for Redress in the most humble Terms: Our repeated Petitions have been answered only by repeated Injury. A Prince, whose Character is thus marked by every act which may define a Tyrant, is unfit to be the Ruler of a free People.

Nor have we been wanting in Attentions to our British Brethren. We have warned them from Time to Time of Attempts by their Legislature to extend an unwarrantable Jurisdiction over us. We have reminded them of the Circumstances of our Emigration and Settlement here. We have appealed to their native Justice and Magnanimity, and we have conjured them by the Ties of our common Kindred to disavow these Usurpations, which would inevitably interrupt our Connections and Correspondence. They too have been deaf to the Voice of Justice and of Consanguinity. We must, therefore, acquiesce in the Necessity, which denounces our Separation, and hold them, as we hold the rest of Mankind, Enemies in War, in Peace, Friends.

We, therefore, the Representatives of the UNITED STATES OF AMERICA, in General Congress Assembled, appealing to the Supreme Judge of the World for the Rectitude of our Intentions, do, in the Name, and by Authority of the good People of these Colonies, solemnly Publish and Declare, That these United Colonies are, and of Right ought to be, Free and Independent States; that they are absolved from all Allegiance to the British Crown, and that all political Connection between them and the State of Great Britain, is and ought to be totally dissolved; and that as Free and Independent States, they have full Power to levy War, conclude Peace, contract Alliances, establish Commerce, and to do all other Acts and Things which Independent States may of right do. And for the support of this declaration, with a firm Reliance on the Protection of divine Providence, we mutually pledge to each other our Lives, our Fortunes, and our sacred Honor.

Constitution of the United States of America[*]

We the people of the United States, in Order to form a more perfect Union, establish Justice, insure domestic Tranquility, provide for the common defence, promote the general Welfare, and secure the Blessings of Liberty to ourselves and our posterity, do ordain and establish this Constitution for the United States of America.

Article I

Section 1. All legislative Powers herein granted shall be vested in a Congress of the United States, which shall consist of a Senate and House of Representatives.

Section 2. The House of Representatives shall be composed of Members chosen every second Year by the People of the several States, and the Electors in each State shall have the Qualifications requisite for Electors of the most numerous Branch of the State Legislature.

No person shall be a Representative who shall not have attained to the Age of twenty-five Years, and been seven Years a Citizen of the United States, and who shall not, when elected, be an Inhabitant of that State in which he shall be chosen.

Representatives and direct [Taxes][1] shall be apportioned among the several States which may be included within this Union, according to their respective Numbers [which shall be determined by adding to the whole Number of free Persons, including those bound to Service for a Term of Years, and excluding Indians not taxed, three fifths of all other Persons].[2] The actual Enumeration shall be made within three Years after the first Meeting of the Congress of the United States, and within every subsequent Term of ten Years, in such Manner as they shall by Law direct. The Number of Representatives shall not exceed one for every thirty Thousand, but each State shall have at Least one Representative; and until such enumeration shall be made, the State of New Hampshire shall be entitled to chuse three, Massachusetts eight, Rhode Island and Providence Plantations one, Connecticut five, New-York six, New Jersy four, Pennsylvania eight, Delaware one, Maryland six, Virginia ten, North Carolina five, South Carolina five, and Georgia three.

When vacancies happen in the Representation from any State, the Executive Authority thereof shall issue Writs of Election to fill such Vacancies.

The House of Representatives shall chuse their Speaker and other Officers; and shall have the sole Power of Impeachment.

Section 3. The Senate of the United States shall be composed of two Senators from each State [chosen by the Legislature thereof],[3] for six Years; and each Senator shall have one Vote.

Immediately after they shall be assembled in Consequence of the first Election, they shall be divided as equally as may be into three Classes. The Seats of the Senators of the first Class shall be vacated at the Expiration of the second year, of the second Class at the Expiration of the fourth Year, and of the third Class at the Expiration of the sixth Year, so that one third may be chosen every second Year [and if Vacancies happen by Resignation, or otherwise, during the Recess of the Legislature of any State, the Executive thereof may make temporary Appointments until the next Meeting of the Legislature, which shall then fill such Vacancies.][4]

No Person shall be a Senator who shall not have attained to the Age of thirty Years, and been nine Years a Citizen of the United States, and who shall not, when elected, be an Inhabitant of that State for which he shall be chosen.

The Vice President of the United States shall be President of the Senate, but shall have no Vote, unless they be equally divided.

The Senate shall chuse their other Officers, and also a President pro tempore, in the Absence of the Vice President, or when he shall exercise the Office of President of the United States.

The Senate shall have the sole Power to try all Impeachments. When sitting for that Purpose, they shall be on Oath or Affirmation. When the President of the United States is tried, the Chief Justice shall preside: And no Person shall be convicted without the Concurrence of two thirds of the Members present.

---

[*]The spelling, capitalization, and punctuation of the original have been retained here. Brackets indicate passages that have been altered by amendments to the Constitution.
1. Modified by the Sixteenth Amendment.
2. Modified by the Fourteenth Amendment.
3. Repealed by the Seventeenth Amendment.
4. Modified by the Seventeenth Amendment.

Judgment in Cases of Impeachment shall not extend further than to removal from Office, and disqualification to hold and enjoy any Office of honor, Trust or Profit under the United States; but the Party convicted shall nevertheless be liable and subject to Indictment, Trial, Judgment and Punishment, according to Law.

Section 4. The Times, Places and Manner of holding Elections for Senators and Representatives, shall be prescribed in each State by the Legislature thereof; but the Congress may at any time by Law make or alter such Regulations, except as to the Places of chusing Senators.

[The Congress shall assemble at least once in every Year, and such Meeting shall be on the first Monday in December, unless they shall by Law appoint a different Day.][5]

Section 5. Each House shall be the Judge of the Elections, Returns and Qualifications of its own Members, and a Majority of each shall constitute a Quorum to do Business; but a smaller Number may adjourn from day to day, and may be authorized to compel the Attendance of absent Members, in such Manner, and under such Penalties as each House may provide.

Each House may determine the Rules of its Proceedings, punish its Members for disorderly Behaviour, and, with the Concurrence of two thirds, expel a Member.

Each House shall keep a Journal of its Proceedings, and from time to time publish the same, excepting such Parts as may in their Judgment require Secrecy; and the Yeas and Nays of the Members of either House on any question shall, at the Desire of one fifth of those present, be entered on the Journal.

Neither House, during the Session of Congress, shall, without the Consent of the other, adjourn for more than three days, nor to any other Place than that in which the two Houses shall be sitting.

Section 6. The Senators and Representatives shall receive a Compensation for their Services, to be ascertained by Law, and paid out of the Treasury of the United States. They shall in all Cases, except Treason, Felony and Breach of the Peace, be privileged from Arrest during their Attendance at the Session of their respective Houses, and in going to and returning from the same; and for any Speech or Debate in either House, they shall not be questioned in any other Place.

No Senator or Representative shall, during the Time for which he was elected, be appointed to any civil Office under the Authority of the United States, which shall have been created, or the Emoluments whereof shall have been encreased during such time; and no Person holding any Office under the United States, shall be a Member of either House during his Continuance in Office.

Section 7. All Bills for raising Revenue shall originate in the House of Representatives; but the Senate may propose or concur with Amendments as on other Bills.

Every Bill which shall have passed the House of Representatives and the Senate, shall, before it become a Law, be presented to the President of the United States; If he approves he shall sign it, but if not he shall return it, with his objections to that House in which it shall have originated, who shall enter the Objections at large on their Journal, and proceed to reconsider it. If after such Reconsideration two thirds of that House shall agree to pass the Bill, it shall be sent, together with the Objections, to the other House, by which it shall likewise be reconsidered, and if approved by two thirds of that House, it shall become a Law. But in all such Cases the Votes of both Houses shall be determined by yeas and Nays, and the Names of the Persons voting for and against the Bill shall be entered on the Journal of each House respectively. If any Bill shall not be returned by the President within ten Days (Sundays excepted) after it shall have been presented to him, the Same shall be a Law, in like Manner as if he had signed it, unless the Congress by their Adjournment prevent its Return, in which Case it shall not be a Law.

Every Order, Resolution, or Vote to which the Concurrence of the Senate and House of Representatives may be necessary (except on a question of Adjournment) shall be presented to the President of the United States; and before the Same shall take Effect, shall be approved by him, or being disapproved by him, shall be repassed by two thirds of the Senate and House of Representatives, according to the Rules and Limitations prescribed in the Case of a Bill.

Section 8. The Congress shall have Power To lay and collect Taxes, Duties, Imposts and Excises, to pay the Debts and provide for the common Defence and general Welfare of the United States; but all Duties, Imposts and Excises shall be uniform throughout the United States;

To borrow Money on the credit of the United States;

To regulate Commerce with foreign Nations, and among the several States, and with the Indian Tribes;

To establish a uniform Rule of Naturalization, and uniform Laws on the subject of Bankruptcies throughout the United States;

To coin Money, regulate the Value thereof, and of foreign Coin, and fix the Standard of Weights and Measures;

To provide for the Punishment of counterfeiting the Securities and current Coin of the United States.

To establish Post Offices and post Roads;

To promote the Progress of Science and useful Arts, by securing for limited Times to Authors and Inventors the exclusive Right to their respective Writings and Discoveries;

To constitute Tribunals inferior to the supreme Court;

To define and punish Piracies and Felonies committed on the high Seas, and Offences against the Law of Nations;

To declare War, grant Letters of Marque and Reprisal, and make Rules concerning Captures on Land and Water;

To raise and support Armies, but no Appropriation of Money to that Use shall be for a longer Term than two Years;

To provide and maintain a Navy;

5. Changed by the Twentieth Amendment.

To make Rules for the Government and Regulation of the land and naval Forces;

To provide for calling forth the Militia to execute the Laws of the Union, suppress Insurrections and repel Invasions;

To provide for organizing, arming, and disciplining the Militia, and for governing such Part of them as may be employed in the Service of the United States, reserving to the States respectively, the Appointment of the Officers, and the Authority of training the Militia according to the discipline prescribed by Congress;

To exercise exclusive Legislation in all Cases whatsoever, over such District (not exceeding ten Miles square) as may, by Cession of particular States, and the Acceptance of Congress, become the Seat of the Government of the United States, and to exercise like Authority over all Places purchased by the Consent of the Legislature of the State in which the Same shall be, for the Erection of forts, Magazines, Arsenals, dock-Yards, and other needful Buildings;—And

To make all Laws which shall be necessary and proper for carrying into Execution the foregoing Powers, and all other Powers vested by this Constitution in the Government of the United States, or in any Department or Officer thereof.

Section 9. The Migration or Importation of such Persons as any of the States now existing shall think proper to admit, shall not be prohibited by the Congress prior to the Year one thousand eight hundred and eight, but a Tax or duty may be imposed on such Importation, not exceeding ten dollars for each Person.

The Privilege of the Writ of Habeas Corpus shall not be suspended, unless when in Cases of Rebellion or Invasion the public Safety may require it.

No Bill of Attainder or ex post facto Law shall be passed.

[No Capitation, or other direct, Tax shall be laid, unless in Proportion to the Census or Enumeration herein before directed to be taken.][6]

No Tax or Duty shall be laid on Articles exported from any State.

No Preference shall be given by any Regulation of Commerce or Revenue to the Ports of one State over those of another; nor shall Vessels bound to, or from, one State, be obliged to enter, clear, or pay Duties in another.

No Money shall be drawn from the Treasury, but in Consequence of Appropriations made by Law; and a regular Statement and Account of the Receipts and Expenditures of all public Money shall be published from time to time.

No Title of Nobility shall be granted by the United States; and no Person holding any Office or Profit or Trust under them, shall, without the Consent of the Congress, accept of any present, Emolument, Office, or Title, of any kind whatever, from any King, Prince, or foreign State.

Section 10. No state shall enter into any Treaty, Alliance, or Confederation; grant Letters of Marque and Reprisal; coin Money; emit Bills of Credit; make any Thing but gold and silver Coin a Tender in Payment of Debts; pass any Bill of Attainder, ex post facto Law, or Law impairing the Obligation of Contracts, or grant any Title of Nobility.

No State shall, without the Consent of the Congress, lay any Imposts or Duties on Imports or Exports, except what may be absolutely necessary for executing its inspection Laws; and the net Produce of all Duties and Imposts, laid by any State on Imports or Exports, shall be for the Use of the Treasury of the United States; and all such Laws shall be subject to the Revision and Controul of the Congress.

No State shall, without the Consent of Congress, lay any duty of Tonnage, keep Troops, or Ships of War in time of Peace, enter into any Agreement or Compact with another State, or with a foreign Power or engage in War, unless actually invaded, or in such imminent Danger as will not admit of delay.

Article II

Section 1. The executive Power shall be vested in a President of the United States of America. He shall hold his Office during the Term of four Years, and, together with the Vice President, chosen for the Same Term, be elected, as follows.

Each State shall appoint, in such Manner as the Legislature thereof may direct, a Number of Electors, equal to the whole Number of Senators and Representatives to which the State may be entitled in the Congress; but no Senator or Representative, or Person holding an Office of Trust or Profit under the United States, shall be appointed an Elector.

[The Electors shall meet in their respective States, and vote by Ballot for two Persons of whom one at least shall not be an Inhabitant of the same State with themselves. And they shall make a List of all the Persons voted for, and of the Number of Votes for each; which List they shall sign and certify, and transmit sealed to the Seat of the Government of the United States, directed to the President of the Senate. The President of the Senate shall, in the Presence of the Senate and House of Representatives, open all the Certificates, and the Votes shall then be counted. The Person having the greatest Number of Votes shall be the President, if such Number be a Majority of the whole Number of Electors appointed; and if there be more than one who have such Majority, and have an equal Number of Votes, then the House of Representatives shall immediately chuse by Ballot one of them for President; and if no Person have a Majority, then from the five highest on the List the said House shall in like Manner chuse the President. But in chusing the President, the Votes shall be taken by States, the Representation from each State having one Vote; A quorum for this Purpose shall consist of a Member or Members from two thirds of the States, and a Majority of all the states shall be necessary to a Choice. In every Case, after the Choice of the President, the Person having the greatest Number of Votes of the Electors shall be the Vice President. But if

6. Modified by the Sixteenth Amendment.

there should remain two or more who have equal Votes, the Senate shall chuse from them by Ballot the Vice President.][7]

The Congress may determine the Time of chusing the Electors, and the Day on which they shall give their Votes; which Day shall be the same throughout the United States.

No person except a natural born Citizen, or a Citizen of the United States, at the time of the Adoption of this Constitution, shall be eligible to the Office of President; neither shall any Person be eligible to that Office who shall not have attained to the Age of thirty five Years, and been fourteen Years a Resident within the United States.

[In Case of the Removal of the President from Office, or of his Death, Resignation, or Inability to discharge the Powers and Duties of the said Office, the same shall devolve on the Vice President, and the Congress may by Law provide for the Case of Removal, Death, Resignation or Inability, both of the President and Vice President, declaring what Officer shall then act as President, and such Officer shall act accordingly, until the Disability be removed, or a President shall be elected.][8]

The President shall, at stated Times, receive for his Services, a Compensation, which shall neither be encreased nor diminished during the Period for which he shall have been elected, and he shall not receive within that Period any other Emolument from the United States, or any of them.

Before he enter on the Execution of his Office, he shall take the following Oath or Affirmation:—"I do solemnly swear (or affirm) that I will faithfully execute the Office of President of the United States, and will to the best of my Ability, preserve, protect and defend the constitution of the United States."

Section 2. The President shall be Commander in Chief of the Army and Navy of the United States, and of the Militia of the several States, when called into the actual Service of the United States; he may require the Opinion, in writing, of the principal Officer in each of the executive Departments, upon any Subject relating to the Duties of their respective Offices, and he shall have Power to grant Reprieves and Pardons for Offences against the United States, except in Cases of Impeachment.

He shall have Power, by and with the Advice and Consent of the Senate, to make Treaties, provided two thirds of the Senators present concur; and he shall nominate, and by and with the Advice and Consent of the Senate, shall appoint Ambassadors, other public Ministers and Consuls, Judges of the supreme Court, and all other Officers of the United States, whose Appointments are not herein otherwise provided for, and which shall be established by Law; but the Congress may by Law vest the Appointment of such inferior Officers, as they think proper, in the President alone, in the Courts of Law, or in the Heads of Departments.

The President shall have Power to fill up all Vacancies that may happen during the Recess of the Senate, by granting Commissions which shall expire at the end of their next Session.

Section 3. He shall from time to time give to the Congress Information of the State of the Union, and recommend to their Consideration such Measures as he shall judge necessary and expedient; he may, on extraordinary Occasions, convene both Houses, or either of them, and in Case of Disagreement between them, with Respect to the Time of Adjournment, he may adjourn them to such Time as he shall think proper; he shall receive Ambassadors and other public Ministers; he shall take Care that the Laws be faithfully executed, and shall Commission all the Officers of the United States.

Section 4. The President, Vice President and all civil Officers of the United States, shall be removed from Office on Impeachment for, and Conviction of, Treason, Bribery, or other high Crimes and Misdemeanors.

Article III

Section 1. The judicial Power of the United States, shall be vested in one supreme Court, and in such inferior Courts as the Congress may from time to time ordain and establish. The Judges, both of the supreme and inferior Courts, shall hold their Offices during good Behaviour, and shall, at stated Times, receive for their Services, a Compensation, which shall not be diminished during their Continuance in Office.

Section 2. The judicial Power shall extend to all Cases, in Law and Equity, arising under this Constitution, the Laws of the United States, and Treaties made, or which shall be made, under their Authority;—to all Cases affecting Ambassadors, other public Ministers and Consuls;—to all Cases of admiralty and maritime Jurisdiction;—to Controversies to which the United States shall be a Party;—to Controversies between two or more States;—[between a State and Citizens of another State;][9]—between Citizens of different States,—between Citizens of the same State claiming Lands under Grants of different States, [and between a state, or the Citizens thereof, and foreign States, Citizens or Subjects.][10]

In all cases affecting Ambassadors, other public Ministers and Consuls, and those in which a State shall be Party, the supreme Court shall have original Jurisdiction. In all the other Cases before mentioned, the supreme Court shall have appellate Jurisdiction, both as to Law and Fact, with such Exceptions, and under such Regulations as the Congress shall make.

The Trial of all Crimes, except in Cases of Impeachment, shall be by Jury; and such Trial shall be held in the State where the said Crimes shall have been committed; but when not

7. Changed by the Twelfth Amendment.
8. Modified by the Twenty-fifth Amendment.

9. Modified by the Eleventh Amendment.
10. Modified by the Eleventh Amendment.

committed within any State, the Trial shall be at such Place or Places as the Congress may by Law have directed.

Section 3. Treason against the United States, shall consist only in levying War against them, or in adhering to their Enemies, giving them Aid and Comfort. No Person shall be convicted of Treason unless on the Testimony of two Witnesses to the same overt Act, or on Confession in open Court.

The Congress shall have Power to declare the Punishment of Treason, but no Attainder of Treason shall work Corruption of Blood, or Forfeiture except during the Life of the Person attainted.

Article IV

Section 1. Full Faith and Credit shall be given in each State to the public Acts, Records, and judicial Proceedings of every other State. And the Congress may by general Laws prescribe the Manner in which such Acts, Records and Proceedings shall be proved, and the Effect thereof.

Section 2. The Citizens of each State shall be entitled to all Privileges and Immunities of Citizens in the several States.

A Person charged in any State with Treason, Felony, or other Crime, who shall flee from Justice, and be found in another State, shall on Demand of the executive Authority of the State from which he fled, be delivered up, to be removed to the State having Jurisdiction of the Crime.

[No Person held to Service or Labour in one State under the Laws thereof, escaping into another, shall, in Consequence of any Law or Regulation therein, be discharged from such Service or Labour, but shall be delivered up on Claim of the Party to whom such Service or Labour may be due.]¹¹

Section 3. New States may be admitted by the Congress into this Union; but no new State shall be formed or erected within the Jurisdiction of any other State; nor any State be formed by the Junction of two or more States, or Parts of States, without the Consent of the Legislatures of the States concerned as well as of the Congress.

The Congress shall have Power to dispose of and make all needful Rules and Regulations respecting the Territory or other Property belonging to the United States; and nothing in this Constitution shall be so construed as to Prejudice any Claimes of the United States, or of any particular State.

Section 4. The United States shall guarantee to every State in this Union a Republican Form of Government, and shall protect each of them against Invasion, and on Application of the Legislature, or of the Executive (when the Legislature cannot be convened) against domestic Violence.

Article V

The Congress, whenever two thirds of both Houses shall deem it necessary, shall propose Amendments to this Constitution, or on the Application of the Legislatures of two thirds of the several States, shall call a Convention for proposing Amendments, which, in either Case, shall be valid to all Intents and Purposes, as Part of this Constitution, when ratified by the Legislatures of three fourths of the several States, or by Conventions in three fourths thereof, as the one or the other Mode of Ratification may be proposed by the Congress; Provided that no Amendment which may be made prior to the Year One thousand eight hundred and eight shall in any Manner affect the first and fourth Clauses in the Ninth Section of the first Article; and that no State, without its Consent, shall be deprived of its equal Suffrage in the Senate.

Article VI

All Debts contracted and Engagements entered into, before the Adoption of this Constitution, shall be as valid against the United States under this Constitution, as under the Confederation.

This Constitution, and the laws of the United States which shall be made in Pursuance thereof; and all Treaties made, or which shall be made, under the Authority of the United States, shall be the supreme Law of the Land; and the Judges in every State shall be bound thereby, any Thing in the Constitution or Laws of any State to the Contrary notwithstanding.

The Senators and Representatives before mentioned, and the Members of the several State Legislatures, and all executive and judicial Officers, both of the United States and of the several States, shall be bound by Oath or Affirmation, to support this Constitution; but no religious Text shall ever be required as a Qualification to any Office or public Trust under the United States.

Article VII

The Ratification of the Conventions of nine States, shall be sufficient for the Establishment of this constitution between the States so ratifying the Same.

Done in Convention by the Unanimous Consent of the States present the Seventeenth Day of September in the Year of our Lord one thousand seven hundred and Eighty seven and of the Independence of the United States of America the Twelfth. IN WITNESS whereof we have hereunto subscribed our Names.

Go. WASHINGTON
Presid't. and deputy from Virginia

Attest
William Jackson
Secretary

---

11. Repealed by the Thirteenth Amendment.

Delaware
Geo. Read
Gunning Bedford jun
John Dickinson
Richard Basset
Jaco. Broon

Massachusetts
Nathaniel Gorham
Rufus King

Connecticut
Wm. Saml. Johnson
Roger Sherman

New York
Alexander Hamilton

New Jersey
Wh. Livingston
David Brearley
Wm. Paterson
Jona. Dayton

Pennsylvania
B. Franklin
Thomas Mifflin
Robt. Morris
Geo. Clymer
Thos. FitzSimons
Jared Ingersoll

James Wilson
Gouv. Morris

Virginia
John Blair
James Madison Jr.

North Carolina
Wm. Blount
Richd. Dobbs Spaight
Hu. Williamson

South Carolina
J. Rutledge
Charles Cotesworth Pinckney
Charles Pinckney
Pierce Butler

Georgia
William Few
Abr. Baldwin

New Hampshire
John Langdon
Nicholas Gilman

Maryland
James McHenry
Dan of St. Thos. Jenifer
Danl. Carroll

Amendment I[12]

Congress shall make no law respecting an establishment of religion, or prohibiting the free exercise thereof; or abridging the freedom of speech, or of the press; or the right of the people peaceably to assemble, and to petition the Government for a redress of grievances.

Amendment II

A well regulated militia, being necessary to the security of a free State, the right of the people to keep and bear arms, shall not be infringed.

Amendment III

No Soldier shall, in time of peace be quartered in any house, without the consent of the owner, nor in time of war, but in a manner to be prescribed by law.

12. The first ten amendments were passed by Congress on September 25, 1789, and were ratified on December 15, 1791.

Amendment IV

The right of the people to be secure in their persons, houses, papers, and effects, against unreasonable searches and seizures, shall not be violated, and no warrants shall issue, but upon probable cause, supported by oath or affirmation, and particularly describing the place to be searched, and the persons or things to be seized.

Amendment V

No person shall be held to answer for a capital, or otherwise infamous crime, unless on a presentment or indictment of a Grand Jury, except in cases arising in the land or naval forces, or in the militia, when in actual service in time of war or public danger; nor shall any person be subject for the same offence to be twice put in jeopardy of life or limb; nor shall be compelled in any criminal case to be a witness against himself, nor be deprived of life, liberty, or property, without due process of law; nor shall private property be taken for public use, without just compensation.

Amendment VI

In all criminal prosecutions, the accused shall enjoy the right to a speedy and public trial, by an impartial jury of the State and district wherein the crime shall have been committed, which district shall have been previously ascertained by law, and to be informed of the nature and cause of the accusation; to be confronted with the witnesses against him; to have compulsory process for obtaining witnesses in his favor, and to have the assistance of counsel for his defence.

Amendment VII

In Suits at common law, where the value in controversy shall exceed twenty dollars, the right of trial by jury shall be preserved, and no fact tried by a jury, shall be otherwise reexamined in any Court of the United States, than according to the rules of the common law.

Amendment VIII

Excessive bail shall not be required, nor excessive fines imposed, nor cruel and unusual punishments inflicted.

Amendment IX

The enumeration in the Constitution, of certain rights, shall not be construed to deny or disparage others retained by the people.

Amendment X

The powers not delegated to the United States by the Constitution, nor prohibited by it to the States, are reserved to the States respectively, or to the people.

Amendment XI
(Ratified February 7, 1795)

The Judicial power of the United States shall not be construed to extend to any suit in law or equity, commenced or prosecuted against one of the United States by Citizens of another State, or by Citizens or Subjects of any Foreign State.

Amendment XII
(Ratified June 15, 1804)

The Electors shall meet in their respective states, and vote by ballot for President and Vice-President, one of whom, at least, shall not be an inhabitant of the same state with themselves; they shall name in their ballots the person voted for as President, and in distinct ballots the person voted for as Vice President, and they shall make distinct lists of all persons voted for as President, and of all persons voted for as Vice-President, and of the number of votes for each, which lists they shall sign and certify, and transmit sealed to the seat of the government of the United States, directed to the President of the Senate;—The President of the Senate shall, in the presence of the Senate and House of Representatives, open all the certificates and the votes shall then be counted;—The person having the greatest number of votes for President, shall be the President, if such number be a majority of the whole number of Electors appointed; and if no person have such majority, then from the persons having the highest numbers not exceeding three on the list of those voted for as President, the House of Representatives shall choose immediately, by ballot, the President. But in choosing the President, the votes shall be taken by states, the representation from each state having one vote; a quorum for this purpose shall consist of a member or members from two-thirds of the states, and a majority of all the states shall be necessary to a choice. [And if the House of Representatives shall not choose a President whenever the right of choice shall devolve upon them, before the fourth day of March next following, then the Vice-President shall act as President, as in the case of the death or other constitutional disability of the President.][13]—The person having the greatest number of votes as Vice-President, shall be the Vice-President, if such number be a majority of the whole number of Electors appointed, and if no person have a majority, then from the two highest numbers on the list, the Senate shall choose the Vice-President; a quorum for the purpose shall consist of two-thirds of the whole number of Senators, and a majority of the whole number shall be necessary to a choice. But no person constitutionally ineligible to the office of President shall be eligible to that of Vice-President of the United States.

Amendment XIII
(Ratified on December 6, 1865)

Section 1. Neither slavery nor involuntary servitude, except as a punishment for crime whereof the party shall have been duly convicted, shall exist within the United States, or any place subject to their jurisdiction.

Section 2. Congress shall have power to enforce this article by appropriate legislation.

Amendment XIV
(Ratified on July 9, 1868)

All persons born or naturalized in the United States, and subject to the jurisdiction thereof, are citizens of the United States and of the State wherein they reside. No State shall make or enforce any law which shall abridge the privileges or immunities of citizens of the United States; nor shall any State deprive any person of life, liberty, or property, without due process of law; nor deny to any person within its jurisdiction the equal protection of the laws.

Section 2. Representatives shall be apportioned among the several States according to their respective numbers, counting the whole number of persons in each State, excluding Indians not taxed. But when the right to vote at any election for the choice of electors for President and Vice President of the United States, Representatives in Congress, the Executive and Judicial officers of a State, or the members of the Legislature thereof, is denied to any of the male inhabitants of such State, being [twenty-one][14] years of age, and citizens of the United States, or in any way abridged, except for participation in rebellion, or other crime, the basis of representation therein shall be reduced in the proportion which the number of such male citizens shall bear to the whole number of male citizens twenty-one years of age in such State.

Section 3. No person shall be a Senator or Representative in Congress, or elector of President and Vice President, or hold any office, civil or military, under the United States, or under any State, who having previously taken an oath, as a member of Congress, or as an officer of the United States, or as a member of any State legislature, or as an executive or judicial officer of any State, to support the Constitution of the United States, shall have engaged in insurrection or rebellion against the same, or given aid or comfort to the enemies thereof. But Congress may by a vote of two-thirds of each House, remove such disability.

Section 4. The validity of the public debt of the United States, authorized by law, including debts incurred for payment of pensions and bounties for services in suppressing insurrection or rebellion, shall not be questioned. But neither the United States nor any State shall assume or pay any debt or obligation incurred in aid of insurrection or rebellion

---

13. Changed by the Twentieth Amendment.
14. Changed by the Twenty-sixth Amendment.

against the United States, or any claim for the loss or emancipation of any slave, but all such debts, obligations and claims shall be held illegal and void.

Section 5. The Congress shall have power to enforce, by appropriate legislation, the provisions of this article.

Amendment XV
(Ratified on February 3, 1870)

Section 1. The right of citizens of the United States to vote shall not be denied or abridged by the United States or by any State on account of race, color, or previous condition of servitude.

Section 2. The Congress shall have power to enforce this article by appropriate legislation.

Amendment XVI
(Ratified on February 3, 1913)

The Congress shall have power to lay and collect taxes on incomes, from whatever source derived, without apportionment among the several States, and without regard to any census or enumeration.

Amendment XVII
(Ratified on April 8, 1913)

The Senate of the United States shall be composed of two Senators from each State, elected by the people thereof, for six years; and each Senator shall have one vote. The electors in each State shall have the qualifications requisite for electors of the most numerous branch of the State legislatures.

When vacancies happen in the representation of any State in the Senate, the executive authority of such State shall issue writs of election to fill such vacancies: *Provided,* That the legislature of any State may empower the executive thereof to make temporary appointments until the people fill the vacancies by election as the legislature may direct.

This amendment shall not be so construed as to affect the election or term of any Senator chosen before it becomes valid as part of the Constitution.

Amendment XVIII
(Ratified on January 16, 1919)

Section 1. After one year from the ratification of this article the manufacture, sale, or transportation of intoxicating liquors within, the importation thereof into, or the exportation thereof from the United States and all territory subject to the jurisdiction thereof for beverage purposes is hereby prohibited.

Section 2. The Congress and the several States shall have concurrent power to enforce this article by appropriate legislation.

Section 3. This article shall be inoperative unless it shall have been ratified as an amendment to the Constitution by the legislatures of the several States, as provided in the Constitution, within seven years from the date of the submission hereof to the States by the Congress.[15]

Amendment XIX
(Ratified on August 18, 1920)

The right of citizens of the United States to vote shall not be denied or abridged by the United States or by any State on account of sex.

Congress shall have power to enforce this article by appropriate legislation.

Amendment XX
(Ratified on January 23, 1933)

Section 1. The terms of the President and Vice President shall end at noon on the 20th day of January, and the terms of Senators and Representatives at noon on the 3rd day of January, of the years in which such terms would have ended if this article had not been ratified, and the terms of their successors shall then begin.

Section 2. The Congress shall assemble at least once in every year, and such meeting shall begin at noon on the 3rd day of January, unless they shall by law appoint a different day.

Section 3. If, at the time fixed for the beginning of the term of the President, the President elect shall have died, the Vice President elect shall become President. If a President shall not have been chosen before the time fixed for the beginning of his term, or if the President elect shall have failed to qualify, then the Vice President elect shall act as President until a President shall have qualified; and the Congress may by law provide for the case wherein neither a President elect nor a Vice President elect shall have qualified, declaring who shall then act as President, or the manner in which one who is to act shall be selected, and such person shall act accordingly until a President or Vice President shall have qualified.

Section 4. The Congress may by law provide for the case of the death of any of the persons from whom the House of Representatives may choose a President whenever the rights of choice shall have devolved upon them, and for the case of the death of any of the persons from whom the Senate may

---

15. The Eighteenth Amendment was repealed by the Twenty-first Amendment.

choose a Vice President whenever the right of choice shall have devolved upon them.

Section 5. Sections 1 and 2 shall take effect on the 15th day of October following the ratification of this article.

Section 6. This article shall be inoperative unless it shall have been ratified as an amendment to the Constitution by the legislatures of three-fourths of the several States within seven years from the date of its submission.

Amendment XXI
(Ratified on December 5, 1933)

Section 1. The eighteenth article of amendment to the Constitution of the United States is hereby repealed.

Section 2. The transportation or importation into any State, Territory, or possession of the United States for delivery or use therein of intoxicating liquors, in violation of the laws thereof, is hereby prohibited.

Section 3. This article shall be inoperative unless it shall have been ratified as an amendment to the Constitution by conventions in the several States, as provided in the Constitution, within seven years from the date of the submission hereof to the States by the Congress.

Amendment XXII
(Ratified on February 27, 1951)

No person shall be elected to the office of the President more than twice, and no person who has held the office of President, or acted as President, for more than two years of a term to which some other person was elected President shall be elected to the office of the President more than once. But this Article shall not apply to any person holding the office of President when this Article was proposed by the Congress, and shall not prevent any person who may be holding the office of President, or acting as President, during the term within which this Article becomes operative from holding the office of President or acting as President during the remainder of such term.

Amendment XXIII
(Ratified on March 29, 1961)

Section 1. The District constituting the seat of Government of the United States shall appoint in such manner as the Congress may direct:

A number of electors of President and Vice President equal to the whole number of Senators and Representatives in Congress to which the District would be entitled if it were a State, but in no event more than the least populous State; they shall be in addition to those appointed by the States, but they shall be considered, for the purposes of the election of President and Vice President, to be electors appointed by a State; and they shall meet in the District and perform such duties as provided by the twelfth article of amendment.

Section 2. The Congress shall have power to enforce this article by appropriate legislation.

Amendment XXIV
(Ratified on January 23, 1964)

Section 1. The right of citizens of the United States to vote in any primary or other election for President or Vice President, for electors for President or Vice President, or for Senator or Representative in Congress, shall not be denied or abridged by the United States or any State by reason of failure to pay any poll tax or other tax.

Section 2. The Congress shall have power to enforce this article by appropriate legislation.

Amendment XXV
(Ratified on February 10, 1967)

Section 1. In case of the removal of the President from office or of his death or resignation, the Vice President shall become President.

Section 2. Whenever there is a vacancy in the office of the Vice President, the President shall nominate a Vice President who shall take office upon confirmation by a majority vote of both Houses of Congress.

Section 3. Whenever the President transmits to the President pro tempore of the Senate and the Speaker of the House of Representatives his written declaration that he is unable to discharge the powers and duties of his office, and until he transmits to them a written declaration to the contrary, such powers and duties shall be discharged by the Vice President as Acting President.

Section 4. Whenever the Vice President and a majority of either the principal officers of the executive departments or of such other body as Congress may by law provide, transmit to the President pro tempore of the Senate and the Speaker of the House of Representatives their written declaration that the President is unable to discharge the powers and duties of his office, the Vice President shall immediately assume the powers and duties of the offices as Acting President.

Thereafter, when the President transmits to the President pro tempore of the Senate and the Speaker of the House of

Representatives his written declaration that no inability exists, he shall resume the powers and duties of his office unless the Vice President and a majority of either the principal officers of the executive department or of such other body as Congress may by law provide, transmit within four days to the President pro tempore of the Senate and the Speaker of the House of Representatives their written declaration that the President is unable to discharge the powers and duties of his office. Thereupon Congress shall decide the issue, assembling within forty-eight hours for that purpose if not in session. If the Congress, within twenty-one days after receipt of the latter written declaration, or, if Congress is not in session, within twenty-one days after Congress is required to assemble, determines by two-thirds vote of both Houses that the President is unable to discharge the powers and duties of his office, the Vice President shall continue to discharge the same as Acting President; otherwise; the President shall resume the powers and duties of his office.

Amendment XXVI (Ratified on July 1, 1971)

Section 1. The right of citizens of the United States, who are eighteen years of age or older, to vote shall not be denied or abridged by the United States or by any State on account of age.

Section 2. The Congress shall have the power to enforce this article by appropriate legislation.

Amendment XXVII (Ratified on May 7, 1992)

No law, varying the compensation for the services of the Senators and Representatives, shall take effect, until an election of Representatives shall have intervened.

Federalist Paper 10

Among the numerous advantages promised by a well-constructed Union, none deserves to be more accurately developed than its tendency to break and control the violence of faction. The friend of popular governments never finds himself so much alarmed for their character and fate as when he contemplates their propensity to this dangerous vice. He will not fail, therefore, to set a due value on any plan which, without violating the principles to which he is attached, provides a proper cure for it. The instability, injustice, and confusion introduced into the public councils have, in truth, been the mortal diseases under which popular governments have everywhere perished, as they continue to be the favorite and fruitful topics from which the adversaries to liberty derive their most specious declamations. The valuable improvements made by the American constitutions on the popular models, both ancient and modern, cannot certainly be too much admired; but it would be an unwarrantable partiality to contend that they have as effectually obviated the danger on this side, as was wished and expected. Complaints are everywhere heard from our most considerate and virtuous citizens, equally the friends of public and private faith and of public and personal liberty, that our governments are too unstable, that the public good is disregarded in the conflicts of rival parties, and that measures are too often decided, not according to the rules of justice and the rights of the minor party, but by the superior force of an interested and overbearing majority. However anxiously we may wish that these complaints had no foundation, the evidence of known facts will not permit us to deny that they are in some degree true. It will be found, indeed, on a candid review of our situation, that some of the distresses under which we labor have been erroneously charged on the operation of our governments; but it will be found, at the same time, that other causes will not alone account for many of our heaviest misfortunes; and, particularly, for that prevailing and increasing distrust of public engagements and alarm for private rights which are echoed from one end of the continent to the other. These must be chiefly, if not wholly, effects of the unsteadiness and injustice with which a factious spirit has tainted our public administration.

By a faction I understand a number of citizens, whether amounting to a majority or minority of the whole, who are united and actuated by some common impulse of passion, or of interest, adverse to the rights of other citizens, or the permanent and aggregate interests of the community.

There are two methods of curing the mischiefs of faction: the one, by removing its causes; the other, by controlling its effects.

There are again two methods of removing the causes of faction: the one, by destroying the liberty which is essential to its existence; the other, by giving to every citizen the same opinions, the same passions, and the same interests.

It could never be more truly said than of the first remedy that it was worse than the disease. Liberty is to faction what air is to fire, an aliment without which it instantly expires. But it could not be a less folly to abolish liberty, which is essential to political life, because it nourishes faction than it would be to wish the annihilation of air, which is essential to animal life, because it imparts to fire its destructive agency.

The second expedient is as impracticable as the first would be unwise. As long as the reason of man continues fallible, and his is at liberty to exercise it, different opinions will be formed. As long as the connection subsists between his reason and his self-love, his opinions and his passions will have a reciprocal influence on each other; and the former will be objects to which the latter will attach themselves. The diversity in the faculties of men, from which the rights of property originate, is not less an insuperable obstacle to a uniformity of interests. The protection of these faculties is the first object of government. From the protection of different and unequal faculties of acquiring property, the possession of different degrees and kinds of property immediately results; and from the influence of these on the sentiments and views of the respective proprietors ensues a division of the society into different interests and parties.

The latent causes of faction are thus sown in the nature of man; and we see them everywhere brought into different degrees of activity, according to the different circumstances of civil society. A zeal for different opinions concerning religion, concerning government, and many other points, as well of speculation as of practice; an attachment to different leaders ambitiously contending for pre-eminence and power; or to persons of other descriptions whose fortunes have been interesting to the human passions, have, in turn, divided mankind into parties, inflamed them with mutual animosity, and rendered them much more disposed to vex and oppress each other than to cooperate for their common good. So strong is this propensity of mankind to fall into mutual animosities that where no substantial occasion presents itself the most frivolous and fanciful distinctions have been sufficient to kindle their unfriendly passions and excite their most violent conflicts. But the most common and durable source of factions has been the various and unequal distribution of property. Those who hold and those who are without property have ever formed distinct interests in society. Those who are creditors, and those who are debtors, fall under a like discrimination. A landed interest, a manufacturing interest, a mercantile interest, a moneyed interest, with many lesser interests, grow up of necessity in civilized nations, and divide them into different classes, actuated by different sentiments and views. The regulation of these various and interfering interests forms the principal task of modern legislation and involves the spirit of party and faction in the necessary and ordinary operations of government.

No man is allowed to be a judge in his own cause, because his interest would certainly bias his judgment, and, not improbably, corrupt his integrity. With equal, nay with greater reason, a body of men are unfit to be both judges and parties at the same time; yet what are many of the most important acts of legislation but so many judicial determinations, not indeed concerning the rights of single persons, but concerning the rights of large bodies of citizens? And what are the different classes of legislators but advocates and parties to the causes which they determine? Is a law proposed concerning private debts? It is a question to which the creditors are parties on one side and the debtors on the other. Justice ought to hold the balance between them. Yet the parties are, and must be, themselves the judges; and the most numerous party, or in other words, the most powerful faction must be expected to prevail. Shall domestic manufacturers be encouraged, and in what degree, by restrictions on foreign manufacturers? are questions which would be differently decided by the landed and the manufacturing classes, and probably by neither with a sole regard to justice and the public good. The apportionment of taxes on the various descriptions of property is an act which seems to require the most exact impartiality; yet there is, perhaps, no legislative act in which greater opportunity and temptation are given to a predominant party to trample on the rules of justice. Every shilling with which they overburden the inferior number is a shilling saved to their own pockets.

It is in vain to say that enlightened statesmen will be able to adjust these clashing interests and render them all subservient to the public good. Enlightened statesmen will not always be at the helm. Nor, in many cases, can such an adjustment be made at all without taking into view indirect and remote considerations, which will rarely prevail over the immediate interest which one party may find in disregarding the rights of another or the good of the whole.

The inference to which we are brought is that the *causes* of faction cannot be removed and that relief is only to be sought in the means of controlling its *effects.*

If a faction consists of less than a majority, relief is supplied by the republican principle, which enables the majority to defeat its sinister views by regular vote. It may clog the administration, it may convulse the society; but it will be unable to execute and mask its violence under the forms of the Constitution. When a majority is included in a faction, the form of popular government, on the other hand, enables it to sacrifice to its ruling passion or interest both the public good and the rights of other citizens. To secure the public good and private rights against the danger of such a faction, and at the same

time to preserve the spirit and the form of popular government, is then the great object to which our inquiries are directed. Let me add that it is the great desideratum by which alone this form of government can be rescued from the opprobrium under which it has so long labored and be recommended to the esteem and adoption of mankind.

By what means is this object attainable? Evidently by one of two only. Either the existence of the same passion or interest in a majority at the same time must be prevented, or the majority, having such coexistent passion or interest, must be rendered, by their number and local situation, unable to concert and carry into effect schemes of oppression. If the impulse and the opportunity be suffered to coincide, we well know that neither moral nor religious motives can be relied on as an adequate control. They are not found to be such on the injustice and violence of individuals, and lose their efficacy in proportion to the number combined together, that is, in proportion as their efficacy becomes needful.

From this view of the subject it may be concluded that a pure democracy, by which I mean a society consisting of a small number of citizens, who assemble and administer the government in person, can admit of no cure for the mischiefs of faction. A common passion or interest will, in almost every case, be felt by a majority of the whole; a communication and concert results from the form of government itself; and there is nothing to check the inducements to sacrifice the weaker party or an obnoxious individual. Hence it is that such democracies have ever been spectacles of turbulence and contention; have ever been found incompatible with personal security or the rights of property; and have in general been as short in their lives as they have been violent in their deaths. Theoretic politicians, who have patronized this species of government, have erroneously supposed that by reducing mankind to a perfect equality in their political rights, they would at the same time be perfectly equalized and assimilated in their possessions, their opinions, and their passions.

A republic, by which I mean a government in which the scheme of representation takes place, opens a different prospect and promises the cure for which we are seeking. Let us examine the points in which it varies from pure democracy, and we shall comprehend both the nature of the cure and the efficacy which it must derive from the Union.

The two great points of difference between a democracy and a republic are: first, the delegation of the government, in the latter, to a small number of citizens elected by the rest; secondly, the greater number of citizens and greater sphere of country over which the latter may be extended.

The effect of the first difference is, on the one hand, to refine and enlarge the public views by passing them through the medium of a chosen body of citizens, whose wisdom may best discern the true interest of their country and whose patriotism and love of justice will be least likely to sacrifice it to temporary or partial considerations. Under such a regulation it may well happen that the public voice, pronounced by the representatives of the people, will be more consonant to the public good than if pronounced by the people themselves, convened for the purpose. On the other hand, the effect may be inverted. Men of factious tempers, of local prejudices, or of sinister designs, may, by intrigue, by corruption, or by other means, first obtain the suffrages, and then betray the interests of the people. The question resulting is, whether small or extensive republics are most favorable to the election of proper guardians of the public weal; and it is clearly decided in favor of the latter by two obvious considerations.

In the first place it is to be remarked that however small the republic may be the representatives must be raised to a certain number in order to guard against the cabals of a few; and that however large it may be they must be limited to a certain number in order to guard against the confusion of a multitude. Hence, the number of representatives in the two cases not being in proportion to that of the constituents, and being proportionally greatest in the small republic, it follows that if the proportion of fit characters be not less in the large than in the small republic, the former will present a greater option, and consequently a greater probability of a fit choice.

In the next place, as each representative will be chosen by a greater number of citizens in the large than in the small republic, it will be more difficult for unworthy candidates to practice with success the vicious arts by which elections are too often carried; and the suffrages of the people being more free, will be more likely to center on men who possess the most attractive merit and the most diffusive and established characters.

It must be confessed that in this, as in most other cases, there is a mean, on both sides of which inconveniencies will be found to lie. By enlarging too much the number of electors, you render the representative too little acquainted with all their local circumstances and lesser interests; as by reducing it too much, you render him unduly attached to these, and too little fit to comprehend and pursue great and national objects. The federal Constitution forms a happy combination in this respect; the great and aggregate interests being referred to the national, the local and particular to the State legislatures.

The other point of difference is the greater number of citizens and extent of territory which may be brought within the compass of republican than of democratic government; and it is this circumstance principally which renders factious combinations less to be dreaded in the former than in the latter. The smaller the society, the fewer probably will be the distinct parties and interests composing it; the fewer the distinct parties and interests, the more frequently will a majority be found of the same party; and the smaller the number of individuals composing a majority, and the smaller the compass within which they are placed, the more easily will they concert and execute their plans of oppression. Extend the sphere and you take in a greater variety of parties and interests; you make it less probable that a majority of the whole will have a common motive to invade the rights of other citizens; or if such a common motive exists, it will be more difficult for all who feel it to discover their own strength and to act in unison with each other. Besides other impediments, it may be remarked that, where there is a consciousness of unjust or dishonorable purposes, communication is always checked by distrust in proportion to the number whose concurrence is necessary.

Hence, it clearly appears that the same advantage which a republic has over a democracy in controlling the effects of faction is enjoyed by a large over a small republic—is enjoyed by the Union over the States composing it. Does this advantage consist in the substitution of representatives whose enlightened views and virtuous sentiments render them superior to local prejudices and to schemes of injustice? It will not be denied that the representation of the Union will be most likely to possess these requisite endowments. Does it consist in the greater security afforded by a greater variety of parties, against the event of any one party being able to outnumber and oppress the rest? In an equal degree does the increased variety of parties comprised within the Union increase this security. Does it, in fine, consist in the greater obstacles opposed to the concert and accomplishment of the secret wishes of an unjust and interested majority? Here again the extent of the Union gives it the most palpable advantage.

The influence of factious leaders may kindle a flame within their particular States but will be unable to spread a general conflagration through the other States. A religious sect may degenerate into a political faction in a part of the Confederacy; but the variety of sects dispersed over the entire face of it must secure the national councils against any danger from that source. A rage for paper money, for an abolition of debts, for an equal division of property, or for any other improper or wicked project, will be less apt to pervade the whole body of the Union than a particular member of it, in the same proportion as such a malady is more likely to taint a particular county or district than an entire State.

In the extent and proper structure of the Union, therefore, we behold a republican remedy for the diseases most incident to republican government. And according to the degree of pleasure and pride we feel in being republicans ought to be our zeal in cherishing the spirit and supporting the character of federalists.

Federalist Paper 51

To what expedient, then, shall we finally resort, for maintaining in practice the necessary partition of power among the several departments as laid down in the Constitution? The only answer that can be given is that as all these exterior provisions are found to be inadequate the defect must be supplied, by so contriving the interior structure of the government as that its several constituent parts may, by their mutual relations, be the means of keeping each other in their proper places. Without presuming to undertake a full development of this important idea I will hazard a few general observations which may perhaps place it in a clearer light, and enable us to form a more correct judgment of the principles and structure of the government planned by the convention.

In order to lay a due foundation for that separate and distinct exercise of the different powers of government, which to a certain extent is admitted on all hands to be essential to the preservation of liberty, it is evident that each department should have a will of its own; and consequently should be so constituted that the members of each should have as little agency as possible in the appointment of the members of the others. Were this principle rigorously adhered to, it would require that all the appointments for the supreme executive, legislative, and judiciary magistracies should be drawn from the same fountain of authority, the people, through channels having no communication whatever with one another. Perhaps such a plan of constructing the several departments would be less difficult in practice than it may in contemplation appear. Some difficulties, however, and some additional expense would attend the execution of it. Some deviations, therefore, from the principle must be admitted. In the constitution of the judiciary department in particular, it might be inexpedient to insist rigorously on the principle: first, because peculiar qualifications being essential in the members, the primary consideration ought to be to select that mode of choice which best secures these qualifications; second, because the permanent tenure by which the appointments are held in that department must soon destroy all sense of dependence on the authority conferring them.

It is equally evident that the members of each department should be as little dependent as possible on those of the others for the emoluments annexed to their offices. Were the executive magistrate, or the judges, not independent of the legislature in this particular, their independence in every other would be merely nominal.

But the great security against a gradual concentration of the several powers in the same department consists in giving to those who administer each department the necessary constitutional means and personal motives to resist encroachments of the others. The provision for defense must in this, as in all other cases, be made commensurate to the danger of attack. Ambition must be made to counteract ambition. The interest of the man must be connected with the constitutional rights of the place. It may be a reflection on human nature that such devices should be necessary to control the abuses of government. But what is government itself but the greatest of all reflections on human nature? If men were angels, no government would be necessary. If angels were to govern men, neither external nor internal controls on government would be necessary. In framing a government which is to be administered by men over men, the great difficulty lies in this: you must first enable the government to control the governed; and in the next place oblige it to control itself. A dependence on the people is, no doubt, the primary control on the government; but experience has taught mankind the necessity of auxiliary precautions.

This policy of supplying, by opposite and rival interests, the defect of better motives, might be traced through the whole system of human affairs, private as well as public. We see it particularly displayed in all the subordinate distributions of power, where the constant aim is to divide and arrange the several offices in such a manner as that each may be a check on the other—that the private interest of every individual may be a sentinel over the public rights. These inventions of prudence cannot be less requisite in the distribution of the supreme powers of the State.

But it is not possible to give to each department an equal power of self-defense. In republican government, the legislative authority necessarily predominates. The remedy for this inconveniency is to divide the legislature into different branches; and to render them, by different modes of election and different principles of action, as little connected with each other as the nature of their common functions and their common dependence on the society will admit. It may even be necessary to guard against dangerous encroachments by still further precautions. As the weight of the legislative authority requires that it should be thus divided, the weakness of the executive may require, on the other hand, that it should be fortified. An absolute negative on the legislature appears, at first view, to be the natural defense with which the executive magistrate should be armed. But perhaps it would be neither altogether safe nor alone sufficient. On ordinary occasions it might not be exerted with the requisite firmness, and on extraordinary occasions it might be perfidiously abused. May not this defect of an absolute negative be supplied by some qualified connection between this weaker department and the weaker branch of the stronger department, by which the latter may be led to support the constitutional rights of the former, without being too much detached from the rights of its own department?

If the principles on which these observations are found be just, as I persuade myself they are, and they be applied as a criterion to the several State constitutions, and the federal Constitution, it will be found that if the latter does not perfectly correspond with them, the former are infinitely less able to bear such a test.

There are, moreover, two considerations particularly applicable to the federal system of America, which place that system in a very interesting point of view.

First. In a single republic, all the power surrendered by the people is submitted to the administration of a single government; and the usurpations are guarded against by a division of the government into distinct and separate departments. In the compound republic of America, the power surrendered by the people is first divided between two distinct governments, and then the portion allotted to each subdivided among distinct and separate departments. Hence a double security arises to the rights of the people. The different governments will control each other, at the same time that each will be controlled by itself.

Second. It is of great importance in a republic not only to guard the society against the oppression of its rulers, but to guard one part of the society against the injustice of the other part. Different interests necessarily exist in different classes of citizens. If a majority be united by a common interest, the rights of the minority will be insecure. There are but two methods of providing against this evil: the one by creating a will in the community independent of the majority—that is, of the society itself; the other, by comprehending in the society so many separate descriptions of citizens as will render an unjust combination of a majority of the whole very improbable, if not impracticable. The first method prevails in all governments possessing an hereditary or self-appointed authority. This, at best, is but a precarious security; because a power independent of the society may as well espouse the unjust views of the major as the rightful interests of the minor party, and may possibly be turned against both parties. The second method will be exemplified in the federal republic of the United States. Whilst all authority in it will be derived from and dependent on the society, the society itself will be broken into so many parts, interests and classes of citizens, that the rights of individuals, or of the minority, will be in little danger from interested combinations of the majority. In a free government the security for civil rights must be the same as that for religious rights. It consists in the one case in the mul-

tiplicity of interests, and in the other in the multiplicity of sects. The degree of security in both cases will depend on the number of interests and sects; and this may be presumed to depend on the extent of country and number of people comprehended under the same government. This view of the subject must particularly recommend a proper federal system to all the sincere and considerate friends of republican government, since it shows that in exact proportion as the territory of the Union may be formed into more circumscribed Confederacies, or States, oppressive combinations of a majority will be facilitated; the best security, under the republican forms, for the rights of every class of citizen, will be diminished; and consequently the stability and independence of some member of the government, the only other security, must be proportionally increased. Justice is the end of government. It is the end of civil society. It ever has been and ever will be pursued until it be obtained, or until liberty be lost in the pursuit. In a society under the forms of which the stronger faction can readily unite and oppress the weaker, anarchy may as truly be said to reign as in a state of nature, where the weaker individual is not secured against the violence of the stronger; and as, in the latter state, even the stronger individuals are prompted, by the uncertainty of their condition, to submit to a government which may protect the weak as well as themselves; so, in the former state, will the more powerful factions or parties be gradually induced, by a like motive, to wish for a government which will protect all parties, the weaker as well as the more powerful. It can be little doubted that if the State of Rhode Island was separated from the Confederacy and left to itself, the insecurity of rights under the popular form of government within such narrow limits would be displayed by such reiterate oppressions of factious majorities that some power altogether independent of the people would soon be called for by the voice of the very factions whose misrule had proved the necessity of it. In the extended republic of the United States, and among the great variety of interests, parties, and sects which it embraces, a coalition of a majority of the whole society could seldom take place on any other principles than those of justice and the general good; whilst there being thus less danger to a minor from the will of a major party, there must be less pretext, also, to provide for the security of the former, by introducing into the government a will not dependent on the latter, or, in other words, a will independent of the society itself. It is no less certain than it is important, notwithstanding the contrary opinions which have been entertained, that the larger the society, provided it lie within a practicable sphere, the more duly capable it will be of self-government. And happily for the *republican cause,* the practicable sphere may be carried to a very great extent by a judicious modification and mixture of the *federal principle.*

Glossary

Abscam A 1981 FBI undercover operation in which six House members and one senator were convicted of taking bribes.

Activist judges Judges who are not reluctant to overrule the other branches of government by declaring laws or actions of government officials unconstitutional.

Adversarial relationship A relationship in which the parties are constantly in conflict with each other.

Affirmative action A policy in job hiring or university admissions that gives special consideration to members of traditionally disadvantaged groups in an effort to compensate for the effects of past discrimination.

Agents of political socialization Sources of information about politics; include parents, peers, schools, the media, political leaders, and the community.

Aid to Families with Dependent Children (AFDC) A program that provides income support for the poor.

American Civil Liberties Union (ACLU) A nonpartisan organization that seeks to protect the civil liberties of all Americans.

Amicus curiae In Latin, "friend of the court." A third party that gives advice in a legal case to which it is not a party.

Antifederalists Those who opposed the ratification of the U.S. Constitution.

Antitrust legislation Laws that prohibit **monopolies**.

Appropriations Budget legislation that specifies the amount of authorized funds that will actually be allocated for agencies and departments to spend.

Articles of Confederation The first constitution of the United States; in effect from 1781 to 1789.

Authorizations Budget legislation that provides agencies and departments with the legal authority to operate; may specify funding levels but do not actually provide the funding (the funding is provided by **appropriations**).

Baker v. Carr A 1962 Supreme Court decision giving voters the right to use the courts to rectify the malapportionment of legislative districts.

Balanced budget amendment A proposed constitutional amendment that would require balancing the federal budget.

Balanced government Refers to the idea that the different branches of government all represent different interests, forcing the various factions to work out compromises acceptable to all.

Bandwagon effect The tendency of voters to follow the lead of the media, which de-clare some candidates winners and others losers, and vote for the perceived winner. The extent of this effect is unknown.

Bay of Pigs invasion The disastrous CIA-backed invasion of Cuba in 1961, mounted by Cuban exiles and intended to overthrow the government of Fidel Castro.

Behavioral approach The study of politics by looking at the behavior of public officials, voters, and other participants in politics, rather than by focusing on institutions or law.

Bible Belt A term used to describe portions of the South and Midwest that were strongly influenced by Protestant fundamentalists.

Bilingual education Programs where students whose native language is not English receive instruction in substantive subjects such as math in their native language.

Bill of Rights The first 10 amendments to the U.S. Constitution.

Bills of attainder Legislative acts that pronounce specific persons guilty of crimes.

Black Codes Laws passed by Southern states following the **Civil War** that denied most legal rights to the newly freed slaves.

Blockbusting The practice in which realtors would frighten whites in a neighborhood where a black family had moved by telling the whites that their houses would decline in value. The whites in panic would then sell their houses to the realtors at low prices, and the realtors would resell the houses to blacks, thereby resegregating the area from white to black.

Block grants A system of giving federal funds to states and localities under which the federal government designates the purpose for which the funds are to be used but allows the states some discretion in spending.

Boll Weevils Conservative Democratic members of Congress, mainly from the South, who vote more often with the Republicans than with their own party.

Brownlow Committee Appointed by Franklin Roosevelt in 1935, the committee recommended ways of improving the management of the federal bureaucracy and increasing the president's influence over it.

Brown v. Board of Education The 1954 case in which the U.S. Supreme Court overturned the **separate-but-equal doctrine** and ruled unanimously that segregated schools violated the Fourteenth Amendment.

Bubble concept A policy that permits flexibility in meeting pollution standards by allowing a company to meet an emissions standard if total emissions from all smoke-stacks at a factory or from all factories in a given area (under an imaginary bubble) meet the standard, even though emissions from individual smokestacks or factories fail to comply.

Budget and Accounting Act of 1921 This act gives the president the power to propose a budget and led to presidential dominance in the budget process. It also created the **Bureau of the Budget,** changed to the **Office of Management and Budget** in 1970.

Bureaucratic continuity The stability provided by career-oriented civil servants, who remain in government for many years while presidents, legislators, and political appointees come and go.

Bureau of the Budget Established in 1921 and later changed to the **Office of Management and Budget,** the BOB was designed as the president's primary means of developing federal budget policy.

Burger Court The U.S. Supreme Court under Chief Justice Warren Burger (1969–1986). Though not as activist as the **Warren Court,** the Burger Court maintained most of the rights expanded by its predecessor and issued important rulings on abortion and sexual discrimination.

Canadian health care plan A single-payer system in which individuals choose their own doctors and the province pays the doctors for services performed; fees are strictly regulated.

Capitalist economy An economic system in which prices, wages, working conditions, and profits are determined solely by the market.

Captured agencies Refers to the theory that regulatory agencies often end up working on behalf of the interests they are supposed to regulate.

Casework The assistance members of Congress provide to their constituents; includes answering questions and doing personal favors for those who ask for help. Also called **constituency service**.

Caucus Today, a meeting of local residents who select delegates to attend county, state, and national conventions where the delegates nominate candidates for public office. Originally, caucuses were limited to party leaders and officeholders who selected the candidates.

Central Intelligence Agency (CIA) Created after World War II, the CIA is a federal agency charged with coordinating overseas intelligence activities for the United States.

Checks and balances The principle of government that holds that the powers of the various branches should overlap to avoid power becoming overly concentrated in one branch.

City-state In ancient Greece, a self-governing state such as Athens or Sparta, consisting of an independent city and its surrounding territory.

Civil case A case in which individuals sue others for denying their rights and causing them harm.

Civil Rights Act of 1964 Major civil rights legislation that prohibits discrimination on the basis of race, color, religion, or national origin in public accommodations.

Civil Rights Act of 1968 Civil rights legislation that prohibits discrimination in the sale or rental of housing on the basis of race, color, religion, or national origin; also prohibits **blockbusting, steering, and redlining.**

Civil Service Commission An agency established by the **Pendleton Act of 1883** to curb **patronage** in the federal bureaucracy and replace it with a merit system.

Civil War The war between the Union and the Confederacy (1861–1865), fought mainly over the question of whether the national or state governments were to exercise ultimate political power. Slavery was the issue that precipitated this great conflict.

Classical democracy A system of government that emphasizes citizen participation through debating, voting, and holding office.

Closed primary A primary election where participation is limited to those who are registered with a party or declare a preference for a party.

Cloture A method of stopping a **filibuster** by limiting debate to only 20 more hours; requires a vote of three-fifths of the members of the Senate.

Coalition A network of **interest groups** with similar concerns that combine forces to pursue a common goal; may be short-lived or permanent.

Coalition building The union of **pressure groups** that share similar concerns.

Cold War The era of hostility between the United States and the Soviet Union that existed between the end of World War II and the collapse of the Soviet Union.

Commercial bias A slant in news coverage to please or avoid offending advertisers.

Committee of the Whole Refers to the informal entity the House of Representatives makes itself into to debate a bill.

Commodity groups Interest groups that represent producers of specific products, such as cattle, tobacco, or milk producers.

Comparable worth The principle that comparable jobs should pay comparable wages.

Concurrent resolutions Special resolutions expressing the sentiment of Congress, passed by one house with the other concurring, but not requiring the president's signature.

Confederal system A system in which the central government has only the powers given to it by the subnational governments.

Conference committee A committee composed of members of both houses of Congress that is formed to try to resolve the differences when the two houses pass different versions of the same bill.

Conflict of interest The situation when government officials make decisions that directly affect their own personal livelihoods or interests.

Conscientious objectors Persons who oppose all wars and refuse military service on the basis of religious or moral principles.

Conservative A person who believes that the domestic role of government should be minimized and that individuals are responsible for their own well-being.

Constituencies The persons a member of Congress represents. For a senator, all the residents of the state; for a member of the House, all the residents of the member's district.

Constituency service The assistance members of Congress provide to residents in their districts (states, if senators); includes answering questions and doing personal favors for those who ask for help. Also called **casework.**

Constitution The body of basic rules and principles that establish the functions, limits, and nature of a government.

Constitutional Convention The gathering in Philadelphia in 1787 that wrote the U.S. Constitution; met initially to revise the **Articles of Confederation** but produced a new national **constitution** instead.

Containment A policy formulated by the Truman administration that aimed to limit the spread of communism by meeting any action taken by the Soviet Union with a countermove; led U.S. decision makers to see most conflicts in terms of U.S.-Soviet rivalry.

Contras Rebels who have fought to overthrow the Sandinista government of Nicaragua.

Cooperative federalism The continuing cooperation among federal, state, and local officials in carrying out the business of government.

Cost-benefit analysis The process of evaluating a **regulation** by weighing its cost against the risk of harm if it is not implemented.

Cost overruns The amount by which the cost of a certain project exceeds the expected cost.

Cost-plus project A project for which the contractor is reimbursed for all of its costs in addition to a set, agreed-upon profit rate.

Court-packing plan President Franklin D. Roosevelt's attempt to expand the size of the U.S. Supreme Court in an effort to obtain a Court more likely to uphold his New Deal legislation.

Courts of appeals Intermediate courts between trial courts (**district courts** in the federal system) and the supreme court (the U.S. Supreme Court in the federal system).

Cracking, stacking, and packing Methods of drawing district boundaries that minimize black representation. With cracking, a large concentrated black population is divided among two or more districts so that blacks will not have a majority anywhere; with stacking, a large black population is combined with an even larger white population; with packing, a large black population is put into one district rather than two so that blacks will have a majority in only one district.

Cradle-to-grave Regulations for dealing with hazardous wastes that require the wastes to be identified as toxic and handled in an environmentally sound manner from the time of creation until disposition.

Credentials committee A body responsible for examining the credentials of political convention delegates.

Criminal case A case in which a government (national or state) prosecutes a person for violating its laws.

Cruel and unusual punishment Torture or any punishment that is grossly disproportionate to the offense; prohibited by the Eighth Amendment.

Cuban Missile Crisis The 1962 stand-off between the United States and the Soviet Union over an offensive missile buildup in Cuba. The Soviets finally agreed to remove all the missiles from Cuban soil.

Cumulative voting A proposed reform to increase minority representation; calls for members of Congress to be elected from at-large districts that would elect several members at once. Each voter would have as many votes as the district had seats and could apportion the votes among the candidates as he or she wished, such as giving all votes to a single candidate.

De facto segregation Segregation that is based on residential patterns and is not imposed by law; because it cannot be eliminated by striking down a law, it is more intractable than **de jure segregation.**

Deficit A condition in which expenditures exceed revenues.

De jure segregation Segregation imposed by law; outlawed by *Brown v. Board of Education* and subsequent court cases.

Delegated legislative authority The power to draft, as well as execute, specific policies; granted by Congress to agencies when a problem requires technical expertise.

Demagogue A leader who obtains political power by appealing to the emotions and biases of the populace.

Democracy A system of government in which authority resides in the people.

Departments Executive divisions of the federal government, such as the Departments of Defense and Labor, each headed by a cabinet officer.

Depression A period of prolonged high unemployment.

Deregulation Ending **regulation** in a particular area.

Detente A policy designed to deescalate **Cold War** rhetoric and promote the notion that relations with the Soviet Union could be conducted in ways other than confrontation; developed by President Richard M. Nixon and Secretary of State Henry Kissinger.

Direct democracy A system of government in which citizens govern themselves directly and vote on most issues; e.g., a New England town meeting.

Direct lobbying Direct personal encounters between lobbyists and the public officials they are attempting to influence.

Direct primary An election in which voters directly choose a party's candidates for office.

Discretionary spending Spending by the federal government where the amount is set by annual **appropriations** bills passed by Congress; includes government operating expenses and salaries of many federal employees.

District courts The trial courts (lower-level courts) in the federal system.

Divided government The situation when one political party controls the presidency and the other party controls one or both houses of Congress.

Dixiecrat A member of a group of southern segregationist Democrats who formed the States' Rights Party in 1948.

Domino theory The idea that if one country fell under communist rule, its neighbors would also fall to communism; contributed to the U.S. decision to intervene in Vietnam.

Dred Scott case An 1857 case in which the U.S. Supreme Court held that blacks, whether slave or free, were not citizens and that Congress had no power to restrict slavery in the territories; contributed to the polarization between North and South and ultimately to the **Civil War.**

Dual federalism The idea that the Constitution created a system in which the national government and the states have separate grants of power with each supreme in its own sphere.

Due process The guarantee that the government will follow fair and just procedures when prosecuting a criminal defendant.

Earned income tax credit (EITC) A negative income tax. Instead of paying tax, persons with low incomes receive a payment from the government or a credit toward their taxes.

Education Amendments of 1972 These forbid discrimination on the basis of sex in schools and colleges that receive federal aid.

Electoral College A group of electors selected by the voters in each state and the District of Columbia; the electors officially elect the president and vice president.

Environmental impact statement An analysis of a project's effects on the environment; required from government agencies under the National Environment Policy Act of 1970 before any new projects could be carried out.

Environmental Protection Agency (EPA) The regulatory agency with responsibility for pollution control; created in 1970 by President Richard M. Nixon.

Equal Credit Opportunity Act This act forbids discrimination on the basis of sex or marital status in credit transactions.

Equal Employment Opportunity Commission (EEOC) The EEOC enforces the **Civil Rights Act of 1964,** which forbids discrimination on the basis of sex or race in hiring, promotion, and firing.

Equal Pay Act A statute enacted by Congress in 1963 that mandates that women and men should receive equal pay for equal work.

Equal protection clause The Fourteenth Amendment clause that is the Constitution's primary guarantee that government will treat everyone equally.

Equal Rights Amendment (ERA) A proposed amendment to the Constitution that would prohibit government from denying equal rights on the basis of sex; passed by Congress in 1972 but failed to be ratified by a sufficient number of states.

Establishment clause The First Amendment clause that prohibits the establishment of a church officially supported by government.

European Union (EU) A union of European nations formed in 1957 to foster political and economic integration in Europe; formerly called the European Economic Community or Common Market.

Exclusionary rule A rule that prevents evidence obtained in violation of the Fourth Amendment from being used in court against the defendant.

Executive leadership The president's control over the bureaucracy in his capacity as chief executive; achieved through budgeting, appointments, administrative reform, lobbying, and mobilizing public opinion.

Executive orders Rules or regulations issued by the president that have the force of law; issued to implement constitutional provisions or statutes.

Executive privilege The authority of the president to withhold information from the courts and Congress.

Exit polls Election-day poll of voters leaving the polling places, conducted mainly by television networks and major newspapers.

Ex post facto law A statute that makes some behavior illegal that was not illegal when it was done.

Externality A cost or benefit of production that is not reflected in the product's market price. **Regulation** attempts to eliminate negative externalities.

Faithless elector A member of the **Electoral College** who votes on the basis of personal preference rather than the way the majority of voters in his or her state voted.

Farm subsidies Government payments to farmers to raise the price they receive for crops to above-market prices.

Federal Communication Commission (FCC) A regulatory agency that controls interstate and foreign communication via radio, television, telegraph, telephone, and cable. The FCC licenses radio and television stations.

Federal Election Campaign Act A 1974 statute that regulates campaign finance; provided for public financing of presidential campaigns, limited contributions to campaigns for federal offices, and established the **Federal Election Commission,** among other things.

Federal Election Commission Created in 1975, the commission enforces federal laws on campaign financing.

Federalism A system in which power is constitutionally divided between a central government and subnational or local governments.

Federalist Papers A series of essays in support of the U.S. Constitution; written for New York newspapers by Alexander Hamilton, James Madison, and John Jay during the debate over ratification.

Federalists Originally, those who supported the U.S. Constitution and favored its ratification; in the early years of the Republic, those who advocated a strong national government.

Federal Register A government publication describing bureaucratic actions and detailing regulations proposed by government agencies.

Federal Reserve Board Created by Congress in 1913, the board regulates the lending practices of banks and plays a major role in determining **monetary policy.**

Felonies Crimes considered more serious than **misdemeanors** and carrying more stringent punishment.

Feminization of poverty The phenomenon that the majority of families living in poverty are headed by females.

Fifteenth Amendment An amendment to the Constitution, ratified in 1870, that prohibits denying voting rights on the basis of race, color, or previous condition of servitude.

Filibuster A mechanism for delay in the Senate in which one or more members engage in a continuous speech to prevent the Senate from taking action.

Fireside chats Short radio addresses given by President Franklin D. Roosevelt to win support for his policies and reassure the public during the Great Depression.

Fiscal policy Government's actions to regulate the economy through taxing and spending policies.

Fixed-cost project A project that a contractor has agreed to undertake for a specified sum.

Flat tax A tax structured so that all income groups pay the same rate.

Food stamp program A poverty program that gives poor people coupons redeemable in grocery stores for food.

Franking The privilege of members of Congress that allows them to send free mail to their constituents.

Freedom of speech The First Amendment guarantee of a right of free expression.

Free exercise clause The First Amendment clause that guarantees individuals the right to practice their religion without government intervention.

Free trade A policy of minimum intervention by government in trade relations.

Frontrunners Candidates whom political pros and the media have portrayed as likely winners.

Full faith and credit A clause in the U.S. Constitution that requires the states to recognize contracts that are valid in other states.

Fundraiser An event, such as a luncheon or cocktail party, hosted by a legislator or candidate for which participants pay an entrance fee.

Game orientation The assumption in political reporting that politics is a game and that politicians are the players; leads to an emphasis on strategy at the expense of substance in news stories.

Gender gap An observable pattern of modest but consistent differences in opinion between men and women on various public policy issues.

General revenue sharing A Reagan administration policy of giving states and cities federal money to spend as they wished, subject to only a few conditions.

Gerrymander A congressional district whose boundaries are drawn so as to maximize the political advantage of a party or racial group; often such a district has a bizarre shape.

Glasnost Mikhail Gorbachev's policy of opening the Soviet Union to the outside world by encouraging foreign investment, allowing more Soviet citizens to emigrate, and permitting multiparty elections in eastern Europe.

Globalization The international dispersion of economic activity through the networking of companies across national borders.

Going public The process in which Congress or its members carry an issue debate to the public via the media; e.g., televising floor debates or media appearances by individual members.

GOP Grand Old Party or Republican Party, which formed in 1856 after the Whig Party split. The GOP was abolitionist and a supporter of the Union.

Grace Commission A special commission established by President Ronald Reagan to recommend ways of cutting government waste.

Grandfather clause A device used in the South to prevent blacks from voting; such clauses exempted those whose grandfathers had the right to vote before 1867 from having to fulfill various requirements that most people could not meet. Since no blacks could vote before 1867, they could not qualify for the exemption.

Grand jury A jury of citizens who meet in private session to evaluate accusations in a given **criminal case** and to determine if there is enough evidence to warrant a trial.

Grants-in-aid Federal money provided to state and, occasionally, local governments to establish programs to help people such as the aged poor or the unemployed; began during the New Deal.

Grassroots lobbying The mass mobilization of members of an **interest group** to apply pressure to public officials, usually in the form of a mass mailing.

Great Compromise The decision of the **Constitutional Convention** to have a bicameral legislature in which representation in one house would be by population and in the other house, by states; also called the Connecticut Compromise.

Habeas corpus Latin for "have ye the body." A writ of habeas corpus is a means for criminal defendants who have exhausted appeals in state courts to appeal to a federal **district court.**

Hatch Act A statute enacted in 1939 that limits the political activities of federal employees in partisan campaigns.

Head of state The president's role as a national symbol of collective unity and pride.

Health maintenance organization (HMO) A group of doctors who agree to provide full health care for a fixed monthly charge.

Home rule The grant of considerable autonomy to a local government.

Honoraria Legal payments made to legislators who speak before **interest groups** or other groups of citizens.

Hyperpluralism The idea that it is difficult for government to arrive at a solution to problems because **interest groups** have become so numerous and so many groups have a "veto" on issues affecting them.

ICBM Intercontinental ballistic missiles, or land-based missiles.

Identity politics The practice of organizing on the basis of sex, ethnic or racial identity, or sexual orientation to compete for public resources and influence public policy.

Ideology A highly organized and coherent set of opinions.

Impeachment and removal A two-step process by which Congress may remove presidents, judges, and other civil officers accused of malfeasance. The House decides questions of impeachment; if a majority favors impeachment, the Senate decides whether to remove the accused from office.

Imperial presidency A term that came into use at the end of the 1960s to describe the growing power of the presidency.

Implied powers clause The clause in the U.S. Constitution that gives Congress the power to make all laws **"necessary and proper"** for carrying out its specific powers.

Impoundment A refusal by the president to spend money appropriated by Congress for a specific program.

Incrementalism A congressional spending pattern in which budgets usually increase slightly from year to year.

Independent A voter who is not aligned with any political party.

Independent agencies Government bureaus that are not parts of **departments.** Their heads are appointed by and responsible to the president.

Independent counsel See **Special prosecutor.**

Independent expenditures Campaign contributions made on behalf of issues or candidates, but not made directly to candidates or political parties.

Independent spending Spending on political campaigns by groups not under the control of the candidates.

Indirect democracy A system of government in which citizens elect representatives to make decisions for them.

Indirect lobbying Attempts to influence legislators through such nontraditional means as letter-writing campaigns.

Individualistic political culture One of three primary political cultures in the United States. One in which politics is seen as a way of getting ahead, of obtaining benefits for oneself or one's group, and in which corruption is tolerated. See also **moralistic** and **traditionalistic political cultures**.

Inflation The situation in which prices increase but wages and salaries fail to keep pace with the prices of goods.

Influence peddling Using one's access to powerful people to make money, as when former government officials use access to former colleagues to win high-paying jobs in the private sector.

Informal norms Unwritten customs that help keep Congress running smoothly by attempting to diminish friction and competition among the members.

Infotainment Television news stories that, without any sacrifice of probity or responsibility, display the attributes of fiction, of drama.

Injunction A court order demanding that a person or group perform a specific act or refrain from performing a specific act.

Inquisition A medieval institution of the Roman Catholic Church used to identify and punish heretics.

Institutional approach An investigation of government that focuses on institutions, such as Congress or the civil service, and their rules and procedures.

Institutional loyalty An **informal norm** of Congress that calls for members to avoid criticizing their colleagues and to treat each other with mutual respect; eroded in recent decades.

Interest groups Organizations that try to achieve at least some of their goals with government assistance.

Investigative reporting In-depth news reporting, particularly that which exposes corruption and wrongdoing on the part of government officials and big institutions.

Iroquois Confederacy An association of Native Americans in what is now New York State that was based on the principles of **checks and balances** and **federalism,** among other things.

Isolationism A policy of noninvolvement with other nations outside the Americas; generally followed by the United States during the nineteenth and early twentieth centuries.

Issue consistency The extent to which individuals who identify themselves as **"liberal"** or **"conservative"** take issue positions that reflect their professed leanings.

Issue voting Refers to citizens who vote for candidates whose stands on specific issues are consistent with their own.

Jeffersonian Republicans (Jeffersonians) Opponents of a strong national government. They challenged the **Federalists** in the early years of the Republic.

Jim Crow laws Laws enacted in southern states that segregated schools, public accommodations, and almost all other aspects of life.

Joint resolutions Measures that have the force of law and must be approved by both houses of Congress and signed by the president.

Judicial review The authority of the courts to declare laws or actions of government officials unconstitutional.

Junkets Trips by members of Congress to desirable locations with expenses paid by lobbyists; the trips are ostensibly made to fulfill a "speaking engagement" or conduct a "fact-finding tour."

Jurisdiction The authority of a court to hear and decide cases.

Justices of the peace Magistrates at the lowest level of some state court systems, responsible mainly for acting on minor offenses and committing cases to higher courts for trial.

Keating 5 Senators Alan Cranston, John McCain, Donald Riegle, John Glenn, and Dennis DeConcini, who were investigated by the Senate for ethics violations in connection with campaign contributions they received from financier/developer Charles Keating. All later intervened on his behalf with federal regulators.

Keynesian economics The argument by John Maynard Keynes that government should stimulate the economy during periods of high unemployment by increasing spending even if it must run **deficits** to do so; the deficits would be made up by higher employment and thus higher tax revenues during periods of prosperity.

Kitchen cabinet A group of informal advisers, usually longtime associates, who assist the president on public policy questions.

Know-Nothing Party An extreme right-wing party in mid-nineteenth-century America that opposed Catholics and immigrants.

Lame duck An officeholder, legislature, or administration that has lost an election but holds power until the inauguration of a successor.

Landslide An election won by a candidate who receives an overwhelming majority of the votes, such as more than a 10-point gap.

Leaks Disclosures of information that some government officials want kept secret.

Legislative calendar An agenda or calendar containing the names of all bills or resolutions of a particular type to be considered by committees or either legislative chamber.

Legislative veto A congressional **oversight** tool that allows one or both houses to block agency actions. Though the legislative veto was held unconstitutional by the Supreme Court in 1983, legislation with provisions for legislative vetoes continues to be passed, and agencies continue to honor the vetoes.

Libel Printed or broadcast statements that are false and tarnish someone's reputation.

Liberal A person who believes in a national government that is active in domestic policies, providing help to individuals and communities in such areas as health, education, and welfare.

Limited government A government that is strong enough to protect the people's rights but not so strong as to threaten those rights; in the view of John Locke, such a government was established through a **social contract.**

Line-Item veto A proposal that would give a president the power to veto one or more provisions of a bill while allowing the remainder of the bill to become law.

Literacy tests Examinations ostensibly carried out to ensure that voters could read and write but actually a device used in the South to disqualify blacks from voting.

Litigation Legal action.

Lobbying The efforts of **interest groups** to influence government.

Majority leader The member of the majority party in the House of Representatives who is second in command to the **Speaker.** Also, the leader of the Senate, who is chosen by the majority party.

Majority-minority district A congressional district whose boundaries are drawn to give a minority group a majority in the district.

Managed competition An aspect of the Clinton health care plan that involved joining employers and individuals into large groups or cooperatives to purchase health insurance.

Mandamus, writ of A court order demanding government officials or a lower court to perform a specified duty.

Mandate A term used in the media to refer to a president having clear directions from the voters to take a certain course of action; in practice, it is not always clear that a president, even one elected by a large majority, has a mandate or, if so, for what.

Mandatory spending Spending by the federal government that is required by permanent laws; e.g., payments for **Medicare.**

Marble cake federalism The idea that different levels of government work together in carrying out policies; governments are intermixed, as in a marble cake.

Marbury v. Madison The 1803 case in which the U.S. Supreme Court enunciated the doctrine of **judicial review.**

Market share The number of members of an **interest group** compared to its potential membership; having a large market share is an advantage.

Markup The process in which a congressional subcommittee rewrites a bill after holding hearings on it.

McCarthyism Methods of combating communism characterized by irresponsible accusations made on the basis of little or no evidence; named after Senator Joseph McCarthy of Wisconsin who used such tactics in the 1950s.

McCulloch v. Maryland An 1819 U.S. Supreme Court decision that broadly interpreted Congress's powers under the **implied powers clause.**

McGovern-Fraser Commission A commission formed after 1968 by the Democratic Party to consider changes making convention delegates more representative of all Democratic voters.

Means test An eligibility requirement for poverty programs under which participants must demonstrate that they have low income and few assets.

Media event An event, usually consisting of a speech and a photo opportunity, that is staged for television and is intended to convey a particular impression of a politician's position on an issue.

Media malaise A feeling of cynicism and distrust toward government and officials that is fostered by media coverage of politics.

Medicaid A federal-state medical assistance program for the poor.

Medicare A public health insurance program that pays many medical expenses of the elderly and the disabled; funded through **Social Security** taxes, general revenues, and premiums paid by recipients.

Merit system A system of filling bureaucratic jobs on the basis of competence instead of **patronage.**

Minimum tax A proposed tax that would require corporations and individuals with high incomes to pay a certain minimum amount in federal taxes.

Minority leader The leader of the minority party in either the House of Representatives or the Senate.

Miranda rights A means of protecting a criminal suspect's **rights against self-incrimination** during police interrogation. Before interrogation, suspects must be told that they have a right to remain silent; that anything they say can be used against them; that they have a right to an attorney; and that if they cannot afford an attorney, one will be provided for them. The rights are named after the case *Miranda v. Arizona.*

MIRV Stands for multiple independently targeted reentry vehicles; an offensive missile system that uses a single rocket to launch a number of warheads, each of which could be aimed at a different target.

"Mischiefs of faction" A phrase used by James Madison in the *Federalist Papers* to refer to the threat to the nation's stability that factions could pose.

Misdemeanors Crimes of less seriousness than **felonies,** ordinarily punishable by fine or imprisonment in a local rather than a state institution.

Missouri Compromise of 1820 A set of laws by which Congress attempted to control slavery in the territories, maintaining the balance between slave and non-slave states.

Mixed economies Countries that incorporate elements of both capitalist and socialist practices in the workings of their economies.

Monetary policy Actions taken by the **Federal Reserve Board** to regulate the economy through changes in short-term interest rates and the money supply.

Monopoly One or a few firms that control a large share of the market for certain goods and can therefore fix prices.

Monroe Doctrine A doctrine articulated by President James Monroe in 1823 that warned European powers not already involved in Latin America to stay out of that region.

Moralistic political culture One of three political cultures in the United States. One in which people feel obligated to take part in politics to bring about change for the better, and in which corruption is not tolerated. See also **individualistic** and **traditionalistic political cultures.**

Most favored nation (MFN) Trade status granted to a trading partner that permits that nation to export goods to the United States under the most advantageous **tariff** arrangements that the United States allows.

Motor voter law A statute that allows people to register to vote at public offices such as welfare offices and drivers' license bureaus.

Muckrakers Reform-minded journalists in the early twentieth century who exposed corruption in politics and worked to break the financial link between business and politicians.

Mutual assured destruction (MAD) The capability to absorb a nuclear attack and retaliate against the attacker with such force that it would also suffer enormous damage; believed to deter nuclear war during the **Cold War** because both sides would be so devastated that neither would risk striking first.

NAACP (National Association for the Advancement of Colored People) An organization founded in 1909 to fight for black rights; its attorneys challenged segregation in the courts and won many important court cases, most notably, *Brown v. Board of Education.*

Nader's Raiders The name given to people who work in any of the "public interest" organizations founded by consumer advocate and regulatory watchdog Ralph Nader.

National chair The head of a political **party organization,** appointed by the **national committee** of that party, usually at the direction of the party's presidential nominee.

National committee The highest level of **party organization;** chooses the site of the national convention and the formula for determining the number of delegates from each state.

National debt The total amount of money owed by the federal government; the sum of all budget **deficits** over the years.

National Organization for Women (NOW) A group formed in 1966 to fight primarily for political and economic rights for women.

NATO (North Atlantic Treaty Organization) A mutual defense pact established by the United States, Canada, and their western European allies in 1949 to protect against Soviet aggression in Europe; later expanded to include other European nations.

Natural rights Inalienable and inherent rights such as the right to own property (in the view of John Locke).

"Necessary and proper" A phrase in the **implied powers clause** of the U.S. Constitution that gives Congress the power to make all laws needed to carry out its specific powers.

Neutral competence The concept that bureaucrats should be uninvolved or neutral in policymaking and should be chosen only for their expertise—not their political affiliation.

New Deal A program of President Franklin D. Roosevelt's administration in the 1930s aimed at stimulating economic recovery and aiding victims of the Great Depression; led to expansion of the national government's role.

New Deal coalition The broadly based coalition of southern conservatives, northern liberals, and ethnic and religious minorities that sustained the Democratic Party for some 40 years.

New federalism During the Nixon administration, the policy under which unrestricted or minimally restricted federal funds were provided to states and localities; during the Reagan administration, a policy of reducing federal support for the states.

News release A printed handout given by public relations workers to members of the media, offering ideas or information for new stories.

Nineteenth Amendment An amendment to the Constitution, ratified in 1920, guaranteeing women the vote.

Nullification A doctrine advocated by supporters of state-centered federalism, holding that a state could nullify laws of Congress.

Obscenity Sexual material that is patently offensive to the average person in the community and that lacks any serious literary, artistic, or scientific value.

Obstruction of justice A deliberate attempt to impede the progress of a criminal investigation or trial.

Occupational Safety and Health Administration (OSHA) An agency formed in 1970 and charged with ensuring safe and healthful working conditions for all American workers.

Office of Management and Budget (OMB) A White House agency with primary responsibility for preparing the federal budget.

Open primary A primary election that is not limited to members of a particular party; a voter may vote in either party's primary.

Overlapping membership The term refers to the tendency of individuals to join more than one group. This tends to moderate a group's appeals, since its members also belong to other groups with different interests.

Oversight Congress's responsibility to make sure the bureaucracy is administering federal programs in accordance with congressional intent.

Parliamentary government A system in which voters elect only their representatives in parliament; the chief executive is chosen by parliament, as in Britain.

Party boss The head of a **political "machine,"** a highly disciplined state or local **party organization** that controls power in its area.

Party convention A gathering of party delegates, on the local, state, or national level, to set policy and strategy and to select candidates for elective office.

Party identification A psychological link between individuals and a political party that leads those persons to regard themselves as members of that party.

Party in government Those who are appointed or elected to office as members of a political party.

Party in the electorate Those who identify with a political party.

Party organization The "professionals" who run a political party at the national, state, and local levels.

Patronage A system in which elected officials appoint their supporters to administrative jobs; used by **political machines** to maintain themselves in power.

Pendleton Act of 1883 This act created the **Civil Service Commission,** designed to protect civil servants from arbitrary dismissal for political reasons and to staff bureaucracies with people who have proven their competence by taking competitive examinations.

Pentagon Papers A top-secret study, eventually made public, of how and why the United States became embroiled in the Vietnam War; the study was commissioned by Secretary of Defense Robert McNamara during the Johnson administration.

Permanent campaign The situation in which elected officials are constantly engaged in a campaign; fund-raising for the next election begins as soon as one election is concluded.

Personal presidency A concept proposed by Theodore Lowi that holds that presidents since the 1930s have amassed tremendous personal power directly from the people and, in return, are expected to make sure the people get what they want from government.

Platform committee The group that drafts the policy statement of a political party's convention.

Plea bargain An agreement between the prosecutor, defense attorney, and defendant in which the prosecutor agrees to reduce the charge or sentence in exchange for the defendant's guilty plea.

Plebiscite A direct vote by all the people on a certain public measure. Theodore Lowi has spoken of the "Plebiscitary" presidency, whereby the president makes himself the focus of national government through use of the mass media.

Plessy v. Ferguson The 1896 case in which the U.S. Supreme Court upheld segregation by enunciating the **separate-but-equal doctrine.**

Pluralism The theory that American government is responsive to groups of citizens working together to promote their common interests and that enough people belong to **interest groups** to ensure that government ultimately hears everyone, even though most people do not participate actively in politics.

Pocket veto A legislative bill dies by pocket veto if a president refuses to sign it and Congress adjourns within 10 working days.

Policy implementation The process by which bureaucrats convert laws into rules and activities that have an actual impact on people and things.

Political action committee (PAC) A committee established by corporation, labor union, or **interest group** that raises money and contributes it to a political campaign.

Political bias A preference for candidates of particular parties or for certain stands on issues that affects a journalist's reporting.

Political culture A shared body of values and beliefs that shapes perceptions and attitudes toward politics and government and, in turn, influences political behavior.

Political equality The principle that every citizen of a democracy has an equal opportunity to try to influence government.

Political machines Political organizations based on **patronage** that flourished in big cities in the late nineteenth and early twentieth centuries. The machine relied on the votes of the lower classes and, in exchange, provided jobs and other services.

Political socialization The process of learning about politics by being exposed to information from parents, peers, schools, the media, political leaders, and the community.

Political tolerance The willingness of individuals to extend procedural rights and liberties to people with whom they disagree.

Political trust The extent to which citizens place trust in their government, its institutions, and its officials.

Politics A means by which individuals and **interest groups** compete, via political parties and other extragovernmental organizations, to shape government's impact on society's problems and goals.

Poll tax A tax that must be paid before a person can vote; used in the South to prevent blacks from voting. The Twenty-fourth Amendment now prohibits poll taxes in federal elections.

Popular sovereignty Rule by the people.

Pork barrel Funding for special projects, buildings, and other public works in the district or state of a member of Congress. Members tend to support such projects because they provide jobs for constituents and enhance the members' reelection chances, rather than because the projects are necessarily wise.

Power to persuade The president's informal power to gain support by dispensing favors and penalties and by using the prestige of the office.

Precedents In law, judicial decisions that may be used subsequently as standards in similar cases.

Precinct The basic unit of the American electoral process—in a large city perhaps only a few blocks—designed for the administration of elections. Citizens vote in precinct polling places.

Presidential immunity Immunity of the president from lawsuits for acts that occur during his term in office and are related to his official responsibilities.

Presidential preference primary A **direct primary** where voters select delegates to presidential nominating conventions; voters indicate a preference for a presidential candidate, delegates committed to a candidate, or both.

Presidential press conference A meeting at which the president answers questions from reporters.

Pressure group An organization representing specific interests that seeks some sort of government assistance or attempts to influence public policy. Also known as an **interest group.**

Pretrial hearings Preliminary examinations of the cases of persons accused of a crime.

Prior restraint Censorship by restraining an action before it has actually occurred; e.g., forbidding publication rather than punishing the publisher after publication has occurred.

Private interest groups Interest groups that chiefly pursue economic interests that benefit their members; e.g., business organizations and labor unions.

Probable cause In law, reasonable grounds for belief that a particular person has committed a particular crime.

Productivity The ratio of total hours worked by the labor force to total goods and services produced.

Professional association A pressure **group** that promotes the interests of a professional occupation, such as medicine, law, or teaching.

Progressive reforms Election reforms introduced in the early twentieth century as part of the Progressive movement; included the secret ballot, primary elections, and voter registration laws.

Progressive tax A tax structured so that those with higher incomes pay a higher percentage of their income in taxes than do those with lower incomes.

Prohibition Party A political party founded in 1869 that seeks to ban the sale of liquor in the United States.

Protectionism Government intervention to protect domestic producers from foreign competition; can take the form of **tariffs,** quotas on imports, or a ban on certain imports altogether.

Public forum A public place such as a street, sidewalk, or park where people have a First Amendment right to express their views on public issues.

Public interest A term generally denoting a policy goal, designed to serve the interests of society as a whole, or the largest number of people. Defining the public interest is the subject of intense debate on most issues.

Public interest groups Interest groups that chiefly pursue benefits that cannot be limited or restricted to their members.

Public opinion The collection of individual opinions toward issues or objects of general interest.

Pure speech Speech without any conduct (besides the speech itself).

Quorum calls Often used as a delaying tactic, quorum calls are demands that all members of a legislative body be counted to determine if a quorum exists.

Realignment The transition from one stable party system to another, as occurred when the **New Deal coalition** was formed.

Reapportionment The process of redistributing the 435 seats in the House of Representatives among the states based on population changes; occurs every 10 years based on the most recent census.

Recession Two or more consecutive three-month quarters of falling production.

Reciprocity An **informal norm** of Congress in which members agree to support each other's bills; also called logrolling.

Reconstruction The period after the **Civil War** when black rights were ensured by a northern military presence in the South and by close monitoring of southern politics; ended in 1877.

Redistricting The process of redrawing the boundaries of congressional districts within a state to take account of population shifts.

Redlining The practice in which bankers and other lenders refused to lend money to persons who wanted to buy a house in a racially changing neighborhood.

"Red Scare" Prompted by the Russian Revolution in 1917, this was a large-scale crackdown on so-called seditious activities in the United States.

Reelection constituency Those individuals a member of Congress believes will vote for him or her. Differs from a geographical, loyalist, or personal constituency.

Regressive tax A tax structured so that those with lower incomes pay a larger percentage of their income in tax than do those with higher incomes.

Regulation The actions of regulatory agencies in establishing standards or guidelines conferring benefits or imposing restrictions on business conduct.

Rehnquist Court The U.S. Supreme Court under Chief Justice William Rehnquist (1986–); a conservative Court, but still has not overturned most previous rulings.

Religious tests Tests once used in some states to limit the right to vote or hold office to members of the "established church."

Republic A system of government in which citizens elect representatives to make decisions for them; an **indirect democracy.**

Reregulation The resumption of regulatory activity after a period of **deregulation**.

Responsiveness The extent to which government conforms to the wishes of individuals, groups, or institutions.

Restrained judges Judges who are reluctant to overrule the other branches of government by declaring laws or actions of government officials unconstitutional.

Restrictive covenants Agreements among neighbors in white residential areas not to sell their houses to blacks.

Retrospective voting Voting for or against incumbents on the basis of their past performance.

Right against self-incrimination A right granted by the Fifth Amendment, providing that persons accused of a crime shall not be compelled to be witnesses against themselves.

Right to a jury trial The Sixth Amendment's guarantee of a trial by jury in any **criminal case** that could result in more than six months' incarceration.

Right to counsel The Sixth Amendment's guarantee of the right of a criminal defendant to have an attorney in any **felony or misdemeanor** case that might result in incarceration; if defendants are indigent, the court must appoint an attorney for them.

Right to privacy A right to autonomy—to be left alone—that is not specifically mentioned in the U.S. Constitution, but has been found by the U.S. Supreme Court to be implied through several amendments.

Rules Committee The committee in the House of Representatives that sets the terms of debate on a bill.

Sandinistas The name of the group that overthrew Nicaraguan dictator Anastasio Somoza in 1978 and governed Nicaragua until 1990.

Scientific polls Systematic, probability-based sampling techniques that attempt to gauge public sentiment based on the responses of a small, selected group of individuals.

Scoop To obtain information before another reporter; also the information so obtained.

Seditious speech Speech that encourages rebellion against the government.

Selective perception The tendency to screen out information that contradicts one's beliefs.

Senatorial courtesy The custom of giving senators of the president's party a virtual veto over appointments to jobs, including judicial appointments, in their states.

Senior Executive Service The SES was created in 1978 to attract high-ranking civil servants by offering them challenging jobs and monetary rewards for exceptional achievement.

Seniority rule The custom that the member of the majority party with the longest service on a particular congressional committee becomes its chair; applies most of the time but is occasionally violated.

Separate-but-equal doctrine The principle, enunciated by the U.S. Supreme Court in *Plessy v. Ferguson* in 1896, that allowed separate facilities for blacks and whites as long as the facilities were equal.

Separation of powers The principle of government under which the power to make, administer, and judge the laws is split among three branches—legislative, executive, and judicial.

Setting the agenda Influencing the process by which problems are deemed important and alternative policies are proposed.

Sharecroppers Tenant farmers who lease land and equipment from landowners, turning over a share of their crops in lieu of rent.

Shays's Rebellion A revolt of farmers in western Massachusetts in 1786 and 1787 to protest the state legislature's refusal to grant them relief from debt; helped lead to calls for a new national **constitution.**

Shield laws Laws that protect news reporters from having to identify their sources of information.

Single-issue groups Interest groups that pursue a single public interest goal and are characteristically reluctant to compromise.

Social choice An approach to political science based on the assumption that political behavior is determined by costs and benefits.

Social contract An implied agreement between the people and their government in which the people give up part of their liberty to the government in exchange for the government protecting the remainder of their liberty.

Social insurance A social welfare program such as **Social Security** that provides benefits only to those who have contributed to the program and their survivors.

Socialism An economic system in which the government owns the country's productive capacity—industrial plants and farms—and controls wages and the supply of and demand for goods; in theory, the people, rather than the government, collectively own the country's productive capacity.

Social issue An important, noneconomic issue affecting significant numbers of the populace, such as crime, racial conflict, or changing values.

Social Security A social welfare program for the elderly and the disabled.

Soft money Contributions to national party committees that do not have to be reported to the federal government (and sometimes not to the states) because they are used for voter registration drives, educating voters on the issues, and the like, rather than for a particular candidate; the national committees send the funds to the state parties, which operate under less stringent reporting regulations than the federal laws provide.

Sound bite A few key words or phrase included in a speech with the intent that television editors will use the phrase in a brief clip on the news.

Speaker of the House The leader and presiding officer of the House of Representatives; chosen by the majority party.

Special interest caucuses Groups of members of the House of Representatives who are united by some personal interest or characteristic; e.g., the Black Caucus.

Specialization An **informal norm** of Congress that holds that since members cannot be experts in every area, some deference should be given to those who are most knowledgeable about a given subject related to their committee work.

Special prosecutor A prosecutor charged with investigating and prosecuting alleged violations of federal criminal laws by the president, vice president, senior govern-

ment officials, members of Congress, or the judiciary.

Speech plus conduct Speech combined with conduct that is intended to convey ideas; e.g., a sit-in (conduct) where the protesters chant slogans (speech).

Stagflation The combination of high inflation and economic stagnation with high unemployment that troubled the United States in the 1970s.

Standing committees Permanent congressional committees.

Standing to sue The principle that individuals or groups must themselves have lost rights and suffered harm before they can bring a lawsuit.

Stare decisis Latin for "stand by what has been decided." The rule that judges should follow **precedents** established in previous cases by their court or higher courts.

"Star Wars" The popular name for former President Reagan's proposed space-based nuclear defense system, known officially as the Strategic Defense Initiative.

States' rights The belief that the power of the federal government should not be increased at the expense of the states' power.

Statistical Abstract Annual summary of reports published by the federal government.

Statutes Laws passed by the legislative body of a representative government.

Steering The practice in which realtors promoted segregation by showing blacks houses in black neighborhoods and whites houses in white neighborhoods.

Straw polls Unscientific polls.

Structural unemployment Joblessness that results from the rapidly changing nature of the economy, which displaces, for example, auto and steel industry workers.

Subcommittee bill of rights Measures introduced by Democrats in the House of Representatives in 1973 and 1974 that allowed members of a committee to choose subcommittee chairs and established a fixed jurisdiction and adequate budget and staff for each subcommittee.

Subgovernment A mutually supportive group comprising a **pressure group,** an executive agency, and a congressional committee or subcommittee with common policy interests that makes public policy decisions with little interference from the president or Congress as a whole and little awareness by the public. Also known as an iron triangle.

Subpoena A court order requiring someone to appear in court to give testimony under penalty of punishment.

Suffrage The right to vote.

Superdelegates Democratic delegates, one-fifth of the total sent to the national convention who are appointed by Democratic Party organizations, in order to retain some party control over the convention. Most are public officials, such as members of Congress.

Superfund Revenue from a tax imposed on industry, along with federal funds, that is used for cleaning up hazardous waste sites.

Super Tuesday The day when most southern states hold **presidential preference primaries** simultaneously.

Supplemental Security Income (SSI) A program that provides supplemental income for those who are blind, elderly, or disabled and living in poverty.

Supply-side economics The argument that tax revenues will increase if tax rates are reduced; supposedly, more money will be available for business expansion and modernization, which will stimulate employment and economic growth and result in higher tax revenues.

Supremacy clause A clause in the U.S. Constitution stating that treaties and laws made by the national government are to be supreme over state laws in cases of conflict.

Symbiotic relationship A relationship in which the parties use each other for mutual advantage.

Symbolic speech The use of symbols, rather than words, to convey ideas; e.g., wearing black armbands or burning the U.S. flag to protest government policy.

Tariff A special tax or "duty" imposed on imported or exported goods.

Tax deductions Certain expenses or payments that may be deducted from one's taxable income.

Tax exemptions Certain amounts deductible from one's annual income in calculating income tax.

Teapot Dome scandal A 1921 scandal in which President Warren Harding's secretary of the interior received large contributions from corporations that were then allowed to lease oil reserves (called the Teapot Dome); led to the Federal Corrupt Practices Act of 1925, which required reporting of campaign contributions and expenditures.

Temporary Assistance for Needy Families (TANF) A program that provides income support for the poor; successor to Aid to Families with Dependent Children (AFDC).

Third party A political party made up of independents or dissidents from the major parties, often advocating radical change or pushing single issues.

Three-fifths Compromise The decision of the **Constitutional Convention** that three-fifths of a state's slave population would be counted in apportioning seats in the House of Representatives.

Ticket splitting Voting for a member of one party for a high-level office and a member of another party for a different high-level office.

Trade association An **interest** or **pressure group** that represents a single industry, such as builders.

Traditionalistic political culture One of three political cultures in the United States. One in which politics is left to a small elite and is viewed as a way to maintain the status quo. See **individualistic** and **moralistic political cultures.**

Tragedy of the commons The concept that although individuals benefit when they exploit goods that are common to all such as air and water, the community as a whole suffers from the pollution and depletion of resources that occur; a reason for **regulation.**

Treason The betrayal of one's country by knowingly aiding its enemies.

Truth in labeling The requirement that manufacturers, lenders, and other business entities provide certain kinds of information to consumers or employees.

Turnout The proportion of eligible citizens who vote in an election.

Unanimous consent agreements Procedures by which a legislative body may dispense with standard rules and limit debate and amendments.

Underdogs Candidates for public office who are thought to have little chance of being elected.

Unfunded mandates Federal laws that require the states to do something without providing full funding for the required activity.

Unitary system A system in which the national government is supreme; subnational governments are created by the national government and have only the power it allocates to them.

United Nations An international organization formed in 1945 for the purpose of promoting peace and worldwide cooperation. It is headquartered in New York.

Unreasonable searches and seizures Searches and arrests that are conducted without a warrant or that do not fall into one of the exceptions to the warrant requirement; prohibited by the Fourth Amendment.

Unscientific polls Unsystematic samplings of popular sentiments; also known as **straw polls.**

Vietnam syndrome An attitude of uncertainty about U.S. foreign policy goals and our ability to achieve them by military means; engendered among the public and officials as a result of the U.S. failure in Vietnam.

Voting Rights Act (VRA) A law passed by Congress in 1965 that made it illegal to interfere with anyone's right to vote. The act and its subsequent amendments have been the main vehicles for expanding and protecting minority voting rights.

War Powers Act A 1973 statute enacted by Congress to limit the president's ability to commit troops to combat.

Warren Court The U.S. Supreme Court under Chief Justice Earl Warren (1953–1969); an activist Court that expanded the rights of criminal defendants and racial and religious minorities.

Watergate scandal The attempt to break into Democratic National Committee headquarters in 1972 that ultimately led to President Richard M. Nixon's resignation for his role in attempting to cover up the break-in and other criminal and unethical actions.

Weber, Max German social scientist, author of pioneering studies on the nature of bureaucracies.

Whigs Members of the Whig Party, founded in 1834 by National Republicans and several other factions who opposed Jacksonian Democrats.

Whips Members of the House of Representatives who work to maintain party unity by keeping in contact with party members and attempting to win their support. Both the majority and the minority party have a whip and several assistant whips.

Whistleblower An individual employee who exposes mismanagement and abuse of discretion in an agency.

White primary A device for preventing blacks from voting in the South. Under the pretense that political parties were private clubs, blacks were barred from voting in Democratic primaries, which were the real elections because Democrats always won the general elections.

Whitewater investigation An investigation conducted by a **special prosecutor** into the activities of President Bill Clinton and Hillary Rodham Clinton in connection with an Arkansas land deal and other alleged wrongdoings.

Wire services News-gathering organizations such as the Associated Press and United Press International that provide news stories and other editorial features to the media organizations that are their members.

Writ of certiorari An order issued by a higher court to a lower court to send up the record of a case for review; granting the writ is the usual means by which the U.S. Supreme Court agrees to hear a case.

Yuppies Young upwardly mobile professionals.

Spanish Equivalents for Important Political Terms

Acid rain: Lluvia acida

Acquisitive model: Modelo adquisitivo

Actionable: Procesable, enjuiciable

Action-Reaction syndrome: síndrome de acción y reacción

Actual malice: Malicia expresa

Administrative agency: Agencia administrativa

Advice and consent: Consejo y consentimiento

Affirm: Afirmar

Affirmative action: Acción afirmativa

Agenda setting: Agenda establecida

Aid to Families with Dependent Children (AFDC): Ayuda para Familias con Niños Dependientes

Amicus curiae brief: Tercer persona o grupo no involucrado en el caso, admitido en un juicio para hacer valer el interés público o el de un grupo social importante

Anarchy: Anarquía

Anti-Federalists: Anti-Federalistas

Appellate court: Corte de apelación

Appointment power: Poder de apuntamiento

Appropriation: Apropiación

Aristocracy: Aristocracia

Attentive public: Público atento

Australian ballot: Voto Australiano

Authority: Autoridad

Authorization: Autorización

Bad-tendency rule: Regla de tendencia-mala

"Beauty contest": Concurso de belleza

Bicameralism: Bicameralismo

Bicameral legislature: Legislatura bicameral

Bill of Rights: Declaración de Derechos

Blanket primary: Primaria comprensiva

Block grants: Concesiones de bloque

Bureaucracy: Burocracia

Busing: Transporte público

Cabinet: Gabinete, consejo de ministros

Cabinet department: Departamento del gabinete

Cadre: El núcleo de activistas de partidos políticos encargados de cumplir las funciones importantes de los partidos políticos americanos

Canvassing board: Consejo encargado con la encuesta de una violación

Capture: Captura, toma

Casework: Trabajo de caso

Categorical grants-in-aid: Concesiones categóricas de ayuda

Caucus: Reunión de dirigentes

Challenge: Reto

Checks and balances: Chequeos y equilibrio

Chief diplomat: Jefe diplomático

Chief executive: Jefe ejecutivo

Chief legislator: Jefe legislador

Chief of staff: Jefe de personal

Chief of state: Jefe de estado

Civil law: Derecho civil

Civil liberties: Libertades civiles

Civil rights: Derechos civiles

Civil service: Servicio civil

Civil Service Commission: Comisión de Servicio Civil

Class-action suit: Demanda en representación de un grupo o clase

Class politics: Política de clase

Clear and present danger test: Prueba de peligro claro y presente

Climate control: Control de clima

Closed primary: Primaria cerrada

Cloture: Cierre al voto

Coattail effect: Effecto de cola de chaqueta

Cold War: Guerra Fría

Commander in chief: Comandante en jefe

Commerce clause: Cláusula de comercio

Commercial speech: Discurso comercial

Common law: Ley común, derecho consuetudinario

Comparable worth: Valor comparable

Compliance: De acuerdo

Concurrent majority: Mayoría concurrente

Concurring opinion: Opinión concurrente

Confederal system: Sistema confederal

Confederation: Confederación

Conference committee: Comité de conferencia

Consensus: Concenso

Consent of the people: Consentimiento de la gente

Conservatism: Calidad de conservador

Conservative coalition: Coalición conservadora

Consolidation: Consolidación

Constant dollars: Dólares constantes

Constitutional initiative: Iniciativa constitucional

Constitutional power: Poder constitucional

Containment: Contenimiento

Continuing resolution: Resolución contínua

Cooley's Rule: Regla de Cooley

Cooperative federalism: Federalismo cooperativo

Corrupt Practices Acts: Leyes Contra Acciones Corruptas

Council of Economic Advisers (CEA): Consejo de Asesores Económicos

Council of Government (COG): Consejo de Gobierno

County: Condado

Credentials committee: Comité de credenciales

Criminal law: Ley criminal

De facto segregation: Segregación de hecho

De jure segregation: Segregación cotidiana

Defamation of character: Defamación de carácter

Democracy: Democracia

Democratic Party: Partido Democrático

Détente: No Spanish equivalent

Dillon's Rule: Regla de Dillon

Diplomacy: Diplomácia

Direct democracy: Democracia directa

Direct primary: Primaria directa

Direct technique: Técnica directa

Discharge petition: Petición de descargo

Dissenting opinion: Opinión disidente

Divisive opinion: Opinión divisiva

Domestic policy: Principio político doméstico

Dual citizenship: Ciudadanía dual

Dual federalism: Federalismo dual

Economic aid: Ayuda económica

Economic regulation: Regulación económica

Elastic clause, or necessary and proper clause: Cláusula flexible, o cláusula propia necesaria

Elector: Elector

Electoral College: Colegio Electoral

Electronic media: Media electronica

Elite: Elite (el selecto)

Elite theory: Teoría elitista (de lo selecto)

Emergency power: Poder de emergencia

Enumerated power: Poder enumerado

Environmental impact statement: Afirmación de impacto ambiental

Equal Employment Opportunity Commission (EEOC): Comisión de Igualdad de Oportunidad en el Empleo

Equality: Igualdad

Equalization: Igualación

Era of good feeling: Era de buen sentimiento

Era of personal politics: Era de política personal

Establishment clause: Cláusula de establecimiento

Euthanasia: Eutanasia

Exclusionary rule: Regla de exclusión

Executive agreement: Acuerdo ejecutivo

Executive budget: Presupuesto ejecutivo

Executive Office of the President (EOP): Oficina Ejecutiva del Presidente

Executive order: Orden ejecutivo

Executive privilege: Privilegio ejecutivo

Expressed power: Poder expresado

Extradite: Entregar por extradición

Faction: Facción

Fairness doctrine: Doctrina de justicia

Fall review: Revisión de otoño

Federalist: Federalista

Federal mandate: Mandato federal

Federal Open Market Committee (FOMC): Comité Federal de Libre Mercado

Federal Register: *Registro Federal*

Federal system: Sistema federal

Federalists: Federalistas

Fighting words: Palabras de provocación

Filibuster: Obstrucción de iniciativas de ley

Fireside chat: Charla de hogar

First budget resolution: Resolución primera presupuesta

First Continental Congress: Primér Congreso Continental

Fiscal policy: Político fiscal

Fiscal year (FY): Año fiscal

Fluidity: Fluidez

Food stamps: Estampillas para comida

Foreign policy: Política extranjera

Foreign policy process: Proceso de política extranjera

Franking: Franqueando

Fraternity: Fraternidad

Free exercise clause: Cláusula de ejercico libre

Full faith and credit clause: Cláusula de completa fé y crédito

Functional consolidation: Consolidación funcional

Gag order: Orden de silencio

Garbage can model: Modelo bote de basura

Gender gap: Brecha de género

General law city: Regla general urbana

General sales tax: Impuesto general de ventas

Generational effect: Efecto generacional

Gerrymandering: División arbitraria de los distritos electorales con fines políticos

Government: Gobierno

Government corporation: Corporación gubernamental

Government in the Sunshine Act: Gobierno en la Acta: Luz del Sol

Grandfather clause: Cláusula del abuelo

Grand jury: Gran jurado

Great Compromise: Grán Acuerdo de Negociación

Hatch Act (Political Activities Act): Acta Hatch (acta de actividades políticas)

Hecklers' veto: Veto de abuchamiento

Home rule city: Regla urbana

Horizontal federalism: Federalismo horizontal

Hyperpluralism: Hiperpluralismo

Ideologue: Ideólogo

Ideology: Ideología

Image building: Construcción de imágen

Impeachment: Acción penal contra un funcionario público

Inalienable rights: Derechos inalienables

Income transfer: Transferencia de ingresos

Incorporation theory: Teoría de incorporación

Independent: Independiente

Independent candidate: Candidato independiente

Independent executive agency: Agencia ejecutiva independiente

Independent regulatory agency: Agencia regulatoria independiente

Indirect technique: Técnica indirecta

Inherent power: Poder inherente

Initiative: Iniciativa

Injunction: Injunción, prohibición judicial

In-kind subsidy: Subsidio de clase

Institution: Institución

Instructed delegate: Delegado con instrucciones

Intelligence community: Comunidad de inteligencia

Intensity: Intensidad

Interest group: Grupo de interés

Interposition: Interposición

Interstate compact: Compacto interestatal

Iron Curtain: Cortina de Acero

Iron triangle: Triángulo de acero

Isolationist foreign policy: Política extranjera de aislamiento

Issue voting: Voto temático

Item veto: Artículo de veto

Jim Crow laws: No Spanish equivalent

Joint committee: Comité mancomunado

Judicial activism: Activismo judicial

Judicial implementation: Implementación judicial

Judicial restraint: Restricción judicial

Judicial review: Revisión judicial

Jurisdiction: Jurisdicción

Justiciable dispute: Disputa judiciaria

Justiciable question: Pregunta justiciable

Keynesian economics: Economía Keynesiana

Kitchen cabinet: Gabinete de cocina

Labor movement: Movimiento laboral

Latent public opinion: Opinión pública latente

Lawmaking: Hacedores de ley

Legislative history: Historia legislativa

Legislative initiative: Iniciativa de legislación

Legislative veto: Veto legislativo

Legislature: Legislatura

Legitimacy: Legitimidad

Libel: Libelo, difamación escrita

Liberalism: Liberalismo

Liberty: Libertad

Limited government: Gobierno limitado

Line organization: Organización de linea

Literacy test: Exámen de alfabetización

Litigate: Litigar

Lobbying: Cabildeo

Logrolling: Práctica legislativa que consiste en incluir en un mismo proyecto de ley temas de diversa índole

Loophole: Hueco legal, escapatoria

Madisonian model: Modelo Madisónico

Majority: Mayoría

Majority floor leader: Líder mayoritario de piso

Majority leader of the House: Líder mayoritario de la Casa

Majority opinion: Opinión mayoritaria

Majority rule: Regla de mayoría

Managed news: Noticias manipuladas

Mandatory retirement: Retiro mandatorio

Matching funds: Fondos combinados

Material incentive: Incentivo material

Media: Media

Media access: Acceso de media

Merit system: Sistema de mérito

Military-industrial complex: Complejo industriomilitar

Minority floor leader: Líder minoritario de piso

Minority leader of the House: Líder minorial de la Casa

Monetary policy: Política monetaria

Monopolistic model: Modelo monopólico

Monroe Doctrine: Doctrina Monroe

Moral idealism: Idealismo moral

Municipal home rule: Regla municipal

Narrow casting: Mensaje dirigído

National committee: Comité nacional

National convention: Convención nacional

National politics: Política nacional

National Security Council (NSC): Concilio de Seguridad Nacional

National security policy: Política de seguridad nacional

National aristocracy: Aristocracia natural

Natural rights: Derechos naturales

Necessaries: Necesidades

Negative constituents: Constituyentes negativos

New England town: Pueblo de Nueva Inglaterra

New federalism: Federalismo nuevo

Nullification: Nulidad, anulación

Office-block (Massachusetts) ballot: Cuadro-oficina (Massachusetts), voto

Office of Management and Budget (OMB): Oficina de Administración y Presupuesto

Oligarchy: Oligarquía
Ombudsman: Funcionario que representa al ciudadano ante el gobierno
Open primary: Primaria abierta
Opinion: Opinión
Opinion leader: Líder de opinión
Opinion poll: Encuesta, conjunto de opinión
Oral arguments: Argumentos orales
Oversight: Inadvertencia, omisión

Paid-for political announcement: Anuncios políticos pagados
Pardon: Perdón
Party-column (Indiana) ballot: Partido-columna (Indiana) voto
Party identification: Identificación de partido
Party identifier: Identificador de partido
Party-in-electorate: Partido electoral
Party-in-government: Partido en gobierno
Party organization: Organización de partido
Party platform: Plataforma de partido
Patronage: Patrocinio
Peer group: Grupo de contemporáneos
Pendleton Act (Civil Service Reform Act): Acta Pendleton (Acta de Reforma al Servicio Civil)
Personal attack rule: Regla de ataque personal
Petit jury: Jurado ordinario
Pluralism: Pluralismo
Plurality: Pluralidad
Pocket veto: Veto de bolsillo
Police power: Poder policiaco
Policy trade-offs: Intercambio de políticas
Political Action Committee (PAC): Comité de acción política
Political consultant: Consultante político
Political culture: Cultura política
Political party: Partido político
Political question: Pregunta política
Political realism: Realismo político
Political socialization: Socialización política
Political tolerance: Tolerancia política
Political trust: Confianza política
Politico: Político
Politics: Política
Poll tax: Impuesto sobre el sufrágio
Poll watcher: Observador de encuesta
Popular sovereignty: Soberanía popular
Power: Poder
Precedent: Precedente
Preferred-position test: Prueba de posición preferida
Presidential primary: Primaria presidencial
President pro tempore: Presidente provisoriamente
Press secretary: Secretaría de prensa
Prior restraint: Restricción anterior
Privileges and immunities: Privilégios e imunidades
Privatization, or contracting out: Privatización

Property: Propiedad
Property tax: Impuesto de propiedad
Public agenda: Agenda pública
Public debt financing: Financiamiento de deuda pública
Public debt, or national debt: Deuda pública o nacional
Public interest: Interés público
Public opinion: Opinión pública
Purposive incentive: Incentivo de propósito

Ratification: Ratificación
Rational ignorance effect: Efecto de ignorancia racional
Reapportionment: Redistribución
Recall: Suspender
Recognition power: Poder de reconocimiento
Recycling: Reciclaje
Redistricting: Redistrictificación
Referendum: Referéndum
Registration: Registración
Regressive tax: Impuestos regresivos
Relevance: Pertinencia
Remand: Reenviar
Representation: Representación
Representative assembly: Asamblea representativa
Representative democracy: Democracia representativa
Reprieve: Tregua, suspensión
Republic: República
Republican party: Partido Republicano
Resulting powers: Poderes resultados
Reverse: Cambiarse a lo contrario
Reverse discrimination: Discriminación reversiva
Rule of four: Regla de cuatro
Rules committee: Comité regulador
Run-off primary: Primaria residual

Safe seat: Asiento seguro
Sampling error: Error de encuesta
Secession: Secesión
Second budget resolution: Resolución segunda presupuestal
Second Continental Congress: Segundo Congreso Continental
Sectional politics: Política seccional
Segregation: Segregación
Select committee: Comité selecto
Selectperson: Persona selecta
Senatorial courtesy: Cortesía senatorial
Seniority system: Sistema señorial
Separate-but-equal doctrine: Separados pero iguales
Separation of powers: Separación de poderes
Service sector: Sector de servicio
Sex discrimination: Discriminación sexual
Sexual harassment: Acosamiento sexual
Slander: Difamación oral, calumnia
Sliding-scale test: Prueba escalonada
Social movement: Movimiento social

Social Security: Seguridad Social
Socioeconomic status: Estado socioeconómico
Solidary incentive: Incentivo de solidaridad
Solid South: Súr Sólido
Sound bite: Mordida de sonido
Soviet bloc: Bloque Soviético
Speaker of the House: Vocero de la Casa
Spin: Girar/giro
Spin doctor: Doctor en giro
Spin-off party: Partido estático
Spoils system: Sistema de despojos
Spring review: Revisión de primavera
Stability: Estabilidad
Standing committee: Comité de sostenimiento
Stare decisis: El principio característico del ley común por el cual los precedentes jurisprudenciales tienen fuerza obligatoria, no sólo entre las partes, sino también para casos sucesivos análogos
State: Estado
State central committee: Comité central del estado
State of the Union message: Mensaje sobre el Estado de la Unión
Statutory power: Poder estatorial
Strategic Arms Limitation Treaty (SALT I): Tratado de Limitación de Armas Estratégicas
Subpoena: Orden de testificación
Subsidy: Subsidio
Suffrage: Sufrágio
Sunset legislation: Legislación sunset
Superdelegate: Líder de partido u oficial elegido quien tiene el derecho de votar
Supplemental Security Income (SSI): Ingresos de Seguridad Suplementaria
Supremacy clause: Cláusula de supremacia
Supremacy doctrine: Doctrina de supremacia
Symbolic speech: Discurso simbólico

Technical assistance: Asistencia técnica
Third party: Tercer partido
Third-party candidate: Candidato de tercer partido
Ticket splitting: División de boletos
Totalitarian regime: Régimen totalitario
Town manager system: Sistema de administrador municipal
Town meeting: Junta municipal
Township: Municipio
Tracking poll: Seguimiento de encuesta
Trial court: Tribunal de primera
Truman Doctrine: Doctrina Truman
Trustee: Depositario
Twelfth Amendment: Doceava Enmienda
Twenty-fifth Amendment: Veinticincoava Enmienda
Two-party system: Sistema de dos partidos

Unanimous opinion: Opinión unánime
Underground economy: Economía subterráea

deregulation by, 606
earned income tax credits, views on, 573
economic policies of, 536
economic sanctions, use of, 661–662
economy during administration of, 549–550
effectiveness of presidency, 362
Equal Rights Amendment, 508
and federal bureaucracy, 373–374, 389
foreign policy of, 636
game orientation media coverage, 135
going public, 348
human rights violations in other countries, 636
image of, 348
INF agreement with Soviets, 650
Iran, sale of arms to, 641
Iran-Contra affair, 249, 251
leaks, criticizing, 118
military intervention in foreign countries, 654
misuse of powers by, 274
moderates, appeal to, 194
new federalism under, 65, 67
news media, relationship with, 118, 123–124
Nicaraguan contras, support of, 92
OMB authority, 601
reelection of, 346
soft money and, 262
South Africa and constructive engagement, 661–662
staff of, 340
State Department, political appointees to, 636
supply-side economics, 534
Supreme Court appointees, 462
taxation under, 540–541
television and, 139
trade policy of, 657
veto exercised by, 354
Rebozo, Bebe, 340
Reed, Thomas, 299
Rehnquist, William, 404–405, 412, 414, 416, 417, 420
Reno, Janet, 333
Revels, Hiram, 214
Robb, Charles, 646
Roberts, Owen, 403, 418
Robertson, Pat, 162, 229

Robinson, Jo Ann, 176
Rockefeller, Nelson, 331, 344
Roe, Jane, 461
Rogers, Will, 535
Roosevelt, Eleanor, 341–343
Roosevelt, Franklin D., 88, 328
    acceptance speech at 1932 convention, 235
    congressional support of, 354
    court-packing plan of, 403
    death of, 331
    federal bureaucracy, growth of, 372–373
    fireside chats, 345
    funeral of, 346
    and the Great Depression, 533
    implied powers, 336
    New Deal, 62, 63
    news media, relationship with, 119, 123
    nomination of, 204
    Pearl Harbor, attack on, 337
    and personal presidency, 345
    photo coverage, 139
    press conferences, 119, 123
    ranking of U.S. presidents, 359, 362
    as secretary of the navy, 337
    Supreme Court appointments, 249
    and tax code, 540
    veto exercised by, 354
Roosevelt, Theodore, 327, 328
    and bully pulpit, 345
    lawsuits over incidents occurring before taking office, 396
    Oliver Wendell Holmes, appointment of, 412
    press conferences, 119
    as secretary of the navy, 337
    Square Deal, 353
Rostenkowski, Daniel, 274
Roukema, Marge, 304
Rudman, Warren, 546
Russell, Benjamin, 217

Salinger, Pierre, 117
Sanford, Edward, 437
Sawyer, Diane, 122
Scalia, Antonin, 420, 450, 508
Schattschneider, E. E., 179, 186, 187, 207
Schlesinger, Arthur, 359
Schmitt, Harrison, 138

Schumer, Charles, 293
Schwarzkopf, Norman, 337
Scott, Dred, 477
Scowcroft, Brent, 640
Shaheen, Jeanne, 219
Shays, Daniel, 29
Sherman, Roger, 337
Shriver, Sargent, 230
Simon, Paul, 368
Simpson, Alan, 122
Simpson, O. J., 133, 134, 413, 496
Sirica, John, 26
Smith, Margaret Chase, 288
Smith, Adam, 529, 530, 594, 595–596
Smith, Alfred, 230, 449
Smith, Howard, 507
Smith, Tubby, 497
Sousa, John Philip, 442
Souter, David, 409–410
Stamaty, Mark Alan, 292
Stanton, Elizabeth Cady, 218, 219
Star, Kenneth, 120
Stevens, John Paul, 396, 398, 423, 426–427, 455
Stevenson, Adlai, 236
Stewart, Potter, 459
Stockman, David, 118, 290, 545, 580
Stone, Harlan, 421
Stovall, Tyler, 580
Stuart, Gilbert, 217
Sununu, John, 352

Taft, William Howard, 407
Taney, Roger, 402, 477
Taylor, Zachary, 359
Thomas, Clarence, 118, 408, 410, 422, 497, 508
Thomas, Evan, 108, 110, 144–145
Thompson, Tommy, 578
Tilden, Samuel, 479
Tillman, Benjamin, 214
Tinker, Mary Beth, 442
Torlino, Tom, 503
Tripp, Linda, 123
Truman, Bess, 341, 343
Truman, Harry S., 233, 242, 328, 331, 350
    approval ratings, 139
    atom bomb, first knowledge of, 344
    containment of Soviet Union, 642–643
    court of appeals appointees, 412

and economists, 533
    Korean War, 338
    lawsuits over incidents occurring before taking office, 396
    nomination of, 204
    pardon power, use of, 336
    ranking of U.S. presidents, 359–360
Tsongas, Paul, 210, 212
Turner, Benjamin, 214
Twain, Mark, 266

Van Buren, Martin, 322
Vanderbilt, Cornelius, 257
Ventura, Jesse, 138
Vidal, Gore, 22
Vinson, Fred, 437
Voltaire, 7
Vowell, Jacob, 602

Wallace, George, 194–195, 216, 376, 484
Walls, Josiah T., 214
Warren, Earl, 403–404, 412, 417
    and communists, conviction of, 437
    desegregation decisions, 483–484
Warren, Mercy Otis, 30
Washington, George, 25, 29, 31, 36, 42, 121, 326
    in the media age, 140
    political parties, view on, 186
    speeches of, 345
    staff of, 338
    vote buying, 256
Washington, Martha, 341, 342
Weber, Max, 369
Webster, Daniel, 299
Weidenbaum, Murray, 545
Whitman, Christine, 219
Whitman, Walt, 5
Whittier, John Greenleaf, 442
Wilder, Douglas, 210, 215
Willkie, Wendell, 232
Wills, Gary, 44
Wilson, Edith, 342
Wilson, Woodrow, 45, 327, 328, 331, 338, 353, 407, 481, 642
    neutral competence, advocate of, 386
Wood, Kimba, 143
Woodhull, Victoria Claflin, 219
Woodward, Bob, 24, 26, 123

Young, Milt, 293

Freedom of Information Act of 1966, 370–372
Freedom of the press, 143
  gathering news, restrictions on, 444–445
  Internet and cyberporn, 448
  libel, 445–446
  obscenity laws, 446–447
  prior restraint, 443–444
  privacy, invasion of, 445
Freedom of religion, 447, 448–450, 453
  animal sacrifices, 432, 434, 468
  establishment of religion, 450–454
  evolution vs. creationism, 453
  minority religions, 450, 451
  prayer in public schools, 450–454
  separation of church and state, 447
Freedom of speech
  belief in, 99
  college campuses, 440
  fighting words, 439
  public forum, 438–442
  seditious speech, 436–438
  speech plus conduct, 439–441
  swearing and vulgarities, 439
  symbolic speech, 441–442
Full faith and credit clause, 72

Gallup poll, 88, 134
Gambling by Native Americans, 504
Game orientation in political reporting, 134–135
Gap between rich and poor, 539, 554, 569–570
Gasoline, regulation of, 604
Gays. See Homosexuality
GDP (gross domestic product), 531–533, 539–540
Gender
  discrimination. See Sex discrimination; Women; Women's movement
  federal judiciary, 409
  political party affiliation, 197
  poverty determined by, 570–571
General Accounting Office, 308, 312
General Motors (GM), 595, 597
General Services Administration, 377
Generational divisions, 97, 98
Genetically altered foods, 611–612, 660, 661
Geographic diversity, 10–11
Geography, poverty and, 571
Germany, 193, 444, 532
  Berlin Wall, tearing down of, 651
  competition between U.S. and, 549
  constitution of, 46
  GDP allocated to government, 539
  Holocaust. See Holocaust
  immigration from, 6
  income inequality, 569
  NATO membership, 655
  productivity rates, 532
Gerrymandering, 214–217, 286
Gettysburg Address, 44, 345
  in the media age, 140
GI Bill of Rights, 296–297
Gideon v. Wainwright, 457
Girls' state, 83
Glasnost policy, 650–651
Glass-Steagall Act, 610
Global economy, 610, 612
  foreign aid and, 663–664
  interest groups influencing trade policy, 640
  labor competition in, 554
  multinational corporations, 554–557
Global warming, 170, 668
Globalization, 554–557, 665, 667
Going public, 294–295, 348–349
GOP. See Republican Party
GOP-TV, 199
Government regulation
  challenges to, 603–605
  cost-benefit analysis, 600–601
  cycles of, 605–612
  deregulation, 605–608, 610–611
  environment. See Environment
  implementing and enforcing, 603–605
  kinds of, 598–599

oversight, 601–602
reasons for, 595–598
reregulation following deregulation, 608–609
responsiveness of, 625
risk analysis, 600–601
time line, 624
tragedy of the commons, 595
writing regulations, 600–601
Gramm-Rudman-Hollings Act, 546
Grandfather clause, 214, 483
Grants, 65, 69, 72
Grassroots/grasstops lobbying, 169–171
Gray lobby, 163–164
Grazing leases, federal lands, 580
Great Britain
  classes in, 477
  elections in, 223
  freedom of press in, 444
  GDP allocated to government, 539
  infant mortality rates, 581
  military alliances with, 654–655
  mixed economies, 529, 531
  parliamentary form of government, 352
  party system in, 193, 198
  shadow cabinets by opposition party, 638
  unitary system of government, 56
  voter turnout in, 222
  writs of assistance in colonies, 455–456
Great Compromise, 31–32
Great Depression, 62–63, 328, 531
  changing U.S. Constitution, 45
  FDR's economic policies, 534
  Hoover's economic policies, 534
  immigration during, 7
  political socialization and, 86
Great Lakes, pollution of, 604
Great Law of Peace (Iroquois), 38
Great Society, 64–65, 353, 569, 570–571
Greece, ancient, 16, 17
Green lobby, 164
Green Party, 195
Greenpeace, 164, 174–175
Grenada, U.S. invasion of, 356, 638, 640, 654
Gridlock, 351–352
Guerrilla warfare, 647
Gulf of Tonkin Resolution, 645–646
Gulf War, 125, 337, 355–356
  Bush gaining support for, 349
  congressional support for, 638
  cost of, 587
  media coverage of, 127
  1992 presidential election, 91
  public opinion on, 641
  success of, 654, 667
Guns
  gun control legislation, 455
  gun lobby, 164–165, 169
  Handgun Control interest group, 165, 178
  Second Amendment, 454–455

Habeas corpus, writ of, 407, 434
  Lincoln suppressing, 337
Haiti, U.S. troops in, 357, 632, 635, 652, 654
Handgun Control interest group, 165, 178
Hanford Nuclear Reservation, 618–619
Harley-Davidson motorcycles, 657, 659
Harris polls, 134
Hatch Act of 1939, 387
Hate speech, 440–441
Hawaii health care reforms, 586
Hazardous waste, 617, 618–619, 620
Head Start, 574, 578, 587
Health and Human Services, Department of, 389
Health care. See also Health care reform
  African Americans, 580–581
  Clinton, Hillary, and reforms. See Health care reform
  federal grants for, 69
  infant mortality rates, 573–574, 580–581
  life expectancy, 580

public opinion on spending for, 95
time line, 586
underinsured and uninsured, 562, 564, 583, 588–589
Health care reform, 20, 135, 348
  and AARP, 163
  access issues, 583–584
  Canadian single-payer system, 564, 585, 589
  Clinton's package for, 562, 564, 588–589
  coalitions on, 172
  commercials to defeat, 171
  congressional hearings on, 168
  cost increases, explanation of, 582–583
  grassroots lobbying and, 170
  managed competition, 564
  responses to crisis, 584, 586–587
  single-payer plan, 564, 585, 589
  socialized medicine, 585
Health Insurance Association of America, 171
Health Maintenance Organizations (HMOs), 584
  health care reform and, 589
Heritage Foundation, 636
Higher education. See Universities and colleges
Highway construction, 65
Hindus, 7
Hiroshima, 643–644
Hispanic Americans, 499, 501–502
  in civil service, 374–375
  Congress, minority power in, 306–307
  discrimination against, 499–500, 502
  elected to office, 215
  immigration from Mexico, 1987–1996, 10
  percentage of population, 518
  political participation, 18, 246
  poverty statistics, 570–571
  race identification in U.S. Census, 13
Holiness Church of God in Jesus' Name, 450
Holocaust
  commercial bias of news media, 132, 135
  denial of, 87, 446
Home rule, 74
Homelessness, 574
Homosexuality
  Christian groups on, 162
  conservative and liberal views on, 96–97
  gay rights, 162–163, 227
  military service, 169, 465–466
  political campaigns and gay issues, 227
  privacy, right to, 465–466
  same-sex marriages, 465
  school clubs, 453
Horatio Alger myth, 228
House of Representatives
  differences between Senate and, 311
  incumbents' losing seats in, 291
  Interior and Insular Affairs Committee, 314
  International Relations Committee, 304
  majority leader, 301–303
  minority leader, 301
  party campaign committees, 199
  Rules Committee, 299, 301, 309–310
  Speaker of the House, 300–303
  specialization in, 294
  standing committees, 303
  subcommittee bill of rights, 304
  two houses, proposal for, 31
  whips, majority and minority, 301
  women in, 288–289
House Ways and Means Committee, 602
Housing
  discrimination in, 489–490, 494–495
  executive order to end discrimination, 335
  low-income housing, 542
  vouchers for, 495
Housing and Urban Development, 373, 374
Howard University Law School, 481

Hudson Foundation, 636
Human life, worth of, 601
Human radiation experiments, 618
Human rights
  foreign policy issues, 632, 659, 660–661, 662
  and trade policy, 659, 660–661, 662
Human Rights Campaign, 163
Hungary, 642, 643, 644
Hunger in America, 576–577
Hurricane Andrew (1992), 66
Hyperpluralism, 19–20

Identity politics, 11–13
Ideology, 94–95
Ignorance, political, 91–92
Immigration, 6, 7, 8–9
  cultural diversity, 5–7, 10
  economy benefiting from, 552–553
  illegal immigrants, 499
  politics and, 7, 10
  population growth and, 568
  social welfare for immigrants, 566
  work visas for college graduates, 9
Immigration and Naturalization Act of 1965, 8
Immigration and Naturalization Service (INS), 552
Immunity, presidential, 396, 398, 426–427
Impeachment, 330
  Clinton, Bill, 96, 330, 357–358
  Nixon and Watergate scandal, 47–49, 330
Implied powers clause, 58
Income taxes, 539–543. See also Taxation
  Amish and Quakers paying, 449
  declining tax burden for families, 539–540
  deductions, 540, 541, 543
  tax code, complexity and reform of, 540–543
Incumbents
  congressional elections, 286–290
  political action committees and, 264, 265
Independent candidates, 194–196, 237
Independent spending, 259, 260
Independent voters, characteristics of, 197–198
India, nuclear testing, 639, 665, 667
Indian Affairs Committee, 303
Indian Claims Commission, 504
Indian Removal Act of 1830, 503
Indiana, Muncie, study of, 62–63
Indifference, political, 11
Indirect democracy, 33
Individual liberties, 15–16
Individualistic political culture, 56–57
Indochina, 643, 645
Industrial revolution, 29
  environmental protection, 613
Industrial safety laws, 62
Industrialization, 62
  children, laws protecting, 62, 402, 403
  safety laws, 62
Infant mortality rates, 573–574, 580–581
Inflation, 531–533
  budget forecasting, 544–545
  during Bush years, 550
  campaign finance and contribution limits, 260
  during Reagan years, 549–550
  Vietnam War, 531, 548–549
Influence peddling, 274–275
Informal norms, 293–294
Information technology, 405
Infotainment, 133
Infrastructure of roads, bridges, etc., 550
Institute for Policy Studies, 636
Institutional loyalty, 293
Insurance risks assumed by government, 553
Integration
  desegregation. See Segregation
  schools and neighborhoods, 98–99
Interest groups, 154–156. See also Lobbying; Public interest groups
  agricultural interests, 159
  bias in representation of, 179, 180

business organizations, 157
competition and goals of, 178
congressional voting and, 298, 315, 317–318
membership in deline, 156–157, 158–159, 160
environmental groups, 621
and federal bureaucracy, 390–392
and federal courts, access to, 413–414
foreign policy, 639–640
formation of, 155–157
health care reform, opposition to, 564
labor unions, 158–159
market share, 177
NAFTA, opposition to, 641
political action committees (PACS), 157
private groups, 157–159
public image of, 178
regulations and, 600
religion, 639
responsiveness of government to, 178–180
success of, 176–178
time line, 179
tobacco industry, 152, 154, 180–181
types of, 157–166
veto power of, 19–20
women, 639–640
Interest rates, 534–536
Interfaith Alliance, 162
Interior and Insular Affairs Committee, 314
Interior Department, 314
Intermarriage, 7, 11–12
Intermediate nuclear forces (INF) agreement, 650–651
Internal Revenue Service (IRS)
auditing low- and middle-income taxpayers, 389
Bush's 1991 budget cuts to, 389
congressional hearings on abuses of, 312–313
and delegated legislative authority, 380
reorganization of, 543
International Atomic Energy Commission, 665
International Monetary Fund (INF), 663
International Relations Committee, 304
International trade. See Trade
Internet, 112, 165, 612
censorship of, 444, 448
cyberporn, 448
and digital divide, 556–557
e-campaigning, 241
and interest groups, 155–156
lobbyists using, 170–171
as news source, 111–112, 114, 117
taxation of Internet activity, 67
Interstate Commerce Commission (ICC), 381, 387, 390, 605
Interstate relations, 72–74
Iodine exposure, 618
Iowa caucuses, 231, 233–234
Iran
foreign policy under Reagan, 636
hostage crisis, 356
sale of arms to, 641, 656
seizure of American embassy in 1980, 136, 137–138
Iran-Contra affair, 68, 101, 119, 249, 250, 272, 327, 336, 340, 349
Iraq
economic sanctions against, 661, 662
Gulf War, 125
Hamdoon, Nizar, as ambassador to U.S., 637
military aid to, 656
UN monitoring of, 665, 667
Irish Americans, 639
Irish Republican Army (IRA), 444
Iron law of oligarchy, 19
Iroquois government, 38–39
Islam, 451
Isolationism, 641–642
Israel, 162, 193
homosexuals in military, 466
military aid to, 656
voter turnout in, 222

Issue voting, 237–239, 247
Italy, 193, 222, 539
Iwo Jima Memorial, 442

Jacksonian Democrats, 188–189
Jamestown settlers, 27
Japan
atomic bombs dropped on, 643–644
competition between U.S. and, 549
defense treaties with, 655
GDP allocated to government, 539
government spending, 539
homosexuals in military, 466
income inequality, 569
infant mortality rates, 581
and military restraints, 655–656
Pearl Harbor, attack on, 337, 642
productivity rates, 532
quotas and tariffs on Japanese goods, 657–659
removal of trade barriers, 657
taxes in, 539
voter turnout in, 222
Japanese internment camps, 337
Jawboning, or persuasion, 536–537
Jeffersonian Republicans, 188–189
Jewish Americans, 7
abortion, right to, 462
and Holocaust. See Holocaust
Israel, support for, 162, 639
percentage of people opposed to jew as president, 230
political party affiliation, 199, 246
Soviet Union, emigration from, 662
Jim Crow laws, 479–480
Joe Camel, 152
Joint Chiefs of Staff, 635
Jordan, military aid to, 656
Journalism. See Media; News Media; Newspapers
Judeo-Christian tradition, 15, 16, 613
Judges. See Judiciary; Supreme Court
Judicial restraint, 417
Judicial review, 390, 399–400, 402, 421–423
Judiciary. See also Federal courts
constitutional interpretation, 44–45, 416–417
deciding cases, 414–421
and divided government, 410
elitism and, 411
gender differences, 409
ideological view of appointees, 407–408
independence of, 412
interpretation of law, 414–417
making laws, 418–419
precedents, following, 418
qualifications of, 412
restraint vs. activism, 417
selection of, 407–411
statutory interpretation, 414–416
tenure of, 411–412
voting record of appointees, 411
Judiciary Act of 1789, 400, 405
Jurisdiction, 406–407, 603
Jury trial, 458
Justice Department, 374, 377
mergers and antitrust regulation, 597
mergers and merger proposals, review of, 610–611

Kenyan constitution, 46
Kerner Commission, 499
Keynesian economics, 534, 547, 558
Kickbacks, 274
Know-Nothings, 7, 194
Korean War, 242, 338, 638, 642. See also North Korea; South Korea
Kosovo crisis, 356–357, 630, 632–633, 652, 654, 668–669
Ku Klux Klan, 438, 480–481, 485, 497–498
Kuwait crisis, 654

Labeling, truth in, 598
Labor and labor unions, 158–159
and campaign financing, 263
child labor laws, 62, 402, 403

membership declining in unions, 160
minimum wage legislation, 269
and PACs, 258
Labor Department, 372, 389, 514
Labor statistics, 551
Lake Erie, pollution of, 604
Land grant colleges, 61
Language, bilingual education, 500–502
Latin America
Monroe Doctrine, 641–642
and U.S. interests, 634
Latinos. See Hispanic Americans
Lawmaking, 309–312
bills becoming law, 309–312
cloture vote, 311–312
conference committee, 282, 312
filibuster, 311–312, 318
House Rules Committee, 309–310
by judiciary, 418–419
legislative veto, 312
lobbyists drafting bills, 167
markup sessions, 303
presidential veto, 312, 353–354
Leadership Conference on Civil Rights, 173
League of Nations, 642
League of Women Voters, 173
Leaks to news media, 118–119
Lebanon, U.S. troops in, 638
Legislative veto, 601
Lesbians. See Homosexuality
Liability, limiting, 599
Libel laws and freedom of press, 445–446
Liberalism, 94–95
Liberals, 58, 84, 94, 95, 98–99
health care reform and, 564
political issues, views on, 96–97
political party affiliation, 197
poverty, causes of, 572–573
Liberty, 15–16
Licensing regulations, 598
Life expectancy, 580
Limited government, 38
Line item veto, 354
Literacy tests and voting, 213–214
Literary Digest poll, 88
Livestock, regulation of, 382
Living will, 466
Lobbying and lobbyists, 154–155, 171.
See also Interest groups; Public interest groups
bureaucrats and policy makers, 168
coalition building, 172–174
Congress, former members of, 315
congressional hearings, testifying at, 167–168
courts and judges, 168–169
expertise and bill drafting, 167
foreign policy matters, 639–640
former federal bureaucrats, 387–388
high-tech, 170–171
litigation as tool of, 168–169
lobbying techniques, 166–169, 169–174
money and campaign contributions, 168
personal contacts, 166–167
public opinion, molding, 171–172
registered agents for foreign countries, 640
states and localities lobbying federal government, 70–71
Ten Commandments of, 169
Local government. See also Cities
number of government units, 68
state-local relations, 74
Lockheed Martin, 171
Logging on federal lands, 579–580
Logrolling, 293
Loral Space and Communication, 264
Love Canal, 618
Low-income housing, 542
Lower class. See Socioeconomic classes
Lynchings of blacks, 480–481, 483

Mad cow disease, 660, 668
Mailing
for dollars, 270
franking privileges, 287

Majority leader, 301–303
Majority-minority congressional districts, 215, 286
Majority rule, 17, 38
Mandamus, writ of, 399–400
Mandates
in presidential elections, 249, 251, 346
unfunded mandates, 69–70
Mandatory spending, 543–544
Manufacturing standards, 598–599
Mapp v. Ohio, 456
Marbury v. Madison, 399–400, 402
March for Women's Lives, 166
Marijuana, ballot initiatives on, 126
Market research and polling, 88
Markup sessions, 303
Marriage
discrimination in custody, 513
interracial dating and marriage, 497, 498
same-sex marriages, 465
Marshall Court, 399–401
Marshall Plan, 643, 663
Maryland health care reforms, 586
Mass media. See Media; Newsmedia
Maternity leave, 511
Mayflower Compact, 27, 33
McCain-Feingold campaign finance reform bill, 273
McCarthyism, 437
McCulloch v. Maryland, 60–61, 402
Media. See Mass media; News media; Radio; Television
as agent of political socialization, 86
declining public trust and, 101
freedom of press. See Freedom of press
presidency, growth of, 328
and presidential campaigns, 238–241
Media events, 120–121, 237, 241
Media malaise, 141
Medicaid, 581–582
abortions under, 462–463
mandatory spending for, 543–544
poor people qualifying for, 551
reforming, 586
SSI recipients eligible for, 573
Medical insurance. See Health care; Medicaid; Medicare
Medicare, 93, 566, 581–582
mandatory spending for, 543–544
percentage of income withheld for, 539–540
reforming, 586
shoring up, 547
Merchant diplomacy, 651–652
Mergers
antitrust regulation, 597
FTC and, 610–611
hospitals and health care institutions, 589
media mergers, 113
Mexican Americans. See Hispanic Americans
Mexico
Hispanic Americans from, 499, 501–502
immigrants returning money to families in, 553
immigration, 1987–1996, 7
Microsoft, 112, 448, 597
Middle class. See Socioeconomic classes
Military, 652–653. See also Armed forces; Nuclear weapons
aid to other countries, 656
alliances, 654–656
arms control negotiations, 636
blowback, 656
intervention in other countries, 630, 632–633, 637–638, 653–654, 668–669
nuclear deterrence, 643–645, 652
post-Vietnam era, 653
sales of arms to other countries, 656
two major theater war (2MTW), 653
Military pensions, 580
Militia and right to bear arms, 454–455
Miller Brewing Company, 508
Minimum wage, 269, 572
Mining
federal land leases, 579–580
regulation of, 601–602

Minor parties, 194–196, 237
Minority leader, 301–303
Minority rights, 17
Miranda rights, 457
Miranda v. Arizona, 457
Misery index, 532
Mississippi
　Freedom Democrats, 474, 476, 518–519
　Neshoba County, 485, 488
　Sovereignty Commission of, 485
Missouri Compromise of 1820, 402
Mitsubishi, 508
Mixed economies, 529–530
Moderates, 94
Mohawk Indians, 38
Monetary policy, 534–536
Money, supply of, 534–536, 546
Money and politics, 256–257, 263, 266,
　270. *See also* Campaign finance laws
　conflicts of interest, 273–275
　corporations, 263
　early reforms, 257–258
　good candidates deterred, 267
　impact of campaign money, 267–272
　independent spending, 259, 260
　labor unions, 263
　McCain-Feingold campaign finance
　　reform bill, 254, 256, 277
　in nineteenth century, 257–258
　PACs. *See* Political action committees
　party organizations, 263
　and public cynicism, 272–273
　public policy changes, 268–272
　responsiveness of government, 275–276
　soft money, 254, 256, 260–264, 277
　sources of campaign funds, 263–266
　special interests, 265–266
　time line, 275
　White House, selling access to,
　　262–263
Monopolies prohibited, 596–597
Monroe Doctrine, 641, 652
Montgomery (Alabama) bus boycott,
　175–177
Moralistic political culture, 56–57
Mormons and polygamy, 449
Mortgages, redlining, 490, 495
Motor voter law, 224–225, 458
Muckrakers, 257, 605
Multilateralism, 651–652
Multinational corporations, 554–557
Multiparty systems, 193–194
Multiple-issue groups, 160
Muslims, 7, 449, 450, 630, 632–633,
　668–669
Mutually assured destruction (MAD),
　644, 665, 667

NAACP. *See* National Association for the
　Advancement of Colored People
NAFTA. *See* North American Free
　Trade Agreement
Nagasaki, 643
Nation of Islam, 177
National Academy of Sciences, 386, 392,
　552
National Aeronautics and Space
　Administration (NASA), 377
National Association for the
　Advancement of Colored People
　(NAACP), 413
　attorneys for, 484
　desegregation of schools, 482–485
　history of, 481–483
　race identification in census, 13
　Rosa Parks and bus boycott, 176
　split and division within, 176–177
National Association of Evangelicals, 162
National Audubon Society, 164, 621
National Cancer Institute, 621
National Conference of State Legislatures,
　70
National Council of Churches, 162
National Council of Senior Citizens, 156
National Council to Control Handguns,
　165, 178
National debt, 545–547
National Economic Council, 333, 533
National Education Association, 264

National Environmental Policy Act, 614
National Farmers' Union, 159
National forests, 613
National Funeral Directors Association, 154
National Governors Association, 156
National Guard, 454–455
National Indian Gaming Association, 504
National Labor Relations Board (NLRB),
　372, 377
　judicial review, 390
National League of Cities, 70
National monuments, 52, 54, 75–76
National Organization for Women
　(NOW), 161, 507
National park system, 613
National party chair, 198
National party committees, 198–199
National party conventions, 202, 203,
　204, 231, 234–236
National Reconnaissance Office, 641
National Rifle Association (NRA),
　154–155, 156, 169
　gun control legislation and, 455
　mailing for dollars, 270
　soft money donors, 264
National Right to Life Committee, 165,
　186
National security, 633–634, 665, 667
National security advisor, 635
National Security News Service, 110, 144
National Smokers Alliance, 169, 186
National Taxpayers Union, 160, 173, 271
National Women's Party, 219
National Women's Political Caucus, 161
Native Americans, 5, 502
　archaeological sites of, 504
　assimilation and citizenship, 503
　citizenship for, 11
　in civil service, 374
　Constitutional Convention, 32
　gambling by, 504
　government policy toward, 502–505
　Iroquois government, 38–39
　Mohawks, Senecas, Oneidas, and
　　Onondagas, 38
　percentage of population, 518
　peyote use by, 449–450
　political party affiliation, 197
　separation, policy of, 502–503
　tribal restoration, 504–505
　uranium mining, 618
Nativist sentiment, 7
Natural disasters, responding to, 66
Natural Resources Defense Council, 164
Natural rights, 37
Navy
　Boorda, Admiral Mike, 108, 110,
　　144–145
　Tailhook convention, 1991, 108
Nazi Party demonstration, 439–440
Necessary and proper clause, 58, 60
Negative campaigning, 242–243
Neighborhoods, integration of, 98–99
Neshoba County, Mississippi, 485, 488
New Deal, 19, 62–65, 339
　Democratic Party and, 190
　liberalism and, 94
　presidency, growth of, 328
　regulatory activity, 605
　social welfare programs, 566
　and Supreme Court rulings, 403
New federalism, 65, 67–68
New Freedom, 353
New Hampshire primary, 204, 233–234
New Jersey Plan, 31
New Republicans, 298
New York Times v. Sullivan, 445
News media. *See also* Media; Newspapers;
　Radio; Television
　adversarial relationship with politicians,
　　121–123
　atomization of, 114–117
　bandwagon effect, 140
　bias of. *See* Bias of news media
　Bush administration, 118, 125
　campaign coverage, 139–141
　concentration of, 112–114
　Congress-media relationship, 125–126,
　　294–295, 303

congressional campaigns and elections,
　287–288, 293
elections, impact of, 138–141
Fairness & Accuracy in Reporting
　(FAIR), 127
FDR's relationship with, 119, 123
freedom of press. *See* Freedom of press
fringe media, 115–117
and Internet, 114, 117
leaks to, 118–119
media events, 120–121, 237, 241
media malaise, 141
political parties, impact on, 138–141
and politicians, 117–123
populist backlash, 114–115
presidential press conferences, 119–120
presidents' going public, 348–349
public agenda, impact of media on,
　137–138
public opinion, impact on, 141
Reagan administration, 123–124
responsiveness of, 142–145
roles of, 111–112
scoops, 119
sound bites, 121, 288, 348
spin by politicians, 122
Supreme Court, relationship with, 126
symbiotic relationship with politicians,
　117–121
time line, 142
U.S. as first media state, 111
Newspapers
　endorsing political candidates, 141
　neutrality of, 129–130
　and straw polls, 87–88
　television's impact on, 111–112
Newsweek, 108, 110, 144–145
Nicaragua, 636
　Contras, 92, 274
　Soviets reducing aid to, 650
　U.S. support of guerrillas in, 355, 641
Nineteenth Amendment, 219, 507
Ninth Amendment, 43
Nominating candidates for political office.
　See Political parties
Nonpoint sources, 617
North American Free Trade Agreement
　(NAFTA), 130, 173, 194, 348, 641,
　659
North Atlantic Treaty Organization
　(NATO), 356–357, 634, 643,
　654–656
　in Kosovo, 356–357
　Serbian armed forces, air strike against,
　　669
North Korea, 655
　Carter in, 635
　denuclearization of, 663
Northwest Ordinance, 28
Northwest Territory, 27
Northwestern University, 21
Norway, voter turnout, 222
Nuclear energy issues, 130
Nuclear Regulatory Commission, 391
Nuclear weapons, 618–619, 643–645
　antiballistic missile (ABM), 649
　antimissile defense system, 650, 667
　atomic bombs dropped on Japan,
　　643–644
　destruction of other countries' arsenals
　　of, 663
　former Soviet Republics, aid to destroy
　　weaponry of, 663
　India and Pakistan testing, 639, 665, 667
　intermediate nuclear forces (INF)
　　agreement, 650
　mutually assured destruction (MAD),
　　644, 665, 667
　removal from Europe, 655
　SALT I and II, 649, 650
　Strategic Defense Initiative (SDI), 650
　and terrorism, 665, 667
Nullification, doctrine of, 62

Obscenity laws, 446–447
Occupational Safety and Health
　Administration (OSHA), 373, 380,
　605
　appointees to, 389

court challenges to, 603
　and deregulation, 606
　and ergonomic injuries, 381
　human life, worth of, 601
　Sikh construction workers and hard
　　hats, 450
Ocean Dumping Act, 621
Office of Management and Budget
　(OMB), 314, 333–334, 339
　budget forecasting, 545
　deregulation, 605–606
　fiscal policies, 533
　regulatory oversight by, 601–602
　toxic waste dumps, cleanup of, 618
Office of Technology Assessment, 308
Office of Vice President, 341, 344–345
Oil prices, 548
Oklahoma City bombing (1995), 66, 174,
　349, 368, 437, 438
Old growth forests, logging in, 592, 594,
　629–630
Oligarchy, iron law of, 19
Oneidas, 38
Onondagas, 38
OPEC oil prices, 548
Operation Rescue, 165, 464
Oregon health care reforms, 586

Pacific Islanders, 306–307, 374
Pacific Northwest, logging in, 592, 594,
　629–630
PACs. *See* Political action committees
Pakistan and nuclear testing, 639, 665
Panama, U.S. troops in, 125, 356, 638,
　654
Panama Canal treaties, 638
Paper bag test, 482
Pardons, 336
Park Service, 314
Parliamentary government, 352
Parochial schools, 454
Partial-birth abortions, 464
Parties. *See* Political parties
Paternity leave, 511
Patronage system, 201, 385
Pearl Harbor, Japanese attack on, 337,
　642
Peer groups and political socialization,
　85–86
Pendleton Act of 1883, 386–387
Pentagon Papers, 443–444
Permanent campaign, 244–245
Permanent normal trading relations
　(PNTR), 641
Persian Gulf War. *See* Gulf War
Personal presidency, 345–346
Persuasion, power of, 346–349
Peyote use, 449–450
Philip Morris, 264
Philippines
　closing U.S. bases in, 655
　U.S. influence in, 642
Phillips Petroleum, 178
Pilgrims, 27
Pink-collar jobs, 510
Planned Parenthood, 166–167
Platforms of political parties, 235
Plea bargains, 460
Pledge of Allegiance, 442
Plessy v. Ferguson, 479–480
Pluralism, 18–20
Plutonium, 665, 667
Plymouth colony, 27
Pocket veto, 353
Pocketbook issues, 237–238, 247–248
Poland, 642
Police officers
　discrimination against blacks,
　　495–496
　racial profiling by, 499
Political action committees (PACs), 157,
　168
　Business-Industry Political Action
　　Committee, 174
　elected officials soliciting funds from,
　　265–266
　Feingold, Russ, and, 254, 256, 277
　527 groups, 262
　incumbents, giving to, 264, 265

Redlining, 490, 495
Reform Party, 1996, 196
Regional conflicts, 11
Regional development grants, 69
Regressive tax, 540
Regulations. *See* Government regulation
Rehnquist Court, 404–405, 414
  affirmative action, 514, 515–516
  capital punishment cases, 460
  civil liberties, interpreting, 468
  desecration of American flag, 442
  desegregation, 490
  free exercise of religion, 449
  free speech issues, 440–441
  Miranda rights, 457
  prior restraint cases, 444
  right to die, 466
  Roe v. Wade, narrowing of, 462–463
  school busing, 487
  school prayer rulings, 452–453
Religion. *See also* Freedom of religion;
    Prayer in schools
  Catholicism. *See* Catholics
  interest groups, 162, 639
  Judeo-Christian beliefs, 15, 16
  Mormons and polygamy, 449
  party loyalties, 246
  Pilgrims, 27
  pluralism, 451, 454
  political party affiliation, 197
  Protestants. *See* Protestants
  Ten Commandments in schools, 451
Religious right, 197
Republic, 17–18, 33–34
Republican Contract with America, 67, 78
Republican Party, 189–190, 197–198
  affirmative action and, 515, 517
  antiabortion lobby, 165
  and campaigns, 200, 238–241
  and Christian Coalition, 162
  in Congress, 200, 284–285
  Contract with America, 67, 78, 575
  corruption in, 274
  and deregulation, 610
  dominance of from 1896–1932, 189,
    190
  economic policies, 537–538
  elephant as symbol of, 191
  environmental policy of, 622
  Equal Rights Amendment, 508
  estate tax, repeal of, 526, 528, 558
  foreign policy issues, 638
  fragmentation within, 194
  gun lobby, 165
  health care reform, opposition to, 564
  and homosexual issues, 227
  mobilizing voters, 225–226
  national committee of, 199–200
  New Republicans, 298
  political action committees (PACs)
    giving to, 264, 265
  religious right and, 197
  role of national government, 187
  soft money donors to, 264
  and taxes, 543
  welfare reform, 575
Reregulation following deregulation,
    608–609
Responsible party government, 198
Restrictive covenants, 489–490
Retrospective voting, 247
Revenue, sources of, 540
Revenue sharing, 65
Revolutionary Communist Youth
    Brigade, 442
Revolutionary War, 17, 401, 547
Right to counsel, 457–458
Right-to-life movement, 462–464
Right to privacy. *See* Privacy rights
Risk analysis, regulations and, 600–601
RJ Reynolds, 152, 154, 169, 180–181, 264
Roe v. Wade, 421, 461–464
Roman Catholics. *See* Catholics
Romania, 642
Ruckus Society, 174
Rural communities
  hospitals in, 581
  poverty, 571

Russia. *See also* Soviet Union
  breakup of Soviet Union, 531
  nuclear weapons, aid to destroy, 663
  revolution in, 436
  uranium and plutonium in, 665, 667
Rutherford Institute, 413
Rwanda, tribal warfare in, 632

Safe Drinking Water Act, 616–617
Sales tax, 540
Same-sex marriages, 465
Sanctions
  and foreign policy, 639, 661–663
  India and Pakistan conducting nuclear
    tests, 639
Santeria religion, 432–434, 468
Saturday Night Massacre, 26
Savings and loan associations
  regulating, 608–609
  scandals affecting, 136, 274
Schools. *See also* Education; Universities
    and colleges
  bilingual education, 500–502
  busing, 130, 485–487
  censorship of school newspapers, 444
  clubs with special interest or affiliation
    in, 453
  desegregation of, 98–99, 482–485
  equalized funding of, 492, 500
  evolution vs. creationism, 453
  ghetto schools, 490–492
  Hispanic Americans in, 499–500
  lunches, federal spending for, 576
  parochial schools, 448, 454
  prayer in. *See* Prayer in schools
  segregation, 98, 490–492
  sex discrimination, 512–513
  Ten Commandments in, 451
  unequal funding, 491–492, 500
Sea Shepherds, 164
Search and seizure, 455–456
Second Amendment, 454
Second party system, 1828–1860,
    188–189
Secretary of defense, 635
Secretary of education, 366, 368
Secretary of state
  advisor to president, 635
  Albright, Madeleine, 630, 632–633,
    668–669
Securities and Exchange Commission,
    377
Sedition Act of 1918, 436
Seditious speech, 436–438
Segregation, 479–480
  busing, 485–487
  de facto vs. de jure, 485–487, 499–500
  desegregation of schools, 483–485
  Latinos experiencing, 499–500
  public opinion on, 98
Self-incrimination, 456–457
Selma, Alabama, march on, 488, 489
Senate
  differences between House and,
    311–312
  Energy and National Resources
    Committee, 314
  Foreign Relations Committee, 303
  impeachment of Clinton, 281
  majority/minority leaders, 301–303
  1998 elections, 249, 254, 256, 276
  party campaign committees, 199
  standing committees, 303
  two houses, proposal for, 31–32
  vice president as presiding officer, 302
  women in, 288–289
Seneca Indians, 38
Senior Executive Service, 389
Separate-but-equal doctrine, 480
Separation of church and state, 447, 450
Separation of powers, 35–36
  checks and balances, 36–37
  legislative veto declared
    unconstitutional, 312
  line item veto and, 354
Sequoia National Forest, 52, 54, 75–76
Serbia and Kosovar Albanians, 630,
    632–633, 668–669

Service Employees International, 264
Seventeenth Amendment, 35
Seventh Amendment, 43
Seventh-Day Adventists, 449
Sewage treatment plants, 615–617
Sex discrimination, 505–506. *See also*
    Women
  Burger Court and, 404
  comparable worth, 510–511
  in education, 511–513
  in employment, 510–511
  Equal Pay Act of 1963, 510
  against men, 509, 513
Sex education, 366, 368, 393
Sexual harassment, 508–509
  Clinton v. Jones, 396, 398, 426–427
Shadow cabinets by opposition party, 638
Shays's Rebellion, 29
Sherman Antitrust Act, 596, 605
Shintoism, 451
Sierra Club, 164, 174, 413
Sikh religion, 450
Silent Spring (Carson), 613
Sin taxes, 539
Single-member districts, winner-take-all,
    193
Sixth Amendment, 43, 457
Slave ship, drawing of, 32
Slavery, 477–478. *See also* African
    Americans; Civil rights movement
  1807 law prohibiting importation, 8
  abolitionist movement, women in, 506
  black slaveholders, 478
  Constitutional Convention, 32
  Dred Scott case, 402, 477
  Senate debates over, 299
  slave trade, 6
  Thirteenth Amendment, 478
  voting rights, 11, 98, 213–217
SLOP surveys, 90
Smith Act, 437
Smog, 595, 596, 604
Smoking, 152, 154, 169, 171, 180, 305
  education programs, 597
  regulations affecting, 604
Social assistance programs, 529
Social classes. *See* Socioeconomic classes
Social clubs, discrimination in, 493
Social contract theory, 15, 33
Social issues
  conservative and liberal views on,
    96–97
  influencing vote, 237–239, 247
Social rootedness, lack of, 223
Social Security, 64, 565, 566–567. *See also*
    Social welfare
  AARP protesting cuts in Social
    Security, 163
  Amish exempt from, 449
  federal monies spent for, 72
  federal revenue sources, 540
  future of, 568–569
  percentage of federal spending for, 566
  percentage of income withheld for,
    539–540
  poverty among elderly since, 571
  privatization of, 568
  problems with, 567–568
  public opinion, 95–96
  revenues from, 566
  shoring up, 547
  Third Rail of Politics, 568
Social Security Administration, 372
Social Security Trust Fund, 545, 546,
    548
Social welfare. *See also* Poverty; Social
    Security
  American Public Welfare Association,
    70
  child support payment mandates,
    71–72
  Clinton administration, 68
  cost comparison of programs, 579
  evolution of, 565–566
  health care programs. *See* Health care
    reform; Medicaid; Medicare
  liberals vs. conservatives, 94, 95
  means test programs, 573

  number receiving direct federal aid,
    565
  policies, 565
  poor people, basic programs for, 573
  pre-1996 programs, assessments of,
    573–575
  public opinion on, 95–96
  responsiveness of, 587
  time line, 586
Socialism, 529–530
  Debs, Eugene, conviction of, 437
  news media bias against, 127
  political tolerance of socialists, 99–100
Socialist Party, 155
Socialization, political. *See* Political
    socialization
Socioeconomic classes
  African Americans, 497–498, 515
  gap between rich and poor, 539, 554
  middle class, decline of, 554
  Native Americans, 504–505
  participation in campaigns, 226
  political participation, 18, 221
  and political parties, 197, 246
Sodomy, 465
Soft money, 254, 256, 260–264, 277
Somalia, U.S. troops in, 355–356
Sound bites, 121, 288, 348
South Africa, 46, 171, 531, 661–662
South America and U.S. interests, 634
South Asia, 664
South Korea, 549,655
Southern Christian Leadership
    Conference (SCLC), 474, 487
Southern states
  and Electoral College, 239
  and party realignment from 1964 to
    present, 192, 198, 489
  segregation in, 479–480
  secession from Union, 62
Sovereignty Commission (Mississippi),
    485
Soviet Union. *See also* Russia
  breakup of, 531, 651, 655
  containment of, 642–643
  and detente, 648–649
  glasnost policy, 650–651
  and Gorbachev, Mikhail, 650–651
  Jews, emigration of, 662
  nuclear deterrence policy, 643–645,
    652
  Sputnik, 643
  Warsaw Pact, 643
Spanish, bilingual education, 500–502
Spanish-American War, 11
Speaker of the House, 300–303
Special interest caucuses, 298
Specialization, 294
Speech, free. *See* Freedom of speech
Speech codes, 440–441
Split ticket, 191–192, 207
Sports, women in, 512–513
Spotted owl, 592, 594, 629–630
Sputnik, 643
Square Deal, 353
Stagflation, 534
Standing committees, 303
Standing to sue, 414
"Star-Spangled Banner," 442
Star Wars program, 650
Stare decisis, 418
State courts, 406
State Department, 372, 657
  and Kosovo crisis, 668
  mission statement for 2000, 633
  specialists in, 636
State governments, 70–71
  competition among states, 73–74
  constitutional restrictions on, 58–59
  constitutions in post-Revolutionary
    era, 28
  federal grants-in-aid to, 65
  federal regulations, 603
  interstate relations, 72–74
  map showing most liberal and most
    conservative states, 58
  National Conference of State
    Legislatures, 70

Welfare. *See* Social welfare
Welfare state, 565
Western Fuels, 170
Western states and Electoral College, 239
Whig Party, 189, 226
Whistleblowers, 392
Whistlestop campaign, 233
White flight to suburbs, 490
White hat organizations, 173
White House
   Office of, 339–340
   selling access to, 262–263
Whitewater affair, 123, 125, 275
Wilderness areas, protection of, 623, 625
Will, living, 466
Winner-take-all, 193
Wiretapping cases, 456
Wisconsin, welfare reform in, 578

Women. *See also* Sex discrimination;
   Women's movement
abolitionist movement, 506
antislavery societies, 506
athletic programs, 512–513
in civil service, 374–375
in Congress, 288–289
draft registration, 513
elected to office, 219
feminization of poverty, 570–571
foreign policy issues, 639–640
Founding Mothers, 30
households headed by black women, 497
interest groups, 161–162, 639–640
as judges, 409
opposition to woman as president, 230
political party affiliation, 197
poverty statistics, 570–571

president, woman as, 97
voting rights, 11, 213, 217–219, 505
Women's movement, 96–97, 506–507
conservative Christian groups on, 162
Equal Rights Amendment, 235, 507–509
protests by, 175
Women's Rights Convention in 1848,
   506
World Bank, 664
World trade. *See* Global economy
World Trade Organization (WTO), 174,
   640, 659–660
World War I, 642
seditious speech and, 436–437
women's contribution to, 218, 219
World War II
   Allied victory in 1945, 642
   economic impact of, 547–548

immigration after, 7
Pearl Harbor, Japanese attack on, 642
president's war powers, 337
seditious speech and, 437
women in labor force, 506
Writ of certiorari, 414
Writs of assistance, 455–456
Wyoming and women's suffrage, 218

Yellowstone National Park fire, 1988,
   136
Yugoslavia
   disintegration of, 655
   ethnic groups in former, 630, 632–633,
     668–669
   Soviet control of, 645

Presidents, Elections, and Congresses, 1789–2000 (cont.)

Year	President	Vice President	Party of President	Election Year	Election Opponent with Most Votes*
1889–1893	Benjamin Harrison	Levi P. Morton	Rep	(1888)	Grover Cleveland
1893–1897	Grover Cleveland	Adlai E. Stevenson	Dem	(1892)	Benjamin Harrison
1897–1901	William McKinley	Garret A. Hobart (to 1901)	Rep	(1896)	William Jennings Bryan
		Theodore Roosevelt (1901)		(1900)	William Jennings Bryan
1901–1909	Theodore Roosevelt	(No VP, 1901–1905)	Rep		Took office upon death of McKinley
		Charles W. Fairbanks (1905–1909)		(1904)	Alton B. Parker
1909–1913	William Howard Taft	James S. Sherman	Rep	(1908)	William Jennings Bryan
1913–1921	Woodrow Wilson	Thomas R. Marshall	Dem	(1912)	Theodore Roosevelt
				(1916)	Charles Evans Hughes
1921–1923	Warren G. Harding	Calvin Coolidge	Rep	(1920)	James Cox
1923–1929	Calvin Coolidge	(No VP, 1923–1925)	Rep		Took office upon death of Harding
		Charles G. Dawes (1925–1929)		(1924)	John Davis
1929–1933	Herbert Hoover	Charles Curtis	Rep	(1928)	Alfred E. Smith
1933–1945	Franklin D. Roosevelt	John N. Garner (1933–1941)	Dem	(1932)	Herbert Hoover
		Henry A. Wallace (1941–1945)		(1936)	Alfred Landon
		Harry S. Truman (1945)		(1940)	Wendell Willkie
				(1944)	Thomas Dewey
1945–1953	Harry S. Truman	(No VP, 1945–1949)	Dem		Took office upon death of Roosevelt
		Alban W. Barkley		(1948)	Thomas Dewey
1953–1961	Dwight D. Eisenhower	Richard M. Nixon	Rep	(1952)	Adlai Stevenson
				(1956)	Adlai Stevenson
1961–1963	John F. Kennedy	Lyndon B. Johnson	Dem	(1960)	Richard M. Nixon
1963–1969	Lyndon B. Johnson	(No VP, 1963–1965)	Dem		Took office upon death of Kennedy
		Hubert H. Humphrey (1965–1969)		(1964)	Barry Goldwater
1969–1974	Richard M. Nixon	Spiro T. Agnew	Rep	(1968)	Hubert H. Humphrey
		Gerald R. Ford (appointed)		(1972)	George McGovern
1974–1977	Gerald R. Ford	Nelson A. Rockefeller (appointed)	Rep		Took office upon Nixon's resignation
1977–1981	Jimmy Carter	Walter Mondale	Dem	(1976)	Gerald R. Ford
1981–1989	Ronald Reagan	George Bush	Rep	(1980)	Jimmy Carter
				(1984)	Walter F. Mondale
1989–1993	George Bush	J. Danforth Quayle	Rep	(1988)	Michael Dukakis
1993–2001	William J. Clinton	Albert Gore	Dem	(1992)	George Bush
				(1996)	Robert Dole
2001–	George W. Bush	Richard Cheney	Rep	(2000)	Albert Gore